Property of Caros.

Excellence
in Business Communication

in Business Communication

Second Canadian Edition

John V. Thill

Chief Executive Officer,
Communication Specialists of America

Courtland L. Bovée

Professor of Business Communication, C. Allen Paul
Distinguished Chair, Grossmont College

Ava Cross

Department of Business and Technical Communication,
Ryerson University

Toronto

To the memory of my mother.

Ava Cross

National Library of Canada Cataloguing in Publication

Thill, John V.
Excellence in business communication / John V. Thill, Courtland L. Bovée, Ava Cross. — 2nd Canadian ed

Includes index.
ISBN 0-13-121142-0

I. Business communication — Case studies. I. Bovée, Courtland L. II. Cross, Ava, 1951-
III. Title.

HF5718.C3T45 2005 658′5 C2003-9058114-5

Copyright © 2005, 2002 Bovée & Thill LLCC and Pearson Education Canada Inc., Toronto, Ontario.

Pearson Prentice Hall All rights reserved. This publication is protected by copyright, and permission should be obtained from the publisher prior to any prohibited reproduction, storage in a retrieval system, or transmission in any form or by any means, electronic, mechanical, photocopying, recording, or likewise. For information regarding permission, write to the Permissions Department.

Original edition published by Prentice Hall, Inc., a division of Pearson Education, Upper Saddle River, NJ 07458. Copyright © 2005 by Bovée & Thill LLC. This edition is authorized for sale in Canada only.

ISBN 0-13-121142-0

Vice President, Editorial Director: Michael J. Young
Executive Editor: Dave Ward
Director of Marketing: Bill Todd
Supervising Developmental Editor: Suzanne Schaan
Production Editor: Judith Scott
Copy Editor: Karen Hunter
Production Coordinator: Patricia Ciardullo
Photo and Persmissions Research: Christina Beamish
Page Layout: Phyllis Seto and Janet Zanette
Art Director: Julia Hall
Interior and Cover Design: Monica Kompter
Cover Image: Todd Davidson

4 5 6 7 09 08 07 06

Printed and bound in the U.S.A.

Contents in Brief

Contents

CHECKLISTS

Preface

Excellence in Business Communication paints a vivid picture of the world of business communication, offering an overview of the wide range of communication skills used by business-people to present ideas clearly and persuasively. It also gives specific examples of the communication techniques that have led to sound decision making and effective teamwork. In addition, the book's insights into the way organizations operate help clarify student career interests by identifying the skills needed for a lifetime of career success.

New Features in This Edition

Streamlined and Reorganized Text

This edition streamlines and reorganizes the text, reducing the number of chapters from 18 to 15, making it easier to cover the entire text in one term. Material previously covered in Chapters 1 and 2 has been combined into Chapter 1. The chapter on writing direct requests has been combined with the chapter on writing routine, good-news, and goodwill letters—shortening the letter-writing chapters from four to three. The discussion of interpersonal communication skills such as listening and working in teams has been expanded and moved to Chapter 2. And the discussion of the writing process now begins in Chapter 1.

A Greater Emphasis on Process and Product

We have reorganized the material in many of the text's chapters into a series of three easy-to-follow steps: planning, writing, and completing business messages. Students will appreciate this practical strategy for solving communication problems and creating well-crafted communication products. The three-step process is explained in detail (Chapters 4–6) before it is applied to specific types of business messages: letters, memos, and e-mail messages (Chapters 7–9); reports and proposals (Chapters 10–12), and speeches and oral presentations (Chapter 13). The three-step writing process even serves as the framework for writing employment messages (Chapters 14–15).

1 Planning	2 Writing	3 Completing
Analyze: Study your purpose, lay out your writing schedule, and then profile your audience. **Investigate:** Gather information through formal or informal research methods. **Adapt:** Choose the right channel and medium; then establish a good relationship with your audience.	**Organize:** Define your main idea, limit the scope, group your points, and choose the direct or indirect approach. **Compose:** Control your style through level of formality and conversational tone. Choose your words carefully so that you can create effective sentences and paragraphs.	**Revise:** Evaluate content and review readability, editing, and rewriting for conciseness and clarity. **Produce:** Use effective design elements and suitable delivery methods. **Proofread:** Review for errors in layout, spelling, and mechanics.

Updates on Technology

This new edition addresses some of the effects that technology has had on business communication:

- *E-mail.* E-mail has evolved into an accepted medium for both personal and business communication. Chapter 4 introduces electronic messages, including a checklist on e-mail etiquette, and Chapter 5 offers expanded coverage of writing effective e-mails.
- *Writing for the Web.* Writing for the Web is quite different from writing for print, so anyone who wants to be an effective Web writer must learn new skills. This new edition offers substantial coverage of writing for the Web (Chapter 5) and looks at real online pages as examples.

➢ *Electronic Presentations.* In most business situations today, the visual aid of choice is the electronic presentation. Information on designing and producing electronic presentations, such as PowerPoint slides, helps bring the discussion of oral presentations up to date (Chapter 13).

Real-World Issues

The boundaries of business communication are always expanding. In addition to covering all the traditional subjects, *Excellence in Business Communication*, Second Canadian Edition, provides material to help students manage these important current issues in business communication:

➢ *Ethics.* Taking an ethical position in the face of pressures and temptations requires more than courage—it requires strong communication skills.
➢ *Communication Barriers.* The shift toward a service economy means that more and more careers will depend on interpersonal skills, making it vital for people to overcome communication barriers.
➢ *Cultural Diversity.* The changing nature of the domestic work force requires strong communication skills to relate to older workers, women, members of various socioeconomic groups, immigrants, and others. Also, strong skills are needed to communicate effectively with people from other cultures.
➢ *Communication Technology.* More and more face-to-face interactions are giving way to interactions with and through computers. And this trend will continue. To survive in today's business world, students must master high-tech communication skills.
➢ *Employment Search.* More and more people are making radical mid-career job changes, whether by choice or because their companies are downsizing and flattening hierarchies. These people need to master new communication skills to compete in today's job market.
➢ *Communication Versatility.* Small businesses create most of the new jobs and employ more people than large corporations do. Since these small businesses are unable to support communication specialists for specific jobs, people working for them need to be versatile in their communication skills.

Trademark Features

"On the Job"

Each chapter opens with the feature "On the Job: Facing a Communication Dilemma." This slice-of-life vignette summarizes a communication problem being faced by an actual company, such as the Royal Bank, McCain Foods, or Indigo Books and Music. The solution to the dilemma is found in the concepts presented in the chapter, and the featured company reappears from time to time throughout the chapter to dramatize the connection between chapter principles and life on the job.

But we don't stop there. Each chapter ends with the follow-up "On the Job: Solving a Communication Dilemma." These simulations expand on the chapter-opening dilemma and are set within the featured company. Students are asked to solve situational problems by applying the principles discussed in the text, by making decisions about the communication process, and by selecting the best alternatives from those offered.

ON THE JOB

Facing a Communication Dilemma at The Forzani Group

Designing a Game Plan for Success

www.forzanigroup.com

Whether it's skateboards, snowboards, skis, or sneakers, you'll probably find the gear you want at one of John Forzani's sporting goods stores across Canada. As the chair and CEO of The Forzani Group Limited (FGL), the former Calgary Stampeder has created a retail empire that includes Sport Chek, Sports Experts, Coast Mountain Sports, Sports Mart, and Atmosphere, his newest chain to serve outdoor enthusiasts. Since opening Forzani's Locker Room in 1974 with three teammates, John Forzani now operates 350 corporate or franchise stores, with net earnings of $20.6 million in 2002, his most profitable year ever. By the end of 2005, Forzani plans on adding 1.5 million square feet of floor space to sell athletic wear and equipment in every city in Canada.

But the future success of The Forzani Group centres on John Forzani's ability to communicate effectively with employees, customers, and suppliers. To keep operations running smoothly, Forzani needs to establish good working relationships with all three audiences. He must find out what each audience needs to know, and he must determine the right way to communicate that information. For example, before Forzani can stock a new product, he must analyze the needs of his audiences and plan appropriate messages for each one. He must assess customer demand, educate employees about product use, and seek vendors that can deliver the right amount of merchandise in a timely manner.

Planning effective messages wasn't as difficult when Forzani opened his first store in Calgary, where he sold athletic footwear in a 1200 square foot space and personally dealt with suppliers and trained employees. But with plans to open or expand to 52 stores by the end of 2003 and to introduce new sports products, Forzani can no longer depend on oral messages to communicate with his audiences. Establishing relationships with 9600 employees, suppliers of almost every major brand of athletic equipment and clothing, and millions of customers has complicated matters. And adapting his messages to serve the needs of each audience requires careful planning.

If you were John Forzani, how would you plan your business messages to different audiences? What factors would you consider as you plan your messages? How would you analyze each audience? And how would you choose the best channel and medium for each of your messages?[1]

ON THE JOB

Solving a Communication Dilemma at The Forzani Group

The Forzani Group's founder, John Forzani, carefully plans his many messages to various audiences. He is also careful to select just the right medium for each message he sends. As Forzani realizes that face-to-face communication with customers is a vital element in his stores' success, he trains owners of franchise outlets such as Atmosphere and Sports Experts and employees of corporate stores, such as SportChek, Save on Sports, and Coast Mountain Sports, to ask specific questions about their customers' needs. This input allows Forzani to gauge his audience's level of understanding so that he can educate his customers about the sports products they purchase. "It's like football," Forzani says about his company's success. "When your people work as a team toward one goal, you can achieve it."

Forzani uses various media to educate his employees. He runs two schools: The Forzani Academy for franchise owners and Forzani's Retail College for corporate employees. Both offer classes in the key areas of management, retail sales, merchandising, customer service, loss prevention, and product knowledge. Forzani also brings factory representatives into stores to do formal presentations, and employees are treated to "sports camps" at such places as Lake Louise, Alberta, where they get to use the gear they will sell, obtaining in-depth product knowledge.

Forzani also uses written media, such as the product catalogue/magazine *Fusion* for franchise owners and flyers and newspaper advertisements to reach consumers. In addition, he established the sportchek.com Web site for selling athletic wear and equipment and promoting awareness of the SportChek chain. Forzani's game plan is to operate in every Canadian city with a population of more than 15 000 people.

Your Mission You have recently joined The Forzani Group's corporate office in Calgary. Two of your major functions in this position are (1) helping store managers and other company executives plan effective business messages for a variety of audiences, and (2) responding to press inquiries about The Forzani Group Ltd. Choose the best alternatives for handling the following situations, and be prepared to explain why your choice is best:

1 You have received a phone call from Ann Mason, a reporter for a local Saskatchewan newspaper. She is planning to write an article about FGL's recent decision to open a Sports Experts store in her community, a small city. Mason has asked you for information about the economic impact of SportChek, Sports Experts, and other chains in Forzani's company in other small Canadian communities. When responding to Mason's request, what should the purpose of your letter be?
   - a The general purpose is to inform. The specific purpose is to provide Mason with a brief summary of the evolution of The Forzani Group over the past 20 years.
   - b The general purpose is to persuade. The specific purpose is to convince Mason that The Forzani Group creates jobs within a community, and that small, existing merchants should not feel threatened by the arrival of a Sports Expert store.
   - c The general purpose is to collaborate. The specific purpose is to work with Mason to develop an article that examines the history of Forzani's entry into new markets.
   - d The general purpose is to respond. The specific purpose is to convey details requested by a journalist.

2 Assume that your purpose is to convince Mason of The Forzani Group's abilities to create new jobs and increase economic activity in small communities. Is your purpose worth pursuing at this time?
   - a Yes. The purpose is realistic, the timing is right, you are the right person to send the message, and the purpose is acceptable to the organization.
   - b Not completely. Realistically, many readers of Mason's newspaper may dread the arrival of a Sports Expert store in their small community, fearing that the giant retailer may force small retailers out of business.
   - c The purpose is fine, but you are not the right person to send this message. John Forzani, the chief executive officer, should respond.
   - d The timing is right for this message. Stress The Forzani Group's involvement in small communities, citing contributions to social causes in other small cities. Show how John Forzani cares about customers on a personal basis.

3 When planning your reply to Mason, what assumptions can you make about your audience?
   - a The audience includes not only Ann Mason but also the readers of the community's newspaper. Given their bias for a simple, rural lifestyle, the readers will probably be hostile to big business in general and to The Forzani Group in particular. They probably know little about large retail operations. Furthermore, they probably mistrust you because you are a Forzani Group employee.
   - b Ann Mason will probably be the only person who reads the letter directly. She is the primary audience; the readers of her article are the secondary audience. Mason will be happy to hear from The Forzani Group and will read the information with an open mind. However, she may not know a great deal about the company. Although she is a stranger to you, she trusts your credibility as a Forzani Group spokesperson.
   - c Ann Mason is probably the sole and primary audience for the letter. The fact that she is writing an article about The Forzani Group suggests that she already knows a great deal about the company and likes the idea of a Sports Expert's outlet in her community. In all likelihood, she will respond positively to your reply and will trust your credibility as a Forzani Group representative.
   - d Ann Mason may be an industrial spy working for a rival home improvement centre. She will show your reply to people who work for your competitor; they will analyze the information and use it to improve their market share of the home improvement industry.

Not only do these simulations give students the opportunity to practise real-world decision making, they also tie the textual information to real-life examples, providing a concrete basis for analyzing the chapter principles.

Special Feature Sidebars

Boxed and strategically placed within each chapter, special-feature sidebars extend the chapter material. We've included discussion questions at the end of each special feature to give students numerous opportunities to analyze business communication principles and practices. These special features centre on four well-integrated themes:

- *Achieving Intercultural Communication.* Tested techniques help students communicate successfully in the global arena and in the culturally diverse business world at home. Cultural issues are well explored in special features such as "Test Your Intercultural Knowledge" (Chapter 3) and "Five Tips for Making Presentations Around the World" (Chapter 13).

- *Promoting Workplace Ethics.* By examining critical ethical issues that face business communicators in today's workplace, students gain instruction on how to identify areas of ethical vulnerability, how to steer clear of ethical perils, and when to seek ethical advice. Special features include a range of topics such as "Ethical Boundaries" (Chapter 1) and "Selling Ethically Online" (Chapter 9).
- *Sharpening Your Career Skills.* Practical pointers and confidence-building guidelines help students improve their writing and speaking skills. Special features help students strengthen their career skills by exploring such topics as "Beating Writer's Block: Nine Workable Ideas to Get Words Flowing" (Chapter 5), "How to Proofread Like a Pro" (Chapter 6), and "Interview Strategies: Answering the 16 Toughest Questions" (Chapter 15).

SHARPENING YOUR CAREER SKILLS 

Improving Your Business Etiquette

Etiquette is knowing how to behave properly in a given situation. Knowing how to interact with people in business will help you appear polished, professional, and confident. Following proper etiquette helps you put fellow employees, business associates, and customers at ease so that they feel comfortable doing business with you.

Consider such common interactions as smiling, shaking hands, and making introductions. When you smile, do so genuinely. An artificial smile is obvious because the timing is off and the expression fails to involve all the facial muscles that a genuine smile would. Repeated false smiling may earn you the reputation of being insincere. Plus, if you smile too long, you make others uncomfortable, because they feel that you're not focused on the present. However, certain occasions require smiling:

- **When you are introduced to someone.** Smiling is courteous and suggests that you are receptive.

- *Using the Power of Technology.* Specific techniques offer students guidance for using technological applications to improve business communication. Special features present a well-balanced selection of technological topics, including "Caution! E-Mail Can Bite" (Chapter 4) and "Netting a Job on the Web" (Chapter 14).

USING THE POWER OF TECHNOLOGY 

Helping Customers Help Themselves

"Problems are opportunities in disguise"—an apt description of how insightful e-businesses approach customer service. Every complaint gives you a chance to strengthen your customer's loyalty, if you make full use of Internet technology to show that you're truly interested in meeting your customer's needs. Web-based businesses offer customers a wide choice of contact methods: e-mail, phone, or regular mail, or instant online customer-service chat. E-businesses can also offer online customers the opportunity to resolve issues through a customer self-care Web site. Here, customers can find FAQs, service information, troubleshooting advice, technical support, and user guides. Providing these features can go a long way toward educating customers about a business's practices—an important way to preserve customer loyalty. Visit Rogers Communications customer care site at **<www.shoprogers.com/Customercare/custcare.asp>** to see how one Canadian company helps customers help themselves.

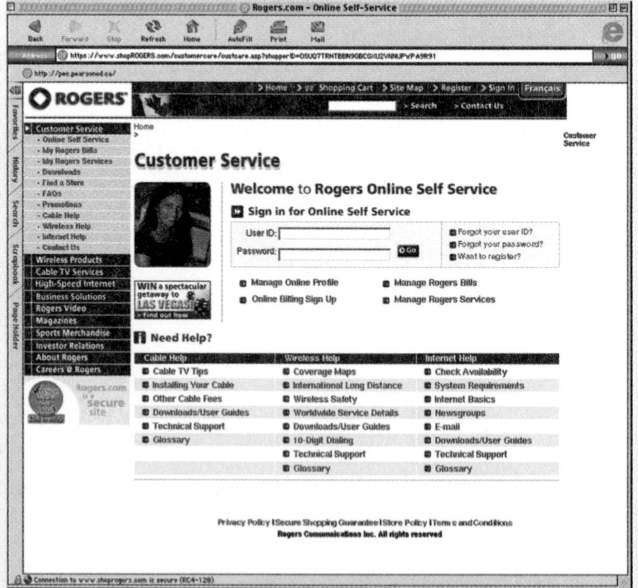

1. By providing online customer care, is a company sidestepping its responsibility to deal with customer complaints? Explain your answer.
2. When you send an e-mail message to update customers whose problems are taking more time than usual to resolve, would the direct or the indirect approach be more appropriate? Why?

Examples of Letters, Memos, E-mail Messages, and Reports

This text contains outstanding examples of documents from numerous types of organizations and from people working in a variety of functional areas. A number of authentic documents from Canadian organizations, such as BCE and The Royal Ontario Museum, are included. Accompanying analyses help students see precisely how to apply the principles discussed in the text. The report-writing chapters give numerous examples too, and illustrate the step-by-step development of a long report, which appears in its entirety to show how all the parts fit together (Chapter 12).

A neatly formatted letterhead and logo can add to a professional appearance.

A contemporary typeface, such as Times New Roman, can make your document inviting to read.

The use of bullets and boldface can make information easily accessible by highlighting it.

Royal Ontario Museum
100 Queen's Park
Toronto, Ontario
Canada
M5S 2C6

Membership
Telephone (416) 586-5700
Facsimile (416) 586-5703
Web Site http://www.rom.on.ca
E-Mail membership@rom.on.ca

January 23, 2005

Ms. Nancy Nau & Mr. Andrew Cheston
1707 Altona Road
Pickering, ON L1V 1M5

Dear Ms. Nau & Mr. Cheston,

One of my greatest pleasures as Head of Membership Services is welcoming new Members to the Royal Ontario Museum. You're now part of a group of over 35 000 individuals who, as Members, contribute so significantly to the Museum's vitality. Most of our Members stay with us for many years. In the hope that you will too, please consider this the first of many welcomes.

You've picked a terrific year to join the ROM, and here are a few reasons why:

- Opening in February is our new expanded **Discovery Centre**. The gallery will be organized in diverse environmental "zones" such as a glittering starlight or an enchanted forest. Older children can dress up in costume, examine minerals under an ultraviolet light, and much more. Families with toddlers and babies have their own special area complete with stroller parking.
- In May the spectacular **Inco Gallery of Earth Sciences** opens. This gallery, which promises to be visually exciting, interactive and educational, will be divided into four major sections: **Dynamic Earth, Restless Earth, Earth: The Alien Planet,** and **Treasures of the Earth**.

Of course, I hope you'll take advantage of all your membership benefits—visit the Members' Lounge, use your discount in all the ROM shops and the ROM restaurant, and enjoy the *Rotunda* magazine and *Atria* newsletter. Also, the next time you visit, inquire at the membership desk about our discounted parking.

But most of all, come to the ROM as often as possible. We truly treasure your attendance and hope you'll be part of the Royal Ontario Museum's great future.

Yours sincerely,

Ania Kordiuk

Ania Kordiuk
Director, Membership and Annual Giving

Checklists

To help students organize their thinking when they begin a communication project, make decisions as they write, and check their own work, we've included numerous checklists throughout the book. Appearing as close as possible to the related discussion, these checklists are reminders, not "recipes." They provide useful guidelines for writing, without limiting creativity.

Checklist: Composing Business Messages

Generate Ideas

✓ Get ideas down as quickly as you can.

✓ Rearrange, delete, and add ideas without losing sight of your purpose.

Vary the Style to Create a Tone That Suits the Occasion

✓ Use the appropriate level of formality.

✓ Avoid being overly familiar, using inappropriate humour (including obvious flattery), sounding preachy, bragging, or trying to be something you're not.

✓ Avoid old-fashioned and pompous language.

Select the Best Words

✓ Use plain English.

✓ Use concrete words that avoid negative connotations.

✓ Rely on nouns, verbs, and specific adjectives and adverbs.

✓ Choose words that are strong and familiar while avoiding clichés.

Create Effective Sentences

✓ Use simple, compound, and complex sentences, choosing the form that best fits the thought you want to express.

✓ Write mainly in the active voice, but use the passive voice to achieve specific effects.

✓ Emphasize key points through sentence style; expand on important points.

✓ Vary the sentence length.

✓ Use lists.

Create Effective Paragraphs

✓ Be sure each paragraph contains a topic sentence, related sentences, and transitional elements.

✓ Choose a method of development that suits the subject: illustration, comparison or contrast, cause and effect, classification, problem and solution.

✓ Vary the length and structure of sentences within paragraphs.

✓ Mix paragraphs of different lengths, try not to write paragraphs; over 100 words.

End-of-Chapter Questions, Exercises, and Cases

The end-of-chapter questions are divided into two types: Test Your Knowledge (review questions) and Apply Your Knowledge (application questions). One application question in each chapter focuses on ethics and is labelled "Ethical Choices." The end-of-chapter questions are designed to get students thinking about the concepts introduced in each chapter. The questions may also prompt students to stretch their learning beyond the chapter content. Not only will students find them useful in studying for examinations, but the instructor may also draw on them to promote classroom discussion of issues that have no easy answers.

A wealth of new exercises and cases provide assignments like those that students will most often face at work. Many of them are memo-writing and e-mail tasks. Icons are used to highlight exercises that require

teamwork  or Internet research. 

The exercises and cases deal with all types and sizes of organizations, both domestic and international, with many of them referring to real organizations such as Ballard Power Systems and ABC Canada.

Additional exercises provide a wide selection of documents that students can critique and revise. Documents include letters, memos, and e-mail messages, a letter of application, and a résumé. This hands-on experience in analyzing and improving sample documents will help students revise their own business messages.

Internet Resources

The Web contains a wealth of valuable resources. To acquaint students with websites that relate to the content of *Excellence in Business Communication*, each chapter includes a Going Online feature that describes an especially useful Web site, with a related exercise provided at the end of the chapter. Students can access the site by using the URL provided or by visiting the Companion Website for this text (www.pearsoned.ca/thill), where live links take students straight to the site of their choice. To give students practice exploring the rich resources of the Web, Going Online Exercises are included at the end of each chapter. These exercises are directly tied to the Going Online sites showcased within the chapters.

Going Online

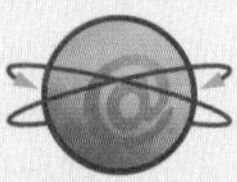

Hone Your Skills for International Business

What do you need to know about international business practices and different social customs? For crucial information that will help you successfully conduct business abroad, preview "Going Global" at **americanexpress.com**. Learn about appropriate business etiquette by accessing information such as negotiation strategies, international business regulations, and reference sources for 78 countries. If you want details on business travel, visa requirements, appropriate attire, accommodations, and language fluency, the research reports at this site will help prepare you to deal internationally.

www.americanexpress.com/smallbusiness

To link directly to this site, visit our Companion Website at **www.pearsoned.ca/thill** and look for the Chapter 3 resources.

Going Online Exercises

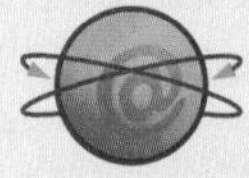

Hone Your Skills for International Business, found on page 61 of this chapter

Procedures and protocol for conducting international business are diverse. Go to the global resources at americanexpress.com to learn why an awareness of differences in business practices is important and how to be culturally correct.

1. Describe several business customs pertaining to etiquette in Korea that differ from customs in Canada. Why is your negotiating style particularly important in establishing a business relationship?
2. What did you discover about cultural differences in Russia that might make it difficult to adapt to Russian business customs such as a dinner meeting?
3. Select a country you might travel to and investigate its customs: what tips and specific information about doing international business did you learn?

Learning Objectives

Chapter-opening learning objectives are clearly stated to signal important concepts that students are expected to master. In addition, the numbered objectives reappear in the text margins, close to the relevant material, and the end-of-chapter "Summary of Learning Outcomes" reinforces basic concepts by capsulizing chapter highlights for students.

AFTER STUDYING THIS CHAPTER, YOU WILL BE ABLE TO

1. Explain why effective communication is important to organizations and how it can help you succeed in business
2. Discuss three changes in the workplace that are intensifying the need to communicate effectively
3. Describe how organizations share information internally and externally
4. Identify and briefly define the six phases of the communication process
5. Identify and briefly discuss four types of communication barriers
6. Discuss four guidelines for overcoming communication barriers
7. Differentiate between an ethical dilemma and an ethical lapse; then list four questions that will help you decide what is ethical

---

Summary of Learning Outcomes

1 Explain why effective communication is important to organizations and how it can help you succeed in business. Communication is the lifeblood of organizations, and effective communication improves an organization's productivity, image, and responsiveness. Communication is effective when it helps people understand each other, stimulates others to take action, and encourages others to think in new ways. It helps you speed problem solution, strengthen decision making, coordinate work flow, cement business relationships, clarify promotional materials, enhance your professional image, and improve your response to stakeholders. Good communication skills increase your chances for career success and your ability to adapt to the changing workplace.

2 Discuss three changes in the workplace that are intensifying the need to communicate effectively. Technological advances such as the Internet and portable communication devices make it possible for employees to telecommute; using such devices also highlights an employee's ability to write and speak clearly. Increased cultural diversity in the workforce requires employees to adapt their communication so that they can be understood by different cultures. Increased use of teams requires mastery of interpersonal skills such as listening, giving feedback, working collaboratively, and resolving conflict.

3 Describe how organizations share information internally and externally. Within an organization, communication occurs formally or informally. The formal communication network can be depicted as an organizational chart, with information flowing downward from managers to employees, upward from employees to managers, and horizontally among peers. The informal network, or grapevine, is sometimes as formal as a communica- tions team or as informal as talking with a customer or letting one's appearance transmit an impression of the organization.

4 Identify and briefly define the six phases of the communication process. The communication process occurs in six phases: First, the sender has an idea (conceives a thought and wants to share it). Second, the sender encodes the idea (puts it into message form). Third, the sender transmits the message (sends the message using a specific channel and medium). Fourth, the receiver gets the message (receives the physical message by hearing or reading it). Fifth, the receiver decodes the message (absorbs and understands the meaning). And sixth, the receiver sends feedback (responds to the message and signals that response to the sender).

5 Identify and briefly discuss four types of communication barriers. First, perceptual differences affect how we see the world; no two people perceive things exactly the same way. Perception also influences how we develop language, which depends on shared definitions for meaning and is shaped by our culture. Second, restrictive structures and management block effective communication. Formal channels tend to cause distortion, as each link in the communication channel holds the potential for misinterpretation. Similarly, if managers aren't diligent in their efforts to communicate down the formal network, their messages can become fragmented so that employees never get the "big picture." Third, distractions can be physical (from poor acoustics to illegible copy), emotional, attributed to poor listening, or the result of information overload. And fourth, deceptive communication tactics are used by unethical communicators to manipulate their receivers.

Margin Notes

To reinforce learning, the book's margins contain short summary statements that highlight key points. These notes are no substitute for reading the chapters, but they help students quickly get the gist of a section, review a chapter, and locate areas of greatest concern.

USE BIAS-FREE LANGUAGE

Most of us think of ourselves as being sensitive, unbiased, ethical, and fair. But being fair and objective isn't enough; to establish a good relationship with your audience, you must also *appear* to be fair.[17] **Bias-free language** avoids unethical, embarrassing blunders in language related to gender, race, ethnicity, age, and disability. Thoughtful communicators make every effort to guard against biased language of any type (see Table 4.2 on page 92).

Avoid biased language that might offend your audience.

- **Gender bias.** Avoid sexist language by using the same label for everyone (for example, don't call a woman *chairperson* and then call a man *chairman*). Reword sentences to use *they* or to use no pronoun at all. Vary traditional patterns by sometimes putting women first (*women and men, she and he, her and his*). Note that the preferred title for women in business is *Ms.*, unless the individual has some other title (such as *Dr.*) or asks to be addressed as *Miss* or *Mrs.*

Replace words that inaccurately exclude women or men.

- **Racial and ethnic bias.** Avoid language suggesting that members of a racial or an ethnic group have stereotypical characteristics. The best solution is to avoid identifying people by race or ethnic origin unless such a label is relevant.

Eliminate references that reinforce racial or ethnic stereotypes.

Appendices and Handbook

Excellence in Business Communication contains three appendices. Appendix A, "Format and Layout of Business Documents," discusses in one convenient place the formatting for all types of documents. Appendix B, "Documentation of Report Sources," gives basic guidelines for handling reference citations, bibliographies, and source notes.

The Handbook, "Fundamentals of Grammar and Usage," is a primer in brief, presenting the basic tools of language. It includes brief exercises for each topic, many of which give practice in proofreading and correcting errors. A list of proofreading marks is provided at the end of the Handbook, and further correction symbols are listed on the inside of the front and back covers.

Mastering Business Communication CD-ROM

Free with every copy of the text!

The Mastering Business Communication CD-ROM is packaged with every copy of *Excellence in Business Communication*, Second Canadian Edition. This CD contains a variety of resources for students:

- *Perils of Pauline, Version 1.1.* Let students learn valuable lessons about communicating effectively in a variety of business situations prior to experiencing them first-hand. *The Perils of Pauline* is an exciting interactive presentation that uses custom video scenarios linked with exercises and activities. These tools allow your students to help Pauline, a recent graduate, deal with real-world communication predicaments on her first job. Twelve individual episodes are featured, each including unique video scenarios that set up the episode, interactive exercises that offer feedback based on student decisions, video conclusions for both good and bad endings, and stimulating discussion questions. The "Interactive Learning" note at the end of each text chapter highlights the segment(s) of particular relevance to that chapter.
- *The Write Stuff.* This grammar tutorial provides students with extra support and exercises (both printable and interactive) on basic grammar topics.
- *Cases.* Case studies offer extra opportunities to consider specific real-life situations and assess how they should be handled.
- *Microsoft Word Templates.* A variety of templates are provided to guide students in creating their own memos and letters.

Additional Student Supplements

Study Guide. The student study guide provides a wide variety of exercises designed to reinforce key concepts and to provide practise in analyzing and correcting documents.

Companion Website (www.pearsoned.ca/thill). The website for *Excellence in Business Communication* offers additional resources such as self-grading quizzes, Internet exercises, and links to websites for those who want to explore business communication further.

Instructor Supplements

Instructor's Resource CD-ROM. This CD-ROM brings together many of the instructor resources for this text, including the following components:

- *Instructor's Manual*, providing chapter outlines, suggested solutions to the exercises, and formatted letters for the cases in the letter-writing chapters. Additional resources include diagnostic tests of English skills and supplementary grammar exercises.
- *Test Item File*, including over 1500 multiple-choice, true/false, and fill-in-the-blank questions. This test bank is offered in both Word and TestGen format.

- *Pearson TestGen*, providing the Test Item File within a testing software that enables instructors to view and edit the existing questions, add questions, generate tests, and print the tests in a variety of formats. Powerful search and sort functions make it easy to locate questions and arrange them in any order desired. TestGen also enables instructors to administer tests on a local area network, have the tests graded electronically, and have the results prepared in electronic or printed reports.
- *PowerPoint Presentations*, covering the key concepts in each chapter.

The Instructor's Manual and PowerPoint Presentations are also available to instructors for downloading from Pearson Education Canada's password-protected Instructor Central site at **www.pearsoned.ca/instructor**. Register for a password online, or contact your local sales representative for further information.

PH Words. An Internet-based practice and assessment program, *PH Words* gives instructors the ability to measure and track students' mastery of all the elements of writing. *PH Words* includes over 100 modules covering grammar, paragraph and essay development, and the writing process, using a three-level questioning strategy—Recall, Apply, and Write. This technology solution allows students to work on their areas of weakness, freeing up class time for instructors to address students' individual needs both in the classroom and one-to-one.

Business Communication Update Newsletter for Faculty. Delivered exclusively by e-mail every month, this newsletter provides interesting materials that can be used in class and offers a wealth of practical ideas about teaching methods. To receive a complimentary subscription, send an e-mail to bovee-thill@uia.net. In the subject line, put "BCU Subscription Request." In the message area, please list your name and institutional affiliation.

Online Learning Solutions. Pearson Education Canada supports instructors interested in using online course management systems. Pearson provides text-related content in WebCT, Blackboard, and our own private label version of Blackboard called CourseCompass. To find out more about creating an online course using Pearson content in one of these platforms, contact your local Pearson Education Canada representative.

ASSET. For qualified adopters, Pearson Education Canada is proud to introduce Instructor's ASSET, the Academic Support and Service for Educational Technologies. ASSET is the first integrated Canadian service program committed to meeting the customization, training, and support needs for your course. Our commitments are made in writing and in consultation with faculty. Your local Pearson sales representative can provide you with more details on this service program.

Innovative Solutions Team. Pearson's Innovative Solutions Team works with faculty and campus course designers to ensure that Pearson Technology products and online course materials are tailored to meet your specific needs. This highly qualified team is dedicated to helping schools take full advantage of a wide range of educational technology, by assisting in the integration of a variety of instructional materials and media formats.

Acknowledgements

At Pearson Education Canada, Michael Young offered me the opportunity to work on this second edition. I am grateful to him, and to Andrew Winton, the sponsoring editor during the early stages. Suzanne Schaan and Judith Scott guided the book through the editorial and production process with tremendous professionalism and graciousness. Thank you also to Karen Hunter for copyediting the text and to Tara Tovell and Joe Zingrone for proofreading.

The following instructors attended an initial focus group that helped shape the plan for the new edition:

George Carere, George Brown College
Thom Dean, Seneca College of Applied Arts and Technology
Katharine Ferguson, Seneca College of Applied Arts and Technology
Marion Hohener, Seneca College of Applied Arts and Technology
Peter Miller, Seneca College of Applied Arts and Technology
Marion Ross, Georgian College
Melanie Rubens, Seneca College of Applied Arts and Technology
Linda Schofield, Ryerson University

Many educators in Canada read my manuscript and made thoughtful suggestions. I would like to thank the following instructors, who commented in detail on the first Canadian edition and/or the manuscript for this new edition:

Margie Clow Bohan, Dalhousie University
Kathy Cocchio, Northern Alberta Institute of Technology
Katharine Ferguson, Seneca College of Applied Arts and Technology
Isobel Findlay, University of Saskatchewan
Martha Finnigan, Durham College
Les Hanson, Red River College
Bruce Harper, Niagara College of Applied Arts and Technology
Don Klepp, Okanagan University College
Shelley Martin, Okanagan University College
David Patient, Simon Fraser University
Laura Reave, University of Western Ontario
Jim Streeter, Seneca College of Applied Arts and Technology
Barry Thorne, Queen's University

Bill Cross was interested, as always. David Cross and Michal Calder Cross supplied some material. My family and friends in the U.S., Leslie Gordon Politzer, Bernetta Gordon, Sharon Barbanel Geier, Hillary Stone Marra, and Ruth Zelig Oppenheimer, always took the time to listen. Finally, my love and affection to John, Miriam, and David, whose unfailing love, support, and good humour kept me going once again.

A Great Way to Learn and Instruct Online

The Pearson Education Canada Companion Website is easy to navigate and is organized to correspond to the chapters in this textbook. Whether you are a student in the classroom or a distance learner you will discover helpful resources for in-depth study and research that empower you in your quest for greater knowledge and maximize your potential for success in the course.

[www.pearsoned.ca/thill]

Enter

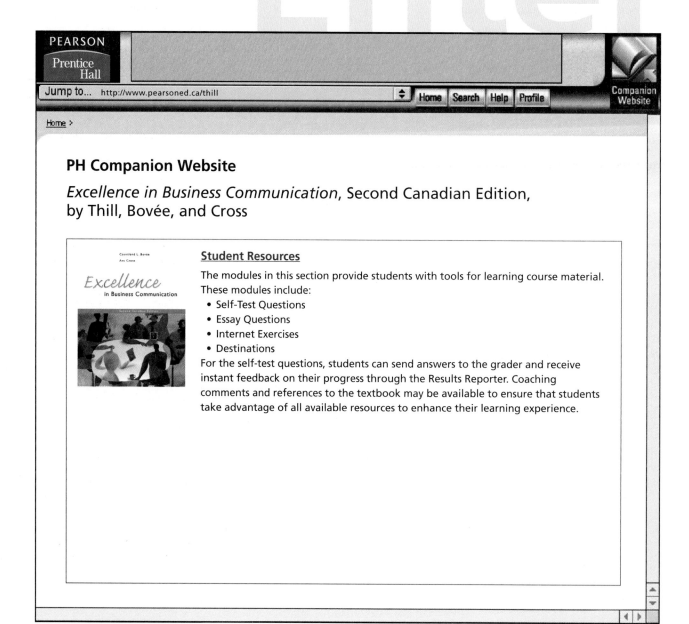

PEARSON Prentice Hall

Jump to... http://www.pearsoned.ca/thill

Home Search Help Profile

Companion Website

Home >

PH Companion Website

Excellence in Business Communication, Second Canadian Edition, by Thill, Bovée, and Cross

Excellence in Business Communication

Student Resources

The modules in this section provide students with tools for learning course material. These modules include:

- Self-Test Questions
- Essay Questions
- Internet Exercises
- Destinations

For the self-test questions, students can send answers to the grader and receive instant feedback on their progress through the Results Reporter. Coaching comments and references to the textbook may be available to ensure that students take advantage of all available resources to enhance their learning experience.

Understanding Business Communication

1. Explain why effective communication is important to organizations and how it can help you succeed in business
2. Discuss three changes in the workplace that are intensifying the need to communicate effectively
3. Describe how organizations share information internally and externally
4. Identify and briefly define the six phases of the communication process
5. Identify and briefly discuss four types of communication barriers
6. Discuss four guidelines for overcoming communication barriers
7. Differentiate between an ethical dilemma and an ethical lapse; then list four questions that will help you decide what is ethical

ON THE JOB

Facing A Communication Dilemma at Suncor Energy Inc.

Working together to find solutions

www.suncor.com

"Once we understand where our organization wants to go, we communicate, communicate, and communicate some more, with our employees, our shareholders, our communities," says Sue Lee, Suncor Energy's senior vice-president of Human Resources and Communications. A leader in Canada's oil industry, Suncor mines the Alberta oil sands, producing 225 000 barrels of crude oil a day. Yet Suncor's objective is to meet the constant need for energy while preserving the environment. A growing part of their business is alternative energy: in 2002, Suncor established the SunBridge wind power project at Gull Lake, Saskatchewan, where wind turbines dotting the prairie landscape generate electricity to 6000 homes.

Fostering an open communication culture, the company works hard to involve their many stakeholders in the process of achieving its goals. Whether they work on the oil fields, in laboratories, or in company offices, management considers employees partners and seeks their input to improve business decisions. The company also asks communities to identify problems that will affect how its activities will impact on residents. In consultation with environmental groups, Suncor determines limits of harmful emissions into the atmosphere.

To communicate effectively with 3400 employees, community and environmental organizations, government agencies, and the general public, Sue Lee and her staff must adapt their messages to their audiences. Avoiding the "one size fits all" approach to Suncor's communications, Lee and her team tailor the strategies. Lee understands that all of Suncor's stakeholders are unique, with their own needs and concerns. To avoid overloading people with too many distractions, she sends only messages that are necessary to their audiences; for example, a message about changes in employee benefits would be distributed to everyone in the company, but information about a specific project would be sent only to the employees involved. According to Lee, Suncor's communication managers "think through and document all our key processes—everything from how we put out a news release to how we develop a comprehensive communication plan."

It's up to Sue Lee to make sure that both internal and external communications not only keep employees and local communities informed of Suncor's activities, but also engage them in shaping the company's direction. If you were in Sue Lee's position, what would you do to keep communication flowing both within and outside of the organization smoothly and efficiently? How would you ensure that everyone receives the information they need? How would you overcome all the possible barriers to communication as you prepare the many messages you send to all of Suncor's stakeholders?[1]

Images are influential communication tools. Suncor Energy uses pictures of alternative power generators in their brochures and on their Web site to communicate their environmental mission.

Achieving Career Success Through Effective Communication

OBJECTIVE 1 Explain why effective communication is important to organizations and how it can help you succeed in business.

Communication enables organizations to function. Effective communication helps you and your organization succeed.

Stakeholders are the groups who are affected by a company's activities and who in return influence the company.

Organizations such as Suncor Energy understand that achieving success in today's workplace is closely tied to the ability of their employees and managers to communicate effectively. **Communication** is the process of sending and receiving messages. However, communication is effective only when people understand each other, stimulate others to take action, and encourage others to think in new ways.

Effective communication offers you and your organization many benefits (see Figure 1-1 below). When you communicate effectively, you increase productivity, both yours and that of the people around you. Effective communication helps you anticipate problems, make decisions, coordinate work flow, supervise others, develop relationships, and promote products. It helps you shape the impressions you make on your colleagues, employees, supervisors, investors, and customers. It assists you to understand and to respond to the needs of these **stakeholders**—the groups that your company affects in some way and who themselves have some influence on your company. For example, as a customer or an employee of a particular business, you are a stakeholder. Other stakeholders include government regulators who create guidelines businesses must observe and the media, who report on business and influence public opinion.

Without effective communication, people misunderstand each other and misinterpret information. "Unclear communication not only results in errors and missed deadlines, but also lies at the root of many other serious workplace issues, such as low morale and poor job performance," says Diane Domeyer, executive director of Office Team, a temporary employment firm.[2] Canada's leading executives believe that 15 percent of each workweek, or almost eight weeks per year, is wasted because of poor communication.[3] Whether you are pitching a business proposal, responding to a customer inquiry, or explaining a new process to your teammates, your ability to communicate effectively increases your chance for career success (see Figure 1-1 below).[4] Moreover, improving your communication skills will help you adapt to the changes occurring in today's workplace.

FIGURE 1-1 The Benefits of Effective Communication

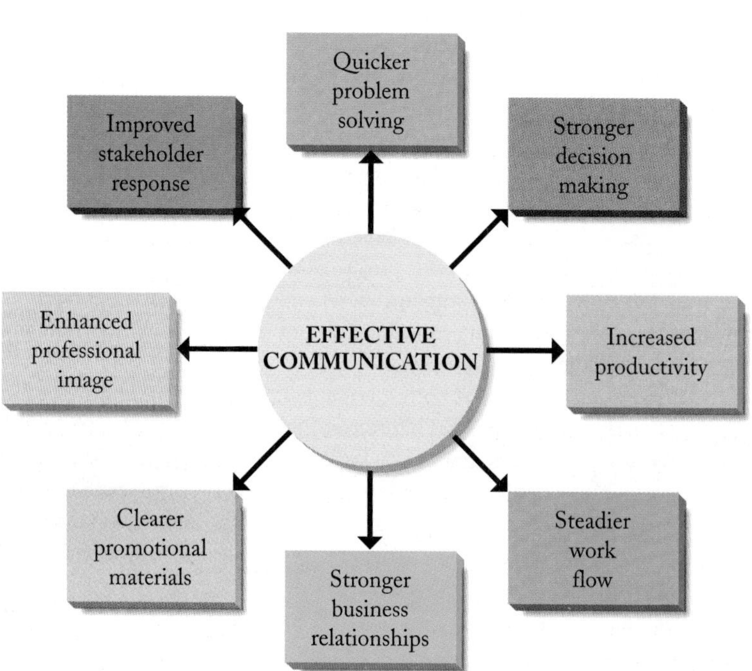

Adapting to the Changing Workplace

OBJECTIVE 2 Discuss three changes in the workplace that are intensifying the need to communicate effectively.

Good communication skills have always been important in the workplace. They are even more vital today. Effective communication helps us adapt to the globalization of the marketplace, the increased use of teams, the continuing advances in technology, and the ability to access vast amounts of information.

COMMUNICATING IN THE TECHNOLOGICAL WORKPLACE

Technology brings new and better tools to the workplace, increasing the speed and frequency of communication and allowing people from opposite ends of the world to work together seamlessly, 24 hours a day. The Internet, e-mail, cell phones, pagers, voice mail, and faxes make it possible for more and more people to telecommute from home, the road, and satellite offices around the globe. Many companies offer telecommuting arrangements for their employees. Bell Canada has about 5000 teleworkers, one of Canada's largest programs, and about 25 percent of IBM Canada's workforce, or, about 2300 people, telework almost full time. The Canadian Telework Association claims that in 2001, 1.5 million Canadians performed their jobs by linking electronically to their offices from home.[5]

The increased use of technology in the workplace not only facilitates new working arrangements but also requires employees to communicate more effectively. Technology showcases your communication skills—your writing skills are revealed in every e-mail message, and your verbal skills are revealed both in telephone conversations and teleconferences.[6] Technology also increases the frequency with which you communicate, and it extends the reach of your messages. **Intranets**, which are private corporate Internets, are an efficient way for employees to access a variety of company information, such as benefit and pension plan updates, company newsletters, and special announcements. **Extranets** are the extension of private networks to certain outsiders such as suppliers; companies use Extranets for such functions as electronic invoicing and ordering. Both Intranets and Extranets facilitate communication among employees, managers, customers, suppliers, and investors. Moreover, the need to communicate effectively with people outside the organization is increased through **electronic commerce (e-commerce)**, the buying and selling of goods and services online. If you work for a company that transacts business electronically, you will be called upon to use e-mail to answer queries, describe new products, or explain delays in filling orders. Your ability to communicate clearly will affect your employer's success in the electronic marketplace.

E-commerce is the buying and selling of goods and services over the Internet.

Electronic commerce intensifies the need to communicate effectively.

The increases in international business dealings and in the diversity of the workforce create communication challenges.

COMMUNICATING WITH A CULTURALLY DIVERSE WORK FORCE

More and more businesses today are crossing national boundaries to compete on a global scale. Over 2 million North Americans now work for foreign employers.[7] Increased globalization and workforce diversity mean that employees must understand the laws, customs, and business practices of many countries besides being able to communicate with people who speak different languages. Between 1991 and 2001, 1.8 million people immigrated to Canada. Altogether, Canadians come from more than 200 different ethnic backgrounds. In Toronto, which attracts the highest percentage of new immigrants, there are 62 different ethnic groups of at least 10 000 people.[8] It has been said that Canada's multiculturalism "makes us so well liked around the world."[9] In 2000 Canada exported 43 percent of its gross domestic product.

Is telecommuting right for you? Can you perform your duties via phone or e-mail? Do you have the self-discipline to work in isolation, away from your colleagues and managers? List the pros and cons of telecommuting to decide if you could work from the comfort of your home.

Overcoming language barriers is just one of the many communication challenges employees face in today's workplace. Chapter 3 discusses intercultural communication in detail and explains how understanding other backgrounds, personalities, and perceptions helps you become a more effective communicator.

COMMUNICATING IN TEAM-BASED ORGANIZATIONS

When working in teams you should be able to clarify, confirm, give feedback, explore ideas, and credit others.

The "command-and-control" style of traditional management structures is ineffective in today's fast-paced, e-commerce environment.[10] Successful companies such as Suncor Energy no longer limit decisions to a few managers at the top of a formal hierarchy. Instead, organizations use teams and collaborative work groups to make the decisions required to succeed in a global and competitive marketplace. The challenges of working in teams increase as more and more team members come from different departments, perform different functions, and have diverse cultural backgrounds. As Chapter 2 discusses in detail, in order to function in a team-based organization, you must be able to clarify, listen to, and understand others. You must also give balanced feedback, explore ideas, keep everyone involved, and credit others' work.[11] Moreover, you must understand how groups interact, reach decisions, work collaboratively, and resolve conflict. Clearly, working in teams requires effective communication, but understanding this need is only the first step toward developing effective communication skills.

Setting Your Course for Effective Communication

Many companies provide employees with a variety of opportunities for communication skills training. Some companies offer seminars and workshops on handling common oral communication situations, such as dealing with customers, managing subordinates, and getting along with co-workers. Others offer training in computers and other electronic means of communication. But even though you may ultimately receive training on the job, don't wait. Start mastering business communication skills right now, during this course. People with good communication skills have an advantage in today's workplace.

Practice helps you improve your communication skills.

One way to improve your communication skills is to practice. Lack of experience may be the only obstacle preventing you from creating effective messages, whether written or spoken. Perhaps you have a limited vocabulary, or maybe you're uncertain about questions of grammar, punctuation, and style. Perhaps you're simply frightened by the idea of writing something or of appearing before a group. People aren't "born" writers or speakers; the more they speak and write, the more their skills improve. Someone who has written ten reports is usually better at the task than someone who has written only two.

Constructive criticism also helps you improve your communication skills.

You learn from experience, and some of the most important lessons are learned through failure. Learning what *not* to do is just as important as learning what *to* do. One of the great advantages of taking a course in business communication is that you get to practice in an environment that provides honest and constructive criticism. A course of this kind also gives you an understanding of practical techniques, so you can avoid making costly mistakes on the job.

This course prepares you to handle communication tasks on the job.

No matter what career you pursue, this course prepares you to handle the communication tasks that await you. This book helps you discover how to collaborate in teams, listen well, deliver effective presentations, and ensure successful meetings. You'll also learn about communicating across cultures and through the Internet. This book presents a three-step process for composing business messages. It gives tips for writing letters, memos, e-mail messages, and reports, and it provides a collection of good and bad communication examples with annotated comments to guide you through your own communication efforts. Finally, it explains how to write effective résumés and application letters and how to handle employment interviews. But before you delve into those topics, it's important that you understand the experience of communicating in an organizational setting.

CAREER OPPORTUNITY IN ALBERTA

Sales & General Manager

SPITZ Sales Inc. has an immediate and exciting opportunity in their rapidly growing International Snack Food Sales and Distribution Company. We are seeking a dynamic goal-oriented and enthusiastic candidate. You will be responsible to the owners of the company and have the opportunity to achieve success through your management of our sales team in Canada and in the USA. If you want an opportunity to grow with a progressive industry, experience and be part of a fast growing community full of opportunity and promise, then we need to talk to you.

REQUIREMENTS:

The successful candidate will have experience in the food industry and be proficient in negotiating national sales contracts, possess excellent verbal and communication skills, and be a leader within a team environment. The ideal individual must be experienced in overall corporate projections and budgeting.

Qualified applicants please apply by email or facsimile with detailed resume and references by Monday, April 2003, to:

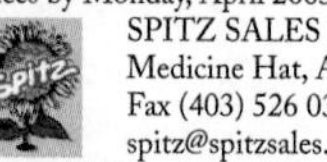

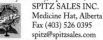

SPITZ SALES INC.
Medicine Hat, Alberta
Fax (403) 526 0395
spitz@spitzsales.com

We would like to thank all interested parties. However, only applicants considered for an interview will be considered.

Most companies want employees who can communicate effectively. What sorts of jobs have you held that required you to communicate with co-workers and with customers or clients? What were your specific communication tasks, both oral and written?

Communicating in Organizations

OBJECTIVE 3 Describe how organizations share information internally and externally.

To succeed, organizations must share information with people both inside and outside of the company.

Whether an organization is large, small, or virtual, sharing information among employees and managers, and with the outside world, is the glue that binds the organization together. When you join a company such as Suncor, you become a link in its information chain. Whether you're a high-level manager or an entry-level employee, you have information that others need to perform their jobs, and others have information that is crucial to you.

In a business with only five or six employees, much information can be exchanged casually and directly by phone, e-mail, or interoffice memo. Short announcements are a typical kind of memorandum. For example, the memo shown in Figure 1-2, below, tells information systems staff about their new director. Notice that while this memo communicates routine information, the tone is friendly, which helps to create an agreeable workplace atmosphere. Large organizations, such as Bata Shoes, have thousands of employees working around the world, and transmitting the right informa-

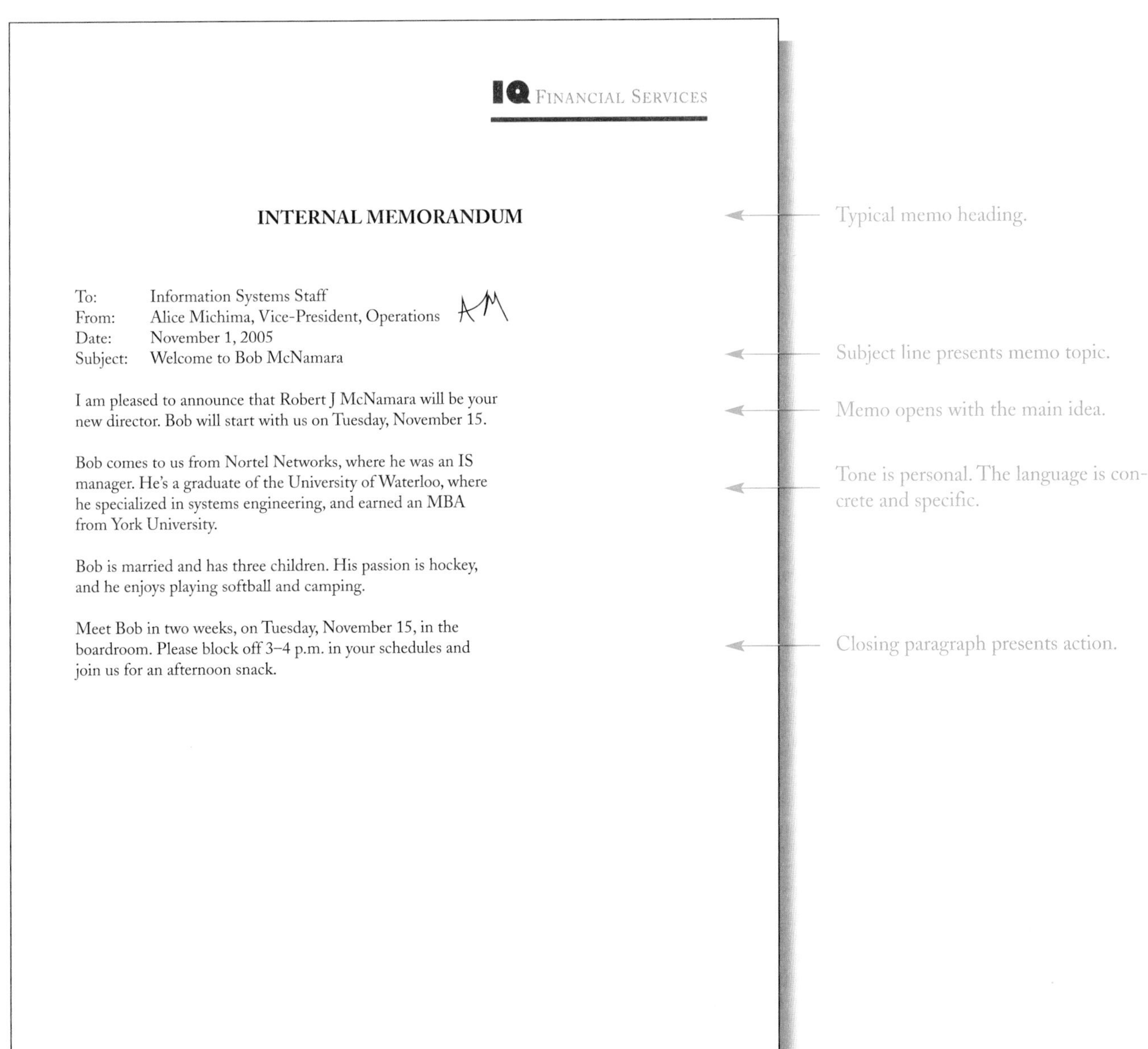
IQ FINANCIAL SERVICES

INTERNAL MEMORANDUM

To: Information Systems Staff
From: Alice Michima, Vice-President, Operations
Date: November 1, 2005
Subject: Welcome to Bob McNamara

I am pleased to announce that Robert J McNamara will be your new director. Bob will start with us on Tuesday, November 15.

Bob comes to us from Nortel Networks, where he was an IS manager. He's a graduate of the University of Waterloo, where he specialized in systems engineering, and earned an MBA from York University.

Bob is married and has three children. His passion is hockey, and he enjoys playing softball and camping.

Meet Bob in two weeks, on Tuesday, November 15, in the boardroom. Please block off 3–4 p.m. in your schedules and join us for an afternoon snack.

FIGURE 1-2 In-Depth Critique: Internal Communication by Memo

tion to the right people at the right time is a real challenge. To meet this challenge, organizations rely on a variety of **channels**, such as memos, reports, faxes, employee newsletters, or Intranets to communicate internally and externally.

Internal Communication

You are a contact point in both the external and internal communication networks.

Internal communication refers to the exchange of information and ideas within an organization. Communication among the members of an organization is essential for effective functioning. As an employee, you are in a position to observe firsthand attitudes and behaviours that your supervisors and co-workers cannot see: a customer's reaction to a product display, a supplier's brief hesitation before agreeing to a delivery date, or a slowdown in the flow of customers. Managers and co-workers need such minute information in order to do their jobs. If you don't pass that information along, nobody will—because nobody else knows. Communicating freely helps employees develop a clear sense of the organization's mission and helps managers identify and react quickly to potential problems. To maintain a healthy flow of information within the organization, effective communicators use both formal and informal channels.

FORMAL COMMUNICATION NETWORK

The formal flow of information follows the official chain of command.

The **formal communication network** is typically shown as an organizational chart such as the one in Figure 1-3, below. Such charts summarize the lines of authority; each box represents a link in the chain of command, and each line represents a formal **channel**, or route, for the transmission of official messages. Information may travel down, up, and across an organization's formal hierarchy.

Information flows up, down, and across the formal hierarchy.

- **Downward flow.** Organizational decisions are usually made at the top and then flow down to the people who will carry them out. Most of what filters downward is geared toward helping employees do their jobs. From top to bottom, each person must understand each message, apply it, and pass it along.
- **Upward flow.** To solve problems and make intelligent decisions, managers must learn what's going on in the organization. Because they must delegate work to be efficient, executives depend on lower-level employees to furnish them with

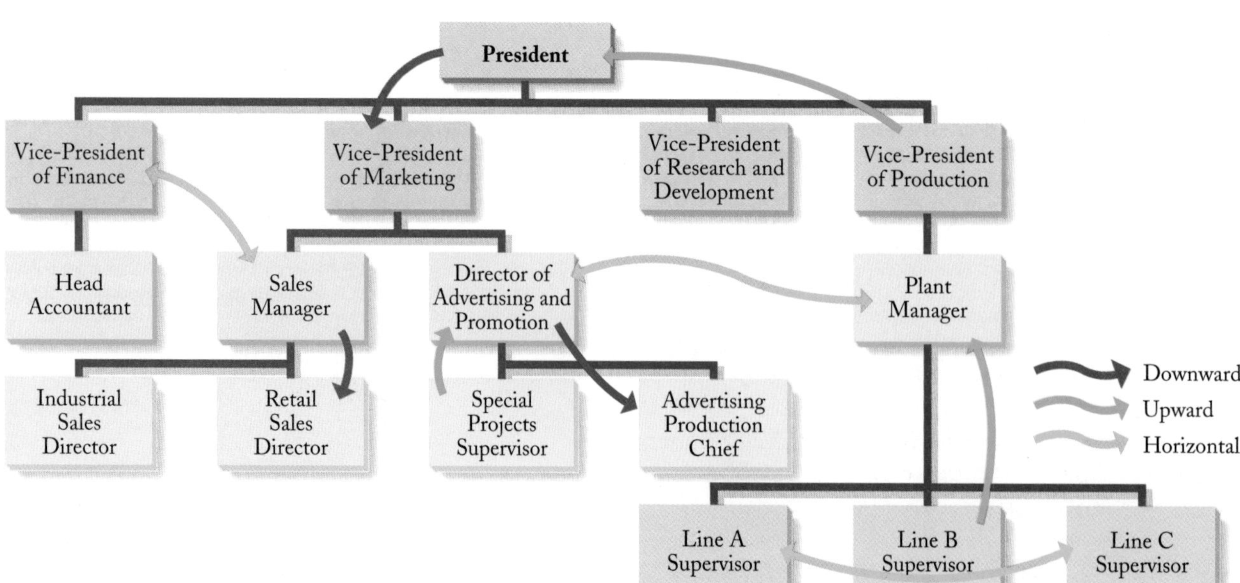

FIGURE 1-3 Formal Communication

accurate, timely reports on problems, emerging trends, opportunities for improvement, grievances, and performance.

- **Horizontal flow.** Communication also flows laterally, from one department to another. This horizontal communication helps employees share information and coordinate tasks. Project teams are one example of horizontal communication: in these teams, employees from different departments work together to solve problems and improve the operation of their company.

Formal organizational charts illustrate how information is supposed to flow. In actual practice, however, employees across the organizational hierarchy communicate with each other informally.

INFORMAL COMMUNICATION NETWORK

Every organization has an **informal communication network**—a **grapevine**—that supplements official channels. As people go about their work, they have casual conversations with their friends in the office. Although many of these conversations deal with personal matters, one study found that about 86 percent of the information that travels along the grapevine pertains to business.[12] Some executives are wary of the informal communication network, possibly because it threatens their power to control the flow of information. However, smart managers tap into the grapevine. It provides them with a sense of employees' concerns and anxieties. The grapevine also helps employers determine if their formal means of communication are effective.[13] Eliminating the grapevine is virtually impossible, so sophisticated companies minimize its importance by making certain that the official word gets out.

The **informal communication network** carries information along the organization's unofficial lines of activity and power.

The **grapevine** is an important source of information in most organizations.

External Communication

Just as internal communication carries information up, down, and across the organization, **external communication** carries it into and out of the organization. Companies constantly exchange messages with customers, vendors, distributors, competitors, investors, journalists, and community representatives. Often this external communication is carefully orchestrated—especially during a crisis. At other times it occurs informally as part of routine business operations.

The **external communication** network links the organization with the outside world of customers, suppliers, competitors, and investors.

FORMAL OUTSIDE COMMUNICATION

Carefully constructed letters convey an important message to outsiders about the quality of your organization. For example, when canoeing enthusiasts request a catalogue from Swift Canoe & Kayak, they also receive a letter summarizing how to select and order products. External messages such as these not only provide useful information, but also establish goodwill between the company and its potential customers, cultivating a relationship that may lead to a purchase (see Figure 1-4 on page 8). Companies use external communication to create a favourable impression.

One important form of communication is the Internet. A company Web site can impart crucial information both inside the organization (using an Intranet) and outside (via the Internet). Web sites can communicate a company's image to the outside world and a company's culture to employees.

Whether by letter, Web, phone, fax, or videotape, good communication is the first step in creating a favourable impression. Extremely careful planning is required for messages such as statements to the press,

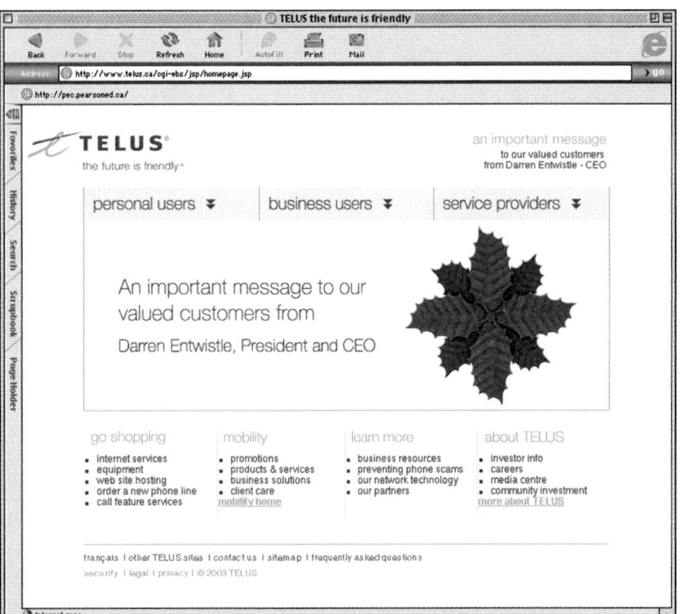

Company Web sites are designed to project a particular image. What image does the Web site of Telus, a telecommunications company, project? How would you describe this image?

The first paragraph establishes the company's credibility by describing its products and affiliation with a nearby outdoor equipment retailer.

The second and third paragraphs provide helpful information about how products can be selected and ordered. The detail provided is meant to reassure readers that their questions will be answered by qualified salespeople.

The fourth and fifth paragraphs continue to reassure readers with detail about shipping and the warranty. The light tone created in the beginning of paragraph five enhances the letter's personal tone.

The final paragraph reinforces key ideas in the message by inviting readers to examine the enclosed catalogue and repeating the company's interest in helping them.

August 16, 2005

Dear Ms. McCallum,

Thank you for your interest in our products. Swift Canoe & Kayak is a canoe and kayak manufacturing and retailing business, located just outside Algonquin Park. Many of our products have been developed in conjunction with our neighbouring business, Algonquin Outfitters.

To purchase a Swift canoe or kayak, you can visit one of our two factory-direct outlets or attend one of the many factory sales we hold throughout the province each spring and fall. Both our Swift stores and all our special events offer on-site test paddling and a tremendous selection. Our annual newsletter about our stores and sales events is available upon request.

Many people choose to order their boat ahead of time or consult with one of our staff members before test paddling and purchasing our canoes and kayaks. In this case, we recommend that you first read through the catalogue, then call us and talk to one of our factory sales representatives. They are all expert paddlers, non-commissioned, and available from 9 AM to 6 PM, seven days a week. You can also visit our Web site and use our interactive canoe selector!

When we receive your order, we will send confirmation and give you a date when your boat will be finished. Most orders can be picked up immediately, while custom orders may take two to four weeks. We can ship your boat to any of the sales events we hold. Factory-direct shipping is also available throughout most of Ontario.

Next is the hard part—waiting for your custom-made Swift craft! When it is ready, it will come with a Swift Owner's Manual and lots of information on how to take care of your boat. For your added assurance, all of our boats are backed with a lifetime warranty and Swift's personal guarantee to provide years of paddling enjoyment.

Please take the time to review our information. We're looking forward to serving your needs.

Happy Paddling,

Karen McDonald
Swift Canoe & Kayak–Algonquin
www.swiftcanoe.com

R.R. #1, Oxtongue Lake, Dwight, ON P0A 1H0
Phone: 705-635-1167 Fax: 705-635-9456 e-mail: swift@bconnex.net

FIGURE 1–4 In-Depth Critique: External Communication by Letter

letters to investors, advertisements, and price announcements. Therefore, such documents are often drafted by a marketing or public relations team—a group of individuals whose sole job is creating and managing the flow of formal messages to outsiders.

The way a company handles a crisis can have a profound effect on the organization's subsequent performance.

One of the most visible tasks of professional business communicators is to help management plan for and respond to crises—which can range from environmental accidents or sabotage situations to strikes, massive product failure, major litigation, or even an abrupt change in management. To minimize the impact of any crisis, expert communicators advise managers to communicate honestly, openly, and often (see Table 1-1 on page 9).[14]

INFORMAL OUTSIDE COMMUNICATION

Although companies often communicate with outsiders in a formal manner, informal contacts with outsiders are important for learning about customer needs. As a member of an organization, you are an important informal channel for communicating with

TABLE 1–1 What to Do in a Crisis

When a Crisis Hits:	
Do	***Don't***
Do prepare for trouble ahead of time by identifying potential problems, appointing and training a response team, and preparing and testing a crisis management plan. **Do** get top management involved as soon as the crisis hits. **Do** set up a news centre for company representatives and the media, equipped with phones, computers, and faxes. • Issue frequent news updates daily, and have trained personnel on call to respond to questions around the clock. • Provide complete information kits to the media as soon as possible. • Prevent conflicting statements and provide continuity by appointing a single person, trained in advance, to speak for the company. • Tell receptionists to direct all calls to the news centre. **Do** tell the whole story-openly, completely, and honestly. If you are at fault, apologize. **Do** demonstrate the company's concern by your statements and your actions.	**Don't** blame anyone for anything. **Don't** speculate in public. **Don't** refuse to answer questions. **Don't** release information that will violate anyone's right to privacy. **Don't** use the crisis to pitch products or services. **Don't** play favourites with media representatives.

the outside world. In the course of your daily activities, you unconsciously absorb bits and pieces of information that add to the collective knowledge of your company. What's more, every time you speak for or about your company, you send a message. Many outsiders may form their impression of your organization on the basis of the subtle, unconscious clues you transmit through your tone of voice, facial expression, and general appearance.

Every employee informally accumulates facts and impressions that contribute to the organization's collective understanding of the outside world.

Top managers rely heavily on informal contacts with outsiders to exchange information that might be useful to their companies. Much of their networking involves interaction with fellow executives. However, plenty of high-level managers recognize the value of keeping in touch with "the real world" by creating opportunities to talk with and get feedback from customers and frontline employees. To facilitate this exchange of information, companies strive to minimize disruptions to the communication process. For the remainder of this chapter we will explain the communication process, the barriers that can block it, and how to overcome these barriers.

Understanding the Communication Process

OBJECTIVE 4 Identify and briefly define the six phases of the communication process.

Communication doesn't occur haphazardly. Nor does it happen all at once. It is more than a single act. Communication is a dynamic, transactional, or two-way, process that can be broken into six phases (See Figure 1-5 on page 10).

The communication process consists of six phases linking sender and receiver.

1. **The sender has an idea.** You conceive an idea and want to share it.

2. **The sender encodes the idea.** When you put your idea into a message that your receiver will understand, you are **encoding** it. In other words, you are deciding on the message's form (word, facial expression, gesture), length, organization, tone, and style—all of which depend on your idea, your audience, and your personal style or mood.

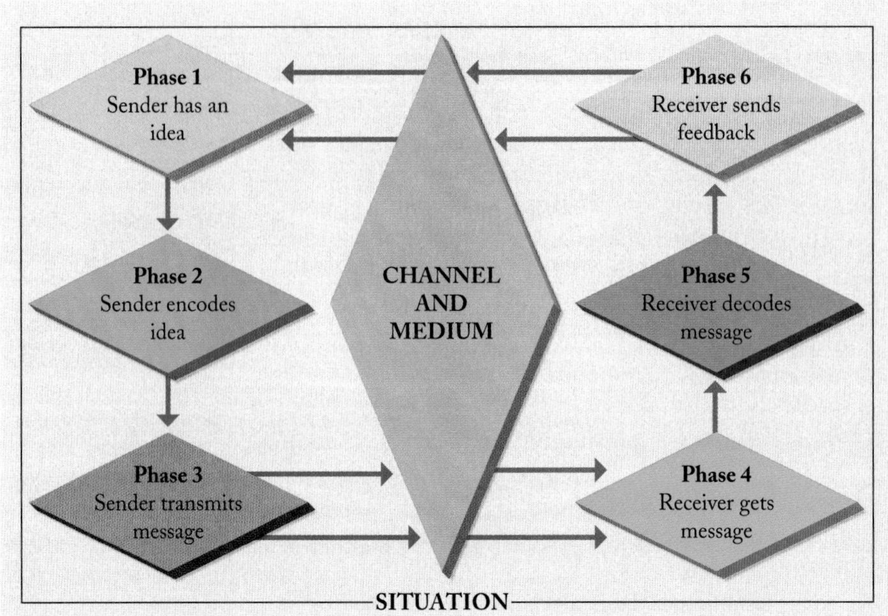

FIGURE 1-5 The Communication Process

3. The sender transmits the message. To physically transmit your message to your receiver, you select a **medium** (telephone, letter, memo, e-mail, report, face-to-face exchange). These choices depend on your message, your audience's location, your need for speed, and the level of formality required.

4. The receiver gets the message. For communication to occur, your receiver must first get the message. If you send a letter, your receiver has to read it before understanding it. If you're giving a speech, your listeners have to be able to hear you, and they have to be paying attention.

5. The receiver decodes the message. Your receiver must **decode**—that is, absorb and understand—your message. The decoded message must then be stored in the receiver's mind. If obstacles do not block the process, the receiver interprets your message correctly; that is, the receiver assigns the same meaning to your words as you intended and responds in the way you desire.

Feedback is your audience's response; it enables you to evaluate your message's effectiveness.

6. The receiver sends feedback. Feedback is your receiver's response. After decoding your message, the receiver responds in some way and signals that response to you. Feedback enables you to evaluate the effectiveness of your message: If your audience doesn't understand what you mean, you can tell by the response and refine your message.

As Figure 1-5 illustrates, the communication process is repeated until both parties have finished expressing themselves.[15]

Recognizing Communication Barriers

OBJECTIVE 5 Identify and briefly discuss four types of communication barriers.

When you send a message, you intend to communicate meaning, but the message itself contains no meaning. The meaning exists in your mind and in the mind of your receiver. To understand each other, you and your receiver must share similar meanings for words, gestures, tone of voice, and other symbols.

The communication process is effective only when each step is successful. Ideas cannot be communicated if any step in this process is blocked (skipped or completed incorrectly). When interference in the communication process distorts or obscures the sender's meaning, it is called a **communication barrier**, or **noise**. Recognizing communication barriers is the first step in overcoming them. Examples of barriers to

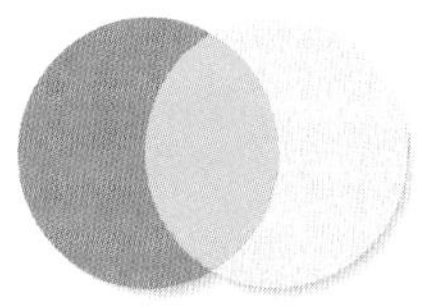

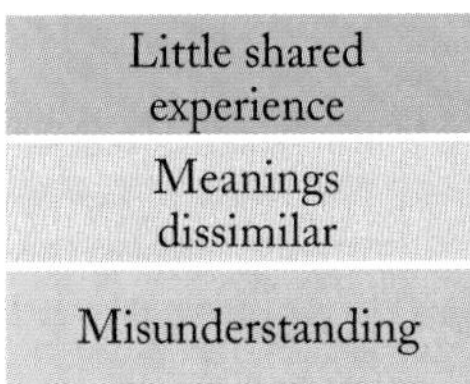

FIGURE 1-6 How Shared Experience Affects Understanding

effective communication include perceptual differences, restrictive environments, distractions, and deceptive communication tactics.

Communication barriers block the communication process.

Perceptual Differences

Even when two people experience the same event, their mental images are not identical. When sending a message, you choose the details that seem important to you. However, when receiving a message, you try to fit new details into your existing pattern, and if a detail doesn't quite fit, you're inclined to distort the information rather than rearrange your pattern.

Our **perception** affects how we see the world and even how we develop language. For example, consider the word *cookie.* You might think of oatmeal, chocolate chip, and sugar cookies. However, someone from Europe may think of meringues, florentines, and spritz. You both agree on the general concept of *cookie,* but your precise images differ.

Perception is people's individual interpretation of the sensory world around them.

Language is only one of the many differences that exist between cultures. Communicating with someone from another country may be the most extreme example of how different cultures can block communication. But even in your own culture, you and the receiver of your message may differ in age, education, social status, economic position, religion, and life experience. The more experiences you share with another person, the more likely you are to share perception and thus share meaning (see Figure 1-6).

Perception is strongly influenced by cultural differences.

Restrictive Environments

Every link in the communication chain is open to error. By the time a message travels all the way up or down the chain, it may bear little resemblance to the original idea. If a company's formal communication network limits the flow of information in any direction (upward, downward, or horizontal), then communication becomes fragmented. Lower-level employees may obtain only enough information to perform their own isolated tasks, learning little about other areas, so only the people at the very top of the organization have an understanding of the entire situation.

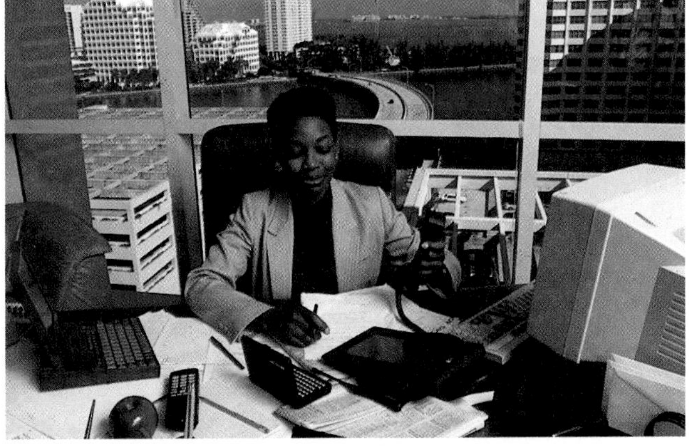

What kinds of communication barriers do you see in this picture? What obstacles might prevent this employee from performing her work productively?

When managers use a directive and authoritarian leadership style, information moves down the chain of command but not up. In a poll of 638 employees, 90 percent said they had good ideas on how their companies could run more successfully. Yet more than 50 percent said they were prevented from communicating these thoughts because of a lack of management interest and a lack of effective means for sharing their ideas.[16]

Distractions

Your audience is more likely to receive your message accurately if nothing physical interrupts or distorts the message.

Communication barriers are often physical distractions: bad connections, poor acoustics, or poorly formatted reports. Although noise of this sort seems trivial, it can block an otherwise effective message. An uncomfortable chair, poor lighting, health problems, or some other irritating condition might distract the person receiving your message.

Listening ability decreases when information is difficult to understand and when it has little meaning for the listener.

Another kind of distraction is poor listening. We all let our minds wander now and then, and we are especially likely to drift off when we are forced to listen to information that is difficult to understand or that has little direct bearing on our own lives. We are even more likely to lose interest if we are tired or concerned about other matters.

Emotions block the communication process.

Emotional distractions can be difficult to overcome. When you are upset, hostile, or fearful, you have a hard time shaping a message objectively. If the person receiving your message is emotional, he or she may ignore or distort your message. It's practically impossible to avoid all communication when emotions are involved, but you must recognize that emotional messages have a greater potential for misunderstanding.

Today's businesspeople are plagued by message overload.

Information overload is the rising volume of messages from all sources, technological and conventional.

The sheer number of messages can also be distracting. One study found that office workers receive about 30 e-mail messages a day and take about two hours to read, forward, and reply to them.[17] With additional types of communication—phone calls, faxes, voice mail, hard-copy letters, memos, and reports—many executives are overwhelmed by **information overload,** the increased volume of messages from all sources.

Going Online

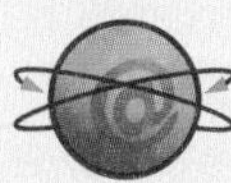

Using the Internet to Explore International Business Communication

Among its many advantages, the International Association of Business Communicators (IABC) offers analyses of issues, case studies, models of communication practices, and advice. All of these can help you develop strategies for managing communication in international business. The IABC is a source for real-world examples, as well as manuals and handbooks on a variety of topics. For students, communicators seeking jobs, and employers, IABC provides a "career and job posting area." When you log on to this site, you'll find an updated list of topics on the IABC homepage, including news items and announcements of conferences and workshops.

www.iabc.com

To link directly to this site, visit our Companion Web site at www.pearsoned.ca/thill and look for the Chapter 1 resources.

Deceptive Tactics

Language itself is made up of words that carry values. So merely by expressing your ideas in a certain way, you influence how others perceive your message, and you shape expectations and behaviors.[18] An organization cannot create illegal or unethical messages and still be credible or successful in the long run. Still, some business communicators try to manipulate their receivers by using deceptive tactics.

Deceptive communicators may exaggerate benefits, quote inaccurate statistics, or hide negative information behind an optimistic attitude. They may state opinions as facts, leave out crucial information, or portray graphic data unfairly. Unscrupulous communicators may seek personal gain by making others look better or worse than they are. And they may allow personal preferences to influence their own perception and the perception of others.

Overcoming Barriers to Improve Communication

Effective communicators work hard at perfecting the messages they deliver. When they make mistakes, they learn from them. If a memo they've written doesn't get the response they hoped for, they change their approach the next time. If a meeting they're running gets out of control or proves unproductive, they will manage the next meeting differently. If they find that they have to explain themselves over and over again, they reevaluate their choice of communication medium or rework their message.

Just think about the people you know. Which of them would you call successful communicators? What do these people have in common? Chances are, the individuals on your list share the following five traits:

1. **Perception.** They are able to predict how you will receive their message. They anticipate your reaction and shape the message accordingly. They read your response correctly and constantly adjust to correct any misunderstanding.
2. **Precision.** They use language accurately. When they finish expressing themselves, you will share the same mental picture with them.

3. **Credibility.** They are believable. You have faith in the substance of their message. You trust their information and their intentions.

4. **Control.** They shape your response. Depending on their purpose, they can make you calm down, change your mind, or take action.

5. **Congeniality.** They maintain friendly, pleasant relations with you. Regardless of whether you agree with them, good communicators command your respect and goodwill. You are willing to work with them again, despite your differences.

OBJECTIVE 6 Discuss four guidelines for overcoming communication barriers.

Effective communication requires perception, precision, credibility, control, and congeniality.

In the coming chapters we present real-life examples of both good and bad communication and explain what's good or bad about them. You'll notice that four themes keep surfacing: (1) adopting an audience-centred approach; (2) fostering an open communication climate; (3) creating lean, efficient messages; and (4) committing to ethical communication. These guidelines will help you overcome barriers and improve your communication. Here's a closer look at them.

Guideline 1: Adopt an Audience-Centred Approach

When you adopt an **audience-centred approach** to communication, you focus on and care about the people receiving your message. You make every effort to get your message across in a way that is meaningful to the receiver. To create an effective message, you need to learn as much as possible about the biases, education, age, status, and style of your audience. When you address strangers, try to find out more about them. If that's impossible, try to project yourself into their position by using your common sense and imagination. Whatever the tactic, you need to write and speak from your audience's point of view to help your audience understand and accept your message.

Using an **audience-centred approach** means keeping your audience in mind at all times when communicating.

By focusing on your audience, you will find it easier to follow the three other guidelines for overcoming barriers that prevent you from communicating effectively. You will work for an open communication climate both inside and outside your organization because you want to know what your audience's needs are and what they think of your message. You will create lean, efficient messages and use communication technology responsibly as you value your audience's time and can anticipate your audience's expectations. And because you sincerely wish to satisfy your audience's needs, you will approach communication situations with good intentions and high ethical standards. Throughout this book, you'll find important advice on how best to use the audience-centered approach to communication. For example, Chapter 4 (Planning Business Messages) presents in-depth information on learning about your audience and focusing on your audience's needs.

The organization's communication climate affects the quantity and quality of the information exchanged.

As anchor of CBC's news program *The National*, Peter Mansbridge addresses a Canada-wide audience daily. He must be careful to use words that mean the same thing to everyone, regardless of background or region of the country. Your chances of being easily understood increase if you are as accurate and as specific as you can be.

Guideline 2: Foster an Open Communication Climate

An organization's communication climate is a reflection of its **corporate culture**: the mixture of values, traditions, and habits that give a company its atmosphere or personality. Successful companies such as Suncor encourage employee contributions by making sure that communication flows freely down, up, and across the organizational chart. They encourage candor and honesty, and their employees feel free to confess their mistakes, disagree with supervisors and managers, and express their opinions. These companies create an open climate in two ways: by modifying the number of organizational levels and by facilitating feedback.

MODIFYING THE NUMBER OF ORGANIZATIONAL LEVELS

One way to foster an open communication climate is to reduce the number of levels in the organization's structure. Having fewer levels, which characterize a flat structure, creates a wide span of control with more people reporting to each supervisor. Consequently, a flat organizational structure is less likely to introduce distortion than

Adjusting organizational levels can improve the communication climate.

a tall structure, which has a narrow span of control. Flatter organizations enable managers not only to share information with colleagues and employees, but also to include employees in decision making, goal setting, and problem solving.[19] A Montreal software company specializing in Internet privacy, Zero-Knowledge keeps its organizational structure relatively flat. New employees work alongside top-level managers, and decisions, whether from upper management or staff, are subject to open and intense scrutiny at all-staff meetings.[20] Although flat is not necessarily better, more and more companies are flattening their structure in an effort to cut costs, boost productivity, and get closer to customers. Still, designing too few formal channels and having too many people report to a single individual can block effective communication by overburdening that key person.

FACILITATING FEEDBACK

Giving your audience a chance to provide feedback is crucial to maintaining an open communication climate. According to an American Express survey, what employees want the most from employers is personal feedback (money was rated second). But many managers are eager to avoid conflict, so they avoid giving frank feedback to underperforming employees. A consequence of this reluctance to criticize is an overall lessening of organizational effectiveness.[21]

Encourage feedback by
- Asking specific questions
- Encouraging your audience to express general reactions
- Being receptive to your audience's responses

To encourage feedback, many companies use techniques such as employee surveys, open-door policies, company newsletters, memos, e-mail, and task forces. Still, feedback isn't always easy to get. You may have to draw out the other person by asking specific questions. Also encourage your audience to express general reactions; you can gain useful information this way. Since taking the helm at Suncor in 1991, CEO Rick George has fostered a culture in which management routinely consults with staff about Suncor's business decisions and performance. This open communication has resulted in early identification of problems and the generation of innovative ideas. Under George's leadership, Suncor's oil production increased from 60 000 barrels a day to 225 000, an increase of almost 400 percent.[22]

Guideline 3: Create Lean, Efficient Messages

You must distinguish between necessary and unnecessary information.

Too much information is as bad as too little; it reduces the audience's ability to concentrate on the most important data. You must realize that some information is unnecessary, and you must make necessary information easily available. Try to give information meaning, rather than just passing it on, and set priorities for dealing with the overall flow of the message. Successful communicators overcome information overload and other communication barriers by reducing the number of messages, decreasing possible distractions, and using technology wisely.

REDUCING THE NUMBER OF MESSAGES

Organizations save time and money by sending only necessary messages.

A good way to make your messages more effective is to send fewer of them. Think twice before sending one. For example, if a written message merely adds to the information overload, it's probably better left unsent or handled some other way—by a quick telephone call or a face-to-face chat. Keeping down the number of messages reduces the chance of information overload.

MINIMIZING DISTRACTIONS

Control physical distractions such as a messy appearance of written messages and poor acoustics in oral presentations.

Although you don't have power over every eventuality, the key to overcoming distracting barriers is control. To overcome physical barriers, exercise as much control as possible over the physical transmission link: If you're preparing a written document, make sure its appearance doesn't detract from your message. If you're delivering an oral presentation, choose a setting that permits the audience to see and hear you without straining. When you're the audience, learn to concentrate on the message rather than on any distractions.

Overcome emotional barriers by recognizing the feelings that arise in yourself and in others as you communicate and by attempting to control these emotions. For example, choose neutral words to avoid arousing strong feelings unduly. Avoid affecting attitudes, placing blame, and generally reacting subjectively. Most important, be aware of the greater potential for misunderstanding that accompanies emotional messages.

Do your best to control emotions before they block the communication process.

As a listener, overcome listening barriers by paraphrasing what you've understood. Try to view the situation through the speaker's eyes, and resist jumping to conclusions. Listen without interrupting, and clarify meaning by asking questions that do not intimidate or demean. As a speaker, help listeners by connecting your subject to their needs, using language that is clear and vivid, and relating your subject to familiar ideas. The greater part of this book focuses on how to control your message and the communication process.

Overcome listening barriers by doing everything you can to understand and provide feedback.

USING TECHNOLOGY RESPONSIBLY

The Internet is just one part of the technological advance in electronic communication. Together with voice mail, teleconferencing, e-mail, and wireless technology, the Internet has revolutionized both oral and written communication. Electronic communication has become a vital element in achieving organizational goals; however, each form of communication has its limitations. Protocols must be followed, and individuals must learn when it is appropriate to use each form.[23] You have to think not only about what you are going to say and how you are going to say it but also about which technological tools you'll use to do so. Throughout this book we present examples of the types of technological tools you'll encounter on the job and how to use those tools effectively and wisely.

Technology has such an impact on business communication that you have no choice but to master it.

PROMOTING WORKPLACE ETHICS

Ethical Boundaries: Where Would You Draw the Line?

At the very least, you owe your employer an honest day's work for an honest day's pay: your best efforts, obedience to the rules, a good attitude, respect for your employer's property, and a professional appearance. Such duties and considerations seem clear-cut, but where does your obligation to your employer end? For instance, where would you draw the line in communication situations such as the following?

- ✧ Writing your résumé so that an embarrassing two-year lapse won't be obvious.
- ✧ Telling your best friend about your company's upcoming merger right after mailing the formal announcement to your shareholders.
- ✧ Hinting to a co-worker (who's a close friend) that it's time to look around for something new, when you've already been told confidentially that she's scheduled to be fired at the end of the month.
- ✧ Saying nothing when you witness one employee taking credit for another's successful idea.
- ✧ Preserving your position by presenting yourself to supervisors as the only person capable of achieving an objective.
- ✧ Pirating computer software; that is, using one copy on more than one computer instead of paying for licences to duplicate the product.
- ✧ Making up an excuse when (for the fourth time this month) you have to pick up your child from school early and miss an important business meeting.
- ✧ Calling in sick because you're taking a few days off and you want to use up some of the sick leave you've accumulated.

The ethics involved in these situations may seem perfectly unambiguous ... until you think about them. But, wherever you are, whatever the circumstances, you owe your employer your best efforts. And time and again, it will be up to you to decide whether those efforts are ethical.

CAREER APPLICATIONS

1. List ethical behaviours you would expect from your employees, and compare your list with those of your classmates.
2. As the supervisor of the office filing clerks, you must deal with several workers who have a tendency to gossip about their colleagues. List five actions you might take to resolve the situation.

Guideline 4: Commit to Ethical Communication

Ethics are the principles of conduct that govern a person or a group.

Ethics are the principles of conduct that govern a person or a group. Unethical people are essentially selfish and unscrupulous, saying or doing whatever it takes to achieve an end. Ethical people are generally trustworthy, fair, and impartial, respecting the rights of others and concerned about the effects of their actions on society. Ethics has been defined as "knowing the difference between what you have a right to do and what is the right thing to do."[24]

Ethical communication includes all relevant information, is true in every sense, and is not deceptive in any way. When sending an ethical message, be accurate and sincere. Avoid language that manipulates, discriminates, or exaggerates. Don't hide negative information behind an optimistic attitude, don't state opinions as facts, and portray graphic data fairly. Be honest with employers, co-workers, and clients, never seeking personal gain by making others look better or worse than they are. Don't allow personal preferences to influence your perception or the perception of others, and act in good faith. On the surface, such ethical practices appear fairly easy to recognize. But deciding what is ethical can be quite complex (see "Promoting Workplace Ethics—Ethical Boundaries: Where Would You Draw the Line?" on page 15).

Ethical communication is truthful and relevant.

RECOGNIZING ETHICAL CHOICES

Every company has responsibilities to various groups: customers, employees, shareholders, suppliers, neighbours, the community, and the nation.

Unfortunately, what's right for one group may be wrong for another.[25] Moreover, as you attempt to satisfy the needs of one group, you may be presented with an option that seems right on the surface but somehow feels wrong. When people must choose between conflicting loyalties and weigh difficult trade-offs, they face a dilemma.

OBJECTIVE 7 Differentiate between an ethical dilemma and an ethical lapse; then list four questions that will help you decide what is ethical.

An **ethical dilemma** involves choosing among alternatives that aren't clear-cut: perhaps two conflicting alternatives are both ethical and valid, or perhaps the alternatives lie somewhere in the vast gray area between right and wrong. Suppose you are president of a company that's losing money. You have a duty to your shareholders to try to reduce your losses and to your employees to be fair and honest. After looking at various options, you conclude that you will have to lay off 500 people immediately. You suspect you may have to lay off another 100 people later on, but right now you need those 100 workers to finish a project. What do you tell them? If you confess that their jobs are shaky, many of them may quit just when you need them most. However, if you tell them that the future is promising, you'll be stretching the truth.

Conflicting priorities and the vast gray areas between right and wrong create ethical dilemmas for an organization's communicators.

Unlike a dilemma, an **ethical lapse** is making a clearly unethical or illegal choice. Suppose you have decided to change jobs and have discreetly landed an interview with your boss's largest competitor. You get along great with the interviewer, who is impressed enough with you to offer you a position on the spot. The new position is a step up from your current job, and the pay is much more than what you're getting now. You accept the job and agree to start next month. Then, as you're shaking hands with the interviewer, she asks you to bring along profiles of your current company's 10 largest customers when you report for work. Do you comply with her request? How do you decide between what's ethical and what is not?

MAKING ETHICAL CHOICES

Laws provide ethical guidance for certain types of messages.

One place to look for guidance is the law. If saying or writing something is clearly illegal, you have no dilemma: You obey the law. However, even though legal considerations will resolve some ethical questions, you will often have to rely on your own judgment and principles. If your intent is honest, the statement is ethical, even though it may be factually incorrect; if your intent is to mislead or manipulate the audience, the message is unethical, regardless of whether it is true. You might look at the consequences of your message and opt for the solution that provides the greatest good to the greatest number of people, and one with which that you can live.[26] You might ask yourself the following set of questions:[27]

- **Is this message legal?** Does it violate civil law or company policy?
- **Is this message balanced?** Does it do the most good and the least harm? Is it fair to all concerned in the short term as well as the long term?
- **Is it a message you can live with?** Does it make you feel good about yourself? Does it make you proud? Would you feel good about your decision if a newspaper published it? If your family knew about it?
- **Is this message feasible?** Can it work in the real world? Have you considered your position in the company? Your company's competition? Its financial and political strength? The likely costs or risks of your decision? The time available?

Asking the right questions can help you decide what is ethical.

MOTIVATING ETHICAL CHOICES

Some companies lay out an explicit ethical policy by using a written **code of ethics** to help employees determine what is acceptable (see the photo of Falconbridge's code of ethics, shown below). In addition, many managers use **ethics audits,** a detailed examination of policies and operatives to monitor ethical progress and to point up any weaknesses that need to be addressed. They know that being ethical is simply the right thing to do and will set a standard. Others will follow your example when they observe you being ethical and see the success you experience both in your interpersonal relationships and in your career.[28]

Organizations can foster ethical behaviour
- By formalizing a written **code of ethics**
- By using **ethics audits**
- By setting a good ethical example

Strengthening Your Communication Skills

Perhaps the best place to begin strengthening your communication skills is with an honest assessment of where you now stand. In the next few days, watch how you handle the communication situations that arise. Try to figure out what you're doing right and what you're doing wrong. Then, as you progress through this course in the months ahead, focus on those areas in which you need the most work.

Focus on building skills in the areas where you've been weak.

This book has been designed to provide the kind of communication practice that will prepare you to get the job you want, to improve your chances for a promotion, to start your own business, or to succeed at whatever you choose to do in the future. As you proceed through this book, you'll meet many business people, such as Sue Lee of Suncor Energy. Their experiences will give you an insight into what it takes to communicate effectively on the job.

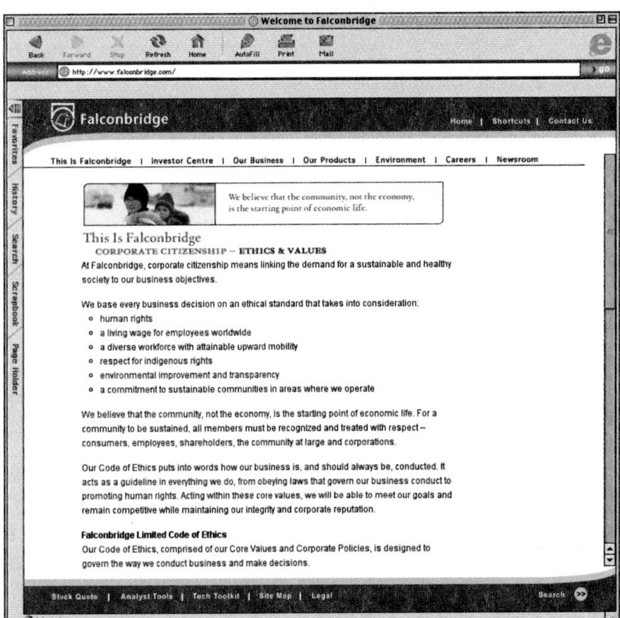

Falconbridge is a Canadian mining company. Like many other Canadian corporations, such as Bank of Montreal, Noranda, and Nexen, Falconbridge posts its code of ethics on its Web site. Why does an organization do so? Find other corporate codes of ethics. What similarities do you find among them? What differences do you see?

Applying What You've Learned

In this chapter, you've met Suncor's Sue Lee, and throughout the book you'll meet a cross-section of real people—men and women who work for some of the most interesting organizations in North America. At the beginning of this chapter, you read about the challenges Lee faced as Suncor's vice president of Human Resources and Communications. Every chapter begins with a similar slice-of-life vignette titled "On the Job: Facing a Communication Dilemma." As you read through each chapter, think about the communication problems faced by the person and the company highlighted in the vignette. Become familiar with the various concepts presented in the chapter, and imagine how they might apply to the featured scenario.

At the end of each chapter, you'll take part in an innovative simulation called "On the Job: Solving a Communication Dilemma." Each simulation starts by explaining how the highlighted company actually solved the communication dilemma profiled. Then you'll play the role of a person working in that organization and you'll face a situation you could encounter there. You will be presented with several communication scenarios, each with several possible courses of action. It's up to you to recommend one course of action from the simulations as homework, as teamwork, as material for in-class discussion, or in a host of other ways. These scenarios let you explore various communication ideas and apply the concepts and techniques from the chapter.

Now you're ready for the first simulation on page 19. As you tackle each problem, think about the material you covered in this chapter and consider your own experience as a communicator. You'll probably be surprised to discover how much you already know about business communication.

Summary of Learning Outcomes

1 Explain why effective communication is important to organizations and how it can help you succeed in business. Communication is the lifeblood of organizations, and effective communication improves an organization's productivity, image, and responsiveness. Communication is effective when it helps people understand each other, stimulates others to take action, and encourages others to think in new ways. It helps you speed problem solution, strengthen decision making, coordinate work flow, cement business relationships, clarify promotional materials, enhance your professional image, and improve your response to stakeholders. Good communication skills increase your chances for career success and your ability to adapt to the changing workplace.

2 Discuss three changes in the workplace that are intensifying the need to communicate effectively. Technological advances such as the Internet and portable communication devices make it possible for employees to telecommute; using such devices also highlights an employee's ability to write and speak clearly. Increased cultural diversity in the workforce requires employees to adapt their communication so that they can be understood by different cultures. Increased use of teams requires mastery of interpersonal skills such as listening, giving feedback, working collaboratively, and resolving conflict.

3 Describe how organizations share information internally and externally. Within an organization, communication occurs formally or informally. The formal communication network can be depicted as an organizational chart, with information flowing downward from managers to employees, upward from employees to managers, and horizontally between departments. The informal communication network, or grapevine, follows the path of casual conversation and has no set pattern of flow. Communication between organizations and the outside world can be as formal as a news release carefully prepared by a marketing or public relations team or as informal as talking with a customer or letting one's appearance transmit an impression of the organization.

4 Identify and briefly define the six phases of the communication process. The communication process occurs in six phases: First, the sender has an idea (conceives a thought and wants to share it). Second, the sender encodes the idea (puts it into message form). Third, the sender transmits the message (sends the message using a specific channel and medium). Fourth, the receiver gets the message (receives the physical message by hearing or reading it). Fifth, the receiver decodes the message (absorbs and understands the meaning). And sixth, the receiver sends feedback (responds to the message and signals that response to the sender).

5 Identify and briefly discuss four types of communication barriers. First, perceptual differences affect how we see the world; no two people perceive things exactly the same way. Perception also influences how we develop language, which depends on shared definitions for meaning and is shaped by our culture. Second, restrictive structures and management block effective communication. Formal channels tend to cause distortion, as each link in the communication channel holds the potential for misinterpretation. Similarly, if managers aren't diligent in their efforts to communicate down the formal network, their messages can become fragmented so that employees never get the "big picture." Third, distractions can be physical (from poor acoustics to illegible copy), emotional, attributed to poor listening, or the result of information overload. And fourth, deceptive communication tactics are used by unethical communicators to manipulate their receivers.

6 Discuss four guidelines for overcoming communication barriers. First, adopting an audience-centred approach to communication means focusing on your audience and caring about their needs—which means finding out as much as you can about audience members, especially if your audience is from a different culture.

Second, fostering an open communication climate means encouraging employee contributions, candor, and honesty. You can create an open climate by modifying the number of organizational levels and by facilitating feedback. Third, creating lean and efficient messages means not communicating unnecessary information and making necessary information easy to get. You can send better messages by reducing the number of messages, minimizing distractions, and using technology responsibly. And fourth, committing to ethical communication means including relevant information that is true in every sense and not deceptive in any way.

7 Differentiate between an ethical dilemma and an ethical lapse; then list four questions that will help you decide what is ethical. An ethical dilemma involves choosing between two or more alternatives that are neither clearly ethical nor clearly unethical, such as alternatives that are all ethical but conflicting or alternatives that lie somewhere in the gray areas between right and wrong. An ethical lapse involves choosing an alternative that is clearly unethical or illegal, perhaps placing your own desire or ambition above the welfare of others. One way to decide whether a decision is ethical is to ask yourself four questions: (1) Is this decision legal? (2) Is this decision balanced? (3) Is it a decision you can live with? (4) Is it feasible?

ON THE JOB

Solving a Communication Dilemma at Suncor Energy Inc.

Suncor relies on effective communication to keep employees informed about company activities, the company's financial status, changes in employee benefits, and so on. To keep Suncor's communication climate open and to ensure that all employees receive the information they need, Sue Lee uses every tool available to her in the formal communication network.

Focusing on all the audiences both within and outside of Suncor, Lee and her team oversee several company publications, both electronic and hard copy. To detail the company's social and environmental performance, Suncor issues the annual *Sustainability Report*. Timely information is provided through news releases and mailouts, as well as special bulletins on the company Web site and Intranet. Residents of communities where Suncor operates receive special newsletters notifying them of events and activities that impact on their lives; *SunBridge* kept residents of Gull Lake and the Nekaneet First Nation in Saskatchewan informed of the Gull Lake wind power project. Another publication is *Stocktalk*, which distributes financial information to investors. Webcasts, live or delayed versions of sound or video broadcasts, allow any stakeholder as well as the general public to listen to presentations delivered by CEO Rick George or other Suncor executives about the company's financial performance or trends in the oil industry. To facilitate feedback from employees, Lee schedules regular face-to-face meetings with company CEO George, who often goes running with staff. Regular meetings with the public are also held to keep them informed of Suncor's operations and their impacts on the environment and their communities.

Communication also occurs throughout the informal network when people chat face-to-face or by telephone, in memos, and by electronic mail. Whether the communication is formal or informal, it's Sue Lee's job to make sure that all necessary information is delivered effectively and efficiently.

Your Mission You are a communications specialist at Suncor's corporate headquarters in Calgary. In this position, you prepare both internal and external communications. Use your knowledge of communication to choose the best response for each of the following situations. Be prepared to explain why your choice is best.

1 The company's medical insurance plan for the next year contains substantial changes from this year's plan. To maintain Suncor's open communication climate, how should this information be distributed to employees?
   a Have Sue Lee, vice president of Human Resources and Communications, present the information at an all-staff meeting so that employees can give their reactions to the changes.
   b Detail the changes in a single e-mail message sent to all staff.
   c Post the details on the corporate Intranet site.
   d Describe the changes in a benefits statement sent to each employee.

2 A manager has asked for your help. Her team is responsible for shipping replacement parts to crews working on the oil rigs in Fort McMurray. Some team members are not filling orders in a timely manner, and she confides that they are not giving their best to the job. As one way of improving performance, she wants to send a memo to everyone in the department, and she's asked you to recommend an approach. Which of the following approaches would be the most ethical and effective?
   a Tell employees that the team's performance is not as good as it could be, and ask for ideas on how to improve the situation.
   b Explain that you'll have to fire the next person you see giving less than 100 percent (even though you know company policy prevents you from actually doing so).
   c Ask employees to monitor one another and report problems to their team leader.
   d Tell all employees that if team performance does not improve, wages will be reduced and evaluations will not be positive.

3 A rumour begins circulating that oil production will be reduced and many workers in the oil sands will be laid off. The rumour is false. What is the first action you should take?
   a Put a notice on the company Intranet denying the rumour.
   b Publish a denial in a memo asking all managers to tell their employees that the rumour is false.

c Schedule a meeting with all employees about working at the oil sands. At the meeting have the company CEO explain the facts and publicly state that the rumour is false.
d Ignore the rumour. Like all false rumours it will eventually die out.

4 Suncor wants its employees to carpool to work with colleagues as a way to save fuel and practice environmental citizenship. What is the best way for the Communications division to introduce this plan to employees?
a Announce the plan on the Intranet, ask for volunteers to carpool, and include a detailed survey to be returned by e-mail to the development team.
b Publish a special newsletter that explains the plan and asks managers to recruit employees and to get their feedback.
c Have the CEO announce the plan at a Corporate Town Hall session and ask for help in getting volunteers.
d Send all employees an individual e-mail message that asks for volunteers and directs interested employees to a download site on the Intranet (which includes a detailed survey to be filled out online).[29]

Test Your Knowledge

1 Define *communication* and list four of the eight benefits of effective communication.
2 How is technology changing communication in the workplace?
3 How does effective communication help employees interact with customers in this age of technology?
4 How does internal communication differ from external communication?
5 In what directions can information travel within an organization's formal hierarchy?
6 What is the grapevine, and why should managers know how it works?
7 In which of the six phases of the communication process do messages get encoded and decoded?
8 What is information overload, and how can it affect communication?
9 Why should communicators take an audience-centred approach to communication?
10 How does corporate culture affect the communication climate within an organization?
11 Define *ethics,* and explain what ethical communication covers.

Interactive Learning 

Visit our Companion Web site at **www.pearsoned.ca/thill**, where you can use the interactive Study Guide to test your chapter knowledge and get instant feedback. Additional resources link you to the sites mentioned in this text and to additional sources of information on chapter topics.

Also check out the resources on the Mastering Business Communication CD, including "Perils of Pauline," an interactive presentation of the business communication challenges within a fictional company.

Apply Your Knowledge

1 Why do you think good communication in an organization improves employees' attitudes and performance? Explain.
2 Under what circumstances might you want to limit the feedback you receive from an audience of readers or listeners? Explain.
3 Would written or spoken messages be more susceptible to noise? Why?
4 As a manager, how can you impress on your employees the importance of including both negative and positive information in messages?
5 **Ethical Choices** Because of your excellent communication skills, your supervisor always asks you to write his reports for him. When you overhear the CEO complimenting him on his logical organization and clear writing style, he responds as if he'd written all those reports himself. What kind of ethical choice does this represent? What can you do in this situation? Briefly explain your solution and your reasoning.

Practice Your Knowledge

Document for Analysis

Read the following document; then (1) analyze the strengths and weaknesses of each sentence and (2) revise the document so that it follows this chapter's guidelines.

> It has come to my attention that many of you are lying on your time cards. If you come in late, you should not put 8:00 a.m. on your card. If you take a long lunch, you should not put 1:00 p.m. on your time card. I will not stand for this type of cheating. I simply have no choice but to institute a time-clock system. Beginning next Monday, all employees will have to punch in and punch out whenever they come and go from the work area.
>
> The time clock will be right by the entrance to each work area, so you will have no excuse for not punching in. Anyone who is late for work or late coming back from lunch more than three times will have to answer to me. I don't care if you had to take a nap or if you girls had to shop. This is a place of business, and we do not want to be taken advantage of by slackers who are cheaters to boot.
>
> It is too bad that a few bad apples always have to spoil things for everyone.

Exercises

1–1 Internal Communication: Planning the Flow For the following tasks, identify the necessary direction of communication (downward, upward, horizontal), suggest an appropriate type of communication (casual conversation, formal interview, meeting, workshop, videotape, newsletter, memo, bulletin board notice, and so on), and briefly explain your suggestion.

- a As personnel manager, you want to announce details about this year's company picnic.
- b As director of internal communication, you want to convince top management of the need for a company newsletter.
- c As production manager, you want to make sure that both the sales manager and the finance manager receive your scheduling estimates.
- d As marketing manager, you want to help employees understand the company's goals and its attitudes toward workers.
- e As a floor supervisor, you want to complain about unsafe procedures in your company's manufacturing facility.

1–2 Communication Networks: Formal or Informal? An old school friend suddenly phoned you to say: "I had to call you. You'd better keep this quiet, but when I heard my company was buying you guys out, I was shocked. I had no idea that a company as large as yours could sink so fast. Your group must be in pretty bad shape over there!" Your stomach turned suddenly queasy, and you felt a chill go up your spine. You'd heard nothing about any buyout, and before you could even get your friend off the phone, you were wondering what you should do. Of the following, choose one course of action and briefly explain your choice.

- a Contact your CEO directly and relate what you've heard.
- b Ask co-workers whether they've heard anything about a buyout.
- c Discuss the phone call confidentially with your immediate supervisor.
- d Keep quiet about the whole thing (there's nothing you can do about the situation anyway).

1–3 Ethical Choices In less than a page explain why you think each of the following is or is not ethical.

- a De-emphasizing negative test results in a report on your product idea.
- b Taking a computer home to finish a work-related assignment.
- c Telling an associate and close friend that she'd better pay more attention to her work responsibilities or management will fire her.
- d Recommending the purchase of excess equipment to use up your allocated funds before the end of the fiscal year so that your budget won't be cut next year.

1–4 The Changing Workplace: Always in Touch Technological devices such as faxes, cell phones, e-mail, and voice mail are making businesspeople easily accessible at any time of day or night, at work and at home. What effects might frequent intrusions have on their professional and personal lives? Please explain your answer in less than a page.

1–5 Internet @ The Conference Board of Canada **www.conferenceboard.ca** is an organization that publishes research reports and holds meetings on current issues in Canadian business, politics, and society. Visit the Conference Board of Canada Web site, and review their Business Ethics Frequently Asked Questions **www.conferenceboard.ca/ccbc/business_ethics/ethics_faq.htm**. Read the answer to question 2, "What is a code of ethics?" Next, find a Canadian corporation that has a code of ethics posted on the Internet (other than Falconbridge, on page 17). Does the code of ethics you found follow the guidelines given in the answer to question 2? Write two or three paragraphs describing the extent to which the code you found follows the guidelines, and describe how it can be improved. Submit your essay to your instructor.

1–6 Communication Process: Know Your Audience Top management has asked you to speak at an upcoming executive meeting to present your arguments for a more open communication climate. Which of the following would be most important for you to know about your audience before giving your presentation? (Briefly explain your choice.)

- a How many top managers will be attending.
- b What management style members of your audience prefer.
- c How firmly these managers are set in their ways.

1–7 Ethical Choices Your boss often uses you as a sounding board for her ideas. Now she seems to want you to act as an unofficial messenger, passing her ideas along to the staff without mentioning her involvement and informing her of what staff members say without telling them you're going to repeat their responses. What questions should you ask yourself as you consider the ethical implications of this situation? Write a short paragraph explaining the ethical choice you will make in this situation.

1–8 Formal Communication: Self-Introduction Write a memo or prepare an oral presentation introducing yourself to your instructor and your class. Include information such as your background, interests, achievements, and goals. If you write a memo, keep it under one page, and use Figure 1-2 on page 5 as a model for the format. If you prepare an oral presentation, plan to speak for no more than two minutes.

1–9 Teamwork Your boss has asked your work group to research and report on corporate childcare facilities. Of course, you'll want to know who (besides your boss) will be reading your report. Working with two team members, list four or five other things you'll want to know about the situation and about your audience before starting your research. Briefly explain why the items on your list are important.

1–10 Communication Process: Analyzing Miscommunication Use the six phases of the communication process to analyze a miscommunication you've recently had with a co-worker, supervisor, classmate, teacher, friend, or family member. What idea were you trying to share? How did you encode and transmit it? Did the receiver get the message? Did the receiver correctly decode the message? How do you know? Based on your analysis, identify and explain the barriers that prevented your successful communication in this instance.

1–11 Ethical Choices You've been given the critical assignment of selecting the site for your company's new plant. After months of negotiations with landowners, numerous cost calculations, and investments in ecological, social, and community impact studies, you are about to recommend building the new plant on the Lansing River site. Now, just 15 minutes before your big presentation to top management, you discover a possible mistake in your calculations: site-purchase costs appear to be $50 000 more than you calculated, nearly 10 percent over budget. You don't have time to recheck all your figures, so you're tempted to just go ahead with your recommendation and ignore any discrepancies. You're worried that management won't approve this purchase if you can't present a clean, unqualified solution. You also know that many projects run over their original estimates, so you can probably work the extra cost into the budget later. On your way to the meeting room, you make your final decision. In a few paragraphs, explain the decision you made.

1–12 Communication Barriers: Eliminating Noise Whenever you report negative information to your boss, she never passes it along to her colleagues or supervisors, even though you think the information is important and should be shared. What barriers to communication are operating in this situation? What can you do to encourage more sharing of this kind of information?

Going Online Exercise

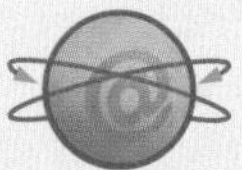

Using the Internet to Explore International Business Communication

Skillful communication is critical to the success of your business or organizational relationships. To help you communicate more effectively, explore IABC's (see page 12) resources, including its links to a global network of communicators. **www.iabc.com**

1 Describe several of IABC's resources. How could the manual "Business Management for Communicators" be useful to you in public relations or organizational communication?
2 What professional benefits does IABC offer to business communicators?
3 What is the IABC code of ethics?

To link directly to this site, visit our Companion Web site at **www.pearsoned.ca/thill** and look for the Chapter 1 resources.

Tips on Using the Web

To reach any of the Web sites listed in this book, visit the Companion Web site for this book at **www.pearsoned.ca/thill**. There, you'll find live links that take you straight to the site of your choice.

If you receive an error message when trying to get to a site mentioned in this text, try using a metasearch engine such as **www.ixquick.com**. If the site you're seeking is still operating, the results of the search will usually provide a live link to it.

As you visit sites around the Internet, be sure to evaluate your online sources before making use of the information you find. For an exhaustive list of sites pertaining to this topic, go to **www.surfwax.com**, and enter "evaluation of information sources" and related phrases in the search box.

Communicating in Teams: Collaboration, Listening, Nonverbal, and Meeting Skills

1 Explain the advantages and disadvantages of using teams

2 Identify the characteristics of effective teams

3 Discuss the tasks involved in preparing effective team messages and list nine guidelines for improvement

4 Describe the listening process and discuss three barriers that interfere with this process

5 Clarify the importance of nonverbal communication and briefly describe six categories of nonverbal expression

6 Explain how you can improve meeting productivity through preparation, leadership, and participation

ON THE JOB

Facing a Communication Dilemma at Royal Bank Financial Group

Taking Charge of Business through Teamwork

www.royalbank.com

With 59 000 employees serving more than 12 million personal, business, and public sector clients, Royal Bank Canada counts on teamwork to keep staff both productive and satisfied. Whether they work in the 1300 Royal Bank branches across Canada, in the investment or insurance divisions, or in one of the 30 global offices, employees can enjoy "flex-work" benefits. Some 30 percent do. Flexible work options include reduced or varied work hours, job sharing, a modified workweek, or working off-site, from home or a satellite office. For example, four employees at Royal Bank's main Halifax branch coordinated schedules so that each person has a long weekend every two weeks. By learning one another's duties and working the occasional longer day, someone is always available to serve clients. High-level bank managers, such as Elisabetta Bigsby, senior executive vice-president, Human Resources and Public Affairs, believe teamwork provides many benefits to employees: they perform better, have more energy, and maintain a better life outside of their job when they have more control over their time.

Job-sharing at Royal Bank is a permanent part of the Bank's culture: teams tend to maintain high performance, and customers report they receive improved service because more people are acquainted with their accounts. If you were a branch manager, how would you develop effective teams? What would you need to know about getting team members to collaborate? And how could you help your team members improve their listening, nonverbal communication, and meeting skills?[1]

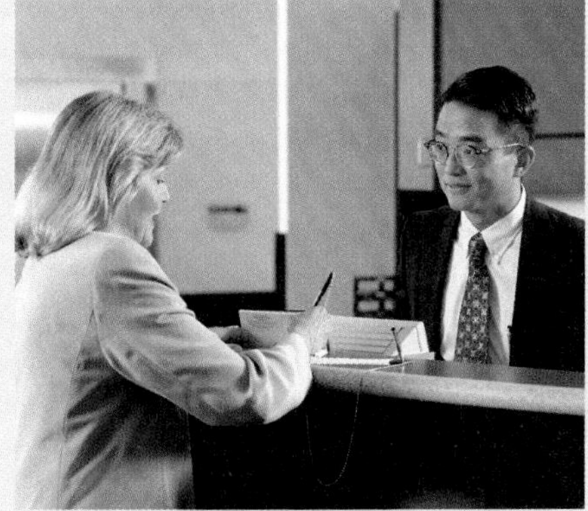

With over 59 000 employees in Canada, the U.S. and more than 30 countries worldwide, Royal Bank Financial Group is recognized as a top corporate employer in the accounting firm KPMG's 2002 Survey of Canada's Most Respected Corporations. Royal Bank helps its employees succeed in their jobs by encouraging teamwork and free-flowing communication throughout the organization.

Working in Teams

Working in teams and small groups puts people's communication skills to the test. A **team** is a unit of two or more people who work together to achieve a goal. Team members share a mission and the responsibility for working to achieve it.[2]

A 2001 Ipso-Reid survey of office workers in Toronto, Vancouver, Calgary, Montreal, Edmonton, and Ottawa revealed that, on average, employees spend 5.2 hours a week in meetings. More than half of the people Ipso-Reid surveyed noted that between 1996 and 2001, opportunities for teamwork have multiplied significantly. When asked about collaborating with colleagues on written communications, 91 percent said they did.[3]

Whether the task is to write reports, give oral presentations, produce a product, solve a problem, or investigate an opportunity, companies look for people who can successfully interact in teams and collaborate with others. Why?

Studies show that teams contribute to an organization's performance.

One reason is performance. A study of 232 organizations across 16 countries and more than eight industries revealed that organizations working in teams experience the highest improvement in performance.[4] Another reason is creativity. Teams encourage creativity in workers through **participative management**, involving employees in the company's decision making. At Ryder Integrated Logistics of Mississauga, Ontario, for example, virtual teams have replaced the "up–down" hierarchy for serving clients. Doug Harrison, vice-president and managing director, says that since the team approach has replaced following a chain of command, "we are able to react more quickly to our customer's needs. We're able to get much quicker decision making because everybody's working together as a team."[5]

Types of Teams

The type, structure, and composition of individual teams vary within an organization. Companies can create *formal teams* that become part of the organization's structure, or they may establish *informal teams.* Informal teams aren't part of the formal organization but are formed to solve a problem, work on a specific activity, or encourage employee participation.

Three popular types of informal teams are cross-functional teams, quality assurance teams, and task forces.

Cross-functional teams are interdisciplinary.

Cross-functional teams bring together people from different areas—information technology, sales, and manufacturing, for example—to create a new product, computer system, long-term organizational strategy, or to combine their talents on some other task. Sometimes as many as eight or more specialties may join a cross-functional team.[6] At Clarica Insurance, information technology specialists are given business training so that they can participate on management and sales teams, bringing their expertise in computers to other areas.[7]

Quality assurance teams make sure products meet predetermined standards.

Quality assurance teams ensure that products and services meet prescribed standards. Typically composed of specialists in a single field, these groups may test automobiles to confirm that they run problem-free before leaving the factory floor or food products to ensure that they meet safety standards.

Task forces are interdisciplinary; they come together to resolve special issues and disband when they achieve their goal.

Committees are long-term teams.

Task forces are informal teams that assemble to resolve specific issues and disband once their goal has been accomplished. Similar to cross-functional teams, task forces often include representatives from many departments so that those who have a stake in the outcome are allowed to provide input. One function of task forces is finding areas where savings can be made. For example, a hospital may bring together people from different departments, such as surgery, nursing, finance, and administration, to find ways to reduce the cost of supplies.[8]

Using advanced communication technology, a **virtual team** brings together employees who live in different parts of a country, or around the world, to work on projects.

Virtual teams bring together geographically distant employees to accomplish goals. Using computer networks, teleconferencing, e-mail, videoconferencing, and web technology, they build teams that are as effective as those in organizations functioning under a single roof. At Texas Instruments, microchip engineers in India, Texas, and Japan are able to pool ideas, design new chips, and collaboratively debug them—even though they're 4000 kilometres and 12 time zones apart.[9]

Teams can play a vital role in helping an organization reach its goals. However, they are not appropriate for every situation. When deciding whether to use teams, managers must weigh both the advantages and disadvantages of doing so.[10]

OBJECTIVE 1 Explain the advantages and disadvantages of using teams.

Advantages and Disadvantages of Teams

At their best, teams can be an extremely useful forum for making key decisions. The interaction of the participants leads to good decisions based on the combined intelligence of the group. An organization's decision making can benefit from the team approach in the following ways:[11]

- **Increased information and knowledge.** By combining the resources of several individuals, teams bring more information to the decision process.
- **Increased diversity of views.** Teams bring many different perspectives to the decision process. People have different backgrounds and experiences, which contribute to a deeper and more thorough examination of the issues the team faces.
- **Increased acceptance of a solution.** Team members who participate in making a decision are more likely to enthusiastically support the decision and encourage others to accept it. Because they share in the final product, they are committed to seeing it succeed.

Teams generally achieve performance levels that exceed what would have been accomplished had the members worked independently, perhaps because teams have the potential to unleash vast amounts of creativity and energy in workers. Motivation and performance are often increased because workers share a sense of purpose and mutual accountability. Teams can also fill the individual worker's need to belong to a group. Furthermore, they can reduce employee boredom, increase feelings of dignity and self-worth, and reduce stress and tension between workers.

Although teamwork has many advantages, it also has a number of potential disadvantages. At their worst, teams are unproductive and frustrating, and they waste everyone's time. Some may actually be counterproductive, because they may arrive at bad decisions. For instance, when people are pressured to conform, they may abandon their sense of personal responsibility and agree to ill-founded plans. Similarly, a team may develop **groupthink,** the willingness of individual members to set aside their personal opinions and go along with everyone else, even if everyone else is wrong. Groupthink develops for several reasons. Group members may be influenced by a dominant personality who controls the discussion. The group may be working under a short deadline, so that participants cannot explore all the dimensions of their problem. And, for some people, simply belonging to the team is more important to them than making the right decision. Groupthink can lead to poor-quality decisions and ill-advised actions, even inducing people to act unethically. Groupthink was one cause of energy company Enron's collapse in 2002 because criticism of accounting practices and the behaviour of senior executives was suppressed.[12]

Some team members may have a **hidden agenda**—private motives that affect the group's interaction. Sam might want to prove that he's more powerful than another member, so he dominates the meeting at the cost of stifling discussion. Dawn might want the group to purchase a product because she's friendly with the salesperson. Each person's hidden agenda can detract from the team's effectiveness.

Going Online

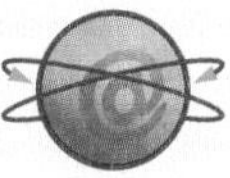

Participate in a Team-Based Organization

At the Center for the Study of Work Teams (CSWT) you'll learn about "collaborative work systems." The site's advantages include links to many other sites about working in teams, a newsletter with articles on teaming tips and communication techniques, and research projects on theoretical and applied knowledge about teams. CSWT lists free publications and information on conferences and workshops. Log on to see what sources are available for career opportunities.

www.workteams.unt.edu

To link directly to this site, visit our Companion Web site at **www.pearsoned.ca/thill** and look for the Chapter 2 resources.

In many of Canada's businesses, such as the Royal Bank, employees voluntarily band together to raise funds for charitable causes. Are the dynamics of voluntary teams similar to those of management-imposed teams? How are they different?

Group members' personal motives can interfere with the group's efforts to accomplish its mission.

The potential disadvantages of teams don't stop there. **Free riders** are team members who don't contribute their fair share to the group's activities because they aren't being held individually accountable for their work. The free-ride attitude can lead to certain tasks remaining unfulfilled. Still another drawback to teamwork is the high cost of coordinating group activities. Aligning schedules, arranging meetings, and coordinating individual parts of a project can eat up a lot of time and money. Finally, teams simply aren't effective for all situations. As management guru Peter Drucker puts it, "When the ship goes down, you don't call a meeting. The captain gives an order or everybody drowns."[13]

Group Dynamics

Group dynamics are the interactions and processes that take place in a team.

The interactions and processes that take place in a team are called **group dynamics**. Some teams are more effective than others simply because the dynamics of the group facilitate member input and the resolution of differences. To keep the task moving forward, productive teams also tend to develop rules that are conducive to business. Often these rules are unstated; they just become standard group practice, or **norms**—informal standards of conduct that members share and that guide member behaviour. For example, there may be an unspoken agreement that it's okay to be 10 minutes late for meetings but not 15 minutes late.

When a team has a strong identity, the members observe team rules rigorously: they're upset by any deviation and feel a great deal of pressure to conform. This loyalty can be positive, giving members a strong commitment to one another and highly motivating them to see that the team succeeds. However, an overly strong identity could lead to negative conditions such as groupthink.

TEAM ROLES

Each member of a group plays a role that affects the outcome of the group's activities.

Members of a team can play various roles, which fall into three categories (see Table 2–1 on page 27). Members who assume **self-oriented roles** are motivated mainly to fulfill personal needs, so they tend to be less productive than other members are. Far more likely to contribute to team goals are those members who assume **team-maintenance roles** to help everyone work well together and those members who assume **task-facilitating roles** to help solve problems or make decisions.

Roles are often determined by status, which can vary from team to team.

To a great extent, the roles that individuals assume in a group depend on their status in that group and their reasons for joining the group. Status depends on many variables, including personal attractiveness, competence in a particular field, past successes, education, age, social background, and organizational position. A person's status also varies from team to team. In most teams, as people try to establish their relative status, an undercurrent of tension can get in the way of the real work. Until roles and status have stabilized, a team may have trouble accomplishing its goals.

FIVE PHASES OF TEAM DECISIONS

While teams grow and evolve in their own ways, research shows that most teams reach a decision by passing through five phases:[14]

- **Orientation.** Team members socialize, establish their roles, and begin to define their task or purpose.
- **Conflict.** Team members begin to discuss their positions and become more assertive in establishing their roles. If members have been carefully selected to represent a variety of viewpoints and expertise, disagreements are a natural part of this phase. Conflict is a positive force because it helps the group to clarify both the ideas and the processes for reaching their decisions. Conflict also works against the danger of groupthink.[15]
- **Brainstorm.** Team members air all the options and discuss the pros and cons fully. At the end of this phase, members begin to settle on a single solution to

TABLE 2-1 Team Roles People Play

Self-Oriented Roles	*Team-Maintenance Roles*	*Task-Facilitating Roles*
Controlling: dominating others by exhibiting superiority or authority	**Encouraging:** drawing out other members by showing verbal and nonverbal support, praise, or agreement	**Initiating:** getting the team started on a line of inquiry
Withdrawing: retiring from the team either by becoming silent or by refusing to deal with a particular aspect of the team's work	**Harmonizing:** reconciling differences among team members through mediation or by using humour to relieve tension	**Information giving or seeking:** offering (or seeking) information relevant to questions facing the team
Attention seeking: calling attention to oneself and demanding recognition from others	**Compromising:** offering to yield on a point in the interest of reaching a mutually acceptable decision	**Coordinating:** showing relationships among ideas, clarifying issues, summarizing what the team has done
Diverting: focusing the team's discussion on topics of interest to the individual rather than on those relevant to the task		**Procedure setting:** suggesting decision-making procedures that will move the team toward a goal

the problem. It's important to avoid judging ideas during brainstorming, so that people feel free to contribute all their thoughts, rather than limit them to ones they believe will win approval.

- **Emergence.** Team members reach a decision. Consensus is reached when the team finds a solution that is acceptable enough for all members to support (even if they have reservations). This consensus happens only after all members have had an opportunity to communicate their positions and feel that they have been listened to.
- **Reinforcement.** Group feeling is rebuilt and the solution is summarized. Members receive their assignments for carrying out the group's decision, and they make arrangements for following up on those assignments.

Group decision making typically passes through five phases: orientation, conflict, brainstorming, emergence, and reinforcement.

These five phases almost always occur regardless of the task or type of decision being considered. Moreover, team members naturally use this process, even when they lack experience or training in team communication.

Developing an Effective Team

OBJECTIVE 2 Identify the characteristics of effective teams.

In effective collaborative relationships, all team members recognize that each individual brings valuable assets, knowledge, and skills to the team. Teams such as those at Royal Bank succeed because members are willing to exchange information, examine issues, and work through conflicts that arise. They trust each other, looking toward the greater good of the team and organization rather than focusing on personal agendas, making unilateral decisions, or exercising power for its own sake.[16]

Developing an effective team is an ongoing process. The characteristics of effective teams include the following:[17]

Effective teams
- understand their purpose
- communicate openly
- build consensus
- think creatively
- stay focused

- **Clear sense of purpose.** Team members clearly understand the task at hand, what is expected of them, and their role on the team.
- **Open and honest communication.** The team culture encourages discussion and debate. Team members speak openly and honestly, without the threat of anger,

resentment, or retribution. They listen to and value feedback from others. As a result, all team members participate.

- **Decision by consensus.** All decisions are arrived at by consensus. No easy, quick votes are taken.
- **Creative thinking.** Effective teams encourage original thinking, considering options beyond the usual.
- **Focused.** Team members get to the core issues of the problem and stay focused on key issues.

Employees can learn effective team skills on the job.

Learning these team skills takes time and practice, so many companies now offer employees training in building their team skills. At Royal Bank, for example, employees can access teamwork courses online through the bank's virtual classroom. Because these courses are available electronically, employees can participate in them at their convenience. For a brief review of characteristics of effective teams, see "Checklist: Developing an Effective Team," below.

Understanding Conflict

Conflict is not necessarily bad, as long as it is handled in a constructive fashion.

Functioning effectively in teams requires many skills. However, none is more important than the ability to handle conflict—clashes over differences in ideas, opinions, goals, or procedures. Conflict can be both constructive and destructive to a team's effectiveness. Conflict is constructive if it increases the involvement of team members and results in the solution to a problem. Conflict is destructive if it diverts energy from more important issues, destroys the morale of teams or individual team members, or polarizes or divides the team.[18]

Checklist: Developing an Effective Team

Build a Sense of Fairness in Decision Making

✓ Encourage debate and disagreement without fear of reprisal

✓ Allow members to communicate openly and honestly

✓ Consider all proposals

✓ Build consensus by allowing team members to examine, compare, and reconcile differences

✓ Avoid quick votes

✓ Keep everyone informed

✓ Present all the facts

Select Team Members Wisely

✓ Involve stakeholders

✓ Limit size to no more than 12 to 15 members

✓ Select members with a diversity of views

✓ Select creative thinkers

Make Working in Teams a Top Management Priority

✓ Recognize and reward individual and group performance

✓ Provide ample training opportunities for employees to develop interpersonal, decision-making, and problem-solving skills

✓ Allow enough time for the team to develop and to learn how to work together

Manage Conflict Constructively

✓ Share leadership

✓ Encourage equal participation

✓ Discuss disagreements

✓ Focus on the issues, not the people

✓ Don't let disagreements turn into angry arguments

Stay on Track

✓ Make sure everyone understands the team's purpose

✓ Communicate what is expected of team members

✓ Don't deviate from the core assignment

✓ Develop and adhere to a schedule

✓ Develop rules and obey norms

Conflict can arise for any number of reasons. Teams and individuals may believe they are competing for scarce or declining resources, such as money, information, and supplies. Team members may disagree about who is responsible for a specific task; this disagreement is usually the result of poorly defined responsibilities and job boundaries. Poor communication can lead to misunderstandings and misperceptions about other team members, and intentionally withholding information can undermine member trust. Basic differences in values, attitudes, and personalities may lead to arguments. Power struggles may result when one person questions the authority of another, or when people or teams with limited authority attempt to increase their power or exert more influence. And conflict can also arise because individuals or teams are pursuing different goals.[19]

Resolving Conflict

Effective teams know how to manage conflict so that it makes a positive contribution.[20] The following measures can help team members successfully resolve conflict:

- **Proaction.** Deal with minor conflict before it becomes major conflict.
- **Communication.** Get those directly involved in the conflict to participate in resolving it.
- **Openness.** Get feelings out in the open before dealing with the main issues.
- **Research.** Seek factual reasons for the problem before seeking solutions.
- **Flexibility.** Don't let anyone lock into a position before considering other solutions.
- **Fair play.** Don't let anyone avoid a fair solution by hiding behind the rules.
- **Alliance.** Get parties to fight together against an "outside force" that is trying to undermine the team instead of against each other.

Overcoming Resistance

When you encounter resistance or hostility, try to maintain your composure and address the other person's emotional needs.

Part of dealing with conflict is learning how to persuade other people to accept your point of view. In a business situation, reason usually prevails—that is, by explaining cost savings, increase in productivity and other benefits of your ideas, you will probably win the agreement of your colleagues. However, you sometimes encounter people who react emotionally. When you face irrational resistance, try to remain calm and detached so that you can avoid destructive confrontations and present your position in a convincing manner.

- **Express understanding.** Most people are ashamed of reacting emotionally in business situations. Show that you sympathize. You might say, "I can understand that this change might be difficult, and if I were in your position, I might be reluctant myself." Help the other person relax and talk about his or her anxiety so that you have a chance to offer reassurance. In addition, sometimes reviewing the details of an initiative or decision will give people confidence.[21]
- **Make people aware of their resistance.** When people are noncommittal and silent, they may be tuning you out without even knowing why. Continuing with your argument is futile. Deal directly with the resistance, without being accusing. You might say, "You seem cool to this idea. Have I made some faulty assumptions?" Such questions force people to face and define their resistance.[22]
- **Evaluate others' objections fairly.** Don't simply repeat yourself. Focus on what the other person is expressing, both the words and the feelings. Get the person to open up so that you can understand the basis for the resistance. Others' objections may raise legitimate points that you'll need to discuss, or they may reveal problems that you'll need to minimize.[23]

- **Hold your arguments until the other person is ready for them.** Getting your point across depends as much on the other person's frame of mind as it does on your arguments. You can't assume that a strong argument will speak for itself. By becoming more audience-centred, you will learn to address the other person's emotional needs first.

The whole purpose of developing a team that's effective is to get members to collaborate on necessary tasks. One of those tasks is communication. Team members must frequently work together on preparing messages.

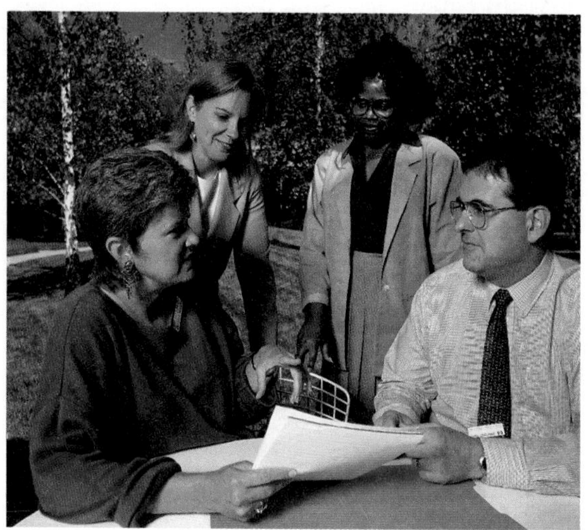

Hewlett-Packard's Industrial Lab investigative team collaborated to write a major report on research-and-development (R&D) contributions to the company. Their team effort produced a document that assessed the impact and value of all future R&D.

Collaborating on Team Messages

Collaborative messages, or team messages, involve working with other writers to produce a single document or presentation. For instance, you might sit down with your manager to plan a memo, work independently during the writing phase, and then ask him or her to review the message and suggest revisions. On the other hand, you might participate in an all-out team effort to write your company's business plan or to prepare and present a major report.

Collaborative messages can involve a project manager, researchers, writers, graphic artists, and editors. Because team messages bring multiple perspectives and various skills to a project, the result is often better than could have been produced by an individual working alone. Still, collaborative messages have their challenges. To begin with, team members often come from different backgrounds and have different work habits or concerns. A technical expert may focus on accuracy and scientific standards; an editor on organization and coherence; and a manager on schedules, cost, and corporate goals. Team members also differ in writing styles and personality traits.

Preparing Effective Team Messages

OBJECTIVE 3 Discuss the tasks involved in preparing effective team messages and list nine guidelines for improvement.

To prepare effective team messages, you must be flexible and open to the opinions of others—focusing on your team's objectives instead of your own.[24] You must also get organized. Select a leader and clarify goals.[25] Before anyone begins to write, team members must agree on the purpose of the project and the audience. Your team must also plan the organization, format, and style of the document—after all, the final message must look and sound as if one writer prepared it. The following guidelines will help you produce team messages that are clear, seamless, and successful:[26]

Make sure the final document "speaks with one voice."

- **Select team members wisely.** Choose team members who have strong interpersonal skills, understand team dynamics, and care about the project.
- **Select a responsible leader.** Identify a group leader who will keep members informed and intervene when necessary.
- **Promote cooperation.** Establish communication standards that motivate accuracy, openness, and trust. Both team leaders and team members should praise each other's achievements. Doing so raises morale and commitment to team goals.
- **Clarify goals.** Make sure team goals are aligned with individual expectations.
- **Elicit commitment.** Create a sense of ownership and shared responsibility for the document.
- **Clarify responsibilities.** Assign specific roles and establish clear lines of reporting. You may need to ask different people to write different sections of a report;

for example, if the committee is cross-functional, the financial specialist would write the financial section, and the marketing specialist the section dealing with demographics and the product launch. Someone with strong writing skills may be the final editor, reviewing the entire report for consistency in writing style and for errors in spelling, punctuation, and grammar.

- **Encourage prompt action.** Establish a timeline and deadlines for every part of the project. Distribute the schedule to all team members, and ask them to contact you if they cannot meet completion dates.
- **Apply technology.** Use electronic tools to communicate quickly and effectively with other team members. You will find the "track changes" feature in word-processing programs handy for viewing how members contribute to and revise the draft versions of the document.
- **Ensure technological compatibility.** Make sure all team members use the same word-processing program to facilitate combining files. Formatting features, for example, can be lost when different word-processing software is used.

Using Technology to Collaborate

Modern technology allows people in several locations to "meet" via video and audio links. In fact, a job candidate may be asked to sit down on the spur of the moment for an interview via videoconference with a prospective employer in another city. Similarly, a salesperson may be required to make a videoconference presentation to a roomful of customers, or a newly formed work team with members in offices around the world may be asked to brainstorm on camera.[27] With the growth of global commerce, teleconferencing is essential to keep global business teams functioning.[28]

Decision-making software offers anonymity, allows honesty, and saves time.

One form of teleconferencing technology is **decision-making software** (also called *groupware* or *electronic meeting systems*). This software offers distinct advantages. For example, participants have the option of anonymity: they can type any message they want, and it flashes on the screen for all to see, but without the writer's name. Such anonymity allows people to be brutally honest without penalty. In addition, electronic meeting systems are much faster than face-to-face meetings because social conversation is eliminated. Still, using decision-making software has its drawbacks. First, you must be good at keyboarding. Also, those with the best ideas don't get credit for them. Finally, the process lacks the rich nonverbal feedback of face-to-face communication.

Web technology also helps team members collaborate. More and more companies are developing large-scale workspaces on the Internet for online discussions, videoconferencing, and data sharing. The primary benefits of Web-based collaboration are that it's easy, it's cost effective, and it allows you to do multiple activities in a seamless fashion. For example, at KPMG Consulting, eight employees scattered around the globe wrote, edited, and commented on a report, using SamePage collaborative software. This software allows users to draft different sections of a document while editing other sections and participating in a Web-based discussion—all at the same time.[29] At IBM, one-third of employees will participate in virtual teams at some point during their careers with the company.[30] Whether sharing information, reaching decisions, or making recommendations, team members can use technology to compose, exchange, and present effective messages.

Web-based collaboration is easy, cost-effective, and efficient, but there are interpersonal obstacles team members must consider.

Web-based collaboration, however, does pose challenges. For virtual teams to work effectively, members must be good communicators and be able to work on their own, without a lot of supervision. Furthermore, different time zones can subvert communication: a message sent at 9 a.m. from a salesperson in Canada to a design specialist in New Zealand will arrive at 4 a.m. the next day. Such time differences must be considered when information is needed to meet a deadline.[31] Building trust is

Collaborative messages benefit from multiple perspectives and various skills; however, team members may have to work hard to overcome differences in background and working habits.

another concern. Without face-to-face communication, nuances in body language and tone of voice are often lost. People like to meet in person at the beginning of a project so that they can get to know one another and establish rapport. After the initial face-to-face meeting, team members will feel more comfortable communicating electronically.[32]

Keep in mind that team presentations can give an organization the opportunity to show off its brightest talent while capitalizing on each person's unique presentation skills. The real advantage is that you can take the collective energy and expertise of the team and create something that transcends what you could do otherwise.[33]

Speaking with Team Members

Most people would rather talk than write.

Given a choice, people would rather talk to each other than write to each other (see Figure 2–1 on the previous page). Talking takes less time and needs no composing, keyboarding, rewriting, duplicating, or distributing. Even more important, oral communication provides the opportunity for feedback. When people communicate orally, they can ask questions and test their understanding of the message; they can share ideas and work together to solve problems.

Spoken words are more difficult to revise than written ones.

However, speaking is such an ingrained activity that we tend to do it without much thought, and that casual approach can be a problem in business. You have far less opportunity to revise your spoken words than to revise your written words. You can't cross out what you just said and start all over.

To improve your speaking skills, be more aware of using speech as a tool for accomplishing your objectives in a business context. Break the habit of talking spontaneously; instead, plan *what* you're going to say and *how* you're going to say it. Before you speak, think about your purpose, your main idea, and your audience. Organize your thoughts, decide on a style that suits the occasion and your audience, and edit your remarks mentally.

Whether speaking or writing, try to predict your audience's reaction.

It is very important that you focus on your audience. Try to predict how your audience will react, and organize your message accordingly. As you speak, watch the other person and judge from verbal and nonverbal feedback whether your message is making the desired impression. If it isn't, revise it and try again.

Now look again at Figure 2–1 below. In addition to underscoring the importance of oral communication, it illustrates that people spend more time *receiving* information than transmitting it. Listening and reading are every bit as important as speaking and writing.

FIGURE 2–1 The Percentage of Communication Time Businesspeople Spend on Various Communication Channels

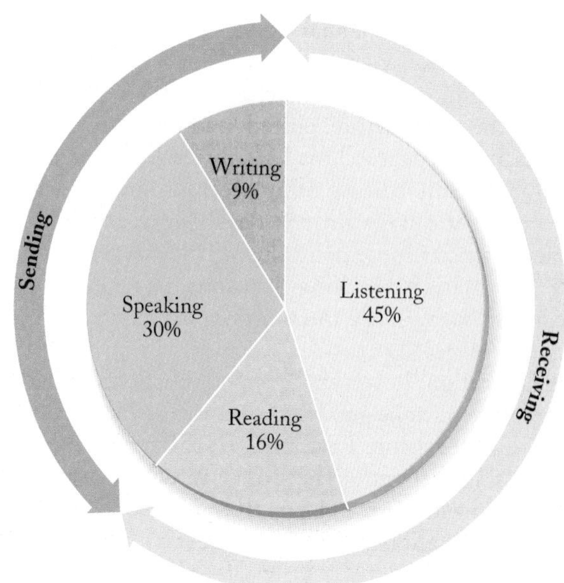

Listening to Team Members

The ability to listen is a vital skill in business.

Because listening is such a routine, everyday activity, few people think of developing their listening skills. Unfortunately, most of us aren't very good listeners. We may hear the words, but that doesn't mean we're actually listening to the message.[34] Most of us face so many distractions that we often give speakers less than our full attention. In fact, businesses lose millions of dollars each year because of a failure to listen to and understand customers' needs.[35]

Most people need to improve their listening skills.

Effective listeners welcome new information and new ideas. They benefit by staying informed and up to date. Good listening gives you an edge and increases your impact when you speak. It strengthens organizational relationships and enhances product delivery. It alerts the organization to innovation from both internal and external sources, and allows the organization to manage growing diversity both in the workforce and in the customers it serves.[36]

Even so, most people listen poorly. In one study, 80 percent of North American executives surveyed believe that listening is a critical workplace skill, yet 28 percent of these executives rated listening as the skill most lacking in employees.[37] In fact, people remember only about half of what's said during a 10-minute conversation, and forget half of that within 48 hours.[38] Furthermore, when questioned about material they've just heard, people are likely to confuse the facts. That's because effective listening requires a conscious effort and a willing mind. Learning to listen effectively can be difficult, but doing so one of the best ways to improve your communication skills. It enhances your performance, which leads to more challenging opportunities at work.[39] At Canadian Imperial Bank of Commerce, financial advisors are evaluated for their listening skills: how effectively can they determine problems customers do not express? How well do they perceive the basic causes of a customer's concerns? At CIBC, listening skills are considered a core competency for employees.[40]

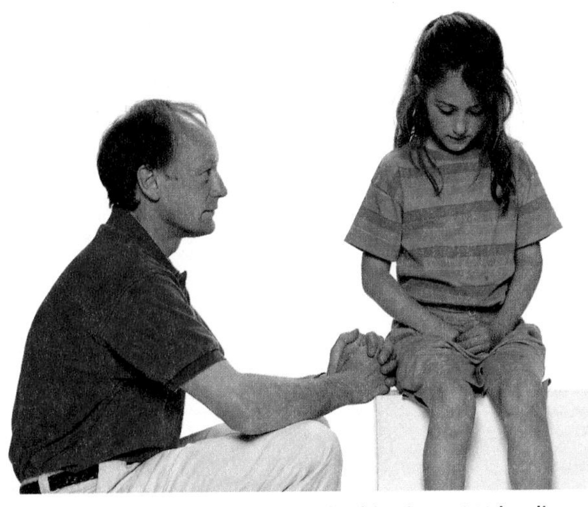

What type of listening is occuring in this picture? What listening skills must the adult apply in this situation?

Types of Listening

To be a good listener, vary the way you listen to suit the situation.

Three types of listening differ not only in purpose but also in the amount of feedback or interaction that occurs. You can improve relationships and productivity by matching your listening style to the speaker's purpose.[41] For example, the goal of **informational listening** is to understand and retain the speaker's message. You may ask questions, but basically information flows from the speaker to you. It doesn't matter that you agree or disagree, approve or disapprove—only that you understand.[42] When you listen to a regional sales manager's monthly report on how many of your products sold that month, you are listening for information. Looking for the main ideas and paraphrasing what the speaker is saying will help you understand and retain the information effectively.[43]

The goal of **critical listening** is to understand and evaluate the meaning of the speaker's message on several levels. You want to consider the logic of the argument, the strength of the evidence, and the validity of the conclusions. You also want to analyze the implications of the message for you and your organization, the speaker's intentions and motives, and the omission of any important or relevant points. Critical listening generally involves interaction as you try to uncover the speaker's point of view and credibility.[44] When the regional sales manager presents sales projections for the next few months, you listen critically, evaluating whether the estimates are valid and what the implications are for your manufacturing department.

The goal of **empathic listening** is to understand the speaker's feelings, needs, and wants so that you can appreciate his or her point of view, regardless of whether you share that perspective. By listening in an empathic way, you help the individual vent the emotions that prevent a dispassionate approach to the subject. Avoid the temptation to give advice. Try not to judge the individual's feelings; just let the other person talk.[45] Listen empathetically when your regional sales manager tells you about a conflict with one of the salespeople who's not meeting his quotas.

Each type of listening is most effective in particular situations. To gain better control of your listening skills, examine what happens when you listen.

OBJECTIVE 4 Describe the listening process and discuss three barriers that interfere with this process.

The Listening Process

By understanding the process of listening, you begin to understand why oral messages are so often lost. Listening involves the following five related activities:[46]

Listening involves five steps: receiving, interpreting, remembering, evaluating, and responding.

- **Receiving:** Physically hearing the message and taking note of it. Noise, impaired hearing, or inattention can block physical reception.
- **Interpreting:** Assigning meaning to sounds according to your own values, beliefs, ideas, expectations, roles, needs, and personal history. The speaker's frame of reference may be quite different from yours, so you may need to determine what the speaker really means.
- **Remembering:** Storing a message for future reference. As you listen, you retain what you hear by taking notes or by making a mental outline of the speaker's key points.
- **Evaluating:** Applying critical-thinking skills to weigh the speaker's remarks. You separate fact from opinion and evaluate the quality of the evidence. You ask, Is the evidence credible? Why is it credible?
- **Responding:** Reacting once you've evaluated the speaker's message. If you're communicating one-on-one or in a small group, the initial response generally takes the form of verbal feedback (see Table 2–2 below). If you're one of many in an audience, your initial response may take the form of applause, laughter, or silence. Later on, you may act on what you have heard.

Because listening requires a mix of physical and mental activities, it is subject to a variety of physical and mental barriers. A large part of becoming a good listener is the ability to recognize and overcome these barriers.

TABLE 2–2 Giving Constructive Feedback

To Give Constructive Feedback
• **Focus on particular behaviours.** Feedback should be specific rather than general.
• **Keep feedback impersonal.** No matter how upset you are, keep feedback job related, and never criticize someone personally.
• **Keep feedback goal oriented.** If you have to say something negative, make sure it's directed toward the recipient's goals. For example, you might have to tell a colleague, "Your frequent absences prevent the team from meeting our deadlines."
• **Make feedback well timed.** Feedback is most meaningful when there is a short interval between the recipient's behaviour and the receipt of feedback about that behaviour. An interval helps create distance, and thus a degree of objectivity. Your colleague will be more open to your remarks.
• **Ensure understanding.** If feedback is to be effective, you need to make sure the recipient understands it. Use language that your colleague comprehends, and avoid terms that might offend.
• **Direct negative feedback toward behaviour that is controllable by the recipient.** There's little value in reminding a person of some shortcoming over which he or she has no control. Be sensitive to such personal factors.

TABLE 2–3 Distinguishing Good Listeners from Bad Listeners

The Bad Listener	The Good Listener	To Listen Effectively
Tunes out dry subjects	Seeks opportunities; asks "What's in it for me?"	1. Find areas of interest
Tunes out if delivery is poor	Judges content; skips over delivery errors	2. Judge content, not delivery
Tends to enter into argument	Doesn't judge until comprehension is complete; interrupts only to clarify	3. Reserve judgment until you are sure you completely understand the speaker.
Listens for facts	Listens for central themes	4. Listen for ideas
Takes extensive notes	Takes fewer notes	5. Take selective notes
Fakes attention	Demonstrates interest; exhibits active body state	6. Work at listening
Is distracted easily	Fights or avoids distractions; knows how to concentrate	7. Block out competing thoughts
Resists difficult material	Uses heavier material as exercise for the mind	8. Paraphrase the speaker's ideas
Reacts to emotional words	Interprets emotional words; does not get hung up on them	9. Stay open-minded
Tends to daydream with slow speakers	Listens between the lines; weighs the evidence; mentally summarizes	10. Capitalize on the fact that thought is faster than speech

Barriers to Effective Listening

Prejudgment is one of the most common barriers to listening and it can be difficult to overcome because it is an automatic process. To operate in life, people must hold some assumptions. However, in new situations, these assumptions can often be incorrect. Moreover, some people listen defensively, viewing every comment as a personal attack. To protect their self-esteem, they distort messages by tuning out anything that doesn't confirm their view of themselves.

When you jump to conclusions, you close your mind to additional information.

Self-centredness causes people to take control of conversations, rather than listening to what's being said. For example, if a speaker mentions a problem (perhaps a manager is trying to deal with conflict between team members), self-centred listeners eagerly relate their own problems with team conflict. They trivialize the speaker's concerns by pointing out that their own difficulties are twice as great and they can top positive experiences as well. No matter what subject is being discussed, they believe they know more than the speaker does—and they're determined to prove it.

Self-centred listeners shift their attention from the speaker to themselves.

When you listen selectively, you let your mind wander to thoughts such as what you will be doing after work. You stay tuned out until you hear a word or phrase that gets your attention once more. The result is that you don't remember what the speaker *actually* said; instead, you remember what you *think* the speaker probably said.[47]

Selective listeners tune the speaker out.

One reason we lose focus from the speaker's message is that we think faster than we speak. Most people speak at about 120 to 150 words per minute. However, studies indicate that, depending on the subject and the individual, people can process information at 500 to 800 words per minute.[48] This disparity between rate of speech and rate of thought can be used to pull your arguments together, but some listeners let their minds wander.

Your mind can process information more than four times faster than the rate of speech.

Recognize these counterproductive tendencies as barriers and work on overcoming them (see Table 2–3 above). Becoming a good listener will help you in many business situations—especially those that are emotion laden and difficult. You can assess your listening skills by paying attention to how you listen. Are you really hearing what is said? Or are you mentally rehearsing how you will respond? For a summary of how to listen better, see this chapter's "Checklist: Improving Your Listening Skills" on page 36.

OBJECTIVE 5 Clarify the importance of nonverbal communication and briefly describe six categories of nonverbal expression.

Understanding Nonverbal Communication

Nonverbal signals often occur unconsciously.

Good listeners pay attention to more than just verbal communication: they look for unspoken messages, the most basic form of communication. Such nonverbal communication consists of all the cues, gestures, facial expressions, spatial relationships, and attitudes toward time that enable people to communicate without words. And it differs from verbal communication in terms of intent and spontaneity. When you say, "Please get back to me on that order by Friday," you have a conscious purpose; you think about the message, if only for a moment. However, you don't mean to raise an eyebrow or to blush. Those actions come naturally. Without a word, and without your consent, your face reveals your emotions. Good communicators recognize the value of nonverbal communication and use it to enhance the communication process (see "Sharpening Your Career Skills—Improving Your Business Etiquette" on page 38).

The Importance of Nonverbal Communication

Nonverbal communication may unintentionally reveal a person's true feelings, motivation, or character.

It's believed that people interpret 65 to 90 percent of each conversation through nonverbal cues.[49] Words are relatively easy to control; it's more difficult to regulate our body language, facial expressions, and vocal characteristics. By paying attention to these nonverbal cues, you can sharpen your perception of the attitude behind a speaker's words.

Because nonverbal communication is often helpful in understanding the spoken message, people generally have more faith in nonverbal cues than they do in verbal messages. If a person says one thing but transmits a conflicting message nonverbally, listeners tend to react more to the nonverbal signal than to the words they are hearing.[50] If you are sensitive to other people's nonverbal messages, you can have insight

Checklist: Improving Your Listening Skills

Look beyond the Speaker's Style

✓ Don't judge the message by the speaker but by the argument

✓ Ask yourself what the speaker knows that you don't

✓ Decrease the emotional impact of what's being said

Fight Distractions

✓ Close doors

✓ Turn off radios and televisions

✓ Move closer to the speaker

✓ Stay ahead of the speaker by anticipating what will be said next and summarizing what's already been said

✓ Don't interrupt—avoid sidetracking solutions and throwing the speaker off course

✓ Hold your rebuttal until you've heard the entire message

Provide Feedback

✓ Let the speaker know you're paying attention by maintaining eye contact and nodding occasionally

✓ Present appropriate facial expressions

✓ Paraphrase what you've heard when the speaker reaches a stopping point

✓ Keep all criticism and feedback positive

Listen Actively

✓ Listen for concepts, key ideas, and facts

✓ Be able to distinguish between evidence and argument, idea and example, fact and principle

✓ Analyze the key points—whether they make sense and are supported by facts

✓ Look for unspoken messages in the speaker's tone of voice or expressions

✓ Keep an open mind

✓ Ask questions that clarify

✓ Reserve judgment until the speaker has finished

✓ Take meaningful notes that are brief and to the point

into their underlying attitudes and intentions and respond appropriately. But keep in mind that you can also misinterpret nonverbal cues. For example, let's imagine you're giving a presentation about your company's new product to potential clients. A member of your audience is sitting with her arms crossed in front of her and she is frowning. You think her appearance indicates that she is opposed to purchasing the product, and you change tactics in your presentation. However, is your perception of her appearance accurate? Her posture and her facial expression can simply be the way she behaves when weighing the pros and cons of an argument. In fact, she may believe that the product is first-rate and that her company should buy it.[51]

Nonverbal communication is important not only because it may help us understand the underlying attitudes of a speaker, but also because it is an efficient form of communication. You can transmit a nonverbal message without even thinking about it, and your audience can register the meaning unconsciously. At the same time, when you have a conscious purpose, you can often achieve it more economically with a gesture than you can with words. A wave of the hand, a pat on the back, a wink—all are streamlined expressions of thought. However, nonverbal communication usually blends with speech to carry part of the message—to augment, reinforce, and clarify that message.

People use nonverbal signals to support and clarify verbal communication.

The Types of Nonverbal Communication

The many forms of nonverbal communication can be grouped into the following general categories: facial expression, gesture and posture, vocal characteristics, personal appearance, touching behaviour, and use of time and space.

FACIAL EXPRESSION

Your face is the primary site for expressing your emotions; it reveals both the type and the intensity of your feelings.[52] Your eyes are especially effective for indicating attention and interest, influencing others, regulating interaction, and establishing dominance. In fact, eye contact is so important in Canadian and U.S. cultures that even when your words send a positive message, averting your gaze can lead your audience to perceive a negative one.[53] However, in some situations maintaining strong eye contact can damage your purpose. Steven Schiffman, president of an international sales training company, says, "If eye contact is held too long with sales prospects, they may be forced into a fight or flight response."[54] To avoid putting pressure on potential customers, Shiffman suggests moving your glance away to let them think about your question and their answer.

The face and eyes command particular attention as sources of nonverbal messages.

Of course, people sometimes manipulate their expressions to simulate an emotion they do not feel or to mask their true feelings. And the interpretation of facial expressions, and of all nonverbal signals, varies from culture to culture (as discussed in Chapter 3). Furthermore, culture is only one influence on our individual body language—other influences are family background and personal habits, and our state of mind at a particular time.[55]

GESTURE AND POSTURE

By moving your body, you can express both specific and general messages, some voluntary and some involuntary. Many gestures—a wave of the hand, for example—have a specific and intentional meaning, such as "hello" or "good-bye." Other types of body movement are unintentional and express a more general message. Slouching, leaning forward, fidgeting, and walking briskly are all unconscious signals that reveal whether you feel confident or nervous, friendly or hostile, assertive or passive, powerful or powerless. For example, if you tend to drum your fingers on your desk or check your watch while listening to a colleague, you will give the impression that you are in a hurry and want to cut the conversation. This body language may inhibit fellow employees from seeking your advice in the future.

Body language and tone of voice reveal a lot about a person's emotions and attitudes.

VOCAL CHARACTERISTICS

Like body language, your voice carries both intentional and unintentional messages. On a conscious level, we can use our voices to create various impressions. Consider the sentence "What have you been up to?" If you repeat this question four or five times, changing your tone of voice and stressing various words, you can convey quite different messages. However, your vocal characteristics also reveal many things of which you are unaware. The tone and volume of your voice, your accent and speaking pace, and all the little um's and ah's that creep into your speech say a lot about who you are, your relationship with the audience, and the emotions underlying your words.

Physical appearance and personal style contribute to one's identity.

PERSONAL APPEARANCE

People respond to others on the basis of their physical appearance. Because you see yourself as others see you, their expectations are often a self-fulfilling prophecy; that is, when people think you're capable and attractive, you feel good about yourself, and that feeling affects your behaviour, which in turn affects other people's perceptions of you. Although an individual's body type and facial features impose limitations, most people are able to control their attractiveness to some degree. Grooming, clothing, accessories, "style"—all modify a person's appearance. If your goal is to make a good impression, adopt the style of the people you want to impress.

When you speak with friends, colleagues at work, or teachers, do you consciously analyze their body language? What does the stance, eye contact, and gesture suggest about the unspoken messages between the people in this photograph?

TOUCHING BEHAVIOUR

Touch is an important vehicle for conveying warmth, comfort, and reassurance. Perhaps because it implies intimacy, touching behaviour is governed in various circumstances by relatively strict customs that establish who can touch whom and how. The accepted norms vary, depending on the gender, age, relative status, and cultural background of the persons involved. In business situations, touching suggests dominance, so a higher-status person is more likely to touch a lower-status person than the other way around. Touching has become controversial, however, because it can sometimes be interpreted as sexual harassment.

Punctuality and comfort zones vary by culture and authority.

USE OF TIME AND SPACE

Like touch, time and space can be used to assert authority. Some people demonstrate their importance by making other people wait; others show respect by being on time. People can also assert their status by occupying the best space. In Canadian companies, the chief executive usually has the corner office and the most scenic view. Apart from serving as a symbol of status, space can determine how comfortable people feel talking with each other. When others stand too close or too far away, we are likely to feel ill at ease.

Again, attitudes toward punctuality and comfort zones vary from culture to culture (see Chapter 3). See this chapter's "Checklist: Improving Nonverbal Communication Skills," below.

SHARPENING YOUR CAREER SKILLS

Improving Your Business Etiquette

Etiquette is knowing how to behave properly in a given situation. Knowing how to interact with people in business will help you appear polished, professional, and confident. Following proper etiquette helps you put fellow employees, business associates, and customers at ease so that they feel comfortable doing business with you.

Consider such common interactions as smiling, shaking hands, and making introductions. When you smile, do so genuinely. An artificial smile is obvious because the timing is off and the expression fails to involve all the facial muscles that a genuine smile would. Repeated false smiling may earn you the reputation of being insincere. Plus, if you smile too long, you make others uncomfortable, because they feel that you're not focused on the present. However, certain occasions require smiling:

- **When you are introduced to someone.** Smiling is courteous and suggests that you are receptive.

- **When you are feeling uncomfortable or out of place.** Smiling masks your concerns, and your confidence level will rise quickly (always being careful that your smile does not appear false).
- **When you give or receive a compliment.** Smiling punctuates your tribute when you give praise. If you're receiving praise, smiling augment's the other person's position. Even if you feel embarrassed or undeserving, don't diminish the praise-giver by revealing those feelings.
- **When you applaud someone.** Smiling is the courteous, gracious thing to do.

In Canada and the United States, most business greetings include a handshake. (Other cultures may have varying approaches or completely different customs.) Extend your hand to greet business associates, regardless of gender. When seated, rise from your chair if you are physically able, and lean into the handshake. Pulling away suggests that something is wrong (people may pull away because of powerful perfume, tobacco residue on breath or clothing, or body odor). Make eye contact, smile, and nod your head to indicate that the person has your full attention. Never extend your hand while turning your head to speak to someone else.

Convey confidence, assurance, interest, and respect by using a firm handshake, without squeezing too hard. Use your right hand. Your hand should touch the other person's extended hand. Thumbs should point upward as you shake hands vertically and face one another squarely. Although your handshake should be brief, it should last long enough for both persons to speak their name and a few words of greeting.

Proper introductions are also an important part of business etiquette. The whole purpose of an introduction is to give people an opportunity to establish a connection, to get to know one another. When introducing yourself to a stranger, include a short, matter-of-fact description of your role, followed by a question about your new acquaintance. When introducing two other people, weave appropriate information into the introduction to help the individuals ease into a comfortable conversation. Try suggesting a subject of mutual interest. Remember that first and last names are mandatory. The people you're introducing need to know what to call each other and how to find each other later. You might say, "Henry Johnson, I would like you to meet Meredith Tucker, our new team member. Ms. Tucker, this is Mr. Johnson, senior manager at Lynco Systems. Ms. Tucker recently canoed the Nahanni River on a four-day trip. Mr. Johnson just returned from sabbatical in London, England."

When making introductions, gender is not a factor in who is introduced to whom. For instance, you should mention the name of the older, more senior person first. Here are some examples of preferred forms of introduction:

- Introduce younger to older ("Mr. *Older Executive,* I would like you to meet Mr. *Younger Executive.*").
- Introduce company peer to a peer in another company (Sam Locker, I'd like to introduce Kelly Martin, our head of engineering. Kelly, this is Sam from Brent & Moran.").
- Introduce junior executive to senior executive ("Ms. *Senior Executive,* I would like to introduce Mr. *Junior Executive.*").
- Introduce fellow executive to a client or customer ("Mrs. Claire Waters, I'd like you to meet Kelly Martin, our head of engineering. Kelly, this is Mrs. Waters, one of our newest clients.").

When you're introduced to someone, take note of the person's name and use it as soon as possible. Try connecting the name with something common to you—perhaps the name is the same as a school friend or a favourite movie character. Knowing and using someone's name is a compliment, and doing so will be useful if you need to contact or refer to this person in the future.

By applying basic business etiquette, you will help create positive working relationships and gain the respect of your peers.

CAREER APPLICATIONS

You are introduced to a new business associate. You extend your hand expecting a handshake, but the person does not extend his. What do you do? Explain your answer.

Should you feel embarrassed if you don't remember someone's name after you are introduced? What should you do?

Source: Dana May Casperson, *Power Etiquette: What You Don't Know Can Kill Your Career,* (New York: AMACOM, 1999), 22; Marilyn Pincus, *Everyday Business Etiquette* (Hauppauge, N.Y.: Barron's Educational Series, 1996), 7, 133; Ellyn Spragins, "Introducing Politeness," *Fortune Small Business,* November 2001, 30.

Increasing Meeting Productivity

OBJECTIVE 6 Explain how you can improve meeting productivity through preparation, leadership, and participation.

Meetings help teams solve problems by providing the opportunity for giving and getting feedback, whether your goal is to develop ideas, identify opportunities, or decide how to maximize resources. Meetings are the lifeblood of business if they run efficiently, and a burden if they are run inefficiently and do not yield the needed results. Unfortunately, many meetings are unproductive. In one study, senior and middle managers reported that only 56 percent of their meetings were actually fruitful and that 25 percent of them could have been handled by a phone call or a memo.[56] Meeting productivity is affected by the way you prepare for them and the way you conduct and participate in them.

Checklist: Improving Nonverbal Communication Skills

Receiving Nonverbal Signals

✓ Pay more attention to the nonverbal signals of others

✓ Be aware that people may give false nonverbal cues

Sending Nonverbal Signals

✓ Avoid giving conflicting signals

✓ Try to be as honest as possible in communicating your emotions

✓ Smile genuinely as faking a smile is obvious to observers

✓ Maintain the eye contact your audience expects

✓ Be aware of your posture and of the gestures you use

✓ Try to use appropriate vocal signals while minimizing unintentional messages

✓ Imitate the appearance of the people you want to impress

✓ Respect your audience's comfort zone

✓ Adopt a handshake that matches your personality and intention

✓ Be aware of varying attitudes toward time

✓ Use touch only when appropriate

Interpreting Nonverbal Signals

✓ Remember that few gestures convey meaning in and of themselves

✓ Remember that the context of situation and culture influences nonverbal communication. Be aware that you might misinterpret nonverbal signals

Preparing for Meetings

The best preparation for a meeting is having a specific goal that would be best handled in a face-to-face situation.

The biggest mistake in holding meetings is not having a specific goal. So before you call a meeting, satisfy yourself that one is truly needed. Perhaps you could communicate more effectively in a memo or through individual conversations. If you do require the interaction of a group, you want to bring the right people together in the right place for just enough time to accomplish your goals. The key to productive meetings is careful planning of purpose, participants, location, and agenda.

DECIDE ON YOUR PURPOSE

Although many meetings combine purposes, most are usually either for informational or decision-making purposes. Information meetings allow participants to share information and perhaps coordinate action. Briefings may come from each participant or from the meeting leader, who then answers questions from attendees. Decision-making meetings mainly involve persuasion, analysis, and problem solving. They often include a brainstorming session, followed by a debate on the alternatives, and they require that each participant is aware of the nature of the problem and the criteria for its solution.

SELECT PARTICIPANTS

Being invited to a particular meeting can be a mark of status, and you may be reluctant to leave anyone out. Nevertheless, try to invite only those people whose presence is essential. If the session is purely informational and one person will be doing most of the talking, you can include a relatively large group. However, if you're trying to solve a problem, develop a plan, or reach a decision, try to limit participation to only those people who must attend. These participants should be invited because they can contribute information essential to the group's deliberations. One suggestion is to limit meetings where analysis takes place to between six and twelve participants.[57]

An agenda, committee reports, and debate are all elements of Canadian parliamentary procedure. Why is an established order important to both political and business meetings?

CHOOSE AN APPROPRIATE LOCATION

Decide where you'll hold the meeting, and reserve the location. For work sessions, morning meetings are usually more productive than afternoon sessions. Also, consider the seating arrangements. Are rows of chairs suitable, or do you need a conference table? Plus, give some attention to details such as room temperature, lighting, ventilation, acoustics, and refreshments. These environmental concerns may seem trivial, but if you ensure that attendees are comfortable, they will be more likely to think sharply and contribute fully.

You might also consider calling a virtual meeting (see the section on Using Technology to Collaborate on page 31 of this chapter for virtual meeting tips). Companies such as WebEx **www.webex.com** offer facilities in cyberspace for meeting with colleagues, customers, and other stakeholders For example, following the WebEx prompts, you enter the meeting date and time, send e-mail announcements to attendees, and request features such as online polling. Then, at meeting time, participants log onto WebEx, click "Join Meeting," and enter a special code to attend your meeting.

SET AND FOLLOW AN AGENDA

Although the nature of a meeting may sometimes prevent you from developing a fixed agenda, at least prepare a list of matters to be discussed. Distribute the agenda (e-mail is very efficient) to the participants several days before the meeting so that they will know what to expect and can come prepared to respond to the issues at hand.

Distribute the agenda ahead of time.

Agendas include the names of the participants, the time, the place, and the order of business (see Appendix A for agenda format). A productive agenda should answer three key questions: (1) What do we need to do in this meeting to accomplish our goals? (2) What conversations will be of greatest importance to all the participants? (3) What information must be available in order to have these conversations?[58]

It's important that your agenda is specific. For example, the phrase "development budget" doesn't reveal much, whereas the longer explanation "Discussion: Proposed reduction of 2005–2006 development budget because of product postponement" helps all committee members prepare in advance with facts and figures.

Apart from providing the meeting's purpose and tasks, agendas help you start and end your meetings on time. As a type of schedule, an agenda sends a signal of good organization and allows attendees to meet other commitments. In fact, one solution for improving meetings is simply telling people what time the meeting will end. Setting a time limit helps people to focus and avoid socializing and digressing.

Conducting and Participating in Meetings

Whether a meeting is conducted electronically or conventionally, its success depends largely on the effectiveness of the leader. If the leader is prepared and has selected participants carefully, the meeting will generally be productive, especially if the leader has good listening skills.

KEEP THE MEETING ON TRACK

A good meeting is not a series of dialogues between individual members and the leader. Instead, it's a cross-flow of discussion and debate, with the leader occasionally guiding, mediating, probing, stimulating, and summarizing, but mostly letting the

Checklist: Improving Meeting Productivity

Preparation

✓ Determine the meeting's objectives
✓ Work out an agenda that will achieve your objectives
✓ Select participants
✓ Determine the location and reserve a room
✓ Arrange for light refreshments, if appropriate
✓ Determine whether the lighting, ventilation, acoustics, and temperature of the room are adequate
✓ Determine seating needs: chairs only or table and chairs

Conduct

✓ Begin and end the meeting on time
✓ Control the meeting by following the announced agenda
✓ Encourage full participation, and either confront or ignore those who seem to be working at cross-purposes with the group
✓ Sum up decisions, actions, and recommendations as you move through the agenda, and restate main points at the end

Follow-Up

✓ Distribute the meeting's notes or minutes on a timely basis
✓ Take the agreed upon follow-up action

others thrash out their ideas. That's why it's important for leaders to avoid being so domineering that they close off suggestions. Of course, they must not be so passive that they lose control of the group. The meeting leader is a facilitator, rather than an autocratic ruler.

Don't be so rigid that you cut off discussion too quickly.

As leader, you're responsible for keeping the meeting moving along. If the discussion lags, call on those who haven't been heard from. Pace the presentation and discussion so that you'll have time to complete the agenda. As time begins to run out, interrupt the discussion and summarize what has been accomplished. However, don't be too rigid. Allow enough time for discussion, and give people a chance to raise related issues. If you cut off discussion too quickly or limit the subject too narrowly, no real consensus can emerge.

FOLLOW PARLIAMENTARY PROCEDURE

Robert's Rules of Order is the most common guide to parliamentary procedure.

One way you can improve the productivity of a meeting is by using **parliamentary procedure**, a time-tested method for planning and running effective meetings. Anyone belonging to a team should understand the basic principles of parliamentary procedure. Used correctly, it can help teams transact business efficiently and accomplish the meeting's goals. Parliamentary procedure also ensures that meetings proceed in a democratic manner, because it protects individual rights, maintains order, and preserves a spirit of harmony.[59] The most common guide to parliamentary procedure is *Robert's Rules of Order,* available in various editions. Also available are less technical guides based on "Robert's Rules" and "plain language" versions that help both newcomers to and experienced users of this system understand and apply it (check out the online "Survival Tips on Robert's Rules of Order" at **www.roberts-rules.com/index.html**). You can determine how strictly you want to adhere to parliamentary procedure. For small groups you may be quite flexible, but for larger groups you'll want to use a more formal approach.

ENCOURAGE PARTICIPATION

Don't let one or two members dominate the meeting.

As the meeting gets under way, you'll discover that some participants are too quiet and others are too talkative. To draw out the quiet ones, ask for their input on issues that particularly pertain to them. You might say something like, "Bob, you've done a lot of work in this area. What do you think?" For the overly talkative, simply say that time is limited and others need to be heard from. The best meetings are those in which everyone participates, so don't let one or two people dominate your meeting while others doodle on their notepads. As you move through your agenda, stop at the end of each item, summarize what you understand to be the feelings of the group, and state the important points made during the discussion.

If you're a meeting participant, try to contribute to both the subject of the meeting and the smooth interaction of the participants. Use your listening skills and powers of observation to size up the interpersonal dynamics of the people, then adapt your behaviour to help the group achieve its goals. Speak up if you have something useful to say, but don't monopolize the discussion.

CLOSE AND FOLLOW UP

Following up with minutes of the meeting allows you to remind everyone of what happened and who needs to take action.

At the conclusion of the meeting, tie up the loose ends. Either summarize the general conclusion of the group or list the suggestions. An overall summary at the end ensures that all participants agree on the outcome and gives them a chance to clear up any misunderstandings. Before people depart, briefly review who has agreed to accept a specific task and when that task will be completed.

Finally, be sure to follow up. As soon as possible after the meeting, make sure all participants receive a copy of the minutes or notes, showing recommended actions, schedules, and responsibilities (see Appendix A, for minutes format). The minutes will remind everyone of what took place and will provide a reference for future actions. To review the tasks that contribute to productive meetings, see this chapter's "Checklist: Improving Meeting Productivity".

Summary of Learning Outcomes

1 Explain the advantages and disadvantages of using teams. Teams can achieve a higher level of performance than individuals because of the combined intelligence and energy of the group. Motivation and creativity flourish in team settings. Moreover, individuals tend to perform better because they achieve a sense of purpose by belonging to a group. Teams also bring more input and a greater diversity of views, which tends to result in better decisions. And because team members participate in the decision-making process, they are committed to seeing the results succeed. Teams do have disadvantages, however. If poorly managed, teams can be a waste of everyone's time. If members are pressured to conform, they may develop groupthink, which can lead to poor-quality decisions and ill-advised actions; some members may let their private motives get in the way. Others may not contribute their fair share, so certain tasks may not be completed.

2 Identify the characteristics of effective teams. Effective team members interact openly and recognize the value that others bring to the group. Members are willing to exchange information, examine issues, and work though conflicts. They focus on the greater good of the team instead of personal agendas. As a group, they understand what is expected of them, stick to the task at hand, and reach decisions by consensus after open, honest debate. All members are encouraged to think creatively and participate. They listen to and value feedback from others, and they don't feel threatened by taking an unpopular stance.

3 Discuss the tasks involved in preparing effective team messages, and list nine guidelines for improvement. Effective team messages require team members to be flexible and open-minded so that they can focus on the team's objectives rather than their own. Team members need to get organized, select a leader, and clarify goals. They must agree on the purpose of their project and on who their audience is. Members must plan how the document will be organized and formatted, and they must choose a writing style. To prepare effective messages, team members can use guidelines such as the following: (1) Select team members wisely, (2) select a responsible leader, (3) promote cooperation, (4) clarify goals, (5) elicit commitment, (6) clarify responsibilities, (7) instill prompt action, (8) apply technology, (9) ensure technological compatibility.

4 Describe the listening process and list three barriers that interfere with this process. The listening process involves five activities: (1) receiving (physically hearing the message), (2) interpreting (assigning meaning to what you hear), (3) remembering (storing the message for future reference), (4) evaluating (thinking about the message), and (5) responding (reacting to the message, taking action, or giving feedback). Three barriers can interfere with the listening process. Prejudgment involves holding assumptions, right or wrong, sometimes even distorting messages if they don't conform with what you want to hear. Self-centredness involves people monopolizing a conversation with their own experience rather than listening to what someone else has to say. And, finally, selective listening involves letting your mind wander away from the speaker and not paying close attention.

5 Clarify the importance of nonverbal communication and briefly describe six categories of nonverbal expression. Nonverbal communication is important because actions may speak louder than words. Body language is more difficult to control than words and may reveal a person's true feelings, motivation, or character. Consequently, people tend to believe nonverbal signals over the spoken message. In addition, nonverbal communication is more efficient; with a wave of your hand or a wink, you can streamline your thoughts—and do so without much thought. Types of nonverbal expression include facial expression, gesture and posture, vocal characteristics, personal appearance, touching behaviour, and use of time and space.

6 Explain how you can improve meeting productivity through preparation, leadership, and participation. When preparing to have a meeting, be sure that your purpose cannot be accomplished better by some other means (e-mail or phone calls). Plan effectively by deciding on your purpose, selecting participants who must attend, choosing a location and time that are conducive to your goals, and developing an agenda that is specific and complete. Conduct productive meetings by guiding, mediating, and summarizing. Pace the discussion, and encourage everyone to participate. Before the end, summarize conclusions and review who has agreed to accept a task and when it will be completed. Follow up with minutes that show recommended actions, schedules, and responsibilities. As a participant in any meeting, do everything you can to contribute to the smooth interaction of attendees as well as to the subject.

ON THE JOB

Solving a Communication Dilemma at Royal Bank Financial Group

As one of Royal Bank's essential values, teamwork permeates all business activities. High-level managers such as Elisabetta Bigsby, senior executive vice-president, Human Resources and Public Affairs, and Charles Coffey, executive vice-president, Government and Community Affairs, believe that teamwork has helped to make Royal Bank become one of Canada's most respected corporations in the areas of human resource management, corporate social responsibility, and corporate governance. In 2002, when the bank re-examined its basic values, each employee received a comprehensive communication package, reinforced by workshops, training, and "e-learning" technologies that imparted the importance and structures of teamwork. Royal Bank's agenda for building a winning team requires: (1) staying close to the customer, (2) having a commitment to excellence, (3) making a difference every day, (4) being accountable for results, and (5) sharing with peers. To promote communication within each team, Royal Bank makes sure that every employee has access to the company's highly efficient computer network. Team members conduct virtual meetings with colleagues around Canada and the world, and they take advantage of e-mail and videoconferencing to brainstorm and collaborate on projects. Office meetings have predetermined agendas and follow regular schedules to reduce wasted meeting time and to allow team members to communicate face to face. One interesting team manages staffing in the Bank's branches in Canada. Under the guidance of Dick Johnson, senior manager of operations and resource optimization, this group uses Planet, a software that helps the Bank to fine-tune employee schedules by tracking the service and transaction times at each of the 1300 branches. This four-person team works in partnership with the branches to determine optimum staffing needs. New employees are introduced to the team concept right away, making sure that everyone at Royal Bank contributes to the company's success through effective teamwork.

Your Mission You have recently been promoted to assistant branch manager at your neighbourhood Royal Bank. Your responsibilities include (1) promoting the team concept among all customer service representatives in your branch, and (2) serving as a team leader on special projects that involve your staff. Choose the best alternatives for handling the following situations, and be prepared to explain why your choice is best.

1 Your district manager has asked you and three other employees at your large urban branch to find a solution to the lack of sufficient office space for the growing number of employees at your location. As leader, you schedule team meetings on Thursday afternoons for four weeks to address the problem. After two meetings with your co-workers, you notice that everyone is making vital contributions to the group's efforts—except Jane. During the meetings, she displays very poor listening skills. She often jumps ahead of the topic or interrupts a speaker's train of thought. At other times, she doodles on her notepad instead of taking constructive notes. And she remains silent after team members deliver lengthy reports about possible solutions to the office space problem. What can you do as team leader to help Jane improve her listening skills?

a Ask Jane to take extensive notes during each meeting. The process of taking detailed notes will improve her concentration and force her to listen more carefully to team members. After the meeting, she can use her notes as a reference to clarify any questions about team decisions or the nature of assignments to individual team members.
b Suggest that Jane mentally summarize the speaker's ideas—or verbally rephrase the ideas in her own words—during the meeting. With some practice, Jane should be able to focus on the topics under discussion and block out distracting thoughts.
c. Schedule future team meetings for Thursday mornings instead of Thursday afternoons. After devoting most of the workday to her regular duties, Jane may be feeling tired or sluggish by the time your team meeting rolls around.
d Prepare a detailed, written summary of each meeting. The summary will clarify any points that Jane may have missed during the meeting and provide her with a complete reference of team decisions and assignments.

2 As assistant branch manager, you schedule a team meeting to discuss new methods of inspiring and motivating customer service representatives to achieve their quarterly goals for selling bank products, such as guaranteed investment certificates. During the meeting, one customer service representative disagrees with every suggestion offered by team members, often reacting with a sneer on his face and a belligerent tone of voice. Which of the following strategies is the best way to overcome the rep's resistance?
a Ignore his remarks. Keep the meeting on track and avoid destructive confrontations by asking for input from other team members.
b Directly confront the sales rep's concerns. Point out the flaws in his arguments, and offer support for the opinions of other team members.
c Remain calm and try to understand his point of view. Ask him to clarify his points, and solicit his suggestions for motivating sales representatives.
d Politely acknowledge his opinions, then repeat the most valid suggestions offered by other team members in a convincing manner.

3 Some employees at your branch want to organize a group to decorate the branch for Thanksgiving. What is the focus of this meeting?
a To find out about competitors' activities for the holiday.
b To inform top managers of the interest in decorating your branch for Thanksgiving.
c To decide which managers/employees should be asked to participate in this project.
d To reach an agreement about the value and practicality of this activity.

4 The district manager realizes his communication skills are important for several reasons: He holds primary responsibility for the region; he needs to communicate with the branch managers who report to him; and his style sets an example for other employees in the region. He asks you to sit in on face-to-face meetings for several days to observe his nonverbal messages. You witness four habits. Which of the following habits do you think is the most negative?
a He rarely comes out from behind his massive desk when meeting people; at one point, he offered a congratulatory handshake to a branch manager, and the manager had to lean way over his desk just to reach him.
b When a manager hands him a report and then sits down to discuss it, he alternates between making eye contact and making notes on the report.
c He is consistently pleasant, even if the person he is meeting is delivering bad news.
d He interrupts meetings to answer the phone, rather than letting an assistant get the phone; then he apologizes to visitors for the interruption.[60]

Test Your Knowledge

Review Questions

1 What are three ways in which an organization's decision making can benefit from teams?
2 What are the main activities that make up the listening process?
3 In what six ways can an individual communicate nonverbally?
4 What questions should an effective agenda answer?
5 How do self-oriented team roles differ from team-maintenance roles and task-facilitating team roles?
6 What is groupthink, and how can it affect an organization?
7 How can organizations help team members successfully resolve conflict?
8 What role does the leader play in helping a team produce effective messages?
9 How does informational listening differ from critical listening and empathic listening?
10 How is nonverbal communication limited?
11 What is the purpose of using parliamentary procedure?

Interactive Learning 

Use this text's online resources.

Visit our Companion Web site at **www.pearsoned.ca/thill**, where you can use the interactive Study Guide to test your chapter knowledge and get instant feedback. Additional resources link you to the sites mentioned in this text and to additional sources of information on chapter topics.

Also check out the resources on the Mastering Business Communication CD, including "Perils of Pauline," an interactive presentation of the business communication challenges within a fictional company. For Chapter 2, see in particular the episodes "Conducting a Meeting," "Verbal and Nonverbal Communication," "Brainstorming Sessions," "Listening Skills," and "Resolving Conflict."

Apply Your Knowledge

Critical Thinking Questions

1 How can nonverbal communication help you run a meeting? How can it help you call a meeting to order and emphasize important topics? How can it help you show approval? How can nonverbal communication help you to express reservations and regulate the flow of conversation?

2 Whenever your boss asks for feedback, she attacks anyone offering criticism, which causes people to agree with everything she says. You want to talk to her about it, but what should you say? List some of the points you want to make when you discuss this issue with your boss.

3 Is conflict in a team good or bad? Explain your answer.

4 At your last department meeting, three people monopolized the entire discussion. What might you do at the next meeting to encourage other department members to voluntarily participate?

5 Your manager wants you to call a face-to-face meeting of your colleagues to review the progress of your project. However, you think that a project review can be handled by a different method. Select at least one other meeting approach, and persuade your manager that it is best for a project review.

6 **Ethical Choices** You've just come from a meeting of your project team, where the marketing representative kept raising objections to points of style in a rough draft of your group's report. Instead of focusing on recommendations, the team spent the time needed for other tasks debating individual words and even punctuation. After the meeting, two members asked you to join them in approaching management to request that the marketing rep be removed from the team. You don't want to make this member look bad, nor do you want to stifle constructive comments and participation. On the other hand, you're concerned about completing the project on time. What should you do? Explain your choice.

Practice Your Knowledge

Document for Analysis

A project leader has made notes about covering the following items at the quarterly budget meeting. Prepare a formal agenda by putting these items into a logical order and rewriting, where necessary, to give phrases a more consistent sound. (See Appendix A for agenda format.)

Budget Committee Meeting to be held on December 12, 2004 at 9:30 a.m.

- I will call the meeting to order.
- Site director's report: A closer look at cost overruns on Greentree site.
- The group will review and approve the minutes from last quarter's meeting.
- I will ask the finance director to report on actual versus projected quarterly revenues and expenses.
- I will distribute copies of the overall divisional budget and announce the date of the next budget meeting.
- Discussion: How can we do a better job of anticipating and preventing cost overruns?
- Meeting will take place in Conference Room 3.
- What additional budget issues must be considered during this quarter?

Exercises

2–1 **Listening Skills: Overcoming Barriers** Identify some of your bad listening habits and make a list of some ways you could correct them. For the next 15 days, review your list and jot down any improvements you've noticed as a result of your effort.

2–2 **Teamwork** With a classmate, attend a local community or campus meeting where you can observe group discussion as well as voting or another group action. Take notes individually during the meeting and then work together to answer the following questions.

a What is your evaluation of this meeting? In your answer, consider (1) the leader's ability to clearly articulate the meeting's goals, (2) the leader's ability to engage members in a meaningful discussion, (3) the group's dynamics, and (4) the group's listening skills.

b How did group members make decisions? Did they vote? Did they reach decisions by consensus? Did people opposed to the decisions get an opportunity to voice their objections?

c How well did the individual participants listen? How could you tell?

d Did any participants change their expressed views or their votes during the meeting? Why might that have happened?

e Did you observe any of the communication barriers discussed in Chapter 1? Identify them.

f Compare the notes you took during the meeting with those of your classmate. What differences do you notice? How do you account for these differences?

2–3 **Team Communication: Overcoming Barriers** Every month, each employee in your department is expected to give a brief oral presentation on the status of his or her project. However, your department has recently hired an employee with a severe speech impediment that prevents people from understanding most of what he has to say. As department manager, how will you resolve this dilemma? Please explain.

2–4 **Nonverbal Communication: Analyzing Written Messages** Select a business letter and envelope that you have received at work or home. Analyze their appearance. What nonverbal messages do they send? Are these messages consistent with the content of the letter? If not, what could the sender have done to make the nonverbal communication consistent with the verbal communication?

2–5 **Internet** Visit the PolyVision Web site at **www.ibidwhite boards.com/index.shtml** and read about electronic whiteboards. What advantages do you see in using this kind of whiteboard during a meeting? Draft a short internal memo to your boss outlining the product's advantages, using the memo format in Figure 1–2 on page 5.

2–6 **Team Development: Resolving Conflict** Describe a recent conflict you had with a team member at work or at school, and explain how you resolved it. Did you find a solution that was acceptable to both of you and to the team?

2–7 **Listening Process: Giving Feedback** Review the guidelines for developing effective feedback skills in Table 2–2 on page 34 and write a brief explanation of why it's important to adopt an audience-centred approach when giving feedback to others.

2–8 **Ethical Choices** During team meetings, one member constantly calls for votes before all the members have voiced their views. As the leader, you asked this member privately about his behaviour. He replied that he was trying to move the team toward its goals, but you are concerned that he is really trying to take control. How can you deal with this situation without removing the member from the group?

2–9 **Meeting Productivity: Analyzing Agendas** Obtain a copy of the agenda from a recent campus or work meeting. Does this agenda show a start time or end time? Is it specific enough that you, as an outsider, would be able to understand what was to be discussed? If not, how would you improve the agenda?

2–10 **Listening Skills: Self-Assessment** How good are your listening skills? Rate yourself on each of the following elements of good listening, using one of the four possible answers provided; then examine your ratings to identify where you are strongest and where you can improve, using the tips in this chapter.

	Always	Frequently	Occasionally	Never
1 I look for areas of interest when people speak.	______	______	______	______
2 I focus on content rather than delivery.	______	______	______	______
3 I wait to respond until I understand the content.	______	______	______	______
4 I listen for ideas and themes, not isolated facts.	______	______	______	______
5 I take notes only when needed.	______	______	______	______
6 I really concentrate on what speakers are saying.	______	______	______	______
7 I stay focused even when the ideas are complex.	______	______	______	______
8 I keep an open mind despite emotionally charged language.	______	______	______	______

Going Online Exercise

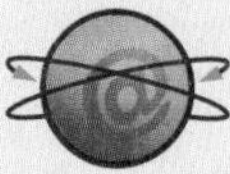

Participate in a Team-Based Organization, page 25 of this chapter

Working in teams to set goals and meet objectives requires cooperation. Collaboration is more than a skill, it's an art. Draw on what you've learned in this chapter and what you find at CSWT to improve your teaming skills.

1 Describe what makes a good or effective team.
2 What information did you learn from a research project about the value of effective teamwork? What was the purpose of the study?
3 In an organizational setting, what is the purpose of dialogue? What did you learn about the benefits of a team approach to solving problems in an organization?

To link directly to this site, visit our Companion Web site at **www.pearsoned.ca/thill** and look for the Chapter 2 resources.

Communicating Interculturally

1 Discuss two trends that have made intercultural business communication so important

2 Define *culture* and *subculture,* and list culture's four basic characteristics

3 Explain the importance of recognizing cultural differences, delineate the differences between high- and low-context cultures, and list four categories of cultural differences

4 Define *ethnocentrism* and *stereotyping;* then discuss three suggestions for overcoming these limiting mind sets

5 Discuss three ways to improve communication with people who speak English as a second language; then discuss three ways to improve communication with people who don't speak your language at all

6 Explain why studying other cultures helps you communicate more effectively, and list at least 7 of the 15 tips offered by successful intercultural businesspeople

7 Illustrate how word choice affects communication with people in other cultures, then list six recommendations for writing more effectively and nine guidelines for speaking across cultures more effectively

ON THE JOB

Facing a Communication Dilemma at Malkam Cross-Cultural Training

Working with Cultural Diversity

www.malkam.com

At a luncheon in Bolivia for the first time, should you immediately begin a business conversation, or build a personal relationship?

Laraine Kaminsky, president of Ottawa-based Malkam Cross-Cultural Training, helps her clients overcome obstacles that might interfere with their adaptation to both the Canadian and international workplace. Her 10 full-time staff and 50 on-call consultants deliver cross-cultural, language, and diversity training programs to new immigrants, Canadians who will work abroad, and Canadians who want to improve their communication skills in the multicultural workplace at home. The rapidly growing global marketplace and Canada's position as a magnet for immigrants from around the world have provided Malkam with many opportunities to help people communicate across cultures.

The unique combination of influences present in one culture can condition people to think, feel, and behave quite differently from people in another culture. Some differences are dramatic, such as the importance of social status. Other differences, such as personal values and decision-making approaches, can be more subtle and more difficult to perceive. Basic language barriers often prevent employees from understanding each other, but the potential for misunderstanding goes beyond language. As one example, Kaminsky cites the employer–employee relationship. In Canada, it is often on a first-name basis. In Korea, she says, the workplace is very formal. Coming from a culture where employees and employers keep their distance, Korean immigrants will find this casual interaction startling.

Cultural differences—and the misconceptions that might result from them—can affect teamwork, productivity, and job satisfaction. If you worked for Malkam, how would you approach teaching clients about the Canadian workplace? How would you help immigrants adapt to Canadian culture? What advice would you give to Canadians to improve their communication with their colleagues from other countries?[1]

By the way, if you answered that cultivating a personal relationship precedes business in Bolivian society, you are correct. As in many countries, in Bolivia it is considered proper etiquette to transact business only after establishing a personal rapport.

South African–born Laraine Kaminsky founded her company in 1989 after an unexpected job transfer to Canada. Her firm helps new immigrants become accustomed to Canadian ways as well as helping employees at all levels to work with people from different cultures within and outside Canada. She says, "These days it's not the transfer of technology that's confusing. It's the transfer of culture. In today's world, what people need to learn is how to be effective in the new culture to which they are exposed."

Understanding the Importance of Communicating across Cultures

More and more Canadian companies are facing the challenges of communicating across cultures. As we saw in Chapter 1, in 2000 Canada exported 43 percent of its gross domestic product; in 1990, the percentage was only 23 percent.[2] And the Canadian workplace itself is highly diverse: Canadians work alongside people from China, India, Pakistan, and the Philippines (cited by Statistics Canada among the top 10 countries of origin for new immigrants) as well as from many other nations.[3] **Intercultural communication** is the process of sending and receiving messages between people whose cultural background leads them to interpret verbal and nonverbal signs differently. Two trends contributing to the rapidly increasing importance of intercultural communication are market globalization and cultural diversity.

OBJECTIVE 1 Discuss two trends that have made intercultural business communication so important.

The Global Marketplace

Market globalization is the increasing tendency of the world to act as one market. Domestic markets are opening to worldwide competition to provide growth opportunities for a company's goods and services. Technological advances in travel and telecommunications are the driving force behind market globalization. New communication technologies allow teams from all over the world to work on projects and share information without leaving their desks. At the same time, advanced technologies allow manufacturers to produce their goods in foreign locations that offer favourable corporate tax rates and low cost-labour.[4] Natural boundaries and national borders disappear as increasing numbers of people work in multicultural settings. Even firms that once thought they were too small to expand into a neighbouring city have discovered that they can tap the sales potential of overseas markets with the help of the Internet, e-mail, fax machines, and overnight delivery services. To be successful in the global marketplace, e-commerce companies must consider offering Web sites in the languages that current Internet users speak. In Canada, businesses such as Royal Bank Financial Group, Bank of Montreal, Canadian National Railway, Bombardier, and Nortel Networks provide Web sites in French and English, as well as other languages spoken in Canada and internationally.

Advances in technology help companies cross national borders to find customers, materials, and money, leading to market globalization.

You need not "go global" or launch a Web site to interact with someone who speaks a foreign language or who thinks, acts, or transacts business differently than you do.[5] Even if your company transacts business locally, you will be communicating at work with people who come from various national, religious, and ethnic backgrounds.

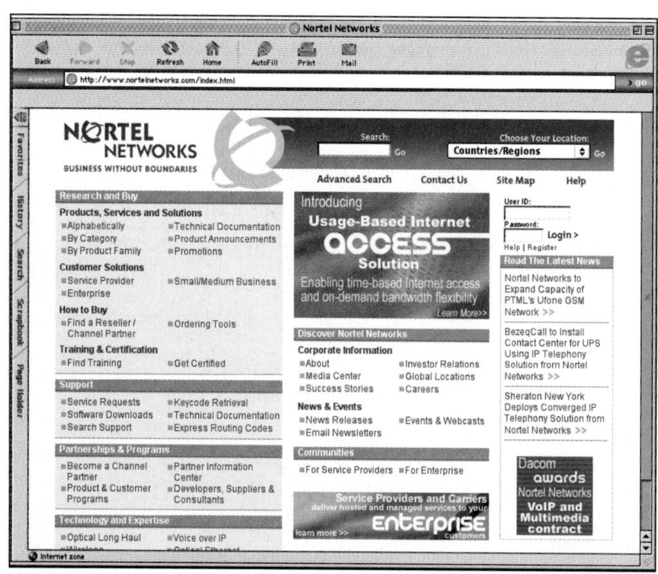

Many multinational Canadian companies, such as Nortel Networks, have created Web sites in the languages of their customers. Use the drop-down "choose your location" menu at **www.nortelnetworks.com** to find international Nortel Web sites.

The Multicultural Work Force

Canada's work force is made up of people who differ in race, gender, age, culture, family structure, religion, and educational background. Such **cultural diversity** is the second trend contributing to the importance of intercultural communication. It affects how business messages are conceived, planned, sent, received, and interpreted in the workplace.

The mosaic of Canadian society can be seen in classrooms, recreation centres, shopping malls, streets, and workplaces. The most recent census figures show that immigrants form almost one-fifth of the Canadian workforce. Recent immigrants—those who have arrived in Canada in the last 10 years—account for 70 percent of labour market growth.[6] The "brain gain" has brought specialists in the fields of information technology, biotechnology, and engineering, from such countries as India, Japan, and the former Yugoslavia. At Toronto's Dalton Chemical Laboratories, about 70 of its 100 employees are new immigrants, and thirty cultures are represented among its workforce.[7] The Cisco Systems unit in Waterloo, Ontario has been offering cross-cultural and language training since 1999, with about seven to 10 employees taking these classes each week.[8] To be successful at your job, you must be sensitive to cultural differences as you communicate with people within your organization and around the world. Glance at the job ads in newspapers and you will find that employers seek people with good intercultural communication skills. Your ability to find an interesting job, and to move ahead at work, will partly depend on your ability to use these skills. Understanding some basics about culture will get you started.

A company's cultural diversity affects how its business messages are conceived, composed, delivered, received, and interpreted.

OBJECTIVE 2 Define *culture* and *subculture,* and list culture's four basic characteristics.

Improving Intercultural Sensitivity

Culture is a shared system of symbols, beliefs, attitudes, values, expectations, and norms for behavior. All members of a culture have similar assumptions about how people should think, behave, and communicate, and they all tend to act on those assumptions in much the same way. You belong to the culture you share with all the people who live in your own country.

Culture is a shared system of symbols, beliefs, attitudes, values, expectations, and norms for behaviour.

In addition, you also belong to other cultural groups, including an ethnic group, probably a religious group, and perhaps a profession that has its own special language and customs. Distinct groups that exist within a major culture are referred to as **subcultures.** For example, Indonesia is home to a wide variety of ethnic and religious subcultures, whereas Japan is much more homogeneous, having only a few subcultures.[9] Groups that might be considered subcultures in Canada are Caribbean Canadians, Métis, hockey fans, Québécois, Russian immigrants, and graduates of the University of Prince Edward Island.

Subcultures are distinct groups that exist within a major culture.

In order to communicate more effectively, you need to understand a few basics about culture:

To better understand culture, remember that culture is learned and that it varies in stability, complexity, and tolerance.

- **Culture is learned.** As we grow up in a culture, we are sometimes told which behaviours are acceptable, and we sometimes observe which values work best in our particular society. But whether conscious or unconscious, culture is transmitted from person to person, from generation to generation, teaching us who we are and how best to function in our society.[10]
- **Cultures vary in stability.** All cultures are changing, but at different rates. Rapid change can interfere with receiving and decoding messages, which requires adjustment from all communicators, both insiders and outsiders. For example, Japan's culture has come to expect the security of lifelong employment. But the downturn in Japan's economy in the 1990s has forced employees to face the possibility of developing their own benefits and even of being laid off. It has also forced some movement away from group identification, an inherent quality of Japanese culture. Seeing the need for individual enterprise to sustain the Japanese economy, the Japanese government has begun to support schools that teach entrepreneurship, deriving the idea from the U.S.[11]
- **Cultures vary in complexity.** The accessibility of information in a culture ranges from explicit verbal codes to implicit body language. Some complex cultures require much more effort from outsiders who wish to communicate clearly with insiders.

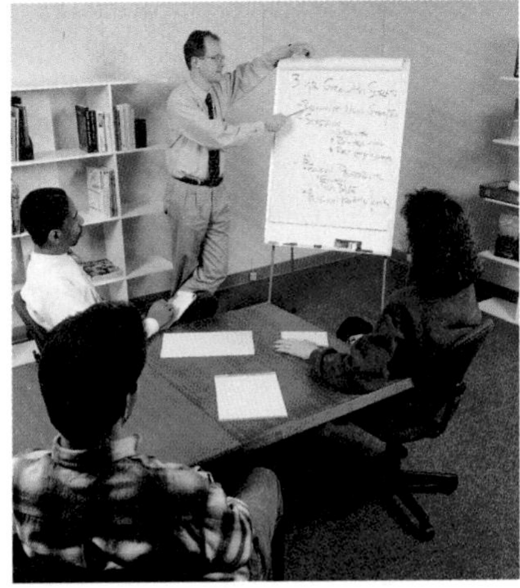
Malkam Cross-Cultural Training provides hands-on opportunities to help new Canadians learn English and French. Courses include "English for Specific Purposes," where students learn the "language" of meetings and the language of negotiation.

Experts such as Laraine Kaminsky recommend that companies transacting business with people from other nationalities find out as much as possible about their customs and religions. What information about your background would be necessary for your business partners?

- **Cultures vary in tolerance.** Some cultures are openly hostile toward outsiders, some maintain a detached aloofness, and others are friendly and cooperative toward strangers. These attitudes can affect the level of trust and open communication that you can achieve with people of other cultures.

As you can see, communication is strongly affected by culture. You can improve your ability to communicate effectively across cultures by recognizing cultural differences and then overcoming ethnocentrism.

Recognize Cultural Differences

OBJECTIVE 3 Explain the importance of recognizing cultural differences, delineate the differences between high- and low-context cultures, and list four categories of cultural differences.

When you write to or speak with someone from another culture, you encode your message using the assumptions of your own culture. However, members of your audience decode your message according to the assumptions of their culture, so your meaning may be misunderstood. The greater the difference between cultures, the greater the chance for misunderstanding.[12] For instance, a nodding gesture indicates understanding in Canada and the United States, but in Japan it means only that the person is listening.[13]

Cultural differences often surface in our assumptions. When Japanese auto manufacturer Mazda opened a plant in the United States, officials passed out company baseball caps and told U.S. employees that they could wear the caps at work, along with their mandatory company uniform (blue pants and khaki shirts). The employees assumed that the caps were a *voluntary* accessory, and many decided not to wear them. Japanese managers were upset, regarding the decision as a sign of disrespect and believing that employees who really cared about the company would want to wear the caps. However, the U.S. employees resented being told what they should want to do.[14] Similarly, exhibitors at a trade show could not understand why Chinese visitors bypassed their booth. Exhibitors were wearing green hats and giving them away as promotional items. But they soon discovered that for many Chinese, green hats are associated with infidelity; the Chinese expression "He wears a green hat" indicates that a man's wife has been cheating on him. So they discarded the green hats (giving out T-shirts instead) and the Chinese visited the booth.[15]

Effective intercultural communication depends on recognizing ways in which people differ.

Problems such as these arise when we assume, wrongly, that other people's attitudes and lives are like ours (see "Achieving Intercultural Communication—Test Your Intercultural Knowledge"). Laraine Kaminsky says, "Most culture is hidden, and that's the part that always gets us into trouble."[16] You can improve intercultural sensitivity by recognizing and accommodating cultural differences, which can be examined in four major categories: contextual, ethical, social, and nonverbal.

CONTEXTUAL DIFFERENCES

Cultural context is the pattern of physical cues, environmental stimuli, and implicit understanding that conveys meaning between members of the same culture.

Culture is subtle and difficult to perceive.

Cultural context is the pattern of physical cues, environmental stimuli, and implicit understanding that convey meaning between two members of the same culture. However, from culture to culture, people convey contextual meaning differently. In fact, correct social behaviour and effective communication can be defined by how much a culture depends on contextual cues (see Table 3–1 on page 54).

High-context cultures rely on implicit nonverbal actions and environmental setting to convey meaning, unlike low-context cultures, which rely heavily on explicit verbal communication.

In a **high-context culture** such as South Korea or Taiwan, people rely less on verbal communication and more on the context of nonverbal actions and environmental setting to convey meaning. A Chinese speaker expects the receiver to discover the essence of a message and uses indirectness and metaphor to provide a web of meaning.[17] In high-context cultures, the rules of everyday life are rarely explicit;

instead, as individuals grow up,they learn how to recognize situational cues (such as gestures and tone of voice) and how to respond as expected.[18]

In a **low-context culture** such as Canada, the United States or Germany, people rely more on verbal communication and less on circumstances and cues to convey meaning. An English speaker feels responsible for transmitting the meaning of the message.[19] In a low-context culture, rules and expectations are usually spelled out through explicit statements such as "Please wait until I'm finished" or "You're welcome to browse." Business people not only explain their own actions but also cue the other person about what to do or what to expect next.[20] Contextual differences are apparent in the way cultures approach situations such as negotiating, decision making, and problem solving.

Differences in Negotiating Styles Canadian, U.S., and German negotiators tend to take a relatively impersonal view of negotiations. Members of these low-context cultures see their goals in economic terms and usually presume trust of the other party, at least at the outset. In contrast, high-context Japanese negotiators prefer a more sociable negotiating atmosphere that is conducive to forging personal ties as the basis

High-context cultures emphasize relationships and a sociable atmosphere when negotiating, whereas low-context cultures view negotiations impersonally and focus on economic goals.

ACHIEVING INTERCULTURAL COMMUNICATION 

Test Your Intercultural Knowledge

Never take anything for granted when you're doing business in a foreign country. All sorts of assumptions that are valid in one place can trip you up elsewhere if you fail to consider that customs may vary. Here are several true stories about businesspeople who blundered by overlooking some simple but important cultural differences. Can you spot the erroneous assumptions that led these people astray?

1. **You're tired of the discussion and you want to move on to a new topic.** You ask your Australian business associate, "Can we table this for a while?" To your dismay, your colleague keeps right on discussing just what you want to put aside. Are Australians that inconsiderate?
2. **You finally made the long trip overseas to meet the new German director of your division.** Despite slow traffic, you arrive only four minutes late. His door is shut, so you knock on it and walk in. The chair is too far away from the desk, so you pick it up and move it closer. Then you lean over the desk, stick out your hand and say, "Good morning, Hans, it's nice to meet you." Of course, you're baffled by his chilly reaction. Why?
3. **Your meeting went better than you'd ever expected.** In fact, you found the Japanese representative for your new advertising agency to be very agreeable; he said yes to just about everything. When you share your enthusiasm with your boss, she doesn't appear very excited. Why?
4. **You've finally closed the deal, after exhausting both your patience and your company's travel budget.** Now, two weeks later, your Chinese customers are asking for special considerations that change the terms of the agreement. How could they do this? Why are they doing it? And, most important, what should you do?

In each case the problems have resulted from inaccurate assumptions. Here are the explanations of what went wrong:

1. To "table" something in Australia means to bring it forward for discussion. This is the opposite of what Americans usually mean. The English that's spoken in Australia is closer to British than to Canadian and U.S. English. If you are doing business in Australia, become familiar with the local vocabulary. Note the tendency to shorten just about any word whenever possible, and adding "ie" to it is a form of familiar slang: for example, *brolly* (umbrella) and *lollie* (candy). And yes, it's true: "G'day" is the standard greeting.
2. You've just broken four rules of German polite behaviour: punctuality, privacy, personal space, and proper greetings. In time-conscious Germany, you should never arrive even a few minutes late. Also, Germans like their privacy and space, and they adhere to formal greetings of "Frau" and "Herr," even if the business association has lasted for years.
3. The word *yes* may not always mean "yes" in the Western sense. Japanese people may say *yes* to confirm they have heard or understood something but not necessarily to indicate that they agree with it. You'll seldom get a direct *no*. Some of the ways that Japanese people say no indirectly include "It will be difficult," "I will ask my supervisor," " I'm not sure," "We will think about it," and "I see."
4. For most Canadian and U.S. businesspeople, the contract represents the end of the negotiation. For Chinese businesspeople, however, it's just the beginning. Once a deal is made, Chinese negotiators view their counterparts as trustworthy partners who can be relied on for special favours—such as new terms in the contract.

Sources: Adapted from David A. Ricks, "International Business Blunders: An Update," *Business & Economic Review*, January–March 1998, 25; Valerie Frazee, "Keeping Up on Chinese Culture," *Global Workforce*, October 1996, 16-17; Valerie Frazee, "Establishing Relations in Germany, " *Global Workforce*, April 1997, 16-17; James Wilfong and Toni Seger, *Taking Your Business Global* (Franklin Lakes, N.J.: Career Press, 1997), 282.

for trust. To high-context negotiators, achieving immediate economic gains are secondary to establishing and maintaining a long-term relationship. In Colombia, businesspeople want to develop a friendship with their business partners before beginning negotiations. If salespeople are changed during the course of their dealings, Colombians will end the association. [21]

High-context cultures encourage lengthy decision making, concentrating on every detail, whereas low-context cultures emphasize quick, efficient decisions on major points while leaving the details to be worked out later.

Differences in Decision-Making Practices In lower-context cultures, executives try to reach decisions as quickly and efficiently as possible. They are concerned with reaching an agreement on the main points, leaving the details to be worked out later by others. However, this approach would be criticized in Japan, a high-context culture, where slow deliberations demonstrate thoughtfulness and prudence.[22]

High-context cultures avoid confrontation and debate, whereas low-context cultures encourage open disagreement.

Differences in Problem-Solving Techniques Cultures differ in their tolerance for open disagreement. Low-context Canadian and U.S. businesspeople typically enjoy confrontation and debate, but high-context Chinese businesspeople try to prevent public conflict, making concessions slowly and staying away from proposal-counterproposal methods. If you try to get members of a Chinese team to back down from their position, you will cause them to lose face—very likely ruining the relationship.[23]

ETHICAL DIFFERENCES

High-context cultures view laws as being more flexible, whereas low-context cultures tend to value written agreements and interpret laws strictly.

Cultural context influences many other cultural areas, including legal and ethical behaviour. For example, because low-context cultures value the written word, they consider written agreements binding. But high-context cultures put less emphasis on the written word and consider personal pledges more important than contracts. They also have a tendency to view law with flexibility, whereas low-context cultures would adhere to the law strictly. [24]

Legal systems differ from culture to culture.

As you conduct business around the world, you'll find that legal systems differ from culture to culture. In Canada, the United Kingdom, and the United States, someone is presumed innocent until proved guilty, a principle rooted in English common law. However, in Mexico and Turkey, someone is presumed guilty until proved innocent, a principle rooted in the Napoleonic code.[25] These distinctions can be particularly important if your firm must communicate about a legal dispute in another country.

Ethical choices can be even more complicated when communicating across cultures; for example, bribing officials is viewed differently from culture to culture.

As discussed in Chapter 1, making ethical choices can be difficult, even within your own culture. When communicating across cultures, ethics can be even more complicated. What happens when a certain behaviour is unethical in Canada but an accepted practice in another culture? In some countries, companies, whether domestic or foreign, are expected to pay government officials extra fees for approving government contracts. These payments aren't always seen as bribes, but as recompense for easing the process of negotiating a contract abroad.

TABLE 3-1 How Cultural Context Affects Business

In Low-Context Companies	In High-Context Companies
Executive offices are separate with controlled access.	Executive offices are shared and open to all.
Workers rely on detailed background information.	Workers do not expect or want detailed information.
Information is highly centralized and controlled.	Information is shared with everyone.
Objective data are valued over subjective relationships.	Subjective relationships are valued over objective data.
Business and social relationships are discrete.	Business and social relationships overlap.
Competence is valued as much as position and status.	Position and status are valued more than competence.
Meetings have fixed agendas and plenty of advance notice.	Meetings are often called on short notice, and key people always accept.

In Canada, bribing officials is illegal, but Kenyans consider paying such bribes a part of life. To get something done right, they pay *kitu kidogo* (or "something small"). In China businesses pay *huilu,* in Russia they pay *vzyatka,* in the Middle East it's *baksheesh,* and in Mexico it's *una mordida* ("a small bite").[26] In 1999, Canada signed an international bribery convention negotiated by nations belonging to the Organization for Economic Cooperation and Development (OECD). In the same year, federal legislation was instituted that would make bribing a foreign official a criminal offence in Canada.[27] Making ethical choices across cultures can seem exceedingly complicated, but doing so actually differs little from the way you choose the most ethical path in your own culture (see Chapter 1).

When communicating across cultures, keep your messages ethical by applying the following four basic principles: [28]

Keep your messages ethical by actively seeking mutual ground, exchanging messages without judgment, sending messages that are honest, and showing respect for cultural differences.

- **Actively seek mutual ground.** To allow the clearest possible exchange of information, both parties must be flexible and avoid insisting that an interaction take place strictly in terms of one culture or another.
- **Send and receive messages without judgment.** To allow information to flow freely, both parties must recognize that values vary from culture to culture, and both must trust one another.
- **Send messages that are honest.** To ensure that the information is true, both parties must see things as they are—not as we would like them to be. In the interest of honesty, we must be fully aware of our personal and cultural biases.
- **Show respect for cultural differences.** To protect the basic human rights of both parties, each must understand and acknowledge the other's needs and preserve each other's dignity by communicating without deception.

SOCIAL DIFFERENCES

Formal rules of etiquette are explicit and well defined, but informal rules are learned through observation and imitation.

In any culture, rules of social etiquette may be formal or informal. Formal rules are the specifically taught "rights" and "wrongs" of how to behave in common social situations, such as table manners at meals. When formal rules are violated, members of a culture can explain why they feel upset. In contrast, informal social rules are more difficult to identify and are usually learned by watching how people behave and then imitating that behaviour. Informal rules govern how males and females are supposed to behave, when it is appropriate to use a person's first name, and so on. When informal rules are violated, members of a culture are likely to feel uncomfortable, although they may not be able to say exactly why.[29]

Respect and rank are reflected differently from culture to culture in the way people are addressed and in their working environment.

Differing Attitudes toward Status Culture dictates how people show respect and signify rank. For example, people in Canada show respect by addressing top managers as "Mr. Roberts" or "Ms. Gutierrez." However, people in China address businesspeople according to their official titles, such as "president" or "manager."[30] Laraine Kaminsky notes that "High-tech people speak in very casual language using first names. But many people from abroad are raised with a different level of formality." A middle-aged engineer from another country would need to adjust to working under a younger manager, particularly if the manager is female.[31]

In addition, a Canadian executive's rank may be reflected by a large corner office, deep carpets, an expensive desk, and handsome accessories. But the highest-ranking executives in France sit in the middle of an open area, surrounded by lower-level employees.[32]

Differing Attitudes toward Manners What is polite in one culture may be considered rude in another. In Arab countries it's impolite to take gifts to a man's wife, but it's acceptable to take gifts to his children. In Germany giving a woman a red rose is considered a romantic invitation—inappropriate if you're trying to establish a business relationship with her.[33] In India, if you're invited to visit someone's home "any time," you should make an unexpected visit without waiting for a definite invitation. Failure to take the "any time" invitation literally would be an insult, a sign that you don't care to develop the friendship.

The rules of polite behaviour vary from country to country.

Although businesspeople in Canada, the United States, Germany, and some other nations see time as a way to organize the business day efficiently, other cultures see time as more flexible.

Differing Attitudes toward Time Conducting business entails schedules, deadlines, and appointments, but these matters are regarded differently from culture to culture. German, Canadian, and U.S. executives see time as a way to plan the business day efficiently, focusing on only one task during each scheduled period and viewing time as limited. However, executives from Latin America and Asia see time as more flexible. Meeting a deadline is less important than building a business relationship; the workday isn't expected to follow a rigid, preset schedule. [34]

NONVERBAL DIFFERENCES

Variations in the meaning of nonverbal communication can cause problems because people are unaware of the messages they are transmitting.

As discussed in Chapter 2, nonverbal communication is extremely reliable when determining meaning, but that reliability is valid only when the communicators belong to the same culture. The simplest hand gestures change meaning from culture to culture, so interpreting nonverbal elements according to your own culture can be dangerous. Nonverbal elements are apparent in attitudes toward personal space and in body language.

People from various cultures have different spatial "comfort zones."

Attitudes toward Personal Space People in Canada and the United States usually stand about an arms' length during a business conversation. However, this distance is uncomfortably close for people from Germany or Japan and uncomfortably far for Arabs and Latin Americans.[35] Because of these differing concepts of personal space, a Canadian manager may react negatively (without knowing exactly why) when an Arab colleague moves closer during their conversation. And the Arab colleague may react negatively (again, without knowing why) when the Canadian manager backs away.

Learning the verbal language of a culture does not mean you understand the body language of that culture.

Use of Body Language Gestures help members of a culture clarify confusing messages, but differences in body language are a major source of misunderstanding during intercultural communication. Don't assume that someone from another culture who speaks your language has mastered your culture's body language. For example, people in Canada and the United States say no by shaking their heads back and forth; people in Bulgaria nod up and down; people in Japan move their right hand; and people in Sicily raise their chin. Similarly, Canadian and U.S. businesspeople assume that a person who won't meet their gaze is evasive and dishonest. However, in many parts of Asia, keeping your eyes lowered is a sign of respect.[36] Hand gestures also communicate different meanings in different cultures. The "thumbs up" gesture commonly used in Canada and the U.S. to celebrate a job well done is considered offensive in Australia and Nigeria (see Figure 3-1 on page 57).[37]

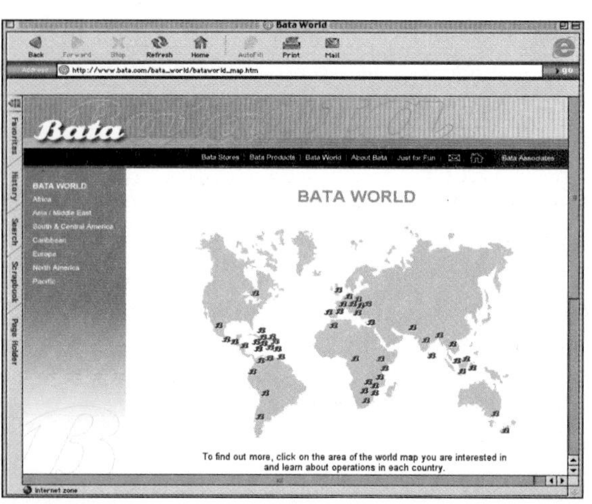

Founded by Tomas Bata, an immigrant from the former Czechoslavakia, Canadian shoe specialist Bata owns over 4700 stores on six continents and employs over 50 000 people. Check out **www.bata.com/about_bata** to learn about the company's operations around the world.

People from different cultures may misread an intentional nonverbal signal, may overlook the signal entirely, or may assume that a meaningless gesture is significant. For example, an Egyptian might mistakenly assume that a Westerner who exposes the sole of his or her shoe is offering a grave insult.[38]

Recognizing cultural differences helps you avoid sending inappropriate signals and helps you correctly interpret the signals from others—an important step toward improving intercultural sensitivity. But simple recognition isn't the whole story. Being aware of cultural differences is only the first step in improving your intercultural communication. To achieve intercultural sensitivity, you need to balance cultural awareness with cultural flexibility. The diagram in Figure 3–2 shows the relationship of language, exposure, and

FIGURE 3-1 Gesture and Meaning Across Cultures

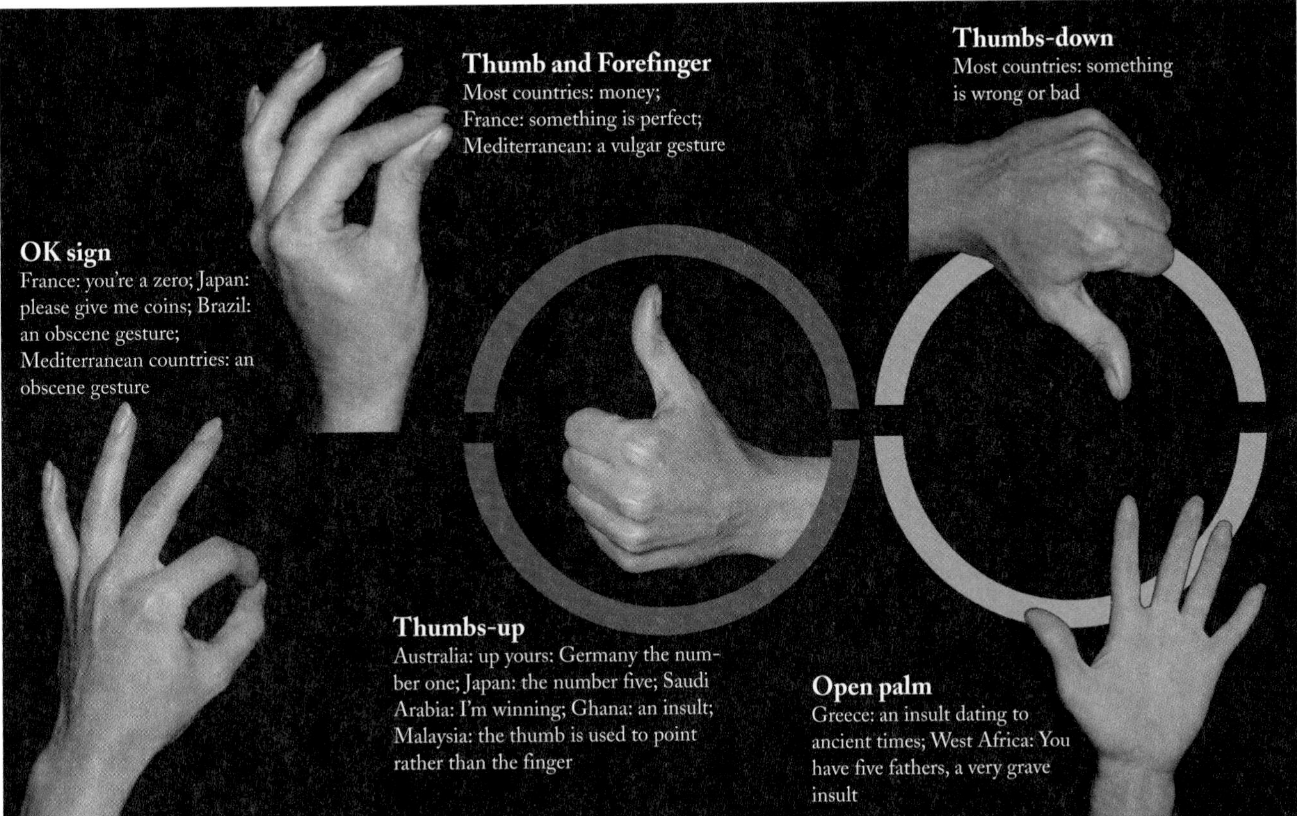

technique to communication skill (all of which are covered in detail in this chapter). To communicate across cultures successfully, you must be able to accommodate these differences without judging them, which means you must be able to overcome the human tendency toward ethnocentrism.

Thumb and Forefinger
Most countries: money;
France: something is perfect;
Mediterranean: a vulgar gesture
Thumbs-down
Most countries: something is wrong or bad
OK sign
France: you're a zero; Japan: please give me coins; Brazil: an obscene gesture;
Mediterranean countries: an obscene gesture
Thumbs-up
Australia: up yours: Germany the number one; Japan: the number five; Saudi Arabia: I'm winning; Ghana: an insult;
Malaysia: the thumb is used to point rather than the finger
Open palm
Greece: an insult dating to ancient times; West Africa: You have five fathers, a very grave insult

Recognizing cultural differences must be followed by the sincere attempt to accommodate those differences.

Overcome Ethnocentrism

OBJECTIVE 4 Define *ethnocentrism* and *stereotyping;* then discuss three suggestions for overcoming these limiting mind sets.

When communicating across cultures, your effectiveness depends on maintaining an open mind. Unfortunately, many people lapse into **ethnocentrism**, the belief that one's own cultural background—including ways of analyzing problems, values, beliefs, and verbal and nonverbal communications—is superior.[39] Enthnocentrists lose sight of the possibility that their words and actions can be misunderstood, and they forget that they are likely to misinterpret the actions of others.

Ethnocentrism is the tendency to judge all other groups according to one's own group's standards, behaviours, and customs and to see other groups as inferior by comparison.

When you first begin to investigate the culture of another group, you may attempt to understand the common tendencies of that group's members by **stereotyping**—predicting individuals' behaviour or character on the basis of their membership in a particular group or class. For example, Japanese visitors often stereotype Americans as people who walk fast, are wasteful in utilizing space, speak directly, ask too many questions in the classroom, don't respect professors, are disrespectful of age and status, lack discipline, and are extravagant.[40]

Stereotyping is the attempt to categorize individuals by trying to predict their behaviour or character on the basis of their membership in a particular group.

Although stereotyping may be useful in the beginning, your next step is to move beyond the stereotypes to relationships with real people. Unfortunately, when ethnocentric people stereotype, they tend to do so on the basis of limited, general, or inaccurate evidence. They frequently develop biased attitudes toward the group, and they

FIGURE 3–2 Components of Successful Intercultural Communication

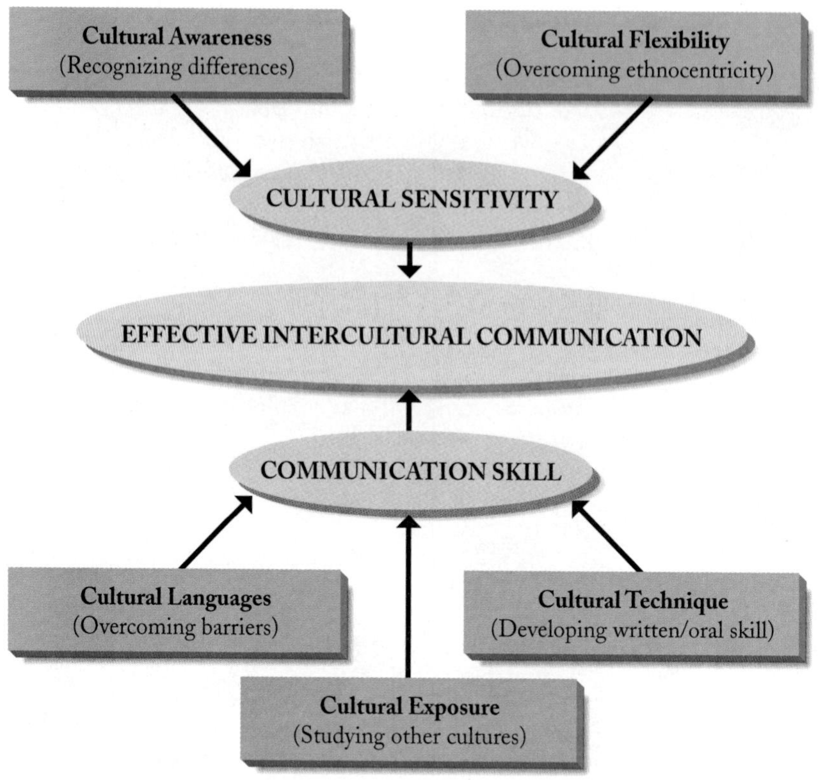

Dining etiquette varies among cultures. If you invite foreign business associates to eat either at your home or in a restaurant, what should you tell them about your culture's customs regarding food and dining?

fail to move beyond that initial step.[41] Instead of talking to someone of another culture as a unique human being, ethnocentric people tend fit that person's actions, attitudes, and behaviour into a preconceived image.

In order to overcome ethnocentrism follow a few simple suggestions:

You can overcome ethnocentrism by acknowledging distinctions, avoiding assumptions, and avoiding judgments.

- **Acknowledge distinctions.** Don't ignore the differences between another person's culture and your own.
- **Avoid assumptions.** Don't assume that others will act the same way you do, that they will operate from the same assumptions, or that they will use language and symbols the same way you do.
- **Avoid judgments.** When people act differently, don't conclude that they are in error, that their way is invalid, or that their customs are inferior to your own.

Too often, both parties in an intercultural exchange are guilty of ethnocentrism and prejudice. It's not surprising, then, that misunderstandings arise when communicating across cultures.

Improving Communication across Cultures

Once you can recognize cultural elements and overcome ethnocentrism, you're ready to focus directly on your intercultural communication skills. To communicate more effectively with people from other cultures, you need to overcome language barriers, study other cultures, develop effective written skills, and develop effective oral skills.

OBJECTIVE 5 Discuss three ways to improve communication with people who speak English as a second language; then discuss three ways to improve communication with people who don't speak your language at all.

Overcome Language Barriers

By choosing specific words to communicate, you signal that you are a member of a particular culture or subculture and that you know the code. The nature of your code—your language and vocabulary—imposes its own barriers on your message. For example, the language of a lawyer differs from that of an accountant or a doctor, and the difference in their vocabularies affects their ability to recognize and express ideas. Barriers also exist because different words can have the same meaning. The influence of British English on Canadian vocabulary is an example. Although such British words as "chesterfield" (for couch or sofa) and "riding" are still used in Canada, vocabulary tends to be more American than British (see Table 3–2).[42]

The barriers become greater still when you're communicating across cultures. You must be able to communicate effectively both with people who speak English as a second language (ESL) and with people who don't speak your language at all.

BREAKING THROUGH ESL BARRIERS

Of the many millions of people who use English as a second language, some are extremely fluent, and others have only an elementary command. When dealing with those less fluent in your own language, you may miss a few subtleties, but you are still able to communicate. Even so, don't assume that the other person understands everything you say. Your message can be confused by slang and idioms, by local accents, and by vocal variations.

English is the most prevalent language in international business, but it's a mistake to assume that everyone understands it.

Avoid Using Slang and Idioms Languages never translate word for word. They are idiomatic—constructed with phrases that mean more than the sum of their literal parts. For example, if a Canadian executive tells an Egyptian executive that a certain product "doesn't cut the mustard" or that making the monthly sales quota will be "a piece of cake," chances are that the communication will fail. When speaking to people less fluent in your language, try to choose words carefully to convey only their most specific denotative meaning, that is, the meaning of the word as defined in a dictionary. Use words that have singular rather than multiple meanings. The word *high* has 20 meanings; the word *expensive* has one.[43]

Slang and idioms, local accents and pronunciation, and vocal variations can pose problems when you're speaking to people from other cultures.

Pay Attention to Local Accents and Pronunciation Even when people speak your language, you may have a hard time understanding their pronunciation. Immigrants with a working knowledge of English would have difficulty understanding that "Jeat yet?" means "Did you eat yet?" and that "Cannahepya?" means "Can I help you?" Some nonnative English speakers don't distinguish between the English sounds *v* and *w*, so they say "wery" for "very." At the same time, Canadians may have trouble pronouncing the German *ch*. Malkam Cross-Cultural Training offers "natural conversation" sessions to help immigrants understand English pronunciation.

Companies such as Toronto-based Dalton Chemical Laboratories provide on-site ESL classes. These classes not only train people in English, but also create cohesive teams.

TABLE 3–2 Canadian and U.S. versus British English

Canadian and U.S. English	British English
eggplant	aubergine
corn	maize
cleaning lady	charwoman
elevator	lift
windshield	windscreen
hood (of an automobile)	bonnet
long-distance call	trunk call
pharmacist	chemist
rare	underdone
roast	joint
string bean	French bean

Be Aware of Vocal Variations Some people use their voices differently from culture to culture. Japanese men tend to speak in clusters of words, and Japanese women seem to vocalize more smoothly. Canadian and American speakers who "uptalk," or raise their voices at the end of sentences (as if they are questions), may project a lack of self-confidence. However, French speakers tend naturally, as a part of the language, to end sentences on a higher pitch than do native speakers of English. This vocal tendency may suggest that the French speaker is uncertain of his or her message, but it would not necessarily be true.[44]

BREAKING THROUGH FOREIGN LANGUAGE BARRIERS

Many companies recognize that they must be able to conduct business in languages other than English.

Even though English is widely spoken in the global business marketplace, the language of business is the language of the customer. When communicating with people who don't speak your language at all, you have three options: You can learn their language, use an intermediary or a translator, or teach them your language.

If you have a long-term business relationship with people of another culture, it is helpful to learn their language.

Learn a Foreign Language If you're planning to live in another country or to do business there repeatedly, you might want to learn the language. The same holds true if you'll be working closely with a subculture that has its own language; in Canada, it's a plus if you are fluent in both national languages. Even if you're doing business in your own language, you show respect by making the effort to learn the subculture's language, or at least to learn a few words. One problem is that language courses may take more time and more money than you can probably afford. However, your customers may be pleased to teach you some common expressions in their native language.

Many companies use translators to help them communicate with people who don't speak English.

Use an Intermediary or a Translator Because so many international business letters are written in English, Canadian firms don't always worry about translating their correspondence. However, many other forms of written communication must be translated. Warranties, repair and maintenance manuals, and product labels require translation. For example, the warranty for a Hewlett-Packard laser jet printer cartridge is written in English, French, Spanish, Italian, and Japanese. In addition, many multinational companies translate policy and procedure manuals for use in overseas offices. Corporate newsletters are translated into the languages of the company's offshore divisions. Bata Shoes has been publishing the Bata World News since 1945 in English, French, and Spanish; however, vital information sent to employees is translated into the language they use most frequently by in-house multilingual staff.[45]

Back-translation helps ensure accuracy by allowing translators to check a second translation against the original message.

An experienced translator can analyze a message, understand its meaning in the cultural context, consider how to convey the meaning in another language, and then use verbal and nonverbal signals to encode or decode the message for someone from another culture. Whenever possible, arrange to meet translators ahead of time to give them a sense of what you are presenting and to discuss specific words or concepts that could be confusing.[46] Some companies use *back-translation* to ensure accuracy. Once a translator encodes a message into another language, a different translator retranslates the same message into the original language. This back-translation is then compared with the original message to discover any errors or discrepancies.

Some companies find it useful to teach their employees to speak English.

Offer English-Language Training Programs for Employees The option of teaching other people to speak your language doesn't appear to be very practical at first glance. However, many companies find it beneficial to offer language-training programs. These programs give companies a degree of freedom from third-party mediators such as interpreters, and they promote more personal and spontaneous communication between the company and its foreign-language employees and clients.[47]

Study Other Cultures

OBJECTIVE 6 Explain why studying other cultures helps you communicate more effectively, and list at least 7 of the 15 tips offered by successful intercultural businesspeople.

Learning all you can about a particular culture is a good way to figure out how to send and receive intercultural messages effectively. Read books and articles about these cultures, and talk to people who have done business with members of these cultures. Concentrate on learning something about each culture's history, religion, politics, values, and customs. Find out about a country's subcultures, especially its business subculture, and any special rules or protocol. Studying culture is especially important if you interact with people from a variety of cultures or subcultures. For example, something as simple as a handshake differs from culture to culture: Germans, Canadians, and Americans shake hands firmly, while the French prefer a gentler handshake.[48]

Learning as much as possible about another culture will enhance your ability to communicate with its members.

This chapter's "Checklist: Doing Business Abroad" on page 62 can help you start your investigation of another culture. Although we cannot understand other cultures completely, we can learn useful general information while remaining aware of and open to variations and individual differences. You can communicate more effectively if you follow the tips from people who have successfully transacted business with their global partners and customers: [49]

- **Assume differences until similarity is proved.** Don't assume that others are more similar to you than they actually are.
- **Take responsibility for communication.** Don't assume it's the other person's job to communicate with you.
- **Withhold judgment.** Learn to listen to the whole story and accept differences in others without judging them.
- **Show respect.** Learn how respect is communicated in various cultures (through gestures, eye contact, and so on).
- **Empathize.** Before sending a message, put yourself in the receiver's shoes. Imagine the receiver's feelings and point of view.
- **Tolerate ambiguity.** Learn to control your frustration when placed in an unfamiliar or confusing situation.
- **Look beyond the superficial.** Don't be distracted by things such as dress, appearance, or environmental discomforts.
- **Be patient and persistent.** If you want to communicate with someone from another culture, don't give up easily.
- **Recognize your own cultural biases.** Learn to identify when your assumptions are different from those of others.
- **Be flexible.** Be prepared to change your habits and attitudes when communicating with someone from another culture.
- **Emphasize common ground.** Look for similarities from which to work.
- **Send clear messages.** Make both your verbal and nonverbal signals clear and consistent.
- **Deal with the individual.** Communicate with each person as an individual, not as a stereotypical representative of another group.
- **Learn when to be direct.** Investigate each culture so that you'll know when to send your message in a straightforward manner and when to be indirect.
- **Treat your interpretation as a working hypothesis.** Once you think you understand a foreign culture, carefully assess the feedback provided by recipients of your communication to see if it confirms your hypothesis.

This advice will help you communicate with anybody, regardless of culture. For more ideas on how to improve communication in the workplace, see this chapter's "Checklist: Communicating with a Culturally Diverse Work Force" on page 63.

Going Online

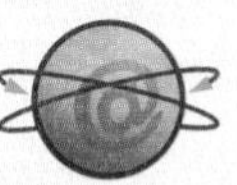

Hone Your Skills for International Business

What do you need to know about international business practices and different social customs? For crucial information that will help you successfully conduct business abroad, preview "Going Global" at **americanexpress.com**. Learn about appropriate business etiquette by accessing information such as negotiation strategies, international business regulations, and reference sources for 78 countries. If you want details on business travel, visa requirements, appropriate attire, accommodations, and language fluency, the research reports at this site will help prepare you to deal internationally.

www.americanexpress.com/small business

To link directly to this site, visit our Companion Website at **www.pearsoned.ca/thill** and look for the Chapter 3 resources.

Learning general intercultural communication skills will help you adapt in any culture, an ability that is especially important if you interact

Checklist: Doing Business Abroad

Understand Social Customs

✓ How do people react to strangers? Are they friendly? Hostile? Reserved?

✓ How do people greet each other? Should you bow? Nod? Shake hands?

✓ How are names used for introductions?

✓ What are the attitudes toward touching people?

✓ How do you express appreciation for an invitation to lunch or dinner or to someone's home?

✓ Should you bring a gift? Send flowers? Write a thank-you note?

✓ How, when, or where are people expected to sit in social or business situations?

✓ Are any phrases, facial expressions, or hand gestures considered rude?

✓ How close do people stand when talking?

✓ How do you attract the attention of a waiter? Do you tip the waiter?

✓ When is it rude to refuse an invitation? How do you refuse politely?

✓ What are the acceptable patterns of eye contact?

✓ What gestures indicate agreement? Disagreement? Respect?

✓ What topics may or may not be discussed in a social setting? In a business setting?

✓ How is time perceived?

✓ What are the generally accepted working hours?

✓ How do people view scheduled appointments?

Learn about Clothing and Food Preferences

✓ What occasions require special clothing? What colours are associated with mourning? Love? Joy?

✓ Are some types of clothing considered taboo for one sex or the other?

✓ What are the attitudes toward human body odors? Are deodorants or perfumes used?

✓ How many times per day do people eat?

✓ How are hands or utensils used when eating?

✓ What types of places, food, and drink are appropriate for business entertainment?

✓ Where is the seat of honour at a table?

Assess Political Patterns

✓ How stable is the political situation? Does it affect businesses in and out of the country?

✓ How is political power manifested? Military power? Economic strength?

✓ What are the traditional government institutions?

What Channels Are Used for Expressing Official and Unofficial Political Opinion?

✓ What information media are important? Who controls them?

✓ Is it appropriate to talk politics in social or business situations?

Understand Religious and Folk Beliefs

✓ To which religious groups do people belong?

✓ How do religious beliefs influence daily activities?

✓ Which places, objects, and events are sacred?

✓ Is there a tolerance for minority religions?

✓ How do religious holidays affect business and government activities?

✓ Does religion affect attitudes toward smoking? Drinking? Gambling?

✓ Does religion require or prohibit eating specific foods? At specific times?

✓ Which objects or actions portend good luck? Bad luck?

Learn about Economic and Business Institutions

✓ Is the society homogeneous?

✓ What minority groups are represented?

✓ What languages are spoken?

✓ Do immigration patterns influence work force composition?

✓ What are the primary resources and principal products?

✓ What vocational/technological training is offered?

✓ What are the attitudes toward education?

✓ Are businesses generally large? Family controlled? Government controlled?

✓ Is it appropriate to do business by telephone? By fax? By e-mail?

✓ Do managers make business decisions unilaterally or do they involve employees?

✓ How are status and seniority shown in an organization? In a business meeting?

✓ Must people socialize before conducting business?

Appraise the Nature of Ethics, Values, and Laws

✓ Is money or a gift expected in exchange for arranging business transactions?

✓ What ethical or legal issues might affect business transactions?

✓ Do people value competitiveness or cooperation?

✓ What are the attitudes toward work? Toward money?

✓ Is politeness more important than factual honesty?

✓ What qualities are admired in a business associate?

Develop Effective Intercultural Skills

Only after you've studied other cultures can you truly begin to develop effective intercultural skills. Once you discover which language barriers must be overcome, and once you understand what sort of cultural differences you'll be facing, you must decide how best to communicate your message, whether using written or oral channels would be best. Then you must adapt your style to make the right impression. For example, your choice of words reflects the relationship between you and your audience. So whether writing or speaking across cultures, be sure to use the appropriate level of formality.

OBJECTIVE 7 Illustrate how word choice affects communication with people in other cultures; then list six recommendations for writing more effectively and nine guidelines for speaking across cultures more effectively.

IMPROVE YOUR WRITTEN SKILLS

In general, Canadian and U.S. businesspeople will want to be somewhat more formal in their international correspondence than they would be when writing to people in their own countries. In many cultures, writers use a more elaborate style, so your audience will expect more formal language in your letter. The letter in Figure 3–3 was written by a supplier in Germany to a nearby retailer. The tone is more formal than would be used in Canada and the United States, but the writer clearly focuses on his audience. In Germany, business letters usually open with a reference to the business relationship and close with a compliment to the recipient. Of course, be careful not to carry formality to extremes, or you'll sound unnatural.

Whether you choose written or oral channels to communicate your message across cultures, you must adapt your style.

International business letters generally have a formal tone and a relatively elaborate style.

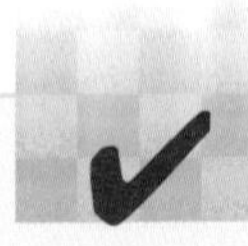

Checklist: Communicating with a Culturally Diverse Work Force

Accept Cultural Differences

- ✓ Adjust your message to employees' education level.
- ✓ Encourage employees to discuss their culture's customs.
- ✓ Create a formal forum to teach employees about the customs of all cultures represented in the firm.
- ✓ Train employees to see and overcome ethnocentric stereotyping.
- ✓ Provide books, articles, and videos about various cultures.
- ✓ Stamp out negative labels by observing how people identify their own groups.

Improve Oral and Written Communications

- ✓ Define the terms people need to know on the job.
- ✓ Emphasize major points with repetition and recap.
- ✓ Use familiar words whenever possible.
- ✓ Don't cover too much information at one time.
- ✓ Be specific and explicit—using descriptive words, exact measurements, and examples when possible.
- ✓ Give the reason for asking employees to follow a certain procedure and explain what will happen if the procedure is not followed.
- ✓ Use written summaries and visual aids (when appropriate) to clarify your points.
- ✓ Demonstrate and encourage the right way to complete a task, use a tool, and so on.
- ✓ Reduce language barriers: Train managers in the language of their employees, train employees in the language of most customers and of most people in the company, ask bilingual employees to serve as translators, print important health and safety instructions in as many languages as necessary.

Assess How Well You've Been Understood

- ✓ Research the nonverbal reactions of other cultures; then be alert to facial expressions and other nonverbal signs that indicate confusion or embarrassment.
- ✓ Encourage employees to ask questions in private and in writing.
- ✓ Observe how employees use the information you've provided, and review any misunderstood points.

Offer Feedback to Improve Communication

- ✓ Focus on the positive by explaining what *should* be done rather than what *shouldn't* be done.
- ✓ Discuss a person's behaviours and the situation, rather than making a judgment about the person.
- ✓ Be supportive as you offer feedback, and reassure individuals that their skills and contributions are important.

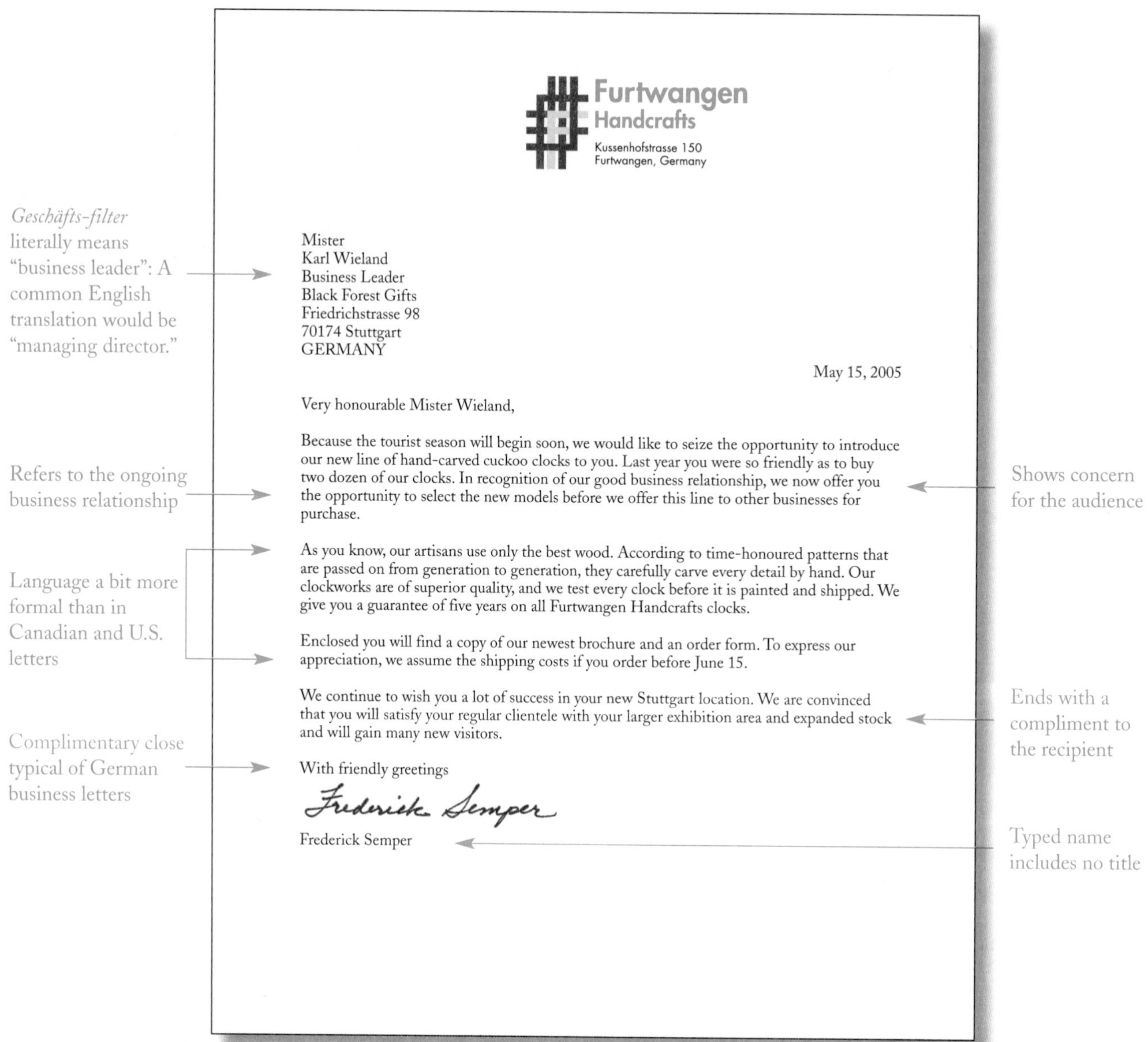

Furtwangen Handcrafts
Kussenhofstrasse 150
Furtwangen, Germany

Mister
Karl Wieland
Business Leader
Black Forest Gifts
Friedrichstrasse 98
70174 Stuttgart
GERMANY

May 15, 2005

Very honourable Mister Wieland,

Because the tourist season will begin soon, we would like to seize the opportunity to introduce our new line of hand-carved cuckoo clocks to you. Last year you were so friendly as to buy two dozen of our clocks. In recognition of our good business relationship, we now offer you the opportunity to select the new models before we offer this line to other businesses for purchase.

As you know, our artisans use only the best wood. According to time-honoured patterns that are passed on from generation to generation, they carefully carve every detail by hand. Our clockworks are of superior quality, and we test every clock before it is painted and shipped. We give you a guarantee of five years on all Furtwangen Handcrafts clocks.

Enclosed you will find a copy of our newest brochure and an order form. To express our appreciation, we assume the shipping costs if you order before June 15.

We continue to wish you a lot of success in your new Stuttgart location. We are convinced that you will satisfy your regular clientele with your larger exhibition area and expanded stock and will gain many new visitors.

With friendly greetings

Frederick Semper

Frederick Semper

Geschäfts-filter literally means "business leader": A common English translation would be "managing director."
Refers to the ongoing business relationship
Language a bit more formal than in Canadian and U.S. letters
Complimentary close typical of German business letters
Shows concern for the audience
Ends with a compliment to the recipient
Typed name includes no title

FIGURE 3–3 In-Depth Critique: Translated German Business Letter

Be aware of various cultures' tendency to organize thoughts differently.

Letter writers in other countries also use various techniques to organize their thoughts. If you are aware of some of these practices, you'll be able to concentrate on the message without passing judgment on the writers. Letters from Japanese businesspeople, for example, are slow to come to the point. They typically begin with a remark about the season or weather, which is followed by an inquiry about your health or congratulations on your success. A note of thanks for your patronage might come next. After these preliminaries, the main idea is introduced. The letter in Figure 3–4 was written by a Japanese banker to a large business customer. Notice how the banker emphasizes developing a long-term business relationship.

To ensure effective written communication, follow these recommendations (all of which are discussed in more detail in Chapter 5, "Composing Business Messages"):[50]

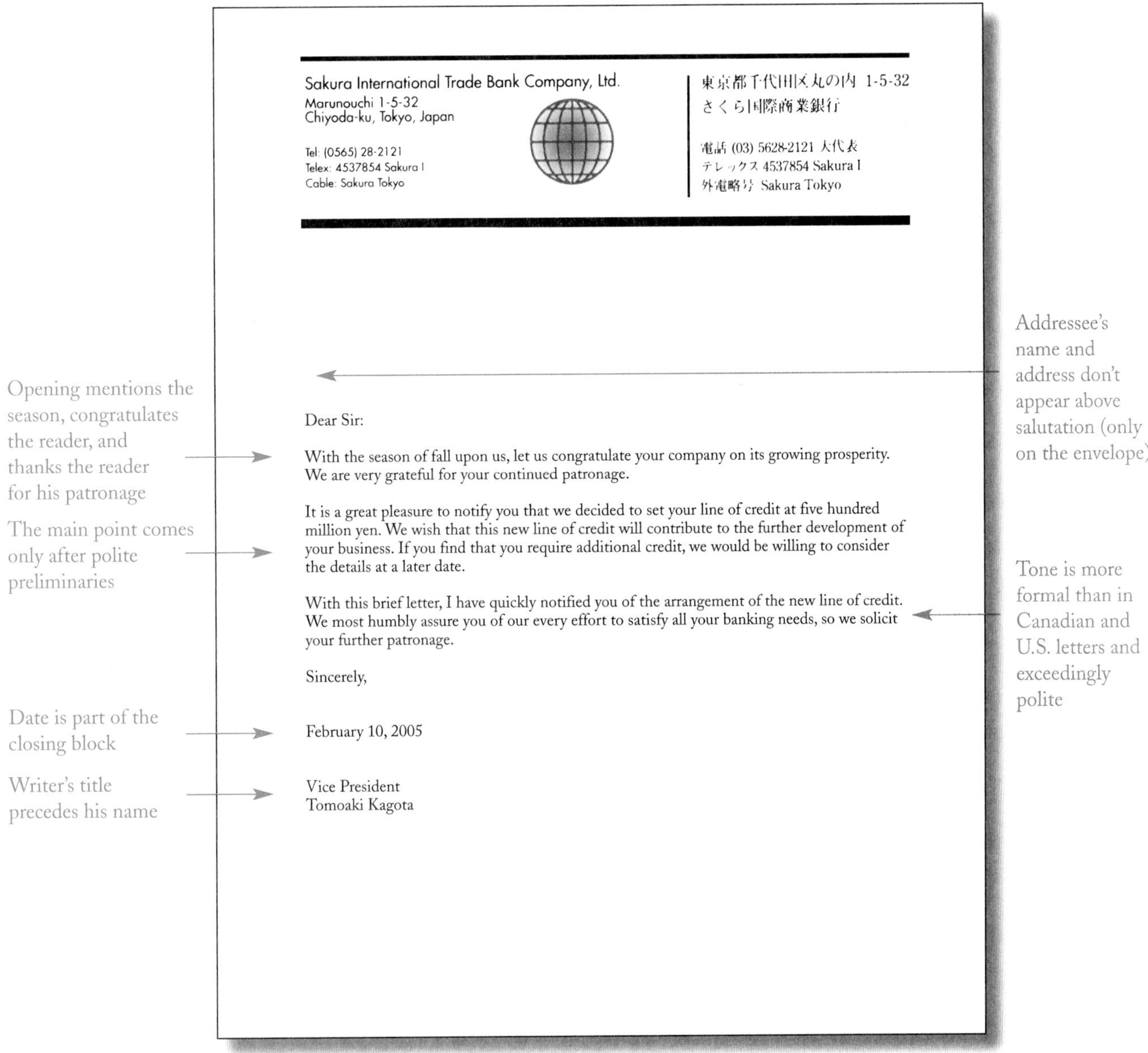

Sakura International Trade Bank Company, Ltd.
Marunouchi 1-5-32
Chiyoda-ku, Tokyo, Japan

Tel: (0565) 28-2121
Telex: 4537854 Sakura I
Cable: Sakura Tokyo

東京都千代田区丸の内 1-5-32
さくら国際商業銀行

電話 (03) 5628-2121 大代表
テレックス 4537854 Sakura I
外電略号 Sakura Tokyo

Dear Sir:

With the season of fall upon us, let us congratulate your company on its growing prosperity. We are very grateful for your continued patronage.

It is a great pleasure to notify you that we decided to set your line of credit at five hundred million yen. We wish that this new line of credit will contribute to the further development of your business. If you find that you require additional credit, we would be willing to consider the details at a later date.

With this brief letter, I have quickly notified you of the arrangement of the new line of credit. We most humbly assure you of our every effort to satisfy all your banking needs, so we solicit your further patronage.

Sincerely,

February 10, 2005

Vice President
Tomoaki Kagota

Addressee's name and address don't appear above salutation (only on the envelope)
Opening mentions the season, congratulates the reader, and thanks the reader for his patronage
The main point comes only after polite preliminaries
Tone is more formal than in Canadian and U.S. letters and exceedingly polite
Date is part of the closing block
Writer's title precedes his name

FIGURE 3-4 In-Depth Critique: Translated Japanese Business Letter

- **Use plain English.** Use short, precise words that say exactly what you mean.
- **Be clear.** Rely on specific terms and concrete examples to explain your points.
- **Avoid slang and idioms.** Avoid using slang, idioms, jargon, and buzzwords. Abbreviations, acronyms (such as CAD/CAM), and unfamiliar product names may also lead to confusion.
- **Be brief.** Construct sentences that are shorter and simpler than those you might use when writing to someone fluent in your own language.
- **Use short paragraphs.** Each paragraph should stick to one topic and be no more than eight to ten lines long.
- **Use transitional elements.** Help readers follow your train of thought by using transitional.

IMPROVE YOUR WEB COMMUNICATION SKILLS

Reaching an international audience on the Web involves more than simply offering translations of the English language. When creating a Web site for your business, address the needs of international customers.[51]

- **Provide both metric and imperial equivalents for weights, measures, sizes, and temperatures.** Use universal terms for times, dates, and geographical names. For example, provide customer service hours in universal time (such as 8:00 to 18:00 instead of 8 a.m. to 6 p.m.), because it will avoid confusion. Since Europeans read "10/04/2005" as April 10, 2005, be sure you spell out the month and year. And offer complete location descriptions, such as "Medicine Hat, Alberta, Canada."
- **Be sensitive to cultural differences.** Since humour is rooted in cultural norms, a touch of Canadian humour may not be funny to Asian or European readers. Avoid idioms and references that aren't universally recognized, such as "putting all your eggs in one basket" or "jumping out of the frying pan into the fire."
- **Keep the message clear.** Use simple words and write in the active voice. Avoid complicated sentence structure to achieve a simple, straightforward tone. Remember to define abbreviations and acronyms.
- **Avoid "e-blunders."** Be careful with translations. A translator at the international courier Fedex learned that the Québécois version of "pick up a parcel" is read in Parisian French as "pick up garbage."[52]
- **Break through language barriers with graphics.** Clarify written concepts with graphics. However, even though most graphical icons are internationally recognized, some images are more widely accepted than others. In some countries, for example, a mailbox doesn't necessarily convey the idea of sending mail. So an envelope might be a more appropriate symbol to reinforce the message "Contact Us."
- **Consult local experts.** Work with local experts and webmasters to develop native-language keywords that will direct international customers to your site. Even simple terms such as "home page" differ from country to country. Spanish readers refer to the "first page," or *pagina inicial,* whereas the French term is "welcome page," or *page d'accueil.*

IMPROVE YOUR ORAL SKILLS

Face-to-face communication lets you establish a personal relationship with people from other cultures and gives you the benefit of immediate feedback.

If you've ever studied another language, you know it's easier to write in that language than to conduct a conversation. However, some transactions simply cannot be handled without face-to-face contact. In many countries, business relationships are based on personal relationships, and until you establish rapport, nothing happens. When speaking in English to people who speak English as a second language, you may find these guidelines helpful:

- **Try to eliminate noise.** Pronounce words clearly, stop at distinct punctuation points, and make one point at a time.
- **Look for feedback.** Be alert to signs of confusion in your listener. Realize that nods and smiles don't necessarily mean understanding. Recognize that gestures and expressions mean different things in different cultures. If the other person's body language seems at odds with the message, take time to clarify the meaning.
- **Rephrase your sentence when necessary.** If someone doesn't seem to understand you, choose simpler words; don't just repeat the sentence in a louder voice.
- **Clarify your true intent with repetition and examples.** Try to be aware of unintentional meanings that may be read into your message.
- **Don't talk down to the other person.** Try not to over-enunciate, and don't "blame" the listener for not understanding. Use phrases such as "Am I going too fast?" rather than "Is this too difficult for you?"
- **Use objective, accurate language.** Avoid throwing around adjectives such as *fantastic* and *fabulous,* which people from other cultures might consider unreal and overly dramatic.

- **Listen carefully and patiently.** Let other people finish what they have to say. If you interrupt, you may miss something important. You'll also show a lack of respect. If you do not understand a comment, ask the person to repeat it.
- **Adapt your conversation style to the other person's.** For instance, if the other person appears to be direct and straightforward, follow suit.
- **Clarify what will happen next.** At the end of the conversation, be sure that you and the other person agree on what has been said and decided. If appropriate, follow up by writing a letter or a memo summarizing the conversation and thanking the person for meeting with you.

In short, take advantage of the other person's presence to make sure that your message is getting across and that you understand his or her message too.

Summary of Learning Objectives

1 Discuss two trends that have made intercultural business communication so important. *Market globalization,* the first trend, is brought about by improvements in communication and transportation technology. Such technological advancements allow companies to sell and produce goods all over the world. As a result, more and more people are working in companies whose employees come from various national, ethnic, racial, and religious backgrounds. This, of course, affects a country's *cultural diversity,* the second trend contributing to the importance of intercultural business communication. The Canadian workforce includes recent immigrants (from Asia, Europe, the U.S., Latin America, and the Caribbean), people from various ethnic backgrounds, and people who differ in other characteristics (such as gender, age, family status, and educational background). Thus, to be successful in today's workplace, you must be sensitive to cultural differences and possess good intercultural skills.

2 Define *culture* and *subculture,* and list culture's four basic characteristics. *Culture* is a shared system of symbols, beliefs, attitudes, values, expectations, and norms for behavior. A *subculture* is a distinct group existing within a major culture, such as Russian immigrants or disabled individuals existing within Canada. Culture has four basic characteristics: (1) culture is learned, (2) cultures vary in stability, (3) cultures vary in complexity, and (4) cultures vary in tolerance.

3 Explain the importance of recognizing cultural differences, delineate the differences between high- and low-context cultures, and list four categories of cultural differences. People from different cultures encode and decode messages differently, increasing the chances of misunderstanding. By recognizing cultural differences, we don't automatically assume that everyone's thoughts and actions are just like ours. For example, *high-context cultures* convey meaning by relying less on verbal communication and more on nonverbal actions and environmental setting. They expect the audience to discover the meaning of a message, and they rarely state the rules of everyday life explicitly. Conversely, *low-context cultures* convey meaning by relying more on verbal communication and less on circumstances and cues. They expect the speaker to transmit the meaning of a message, and they usually spell out rules and expectations in explicit statements. The four categories of cultural differences are contextual differences, ethical differences, social differences, and nonverbal differences.

4 Define *ethnocentrism* and *stereotyping;* then discuss three suggestions for overcoming these limiting mind sets. *Ethnocentrism* is the tendency to judge all other groups according to one's own standards, behaviours, and customs. *Stereotyping* is predicting individuals' behaviour or character on the basis of their membership in a particular group or class. To overcome ethnocentrism, follow three suggestions: (1) acknowledge distinctions, (2) avoid assumptions, and (3) avoid judgments.

5 Discuss three ways to improve communication with people who speak English as a second language; then discuss three ways to improve communication with people who don't speak your language at all. When communicating with people who speak English as a second language, clarify your meaning in three ways. First, since language never translates word for word, avoid using slang and idioms. Choose words that will convey only the most specific denotative meaning. Second, listen carefully and pay close attention to local accents and pronunciation. Third, don't assume that people from different cultures use their voice the same way you do. Be aware of vocal variations across cultures. When communicating with someone who doesn't speak your language at all, you have three choices. First, you can learn a foreign language or at least show respect by learning a few words. Second, you can use an intermediary or a translator to analyze a message, understand its cultural context, and convey its meaning in another language. Back-translation helps ensure accuracy and avoid embarrassing mistakes. Third, you can teach others your language. Many companies offer language-training programs to employees who speak little or no English.

6 Explain why studying other cultures helps you communicate more effectively, and list at least 7 of the 15 tips offered by successful intercultural businesspeople. Studying other cultures helps you send and receive intercultural messages more effectively. Even though you can't expect to understand another culture completely, you can increase your intercultural knowledge by reading books and articles about other cultures and by talking to people who do business in other cultures. Tips offered by successful intercultural businesspeople include the following: (1) take responsibility for communication, (2) withhold judgment, (3) show respect, (4) empathize, (5) look beyond the superficial, (6) be patient and persistent, and (7) be flexible.

7 Illustrate how word choice affects communication with people from other cultures; then list six recommendations for writing more effectively and nine guidelines for speaking across cultures more effectively. Word choice reflects the relationship between you and your audience; for example, the appropriate level of formality is achieved by word choice. To write more effectively, follow six recommendations: (1) use plain English, (2) be clear, (3) avoid slang and idioms, (4) be brief, (5) use short paragraphs, and (6) use transitional elements. To communicate through Web sites (1) provide both metric and imperial equivalents for weights, measures, sizes, and temperatures, (2) be sensitive to cultural differences, including humour, (3) be careful with translations, (4) use graphics to overcome language barriers, (5) and consult local webmasters for tips. To speak across cultures more effectively, follow these nine guidelines: (1) try to eliminate noise, (2) look for feedback, (3) rephrase your sentence when necessary, (4) clarify your true intent with repetition and examples, (5) don't talk down to the other person, (6) use objective and accurate language, (7) listen carefully and patiently, (8) adapt your conversation style to the other person's, and (9) clarify what will happen next.

ON THE JOB

Solving a Communication Dilemma at Malkam Cross-Cultural Training

Malkam Cross-Cultural Training provides diversity, cultural awareness, and language training services to individual and corporate clients. Their diversity-training program, for example, teaches how culture may affect decisions and communication in the workplace. Their communication seminars help employees at all levels to improve their written, oral, and behavioural skills when dealing with people from other cultures.

Malkam's cultural awareness program educates organizations about etiquette and protocols when dealing with business people from different cultures, abroad or at home, and provides insight into different communication styles. Malkam also trains managers and executives to negotiate effectively with different cultures, teaching them about a host country's specific negotiating style and providing strategies that can help a Canadian firm conclude a contract successfully with its foreign counterpart. Furthermore, Malkam assists companies in developing strategies to settle intercultural conflicts by teaching employees about gender and psychological factors of other cultures. Malkam's language training programs for non-native speakers of English help them develop their written and oral skills. The staff offers group and individual programs in effective business writing style, mastering the mechanics of English, and speaking idiomatically and confidently.

Malkam works with government, industry, banking and finance, small businesses and major corporations, so they can take advantage of growing opportunities in the global marketplace. Their facilities include up-to-date language laboratories, several classrooms, as well as a supervised on-site daycare and an employment opportunity program to assist newcomers to Canada while they study with Malkam's specialists.

Your Mission Imagine you are a trainer at Malkam Consultants working with a variety of classes: one is composed of newcomers who are learning English and about Canadian ways, another is made up of managers who will be travelling abroad for business. You want to foster cooperation among your students and encourage them to interact effectively with each other. Use your skill in intercultural communication to choose the best response in each of the following situations. Be prepared to explain why your choice is best.

1 It's important that students in your class for English as a second language develop their ability in speaking conversational English. How do you accomplish this?

a You have each student prepare at least two presentations in English on aspects of their culture that they will deliver to the class.

b From time to time you take the class to a coffee shop and have them order food in English and speak English while they are there.

c You pair off students and have them prepare scenarios in English, such as job interviews, to present in front of the class.

d From time to time you invite the class to your home where you lead conversations in English.

2 One of your students is having trouble following the instructions for using the audiotape machine in the language laboratory. It is obvious to you that she does not understand the instructions, even though she insists that she does. How do you help her?

a You have her memorize the instructions and have her recite them to you.

b You ask a student who speaks her language to help her through the instructions.

c You repeat the instructions several times in front to the entire class.

d You demonstrate how the machine is used and have her repeat the process until she is able to operate it easily.

3 Several of your students in your class for English as a second language do not make eye contact when delivering speeches because in their cultures it is considered rude to make eye contact when speaking to other people. How do you persuade them to look at the audience?

a You gently encourage the students to make eye contact. You explain that in Canada it is common for businesspeople to make eye contact when giving a presentation, and that people who don't are not considered effective speakers.

b You don't discuss the issue with the students at all and let them avoid making eye contact. You believe they will understand the importance of eye contact when they give presentations in their jobs in Canada.

c You show videos about making effective presentations, hoping the students will be encouraged to make eye contact after watching them.

d You set up team presentations, creating teams with students who are comfortable making eye contact with the audience and those who are not. You expect that while these teams rehearse their presentations, students who avoid looking at the audience will be persuaded to make eye contact after working with peers who do.

4 Your students are breaking into ethnically based cliques. Members of individual ethnic groups eat and socialize together, and chat in their native language. Some other students feel left out and alienated. How do you encourage a unified class attitude?

a Ban the use of languages other than English in class.

b Do nothing. This is normal behaviour.

c Encourage people to mingle and get to know each other better.

d Send all of your students to diversity training classes.[53]

Test Your Knowledge

Review Questions

1 How have market globalization and cultural diversity contributed to the increased importance of intercultural communication?

2 What is the relationship between culture and subculture?

3 What are the four basic characteristics of culture?

4 How do high-context cultures differ from low-context cultures?

5 In addition to contextual differences, what other categories of cultural differences exist?

6 What four principles apply to ethical intercultural communication?

7 What is ethnocentrism, and how can it be overcome in communication?

8 Why is it a good idea to avoid slang and idioms when addressing a multicultural audience?

9 What are some ways to improve communication using the World Wide Web?

10 What are some ways to improve oral skills when communicating with people of other cultures?

11 What is the purpose of back-translation when preparing a message in another language?

Interactive Learning 

Use this text's online resources.

Visit our Companion Web site at **www.pearsoned.ca/thill**, where you can use the interactive Study Guide to test your chapter knowledge and get instant feedback. Additional resources link you to the sites mentioned in this text and to additional sources of information on chapter topics.

Also check out the resources on the Mastering Business Communication CD, including "Perils of Pauline," an interactive presentation of the business communication challenges within a fictional company. For Chapter 3, see in particular the episode "Intercultural Communication."

Apply Your Knowledge

Critical Thinking Questions

1 What are some of the intercultural differences that managers of a Canadian-based firm might encounter during a series of business meetings with a China-based company whose managers speak English fairly well?
2 What are some of the intercultural communication issues to consider when deciding whether to accept an overseas job with a firm that's based in your own country? A job in your own country with a local branch of a foreign-owned firm? Explain.
3 How do you think company managers from a country that has a relatively homogeneous culture might react when they do business with the culturally diverse staff of a company based in a less homogeneous country? Explain your answer.
4 Your company has relocated to a Canadian city where a Vietnamese subculture is strongly established. Many of your employees will be from this subculture. What can you do to improve communication between your management and the Vietnamese Canadians you are currently hiring?
5 **Ethical Choices** Your office in Turkey desperately needs the supplies that have been sitting in Turkish customs for a month. Should you bribe a customs official to speed up delivery? Explain your decision.

Practice Your Knowledge

Document for Analysis

Your boss wants to send a brief e-mail message welcoming employees recently transferred to your department from your Hong Kong branch. They all speak English, but your boss asks you to review his message for clarity. What would you suggest your boss change in the following e-mail message—and why? Would you consider this message to be audience centred? Why or why not?

> I wanted to welcome you ASAP to our little family here in Canada. It's high time we shook hands in person and not just across the sea. I'm pleased as punch about getting to know you all, and I for one will do my level best to sell you on Canada.

Exercises

3–1 **Intercultural Sensitivity: Recognizing Differences** You represent a Canadian toy company that's negotiating to buy miniature truck wheels from a manufacturer in Osaka, Japan. In your first meeting, you explain that your company expects to control the design of the wheels as well as the materials that are used to make them. The manufacturer's representative looks down and says softly, "Perhaps that will be difficult." You press for agreement, and to emphasize your willingness to buy, you show the prepared contract you've brought with you. However, the manufacturer seems increasingly vague and uninterested. What cultural differences may be interfering with effective communication in this situation? Explain.

3–2 **Ethical Choices** A Canadian manager wants to export T-shirts to a West African country, but a West African official expects a special payment before allowing the shipment into his country. How can the two sides resolve their different approaches without violating Canadian rules against bribing foreign officials? On the basis of the information presented in Chapter 1, would you consider this situation an ethical dilemma or an ethical lapse? Please explain.

3–3 **Teamwork** Working with two other students, prepare a list of ten examples of slang (in your own language) that would probably be misinterpreted or misunderstood during a business conversation with someone from another culture. Next to each example, suggest other words you might use to convey the same message. Do the alternatives mean *exactly* the same as the original slang or idiom?

3–4 **Intercultural Communication: Studying Cultures** Choose a specific country, such as India, Portugal, Bolivia, Thailand, or Nigeria, with which you are not familiar. Research the culture and write a brief summary of what a Canadian manager would need to know about concepts of personal space and rules of social behaviour in order to conduct business successfully in that country.

3–5 **Multicultural Work Force: Bridging Differences** Differences in gender, age, and physical abilities contribute to the diversity of today's work force. Working with a classmate, role-play a conversation in which

a A woman is being interviewed for a job by a male personnel manager
b An older person is being interviewed for a job by a younger personnel manager
c A person using a wheelchair is being interviewed for a job by a person who can walk

How did differences between the applicant and the interviewer shape the communication? What can you do to improve communication in such situations?

3–6 **Intercultural Sensitivity: Understanding Attitudes** As the director of marketing for a telecommunications firm based in Germany, you're negotiating with an official in Guangzhou, China, who's in charge of selecting a new telephone system for the city. You insist that the specifications be spelled out in detail in the contract. However, your Chinese counterpart argues that in developing a long-term business relationship, such minor details are unimportant. What can you do or say to break this intercultural deadlock and obtain the contract without causing the official to lose face?

3–7 Culture and Language: Understanding Differences Germany is a low-context culture; by comparison, France and England are more high context. These three translations of the same message were posted on a lawn in Switzerland: the German sign read, "Walking on the grass is forbidden"; the English sign read, "Please do not walk on the grass"; and the French sign read, "Those who respect their environment will avoid walking on the grass."[54] How does the language of each sign reflect the way information is conveyed in the cultural context of each nation? Write a brief (two- to three-paragraph) explanation.

3–8 Culture and Time: Dealing with Differences When a company knows that a scheduled delivery time given by an overseas firm is likely to be flexible, managers may buy in larger quantities or may order more often to avoid running out of product before the next delivery. Identify three other management decisions that may be influenced by differing cultural concepts of time, and make notes for a short (two-minute) presentation to your class.

3–9 Intercultural Communication: Using Translators Imagine that you're the lead negotiator for a company that's trying to buy a factory in Prague, capital of the Czech Republic. Your parents grew up near Prague, so you understand and speak the language fairly well. However, you wonder about the advantages and disadvantages of using a translator anyway. For example, you may have more time to think if you wait for an intermediary to translate the other side's position. Decide whether to hire a translator, and then write a brief (two- or three-paragraph) explanation of your decision.

3–10 Internet @ Some companies are experimenting with software that automatically translates business messages and Web sites. To see how this works, go to the Google at **www.google.com**. Click on "translation tools" and enter a sentence such as "We are enclosing a purchase order for four dozen computer monitors." Select "English to Spanish" from the drop-down menu and click to translate. Once you've read the Spanish version, select "Spanish to English.". Try translating the same English sentence into German, French, or Italian and then back into English. How do the results of each translation differ? What are the implications for the use of automated translation services and back-translation? How could you use this Web site to sharpen your intercultural communication skills?

3–11 Intercultural Communication: Improving Skills You've been assigned to host a group of Swedish college students who are visiting your college for the next two weeks. They've all studied English but this is their first trip to your area. Make a list of at least eight slang terms and idioms they are likely to hear on campus. How will you explain each phrase? When speaking with the Swedish students, what word or words might you substitute for each slang term or idiom?

Going Online Exercises

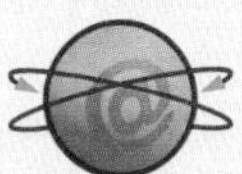

Hone Your Skills for International Business, found on page 61 of this chapter

Procedures and protocol for conducting international business are diverse. Go to the global resources at americanexpress.com to learn why an awareness of differences in business practices is important and how to be culturally correct.

1 Describe several business customs pertaining to etiquette in Korea that differ from customs in Canada. Why is your negotiating style particularly important in establishing a business relationship?
2 What did you discover about cultural differences in Russia that might make it difficult to adapt to Russian business customs such as a dinner meeting?
3 Select a country you might travel to and investigate its customs: what tips and specific information about doing international business did you learn?

1 Describe the three-step writing process

2 Explain why it's important to define your purpose carefully and then list four questions that can help you test that purpose

3 Justify the importance of creating an audience profile and then list four ways of developing one

4 Outline how you can collect information informally, clarify what your audience wants to know, and test the thoroughness of your information

5 Define *media richness* and then list other factors to consider when choosing the most appropriate channel and medium for your message

6 Discuss how you can establish a good relationship with your audience

Planning Business Messages

ON THE JOB

Facing a Communication Dilemma at The Forzani Group

Designing a Game Plan for Success

www.forzanigroup.com

Whether it's skateboards, snowboards, skis, or sneakers, you'll probably find the gear you want at one of John Forzani's sporting goods stores across Canada. As the chair and CEO of The Forzani Group Limited (FGL), the former Calgary Stampeder has created a retail empire that includes Sport Chek, Sports Experts, Coast Mountain Sports, Sports Mart, and Atmosphere, his newest chain to serve outdoor enthusiasts. Since opening Forzani's Locker Room in 1974 with three teammates, John Forzani now operates 350 corporate or franchise stores, with net earnings of $20.6 million in 2002, his most profitable year ever. By the end of 2005, Forzani plans on adding 1.5 million square feet of floor space to sell athletic wear and equipment in every city in Canada.

But the future success of The Forzani Group centres on John Forzani's ability to communicate effectively with employees, customers, and suppliers. To keep operations running smoothly, Forzani needs to establish good working relationships with all three audiences. He must find out what each audience needs to know, and he must determine the right way to communicate that information. For example, before Forzani can stock a new product, he must analyze the needs of his audiences and plan appropriate messages for each one. He must assess customer demand, educate employees about product use, and seek vendors that can deliver the right amount of merchandise in a timely manner.

Planning effective messages wasn't as difficult when Forzani opened his first store in Calgary, where he sold athletic footwear in a 1200 square foot space and personally dealt with suppliers and trained employees. But with plans to open or expand to 52 stores by the end of 2003 and to introduce new sports products, Forzani can no longer depend on oral messages to communicate with his audiences. Establishing relationships with 9600 employees, suppliers of almost every major brand of athletic equipment and clothing, and millions of customers has complicated matters. And adapting his messages to serve the needs of each audience requires careful planning.

If you were John Forzani, how would you plan your business messages to different audiences? What factors would you consider as you plan your messages? How would you analyze each audience? And how would you choose the best channel and medium for each of your messages?[1]

As Canada's largest sporting goods retailer, The Forzani Group operates stores coast to coast—with plans to expand to every Canadian city and increase product offerings. The company must keep operations running smoothly by constantly refining its communication, much of which must be in writing.

Understanding the Three-Step Writing Process

Like sporting goods retailer John Forzani, you will face a variety of communication assignments in your career, both oral and written. Some of your tasks will be routine, needing little more than jotting down a few sentences on paper or keyboarding a brief e-mail message. Others will be more complex, requiring reflection, research, and careful document preparation. Because your audience is exposed to an increasing number of business messages each day, your messages must be livelier, easier to read, more concise, and more interesting than ever before.

Of course, making your business messages interesting doesn't mean using the dramatic techniques of creative writing. Your purpose is not to dazzle your readers with your extensive knowledge or powerful vocabulary. Instead, your messages must be

- **Purposeful.** Business messages provide information, solve a problem, or request the resources necessary to accomplish a goal. Every message you prepare will have a specific purpose.
- **Audience-centred.** Business messages help audiences understand an issue, ask them to collaborate on accomplishing a goal, or take some action. So every message you prepare must consider the audience's point of view.
- **Concise.** Business messages respect everyone's time by presenting information clearly and efficiently. Every message you prepare will be as short as it can be without omitting essential facts or ideas.

To compete for attention, business messages must be purposeful, audience-centred, and concise.

What Is the Three-Step Process?

OBJECTIVE 1 Describe the three-step writing process.

The specific actions you take to write business messages will vary with each situation, audience, and purpose. However, following a process of generalized steps will help you write more effective messages. As Figure 4–1 below shows, this **writing process** may be viewed as comprising three simple steps: (1) planning, (2) writing, and (3) completing your business messages.

The goal of effective business writing is to express your ideas rather than to impress your audience. One of the best ways to do so is to follow a systematic writing process.

- **Planning.** The first stage is to think about the fundamentals of your message. Study your purpose to make sure your reasons for communicating are clear and necessary. Schedule enough time to complete all three steps of the writing process. Analyze audience members so that you can tailor your message to their needs, and then gather the information that will inform, persuade, or motivate them. Don't

Figure 4–1 The Three-Step Writing Process

1 Planning	2 Writing	3 Completing
Analyze: Study your purpose, lay out your writing schedule, and then profile your audience.	**Organize:** Define your main idea, limit the scope, group your points, and choose the direct or indirect approach.	**Revise:** Evaluate content and review readability, editing, and rewriting for conciseness and clarity.
Investigate: Gather information through formal or informal research methods.	**Compose:** Control your style through level of formality and conversational tone. Choose your words carefully so that you can create effective sentences and paragraphs.	**Produce:** Use effective design elements and suitable delivery methods.
Adapt: Choose the right channel and medium; then establish a good relationship with your audience.		**Proofread:** Review for errors in layout, spelling, and mechanics.

Is playing chess similar to planning business messages? How does the three-step process apply to this challenging game?

forget to adapt your message: select the best channel and medium and establish a good audience relationship. Planning business messages is the focus of this chapter.

- **Writing.** Once you've planned your message, organize your ideas and begin composing your first draft. This is the stage when you commit your thoughts to words, create sentences and paragraphs, and select illustrations and details to support your main idea. Writing business messages is discussed in Chapter 5.
- **Completing.** Now that you have your first draft, step back to review the content and organization for overall style, structure, and readability. Revise and rewrite until your message comes across clearly and effectively. Next, edit your message, checking for correct grammar, punctuation, and format. Then produce it, putting your message into the form that your audience will receive. And finally, proofread the final draft for typos, spelling errors, and other mechanical problems. Completing business messages is discussed in Chapter 6.

How Does the Three-Step Process Work?

Because so many of today's business messages are composed under pressure and on a schedule that is often tight, allocating your time among these three steps can be challenging. In some cases, your audience may expect you to get your message out in record time—sometimes only minutes after speaking with a client or attending a meeting. But whether you have 30 minutes or two days, try to give yourself enough time to plan, write, and complete your message.

As a general rule, try using roughly half of your time for planning—for deciding on your purpose, getting to know your audience, and immersing yourself in your subject matter. Use less than a quarter of your time for writing your document. Then use the remaining time for completing the project—you don't want to shortchange important final steps such as revising and proofing.[2]

FGL's John Forzani understands that there is no right or best way to write all business messages. As you work through the writing process presented in Chapters 4, 5, and 6, try not to view it as a list of how-to directives but as a way to understand the various tasks involved in effective business writing.[3] The three-step process will help you avoid the risky "rush in and start writing" routine.

Remember that the writing process is flexible. Effective communicators may not necessarily complete the steps in a predetermined order. Some jump back and forth from one step to another; some compose quickly and then revise; others revise as they go along. However, to communicate effectively, you must ultimately complete all three steps.

Analyzing Your Purpose and Audience

OBJECTIVE 2 Explain why it's important to define your purpose carefully and then list four questions that can help you test that purpose.

When planning a business message, your first step is to think about your purpose, your schedule, and your audience. For a business message to be effective, its purpose and its audience must complement one another. You must know enough about your purpose and audience to shape your message in a way that serves both.

Define Your Purpose

Your **general purpose** may be to inform, to persuade, or to collaborate.

The general purpose of a message influences how much your audience will participate in your message and how much you will control it.

When planning a business message, you must decide on the general and specific purpose of the message. All business messages have a **general purpose**: to inform, to persuade, or to collaborate with your audience. This overall purpose determines both the amount of audience participation you need and the amount of control you have over your message. To inform your audience, you need little interaction. Audience members absorb the information and accept or reject it, but they don't contribute to message content; you control the message. To persuade your audience, you require a moderate amount of participation, and you need to retain a moderate amount of message control. Finally, to collaborate with audience members, you need maximum participation. Your control of the message is minimal because you must adjust to new input and unexpected reactions.

Business messages also have a **specific purpose**. That purpose may be clear and straightforward (such as placing an order or communicating survey responses) or it may be more complicated (such as convincing management to hire more part-time employees during the holiday season). To help you define the specific purpose of your message, decide what you hope to accomplish with your message and what your audience should do or think after receiving your message. For instance, is your goal simply to update your audience on an event, or do you want them to take immediate action? State your specific purpose as precisely as possible, even identifying which audience members should respond.

To determine the **specific purpose**, think of how the audience's ideas or behaviour should be affected by the message.

You must also consider whether your purpose is worth pursuing at this time. Too many business messages serve no practical purpose, and writing useless memos can destroy your **credibility**. So if you suspect that your ideas will have little impact, wait until you have a more practical purpose. To help you decide whether to proceed, ask yourself four questions:

- **Is your purpose realistic?** If your purpose involves a radical shift in action or attitude, go slowly. Consider proposing the first step and viewing your message as the beginning of a learning process.
- **Is this the right time?** If an organization is undergoing changes of some sort, you may want to defer your message until the situation stabilizes and people can concentrate on your ideas.
- **Is the right person delivering your message?** Even though you may have done all the work, achieving your objective is more important than taking the credit. You may want to play a supporting role in delivering your message if, for example, your boss's higher status could get better results.
- **Is your purpose acceptable to your organization?** If you receive an abusive letter that unfairly attacks your company, you might wish to fire back an angry reply. But your supervisors might prefer that you regain the customer's goodwill. Your response must reflect the organization's priorities.

Defer a message, or do not send it at all if

- The purpose is not realistic
- The timing is not right
- You are not the right person to deliver the message
- The purpose is not acceptable to the organization

Once you are satisfied that you have a legitimate purpose in communicating, you must take a good look at your intended audience.

Develop an Audience Profile

Who are your audience members? What are their attitudes? What do they need to know? And why should they care about your message? The answers to such questions will indicate which material you'll need to present and how to develop it.

If you're communicating with someone you know well, perhaps your boss or a co-worker, audience analysis is relatively easy. You can predict this person's reaction quite accurately, without a lot of research. On the other hand, your audience could be made up of strangers—customers or suppliers you've never met, a new boss, or new employees. Just like FGL's Forzani, you'll have to learn about the members of your audience before you can adjust your message to serve them (see Figure 4–2 on page 74). The following steps will help you analyze your audience:

- **Identify the primary audience.** If you can pinpoint the decision makers or opinion moulders in your audience, you'll also be able to determine other members who are important. Key people ordinarily have the most organizational clout, but occasionally a person of relatively low status may have influence in one or two particular areas.
- **Identify the secondary audience.** The secondary audience is composed of people who are given some details your message—or the entire message itself—by

Going Online

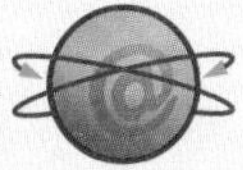

Learn about Your Audience

How can you use an audience profile to write a message that promotes your product? What type of information would you need about your audience? What audience characteristics would be most helpful? Asking the right questions is one way to analyze a specific group. You can learn what sources of information people use, where they live, and what they do for a living. You can learn their age, sex, educational level, marital status, economic level, and cultural background. At the Games.net Audience Profile, you'll learn about the characteristics of Games.net customers.

Marketing.pcworld.com/surveys/gamesnetaudienceprofile.html

To link directly to this site, visit our Companion Web site at **www.pearsoned.ca/thill** and look for the Chapter 4 resources.

OBJECTIVE 3 Justify the importance of creating an audience profile and then list four ways of developing one.

Ask yourself some key questions about your audience:

- Who are they?
- What is their probable reaction to your message?
- How much do they already know about the subject?
- What is their relationship to you?

Focus on the common interests of the audience, but be alert to their individual concerns.

A gradual approach and plenty of evidence are required to win over a skeptical audience.

the primary audience. For example, perhaps you are a sales representative who sees the need for new laptop computers for the sales team. You compose a memo suggesting this purchase and send it to your director— she is your primary audience. To determine whether the sales department's budget can accommodate the purchase, she will send a copy of your memo to a manager in the finance department. He is the secondary audience. Although he is not the person to whom you addressed your memo, he receives the message because he has some influence on the purchase decision.

- **Determine audience size.** A report meant for wide distribution requires a more formal style, organization, and format than one directed to three or four people in your department. Also, be sure to respond to the particular concerns of key individuals. The head of marketing would need different facts than the head of production or finance would need.
- **Determine audience composition.** Look for common denominators that tie audience members together across differences in culture, education, status, or attitude. Include evidence that touches on everyone's area of interest. To be understood across cultural barriers, consider how audience members think and learn, as well as what style they expect.[4]
- **Gauge your audience's level of understanding.** If audience members share your general background, they'll understand your material without difficulty. If not, you must educate them. But deciding how much information to include can be a challenge. As a guideline, include only enough information to accomplish your objective. Other material is irrelevant and must be eliminated; otherwise it will overwhelm your audience and divert attention from the important points. If audience members do not have the same level of understanding, gear your coverage to your primary audience (the key decision makers).
- **Consider your audience's expectations and preferences.** Will members of your audience expect complete details, or will a summary of the main points suffice? Do they want an e-mail or will they expect a formal memo? Should the memo be a brief one- to three-page message or a comprehensive 10- to 15-page report?
- **Estimate your audience's probable reaction.** Chapter 5 discusses how audience reaction affects the organization of your message. If you expect a favourable response, you can state conclusions and recommendations up front and offer minimal supporting evidence. If you expect skepticism, you can introduce conclusions gradually, with more proof. By anticipating the primary audience's response to certain points, you can include evidence to address those issues.

FIGURE 4–2 Audience Analysis Helps You Plan Your Message

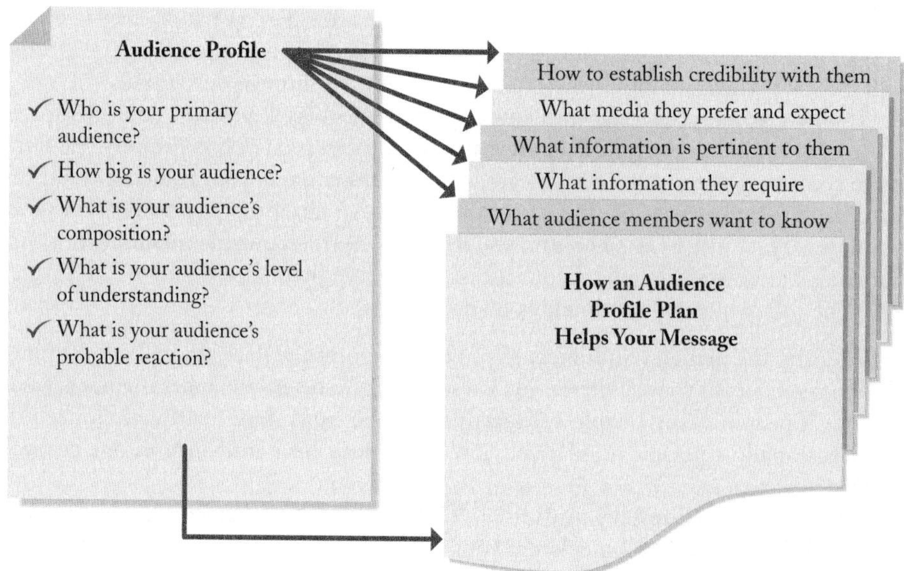

Collecting Information

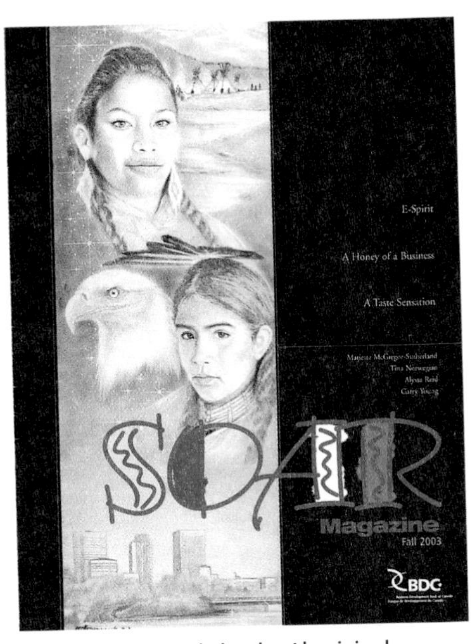

Published quarterly by the Aboriginal Banking Unit of the Business Development Bank of Canada (BDC), *Soar Magazine* includes success stories about Aboriginal entrepreneurs, articles relating to achievements of Aboriginal college and university students, and other items that relate to Aboriginal entrepreneurism. How do you think staff generate story ideas for this magazine?

When writing long, formal reports, you'll need to conduct formal research to locate and analyze all the information relevant to your purpose and your audience. Formal techniques for finding, evaluating, and processing information are discussed in Chapter 10 (Planning Business Reports and Proposals). Other kinds of business messages, however, require much less-formal information gathering.

Whether you're preparing for an informational interview with your supervisor, writing an e-mail message to a close colleague, or gathering opinions for an article to appear in your organization's monthly newsletter, you can collect information informally by

- **Considering others' viewpoints.** You might put yourself in someone else's position to consider what others might be thinking, feeling, or planning.
- **Browsing through company files.** Your own filing cabinet may be a rich source of the information you need for a particular memo or e-mail message. Consider company annual reports, financial statements, news releases, memos, marketing reports, and customer surveys for helpful information.
- **Chatting with supervisors or colleagues.** Fellow workers may have information you need, or they may know what will be of interest to your audience. Conducting telephone or personal interviews is a convenient way to gather information.
- **Asking your audience for input.** If you're unsure of what audience members need from your message, ask them—whether through casual conversation (face-to-face or over the phone), informal surveys, or unofficial interviews.

A good message answers all audience questions. But if you don't know what audience members want to know you won't be helping them complete their assigned tasks. The key to satisfying your audience's informational needs is finding out what questions your audience has and then providing answers that are thorough, accurate, ethical, and pertinent.

OBJECTIVE 4 Outline how you can collect information informally, clarify what your audience wants to know, and test the thoroughness of your information.

For many messages, you may need to collect information only informally.

Find Out Exactly What Your Audience Wants To Know

In many cases your audience's informational needs are readily apparent; for example, a consumer may send you a letter asking a specific question. In other cases, your audience may not be particularly good at telling you what's needed. When your audience makes a vague request, try restating the request in more specific terms. If your boss says, "Find out everything you can about Polaroid," you might respond, "You mean, you want me to track their market position by product line?" Another way to handle a vague request is to get a fix on its priority. You might ask, "Should I drop everything else and devote myself to this for the next week?" Asking a question or two forces the person to think through the request and define more precisely what is required.

By restating a vague request in specific terms, you can get the person seeking information to define his or her needs more precisely.

Also, try to think of information needs that your audience may not even be aware of. Suppose your company has just hired a new employee from out of town, and you've been assigned to coordinate this person's relocation. At a minimum, you would write a welcoming letter describing your company's procedures for relocating employees. With a little extra thought, however, you might include some information about the city: perhaps a guide to residential areas, a map or two, brochures about cultural activities, or information on schools and transportation facilities. In some cases, you may be able to tell your audience something they consider important but wouldn't have thought to ask. Although adding information of this sort lengthens your message, doing so creates goodwill.

Include any additional information that might be helpful, even though the requester didn't specifically ask for it.

Provide All Required Information

Test the completeness of your document by making sure it answers all the important questions: who, what, when, where, why, and how.

Once you've defined your audience's informational needs, be sure you satisfy those needs completely. One good way to test the thoroughness of your message is to use the **journalistic approach**: Check to see whether your message answers *who, what, when, where, why,* and *how.* Many messages fail to pass the test—such as this letter requesting information from a large hotel:

> Dear Ms. Hill:
>
> I just got back from a great vacation in Hawaii. However, this morning I discovered that my favourite black leather shoes are missing. Since I wore them in Hawaii, I assume I left them at the Hawaii Sands Hotel. Please check the items in your "lost and found" and let me know whether you have the missing shoes.

The letter fails to tell Hill everything she needs to know. The *what* could be improved by a detailed description of the missing shoes (size, brand, distinguishable style or trim). Hill doesn't know *when* the writer stayed at the Hawaii Sands, *where* (in what room) the writer stayed, or *how* to return the shoes. Hill will have to write or call the writer to get the missing details, and the inconvenience may be just enough to prevent her from complying with the request.

BE SURE THE INFORMATION IS ACCURATE

Be certain that the information you provide is accurate and that the commitments you make can be kept.

There's no point in answering all your audience's questions if the answers are wrong. Whether you're promising delivery by a given date or agreeing to purchase an item, if you have any doubt about the organization's ability or willingness to back up your promises, check with the appropriate people *before* you make the commitment.

Double-check everything.

You can minimize mistakes by double-checking everything you write or say. If you are using outside sources, ask yourself whether they are current and reliable. Be sure to review any mathematical or financial calculations. Check all dates and schedules, and examine your own assumptions and conclusions to be certain they are valid.

BE SURE THE INFORMATION IS ETHICAL

Honest mistakes are certainly possible. You may sincerely believe that you have answered someone's questions correctly and then later realize that your information was incorrect. If that happens, the most ethical thing for you to do is to contact the person immediately and correct the error. Most people will respect you for your honesty.

Good ethics will help you determine how much detail to include in your message.

Messages can be unethical simply because information is omitted. Of course, as a business professional, you may have legal or other sound business reasons not to include every detail about every matter. So just how much detail should you include? Even though most people don't want to be buried in an avalanche of paperwork, include enough detail to avoid misleading your audience. If you're unsure about how much information your audience needs, offer as much as you believe best fits your definition of complete, and then offer to provide more upon request.

BE SURE THE INFORMATION IS PERTINENT

Try to figure out what points will especially interest your audience, then give those points the most attention.

When deciding how to respond to your audience's informational needs, remember that some points will be of greater interest and importance to your audience than others. If you're summarizing a recent conversation you had with one of your company's oldest and best customers, the emphasis you give each point of the conversation will depend on your audience's concerns. The head of engineering might be most interested in the customer's reaction to your product's new design features. The shipping manager might be most concerned about the customer's comments on recent delivery schedules. In other words, you must choose and emphasize the points that will have the most impact on your audience.

If you don't know your audience, or if you're communicating with a large group of people, use your common sense to identify points of particular interest. Audience factors such as age, job, location, income, or education can give you a clue. If you were trying to sell memberships in the Book-of-the-Month Club, you would adjust your message for college or university students, homemakers, retired people, travelling sales representatives, and auto mechanics. All these people would need to know the same facts about membership, but each group would be more interested in some facts than in others. Economy might be important to college and university students or retired people, and convenience might attract sales reps or homemakers. Remember that your main goal is to tell audience members what they need to know. As Figure 4.3 below shows, your main goal is to tell audience members what they need to know.

Your knowledge of your audience members can help you figure out what will most interest them.

MOTT'S

MOTT'S CANADA

2700 MATHESON BOULEVARD EAST
EAST TOWER, SUITE 500
MISSISSAUGA, ONTARIO L4W 4X1
PHONE (905) 629-1899
FAX (905) 629-3534

September 19, 2005

Ms. Mita Nemani
84 Apple Crescent
Toronto, ON M2R 3J2

Dear Ms. Nemani:

Thank you very much for your interest in our Mott's Bake Lite program.

We have enclosed our free recipe pamphlet which contains a selection of tested and proven recipes which replace the butter and oil in baking with Mott's Apple Sauce.

Many consumers have asked us if they can use Mott's Apple Sauce as a substitute in all their baking recipes. We can only recommend the recipes we have developed in our test kitchens, because they are proven to succeed very well and to produce excellent, healthy results.

We can, however, provide a rule of thumb for those wanting to experiment with their own favourite recipes; butter and oil can normally be substituted with equal amounts of apple sauce. However, you must consider that apple sauce is sweeter, and thinner, which may call for less sugar, and more flour.

Again, we would like to thank you for your interest in Mott's and wish you the best of luck and enjoyment in your baking.

Sincerely,

Holly Prentice

Holly Prentice
Consumer Affairs Specialist

encl.

A MEMBER OF THE CADBURY SCHWEPPES PLC GROUP

The formal salutation indicates Prentice's respect for a customer she doesn't know.

The body of the letter includes advice for using the product. Additional information in a response to a request for a pamphlet or other company publication is included to maintain goodwill and to help sell the product or service.

The close is cordial and alludes to the main idea of the message.

FIGURE 4–3 In-Depth Critique: An Audience-Centred Letter

Adapting Your Message to Serve Your Audience

By now you know why you're writing, you know the audience you're writing to, and you have most of the information you need. But before actually beginning to write your message, you need to figure out how to tailor it to your audience and your purpose. To adapt your message, you need to select a channel and a medium appropriate to audience members, and you need to plan how you will establish a good relationship with them.

Select the Appropriate Channel and Medium

OBJECTIVE 5 Define **media richness** and then list other factors to consider when choosing the most appropriate channel and medium for your message.

Different types of messages require different communication channels and media.

Selecting the best channel and medium for your message can make the difference between effective and ineffective communication.[5] A communication channel can be either oral or written. Each channel includes specific media. The oral channel includes media such as telephone conversations, face-to-face exchanges, and videotaped addresses. The written channel includes media such as letters, memos, e-mail messages, and reports. When selecting a channel and medium, you must consider how your choice will affect the style, tone, and impact of your message. To do so, you need to consider a number of important factors.

The first factor to consider is **media richness**, the value of a medium in a given communication situation. Richness is determined by a medium's ability to

- Convey a message by means of more than one informational cue (visual, verbal, vocal)
- Facilitate feedback
- Establish personal focus

The more complicated the message, the richer the medium necessary.

The richest media aren't always the best choice for every situation.

Face-to-face communication is the richest medium because it is personal, it provides both immediate verbal and nonverbal feedback, and it conveys the emotion behind the message. But it's also one of the most restrictive media because you and your audience must be in the same place at the same time.[6] At the other end of the continuum are unaddressed documents such as fliers (see Figure 4.4 below). Choose the richest media for nonroutine messages intended to extend and humanize your presence throughout the organization, communicate your caring to employees, and gain employee commitment to organizational goals. Use leaner media to communicate more routine messages such as those conveying day-to-day information. For example, Home Depot uses a rich medium (satellite video broadcasts) to educate employees and to introduce new hires to the company's culture. The company educates customers in specific home-improvement skills by using a leaner medium (how-to articles in its magazine, *Weekend*).

Other factors are also important to consider when selecting channel and medium. If you want to emphasize the formality of your message, use a more formal medium, such as a memo, letter, or formal presentation. If you want to emphasize the confidentiality of your message, use voice mail rather than a fax, send a letter rather than

FIGURE 4–4 Media Richness

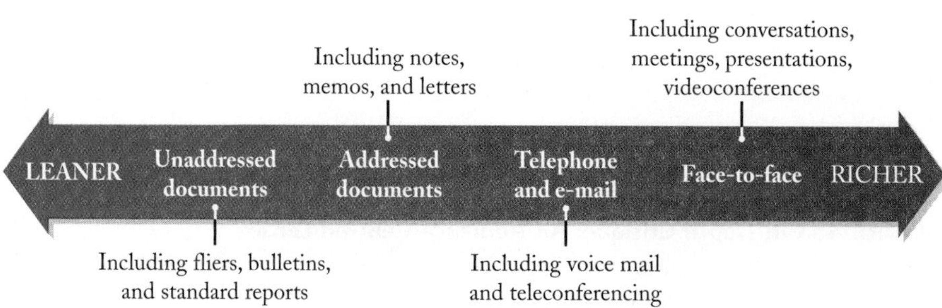

an e-mail, or address the matter in a private conversation rather than during a meeting. If you want to instill an emotional commitment to corporate values, consider a visual medium (a speech, videotape, or videoconference). If you require immediate feedback, face-to-face conversation is your best choice.[7] However, if you'll need a written record, you'll probably want to write a memo or a letter.

Your intentions heavily influence your choice of medium.

Time is another factor you must consider when selecting a medium. If your message is urgent, you'll probably choose to use the phone, fax, or next-day mail. Plus you'll need to consider cost. For instance, you wouldn't think twice about telephoning an important customer overseas if you just discovered your company erroneously sent the customer the wrong shipment. But you'd probably choose to e-mail or fax a routine order acknowledgment to your customer in Australia.

Time and cost also affect medium selection.

Finally, before choosing a channel and medium, consider which media your audience expects or prefers.[8] What would you think if your college or university tried to deliver your diploma by fax? You'd expect the school to hand it to you at graduation or mail it to you. In addition, some cultures tend to favour one channel over another. For example, Canada, the United States, and Germany emphasize written messages, whereas Japan emphasizes oral messages—perhaps because its high-context culture carries so much of the message in nonverbal cues and "between the lines" interpretation.[9]

When choosing the appropriate medium, don't forget to consider your audience's expectations.

From media richness to audience preference—all of these factors are important to consider before choosing a channel and medium. Every medium has limitations that filter out parts of your message, and every medium influences your audience's perception of your intentions. Consider carefully and do your best to match your selection to you audience and your purpose, whether that choice is an oral or a written medium.

ORAL MEDIA

Oral media traditionally include face-to-face conversation (the richest medium), telephone calls, speeches, presentations, and meetings (see Table 4.1 below). Your choice between a face-to-face conversation and a telephone call would depend on audience location, message importance, and your need for the sort of nonverbal feedback that only body language can reveal.

The chief advantage of oral communication is the opportunity it provides for immediate feedback. This is the channel to use when you want the audience to ask questions and make comments or when you're trying to reach a group decision. It's

In general, use an oral channel if your purpose is to collaborate with the audience.

TABLE 4–1 Choosing the Most Appropriate Channel and Medium

A Written Channel Is Best When	An Oral Channel Is Best When
You need no immediate feedback	You want immediate feedback from the audience
Your message is detailed and complex, and it requires careful planning	Your message is relatively simple and easy to accept
You need a permanent, verifiable record	You need no permanent record
Your audience is large and geographically dispersed	You can assemble your audience conveniently and economically
You want to minimize the distortion that can occur when a message passes orally from person to person	You want to encourage interaction to solve a problem or reach a decision
Written Media Include	**Oral Media Include**
• Letters and memos	• Face-to-face conversation, speeches, meetings
• Reports and proposals	• Telephone and voice mail
• Electronic mail	• Audiotape and videotape
• Faxes	• Teleconferences and videoconferences

also the best channel if there's an emotional component to your message and you want to read the audience's body language or hear the tone of their response.[10]

If you need to reach a decision or solve a problem, stick with a smaller audience to get the job done.

Small Meetings, Conversations, and Interviews In general, the smaller the audience, the more interaction among the members. If your purpose involves reaching a decision or solving a problem, select an oral medium geared toward a small audience. Be sure the program is relatively informal and unstructured so that ideas can flow freely.

If your purpose is strictly to inform, a larger audience may be appropriate.

Large Meetings, Conventions, and Presentations At the opposite extreme are formal presentations to large audiences, which are common at events such as sales conventions, shareholder meetings, and ceremonial functions. Often, these major presentations take place in a big facility, where the audience is seated auditorium style. Their formality makes them unsuitable for collaborative purposes that require audience interaction.

WRITTEN MEDIA

A written channel increases the sender's control but eliminates the possibility of immediate feedback.

Written messages take many forms, both traditional and electronic. At one end are the scribbled notes people use to jog their own memories; at the other are elaborate, formal reports that rival magazines in graphic quality. Regardless of the form, written messages have one major advantage: they let you plan and control the message. However, a serious drawback to written messages is that you miss out on the immediate feedback you would receive with many oral media. A written format is appropriate when the information is complex, when a permanent record is needed for future reference, when the audience is large and geographically dispersed, and when immediate interaction with the audience is either unimportant or undesirable.

The most common written media are letters, memos, e-mail messages, reports, and proposals, but this channel also includes faxing, computer conferencing (with groupware), and Web sites.

Use memos and e-mail messages for internal communication.

Letters, Memos, and E-Mail Messages You use memos and e-mail for the routine, day-to-day communication with people inside the organization. Such internal communication helps you do your job. It helps you and other employees develop a clear sense of the organization's mission, identify potential problems, and react quickly to ever-changing circumstances.

Use letters for external communication.

You use letters for communicating with outsiders. Letters not only convey a particular message but also perform an important public relations function. You may also use e-mail for external communication (1) in response to e-mail messages that you receive, (2) when the purpose of your message is informal, and (3) when your audience accepts e-mail as appropriate. External communication helps employees create a favourable impression of their company, plan for and respond to crises, and gather useful information (such as feedback from customers and other stakeholders).

Letters, memos, and e-mail messages differ in format and formality.

Most letters, memos, and e-mail messages are relatively brief, generally less than two pages (often less than a page for e-mail). Letters are the most formal of the three. Memos are less formal, and e-mail messages are the least formal. For in-depth format information, see Appendix A: Format and Layout of Business Documents. But to distinguish between these three types of written documents, keep the following format differences in mind.

- **Letters** Most letters appear on letterhead stationery (which includes a company's name and contact information). After the letterhead comes the date, followed by the inside address and the salutation (*Dear Mr.* or *Ms. Name*). Next is the message (often several paragraphs and sometimes running on to a second page). After the message come the complimentary close (*Sincerely* or *Yours truly*) and the signature block (space for the signature, followed by the sender's printed name and title).

- **Memos** Less formal than letters, memos begin with a title (*Memo, Memorandum,* or *Interoffice Correspondence*) and use a *To, From, Date,* and *Subject* heading (for readers who have time only to skim messages). Memos have no salutation, discuss only one topic, use a conversational tone, and have no complimentary close or signature. Because of their open construction and delivery by interoffice mail or e-mail, they are less private than letters. However, to document all correspondence on a particular in-house issue, printed memos provide paper trails that e-mail messages do not.
- **E-mail messages** Similar to memos, e-mail messages have a heading. Particulars depend on the software you use, but most programs include *To, From,* and *Subject* information, at minimum. Heading information is brief (the *To* and *From* lines sometimes show no names or titles, just e-mail addresses), and often includes information about copies and attachments. The software automatically inserts the date. After the salutation (optional but highly recommended) comes the message, followed by the complimentary close and the typed name of the sender. Contact information is sometimes included after the sender's name.

Chapters 7–9 discuss letters, memos, and e-mail messages in detail.

Reports and Proposals Reports and proposals are factual, objective documents that communicate information about some aspect of the business. They may be distributed to insiders or outsiders, depending on their purpose and subject. They come in many formats, including preprinted forms, letters, memos, and manuscripts. In length, they range from a few to several hundred pages, and they are generally more formal in tone than a typical business letter or memo. (Chapters 10 to 12 discuss reports and proposals in detail.)

Reports are generally longer and more formal than letters and memos, and they have more components.

ELECTRONIC MEDIA

The availability of electronic media increases your communication options in both oral and written channels. The trick is to use the tool that does the best overall job in each situation. Choose an electronic medium when you need speed, when you're physically separated from your audience, when time zones differ, when you must reach a dispersed audience personally, and when you're unconcerned about confidentiality. Although no hard rules dictate which tool to use in each case, here are a few pointers that will help you determine when to select electronic over more traditional forms:[11]

- **Voice mail** can be used to replace short memos and phone calls that need no response. It is most effective for short, unambiguous messages. It solves time-zone difficulties and reduces a substantial amount of interoffice paperwork.[12] Voice mail is a powerful tool when you need to communicate your emotion or tone. It is especially useful for goodwill and other positive messages. (See this chapter's "Checklist: Observing Voice-Mail and Fax Etiquette" on page 86.)
- **Teleconferencing** is an efficient alternative to a face-to-face meeting. Best for informational meetings, it is less effective for decision-making meetings and ineffective for negotiation. Teleconferencing discourages the "secondary" conversations that occur during meetings of more than four or five people. Although participants are better able to focus on a topic without such secondary conversations, they are prevented from sharing documents because the medium is only aural.
- **Videotape** is often effective for getting a motivational message out to a large number of people. By communicating nonverbal cues, video can strengthen the sender's image of sincerity and trustworthiness; however, it offers no opportunity for immediate feedback.
- **Computer conferencing** allows users to meet and collaborate in real time while viewing and sharing documents electronically. It offers democracy because more attention is focused on ideas that appear on the participant's computer monitor than on who communicates them. But overemphasizing a message (to the neg-

lect of the person communicating it) can threaten corporate culture, which needs a richer medium.

- **Faxing** can be used to overcome time-zone barriers when a hard copy is required. It has all the characteristics of a written message, except that (1) it may lack the privacy of a letter, and (2) the message may appear less crisp—even less professional—depending on the quality of the copies output from the receiving machine. (See this chapter's "Checklist: Observing Voice-Mail and Fax Etiquette" on page 86.)
- **E-mail** offers speed, increased access to other employees, portability, and convenience (not just overcoming time-zone problems but carrying a message to many receivers at once). It's best for communicating brief, noncomplex information that is time sensitive, but its effectiveness depends on user skill (see Figure 4.5 below). Because the turnaround time can be quite fast, e-mail tends to be more conversational than traditional paper-based media.

In general, use electronic forms of oral and written communication for speed, to reach a widely dispersed audience personally, to overcome time-zone barriers, and when confidentiality is not a concern.

- **Instant messaging** (IM) allows people to carry on real-time, one-on-one, and small-group text conversations. More versatile than a phone call and quicker than e-mail, IM is becoming a valuable business tool. You can send your boss a text message that is immediately displayed on her or his computer screen, and you can have your response within seconds. Similarly, co-workers in branch offices can use IM to exchange documents or hold a virtual meeting online in a private chat area. Because messages generated via instant messaging aren't recorded or saved, they don't clog the company's network system; however, they don't create a permanent record either.[13]

The addressing information shows that a company may employ an outside firm to manage electronic functions, such as e-mail subscriptions, related to the business's Web site.

The first sentence gives useful advice to the reader. The second paragraph confirms the subscription request and offers information about the content and frequency of outgoing messages.

The message uses humour to establish a light tone and to project a particular image of the company. The message's layout makes it easy for the reader to follow instructions regarding removal from the list or accessing the firm's Web site. The recipient can usually go directly to the Web site by clicking on the Web address.

The e-mail ends courteously.

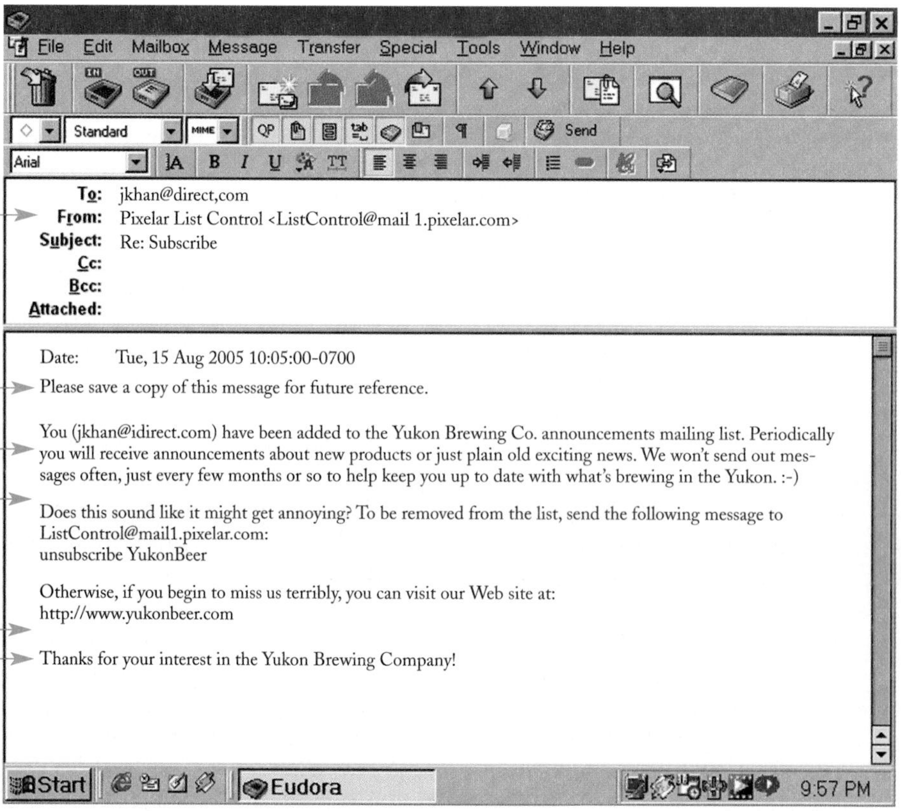

File Edit Mailbox Message Transfer Special Tools Window Help

To: jkhan@direct,com
From: Pixelar List Control <ListControl@mail 1.pixelar.com>
Subject: Re: Subscribe
Cc:
Bcc:
Attached:

Date: Tue, 15 Aug 2005 10:05:00-0700

Please save a copy of this message for future reference.

You (jkhan@idirect.com) have been added to the Yukon Brewing Co. announcements mailing list. Periodically you will receive announcements about new products or just plain old exciting news. We won't send out messages often, just every few months or so to help keep you up to date with what's brewing in the Yukon. :-)

Does this sound like it might get annoying? To be removed from the list, send the following message to ListControl@mail1.pixelar.com:
unsubscribe YukonBeer

Otherwise, if you begin to miss us terribly, you can visit our Web site at:
http://www.yukonbeer.com

Thanks for your interest in the Yukon Brewing Company!

Start Eudora 9:57 PM

FIGURE 4–5 Effective E-Mail Message

➤ **Web sites** offer interactive communication through hyperlinks, allowing readers to absorb information nonsequentially; that is, readers take what they need and skip everything else. A Web site can tailor the same information for numerous readers by breaking up the information into linked pages. Writing for the Web can be a specialized skill, as briefly discussed at the end of Chapter 5.

Electronic forms also have disadvantages, such as tactless remarks causing tension and overuse leading to information overload.

Even though electronic messages offer innumerable advantages, they aren't problem-free. Consider e-mail, for example. People sometimes include comments in e-mail messages that they would never say in person or typing in a document. So although e-mail's new openness can help companies get input from a wider variety of people, it can also create tension and interpersonal conflict. Furthermore, because e-mail is so easy to send, people tend to overuse it, distributing messages more widely than necessary and contributing to the hundreds of junk-mail messages that some executives receive every day. Overusing e-mail can also overload company networks, resulting in lost messages or even system crashes. People can also unintentionally send along viruses, which can disable entire networks and be very costly to control.

Electronic forms lack privacy.

Another drawback is lack of privacy. Some people negate their own privacy by being careless about screening their electronic distribution lists and sending information to receivers who shouldn't have it or don't need it. Of course, even if your message goes only where you originally intended, any recipient can easily forward it to someone else. In addition, e-mail and voice mail can legally be monitored by employers, and both can be subpoenaed for court cases (see "Using the Power of Technology: Caution! E-Mail Can Bite" below).

Electronic forms can reduce productivity.

Furthermore, employee productivity is constantly interrupted by e-mail, voice mail, conference calls, and faxes. Employees can also diminish their productivity by surfing the Web and visiting nonbusiness-related Web sites during working hours. In

USING THE POWER OF TECHNOLOGY

Caution! E-Mail Can Bite

Gone are the days when memos were dictated, typed, revised, retyped, photocopied, and circulated by interoffice "snail" mail. Today, e-mail messages are created, sent, received, and forwarded in the blink of an eye and at the stroke of a key. Despite its benefits, this quick, efficient method of communication can cause a great deal of trouble for companies.

One of the greatest features—and dangers—of e-mail is that people tend to treat it far more informally than they do other forms of business communication. They think of e-mail as casual conversation and routinely make unguarded comments. Moreover, they are led to believe that "deleting" e-mail destroys it permanently. But that's a dangerous misunderstanding of technology.

Even after you delete an e-mail message, it can still exist on the system's hard drive and backup storage devices at both the sender's and the recipient's locations. Deleting files only signals to the computer that the space required for storing the message is no longer needed. The space is so marked, but the data that occupy it continue to exist until the computer overwrites the space with new data. Thus, deleted messages are recoverable—even though data recovery is an involved and expensive process—and they can be used as court evidence against you. Embarrassing e-mail has played a big role in corporate battles. In the high-profile court battle between the U.S. Justice Department and Microsoft, for instance, e-mail emerged as the star witness. Other cases using e-mail as evidence include claims of sexual harassment, discrimination, employee productivity, information leaks, and more.

So how can companies guard against potential e-mail embarrassment and resulting litigation? Besides restricting the use of e-mail by employees, monitoring employees' e-mail, developing company e-mail policies, and reprimanding or terminating offenders, they can train employees to treat e-mail as any other form of written communication. Perhaps one of the best ways to ensure that employees' messages won't come back to haunt the company is to teach employees that e-mail messages are at least as permanent as, if not more so than, letters and memos.

CAREER APPLICATIONS

1. Why do most people treat e-mail so casually? Explain in an e-mail message to your instructor.
2. What kinds of issues should a company address in an e-mail policy? List and explain at least three items.

Sources: Adapted from "E-Mail as Evidence: Threat or Opportunity?" *Africa News Service*, January 10, 2001 (accessed June 11, 2002), premium.search.yahoo.com/search/premium; John J. DiGilio, "Electronic Mail: From Computer to Courtroom," *Information Management Journal*, April 2000, 32–44; Mary Beth Currie and Daniel Black, "E-merging Issues in the Electronic Workplace," *Ivey Business Journal*, January-February 2001, 18–29; Mike Elgan, "The Trouble with E-Mail," *Windows Magazine*, November 1998, 31; Jerry Adler, "When E-Mail Bites Back," Newsweek, November 23, 1998, 45–46; Amy Harmon, "Corporate Delete Keys Busy as E-Mail Turns Up in Court," *New York Times*, November 12, 1998, A1, C2, 95.

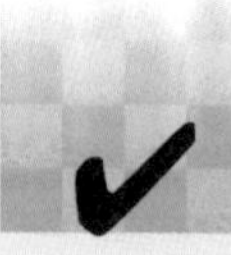

Checklist: Observing Voice-Mail and Fax Etiquette

Leaving Messages on Answering Machines and Voice Mail

✓ State whom you are calling, your first and last name, your company and title, the reason for your call, and your phone number (with area code and extension).

✓ Be brief when stating your message, and indicate specific callback times.

✓ Speak slowly.

✓ Deliver bad news personally.

✓ Follow up on important messages to make sure they were received.

Recording Messages on Answering Machines and Voice Mail

✓ Limit menus and options.

✓ Give callers an easy way to reach a live person.

✓ Test your message.

✓ Update greetings frequently and change your message when going on vacation.

Faxing Messages

✓ Fax nonpersonal messages only.

✓ Use a cover sheet stating the date, number of pages, recipient's name, sender's name, and a phone number to call if there is a transmission error.

✓ Sign your fax for a more personal message.

✓ Call before faxing urgent messages or before faxing long documents.

✓ Check your fax machine regularly to make sure it has adequate paper and cartridges.

one report, 31 percent of the businesses surveyed cited financial losses from reduced employee productivity as a result of Internet misuse alone.[14]

Still, the advantages of electronic media often outweigh the drawbacks, so businesses are selecting electronic forms over traditional ones more and more often (see this chapter's "Checklist: Observing E-Mail Etiquette" below).

Checklist: Observing E-Mail Etiquette

Plan your e-mail carefully.

✓ Limit your purpose to sharing information such as goals, schedules, research, and company news—don't deliver tragic news or discipline via e-mail.
  ✓ Avoid personal messages at work.
  ✓ Follow the chain of command—don't abuse the convenience of e-mail by sending unnecessary messages straight to the top.

✓ Work offline to conserve network resources and cut the costs of Internet connect charges.

Respect your readers.

✓ Send only necessary messages.

✓ Know who your audience is, who actually needs to hear what you have to say.
  ✓ Double-check addressees to include everyone necessary and no one else.
  ✓ Know your audience's culture before you begin composing.
  ✓ Use 24-hour military time in international e-mail (28:00 rather than 6:00 p.m.), and indicate the appropriate time zone.
  ✓ Respect your audience's schedule by making your e-mail worth reading and not sending jokes, chain letters, or derogatory comments.
  ✓ Don't send negative, insensitive, insulting, or critical e-mail: if you're upset about something or angry with someone, compose yourself before composing your e-mail.
  ✓ Don't use the *high priority* feature, unless your message is truly urgent.

Don't let incoming mail run your life.

✓ Check your e-mail frequently, but don't become constantly distracted by overchecking it.
  ✓ Avoid checking e-mail while on vacation—everyone needs a little time away from the office now and again.

✓ Use appropriate filters to screen out unimportant or less-than-critical messages.

✓ Read e-mail in a last-in, first-out order; otherwise, you may respond to issues that have been resolved in later messages. The last e-mail may summarize all previous issues.

Sources: Adapted from Dianna Booher, *E-Writing*, (New York: Pocket Books, 2001, 6; Eve Milrod and Arthur VanDam, *Mastering Communication Through Technology* (Woodmere, N.Y.: Career Advance Center, Inc., 2001) 13–14, 20–22, 24–29, 30–32, 37, 39, 40, 43; Nancy Flynn and Tom Flynn, *Writing Effective E-Mail* (Menlo Park, C.A.: Crisp Publications, 1998), 3, 5-6, 10, 14–15, 17, 29, 47, 55, 61, 62, 71; Diana Booher, *E-Writing* (New York: Pocket Books, 2001), ix, 2, 6–7, 16, 19, 23, 25–27, 30, 33, 36, 39, 41–42, 49; Morey Stettner, "The Right Way to Write: Composing Clear, Crisp Memos and E-Mail," *The Edward Lowe Report*, June 2000, 2; Karen Kalis, "Make Your E-Mail More Effective," *Supervision* 62, no. 9 (September 2001), 23–25; T.L. Aardsma, "Improve Your E-Mail Etiquette," *Inside the Internet* 8, no.7 (July 2001): 6-9; Andrea C. Poe, "Don't Touch that 'Send' Button!" *HRMagazine* 46, no. 7 (July 2001): 74–80.

Establish a Good Relationship with Your Audience

OBJECTIVE 6 Discuss how you can establish a good relationship with your audience.

Effective communicators do more than convey information. They make sure that they establish a good relationship with their audience. The first step is to think about who you are and who your audience is. Are you friends with common interests, or are you total strangers? Are you equal in status, experience, and education, or are you clearly unequal? Your answers to these questions will help you give the right impression in your message.

To establish a good relationship, be yourself.

An important aspect of establishing a good relationship with your audience is to avoid trying to be someone you're not. People can spot falseness very quickly, be yourself and be sincere. FGL's John Forzani will tell you that as in any undertaking, a good relationship is based on respect and courtesy. So when trying to establish good relationships in your business messages, remember to use the "you" attitude, emphasize the positive, establish your credibility, be polite, use bias-free language, and project the company's image.

USE THE "YOU" ATTITUDE

The "you" attitude is best implemented by expressing your message in terms of the audience's interests and needs.

You are already becoming familiar with the audience-centred approach, trying to see a subject through your audience's eyes. Now you want to project this approach in your messages by adopting a **"you" attitude**—that is, by speaking and writing in terms of your audience's wishes, interests, hopes, and preferences. When you talk about the other person, you're talking about what most interests him or her.

Don't overdo the "you" attitude.

Too many business messages have an "I" or "we" attitude, which sounds selfish. The message loses the audience's interest by telling what the sender wants and then expecting the audience to go along with that desire. On the simplest level, you can adopt the "you" attitude by replacing terms that refer to yourself and your company with terms that refer to your audience. In other words, use *you* and *yours* instead of *I, me, mine, we, us,* and *ours:*

INSTEAD OF THIS	USE THIS
To help us process this order, we must ask for another copy of the requisition.	So that your order can be filled promptly, please send another copy of the requisition.
We are pleased to announce our new flight schedule from Montreal to Calgary, which is on the hour.	Now you can take a plane from Montreal to Calgary any hour on the hour.
We offer the printer cartridges in three colours: black, blue, and green.	Select your printer cartridge from three colours: black, blue, and green.

Under the guidance of CEO Firoz Rasul, Ballard Power Systems, Inc. is developing fuel-cell technology as a viable energy alternative Rasul's efforts include informing, persuading, and collaborating with the transportation industry so that his company's research can be transformed into reality.

Using *you* and *yours* requires finesse. If you overdo it, you're likely to create some rather awkward sentences, and you run the risk of sounding manipulative or insincere.[15] The "you" attitude is an extension of the audience-centred approach. In fact, the best way to implement the "you" attitude is to be sincere in thinking about your audience.

Far from simply replacing one pronoun with another, the "you" attitude is a matter of genuine empathy. You can use *you* 25 times in a single page and still ignore your audience's true concerns. Your sincere concern for your audience is what counts, not the pronoun. If you're talking to a retailer, try to think like a retailer; if you're writing to a dissatisfied customer, imagine how you would feel at the other end of the transaction. Avoid using you and yours when doing so

- Makes you sound dictatorial
- Makes someone else feel guilty
- Goes against your organization's style

In fact, on some occasions you'll do better to avoid using *you.* For instance, using *you* in a way that sounds dictatorial is impolite. Or, when someone makes a mistake, you may want to minimize ill will by pointing out the error impersonally. You might say, "We have a problem," instead of "You caused a problem."

INSTEAD OF THIS	USE THIS
You should never use that type of paper in the copy machine.	That type of paper doesn't work very well in the copy machine.
You must correct all five copies by noon.	All five copies must be corrected by noon.

As you practice using the "you" attitude, be sure to consider the attitudes and policies of your organization, as well. In some cultures, it is improper to single out one person's achievements because the whole team is responsible for the outcome; thus, using the pronouns *we* or *our* would be more appropriate. Similarly, some companies have a tradition of avoiding references to *you* and *I* in their memos and formal reports. If you work for a company that expects a formal, impersonal style, confine your use of personal pronouns to informal letters and memos.

EMPHASIZE THE POSITIVE

Explain what you have done, what you can do, and what you will do—not what you haven't done, can't do, or won't do.

Another way of establishing a good relationship with your audience is to emphasize the positive side of your message.[16] Stress what is or will be instead of what isn't or won't be. Most information, even bad news, has some redeeming feature. If you can make your audience aware of that feature, your message will be more acceptable.

INSTEAD OF THIS	USE THIS
It is impossible to repair your vacuum cleaner today.	Your vacuum cleaner will be ready by Tuesday.
We apologize for inconveniencing you during our remodelling.	The renovations now underway will help us serve you better.
We never exchange damaged goods.	We are happy to exchange merchandise that is returned to us in good condition.

When you are offering criticism or advice, focus on what the person can do to improve.

In addition, when you're criticizing or correcting, don't hammer on the other person's mistakes. Avoid referring to failures, problems, or shortcomings. Focus instead on what the person can do to improve:

INSTEAD OF THIS	USE THIS
The problem with this department is a failure to control costs.	The performance of this department can be improved by tightening up cost controls.
You filled out the order wrong. We can't send you the paint until you tell us what colour you want.	So that your order can be processed properly, please check your colour preferences on the enclosed card.

If you're trying to persuade the audience to buy a product, pay a bill, or perform a service for you, emphasize what's in it for them. Don't focus on why *you* want them to do something. An individual who sees the possibility for personal benefit is more likely to respond positively to your appeal.

Show your audience how they will benefit from complying with your message.

INSTEAD OF SAYING	SAY
Please buy this book so that I can make my sales quota.	The plot of this novel will keep in suspense to the last page.
We need your contribution to the Boys and Girls Club.	You can help a child make friends and build self-confidence through your donation to the Boys and Girls Club.

In general, try to state your message without using words that might hurt or offend your audience. Substitute euphemisms (mild terms) for those that have unpleasant connotations. You can be honest without being harsh. Gentle language won't change the facts, but it will make them more acceptable:

Avoid words with negative connotations; use meaningful euphemisms instead.

INSTEAD OF THIS	USE THIS
cheap merchandise	bargain prices
toilet paper	bathroom tissue
used cars	resale cars
elderly	senior citizen
pimples and zits	complexion problems

On the other hand, don't carry euphemisms to extremes. If you're too subtle, people won't know what you're talking about. "Derecruiting" workers to the "mobility pool" instead of telling them that they have six weeks to find another job is unethical. When using euphemisms, you walk a fine line between softening the blow and hiding the facts. It would be immoral to speak to your community about "relocating refuse" when you're really talking about your plans for disposing of toxic waste. Such an attempt to hide the facts would very likely backfire, damaging your business image and reputation. In the end, people respond better to an honest message delivered with integrity than they do to sugar-coated double-talk.

ESTABLISH YOUR CREDIBILITY

If you're unknown to your audience members, you'll have to earn their confidence before you can win them to your point of view. Their belief in your competence and integrity is important. You want people to trust that your word is dependable and that you know what you're doing.

People are more likely to react positively to your message when they have confidence in you.

Credibility (or your believability) is based on how reliable you are and how much trust you evoke in others. If you're communicating with a familiar group, your credibility has already been established, so you can get right down to business. Of course, even in this case some audience members may have preconceptions about you and may have trouble separating your arguments from your personality or your profession. If they think of you as, say, a "numbers person," they may question your competence in other areas. But what if audience members are complete strangers? Or worse, what if they start off with doubts about you? In a new or hostile situation, devote the initial portion of your message to gaining credibility, and try the following techniques:

- **Call attention to what you have in common with your audience.** For example, when communicating with someone who shares your professional background, point out your connection: "As a fellow engineer (or manager or small business owner, for example), I'm sure you can appreciate this situation." Also, try using technical or professional terms that identify you as a peer.
- **Explain your credentials.** Being careful not to sound pompous, mention one or two aspects of your background. Your title or the name of your organization might be enough to impress your audience with your abilities.

To enhance your credibility
- Show that you understand the other person's situation
- Explain your own credentials or ally yourself with a credible source
- Back up your claims with evidence, not exaggerations
- Use words that express confidence
- Believe in yourself and your message

- **Mention the name of someone your audience trusts or views as an authority.** You could begin a letter with "Professor Goldberg suggested that I contact you," or you could quote a recognized authority on your subject, even if you don't know the authority personally. The fact that your ideas are shared by a credible source adds prestige to your message.
- **Provide ample evidence.** Back up your arguments, especially any material outside your usual area of expertise. Make sure your evidence can be confirmed through observation, research, experimentation, or measurement. If audience members recognize that you have the facts, they'll respect you.

On the other hand, if audience members find your evidence insufficient or lacking, your credibility will vanish. For example, avoid exaggerated claims. They are unethical and do more harm than good. A mail-order catalogue might promise: "You'll be absolutely amazed at the remarkable blooms on this healthy plant. Gorgeous flowers with brilliant colour and an intoxicating aroma will delight you week after week." Terms such as *amazing, incredible, extraordinary, sensational,* and *revolutionary* exceed the limits of believability, unless they're supported with some sort of proof.

You also risk losing credibility if you seem to be currying favour with insincere compliments. So support compliments with specific points:

INSTEAD OF THIS	USE THIS
My deepest heartfelt thanks for the excellent job you did. It' s hard these days to find workers like you. You are just fantastic! I can't stress enough how happy you have made us with your outstanding performance. Thanks for the fantastic job, it was much appreciated.	Thanks for the fantastic job you did in filling in for Gladys at the convention with just an hour's notice. Despite the difficult circumstances, you managed to attract several new orders with your demonstration of the new line of coffeemakers. Your dedication and sales ability are truly appreciated.

Another threat to credibility is too much modesty and not enough confidence. You express a lack of confidence when you use words such as *if, hope,* and *trust.* Try not to undermine your credibility with vague sentiments:

INSTEAD OF THIS	USE THIS
We hope this recommendation will be helpful.	We're glad to make this recommendation.
If you'd like to order, mail us the reply card.	To order, mail the reply card.
We trust that you'll extend your service contract.	By extending your service contract, you can continue to enjoy top-notch performance from your equipment.

If you lack faith in yourself, you're likely to communicate an uncertain attitude that undermines your credibility. The key to being believable is to believe in yourself. If you are convinced that your message is sound, you can state your case with authority so that your audience has no doubts.

BE POLITE

Although you may be tempted now and then to be brutally frank, try to express the facts in a kind and thoughtful manner.

Being polite is another good way to earn your audience's respect. By being courteous to members of your audience, you show consideration for their needs and feelings. Express yourself with kindness and tact.

You will undoubtedly be frustrated and exasperated by other people many times in your career. When that happens, you'll be tempted to say what you think in blunt terms. But venting your emotions rarely improves the situation and can jeopardize your audience's goodwill. Instead, be gentle when expressing yourself:

INSTEAD OF THIS	USE THIS
You really fouled things up with that last computer run.	Let's go over what went wrong with the last computer run so that the next run goes smoothly.
You've been sitting on my order for two weeks, and we need it now!	We are eager to receive our order. When can we expect delivery?

Of course, some situations require more diplomacy than others. If you know your audience well, you can get away with being less formal. However, when you are communicating with people who outrank you or with people outside your organization, an added measure of courtesy is usually needed.

Use extra tact when writing and when communicating with higher-ups and outsiders.

In general, written communication requires more tact than oral communication. When you're speaking, your words are softened by your tone of voice and facial expression. Plus, you can adjust your approach according to the feedback you get. But written communication is stark and self-contained. If you hurt a person's feelings in writing, you can't soothe them right away. In fact, you may not even know that you have hurt the other person, because the lack of feedback prevents you from seeing his or her reaction.

Another simple but effective courtesy is to be prompt in your correspondence. If possible, answer your mail within two or three days. If you need more time to prepare a reply, call or write a brief note to say that you're working on an answer. Most people are willing to wait if they know how long the wait will be. What annoys them is the suspense.

Promptness is a form of courtesy.

USE BIAS-FREE LANGUAGE

Most of us think of ourselves as being sensitive, unbiased, ethical, and fair. But being fair and objective isn't enough; to establish a good relationship with your audience, you must also *appear* to be fair.[17] **Bias-free language** avoids unethical, embarrassing blunders in language related to gender, race, ethnicity, age, and disability. Thoughtful communicators make every effort to guard against biased language of any type (see Table 4.2 on page 92).

Avoid biased language that might offend your audience.

- **Gender bias.** Avoid sexist language by using the same label for everyone (for example, don't call a woman *chairperson* and then call a man *chairman*). Reword sentences to use *they* or to use no pronoun at all. Vary traditional patterns by sometimes putting women first (*women and men, she and he, her and his*). Note that the preferred title for women in business is *Ms.*, unless the individual has some other title (such as *Dr.*) or asks to be addressed as *Miss* or *Mrs.*

Replace words that inaccurately exclude women or men.

- **Racial and ethnic bias.** Avoid language suggesting that members of a racial or an ethnic group have stereotypical characteristics. The best solution is to avoid identifying people by race or ethnic origin unless such a label is relevant.

Eliminate references that reinforce racial or ethnic stereotypes.

- **Be correct when you refer to Canada's Aboriginal peoples.** The Canadian constitution recognizes three groups of Aboriginal peoples: Indians, Métis, and Inuit. They each have their own heritage, language, cultural practices, and spiritual beliefs. The term "Indian" describes all the Aboriginal people in Canada who are not Inuit or Métis. Many Aboriginal people today are offended by the term "Indian" and prefer "First Nation." Many First Nations peoples have adapted the term "First Nation" to replace the term "band" to designate their community. As an accurate and ethical communicator, be sure to use the terms Canada's Aboriginal peoples prefer.
- **Age bias.** As with gender, race, and ethnic background, mention the age of a person only when it is relevant. When referring to older people, avoid such stereotyped adjectives as *spry* and *frail.*

Avoid references to an individual's age or physical limitations.

- **Disability bias.** No painless label exists for people with a physical, mental, sensory, or emotional impairment. Avoid mentioning a disability unless it is pertinent. However, if you must refer to someone's disability, avoid terms such as handicapped,

Always refer to people first and their disabilities second.

TABLE 4–2 Overcoming Bias in Language

Examples	Unacceptable	Preferable
GENDER BIAS		
Using words containing "man"	Mankind	Humanity, human beings, human race, people
	Man-made	Artificial, synthetic, manufactured, constructed
	Manpower	Human power, human energy, workers, work force
	Businessman	Executive, business manager, businessperson
	Salesman	Sales representative, salesperson, clerk, sales agent
	Foreman	Supervisor
Using female-gender words	Authoress, actress, stewardess flight attendant	Author, actor, cabin attendant
Using special designations	Woman doctor, male nurse	Doctor, nurse
Using *he* to refer to *everyone*	The average worker, he	The average worker, he or she
Identifying roles with gender	The typical executive spends four hours of his day in meetings.	Most executives spend four hours each day in meetings
	Consumer, she	Consumers, they
	The nurse/teacher, she	Nurses/teachers, they
Identifying women by marital status	Don Harron and Catherine	Don Harron and Catherine McKinnon
	Don Harron and Ms. McKinnon	Mr. Harron and Ms. McKinnon
RACIAL/ETHNIC BIAS		
Assigning	My black assistant speaks more articulately than I do.	My assistant speaks more articulately than I do.
	Jim Wong is an unusually tall Asian.	Jim Wong is unusually tall.
Identifying people by race or ethnicity	Frank Clementi, Italian-Canadian CEO	Frank Clementi, CEO
AGE BIAS		
Including age when irrelevant	Mary Kirazy, 58, has just joined our trust department.	Mary Kirazy has just joined our trust department.
DISABILITY BIAS		
Putting the disability before the person	Crippled workers face many barriers on the job.	Workers with physical disabilities face many barriers on the job.
	An epileptic, Tracy has no trouble doing her job.	Tracy's epilepsy has no effect on her job performance.

crippled, or retarded. Put the person first and the disability second.[18] Present the whole person, not just the disability, by referring to the limitation in an unobtrusive manner. The Canadian Human Rights Commission guarantees equal opportunities for people who have or have had a condition that might handicap them. The goal of bias-free communication is to abandon stereotyped assumptions about what a person can do or will do and to focus on an individual's unique characteristics.

PROJECT THE COMPANY'S IMAGE

Subordinate your own style to that of the company.

Even though establishing a good relationship with the audience is your main goal, give some thought to projecting the right image for your company. When you communicate with outsiders, on even the most routine matter, you serve as the spokesperson for your organization. The impression you make can enhance or damage the reputation of the entire company. Thus, your own views and personality must be subordinated, at least to some extent, to the interests and style of your company.

Say you have just taken a job with a hip, young retail organization called Rappers. One of your first assignments is to write a letter cancelling additional orders for clothing items that haven't been selling well.

Dear Ms. Bataglia:

I am writing to cancel our purchase order 092397AA for the amount of $12,349. Our contract with your organization specifies that we have a 30-day cancellation clause, which we wish to invoke. If any shipments went out before you received this notification, they will be returned; however, we will remunerate freight charges as specified in the contract.

I am told we have ordered from you since our inception in 1993. Your previous service to us has been quite satisfactory; however, recent sales of the "Coloured Denim" line have been less than forecast. We realize that our cancellation may have a negative impact, and we pledge to more accurately predict our needs in the future.

We maintain positive alliances with all our vendors and look forward to doing further business with you. Please keep us informed of new products as they appear.

After reading your draft, you realize that its formal tone may leave a feeling of ill will. Moreover, it certainly doesn't reflect the corporate culture of your new employer. You try again.

Dear Ms. Bataglia:

We appreciate the relationship we've had with you since 1993. Your shipments have always arrived on time and in good order.

However, our recent store reports show a decline in sales for your "Coloured Denim" line. Therefore, we're cancelling our purchase order 092397AA for $12,349. If you'll let us know the amounts, we'll pay the shipping charges on anything that has already gone out.

We're making a lot of changes at Rappers, but one thing remains the same—the positive relationship we have with vendors such as you. Please keep us informed of your new lines as they appear. We look forward to doing business with you in the future.

This version reflects the more relaxed image of your new company. You can save yourself a great deal of time and frustration if you master your company's style early in your career.

The planning step helps you get ready to write business messages. This chapter's "Checklist: Planning Business Messages" below is a reminder of the tasks and choices you address during the planning process.

Checklist: Planning Business Messages

Analyze Your Purpose and Audience

- ✓ Determine whether the purpose of your message is to inform, persuade, or collaborate.
- ✓ Identify the specific behaviour you hope to induce in the audience.
- ✓ Make sure that your purpose is worthwhile and realistic.
- ✓ Make sure that the time is right for your purpose.
- ✓ Make sure the right person is delivering your message.
- ✓ Make sure your purpose is acceptable to your organization.
- ✓ Identify the primary audience.
- ✓ Determine the size of your audience.
- ✓ Determine the composition of your audience.
- ✓ Determine your audience's level of understanding.
- ✓ Estimate your audience's probable reaction to your message.

Collect Information

- ✓ Decide whether to use formal or informal techniques for gathering information.
- ✓ Find out what your audience wants to know.
- ✓ Provide all required information and make sure it's accurate, ethical, and pertinent.

Adapt Your Message to Serve Your Audience and Your Purpose

- Select a channel and medium for your message by matching media richness to your audience and purpose.
- Select the right medium for your message by considering factors such as urgency, formality, complexity, confidentiality, emotional content, cost, audience expectation, and your need for a permanent record.
- Consider the problems as well as the advantages of using electronic forms.
- Adopt an audience-centred approach by using the "you" attitude.
- Emphasize the positive aspects of your message.
- Gain audience confidence by establishing your credibility.
- Show respect for your audience by using a polite tone.
- Show your sensitivity and fairness by using bias-free language.
- Project your company's image to make sure your audience understands that you are speaking for your organization.

Summary of Learning Outcomes

1 Describe the three-step writing process. (1) Planning consists of analyzing your purpose and your audience collecting information (whether formally or informally), and adapting your message by selecting the appropriate channel and medium and by establishing a good relationship with your audience. (2) Writing consists of organizing your ideas and actually composing words, sentences, paragraphs, and visual graphics. (3) Completing your message consists of revising your message by evaluating content and then rewriting and editing for clarity, producing your message by using effective design elements and suitable delivery methods, and proofreading your message for typos and errors in spelling and mechanics.

2 Explain why it's important to define your purpose carefully, and list four questions that can help you test that purpose. You must know enough about the purpose of your message to shape that message in a way that will achieve your goal. To decide whether you should proceed with your message, ask four questions: (1) Is my message realistic? (2) Is my message acceptable to my organization? (3) Is my message being delivered by the right person? (4) Is my message being delivered at the right time?

3 Justify the importance of creating an audience profile, and then list four ways of developing one. Analyzing your audience helps you discover who the members of your audience are, what their attitudes are, what they need to know, and why they should care about your purpose in communicating. An effective profile helps you predict how your audience will react to your message. It also helps you know what to include in your message and how to include it. To develop an audience profile, you need to determine your primary audience (key decision makers), your secondary audience the size of your audience, the make-up of your audience, the level of your audience's understanding, and your audience's probable reaction.

4 Outline how you can collect information informally, clarify what your audience wants to know, and test the thoroughness of your information. You can collect relevant information informally by considering others' viewpoints, browsing through company files, chatting with supervisors or colleagues, or asking your audience for input. You can clarify what your audience wants to know by restating questions, establishing assignment priorities, and trying to think of informational needs that your audience may not even be aware of. Finally, you can test the thoroughness of your information by checking whether your message answers *who, what, when, where, why,* and *how.* You also want to be sure that your information is accurate, ethical, and pertinent.

5 Define *media richness* and list other factors to consider when choosing the most appropriate channel and medium for your message. Media richness is the value of a medium for communicating a message. Richness is determined by the medium's ability to (1) convey a message using more than one informational cue (visual, verbal, vocal), (2) facilitate feedback, and (3) establish personal focus. Other factors to consider when selecting media include complexity, formality, confidentiality, emotional commitment, and feedback needs. You must also consider whether a written record is needed, urgency of the message, cost, and audience expectation. Electronic media are best for speed, to overcome physical separation and differing time zones, to reach a dispersed audience personally, and when confidentiality is not an issue.

6 Discuss how you can establish a good relationship with your audience. Most important, be yourself and be sincere so that your audience won't be put off by falseness. Use the "you" attitude to project your audience focus and highlight audience benefits. Emphasize the positive by talking about what is possible, by not focusing on another person's mistakes, and by using euphemisms when appropriate. Establish your credibility by providing ample supporting evidence for material outside your field of expertise, calling attention to what you have in common with your audience, explaining your credentials when necessary, and always providing the highest-quality information. Be polite by expressing yourself with courtesy, kindness, and tact and by being prompt in your correspondence. Use bias-free language to demonstrate your consideration of your audience's gender, race and ethnicity, age, and disability. And finally, be sure that you establish the right relationship with your audience by projecting your company's image.

ON THE JOB

Solving a Communication Dilemma at The Forzani Group

The Forzani Group's founder, John Forzani, carefully plans his many messages to various audiences. He is also careful to select just the right medium for each message he sends. As Forzani realizes that face-to-face communication with customers is a vital element in his stores' success, he trains owners of franchise outlets such as Atmosphere and Sports Experts and employees of corporate stores, such as SportChek, Save on Sports, and Coast Mountain Sports, to ask specific questions about their customers' needs. This input allows Forzani to gauge his audience's level of understanding so that he can educate his customers about the sports products they purchase. "It's like football," Forzani says about his company's success. "When your people work as a team toward one goal, you can achieve it."

Forzani uses various media to educate his employees. He runs two schools: The Forzani Academy for franchise owners and Forzani's Retail College for corporate employees. Both offer classes in the key areas of management, retail sales, merchandising, customer service, loss prevention, and product knowledge. Forzani also brings factory representatives into stores to do formal presentations, and employees are treated to "sports camps" at such places as Lake Louise, Alberta, where they get to use the gear they will sell, obtaining in-depth product knowledge.

Forzani also uses written media, such as the product catalogue/magazine *Fusion* for franchise owners and flyers and newspaper advertisements to reach consumers. In addition, he established the sportchek.com Web site for selling athletic wear and equipment and promoting awareness of the SportChek chain. Forzani's game plan is to operate in every Canadian city with a population of more than 15 000 people.

Your Mission You have recently joined The Forzani Group's corporate office in Calgary. Two of your major functions in this position are (1) helping store managers and other company executives plan effective business messages for a variety of audiences, and (2) responding to press inquiries about The Forzani Group Ltd. Choose the best alternatives for handling the following situations, and be prepared to explain why your choice is best:

1 You have received a phone call from Ann Mason, a reporter for a local Saskatchewan newspaper. She is planning to write an article about FGL's recent decision to open a Sports Experts store in her community, a small city. Mason has asked you for information about the economic impact of SportChek, Sports Experts, and other chains in Forzani's company in other small Canadian communities. When responding to Mason's request, what should the purpose of your letter be?
   a The general purpose is to inform. The specific purpose is to provide Mason with a brief summary of the evolution of The Forzani Group over the past 20 years.
   b The general purpose is to persuade. The specific purpose is to convince Mason that The Forzani Group creates jobs within a community, and that small, existing merchants should not feel threatened by the arrival of a Sports Expert store.
   c The general purpose is to collaborate. The specific purpose is to work with Mason to develop an article that examines the history of Forzani's entry into new markets.
   d The general purpose is to respond. The specific purpose is to convey details requested by a journalist.

2 Assume that your purpose is to convince Mason of The Forzani Group's abilities to create new jobs and increase economic activity in small communities. Is your purpose worth pursuing at this time?
   a Yes. The purpose is realistic, the timing is right, you are the right person to send the message, and the purpose is acceptable to the organization.
   b Not completely. Realistically, many readers of Mason's newspaper may dread the arrival of a Sports Expert store in their small community, fearing that the giant retailer may force small retailers out of business.
   c The purpose is fine, but you are not the right person to send this message. John Forzani, the chief executive officer, should respond.
   d The timing is right for this message. Stress The Forzani Group's involvement in small communities, citing contributions to social causes in other small cities. Show how John Forzani cares about customers on a personal basis.

3 When planning your reply to Mason, what assumptions can you make about your audience?
   a The audience includes not only Ann Mason but also the readers of the community's newspaper. Given their bias for a simple, rural lifestyle, the readers will probably be hostile to big business in general and to The Forzani Group in particular. They probably know little about large retail operations. Furthermore, they probably mistrust you because you are a Forzani Group employee.
   b Ann Mason will probably be the only person who reads the letter directly. She is the primary audience; the readers of her article are the secondary audience. Mason will be happy to hear from The Forzani Group and will read the information with an open mind. However, she may not know a great deal about the company. Although she is a stranger to you, she trusts your credibility as a Forzani Group spokesperson.
   c Ann Mason is probably the sole and primary audience for the letter. The fact that she is writing an article about The Forzani Group suggests that she already knows a great deal about the company and likes the idea of a Sports Expert's outlet in her community. In all likelihood, she will respond positively to your reply and will trust your credibility as a Forzani Group representative.
   d Ann Mason may be an industrial spy working for a sporting goods retailer. She will show your reply to people who work for your competitor; they will analyze the information and use it to improve their market share of the sporting goods industry.

4 A skateboard manufacturer is unable to keep up with consumer demand for his product in SportChek stores. Customers and store managers are complaining about the shortage of skateboards on the shelves. The Forzani Group's merchandising manager decides that the manufacturer must correct the supply problem within 30 days or FGL will have to find another, more reliable supplier that can meet the high demand. The merchandising manager asks you to suggest the best method of communicating this message to the skateboard manufacturer. Which communication medium would you recommend?

a Call the manufacturer on the phone to discuss the problem; then follow up with a letter that summarizes the conversation.
b Call the manufacturer on the phone to discuss the issue, and inform the company of The Forzani Group's course of action if the problem cannot be corrected within 30 days.
c Send a fax asking for correction of the problem within 30 days, explaining the consequences of noncompliance.
d Send a form letter that states the consequences of failing to meet FGL's demand for products.[19]

Test Your Knowledge

Review Questions

1 What are the three steps in the writing process?
2 What two types of purposes do all business messages have?
3 What do you need to know in order to develop an audience profile?
4 How can you test the thoroughness of the information you include in a message?
5 What is media richness and how is it determined?
6 What is the "you" attitude and how does it differ from an "I" attitude?
7 Why is it important to establish your credibility when communicating with an audience of strangers?
8 How does using bias-free language help communicators to establish a good relationship with their audiences?
9 What are the main advantages of oral communication? Of written media?

Interactive Learning 

Use This Text's Online Resources

Visit our Companion Web site at **www.pearsoned.ca/thill**, where you can use the interactive Study Guide to test your chapter knowledge and get instant feedback. Additional resources link you to the sites mentioned in this text and to additional sources of information on chapter topics.

Also check out the resources on the Mastering Business Communication CD, including "Perils of Pauline," an interactive presentation of the business communication challenges within a fictional company. For Chapter 4, see in particular the episode "Using E-Mail Effectively."

Apply Your Knowledge

Critical Thinking Questions

1 Some writers argue that planning messages wastes time because they inevitably change their plans as they go along. How would you respond to this argument? Briefly explain.
2 As a member of the public relations department, what medium would you recommend using to inform the local community that your toxic-waste cleanup program has been successful? Why?
3 When composing business messages, how can you be yourself and project your company's image at the same time?
4 Considering how fast and easy it is, should e-mail replace meetings and other face-to-face communication in your company? Why or why not?
5 **Ethical Choices** The company president has asked you to draft a memo to the board of directors informing them that sales in the newly acquired line of gourmet fruit jams have far exceeded anyone's expectations. As purchasing director, you happen to know that sales of moderately priced jams have declined substantially (many customers have switched to the more expensive jams). You were not directed to add that tidbit of information. What should you do?

Practice Your Knowledge

Document for Analysis

Read the following document; then (1) analyze the strengths and weaknesses of each sentence and (2) revise the document so that it follows this chapter's guidelines.

> I am a new publisher with some really great books to sell. I saw your announcement in *Publishers Weekly* about the bookseller's show you're having this summer, and I think it's a great idea. Count me in, folks! I would like to get some space to show my books. I thought it would be a neat thing if I could do some airbrushing on T-shirts live to help promote my hot new title, *T-Shirt Art.* Before I got into publishing, I was an airbrush artist, and I could demonstrate my techniques. I've done hundreds of advertising illustrations and have been a sign painter all my life, so I'll also be promoting my other book, hot off the presses, *How to Make Money in the Sign Painting Business.*
>
> I will be starting my PR campaign about May 2005 with ads in *PW* and some art trade papers, so my books should be well known by the time the show comes around in August. In case you would like to use my appearance there as part of your publicity, I have enclosed a biography and photo of myself.
>
> P.S. Please let me know what it costs for booth space as soon as possible so that I can figure out whether I can afford to attend. Being a new publisher is mighty expensive!

Exercises

4–1 **Planning Messages: Specific Purpose** For each of the following communication tasks, state a specific purpose (if you have trouble, try beginning with "I want to...").

a A report to your boss, the store manager, about the outdated items in the warehouse
b A memo to clients about your booth at the upcoming trade show
c A letter to a customer who hasn't made a payment for three months
d A memo to employees about the office's high water bills
e A phone call to a supplier checking on an overdue parts shipment
f A report to future users of the computer program you have chosen to handle the company's mailing list

4–2 **Planning Messages: General and Specific Purpose** Make a list of communication tasks you'll need to accomplish in the next week or so (for example, a job application, a letter of complaint, a speech to a class, an order for some merchandise). For each, determine a general and a specific purpose.

4–3 **Adapting Messages: Media and Purpose** List five messages you have received lately, such as direct-mail promotions, letters, e-mail messages, phone solicitations, and lectures. For each, determine the general and the specific purpose; then answer the following questions: (a) Was the message well timed? (b) Did the sender choose an appropriate medium for the message? (c) Did the appropriate person deliver the message? (d) Was the sender's purpose realistic?

4–4 **Adapting Messages: Media Selection** Barbara Lin is in charge of public relations for a cruise line that operates out of Vancouver. She is shocked to read a letter in a local newspaper from a disgruntled passenger, complaining about the service and entertainment on a recent cruise. Lin will have to respond to these publicized criticisms in some way. What audiences will she need to consider in her response? What medium should she choose? If the letter had been published in a travel publication widely read by travel agents and cruise travellers, how might her course of action differ?

4–5 **Planning Messages: Audience Profile** For each communication task below, write brief answers to three questions: Who is my audience? What is my audience's general attitude toward my subject? What does my audience need to know?

a A final-notice collection letter from an appliance manufacturer to an appliance dealer, sent 10 days before initiating legal collection procedures
b An unsolicited sales letter asking readers to purchase computer disks at near-wholesale prices
c An advertisement for peanut butter
d Fliers to be attached to doorknobs in the neighbourhood, announcing reduced rates for replacement windows
e A cover letter sent along with your résumé to a potential employer
f A request (to the seller) for a price adjustment on a piano that incurred $150 in damage during delivery to a banquet room in the hotel you manage

4–6 **Teamwork** Your team has been studying a new method for testing the durability of your company's running shoes. Now the team needs to prepare three separate reports on the findings: first, a report for the administrator who will decide whether to purchase the equipment needed for this new testing method; second, a report for the company's designers who develop the running shoe; and third, a report for store managers who will be showing employees the shoe's features. To determine the audience's needs for each of these reports, the team has listed the following questions: (1) Who are the readers? (2) Why will they read my report? (3) Do they need introductory or background material? (4) Do they need definitions of terms? (5) What level or type of language is needed? (6) What level of detail is needed? (7) What result does my report aim for? Working with two other students, answer the questions for each of these audiences:

a The administrator
b The designers
c The store managers

4–7 **Meeting Audience Needs: Relevant Information** Choose an electronic device (DVD player, personal computer, telephone answering machine) that you know how to operate well. Write two sets of instructions for operating the device: one set for a reader who has never used that type of machine and one set for someone who is generally familiar with that type of machine but has never operated the specific model. Briefly explain how your two audiences affect your instructions.

4–8 **Internet** More companies are reaching out to audiences through their Web sites. Go to the Bombardier Web site at **www.bombardier.com** and follow the link to the latest annual report. Then locate and read the chairperson's letter. Who is the audience for this message? What is the general purpose of the message? What do you think this audience wants to know from the chairperson of Bombardier? How does the chairperson explain the negative news in this letter and emphasize the positive news? Summarize your answers in a brief (one page) memo or oral presentation.

4–9 **Audience Relationship: Courteous Communication** Substitute a better phrase for each of the following:

a You claim that
b It is not our policy to
c You neglected to
d In which you assert
e We are sorry you are dissatisfied
f You failed to enclose
g We request that you send us
h Apparently you overlooked our terms
i We have been very patient
j We are at a loss to understand

4–10 **Audience Relationship: The "You" Attitude** Rewrite these sentences to reflect your audience's viewpoint.

a We request that you use the order form supplied in the back of our catalogue.
b We insist that you always bring your credit card to the store.
c We want to get rid of all our 15-inch monitors to make room in our warehouse for the 19-inch screens. Thus we are offering a 25 percent discount on all sales this week.
d I am applying for the position of bookkeeper in your office. I feel that my grades prove that I am bright and capable, and I think I can do a good job for you.
e As requested, we are sending the refund for $25.
f We want you to read the warranty, which states the return policy on page 3.

4–11 **Audience Relationship: Emphasize the Positive** Revise these sentences to be positive rather than negative.

a To avoid the loss of your credit rating, please remit payment within 10 days.
b We don't make refunds on returned merchandise that is soiled.
c Because we are temporarily out of Baby Cry dolls, we won't be able to ship your order for 10 days.
d You failed to specify the colour of the blouse that you ordered.
e You should have realized that waterbeds will freeze in unheated houses during winter. Therefore, our guarantee does not cover the valve damage and you must pay the $9.50 valve-replacement fee (plus postage).
f You were not home when our repair technician called to service your refrigerator.

4–12 **Audience Relationship: Emphasize the Positive** Provide euphemisms for the following words and phrases:

a stubborn
b wrong
c stupid
d incompetent
e loudmouth
f thoughtless

4–13 **Audience Relationship: Bias-Free Language** Rewrite each of the following to eliminate bias:

a For an Indian, Maggie certainly is outgoing.
b He needs a wheelchair, but he doesn't let his handicap affect his job performance.
c A pilot must have the ability to stay calm under pressure, and then he must be trained to cope with any problem that arises.
d Candidate Renata Parsons, married and the mother of a teenager, will attend the debate.
e Senior citizen Sam Nugent is still an active salesman.
f A secretary must know how to use her computer for e-mail minutes of meetings.
g A skilled artisan, the Indian Alice Beaver is especially known for her beadwork.

4–14 **Ethical Choices** Your supervisor, whom you respect, has asked you to withhold important information that you think should be included in a report you are preparing. Disobeying him could be disastrous for your relationship and your career. Obeying him could violate your personal code of ethics. What should you do? On the basis of the discussion in Chapter 1, would you consider this situation to be an ethical dilemma or an ethical lapse? Please explain.

4–15 **Three-Step Process: Other Applications** How can the material discussed in this chapter also apply to meetings as discussed in Chapter 2? (Hint: Review the section headings in Chapter 4 and think about making your meetings more productive.)

4–16 **Message Planning Skills: Self-Assessment** How good are you at planning business messages? Rate yourself on the elements of planning an audience-centred business message by answering the questions below. Then examine your ratings to identify where you are strongest and where you can improve, using the tips in this chapter.

		Always	Frequently	Occasionally	Never
1	I start by defining my purpose.	_______	_______	_______	_______
2	I analyze my audience before writing a message.	_______	_______	_______	_______
3	I investigate what my audience wants to know.	_______	_______	_______	_______
4	I check that my information is accurate, ethical, and pertinent.	_______	_______	_______	_______
5	I consider my audience and purpose when selecting media.	_______	_______	_______	_______
6	I adopt the "you" attitude in my messages.	_______	_______	_______	_______
7	I emphasize the positive aspects of my message.	_______	_______	_______	_______
8	I establish my credibility with audiences of strangers.	_______	_______	_______	_______
9	I express myself politely and tactfully.	_______	_______	_______	_______
10	I use bias-free language.	_______	_______	_______	_______
11	I am careful to project my company's image.	_______	_______	_______	_______

Going Online Exercises

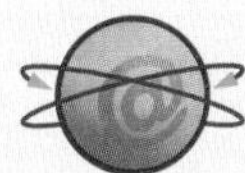

Learn about Your Audience, found on page 75 of this chapter

Messages that produce results require audience analysis. You need to know who your audience members are, determine their interests, and satisfy their needs. Practice using data from audience profiles. Log on to Games.net Audience Profile.

1 To get information to the Games.net audience, would it be effective to place a message in the *Wall Street Journal?* Explain your answer.

2 Check out PC World's summary of its own audience at **marketing.pcworld.com/temp/ main8audprofsummary.html**. Based on the information listed, give reasons why you would develop a Web site to reach an audience rather than send a mass mailing.

3 The URL for PC World's audience profile indicates that it is located in the marketing pages of the magazine's Web site. How do you think PC World uses the data in its audience profile? How might it help PC World attract new readers? New advertisers?

1 Explain why good organization is important to both the communicator and the audience

2 Summarize the process for organizing business messages effectively

3 Discuss two ways of achieving a tone that is businesslike and a style that is clear and concise

4 Briefly describe how to select words that are not only correct but also effective

5 Explain four guidelines that help you achieve clarity and efficiency in your sentences

6 List five ways to develop a paragraph and discuss three factors that increase paragraph readability

7 Explain how to write e-mail messages that capture and keep audience attention.

Writing Business Messages

ON THE JOB

Facing a Communication Dilemma at McCain Foods

No Small Fry

www.mccain.com

From a single plant in Florenceville, New Brunswick to multinational giant, McCain Foods is no small fry in the potato product industry. The largest French-fry producer in the world, with 32 percent of the global market, McCain sells its frozen fries and specialty potato products, as well as green vegetables, desserts, pizzas, juices and beverages, and oven meals in over 120 countries. Headquartered in Florenceville since its founding in 1957, McCain Foods (Canada) has 11 processing facilities and 3300 employees domestically. Worldwide, McCain workforce numbers more than 20 000 people on six continents. The company operates more than 55 food-processing facilities in countries such as France, New Zealand, Argentina, Poland, and South Africa. All told, McCain has the capacity to produce more than 453 000 kilograms of potato products an hour.

Product development, leading to such specialty foods as "Brew City Spicy Pub Pickles" (crunchy pickles in a beer-based crust), sensitivity to local tastes, and attention to consumer feedback have all contributed to McCain success. CEO and President Howard Mann notes that North Americans prefer their fries crispy and thin, while the British like theirs thick and fat for soaking up vinegar. A company motto, "drink the local wine," guides local managers to study local markets and adapt recipes and products. Under McCain's flattened hierarchy, regional executives create and execute their own strategies once they've received approval from head office.

At McCain, feedback is continually sought from employees, suppliers, and customers as products are developed. If you worked for McCain Foods, how would you write messages that solicit advice from both inside and outside the company? How would select information and organize your ideas? What style and tone would you use?[1]

The largest French-fry producer in the world, McCain Foods uses its Web site and brochures such as "The Making of a French Fry" to show consumers how potatoes are processed into fries and specialty items. Whether soliciting input from staff, suppliers, and customers, or educating the public about the company's products, McCain managers must compose messages that are clear, concise, and well organized.

Organizing Your Message

All businesspeople face the challenge of composing messages that their audiences can easily understand. It's difficult for us to remember unconnected facts and figures, so successful communicators rely on organization to make their messages meaningful. Before considering how to achieve good organization, let's look at why it's important.

Wendy MacNair is the editor of the *Aboriginal Banking NEWSLETTER*, published by the Aboriginal Banking Unit of the Business Development Bank of Canada. She helps contributors to the newsletter bring out the best in their writing by reading their drafts and commenting on matters of style and expression. What sort of advice do you think MacNair gives to her authors to help them become effective communicators?

Why Good Organization Is Important

Does it matter whether a message is well organized as long as its point is eventually made? Why not just let your ideas flow naturally and trust your audience to grasp your meaning? If you took this approach, your messages would appear disordered and jumbled. Your readers would waste time reading and rereading to grasp your meaning. It would be difficult for them to make decisions. And, both your image as a professional and your business relationships with your readers would suffer. When you consider such costs, you begin to realize the value of clear writing and good organization.[2]

Moreover, effective organization saves time. You will draft your messages more quickly and efficiently because you won't waste time putting ideas in the wrong places or composing material you don't need. In addition, you can use your organizational plan to get some advance input from your audience. That way, you can be sure you're on the right track *before* you spend hours working on your draft. And if you're working on a large, complex project that involves several people, you can use your organizational plan to delegate writing tasks.

In addition to helping you, good organization helps your audience by

OBJECTIVE 1 Explain why good organization is important to both the communicator and the audience.

Good organization saves time, strengthens relationships, and improves efficiency.

- **Increasing reader understanding.** Effective organization makes your message user friendly and understandable. By arranging your ideas to suit your purpose and your audience's needs, and by expressing your ideas precisely, you message will satisfy your audience's need for information.
- **Making readers more receptive to your message.** Even when your message is logical, you need to select and organize your points in a diplomatic way. By softening refusals and leaving a good impression, you enhance your credibility and add authority to your messages. When ComputerTime responds to the Boswell & Sons inquiry, the message is negative, but the letter is diplomatic and positive (see Figure 5–2 on page 103).
- **Saves readers time.** Well-organized messages are efficient. They contain only relevant ideas, and they are concise. Moreover, all the information in a well-organized message is in a logical place. Audience members receive only the information they need, and because that information is presented as accessibly and succinctly as possible, audience members can follow the thought pattern without a struggle.

Good organization helps audience members understand your message, accept your message, and save time.

The letter from Boswell & Sons asking for a refund (Figure 5–1 on page 102) is organized to give all needed information in a sequence that helps the reader understand the message.

How Good Organization Is Achieved

As you see, there are important benefits to good organization. You can develop a well-structured message by defining the main idea, limiting the scope, grouping supporting points, and establishing their sequence by selecting either a direct or an indirect approach.

OBJECTIVE 2 Summarize the process for organizing business messages effectively.

DEFINE THE MAIN IDEA

In addition to having a general purpose and a specific purpose, all business messages can be reduced to one main idea—one central point that sums up everything. The rest of your message supports, explains, or demonstrates this point. Your main idea is

To organize a message

- Define your main idea
- Limit the scope
- Group your points
- Choose the direct or indirect approach

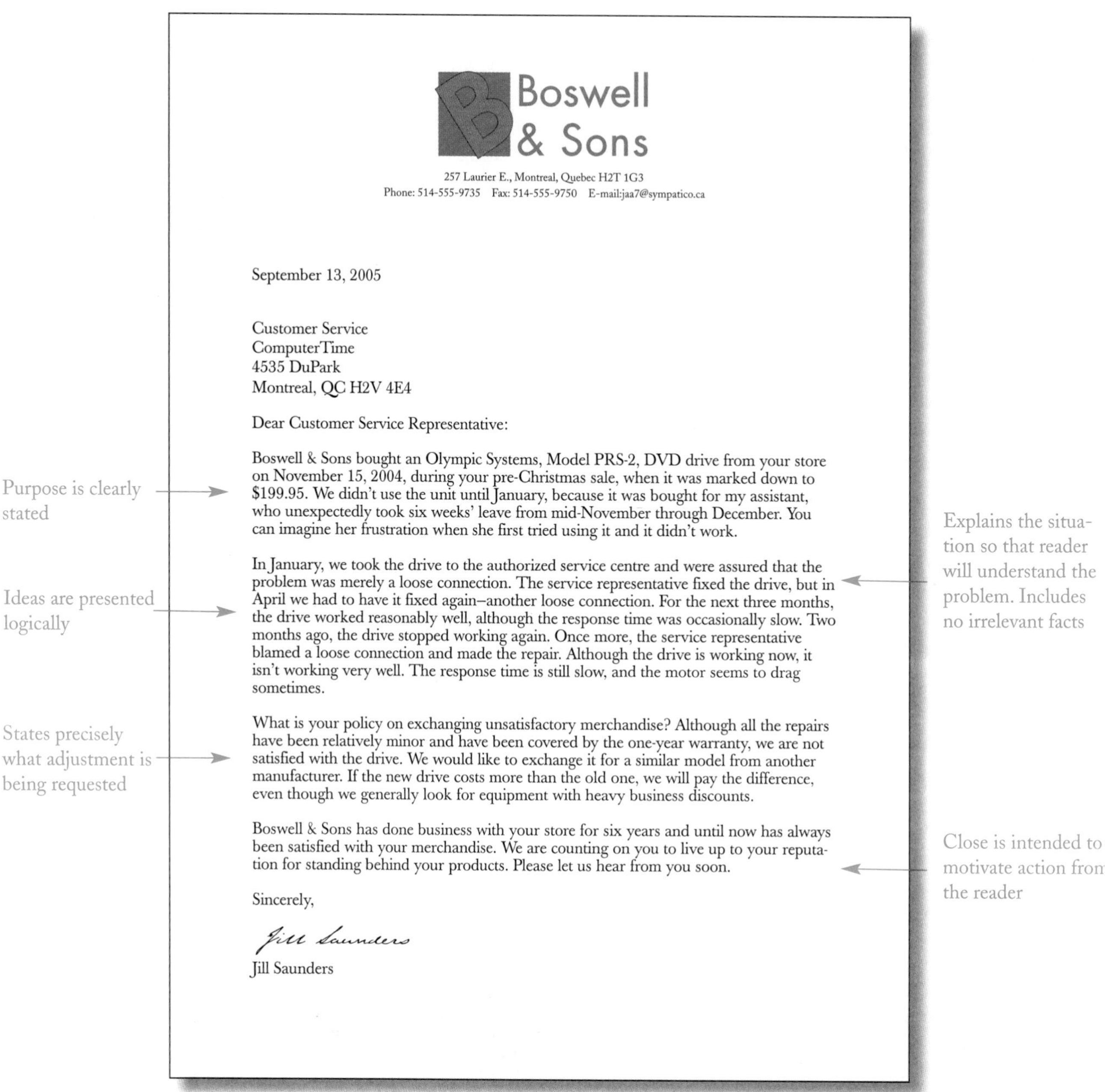
Boswell & Sons

257 Laurier E., Montreal, Quebec H2T 1G3
Phone: 514-555-9735 Fax: 514-555-9750 E-mail:jaa7@sympatico.ca

September 13, 2005

Customer Service
ComputerTime
4535 DuPark
Montreal, QC H2V 4E4

Dear Customer Service Representative:

Boswell & Sons bought an Olympic Systems, Model PRS-2, DVD drive from your store on November 15, 2004, during your pre-Christmas sale, when it was marked down to $199.95. We didn't use the unit until January, because it was bought for my assistant, who unexpectedly took six weeks' leave from mid-November through December. You can imagine her frustration when she first tried using it and it didn't work.

In January, we took the drive to the authorized service centre and were assured that the problem was merely a loose connection. The service representative fixed the drive, but in April we had to have it fixed again–another loose connection. For the next three months, the drive worked reasonably well, although the response time was occasionally slow. Two months ago, the drive stopped working again. Once more, the service representative blamed a loose connection and made the repair. Although the drive is working now, it isn't working very well. The response time is still slow, and the motor seems to drag sometimes.

What is your policy on exchanging unsatisfactory merchandise? Although all the repairs have been relatively minor and have been covered by the one-year warranty, we are not satisfied with the drive. We would like to exchange it for a similar model from another manufacturer. If the new drive costs more than the old one, we will pay the difference, even though we generally look for equipment with heavy business discounts.

Boswell & Sons has done business with your store for six years and until now has always been satisfied with your merchandise. We are counting on you to live up to your reputation for standing behind your products. Please let us hear from you soon.

Sincerely,

Jill Saunders

Jill Saunders

Purpose is clearly stated
Ideas are presented logically
States precisely what adjustment is being requested
Explains the situation so that reader will understand the problem. Includes no irrelevant facts
Close is intended to motivate action from the reader

FIGURE 5–1 In-Depth Critique: Effectively Organized Letter

The topic is the broad subject; the main idea makes a statement about the topic.

not the same as your topic. The broad subject of your message is the topic, and your main idea makes a statement about that topic. Consider the examples in Table 5–1 on page 103.

Your main idea may be obvious when you're preparing a brief message with simple facts that have little emotional impact on your audience. If you're responding to a request for information, your main idea may be simply, "Here is what you wanted." However, defining your main idea is more complicated when you're trying to persuade someone or when you have disappointing information to convey. In these situations, try to define a main idea that will establish a good relationship between you and your audience. For example, you may choose a main idea that highlights a common interest you share with your audience or that emphasizes a point that you and your audience can agree on.

TABLE 5-1 Defining Business Messages

General Purpose	Specific Purpose	Topic	Main Idea
To inform	Teach customer service reps how to file insurance claims	Insurance claims	Proper filing by reps saves the company time and money
To persuade	Get top managers to approve increased spending on research and development	Funding for research and development	Competitors spend more than we do on research and development
To collaborate	Get Information Technology and Sales to devise a computer program that tracks sales by geographical region	Sales	Using a computer program that tracks sales by region will easily highlight geographical areas that need improved representation of products.

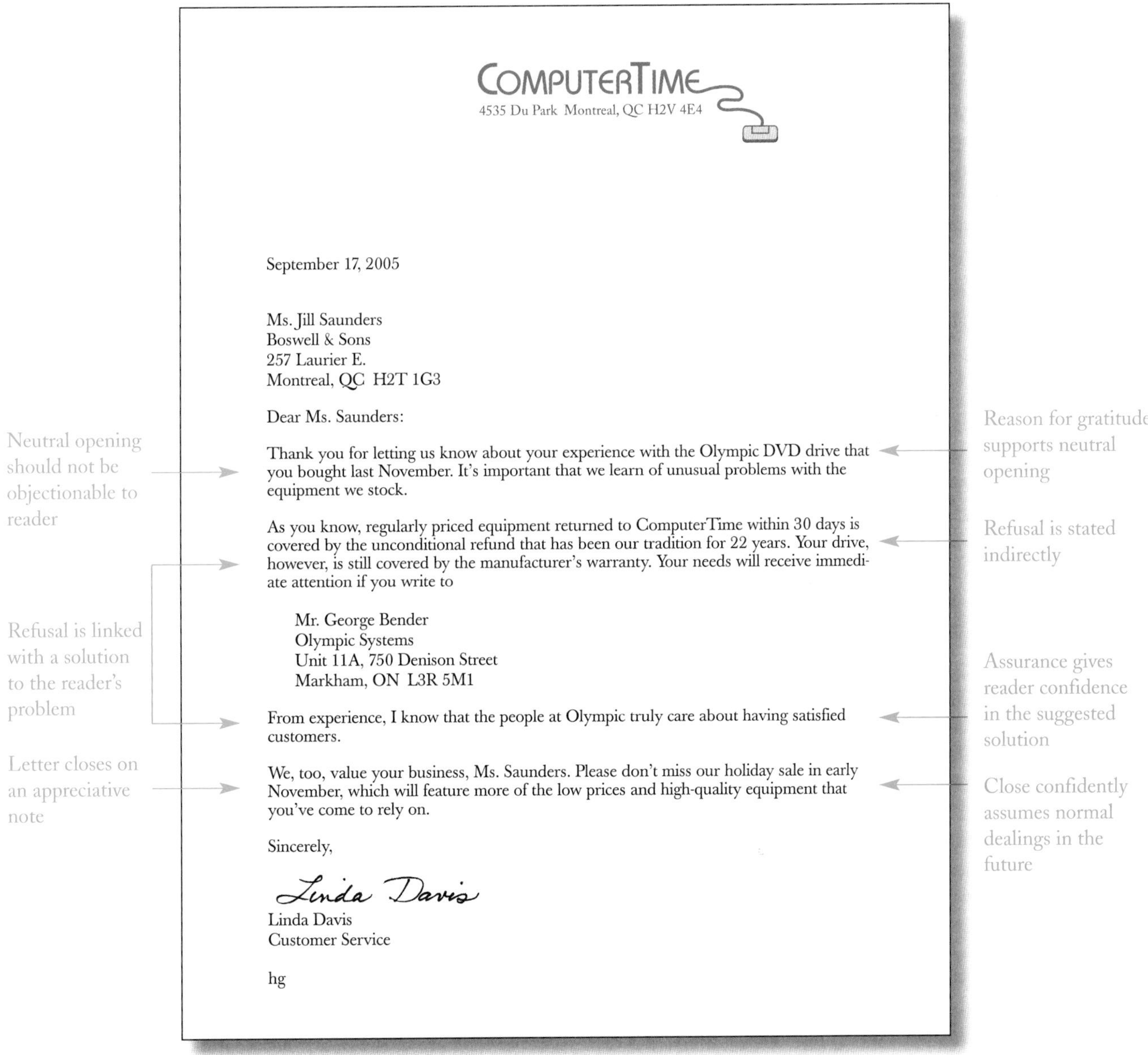

COMPUTERTIME
4535 Du Park Montreal, QC H2V 4E4

September 17, 2005

Ms. Jill Saunders
Boswell & Sons
257 Laurier E.
Montreal, QC H2T 1G3

Dear Ms. Saunders:

Thank you for letting us know about your experience with the Olympic DVD drive that you bought last November. It's important that we learn of unusual problems with the equipment we stock.

As you know, regularly priced equipment returned to ComputerTime within 30 days is covered by the unconditional refund that has been our tradition for 22 years. Your drive, however, is still covered by the manufacturer's warranty. Your needs will receive immediate attention if you write to

Mr. George Bender
Olympic Systems
Unit 11A, 750 Denison Street
Markham, ON L3R 5M1

From experience, I know that the people at Olympic truly care about having satisfied customers.

We, too, value your business, Ms. Saunders. Please don't miss our holiday sale in early November, which will feature more of the low prices and high-quality equipment that you've come to rely on.

Sincerely,

Linda Davis
Customer Service

hg

Neutral opening should not be objectionable to reader
Refusal is linked with a solution to the reader's problem
Letter closes on an appreciative note
Reason for gratitude supports neutral opening
Refusal is stated indirectly
Assurance gives reader confidence in the suggested solution
Close confidently assumes normal dealings in the future

FIGURE 5-2 In-Depth Critique: Letter Demonstrating a Diplomatic Organizational Plan

For longer messages, determining the main idea often requires creative thinking.

In longer documents and presentations, in which you need to unify a mass of material, you need to define a main idea that encompasses all the individual points you want to make. For tough assignments like these, you may want to take special measures to define your main idea. One way to generate ideas is to **brainstorm**—letting your mind wander over the possibilities and testing various alternatives against your purpose, your audience, and the facts you've gathered. To brainstorm effectively, don't censor your thoughts: leave editing and polishing until later (see "Sharpening Your Career Skills—Beating Writer's Block: Nine Workable Ideas to Get Words Flowing" below). Successful communicators use a number of approaches to define the main idea in a message.

Some techniques for establishing the main idea:

- Storyteller's tour
- Random list
- FCR worksheet
- Journalistic approach
- Question-and-answer chain

Storyteller's Tour Turn on your tape recorder and pretend that you've just met an old friend on the street. Give an overview of your message, focusing on your reasons for communicating, your major points, your rationale, and the implications for your intended audience. Listen critically to the tape then repeat the exercise until you are able to give a smooth, two-minute summary that conveys the gist of your message. The summary should reveal your main idea.

SHARPENING YOUR CAREER SKILLS

Beating Writer's Block: Nine Workable Ideas to Get Words Flowing

Putting words on a page or on screen can be a real struggle. Some people get stuck so often that they develop a mental block. If you get writer's block, here are some ways to get words flowing:

- *Use positive self-talk.* Stop worrying about how well or easily you write, and stop thinking of writing as difficult, time consuming, or complicated. Tell yourself that you're capable and that you can do the job. Also, recall past examples of your writing that were successful.
- *Know your purpose.* Be specific about what you want to accomplish with this particular assignment. Without a clear purpose, writing can indeed be impossible.
- *Visualize your audience.* Picture audience backgrounds, interests, subject knowledge, and vocabulary (including the technical jargon they use). Such visualization can help you choose an appropriate style and tone for your writing.
- *Create a productive environment.* Write in a location that's meant for writing only, and make that setting pleasant. Set up "writing appointments." Scheduling a session from 9:30 a.m. to noon is less intimidating than an indefinite session. Also, keep your mind fresh with scheduled breaks.
- *Make an outline or a list.* Even if you don't create a formal outline, at least jot down a few notes about how your ideas fit together. As you go along, you can revise your notes, as long as you end up with a plan that gives direction and coherence.
- *Just start.* Put aside all worries, fears, distractions—anything that gives you an excuse to postpone writing. Then start putting down any thoughts you have about your topic. Don't worry about whether these ideas can actually be used; just let your mind range freely.
- *Write the middle first.* Start wherever your interest is greatest and your ideas are most developed. You can follow new directions, but note ideas to revisit later. When you finish one section, choose another without worrying about sequence. Just get your thoughts down.
- *Push obstacles aside.* If you get stuck at some point, don't worry. Move past the thought, sentence, or paragraph, and come back to it later. Get started simply by writing or talking about why you're stuck: "I'm stuck because ..." Also try brainstorming. Before you know it, you'll be writing about your topic.
- *Read a newspaper or magazine.* Try reading an article that uses a style similar to yours. Choose one you'll enjoy so that you'll read it more closely.

When deadlines loom, don't freeze in panic. Concentrate on the major ideas first, and save the details for later, after you have something on the page. If you keep things in perspective, you'll succeed.

CAREER APPLICATIONS

1. List the ways you procrastinate, and discuss what you can do to break these habits.
2. Analyze your own writing experiences. What negative self-talk do you use? What might you do to overcome this tendency?

Random List On a computer or a clean sheet of paper, list everything you can think of that pertains to your message. Once you begin your list, your thoughts will start to flow. When you've exhausted the possibilities, study the list for relationships. Sort the items into groups, as you would sort a deck of cards into suits. Look for common denominators; the connection might be geographic, sequential, spatial, chronological, or topical. Part of the list might break down into problems, causes, and solutions; another part, into pros and cons. Regardless of what categories finally emerge, the sorting process will help you sift through your thoughts and decide what's important—thus clarifying your main idea. The best way to decide importance is to concentrate on the points that will benefit your audience most.

FCR Worksheet If your subject involves the solution to a problem, you might try using an FCR worksheet to help you visualize the relationships among your findings (F), your conclusions (C), and your recommendations (R). For example, you might find that you're losing sales to a competitor who offers lower prices than you do (F). From this information, you might conclude that your loss of sales is due to your pricing policy (C). This conclusion would lead you to recommend a price cut (R). To make an FCR worksheet, divide a computer screen or a sheet of paper into three columns. List the major findings in the first column, then draw out conclusions and write them in the second column. These conclusions form the basis for the recommendations, which are listed in the third column. An analysis of the three columns should help you define the main idea.

Journalistic Approach For informational messages, such as progress reports, the journalistic approach may provide a good point of departure. Find the answers to six questions—who, what, when, where, why, and how. The answers you come up with should clarify your main idea.

Question-and-Answer Chain Perhaps the best approach is to look at the subject of your message from your audience's point of view. Ask yourself: "What is the audience's main question? What do audience members need to know?" Write down and examine your answers. As additional questions emerge, write down and examine those answers. Follow the chain of questions and answers until you have replied to every conceivable question that might occur to your audience. By thinking about your material from your audience's perspective, you are likely to define your main idea.

LIMIT THE SCOPE

Gear your main idea to the length of the message.

The scope of your message (its length and detail) must match your main idea. Whether your audience expects a one-page memo or a 40-minute presentation, you must develop your main idea within that framework. Once you have a tentative statement of your main idea, test it against the length limitations that have been imposed for your message. If you lack the time and space to develop your main idea fully, or if your main idea won't fill up the time and space allotted, you'll need to redefine the main idea of your message.

How much you can communicate in a given number of words depends on the nature of the subject, your audience members' familiarity with the topic, their receptivity to your conclusions, and your credibility. You'll need fewer words to present routine information to a knowledgeable audience that already knows and respects you. You'll need more time to build consensus about a complex and controversial subject, especially if the audience is composed of skeptical or hostile strangers.

Deal with three or four major points (not more than five), regardless of message length.

As you adjust your message to fit the time or space available, don't change the number of major points. Regardless of how long the message will be, limit it to three or four major points, five at the very most. According to communication researchers, your audience can't remember much more.[3]

If your message is brief—five minutes for a brief speech, or one page for a memo or letter—you'll have only a minute, or a paragraph, each for the introduction,

Marie Delorme is President of ImagiNATION Cards, Inc., a small business that sells Aboriginal art cards to corporate and retail markets. She contributes her time and expertise to the Boards of the Canadian Youth Business Foundation, the Canadian Council for Aboriginal Business, and the University of Calgary Cultural Diversity Institute. What factors must Delorme consider when organizing messages about her products?

conclusion, and major points. Because the amount of evidence you can present is limited, your main idea will have to be easy to understand. However, if you're delivering a long message—say, a 40-minute presentation or a 20-page report—you can develop the major points in detail. You can spend about 10 minutes or 10 paragraphs (more than three pages of double-spaced, typewritten text) on each of your key points, and you'll still have room for your introduction and conclusion. Instead of introducing additional points, you can deal more fully with complex issues, offer a variety of evidence, and overcome resistance.

The overall scope of your message also determines the amount and depth of investigation you can conduct. You may need only to glance at your calendar to confirm a meeting, or you may need to spend weeks conducting formal research for a complicated report. Gathering information for reports and proposals is discussed in Chapter 10.

GROUP YOUR POINTS

Although these techniques will help generate your main idea, they won't necessarily tell you how to develop it or how to group the supporting details in the most logical and effective way. To decide on the final structure of your message, you need to visualize how all the points fit together. One way to do so is to construct an outline. Whether you use the outlining features provided with word-processing software or simply jot down three or four points on the back of an envelope, making a plan and sticking to it will help you cover the important details.

An outline or a schematic diagram will help you visualize the relationship among parts of a message.

When you're preparing a longer, more complex message, an outline is indispensable because it helps you visualize the relationships among the various parts. Without an outline, you may be inclined to ramble, and you may forget your original point. With an outline to guide you, however, you can prepare messages in a systematic way. Following an outline also helps you insert transitions in appropriate places, so that your message is coherent and your audience can understand the relationships among your ideas.

Outlines can appear in various formats.

You're no doubt familiar with the basic outline formats, which (1) use numbers or numbers and letters to identify each point and (2) indent points to show which ideas are of equal status. An effective outline divides a topic into at least two parts (see Figure 5-4 on page 107), restricts each subdivision to one category, and ensures that each group is separate and distinct. Figure 5-3 below shows the common forms and Figure 11-6 in Chapter 11(Writing Business Reports and Proposals) shows how the alphanumeric form is applied.

FIGURE 5-3 Two Common Outline Forms

ALPHANUMERIC OUTLINE

I. First Major Part
  A. First subpoint
  B. Second subpoint
    1. Evidence
    2. Evidence
      a. Detail
      b. Detail
    3. Evidence
  C. Third subpoint
II. Second Major Point
  A. First subpoint
    1. Evidence
    2. Evidence
  B. Second subpoint

DECIMAL OUTLINE

1.0 First Major Part
  1.1 First subpoint
  1.2 Second subpoint
    1.2.1 Evidence
    1.2.2 Evidence
      1.2.2.1 Detail
      1.2.2.2 Detail
    1.2.3 Evidence
  1.3 Third subpoint
2.0 Second Major Point
  2.1 First subpoint
    2.1.1 Evidence
    2.1.2 Evidence
  2.2 Second subpoint

FIGURE 5-4 Topic Division In Outlines

RIGHT:	WRONG:
I. Alternatives for Improving Profits A. Increasing sales 1. Radio advertising 2. Internet advertising B. Reducing production costs 1. Modernizing plants 2. Using more off-shore labour	I. Alternatives for Improving Profits A. Increasing sales 1. Radio Advertising B. Reducing production costs 1. Modernizing plants 2. Using more off-shore labour

When dividing a topic in an outline, be sure to divide it into at least two parts. A topic cannot be divided into only one part.

In the second (wrong) example, subtopic A. is only divided once. Either the writer hasn't developed her ideas sufficiently, or has only one idea (radio advertising) for increasing sales. If she only has one idea for increasing sales, then that idea should be subtopic A.

Note in the second example in Figure 5–4, that subtopic A. is only divided once. Either the writer hasn't developed her ideas sufficiently, or has only one idea for increasing sales: radio advertising. If she only has one idea for increasing sales, then it should be subtopic A.

A more schematic format illustrates the structure of your message in an organizational chart similar to the charts used to show a company's management structure (see Figure 5-5 on page 108). The main idea is shown in the highest-level box, and like the CEO, it establishes overall vision, or the big picture. The lower-level ideas, like lower-level employees, provide the details. All the ideas are logically organized into divisions of thought, just as a company is organized into divisions and departments.[4] To develop this type of outline, you must start with the main idea, state the major supporting points, then illustrate these points with evidence.

The main idea is the starting point for constructing an outline.

Start with the Main Idea The main idea (placed at the top of the organizational chart in Figure 5-5), helps you establish the goals and general strategy of the message. This main idea expresses two purposes: (1) what you want your audience to do or think and (2) why they should do so. Everything in the message should either support the main idea or explain its implications

Major supporting points clarify your main idea.

State the Major Points In an organizational chart, the boxes directly below the top box represent the major supporting points (corresponding to the main headings in a conventional outline). These first-level ideas clarify the message by expressing it in more concrete terms. When dividing the main idea into these smaller units, try to identify between three and five major points. If you come up with more, go back and look for opportunities to combine some of your ideas.

Sometimes the points that go into these boxes are fairly obvious. But at other times, you may have at least a dozen ideas to sort through and group together. Be sure to keep in mind your purpose and the nature of the material.

The division of major points may be based on physical relationships, the description of a process, the components of an object, or a historical chronology.

If your purpose is to inform and the material is factual, divisions are generally suggested by the subject itself. Major points are often based on something physical—something you can visualize or measure, such as activities to be performed, functional units, spatial or chronological relationships, or parts of a whole. When you're describing a process, the major points are almost inevitably steps in the process. When you're describing an object, perhaps equipment used in a manufacturing process, the major points correspond to the components of the object. When you're giving a historical account, major points represent events in the chronology.

FIGURE 5-5 Organizational Chart for Organizing a Message

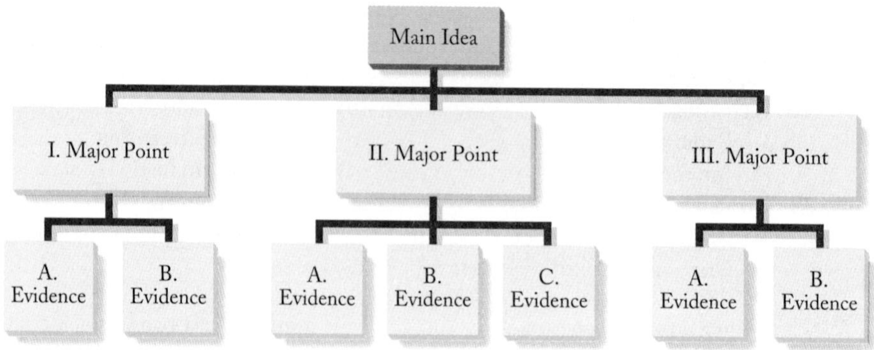

Major points may also be based on the elements of a logical argument.

If your purpose is to persuade or to collaborate, the major supporting points may be more difficult to identify. Instead of relying on a natural order imposed by the subject, develop a line of reasoning that proves your central message and motivates your audience to act. The boxes on the organizational chart then correspond to the major elements in a logical argument. The supporting points are the main reasons your audience should accept your message.

Illustrate with Evidence The third level on the organization chart shows the specific evidence you'll use to illustrate your major points. This evidence is the concrete detail that helps your audience understand and remember the more abstract concepts you're presenting. For example, if you're advocating that your company increase its advertising budget, you can support your major point by providing evidence that your most successful competitors spend more on advertising than you do. You can also describe a case in which a particular competitor increased its ad budget and achieved an impressive sales gain. And then you can show that over the past five years, your firm's sales have gone up and down in response to the amount spent on advertising.

If you're developing a long, complex message, you may need to carry the organizational chart (or outline) down several levels. Remember that every level is a step along the chain from the abstract to the concrete, from the general to the specific. The lowest level contains the individual facts and figures that tie the generalizations to the observable, measurable world. The higher levels are the concepts that reveal why those facts are significant.

Each major point must be supported with enough specific evidence to be convincing, but not so much that it's boring.

The more evidence you provide, the more conclusive your case will be. If your subject is complex and unfamiliar or if your audience is skeptical, you'll need a lot of facts and figures to demonstrate your points. On the other hand, if your subject is routine and the audience is positively inclined, you can be more sparing with the evidence. You want to provide enough support to be convincing but not so much that your message becomes boring or inefficient.

CHOOSE BETWEEN THE DIRECT AND INDIRECT APPROACHES

Once you've defined and grouped your ideas, you're ready to decide on their sequence. When you're addressing Canadian or U.S. audiences, individuals who are accustomed to messages that proceed in a linear fashion, or point by point,[5] you have two basic options:

Use direct order if the audience's reaction is likely to be positive and indirect order if it is likely to be negative.

- **Direct approach (deductive).** The main idea comes first, followed by the evidence. Use this approach when your audience will be neutral about your message or pleased to hear from you.
- **Indirect approach (inductive).** The evidence comes first, and the main idea comes later. Use this approach when your audience will be displeased about what you have to say.

To choose between these two alternatives, you must analyze your audience's likely reaction to your purpose and message. Audience reaction will fall somewhere between being eager to accept your message and being unwilling to accept your message (see Figure 5-6 below). The direct approach is generally fine when audience members will be receptive—if they are eager, interested, pleased, or even neutral. But you may have better results with the indirect approach if audience members are likely to resist your message—if they are displeased, uninterested, or unwilling.

Audience reaction can range from eager to unwilling.

Bear in mind, however, that each message is unique. No simple formula will solve all your communication problems. For example, if you're sending bad news to outsiders, an indirect approach may be best. On the other hand, if you're writing a memo to an associate, you may want to get directly to the point, even if your message is unpleasant. The direct approach might also be a good choice for long messages, regardless of your audience's attitude, because delaying the main idea could cause confusion and frustration. To summarize, your choice of a direct or an indirect approach depends on the following factors:

Avoid simple formulas: analyze your audience and purpose carefully before applying an approach.

- **Audience reaction:** (1) positive, (2) neutral, or (3) negative
- **Message length:** (1) short (memos and letters), or (2) long (reports, proposals, and presentations—discussed in Part 4)
- **Message type:** (1) routine, good-news, and goodwill messages, (2) bad-news messages, or (3) persuasive messages

Choice of approach also depends on message length and type.

When used with good judgment, the three basic types of business messages can be powerful communication tools.[6] Just remember: your first priority is to make your message clear. In the following brief discussions, note how the opening, body, and close all play an important role in getting your message across, regardless of message type.

The direct approach is effective for messages that will please the audience or will cause no particular reaction.

Routine, Good-News, and Goodwill Messages The most straightforward business messages are routine, good-news, and goodwill messages. If you're inquiring about

FIGURE 5-6 Audience Reaction Affects Organizational Approach

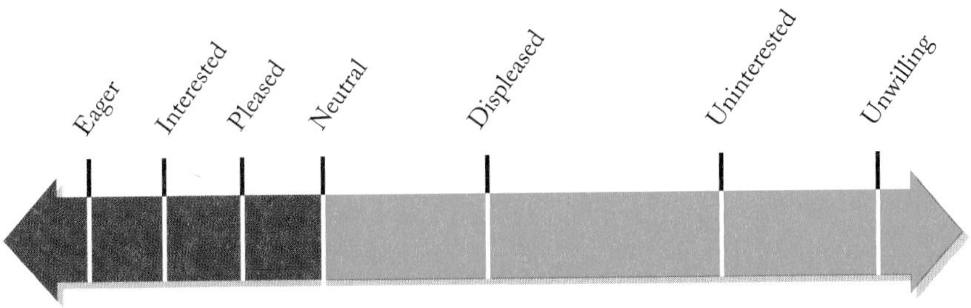

Eager — Interested — Pleased — Neutral — Displeased — Uninterested — Unwilling

	Direct approach	Indirect approach	
Audience reaction	Eager/interested/pleased/neutral	Displeased	Uninterested/unwilling
Message type	Routine, good news, goodwill	Bad news	Persuasive
Message opening	Start with the main idea, the request or the good news.	Start with a neutral statement that acts as a transition to the bad news.	Start with a statement or question that captures attention.
Message body	Provide necessary details.	Give reasons to justify a negative answer. State or imply the bad news, and make a positive suggestion.	Arouse the audience's interest in the subject. Build the audience's desire to comply.
Message close	Close with a cordial comment, a reference to the good news, or a statement about the specific action desired.	Close cordially.	Request action.

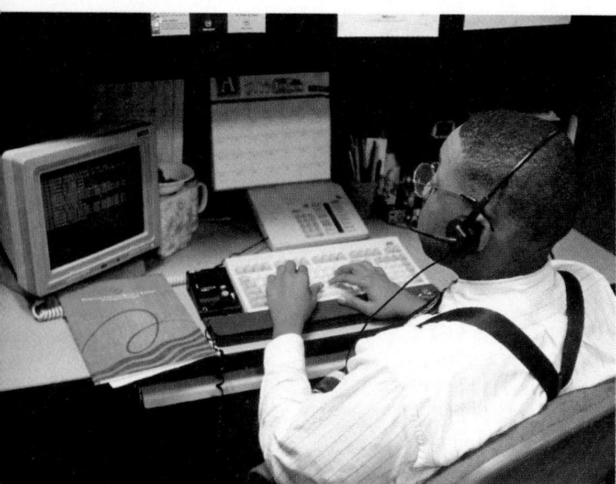

When telemarketers take orders from phone customers, they ask for the same information that a writer would need to include in an order letter: contact information (name, address, phone, e-mail), payment information (cheque, credit card type and number), and item information (item description, how many, etc.). Because such orders are routine, the information is presented in a direct and straightforward manner.

products or placing an order, your audience will usually want to comply. If you're announcing a price cut, granting an adjustment, accepting an invitation, or congratulating a colleague, your audience will most likely be pleased to hear from you. If you're providing routine information as part of your regular business, your audience will probably be neutral, neither pleased nor displeased.

Aside from being easy to understand, these kinds of messages are often easy to prepare. In the opening, you state your main idea directly, without searching for some creative introduction. The body of your message can then provide all necessary detail. The close is cordial and emphasizes your good news or makes a statement about the specific action desired.

By starting off with your positive idea, you put your audience in a good frame of mind and encourage them to be receptive to whatever else you have to say. This approach also emphasizes the pleasing aspect of your message by putting it right up front, where it's the first thing recipients see. Routine, good-news, and goodwill messages are discussed in greater detail in Chapter 7.

Bad-News Messages If you're refusing credit or denying a request for an adjustment, your audience will be disappointed. In such cases, it may be best to use the indirect approach—putting the evidence first and the main idea later. Astute businesspeople know that every person they encounter could be a potential customer, supplier, or contributor, or could influence someone who might become one.

If you have bad news, try to put it somewhere in the middle, cushioned by other, more positive ideas.

Successful communicators take a little extra care with their bad-news messages. They open with a neutral statement that acts as a transition to the reasons for the bad news.

In the body they give the reasons that justify a negative answer before stating or implying the bad news. And they are always careful to close cordially. Bad-news messages are discussed further in Chapter 8.

Using the indirect approach gives you an opportunity to get your message across to an uninterested or skeptical audience.

Persuasive Messages The indirect approach is also useful when you know that your audience will resist your message: they will be uninterested in your request or unwilling to comply. You might find an audience resistant to a sales letter, a collection letter, an unsolicited job application, or a request for a favour of some kind. In such cases, your message has a better chance of getting noticed if you lead off with an

Checklist: Organizing Business Messages

Recognize Good Organization

✓ Subject and purpose are clear.

✓ Information is directly related to subject and purpose.

✓ Ideas are grouped and presented logically.

✓ All necessary information is included.

Define the Main Idea

✓ Stimulate your creativity with brainstorming techniques.

✓ Identify a "hook" to motivate your audience to respond in the way you intend.

✓ Evaluate whether the main idea is realistic, given the imposed length limitations.

✓ Collect any necessary information.

Decide What to Say

✓ Start with the main idea.

✓ State the major points.

✓ Illustrate with evidence.

Organize the Message to Respond to the Audience's Probable Reaction

✓ Use the direct approach when your audience will be neutral, pleased, interested, or eager.

✓ Use the indirect approach when your audience will be displeased, uninterested, or unwilling.

attention-getting statement, one that makes your audience sit up and be receptive to what you have to say. For example, you may begin a persuasive message by mentioning a possible benefit, referring to a problem that the recipient might have, or posing a question. Then the body builds interest in the subject and arouses your audience's desire to comply. Once you have them thinking, you can introduce your main idea. The close is cordial and requests the desired action. Persuasive messages are discussed at greater length in Chapter 9. For a reminder of the organization tasks involved in preparing your messages, see "Checklist: Organizing Business Messages" on page 110.

Persuasive messages have their own indirect pattern.

Composing Your Message

Once you've completed the planning process and organized your message, you're ready to begin composing your first draft. If your schedule permits, put aside your outline for a day or two. Then review it with a fresh eye, looking for opportunities to improve the flow of ideas.

Composition is easiest if you've already figured out what to say and in what order, although you may need to pause now and then to find the right word. You may also discover as you go along that you can improve on your outline. Feel free to rearrange, delete, and add ideas, as long as you don't lose sight of your purpose.

Composition is the process of drafting your message; polishing it is a later step.

Although an outline is crucial to good organization, don't let it restrict you from changing the order of your ideas as you compose your message.

As you compose your first draft, pay attention to your style and tone, and try to select words that match the tone you want to achieve. Try to create effective sentences and to develop coherent paragraphs. But don't strive for perfection. Just put down your ideas as quickly as you can. You'll have time to revise and refine the material later.

Good business writing is learned by expanding your familiarity with business writers and by practice. Read business journals and newspapers, and become sensitive to language, sentence structure, and paragraph development. Write your own business messages: for example, if you're dissatisfied with a product you bought, send a complaint letter to the company. And complete cases in this book that your instructor hasn't assigned. You will be surprised—and pleased—with the progress you will make as a business communicator.

Control Your Style and Tone

Style is the way you use words to achieve a certain **tone**, or overall impression. You can vary your style—your sentence structure and vocabulary—to sound forceful or objective, personal or formal, colourful or dry. The right choice depends on the nature of your message and your relationship with the reader. Although style can be refined during the revision phase (see Chapter 6), you'll save time and a lot of rewriting if you use a style that allows you to achieve the desired tone from the start.

When composing your message, you can vary the style to create a tone that suits the occasion.

OBJECTIVE 3 Discuss two ways of achieving a tone that is businesslike and a style that is clear and concise.

Your use of language is one of your credentials. Try to make your style clear, concise, and grammatically correct, and try to make it conform to the norms of your group. Your company or industry will have its own stylistic conventions, and many occupational groups share a particular vocabulary. In general, try to make your tone conversational, and keep your message clear by using plain English.

Most business messages aim for a conversational style. To achieve a warm but businesslike tone

- Don't use old-fashioned language.
- Don't use pompous phrases.
- Don't be too familiar.
- Use humour only with great care.
- Don't preach.
- Don't brag.

USE A CONVERSATIONAL TONE

The tone of your business messages may span a continuum from informal to conversational to formal. Most business messages aim for a conversational tone, using plain language that sounds businesslike without being stuffy, stiff, wordy, or full of jargon. Rather than trying to impress audiences with an extensive vocabulary, good

Going Online

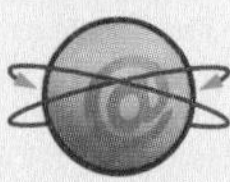

Compose a Better Business Message

At Purdue's Online Writing Lab (OWL) you'll find tools to help you improve your business messages. For advice on composing written messages, for help with grammar, and for referrals to other information sources, you'll be wise to visit this site. Purdue's OWL offers online services and an introduction to Internet search tools. You can also download a variety of handouts on writing skills. Check out the resources at the OWL home page and learn how to write a professional business message.

owl.english.purdue.edu

To link directly to this site, visit our Companion Web site at **www.pearsoned.ca/thill** *and look for the Chapter 5 resources.*

communicators focus on being sensible, logical, and objective; they provide supporting facts and a rationale. To achieve such a conversational tone in your messages, try to avoid obsolete and pompous language, intimacy, humour, and preaching or bragging:

- **Avoid obsolete and pompous language.** Business language used to be much more formal than it is today, and some old-fashioned phrases (such as "kindly advise") are still used in certain occupations, such as law. In general, however, avoid using such outdated language by asking yourself, "Would I say this if I were talking with someone face to face?" Similarly, avoid using big words, trite expressions, and overly complicated sentences to impress others. Such pompous language sounds puffed up and roundabout (see Table 5–2 on page 113).
- **Avoid intimacy.** Avoid phrases that imply intimacy, such as "just between you and me" and "as you and I are well aware." Be careful about sounding too familiar or chatty; such a tone may be seen as an attempt to seem like an old friend when, in fact, you're not.
- **Avoid humour.** Using humour can backfire, especially if you don't know your audience very well. What seems humourous to you may be serious to others. And when you're communicating across cultures, your audience may not appreciate your humour or even realize that you're trying to be funny.[7] Also, humour changes too quickly. What's funny today may not be in a week or a month from now.
- **Avoid preaching and bragging.** People who think that they know everything and others know nothing are irritating. If you must tell your audience something obvious, try to place the information in the middle of a paragraph, where it will sound like a casual comment rather than a major revelation. You can also preface the obvious with a comment like, "As you know." Also, avoid bragging about your accomplishments or about the size or profitability of your organization (though you may consider highlighting your company's success if your audience is a part of your organization).

Your conversational tone may become less or more formal, depending on the situation. For instance, if you're addressing an old friend, your conversational tone may lean more toward an informal level. In business messages, however, your tone would never be as informal as it would with family members or school friends. On the other hand, if you're in a large organization and you're communicating with your superiors or if you're communicating to customers, your conversational tone would tend to be more formal and respectful.

USE PLAIN ENGLISH

Plain English is close to spoken English and can be easily understood.

Plain English is a way of writing so that your audience can easily understand your meaning. Plain English avoids jargon and unnecessary technical terms. Because it's close to the way people normally speak, plain English is easily understood. If you've ever tried to make sense of an overwritten or murky passage in a legal document or credit agreement, you can understand why many governments and corporations today are endorsing the plain-English movement. Revenue Canada has been improving the readability of its publications and forms.[8] The Government of Nova Scotia Web site has a link dedicated to communication that includes advice to government agencies (and the interested public) on plain language (see **www.gov.ns.ca/cmns/plainlanguage).**

Plain English is already being used in many areas.

It's been shown there's a link between confusing jargon and corporate performance. A New York investor relations firm studied letters to shareholders in annual reports. The firm discovered that corporations that used a lot of jargon in these letters performed worse financially than corporations that communicated in plain English.[9]

Not every application is appropriate for plain English.

Of course, plain English has some limitations. It lacks the precision necessary for scientific research, intense feeling, and personal insight. Moreover, it fails to embrace all cultures and dialects equally. But even though it's intended for audiences who speak English as their primary language, plain English can also help you simplify the messages you prepare for audiences who speak English only as a second or

TABLE 5–2 Staying Up to Date and Accessible with Business Language

Old-fashioned	Up to Date
in due course	today, tomorrow (or a specific time)
permit me to say that	(permission is not necessary)
we are in receipt of	we have received
pursuant to	(omit)
in closing, I'd like to say	(omit)
the undersigned	I; me
kindly advise	please let us know
we wish to inform you	(just say it)
attached please find	enclosed is
it has come to my attention	I have just learned; or, Ms. Garza has just told me
our Mr. Lydell	Mr. Lydell, our credit manager
please be advised that	(omit)
Pompous	**Accessible**
Upon procurement of additional supplies, I will initiate fulfillment of your order.	I will fill your order when I receive more supplies.
Perusal of the records indicates a substantial deficit for the preceding accounting period due to the utilization of antiquated mechanisms.	The records show a company loss last year due to the use of old equipment.

even third language. For example, by choosing words that have only one interpretation, you will surely communicate more clearly with your intercultural audience.[10]

Use Precise Vocabulary

OBJECTIVE 4 Briefly describe how to select words that are not only correct but also effective.

To compose effective messages, you must choose your words carefully.[11] First, pay close attention to correctness. The "rules" of grammar and usage are constantly changing to reflect changes in the way people speak. So even editors and grammarians occasionally have questions about correct usage, and they sometimes disagree about the answers. For example, the word *data* is the plural form of *datum,* yet some experts now prefer to treat *data* as a singular noun when it's used in nonscientific material to refer to a body of information. You be the judge: Which of the following sentences sounds better?

Correctness is the first consideration when choosing words.

> The data on our market share is consistent from region to region.
> The data on our market share are consistent from region to region.

Although debating the finer points of usage may seem like nitpicking, using words correctly is important. If you make grammatical or usage errors, you lose credibility with your audience. Poor grammar implies that you're unaware or uninformed, and audiences put little faith in an uninformed source. Even if an audience is broad-minded enough to withhold such a judgment, grammatical errors are distracting.

Correct grammar enhances your image.

If you have doubts about what is correct, don't be lazy. Look up the answer and use the proper form of expression. Check the grammar and usage guide in Appendix C, or consult any number of special reference books and resources available in libraries, in bookstores, and on the Internet. Most authorities agree on the basic conventions.

If in doubt, check it out.

Effectiveness is the second consideration when choosing words.

Just as important as selecting the correct word is selecting the most suitable word for the job at hand. Word effectiveness is generally more difficult to achieve than correctness, particularly in written communication. Writers have to work at their craft, using functional and content words correctly and finding the words that communicate.

USE FUNCTIONAL AND CONTENT WORDS CORRECTLY

Functional words (conjunctions, prepositions, articles, and pronouns) express relationships among **content words** (nouns, verbs, adjectives, and adverbs).

Words can be divided into two main categories. **Functional words** express relationships and have only one unchanging meaning in any given context. They include conjunctions, prepositions, articles, and pronouns. Your main concern with functional words is to use them correctly. **Content words** are multidimensional and therefore subject to various interpretations. They include nouns, verbs, adjectives, and adverbs. These words carry the meaning of a sentence. In your sentences, content words are the building blocks, and functional words are the mortar that holds them together. In the following sentence, all the content words are underlined:

> Some objective observers of the cookie market give Christie's the edge in quality, but President's Choice is lauded for superior distribution.

Both functional words and content words are necessary, but your effectiveness as a communicator depends largely on your ability to choose the right content words for your message. Content words can be classified (1) by denotation and connotation and (2) by abstraction and concreteness.

Content words have both a denotative (explicit, specific) meaning and a connotative (implicit, associative) meaning.

Denotation and Connotation Content words have both a denotative and a connotative meaning. The denotative meaning is the literal, or dictionary, meaning. The connotative meaning includes all the associations and feelings evoked by the word.

The denotative meaning of *desk* is "a table used for writing." Some desks may have drawers or compartments, and others may have a flat top or a sloping top, but the literal meaning is generally well understood. The connotative meaning of *desk* may include thoughts associated with work or study, but the word *desk* has fairly neutral connotations—neither strong nor emotional. However, some words have much stronger connotations than others. For example, if you say that a student *failed* to pass a test, the connotative meaning suggests that the person is inferior, incompetent, below some standard of performance. The connotations of the word *fail* are negative and can carry strong emotional meaning.

Business communicators avoid words with negative connotations.

In business communication, avoid using terms that are high in connotative meaning. By saying that a student achieved a score of 65 percent, you communicate the facts and avoid a heavy load of negative connotations. If you use words that have relatively few possible interpretations, you are less likely to be misunderstood. In addition, because you are trying to communicate in an objective, rational manner, you want to avoid emotion-laden comments.

The more abstract a word, the more it is removed from the tangible, objective world of things that can be perceived with the senses.

Abstraction and Concreteness An **abstract word** expresses a concept, quality, or characteristic. Abstractions are usually broad, encompassing a category of ideas. They are often intellectual, academic, or philosophical. Love, honour, progress, tradition, and beauty are abstractions.

A **concrete word** stands for something you can touch or see. Concrete terms are anchored in the tangible, material world. *Chair, table, horse, rose, kick, kiss, red, green,* and *two* are concrete words; they are direct, clear, and exact.

You might assume that concrete words are better than abstract words, because they are more precise, but you would sometimes be wrong. However, imagine trying to talk about business without referring to such concepts as *morale, productivity, profits, quality, motivation,* and *guarantees.* Abstractions permit us to rise above the common and tangible. Even though they're indispensable, abstractions can be troublesome. They tend to be fuzzy and subject to many interpretations. They also tend to be boring. It isn't always easy to get excited about ideas, especially if they're unrelated to con-

TABLE 5-3 Thinking Like a Wordsmith

Avoid Unfamiliar Words	Use Familiar Words
ascertain	find out, learn
consummate	close, bring about
peruse	read, study
circumvent	avoid
increment	growth, increase
unequivocal	certain
Avoid Clichés	**Use Plain Language**
scrape the bottom of the barrel	strain shrinking resources
an uphill battle	a challenge
writing on the wall	prediction
call the shots	be in charge
take by storm	attack
cost an arm and a leg	expensive
a new ballgame	fresh start
worst nightmare	strong competitor, disaster
fall through the cracks	be overlooked

crete experience. The best way to minimize such problems is to blend abstract terms with concrete ones, the general with the specific. State the concept, then pin it down with details expressed in more concrete terms. Save the abstractions for ideas that cannot be expressed any other way.

In business communication, use concrete, specific terms whenever possible; use abstractions only when necessary.

Take a moment to look at a sample of your writing. Circle all the nouns. How many of them stand for a specific person, place, or object? The ones that do are concrete. Look at the vague nouns; can you replace them with terms that are more vivid? Now underline all the adjectives. How many of them describe the exact color, size, texture, quantity, or quality of something? Remember that words such as *small, numerous, sizable, near, soon, good,* and *fine* are imprecise. Try to replace them with terms that are more accurate. Instead of referring to a *sizable loss,* talk about a *loss of $32 million.*

FIND WORDS THAT COMMUNICATE

Anyone who earns a living by crafting words is a *wordsmith*—including journalists, public relations specialists, editors, and letter and report writers. Unlike poets, novelists, or dramatists, wordsmiths don't strive for dramatic effects. Instead, they are concerned with using language to be clear, concise, and accurate. To reach their goal, they emphasize words that are strong and familiar. When you compose your business messages, do your best to think like a wordsmith (See Table 5–3 above).

Business communicators aim for clarity and accuracy rather than dramatic effect.

- **Choose strong words.** Choose words that express your thoughts most clearly, specifically, and dynamically. Nouns and verbs are the most concrete, so use them as much as you can. Adjectives and adverbs have obvious roles, but use them sparingly—they often evoke subjective judgments. Verbs are especially powerful because they tell what's happening in the sentence, so make them dynamic and specific; for example, replace *rise* or *fall* with *soar* or *plummet.*
- **Choose familiar words.** You'll communicate best with words that are familiar to your readers. However, keep in mind that words familiar to one reader might be unfamiliar to another.
- **Avoid clichés.** Although familiar words are generally the best choice, beware of terms and phrases so common that they have become virtually meaningless.

Wordsmiths choose strong words, choose familiar words, avoid clichés, and use jargon carefully.

Because clichés are used so often, they don't make a strong impression on readers. Most people use these phrases not because they think it makes their message more vivid and inviting but because they don't know how to express themselves otherwise.[12]

➤ **Use jargon carefully.** Handle technical or professional terms with care. These words can add precision and authority to a message, but many people don't understand them (even an audience familiar with the jargon can be lulled to sleep by too much). Let your audience's vocabulary guide you. When addressing a group of engineers or scientists, refer to *meteorological effects on microwave propagation;* otherwise, refer to the *effects of weather on radio waves.*

Create Effective Sentences

In English, word order is important when constructing sentences.

In English, words don't make much sense until they're combined in a sentence to express a complete thought. Thus the words *Jill, receptionist, the, smiles,* and *at* can be organized into "Jill smiles at the receptionist." Now that you've constructed the sentence, you can begin exploring the possibilities for improvement, looking at how well each word performs its particular function. Nouns and noun equivalents are the topics (or subjects) you're communicating about, and verbs and related words (or predicates) make statements about those subjects. In a complicated sentence, adjectives and adverbs modify the subject and the statement, and various connectors hold the words together.

Every sentence contains a subject (noun or noun equivalent) and a predicate (verb and related words).

THE FOUR TYPES OF SENTENCES

A **simple sentence** has one main clause.

Sentences come in four basic varieties: simple, compound, complex, and compound-complex. A **simple sentence** has one main clause (a single subject and a single predicate), although it may be expanded by nouns and pronouns serving as objects of the action and by modifying phrases. Here's a typical example (with the subject underlined once and the predicate verb underlined twice):

Profits have increased in the past year.

A **compound sentence** has two main clauses.

A **compound sentence** has two main clauses that express two or more independent but related thoughts of equal importance, usually joined by *and, but,* or *or.* In effect, a compound sentence is a merger of two or more simple sentences (independent clauses) that are related. For example:

Wage rates have declined by 5 percent, and employee turnover has been high.

The independent clauses in a compound sentence are always separated by a comma or by a semicolon (in which case the conjunction—*and, but, or*—is dropped).

A **complex sentence** has one main clause and one subordinate clause.

A **complex sentence** expresses one main thought (the independent clause) and one or more subordinate thoughts (dependent clauses) related to it, often separated by a comma. The subordinate thought, which comes first in the following sentence, could not stand alone:

Although you may question Gerald's conclusions, you must admit that his research is thorough.

A **compound-complex sentence** has two main clauses and at least one dependent clause.

A **compound-complex sentence** has two main clauses and at least one subordinate clause:

Profits have increased in the past year, and although you may question Gerald's conclusions, you must admit that his research is thorough.

When constructing a sentence, choose the form that matches the relationship of the ideas you want to express. If you have two ideas of equal importance, express them as two simple sentences or as one compound sentence. However, if one of the ideas is less important than the other one, place it in a dependent clause to form a complex sentence. For example, although the following compound sentence uses a conjunction to join two ideas, they aren't truly equal:

> The chemical products division is the strongest in the company, and its management techniques should be adopted by the other divisions.

By making the first thought subordinate to the second, you establish a cause-and-effect relationship. So the following complex sentence is much more effective:

> Because the chemical products division is the strongest in the company, its management techniques should be adopted by the other divisions.

In complex sentences, the placement of the dependent clause hinges on the relationship between the ideas expressed. If you want to emphasize the idea, put the dependent clause at the end of the sentence (the most emphatic position) or at the beginning (the second most emphatic position). If you want to downplay the idea, bury the dependent clause within the sentence.

Dependent clauses can determine emphasis.

> **Most emphatic:** The electronic parts are manufactured in Mexico, *which has lower wage rates than Canada.*
> **Emphatic:** *Because wage rates are lower there,* the electronic parts are manufactured in Mexico.
> **Least emphatic:** Mexico, *which has lower wage rates,* was selected as the production point for the electronic parts.

To make your writing as effective as possible, balance all four sentence types. If you use too many simple sentences, you won't be able to properly express the relationships among your ideas. If you use too many long, compound sentences, your writing will sound monotonous. On the other hand, an uninterrupted series of complex or compound-complex sentences is hard to follow.

SENTENCE STYLE

OBJECTIVE 5 Explain four guidelines that help you achieve clarity and efficiency in your sentences.

Sentence style varies from culture to culture. For example, German sentences are extremely complex, with many modifiers and appositives; Japanese and Chinese languages don't have sentences in the same sense that Western languages do.[13] In English try to make your sentences grammatically correct, concise, readable, and appropriate for your audience. In general, strive for straightforward simplicity. For most business audiences, clarity and conciseness take precedence over literary style. The following guidelines will help you achieve these qualities in your own writing.

Business communicators strive for a clear and efficient style.

Select Active or Passive Voice You're using active voice when the subject (the "actor") comes before the verb and the object of the sentence (the "acted upon") follows the verb, as in the sentence, "John rented the office." You're using passive voice when the subject follows the verb and the object precedes it: "The office was rented by John." As you can see, the passive voice combines the helping verb to be with a form of the verb that is usually similar to the past tense.

Active sentences are stronger than passive ones.

Active verbs produce shorter, stronger sentences, making your writing more vigorous and concise and generally easier to understand (see Table 5–4 on page 118). Passive verbs make sentences longer and de-emphasize the subject. Nevertheless, because you always focus on your audience and demonstrate the "you" attitude, using the passive voice makes sense in some situations:

1. When you want to be diplomatic about pointing out a problem or error of some kind: using the passive version makes your criticism seem less like an accusation
2. When you want to point out what's being done without taking or attributing either the credit or the blame: the passive version leaves the actor completely out of the sentence and focuses on the action itself
3. When you want to avoid personal pronouns in order to create an objective tone (the passive version may be used in a formal report, for example)

Use passive sentences to soften bad news, to put yourself in the background, or to create an impersonal tone.

TABLE 5-4 Choosing Active or Passive Voice

Passive	Active
Use the active voice to emphasize the subject (or "actor")	
The new procedure is thought by the president to be superior.	The president thinks the new procedure is superior.
There are problems with this contract.	This contract has problems.
Use the active voice to write concisely	
It is necessary that the report be finished by next week.	You must finish the report by next week.
Use the passive voice to avoid placing blame	
The shipment was lost.	You lost the shipment.
Use the passive voice to create an impersonal tone	
The production line is being analyzed to determine the problem.	I am analyzing the production line to determine the problem.
Criteria have been established to evaluate capital expenditures.	We have established criteria to evaluate capital expenditures.

Emphasize parts of a sentence by
- Amplifying them through description
- Putting them at the beginning or at the end of the sentence
- Making them the subject of the sentence

Emphasize Key Thoughts In every message, some ideas are more important than others are. You can emphasize these key ideas through your sentence style. One technique is amplification. When you want to call attention to a thought, use extra words to describe it. Consider this sentence:

> The chairperson of the board called for a vote of the shareholders.

To emphasize the importance of the chairperson, you might describe her more fully:

> Having considerable experience in corporate takeover battles, the chairperson of the board called for a vote of the shareholders.

You can increase the emphasis even more by adding a separate, short sentence to augment the first:

> The chairperson of the board called for a vote of the shareholders. She has considerable experience in corporate takeover battles.

You can also call attention to a thought by making it the subject of the sentence. In the following example, the emphasis is on the person:

> *I* can write letters much more quickly using a computer.

However, by changing the subject, the computer is the focus of attention:

> The *computer* enables me to write letters much more quickly.

Of course, another way to emphasize an idea is to place it at either the beginning or the end of a sentence:

> **Less Emphatic:** *We are cutting the price* to stimulate demand.
> **More Emphatic:** To stimulate demand, *we are cutting the price.*

Techniques like these give you a great deal of control over the way your audience interprets what you have to say.

To keep readers' interest, use both long and short sentences.

Vary Sentence Length Variety is the key to making your message interesting. Using words and sentence structure skillfully, you can create a rhythm that emphasizes important points, enlivens your writing style, and makes your information appealing to your reader. Although good business writers often use short sentences, too many short sentences in a row can make your writing choppy. Conversely, if all your sentences move at the same plodding gait, you're likely to bore your reader. So to be interesting, use a variety of both short and long sentences.

Long sentences are usually harder to understand than short sentences because they are packed with information that must all be absorbed at once. On the other hand, long sentences are especially well suited for grouping or combining ideas, listing points, and summarizing or previewing information. Medium-length sentences (those with about 20 words) are useful for showing the relationships among ideas. Short sentences emphasize important information.

Lists are effective tools for highlighting and simplifying material.

Use Bullets and Lists An effective alternative to using straight sentences is to set off important ideas in a list—a series of words, names, or items. Lists can show the sequence of your ideas or heighten their impact visually. In addition, they ease the skimming process for busy readers, simplify complex subjects, highlight the main point, and break up the page visually.

When creating a list, you can separate items with numbers, letters, or bullets. Use numbers if the sequence of events is critical, for example, if your are describing steps in a process that must be completed in a specific order. The following three steps need to be performed in the order indicated, and the numbers make that clear:

1. Find out how many employees would like on-site daycare facilities.
2. Determine how much space the daycare centre would require.
3. Estimate the cost of converting a conference room for the on-site facility.

When using lists, make sure to introduce them clearly so that people know what they're about to read. Consider the following example:

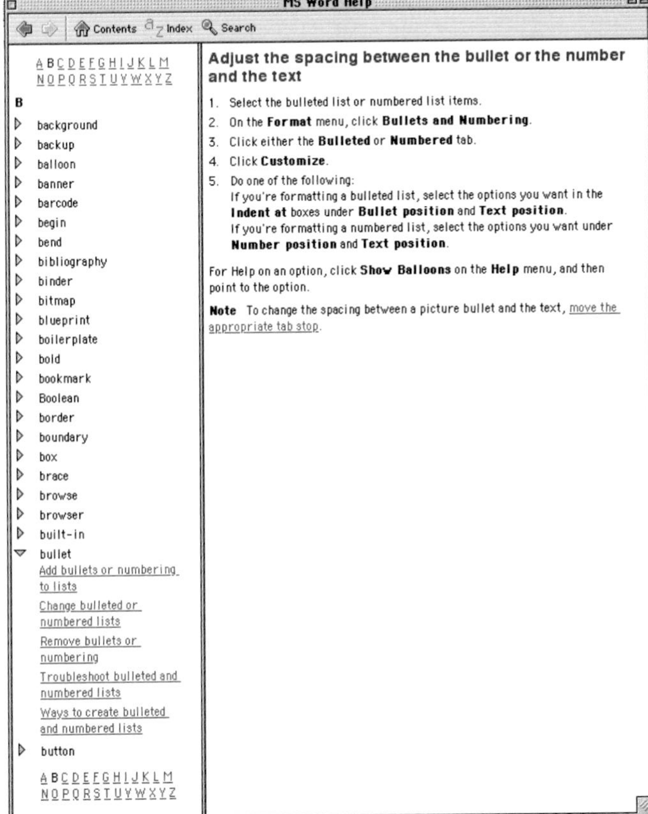

FIGURE 5-7: Example of Numbered List
"Help" screens, such as this example from Microsoft Word, use numbered lists to explain features clearly. Note that the list is introduced by a statement.

The board of directors met to discuss the revised annual budget. To keep expenses in line with declining sales, the directors voted to

- Cut everyone's salary by 10 percent
- Close the employee cafeteria
- Reduce travel expenses

Lists should follow the rules of parallelism.

Note that the items in the sample lists are phrased in parallel form. In other words, if one item begins with a verb, all subsequent items begin with a verb. If one is a noun phrase, all should be noun phrases; for example,

This report discusses the following topics:

- Labour costs
- Equipment costs
- Travel costs

Your bullet charts for oral presentation should also be phrased in parallel form (see Figure 13-5 in Chapter 13, Giving Speeches and Oral Presentations for examples).

Develop Coherent Paragraphs

Paragraphs are functional units that revolve around a single thought.

A paragraph is a cluster of sentences all related to the same general topic. It is a unit of thought. A series of paragraphs makes up an entire composition. Each paragraph is an important part of the whole, a key link in the train of thought. As you compose your message, think about the paragraphs and their relationship to one another.

When you're talking with someone face to face, you develop your paragraphs informally, using tone of voice and gestures to signal the relationships among ideas. You pause to indicate that you have completed one topic and are ready to begin another, a new "paragraph." In a written document, on the other hand, paragraphs are developed more formally. Each paragraph is separated from other units of thought by skipping a line or indenting the first line.

ELEMENTS OF THE PARAGRAPH

Most paragraphs consist of a topic sentence, related sentences, and transitional elements.

Paragraphs vary widely in length and form. You can communicate effectively in one short paragraph or in pages of lengthy paragraphs, depending on your purpose, your audience, and your message. The typical paragraph contains three basic elements: a topic sentence, related sentences that develop the topic, and transitional words and phrases.

The topic sentence

- Reveals the subject of the paragraph
- Indicates how the subject will be developed

Topic Sentence Every properly constructed paragraph is unified; it deals with a single topic. The sentence that introduces that topic is called the topic sentence. In informal and creative writing, the topic sentence may be implied rather than stated. In business writing, the topic sentence is generally explicit and is often the first sentence in the paragraph. The topic sentence gives readers a summary of the general idea that will be covered in the rest of the paragraph. The following examples show how a topic sentence can introduce the subject and suggest the way that subject will be developed:

The medical products division has been troubled for many years by public relations problems. [In the rest of the paragraph, readers will learn the details of the problems.]

Relocating the plant in Regina has two main disadvantages. [The disadvantages will be explained in subsequent sentences.]

To get a refund, you must supply us with some additional information. [The details of the necessary information will be described in the rest of the paragraph.]

Paragraphs are developed through a series of related sentences that provide details about the topic sentence.

Related Sentences The sentences that explain the topic sentence round out the paragraph. These related sentences must all have a bearing on the general subject and must provide enough specific details to make the topic clear:

The medical products division has been troubled for many years by public relations problems. Since 2001 the local newspaper has published 15 articles that portray the division in a negative light. We have been accused of everything from mistreating laboratory animals to polluting the local groundwater. Our facility has been described as a health hazard. Our scientists are referred to as "Frankensteins," and our profits are considered "obscene."

The developmental sentences are all more specific than the topic sentence. Each one provides another piece of evidence to demonstrate the general truth of the main thought. Also, each sentence is clearly related to the general idea being developed; the relation between the sentences and the idea is what gives the paragraph its unity. A paragraph is well developed when it contains enough information to make the topic sentence convincing and interesting.

Transitional Elements In addition to being unified and well developed, effective paragraphs are coherent; that is, they are arranged in a logical order so that the audience can understand the train of thought. When you complete a paragraph, your readers automatically assume that you've finished with a particular idea. You achieve coherence by using transitions that show the relationship between paragraphs and among sentences within paragraphs. Transitions show how one thought is related to another, and they help readers understand the connections you're trying to make. You can establish transitions in various ways:

Because each paragraph covers a single idea, use transitional words and phrases to show readers how paragraphs relate to each other.

- Use connecting words: *and, but, or, nevertheless, however, in addition,* and so on.
- Echo a word or phrase from a previous paragraph or sentence: "A system should be established for monitoring inventory levels. *This system* will provide ..."
- Use a pronoun that refers to a noun used previously: "Ms. Arthur is the leading candidate for the president's position. *She* has excellent qualifications."
- Use words that are frequently paired: "The machine has a *minimum* output of ... Its *maximum* output is ..."

Some transitional devices include
- Connecting words (conjunctions)
- Repeated words or phrases
- Pronouns
- Words that are frequently paired

Some transitions alert the reader to a change in mood from the previous paragraph. Some announce a complete contrast with what's gone on before, and some announce a causal relationship. Other transitions signal a change in time. At least a dozen words will do this job for you: *but, yet, however, nevertheless, still, instead, thus, therefore, meanwhile, now, later, today, subsequently,* and several more. Look in Chapter 11 (Writing Business Reports and Proposals) for more transitions.

FIVE WAYS TO DEVELOP A PARAGRAPH

OBJECTIVE 6 **List five ways to develop a paragraph and discuss three factors that increase paragraph readability.**

Paragraphs can be developed in many ways. Five of the most common techniques are illustration, comparison or contrast, cause and effect, classification, and problem and solution (see Table 5–5 on page 122). Your choice of technique depends on your subject, your intended audience, and your purpose.

In actual practice, you'll often combine two or more methods of development in a single paragraph. To add interest, you might begin by using illustration, shift to comparison or contrast, and then shift to problem and solution. However, before settling for the first approach that comes to mind, consider the alternatives. Think through various methods before committing yourself. If you fall into the easy habit of repeating the same old paragraph pattern time after time, your writing will lack interest.

Five ways to develop paragraphs:
- Illustration
- Comparison or contrast
- Cause and effect
- Classification
- Problem and solution

PARAGRAPH READABILITY

Making your message easier to read helps audience members move through your material more quickly and helps them understand what you're trying to say. To increase readability, consider using shorter paragraphs, effective headings, and occasional questions.

Length Short paragraphs (of 100 words or fewer) are easier to read than long ones, and they make your writing look inviting. Direct-mail letters almost always use very short paragraphs because the writers know that their letters will be read more

Short paragraphs are easier to read than long ones.

TABLE 5–5 Five Techniques for Developing Paragraphs

Technique	Description	Sample
Illustration	Giving examples that demonstrate the general idea	Some of our most popular products are available through local distributors. For example, Everett & Lemmings carries our frozen soups and entrees. The J. B. Green Company carries our complete line of seasonings, as well as the frozen soups. Wilmont Foods, also a major distributor, now carries our new line of frozen desserts.
Comparison or Contrast	Using similarities or differences to develop the topic	In previous years, when the company was small, the recruiting function could be handled informally. The need for new employees was limited, and each manager could comfortably screen and hire her or his own staff. Today, however, Gambit Products must undertake a major recruiting effort. Our successful bid on the Owens contract means that we will be doubling our labour force over the next six months. To hire that many people without disrupting our ongoing activities, we will create a separate recruiting group within the human resources department.
Cause and Effect	Focusing on the reasons for something	The heavy-duty of your Wanderer tent probably broke down for one of two reasons: (1) a sharp object punctured the fabric, and without reinforcement, the hole was enlarged by the stress of erecting the tent daily for a week, or (2) the fibres gradually rotted because the tent was folded and stored while still wet.
Classification	Showing how a general idea is broken into specific categories	Successful candidates for our supervisor trainee program generally come from one of several groups. The largest group, by far, consists of recent graduates of accredited data-processing programs. The next largest group comes from within our own company, as we try to promote promising clerical workers to positions of greater responsibility. Finally, we do occasionally accept candidates with outstanding supervisory experience in related industries.
Problem and Solution	Presenting a problem and then discussing the solution	Selling handmade toys by mail is a challenge because consumers are accustomed to buying heavily advertised toys from major chains. However, if we develop an appealing catalogue, we can compete on the basis of product novelty and quality. In addition, we can provide craftsmanship at a competitive price: a rocking horse of birch, with a hand-knit tail and mane; a music box with the child's name painted on the top; a real teepee, made by First Nations artisans.

carefully that way. Even in memos, letters, and reports, you may want to emphasize an idea from time to time by isolating it in a short, forceful paragraph.

However, some ideas are simply too big to be handled conveniently in one paragraph. Unless you break up your thoughts, you'll end up with a three-page paragraph that's guaranteed to intimidate even the most dedicated reader. When you want to package a big idea in short paragraphs, break the idea into subtopics and treat each subtopic in a separate paragraph—being careful to provide plenty of transitional elements.

By breaking a large single paragraph into several shorter ones, a writer can make the material more readable. Of course, many other approaches might be as effective. There is no "right" way to develop a paragraph. As you write your message, try to use a variety of paragraph lengths. But be careful to use one-sentence paragraphs only occasionally and only for emphasis.

Headings Headings are another effective tool for organizing your material into short sections. They act as labels to group related paragraphs together. They not only help the reader understand you but can also serve as shortcuts, highlighting material so that your reader can decide whether to read or skip it. Effective headings grab the reader's attention and make your text easier to read. Headings are similar to the subject line in memos and e-mail correspondence. However, subject lines identify the purpose of the memo or e-mail, whereas headings also advise the reader about the material included in the paragraph. Keep your headings brief, and try to put your reader right into the context of your message. Chapter 11 discusses headings in more detail.

Use headings to grab the reader's attention and divide material into short sections.

Questions Questions are another way to enliven your writing. They stop the motion, and then the answer starts it up again. By asking questions of your readers, you engage their interest and help guide them through your message. Consider the following:

Questions help readers by increasing their interest.

> Frank Deitch is an excellent employee who fully deserves the Employee of the Year Award. Why? The answer is simple. He understands every aspect of his position and is results driven.

Together with paragraph length and descriptive headings, questions make your message more readable and thus more effective. For a reminder of the tasks involved in composing your message, see "Checklist: Composing Business Messages" below.

Compose Efficient E-Mail Messages

OBJECTIVE 7 Explain how to write e-mail messages that capture and keep audience attention.

E-mail can be as informal and casual as a conversation between friends. But it can also emulate "snail mail" by using conventional business language, a respectful style, and a more formal format—such as a traditional greeting, headings, lists, and a formal closing and signature.[14] (For a discussion of e-mail etiquette, see Chapter 4, "Checklist:

E-mail messages need as much care and attention as other business messages.

Checklist: Composing Business Messages

Generate Ideas

✓ Get ideas down as quickly as you can.

✓ Rearrange, delete, and add ideas without losing sight of your purpose.

Vary the Style to Create a Tone That Suits the Occasion

✓ Use the appropriate level of formality.

✓ Avoid being overly familiar, using inappropriate humour (including obvious flattery), sounding preachy, bragging, or trying to be something you're not.

✓ Avoid old-fashioned and pompous language.

Select the Best Words

✓ Use plain English.

✓ Use concrete words that avoid negative connotations.

✓ Rely on nouns, verbs, and specific adjectives and adverbs.

✓ Choose words that are strong and familiar while avoiding clichés.

Create Effective Sentences

✓ Use simple, compound, and complex sentences, choosing the form that best fits the thought you want to express.

✓ Write mainly in the active voice, but use the passive voice to achieve specific effects.

✓ Emphasize key points through sentence style; expand on important points.

✓ Vary the sentence length.

✓ Use lists.

Create Effective Paragraphs

✓ Be sure each paragraph contains a topic sentence, related sentences, and transitional elements.

✓ Choose a method of development that suits the subject: illustration, comparison or contrast, cause and effect, classification, problem and solution.

✓ Vary the length and structure of sentences within paragraphs.

✓ Mix paragraphs of different lengths, try not to write paragraphs; over 100 words.

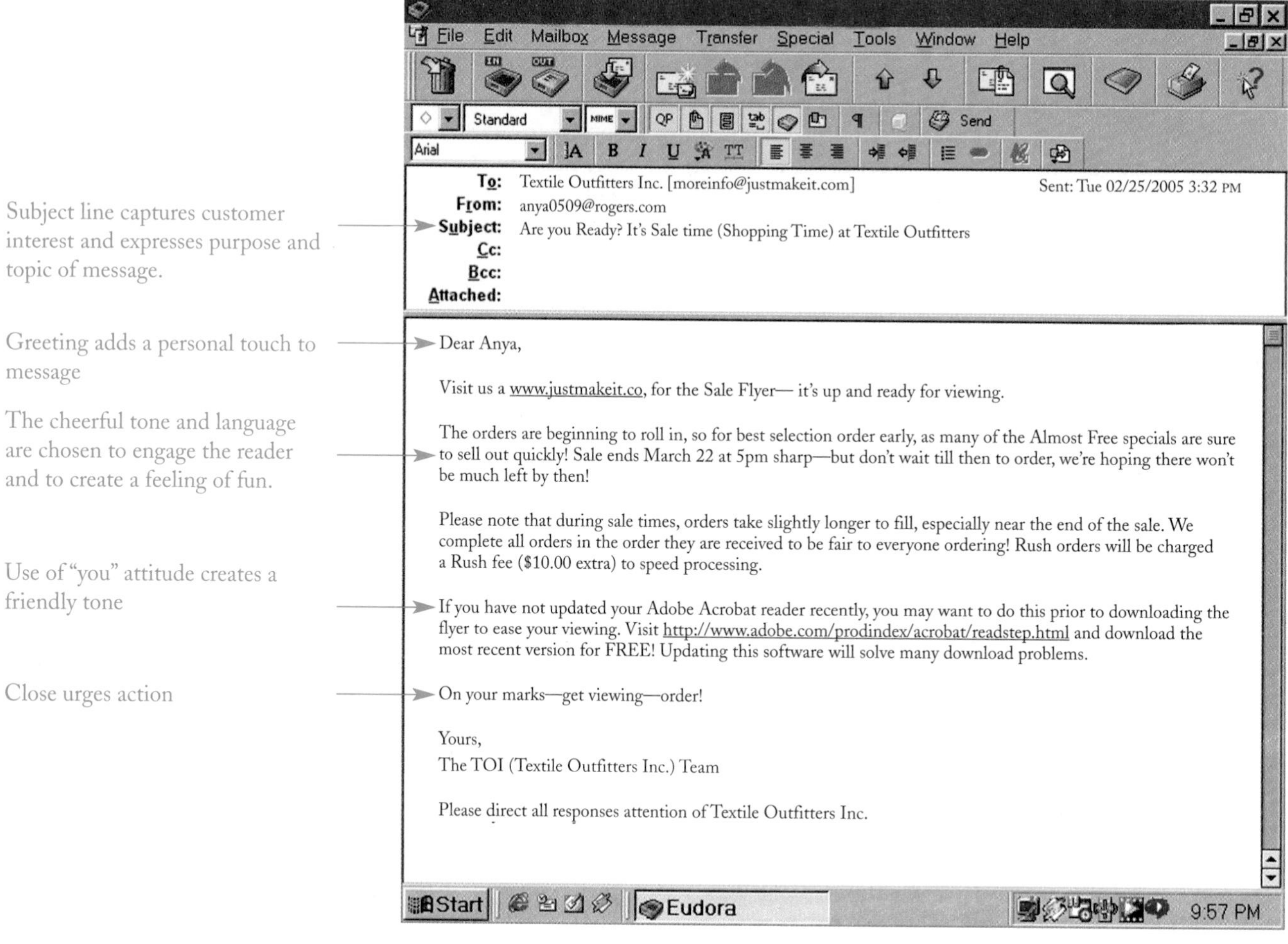

FIGURE 5–8 In-Depth Critique: On-Screen E-Mail Message

The formality of your e-mail depends on your audience and your purpose.

Make responding easy.

Make your e-mail easy to process by
- referring to the sender's message
- using the PDF method
- top loading
- assigning one purpose per e-mail
- providing an informative subject line

Observing E-Mail Etiquette"). As with any business communication, how formal you make your message depends on your audience and your purpose. Just be sure that the style you select is appropriate for the situation.

Also, be sure you use correct spelling and proper grammar in your electronic messages. Although we may be a bit untidy about spelling, grammar, and punctuation when sending e-mail to friends and family, in business situations we must be correct, clear, and easy to understand. Keep in mind that e-mail projects your reputation and the image of your company just as verbal conversations and hard-copy messages do. Like these communication forms, a poorly written e-mail has the same potential to damage your relationship with your customers and clients.

Your e-mail messages should make responding easy. To write e-mail that saves your audience time, follow the guidelines described below. To be sure, companies have different practices regarding e-mail tone and format. Furthermore, e-mail has many uses. It may be routine (such as scheduling meetings or seeking information) or sales-oriented (such as advertising products). In some situations, businesspeople use e-mail to debate an important organizational issue or to convey condolences to a co-worker.[15] For the more routine and positive situations, however, some common rules have evolved to ease the demands that e-mail makes on employees' time. As Chapter 1 mentioned, office workers may receive about 30 e-mail messages a day and take about two hours read, forward, and reply to them.[16]

➤ **Refer to sender's message in your reply** If you are responding to a question or a request for information, be sure to start your e-mail by inserting the original question into your reply. You can preprogram most e-mail software packages to automatically include the sender's original message in your e-mail replies and forwards. Or you can cut and paste the message yourself. Either way, use this feature with care. Save your reader time by editing the original message and including only enough to refresh your readers' memory about why you are sending the e-mail and how it addresses their specific needs.

➤ **Follow the PDF approach for single-screen e-mails.** "PDF" means "purpose, details, and follow-through."[17] When composing an e-mail, give your purpose in the opening paragraph, the details in the body of the message, and the desired action in the close. By observing this method, you are helping your reader understand your point quickly and respond in a timely manner. Figure 5-8 on page 124, an e-mail from a firm that sells sportswear fabrics, follows the PDF approach: the purpose is to motivate the reader to purchase fabric through the firm's sale flyer; the body gives details about selection, timing, ordering, and viewing the sale flyer; and the close urges the reader to place an order. Figure 5-9 on page 126 is an internal e-mail message that uses the PDF approach.

➤ **Top load two-screen e-mails** Reading a long e-mail is cumbersome, especially if it flows onto a second screen. When preparing lengthy e-mails, position not only your purpose, but also your request for action and request for a reply (if needed) near the top of your message. Also preview the body of the e-mail—that is, highlight the topics that will be discussed. Top loading helps ensure that your reader will review your entire message and act on it.[18]

Consider your audience's ease of reading your e-mail on-screen.

➤ **Give your messages a single purpose.** Effective e-mails avoid confusing readers with several purposes. Don't ask your reader to attend a meeting and also congratulate her on surpassing her sales quota in the same e-mail; develop each purpose in separate messages.[19]

➤ **Make your subject line informative.** Effective e-mail subject lines grab audience attention. When e-mail recipients are deciding which messages to read first, they look at who sent each message, they check the subject line, and then they may or may not scan the first few lines. A message with a blank subject line or a general one (such as "Question" or "Read This!") will probably go unread and will perhaps be deleted.

Grab audience attention by making your subject line informative.

Do more than just describe or classify message content. If you need to seek action from your readers, word subject lines to tell them what to do: Saying *Send figures for July sales* is more informative than saying just *July sales figures.* If you are sending information, your subject line should also be informative: Say "Revised Vacation Policy Statement," instead of "Vacation Policy."[20] Here are some other examples:

Tomorrow's meeting	Bring consultant's report to Friday's meeting
Marketing report	Need budget for marketing report
Status report	Warehouse remodelling is on schedule

If you are exchanging multiple e-mails with someone on the same topic, be sure to periodically modify the subject line of your message to reflect the revised message content. Most e-mail programs will copy the subject line when you press the Reply key. However, multiple messages with the same subject line can be confusing. In fact, newer messages may have evolved so that they now have nothing to do with the original topic. Modifying the subject line with each new response can make it easier not only for your audience but also for you to locate a message at a later date.

Change subject lines in multiple e-mails on the same topic.

➤ **Personalize your e-mail message and use a signature file.** Adding a greeting and a closing makes your e-mail more personal.[21] Naturally, whether you use a formal greeting (*Dear Professor Ingersol*) or a more casual one (*Hi Marty*) depends on your audience and your purpose. Your closing and signature also personalize your

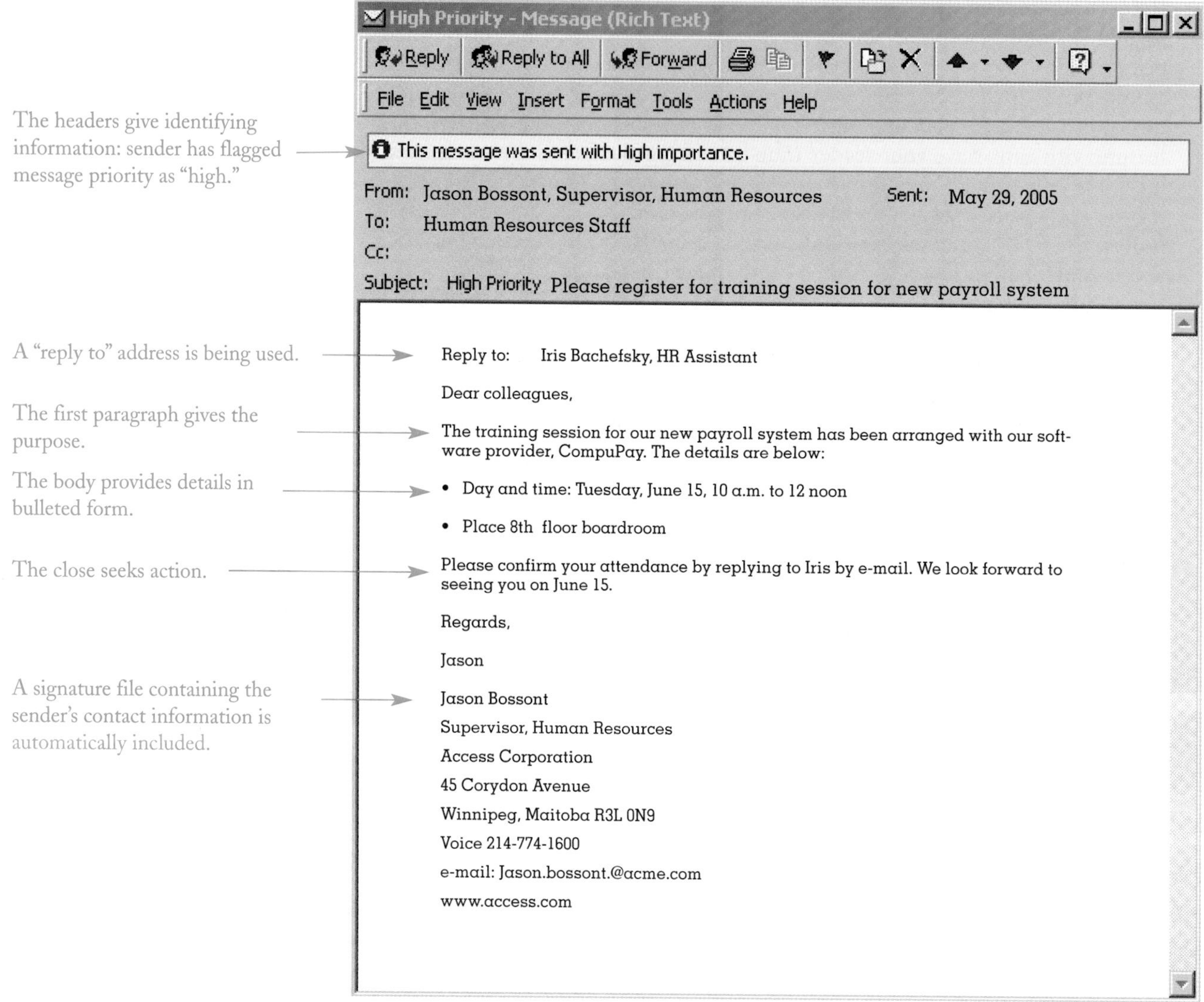

FIGURE 5-9 PDF Structure for E-Mail

e-mail message. In most cases, select simple closings, such as *Thanks* or *Regards,* rather than traditional business closings such as *Sincerely yours.* However, you may want to use a more formal closing for international e-mail.

After a simple closing, you can include a signature in several ways.

For your signature, you can simply type your name on a separate line. Or you may want to use a *signature file,* a short identifier that can include your name, company, postal address, fax number, other e-mail addresses (see Figure 5-9 above). Follow the software's instructions for setting up a signature file, and it will be inserted automatically into your messages. (Avoid emoticons [such as **;)** or **:(**]to personalize your message: they are inappropriate for business.) You can also use a digital copy of your handwritten signature, which is becoming acceptable as legal proof in business transactions, especially when accompanied by a date stamp, which is automatically inserted by your mail program.

Use short paragraphs, lists, headings, and white space to improve the readability of your e-mail messages.

➤ **Make your e-mail easy to follow.** Paragraph length, topic sentences, headings and lists, and white space will ensure your message is read. Write short, focused, logically organized paragraphs, and use topic sentences at the beginning of each paragraph to make your e-mail easy to follow. Skip two lines between paragraphs so that each paragraph stands out. By using bulleted or numbered lists (use a hyphen if your reader's e-mail system will not accept graphical bullets) you will also improve the readability of your message. Headings for lengthy e-mails (use capital letters so that headings are distinct) at the top if main sections will also make your text easy to review.[22]

For an overview of e-mail strategies and etiquette, consult "Checklist: Composing E-mail with Style" below.

Writing Effectively for the Web

The Web is unlike any other medium for which you may be required to write. Whenever readers visit a Web site, they have more than 5 million other cyber-places they could be.[23] More than any other medium, the Web demands that you grab reader

Checklist: Composing E-mail with Style

Create the Right Tone

- ✓ Don't use cyberspace shorthand or offbeat acronyms such as *bcnu* ("be seeing you"), *fwiw* ("for what it's worth"), and *obo* ("or best offer").
- ✓ Avoid smileys and other gimmicks—rely on the strength of your writing to convey your message in the appropriate tone.
- ✓ Use exclamation points sparingly, if at all.

Cultivate Good Communication Skills

- ✓ Keep subject lines truthful—be careful you don't stretch the truth to grab attention.
- ✓ Limit the scope—each e-mail message should have only one purpose.
- ✓ Craft tight, meaningful messages by covering only what is necessary.
- ✓ Write short, direct messages that include all the relevant information.
- ✓ Rely on short, concise sentences to make your message easier to read on screen.
- ✓ Aim for clarity over hype—don't include thinly disguised marketing material.

Make E-mail Easy to Read

- ✓ Use a plain typeface (Times New Roman, Courier, Arial) with a 10- to 12-point font size.
- ✓ Don't yell—avoid writing messages in all uppercase letters.
- ✓ Don't whisper—avoid writing messages in all lowercase letters.
- ✓ Use ample white space—avoid great amounts of text; separate paragraphs with a blank line.
- ✓ Use bullets and headings for clarity and ease of reading.
- ✓ Avoid double spacing.

Make Responsible, Careful Replies

- ✓ Avoid carelessly hitting the "reply to all" button.
- ✓ When you do choose to "reply to all," do so wisely.
- ✓ Keep subject lines relevant—modify them after a few rounds of replies.
- ✓ Slow down—avoid instantaneous responses and think about what you want to say.
- ✓ Re-read your message to ensure it will convey exactly what you want.
- ✓ Carefully edit content, completeness, fluency, grammar, punctuation, and spelling.
- ✓ Correct misspelled proper names.

Handle Attachments Appropriately

- ✓ Ask permission to send long attachments—downloads may impose on recipients' time and could even choke their mailbox so that no other messages can be delivered.
- ✓ Use as few resources as possible by compressing attachments with WinZip or Netzip.
- ✓ In the body of your message, include a synopsis of lengthy attachments.
- ✓ Mention the attachment file name in your e-mail message so that recipients can locate it.
- ✓ Don't forget to attach your attachment.
- ✓ Send virus-free attachments (for short messages, cut and paste attachment contents directly into your e-mail message).

attention quickly, write concisely, and get directly to your point. Although many organizations hire Web designers to create graphics and text for their sites, small business owners with limited resources can set up their own. For people with little or no expertise, products such as Contribute, made by Macromedia **www.macromedia.com** or tools available on Homestead Technologies' Web site **www.homestead.com** help the non-expert create an attractive Internet presence.[24]

Understand the Unique Needs and Expectations of Web Readers

Web readers are impatient to get the information they need.

The rapid pace of business today and the sheer amount of information available have made business readers impatient. As these readers turn to the Internet for information, they develop needs and expectations that are unique to the Web environment. The following terms describe the experience of reading online:

The Web is physically demanding, nonlinear, interactive, and three-dimensional.

- **Cursory.** Racing to digest mountains of information, online readers hunger for instant gratification. They have hundreds of millions of pages to choose from—each page competing for attention.[25] Thus, these Web readers tend to move from Web page to Web page, seeking the most appealing segments of each one in as little time as possible. This skim-and-scan style demands extreme brevity. Web writers must hook readers quickly, write concisely, and get directly to the point.
- **Difficult.** Reading speeds are about 25 percent slower on a monitor than on paper.[26] Screen settings and quality vary, but even using the best monitors, people find reading from a screen to be tiring on the eyes. Moreover, one page of written information can take up multiple screens on the Web, forcing readers to scroll through a document.
- **Nonlinear and interactive.** Although most readers move through a printed document in a fairly linear path, Web readers choose their own path and move about a document in any order they please. This nonlinear interactivity is possible because of **hyperlinks**—the in-text tags that let readers click on a screen element and be instantly transported to information that may be on the same Web page, on a different page in the same Web site, on a page in a different Web site, or just about anywhere on the Web.
- **Three-dimensional.** The ability to jump into, out of, and all around a document gives the Web its three-dimensional format. Consider the Orbitz site. Visitors may arrive from search engines, from the sites of Orbitz alliance partners (such as American or Northwest Airlines), or from online newspaper articles, financial sites, travel sites, and so on. Once visitors arrive (at a page that may or may not be the site's homepage), they decide whether to visit other pages on this site, return to the site later, or go elsewhere.[27]

Being able to access information from all directions is a powerful benefit for readers. But it also makes it difficult for them to judge the depth and scope of a Web site. Moreover, cyber content is always changing. So effective Web writers help readers along by developing a hyperlink structure that is well organized.

Develop a Well-Organized Hyperlink Structure

Your hyperlink structure should help readers find what they need easily.

When writing for the Web, you must incorporate the effective writing skills discussed in this book, but that's not all. You must also coordinate your words with your navigational elements. Your goal is to help readers either find the information they want or bypass the information that is of no interest to them. The following tips will help you develop a well-organized hyperlink structure:

- **Plan your navigation first.** Incorporate navigation as an integral part of your written material, not as an afterthought or an element to be left to a designer or developer.[28] Think about who your readers are and what paths they will follow to get key information.[29] Decide up front how much information you will actually

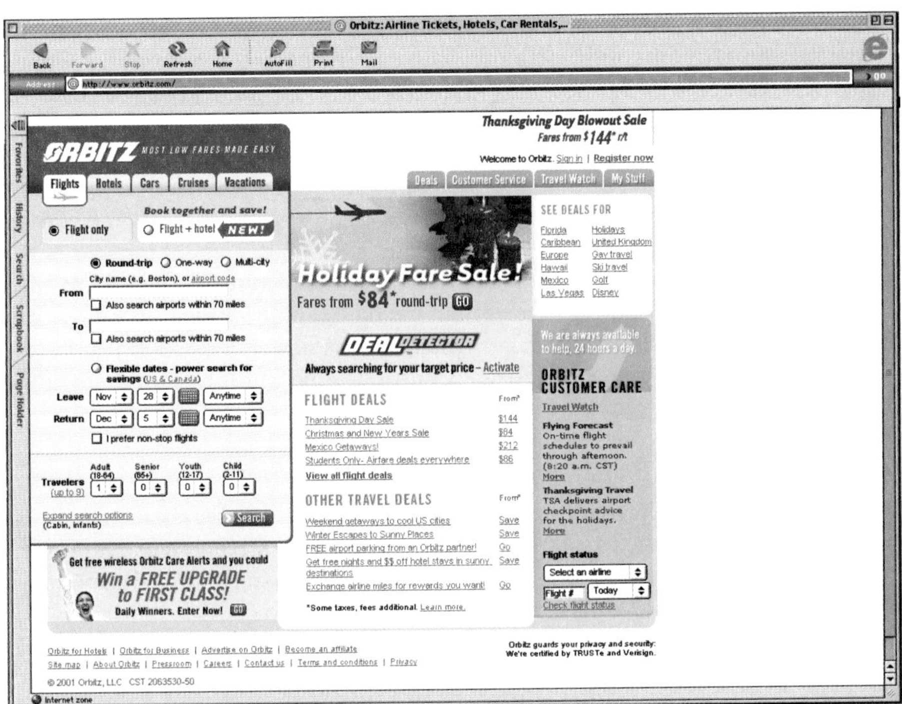

Regardless of how or why visitors arrive at the Orbitz homepage, their initial evaluation of this site determines whether they will explore further or go somewhere else.

write and how much your readers will access via links to other sites. This knowledge saves you writing information that your readers can obtain elsewhere.

➢ **Let your readers be in control.** Help readers move about your document in a smooth, intuitive fashion. Be sure that each step on your navigational path makes sense and leads naturally to the next step. Also, avoid forcing readers to follow a specific path. Let them explore on their own. Consider including a search engine, a site map (an outline of your site's layout that helps readers understand the structure and depth of your site), and an index or a table of contents (placed at the top, side, or bottom margin of your Web page).

➢ **Write effective links.** Links can be words, graphics, phrases, or even complete sentences. You will most likely use a mixture of textual and graphical hyperlinks. If you choose to use graphical links, be careful not to overdo it. Including too many images can slow down the loading time of your Web pages, and you need to accommodate those readers who conserve downloading time by turning off the graphic capabilities in their Web browsers.

Modify Your Message Style and Format

Once you have established a navigational structure for your message, begin composing it in a style and format suitable for the Web. Even though a good design is important for effective Web messages, substantive content is what drives a site's success. One of the most common errors found on corporate Web sites is lackluster copy—messages written without interesting and specific details.[30]

For all the interest in graphics, the Web is content-driven.

MODIFY YOUR MESSAGE FOR GLOBAL AUDIENCES

Web material speaks to everyone around the globe, including people who may speak English only as a second language or not at all. Generally use a lighter, less formal tone—but without being chatty. Also, infuse as much of your organization's or your own personality into your text as possible. But be careful to avoid clever, humorous, or jargon-filled phrases that can be misunderstood by readers from other cultures.

The Web is a global medium

If many of your visitors are overseas, it may pay to have your site and material "localized" to reflect not only a region's native language but local norms, weights, measures, time, currency, and so on. Much more than simply translating your material into another language, localization makes your site and material appear as if it were originally developed in that language.

This process demands a keen understanding of your target audience. You must adapt your style and tone, translate your text, include appropriate design elements (colours, icons, imagery), and develop a navigation system that works for your target culture. For example, local teams would know that the picture of a raised flag on a mailbox indicates mail waiting in Canada but has no meaning for many in Europe and Asia. Such teams would also understand that, in Canadian address books, names are sorted alphabetically, but in some Asian countries, names must be sorted according to the number of keystrokes.[31]

BREAK YOUR INFORMATION INTO CHUNKS

Because reading online is so difficult, you need to help Web readers scan and absorb information more easily. Break text into self-contained, screen-sized chunks (or pages) that may be accessed in any order. Each chunk includes several paragraphs that are brief, are focused, and stick to a single theme.

These theme-related chunks make up one Web page, but that Web page may not necessarily be viewable all at once on your computer screen (readers may have to scroll the screen to see your entire message). Breaking information into manageable chunks and then linking them to other chunks allows you to provide comprehensive coverage in a concise way. Consider these tips:

Carefully divide Web information into chunks.

- **Make the content of each Web page independent.** Don't assume that readers approach your material in a linear order, as they might in a book. Present your message so that readers can understand the subject matter of a Web page regardless of the navigational path they followed to get there.
- **Don't force subdivisions.** Be careful not to make your readers tunnel through too many links to get the information they need. If the information can be succinctly presented in a short paragraph or on a single Web page, hyperlinks aren't necessary.
- **Reduce the length of your text.** Online text should be at least 50 percent shorter than printed text.[32] Try to limit your Web articles to one computer screen. But if doing so is impossible, try not to exceed three full screens of text.
- **Handle longer documents with care.** If your written material is longer than three screens and you cannot break down your concept any further, do not randomly divide it into several Web pages. Illogical interruptions in a single piece of linear material can irritate readers.[33]
- **Provide a printable version of longer documents.** Most readers prefer to print out lengthy documents and read them offline. Provide a print-ready version of your document to which readers can link. Indicate the file size so that readers can gauge how long it will take to download. Also, put your URL in the document title so that the source will print on the page.

ADOPT AN INVERTED PYRAMID STYLE

Make sure your online messages get right to the point and give your readers all the information they need in as little time as possible. One way to do so is to write your material using an inverted pyramid style. Journalists have long used this inverse approach—writing the main idea first and providing the details later. Then readers can stop at any time and still get the most important parts of the article.

Using the inverted pyramid style lets your readers move on quickly without missing the most important information.

The inverted pyramid becomes even more important on the Web, since users don't like to scroll and frequently read only the top portion of an article. This inverted style allows you to place your most important information above the scroll. As with newspapers, this top-level space is prime property, so use it economically. *The Wall Street*

Journal, for example, reserves its front page for short summaries of articles that are discussed in detail on interior pages.

Writing for the Web is a specialized area; if you're given the opportunity to work on a Web page for your company, consult recent books on this intriguing process.

Summary of Learning Outcomes

1 Explain why good organization is important to both the communicator and the audience. Audiences benefit from good organization in several ways. When audience members receive a message that is well organized, they don't have to read and reread a message to make sense of it, so they save time. They are also better able to understand the content, so they can accept the message more easily and can make better decisions based on its information. Communicators also benefit from good organization. When a message is well organized, communicators save time because preparing the message is quicker. Communicators can also use their organization plan to get advance input from their colleagues, making sure they're on the right track. Finally, good organization allows communicators to divide portions of the writing assignment among co-workers.

2 Summarize the process for organizing business messages effectively. The process for organizing messages effectively has four parts, or steps. First, define the main idea of the message by making a specific statement about the topic. Second, limit the scope of the message by adjusting the space and detail you allocate to major points (which should number three to five, regardless of message length). Third, group the points by constructing an outline to visualize the relationship between the ideas and the supporting material. Fourth, choose either a direct or an indirect approach by anticipating the audience's reaction to the message (positive, neutral, or negative) and by matching the approach to message length (short or long) and message type (routine, good-news, and goodwill; bad-news; or persuasive).

3 Discuss two ways of achieving a businesslike tone with a style that is clear and concise. To ensure that messages are businesslike, clear, and concise, start by using a conversational tone: (1) focus on the facts, (2) construct rational arguments, and (3) try to avoid old-fashioned and pompous language, intimacy, humour, and preaching and bragging. Support this conversational tone by using plain English, which is easily understood by anyone with an eighth- or ninth-grade education.

4 Briefly describe how to select words that are not only correct but also effective. To select the best words, first make sure they are correct by checking grammar and usage guides. Next, make sure the words you select are effective by knowing how to use functional and content words. Choose words that have fewer connotations and no negative connotations. Blend abstract words with concrete ones, narrowing from the general to the specific, and select words that communicate clearly, specifically, and dynamically. Select words that are strong, familiar and avoid clichés, and use jargon only when your audience will understand it.

5 Explain four guidelines that help you achieve clarity and efficiency in your sentences. To create effective sentences, follow four guidelines: First, use the active voice to produce shorter, stronger sentences, and use the passive voice to be diplomatic, to avoid taking credit or placing blame, or to create an objective tone. Second, emphasize key ideas by using more words to describe them, by making them the subject of sentences, or by placing them at the beginning or end of sentences. Third, vary sentence length to emphasize points, to enliven the writing, and to make information more appealing to readers. And, fourth, use lists and bullets to set off important ideas, to show the sequence of a process, or to heighten visual impact.

6 List five ways to develop a paragraph and discuss three factors that increase paragraph readability. Paragraphs can be developed by illustration (giving examples), by comparison and contrast (pointing out similarities or differences), by focusing on cause and effect (giving reasons), by classification (discussing categories), and by focusing on the solution to a problem (stating a problem and showing how to solve it). Paragraphs are easier to read when they are short (100 words or fewer), when they are broken up by headings (which highlight and summarize the material covered), and when they occasionally contain questions (which engage reader interest).

7 Explain how to write e-mail messages that capture and keep audience attention. To grab your audience's attention, make your subject lines specific and concrete. Then, organize your message by using the PDF approach: put your purpose in the opening, details in the body, and action in the close. If your message will cover more than one screen, place both the purpose and desired action at the beginning and also preview the topics you'll discuss in the body of the e-mail. Be sure to assign only a single purpose to each e-mail you send, and no more.

ON THE JOB

Solving a Communication Dilemma at McCain Foods

McCain Foods is one of Canada's truly homegrown multinational companies. Founded in 1957 by Harrison McCain, this family-owned firm started in New Brunswick with 30 employees producing about 680 kilograms of potato product an hour. In 2001, the company's annual sales reached 5.3 billion dollars. CEO Howard Mann attributes the firm's success to the independence of its local managers, teamwork, and open communication. "Autonomy has proven to be a breeding ground for creativity," says Mann. "Marketing, sales, and most other decisions are left to our managers who understand their markets." One best practice is frequent meetings among employees with technical skills to brainstorm for better ways to manufacture products and bring them to market. Another is collaboration between customers and suppliers to help the company innovate and maintain quality.

About 60 percent of McCain products are sold through grocery stores and 40 percent through food service outlets, such as restaurants and hospital and corporate cafeterias. The company's communication channels include its extensive multilingual Web site. Divided into separate sites for both the general public and the foodservice trade, it contains information about the company history, leadership, and operations in Canada and worldwide. At both sites, visitors can download brochures about career opportunities and the manufacturing of French fries, enter contests, pick up food preparation tips and recipes, and register at the "Click 'n' Save" link for promotions. At the foodservice site, industry professionals can register at the "Resource Zone" to receive trade-related information and opt to participate in surveys.

In 2000, food industry analysts proclaimed McCain Foods Ltd. as the "Processor of the Century."

Your Mission As a communications assistant at McCain's media office in Florenceville, New Brunswick, you have been asked to compose an e-mail to be sent to middle-level managers in Canada and at McCain's worldwide operations seeking their feedback about the McCain Web site. You have drafted the following e-mail, leaving the to/from/date headers blank until you send it.

> Subject: Web Site
>
> Greetings,
>
> What do you think about the McCain Web site? It's divided into two separate sites; do you think both are equally useful for visitors?
>
> Head office is doing a review of the McCain Web site. Please answer the following questions. Your responses will guide us in improving the site and making it even better for both consumers and industry professionals. Also, please look at our latest news on the Web site for information about our acquisition of Wong Wing Foods of Montreal. The company is Canada's leading manufacturer of authentic Chinese entrées, egg rolls, and dim sum.
>
> What are your favourite features about our Web site? What do you think about the links? Are there any links we should add? What do you think about the design of the site? Do you think we should make it more interactive?
>
> Thanks for taking the time to answer these questions. Please reply to me by June 30. We'll send everyone a summary of suggestions after we've received them.
>
> Regards,
>
> Jim

Now select the best responses to the questions that follow. Be prepared to explain why your choice is best.

1 Is the subject line effective for this e-mail?
- a Yes. Recipients will tell what the e-mail is about after reading it.
- b No, the subject line should express the purpose of the e-mail more effectively.
- c The subject line is fine: because the message comes from head office, receivers will open it, even if the subject line is left blank.
- d The subject line neglects to mention the acquisition of Wong Wing Foods.

2 Does the message conform to the guidelines for good organization?
- a No. The opening paragraph does not directly state the purpose of the message. The e-mail does not get to the point until the second paragraph, and even then the message is confusing.
- b The e-mail includes unnecessary information. It mentions the acquisition of a company in a message that also asks readers to evaluate the company Web site.
- c The message is not well organized. The questions are presented in a confused manner without any plan.
- d The letter is well organized. The subject and purpose are clear. All necessary information is included, and the information is directly related to subject and purpose. Information is grouped and presented logically.

3 Is the message effectively formatted?
- a Yes. Because the message is short, special formatting is needed.
- b No. It should list all the questions using numbers. It should also introduce the list with a statement.
- c No. It should list all questions using bullets.
- d No. It should divide the questions into two separate lists, and use bullets before each one.

4 Which organizational plan should the e-mail follow?
- a Direct. Open with the request, followed by the reasons for it. Organize the questions effectively, end with the statement that employees will receive a summary of the results, and follow with thanks.
- b Indirect. Employees will not want to spend the time answering the questions, so the e-mail will have to persuade them. The first paragraph should give the benefits of answering the questions.
- c Indirect. Start by describing the Web site. Then give the benefits of answering questions, followed by the questions themselves. End with thanks, followed by the statement that employees will receive a summary of the results.[34]

Test Your Knowledge

Review Questions

1 What are the four steps in the process for organizing messages?
2 How does the denotative meaning of a word differ from its connotative meaning?
3 What three elements do you consider when choosing between a direct and an indirect approach?
4 How does the audience benefit from a well-organized message?
5 What is style, and how do you decide on the appropriate style for a message?
6 How does an abstract word differ from a concrete word?
7 In what three situations is passive voice appropriate?
8 What is the purpose of the topic sentence?
9 How do you use the subject line in an e-mail?
10 How can you increase the readability of your paragraphs?
11 What special concerns must you keep in mind when writing for the Web?

Interactive Learning 

Use This Text's Online Resources

Visit our Companion Web site at **www.pearsoned.ca/thill**, where you can use the interactive Study Guide to test your chapter knowledge and get instant feedback. Additional resources link you to the sites mentioned in this text and to additional sources of information on chapter topics.

Also check out the resources on the Mastering Business Communication CD, including "Perils of Pauline," an interactive presentation of the business communication challenges within a fictional company. For Chapter 5, see in particular the episode "Using E-Mail Effectively".

Apply Your Knowledge

Critical Thinking Questions

1 When organizing the ideas for your business message, how can you be sure that what seems logical to you will also seem logical to your audience?
2 Would you use a direct or an indirect approach to ask employees to work overtime to meet an important deadline? Please explain.
3 Which approach would you use to let your boss know that you'll be out half a day this week to attend a close friend's funeral—direct or indirect? Why?
4 Is it ever okay to use an indirect approach when writing e-mail? How can you put off the bad news when you have to state your purpose in the subject line? Explain.
5 **Ethical Choices** Do you think that using an indirect approach to cushion bad news is manipulative? Discuss the ethical issues in your answer.

Practice Your Knowledge

Document for Analysis

A writer is working on an insurance information brochure and is having trouble grouping the ideas logically into an outline. Prepare the outline, paying attention to appropriate subordination of ideas. If necessary, rewrite phrases to give them a more consistent sound.

Accident Protection Insurance Plan

- Coverage is only pennies a day
- Benefit is $100 000 for accidental death on common carrier
- Benefit is $100 a day for hospitalization as result of motor vehicle or common carrier accident
- Benefit is $20 000 for accidental death in motor vehicle accident
- Individual coverage is only $17.85 per quarter; family coverage is just $26.85 per quarter
- No physical exam or health questions
- Convenient payment—billed quarterly
- Guaranteed acceptance for all applicants
- No individual rate increases
- Free, no-obligation examination period
- Cash paid in addition to any other insurance carried

- Covers accidental death when riding as fare-paying passenger on public transportation, including buses, trains, jets, ships, trolleys, subways, or any other common carrier
- Covers accidental death in motor vehicle accidents occurring while driving or riding in or on automobile, truck, camper, motor home, or nonmotorized bicycle

Exercises

5–1 Message Organization: Limiting Scope Suppose you are preparing to recommend that top management install a new heating system (using the cogeneration process). The following information is in your files. Eliminate topics that aren't essential; then arrange the other topics so that your report will give top managers a clear understanding of the heating system and a balanced, concise justification for installing it.

History of the development of the cogeneration heating process
Scientific credentials of the developers of the process
Risks assumed in using this process
Your plan for installing the equipment in your building
Stories about its successful use in comparable facilities
Specifications of the equipment that would be installed
Plans for disposing of the old heating equipment
Costs of installing and running the new equipment
Advantages and disadvantages of using the new process
Detailed 10-year cost projections
Estimates of the time needed to phase in the new system
Alternative systems that management might wish to consider

5–2 Message Organization: Choosing the Approach Indicate whether the direct or the indirect approach would be best in each of the following situations; then briefly explain why. Would any of these messages be inappropriate for e-mail? Explain.

a A letter asking when next year's automobiles will be put on sale locally
b A letter from a recent college graduate requesting a letter of recommendation from a former instructor
c A letter turning down a job applicant
d An announcement that because of high air-conditioning costs, the plant temperature will be held at 78 degrees during the summer
e A final request to settle a delinquent debt

5–3 Message Organization: Planning Persuasive Messages If you were trying to persuade people to take the following actions, how would you organize your argument?

a You want your boss to approve your plan for hiring two new people.
b You want to be hired for a job.
c You want to be granted a business loan.
d You want to collect a small amount from a regular customer whose account is slightly past due.
e You want to collect a large amount from a customer whose account is seriously past due.

5–4 Message Composition: Creating Sentences Suppose that end-of-term frustrations have produced this e-mail message to Professor Anne Brewer from a student who believes he should have received a B in his accounting class. If this message were recast into three or four clear sentences, the teacher might be more receptive to the student's argument. Rewrite the message to show how you would improve it:

> I think I was unfairly awarded a C in your accounting class this term, and I am asking you to change the grade to a B. It was a difficult term. I don't get any money from home, and I have to work mornings at the Pancake House (as a cook), so I had to rush to make your class, and those two times that I missed class were because they wouldn't let me off work because of special events at the Pancake House (unlike some other students who just take off when they choose). On the midterm examination, I originally got a 75 percent, but you said in class that there were two different ways to answer the third question and that you would change the grades of students who used the "optimal cost" method and had been counted off 6 points for doing this. I don't think that you took this into account, because I got 80 percent on the final, which is clearly a B. Anyway, whatever you decide, I just want to tell you that I really enjoyed this class, and I thank you for making accounting so interesting.

5–5 Message Composition: Controlling Style Rewrite the following letter to Mrs. Bruce Crandall (RR #1 New Norway, AB TOB 3L0) so that it conveys a helpful, personal, and interested tone:

> We have your letter of recent date to our Ms. Dobson. Owing to the fact that you neglected to include the size of the dress you ordered, please be advised that no shipment of your order was made, but the aforementioned shipment will occur at such time as we are in receipt of the aforementioned information.

5–6 Message Composition: Selecting Words Write a concrete phrase for each of these vague phrases:

a sometime this spring
b a substantial saving
c a large number attended
d increased efficiency
e expanded the work area
f an incredible computer

5–7 Message Composition: Selecting Words List terms that are stronger than the following:

a ran after
b seasonal ups and downs
c bright
d suddenly rises

5–8 **Message Composition: Selecting Words** As you rewrite these sentences, replace the clichés with fresh, personal expressions:

a Being a jack-of-all-trades, Dave worked well in his new selling job.
b Moving Leslie into the accounting department, where she was literally a fish out of water, was like putting a square peg into a round hole, if you get my drift.
c I knew she was at death's door, but I thought the doctor would pull her through.
d Movies aren't really my cup of tea; as far as I am concerned, they can't hold a candle to a good book.
e It's a dog-eat-dog world out there in the rat race of the asphalt jungle.

5–9 **Message Composition: Selecting Words** Suggest short, simple words to replace each of the following.

a inaugurate
b consummate
c terminate
d advise
e utilize
f alteration
g anticipate
h forwarded
i assistance
j fabricate
k endeavour
l nevertheless
m ascertain
n substantial
o procure

5–10 **Message Composition: Creating Sentences** Rewrite each sentence so that it is active rather than passive:

a The raw data are submitted to the data processing division by the sales representative each Friday.
b High profits are publicized by management.
c The policies announced in the directive were implemented by the staff.
d Our computers are serviced by the Santee Company.
e The employees were represented by Janet Hogan.

5–11 **Message Composition: Selecting Words** Write up-to-date versions of these phrases; write *none* if you think there is no appropriate substitute:

a as per your instructions
b attached herewith
c in lieu of
d in reply I wish to state
e please be advised that

5–12 **Message Composition: Writing Paragraphs** Rewrite the following paragraph to vary the length of the sentences and to shorten the paragraph so it looks more inviting to readers.

> Although major league hockey remains popular, more people are attending women's league hockey games because they can spend less on admission, snacks, and parking and still enjoy the excitement of Canada's pastime. British Columbia has the Vancouver Griffins, the Richmond Steelers, and the North Island Eagles; Quebec has Laval Mistral and Montreal Wingstar; southern Ontario has the Toronto Sting, the Beatrice Aeros, and the Brampton Thunder. These teams play in relatively small arenas, so fans are close enough to see and hear everything, from the smack of the stick hitting the puck to the crash of a body check. Best of all, the cost of a family outing to see rising stars play in a local women's league game is just a fraction of what the family would spend to attend a major league game in a much larger, more crowded arena.

5–13 **Message Composition: Writing Paragraphs** In the following paragraph, identify the topic sentence and the related sentences (those that support the idea of the topic sentence):

> Each year Greet's Great Hamburger Restaurants sponsors the All-Canadian Band, made up of two high-school students from 50 cities. The band marches in Ottawa on Canada Day. Franchisees are urged to join their local Chamber of Commerce, United Way, and the Canadian Legion and other important institutions of Canadian society. Greet's tries hard to project an image of almost a charitable organization. Local outlets sponsor campaigns on fire prevention, bicycle safety, and litter cleanup, with advice from Hamburger Central on how to extract the most publicity from their efforts.[35]

Now add a topic sentence to this paragraph:

> Your company's image includes what a person sees, hears, and experiences in relation to your firm. Every business letter you write is therefore important. The quality of the letterhead and typing, the position of the copy on the page, the format, the kind of typeface used, and the colour of the typewriter ribbon—all these factors play a part in creating an impression of you and your company in the mind of the person to whom you are writing.[36]

5–14 **Teamwork** Working with four other students, divide the following five topics and write one paragraph on your selected topic. Be sure one student writes a paragraph using the illustration technique, one using the comparison-or-contrast technique, one using a discussion of cause and effect, one using the classification technique, and one using a discussion of problem and solution. Then exchange paragraphs within the team and pick out the main idea and general purpose of the paragraph one of your teammates wrote. Was everyone able to correctly identify the main idea and purpose? If not, suggest how the paragraph might be rewritten for clarity.

a Types of cameras (or dogs or automobiles) available for sale
b Advantages and disadvantages of eating at fast-food restaurants
c Finding that first full-time job

d Good qualities of my car (or house, or apartment, or neighbourhood)
e How to make a dessert recipe (or barbecue a steak or make coffee)

5–15 Internet Visit the Security Exchange Commission's (SEC) plain-English Web site at **www.sec.gov**, click on "Online Publications," and review the online handbook. In one or two sentences, summarize what the SEC means by the phrase "plain English." Now read the SEC's online advice about how to invest in mutual funds. Does this document follow the SEC's plain-English guidelines? Can you suggest any improvements to organization, words, sentences, or paragraphs?

5–16 Message Composition: Using Bullets Rewrite the following paragraph using a bulleted list:

> With our alarm system, you'll have a 24-hour security guard who signals the police at the suggestion of an intruder. You'll also appreciate the computerized scanning device that determines exactly where and when the intrusion occurred. No need to worry about electrical failure, either, thanks to our backup response unit.[37]

5–17 Message Organization: Grouping Points Using the Boswell & Sons letter in Figure 5–1 on page 102, draw an organizational chart similar to the one shown in Figure 5–4 on page 107, filling in the main idea, the major points, and the evidence provided in this letter. (Note: Your diagram may be smaller.)

5–18 Ethical Choices Under what circumstances would you consider the use of terms that are high in connotative meaning to be ethical? When would you consider it to be unethical? Explain your reasoning.

Going Online Exercises

Compose a Better Business Message, found on page 112 of this chapter

To be effective, the ideas you express in a written message must be logically organized. The style and tone of your business message are equally important and should fit the occasion and the intended audience. To reinforce what you've learned in this chapter about writing a business message, log on to Purdue University's OWL.

1 Explain why positive wording in a message is more effective than negative wording. Why should you be concerned about the position of good news or bad news in your written message?
2 What six factors of tone should you consider when conveying your message to your audience?
3 What points should you include in the close of your business message? Why?

Completing Business Messages

1 Explain why revision is so important in business, list its three main tasks, and discuss when revision is performed

2 Discuss why it's important to make your message concise and give four tips on how to do so

3 List nine tips for making your writing clear

4 Identify seven issues to keep in mind when critiquing someone else's writing

5 Describe five design elements, explain how they can change a document's appearance, and tell how to use them effectively

6 Outline some of the ways technology helps you produce and distribute your messages

7 Define the types of errors to look for when proofreading

ON THE JOB

Facing a Communication Dilemma at the Confederation Centre of the Arts

Celebrating Canadian Heritage and Culture

www.confederationcentre.com

Gathering information and images, writing, editing, and proofreading copy for brochures and publications, advising spokespeople on media-related issues—these are just some of Anna MacDonald's tasks as publicist for the Confederation Centre of the Arts. Located in Charlottetown, Prince Edward Island, the centre is best known across Canada for its summer-long Charlottetown Festival, featuring the famous *Anne of Green Gables–The Musical*™, the Charlottetown Festival Young Company, and other productions. But the public can also experience the centre's eclectic mix of art forms year-round—plays, such as *Anne of Green Gables, the Musical,* or Young Company and community theatre productions; contemporary and visual art exhibitions in its gallery; performances by popular and classical musicians and dancers.

The primary audience for the messages generated by the publicity office, MacDonald explains, "is the general public—local, national, and international. We hope that the documents we produce will act as a call to action to people, prompting them to purchase tickets to our events and to visit the entire centre, and also to keep the centre in the public eye."

A typical day workday is "never boring and never the same," says MacDonald. Her activities are both individual and collaborative. She works with staff involved in programming to "search out any angles or special features that might be of interest to the media, and draft a press release based on that information." As one example, "local media usually are interested in the 'Island connection'—if a lead actor in one of our productions is from the Island, or an artist whose work is shown in the gallery." Press releases are one way Macdonald reaches her audiences. Usually distributed by e-mail, press releases are typically limited to 500 words and include an "in brief" version for on-air public service announcements and a longer version for print media.

Put yourself in the position of Anna MacDonald. As a publicist for the Confederation Centre of the Arts, how would you polish the documents you create? What details would you look at for revision? What process would you follow to assess your own writing and that of your colleagues?[1]

P.E.I.'s Confederation Centre of the Arts fulfills its mandate to inspire all Canadians to celebrate Canadian heritage and culture through theatre, music, and the visual arts. The Centre's communications make Canadians aware of this important institution, established in 1964 as Canada's National Memorial to the Fathers of Confederation.

Moving Beyond Your First Draft

Once you've completed the first draft of your message, you may be tempted to breathe a sigh of relief and get on with the next project. Resist the temptation. As professional communicators such as Anna MacDonald are aware, the first draft is rarely good enough. In a first attempt, most writers don't say what they want to say—or don't say it as well as they could. You owe it to yourself and to your audience to review and refine your messages before sending them. Plan to go over a document at least three times: one pass for content and organization, one for style and readability, and one for mechanics and format.

You might wonder whether all this effort to fine-tune a message is worthwhile. The fact is, people in business care very much about saying precisely the right thing in precisely the right way. Multiple review of the same message helps to ensure that the receiver will be able to understand and act exactly as the sender intends.

After revising, producing, and proofreading a message, you must also check its design and mechanics.

Even after you've fine-tuned your written message, your work is not finished. Look back at the diagram of the three-step writing process (Figure 4.1 on page 73). Notice that completing your message consists of three tasks: revising, producing, and proofreading. To complete your business message, check its design and mechanics, and distribute it to your audience. Start by evaluating the document as a whole before looking at details. Focusing on the big picture first is more efficient, since you won't be wasting time perfecting sections that you may eventually eliminate or change substantially.

Revising Your Message

OBJECTIVE 1 Explain why revision is so important in business, list its three main tasks, and discuss when revision is performed.

Although the tendency is to separate revision from composition, revision is an ongoing activity that occurs throughout the writing process. Revise as you go along, then revise again after you've completed the first draft. Constantly search for the best way to say something, probe for the right words, test alternative sentences, reshape, tighten, and juggle the elements that already exist. The draft in Figure 6–1 on page 139 responds to Beverly Friesen's request for information about the Commerce Hotel's frequent-guest program. It has been edited using the proofreading marks shown in Appendix D. Figure 6–2 on page 140 shows how the letter looks with all the revisions incorporated—providing the requested information in a more organized fashion, in a friendlier style, and with clearer mechanics.

Evaluate Your Content and Organization

After a day or two, review your message for content and organization.

Ideally, let your draft age a day or two before you begin the revision process so that you can approach the material with a fresh eye. Then read through the document quickly to evaluate its overall effectiveness. Focus mainly on content, organization, and flow. Compare the draft with your original plan. Have you covered all your points in the most logical order? Is there a good balance between the general and the specific? Are the most important ideas developed adequately? Have you provided enough support and double-checked the facts? Would the message be more convincing if it were arranged in another sequence? Do you need to add anything? Be sure to consider the effect your words will actually have on readers, not just the effect you *plan* for them to have.

The beginning and end of a message have the greatest impact on readers.

In this first pass, spend a few extra moments on the beginning and ending of the message. These are the sections that have the greatest impact on the audience. Be sure that the opening of a letter or memo is relevant, interesting, and geared to the reader's probable reaction. In longer messages, check to see that the first few paragraphs establish the subject, purpose, and organization of the material. Review the conclusion to be sure that it summarizes the main idea and leaves the audience with a positive impression. Make sure you achieve the right tone and interest level.

November 11, 2005

Ms. Beverley Friesen
Corporate Travel Department
Brother's Electric Corporation
633 Bay Street
Toronto, ON M5G 2G4

Dear Ms. Friesen:

I enjoyed our recent conversation regarding the FG program and am delighted to hear that the people at Brother's Electric are thinking about joining. Incidentally, we are planning a special Thanksgiving weekend rate, so keep that in mind in case you happen to be in San Francisco for the holiday.

The enclosed brochure explains the details of the FG program. Your FG ID card is enclosed. Use it whenever you make reservations with us to obtain a corporate discount. We will see to it that your executives are treated with special courtesy and that they get to use the health club free. We also have excellent convention facilities and banquet rooms should you want to book a convention or meeting here. We hope you and your company will take advantage of these outstanding world class amenities. Please call me if you have any questions. I will be happy to answer them.

Sincerely,

Mary Cortez
Account Representative

Content and organization: In the first paragraph, keep to the main idea. In the middle highlight the key advantage of the frequent-guest program, and discuss details in a subsequent paragraph. Eliminate redundancies.

Style and readability: Reword to stress the "you" viewpoint. Clarify the relationships among ideas through placement and combination of phrases. Moderate the excessive enthusiasm, and eliminate words (such as *amenities*) that might be unfamiliar to your reader.

Mechanics and format: To prevent confusion, spell out the abbreviated phrase FG.

FIGURE 6–1 In-Depth Critique: Sample Edited Letter

Review Your Style and Readability

Once you're satisfied with the content and structure of your message, make a second pass to look at its style and readability, editing for conciseness and clarity. Ask yourself whether you have achieved the right tone for your audience. Look for opportunities to make the material more interesting through the use of strong words and phrases, as discussed in Chapter 5.

At the same time, be particularly conscious of whether your message is readable. You want your audience to understand you with a minimum of effort. Check your vocabulary and sentence structure to be sure you're relying mainly on familiar terms and simple, direct statements. You might even apply a readability formula to gauge the difficulty of your writing.

333 Sansome Street ➢ San Francisco, CA 94104
(800) 323-7347 ➢ (415) 854-2447 ➢ Fax (415) 854-7669
www.CommerceHotel.com

November 11, 2005

Ms. Beverley Friesen
Corporate Travel Department
Brother's Electric Corporation
633 Bay Street
Toronto, ON M5G 2G4

Dear Ms. Friesen:

The first paragraph now provides a "you" attitude, spells out what was previously abbreviated, and contains only relevant material.

Thank you for your interest in the frequent-guest program at the Commerce Hotel. We are delighted to hear that the people at Brother's Electric are thinking about joining.

The second paragraph now clarifies the benefits of the frequent-guest program and personalizes those benefits with the "you" style.

The enclosed brochure explains the details of the frequent-guest program. As a corporate member, Brother's Electric will be entitled to a 20 percent discount on all rooms and services. To obtain your corporate discount, use the enclosed ID card whenever you make reservations with us. Your executives will receive special courtesy, including free use of the health club.

The last paragraph now combines a final benefit with more information about services available. It also concludes with a friendly tone.

Organizations enrolled in the frequent-guest program also qualify for discounts on convention facilities and banquet rooms. We hope you and your company will take advantage of these facilities the next time you book a convention. Please call me if you have any questions. I will be happy to answer them.

Sincerely,

Mary Cortez

Mary Cortez
Account Representative

FIGURE 6–2 In-Depth Critique: Final Revised Letter

GAUGE READING LEVEL

Readability formulas gauge reading level.

The most common readability formulas measure the length of words and sentences to give you a rough idea of how well educated your audience must be to understand your message. Figure 6–3 on page 142 shows how one readability formula, the Fog Index, has been applied to an excerpt from a memo. (For more on this topic, visit **www.profusion.com**, and enter "Fog Index" in the search box.) As the calculation shows, anyone who reads at a grade nine level should be able to read this passage with ease. For technical documents, you can aim for an audience that reads at a grade twelve level or higher; for general business messages, your writing should be geared to readers at the grade eight to grade eleven level. The Fog Index of popular business publications such as *Canadian Business*, the *Wall Street Journal*, and *Forbes* magazine is somewhere between 10 and 11.

Of course, readability indexes can't be applied to languages other than English. Counting syllables makes no sense in other languages. For example, compare the

English *forklift driver* with the German *Gabelstaplerfahrer.* Also, Chinese and Japanese characters don't lend themselves to syllable counting at all.[2]

Readability formulas are easy to apply; many are commonly done by computer. However, they ignore some important variables that contribute to reading ease, such as sentence structure, the organization of ideas, the appearance of the message on the page, and word choice.[3] To fully evaluate the readability of your message, ask yourself whether you have effectively emphasized the important information. Are your sentences easy to understand? Do your paragraphs have clear topic sentences? Are the transitions between ideas obvious?

Readability depends on word choice, sentence length, sentence structure, organization, and the message's physical appearance.

EDIT AND REWRITE YOUR MESSAGE

Once most businesspeople produce a first draft, they make one of two mistakes: they shuffle words around on the page rather than actually make improvements, or they think rewriting is too time consuming and send the document out the moment that last period hits the page.[4]

With a minimal amount of solid rewriting, you will end up with a stronger document. As you edit your business message, you'll find yourself rewriting sentences, passages, and even whole sections to improve their effectiveness. Of course, you're probably also facing a deadline, so try to stick to the schedule you set during the planning stage of the project. Do your best to revise and rewrite thoroughly but also economically.

As you rewrite, concentrate on how each word contributes to an effective sentence and how that sentence develops a coherent paragraph. Sometimes you'll find that the most difficult problem in a sentence can be solved by simply removing the problem itself. When you find yourself with a troublesome element, ask, "Do I need it at all?" Probably not. In fact, you may find that it was giving you so much grief because it was trying to do an unnecessary job.[5] Once you remove the troublesome element, the afflicted sentence will spring to life. Before you delete anything, keep copies of your previous versions as a paper trail for future reference. If you don't know already, learn how to use the "compare documents" or "versions" features on your wordprocessing software: it's a handy way to save drafts of your letters, memos, and reports.

OBJECTIVE 2 Discuss why it's important to make your message more concise and give four tips on how to do so.

Revise for Conciseness Many business documents are swollen with unnecessary words and phrases. In fact, most first drafts can be cut substantially. Your supervisors, as well as fellow employees, are more likely to read documents that efficiently say what needs to be said, so it's important to weed out unnecessary material. Examine every word you put on paper, and strip every sentence to its cleanest components: eliminate every word that serves no function, replace every long word that could be a short word, and remove every adverb that adds nothing to the meaning already carried in the verb. For instance, *very* can be a useful word to achieve emphasis, but more often it's clutter. There's no need to call someone *very* methodical. Either someone is methodical or not. As you begin your editing task, simplify, prune, and strive for order. See Table 6–1 on page 143 for examples of the following tips:

Conciseness means efficiency.

- **Delete unnecessary words and phrases.** Some combinations of words have more efficient, one-word equivalents. In addition, too many or poorly placed relative pronouns (*who, that, which*) can cause clutter. Even articles can be excessive (too many *the*'s). However, well-placed relative pronouns and articles prevent confusion.
- **Shorten long words and phrases.** Short words are generally more vivid and easier to read than long ones are. The idea is to use short, simple words, *not* simple concepts.[6] Also, by using infinitives in place of some phrases, you not only shorten your sentences, but also make them clearer.
- **Eliminate redundancies.** In some word combinations, the words tend to say the same thing. For instance, "visible to the eye" is redundant because *visible* is enough; nothing can be visible to the ear.

Remove unneeded repetition.

Short words and infinitives are generally more vivid than long words and phrases, and they improve the readability of a document.

FIGURE 6–3 The Fog Index

1. **Select a writing sample.**
   Keep the sample between 100 and 125 words long.

   I called Global Corporation to ask when we will receive copies of its insurance policies and engineering reports. Cindy Turner of Global said that they are putting the documents together and will send them by Express Mail next week. She told me that they are late because most of the information is in the hands of Global's attorneys in Montreal. I asked why it was in Montreal; we had understood that the account is serviced by the client's Halifax branch. Turner explained that the account originally was sold to Global's Montreal division, so all paperwork stays there. She promised to telephone us when the package is ready to ship.

2. **Determine average sentence length.**
   Count the number of words in each sentence. Treat independent clauses (stand-alone word groups containing subject and predicate) as separate sentences. For example, "In school we studied; we learned; we improved" counts as three sentences. Then add the word counts for all the sentences to get the total word count, and divide that by the number of sentences. This excerpt has an average sentence length of 14 words:

   $$18 + 21 + 21 + 7 + 13 + 12 + 5 + 12 = 109$$
   $$109 \text{ words} - 8 \text{ sentences} = 14$$

3. **Determine percentage of long words.**
   Count the number of long words—that is, all words that have three or more syllables (underlined in excerpt). Do not count proper nouns, combinations of short words (such as *paperwork* and *anyway*), and verbs that gain a third syllable by adding -es or -ed (as in *trespasses* and *created*). Divide the number of long words by the total number of words in the sample and multiply the answer by 100. The percentage of long words in this excerpt is 10 percent:

   $$11 \text{ long words} \div 109 \text{ total words} = 10 \text{ percent}$$

4. **Determine the grade level required to read the passage.**
   Add the numbers of average sentence length and percentage of long words. Multiply the sum by 0.4, and drop the number following the decimal point (if there is one). The grade level required to easily read this excerpt is 9:

   $$14 \text{ words per sentence} + 10 \text{ percent long words} = 24$$
   $$24 \times 0.4 = 9.6 - 0.6 = 9 \text{ (Fog Index)}$$

Avoid starting sentences with *it* and *there*.

➤ **Recast *It is/There are* starters.** If you begin a sentence with an indefinite pronoun such as *it* or *there,* the sentence could probably be shorter.

OBJECTIVE 3 List nine tips for making your writing clear.

Revise for Clarity Good writing doesn't come naturally, though most people think it does. Writers must constantly ask, "What am I trying to say?" Surprisingly, they often don't know. Then they must look at what they have written and ask, "Have I said what I wanted to say? Will the message be clear to someone encountering the subject for the first time?" If either answer is no, it's usually because the writer hasn't been careful enough.[7]

Clarity avoids confusion.

Carelessness can take any number of forms. Perhaps the sentence is so cluttered that the reader can't unravel it; perhaps it's so poorly constructed that the reader can interpret it in several ways. Perhaps the writer switches pronouns or tense in the

TABLE 6–1 Revising for Conciseness

Examples	Unacceptable	Preferable
Unnecessary Words and Phrases		
Using wordy phrases	for the sum of	for
	in the event that	if
	on the occasion of	on
	prior to the start of	before
	in the near future	soon
	have the capability of	can
	at this point in time	now
	due to the fact that	because
	in view of the fact that	because
	until such time as	when
	with reference to	about
Using too many relative pronouns	Cars sold that are after January will not have a six-month warranty.	Cars sold after January will not have a six-month warranty.
	Employees who are driving to work should park in the underground garage.	Employees driving to work should park in the underground garage.
Using too few relative pronouns	The project manager told the engineers last week the specifications were changed.	The project manager told the engineers last week *that* the specifications were changed.
Long Words and Phrases		
Using overly long words	During the preceding year, the company accelerated productive operations.	Last year the company sped up operations.
	The action was predicated on the assumption that the company was operating at a financial deficit.	The action was based on the belief that the company was losing money.
Using wordy phrases rather than infinitives	If you want success as a writer, you must work hard.	To be a successful writer, you must work hard.
	He went to the library for the purpose of studying.	He went to the library to study.
	The employer increased salaries so that she could improve morale.	The employer increased salaries to improve morale.
Redundancies		
Repeating meanings	absolutely complete	complete
	basic fundamentals	fundamentals
	follows after	follows
	reduce down	reduce
	free and clear	free
	refer back	refer
	repeat again	repeat
	collect together	collect
	future plans	plans
	return back	return
	important essentials	essentials
	midway between	between
	end result	result
	actual truth	truth
	final outcome	outcome
	uniquely unusual	unique
	very unique	unique
	surrounded on all sides	surrounded
Using double modifiers	modern, up-to-date equipment	modern equipment
"It Is/There Are" Starters		
Starting sentences with *it* or *there*	It would be appreciated if you would sign the lease today.	Please sign the lease today.
	There are five employees in this division who were late to work today.	Five employees in this division were late to work today.

middle of the sentence, so that the reader loses track of who is talking or when the event took place. Perhaps sentence B does not logically follow sentence A; or perhaps the writer uses a word incorrectly by not taking the trouble to look it up.[8]

Writing is hard work and takes practice. The more you write, whether on the job or for pleasure, the better writer you'll become. A clear sentence is no accident. Few sentences come out right the first time, or even the third time. See Table 6–2 on the next page for examples of the following tips:

In many cases, the parts of a compound sentence should be separated into two sentences.

- **Divide overly long sentences.** Don't connect too many clauses by *and.* If you find yourself stuck in a long sentence, you're probably trying to make the sentence do more than it can reasonably do, such as express two dissimilar thoughts. You can often clarify your writing style by separating the string into individual sentences.

Don't be afraid to present your opinions without qualification.

- **Rewrite hedging sentences.** Sometimes you have to write *may* or *seems* to avoid stating a judgment as a fact. Nevertheless, when you have too many such hedges, you aren't really saying anything.

When you use the same grammatical pattern to express two or more ideas, you show that they are comparable thoughts.

- **Impose parallelism.** When you have two or more similar (parallel) ideas to express, use the same grammatical pattern for each related idea—parallel construction. Repeating the pattern makes your message more readable by telling readers the ideas are comparable and adding rhythm. Parallelism can be achieved by repeating the pattern in words, phrases, clauses, or entire sentences (see Table 6–3 on page 146).

Make sure that modifier phrases are really related to the subject of the sentence.

- **Correct dangling modifiers.** Sometimes a modifier is not just an adjective or an adverb but an entire phrase modifying a noun or a verb. Be careful not to leave this type of modifier dangling with no connection to the subject of the sentence. The first unacceptable example under "Dangling Modifiers" in Table 6–2 on page 145 implies that the red sports car has both an office and the legs to walk there. The second example shows one frequent cause of dangling modifiers: passive construction.

Stringing together a series of nouns may save a little space, but it causes confusion.

- **Reword long noun sequences.** When nouns are strung together as modifiers, the resulting sentence is hard to read. You can clarify the sentence by putting some of the nouns in a modifying phrase. Although you add a few more words, your audience won't have to work as hard to understand the sentence.

Turning verbs into nouns or adjectives weakens your writing style.

- **Replace camouflaged verbs.** Watch for word endings such as *-ion, -tion, -ing, -ment, -ant, -ent, -ence, -ance,* and *-ency.* Most of them change verbs into nouns and adjectives. Delete them. Another bad habit is to transform verbs into nouns (writing "we performed an analysis of" rather than "we analyzed"). To prune and enliven your messages, use verbs instead of noun phrases.

Subject and predicate should be placed as close together as possible, as should modifiers and the words they modify.

- **Clarify sentence structure.** Keep the subject and predicate of a sentence as close together as possible. When subject and predicate are far apart, readers have to read the sentence twice to figure out who did what. Similarly, adjectives, adverbs, and prepositional phrases usually make the most sense when they're placed as close as possible to the words they modify.

Be specific in your references.

- **Clarify awkward references.** To save words, business writers sometimes use expressions such as *the above-mentioned, as mentioned above, the aforementioned, the former, the latter,* and *respectively.* These words cause readers to jump from point to point, which hinders effective communication. Use specific references, even if you must add a few more words.

Business writing shouldn't be gushy.

- **Moderate your enthusiasm.** An occasional adjective or adverb intensifies and emphasizes your meaning, but too many can ruin your writing. And, when using an adjective or adverb to enhance your meaning, be accurate and concrete. The word "incredibly" is often used incorrectly to describe a quality. One example is the sentence "This chocolate ice cream is incredibly good." The word "incredible" means "not to be believed." A better way of expressing the idea is "This delicious ice cream is made from Dutch chocolate and with more cream than the leading brand."

TABLE 6–2 Revising for Clarity

Examples	Unacceptable	Preferable
Overly Long Sentences		
Taking compound sentences too far	The magazine will be published January 1, and I'd better meet the deadline if I want my article included.	The magazine will be published January 1. I'd better meet the deadline if I want my article included.
Hedging Sentences		
Overqualifying sentences	I believe that Mr. Johnson's employment record seems to show that he may be capable of handling the position.	Mr. Johnson's employment record shows that he is capable of handling the position.
Unparallel Sentences		
Using dissimilar construction for similar ideas	Miss Simms had been drenched with rain, bombarded with telephone calls, and her boss shouted at her.	Miss Simms had been drenched with rain, bombarded with telephone calls, and shouted at by her boss.
	Ms. Singh dictated the letter, and next she signed it and left the office.	Ms. Singh dictated the letter, signed it, and left the office.
	To waste time and missing deadlines are bad habits.	Wasting time and missing deadlines are bad habits.
	Interviews are a matter of acting confident and to stay relaxed.	Interviews are a matter of acting confident and staying relaxed.
Dangling Modifiers		
Placing modifiers close to the wong nouns and verbs	Walking to the office, a red sports car passed her.	A red sports car passed her while she was walking to the office.
	Working as fast as possible, the budget was soon ready.	Working as fast as possible, the committee soon had the budget ready.
	After a three-week slump, we increased sales.	After a three-week slump, sales increased.
Long Nouns Sequences		
Stringing too many nouns together	The window sash installation company will give us an estimate on Friday.	The company that installs window sashes will give us an estimate on Friday.
Camouflaged Verbs		
Changing verbs and nouns into adjectives	The manager undertook implementation of the rules.	The manager implemented the rules.
	Verification of the shipments occurs weekly.	Shipments are verified weekly.
Changing verbs into nouns	reach a conclusion about make a discovery of give consideration to	conclude discover consider
Sentence Structure		
Separating subject and predicate	A 10 percent decline in market share, which resulted from quality problems and an aggressive sales campaign by Armitage, the market leader in the Northeast, was the major problem in 2004.	The major problem in 2004 was a 10 percent loss of market share, which resulted from both quality problems and an aggressive sales campaign by Armitage, the market leader in the Northeast.
Separating adjectives, adverbs, or prepositional phrases from the words they modify	Our antique desk is suitable for busy executives with thick legs and large drawers.	With its thick legs and large drawers, our antique desk is suitable for busy executives.
Awkward References	The Law Office and the Accounting Office distribute computer supplies for legal secretaries and beginning accountants, respectively.	The Law Office distributes computer supplies for legal secretaries; the Accounting Office distributes those for beginning accountants.
Too Much Enthusiasm	We are extremely pleased to offer you a position on our staff of exceptionally skilled staff and highly educated employees. The work offers extraordinary challenges and a very large salary.	We are pleased to offer you a position on our staff of skilled and well-educated employees. The work offers challenges and an attractive salary.

TABLE 6–3 Achieving Parallelism

Method	Example
Parallel words:	The letter was approved by Clausen, Whittaker, Merlin, and Carlucci.
Parallel phrases:	We have beaten the competition in supermarkets, in department stores, and in specialty stores.
Parallel clauses:	I'd like to discuss the issue after Vicki gives her presentation but before Raj shows his slides.
Parallel sentences:	In 1998 we exported 30 percent of our production. In 1999 we exported 50 percent.

Give Others Specific, Constructive Criticism

OBJECTIVE 4 Identify seven issues to keep in mind when critiquing someone else's writing.

In Chapter 2, we discussed guidelines and challenges for effective team writing. We explained that before you begin writing collaboratively, your team must agree on the purpose of the project and on the audience, as well as on the organization, format, and style of the document.

Whether you're writing in teams or reviewing a document prepared by someone else for your signature, you will need to assess the writing of another. When doing so, be sure to provide specific, constructive comments. To help the writer make meaningful changes, you need to say more than simply "This doesn't work" or "This isn't what I wanted" or "I don't see what you're trying to say."[9] Keep in mind that as a team member, you are as responsible for the message's content and style as the actual author.

When critiquing the writing of another, make constructive comments in four areas:

- Assignment instructions
- Intended purpose
- Factual material
- Language clarity

When evaluating a document, concentrate on four elements:[10]

- **Are the assignment instructions clear?** Be sure to determine whether the directions given with the initial assignment were clear and complete. Making sure that directions are specific and understandable saves time for both the writer and the person giving the critique.
- **Does the document accomplish the intended purpose?** Is the purpose clearly stated? Does the body support the stated purpose? You could outline the key points to see whether they support the main idea. Is the conclusion supported by the data? Are the arguments presented logically? If the document fails to accomplish its purpose, it must be rewritten.
- **Is the factual material correct?** A proposal to provide a company with computer-training services for $750 000 would be disastrous if your intention was to provide those services for $75 000. Be sure you pay strict attention to detail. Professionals such as the Confederation Centre's Anna MacDonald know that factual errors, such as the wrong dates for a play's run, will affect ticket sales as well as the image of the organization.
- **Does the document use unambiguous language?** Readers must not be allowed to interpret the meaning in any way other than intended. If you interpret a message differently from what the writer intended, the writer is at fault, and the document must be revised to clarify problem areas.

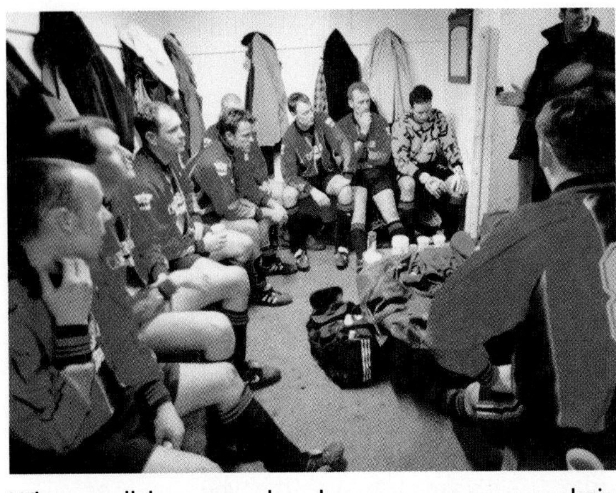

What parallels can you draw between post-game analysis and editing business messages? What do coaches look for when reviewing a game that their team either won or lost? Can you adapt the process coaches use to editing your own work?

If any of these elements needs attention, the document must be rewritten or revised. However, once these elements are deemed satisfactory, the question is whether to request other changes. Minor changes can be made at any time in the critiquing process. But if these criteria are in fact met, consider these additional points before requesting a major revision:[11]

- **Can the document truly be improved?** The answer to this question is usually yes—given enough time.

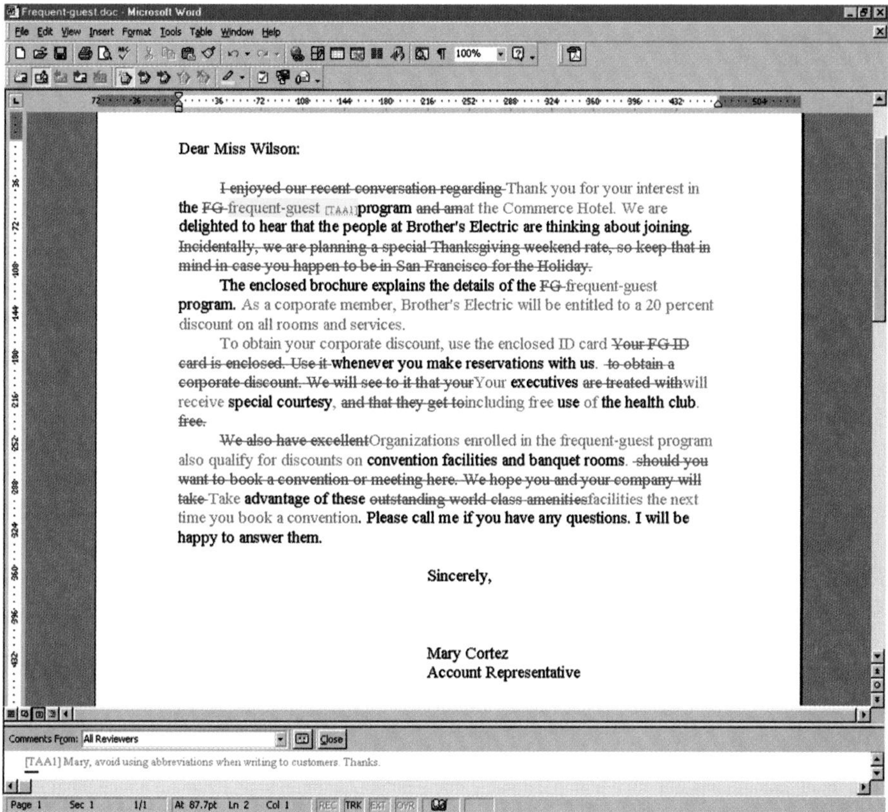

Dear Miss Wilson:

~~I enjoyed our recent conversation regarding~~ Thank you for your interest in the ~~FG~~ frequent-guest [TAA1] program ~~and am~~at the Commerce Hotel. We are delighted to hear that the people at Brother's Electric are thinking about joining. ~~Incidentally, we are planning a special Thanksgiving weekend rate, so keep that in mind in case you happen to be in San Francisco for the Holiday.~~

The enclosed brochure explains the details of the ~~FG~~ frequent-guest program. As a corporate member, Brother's Electric will be entitled to a 20 percent discount on all rooms and services.

To obtain your corporate discount, use the enclosed ID card ~~Your FG ID card is enclosed. Use it~~ whenever you make reservations with us. ~~to obtain a corporate discount. We will see to it that your~~Your executives ~~are treated with~~will receive special courtesy, ~~and that they get to~~including free use of the health club. ~~free.~~

~~We also have excellent~~Organizations enrolled in the frequent-guest program also qualify for discounts on convention facilities and banquet rooms. ~~should you want to book a convention or meeting here. We hope you and your company will take~~ Take advantage of these ~~outstanding world class amenities~~facilities the next time you book a convention. Please call me if you have any questions. I will be happy to answer them.

Sincerely,

Mary Cortez
Account Representative

[TAA1] Mary, avoid using abbreviations when writing to customers. Thanks.

FIGURE 6–4 Computer-Edited Text.

Going Online

Write It Right: Rethink and Revise

Are you sure that readers perceive your written message as you intended? If you want help revising a message that you're completing, use the Paradigm Online Writing Assistant (POWA). With this interactive writer's guide, you can select topics to get tips on how to edit your work, reshape your thoughts, and rewrite for clarity. Read discussions about perfecting your writing skills, and for practice, complete one of the many online activities provided to reinforce what you've learned. Or select the Forum to "talk" about writing. At POWA's Web site, you'll learn how to improve the final draft of your message.

www.powa.org

To link directly to this site, visit our Companion Web site at **www.pearsoned.ca/thill** *and look for the Chapter 6 resources.*

- **Can you justify the time needed for a rewrite or a revision?** Will deadlines be missed? Will other priorities suffer from a delay? For example, if a production line is down and the document in question is a description of what's wrong or how to fix it, any polishing beyond accuracy and clarity is secondary to getting the production line running again.
- **Will your request have a negative impact on morale?** Are the changes to be made a purely personal preference? If you regularly make unexplained or inconsistent changes to a person's writing, that writer can become demoralized. (Of course, consistent style preferences can always be suggested for future use.)

Evaluating the work of another is often accomplished using *groupware.* As mentioned in Chapter 2, this sort of software allows many people to compose and edit a single document at the same time from different locations. In addition, groupware tracks each person's revisions so that if you later have a question or recommendation, you can easily identify the author of that revision. Figure 6–4 above shows a screen of text edited by a wordprocessor, which keeps track of proposed changes and provides a history of a document's revisions. For a reminder of the tasks involved in revision, see this chapter's "Checklist: Revising Business Messages" on page 148.

Producing Your Message

Even after you have rewritten your message from start to finish, you're not finished. Once you're satisfied with your message's content and organization, style and readability, word choice, sentence style, and paragraph development, you'll want to produce your message in some form that allows you to check it for appearance, accuracy, and mechanics.

OBJECTIVE 5 Describe five design elements, explain how they can change a document's appearance, and tell how to use them effectively.

Design Your Message Carefully

Design affects the impression your message makes.

An attractive, professional appearance can help you get your message across effectively. When designing your message, balancing graphics and text is important. Consider the letter in Figure 6–5 on page 149. The use of boldface and bullets, as well as the short- and medium-length paragraphs, invite the reader's attention and respect. The way you package your ideas has a lot to do with how successful your communication will be. Your readers will notice the appearance of your message. If your document looks out of date, it will give that impression to your readers—even if your ideas are innovative. So choose design elements that will help your message look professional, accessible, and up to date.

SELECT THE RIGHT DESIGN ELEMENTS

Most readers have trouble comprehending long, uninterrupted pages of text. Design elements such as white space, headings, bullets, and boldface type help readers by providing visual clues to the importance and relationship of ideas.[12] Of course, always keep in mind that if you're composing a half-page memo or a short letter, too many design elements will only confuse your audience.

White space is free of text and artwork.

White Space Space free of text or artwork is known as *white space*. It provides contrast, and perhaps even more important, it gives readers a resting point. White space includes the open area surrounding headings, the margin space, the vertical space between columns, and the space created by ragged line endings. It also includes paragraph indentations or extra space between unindented, or full-block paragraphs, and the horizontal space between lines of type. You need to decide how much white space to allow for each of these areas.

Margins frame your text.

Margins and Line Justification Margins define the space around your text and between text columns. They're influenced by the way you place lines of type, which can be set (1) justified (flush on the left and flush on the right), (2) flush left with a ragged right margin, (3) flush right with a ragged left margin, or (4) centred.

Checklist: Revising Business Messages

Evaluate Content and Organization

- ✓ Review your draft against the message plan.
- ✓ Check that all necessary points appear in logical order.
- ✓ Make sure your message is organized according to the audience's probable reaction.
- ✓ Verify that you present enough support to make the main idea convincing and interesting.
- ✓ Eliminate unnecessary material, and add useful material.
- ✓ Be sure the beginning and ending are effective.

Review Style and Readability

- ✓ Make sure you've achieved the right tone.
- ✓ Increase interest with strong words and phrases.
- ✓ Make sure your message is readable—check vocabulary and sentence structure.
- ✓ Consider using a readability index.

Edit for Conciseness

- ✓ Delete unnecessary words and phrases.
- ✓ Shorten long words and phrases.
- ✓ Eliminate redundancies.
- ✓ Recast "It is/There are" starters.
- ✓ Clarify awkward references.

Edit for Clarity

- ✓ Break up overly long sentences.
- ✓ Rewrite hedging sentences.
- ✓ Impose parallelism.
- ✓ Correct dangling modifiers.
- ✓ Reword long noun sequences.
- ✓ Replace camouflaged verbs.
- ✓ Clarify sentence structure.
- ✓ Moderate your enthusiasm.

Justified type "darkens" your message's appearance, because the uniform line lengths lack the white space created by ragged margins. It also tends to make your message look more like a form letter and less like a customized message. Justified type is often considered more difficult to read, because large gaps can appear between words and because more words are hyphenated. Excessive hyphenation is distracting and hard to follow. Even so, many magazines and newspapers use justified type because word density is higher.

Flush-left–ragged-right text "lightens" your message's appearance. It gives a document an informal, contemporary feeling of openness. The space between words is the same, and only long words that fall at the ends of lines are hyphenated.

Flush-left–ragged-right text gives your message an open feeling.

Centred text lends a formal tone to your message. However, centring long blocks of text slows reading because your audience has to search for the beginning of each line. The same problem is true of text that is formatted with a right-justified margin, which creates ragged-left text. These two approaches should be avoided unless there

A neatly formatted letterhead and logo can add to a professional appearance.

A contemporary typeface, such as Times New Roman, can make your document inviting to read.

The use of bullets and boldface can make information easily accessible by highlighting it.

Royal Ontario Museum
100 Queen's Park
Toronto, Ontario
Canada
M5S 2C6

Membership
Telephone (416) 586-5700
Facsimile (416) 586-5703
Web Site http://www.rom.on.ca
E-Mail membership@rom.on.ca

January 23, 2005

Ms. Nancy Nau & Mr. Andrew Cheston
1707 Altona Road
Pickering, ON L1V 1M5

Dear Ms. Nau & Mr. Cheston,

One of my greatest pleasures as Head of Membership Services is welcoming new Members to the Royal Ontario Museum. You're now part of a group of over 35 000 individuals who, as Members, contribute so significantly to the Museum's vitality. Most of our Members stay with us for many years. In the hope that you will too, please consider this the first of many welcomes.

You've picked a terrific year to join the ROM, and here are a few reasons why:

- Opening in February is our new expanded **Discovery Centre**. The gallery will be organized in diverse environmental "zones" such as a glittering starlight or an enchanted forest. Older children can dress up in costume, examine minerals under an ultraviolet light, and much more. Families with toddlers and babies have their own special area complete with stroller parking.
- In May the spectacular **Inco Gallery of Earth Sciences** opens. This gallery, which promises to be visually exciting, interactive and educational, will be divided into four major sections: **Dynamic Earth, Restless Earth, Earth: The Alien Planet,** and **Treasures of the Earth**.

Of course, I hope you'll take advantage of all your membership benefits—visit the Members' Lounge, use your discount in all the ROM shops and the ROM restaurant, and enjoy the *Rotunda* magazine and *Atria* newsletter. Also, the next time you visit, inquire at the membership desk about our discounted parking.

But most of all, come to the ROM as often as possible. We truly treasure your attendance and hope you'll be part of the Royal Ontario Museum's great future.

Yours sincerely,

Ania Kordiuk

Ania Kordiuk
Director, Membership and Annual Giving

FIGURE 6–5 In-Depth Critique: The Importance of Appearance

is an unusual need for them; for example, you may want to highlight certain information in a sales letter by centring it.

Headings help your readers quickly identify the content and organization of your message.

Headings and Captions Headings and subheadings can be set in the same font size and type used for text, but treated differently. For example, for a short memo that uses only one level of headings, all headings can be positioned flush-left. However, they should be bolded and capitalized to set them off from the text. If you have prepared a document that uses two or more levels of headings, consider placing the second level in normal upper- and lower-case font but underlining this heading to distinguish it from the higher-level heading. Because they invite readers to become involved in your message, avoid headings that contain more than two lines. The figures in Chapter 12 show several examples of heading design and placement.

Because headings and subheadings clue readers into the organization of your message's content, place them close to the text that they introduce. You can do so by putting more space above the heading than below it; for example, use three blank lines above the heading, and two blank lines beneath it.

Next to headings, captions are the most widely read part of a document. They tie photographs and illustrations into the rest of your message. Although usually placed below the figures they describe, captions can also be placed beside or above them. Make sure that the width of your captions is pleasing in proportion to the width of the figure, the surrounding white space, and the text.

Fonts Font refers to type style and type size. Your wordprocessor offers a wide choice of fonts. Each font influences the tone of your message, making it look authoritative, friendly, expensive, sophisticated, casual, and so on. Choose fonts that are appropriate for your message.

Serif fonts are commonly used for text.

Serif fonts have small crosslines, called *serifs*, at the ends of each letter stroke.[13] (See Table 6–4 below.) Use serif fonts such as Times Roman for text; avoid them for headings or other display treatments, such as PowerPoint slides, because they tend to look busy and cluttered when set in large sizes. Fonts with rounded serifs can look friendly and casual; those with squared serifs can look official.

Sans serif fonts are commonly used for headings.

Sans serif fonts have no serifs. Fonts such as Helvetica are ideal for display treatments that use a larger font. Sans serif fonts can be difficult to read in long blocks of text. They look best when surrounded by plenty of white space—as in headings or in widely spaced lines of text.

Limit the number of fonts used in a single document.[14] In general, avoid using more than two fonts on a page. Many attractive documents are based on single sans serif fonts for headings and subheadings, with a second serif font for text and captions. Using too many fonts clutters the document and reduces your audience's comprehension.

Font Styles Font style refers to any modification that lends contrast or emphasis to type. Your computer offers not only underlining but also boldface, italic, and other highlighting and decorative styles. Using boldface fonts for subheadings breaks up long expanses of text. Just remember that too much boldfacing will darken the appearance of your message and make it look heavy. You can set isolated words in boldface type

TABLE 6–4 Common Fonts

Sample Serif Font	Sample Sans Serif Font
Times Roman is often used for text.	Helvetica is often used for headings.
TIMES ROMAN IS HARDER TO READ IN ALL CAPS.	HELVETICA IS A CLEANER TYPE FACE, EVEN IN ALL CAPS.

in the middle of a text block to draw more attention to them. If you draw more attention than a word warrants, however, you might create a "checkerboard" appearance.

Use italic font for emphasis. Although italics are sometimes used when irony or humour is intended, quotation marks are usually best for that purpose. Italics can also be used to indicate a quote and are often used in captions.

Avoid any font style that slows your audience's progress through your message. Underlining can interfere with your reader's ability to recognize the shapes of words, and using all capitals slows reading.[15] Shadowed or outlined type can seriously hinder legibility, so use these styles judiciously.

Avoid using font styles that slow your readers down.

A small font in a sea of white space appears lost. A large font squeezed into a small area is hard to read and is visually claustrophobic.

MAKE DESIGN ELEMENTS EFFECTIVE

Effective design guides your readers through your message, so be sure to be consistent, balanced, restrained, and detail-oriented:

For effective design, pay attention to
- Consistency
- Balance
- Restraint
- Detail

- **Consistency.** Throughout a message (and usually even from message to message), be consistent in your use of margins, font type, font size, and spacing (for example, in paragraph indentations, between columns, and around photographs). Also be consistent when using recurring design elements, such as vertical lines, columns, and borders.
- **Balance.** To create a pleasing design, balance the space devoted to text, artwork, and white space.
- **Restraint.** Strive for simplicity in design. Don't clutter your message with too many design elements, too much highlighting, or too many decorative touches.
- **Detail.** Track all details that affect your design and thus your message. Headings and subheadings that appear at the bottom of a column or a page can offend readers when the promised information doesn't appear until the next column or page. A layout that appears off balance can be distracting, and any typographical errors can sabotage an otherwise good-looking design.

Avoid last-minute compromises. Don't reduce font size or white space to squeeze in text. On the other hand, avoid increasing type size or white space to fill space (see Figure 6-6 on page 152). If you've planned your message so that your purpose, your audience, and your message are clear, you can design your document to be effective.[16] Start by thinking about your medium: press release, magazine or newsletter article, brochure, direct-mail package, slide presentation, formal report, business letter, or internal memo. Once you've decided on a medium, try to make it look as interesting as you can while making it as easy as possible to read and understand.

Using Technology to Produce and Distribute Your Messages

OBJECTIVE 6 Outline some of the ways technology helps you produce and distribute your messages.

Wordprocessing software is the dominant tool for writing business messages. It provides you with many options to ease the writing process. Using software tools selectively will help ensure that your documents engage your reader's interest and project a professional image of you as a business writer.

The most common means for creating printed documents is word-processing software.

Entering Text

The *delete* and *move* functions of your wordprocessor help make writing your document a smooth process. But in addition to these frequently used features, also become familiar with others. They will help you create a more business-like message and project a more professional image.

Royal Ontario Museum **Membership**

100 Queen's Park
Toronto, Ontario
Canada
M5S 2C6

Telephone (416) 586-5700
Facsimile (416) 586-5703
Web Site http://www.rom.on.ca
E-Mail membership@rom.on.ca

January 23, 2005

Ms. Nancy Nau & Mr. Andrew Cheston
1707 Altona Road
Pickering, ON L1V 1M5

Dear Ms. Nau & Mr. Cheston,

One of my greatest pleasures as Head of Membership Services is welcoming new Members to the Royal Ontario Museum. **YOU'RE NOW PART OF A GROUP OF OVER 35 000 INDIVIDUALS WHO, AS MEMBERS, CONTRIBUTE SO SIGNIFICANTLY TO THE MUSEUM'S VITALITY**. Most of our Members stay with us *for many years*. In the hope that you will too, *please* consider this the first of many *welcomes*.

You've picked a terrific year to join the ROM, and here are a few reasons why:

☺ Opening in February is our new expanded **Discovery Centre.** The gallery will be organized in diverse environmental "zones" such as a glittering starlight or an enchanted forest. Older children can dress up in costume, examine minerals under an ultraviolet light, and much more. Families with toddlers and babies have their own special area complete with stroller parking.

☺ In May the spectacular **Inco Gallery of Earth Sciences** opens. This gallery which promises to be visually exciting, interactive and educational will be divided into four major sections: **Dynamic Earth, Restless Earth, Earth: The Alien Planet**, and **Treasures of the Earth**.

Of course, I hope you'll take advantage of all your membership benefits—visit the Members' Lounge, use your discount in all the ROM shops and the ROM restaurant, enjoy the *Rotunda* magazine and *Atria* newsletter. Also, the next time you visit, inquire at the membership desk about our discounted parking.

But most of all, come to the ROM as often as possible. We truly treasure your attendance and hope you'll be part of the Royal Ontario Museum's great future.

Yours sincerely,

Ania Kordiuk

Ania Kordiuk
Director, Membership and Annual Giving

FIGURE 6-6 Poorly Designed Document.
What design problems do you see in this version of the letter in Figure 6-6?

Wordprocessing software provides specific functions for numbering and formatting lists, inserting page numbers and dates, creating customized headers and footers, inserting footnotes and merging files.

➢ **Numbered lists.** When composing a numbered list, the software will automatically renumber the remaining segments if an entry is removed. You can customize the list by formatting the indentation and changing the number style (such as using Roman numerals instead of Arabic numerals).
➢ **Automatic page numbering and dating.** When inserting a date code into a document, the software automatically fills in today's date each time you open or print that document. This feature is especially handy when you write form letters. However, be careful: sometimes you'll want to keep the original date intact, especially if you're keeping a history of your correspondence.
➢ **Headers and footers.** Learn how to use headers and footers, which automatically repeat specific text on each page of your document, either at the top or at the bottom. As a business writer, you may need to include certain information on each page of a report, such as the title. By creating a header or footer, your software will do the job for you.

- **Footnotes and endnotes.** Your software will position your documentation for you, either at the bottom of each page or at the end of your document. Numbering can be continuous, restarted at each section, or restarted on each page. If you delete a note, the software will renumber the list for you.
- **Merge files.** Some of the text that businesspeople use in their documents is "prewritten." For example, say that you want to announce to the media that you've developed a new product. Such announcements, called *press releases*, usually end with a standard paragraph about the company and its line of business. Any standard block of text used in various documents without being changed is called a *boilerplate*. With a wordprocessor, you simply store the paragraph the first time you write it and then insert it into a document whenever you need it. Using boilerplates saves time and reduces mistakes because you're not retyping the paragraph every time you use it.

  A related concept applies to manipulating existing text. If you're a national sales manager compiling a report that includes summaries from your four regional managers, you can use your word processor's *file merge* capability to combine the four documents into one, saving yourself the trouble of retyping all four. Along the same line, *mail merge* will combine a form letter with a list of addresses stored in a database or table.

Some of the latest technology lets you enter text without keyboarding. With pen-based computers, you can write on regular paper. The pen stores your data, which you can download onto your desktop or laptop at your convenience.

A *boilerplate* is any standard block of text used in various documents without being changed.

Revising Text

When it's time to revise and polish your message, your wordprocessor helps you add, delete, and move text using functions such as *cut and paste*—that is, taking a block of text out of one section of a document and pasting it in somewhere else. Several other functions will also help you revise efficiently.

Electronic tools such as search and replace, bookmarks, and track changes facilitate the revision process.

- **Search and replace.** *Search and replace* quickly tracks down words or phrases and changes them if you need to. Be careful, though—choosing the "replace all" option can result in some unintended errors. For example, finding *power* and replacing all occurrences with *strength* will also change the word *powerful* to *strengthful*. In addition, the AutoCorrect feature allows you to store words you commonly misspell or mistype, along with their correct spelling. So if you frequently type *teh* instead of *the*, AutoCorrect will automatically correct your typo for you.
- **Bookmarks.** Consider using the *bookmark* feature when preparing long documents. When revising a lengthy document, such as a 20-page recommendation report, you may need to return to specific places to check facts and phrasing. Instead of scrolling through the document, you can place a bookmark at spots you frequently review (see Figure 6-7 on page 154). Bookmarks save you valuable time when editing long business messages.
- **Track changes, versions, and comments.** Figure 6-4 on page 147 shows an example of computer-edited text, using the *track changes* function. By turning this function on, you can easily see how you revised your message. Remember to save versions of your document using the "compare documents" feature so that you can retrieve a phrase you had deleted. A similar feature also permits you to save versions of your document, by date and time. Called *version* or *version control*, this tool lets you save drafts of your document under the same name, instead of different file names; you distinguish each separate draft by including a comment in the comment column. If you are collaborating on a document, you can attach comments to different sections of the text using the *comment* function. Each team member's remarks can be displayed separately, or all at once.
- **Spelling and grammar checkers.** Your wordprocessor's *spell checker* weeds major typos out of your documents, but don't use it as a replacement for good spelling

Spell checkers, grammar checkers, and computerized thesauruses can all help with the revision process, but they can't take the place of good writing and editing skills.

skills. For example, if you use *their* when you mean to use *there,* your spell checker will ignore the error, because *their* is spelled correctly. If you're in a hurry and accidentally omit the *p* at the end of *top,* your spell checker will read *to* as correct. Or if you mistakenly type the semicolon instead of the *p,* your spell checker will read *to;* as a correctly spelled word. Furthermore, some of the "errors" detected may actually be proper names, technical words, words that you misspelled on purpose, or simply words that weren't included in the spell checker's dictionary. It's up to you to decide whether each flagged word should be corrected or left alone, and it's up to you to find the errors that your spell checker has overlooked.

Your *grammar checker* performs some helpful review tasks and points out stylistic weaknesses you should consider changing, such as passive voice, long sentences, and words that tend to be misused or overused. But avoid over-relying on your grammar checker. For example, as a business writer, you will want to use the passive voice in certain situations, as Chapter 5 points out. Your grammar checker's function is to determine whether you're using words correctly and constructing sentences according to the complex rules of composition. Because the program can't determine what you're trying to say, it can't tell whether you've said it correctly. Moreover, even if you've used all the rules correctly, a grammar checker still can't tell whether your document communicates clearly.

- **Thesaurus.** Your wordprocessor's *thesaurus* gives you alternative words, just as your printed thesaurus does. You can also access an online thesaurus, at **www.vancouver-webpages.com/wordnet**, which finds words have the same meaning, are more general, or more specific than the original word.

Spell checkers and grammar checkers have their limitations.

When revising your documents use any software that you find helpful. Just remember that it's unwise to rely on grammar or spell checkers to do all your revision work. What these programs can do is identify "mistakes" you may overlook on your own. It's up to you to decide what, if anything, needs to be done, and it's up to you to catch the mistakes that these computer programs can't.[17]

Adding Graphics, Sound, and Hypertext

You can use graphics software to add visual elements to your message.

With advances in computer technology, it's easy to illustrate and enliven your text with full-colour pictures, sound recordings, and hypertext links. The software for creating business visuals falls into two basic groups: *Presentation software* helps you create overhead transparencies and computerized slide shows (presentations are discussed

FIGURE 6–7
Example of a Bookmark List

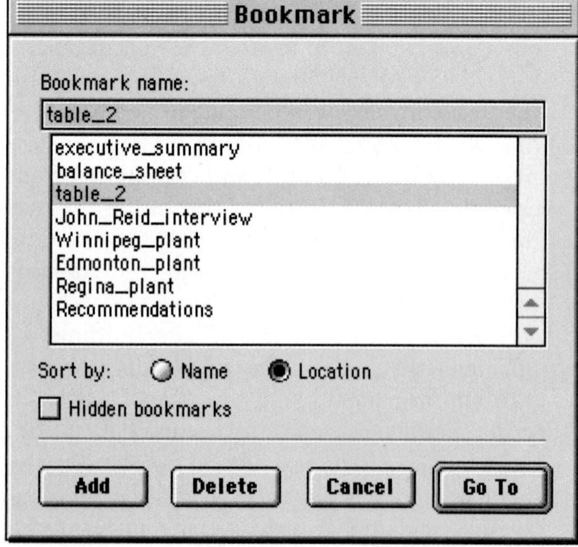

in Chapter 13). *Graphics software* ranges from products that can create simple diagrams and flowcharts (see Chapter 11) to comprehensive tools geared to artists and graphic designers. You can create your pictures from scratch, use *clip art* (collections of uncopyrighted images), or scan in drawings or photographs. A word of caution about clip art: these images look artificial and "canned," so use them only if they serve your purpose.

Hypertext links are a common feature of online annual reports.

Adding *sound bites* to your documents is an exciting way to get your message across. You record a brief message or other sound (or use a sound provided by your software) and attach it to particular places in a document. For instance, you can add sound annotations, instead of written ones. Then, clicking on the speaker icon plays a recorded comment, such as "Please convert this paragraph to a bulleted list." However, remember that most of your readers want to review your document quickly and may be irritated by unnecessary sounds. So, be cautious when inserting sound clips into your document.

You can also use HyperText Markup Language (HTML) to *insert hyperlinks* into your message. Readers can easily jump from one document to another by clicking on such a link. They can go directly to a Web site, jump to another section of your document, or go to a different document altogether. For example, if you were preparing a report on this year's budget, rather than including pages of budget details from prior years, submit your report on disk and include a hyperlink in the file. Then, when readers click on the hyperlink, they enter a document containing details of the prior years' budget. By using hyperlinks, you can customize your documents to meet the individual information needs of your readers—just as you can on a Web page. Of course, you'll have to make sure that the file, or the software program used to open that file, is either included with your electronic document or installed on the recipient's computer.

Your document can have live links to other documents and to the Internet.

Distributing Your Message

Technology gives us the benefits of speed and low cost when distributing business messages, but sometimes a low-tech form, such as regular mail or courier, is best. Before attaching a memo or report to your e-mail and hitting the "send" button, ask yourself if e-mail is the best transmission tool. Do document size and audience preference require a different transmission mode? Is e-mail sufficiently secure for your message?

- **E-mail.** E-mail is an excellent tool for sending memos and reports as attachments to your message. Your receivers need only open the attachment and print out the document, and they can save the electronic copy on their computers. E-mail is an economical transmission choice, because it is included in the cost of your company's Internet connection.

  However, when sending documents by e-mail, be sure that your receiver's software is compatible with yours; while some systems may open an attachment prepared by one wordprocessing software, others may not. In addition, your audience may not want to receive a long attachment by e-mail. Consider calling (or e-mailing) your reader before sending your document to determine if another transmission means, such as interoffice mail, or courier for external audiences, is preferred.[18]

  Another caution for e-mail is security. You may inadvertently send a virus with your e-mail, and infect your receiver's computer (or the company's entire system). Be sure your system has updated virus detection software to detect viruses. Even with virus protection, some recipients prefer receiving hard copy only.

- **Fax.** Despite the economy of e-mail, the fax machine is still a popular tool for distributing business messages. Fax transmission is not only fast, but also more secure than e-mail because viruses cannot attach to the document. Another benefit is that senders receive immediate confirmation, with the fax receipt, that the material has been transmitted. In industries that frequently use forms, such as finance and medicine, fax is the only choice for "real time" transmission. With multifunction products, which are all-in-one units that can photocopy, scan, and fax, the user can program the machine to "scan to fax."[19] However, only fax documents that are short to medium-length, say one page to 25 pages. Anything much longer should be sent by conventional means unless your recipient would prefer fax transmission.

Cost, audience preference, document size, and security determine the distribution channel for your messages.

- **Regular mail and courier.** Less economical and slower than e-mail and fax, conventional mail and courier are the only choices for sending long documents or optical media, such as CD-ROMs and DVDs. Hard copy annual reports, or documents burned onto a compact disc, for example, can only be delivered by traditional mail. If time is essential, select a courier for same-day or next-day service.

Proofreading Your Message

Your credibility is affected by your attention to the details of mechanics and form.

Although spelling, punctuation, and typographical errors seem trivial to some people, most readers view your attention to detail as a sign of your professionalism. Whether you're writing a one-paragraph memo or a 200-page report, if you let mechanical errors slip through, your readers wonder whether you're unreliable in more important ways.

What to Look for When Proofreading

OBJECTIVE 7 Define the types of errors to look for when proofreading.

Proofread your message to ensure that it's letter perfect. Begin by refreshing your memory about the details of grammar, usage, and punctuation (by reviewing Appendix C). Then, in addition to these language errors, be on the lookout for common spelling errors and typos. Also watch for missing material: a missing source note, a missing figure, or even a missing paragraph.

The types of details to look for when proofreading include language errors, missing material, design errors, and typographical errors.

Look for design errors. For example, some headings and text might appear in the wrong font (Helvetica rather than Times New Roman, or **Arial Black** rather than Arial Narrow). One or two special elements may appear in the wrong font style (**boldface** instead of *italic*, or *italic* instead of underlined). Columns within tables and exhibits on a page might be misaligned. Graphical characters such as ampersands and percent signs may appear when they should be spelled out, and numerical symbols might be incorrect. Also look for typographical errors, such as extra spacing between lines or between words, crowded type, a short line of type carried over to the top of a new page, a heading left hanging at the bottom of a page, or incorrect hyphenation. (See "Sharpening Your Career Skills—How to Proofread Like a Pro: Tips for Creating the Perfect Document" on page 157.)

Give attention to your overall format. Have you followed accepted conventions and company guidelines for laying out the document on the page (margin width, number of columns, heading placement)? Have you included all the traditional elements that belong in the type of document you're creating? Have you been consistent in handling page numbers, heading styles, figure titles, source notes?

Proofreading e-mail messages takes special attention.

Special considerations apply to proofreading e-mail messages. Review the addresses in the "to" box and check that your message goes only to the people who must read it. It's important to limit your distribution list so that you don't overload colleagues with unnecessary e-mail. Reread your message for accuracy in content and for tone. If you are uncomfortable about anything you say in your message, don't send it until you rewrite it. Remember that no e-mail message is truly confidential: recipients can download, print, or forward your message; even deleted messages can be retrieved. And, if you're sending the e-mail to non-native speakers, revise language that is unfamiliar and avoid using slang.[20]

How to Adapt the Proofreading Process

The number and kind of errors you catch when proofreading depends on the amount of time you have to proofread and the sort of document you're preparing. The more routine your document the less time you'll need to proofread, because routine documents have fewer elements to check. Moreover, the more often you prepare one type of document, the more you'll know about the sorts of errors to look for.

Longer, more complex documents can have many more components that need checking. For complicated documents, you may feel pressed for enough time to do a good proofreading job. Back in step one of the writing process (look back at Figure 4–1 on page 73), you planned out how you would approach this message and you allotted a certain amount of time for each task. Try your best to keep to your schedule. You want to create a letter-perfect document, but you also want to meet your deadline and turn in your work promptly. As with every task in the writing process, practice helps—you not only become more familiar with what errors to look for, but you also become more skilled in identifying those errors.

Even when you're pressed for time, try to maintain the schedule you laid out during the planning step of the writing process.

SHARPENING YOUR CAREER SKILLS

How to Proofread Like a Pro: Tips for Creating the Perfect Document

You've carefully revised and polished your document, but to ensure it's error free, always proofread the final version before you distribute your work. Following are some hints to help make your proofreading more effective.

- **Multiple passes.** Go through the document several times, focusing on a different aspect each time. The first pass might be to look for omissions and errors in content; the second pass could be for layout, spacing, and other aesthetic features; a final pass might be to check for typographical, grammatical, and spelling errors.
- **Perceptual tricks.** Your brain has been trained to ignore transposed letters, improper capitalization, and misplaced punctuation. Try (1) reading each page from the bottom to the top (starting at the last word in each line), (2) placing your finger under each word and reading it silently, (3) making a slit in a sheet of paper that reveals only one line of type at a time, and (4) reading the document aloud and pronouncing each word carefully.
- **Impartial reviews.** Have a friend or colleague proofread the document for you. Others are likely to catch mistakes that you continually fail to notice. All of us have blind spots when it comes to reviewing our own work.
- **Typos.** Look for the most common typographical errors (typos): transposition (such as *teh*), substitution (such as *ecomonic*), and omission (such as *productvity*).
- **Mechanics.** When looking for errors in spelling, grammar, punctuation, and capitalization, if you're unsure about something, look it up in a dictionary, a usage book, or another reference work.
- **Accuracy.** Double-check the spelling of names and the accuracy of dates, addresses, and all numbers (quantities ordered, prices, and so on). People are offended when their names are misspelled, and numerical and other errors can be costly.
- **Distance.** If you have time, set the document aside and proofread it the next day.
- **Vigilance.** Avoid reading large amounts of material in one sitting, and try not to proofread when you're tired.
- **Focus.** Concentrate on what you're doing. Try to block out distractions, and focus as completely as possible on your proofreading task.
- **Caution.** Take your time. Quick proofreading is not careful proofreading.

Proofreading may require patience, but it adds credibility to your document.

CAREER APPLICATIONS

1 What qualities does a person need to be a good proofreader? Are such qualities inborn, or can they be learned?

2 Proofread the following sentence: aplication of thse methods in stores in Vancouver nd Winnipeg have resultted in a 30 drop in roberies an a 50 percent decling in violnce there, acording ot thedevelpers if the securty sytem, Hanover brothrs, Inc.

Sources: Adapted from Philip C. Kolin, *Successful Writing at Work*, 2d ed., 102. Used with permission of D. C. Heath & Company; Dennis Hensley, "A Way with Words: Proofreading Can Save Cash and Careers," Dallas Magazine, May 1986, 57–58.

Summary of Learning Outcomes

1 Explain why the revision of written material is so important in business, list its three main tasks, and discuss when revision is performed. Revision consists of three main tasks: (1) evaluating content and organization, (2) reviewing style and readability, and (3) proofreading the final version after it has been produced. Revision is an ongoing activity. It occurs throughout the writing process, again after you complete the first draft of your business message, and again after you produce the final version.

2 Discuss why it's important to make your message concise, and give four tips on how to do so. Businesspeople are more likely to read documents that give information efficiently. To make business messages more concise, try to include only necessary material and to write clean sentences by (1) deleting unnecessary words and phrases, (2) shortening overly long words and phrases, (3) eliminating redundancies, and (4) recasting *It is* and *There are* starters.

3 List nine tips for making your writing clear. Clear writing doesn't happen the first time, so you need to revise your work. As you try to clarify your message, (1) divide overly long sentences, (2) rewrite hedging sentences, (3) impose parallelism, (4) correct dangling modifiers, (5) reword long noun sequences, (6) replace camouflaged verbs, (7) clarify sentence structure, (8) clarify awkward references, and (9) moderate your enthusiasm.

4 Identify seven issues to keep in mind when evaluating someone else's writing. When evaluating someone else's writing style, you should first make sure that the document accomplishes its intended purpose, verify that the factual material is correct, and point out all ambiguous language so that it can be eliminated. Then ask yourself whether the document can truly be improved, whether the time needed to rewrite it can be justified, and whether asking for a rewrite could have a negative effect on morale. Finally, make sure your comments are specific and constructive.

5 Describe five design elements, explain how they can change a document's appearance, and tell how to use them effectively. White space provides contrast and gives readers a resting point. Margins define the space around the text and contribute to the amount of white space. Headings and captions invite readers to become involved in the message. Fonts influence the tone of the message. Font styles provide contrast or emphasis. When selecting and applying design elements, you can ensure their effectiveness by being consistent throughout your document; balancing your space between text, art, and white space; showing restraint in the number of elements you use; and paying attention to every detail.

6 Outline some of the ways technology helps you produce and distribute your messages. Wordprocessors help you enter, delete, replace, and move text easily. They can automatically number lists, notes, and pages, and fill in the current date. They also simplify creating headers and footers, inserting footnotes and endnotes, writing boilerplate, and merging files. As you revise messages, computers help you manipulate text with *cut and paste* as well as *search and replace* commands. Revision tools include the *spell checker*, *thesaurus*, and *grammar checker*. Using such features as *bookmarks*, *track changes*, and *comments* will also speed the revision process. Technology helps you illustrate your text with *presentation software*, *graphic software*, and *HTML*. Technology also helps you distribute messages with e-mail and fax machines, though there will be many occasions when regular mail and courier will be used.

7 Define the types of errors to look for when proofreading. When proofreading the final version of your document, always look for errors in grammar, usage, and punctuation. In addition, watch for spelling errors and typos. Make sure that nothing is missing (whether a source note, a figure, or text). Correct design errors such as elements that appear in the wrong font, elements that appear in the wrong font style, misaligned elements (columns in a table, figures on a page, etc.), and graphical characters (such as ampersands and percent signs) that appear in both symbol and spelled-out form. Look for typographical errors such as uneven spacing between lines and words, a short line of type at the top of a page, a heading at the bottom of a page, or incorrect hyphenation. In addition, make sure your layout conforms to company guidelines. When proofreading e-mail, check the "to" box for appropriate recipients, and reread your e-mail for accuracy in content, the right tone, and language that would confuse non-native speakers.

ON THE JOB

Solving a Communication Dilemma at the Confederation Centre of the Arts

"Working in the publicity office, one has the opportunity to meet fascinating people, including world-class Canadian visual and performing artists, from all works of life and from around the world," comments Anna MacDonald, publicist for Charlottetown's Confederation Centre of the Arts. In 2003, her office's copy for *Dracula: A Chamber Musical* ("the story of the triumph of good over evil and love over death"), the whimsical art of Elisabeth Belliveau, and the Halifax-based band Afro-Musica drew thousands of visitors from across North America and internationally to the Charlottetown institution.

Besides press releases, MacDonald also writes, edits, and proofreads both in-house material and external brochures and publications, such as theatre and music programmes and the membership brochure. MacDonald also contributes to the *Guide to Charlottetown* and travel trade magazines, writes remarks for the CEO, and assists with the organization of special events. "For all the documents I write, I try to maintain a concise style that is easy to read and understand by the reader," she says. While press releases follow the "who, what, when, where, why, and how" of newspapers and magazines, promotional documents, such as the Charlottetown Festival seasonal brochure "are written in more punchy, upbeat language designed to create excitement in readers for the programming we offer." The number of people who revise and proofread material depends on the nature of the piece. After Macdonald proofreads, she sends the document to the director of the marketing department, here the publicity office is located, and to the director or organizer of the program or event for further comments and approval. "Press releases and documents that involve the CEO are approved by him as well," MacDonald explains.

Press releases and most Confederation Centre documents are sent to the centre's French translator. The Web site (www.confederationcentre.ca) is also bilingual. Completely redesigned in 2001, the Confederation Centre Web site gives visitors the option to buy tickets online, select seats, take a virtual tour of the art gallery, and learn everything they want to know about the centre's programs and activities.[21]

Your Mission You have recently joined the Confederation Centre of the Arts marketing department as an intern. You are asked to write a message that will appear on the Centre's Web site, under the signature of David MacKenzie, the Chief Executive Officer. Here is the first draft. Using the questions that follow, analyze it according to the material in this chapter. Be prepared to explain your analysis.

> With your support and participation, we at your Confederation Centre of the Arts are looking forward to a great Festival season. As always, we welcome your comments and suggestions about the programming and services we offer to you.
>
> The Confederation Centre Art Gallery's exhibition programme offers food for thought, with stimulating exhibitions ranging from the contemporary to the historical, the beautiful and contemplative, and local and the international. Be sure to drop by and watch our artists-in-residence as they create their works in full public view.
>
> Fresh from a phenomenally successful tour of Ottawa in April, *Anne of Green Gables—The Musical*™, Canada's greatest, most fantastic, and longest running musical, will run until September 27—its most ambitious and overwhelmingly great season ever. With its incredible music and talented cast, *Dracula: A Chamber Musical* has quickly become the talk of the town and a must-see for everyone. Following the successful run of *Fire*, the MacKenzie Theatre showcases the truly hilarious adult comedy *Eight to the Bar*, back for a 25th anniversary production.
>
> In addition to our theatre and art exhibitions, we are again offering our popular theatre and art camps for children. We are pleased to say that the theatre camp is now full!
>
> We are so excited about the 2003 Charlottetown Festival, a feast for the senses! The Festival, which started on May 15, will run until October 11—our longest season ever.
>
> See you at the Festival!

1 How would you rate this draft in terms of its content and organization?
- a Although the style of the message needs work, the content and organization are basically okay.
- b The draft is seriously flawed in both content and organization. Extensive editing is required.
- c The content is fine, but the organization is poor.
- d The organization is fine, but the content is poor.

2 Should the third paragraph be revised?
- a Yes. The paragraph needs more concrete detail to fill in the reader about more of the Confederation Centre's activities.
- b No. The paragraph is fine the way it is. It is a promotional message.
- c Yes. All adjectives and adverbs should be removed.
- d Yes. The tone should be moderated, but some adjectives and adverbs should be retained.

3 Because this message will appear on the Confederation Centre's Web site, it will be read by people whose first language is not English. Will these readers understand the language of this draft?
- a Yes. There is no slang or jargon in the message. Everyone who reads it, no matter what their educational level or language, will understand the message entirely.
- b Yes. While terms such as "talk of the town" and "food for thought" are idiomatic to English, second-language readers will understand it.
- c No. Terms such as "talk of the town" and "food for thought" will be unfamiliar to second-language readers and these terms should be rewritten.
- d Yes. Terms such as "talk of the town" and "food for thought" are idiomatic, but second-language readers should look them up in a dictionary. These terms add colour to the message and should not be changed.

4 Take a look at the last paragraph of this letter. What is its chief flaw?
- a It is only one sentence. A message cannot end with a single sentence.
- b It lacks an action for the reader to take. Readers should be told how to get in touch with the Confederation Centre of the Arts if they want to order tickets for a production.
- c The statement should not end with an exclamation mark. A period is more effective.
- d. A message can end with a single sentence, but this sentence is too short and makes the message looks visually unbalanced.
- e The final paragraph is fine as it is.

Test Your Knowledge

Review Questions

1 What are the three main tasks involved in revising a business message?
2 How do readers benefit from white space and headings?
3 What wordprocessing tools can you use when revising messages?
4 What is the purpose of the Fog Index and similar formulas?
5 What is parallel construction, and why is it important?
6 What are some of the issues to focus on when evaluating someone else's document?
7 What are some ways you can make a document more concise?
8 Why is proofreading an important part of the writing process?
9 What happens when you use too many hedging sentences in one document?
10 Why is it a good idea to use verbs instead of noun phrases?

Interactive Learning 

Use This Text's Online Resources

Visit our Companion Web site at **www.pearsoned.ca/thill**, where you can use the interactive Study Guide to test your chapter knowledge and get instant feedback. Additional resources link you to the sites mentioned in this text and to additional sources of information on chapter topics.

Also check out the resources on the Mastering Business Communication CD, including "Perils of Pauline," an interactive presentation of the business communication challenges within a fictional company. For Chapter 6, see in particular the episode "Using E-Mail Effectively."

Apply Your Knowledge

Critical Thinking Questions

1 Why is it important to let your draft "age" a day before you begin the editing process?
2 What are some challenges you might encounter when evaluating the work of others?
3 Given the choice of only one, would you prefer to use a grammar checker or a spell checker? Why?
4 When you are designing a formal business letter, which design elements do you have to consider and which are optional?
5 What issues are involved in faxing long documents?
6 Should editing and proofreading business messages be done only by computer? Why? Why not?
7 **Ethical Choices** What are the ethical implications of using underlining, all capitals, and other hard-to-read type styles in a document explaining how customers can appeal the result of a decision made in the company's favour during a dispute?

Practice Your Knowledge

Documents for Analysis

Read the following documents; then (1) analyze the strengths and weaknesses of each sentence and (2) revise each document so that it follows the guidelines in Chapters 4 through 6.

Document 6.A

The move to our new offices will take place over this coming weekend. For everything to run smooth, everyone will have to clean out their own desk and pack up the contents in boxes that will be provided. You will need to take everything off the walls too, and please pack it along with the boxes.

If you have a lot of personal belongings, you should bring them home with you. Likewise with anything valuable. I do not mean to infer that items will be stolen, irregardless it is better to be safe than sorry.

On Monday, we will be unpacking, putting things away, and then get back to work. The least amount of disruption is anticipated by us, if everyone does their part. Hopefully, there will be no negative affects on production schedules, and current deadlines will be met.

Document 6.B

Dear Ms. Giraud:

Enclosed herewith please find the manuscript for your book, *Careers in Woolgathering*. After perusing the first two chapters of your 1500-page manuscript, I was forced to conclude that the subject matter, handicrafts and artwork using wool fibres, is not coincident with the publishing program of Caribou Press, which to this date has issued only works on business endeavours, avoiding all other topics completely.

Although our firm is unable to consider your impressive work at the present time, I have taken the liberty of recording some comments on some of the pages. I am of the opinion that any feedback that a writer can obtain from those well versed in the publishing realm can only serve to improve the writer's authorial skills.

In view of the fact that your residence is in the Winnipeg area, might I suggest that you secure an appointment with someone of high editorial stature at the Red River Press, which I believe might have something of an interest in works of the nature you have produced.

Wishing you the best of luck in your literary endeavours, I remain

Arthur J. Cogswell
Editor

Document 6.C

For delicious, air-popped popcorn, please read the following instructions: the popper is designed to pop 120 mL of popcorn kernels at one time. Never add more than 120 mL. One hundred and twenty mL of corn will produce 3.4 to 4.5 litres of popcorn. More batches may be made separately after completion of the first batch. Popcorn is popped by hot air. Oil or shortening is not needed for popping corn. Add only popcorn kernels to the popping chamber. Standard grades of popcorn are recommended for use. Premium or gourmet type popping corns may be used. Ingredients such as oil, shortening, butter, margarine, or salt should never be added to the popping chamber. The popper, with popping chute in position, may be preheated for two minutes before adding the corn. Turn the popper off before adding the corn. Use electricity safely and wisely. Observe safety precautions when using the popper. Do not touch the popper when it is hot. The popper should not be left unattended when it is plugged into an outlet. Do not use the popper if it or its cord has been damaged. Do not use the popper if it is not working properly. Before using the first time, wash the chute and butter/measuring cup in hot soapy water. Use a dishcloth or sponge. Wipe the outside of the popper base. Use a damp cloth. Dry the base. Do not immerse the popper base in water or other liquid. Replace the chute and butter/measuring cup. The popper is ready to use.

Exercises

6–1 Revising Messages: Conciseness Revise the following sentences, using shorter, simpler words:

a The antiquated calculator is ineffectual for solving sophisticated problems.

b It is imperative that the pay increments be terminated before an inordinate deficit is accumulated.

c There was unanimity among the executives that Mr. MacTavish's idiosyncrasies were cause for a mandatory meeting with the company's personnel director.

d The impending liquidation of the company's assets was cause for jubilation among the company's competitors.

e The expectations of the president for a stock dividend were accentuated by the preponderance of evidence that the company was in good financial condition.

6–2 Revising Messages: Camouflaged Verbs Rewrite each sentence so that the verbs are no longer camouflaged:

a Adaptation to the new rules was performed easily by the employees.

b The assessor will make a determination of the tax due.

c Verification of the identity of the employees must be made daily.

d The board of directors made a recommendation that Ms. Habibi be assigned to a new division.

e The auditing procedure on the books was performed by the vice-president.

6–3 Revising Messages: Clarity Divide these long sentences into shorter, grammatical sentences:

a The next time you write something, check your average sentence length in a 100-word passage, and if your sentences average more than 16 to 20 words, see whether you can break up some of the sentences.

b Don't do what the village blacksmith did when he instructed his apprentice as follows: "When I take the shoe out of the fire, I'll lay it on the anvil, and when I nod my head, you hit it with the hammer." The apprentice did just as he was told, and now he's the village blacksmith.

c Unfortunately, no gadget will produce excellent writing, but using a yardstick like the Fog Index gives us some guideposts to follow for making writing easier to read because its two factors remind us to use short sentences and simple words.

d Know the flexibility of the written word and its power to convey an idea, and know how to make your words behave so that your readers will understand.

e Words mean different things to different people, and a word such as *block* may mean city block, butcher block, engine block, auction block, or several other things.

6–4 Revising Messages: Conciseness Cross out unnecessary words in the following phrases:

a consensus of opinion

b new innovations

c long period of time

d at a price of $50

e still remains

6–5 Revising Messages: Conciseness Use infinitives as substitutes for the overly long phrases in these sentences:

a For living, I require money.

b They did not find sufficient evidence for believing in the future.

c Bringing about the destruction of a dream is tragic.

6–6 Revising Messages: Conciseness Rephrase the following in fewer words:

a in the near future

b in the event that

c in order that

d for the purpose of
e with regard to
f it may be that
g in very few cases
h with reference to
i at the present time
j there is no doubt that

6–7 Revising Messages: Conciseness Condense these sentences to as few words as possible:

a We are of the conviction that writing is important.
b In all probability, we're likely to have a price increase.
c Our goals include making a determination about that in the near future.
d When all is said and done at the conclusion of this experiment, I'd like to summarize the final windup.
e After a trial period of three weeks, during which time she worked for a total of 15 full working days, we found her work was sufficiently satisfactory so that we offered her full-time work.

6–8 Revising Messages: Modifiers Remove all the unnecessary modifiers from these sentences:

a Tremendously high pay increases were given to the extraordinarily skilled and extremely conscientious employees.
b The union's proposals were highly inflationary, extremely demanding, and exceptionally bold.

6–9 Revising Messages: Hedging Rewrite these sentences so that they no longer contain any hedging:

a It would appear that someone apparently entered illegally.
b It may be possible that sometime in the near future the situation is likely to improve.
c Your report seems to suggest that we might be losing money.
d I believe Nancy apparently has somewhat greater influence over employees in the marketing department.
e It seems as if this letter of resignation means you might be leaving us.

6–10 Revising Messages: Indefinite Starters Rewrite these sentences to eliminate the indefinite opening phrases:

a There are several examples here to show that Marcelle can't hold a position very long.
b It would be greatly appreciated if every employee would make a generous contribution to Mildred Cook's retirement party.
c It has been learned in Ottawa today from generally reliable sources that an important announcement will be made shortly by the Prime Minister's Office.
d There is a rule that states that we cannot work overtime without permission.
e It would be great if you could work late for the next three Saturdays.

6–11 Revising Messages: Parallelism Present the ideas in these sentences in parallel form:

a Mr. Blackbird is expected to lecture three days a week, to counsel two days a week, and must write for publication in his spare time.
b She knows not only accounting, but she also reads Spanish.
c Both applicants had families, college degrees, and were in their thirties, with considerable accounting experience but few social connections.
d This book was exciting, well written, and held my interest.
e Dragan is both a hard worker and he knows bookkeeping.

6–12 Revising Messages: Awkward References Revise the following sentences to delete the awkward references:

a The vice-president in charge of sales and the production manager are responsible for the keys to 34A and 35A, respectively.
b The keys to 34A and 35A are in executive hands, with the former belonging to the vice-president in charge of sales and the latter belonging to the production manager.
c The keys to 34A and 35A have been given to the production manager, with the aforementioned keys being gold embossed.
d A laser printer and an ink-jet printer were delivered to John and Megan, respectively.
e The walnut desk is more expensive than the oak desk, the former costing $300 more than the latter.

6–13 Revising Messages: Dangling Modifiers Rewrite these sentences to clarify the dangling modifiers:

a Running down the railroad tracks in a cloud of smoke, we watched the countryside glide by.
b Lying on the shelf, Ruby saw the seashell.
c Based on the information, I think we should buy the property.
d Being cluttered and filthy, Phillipe took the whole afternoon to clean up his desk.
e After proofreading every word, the memo was ready to be signed.

6–14 Revising Messages: Noun Sequences Rewrite the following sentences to eliminate the long strings of nouns:

a The focus of the meeting was a discussion of the bank interest rate deregulation issue.
b Following the government task force report recommendations, we are revising our job applicant evaluation procedures.
c The production department quality assurance program components include employee training, supplier cooperation, and computerized detection equipment.
d The supermarket warehouse inventory reduction plan will be implemented next month.
e The Rotman School of Business graduate placement program is one of the best in the country.

6–15 Revising Messages: Sentence Structure Rearrange the following sentences to bring the subjects closer to their verbs:

a Trudy, when she first saw the bull pawing the ground, ran.
b It was Terri who, according to Ted, who is probably the worst gossip in the office (Tom excepted), mailed the wrong order.

c William Oberstreet, in his book *Investment Capital Reconsidered,* writes of the mistakes that bankers through the decades have made.

d Judy Schimmel, after passing up several sensible investment opportunities, despite the warnings of her friends and family, invested her inheritance in a jojoba plantation.

e The president of U-Stor-It, which was on the brink of bankruptcy after the warehouse fire, the worst tragedy in the history of the company, prepared a press announcement.

6–16 **Internet** Visit the Web site of StockHouse Canada **www.stockhouse.ca** and evaluate the design of the home page. What design improvements can you suggest to enhance readability of the information posted on this page?

6–17 **Teamwork** Team up with another student and exchange your revised versions of Document 6.A, 6.B, or 6.C (see exercise under Documents for Analysis). Review the assignment to be sure the instructions are clear. Then read and critique your teammate's revision to see whether it can be improved. After you have critiqued each other's work, take a moment to examine the way you expressed your comments and the way you felt listening to the other student's comments. Can you identify ways to improve the critiquing process in situations such as this?

6–18 **Producing Messages: Design Elements** Look back at your revised version of Document 6.C (see exercise under Documents for Analysis). Which design elements could you use to make this document more readable? Produce your revision of Document 6.C using your selected design elements. Then experiment by changing one of the design elements. How does the change affect readability? Exchange documents with another student and critique each other's work.

6–19 **Proofreading Messages: E-Mail** Proofread the following e-mail message and revise it to correct any problems you find:

> Our final company orientation of the year will be held on Dec. 20. In preparation for this sesssion, please order 20 copies of the Policy handbook, the confindentiality agreement, the employee benefits Manual, please let me know if you anticipate any delays in obtaining these materials.

6–20 **Ethical Choices** Three of your company's five plants exceeded their expense budgets last month. You want all the plants to operate within their budgets from now on. You were thinking of using broadcast faxing to let all five plants see the memo you are sending to the managers of the three over-budget plants. Is this a good idea? Why or why not?

Going Online Exercises

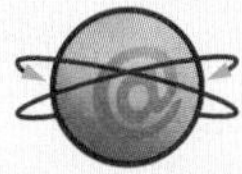

Write It Right: Rethink and Revise, found on page 147 of this chapter

Before completing a message, go to **www.powa.org** for advice on organizing ideas, choosing the best word and appropriate style, and placing each paragraph effectively so that your message achieves its purpose.

1. Why is it better to write out ideas in a rough format and later reread your message to revise its content? When revising your message, what two questions can you ask about your writing?
2. Name the four elements of the "writing context." Imagine that you're the reader of your message. What questions might you ask?
3. When you revise a written message, what is the purpose of "tightening"? What is one way to tighten your writing as you complete a message?

1 Apply the three-step writing process to routine positive messages

2 Illustrate the strategy for writing routine requests

3 Discuss the differences among the four types of routine requests

4 Explain the main differences in messages granting a claim when the company, the customer, or a third party is at fault

5 Clarify the importance of goodwill messages, and describe how to make them effective

Writing Routine, Good-News, and Goodwill Messages

ON THE JOB

Facing a Communication Dilemma at Indigo Books and Music

Becoming Canada's Bookseller

www.chapters.indigo.ca

Considered the most powerful figure in Canadian bookselling, Heather Reisman, CEO of Indigo Books and Music, has been facing a flat book market in recent years. The 1990s saw booming book sales as "big-box" bookstores opened across Canada. Reisman created Indigo Books and Music in 1996 as the "world's first cultural department store," where consumers can buy books, CDs, DVDs, videos, gift items, and fine stationery. At that time, her chief competitor was Chapters Books, another superstore chain, which merged with Indigo in 2000, with Reisman becoming the controlling shareholder. Today, Indigo is Canada's largest retail bookstore, with 88 superstores and 187 mall stores (under the Coles and Smith Books banners). A "bricks and clicks" company, Indigo also maintains an online presence, **www.chapters.indigo.ca**, reaching consumers domestically and around the world.

Reisman's challenge is to revive Canadian interest in books. While the wildly popular Harry Potter series has contributed to sales, the economic downturn in 2000 and the entry of Amazon, the major U.S. online book and music retailer, into the Canadian scene, have prevented Reisman from achieving the profits her firm saw in the 1990s. Reisman also faces competition from Canada's independent booksellers and specialty bookstores.

Reisman's business is her passion. A book lover herself, she holds literacy fundraisers in her home and includes her "personal picks" in Indigo's holiday gift catalogue. She promotes the "Get Caught Reading" program to encourage "the joy of reading" and regularly holds book readings, cooking demonstrations, and book club meetings in her stores. Indigo stores are intended to be more than retail outlets: Reisman envisions them as "cultural havens for book lovers to meet local, national, and international artists."

As you read this chapter, put yourself in Heather Reisman's position. To maintain and improve your market share, you must send clear messages to customers and store managers, requesting both information and action. How can you obtain the information you need to make your decisions? How will you phrase your requests so that store managers will respond with positive action in the race against competitors, both the bookstores that occupy physical building space and those that occupy the virtual space of the Internet?[1]

As Indigo's founder and CEO, Heather Reisman is the primary decision-maker when it comes to her firm's image and activities. Her goal is to create an environment where book lovers can enjoy "the best of a proprietor-run shop combined with the selection of a true emporium." Indigo's position in the Canadian book market is testimony to her ability to communicate her vision clearly to Indigo executives, front-line staff, and customers.

Using the Three-Step Writing Process for Routine Messages

Whether you're answering consumer correspondence, congratulating an employee on a job well done, or requesting information from another firm, in the course of everyday business you'll compose a lot of routine, good-news, and goodwill messages. In fact, most of a typical employee's communication is about routine matters: orders, information, claims, credit, products, operations, and so on. These messages are rarely long or complex. Yet, these short messages, like longer ones, convey an impression of you as a business writer and of your organization. To ensure that the image you project is professional, you'll want to apply the three-step writing process.

Step 1: Planning Routine Messages

OBJECTIVE 1 Apply the three-step writing process to routine positive messages.

As with longer, complex messages, you need to analyze, investigate, and adapt. However, for routine messages, this planning step may take only a few moments. First, analyze your purpose to make sure that it's specific, that the message should indeed be sent, and that the message should be written, rather than handled by a quick phone call or face-to-face. Also, think a moment about your readers. Are you sure they'll receive your message positively (or at least neutrally)? Most routine messages are of interest to your readers because they contain information necessary to conduct day-to-day business. Even so, you may need to discover more about audience attitudes or needs.

Even for routine situations, you need to analyze, investigate, and adapt your messages.

Second, investigate to learn exactly what your audience needs to know. Do you have all the relevant information? Do you need to take a little time to gather more?

Third, adapt your routine messages to your readers. Select the most appropriate medium, and establish or maintain a good relationship with them. Use the "you" attitude and be sure to keep your language positive and polite.

Step 2: Writing Routine Messages

Organize your routine messages according to the direct approach.

Organizing and composing routine messages can go rather quickly. Your main idea may already be fairly well defined. Just be sure you stick to it by limiting the scope of your message. Cover only relevant points, and group them in the most logical fashion. Because your readers will be interested or neutral, you can usually adopt the direct approach for routine messages: Open with a clear statement of the main idea, include all necessary details in the body, and then close cordially.

However, even though these messages are the least complicated business messages to write, communicating across cultural boundaries can be challenging. (See "Achieving Intercultural Communication—How Direct Is Too Direct?" on page 166.) To help your reader understand your message, keep your tone conversational and use plain English.

The Internet has simplified some routine communications, such as product ordering. By merely clicking on the item and quantity, buyers fill their electronic shopping carts and "check out" with the totals, shipping, and taxes automatically completed. However, "cottage industries" that operate out of home offices or small factories may not have Web sites that accommodate online ordering. In situations such as these, you may need to compose your own order letters.

Step 3: Completing Routine Messages

No matter how short or straightforward your message, make it professional by allowing plenty of time to revise, produce, and proofread it. First, revise your routine message for overall effect. Evaluate your content and organization to make sure you've said what you want in the order you wanted to say it. Review your message's readability. Edit and

Just as you do for other messages, you need to revise, produce, and proofread routine messages.

rewrite routine messages for conciseness and clarity. Second, design your document to suit your audience. Choose effective design elements and appropriate delivery methods. Finally, proofread the final version of your routine message. Look for typos, errors in spelling and mechanics, alignment problems, poor print quality, and so on.

Making Routine Requests

OBJECTIVE 2 **Illustrate the strategy for writing routine requests.**

Whenever you ask for something—information, action, products, adjustments, references—you are making a request. A request is routine if it's part of the normal course of business and you anticipate that your audience will want to comply. Be careful not to make unnecessary requests. If you can find information yourself, don't burden others and risk your credibility by asking someone else to find it for you. But when you must make a routine request, make sure it's efficient and effective.

For routine requests and positive messages

- State the request or main idea
- Give necessary details
- Close with a cordial request for specific action

Strategy for Routine Requests

Like all routine messages, routine requests have three parts: an opening, a body, and a close. Using the direct approach, you place your main idea (the request) in the opening. You use the middle to explain details and justify your request. Then you close by requesting specific action and concluding cordially (see Figure 7–1 on page 167).

ACHIEVING INTERCULTURAL COMMUNICATION

How Direct Is Too Direct?

Being direct is civil, considerate, and honest—or so say people in Canada and the United States. Other folks view that same directness as being abrupt, rude and intrusive—even dishonest and offensive. Countries such as France, Mexico, Japan, Saudi Arabia, Italy, and the Philippines all tend to be high-context cultures (see discussion in Chapter 3). That is, the people in these countries depend on shared knowledge and inferred messages to communicate; they gather meaning more from context and less from direct statement.

Offering a little constructive criticism may actually hurt your Japanese assistant's dignity. In fact, in high-context cultures, avoid saying outright, "You are wrong." You could cause the other person to lose face. When making requests, determine whether to use a direct or an implied message by considering audience attitudes toward destiny, time, authority, and logic:

- *Destiny.* Do audience members believe they can control events themselves or do they see events as predetermined and uncontrollable? If you're supervising employees who believe that fate controls a construction deadline, your crisp e-mail message requesting them to stay on schedule may be hard for them to understand. It may even be insulting.
- *Time.* Do audience members view time as exact, precise, and not to be wasted, or do they see time as relative, relaxed, and necessary for developing interpersonal relationships? If you see time as money and you get straight to business in your memo to your Mexican manager, your message may be overlooked in the confusion over your disregard for social propriety.
- *Authority.* Do audience members conduct business more autocratically or more democratically? In Japan, rank and status are highly valued, so when communicating downward, you may need to be even more direct than you're used to being in Canada. And when communicating upward, you may need to be much less direct than usual.
- *Logic.* Do audience members pursue logic in a straight line, from point *a* to point *b*, or do they communicate in circular or spiral patterns of logic? If you organize a speech or letter in a straightforward and direct manner, your message may be considered illogical, unclear, and disorganized.

You may want to decide not only how direct to be in written messages but also whether to write at all. Perhaps a phone call or a visit would be more appropriate. By finding out how much or how little a culture tends toward high-context communication, you'll know whether to be direct or to rely on nuance when communicating with the people there.

CAREER APPLICATIONS

1. Research a high-context culture such as Japan, Korea, or China, and write a one- or two-paragraph summary of how someone in that culture would go about requesting information.
2. When you are writing to someone in a high-context culture, would it be better to (a) make the request directly in the interest of clarity or (b) try to match your audience's unfamiliar logic and make your request indirectly? Explain your answer.

Sources: Adapted from Mary A. DeVries, *Internationally Yours* (Boston: Houghton Mifflin, 1994), 195; Myron W. Lustig and Jolene Koester, *Intercultural Competence* (New York: HarperCollins, 1993), 66–72; Mary Munter, "Cross-Cultural Communication for Managers," *Business Horizons,* May–June 1993, 69–78; David A. Victor, *International Business Communication* (New York: HarperCollins, 1992), 137–168; Larry A. Samovar and Richard E. Porter, *Intercultural Communication: A Reader,* 6th ed. (Belmont, Calif.: Wadsworth, 1991), 109–110; Larry A. Samovar and Richard E. Porter, *Communication between Cultures* (Belmont, Calif.: Wadsworth, 1991), 235–244; Carley H. Dodd, *Dynamics of Intercultural Communication,* 3d ed. (Dubuque, Iowa: Wm. C. Brown, 1989), 69–73.

STATE YOUR REQUEST UP FRONT

Begin routine requests by placing your request first. Up front is where it stands out and gets the most attention. Of course, getting right to the point should not be interpreted as a licence to be abrupt or tactless:

- **Pay attention to tone.** Even though you expect a favourable response, the **tone** of your initial request is important. Instead of demanding action ("Send me your catalog no. 33A"), soften your request with words such as *please* and *I would appreciate.*
- **Assume your audience will comply.** An impatient demand for rapid service isn't necessary. Generally make the assumption that your audience will comply with your request once the reason for it is clearly understood.
- **Avoid beginning with personal introductions.** Don't be tempted to begin your request with a personal introduction such as "I am the assistant manager at an Indigo Books and Music store, and I am looking for information that ..." This type of beginning buries the main idea, so the request may get lost.
- **Punctuate questions and polite requests differently.** A polite request in question form requires no question mark ("Would you please help me determine if the Mechstart 2000 magnetic tape is sufficient for backing up our data.") A direct question within your message does require a question mark ("Is the Mechstart 2000 magnetic tape sufficient for backing up our data?")
- **Be specific.** State precisely what you want. For example, if you request "the latest computer catalogue" from a vendor, be sure to say whether you want the catalogue for PC users or for Macintosh users if you know the vendor has two separate catalogues for these different systems.

Going Online

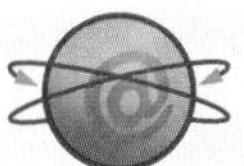

The Medium and the Message

Explore About.com's numerous links to sources of information on a variety of subjects. You can find tips on business writing with examples of letters, memos, and press releases. You'll find Web-design ideas and help from numerous guides on many business-related topics. You can even get online help with setting standards for a company's online communication.

www.about.com

To link directly to this site, visit our Companion Web site at **www.pearsoned.ca/thill** *and look for the Chapter 7 resources.*

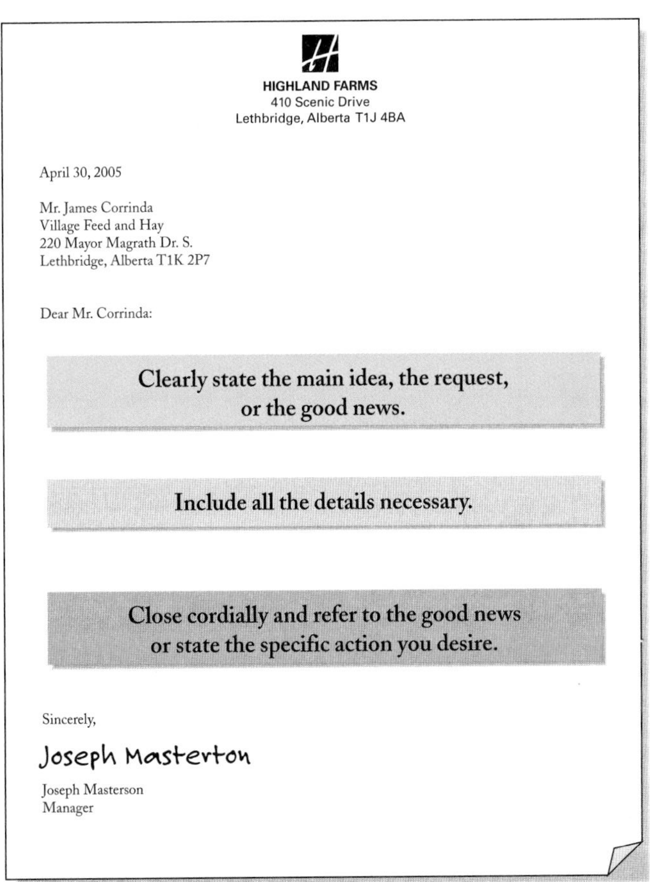

HIGHLAND FARMS
410 Scenic Drive
Lethbridge, Alberta T1J 4BA

April 30, 2005

Mr. James Corrinda
Village Feed and Hay
220 Mayor Magrath Dr. S.
Lethbridge, Alberta T1K 2P7

Dear Mr. Corrinda:

Clearly state the main idea, the request, or the good news.

Include all the details necessary.

Close cordially and refer to the good news or state the specific action you desire.

Sincerely,

Joseph Masterton

Joseph Masterson
Manager

FIGURE 7–1 The Parts of Routine, Good-News, and Goodwill Messages

In the middle section of the request, give the details of your request.

EXPLAIN AND JUSTIFY YOUR REQUEST

Use the body of your message to explain and develop your initial request. Make the explanation a smooth and logical outgrowth of your opening remarks. For example, you might show how your readers could benefit from complying. Figure 7-2 below is a letter to a potential supplier. The writer is looking for product information, but she's also (1) telling her reader why she needs the information, and (2) suggesting that a long-term business relationship might evolve when she mentions her customer's interest in the product.

As Figure 7-2 below shows, the middle section of routine requests can be handled as a series of questions—a method particularly useful whether your inquiry concerns simple products or complex equipment. For instance, you might ask about technical specifications, exact dimensions, and the precise use of a complex tool. Even if your request is relatively simple, you can use a list of questions in the body of your message. Be sure to divide multiple requests. When requesting several items or answers, num-

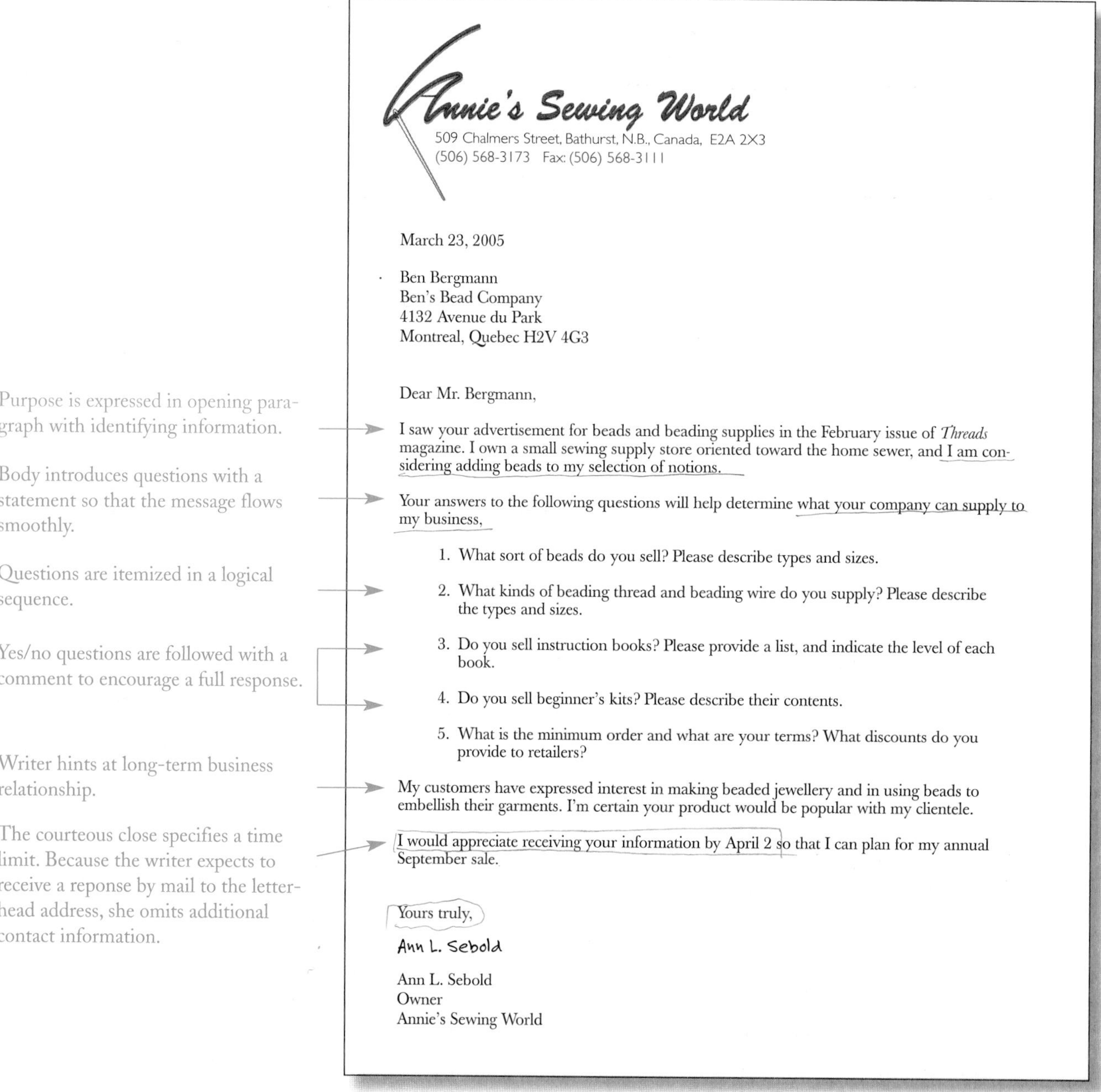
Annie's Sewing World
509 Chalmers Street, Bathurst, N.B., Canada, E2A 2X3
(506) 568-3173 Fax: (506) 568-3111

March 23, 2005

Ben Bergmann
Ben's Bead Company
4132 Avenue du Park
Montreal, Quebec H2V 4G3

Dear Mr. Bergmann,

I saw your advertisement for beads and beading supplies in the February issue of *Threads* magazine. I own a small sewing supply store oriented toward the home sewer, and I am considering adding beads to my selection of notions.

Your answers to the following questions will help determine what your company can supply to my business,

1. What sort of beads do you sell? Please describe types and sizes.
2. What kinds of beading thread and beading wire do you supply? Please describe the types and sizes.
3. Do you sell instruction books? Please provide a list, and indicate the level of each book.
4. Do you sell beginner's kits? Please describe their contents.
5. What is the minimum order and what are your terms? What discounts do you provide to retailers?

My customers have expressed interest in making beaded jewellery and in using beads to embellish their garments. I'm certain your product would be popular with my clientele.

I would appreciate receiving your information by April 2 so that I can plan for my annual September sale.

Yours truly,

Ann L. Sebold

Ann L. Sebold
Owner
Annie's Sewing World

Purpose is expressed in opening paragraph with identifying information.
Body introduces questions with a statement so that the message flows smoothly.
Questions are itemized in a logical sequence.
Yes/no questions are followed with a comment to encourage a full response.
Writer hints at long-term business relationship.
The courteous close specifies a time limit. Because the writer expects to receive a reponse by mail to the letterhead address, she omits additional contact information.

FIGURE 7-2 In-Depth Critique: Request for Information

ber the items and list them in logical order or in descending order of importance. When using a series of questions, keep a few basics in mind:

Numbered lists may help readers sort through multiple related items or multiple requests.

- **Ask the most important questions first.** If cost is your main concern, you might begin with a question such as "What is the cost for shipping the DVDs by express post?" Then you may want to ask more specific but related questions about the cost of shipping partial orders.
- **Ask only relevant questions.** So that your request can be handled quickly, ask only questions central to your main request. If your questions require simple yes-or-no answers, you might provide readers with a form or with boxes to check. If you need more elaborate answers, pose open-ended questions. "How fast can you ship the DVDs?" is more likely to elicit the information you want than "Can you ship the DVDs?"
- **Deal with only one topic per question.** If you have an unusual or complex request, list the request and provide supporting details in a separate, short paragraph. You may even use paragraph headings to make your reader's job easier.

REQUEST SPECIFIC ACTION IN A COURTEOUS CLOSE

Close your letter with three important elements: (1) a specific request, (2) information about how you can be reached, and (3) an expression of appreciation or goodwill. Use the closing to request a specific action, and ask that readers respond by a specific and appropriate time limit ("Please send the figures by April 5 so that I can return quarter results to you before the May 20 conference"). Help your reader respond easily by including your e-mail address, phone extension, office hours, and other contact information.

Close with
- A request for some specific response
- Information about how you can be reached
- An expression of appreciation

Conclude your message by sincerely expressing your goodwill and appreciation. However, don't thank the reader "in advance" for cooperating. If the reader's reply warrants a word of thanks, send it after you've received the reply. To review, see this chapter's "Checklist: Writing Routine Requests", below.

Types of Routine Requests

At work you will be writing many types of routine requests: asking favours, requesting credit, seeking scheduling changes, asking for progress reports, and many more.

OBJECTIVE 3 Discuss the differences among four types of routine requests.

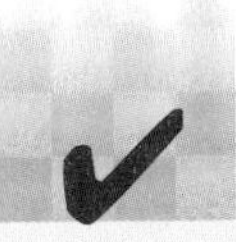

Checklist: Writing Routine Requests

Direct Statement of the Request

✓ Use the direct approach, since your audience will respond favourably to your request.

✓ Phrase the opening clearly and simply so that the main idea cannot be misunderstood.

✓ Write in a polite, undemanding, personal tone.

✓ Preface complex requests with a sentence or two of explanation.

Justification, Explanation, and Details

✓ Justify the request or explain its importance.

✓ Explain the benefit of responding.

✓ State desired actions in a positive and supportive (not negative or dictatorial) manner.

✓ Itemize parts of a complex request in a logical or numbered series.

✓ List specific questions that you can't answer through your own efforts.

✓ Limit any question to one topic.

✓ Word any questions to get the type of answers you need.

Courteous Close with Request for Specific Action

✓ Courteously request a specific action.

✓ Make it easy to comply by including your contact information: name, address, phone and fax numbers (with area code), and e-mail address.

✓ Indicate gratitude.

✓ Clearly state any important deadline or time frame for the request.

The following sections discuss four categories: placing orders, requesting information and action, making claims and requesting adjustments, and requesting recommendations and references.

PLACING ORDERS

Messages placing orders are considered some of the simplest types of routine messages. When placing an order, you need not excite your reader's interest, just state your needs clearly and directly. Your readers will of course welcome your orders, because they increase their business.

Most companies today use computer-generated order forms.

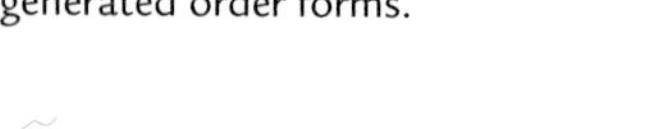

Many large and medium-size companies today provide online ordering, either through their Internet site or, for regular customers, an Intranet. For paper-based orders, firms typically provide forms listing products with descriptions of each item and information such as the catalogue number, name or trade name, colour, size, and unit price. Your job is simple: fill in the quantity, compute the total amount due, and provide the shipping address.

Small firms, such as those making handcrafts, may not offer online ordering on their Web site (they may not have a Web site at all). Consequently, you may face instances where you need to draft an order letter; for example, you may be dealing with a company that e-mails you a list of end-of-stock specials, and you will have to write your own order message to obtain the materials you want. In situations such as these, follow the same format as you would on an order blank. Open with the general request. In the body, include specific information about the items that you want. Present this information in column form, double-space between the items, and total the price at the end. (Alternatively, you can use the table feature of your wordprocessing software.) In the close be sure to specify the delivery address, since it may differ from the billing address. Also indicate how the merchandise is to be shipped: by priority post, parcel post, air express, or courier. Otherwise, the seller chooses the mode of transportation. In any letter including a payment, mention the amount enclosed, explain

Checklist: Placing Orders, Making Claims, and Requesting Adjustments*

Placing Orders

- ✓ Provide a general description of the order in the opening.
- ✓ Include all order specifications in the body: quantity, price (including discounts), size, catalogue or product number, product description, delivery instructions, arrangements for payment (method, time, deposits), and total cost.
- ✓ Indicate how and where to send the shipment (sometimes billing and delivery addresses are different).
- ✓ Use a format that presents information clearly and makes it easy to total the amounts.
- ✓ Double-check the completeness of your order and the total cost.
- ✓ Mention any payment you've enclosed, along with cheque number and amount.
- ✓ In the close, state when you expect delivery and specify any time limits in the closing.

Making Claims and Requesting Adjustments

- ✓ Write a claim letter as soon as possible after the problem has been identified.
- ✓ Maintain a confident, factual, fair, unemotional tone.
- ✓ Present facts honestly, clearly, and politely.
- ✓ Eliminate threats, sarcasm, exaggeration, and hostility, and use a nonargumentative tone to show confidence in the reader's fairness.
- ✓ Make no accusation against any person or company, unless you can back it up with facts.
- ✓ To gain the reader's understanding, praise some aspect of the good or service, or at least explain why the product was originally purchased.
- ✓ If appropriate, clearly state what you expect as a fair settlement, or ask the reader to propose a fair adjustment.
- ✓ Provide copies of necessary documents (invoices, cancelled cheques, confirmation letters, and the like); keep the originals.
- ✓ In the closing, briefly summarize desired action.

*These items are in addition to the basic tasks associated with writing routine requests.

how the amount was calculated, and if necessary, explain to what account the amount should be charged. Here's an example:

When placing orders, be thorough and clear.

General request is stated first.

Please send the following items to the above address by air freight. I am ordering from your current spring–summer catalogue:

Quantity	Stock I.D.	Description	Item Price	Total Price
3	139-24	Daily appointment books (black)	$ 8.95	$26.85
50	289-90	Mechanical pencils (0.5 mm/black)	1.69	84.50
5	905-18	Wrist pads (gray)	6.99	34.95
10	472-67	Bulk IBM-format 3" diskettes 50/box)	17.99	179.90
		Total Sale		$326.20
		Shipping		Free
		Amount Due		$326.20

All necessary details provided in a format similar to an order form.

Writer calculates amount due (information on tax and shipping was provided in catalogue).

My cheque #1738 for $326.20 is enclosed. Please ship these supplies by priority post to the address in the letterhead.

Additional important information is included in the close.

When placing orders with international companies, remember that in most countries, the day is placed before the month: 15 March 2005 (15.3.05) rather than March 15, 2005 (3/15/05). To review the tasks involved in placing orders, see this chapter's "Checklist: Placing Orders, Making Claims, and Requesting Adjustments" on page 170.

When making a routine request, say
- What you want to know
- Why you want to know
- Why it is in the reader's interest to help you

REQUESTING INFORMATION AND ACTION

When you need to know about something, to obtain an opinion from someone, or to suggest a simple action, you usually need only ask. In essence, simple requests say, "This is what I want to know or what I want you to do, why I'm making the request, and why it may be in your interest to help me." If your reader can do what you want, such a straightforward request gets the job done easily. Follow the direct approach: Start with a clear statement of your reason for writing. In the middle, provide whatever explanation is needed to justify your request. Then close with a specific account of what you expect, and include a deadline if appropriate.

Despite the simple organization of routine requests, they can cause ill will through ambiguous wording or a discourteous tone. When you prepare your request, remember that even the briefest note can create confusion and hard feelings. As with any business message, keep your purpose in mind. Ask yourself what you want readers to do or to understand as a result of reading your message.

Customer relationship software (CRM) stores varied customer information—addresses and phone numbers, previous orders, personal facts like birthdates, hobbies, and interests. This information helps companies generate routine, good-news, and goodwill messages, such as product announcements, special deals, and business events, to selected customers. While CRM software helps business retain customers and raise profits, does it also pose the danger of violating one of our most prized possessions, our privacy?

Asking Company Insiders Requests to fellow employees are often oral and rather casual. However, as long as you avoid writing frequent, long, or unneeded messages, a clear, thoughtfully written memo or e-mail message can save time and questions by helping readers understand precisely what is required. For information on formatting memos and other business messages, see Appendix A. In the following single-screen e-mail, the writer describes a concern and requests a response from employees:

To: All staff
From: Michelle Charest, Director, Human Resources
Reply to: f.karpulin@timken.com
Date: July 13, 2005 9:00 AM

Are you interested in having a daycare centre on site? Please answer the following questions to help us determine the feasibility of establishing a daycare centre at Timken Manufacturing.

The e-mail begins with the central question.

A little background information orients the reader.

Several suggestions in the cafeteria suggestion box indicate that parents at Timken want convenient, affordable childcare. Therefore, your answers to the following questions will make us aware of your needs.

The numbered questions focus responses to simplify recording them.

1. How many children would you enroll in the new centre?
2. How much do you currently pay each week for each child in daycare?
3. Do you think the cost is too high? In your opinion, what would be a reasonable weekly charge for each child?
4. What qualities do you look for in a daycare centre?
5. What qualifications do you expect of the caregivers?

Specific instructions for replying close the memo. The courteous tone helps ensure a prompt response.

Please respond to Felix (f.karpulin@timken.com) in Human Resources by Friday, July 23. We appreciate your prompt response so that we may begin analyzing the possibilities.

The memo in Figure 7-3 (on page 173) was sent to all employees of a small interior design firm. It seeks employee input about a new wellness and benefits program and about a new fee. The tone is matter-of-fact, and the memo assumes some shared background, which is appropriate when you're communicating about a routine matter to someone in the same company.

Asking Company Outsiders Businesspeople often ask businesses, customers, or others outside their organization to provide information or to take some simple action: attend a meeting, return an information card, endorse a document, confirm an address, or supplement information on an order. Such requests are in letter form (see Appendix A) or e-mail. These messages are usually short and simple, like the request for information in Figure 7-2 on page 168.

Requests to outsiders often spell out in detail how filling the request will benefit readers.

In more complex situations, readers might be unwilling to respond unless they understand how the request benefits them. Be sure to include this information in your explanation.

The purpose of some routine requests to customers is to reestablish communication.

Sometimes businesses need to re-establish a relationship with former customers or suppliers. Frequently, customers don't complain when they are unhappy about some purchase or about the way they were treated: They simply stay away from the business. A letter of inquiry might, for example, encourage readers to use idle credit accounts, offering them an opportunity to register their displeasure and then move on to a good relationship. In addition, a customer's response to such an inquiry may provide the company with insights into ways to improve its products and customer service. Even if they have no complaint, customers still welcome the personal attention. Such an inquiry to a customer might begin this way:

> When a good charge customer like you has not bought anything from us in six months, we wonder why. Is there something we can do to serve you better?

Similar inquiry letters are sent from one business to another. For example, a sales representative of a housewares distributor might send the same type of letter to a retailer. To review the tasks involved in requesting information and action, see this chapter's "Checklist: Writing Routine Requests" on page 169.

MAKING CLAIMS AND REQUESTING ADJUSTMENTS

Putting your claim in writing
- Documents your dissatisfaction
- Requires courtesy, clarity, and conciseness

When you're dissatisfied with a company's product or service, you make a **claim** (a formal complaint) or request an **adjustment** (a claim settlement). Although a phone call or visit may solve the problem, a written claim letter is sometimes necessary because it documents your dissatisfaction. If you have to pursue your claim with legal assistance, your claim letter establishes a formal record of the problem and your attempts to seek some sort of compensation. Even though your first reaction to poor service or a defective product is likely to be anger or frustration, remember that a courteous, clear, concise explanation will impress your reader much more favourably than an abusive, angry letter.

1 Planning

Analyze: Purpose is to request feedback from fellow employees.

Investigate: Gather accurate, complete information on program benefits and local gym.

Adapt: Office memo or e-mail is appropriate medium. Use "you" attitude, and make responding easy.

2 Writing

Organize: Main idea is saving money while staying healthy. Save time and meet audience expectations using the direct approach.

Compose: Keep style informal but businesslike. Using a "we" attitude includes readers in the decision-making processes.

3 Completing

Revise: Keep it brief—weed out overly long words and phrases. Avoid unnecessary detail.

Produce: No need for fancy design elements in this memo. Include a response form.

Proofread: Review carefully for both content and typographical errors.

Hydel Interior Alternatives

INTERNAL MEMORANDUM

To: All Employees
From: Mike Ortega, Human Resources
Date: October 15, 2005
Subj: New Wellness Program Opportunity

Routes message efficiently, with all needed information.

The benefits package committee wants you to consider participating in a wellness program. As you know, we've been meeting to decide on changes in our benefits package. We need your response on this matter, so please read the following information carefully and complete the bottom half of this memo.

States purpose in opening to avoid wasting readers' time.

Last week, we sent you a memo detailing the Synergy Wellness Program. In addition to the package as described in the memo (life, major medical, dental, hospitalization), Synergy offered HIA a 10 percent discount in our premiums. To meet the requirements for the discount, we have to show proof that at least 25 percent of our employees participate in aerobic exercise at least three times a week for at least 20 minutes. (Their actuarial tables show a resulting 10 percent reduction in claims.)

During warm weather, many of us walk the nature trail on our lunch break. Those walks will satisfy Synergy's requirements, but we have those nasty winters when few of us venture outside. After investigating, we found a gymnasium with an indoor track just a few blocks south on Grant Street. The Keep Fit Sports Centre will give our employees unlimited daytime access to their indoor track, gym, and pool for a group fee that comes to approximately $4.50 per month per employee if at least half of us sign up. Payroll says you can have the amount automatically deducted, if you wish.

Presents the situation that makes the inquiry necessary.

In addition to walking, we can swim, play volleyball, take dance, yoga, and Pilates classes, form our own intramural basketball teams, and much more. Partners and children can also participate at a deeply discounted monthly fee. If you have questions, please e-mail or call me. Let us know your wishes on the following form.

Lists reader benefits and requests action.

Sign and return the following no later than Friday, October 27.

==

______ Yes, I will participate in the Synergy Wellness program and pay $4.50 a month.
______ Yes, I am interested in a discounted family membership.
______ No, I prefer not to participate.

Signature ______________________________

Employee ID Number ______________________________

Provides an easy-to-use response form.

FIGURE 7–3 In-Depth Critique: Memo Requesting Action from Company Insiders

In your claim letter
- Explain the problem and give details
- Provide backup information
- Request specific action

In most cases, and especially in your first letter, assume that a fair adjustment will be made, and follow the plan for direct requests. Begin with a straightforward statement of the problem. In the body, give a complete, specific explanation of the details. Provide any information the reader would need to verify your complaint about faulty merchandise or unsatisfactory service. In your closing, politely request specific action or convey a sincere desire to find a solution. You can also suggest that the business relationship will continue if the problem is solved satisfactorily.

Be prepared to document your claim. Send copies and keep the original documents.

It's essential to be entirely honest when filing claims. Be prepared to back up your claim with invoices, sales receipts, cancelled cheques, dated correspondence, catalogue descriptions, and any other relevant documents. Send copies and keep the originals for your files.

If the remedy is obvious, tell your reader exactly what will return the company to your good graces—for example, an exchange of merchandise for the right item or a refund if the item is out of stock. In some cases you might ask the reader to resolve the problem. If you're uncertain about the precise nature of the trouble, you could ask the company to make an assessment. But be sure to supply your contact information and the best time to call so that the company can discuss the situation with you if necessary.

Be as specific as possible about what you want to happen next.

The following letter was written to an office cleaning company. As you read it, compare the tone with the one in Figure 7-4. If you were the person receiving the complaint, which version would you respond to more favorably?

First Draft

We have used your service since March 2002, and we are disgusted by the condition the shop has been left in this week. I found full wastebaskets, smudge marks on the countertops, and coffee cups on the desks. Furthermore, the floor was full of scuff marks and dirt; remember that we contracted with your firm to polish the floors on Wednesday and Friday nights. This carelessness is very disappointing. I expect you to hire good workers, and to check up on them.

Most people would react much more favorably to the version in Figure 7–4. A rational, clear, and courteous approach is best for any routine request. To review the tasks involved in making claims and requesting adjustments, see this chapter's "Checklist: Placing Orders, Making Claims, and Requesting Adjustments" on page 169.

REQUESTING RECOMMENDATIONS AND REFERENCES

The need to inquire about people arises often in business. For example, before awarding credit, contracts, jobs, promotions, scholarships, and so on, some companies ask applicants to supply references. If you're applying for a job and your potential employer asks for references, you may want to ask a close personal or professional associate to write a letter of recommendation. Or, if you're an employer considering whether to hire an applicant, you may want to write directly to the person the applicant named as a reference.

Always ask for permission before using someone's name as a reference.

Companies ask applicants to supply references who can vouch for their ability, skills, integrity, character, and fitness for the job. Before you volunteer someone's name as a reference, ask that person's permission. Some people prefer not to serve as a reference, perhaps because they don't know enough about you to feel comfortable writing a letter or because they have a policy of not providing recommendations. Some companies will only supply the job candidate's date of hire, position, duties, salary, and date of termination to prospective employers.[2] In any event, you are likely to receive the best recommendation from persons who agree to write about you, so check first.

Refresh the memory of any potential reference you haven't been in touch with for a while.

Because requests for recommendations and references are routine, you can assume your reader will honour your request and organize your inquiry using the direct approach. Begin your message by clearly stating that you're applying for a position and that you would like your reader to write a letter of recommendation. If you haven't had contact with the person for some time, use the opening to recall the nature of the relationship you had, the dates of association, and any special events that might bring a clear, favourable picture of you to mind.

Baltic Instaprint
620 Broadway Ave • Saskatoon, SK S7N 1A8
306-555-6543
pol@baltprint.com

June 10, 2005

Stephan Mikolovic, Manager
Brightspot Cleaning and Maintenance
1515 Arlington Ave
Saskatoon, SK S7Y 2Y3

Dear Mr. Mikolovic:

For the last two weeks, my store has not been properly cleaned. I am asking you to replace the current staff with new cleaners.

I have contracted with you since March 2002, and had been very satisfied with your service. The contract specified that the store would be cleaned thoroughly and vacuumed each night and that Tuesday and Friday the floor would be polished.

However, when I opened the store on Tuesday, Wednesday, and Thursday mornings this week, I found full wastebaskets, smudge marks on the countertops, and coffee cups on the desks. Furthermore, the floor showed scuffmarks and was littered with paper. This lack of care is very unusual. Until this past week your cleaners had been meticulous in looking after our shop.

Assigning new cleaners to our store may solve the problem. We are a very busy photocopy and print shop and see a steady stream of customers from the time we open until we close. Our customers expect us to do clean and neat work; accordingly, the appearance of our shop must reflect our high standards.

Thank you for looking into this matter; I hope to hear from you by the end of next week about the change of cleaners. You can reach me at 555-6543 between 8 a.m. and 7 p.m.

Yours truly,

Vassily Polikoff
Owner

Opening clearly and calmly states the problem.

Important background information helps to highlight the problem.

Details are presented clearly, concisely, and completely.

Body explains details so that reader can understand why writer believes a problem exists.

Closing requests specific action and provides contact information to make responding easy.

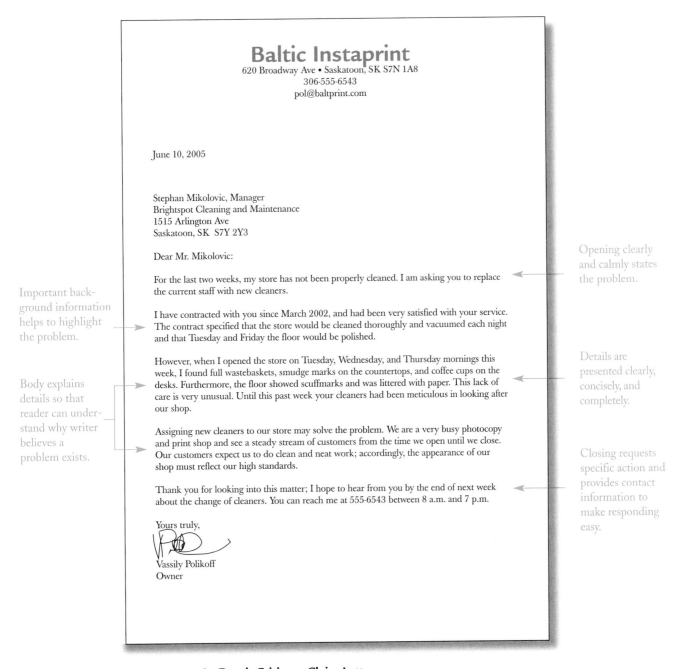

FIGURE 7–4 In-Depth Critique: Claim Letter

If you're applying for a job, a scholarship, or the like, include a copy of your résumé to give the reader an idea of the direction your life has taken. After reading the résumé, your reader will know what favourable qualities to emphasize and will be able to write the recommendation that best supports your application. If you don't have a résumé, use the body of your letter to include any information about yourself that the reader might use to support a recommendation, such as a description of related jobs you've held.

Provide your reader with as much information as possible about your qualifications.

Close your letter with an expression of appreciation and the full name and address of the person to whom the letter should be sent. When asking for an immediate recommendation, you should also mention the deadline. You'll make a response more likely if you enclose a stamped, pre-addressed envelope. The letter in Figure 7–5 on page 176 covers all these points and adds important information about some qualifications that might be of special interest to her potential employer.

1 Planning

Analyze: Purpose is to request a recommendation letter from your university professor.

Investigate: Gather information to help reader recall you and to clarify the position you want.

Adapt: A letter format will give your message the formality you need. Be polite.

2 Writing

Organize: Main idea is to convince your professor to send a glowing recommendation to potential employer. Use the direct approach.

Compose: Make message friendly but businesslike and slightly more formal than usual. Use plain English and an active voice.

3 Completing

Revise: Be concise but thorough. Make sure that concrete detail flows logically.

Produce: Use simple typeface with ample margins and spacing between text. Enclose your résumé.

Proofread: Review letter and enclosures for errors.

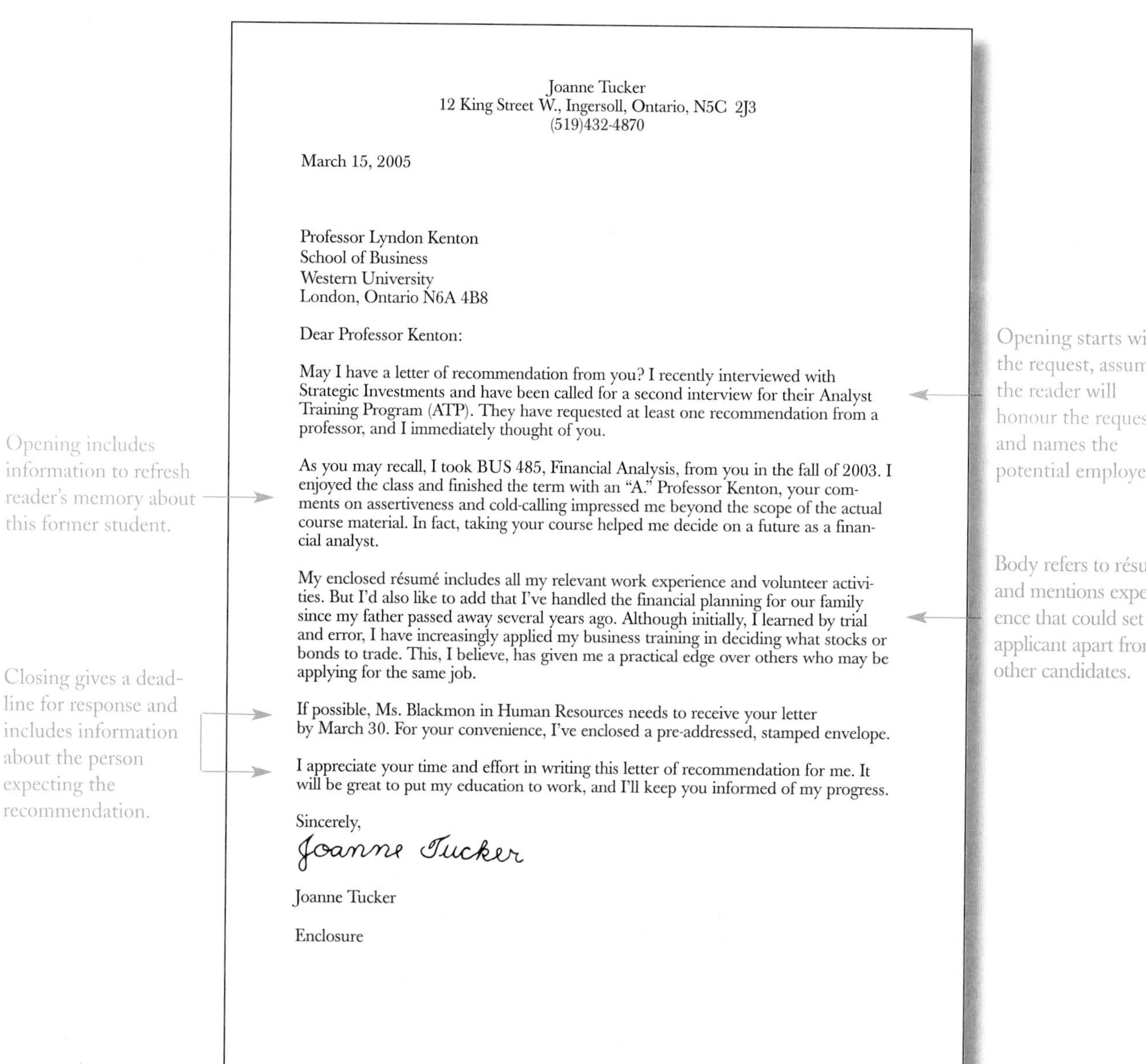

Joanne Tucker
12 King Street W., Ingersoll, Ontario, N5C 2J3
(519)432-4870

March 15, 2005

Professor Lyndon Kenton
School of Business
Western University
London, Ontario N6A 4B8

Dear Professor Kenton:

May I have a letter of recommendation from you? I recently interviewed with Strategic Investments and have been called for a second interview for their Analyst Training Program (ATP). They have requested at least one recommendation from a professor, and I immediately thought of you.

As you may recall, I took BUS 485, Financial Analysis, from you in the fall of 2003. I enjoyed the class and finished the term with an "A." Professor Kenton, your comments on assertiveness and cold-calling impressed me beyond the scope of the actual course material. In fact, taking your course helped me decide on a future as a financial analyst.

My enclosed résumé includes all my relevant work experience and volunteer activities. But I'd also like to add that I've handled the financial planning for our family since my father passed away several years ago. Although initially, I learned by trial and error, I have increasingly applied my business training in deciding what stocks or bonds to trade. This, I believe, has given me a practical edge over others who may be applying for the same job.

If possible, Ms. Blackmon in Human Resources needs to receive your letter by March 30. For your convenience, I've enclosed a pre-addressed, stamped envelope.

I appreciate your time and effort in writing this letter of recommendation for me. It will be great to put my education to work, and I'll keep you informed of my progress.

Sincerely,

Joanne Tucker

Joanne Tucker

Enclosure

Opening starts with the request, assumes the reader will honour the request, and names the potential employer.
Opening includes information to refresh reader's memory about this former student.
Body refers to résumé and mentions experience that could set applicant apart from other candidates.
Closing gives a deadline for response and includes information about the person expecting the recommendation.

FIGURE 7–5 In-Depth Critique: Letter Requesting a Recommendation

Sending Routine Replies and Positive Messages

When responding positively to a request or sending a good-news or goodwill message, you have several goals: to communicate the good news, answer all questions, provide all required details, and leave your reader with a good impression of you and your firm. This sort of message can be quite brief and to the point. However, even though you may be doing someone a favour by responding to a request, you want to be courteous and upbeat and maintain a you-oriented tone.

Strategy for Routine Replies and Positive Messages

Like requests, routine replies and positive messages have an opening, a body, and a close. Readers receiving these messages will generally be interested in what you have to say, so you'll usually use the direct approach. Place your main idea, the positive reply or the good news, in the opening. Use the middle to explain all the relevant details, and close cordially, perhaps highlighting a benefit to your reader.

Use the direct organizational plan for positive messages.

START WITH THE MAIN IDEA

By beginning your positive message with the main idea or good news, you're preparing your audience for the detail that follows. Try to make your opening clear and concise. Although the following introductory statements make the same point, one is cluttered with unnecessary information that buries the purpose, whereas the other is brief and to the point:

INSTEAD OF THIS	WRITE THIS
I am pleased to inform you that after deliberating the matter carefully, our human resources committee has recommended you for appointment as a staff accountant.	Congratulations! You've been selected to join our firm as a staff accountant, beginning March 20.

The best way to write a clear opening is to have a clear idea of what you want to say. Before you put one word on paper, ask yourself, "What is the single most important message I have for the audience?"

Before you begin, have a clear idea of what you want to say.

PROVIDE NECESSARY DETAILS AND EXPLANATION

The body of a positive message is typically the longest section. You need the space to explain your point completely so that the audience will experience no confusion or lingering doubt. In addition to providing details in the body of your message, maintain the supportive tone established at the beginning. This tone is easy to continue when your message is purely good news, as in this example:

> Your educational background and internship have impressed us, and we believe you would be a valuable addition to Green Valley Properties. As discussed during your interview, your salary will be $36 000 per year, plus benefits. We have arranged for you to meet with our benefits manager, Paula Sanchez, at 8:00 a.m. on Monday, March 20. She will assist you with all the paperwork necessary to tailor our benefit package to your family situation. She will also arrange various orientation activities to help you acclimate to our company.

However, if your routine message is mixed and must convey mildly disappointing information, put the negative portion of your message into as favourable a context as possible:

Embed negative information in a positive context.

INSTEAD OF THIS	WRITE THIS
No, we no longer carry the Sportsgirl line of sweaters.	The new Olympic line has replaced the Sportsgirl sweaters that you asked about. Olympic features a wider range of colours and sizes and more contemporary styling.

Checklist: Writing Routine Replies and Positive Messages

Initial Statement of the Good News or Main Idea

- ✓ If the message is mixed, present the good news first.
- ✓ Respond promptly.
- ✓ Avoid trite and obvious statements such as "I am pleased to," "We have received," "This is in response to," or "Enclosed please find."
- ✓ Convey an upbeat, courteous, you-oriented tone.

Middle, Informational Section

- ✓ Imply or express interest in the request, or provide details of the good news.
- ✓ List all information in an orderly manner.
- ✓ If possible, answer all questions and requests in the order posed.
- ✓ Adapt replies to the reader's needs.
- ✓ Indicate what you have done and what you will do.
- ✓ Include any necessary details or interpretations that the reader may need in order to understand your answers.
- ✓ If you cannot comply with part of the request (perhaps because the information is unavailable or confidential), tell the reader why and then offer other assistance, if possible.
- ✓ Embed negative statements in positive contexts or balance them with positive alternatives.
- ✓ Inform or remind the reader of the general benefits of doing business with your firm. Avoid exaggerations or flamboyant language.

Warm, Courteous Close

- ✓ If further action is required, tell the reader how to proceed and encourage the reader to act promptly.
- ✓ Avoid clichés (such as "Please feel free to").
- ✓ Offer additional service, but avoid implying that your answer is inadequate by using doubtful statements such as "I trust that" or "I hope."
- ✓ Express goodwill or take an optimistic look into the future, if appropriate.

Make sure the audience understands what to do next and how that action will benefit them.

The more complete description is less negative and emphasizes how the audience can benefit from the change. Be careful, though: You can use negative information in this type of message *only* if you're reasonably sure the audience will respond positively. Otherwise, use the indirect approach (discussed in Chapter 8).

END WITH A COURTEOUS CLOSE

Many companies use form responses to reply to similar requests.

Your message is most likely to succeed if your readers are left feeling that you have their personal welfare in mind. You accomplish this goal either by highlighting a benefit to the audience or by expressing appreciation or goodwill. If follow-up action is required, clearly state who will do what next. See this chapter's "Checklist: Writing Routine Replies and Positive Messages" to review the primary tasks involved in this type of business message.

Letters of reference are sensitive messages because you may need to describe the job candidate's shortcomings as well as strengths. In your letter, you must, of course, include such details as the position the employee held in your organization, the duties, and the number of years of service. However, seek advice from your company's human resources department, as they may have specific guidelines for writing reference letters.

Types of Routine Replies and Positive Messages

Many types of routine replies and positive messages are used in business everyday. The routine positive messages that you'll be writing will likely fall into four major categories; (1) granting requests for information and action, (2) granting claims and requests for adjustments, (3) announcing good news, and (4) sending goodwill messages.

GRANTING REQUESTS FOR INFORMATION AND ACTION

If your answer to a request is yes or is straightforward information, the direct plan is appropriate. Your prompt, gracious, and thorough response will positively influence how people think about your company, its products, your department, and you.

Many requests are similar. For example, a human resources department frequently receives routine inquiries about job openings. To handle repetitive queries like these, companies usually develop form responses. Although these messages are often criticized as being cold and impersonal, you can put a great deal of thought into wording them, and you can use computers to personalize and adapt your text. Thus, a computerized form letter prepared with care may actually be more personal and sincere than a quickly dictated, hastily typed "personal" reply. Figure 7-6, on page 181, shows a reply to a person prospecting for a position in retail management.

When you're answering requests and a potential sale is involved, you have three main goals: (1) to respond to the inquiry and answer all questions, (2) to leave your reader with a good impression of you and your firm, and (3) to encourage the future sale. The letter in Figure 7-7, on page 181, which accompanies product information, succeeds in meeting all three objectives.

Three main goals when a potential sale is involved:

- Respond to the immediate request
- Convey a good impression of you and your firm
- Encourage a sale

GRANTING CLAIMS AND REQUESTS FOR ADJUSTMENT

OBJECTIVE 4 Explain the main differences in messages granting a claim when the company, the customer, or a third party is at fault.

Satisfied customers bring additional business to a firm; angry or dissatisfied customers do not. In addition, angry customers complain to anyone who'll listen, creating poor public relations. So even though claims and adjustments may seem unpleasant, they are opportunities to build customer loyalty.[3]

Few people go to the trouble of requesting an adjustment unless they actually have a problem. So the most sensible reaction to a routine claim is to assume that the claimant's account of the transaction is an honest statement of what happened—unless the same customer repeatedly submits dubious claims or the dollar amount is very large. When you receive a complaint, respond promptly. You'll want to investigate the problem first to determine what went wrong and why. You'll also want to determine whether your company, your customer, or a third party is at fault.

In general, it pays to give customers the benefit of the doubt.

When Your Company Is at Fault Reputable businesspeople eagerly investigate claims to find out if their firm is responsible for poor product performance or poor service. When your company is at fault and your response to a claim is positive, you must protect your company's image and try to regain the customer's goodwill by referring to company errors carefully. Don't blame an individual or a specific department. And avoid lame excuses such as "Nobody's perfect" or "Mistakes will happen." Don't promise that problems will never happen again; such guarantees are unrealistic and often beyond your control. Instead, explain your company's efforts to do a good job, implying that the error was an unusual incident.

An ungracious adjustment may increase customer dissatisfaction.

For example, a large mail-order clothing company has created the following form letter to respond to customers who claim they haven't received exactly what was ordered. The form letter can be customized through word processing and then individually signed:

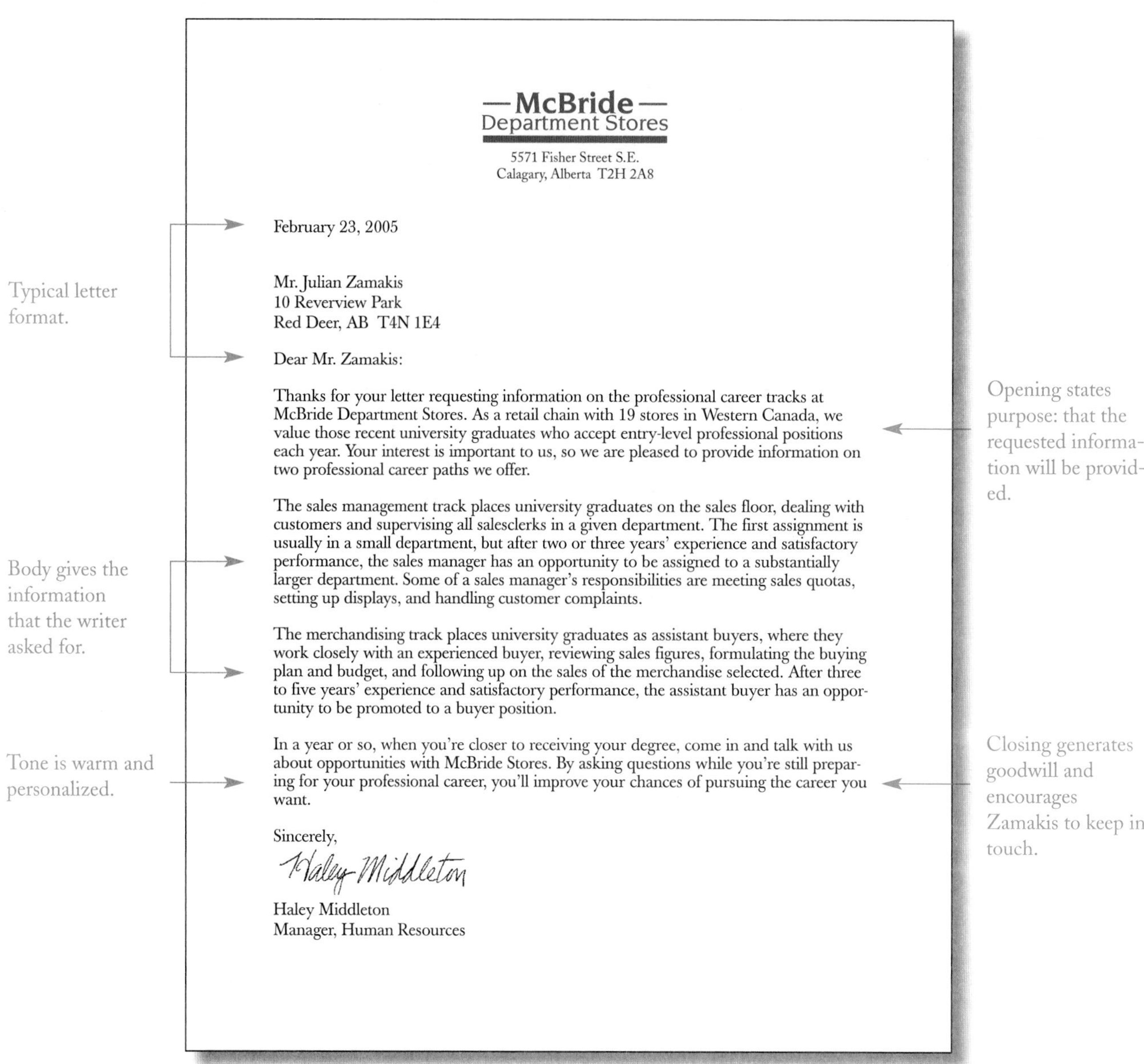
Typical letter format.
Body gives the information that the writer asked for.
Tone is warm and personalized.
Opening states purpose: that the requested information will be provided.
Closing generates goodwill and encourages Zamakis to keep in touch.

—McBride—
Department Stores

5571 Fisher Street S.E.
Calagary, Alberta T2H 2A8

February 23, 2005

Mr. Julian Zamakis
10 Reverview Park
Red Deer, AB T4N 1E4

Dear Mr. Zamakis:

Thanks for your letter requesting information on the professional career tracks at McBride Department Stores. As a retail chain with 19 stores in Western Canada, we value those recent university graduates who accept entry-level professional positions each year. Your interest is important to us, so we are pleased to provide information on two professional career paths we offer.

The sales management track places university graduates on the sales floor, dealing with customers and supervising all salesclerks in a given department. The first assignment is usually in a small department, but after two or three years' experience and satisfactory performance, the sales manager has an opportunity to be assigned to a substantially larger department. Some of a sales manager's responsibilities are meeting sales quotas, setting up displays, and handling customer complaints.

The merchandising track places university graduates as assistant buyers, where they work closely with an experienced buyer, reviewing sales figures, formulating the buying plan and budget, and following up on the sales of the merchandise selected. After three to five years' experience and satisfactory performance, the assistant buyer has an opportunity to be promoted to a buyer position.

In a year or so, when you're closer to receiving your degree, come in and talk with us about opportunities with McBride Stores. By asking questions while you're still preparing for your professional career, you'll improve your chances of pursuing the career you want.

Sincerely,

Haley Middleton

Haley Middleton
Manager, Human Resources

FIGURE 7–6 In-Depth Critique: Letter Replying to Request for Information

Starts with a "good attitude" statement (not the usual good-news statement), because it goes to people with various complaints.

Puts customer at ease with "you" attitude.

Never suggests that customer was wrong to write to Klondike.

Includes resale and sales promotion.

Closes with statement of company's concern for all its customers.

Your letter concerning your recent Klondike order has arrived and has been forwarded to our customer service supervisor. Your complete satisfaction is our goal; when you are satisfied, we are satisfied. A representative will contact you soon to assist with the issues raised in your letter.

Whether you're skiing or driving a snowmobile, Klondike Gear offers you the best protection from wind, snow, and cold—and Klondike has been taking care of your outdoor needs for over 27 years! Because you're a loyal customer, enclosed is a $5 gift certificate. You may wish to consider our new line of quality snow goggles.

Thank you for taking the time to write to us. Your input helps us better serve you and all our customers.

Piano
LIFE SAVER SYSTEM
from
DAMPP-CHASER

Phone: 800-438-1524 828-892-8271
Fax: 828-892-8272
Post Office Box 1810
Hendersonville, NC 28793 USA
www.dampp-chaser.com
e-mail: piano@dampp-chaser.com

June 19, 2005

Giulio Ferrante
2 Campbell Avenue
St. John's, Newfoundland A1E 2S6

Dear Mr. Ferrante:

Thank you for visiting the Dampp-Chaser homepage. You will find enclosed the information you requested about the Dampp-Chaser Piano Climate Control System.

Established in 1974, Dampp-Chaser Corporation manufactures and supports products which provide climate control for small enclosed spaces. With the installation of the Dampp-Chaser Piano Climate Control System, application of Dampp-Chaser's unique technology protects pianos from the damaging effects of environmental changes.

From our headquarters and manufacturing facility in Hendersonville, North Carolina we serve an international market. We have cultivated a corporate environment where pride in our product flourishes, where creativity and ingenuity are rewarded, and where the best interest of the customer is our primary consideration.

Please read through the enclosed literature. Our Piano Climate Control Systems are sold by piano dealers and piano technicians. To activate the 5-year warranty we extend on each System, it must be installed by a professional piano technician. If your piano technician is not a Dampp-Chaser installer, please call us to get the name of a technician in your area who currently installs Dampp-Chaser Systems. Or, ask your technician to contact us for detailed installation instructions. With his/her exceptional knowledge of the piano, your technician can easily follow the instructions we provide.

Call us with any questions you may have at our toll-free number: (800) 438-1524.

Thank you again for your interest in the Dampp-Chaser System which extends the life of your piano, and over time, will provide you substantial cost savings for repairs and pitch adjustments.

Best regards,
Dampp-Chaser Corporation

Brenda Robbins

Brenda Robbins
Customer Service

Enclosures

Opens with a clear statement of the main point.

Presents both product and company information which educate the reader and heighten the credibility of the message.

Message provides essential information about the warranty and installation.

Close offers reader customer service for more information and end by citing product benefits.

FIGURE 7-7: In-Depth Critique: Letter Accompanying Product Information

In contrast, a response letter written as a personal answer to a unique claim would start with a clear statement of the good news: the settling of the claim according to the customer's request. Here is a more personal response from Klondike Gear:

> Here is your heather-blue wool-and-mohair sweater (size large) to replace the one returned to us with a defect in the knitting on the left sleeve. Thanks for giving us the opportunity to correct this situation. Customers' needs have come first at Klondike Gear for 27 years. Our sweaters are handmade by the finest knitters in this area.
>
> Our newest catalogue is enclosed. Browse through it and see what wonderful new colours and patterns we have for you. Whether you are skiing or driving a snowmobile, Klondike Gear offers you the best protection available from wind, snow, and cold. Let us know how we may continue to serve you and your sporting needs.

When the Customer Is at Fault When your customer is at fault (perhaps washing a dry-clean-only sweater in hot water), you can (1) refuse the claim and attempt to justify your refusal or (2) simply do what the customer asks. But remember, if you refuse the claim, you may lose your customer—as well as many of the customer's friends, who will hear only one side of the dispute. You must weigh the cost of making the adjustment against the cost of losing future business from one or more customers.

When complying with an unjustified claim, let the customer know that the merchandise was mistreated, but maintain a respectful and positive tone.

If you choose to grant the claim, you can start off with the good news: you're replacing the merchandise or refunding the purchase price. However, the middle section needs more attention. Your job is to make the customer realize that the merchandise was mistreated, but you want to avoid being condescending ("Perhaps you failed to read the instructions carefully") or preachy ("You should know that wool shrinks in hot water"). Keep in mind that a courteous tone is especially important to the success of your message, regardless of the solution you propose. For example, an explanation of correct handling might be phrased in the following way:

> Our washing instructions, included on the tag attached to the sweater as well as the label sewn into the seam, indicate that the sweater should be washed by hand in cold water using a detergent specially formulated for wool garments, or dry cleaned. Following these methods ensures that the sweater will retain its original shape.

Note that the explanation is straightforward and objective; it doesn't cast blame on the customer.

The dilemma is this: If the customer fails to realize what went wrong, you may commit your firm to an endless procession of returned merchandise; but if you insult the customer, your cash refund will have been wasted because you'll lose your customer anyway. Without being offensive, the letter in Figure 7-8 on page 184 educates a customer about how to treat his inline skates.

When a Third Party Is at Fault Sometimes neither you nor the claimant is at fault. Perhaps the carrier damaged merchandise in transit. Or perhaps the original manufacturer is responsible for some product defect. When a third party is at fault, you have three options:

1. **Simply honour the claim.** This option is the most attractive. You can satisfy your customer with the standard good-news letter and no additional explanation. This way you maintain your reputation for fair dealing and bear no cost, because the carrier, manufacturer, or other third party will reimburse you for the damage.
2. **Honour the claim, but explain you're not at fault.** This option corrects any impression that the damage was caused by your negligence. You can still write the standard good-news letter, but stress the explanation.
3. **Refer the claimant to the third party.** This option is almost always a bad choice. When you suggest filing a claim with the firm that caused the defect or damage, you fail to satisfy the claimant's needs. The exception is when you're trying to dissociate yourself from any legal responsibility for the damaged merchandise, especially if it has caused a personal injury. In this case, it would be best to consult a lawyer for advice in preparing your message.

This chapter's "Checklist: Granting Claims and Adjustment Requests, and Sending Goodwill Messages" on page 183 reviews the tasks involved in granting claims and requests for adjustments.

ANNOUNCING GOOD NEWS

To develop and maintain good relationships, smart companies such as Indigo Books and Music recognize that it's good business to spread the word about positive developments such as opening new facilities, appointing a new executive, introducing new products or services, or sponsoring community events. Because good news is welcomed by all, use the direct approach.

Checklist: Granting Claims and Adjustment Requests, and Sending Goodwill Messages*

Granting Claims and Adjustment Requests

- ✓ In the opening, state your willingness to honour the reader's claim, without negative comment.
- ✓ Thank the claimant for taking the time to write.
- ✓ In the body, explain how you will remedy the problem.
- ✓ Minimize or, if possible, omit any disagreements with your reader's interpretation of events.
- ✓ Make your explanation objective, nonvindictive, and impersonal.
- ✓ Apologize only when appropriate; then do so crisply and without an overly dramatic tone.
- ✓ Maintain a supportive tone: "Thank you for," "May we ask," and "We are glad to work with you."
- ✓ Admit your firm's faults carefully: Don't shift blame, imply inefficiency, or make unrealistic promises.
- ✓ Be careful when discussing the claimant's role in creating the problem.
- ✓ In the closing, remind the reader how you are honouring the claim.
- ✓ Encourage the claimant to look favourably on your company or the product in question.
- ✓ Clarify any actions that your reader must take.

Sending Goodwill Messages

- ✓ Be prompt when sending out goodwill messages so that they lose none of their impact.
- ✓ Send a written message whenever possible (it is more enduring than a verbal message), but a telephone call is better than no message at all.
- ✓ Use letter format for all condolences and any other goodwill message sent to outsiders or mailed to an employee's home.
- ✓ Except for condolences, use the memo format for any goodwill messages sent through interoffice mail.
- ✓ Hand-write condolences and replies to handwritten invitations.
- ✓ When possible, present congratulations in a folder with a clipping or photo commemorating the special event.
- ✓ In the opening paragraph, incorporate a friendly statement that builds goodwill.
- ✓ Focus on the good qualities of the person or situation.
- ✓ In the body, express personalized details in sincere, restrained, language.
- ✓ Be warm but concise.
- ✓ Make the reader the focus of all comments.
- ✓ Close with a positive or forward-looking statement.
- ✓ Restate the important idea in the close, when appropriate.

*These items are in addition to the basic tasks associated with writing positive responses.

About Employment Writing a letter to the successful job applicant is a pleasure. Such a letter is eagerly awaited, so the direct approach is appropriate:

> Welcome to Lake Valley Rehabilitation Centre. A number of excellent candidates were interviewed, but your educational background and recent experience at Memorial Hospital make you the best person for the position of medical records coordinator.
>
> As we discussed, your salary is $34 000 per year. We would like you to begin on Monday, February 1. Please come to my office at 8:00 a.m. I will give you an in-depth orientation to Lake Valley and discuss the various company benefits available to you. You can also sign all the necessary employment documents.
>
> After lunch, Vanessa Jackson will take you to the medical records department and help you settle into your new responsibilities at Lake Valley Rehabilitation Centre. I look forward to seeing you on February 1.

← Announces news in a friendly, welcoming tone.

← Explains all necessary details.

← Explains first day's routine to ease new employee's uncertainty.

Although letters like these are pleasant to write, they constitute a legal job offer. In many large firms, the human resources department handles messages such as these, but in smaller firms the owner or a department manager may write the message. Remember that you and your company may be held to any promises you make, so obtain legal advice before sending an employment offer to the new employee.

A letter telling someone that she or he got the job is a legal document, so make sure all statements are accurate.

1 Planning

Analyze: Purpose is to grant a customer's claim, gently educate him, and encourage further business.

Investigate: Gather information on product care, warranties, and resale information.

Adapt: Use letter format to reinforce businesslike tone. Give customer relationship utmost attention.

2 Writing

Organize: Main idea is that you're replacing the wheel assembly—even though you are not required to do so.

Compose: Use an upbeat conversational style, but remain businesslike. Choose words carefully, especially when educating customer. Include resale information to reinforce future business.

3 Completing

Revise: Revise for tone, focusing on conciseness, clarity, and the "you" attitude.

Produce: Avoid confusing your positive message with fussy design elements. Keep it simple.

Proofread: Review for the usual errors, and include all promised enclosures.

20901 El Dorado Hills
Laguna Niguel, CA 92677
(714) 332-7474 • Fax: (714) 336-5297
skates@speed.net

February 6, 2004

Mr. Steven Cox
5 Main Street
Brackley Beach, PEI C1E 1Z3

Dear Mr. Cox:

Thank you for letting us know about the problem with your in-line skates. Although your six-month warranty has expired, we are mailing you a complete wheel assembly replacement free of charge. The enclosed instructions make removing the damaged wheel line and installing the new one relatively easy.

Opening acknowledges the problem and conveys the good news.

The "Fastrax" (model NL 562) you purchased is our best-selling and most reliable skate. However, wheel jams may occur when fine particles of sand block the smooth rotating action of the wheels. These skates perform best when used on roadways and tracks that are relatively free of sand. We suggest that you remove and clean the wheel assemblies (see enclosed directions) once a month and have them checked by your dealer about every six months.

Body explains problem without blaming customer, suggesting ways to avoid future problems.

Because of your Maritimes location, you may want to consider our more advanced "Glisto" (model NL 988) when you decide to purchase new skates. Although more expensive than the Fastrax, the Glisto design helps shed sand and dirt quite efficiently and should provide years of trouble-free skating.

Body also includes resale information, encouraging the customer to "trade up."

Enjoy the enclosed copy of "Rock & Roll" with our compliments. Inside, you'll read about new products, hear from other skaters, and have an opportunity to respond to our customer questionnaire.

Adds value by enclosing a newsletter that invites future response from customer.

We love hearing from our skaters, so keep in touch. All of us at Skates Alive! wish you good times and miles of healthy skating.

Close is positive, ending on a "feel good" note that conveys an attitude of excellent customer service.

Sincerely,

Candace Parker

Candace Parker
Customer Service Representative

Enclosure

FIGURE 7–8 In-Depth Critique: Letter Responding to a Claim When the Buyer Is at Fault

About Products and Operations A company announcing a new discount program to customers would begin the letter by trumpeting the news. The body would fill in the details of the discount program, and the close would include a bit of resale information and a confident prediction of a profitable business relationship.

Specially formatted news releases convey good news to the media, which in turn disseminate it to the public.

However, when the audience for a good-news message is large and scattered, companies often communicate through the mass media. When McDonald's opened its first restaurant in Moscow, it sent announcements to newspapers, magazines, radio stations, and television networks. The specialized documents used to convey such information to the media are called **news releases**. Written to match the style of the medium they are intended for, news releases are prepared on plain 21.5-by-28.0-cm paper or on special letterhead (not on regular letterhead). They are often double-spaced for print media or triple-spaced for reading on television and radio. You can view news releases on many company Web sites.

Figure 7-9 on page 186 illustrates a common format for print media. The content follows the customary pattern for a good-news message: good news, followed by details and a positive close. However, it avoids explicit references to any reader and displays the "you" attitude by presenting information presumed to be of interest to all readers. To write a successful news release, keep the following points in mind: [4]

- Include no marketing or sales material in your news release.
- Put your most important idea first (Don't say "Calco's president James Grall announced today that the company will move its headquarters to the Main Street office." Instead, start with the news: "Calco will move its headquarters to the Main Street office, President James Grall announced today.").
- Be brief: divide long sentences and keep paragraphs short.
- Eliminate clutter such as redundancy and extraneous facts.
- Be as specific as possible.
- Avoid adjectives and adverbs: understatement impresses the media rather than overstatement, so let the facts speak for themselves.

In addition to issuing written news releases, many large companies hold news conferences or create their own videotapes, which are sent to television stations and networks and sometimes shown on their Web sites.

SENDING GOODWILL MESSAGES

OBJECTIVE 5 Clarify the importance of goodwill messages, and describe how to make them effective.

You can enhance your relationships with customers, colleagues, and other businesspeople by sending friendly, unexpected notes with no direct business purpose. Effective goodwill messages must be sincere and honest. Otherwise, the writer appears interested in personal gain rather than in benefiting customers or fellow workers. To come across as sincere, avoid exaggeration and back up any compliments with specific points. In addition, readers often regard more restrained praise as being more sincere:

Goodwill is the positive feeling that encourages people to maintain a business relationship.

Make sure your compliments are grounded in reality

INSTEAD OF THIS	WRITE THIS
Words cannot express my appreciation for the great job you did. Thanks. No one could have done it better. You're terrific! You've made the whole firm sit up and take notice, and we are ecstatic to have you working here.	Thanks again for taking charge of the meeting in my absence. You did an excellent job. With just an hour's notice, you managed to pull the legal and public relations departments together so that we could present a united front in the negotiations. Your dedication and communication abilities have been noted and are truly appreciated.

Congratulations One prime opportunity for sending goodwill messages is to congratulate employees for volunteer work, fundraising for a charity, or an athletic achievement. Figure 7-10 on page 187 shows an e-mail congratulating an organization's team that participated in the International Dragon Boat race on Lake Ontario (see photo on page 187).

FIGURE 7–9 In-Depth Critique: Online News Release

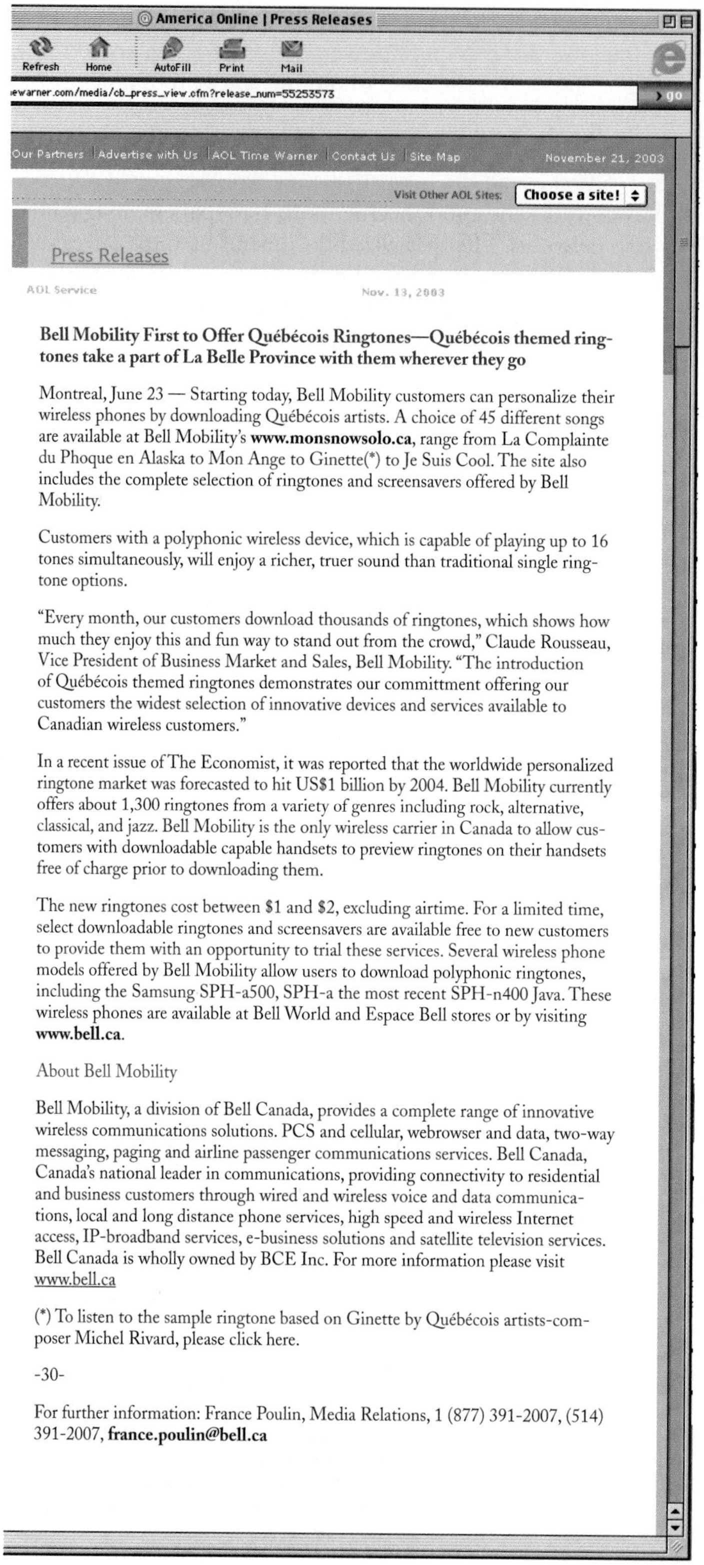

@America Online | Press Releases

Refresh Home AutoFill Print Mail

ewarner.com/media/cb_press_view.cfm?release_num=55253573

Our Partners | Advertise with Us | AOL Time Warner | Contact Us | Site Map November 21, 2003

Visit Other AOL Sites: Choose a site!

Press Releases

AOL Service Nov. 13, 2003

Provides a suggestion for a title (otherwise you leave two inches for editor to insert headline) →

Bell Mobility First to Offer Québécois Ringtones—Québécois themed ringtones take a part of La Belle Province with them wherever they go

Opening begins with a dateline and summary →

Montreal, June 23 — Starting today, Bell Mobility customers can personalize their wireless phones by downloading Québécois artists. A choice of 45 different songs are available at Bell Mobility's **www.monsnowsolo.ca**, range from La Complainte du Phoque en Alaska to Mon Ange to Ginette(*) to Je Suis Cool. The site also includes the complete selection of ringtones and screensavers offered by Bell Mobility.

Body fleshes out details in descending order of importance →

Customers with a polyphonic wireless device, which is capable of playing up to 16 tones simultaneously, will enjoy a richer, truer sound than traditional single ringtone options.

"Every month, our customers download thousands of ringtones, which shows how much they enjoy this and fun way to stand out from the crowd," Claude Rousseau, Vice President of Business Market and Sales, Bell Mobility. "The introduction of Québécois themed ringtones demonstrates our committment offering our customers the widest selection of innovative devices and services available to Canadian wireless customers."

In a recent issue of The Economist, it was reported that the worldwide personalized ringtone market was forecasted to hit US$1 billion by 2004. Bell Mobility currently offers about 1,300 ringtones from a variety of genres including rock, alternative, classical, and jazz. Bell Mobility is the only wireless carrier in Canada to allow customers with downloadable capable handsets to preview ringtones on their handsets free of charge prior to downloading them.

The new ringtones cost between $1 and $2, excluding airtime. For a limited time, select downloadable ringtones and screensavers are available free to new customers to provide them with an opportunity to trial these services. Several wireless phone models offered by Bell Mobility allow users to download polyphonic ringtones, including the Samsung SPH-a500, SPH-a the most recent SPH-n400 Java. These wireless phones are available at Bell World and Espace Bell stores or by visiting **www.bell.ca**.

About Bell Mobility

News release ends with company information →

Bell Mobility, a division of Bell Canada, provides a complete range of innovative wireless communications solutions. PCS and cellular, webrowser and data, two-way messaging, paging and airline passenger communications services. Bell Canada, Canada's national leader in communications, providing connectivity to residential and business customers through wired and wireless voice and data communications, local and long distance phone services, high speed and wireless Internet access, IP-broadband services, e-business solutions and satellite television services. Bell Canada is wholly owned by BCE Inc. For more information please visit www.bell.ca

(*) To listen to the sample ringtone based on Ginette by Québécois artists-composer Michel Rivard, please click here.

A conventional symbol for the end of the news release →

-30-

For further information: France Poulin, Media Relations, 1 (877) 391-2007, (514) 391-2007, **france.poulin@bell.ca**

Taking note of significant events in someone's personal life helps cement the business relationship.

Other reasons for sending congratulations include significant business achievement—perhaps for being promoted or for attaining an important civic position. The congratulatory note in Figure 7–11, on page 188, moves swiftly to the subject: the good news. It gives reasons for expecting success and avoids extravagances such as "Only you can do the job!" Congratulations messages can also recognize highlights in people's personal lives—weddings, births, graduations.

Some companies even develop a mailing list of potential customers by assigning an employee to clip newspaper announcements of births, engagements, weddings, and graduations or to obtain information on real estate transactions in the local community. Then they introduce themselves by sending out a form letter that might read like this:

> Congratulations on your new home! Our wish is that it brings you much happiness.
>
> To help you commemorate the occasion, we've enclosed a key chain with your new address engraved on the leather tab. Please accept this with our best wishes.

In this case, the company's letterhead and address are enough of a sales pitch. This simple message has a friendly tone, even though the sender has never met the recipient.

Both oral and written messages from organizations can promote good relationships with colleagues, customers, and the community. Well-written congratulations, thank-you notes, or condolences to associates inside or outside the organization don't boast about all the good their organization accomplishes; they focus on the situation of the person receiving the message.

Messages of Appreciation An important business quality is the ability to recognize the contributions of employees, colleagues, suppliers, and other associates. Your praise doesn't just make the person feel good; it also encourages further excellence. Moreover, a message of appreciation may become an important part of someone's personnel file. So when you write a message of appreciation, try to specifically mention the person or people you want to praise. The brief message that follows expresses gratitude and reveals the happy result:

A message of appreciation documents a person's contributions.

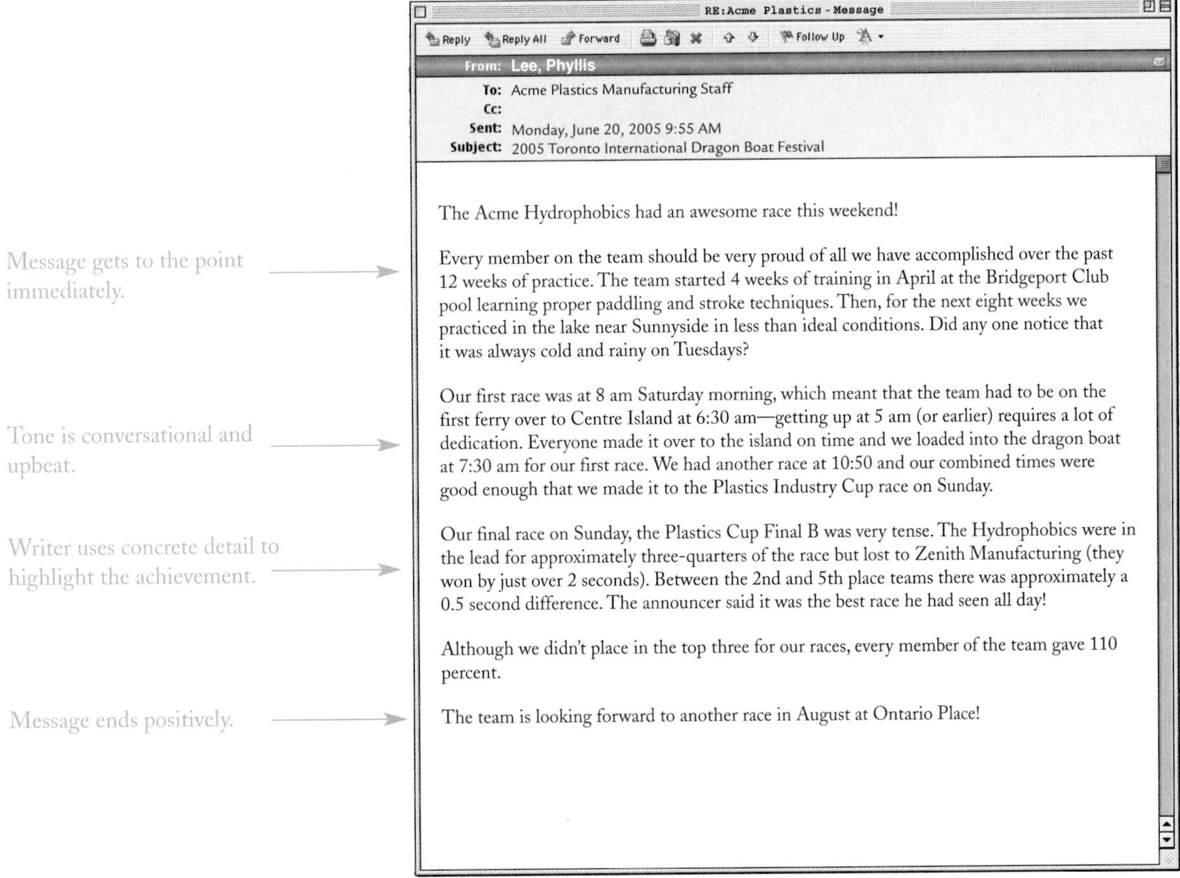

RE:Acme Plastics - Message

Reply | Reply All | Forward | Follow Up

From: Lee, Phyllis
To: Acme Plastics Manufacturing Staff
Cc:
Sent: Monday, June 20, 2005 9:55 AM
Subject: 2005 Toronto International Dragon Boat Festival

The Acme Hydrophobics had an awesome race this weekend!

Every member on the team should be very proud of all we have accomplished over the past 12 weeks of practice. The team started 4 weeks of training in April at the Bridgeport Club pool learning proper paddling and stroke techniques. Then, for the next eight weeks we practiced in the lake near Sunnyside in less than ideal conditions. Did any one notice that it was always cold and rainy on Tuesdays?

Our first race was at 8 am Saturday morning, which meant that the team had to be on the first ferry over to Centre Island at 6:30 am—getting up at 5 am (or earlier) requires a lot of dedication. Everyone made it over to the island on time and we loaded into the dragon boat at 7:30 am for our first race. We had another race at 10:50 and our combined times were good enough that we made it to the Plastics Industry Cup race on Sunday.

Our final race on Sunday, the Plastics Cup Final B was very tense. The Hydrophobics were in the lead for approximately three-quarters of the race but lost to Zenith Manufacturing (they won by just over 2 seconds). Between the 2nd and 5th place teams there was approximately a 0.5 second difference. The announcer said it was the best race he had seen all day!

Although we didn't place in the top three for our races, every member of the team gave 110 percent.

The team is looking forward to another race in August at Ontario Place!

Message gets to the point immediately.
Tone is conversational and upbeat.
Writer uses concrete detail to highlight the achievement.
Message ends positively.

FIGURE 7–10 In-Depth Critique: E-Mail Congratulations Message

1 Planning

Analyze: Purpose is to create goodwill with industry business associates.

Investigate: Gather information on specific accomplishments of the reader's firm.

Adapt: A letter format lets reader use your message (perhaps reproduce it) as an industry testimonial.

2 Writing

Organize: Main idea is to congratulate the reader. The direct approach is perfect for this welcome news.

Compose: A conversational tone complements the slightly formal style, since this is your first contact with the reader. Avoid generalized praise by mentioning specific, concrete accomplishments.

3 Completing

Revise: Review for consistency in tone, word choice, and sentence structure.

Produce: A simple design avoids distracting your reader from the message.

Proofread: Create a positive first impression by being especially careful to send an error-free message.

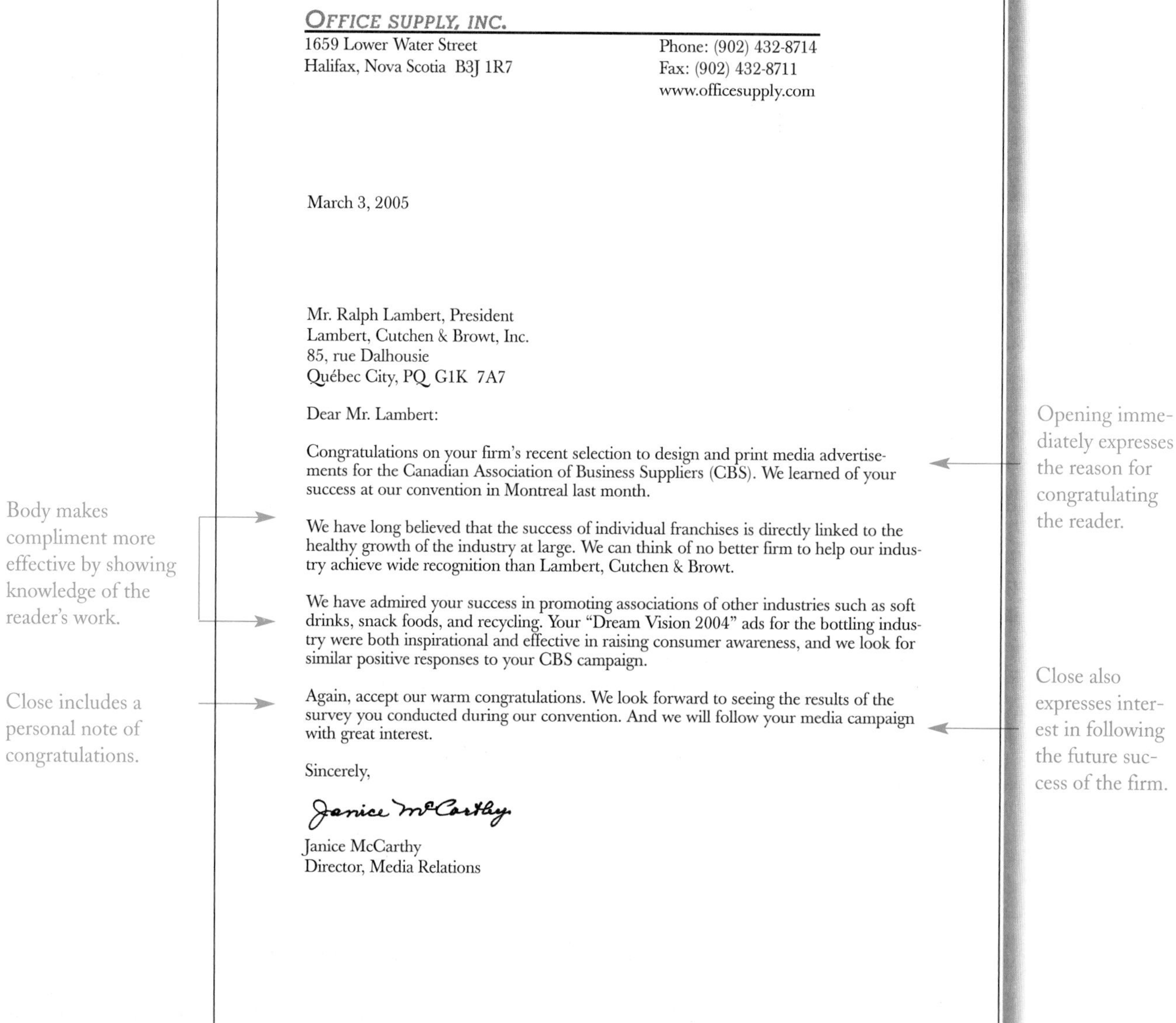

OFFICE SUPPLY, INC.
1659 Lower Water Street
Halifax, Nova Scotia B3J 1R7

Phone: (902) 432-8714
Fax: (902) 432-8711
www.officesupply.com

March 3, 2005

Mr. Ralph Lambert, President
Lambert, Cutchen & Browt, Inc.
85, rue Dalhousie
Québec City, PQ G1K 7A7

Dear Mr. Lambert:

Congratulations on your firm's recent selection to design and print media advertisements for the Canadian Association of Business Suppliers (CBS). We learned of your success at our convention in Montreal last month.

We have long believed that the success of individual franchises is directly linked to the healthy growth of the industry at large. We can think of no better firm to help our industry achieve wide recognition than Lambert, Cutchen & Browt.

We have admired your success in promoting associations of other industries such as soft drinks, snack foods, and recycling. Your "Dream Vision 2004" ads for the bottling industry were both inspirational and effective in raising consumer awareness, and we look for similar positive responses to your CBS campaign.

Again, accept our warm congratulations. We look forward to seeing the results of the survey you conducted during our convention. And we will follow your media campaign with great interest.

Sincerely,

Janice McCarthy

Janice McCarthy
Director, Media Relations

Opening immediately expresses the reason for congratulating the reader.
Body makes compliment more effective by showing knowledge of the reader's work.
Close includes a personal note of congratulations.
Close also expresses interest in following the future success of the firm.

FIGURE 7–11 In-Depth Critique: Letter Congratulating a Business Acquaintance

> Thank you for sending the air-conditioning components via overnight delivery. You allowed us to satisfy the needs of two customers who were getting very impatient with the heat.
>
> Special thanks to Susan Brown, who took our initial call and never said, "It can't be done." Her initiative on our behalf is greatly appreciated.

Condolences In times of serious trouble and deep sadness, written condolences and expressions of sympathy leave their mark. This type of message is difficult to write, but don't let the difficulty of the task keep you from responding promptly. Those who have experienced a health problem, the death of a loved one, or a business misfortune like to know that they're not alone.

Begin condolences with a brief statement of sympathy, such as "I was deeply sorry to hear of your loss." In the middle, mention the good qualities or the positive contributions made by the deceased. State what the person or business meant to you. In closing, you can offer your condolences and your best wishes. One considerate way to end this type of message is to say something that will give the reader a little lift, such as a reference to a brighter future. Here are a few general suggestions for writing condolence messages:

In condolence messages, try to find a middle path between being superficial and causing additional distress.

- **Keep reminiscences brief.** Recount a memory or an anecdote (even a humorous one), but don't dwell on the details of the loss, lest you add to the reader's anguish.
- **Write in your own words.** Write as if you were speaking privately to the person. Don't quote "poetic" passages or use stilted or formal phrases. If the loss is a death, refer to it as such rather than as "passing away" or "departing."
- **Be tactful.** Mention your shock and dismay, but remember that bereaved and distressed loved ones take little comfort in lines such as, "Richard was too young to die" or "Starting all over again will be so difficult." Try to strike a balance between superficial expressions of sympathy and heart-rending references to a happier past or the likelihood of a bleak future.
- **Take special care.** Be sure to spell names correctly and to be accurate in your review of facts. Try to be prompt.
- **Write about special qualities of the deceased.** You may have to rely on reputation to do this, but let the grieving person know you valued his or her loved one.
- **Write about special qualities of the bereaved person.** A few kind words may help a bereaved family member feel more confident about handling things during such a traumatic time.[5]

Supervisor George Bigalow sent the following condolence letter to his administrative assistant, Janice Case, after learning of the death of Janice's husband:

> My sympathy to you and your children. All your friends at Carter Electric were so very sorry to learn of John's death. Although I never had the opportunity to meet him, I do know how very special he was to you. Your tales of your family's camping trips and his rafting expeditions were always memorable.

To review the tasks involved in writing goodwill messages, see the "Checklist: Granting Claims and Adjustment Requests, and Sending Goodwill Messages" on page 183.

Summary of Learning Outcomes

1 Apply the three-step writing process to routine positive messages. Even though routine messages are usually short and simple, they benefit from the three-step writing process. Planning routine messages may take only a few moments to (1) analyze your purpose and audience, (2) investigate your readers' needs and make sure that you have all the facts to satisfy them, and (3) adapt your message through your choice of medium and your "you" attitude. When writing routine messages, use the direct approach, as long as your readers will be positive (or neutral), and plain language for non-native speakers. Completing routine messages means making them as professional as possible by (1) revising for clarity and conciseness; (2) selecting appropriate design elements and delivery methods; and (3) proofreading carefully.

2 Illustrate the strategy for writing routine requests. When writing a routine request, open by stating your specific request. At the same time, avoid being abrupt or tactless: pay attention to tone, assume your audience will comply, avoid personal introductions, end polite requests with a period, and be specific. Use the body of a routine request to justify your request and explain its importance. Close routine requests by asking for specific action (including a deadline as often as possible) and expressing goodwill. Be sure to include all contact information so that your reader can respond easily.

3 Discuss the differences among four types of routine requests. Each type of routine request has distinguishing features. All start with a statement of the main idea. But when placing orders, the body includes columns for product information, just like any good order blank. The close includes the delivery address, the preferred method of shipment, and information about any enclosed payment. When the request is for information or action, the middle explains or justifies your request and the close specifies what you need and when you need it. When the message is a claim or request for an adjustment, the middle includes whatever facts your reader needs to verify your complaint. The close requests a specific solution or conveys a sincere desire to find one, and it suggests that future business depends on a satisfactory resolution. In a request for a recommendation, the opening states the position or award being applied for and, if necessary, recalls the nature and dates of your relationship with the reader. The middle refers to your résumé or includes information that would support a recommendation, and the appreciative close includes the name and address of the person to whom the recommendation will be sent.

4 Explain the main differences in messages granting a claim when the company, the customer, or a third party is at fault. In messages granting a claim, the explanatory section differs, depending on who is at fault. If your company is at fault, avoid reacting defensively, and be careful when referring to company errors. Rather than placing blame, explain your company's efforts to do a good job. Remember not to make any unrealistic promises or guarantees. If your customer is at fault, you must help your reader realize what went wrong so that it won't happen again and again. However, you don't want to sound condescending, preachy, or insulting. If a third party is at fault, you can honour the claim with no explanation, or you can honour the claim and explain that the problem was not your fault.

5 Clarify the importance of goodwill messages, and describe how to make them effective. Goodwill messages are important for building relationships with customers, colleagues, and other businesspeople. These friendly, unexpected notes have no direct business purpose, but they make people feel good about doing business with the sender. To make goodwill messages effective, be honest and sincere. Avoid exaggerating, back up compliments with specific points, and give restrained praise.

ON THE JOB

Solving A Communication Dilemma at Indigo Books and Music

Since 1997, Heather Reisman has been building an impressive presence on the Canadian book scene with Indigo Books and Music. Reisman has achieved her prominence as a Canadian bookseller through a mix of the right locations, books, and gift items that makes her chain distinctive, and the ability to communicate her business vision effectively to employees and customers. As Indigo's chief manager, she must also request information. Reisman uses feedback from her executive team, store managers, and service staff to help her company grow.

In Canada, the battle for the book-reading public is between Reisman's Indigo stores; independents such as Nicholas Hoare Booksellers, with locations in Montreal, Ottawa, and Toronto, and McNally Robinson in Winnipeg; and online stores, such as Reisman's main competitor, Amazon.ca. Reisman's Indigo tries to be a megastore with the personal appeal of the smaller booksellers. Indigo is targeted toward an upscale market, with an emphasis on travel, home decor, gardening, and art books, as well as trade fiction, rather than mass-market paperbacks. The atmosphere of each Indigo outlet speaks refinement in the large, portico windows, uncluttered floor space, and winding staircases. In the competitive arena of the Internet, the chapters.indigo.ca Web site is designed as a convenient location to browse for and order books, music, and gifts. Visitors can browse "Heather's Picks," sign up for "iREWARDS," and take advantage of online discounts.

Reisman wants to offer Canada's book lovers "the best of a small proprietor-run shop combined with the selection of a true emporium." The impact she has made in only a few years demonstrates her ability to communicate with customers and employees.

Your Mission You have recently taken a job at Indigo's head office as an administrative assistant on the management team. One of your jobs entails drafting letters to Indigo store managers and outside contacts. Using the principles outlined in this chapter for writing direct requests, handle each of the following letters to the best of your ability. Be prepared to explain your choices.

1 You are asked to contact the store managers to find out whether the company's Web site is affecting sales in retail stores. Which of the following is the best opening for this e-mail?

a I have recently joined Heather Reisman's staff as an administrative assistant. She has asked me to write to you to obtain your feedback on the impact of the company's new Web site on store sales. Please reply to the following questions within five working days. (List of questions follows.)

b Please tell us what you think of Indigo.ca. Ms. Reisman is trying to evaluate its impact on our business. Within the next few days, can you take a few moments to jot down your thoughts on its impact. Specifically, Ms. Reisman would like to know ... (List of questions follows.)

c By April 15, please submit written answers to the following questions on the new Indigo Web site. (List of questions follows.)

d Is the new Web site affecting sales in your store? We're polling all store managers for their reaction to online retailing. Is it thumbs up or thumbs down on the Web?

2 Which of the following is the best choice for the middle section of the e-mail?

a Specifically, has store business decreased since the Web site went online? If so, what is the percentage decrease in sales over the previous six months? Over the comparable period last year? Have customers mentioned the Web site? If so, have their comments been positive or negative? Has employee morale been affected by the site? How?

b By replying to the following questions, you will help us decide whether to continue with the Web site as is, revise it, or drop it entirely:

1 Has business decreased in your store since the Web site went live? If it has, what is the percentage decrease in sales over the previous six months? Over the comparable period last year?

2 Have customers mentioned the site? If so, have their comments been positive or negative? Give some typical examples.

3 Has employee morale been affected by the Web site initiative? How?

c By circling the response that most accurately reflects your store's experience, please answer the following questions regarding the company's new Web site:

1 Since the Web site went live, sales have

a increased

b decreased

c remained about the same

2 Customers (have/have not) mentioned the Web site. Their comments have been primarily positive/negative).

3 Employee morale (has/has not) been affected by the Web site.

4 Ms. Reisman needs to know the following: (1) How have overall store sales changed since the company's new Web site went live? (2) What do customers think of the site? Attach complimentary customer comments. (3) What do employees think of the site? Attach complimentary employee comments.

3 For a courteous close with a request for specific action, which of the following paragraphs is the best?

a Thank you for your cooperation. Please submit your reply in writing by April 15.

b Ms. Reisman is meeting with her senior staff on April 17 to discuss the Web site. She would like to have your reaction in writing by April 15 so that she can present your views during that meeting. If you have any questions, please contact me at (416) 697-2886.

c You may contact me at (416) 697-2886 if you have any questions or need additional information about this survey. Ms. Reisman requires your written response by April 15 so she can discuss your views with her senior staff on April 17.

d Thank you for your input. As the frontline troops in the battle for sales, you are in a good position to evaluate the impact of the new Web site. We here at corporate headquarters want to increase overall company sales, but we need your feedback. Please submit your written evaluation by April 15 so that Ms. Reisman can use the results as ammunition in her meeting with senior staff on April 17.

4 To promote the Harry Potter series, your supervisor has ordered 30 large cutout cardboard displays of the most recent cover. The Indigo warehouse has received the shipment; however, seven of the displays are bent and cannot be used in promoting the book. You have been asked to prepare a letter requesting an adjustment. Select the best version.

a On March 25, we ordered 30 cardboard cutouts (item #90067-C in your April catalogue). When the shipment arrived last week, we discovered that seven of the cutouts were bent.

Whether the damage occurred during shipping or at your place of business, I do not know. However, I do know that we cannot use the cutouts in their present form. If you can replace them before April 25, please do so. We are withholding payment until the matter is straightened out.

b Please call me immediately at (416) 697-2886 to discuss a problem with the Harry Potter cutouts that we ordered from you. Seven of them are bent and cannot be used in our nationwide book promotion scheduled for May 1.

Time is running short, I know, but we would really like you to replace the seven damaged cutouts if you can do so in time for our promotion. If that is not possible, we will adjust our payment to reflect a sale of 23 cutouts as opposed to 30. Thanks for your cooperation. The good cutouts are really cute, and we expect they will boost our book sales.

c Of the 30 Harry Potter cardboard cutouts received last week, seven are not in good condition. I inspected them myself, and several of us tried to fix the cutouts, but they don't look very good. Therefore, please replace these seven before April 25.

d Seven of the Harry Potter cardboard cutouts that we ordered from your firm on March 25 arrived in poor condition. Can you replace them before April 25? If so, we would still like to use them in our May 1 book promotion. I am enclosing a copy of the invoice for your convenience. As you can see, our original order was for 30 cutouts (catalogue item #90067-C), priced at $35.00 each. Our bill for the total order is $1050.00. We will send payment in full when we receive the seven undamaged cutouts. If replacements are not available by April 25, we will send you a cheque for the 23 good cutouts, which we plan to use in any case. Including tax and handling costs, the adjusted total would be $955.75. Would you like us to return the damaged items? Perhaps they can be salvaged for another purpose.

Please call me at (416) 697-2886 any time this week to discuss the situation. We are eager to receive the replacement cutouts so that our bookstores can benefit from the Harry Potter display during our nationwide book promotion scheduled for May 1.[6]

Test Your Knowledge

Review Questions

1. Should you use the direct or indirect approach for most routine messages? Why?
2. Where in a routine message should you state your actual request?
3. How does the question of fault affect what you say in a message granting a claim?
4. When is a request routine?
5. What are some of the guidelines for asking a series of questions in a routine request?
6. What information should be included in an order request?
7. How does a claim differ from an adjustment?
8. How can you avoid sounding insincere when writing a goodwill message?
9. What are some of the guidelines for writing condolence messages?
10. Why is tone important in routine messages?

Interactive Learning 

Use This Text's Online Resources

Visit our Companion Web site at **www.pearsoned.ca/thill**, where you can use the interactive Study Guide to test your chapter knowledge and get instant feedback. Additional resources link you to the sites mentioned in this text and to additional sources of information on chapter topics.

Also check out the resources on the Mastering Business Communication CD, including "Perils of Pauline," an interactive presentation of the business communication challenges within a fictional company. For Chapter 7, see in particular the episode "Using E-Mail Effectively."

Apply Your Knowledge

Critical Thinking Questions

1. When organizing your requests, why is it important to know whether any cultural and language differences exist between you and your audience? Explain.
2. Your company's error cost an important business customer a new client; you know it and your customer knows it. Do you apologize or do you refer to the incident in a positive light without admitting any responsibility? Briefly explain.
3. Every time you send a direct-request memo to Ted Jackson, he delays or refuses to comply. You're beginning to get impatient. Should you send Jackson a memo to ask what's wrong? Complain to your supervisor about Jackson's uncooperative attitude? Arrange a face-to-face meeting with Jackson? Bring up the problem at the next staff meeting? Explain.
4. **Ethical Choices** A competitor has been honoured for supporting a local charity. Should you send her a letter of congratulations? Why or why not?
5. **Ethical Choices** You have a complaint against one of your suppliers, but you have no documentation to back it up. Should you request an adjustment anyway? Why or why not?

Practice Your Knowledge

Documents for Analysis

Read the following documents; then (1) analyze the strengths and weaknesses of each sentence and (2) revise each document so that it follows this chapter's guidelines.

Document 7.A: Requesting Routine Information from a Business

Our university is closing its dining hall for financial reasons, so we want to do something to help the students prepare their own food in their residence rooms if they so choose. Your colourful ad in *University Management Magazine* caught our eye. We need the following information before we make our decision.

1. Would you be able to ship the microwaves by August 15? I realize this is short notice, but our board of trustees just made the decision to close the dining hall last week and we're scrambling around trying to figure out what to do.
2. Do they have any kind of a warranty? Students can be pretty hard on things, as you know, so we will need a good warranty.
3. How much does it cost? Do you give a discount for a big order?
4. Do we have to provide a special outlet?
5. Will students know how to use them, or will we need to provide instructions?

As I said before, we're on a tight time frame and need good information from you as soon as possible to help us make our decision about ordering. You never know what the board might come up with next. I'm looking at several other companies also, so please let us know ASAP.

Document 7.B: Making Claims and Requests for Adjustment

At a local business-supply store, I recently purchased your "Negotiator Pro" for my computer. I bought the CD because I saw your ad for it in *MacWorld* magazine, and it looked as if it might be an effective tool for use in my corporate seminar on negotiation.

Unfortunately, when I inserted it in my office computer, it wouldn't work. I returned it to the store, but since I had already opened it, they refused to exchange it for a CD that would work or give me a refund. They told me to contact you and that you might be able to send me a version that would work with my computer.

You can send the information to me at the letterhead address. If you cannot send me the correct disk, please refund my $79.95. Thanks in advance for any help you can give me in this matter.

Document 7.C: Responding to Claims and Adjustment Requests When the Customer Is at Fault

We read your letter requesting your rental deposit refund. We couldn't figure out why you hadn't received it, so we talked to our maintenance engineer as you suggested. He said you had left one of the doors off the hinges in your apartment in order to get a large sofa through the door. He also confirmed that you had paid him $26.00 to replace the door since you had to turn in the U-Haul trailer and were in a big hurry.

This entire situation really was caused by a lack of communication between our housekeeping inspector and the maintenance engineer. All we knew was that the door was off the hinges when it was inspected by Sally Tarnley. You know that our policy states that if anything is wrong with the apartment, we keep the deposit. We had no way of knowing that George just hadn't gotten around to replacing the door.

But we have good news. We approved the deposit refund, which will be mailed to you from our home office in Halifax, N.S. I'm not sure how long that will take, however. If you don't receive the cheque by the end of next month, give me a call.

Next time, it's really a good idea to stay at your apartment until it's inspected as stipulated in your lease agreement. That way, you'll be sure to receive your refund when you expect it. Hope you have a good summer.

Exercises

7–1 Revise the following short e-mail messages so that they are more direct and concise; develop a subject line for each revised message.

a I'm contacting you about your recent order for a High Country backpack. You didn't tell us which backpack you wanted, and you know we make a lot of different ones. We have the canvas models with the plastic frames and vinyl trim and we have the canvas models with leather trim, and we have the ones that have more pockets than the other ones. Plus they come in lots of different colours. Also they make the ones that are large for a big-boned person and the smaller versions for little women or kids.

b Thank you for contacting us about the difficulty you had collecting your luggage at the Denver airport. We are very sorry for the inconvenience this has caused you. As you know, travelling can create problems of this sort regardless of how careful the airline personnel might be. To receive compensation, please send us a detailed list of the items that you lost and complete the following questionnaire. You can e-mail it back to us.

c Sorry it took us so long to get back to you. We were flooded with résumés. Anyway, your résumé made the final ten, and after meeting three hours yesterday, we've decided we'd like to meet with you. What is your schedule like for next week? Can you come in for an interview on June 15 at 3:00 p.m? Please get back to us by the end of this workweek and let us know if you will be able to attend. As you can imagine, this is our busy season.

d We're letting you know that because we use over a ton of paper a year and because so much of that paper goes into the wastebasket to become so much more environmental waste, starting Monday, we're placing white plastic bins outside the elevators on every floor to recycle that paper and in the process, minimize pollution.

7–2 Rewrite the following sentences so that they are direct and concise.

a We wanted to invite you to our special 40% off by-invitation-only sale. The sale is taking place on November 9.

b We wanted to let you know that we are giving a tote bag and a free Phish CD with every $50 donation you make to our radio station.

c The director planned to go to the meeting that will be held on Monday at a little before 11:00 a.m.

d In today's meeting, we were happy to have the opportunity to welcome Paul Eccelson. He reviewed some of the newest types of order forms. If you have any questions about these new forms, feel free to call him at his office.

7–3 **Teamwork** With another student, identify the purpose and select the most appropriate format for communicating these written messages. Next, consider how the audience is likely to respond to each message. Based on this audience analysis, determine whether the direct or indirect approach would be effective for each message, and explain your reasoning.

a A notice to all employees about the placement of recycling bins by the elevator doors.

b The first late-payment notice to a good customer who usually pays his bills on time.

7–4 **Internet** Visit the business section of the Blue Mountain site at **www.bluemountain.com/eng3/business** and analyze one of the electronic greeting cards bearing a goodwill message of appreciation for good performance. Under what circumstances would you send this electronic message? How could you personalize it for the recipient and the occasion? What would be an appropriate close for this message?

7–5 Evaluate the following closing paragraphs. How would you rewrite each to be concise, courteous, and specific?

a I need your response sometime soon so I can order the parts in time for your service appointment. Otherwise your air conditioning system may not be in tip-top condition for the start of the summer season.

b Thank you in advance for sending me as much information as you can about your products. I look forward to receiving your package in the very near future.

c To schedule an appointment with one of our knowledgeable mortgage specialists in your area, you can always call our hotline at 1-800-555-8765. This is also the number to call if you have more questions about mortgage rates, closing procedures, or any other aspect of the mortgage process. Remember, we're here to make the home-buying experience as painless as possible.

7–6 **Ethical Choices** Your small supermarket chain has received dozens of complaints about the watery consistency of the ketchup sold under the chain's brand name. You don't want your customers to stop buying other store-brand foods, which are made and packaged for your chain by various suppliers, but you do want to address their concerns about the ketchup. In responding to these complaints, should you explain that the ketchup is actually manufactured by a local supplier and then name the supplier, who has already started bottling a thicker ketchup?

Cases

Applying the Three-Step Writing Process to Cases

Apply each step to the following cases, as assigned by your instructor

1 Planning Cases

Analyze

1 What is your general purpose?
2 What is your specific purpose?
3 What do you want readers to do?
4 Who are your readers? (Who is the primary audience? Who is the secondary audience? What do readers have in common? What is their general background? How will they react?)

Investigate

5 What information do readers need?
6 What facts must you gather?

Adapt

7 How will you establish credibility?

2 Writing Cases

Organize

1 What is your main idea?
2 Will you usew the direct or indirect approach? Why?

Compose

3 Will your tone be informal or more formal?
4 Draft the message as discussed in the "Your Task" section of the case.

3 Completing Cases

Revise

1 Use the "Checklist for Revising Business Messages" in Chapter 6 to edit and revise your message for clarity.

Produce

2 What is the best way to distribute your message? By fax? By e-mail? By sealed envelope?

Proofread

3 Proofread your message for errors in layout, spelling, and mechanics.

Routine Requests

1 Step on it: Letter to Floorgraphics requesting information about underfoot advertising You work for Mary Utanpitak, owner of Better Bike and Ski Shop. Yesterday, Mary met with the Schwinn sales representative, Tom Beeker, who urged her to sign a contract with Floorgraphics. That company leases floor space from retail stores, then creates and sells floor ads to manufacturers like Schwinn. Floorgraphics will pay Mary a fee for leasing the floor space, as well as a percentage for every ad it sells. Mary was definitely interested, and turned to you after Beeker left.

"Tom says that advertising decals on the floor in front of the product reach consumers right where they're standing when making a decision," explained Mary. "She says the ads increase sales from 25 to 75 percent."

You both look down at the dusty floor, and Mary laughs. "It seems funny that manufacturers will pay hard cash to put their names where customers are going to track dirt all over them! But if Tom's telling the truth, we could profit three ways: from the leasing fee, the increased sales, and the share in ad revenues. That's not so funny."

Your Task: Mary Utanpitak wants you to write a letter to CEO Richard Rebh at Floorgraphics, Inc. (1725 E. 3rd Avenue, Vancouver, BC, V5M 5R6) asking for financial details and practical information about the ads. For example, how will you clean your floors? Who installs and removes the ads? Can you terminate the lease if you don't like them? She'll sign the letter, but since you've been studying business communication, she thinks you'll do a better job writing the request.[7]

2 Blockbuster Video shake-up: Memo from top brass requesting info from retail managers Everyone knew there was trouble at Blockbuster's new headquarters in Dallas when CEO Bill Fields, a former Wal-Mart whiz, suddenly resigned. Then Sumner Redstone and Tom Dooley (chair and deputy chair of Blockbuster's parent company, Viacom) flew in to assess the damage wrought by Fields' departure. They started by giving orders, particularly to you, Fields' former executive assistant.

Before he resigned to take a position with Hudson's Bay Company in Canada, Fields' strategy had been to boost Blockbuster's revenues and profits by establishing a new niche as a "neighbourhood entertainment centre." Using tricks he'd learned at Wal-Mart, he ordered the reconfiguration of more than 1000 Blockbuster outlets, surrounding the cash registers with flashy displays of candy, potato chips, new and used videotapes for sale, magazines, and tie-in toys. His stated goal was to add $1 in retail purchases to every video rental transaction. Meanwhile, he also moved Blockbuster's headquarters from Florida to Dallas, losing some of the company's top staff when they declined to make the

move. Then Fields started construction on an 818 000 square-foot warehouse 40 km outside Dallas to centralize a new, sophisticated distribution operation for Blockbuster's North American outlets. But revenues were still falling.

Redstone and Dooley's new plan is to get Blockbuster back into its core business—video rentals—ignoring gloomy analysts who say satellite dishes and cheap tape sales are slowly sinking the rental industry. "This is still a healthy, growing business," Dooley insists. He believes that consumers coming in to rent videos were confused by the array of retail products they saw. "We want people to think of Blockbuster as the place to go to rent tapes," he says. Dooley and Redstone have brought in new management and are making changes in everything from store format to marketing and advertising to inventory control and overhead reduction. Now they've turned to you. "We've got a job you'll love," Dooley smiles. "We know you can handle it."

Your Task: "Draft a memo that will pick the brains of retail managers in the stores that Fields reconfigured," Dooley orders. "I want to know whether customers walk out when current hits aren't available, whether the emphasis on retail products affected cash flow, and whether sales and rental figures have changed now that we've ordered all that clutter out of the limelight. Ask them where the cash is coming from: tape rentals, tape sales, or candy bars? More importantly, what about profit margins? I want a full report from every manager by the end of next week!" To get that kind of cooperation, you'd better organize your questions effectively. [8]

3 Please tell me: Letter requesting routine information about a product As a consumer, you've probably seen hundreds of products that you'd like to buy (if you haven't, look at the advertisements in your favourite magazine for ideas). Choose a big-ticket item that is rather complicated, such as a stereo system or a vacation in the Caribbean.

Your Task: You surely have some questions about the features of your chosen product or about its price, guarantees, local availability, and so on. Write to the company or organization that's offering it, and ask four questions that are important to you. Be sure to include enough background information for the reader to answer your questions satisfactorily.

If requested to do so by your instructor, mail a copy of your letter (after your instructor has had an opportunity to review it) to the company or organization. After a few weeks, you and your classmates may wish to compare responses and to answer this question: How well do companies or organizations respond to unsolicited inquiries?

4 Couch potato. Letter requesting refund from House of Couches Furniture Store You finally saw the couch you need: the colour is perfect (royal blue), the length just right (it could seat you, your husband, and the kids), and the styling ideal for your furnishings (modern but classic). With the scratch-and-save card, you bought it at a 40 percent discount, bringing the price to a mere $600.00, plus delivery and taxes.

The salesperson who served you said that for an extra $10.00 you can have "deluxe delivery": the new couch will be taken out of its box and put into place, and the cardboard and your old couch removed. You wouldn't have to arrange removal on your own. "Deluxe delivery" sounded great, and the price was right. You decided to pay for it.

The day of delivery, your couch arrived wrapped in plastic. The deliverymen dropped it in the middle of your living room, and started to leave, with their hands out for a tip. You reminded them about "deluxe delivery." They removed the plastic covering, took your old, sagging couch to the garage after you asked them twice, saying they didn't remove couches from the owner's property. They left grumbling. You could have done everything with the help of your spouse, and saved the $10.00.

That afternoon you called customer service at House of Couches seeking a refund of the $10.00 you paid for "deluxe delivery." The representative refused to honour your request, saying that the deliverers fulfilled the "deluxe delivery" conditions.

Your Task: You feel that the salesperson lied to you and that the customer service representative was rude. You decide to write to the owner of House of Couches, Fritz Wegman, to seek satisfaction. His address is: House of Couches, 975 Broad Street, Regina, Saskatchewan Canada, S4P 1Y2.

5 Bolga mix-up: E-mail to Getrade (Ghana) Ltd. from Pier 1 Imports The way you heard it, in 1993 your employer, Pier 1 Imports, sent a buyer to Accra, Ghana, to find local handicrafts. Free-market reforms in Ghana during the 1980s helped ease export procedures, but so far the Ghanaian entrepreneurs who sprang forward to take advantage of the change are having trouble meeting demand from large-quantity buyers like Pier 1. The shipment that just arrived from Getrade (Ghana) Ltd., one of your best Ghanaian suppliers, is a good example of what's been going wrong.

Your customers love the bowl-shaped Bolga baskets woven by the Fra-Fra people of northern Ghana; you can't keep them in stock. This was to be a huge shipment of 3000 Bolga baskets. You requested baskets in the traditional Bolga shape but woven in solid colours, since your customers prefer solid to mixed colours. Getrade was to ship 1000 green, 1000 yellow, and 1000 magenta. Your overseas buyer heard that the Body Shop ordered similar baskets with traditional mixed-colour patterns and a flatter shape. You sympathize with Ladi Nylander, chair and managing director of Getrade, who is trying hard to adapt to the specific tastes of his North American buyers. He's hiring local artisans to carve, shape, and weave all sorts of items—often from designs provided by Pier 1. Personally, you can understand how Getrade got confused. But you know Pier 1 can't sell the 3000 mixed-colour, flat Bolga baskets that you've been shipped.

Your Task: As assistant buyer, it's your job to compose the e-mail message alerting Getrade to the mix-up. You decide that if you want the mistake corrected, you'd better direct your message to Nylander at **Nylander@Getrade.co.za.** If you're lucky, it may be simply that the Body Shop's order got mixed up with yours.[9]

6 Web site: E-mail message from Knitsmart Yarn and Needles requesting additional information An enjoyable hobby that whiled away cold winter evenings in Corner Brook, Newfoundland has given cousins Lee O'Reilly and Siobhan Gavin a local following and fame throughout the handknitting community in the Maritimes as well as in fashionable shops in Canada's large cities. First teaching their young relatives and neighbours the art of knitting, they soon branched into selling yarn out of Lee's basement and then running small classes for different skill levels. After opening a small yarn shop in Corner Brook's shopping district, they began creating their own knitwear designs and selling them as kits, supplied with yarn and knitting needles, through their shop and catalogue. After their designs caught the eye of a Holt Renfrew buyer, their business took off beyond what the cousins ever imagined. Their colourful sweater and hat designs are worn by not only socialites but also film and stage performers attracted to their uniqueness. Little did the cousins think that their hobby would become a cottage industry and then a major business.

You've been working at Knitsmart Yarn and Needles during your summer break from university, and you think it's time that Lee and Siobhan branch into new territory: the World Wide Web. You think that the cousins should build a Web site where they can gain new customers, interest other people in their craft, and inspire knitters around the world with their patterns. You find an advertisement in the local newspaper for a company that creates Web sites (Webtech), but the classified ad gives little information beyond a phone number and an e-mail address.

Your Task: You will be setting aside time next week to discuss the opportunities a Knitsmart Web site offers to the Lee and Siobhan. Write an e-mail message requesting more information from Webtech about what the company can do for Knitsmart Yarn and Needles.

7 Helping out: E-mail request about donations to the Computers for Schools Initiative As a computer-literacy volunteer at a local high school, you have heard of the Computers for Schools Initiative, an Industry Canada program that works with private business, industry, and volunteer organizations to collect, refurbish, and distribute "retired" computers to Canada's schools and public libraries free of charge. Since its creation in 1993 by Industry Canada and the Telephone Pioneers, the largest industry-related volunteer organization globally, more than 230 000 computers have been placed across Canada. There are many benefits: older technology is recycled, saving it from the dump; kids develop skills they can use for education and the job market; and the donors do something beneficial for society.

You are intrigued and inspired by this national initiative, and you get thinking. At your part-time job as a customer service representative at a local bank you've already seen the desktop computers replaced twice in the last three years. You've also seen the laptops used by managers replaced with newer, faster ones with more bells and whistles. Where does this old equipment go, you wonder. Is it used as landfill, or just taking up space in a warehouse? You want to find out.

Your Task: Visit the Computers for Schools Web site at **www.schoolnet.ca** to learn about this worthy project. Then go to the Web site of a bank of your choice, and compose an e-mail message to their contact address. Asking suitable questions, find out about the bank's computer recycling program, if any, and tell them about the Computers for Schools project.[10]

Routine Replies

8 Window shopping at Wal-Mart: Writing a positive reply via e-mail The Wal-Mart chain of discount stores is one of the most successful in the world: designing, importing, and marketing across national borders. In particular, Wal-Mart rarely fails to capitalize on a marketing scheme, and its online shopping page is no exception. To make sure the Web site remains effective and relevant, the Webmaster asks various people to check out the site and give their feedback. As administrative assistant to Wal-Mart's director of marketing, you have just received a request from the Webmaster to visit Wal-Mart's Web site and give feedback on the shopping page.

Your Task: Visit Wal-Mart at **www.wal-mart.com** and do some online "window shopping." As you browse through the shopping page, consider the language, layout, graphics, ease of use, and background noise. Compose a positive reply to the Webmaster, and send your feedback to cserve@wal-mart.com. Print a copy of your e-mail message for submission to your instructor.

9 Red dirt to go: Positive reply by e-mail from Paradise Sportswear Robert Hedin would agree with whoever said that it's possible to turn a failure into a success. But he'd probably add with a chuckle that it could take several failures before you finally hit "pay dirt." As the owner of Paradise Sportswear in Hawaii, Hedin was nearly done in by Hurricane Iniki in 1992, which wiped out his first silk-screened and airbrushed T-shirt business. He tried again, but then Hawaii's red dirt started seeping into his warehouse and ruining his inventory. Finally, a friend suggested that he stop trying to fight Mother Nature. Hedin took the hint: He mortgaged his condo and began producing Red Dirt Shirts, all made with dye created from the troublesome local dirt.

Bingo: So popular are Hedin's Red Dirt Sportswear designs, they're being snapped up by locals and tourists in Hedin's eight Paradise Sportswear retail outlets and in every Kmart on the islands. Last year Hedin added a new line: Lava Blues, made with real Hawaiian lava rock.

"You can make 500 shirts with a bucket of dirt" grins Hedin as he shows you around the operation on your first day. He's just a few years away from the usual retirement age, but he looks like a kid who's finally found the right playground.

Recently Hedin decided to capitulate to all the requests he's received from retail outlets on the mainland. Buyers kept coming to the islands on vacation, discovering Hedin's "natural" sportswear, and plaguing him in person, by mail, and by e-mail, trying to set up a deal. For a long time, his answer was no; he simply couldn't handle the extra work. But now he's hired you.

As special sales representative, you'll help Hedin expand slowly into this new territory, starting with one store. Wholesaling to the local Kmarts is easy enough, but handling all the arrangements for shipping to the mainland would be too much for the current staff. So you'll start with the company Hedin has chosen to become the first mainland retailer to sell Red Dirt and Lava Blues sportswear: Surf's Up in Chicago, Illinois—of all places. The boss figures that with less competition than he'd find on either coast, his island-influenced sportswear will be a big hit in Chicago, especially in the dead of winter.

Your Task: Write a positive response to the e-mail received from Surf's Up buyer Ronald Draeger, who says he fell in love with the Paradise clothing concept while on a surfing trip to Maui. Let him know he'll have a temporary exclusive and that you'll be sending a credit application and other materials by snail mail. His e-mail address is surfsup@insnet.com.[11]

10 Satellite farming: Letter granting credit from Deere & Company The best part of your job with Deere & Co., a heavy machinery manufacturer, is saying yes to a farmer. In this case, it's Arlen Ruestman in Broadview, Saskatchewan.

Ruestman wants to take advantage of new farming technology. Your company's new GreenStar system uses satellite technology: the Global Positioning System (GPS). By using a series of satellites orbiting Earth, the system can pinpoint (to the metre) exactly where a farmer is positioned at any given moment as he drives his GreenStar-equipped combine over a field. For farmers like Ruestman, that means a new ability to micromanage even as much as 10 000 acres of corn or soybeans.

For instance, using the GreenStar system, farmers can map crop yields from a given area and then examine potential causes of yield variations. After careful analysis, they can determine exactly how much herbicide or fertilizer to spread over precisely which spot—eliminating waste and achieving better results. With cross-referencing and accumulated data, farmers can analyze why crops are performing well in some areas and not so well in others.

Then they can program farm equipment to treat only the problem area—for example, spraying a new insect infestation two meters wide, 300 yards down the row.

Some farms have already saved as much as $10 an acre on fertilizers alone. For 10,000 acres, that's $100,000 a year. Once Ruestman retrofits your GreenStar precision package on his old combine and learns all its applications, he should have no problem saving enough to pay off the $7,350 credit account you're about to grant him.

Your Task: Write a letter to Mr. Ruestman (P.O. Box 4067, Broadview, Saskatchewan.[12]

Positive Messages

11 Cold comfort: Letter offering a regional sales position with Golight Winter in Saskatchewan ranch country is something to sneeze at—and to shiver over. That's why rancher Jerry Gohl invented the Golight, a portable spotlight that can be mounted on a car or truck roof and rotated 360 degrees horizontally and 70 degrees vertically by remote control. No more getting out of the truck in freezing, pre-dawn temperatures to adjust a manual spotlight in order to check on his livestock in the dark. In fact, Gohl hardly has any time left to check the livestock at all these days: his invention has become so popular that three-year-old Golight, Inc., expects to sell more than $2 million worth of the remote-controlled lights next year.

The company expanded fast, with Golights becoming popular all over the world among hunters, boaters, commuters who fear dark-of-night roadside tire changes, and early morning fishing enthusiasts who can scope out the best shoreline sites by controlling the spotlight from inside their warm and cozy vehicles. Sales reps have been hired for every part of the country and overseas, but Gohl has been holding out for just the right person to replace him in Saskatchewan. After all, the company president knows better than anyone what the local ranchers need and how they think—that's why his invention was such a success there. He didn't want to jinx his good fortune by choosing the wrong replacement.

Finally, last week he met a young man named Robert Victor who seems to fit the bill. Robert grew up on a Saskatchewan ranch, helping his dad with those 4 a.m. chores. He's young, but he's felt the bite of the Prairie's cold, he knows the rancher mind, and best of all, he's been bringing in top dollar selling agricultural equipment in Alberta for the past few years. Now he wants to return to his home province. Jerry liked him from the first moment they shook hands. "He's got the job if he wants it," the boss tells you. "Better send him some e-mail before someone else grabs him. He can start as soon as he's settled."

Your Task: Compose the message communicating Gohl's offer to Robert Victor: salary plus commission as discussed.[13]

12 Learn while you earn: Memo announcing Burger King's educational benefits Your boss, Mike Andrade, owner of three Burger King stores in downtown Montreal, is worried about employee turnover. He needs to keep 50 people on his payroll to operate the outlets, but recruiting and retaining those people is tough. The average employee leaves after about seven months, so Andrade has to hire and train 90 people a year just to maintain a 50-person crew. At a cost of $1500 per hire, the price tag for all that turnover is approximately $62 000 a year.

Andrade knows that a lot of his best employees quit because they think that flipping burgers is a dead-end job. But what if it weren't a dead end? What if a person could really get someplace flipping burgers? What if Andrade offered to pay his employees' way through college if they remained with the store? Would that keep them behind the counter?

He's decided to give educational incentives a try. Employees who choose to participate will continue to earn their usual salary, but they will also get free books and tuition, keyed to the number of hours they work each week. Those who work from 10 to 15 hours a week can take one free course at any local college or university; those who work 16 to 25 hours can take two courses; and those who work 26 to 40 hours can take three courses. The program is open to all employees, regardless of how long they have worked for Burger King, but no one is obligated to participate.

Your Task: Draft a memo for Mr. Andrade to send out announcing the new educational incentives.[14]

13 Midnight mission: Thank-you letter at The Blue Marble bookstore As owner of The Blue Marble bookstore in Fort Garry, Manitoba, Tina Blackfeather won't be outdone this time. You are store manager, and along with the rest of the staff, you've been working hard to prepare for the biggest book-sales party your store has ever hosted. Tonight's the night. Last time you blew it with the popular *Harry Potter* series (about a boy who discovers he's not only a wizard-in-training, but a famous one). Book #5 was to be released at 12:01 a.m. on Friday, June 21, a "strict on sale" date in Canada, the United States, and Britain. Like thousands of other adults, you've enjoyed the cleverly written stories of Harry and his friends at Hogwarts School of wizardry. But you and Blackfeather agreed that customers would probably be content to come in for a copy on Saturday morning. Who would let their kids stay up past midnight for a book party?

Apparently, tens of thousands of parents did—all grateful to see their kids reading so avidly. On Friday night, bookstores all over the country opened up at midnight—especially the chains, your biggest competitors. By morning, very few copies of "HP5" were left. British author J. K. Rowling had done it again. Even well-known adult critics loved the new book.

Of course, that morning you still had copies available, but your customers felt cheated. "Why didn't you have a pajama party last night?" they complained. "My kids saw the crowds on TV and wanted to go—but the nearest chain store is miles from here!" Some fans even called your staff "clueless muggles!" (nonwizards—usually the last to know about anything truly interesting). But that was last time.

This time, when the clock chimes midnight and you're allowed to sell *Harry Potter* #6, your customers will be ushered in by staff members in costume. A local trainer will stroll the store with a pet owl (favourite messengers in Harry's world). From the big black cauldrons your staff built, you'll serve oatmeal and Harry's favorite "butter beer" (apple juice and ginger ale over dry ice). The first kids in line will get free lightning-bolt stickers to create forehead scars like Harry's, and some will receive black, round-rimmed imitation "Harry Potter spectacles." It's going to be great fun.

Your Task: Your staff has been working on their own time sewing costumes, making hats, and inventing butter-beer recipes. Write a thank-you letter to them from both you and Blackfeather, and enclose a $25 gift certificate in each one. You plan to distribute the letters before tonight's party.[15]

14 ABCs: Form letter thanking volunteers Working together with government, educators, labour, and business, ABC Canada, a national literacy organization, promotes awareness of literacy and works to involve the private sector in supporting literacy. Its aim is "to promote a fully literate Canadian population." People in your firm, Fine Paper Company, participated in the annual PGI Golf Tournament for Literacy, which was founded by Peter Gzowski, one of Canada's great broadcasters and writers, and best known for his morning show on the CBC. The PGI is a very successful fundraising event, having generated $5 million over more than a decade. PGI tournaments are held in every province and territory.

Statistics Canada's report, *Literary Skills for the Knowledge Society*, notes that "22 percent of adult Canadians have serious problems with printed materials" and that "24 to 26 percent of Canadians can only deal with simple reading tasks."

Not only does your firm support the PGI Golf Tournament with monetary donations—and golf lovers—but the CEO, Laurent DesLauriers, established a volunteer program for employees to donate their time at local community centres to help adults learn to read. This program has become a success at Fine Paper Company.

Your Task: As a human resources specialist at Fine Paper Company, you are sometimes asked to write goodwill letters to employees, a job you enjoy doing. Mr. DesLauriers has directed the office to send a thank-you letter to all the volunteers, those who participated in the golf tournament and those who volunteer their time at the community centres. You will compose a form letter, which will be merged with individual employee's names and addresses.[16]

15 Cable hiccups: E-mail reply to an unhappy cable Internet customer As a customer service agent working for your local cable company, you've received the occasional complaint like the one you're looking at on your computer monitor. The writer says,

> I'm fed up with the your cable Internet service. I've had my new computer for about a year and used the slow dial-up ISP service only because the manufacturer included it for free. I got your

> high-speed cable Internet service because your advertising promised it was 30 times faster than dial-up. I've used it since March, and I'm very disappointed. I'm paying $39.95 a month, plus taxes, but twice in the last month I've been unable to connect and service is a lot slower than advertised. What a rip-off!
>
> I'm a student and I work part-time. I do a lot of my research for essays and reports over the Internet. Not to mention e-mail. I have deadlines to meet. I want you to cancel my service and refund me my last two months' payments.

You know that many people complain that the cable line is shared with neighbours, which might slow down service. But slowdowns are rare with cable and happen with high-speed phone lines too. Cable Internet service has a lot of capacity and can provide rapid access to the Internet, even though lines are shared. You think the writer is exaggerating and just wants to get his money back because the message is dated April 6, near the end of the school term.

Your Task: You'll be sending a positive e-mail to the writer indicating that your company will refund the amount he requests. Write to TopGuy@ihome.com You've been trained to educate consumers about cable Internet service

16 A rising star: Letter congratulating award recipient You read in your university alumni magazine, *McGill News*, that Melissa Thanh won this year's Student Entrepreneur of the Year Award from ACE, the Association of Canadian Entrepreneurs. Melissa worked in your desktop publishing firm part-time during her high school years to help with family expenses. She was a very diligent employee and caught on very fast to the technology. You check out the ACE Canada Web site and learn that the CIBC Student Entrepreneur of the Year Award is "presented annually to a full-time Canadian university or college student running a business." Finalists are chosen based on "operating success, job creation, involvement in new economy activities, innovation, community involvement, and school performance." Melissa wins a package of products and services that will be useful for her business, and $1000 cash.

You've heard through a friend in the industry that Melissa started her own desktop-publishing firm out of her family's basement and created a Web site to advertise her business—putting together newsletters, brochures, letterheads, and other documents. As long as a client provides the text, she is able create an attractive package. Obviously her skills are known, for as your friend tells you, she has many clients. She's also been a straight-A student at McGill University, captain of the women's soccer team, and a volunteer in soup kitchens.

Your Task: Write a letter of congratulation to Melissa. Address it to 2505 35th Ave. W, Vancouver B.C. V6N 2L9.[17]

Going Online Exercises

The Medium and the Message, found on page 167 of this chapter

Choosing what to include in a message, deciding how to effectively express it, and selecting an appropriate format are all important considerations when you write. Go to **www.about.com** and add to what you've already learned in this chapter about writing requests and other messages.[18]

1 Both the chapter and this site offer guidelines for writing effective messages. List the "seven C's" that characterize good letters and memos. If you use clear language in a routine message, is it still important to restrict yourself to one topic? Why or why not?
2 Even the best-run businesses sometimes disappoint their customers. Imagine that you have been asked to write a response to an angrily worded e-mail message that charges your company with fraud because a product ordered through the Web has not arrived. Which of the ten "secrets" of writing business letters do you think would be most useful in shaping your reply?
3 Describe some similarities and differences between a memo and a letter.

Writing Bad-News Messages

1 Apply the three-step writing process to bad-news messages

2 Show how to achieve an audience-centred tone and explain why it helps readers

3 Differentiate between the direct and indirect organizational approaches to bad-news messages and discuss when it's appropriate to use each one

4 Discuss the three techniques for saying "no" as clearly and kindly as possible

5 Define *defamation* and explain how to avoid it in bad-news messages

6 Outline the main purpose of performance reviews, give three ways to accomplish that purpose, and list six guidelines to follow when communicating a negative assessment

ON THE JOB

Facing a Communication Dilemma at Wal-Mart

When Saying "No" Is Part of Your Job

www.wal-mart.com

With 213 discount department stores across Canada and more than 70 000 products, Wal-Mart is a shopper's paradise and a suppliers dream. Wal-Mart's relationship with its suppliers accounts in large part for the chain's success. To deliver its "everyday low price," or "EDLP" in Wal-Mart jargon, the store works with manufacturers and service providers to lower costs—and still be profitable—through reduced packaging and streamlined distribution systems. In 1994, when Wal-Mart first established its Canadian outlets, the firm also launched its "buy Canadian" program, forming vendor–partner agreements with Canadian suppliers, stocking its shelves with Canadian-made goods, and creating thousands of jobs.

Suppliers are eager to work with Wal-Mart, but they must meet Wal-Mart's stringent criteria in order to get their wares onto Wal-Mart's shelves and their services to Wal-Mart's customers. To start the process of becoming a Wal-Mart supplier, manufacturers and service providers must complete a comprehensive proposal. They must answer key questions about their customers' demographics—age, family size, income, geographical location. Potential suppliers must discuss how their product will help Wal-Mart gain market share while controlling costs. They must analyze product benefits, direct and indirect competition, and their product's impact on other related products sold at Wal-Mart. Along with their answers, potential suppliers must provide financial statements, product literature and price lists, and samples. To become a Wal-Mart supplier is a demanding process, with no guarantee of success.

How would you say "no" to Canadian businesses, large and small, whose products don't meet Wal-Mart's standards? What strategy would you use to communicate your decision, yet try to retain the good will of your audience?[1]

Although Wal-Mart will reject some potential suppliers, the firm still wants to maintain good relationships with them. By explaining the reasons for the refusal in a clear and helpful way, Wal-Mart communicates their understanding and goodwill—essential elements for maintaining a positive link in a difficult situation.

Using the Three-Step Writing Process for Bad-News Messages

Nobody likes bad news. People don't like to get it, and they don't like to give it. Saying "no" to an idea, a proposition, or a request from a customer, an employee, a shareholder, a salesperson—or even your boss—can put knots in your stomach and cost you hours of sleep. The challenge lies in being honest but kind.

The word "no" is terse and abrupt, so negative that a lot of people have trouble saying it. And for most, it's the most difficult word to hear or understand. The delivery can be far more damaging than the answer itself. The most painful no is usually the one you don't explain.[2] That's why you must be careful whenever you deliver bad news. You don't want to sacrifice ethics and mislead your audience; nor do you want to be overly blunt. The three-step process can help you write bad-news messages that are more effective and less hurtful.

Step 1: Planning Your Bad-News Messages

OBJECTIVE 1 Apply the three-step writing process to bad-news messages.

Analysis, investigation, and adaptation help you avoid alienating your readers.

When your message is a negative one, analysis becomes extremely important. If your purpose is specific, you are able to word it in the best possible way. You want to be sure that a bad-news message should indeed be sent and should definitely be sent in writing. And more than ever, you need to know how your audience will receive your message. Do readers prefer to receive negative news up front, without delay? Or would they accept the news more readily if you explained your reasons first?

Any investigation or research must yield reliable, unmistakable facts that will support your negative decision. You'll want to be sure that you have all the facts your audience will need. After sending your bad news, you don't want to face a barrage of questions from confused readers.

Finally, you'll want to pay particular attention to maintaining a good relationship with your audience. Be sure to adapt your medium and tone to your audience. Careful attention to adaptation can help you avoid alienating your readers.

Step 2: Writing Your Bad-News Messages

The appropriate organization helps readers accept your negative news.

In a bad-news message, your main idea is a refusal, a rejection, or a negative announcement, so you want to be careful about defining that main idea and about covering relevant points thoroughly and logically. Choosing between the direct and indirect approaches takes on added importance in bad-news messages. You need to know whether it will be better to open with the bad news or to prepare your readers with a cogent explanation before giving them the negative bits. You also need to pay special attention to word choice so that you can create your sentences and paragraphs carefully.

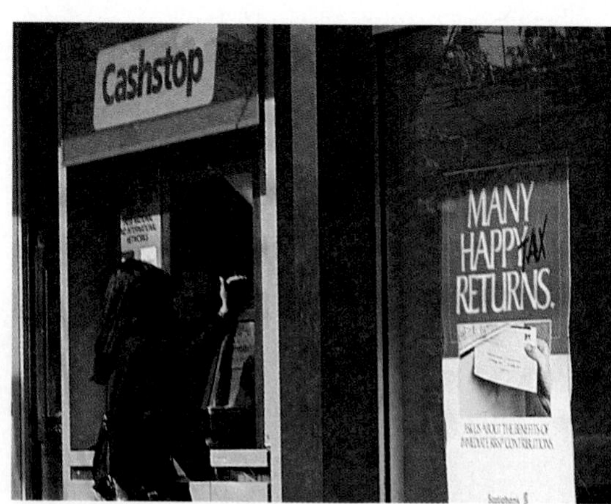

Higher fees or loan refusals are two examples of bad-news messages that banks send to customers. Bankers face the same challenges confronting many businesspeople who must communicate bad news—how to retain the customer's business and goodwill while justifying negative decisions.

Step 3: Completing Your Bad-News Messages

Revision is as important as the other steps in the writing process; it helps you make sure that your bad-news messages are organized properly, that they say what you want them to say, and that they do so concisely and clearly. You'll want to make sure that your design doesn't detract from the bad news or from your efforts to be sensitive. And as always, proofreading bad-news messages guarantees that there are no misunderstandings from typos or from errors in spelling or mechanics.

Sending Bad-News Messages

You are sending a bad-news message when you refuse to grant a claim, encounter problems filling an order, announce that quarterly profits are down, or refuse a favour. Whatever the details of your particular message, when you have bad news, make your readers feel that they are being taken seriously. You want them to understand that your news is fair and reasonable.

Strategies for Bad-News Messages

When delivering bad news, you have five main goals: (1) to convey the bad news, (2) to gain acceptance for it, (3) to maintain as much goodwill as possible with your audience, (4) to maintain a good image for your organization, and (5) to reduce or eliminate the need for future correspondence on the matter. Accomplishing so many goals in a single message is not easy. But you can make your bad-news messages effective. First, adopt an audience-centred tone. Second, organize your message to meet your audience's needs and expectations by using either the direct approach, which presents the main idea before the supporting information (fully described in Chapter 7), or the indirect approach, which presents the supporting data before the main idea.

Five goals of bad-news messages:
- Give the bad news
- Ensure its acceptance
- Maintain reader's goodwill
- Maintain organization's good image
- Reduce future correspondence on the matter

CREATING AN AUDIENCE-CENTRED TONE

OBJECTIVE 2 Show how to achieve an audience-centred tone and explain why it helps readers.

You've probably heard the saying "It's not what you say but how you say it that counts." That idea couldn't be truer with bad-news messages. Your tone contributes to your message's effectiveness by helping your readers

- Accept that your bad-news represents a firm decision
- Understand that, under the circumstances, your decision was fair and reasonable
- Remain well disposed toward your business
- Preserve their pride

When establishing tone, strive for
- Firmness
- Fairness
- Goodwill
- Respect.

Be sure to use a you-centred approach, positive words, and respectful language in your bad-news messages. When communicating across cultures, be aware of the tone, organization, and other cultural conventions of the culture. Only then can you avoid the inappropriate or even offensive approaches that could jeopardize your business relationship.[3]

Use the "You" Attitude Being sensitive to the feelings and state of mind of your audience is crucial to every message you write, but it's especially important in bad-news messages. In these messages, using the "you" attitude does not necessarily mean directly addressing the reader. As Chapter 5 explains, use the passive voice when you must criticize your audience or place blame, because using the active voice makes your criticism sound like an accusation. To achieve a diplomatic tone, also try to focus on some aspect of the situation that makes the bad news easier to accept. For example, point out how your decision might actually further your audience's goals. Convey concern by looking for the best in your audience. And assume that your audience is interested in being fair, even when they are at fault.

The "you" attitude is especially important in bad-news messages.

Choose Positive Words You can ease disappointment by using positive words rather than negative, counterproductive words. Just be sure that your positive tone doesn't hide the bad news behind language that is misleading.[4] Remember, you want to convey the bad news, not conceal it.

Use positive rather than negative phrasing in bad-news messages.

INSTEAD OF THIS	SAY THIS
I cannot understand what you mean.	Please clarify your request.
The damage won't be fixed for a week.	The item will be repaired next week.
There will be a delay in your order.	We will ship your order as soon as possible.

You are clearly dissatisfied.	We are doing what we can to make things right.
Your account is in error.	Corrections have been made to your account.
The breakage was not our fault.	The merchandise was broken during shipping.
Sorry for your inconvenience.	The enclosed coupon will save you $5 next time.
We regret the misunderstanding.	I'll try my best to be clearer from now on.
I was shocked to learn that you're unhappy.	Your letter reached me yesterday.
Unfortunately, we haven't received it.	It hasn't arrived yet.
The enclosed statement is wrong.	Please recheck the enclosed statement.

Use Respectful Language When you use language that conveys respect and avoids an accusing tone, you protect your audience's pride. For instance, when refusing an adjustment or a claim, try using third-person, impersonal, passive language to explain your audience's mistakes in an inoffensive way. This approach downplays the doer of the action because the doer is not specified. Say, "The appliance won't work after being immersed in water" instead of "You shouldn't have immersed the appliance in water." When your audience is at fault, the "you" attitude is better observed by avoiding the word "you."

Sometimes the "you" attitude is best observed by avoiding the word you.

USING THE DIRECT APPROACH

OBJECTIVE 3 Differentiate between the direct and indirect organizational approaches to bad-news messages and discuss when it's appropriate to use each one.

As with most business messages, the key to choosing the best approach for bad-news messages is to analyze audience members first. Try to see the situation from their viewpoint. What is their likely reaction to the news? How important is the message? How well do you know them? Some people like to know the bad news right away. Similarly, some situations are more appropriate for directness than others. If you know that your audience is likely to prefer the bad news first, or if the situation is minor and the news will cause your audience little pain or disappointment, then use the direct approach.

Audience analysis is crucial for determining the organization of bad-news messages.

A bad-news message organized using the direct approach starts with a clear statement of the bad news, proceeds to the reasons for the decision (perhaps offering alternatives), and ends with a positive statement aimed at maintaining a good relationship with the audience (see Figure 8–1 below). Stating the bad news at the beginning can have two advantages: (1) it makes a shorter message possible, and (2) the audience needs less time to reach the main idea of the message, the bad news itself.

Memos are often organized so that the bad news comes before the reasons. Some managers expect all internal correspondence to be brief and direct, regardless of

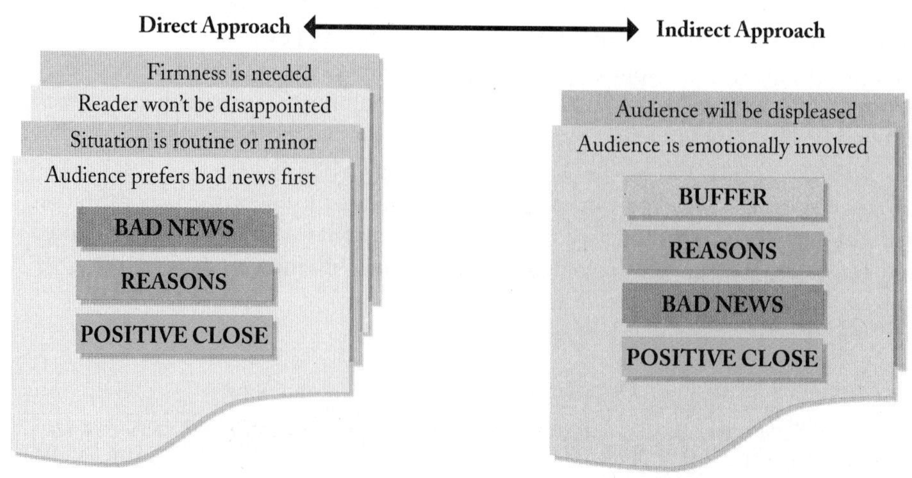

FIGURE 8–1
Differences between the Indirect and Direct Organizational Plans for Bad-News Messages

whether the message is positive or negative. Routine bad-news messages to other companies often follow the direct approach, especially if they relay decisions that have little or no personal impact. The indirect approach can actually cause ill will in people who see bad news frequently, such as people searching for employment.[5] In addition, you'll sometimes know from experience that your audience simply prefers reading the bad news first in any message. The direct approach is also appropriate when you want to present an image of firmness and strength; for example, the last message in a debt collection series (just before the matter is turned over to an attorney) usually gets right to the point.

You may want to use the direct approach in a variety of circumstances, saving your positive comments for the close. Even so, remember that a tactful tone and a focus on reasons will help make any bad-news message easier to accept. However, you'll find that many businesspeople prefer using an indirect approach for delivering bad news.

Should you use the indirect or direct strategy when communicating all bad news? Many people in finance believe that, when communicating the falling fortunes of one's investments, the direct strategy is best. Why?

USING THE INDIRECT APPROACH

Beginning a bad news message with a blunt "no" could well prevent your audience from reading or listening to your reasons. Some prefer preparation or explanation first. The indirect approach eases your audience into your message by explaining your reasons before delivering the bad news. Presenting the reasons first increases your chances of gaining audience acceptance by gradually preparing readers for the negative news to come. The indirect approach follows a four-part sequence (as shown in Figure 8–1 on page 204): (1) Open with a buffer, (2) continue with a logical, neutral explanation of the reasons for the bad news, (3) follow with a clear but diplomatic statement of the bad news, emphasizing any good news and de-emphasizing the bad, and (4) close with a positive forward-looking statement that is helpful and friendly.

Use the direct approach when your negative answer or information will have little personal impact.

Use the indirect approach when some preparation will help your audience accept your bad news.

Begin with a Buffer The first step in using the indirect approach is to make a neutral, noncontroversial statement that is closely related to the point of the message; this statement is called a **buffer**. A good buffer is demanding to write. Some critics believe that using a buffer is manipulative, dishonest, and thus unethical. In fact, buffers are unethical only if they're insincere. Breaking bad news with kindness and courtesy is the humane way. Consideration for the feelings of others is never dishonest, and that consideration helps your audience accept your message.

A **buffer** is a neutral lead-in to bad news.

Use a buffer that is
- Neutral
- Relevant
- Not misleading
- Assertive
- Succinct

A good buffer expresses your appreciation for being thought of, assures the reader of your attention to the request, compliments the reader, or indicates your understanding of the reader's needs. A buffer must not insult the audience with insincere flattery or self-promoting blather. It sets the stage for the bad news to follow, and it must be both sincere and relevant so that readers don't feel they are being set up or deceived. For example, in a memo telling another supervisor that you can't spare anyone from your staff for a temporary assignment to the order fulfillment department, you might begin with a sentence like this:

> Our department shares your goal of processing orders quickly and efficiently.

If possible, base your buffer on statements made by the person you're responding to. This type of buffer shows the person that you have listened well. If you use an unrelated buffer, you will seem to be avoiding the issue; that is, you'll appear manipulative and unethical, and you'll lose your audience's respect.

Another goal when composing your buffer is to avoid giving the impression that good news will follow. Building up your audience's expectations at the beginning only makes the actual bad news even more surprising. Imagine your reaction to the following openings:

To write an effective buffer, avoid giving the impression that good news will follow.

> Your résumé indicates that you would be well suited for a management trainee position with our company.

> Your résumé shows very clearly why you are interested in becoming a management trainee with our company.

USING THE POWER OF TECHNOLOGY

Helping Customers Help Themselves

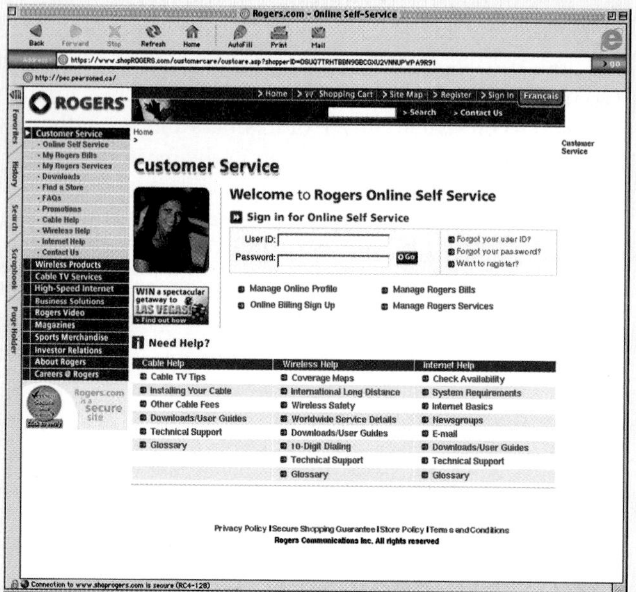

"Problems are opportunities in disguise"—an apt description of how insightful e-businesses approach customer service. Every complaint gives you a chance to strengthen your customer's loyalty, if you make full use of Internet technology to show that you're truly interested in meeting your customer's needs. Web-based businesses offer customers a wide choice of contact methods: e-mail, phone, or regular mail, or instant online customer-service chat. E-businesses can also offer online customers the opportunity to resolve issues through a customer self-care Web site. Here, customers can find FAQs, service information, troubleshooting advice, technical support, and user guides. Providing these features can go a long way toward educating customers about a business's practices—an important way to preserve customer loyalty. Visit Rogers Communications customer care site at **<www.shoprogers.com/Customercare/custcare.asp>** to see how one Canadian company helps customers help themselves.

1. By providing online customer care, is a company sidestepping its responsibility to deal with customer complaints? Explain your answer.
2. When you send an e-mail message to update customers whose problems are taking more time than usual to resolve, would the direct or the indirect approach be more appropriate? Why?

The second opening emphasizes the applicant's interpretation of her qualifications rather than the company's evaluation, so it's less misleading but still positive. Here are other points to remember when writing buffer:

- **Avoid saying "no."** An audience encountering the blunt refusal right at the beginning usually reacts negatively to the rest of the message, no matter how reasonable and well phrased it is.
- **Avoid using a know-it-all tone.** When you use phrases such as "you should be aware that," readers expect your lecture to lead to a negative response, so they resist the rest of your message.
- **Avoid wordy and irrelevant phrases and sentences.** Sentences such as "We have received your letter," "This letter is in reply to your request," and "We are writing in response to your request" are irrelevant. Make better use of the space by referring directly to the subject of the letter.
- **Avoid apologizing.** Unless warranted by extreme circumstances, an apology only weakens the following explanation of your unfavourable news.
- **Avoid writing a buffer that is too long.** Be brief. Identify something that both you and your audience are interested in and agree on before proceeding in a businesslike way.

Table 8–1 on page 207 shows several types of buffers you could use to open a bad-news message tactfully.

After you've composed a buffer, evaluate it by asking yourself four questions: Is it pleasant? Is it relevant? Is it neutral, saying neither yes nor no? Does it provide for a smooth transition to the reasons that follow? If you can answer yes to every question, you can proceed confidently to the next section of your message.

TABLE 8–1 Types of Buffers

Buffer	Strategy	Example
Agreement	Find a point on which you and the reader share similar views.	We both know how hard it is to make a profit in this industry.
Appreciation	Express sincere thanks for receiving something.	Your cheque for $127.17 arrived yesterday. Thank you.
Cooperation	Convey your willingness to help in any way you realistically can.	Employee Services is here to smooth the way for all of you who work to achieve company goals.
Fairness	Assure the reader that you've closely examined and carefully considered the problem, or mention an appropriate action that has already been taken.	For the past week, we have carefully monitored to those using the photocopying machine see whether we can detect any pattern of use that might explain its frequent breakdowns.
Good news	Start with the part of your message that is favourable.	A replacement knob for your range is on its way, shipped February 10 via XpressPost.
Praise	Find an attribute or an achievement to compliment.	Your résumé shows an admirable breadth of experience, which should serve you well as you progress in your career.
Resale	Favourably discuss the product or company related to the subject of the letter.	With their heavy-duty, full-suspension hardware and fine veneers, the desks and file cabinets in our Montclair line have become a hit with value-conscious professionals.
Understanding	Demonstrate that you understand the reader's goals and needs.	So that you can more easily find the printer with the features you need, we are enclosing a brochure that describes all the Panasonic printers currently available.

Follow with Reasons If you've done a good job of composing the buffer, the reasons will follow naturally. Cover the more positive points first; then move to the less positive ones. Provide enough detail for the audience to understand your reasons, but be concise; a long, roundabout explanation may make your audience impatient. Your goal is to explain why you have reached your decision before you explain what that decision is. If you present your reasons effectively, they should convince your audience that your decision is justified, fair, and logical.

Present reasons to show that your decision is reasonable and fair.

One way to be tactful when giving your reasons is to highlight how your negative decision benefits your readers (rather than focusing on why the decision is good for you or your company). For example, when denying a credit request, you can show how your decision will keep the person from becoming overextended financially. Facts and figures are often helpful in convincing members of your audience that you're acting in their best interests.

Focus on how the audience might benefit from your negative message.

Avoid hiding behind company policy to cushion the bad news. If you say, "Company policy forbids granting adjustments on products that are out of warranty," you seem to imply that you haven't considered the case on its own merits. Skilled and sympathetic communicators explain company policy (without referring to it as "policy") so that the audience can understand company practice and try to meet the requirements at a later time.

Well-written reasons are

- Detailed
- Tactful
- Individualized
- Unapologetic
- Positive

Similarly, avoid apologizing when giving your reasons. Apologies are appropriate only when someone in your company has made a severe mistake or has done something terribly wrong. If no one in the company is at fault, an apology gives the wrong impression. For example, say that you're refusing a manufacturer's proposal to sell a line of lightweight backpacks in your sporting supply store. A tactfully worded letter might give these reasons for the decision to reject the product:

> Many of Sportworld's customers are outdoor enthusiasts who camp from early spring through late fall. Our research shows that backpacks manufactured from 630-denier superpack nylon or a stronger fabric will withstand all weather conditions.

The paragraph does a good job of stating the reasons for the refusal:

- It provides enough detail to make the reason for the refusal logically acceptable.
- It implies that the manufacturer is better off finding a different type of sporting goods retailer that sells to different clientele.
- It explains the company's decision as logical rather than rigid.
- It offers no apology for the decision.
- It avoids negative personal expressions ("Your product is manufactured from weak fabric.").

Sometimes detailed reasons should not be provided.

However, even though specific reasons help audiences accept bad news, reasons cannot always be given. Don't include reasons when they involve confidential, excessively complicated, or purely negative information or when they benefit only you or your firm (by enhancing the company's profits, for example). Instead, move directly to the next section.

OBJECTIVE 4 Discuss the three techniques for saying "no" as clearly and kindly as possible.

State the Bad News When the bad news is a logical outcome of the reasons that come before it, the audience is psychologically prepared to receive it. However, the audience may still reject your message if the bad news is handled carelessly. Three techniques are especially useful for saying no as clearly and as kindly as possible. First, de-emphasize the bad news:

To handle bad news carefully
- De-emphasize the bad news visually and grammatically
- Use a conditional statement
- Tell what you did do, not what you didn't do

- Minimize the space or time devoted to the bad news.
- Subordinate bad news in a complex or compound sentence ("My department is already shorthanded, so I'll need all my staff for at least the next two months"). This construction pushes the bad news into the middle of the sentence, the point of least emphasis.
- Embed bad news in the middle of a paragraph or use parenthetical expressions ("Our profits, *which are down*, are only part of the picture").

Second, use a conditional (*if* or *when*) statement to imply that the audience could have received, or might someday receive, a favourable answer ("When you have more managerial experience, you are welcome to reapply."). Such a statement could motivate applicants to improve their qualifications.

Third, tell the audience what you did do, can do, or will do rather than what you did not do, cannot do, or will not do. Say "We sell exclusively through retailers, and the one nearest you that carries our merchandise is ..." rather than "We are unable to serve you, so please call your nearest dealer." By implying the bad news, you may not need to actually state it ("Our line of camping stoves is currently being supplied by two manufacturers."). By focusing on the positive and implying the bad news, you soften the blow.

Don't let the bad news get lost by overemphasizing the positive.

When implying bad news, be sure your audience understands the entire message—including the bad news. It would be unethical to overemphasize the positive. So if an implied message might leave doubt, state your decision in direct terms. Just be sure to avoid overly blunt statements that are likely to cause pain and anger:

INSTEAD OF THIS	USE THIS
I must refuse your request.	I won't be in town on the day you need me.
We must deny your application.	The position has been filled.
I am unable to grant your request.	Contact us again when you have established ...
We cannot afford to continue the program.	The program will conclude on May 1.
Much as I would like to attend ...	Our budget meeting ends too late for me to attend.
We must reject your proposal.	We've accepted the proposal from AAA Builders.
We must turn down your extension request.	Please send in your payment by June 14.

End with a Positive Close After giving your audience the bad news, your job is to end your message on an optimistic note. You might propose an attainable solution to the audience's problem ("The human resources department has offered to bring in temporary workers when I need them, and they would probably consider doing the same for you." "I suggest that you contact less specialized sporting goods retailers, such as MegaSports and WorldSport, which serve a general market."). In a message to a customer or potential customer, an off-the-subject ending that includes resale information or sales promotion may also be appropriate. If you've asked readers to decide between alternatives or to take some action, make sure that they know what to do, when to do it, and how to do it with ease. Whatever type of close you choose, follow these guidelines:

- **Keep it positive.** Don't refer to, repeat, or apologize for the bad news, and refrain from expressing any doubt that your reasons will be accepted (avoid statements such as "I trust our decision is satisfactory.").
- **Limit future correspondence.** Encourage additional communication only if you're willing to discuss your decision further (avoid phrases such as "If you have further questions, please write.").
- **Be optimistic about the future.** Don't anticipate problems (avoid statements such as "Should you have further problems, please let us know.").
- **Be sincere.** Steer clear of clichés that are insincere in view of the bad news (avoid saying, "If we can be of any help, please contact us.").
- **Be confident.** Don't show any doubt about keeping the person as a customer (avoid phrases such as "We hope you will continue to do business with us.").

Keep in mind that the close is the last thing the audience has to remember you by. Try to make the memory a positive one. For a reminder of the strategies for delivering bad-news messages, see this chapter's "Checklist: Bad-News Messages" on page 210.

Types of Bad-News Messages

During your careers, you will write various types of bad-news messages: you may be refusing a claim or a favour, or refusing to give a job reference. In the following sections, we discuss some specific examples within three major categories: sending negative answers to routine requests, sending negative organizational news, and sending negative employment messages.

SENDING NEGATIVE ANSWERS TO ROUTINE REQUESTS

The businessperson who tries to say "yes" to everyone probably won't win many promotions or stay in business for long. Occasionally, your response to requests must simply be "no." It's a mark of your skill as a communicator to be able to say "no" clearly yet not cut yourself off from future dealings with other people.

Refusing Requests for Information When people ask you for information and you can't honour the request, you may answer with either the direct approach or the indirect approach. Say that you've asked a company to participate in your research project concerning sales promotion. However, that company has a policy against disseminating any information about projected sales figures. In the following letter, the direct approach is used even though the reader is outside the company and may be emotionally involved in the response. This letter would offend most readers:

Use either the direct or the indirect approach to tell someone you cannot provide what has been requested.

> Our company policy prohibits us from participating in research projects where disclosure of discretionary information might be necessary. Therefore, we decline your invitation to our sales staff to fill out questionnaires for your study.
>
> Thank you for trying to include Qualcomm Corporation in your research. If we can be of further assistance, please let us know.

The writer hides behind the blanket "company policy," a policy that the reader may find questionable.

Tone is unnecessarily negative and abrupt.

The offer to help is an unpleasant irony, given the writer's unwillingness to help in this instance.

Checklist: Bad-News Messages

Overall Strategy

✓ Use the direct approach when the situation is between employees of the same company, when the reader is not emotionally involved in the message, when you know that the reader would prefer the bad news first, or when you know that firmness is necessary.

✓ Use the indirect approach in all other cases.

✓ Adopt an audience-centred tone by being sincere, being aware of cultural differences, using the "you" attitude, choosing positive words, and using respectful language.

Buffer

✓ Express appreciation, cooperation, fairness, good news, praise, resale, or understanding.

✓ Introduce a topic that is relevant to the subject and that both you and the reader can agree on.

✓ Avoid apologies and negative-sounding words (*won't, can't, unable to*).

✓ Be brief and to the point.

✓ Maintain a confident, positive, supportive tone.

Reasons

✓ Check the lead-in from the buffer for a smooth transition from the favourable to the unfavourable.

✓ Show how the decision benefits your audience.

✓ Avoid apologies and expressions of sorrow or regret.

✓ Offer enough detail to show the logic of your position.

✓ Include only factual information.

✓ Include only business reasons, not personal ones.

✓ Carefully word the reasons so that readers can anticipate the bad news.

✓ Work from the general to the specific.

Bad News

✓ State the bad news as positively as possible, using tactful wording.

✓ De-emphasize bad news by minimizing the space devoted to it, subordinating it, or embedding it.

✓ Emphasize what the firm did do or is doing rather than what it can't or won't do.

Positive, Friendly, Helpful Close

✓ Remind the reader of how his or her needs are being met.

✓ Keep the close as positive as possible by eliminating any reference to the bad news, avoiding apologies and words of regret, and eliminating words suggesting uncertainty.

✓ Suggest actions the reader might take.

✓ Keep a positive outlook on the future.

✓ Be confident about keeping the person as a customer.

Wording and tone combine to make a letter either offensive or acceptable.

The letter in Figure 8.2 on page 211 conveys the same negative message as the previous letter but without sounding offensive.

As you think about the different impact the first draft and the revised letter in Figure 8-2 might have on you, you can see why effective business writers take the time and the trouble to give negative messages the attention they deserve.

When turning down an invitation or a request for a favour, consider your relationship to the reader.

Refusing Invitations and Requests for Favours When you must say "no" to an invitation or a request for a favour, your use of the direct or the indirect approach depends on your relationship with the reader. For example, suppose your former business-management professor wants to take her students on a tour of your company's facilities, and she contacts you to arrange it. However, the company-wide sales meeting will take place at the requested time. If you didn't know the teacher, you would probably use the indirect plan. But if you are friendly with her, and keep in touch, you might use the direct approach, as Figure 8-3 on page 212 demonstrates. The letter gets to the point in the first paragraph, but presents both the reason for the refusal and an alternative, thus softening the rejection and maintaining goodwill.

Quallcom Corporation

687 Portage Ave, Suite 1700, Winnipeg, MB R3G 0M5
204-555-2354/fax 204-555-2349
www.quallcom.net
contact@quallcom.net

February 14, 2005

Phillippe DiCastro
Analyst
Morrissey Financial Advisors
30 Cumberland St N
Thunder Bay, ON P7A 4K9

Dear Mr. DiCastro:

We at Quallcom Corporation appreciate and benefit from the research conducted by companies such as yours. Your study sounds interesting, and we are certainly able to help within the guidelines of our firm's policies governing outside researchers.

Our board requires strict confidentiality of all sales information until quarterly reports are mailed to shareholders. As you know, we release news reports at the same time quarterly reports go out. We will include you in all our future mailings.

Although we cannot release projected figures, we are, of course, able to share data that are part of the public record. I've enclosed several of our past earnings reports for your inspection.

We look forward to the results of your study. Please let us know if there is any additional way we can help.

Yours truly,

Lisa McKinnon

Lisa McKinnon
Customer Service
Investor Relations

Enclosure

1 Buffer is supportive and appreciative.

2 Bad news is implied, not stated explicitly.

3 Fully explains reason for decision without falling back on a blanket reference to company policy

4 The close is friendly, positive, and helpful.

FIGURE 8–2 In-Depth Critique: Letter Refusing a Routine Request for Information

Handling Bad News about Orders For several reasons, businesses must sometimes convey bad news concerning orders. Also, when delivering bad news to existing or would-be customers, you have an additional challenge—resale. To make readers feel good about continuing to do business with your firm, you want to

The basic goal of a bad-news letter about orders is to protect or make a sale.

- Work toward an eventual sale along the lines of the original order
- Keep instructions or additional information as clear as possible
- Maintain an optimistic, confident tone so that your reader won't lose interest

When you must back order for a customer, you have one of two types of bad news to convey: (1) You're able to send only part of the order, or (2) you're able to send none of the order. When sending only part of the order, you actually have both good

1 Planning

Analyze: Study the audience and analyze your purpose: Define the problem, limit the scope, outline the investigation, write the statement of purpose, and prepare the work plan.

Investigate: Research secondary or primary sources.

Adapt: Establish a good audience relationship and choose the right medium.

2 Writing

Organize: Decide format, length, order, and structure. Prepare the final outline, and organize any visual aids

Compose: Control your style through level of formality and tome. Establish a time perspective and help readers find their way with devices such as headings, lists, and transitions.

3 Completing

Revise: Evaluate content and review readability, editing and rewriting for conciseness and clarity.

Produce: Use effective design elements. Include all required formal components.

Proofread: Review text and visuals for errors in layout, spelling, and mechanics.

Plastics Injections Inc.

33 Research Court, Saskatoon, SK, Canada S7N 3R1
Phone (306) 963-1265 Fax (306) 963-1166
www.plasticsinjections.ca info@plasticsinj.ca

December 2, 2005

Professor Ning Wong
Department of Chemistry
62 Campus Drive
Western Technical University
Saskatoon, Saskatchewan S8N 0H2

Dear Ning,

Thank you for asking Plastics Injection Inc. to host a plant tour for your students. In past years, students have learned a great deal about how a business like ours operates. This year, however, I will have to book a date other than the one you have suggested.

States the bad news in opening.

Our company-wide sales meeting takes place from March 13 to 14. During this time, our auditorium is fully booked for presentations, and the staff who conduct the tours will be updating the sales reps on current projects.

Buffers bad news by presenting reason.

Suggests an alternative—showing that the writer cares about the tour and has given the matter some thought

Can your class take the tour the following week, on March 21? As usual, a tour guide will meet your group at 10:00 a.m. at the main entrance. Let me know if this date is good for you and how many students to expect. As in the past, the tour lasts two hours, and the students can enjoy lunch in the staff cafeteria. Please call me at 555-2232 (my direct line) to discuss the new date.

Ning, I appreciate your understanding and look forward to speaking with you.

Closing paragraphs seek action and express goodwill.

Sincerely,

Mohammed Mansour

Mohammed Mansour
Manager
Manufacturing Division

FIGURE 8-3 In-Depth Critique: Letter Refusing a Favour Using the Direct Strategy

news and bad news. In such situations, the indirect approach works very well. The buffer contains the good news (that part of the order is en route) along with a resale reminder of the product's attractiveness. After the buffer come the reasons for the delay of the remainder of the shipment. A strong close encourages a favourable attitude toward the entire transaction. For a customer whose order for a recliner and ottoman will be only partially filled, your letter might read like the one in Figure 8-4 on page 214.

When you're unable to send the customer any portion of an order, you still use the indirect approach. However, because you have no good news to give, your buffer only confirms the sale, and the explanation section states your reasons for not filling the order promptly. For a brief outline of back-order tasks, see this chapter's "Checklist: Bad News about Orders" below.

Use the indirect approach in most cases of refusing a claim.

Refusing Claims and Requests for Adjustment Almost every customer who makes a claim is emotionally involved; therefore, the indirect approach is usually the best approach for a refusal. Your job as a writer is to avoid accepting responsibility for the unfortunate situation and yet avoid blaming or accusing the customer. To steer clear of these pitfalls, pay special attention to the tone of your letter. Keep in mind that a tactful and courteous letter can build goodwill even while denying the claim. For example, Brodie's Stereo/Video has received a letter from George Pulkinen, who purchased a portable CD player more than a year ago. He wrote to say that the unit doesn't work correctly and to inquire about the warranty. Pulkinen believes that the warranty covers two years, but it actually covers only one year (see Figure 8–5 on page 215).

When refusing a claim
- Demonstrate your understanding of the complaint
- Explain your refusal
- Suggest alternative action

When refusing a claim, avoid language that might have a negative impact on the reader. Instead, demonstrate that you understand and have considered the complaint. Then, even if the claim is unreasonable, rationally explain why you are refusing the request. Remember, don't apologize, and don't rely on company policy. End the letter on a respectful and action-oriented note.

Checklist: Bad News about Orders*

Buffer

✓ Include any details identifying the order.

✓ Extend a welcome to a new customer.

✓ Use resale information on the ordered merchandise to build the customer's confidence in the original choice (except for unfillable orders).

✓ For partial shipments, include the good news about the fulfilled part.

Reasons

✓ State the facts without laying blame.

✓ Specify shipping dates.

✓ Explain why the item is out of stock, such as high popularity or exceptional demand, which may stimulate the customer's desire for the item.

✓ Reinforce the customer's confidence (for consumers, emphasize resale information such as personal attention, credit, repair services, free delivery, special discounts, telephone shopping, and other services; for dealers, emphasize free counter and window displays, advertising materials, sales manuals, factory guarantees, and nearby warehousing).

✓ Refer to sales promotion material, if desirable.

The Bad News

✓ Stress the reader benefit of the decision to buy.

✓ Offer a substitute product, if available.

Positive, Friendly, Helpful Close

✓ Adopt a tone that shows you remain in control of the situation and will continue to give customers' orders personal attention.

✓ Use resale information to secure the sale, especially for back orders.

*These items are in addition to the material included in "Checklist: Bad-News Messages" on page 210.

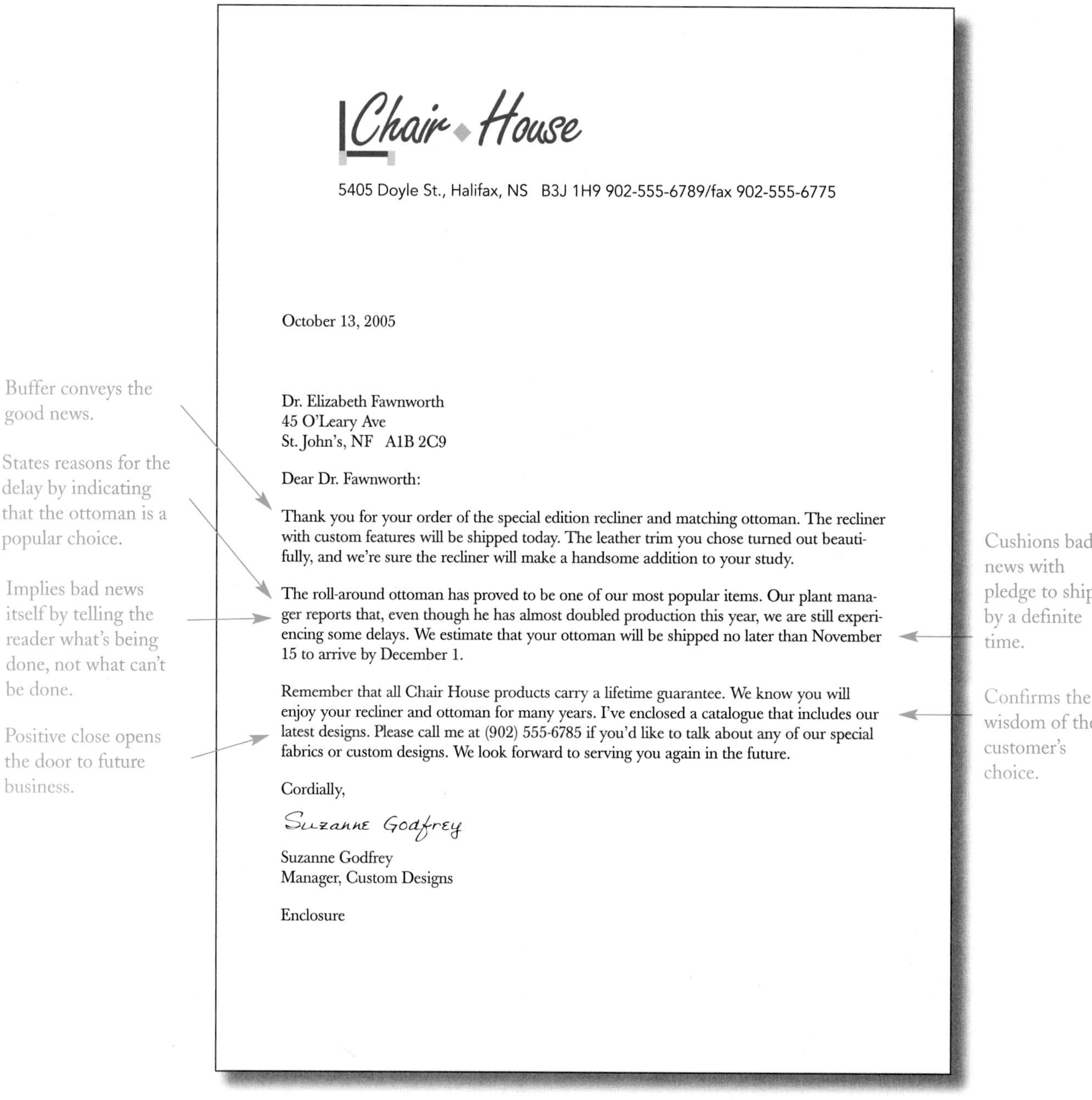

FIGURE 8–4 In-Depth Critique: Letter Advising of a Back Order

OBJECTIVE 5 Define *defamation* and explain how to avoid it in bad-news messages.

You may be tempted to respond to something particularly outrageous by calling the person responsible a crook or an incompetent. Don't. If you use such language, you could be sued for defamation a false statement that tends to damage someone's character or reputation. (Written defamation is called *libel*; spoken defamation is called *slander*.) By this definition, someone suing for defamation would have to prove (1) that the statement is false, (2) that the language is injurious to the person's reputation, and (3) that the statement has been "published."

If you can prove that your accusations are true, you haven't defamed the person. The courts are likely to give you the benefit of the doubt because our society believes that ordinary business communication should not be hampered by fear of lawsuits. However, beware of the irate letter intended to let off steam: If the message has no necessary business purpose and is expressed in abusive language that hints of malice, you'll lose the case. To avoid being accused of defamation, follow these guidelines:

1 Planning

Analyze: Purpose is to explain that warranty has expired and to offer repairs that the reader can pay for.

Investigate: Briefly gather information on product warranties, terms for repair, and resale information.

Adapt: Use letter format and focus on customer relationship.

2 Writing

Organize: Main idea is that you're offering repairs, even though the warranty has expired. Use the indirect approach to help reader accept your message.

Compose: Make the style conversational. Choose your words carefully, and enclose a catalog to encourage future business.

3 Completing

Revise: Review for logical order and tone. Be clear but friendly.

Produce: Use a clean letter format on letterhead.

Proofread: Review for accuracy and correctness. Be sure to include promised enclosures.

NUMBER ONE IN ENTERTAINMENT

BRODIE'S

STEREO
VIDEO

415 Main St. ¥ Whitehorse, YT Y1A ZB6
Voice: (867) 555-1312 ¥ Fax: (867) 555-1316
www.brodiestereo.com

May 3, 2005

Mr. George Pulkinen
General Delivery
Cassiar, BC V0C 1E0

Dear Mr. Pulkinen:

Thank you for your letter describing the problem with your portable Sony CD Walkman. We believe, as you do, that electronic equipment should be built to last. That's why we support our products with a free in-store repair service for the length of the product warranty.

Even though your Walkman is 8 months old and therefore out of warranty, we can still help. Please package your CD player carefully and ship it to our store in Whitehorse. Include your complete name, address, phone number, and a brief description of the problem along with a cheque for $35. After examining the unit, we will give you a written estimate of the needed parts and labour. Then just let us know–either by phone or by filling out the prepaid card we will provide–whether you want us to make the repairs.

If you choose to repair the unit, the $35 will be applied toward your bill, payable by cheque or major credit card. If you decide not to repair the unit, the $35 will pay for the technician's time in examining the unit. Sony also has service centres available in your area. If you would prefer to take the unit to one of them, please see the enclosed list.

Thank you again for inquiring about our service. I've also enclosed a catalogue of our latest high-tech electronic gear. For the month of June, Sony is offering a 10 percent discount on new-model digital camcorders. Please visit Brodie's again soon.

Sincerely,

Walter Brodie

Walter Brodie
Proprietor

Enclosure

Buffer emphasizes a point that reader and writer both agree on.

Puts company's policy in a favourable light.

States bad news indirectly, tactfully leaving the repair decision to the customer.

Helps soothe reader with a positive alternate action.

Close blends sales promotion with acknowledgement of the customer's interests.

FIGURE 8–5 In-Depth Critique: Letter Refusing a Claim

Checklist: Refusing Claims*

Buffer

✓ Indicate your full understanding of the nature of the complaint.
✓ Avoid all areas of disagreement.
✓ Avoid any hint of your final decision.

Reasons

✓ Provide an accurate, factual account of the transaction.
✓ Emphasize ways the situation should have been handled, rather than dwelling on reader's negligence.
✓ Avoid using a know-it-all tone.
✓ Use impersonal, passive language.
✓ Avoid accusing, preaching ("you should have"), blaming, or scolding the reader.
✓ Do not make the reader appear or feel demeaned.

The Bad News

✓ Make the refusal clear, using tactful wording.
✓ Avoid any hint that your decision is less than final.
✓ Avoid words such as *reject* and *claim*.
✓ Make a counterproposal, offer a compromise, or make a partial adjustment (if desirable).
✓ Make your tone willing, not begrudging, in a spirit of honest cooperation.
✓ Include resale information for the company or product.
✓ Emphasize a desire for a good relationship in the future.
✓ Extend an offer to replace the product or to provide a replacement part at the regular price.

Positive, Friendly, Helpful Close

✓ Make no reference to your refusal.
✓ Refer to enclosed sales material.
✓ Make any suggested action easy for readers to comply with.

*These items are in addition to the material included in the "Checklist: Bad-News Messages" on page 210.

- Avoid defamation by not responding emotionally.
- Avoid using any kind of abusive language or terms that could be considered defamatory.
- If you wish to express your own personal opinions about a sensitive matter, use your own stationery (not company letterhead), and don't include your job title or position. Take responsibility for your own actions without involving your company.
- Provide accurate information and stick to the facts.
- Never let anger or malice motivate your messages.
- Consult your company's legal department or a lawyer whenever you think a message might have legal consequences.
- Communicate honestly, and make sure that what you're saying is what you believe to be true.

For a brief review of the tasks involved when refusing claims, see this chapter's "Checklist: Refusing Claims" on the following page.

SENDING NEGATIVE ORGANIZATIONAL NEWS

Bad news doesn't only result from refusing requests. At times you may have bad news about your company's products or about its operations. Whether you're reporting to a supervisor or announcing your news to the media, the particular situation dictates whether you will use the direct or the indirect approach.

Use either the direct or the indirect approach when providing bad news about a product.

Providing Bad News about Products Imagine that you have to provide bad news about a product. If you were writing to tell your company's accounting department about increasing product prices, you'd use the direct approach. Your audience would have to make some arithmetical adjustments once the increases are put into effect, but readers would presumably be unemotional about the matter. On the other hand, if you

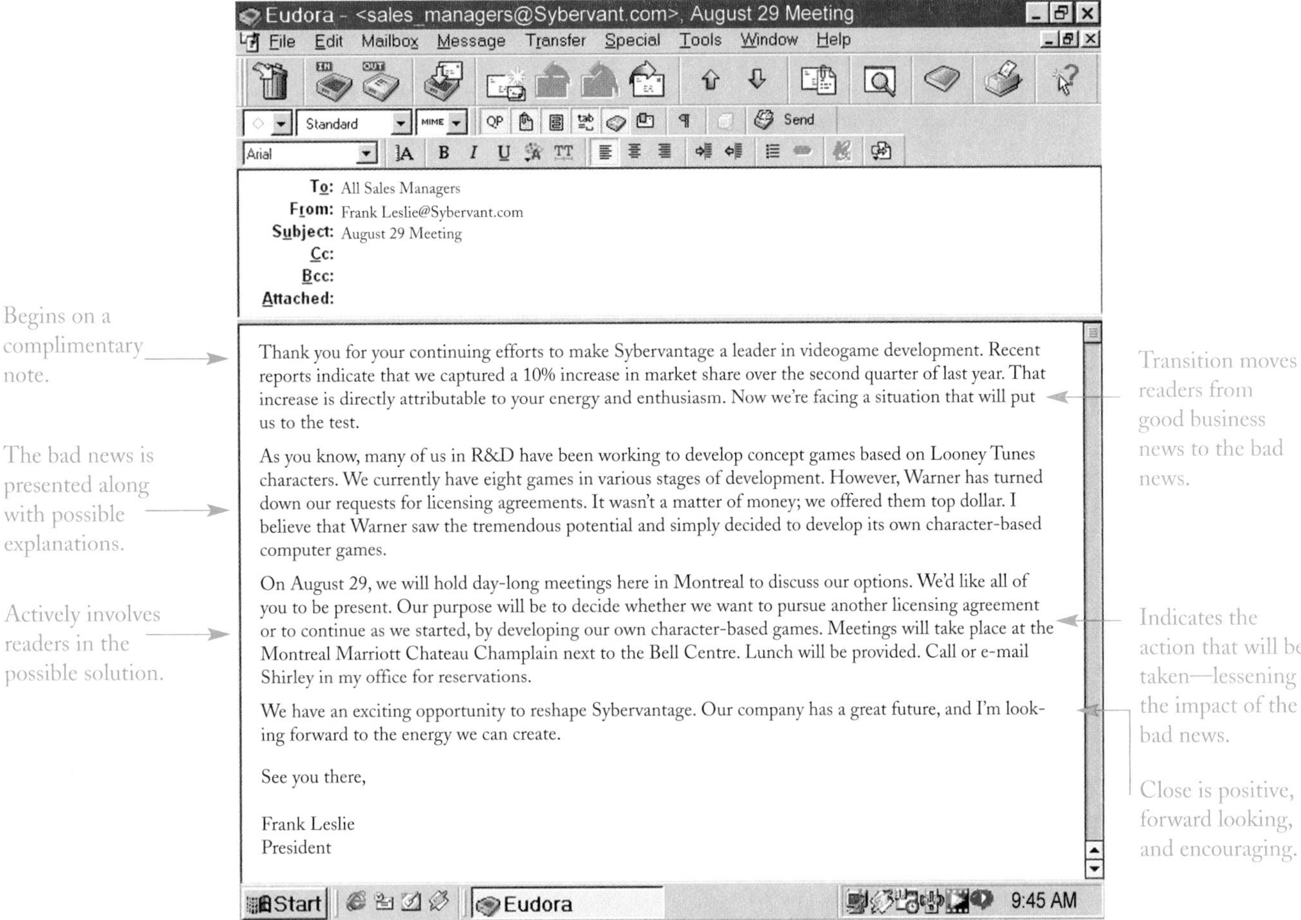
Eudora - <sales_managers@Sybervant.com>, August 29 Meeting

To: All Sales Managers
From: Frank Leslie@Sybervant.com
Subject: August 29 Meeting
Cc:
Bcc:
Attached:

Thank you for your continuing efforts to make Sybervantage a leader in videogame development. Recent reports indicate that we captured a 10% increase in market share over the second quarter of last year. That increase is directly attributable to your energy and enthusiasm. Now we're facing a situation that will put us to the test.

As you know, many of us in R&D have been working to develop concept games based on Looney Tunes characters. We currently have eight games in various stages of development. However, Warner has turned down our requests for licensing agreements. It wasn't a matter of money; we offered them top dollar. I believe that Warner saw the tremendous potential and simply decided to develop its own character-based computer games.

On August 29, we will hold day-long meetings here in Montreal to discuss our options. We'd like all of you to be present. Our purpose will be to decide whether we want to pursue another licensing agreement or to continue as we started, by developing our own character-based games. Meetings will take place at the Montreal Marriott Chateau Champlain next to the Bell Centre. Lunch will be provided. Call or e-mail Shirley in my office for reservations.

We have an exciting opportunity to reshape Sybervantage. Our company has a great future, and I'm looking forward to the energy we can create.

See you there,

Frank Leslie
President

Begins on a complimentary note.
The bad news is presented along with possible explanations.
Actively involves readers in the possible solution.
Transition moves readers from good business news to the bad news.
Indicates the action that will be taken—lessening the impact of the bad news.
Close is positive, forward looking, and encouraging.
Start
Eudora
9:45 AM

FIGURE 8-6 In-Depth Critique: E-Mail Message Providing Bad News about Products

were writing to convey the same information to customers or even to your own sales department, you would probably use the indirect approach. Customers never like to pay more, and your sales reps would see the change as weakening your products' competitive edge, threatening their incomes, and possibly threatening their jobs.

For example, when Sybervantage pursued licensing agreements with Warner, it expected to be entering into a lucrative arrangement in which both companies would profit. But Warner rejected the request, and now Sybervantage must adjust its strategic planning and must keep its sales force both motivated and involved (see Figure 8-6 on page 217). The middle section of the e-mail message presents an honest statement of the bad news. However, the effect of the bad news is diminished by the problem-solving tone, by the lack of any overt statement that such a setback may affect commissions, and by the optimistic close.

Handling Bad News about Company Policies and Practice Businesses frequently have to modify their policies and practices: For example, a firm may prohibit personal e-mail on company computers when it was previously allowed. Or, perhaps a company must enforce stricter security measures when outsiders visit. If an apology is appropriate when a change in company policy will not be well received or when it inconveniences customers and clients, good writers usually make it brief and place it in the middle of the letter in a subordinate position. Moreover, they try to leave readers with a favourable impression by closing on a positive note.

When conveying bad news about your company, focus on the reasons and on possible benefits.

When a change in company policy will have a negative effect on your audience, state the reasons for the change clearly and carefully. The explanation section of the letter convinces readers that the change was necessary and, if possible, describes how

122 John Street South, Arnprior, Ontario K7S 2N5
Phone: 1-800-512-5643 (613) 512-2324
Fax: (613) 512-8600
www.fleur-essence.com
e-mail service@fleuressence.com

May 27, 2005

Dear Customer:

Beginning July 15, Fleur-Essence Wall Coverings, Inc. will no longer accept orders by telephone. We are switching entirely to online ordering through our Web site: www.fleur-essence.com.

On our Web site you can browse the Fleur-Essence wall covering collections by style, colour, pattern, finish effect, print size, and other options. Simply choose the item your customer wants, select the quantity from the drop-down menu, and click on the "order pencil" to place the item in your shopping cart. After you complete your first selection, you will be asked to provide your client number and password. Then you can continue adding items.

Our online ordering system provides several advantages over our phone system. You will be able to

- check our inventory status and in-stock dates for backordered items
- check the status of your orders
- track your shipment
- examine your order history
- purchase closeouts as soon as they are announced
- access the most current wholesale price lists
- request our newest pattern books

Our online system will automatically calculate your costs (including shipping and taxes). It is accurate and quick, and available 24/7 (except from midnight to 7 a.m. on Sundays). With Fleur-Essence online ordering, you will be able to place orders at your convenience, with no waiting during busy periods. And all in-stock items will be shipped within 48 to 72 hours.

Again, remember that until July 15, you can still place orders by telephone during our business hours: Monday through Wednesday, 9–5; Thursday, 9–8, and Friday 9–4.

If you have any questions about our online ordering system, please call the technical support line at 1-800-512-9887. For questions about our selection, our service representatives are waiting to help you at 1-800-512-5643.

We look forward to serving you online.

Sincerely,

Piers Thorvold

Piers Thorvold
President
Fleur-Essence Wall Coverings, Inc.

Letter begins with the main idea because the change in practice will benefit most readers.

Body describes the user-friendly interface to acquaint telephone users with the online system.

Body also describes benefits of the online ordering system to counteract resistance.

References to negative aspects of telephone ordering system further imply benefits of automated system.

Ends cordially with contact information.

FIGURE 8-7 In-Depth Critique: Letter Describing Change in Company Practice

the change will benefit them. The letter in Figure 8-7 on page 218 is a mass mailing to trade customers, such as interior designers and owners of home decor stores, from a wallpaper manufacturer. It announces a change in practice that might inconvenience some readers, but provides overriding benefits.

SENDING NEGATIVE EMPLOYMENT MESSAGES

Negative employment messages are best handled with the advice of experts.

Most managers must convey bad news about people. Negative employment messages are sensitive communications because they have legal implications. When writing these messages, seek the advice of a human resources specialist in your organization, or a lawyer who specializes in employment matters.[6] Companies often have policies on reference letters and other negative employment messages that managers are required to follow.[7]

In letters informing prospective employers that you will not provide a recommendation, be direct, brief, and factual.

Refusing Requests for Recommendation Letters Be familiar with your firm's policy regarding reference requests.[8] Many former employers refuse to write recommendation letters, especially for people whose job performance has been unsatisfactory. Generally speaking, letters written to a prospective employer that refuse to provide a recommendation are typically brief and direct:[9]

> We received your request for a recommendation for Yolanda Johnson. According to the guidelines from our human resources department, we are authorized to confirm only that Ms. Johnson worked for Freemont Inc. for three years, from June 1999 to July 2003.

Experts also suggest prudence in letters to applicants themselves. Any refusal to cooperate may seem a personal slight and a threat to the applicant's future. To avoid potential ill feeling, it is important to handle the situation with diplomacy. The following example is brief but polite:

> Although I am unable to write a formal recommendation for your position, I can send Freemont Inc. a confirmation of your employment dates. You may want to consult with your professors at university for detailed references. Best of luck in your career.

By suggesting an alternative avenue for assistance, this message attempts to maintain good will while refusing the recipient's request for a job reference.

OBJECTIVE 6 **Outline the main purpose of performance reviews, give three ways to accomplish that purpose, and list six guidelines to follow when communicating a negative assessment.**

Giving Performance Reviews A performance review is a manager's formal or informal evaluation of an employee. Few other communication tasks require such a broad range of skills and strategy as that needed for performance reviews, whether positive or negative. The main purpose of these reviews is to improve employee performance by (1) emphasizing and clarifying job requirements, (2) giving employees feedback on their efforts toward fulfilling those requirements, and (3) guiding continued efforts by developing a plan of action, along with its rewards and opportunities. In addition to improving employee performance, performance reviews help companies set organizational standards and communicate organizational values.[10]

Positive and negative performance reviews share several characteristics: The tone is objective and unbiased, the language is nonjudgmental, and the focus is problem resolution.[11] To increase objectivity, more organizations are giving their employees feedback from multiple sources. In these "360-degree reviews," employees get feedback from all directions in the organization: above, below, and horizontally.[12]

Performance reviews must be well balanced and honest. It's recommended that employees undergoing a formal review be told well in advance of the meeting, so that they will be prepared. Furthermore, managers should discuss the all criteria used to evaluate the employee's performance, and not limit them to one or two.[13] When you need to communicate negative information in a performance review, remember these guidelines:[14]

- **Be calm and objective.** Anger interferes with the ability to communicate clearly and listen effectively. So when you discuss sensitive issues, be calm: you will encourage communication, project professionalism, and receive respect.
- **Plan your message.** Be clear about your concerns, and include concrete examples of the employee's specific actions. Think about any possible biases You may have, and get feedback from others. Collect all relevant facts about the employee's strengths as well as weaknesses.
- **Deliver the performance review in private.** Whether in writing or in person, be sure to address the performance privately. When you are sending a written performance review, do not send it by e-mail or fax. If you're reviewing an employee's performance face-to-face, conduct that review in a meeting arranged expressly for that purpose. Hold the meeting in a place where you will not be interrupted,

Going Online

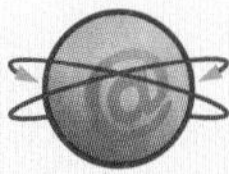

Protect Yourself When You Write a Job Reference

Learn about exit interviews and guidelines for terminating employment by examining Employers Online, a Government of Canada sponsored Web site that informs small business owners and entrepreneurs about hiring and firing employees. Find out about employment standards legislation, just cause, constructive dismissal, and other topics related to employment termination. At the Government of Canada site for employers, start with Human Resource Management and then look at the Layoffs and Terminations page. You can also see regulations for particular provinces on this site:
employers.gc.ca

To link directly to this site, visit our Companion Web site at **www.pearsoned.ca/thill** and look for the Chapter 8 resources.

such as a conference room or some other neutral area that you have booked ahead of time for the appraisal.

- **Place performance problems in an organizational context.** When you discuss weak performance, show the employee how it affects overall organizational performance. Compare the employee's performance with what's expected, with company goals, or with job requirements (not with the performance of other employees). Identify the consequences of continuing poor performance, and show that you're committed to helping solve the problem.
- **Use plain language.** When discussing performance, be direct and make sure your vocabulary is concrete and easy to understand. Be certain to have the facts on hand to support your appraisal. Show in specific and clear terms where the employee achieved, and where improvement is needed.
- **Ask for a commitment from the employee.** Help the employee understand that planning for and making improvements are the employee's responsibility. However, set goals jointly so that you can be sure any action to be taken is achievable. Demonstrate how improvement can be accomplished. Set a schedule and follow up with discussions of that improvement. Even if the employee's performance has been disappointing, be sure to reinforce strengths rather than weaknesses at the end of the review. The goal is to help the employee succeed.

Summary of Learning Outcomes

1 Apply the three-step writing process to bad-news messages. Because the way you say "no" can be far more damaging than the fact that you're saying it, planning your bad-news messages is crucial. Make sure your purpose is specific, necessary, and appropriate for written media. Find out how your audience prefers to receive bad news. Collect all the facts necessary to support your negative decision, and adapt your tone to the situation as well as to your audience. Bad-news messages may be organized according to the direct or the indirect approach, and your choice depends on audience preference as well as on the situation. In addition, carefully choose positive words to construct diplomatic sentences. Finally, revision, design, and proofreading are necessary to ensure that you are saying exactly what you want to say in the best possible way.

2 Show how to achieve an audience-centred tone and explain why it helps readers. To create an audience-centred tone, see the situation from the audience's viewpoint. Choose positive words and use language that is respectful. Adopting this tone helps your readers accept that your decision is firm, understand that your decision is fair and reasonable, remain well-disposed toward your company, and preserve their pride.

3 Differentiate between the direct and indirect organizational approaches to bad-news messages, and discuss when it's appropriate to use each one. The direct approach to bad-news messages puts the bad news up front, follows with the reasons (and perhaps offers an alternative), and closes with a positive statement. On the other hand, the indirect approach begins with a buffer (a neutral or positive statement), explains the reasons, clearly states the bad news (de-emphasizing it as much as possible), and closes with a positive statement. It's best to use the direct approach when you know your audience prefers receiving bad news up front or if the bad news will cause readers little pain or disappointment. Otherwise, the indirect approach is best.

4 Discuss the three techniques for saying "no" as clearly and kindly as possible. To say "no" and still be diplomatic, use three techniques. First, de-emphasize the bad news by minimizing the space (or time) devoted to it, subordinating it in a complex or compound sentence, or embedding it mid-paragraph. Second, relate the bad news in a conditional (*if* or *when*) statement to imply that readers could have received or might someday receive a favourable answer. Third, imply the bad news by saying what you will do, not what you won't do.

5 Define *defamation* and explain how to avoid it in bad-news messages. Defamation is a false statement that is damaging to a person's character or reputation. When written, defamation is called *libel*. When spoken, it is called *slander*. To avoid being accused of defamation, (1) never use abusive language, (2) express personal opinions without involving your company (using your own personal letterhead and excluding your title or position), (3) stick to the facts, (4) never write a message in anger, (5) seek legal advice about questionable messages, and (6) communicate honestly.

6 Outline the main purpose of performance reviews, give three ways to accomplish that purpose, and list six guidelines to follow when communicating a negative assessment. The main purpose of a performance review is to improve employee performance. To accomplish this purpose, be sure to emphasize and clarify job requirements, give feedback on employee efforts, and develop a plan of action to guide continuing efforts. When giving negative reviews, deliver your message in private, focus on the problem (not on the employee), and ask for a commitment from the employee.

ON THE JOB

Solving a Communication Dilemma at Wal-Mart

Manufacturers who want to sell their products through Wal-Mart undergo a gruelling process to receive the approval that will put their goods on the shelves of a major multinational retailer. The *Wal-Mart Supplier Proposal Guide*, which all potential suppliers must read before submitting their products, gives them the facts about Wal-Mart's philosophy, standards, and practices—the policies and rules suppliers must observe if they are chosen to sell their products through Wal-Mart stores.

When Wal-Mart receives a proposal, the supplier-development staff direct the products to the appropriate buyers for review and evaluation. Potential suppliers are guaranteed a reply by phone or letter from Wal-Mart within 90 days of receipt of the completed proposal package, but are not guaranteed a supplier number. Final judgment lies in the office of the purchasing agent at head office, with no certainty of success.

The proposal process benefits Wal-Mart by giving them suppliers whose products and services can enhance the giant retailer's bottom line. But the process also benefits companies, even if Wal-Mart rejects them, because it helps the firms to analyze their own business practices and improve them. Undoubtedly, effective communication is one of the key skills Wal-Mart's purchasing agents must have to refuse potential suppliers after they have worked hard to become a Wal-Mart partner and still maintain their goodwill.

Your Mission You're on the purchasing staff at Wal-Mart at the home office. Your job includes responding to requests and proposals from companies that would like to become Wal-Mart suppliers. These requests cover a variety of topics, from meetings to making sales presentations.

1 You have received a proposal from a company whose product, you believe, would be attractive to current Wal-Mart customers. But the applicant has not effectively discussed future demand for the product, one of the key questions in the proposal package. You'd like the applicant to resubmit the proposal, but he will have to wait an additional 90 days for a response. Which of the following paragraphs does the best job of presenting the bad news?
   - a It's too bad you neglected to answer fully the key question about future demand for your product. If you want us to consider your product for display at Wal-Mart, you'd better fill out the questionnaire completely.
   - b We know completing the supplier proposal is a demanding and time-consuming process. As the instructions indicate, all key questions must be fully answered if the proposal is to receive consideration. We are returning your proposal package so that you can review your answer to Question #2, dealing with future competition for your product.
   - c We appreciate the work you put into completing your supplier proposal. You did a thorough job. But please expand on Question #2.

2 Continuing with the case of the incomplete proposal, which of the following closing paragraphs would you choose and why?
   - a We do appreciate that you took a lot of time to work on the proposal, but we can't read it until you complete it. And you won't be hearing from us for another 90 days.
   - b If you need further assistance in completing your proposal, please consult the Internet bookmarks listed in the guidebook. We look forward to receiving your revised supplier proposal.
   - c Thank you for your attention to this matter.

3 Personal contacts are an important source of new business opportunities in many industries. In some cases, businesspeople develop these contacts through active participation in industry or professional groups, visits to trade shows, alumni societies, and other groups. You've recently received a request from a former classmate (Marcia DeLancey) who is now a sales manager for a plastics manufacturer. She wants to visit your office to present her company's plastic containers. However, you are already familiar with the company and know that it is too small to meet your needs for on-time global deliveries. You didn't know DeLancey all that well; in fact, you had to think for a minute to remember who she was (this is the first contact you've had with her since you both graduated five years ago). Which of the following openings would be most appropriate, keeping in mind that you know her company can't make the grade?
   - a Congratulations on reaching such an impressive position at your new company. I hope you enjoy your work as much as I enjoy mine. Thank you for your recent inquiry—evaluating such requests is one of my key responsibilities.
   - b Great to hear from you; I'd love to catch up on old times with you and find out how you're doing in your new job. I bounced around a bit after university, but I really feel that I've found my niche here at Wal-Mart.
   - c I'm sorry to say that Wal-Mart has already evaluated your company and found its resources were not a good match for our international delivery needs. However, I do appreciate your getting in touch, and I hope all is well with you.

4 Wal-Mart, like many corporate buyers, wants to establish stable, dependable relationships with suppliers. Having a supplier falter on the job or even go out of business without warning would be a huge disruption for Wal-Mart. As a result, your department is concerned about every supplier's financial health. The company that provides Wal-Mart with linens has done a good job for years, but recent events have left the company in precarious financial shape. Your office has already told the company that Wal-Mart would be forced to find another linen source if the company's finances didn't improve. Unfortunately, they've gotten even worse, and it's time to act. You've already written the buffer, reasons, and bad news, and now you need a positive close. Which of these would you choose?

a Thank you very much for the products you've provided in the past. All of us here at Wal-Mart wish you the best in resolving your current situation. If you are able to meet our financial criteria in the future, by all means please get back in touch with us.

b I understand that you're bound to be disappointed by our decisions. If you don't think our decision was valid or if there is more information that you believe we need to evaluate, please feel free to call me or my immediate supervisor to discuss the situation. We have to deal with quite a few suppliers, as you know, and I suppose there is a chance that we missed something in our initial evaluation.

c I'm very sorry that we have to terminate our purchasing agreement with you. We relied on your company's products for many years, and it's a shame that we won't be able to in the future. I hope this decision doesn't affect your workforce too negatively. If there's anything we can do to help, please don't hesitate to call.[15]

Test Your Knowledge

Review Questions

1 Why is it particularly important to adapt your medium and tone to your audience's needs and preferences when writing a bad-news message?
2 What are the five main goals in delivering bad news?
3 What are the advantages of using the direct approach to deliver the bad news at the beginning of a message?
4 What is the sequence of elements in a bad-news message organized using the indirect approach?
5 What is a buffer, and why do some critics consider it unethical?
6 When using an indirect approach to announce a negative decision, what is the purpose of presenting your reasons before explaining the decision itself?
7 What are three techniques for de-emphasizing bad news?
8 What is defamation, and how does libel differ from slander?
9 When giving a negative review to an employee, what six guidelines should you follow?

Interactive Learning 

Use This Text's Online Resources

Visit our Companion Web site at **www.pearsoned.ca/thill**, where you can use the interactive Study Guide to test your chapter knowledge and get instant feedback. Additional resources link you to the sites mentioned in this text and to additional sources of information on chapter topics.

Also check out the resources on the Mastering Business Communication CD, including "Perils of Pauline," an interactive presentation of the business communication challenges within a fictional company. For Chapter 8, see in particular the episode "Writing Bad News Messages."

Apply Your Knowledge

Critical Thinking Questions

1 Why is it important to end your bad-news message on a positive note? Explain.
2 If company policy or practice changes, should you explain those changes to employees and customers at about the same time, or should you explain them to employees first? Why?
3 If the purpose of your letter is to convey bad news, should you take the time to suggest alternatives to your reader? Why or why not?
4 When a company suffers a setback, should you soften the impact by letting out the bad news a little at a time? Why or why not?
5 What are your responsibilities when you deliver negative information during a performance review?
6 **Ethical Choices** Is intentionally de-emphasizing bad news the same as distorting graphs and charts to de-emphasize unfavourable data? Why or why not?

Practice Your Knowledge

Documents for Analysis

Read the following documents; then (1) analyze the strengths and weaknesses of each sentence and (2) revise each document so that it follows this chapter's guidelines.

Document 8.A: Providing Bad News about Products

Your spring fraternity party sounds like fun. We're glad you've again chosen us as your caterer. Unfortunately, we have changed a few of our policies, and I wanted you to know about these changes in advance so that we won't have any misunderstandings on the day of the party.

We will arrange the delivery of tables and chairs as usual the evening before the party. However, if you want us to set up, there is now a $100 charge for that service. Of course, you might want to get some of the brothers and pledges to do it, which would save you money. We've also added a small charge for cleanup. This is only $3 per person (you can estimate because I know a lot of people come and go later in the evening).

Other than that, all the arrangements will be the same. We'll provide the skirt for the band stage, tablecloths, bar setup, and of course, the barbecue. Will you have the tubs of ice with soft drinks again? We can do that for you as well, but there will be a fee.

Please let me know if you have any problems with these changes and we'll try to work them out. I know it's going to be a great party.

Document 8.B: Refusing Requests for Claims and Adjustments

I am responding to your letter of about six weeks ago asking for an adjustment on your all-in-one fax/scanner/printer, model FM39Z. We test all our products before they leave the factory; therefore, it could not have been our fault that your fax/scanner didn't work.

If you or someone in your office dropped the unit, it might have caused the damage. Or the shipper could have caused the damage if he dropped it. If so, you should file a claim with the shipper. At any rate, it wasn't our fault. The parts are already covered by warranty. However, we will provide labour for the repairs for $50, which is less than our cost since you are a valued customer.

We will have a booth at the upcoming trade fair there and hope to see you or someone from your office. We have many new models of office machines that we're sure you'll want to see. I've enclosed our latest catalogue. Hope to see you there.

Document 8.C: Conveying Bad News about Orders

We want to take this opportunity to thank you for your past orders. We have included our new catalogue of books, videos, films, and slides to let you know about our great new products. We included our price list also. Please use this list rather than the old one as we've had a slight increase in prices.

Per your request, we are sorry we can't send you the free examination copies of the textbooks you requested. The books, *Communication for Business* and *Winning the Presentation Game*, are two of our new titles that are enjoying brisk sales. It seems everyone is interested in communication skills these days.

We do apologize for not sending the exam copies for free. Our prices continue to rise along with everyone else's, and it's just not feasible to send everyone free copies. If you'd still like to have a look, please notice the prices in the list I've included and don't forget shipping and handling. You can also fax your order to the number shown on the sheet or e-mail your order over the Internet.

I'm sure these books would make a great addition to your collection. Again, we are sorry we couldn't grant your request, but we hope you order anyway.

Exercises

8–1 Select which approach you would use (direct or indirect) for the following bad-news messages:

a A memo to your boss informing her that one of your key clients is taking its business to a different accounting firm

b An e-mail message to a customer informing her that one of the books she ordered over the Internet is temporarily out of stock

c A letter to a customer explaining that the tape backup unit he ordered for his new custom computer is on back order and that, as a consequence, the shipping of the entire order will be delayed

d A letter from the telephone company rejecting a customer's claim that the phone company should reimburse the customer for the costs of a new high-speed modem (apparently, the phone lines will carry data at only half the modem's speed)

e A memo to all employees notifying them that the company parking lot will be repaved during the first week of June and that the company will provide a shuttle service from a remote parking lot during that period

f A letter from a travel agent to a customer stating that the airline will not refund her money for the flight she missed but that her tickets are valid for one year

g A form letter from a Canadian airline to a customer explaining that they cannot extend the expiration date of the customer's frequent flyer miles even though the customer was living overseas for the past three years

h A letter from an insurance company to a policyholder denying a claim for reimbursement for a special medical procedure that is not covered under the terms of the customer's policy

i A letter from an electronics store stating that the customer will not be reimbursed for a malfunctioning cell phone still under warranty (the terms of the warranty do not cover damages to phones that were accidentally run over by inline skates)

j An announcement to the repairs department listing parts that are on back order and will be three weeks late.

8–2 Teamwork Working alone, revise the following statements to de-emphasize the bad news. (Hint: Minimize the space devoted to the bad news, subordinate it, embed it, or use the passive voice.) Then team up with a classmate and read each other's revisions. Did you both use the same approach in every case? Which approach seems to be most effective for each of the revised statements?

a The airline can't refund your money. The "Conditions" segment on the back of your ticket states that there are no refunds for missed flights. Sometimes the airline makes exceptions, but only when life and death are involved. Of course, your ticket is still valid and can be used on a flight to the same destination.

b I'm sorry to tell you, we can't supply the custom decorations you requested. We called every supplier and none of them can do what you want on such short notice. You can, however, get a standard decorative package on the same theme in time. I found a supplier that stocks these. Of course, it won't have quite the flair you originally requested.

c We can't refund your money for the malfunctioning lamp. You shouldn't have placed a 150-watt bulb in the fixture socket; it's guaranteed for a maximum of 75 watts.

8–3 Answer the following questions pertaining to buffers:

a You have to tell a local restaurant owner that your plans have changed and you have to cancel the 90-person banquet scheduled for next month. Do you need to use a buffer? Why or why not?

b Write a buffer for a letter declining an invitation to speak at an association's annual fund-raising event. Show your appreciation for being asked.

c Write a buffer declining a high school group a visit to your factory because it does not provide access to the two students who are in wheelchairs.

d Write a memo cancelling the office end-of-year party because the company does not have enough money to hold it this year. Do you need to use a buffer? Why or why not?

e Write a buffer for a letter cancelling a school group's reservation to attend a theatre's musical show in two months. It's been cancelled because box office sales have been generally poor.

8–4 Internet Public companies sometimes have to issue news releases announcing or explaining downturns in sales, profits, demand, or other business factors. Visit the Web site of a company that has recently reported lower earnings or other bad news, and access the news release on that firm's site. How does the headline relate to the main message of the release? Is the release organized according to the direct or the indirect approach? What does the company do to present the bad news in a favourable light?

8–5. Ethical Choices The insurance company where you work is planning to raise all premiums for health-care coverage. Your boss has asked you to read a draft of her letter to customers announcing the new, higher rates. The first two paragraphs discuss some exciting medical advances and the expanded coverage offered by your company. Only in the final paragraph do customers learn that they will have to pay more for coverage starting next year. What are the ethical implications of this draft? What changes would you suggest?

Cases

Applying the Three-Step Writing Process to Cases

Apply each step to the following cases, as assigned by your instructor.

1 Planning Cases

Analyze

1 What's your general purpose?
2 What's your specific purpose?
3 What do you want readers to do?
4 Who are your readers? (Who is the primary audience? Who is the secondary audience? What do readers have in common? What is their general background? How will they react?)

Investigate

5 What information do readers need?
6 What facts must you gather?

Adapt

7 How will you establish credibility?

2 Writing Cases

Organize

1 What's your main idea?
2 Will you use the direct or indirect approach? Why?

Compose

3 Will your tone be informal or more formal?
4 Draft the message as discussed in the "Your Task" section of the case.

3 Completing Cases

Revise

1 Use the "Checklist for Revising Business Messages" in Chapter 6 to edit and revise your message for clarity.

Produce

2 What's the best way to distribute your message? By fax? By e-mail? By sealed envelope?

Proofread

3 Proofread your message for errors in layout, spelling, and mechanics.

Negative Answers to Routine Requests

1 Tethered SwimCords: Letter to Italian sports retailer returning order Kelly Greene loved to swim; more than that, she loved the all-over exercise that swimming provides, without the joint hammering of jogging or aerobics. Unfortunately, it took only six strokes to swim across the small pool at her apartment complex. She spent turning and pushing off, so she was actually gliding most of the time and she wasn't getting much exercise. What could she do? She invented SwimCords.

Taking her cue from surfers who use ankle tethers to keep their boards from getting lost in the waves, Greene developed an elastic, Bungee-like leash she could attach to her ankle and the pool's edge. She could swim and swim—and go nowhere. After a few design improvements and an enthusiastic endorsement from the swim team at the University of California at Los Angeles, Greene opened her new manufacturing business.

As she explained when she hired you to help process orders, it wasn't an overnight success. She first spent two years as a member of an inventors' guild, learning her way through the patenting process. But now orders for the $29.95 SwimCords are pouring in from all over the United States and Canada.

Today you opened a letter from Isabella Caparelli, owner of Sports Italia in Milan, eagerly requesting a sizable shipment of SwimCords. Caparelli spotted them in a Canadian sporting goods store and "has to have them," she writes. You took the letter straight to Greene's office.

"We're not ready to ship overseas," the inventor fretted. "I knew it would happen soon, but right now—you'll just have to tell her no." She hesitated for a moment, glanced at the letter again, then added, "But mention that we're growing fast and we might be ready to ship them internationally in, say," she glanced at the calendar on her wall, "six months. I just hate to lose an order that big. Do what you can to keep her interest, but don't mislead her, either. I'm learning that honesty pays off faster than any big-ticket sales in this business," she smiled. "Oh, and be sure to send her a free sample."

Your Task: Back at your desk, write a polite and encouraging refusal to Isabella Caparelli, the owner of Sports Italia, Via Arimondi 29-20121, Milan, Italy. Enclose a sample SwimCord.[16]

2 Disappearing soaps: E-mail from Craftopia.com At Craftopia.com, orders for the Seaside Soaps kit have been flying in faster than you can fill them. Consumers are ordering the kit over your 800-line and from your Web site, through the SSL (Secure Socket Layering) encrypted ordering service. The frenzy started with a national magazine ad campaign—Craftopia's first.

The print ad for the "soap-making" kits featured a luscious summer beach scene with a sun-drenched little girl playing in the surf. Next to this warm image, an inset photo displayed the translucent blue, yellow, and green "sea-life" soaps spilling from a bucket onto the sand like coloured ice cubes. The kit includes molds (for conch and scallop shells, bubbles, starfish, and a porpoise), a two-pound block of glycerine soap (enough for 52 soaps), lavender scent, colour dyes, and eyedroppers. Although your site sells some 75 000 products for creative crafts projects, the soap kit is the biggest seller the company has had. With deep-pocketed funding from an impressive array of investors, Craftopia.com offers an extensive variety of products for the growing number of crafters now shopping online. People have ordered 50 of a single item at one time; many stores don't carry that much in stock.

At www.craftopia.com, consumers can read Craftopia's online magazine, share tips and ideas with others on the bulletin board, search for projects by level of skill required, and read instructions and tips for using the products they order. If they're reluctant to transmit credit card information over the Internet, they can call 1-800-373-0343, Monday through Friday, 9 a.m. to 5 p.m. ET, and speak to an operator.

Yarn, ribbon, candles, stencils; you name it, Craftopia.com can deliver it to your door. Everything a creative dabbler could ask for—except for those cool Seaside Soap kits so enticingly displayed on your Web site "for the hot price of just $39.00." Your supplier has just informed you that the stock has run out. Regardless of the scramble to speed up production, the new kits won't be ready to ship until six weeks from today.

Your Task: As customer service supervisor, you've been asked to break the bad news in an e-mail message notifying customers of the delay. Craftopia will offer refunds or merchandise credit to customers who make such a request. Also, because the soap kits are reaching the kind of numbers that investors want to see, your message will be reviewed by the company's CEO before it's released. Try make it your best work.[17]

3 More to come: Letter explaining delay of Anne of Green Gables T-shirt Each year thousands of people attend the Charlottetown Festival to see plays featuring Lucy Maud Montgomery's fictional characters. Montgomery's stories have been loved by Canadians and by millions around the world, since the publication of her first novel, *Anne of Green Gables*, in 1908. Prince Edward Island has benefited immensely from tourists who travel there during the Festival season to enjoy not only the theatre but the sea, beaches, and Montgomery's birthplace. Souvenirs are popular among both Canadian and foreign visitors, who buy them for friends and relatives back home.

This summer's Festival was so successful that your local store, Little Things, has sold out its stock of child and youth size T-shirts featuring Anne's image. You've received a letter from a German tourist explaining that when his nieces and nephews saw his daughter's T-shirt, they each wanted one too. He's included his credit card number and expiry date, and wants two green T-shirts in size 6X, three white shirts in size 10–12, and two in size 14–16. His letter is dated October 6, 2005, and he is hoping to get the shirts in time for Christmas. Your problem is that you only have two blue shirts, size 6X—no green—in stock, and one white shirt, size 10–12. You do have lots of white shirts in size 14-16. More T-shirts won't be available until March 2005 as the product is seasonal. You also have some other items in stock, such as stickers, always popular with kids, and buttons.

Your Task: Write to Josef Mandelheim, Sonnenstrasse 4, 86669 Erlingshofen, Germany. Explain what you can do. Child-size shirts are $8.95 each, youth size $10.95, duty is 12 percent of the total, there is no GST, and shipping is $32.00.

4 Cyber-surveillance: Memo refusing claim from "Silent Watch" victim Next week you're going to write a thank-you letter to Roy Young of Adavi, Inc., makers of "Silent Watch" software, for solving an impossible management task. But right now you've got an employee's claim on your desk, and you're trying to calm yourself before you reply.

Your business is called Advertising Inflatables, and your specialty is designing and building the huge balloon replicas used for advertising atop retail stores, tire outlets, used car lots, fast-food outlets, fitness clubs, etc. You've built balloon re-creations of everything from a 15-metre King Kong to a "small" 3-metre pizza. When your business grew from two employees to 25, you thought your biggest concern would be finding enough work to support them.

Your fame spread after local newspapers wrote about your company building giant soft drink "cans" for a Pepsi Superbowl commercial, set in outer space with real cosmonauts. The commercial never aired, but your business boomed. You hired more designers, salespeople, customer service reps, and additional painters and builders to work in the shop. Today, even design work is done on computers, and it turns out the hardest part of your job is managing the people who run them.

As business increased, you started spending your days outside the office, attending business events and making presentations. That's when productivity began to slip. If you showed up at the office unexpectedly, you noticed computer screens suddenly switching to something else. You got suspicious.

You decided to install the "cyber-surveillance" software, "Silent Watch," to record your employees' every keystroke. You sent around a memo informing your staff that their computer use should be limited to work projects only and that their e-mail should not include personal messages. You also informed them that their work would be monitored. You didn't tell them that "Silent Watch" would record their work while you were gone or that you could now monitor them from a screen in your office.

Sure enough, "Silent Watch" caught two of your sales staff spending between 50 and 70 percent of their time surfing Internet sites unrelated to their jobs. You docked their pay accordingly, without warning. You notified them that they were not fired but were on probation. You considered this extremely generous, but also wise. When they work, both of them are very good at what they do, and talent is hard to find.

Now salesman Jarod Harkington is demanding reinstatement of his pay because he claims you "spied on him illegally." On the contrary, your lawyers have assured you that the courts almost always side with employers on this issue, particularly after employees receive a warning such as the one you gave your workers. The computer equipment is yours, and you're paying a fair price for your employees' time.

Your Task: Write a memo refusing Mr. Harkington's claim.[18]

5 Music Mania: Letter rejecting Web site proposal Your amateur band, Four Guys, plays at parties and in clubs. You have a lot of fun entertaining your audience with popular rock and original compositions, and your group usually has a gig. All the members have thought that getting a Web site would be great for business—you can advertise your band, the music you play, who you are—as well as provide references from previous customers and give contact numbers. You also thought links to other musical sites would draw interest to your band's Web site. A Web site would be a great opportunity for more exposure. Who knows? Maybe you'd get the attention of a music producer, and get a recording contract! One of the guys, Jim McKay, has a buddy who wants to start his own Web site company and is happy to create a site for the band on spec.

The result isn't exactly what you and your band expected. Colours are black, purple, and green. The text is very small and hard to read. The site is difficult to navigate. Jim's friend neglected to include a contact e-mail address and links to other sites. The guys are really disappointed. At least they didn't have to put down a deposit for the work.

Your Task: Since you are the band's manager, you've been designated as the bearer of bad news. Write a letter to Jim's buddy, Grant Roberts, telling him you won't be needing his services.

6 Suffering artists: Memo declining high-tech shoes at Centennial Ballet Theatre Here at the Centennial Ballet Theatre (CBT), where you're serving as assistant to Artistic Director Kenneth MacLachlan, the notion of suffering for the art form has been ingrained since the early 1800s, when the first ballerina rose up en pointe. Many entrepreneurs are viewing this painful situation with hopeful enthusiasm, especially when they discover that dancers worldwide spend about $150 million annually on their shoes—those "tiny torture chambers" of cardboard and satin (with glued linen or burlap to stiffen the toes). The pink monstrosities (about $75 a pair) rarely last beyond a single hard performance.

A company the size of CBT spends about $500,000 a year on ballet slippers—plus the cost of their staff physical therapist and all those trips to chiropractors, podiatrists, and surgeons to relieve bad necks, backs, knees, and feet. Entrepreneurs believe there must be room for improvement, given the current advantages of orthopedics, space-age materials, and high-tech solutions for contemporary athletes. There's no denying that ballerinas are among the hardest-working athletes in the world.

The latest entrepreneur to approach CBT is Melinda Ellis of Gray Ellis, Inc. No one in the ballet company blames her for wanting to provide a solution to the shoe problem. She buttonholed Marvin King, executive director and a member of CBT's Board of Governing Trustees, with a proposal for providing new, high-performance pointe shoes in exchange for an endorsement. It truly is a good idea. It's just a hard sell among the tradition-oriented dancers.

Ellis' alternative pointe shoes offer high-impact support and toe cushions. They're only $70 a pair, and supposedly they can be blow-dried back into shape after a performance. When the cost-conscious board member urged the company to give them a try, you were assigned to collect feedback from dancers.

So far, not good. For example, principal ballerina Grace Durham: She'd rather numb her feet in icy water, dance through "zingers" of toe pain, and make frequent visits to the physical therapist than wear Ellis' shoes, she insisted after a brief trial. The others agree. Apparently, they like breaking in the traditional satin models with hammers and door slams and throwing them away after a single performance of Swan Lake. Too stiff, they say of the new shoes. Adds Durham, "I'm totally settled into what I'm doing."

You've seen those sinewy, wedge-shaped feet bleeding backstage. You feel sorry for Ellis; it was a good idea. Maybe she should try younger dancers.

Your Task: MacLachlan has asked you to write an internal memo in his name to Marvin King, executive director of the Centennial Ballet Theatre, explaining the dancers' refusal to use the new high-tech Gray Ellis pointe shoes. In your memo be sure to include the dancers' reasons as well as your own opinion regarding the matter. You'll need to decide whether to use the direct or the indirect approach; include a separate short note to your instructor justifying your selection.[19]

7 Photo finish: No credit to Tod Rooker, photographer You've dealt with Tod Rooker, a photographer of weddings and family events, for the last 13 years with no problem. He's sent numerous jobs to you for developing and has always paid on time. But for the last two jobs he has asked your company, Best Photo Labs, to extend credit. He says the wedding and special events market is drying up in his neighbourhood, and he's getting few referrals from old customers. He has to work as an industrial photographer during the day for a friend's firm, and can only work evenings at his own business. He isn't making the money he used to, but he hopes to get enough cash flowing from his day job to pay Best Labs for developing his photos. He sure can't ask for money from his customers until they see the finished pictures.

But Best Photo Labs has a business to run, and they can't rely on goodwill to pay their technicians, rent, and utilities, as well as for developing chemicals and photographic paper.

Your Task: As the office manager for Best Photo Labs, you've dealt with Tod Rooker's account for several years. You know he's a nice guy, and a good photographer. Write Tod a tactful letter refusing credit. Tod's address is Tod Rooker, Professional Photographer, 195 Argyle St., Fredericton, NB E3B 1T6.

8 Pay or sell: Last chance to settle condo management fees You don't like writing such letters, but during your five years as a property manager for Provide Corporation you've had to tell condo owners that if they don't pay their monthly maintenance fees, Provide will attach a lien to their bank accounts, as they are permitted to do by provincial law. The problem you're having now is with Mrs. Edith Bookman, a recent widow who has fallen behind two months in her maintenance fees. The money she—and all the other apartment owners—pay each month goes towards maintaining the building and grounds in order to keep the property healthy and attractive. Without the monthly maintenance fee from each owner, the condo would fall into disrepair, and everyone would have to pay a special assessment to bring it back to standard. No one wants that to happen.

You know that things are difficult for Mrs. Bookman right now. You've consulted with the condo's board of directors, made up of owners who give direction to the property manager when needed. They've told you not to attach Mrs. Bookman's account now, although provincial law says you could. Instead, they want to give her another month to pay the arrears.

Your Task: Write a letter to Mrs. Bookman following the Board's direction. Explain that she must pay her two months arrears with her third payment, and why doing so is important. If she doesn't, Provide will attach her bank account for the balance owed as well as a $500 administrative lien fee, which they are legally allowed to do. Mrs. Bookman lives at 1335 St. Albert Trail NW, Suite 3E, Edmonton, AB T5L 4R3.

9 Your monkey, your choice: Letter from Choquette's Exotic Pets refusing a damage claim As a well-known exotic animal dealer in the Montreal area, your boss, Roger Choquette, has dealt with his share of customers experiencing buyer's regret. Despite his warnings, many of them still buy their exotic pets for the wrong reasons. When Lisa Carpenter bought Binky, a red-tailed guenon monkey, she begged Mr. Choquette to reduce his price to $10 000 because she had "fallen in love with Binky's soulful eyes and adorable button nose." Now she wants to return poor Binky, and you have never seen your boss so angry.

"Listen to this!" fumes Mr. Choquette as he reads Carpenter's letter:

> While I was at work, I locked your monkey in his own room—which I equipped with his own colour TV (with cable) and which I spent days wallpapering with animal pictures. Then last night your monkey somehow unlocked the door, ripped out my telephone, opened the refrigerator, smashed eggs all over my kitchen and my new Persian carpet, broke 14 of the china dishes my mother gave me when I got married, and squeezed toothpaste all over the Louis XIV settee I inherited from my grandmother!

"Not only does she demand that I take poor Binky back after she's abused him through her ignorance and neglect," snapped Mr. Choquette, "but she wants me to pay $150 000 in damages for her car, her apartment, and her state of mind."

Your boss is so upset that you decide to write Ms. Carpenter yourself.

Your Task: Write to Lisa Carpenter (22 Oakland Ave, Westmount, QC H3Y 1N9) and include a copy of her contract. It clearly states Roger Choquette's policy: refunds only if animals are returned in good health, and absolutely no warranty against damages. Each pet comes with specific care instructions, including warnings about certain idiosyncrasies that could cause problems in the wrong environment. Despite the fact that Binky is probably traumatized by his experiences, Mr. Choquette has generously agreed to accept his return, refunding Ms. Carpenter's $10 000. However, he will not accept liability for any loss of property or for any claims of mental duress on the part of Ms. Carpenter.[20]

10 No deal: Letter from Home Depot to faucet manufacturer As assistant to the vice-president of sales for Home Depot, you were present at Home Depot's biannual product-line review. Also present were hundreds of vendor hopefuls, eager to become one of the huge retail chain's 25 303 North American suppliers. These suppliers did their best to win, keep, or expand their spot in the Home Depot product lineup, in individual meetings with a panel of regional and national merchandisers for the chain.

Product suppliers know that Home Depot holds all the cards, so if they want to play, they have to follow Home Depot rules, offering low wholesale prices and swift delivery. Once chosen, they're constantly re-evaluated—and quickly dropped for infractions such as requesting a price increase or planning to sell directly to consumers via the Internet. They'll also hear sharp critiques of their past performance, which are not to be taken lightly.

A decade ago, General Electric failed to keep Home Depot stores supplied with lightbulbs, causing shortages. Co-founder Bernard Marcus immediately stripped GE of its exclusive, 80-foot shelf-space and flew off to negotiate with its Netherlands competitor, Phillips. Two years later, after high-level negotiations, GE bulbs were back on Home Depot shelves—but in a position inferior to Phillips's.

Such cautionary tales aren't lost on vendors. But they know that despite tough negotiating, Home Depot is always looking for variety to please its customers' changing tastes and demands. The sales potential is so enormous that the compromises and concessions are worthwhile. If selected, vendors get immediate distribution in more than 1000 stores (a number that Home Depot plans to double in the next few years).

Still, you've seen the stress on reps' faces as they explain product enhancements and on-time delivery ideas in the review sessions. Their only consolation for this gruelling process is that, although merchandisers won't say yes or no on the spot, they do let manufacturers know where they stand within a day or two. And the company is always willing to reconsider at the next product-line review—wherever it's held.

Your Task: You're drafting some of the rejection letters, and the next one on your stack is to a faucet manufacturer, Brightway Manufacturing, 2001 Lasalle Blvd., Sudbury, ON P3A 2A3. "Too expensive," "substandard plastic handles," and "a design not likely to appeal to Home Depot customers," say the panel's notes. (And knowing what its customers want has put Home Depot in the top 10 of the Fortune 500 list, with $40 billion in annual sales.) Find a way to soften the blow in your rejection letter to Brightway. After all, consumer tastes do change. Direct your letter to Pamela Wilson, operations manager.[21]

Negative Organizational News

11 The cheque's in the mail—almost: Letter from Sun Microsystems explaining late payments You'd think that a computer company could install a new management information system without a hitch, wouldn't you? The people at Sun Microsystems thought so too, but they were wrong. When they installed their own new computerized system for getting information to management, a few things, such as payments to vendors, fell through the cracks.

It was embarrassing when Sun's suppliers started clamouring for payment. Terence Lenaghan, the corporate controller, found himself in the unfortunate position of having to tell 6000 vendors why Sun Microsystems had failed to pay its bills on time—and why it might be late with payments again. "Until we get these bugs ironed out," Lenaghan confessed, "we're going to have to finish some of the accounting work by hand. That means that some of our payments to vendors will probably be late next month too. We'd better write to our suppliers and let them know that there's nothing wrong with the company's financial performance. The last thing we want is for our vendors to think our business is going down the tubes."

Your Task: Write a form letter to Sun Microsystem's 6000 vendors explaining that bugs in their new management information system are responsible for the delays in payment.[22]

12 Not so good: Bill 180 says no way As a Campbell's Soup Canada corporate affairs employee, you've been working on the Labels for Education program since its start here in the fall of 1998. You've enjoyed watching schools across the country receive free audio-visual, computer, sports, and electronic equipment as well as books, videocassettes, and CD-ROMs in exchange for the labels the kids save from Campbell's Soup tins and packages. The program has been in place in U.S. schools since 1973, and now cash-strapped Canadian schools can obtain much-needed equipment to enhance their students' education. Although it takes thousands of labels to exchange for products, kids, parents, teachers, and administrators think the program is very worthwhile, especially with limited funding for education.

But Campbell's has to discontinue the program in Quebec. The company didn't know that Bill 180, passed by the provincial legislature in 1998, the same year Campbell's Labels for Education began in Canada, prohibits commercial solicitation in public schools. Said Alain Leclerc, press attaché to Quebec's Minister of Education, Bill 180 makes it unacceptable for companies to "incite or put pressure on children to consume products." You saw Kellogg's end its Education is Tops program in Quebec, for which kids brought Kellogg's box tops to their schools, giving educators the pleasure of seeing 10 cents from each top going to educational materials. Now, Campbell's has received notice from Ministry of Education officials on February 22 to end the program in two weeks. "If you don't do anything, we will," Campbell's was told. In Canada, 3600 schools have registered for Labels for Education, and only 70 are in Quebec. Yet, although Campbell's must pull the plug on their educational program, companies like Scholastic Books of Markham, Ontario continue to sell their products through catalogues distributed in the classroom, and chocolate manufacturers have kids sell their candies door-to-door for fundraising programs, with the companies reaping the profits. You don't see the fairness.

Your Task: As a public affairs specialist with Campbell's, compose a form letter, to be mailed to Quebec parents, who want to know what's happening with Campbell's Labels for Education program.[23]

13 Cell phone violations: E-mail message to associates at Smith Rooney law firm "Company policy states that personnel are not to conduct business using cell phones while driving," David Finch reminds you. He's a partner at the law firm of Smith Rooney in St. John's, Newfoundland, where you work as his administrative assistant.

You nod, waiting for him to explain. He already issued a memo about this rule last year, after that 15-year-old girl was hit and killed by an attorney from another firm. Driving back from a client meeting, the attorney was distracted while talking on her cell phone. The girl's family sued the firm and won $10 million, but that's not the point. The point is that cell phones can cause people to be hurt, even killed.

Finch explains, "Yesterday one of our associates called his secretary while driving his car. We can't allow this. Recently in Windsor a driver caused a fatal accident when reaching for his cell phone; his van turned over, and the accident killed his nephew and two friends. The van caught on fire because they were transporting a canister of gasoline to a farm. From now on, any violation of our cell phone policy will result in suspension without pay, unless the call is a genuine health or traffic emergency."

Your Task: Finch asks you to write an e-mail message to all employees, announcing the new penalty for violating company policy.[24]

14 Product recall: Letter from Perrigo to retailers about children's painkiller Discovering that a batch of your company's cherry-flavoured children's painkiller contains more than the label-indicated amount of acetaminophen was not a happy occasion around Perrigo Company. But such errors do happen, and the best move is immediate and direct, being completely honest with retailers and the public—so say your superiors in the Customer Support and Service Department. Full and prompt disclosure is especially crucial when consumers' health is involved, as it always is in your line of business.

Perrigo is the leading manufacturer of store-brand, over-the-counter (OTC) pharmaceuticals and nutritional products, producing more than 900 products. These are the items found beside brand-name products such as Tylenol, Motrin, Aleve, Benadryl, NyQuil, Centrum, or Ex-Lax, but they're packaged under the name of the store in which customers are shopping. They're priced a bit lower and offer "comparable quality and effectiveness," as your sales literature proclaims.

For retailers, selling Perrigo products yields a higher profit margin than name brands. For consumers, buying the store brands can mean significant savings.

As of this morning, your marketing department calculates that 6500 113-milliletres bottles of the "children's nonaspirin elixir" (a Tylenol look-alike) are already in the hands of consumers. That leaves some 1288 bottles still on store shelves. The problem is that the acetaminophen contained in the painkilling liquid is up to 29 percent more than labels state, enough to cause an overdose in the young children the product is designed for. Such overdoses can cause liver failure. No one is telling you how this error happened, and it's only been found in lot number 1AD0228, but frankly, finding a guilty party is not so important to your job. You're more concerned about getting the word out fast.

The painkiller has been sold under the T-Mart label at stores in British Columbia, the Northwest Territories, Saskatchewan, Manitoba, and Alberta. It was sold under the Good Life label in Ontario, Quebec, Newfoundland and Labrador, New Brunswick, Nova Scotia, and Prince Edward Island. It was sold under the Healthy Living label in independent retail chains throughout Canada. Perrigo needs to notify consumers throughout Cananda that they should not give the product to children, but rather should check the lot number and return the bottle to the store they bought it from for a refund if it's from the affected batch.

Your Task: As Perrigo's customer service supervisor, you must notify retailers by letter. They've already been told verbally, but legal requirements mandate a written notification. That's good, because a form letter to your retail customers can also include follow-up instructions. Explain the circumstances behind the recall, and instruct stores to pull bottles from the shelves immediately for return to your company. Perrigo will, of course, reimburse refunds provided to consumers. Questions should be directed to Perrigo at 1-800-622-0206—and it's okay if they give that number to consumers. Be sure to mention all that your company is doing, and use resale information.[25]

15 Performance review. Team up with someone in your class and interview each other about a job you currently have or had in the past. Get details about the organization that employed your partner, the organization's objectives and goals, and your partner's responsibilities and duties. Ask your partner about the strengths and weaknesses of his or her performance in that job (be sure to get concrete details). Using the guidelines in this chapter, write a performance review for your partner in memo format.

Going Online Exercises

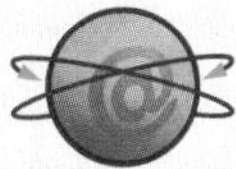

Protect Yourself When You Write a Job Reference, found on page 219 of this chapter

As you explore the Layoffs and Terminations section at **employers.gc.ca** you'll see how complicated the ins and outs of reference writing have become. Do you think these constraints are good for employees? For employers? Why or why not?

1 Discuss the planning tasks that need extra attention when preparing persuasive messages

2 Distinguish between emotional and logical appeals, and discuss how to balance them

3 Describe the AIDA plan for persuasive messages

4 Explain the best way to overcome resistance to your persuasive message, and list four common mistakes

5 Compare sales messages with fundraising messages

6 List eight guidelines that will help you strengthen your fundraising messages

Writing Persuasive Messages

ON THE JOB

Facing a Communication Dilemma at the Young Entreprenuers' Association

Gearing Up for Business

www.yea.ca

It started as a thought, and grew into a nation-wide support group for young businesspeople who had original ideas and the need for advice and encouragement. After meeting the fellow winners of the 1991 Young Entrepreneur of the Year Awards— sponsored by the Federal Business Development Bank—Robert French established the Young Entrepreneurs' Association. Founded in 1992, the group provides members with peer support, business contacts, and the opportunity to develop lifelong friendships, by taking advantage of the YEA's many educational and social programs. Currently, the YEA has local chapters in British Columbia, Alberta, Manitoba, Ontario, Nova Scotia, New Brunswick, and Newfoundland, with more being established.

With 11 chapters nationwide, the YEA certainly has room to grow and to provide numerous benefits to young Canadian businesspeople. The non-profit organization offers a pitch-free environment where members can discuss their achievements and challenges, and share knowledge and information that can help other entrepreneurs, seasoned or new, to attain success. In addition to peer-mentoring groups, YEA members also receive referrals to the media that will give them publicity and recognition and invitations to many social occasions where they can both relax and make important contacts for growing their businesses.

The YEA itself, however, is still in its infancy. Open to anyone under 35 who owns a business, the YEA also offers associate and student memberships. Creating a grassroots network of young businesspeople is a challenge because YEA staff, like president Jason Guille and sponsorship director Rodney De Freitas, must persuade busy students and entrepreneurs to join in order to gain both the personal and professional benefits that participation offers. As YEA has limited resources, Guille and De Freitas must also persuade established companies, such as Royal Bank, to provide financial support, guest speakers, and in-kind services.

The entire eight-member board of directors is acutely aware of the need for members and sponsors to keep the organization alive. If you worked as YEA director, how would you persuade students and business people of the group's value? How would you convince companies to support the YEA? How would you organize such messages? What would you do to get your audience's attention?[1]

To encourage students and young entrepreneurs to join the YEA, staff must craft messages that get attention, create interest, encourage desire, and motivate action. Strong persuasive skills are essential for members of the non-profit organization's board of directors.

Using the Three-Step Writing Process for Persuasive Messages

When consumers are asked to spend their hard-earned money on a product, or employees to perform a non-routine task, they want to know why they should do it. An essential skill of any businessperson is **persuasion**—the ability to change an audience's attitudes, beliefs, or actions.[2] The most effective business leaders, managers, and salespeople have a knack for putting together a persuasive argument. They know how to determine the mood of a group and communicate with people in terms they can both understand and accept.[3] Whether you're selling an MP3 player, real estate, or an idea to your manager, writing effective persuasive messages is a vital skill. Applying the three-step writing process to your persuasive messages will help you make them as effective as possible.

Step 1: Planning Persuasive Messages

OBJECTIVE 1 Discuss the planning tasks that need extra attention when preparing persuasive messages.

Unlike routine positive messages (discussed in Chapter 7), persuasive messages aim to influence audiences who are inclined to resist. Therefore, persuasive messages are generally longer, are usually more detailed, and often depend heavily on strategic planning. Persuasive messages require that you pay particular attention to several planning tasks. For example, you must decide whether your persuasive message is best communicated through a written form or orally (or, as is sometimes the case with formal business proposals, both). When analyzing your audience for a persuasive message, you may want to delve more deeply than you would for other messages. Your credibility takes on extra importance in a persuasive message: whenever you're trying to persuade someone, you must make sure your ethics are above reproach.

For a persuasive message, some planning tasks require more effort.

ANALYZE YOUR PURPOSE

Although many business messages are routine, as you advance in your careers you will be writing more and more messages designed to motivate or persuade others. An external persuasive message is one of the most difficult tasks you could undertake. First, people are busy, so they're reluctant to do something new, especially if it takes time and offers no guarantee of any reward in return. Secondly, competing requests are plentiful—mailboxes are filled with numerous requests from organizations selling products and services, or raising money for charitable causes. Given the complexity and sensitivity of persuasive messages, making sure of your purpose is perhaps the most important planning task.

Persuasive requests encounter two problems:

- Audiences are busy.
- Audiences receive many competing requests.

ANALYZE YOUR AUDIENCE

Chapter 4 discusses the basics of audience analysis, but the process can become much more involved for persuasive messages. Learning about your audience and the position you intend to argue can take weeks—sometimes months. Why? Because everyone's needs differ, so everyone responds differently to any given message. For instance, not every reader is interested in economy or even in fair play; you may even find that satisfying someone's need for status or appealing to someone's greed may at times be much more effective than emphasizing human generosity or civic duty.

You must appeal to the specific needs of your audience, especially in persuasive messages.

Gauging Audience Needs The best persuasive messages are closely connected to your audience's existing desires and interests.[4] Consider these important questions: Who is my audience? What are their needs? What do I want them to do? How might they resist? Are there alternative positions I need to examine? What does the decision-maker consider the most important issue? How might the organization's culture influence my strategy?

The questions you ask before writing a persuasive message go beyond those you would ask for other types of messages.

For example, suppose you supervise someone who meets his goals and is pleasant to you but is short-tempered with co-workers.[5] You must either persuade the employee to change his behaviour or risk losing staff. To prepare for a meeting with him, first try to understand what motivates his conduct. If possible, determine if he has a personal problem that is causing stress. Also examine his duties: is he burdened with too many projects and employees to supervise? Once you have tried to discover reasons for his behaviour, you can craft an appeal to him to change it. Perhaps you can begin a conversation by saying, "I understand a family member is ill. Do you want to tell me about this, so that we can help you?" Or, you can say, "I've examined your work record, and noticed that over the past year you've managed three major projects involving 15 employees. You're doing more than others in your position. Let's talk about how we can lighten your load." By understanding your audience's situation and needs, you would be able to get him to listen to you and be open to resolving the problem.

Demographics include characteristics such as age, gender, occupation, income, and education.

Psychographics include characteristics such as personality, attitudes, and lifestyle.

To assess various individual needs, you can refer to specific information such as **demographics** (the age, gender, occupation, income, education, and other quantifiable characteristics of the people you're trying to persuade) and **psychographics** (the personality, attitudes, lifestyle, and other psychological characteristics of an individual). Both types of information are strongly influenced by culture. When analyzing your audience, take into account their cultural expectations and practices so that you don't undermine your persuasive message by using an inappropriate appeal or by organizing your message in a way that seems unfamiliar or uncomfortable to your audience.

Cultural differences influence your persuasion attempts.

Considering Cultural Differences Your understanding and respect for cultural differences will help you satisfy the needs of your audience and will help your audience respect you. That's because persuasion is different in different cultures. In France, using an aggressive, hard-sell technique is no way to win respect. Such an approach would probably antagonize your audience. In Germany, where people tend to focus on technical matters, plan on verifying any figures you use for support, and make sure they are exact. In Sweden, audiences tend to focus on theoretical questions and strategic implications, whereas Canadian and U.S. audiences are usually concerned with more practical matters.[6]

Every message written for a corporation adds to the corporate tradition.

As with individuals, an organization's culture or subculture heavily influences the effectiveness of messages. All the previous messages in an organization have established a tradition that defines persuasive writing within that culture. When you accept and use these traditions, you establish one type of common ground with your audience. If you reject or never learn these traditions, you'll have difficulty achieving that common ground, which damages both your credibility and your persuasion attempts.

ESTABLISH YOUR CREDIBILITY

To persuade a skeptical or hostile audience, you must convince people that you know what you're talking about and that you're not trying to mislead them. Your *credibility* is your capability of being believed because you're reliable and worthy of confidence. Without such credibility, your efforts to persuade will seem manipulative. Research strongly suggests that most managers overestimate their own credibility—considerably.[7] Establishing your credibility is a process, so it takes time to earn your audience's respect. Some of the best ways to gain credibility include the following:

- **Support your message with facts.** Testimonials, documents, guarantees, statistics, and research results all provide seemingly objective evidence for what you have to say, which adds to your credibility. The more specific and relevant your proof, the better.
- **Name your sources.** Telling your audience where your information comes from and who agrees with you always improves your credibility, especially if your sources are already respected by your audience.

- **Be an expert.** Your knowledge of your message's subject area (or even of some other area) helps you give your audience the quality information necessary to make a decision.
- **Establish common ground.** Those beliefs, attitudes, and background experiences that you have in common with members of your audience will help them identify with you.

STRIVE FOR HIGH ETHICAL STANDARDS

The word *persuasion* is viewed by some as negative. They associate persuasion with dishonest and unethical practices, such as coaxing, urging, and sometimes even tricking people into accepting an idea, buying a product, or taking an unwanted or unneeded action. However, the best businesspeople make persuasion positive. They influence audience members by providing information and aiding understanding, which allows audiences the freedom to choose.[8] Ethical businesspeople inform audiences of the benefits of an idea, an organization, a product, a donation, or an action so that these audiences can recognize just how well the idea, organization, product, donation, or action will satisfy a need they truly have.

Positive persuasion leaves your audience free to choose.

For anyone trying to influence people's actions, knowing the law is crucial. However, merely avoiding what is illegal may not always be enough. To maintain the highest standards of business ethics, make every attempt to persuade without manipulating. Choose words that won't be misinterpreted, and be sure you don't distort the truth. Adopt the "you" attitude by showing honest concern for your audience's needs and interests. Your consideration of audience needs is more than ethical; it's the proper use of persuasion. That consideration is likely to achieve the response you intended and to satisfy your audience's needs.

To maintain the highest ethics, try to persuade without manipulating.

Step 2: Writing Persuasive Messages

When applying Step 2 to your persuasive messages, you will define your main idea, limit the scope of your message, and group your points in a meaningful way. But you must focus even more effort on choosing the direct or indirect approach.

As with routine and bad-news messages, the best organizational approach is based on your audience's likely reaction to your message. However, because the nature of persuasion is to convince your audience or to change their attitudes, beliefs, or actions, most persuasive messages use the indirect approach. So you'll want to explain your reasons and build interest before revealing your purpose. Nevertheless, many situations do call for the direct approach.

Use the indirect approach when your audience will react unfavourably to your message. Use the direct approach when your message is long or complex, or when your reader prefers directness.

If audience members are objective, or if you know they prefer the "bottom line" first (perhaps because it saves them time), the direct approach might be the better choice. You'll also want to use the direct approach when your corporate culture encourages directness. In addition, when a message is long or complex, your readers may become impatient if the main idea is buried seven pages in, so you may want to choose the direct approach for these messages as well.

Bette McGiboney is administrative assistant to the athletic director of Central Alberta Institute of Technology. Each year, after season tickets have been mailed out, the cost of the athletic department's toll-free number skyrockets as fans call to complain about their seats, or about receiving the wrong number of tickets, or to order last-minute tickets. The August phone bill is usually over $1500, in part because each customer is put on hold while operators serve others. McGiboney has an idea that may solve the problem (see Figure 9–1 on page 237).

If you use the direct approach, keep in mind that even though your audience may be easy to convince, you'll still want to include at least a brief justification or explanation. Don't expect your reader to accept your idea on blind faith. For example, consider the following two openers:

POOR	IMPROVED
I recommend building our new retail outlet on the West Main Street site.	After comparing the four possible sites for our new retail outlet, I recommend West Main Street as the only site that fulfills our criteria for visibility, proximity to mass transportation, and square footage.

Choice of approach is also influenced by your position (or authority within the organization) relative to your audience's.

Your choice between the direct and indirect approach is also influenced by the extent of your authority, expertise, or power in an organization. As a first-line manager writing a persuasive message to top management, you may try to be diplomatic and use an indirect approach. But your choice could backfire if some managers perceive your indirectness as manipulative and time wasting. On the other hand, you may consciously try to save your supervisors time by using a direct approach, which might be perceived as brash and presumptuous. Similarly, when writing a persuasive message to employees, you may use the indirect approach to ease into a major change, but your audience might see your message as weak and unconvincing. You need to think carefully about your corporate culture and what your audience expects before you select your approach.

Step 3: Completing Persuasive Messages

As with other business messages, Step 3 of the writing process helps guarantee the success of your persuasive messages.

Because persuasive messages are longer and more complex than routine and bad-news messages, applying Step 3 is even more crucial to your success. When you evaluate your persuasive content, be sure to judge your argument objectively and to seriously appraise your credibility. When revising persuasive messages, you must carefully match purpose and organization to audience needs.

Your design elements must complement, and not detract from, your argument. In addition, make sure your delivery methods fit your audience's expectations as well as your purpose. Finally, meticulous proofreading will identify any mechanical or spelling errors that would weaken your persuasive message.

Sending Persuasive Messages

Like routine messages, persuasive messages must develop their main idea with concrete information. But persuasive messages differ from routine messages in one important way: in addition to communicating your main idea and reasons, you need to motivate your audience to do something. So before looking at specific types of persuasive messages, let's examine some special persuasive strategies.

Strategies for Persuasive Messages

Four essential persuasion strategies:
- Balancing your appeals
- Framing your argument
- Reinforcing your position
- Overcoming audience resistance

Whether you use a direct or an indirect approach, you must convince your reader that your request or idea is reasonable. Effective persuasion involves four distinct and essential strategies: balancing emotional and logical appeals, framing your arguments, reinforcing your position, and dealing with resistance. The amount of detail you pursue in each of these strategies varies according to the complexity of your idea or request.

BALANCING EMOTIONAL AND LOGICAL APPEALS

OBJECTIVE 2 Distinguish between emotional and logical appeals, and discuss how to balance them.

How do you actually convince an audience that your position is the right one, that your plan will work, or that your charitable organization will do the most with readers' donations? One way is to appeal to the audience's minds and hearts. Most persuasive messages include both emotional and logical appeals. Together, these two elements have a good chance of persuading your audience to act.

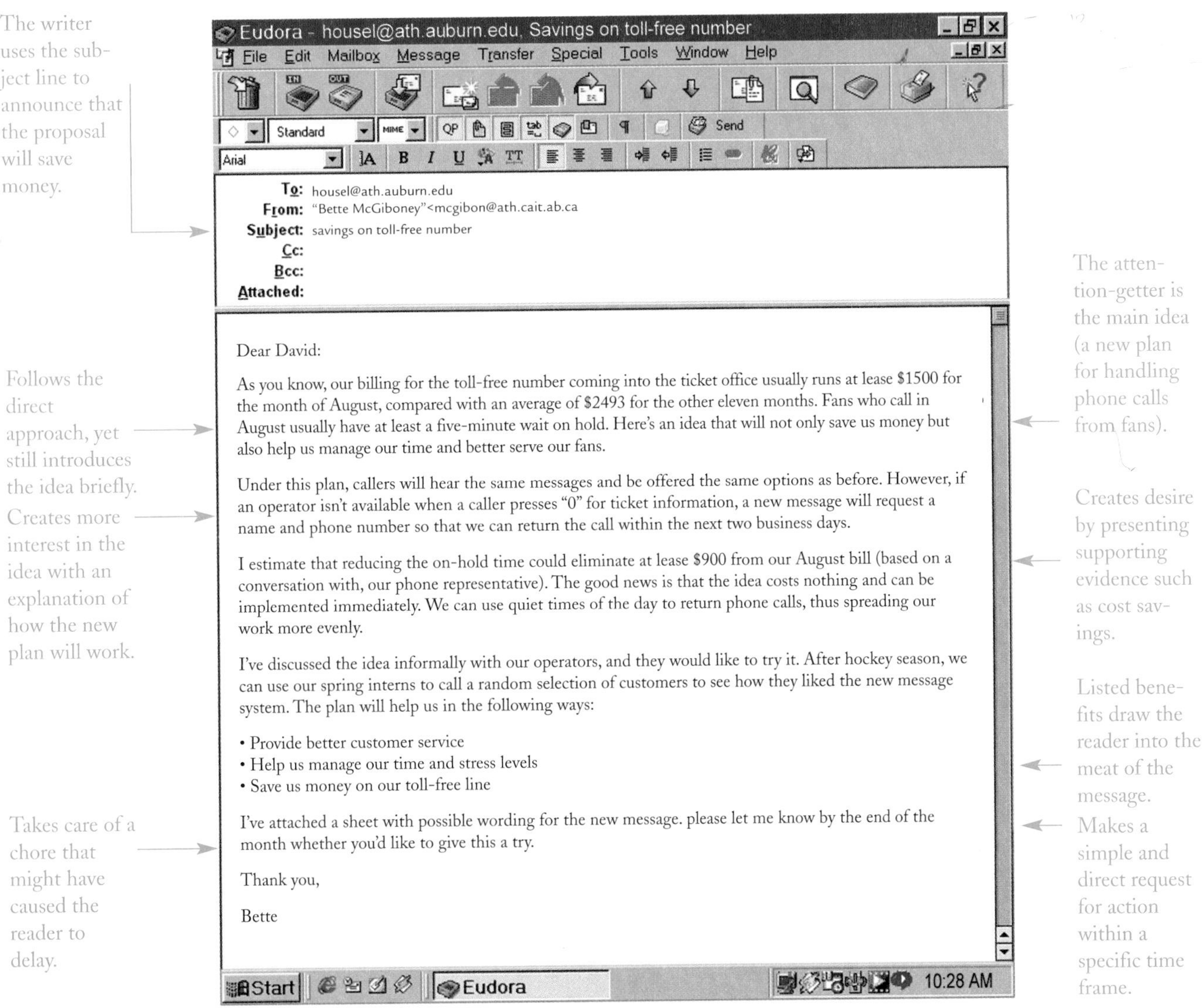

Eudora - housel@ath.auburn.edu, Savings on toll-free number
File Edit Mailbox Message Transfer Special Tools Window Help
The writer uses the subject line to announce that the proposal will save money.
Follows the direct approach, yet still introduces the idea briefly.
Creates more interest in the idea with an explanation of how the new plan will work.
Takes care of a chore that might have caused the reader to delay.
The attention-getter is the main idea (a new plan for handling phone calls from fans).
Creates desire by presenting supporting evidence such as cost savings.
Listed benefits draw the reader into the meat of the message.
Makes a simple and direct request for action within a specific time frame.
Start
Eudora
10:28 AM

To: housel@ath.auburn.edu
From: "Bette McGiboney"<mcgibon@ath.cait.ab.ca
Subject: savings on toll-free number
Cc:
Bcc:
Attached:

Dear David:

As you know, our billing for the toll-free number coming into the ticket office usually runs at lease $1500 for the month of August, compared with an average of $2493 for the other eleven months. Fans who call in August usually have at least a five-minute wait on hold. Here's an idea that will not only save us money but also help us manage our time and better serve our fans.

Under this plan, callers will hear the same messages and be offered the same options as before. However, if an operator isn't available when a caller presses "0" for ticket information, a new message will request a name and phone number so that we can return the call within the next two business days.

I estimate that reducing the on-hold time could eliminate at lease $900 from our August bill (based on a conversation with, our phone representative). The good news is that the idea costs nothing and can be implemented immediately. We can use quiet times of the day to return phone calls, thus spreading our work more evenly.

I've discussed the idea informally with our operators, and they would like to try it. After hockey season, we can use our spring interns to call a random selection of customers to see how they liked the new message system. The plan will help us in the following ways:

- Provide better customer service
- Help us manage our time and stress levels
- Save us money on our toll-free line

I've attached a sheet with possible wording for the new message. please let me know by the end of the month whether you'd like to give this a try.

Thank you,

Bette

FIGURE 9–1 In-Depth Critique: E-Mail Message Selling an Idea to a Supervisor

Finding the right balance between the two types of appeals depends on four factors: (1) the actions you wish to motivate, (2) your reader's expectations, (3) the degree of resistance you must overcome, and (4) how far you feel empowered to go in selling your point of view.[9] When you're persuading someone to accept a complex idea, take a serious step, or make a large and important decision, lean toward logic and make your emotional appeal subtle. However, when you're persuading someone to purchase a product, join a cause, or make a donation, you'll rely a bit more heavily on emotion.

Both emotional and logical appeals are needed to write successful persuasive messages.

Emotional Appeals An emotional appeal calls on human feelings, basing the argument on audience needs or sympathies; however, such an appeal must be subtle.[10] For instance, you can make use of the emotion surrounding certain words. The word *freedom* evokes strong feelings, as do words such as *success, prestige, credit record, savings, free, value,* and *comfort*. Words such as these put your audience in a certain frame of mind and help them accept your message. But be careful. Emotional appeals aren't necessarily effective by themselves. Emotion works with logic in a unique way: People need to find rational support for an attitude they've already embraced emotionally.

Emotional appeals are best if subtle.

Logical Appeals A logical appeal calls on human reason. In any argument you might use to persuade an audience, you make a claim and then support your claim with

Logical appeals can use
- Analogy
- Induction
- Deduction

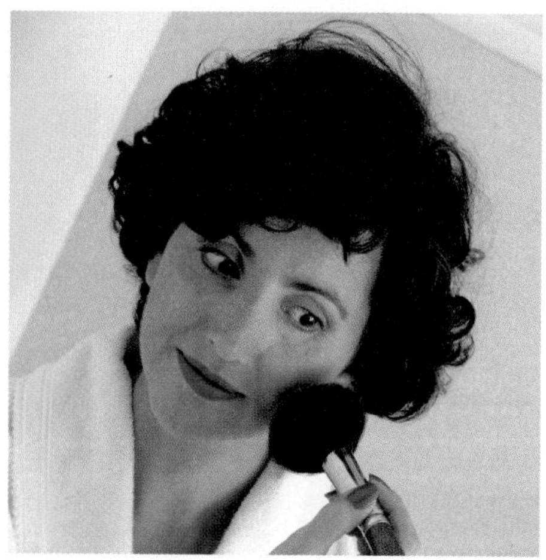

Companies work hard to persuade consumers to buy their products. What appeals do manufacturers of cosmetics make? Are these appeals successful? Are they ethical?

reasons or evidence. When appealing to your audience's logic, you might use three types of reasoning:

➤ **Analogy.** You might reason from specific evidence to specific evidence. In order to persuade employees to attend a planning session, you might use a town meeting analogy, comparing your company to a small community and your employees to valued members of that community.

➤ **Induction.** You might reason from specific evidence to a general conclusion. To convince potential customers that your product is best, you might report the results of test marketing in which individuals preferred your product over others. After all, if some individuals prefer it, so will others.

➤ **Deduction.** You might reason from a generalization to a specific conclusion. To persuade your boss to hire additional employees, you might point to industry-wide projections and explain that industry activity (and thus your company's business) will be increasing rapidly over the next three months, so you'll need more employees to handle increased business.

No matter what reasoning method you use, any argument or statement can easily appear to be true when it's actually false. Whenever you appeal to your audience's reason, do everything you can to ensure that your arguments are logically sound. To avoid faulty logic, practice the following guidelines:[11]

Avoid faulty logic such as hasty generalizations, begging the question, attacking your opponent, oversimplifying, assuming a false cause, using faulty analogies, and using illogical support.

- **Avoid hasty generalizations.** Make sure you have plenty of evidence before drawing conclusions.
- **Avoid begging the question.** Make sure you can support your claim without simply restating it in different words.
- **Avoid attacking your opponent.** Be careful to address the real question. Attack the argument your opponent is making, not your opponent's character.
- **Avoid oversimplifying a complex issue.** Make sure you present all the facts rather than relying on an "either/or" statement that makes it look as if only two choices are possible.
- **Avoid assuming a false cause.** Use cause-and-effect reasoning correctly; do not assume that one event caused another just because it happened first.
- **Avoid faulty analogies.** Be sure that the two objects or situations being compared are similar enough for the analogy to hold. Even if A resembles B in one respect, it may not in all respects.
- **Avoid illogical support.** Make sure the connection between your claim and your support is truly logical and not based on a leap of faith, a missing premise, or irrelevant evidence.

FRAMING YOUR ARGUMENTS

Whether you emphasize emotion or logic, and whether you decide to use a direct or an indirect approach, you still need to frame your argument in the most effective way. You want to present the advantages of your decision, idea, or product. You want

TABLE 9–1 The AIDA Organizational Plan

Phase	Objective
Attention	Get the reader's attention with a benefit that is of real interest or value.
Interest	Build the reader's interest by further explaining benefits and appealing to his or her logic or emotions.
Desire	Build desire by showing how your offer can truly help the reader.
Action	Give a strong and simple call to action and provide a convenient means for the reader to take the next step.

to support your main point. You need room to anticipate and answer any objections, as well as to motivate action at the close.

Using the AIDA Plan Most persuasive messages follow an organizational plan that goes beyond the indirect approach used for negative messages. The opening does more than serve as a buffer; it grabs your audience's attention. The explanation section does more than present reasons, and it is expanded to two sections. The first incites your audience's interest, and the second changes your audience's attitude. Finally, your close does more than end on a positive note with a statement of what action is needed; it emphasizes reader benefits and motivates readers to take specific action. Although similar to the indirect approach of negative messages, this new persuasive approach builds on it in each of four phases: (1) Attention, (2) Interest, (3) Desire, and (4) Action. Table 9–1 summarizes this AIDA plan.

OBJECTIVE 3 Describe the AIDA plan for persuasive messages.

Organize persuasive messages using the AIDA plan:

- Attention
- Interest
- Desire
- Action

- **Attention.** Make your audience want to hear about your problem or idea. Write a brief and engaging opening sentence, with no extravagant claims or irrelevant points. And be sure to find some common ground on which to build your case. In Figure 9-2 on page 240, Randy Thumwolt uses the AIDA plan in a persuasive memo about his program to reduce Host Marriott's annual plastics costs and to curtail consumer complaints about the company's recycling record.
- **Interest.** Explain the relevance of your message to your audience. Continuing the theme you started with, paint a more detailed picture with words. Get your audience thinking, "This is an interesting idea; could it possibly solve my problems?" Thumwolt's interest section ties a factual description to the benefits of instituting his new recycling plan. Also, Thumwolt relates benefits specifically to the attention phase that precedes this section.
- **Desire.** Make audience members want to change by explaining how the change will benefit them. Reduce resistance by predicting and answering in advance any questions your audience might have. If your idea is complex, explain how you would implement it. Back up your claims to increase audience willingness to take the action that you suggest in the next section. Just remember to make sure that all evidence is directly relevant to your point.
- **Action.** Suggest the action you want readers to take. Make it more than a statement such as "Please institute this program soon" or "Send me a refund." This is the opportunity to remind readers of the benefits of taking action. The secret of a successful action phase is making the action easy. Ask readers to call a toll-free number for more information, to use an enclosed order form, or to use a prepaid envelope for donations. Include a deadline when applicable.

Begin every persuasive message with an attention-getting statement that is

- Personalized
- "You"-oriented
- Straightforward
- Relevant

In the interest section

- Continue the opening theme in greater detail
- Relate benefits specifically to the attention-getter

In the desire section

- Provide evidence to prove your claim
- Draw attention to any enclosures

End by

- Suggesting a specific step the audience can take
- Restating how the audience will benefit by acting as you wish
- Making action easy

Making the AIDA Plan Work The AIDA plan is tailor-made for using the indirect approach, allowing you to save your main idea for the action phase. However, it can also be used for the direct approach. In this case, you use your main idea as an attention-getter. You build interest with your argument, create desire with your evidence, and emphasize your main idea in the action phase with the specific action you want your audience to take.

Using AIDA with the indirect approach allows you to save your idea for the action phase; using it with the direct approach allows you to use your main idea as your attention-getter.

When your AIDA message uses an indirect approach and is delivered by memo or e-mail, keep in mind that your subject line usually catches your readers' eye first. Your challenge is to make it interesting and relevant enough to capture reader attention without revealing your proposal. If you put your request in the subject line, you're likely to get a quick "no" before you've had a chance to present your arguments.

When using the indirect approach, make subject lines interesting without revealing your purpose.

INSTEAD OF THIS	TRY THIS
Proposal to Install New Phone Message System	Savings on Toll-Free Number

When using the AIDA plan, also remember to narrow your objectives. Focus on your primary goal when presenting your case, and concentrate your efforts on accomplishing that one goal. For example, if your main idea is to convince your company to

1 Planning

Analyze: The purpose is to help solve an ongoing problem. The audience will be receptive.

Investigate: Gather information on recycling problem areas.

Adapt: Use a memo, and strengthen the point by reviewing the bulk-purchase idea, which has already been instituted.

2 Writing

Organize: Follow the indirect approach by using background information to introduce the continuing problems. Then list the new recycling ideas.

Compose: Make your style businesslike and your appeal logical. Use a conversational tone, and respect the reader's time by avoiding wordiness.

3 Completing

Revise: Be sure the flow of this memo is logical. Edit and rewrite for conciseness and clarity.

Produce: Minimal design is needed for an internal memo. Send the message either as a printed memo or via e-mail.

Proofread: Review for accuracy and typos.

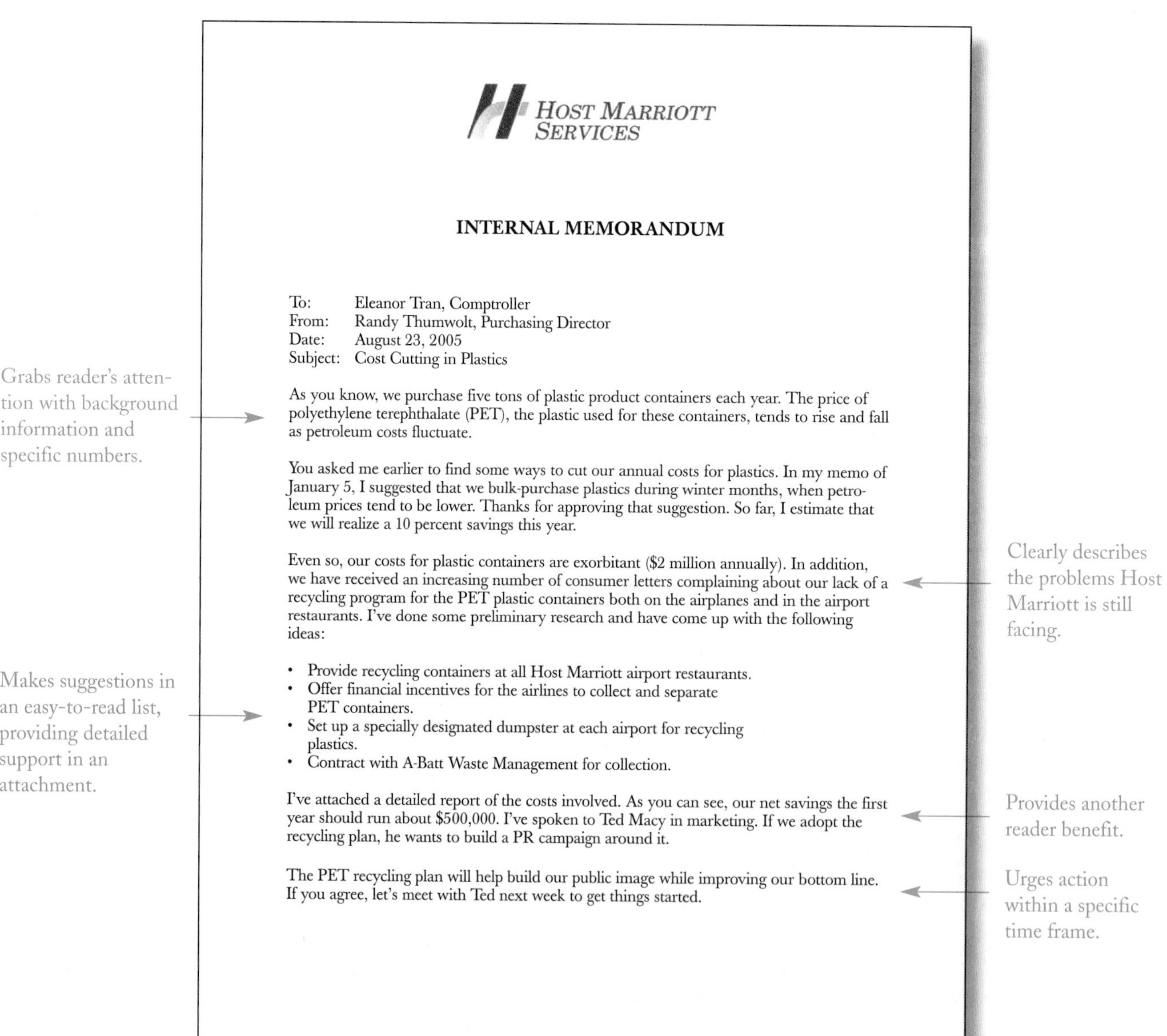

HOST MARRIOTT SERVICES

INTERNAL MEMORANDUM

To: Eleanor Tran, Comptroller
From: Randy Thumwolt, Purchasing Director
Date: August 23, 2005
Subject: Cost Cutting in Plastics

As you know, we purchase five tons of plastic product containers each year. The price of polyethylene terephthalate (PET), the plastic used for these containers, tends to rise and fall as petroleum costs fluctuate.

You asked me earlier to find some ways to cut our annual costs for plastics. In my memo of January 5, I suggested that we bulk-purchase plastics during winter months, when petroleum prices tend to be lower. Thanks for approving that suggestion. So far, I estimate that we will realize a 10 percent savings this year.

Even so, our costs for plastic containers are exorbitant ($2 million annually). In addition, we have received an increasing number of consumer letters complaining about our lack of a recycling program for the PET plastic containers both on the airplanes and in the airport restaurants. I've done some preliminary research and have come up with the following ideas:

- Provide recycling containers at all Host Marriott airport restaurants.
- Offer financial incentives for the airlines to collect and separate PET containers.
- Set up a specially designated dumpster at each airport for recycling plastics.
- Contract with A-Batt Waste Management for collection.

I've attached a detailed report of the costs involved. As you can see, our net savings the first year should run about $500,000. I've spoken to Ted Macy in marketing. If we adopt the recycling plan, he wants to build a PR campaign around it.

The PET recycling plan will help build our public image while improving our bottom line. If you agree, let's meet with Ted next week to get things started.

Grabs reader's attention with background information and specific numbers.
Clearly describes the problems Host Marriott is still facing.
Makes suggestions in an easy-to-read list, providing detailed support in an attachment.
Provides another reader benefit.
Urges action within a specific time frame.

FIGURE 9–2 In-Depth Critique: Persuasive Letter Using the AIDA Plan

install a new phone messaging system, leave discussions about switching long-distance carriers until another day—unless it's relevant to your argument.

To make the AIDA plan more successful, focus closely on one goal only.

REINFORCING YOUR POSITION

The facts alone may not be enough to persuade your audience. Effective persuaders such as the YEA's directors supplement numerical data with examples, stories, metaphors, and analogies to make their position come alive. They use language to paint a vivid picture of the persuader's point of view.[12]

Your language helps reinforce your position.

Semantics Say that you're trying to build your credibility. How do you let your audience know that you're enthusiastic and trustworthy? Simply making an outright claim that you have these traits is sure to raise suspicion. However, you can use **semantics**, the meaning of words and other symbols, to do much of the job for you. The words you choose to state your message say much more than their dictionary definition.[13]

Semantics is the meaning of words and other symbols.

INSTEAD OF THIS	SAY THIS
I think we should attempt to get approval on this before it's too late.	Let's get immediate approval on this.
It seems to me that ...	I believe ...
I've been thinking lately that maybe someone could ...	After careful thought over the past two months, I've decided that ...
This plan could work if we really push it.	With our support, this plan will work.

Another way semantics can affect persuasive messages is in the variety of meanings that people attribute to certain words. As discussed in Chapter 5, abstract words are subject to interpretation because they refer to things that people cannot experience with their senses. So you can use abstractions to enhance the emotional content of a persuasive message. For example, you may be able to sell more flags by appealing to your audience's patriotism than by describing the colour and size of the flags. You may have better luck collecting an overdue bill by mentioning honesty and fair play than by repeating the sum owed and the date it was due. However, be sure to include the details along with the abstractions; the very fact that you're using abstract words leaves room for misinterpretation.

Two ways of using semantics are choosing your words carefully and using abstractions to enhance emotional content.

Other Tools Using semantics skillfully isn't your only persuasive tool. Here are some additional techniques you can use to strengthen your persuasive messages:[14]

In addition to semantics, you have other persuasive tools at your disposal.

- **Be moderate.** Asking your audience to make major changes in attitudes or beliefs will most likely evoke a negative response. However, asking audience members to take one step toward that change may be a more reasonable goal.
- **Focus on your goal.** Your message will be clearest if you shift your focus away from changing minds and emphasize the action you want your audience to take.
- **Use simple language.** In most persuasive situations, your audience will be cautious, watching for fantastic claims, insupportable descriptions, and emotional manipulation. So speak plainly and simply.
- **Anticipate opposition.** Think of every possible objection in advance. In your message, you might raise and answer some of these counter arguments.
- **Provide sufficient support.** It is up to you to prove that the change you seek is necessary.
- **Be specific.** Back up your claims with evidence, and when necessary cite actual facts and figures. Let your audience know that you've done your homework.
- **Create a win-win situation.** Make it possible for both you and your audience to gain something. Audience members will find it easier to deal with change if they stand to benefit.

- **Time your messages appropriately.** The time to sell roofs is right after the tornado. Timing is crucial in persuasive messages.
- **Speak metaphorically.** Metaphors create powerful pictures. One metaphor can depict a crucial idea or image to communicate your purpose forcefully.
- **Use anecdotes and stories to make your points.** Anecdotes tie it all together—the logic and the emotions. For example, don't tell your audience what kinds of problems they can have if their computer system crashes. Tell them what happened to your company's sales representative when her hard drive crashed in the middle of her annual sales presentation.

All of these tools will help your persuasive message be accepted, but none of them will actually overcome your audience's resistance. Whether based on emotion or logic, your argument must be strong enough to persuade people to act.

DEALING WITH RESISTANCE

OBJECTIVE 4 Explain the best way to overcome resistance to your persuasive message, and list four common mistakes.

The best way to deal with audience resistance is to eliminate it. If you expect a hostile audience, one biased against your plan from the beginning, present all sides—cover all options, explaining the pros and cons of each. You'll gain additional credibility if you present these options before presenting the decision.[15]

You can overcome resistance by presenting the pros and cons of all sides of your argument.

To uncover audience objections, try some "What if?" scenarios. Poke holes in your own theories and ideas before your audience does. Then find solutions to the problems you've uncovered. You can also ask your audience for their thoughts on the subject before you put your argument together. Let your audience recommend some solutions; people often support what they help to create.

"What if?" scenarios help you see the holes in your argument.

Furthermore, with enough thought and effort, you may even be able to turn problems into opportunities; for example, you may show how your plan will be more economical in the long run, even though it may cost more now. Just be sure to be thorough, open, and objective about all the facts and alternatives. When putting together persuasive arguments, avoid common mistakes such as these:[16]

Avoiding common mistakes helps you overcome resistance.

- **Don't use an up-front hard sell.** Setting out a strong position at the start of a persuasive message gives potential opponents something to grab onto—and fight against.
- **Don't resist compromise.** Persuasion is a process of give and take. A persuader rarely changes another person's behaviour or viewpoint without altering his or her own in the process.
- **Don't rely solely on arguments.** In persuading people to change their minds, effective arguments matter, but they are only one element of your persuasive message. Your ability to create a mutually beneficial framework for your position, to connect with your audience on the right emotional level, and to communicate through vivid language are all just as important; they bring your argument to life.
- **Don't assume persuasion is a one-shot effort.** Persuasion is a process, not a one-time event. More often than not, persuasion involves listening to people, testing a position, developing a new position that reflects new input, more testing, more compromise, and so on.

Remember, successful persuasive messages depend on your ability to balance emotional and logical appeals, frame your argument, reinforce your position, and overcome resistance. Using these strategies will help you craft strong persuasive messages, no matter what the situation. To review the steps involved in developing persuasive messages, see this chapter's "Checklist: Developing Persuasive Messages" on page 243.

Types of Persuasive Requests

Persuasive requests are used both inside and outside the organization.

People write many different kinds of persuasive messages within an organization: selling a supervisor on an idea for cutting costs, suggesting more efficient operating procedures, eliciting cooperation from competing departments, winning employee

Checklist: Developing Persuasive Messages

Balance Emotional and Logical Appeals

✓ Use emotional appeals to help the audience accept your message.

✓ Use logical appeals when presenting facts and evidence for complex ideas or recommendations.

✓ Avoid faulty logic.

Get Your Reader's Attention

✓ Open with a reader benefit, a stimulating question, a problem, or an unexpected statement.

✓ Discuss something your audience can agree with; in other words, establish common ground.

✓ Demonstrate that you understand the audience's concerns.

Build Your Reader's Interest

✓ Elaborate on the main benefit.

✓ Explain the relevance of your message to your audience.

Increase Your Reader's Desire

✓ Make audience members want to change by explaining how the change will benefit them.

✓ Back up your claims with relevant evidence.

Reinforce Your Position

✓ Use semantics to build credibility and enhance the emotional content of your message.

✓ Use a variety of critical thinking and effective writing tools to strengthen your case.

Deal with Resistance

✓ Anticipate and answer possible objections. Turn them into opportunities when possible. Otherwise, give assurance that you will handle them as best you can.

✓ Try "What if?" scenarios to poke holes in your theories and then find solutions.

✓ Let others help you find solutions to problems that you uncover.

✓ Present the pros and cons of all options.

✓ Avoid common mistakes such as using a hard sell up front, resisting compromise, relying solely on arguments, and assuming persuasion is a one-shot effort.

Motivate Your Reader to Take Action

✓ Confidently ask for the audience's cooperation.

✓ Stress the positive results of the action.

✓ Include the date (if any) for a response, and tie it in with audience benefits.

✓ Include one last reminder of the audience benefit.

✓ Make the desired action clear and easy.

Increase the Effectiveness of Your AIDA Plan

✓ Use the AIDA plan for both direct and indirect approaches.

✓ Write an attention-getting subject line without revealing your purpose.

✓ Limit your objectives by focusing on your primary goal.

support for a new benefits package, requesting money for new equipment or funding for a special project, or requesting a favour. Similarly, people may send a variety of persuasive messages to individuals or groups outside the organization: requesting favours, demanding adjustments, asking for information, or soliciting funds and cooperation.

Make only reasonable requests.

The most important thing to remember when preparing a persuasive request is to keep your request within bounds. Nothing is as distressing as a request so general, so all encompassing, or so inconsiderate that it seems impossible to grant, no matter how worthy the cause. Therefore, when making a persuasive request, take special care to highlight both the direct and the indirect benefits of fulfilling the request.

Highlight the direct and indirect benefits of complying with your request.

For example, if you want to persuade your supervisor to institute flexible working hours, a direct benefit for that person might be the reduced workload or the enhanced prestige. An indirect benefit might be better employee morale, once flextime is instituted. If you are asking someone to respond to a survey, you might offer a premium as the direct benefit and a chance to make a meaningful contribution as the indirect benefit. As examples of persuasive requests, let's look at two specific types: persuasive requests for action and persuasive claims and requests for adjustments.

Going Online

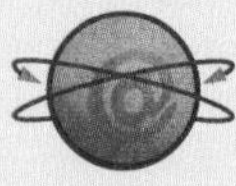

Lobby Your Leaders

A Canadian Government site offers information about the structure of the Canadian government. It identifies ministers and their portfolios, and how to contact them. Persons wishing to persuade a minister or other official about an issue of importance can have direct access through this site. It provides easy access in several ways: by the ministers' names, by their areas of responsibility, and by government departments. This site also leads to members of parliament.

canada.gc.ca/howgoc/glance_e.html

To link directly to this site, visit our Companion Web site at **www.pearsoned.ca/thill** *and look for the Chapter 9 resources.*

PERSUASIVE REQUESTS FOR ACTION

Whether you're requesting a favour or a budget increase, remember to use the AIDA plan to frame your message. Begin with an attention-getting device. Show readers that you know something about their concerns and that you have some reason for making such a request. In this type of persuasive message, more than in most others, a flattering comment about your reader is acceptable, as long as it's sincere.

Use the interest and desire sections of your message to cover what you know about the situation you're requesting action on: the facts and figures, the benefits of helping, and any history or experience that will enhance your appeal. Your goals are (1) to gain credibility for you and your request and (2) to make your readers believe that helping you will indeed help solve a significant problem. Be careful not to doom your request to failure by asking your reader to do all your work for you. For example, don't ask your readers to

- Provide information that you were too lazy to seek
- Take action that will save you from embarrassment or inconvenience
- Provide total financial support for a cause that nobody else is supporting

Once you've demonstrated that your message is relevant to your reader, you can close with a request for some specific action. Be aware, however, that a persuasive memo to a colleague is somewhat more subdued than a persuasive letter to an outsider would be. Ed Alvarez wrote the memo in Figure 9-3 on page 245. He's excited about a new method of packaging bananas to decrease shipping damage and reduce costs. He not only needs his boss's approval to proceed but also needs her cooperation in coordinating with another department.

When requesting a favour that is routine (such as asking someone to attend a meeting in your absence), use the direct approach and the format for routine messages (see Chapter 7). However, when asking for a special favour (such as asking someone to chair an event or to serve as the team leader because you can no longer fill that role), use persuasive techniques to convince your reader of the value of the project. Include all necessary information about the project and any facts and figures that will convince your reader that his or her contribution will be enjoyable, easy, important, and of personal benefit.

When making a persuasive request for action, be sure to use the AIDA plan to frame your argument.

PERSUASIVE CLAIMS AND REQUESTS FOR ADJUSTMENTS

The goal of a persuasive claim or request for adjustment is to convince someone to make an adjustment in your favour.

Although persuasive claims and adjustment requests are sometimes referred to as complaint letters, your goal is to persuade someone to make an adjustment in your favour; you're not complaining merely in order to feel better. You reach your goal by demonstrating the difference between what you expected and what you actually got.

Most claim letters are routine messages and use the direct approach discussed in Chapter 7. However, suppose you purchase something, and after the warranty expires, you discover that it was defective. You write the company a routine request asking for a replacement, but your request is denied. You're not satisfied, and you still feel you have a strong case. Perhaps you just didn't communicate it well enough the first time. Persuasion is necessary in such cases.

You can't threaten to withhold payment, so try to convey the essentially negative information in a way that will get positive results. Fortunately, most people in business are open to settling your claim fairly. It's to their advantage to maintain your goodwill and to resolve your problem quickly.

Make your persuasive claims
- Complete and specific when reviewing the facts
- Confident and positive in tone

The key ingredients of a good persuasive claim are a complete and specific review of the facts and a confident and positive tone. Assume that the other person is not trying to cheat you but that you also have the right to be satisfied with the transaction. Talk only about the complaint at hand, not about other issues involving similar products or other complaints about the company. Your goal is to solve a particular problem, and your audience is most likely to help if you focus on the audience benefits of doing so, rather than focusing on the disadvantages of neglecting your complaint.

MEMORANDUM

To: Kia Miamoto
From: Ed Alvarez
Date: September 4, 2005
Subject: Money-saving packaging

Earlier this year you expressed concern about our damage problems in transporting our bananas from Chile using wooden crates. Recently, I came across information on plastic-lined reusable boxes that may solve our problem and save us money.

TexCrate, Inc., manufactures the corrugated boxes to any specifications. A heat process is used to affix the 6 ml polyethylene lining to the walls of the boxes. A metal U-bar inside the box provides a hanger for the bananas.

The boxes feature slip-on lids that make stacking them in our containers quite easy. They can be fork-lifted using wooden pallets that we already own. We would place a desiccant pouch in each box to prevent "sweating." In addition, small vents can be cut into the lids and sides.

Because of the recent increase in lumber costs, the boxes cost less than the wooden crates. The boxes are also fully recyclable, so they fit in with our "Earth-Friendly" campaign. Randy Farney of TexCrate says we should be able to ship repeatedly in the same boxes for several years.

Farney would like to provide us with six sample boxes to test before our peak season, and he wants our specifications as soon as possible. He'll work up a dollar amount depending on the size we'll need. If we decide to use TexCrate's boxes, we can donate our wooden crates to Habitat for Humanity.

If you agree, I'd like to proceed with the test. Can you authorize someone from R&D to work with me on developing the specs for TexCrate? Please let me hear from you by Wednesday.

If we can get the information to TexCrate within the week, we'll be able to conduct the tests and have results by early November. At that time I'll also be able to give you an estimate of our dollar savings so that we'll be ready to make a decision before mid-November–in plenty of time to make any needed changes before our peak season begins in late December.

Gets the reader's attention by solving an ongoing problem and including an additional benefit.

Details advantages and adaptability of the boxes to give the request credibility while increasing interest.

Builds the reader's desire to try the new method by emphasizing cost and environmental benefits.

Tells the reader exactly what must be done and emphasizes the need to act now.

FIGURE 9-3 In-Depth Critique: Persuasive Memo Requesting Action

Begin persuasive claims by stating the basic problem (or with a sincere compliment, rhetorical question, agreeable assertion, or brief review of what's been done about the problem). Include a statement that both you and your audience can agree with or that clarifies what you wish to convince your audience about. Be as specific as possible about what you want to happen.

Next, give your reader a good reason for granting your claim. Show how your audience is responsible for the problem, and appeal to your readers' sense of fair play, goodwill, or moral responsibility. Tell your audience how you feel about the problem, but don't get carried away, don't complain too much, and don't make threats. Make sure your request is calm and reasonable.

Finally, state your request specifically and confidently. Make sure your request proceeds logically from the problem and the facts you've explained. Remember to specify a deadline for action when necessary or desirable. And remind your audience of the main benefit of granting your claim. Look at the following letter, and note the improvements that could be made:

The CEO of Habitat for Humanity, Bobbye Goldenberg must effectively communicate Habitat's mission: to build affordable housing with families in need. Her organization works in partnership with their clients and local communities, supported by donations of goods and services from suppliers and volunteers.

Opening fails to clarify the details of the purchase, the exact product involved, and the problem.

I bought an Audio-Tech sound system a few months ago to provide background music at my gift shop. Now one of the components, the CD player, does not work right. When we play a CD, it repeats and repeats. This is very irritating to me and my customers, and Audio-Tech needs to fix this problem.

Doesn't include any acceptable reasons for Audio-Tech to consider making an adjustment.

My clerks and I noticed this major mess about a month or so after I bought this fancy unit at the McNally Sound and Light Store in Burnaby, where I buy most of my video and CD stuff—although sometimes I buy through catalogues. When one of the clerks first heard the CD repeat, she tried another CD, and sure enough, it did the same thing, so it is a player problem, not a CD problem.

Captures the store owner's frustration, but fails to persuade the reader—who is still trying to grasp the dimensions of the problem.

When I finally brought the unit back to the store, Henry McNally said that the 60-day warranty had expired, and it was my gift shop's problem, but definitely not his problem. He said I probably had a "lemon."

Touches on what the writer expected from the product, but doesn't state what she wants done; contains only additional complaining and a vague threat.

This CD unit probably never did work right. I would think that, since I paid hundreds of dollars for this component, it would work for many years. Other stores here on Main Street cannot believe how irritating it is to hear irritating background music on this Audio-Tech player. They say they will not buy the Audio-Tech brand if you don't replace my unit.

Figure 9-4 on page 247 is a revised version of this letter that should yield much more favourable results. As the figure illustrates, resolving problems is more a reasonable exchange than a struggle between adversaries. For a review of the tasks involved here, see this chapter's "Checklist: Persuasive Claims and Requests for Adjustments" on page 248.

Sending Sales and Fundraising Messages

OBJECTIVE 5 Compare sales messages with fundraising messages.

Two distinctive types of persuasive messages are sales and fundraising messages. These messages are often sent in special direct-mail packages that can include brochures, reply forms, or other special inserts. Both types of messages are often written by specialized and highly skilled professionals.

Sales and fundraising letters are distinctive types of persuasive messages that often come in special direct-mail packages.

How do sales messages differ from fundraising messages? Sales messages are usually sent by for-profit organizations persuading readers to spend money on products for themselves. However, fundraising messages are usually sent by non-profit organizations persuading readers to donate money or time to help others. In other words, sales and fundraising messages are quite similar: Both compete for business and public attention, time, and dollars.[17] Both attempt to persuade readers to spend their time or money on the value being offered—whether that value is the convenience of a more efficient vacuum cleaner or the satisfaction of helping save children's lives. Both require a few more steps than other types of persuasive messages, and both generally use the AIDA sequence to deliver their message.

Strategies for Sales Messages

When planning a sales message, know your product.

Your purpose in writing a sales message is to sell a product. One of the first things to do is gain a thorough understanding of that product. What does it look like? How does it work? How is it priced? Are there any discounts? How is it packaged? How is it delivered?

Before writing your sales message, decide what sort of campaign you'll conduct.

You'll also need to think about the type of sales campaign you'll conduct. Will you send a letter only, or will you include brochures, samples, response cards, and the like? If you send a brochure, how many pages will it run? Will you conduct a multistage campaign, with several mailings and some sort of telephone or in-person follow-up? Or will you rely on a single hard-hitting mailing? Expensive items and hard-to-accept propositions call for a more elaborate campaign than low-cost products and simple actions.

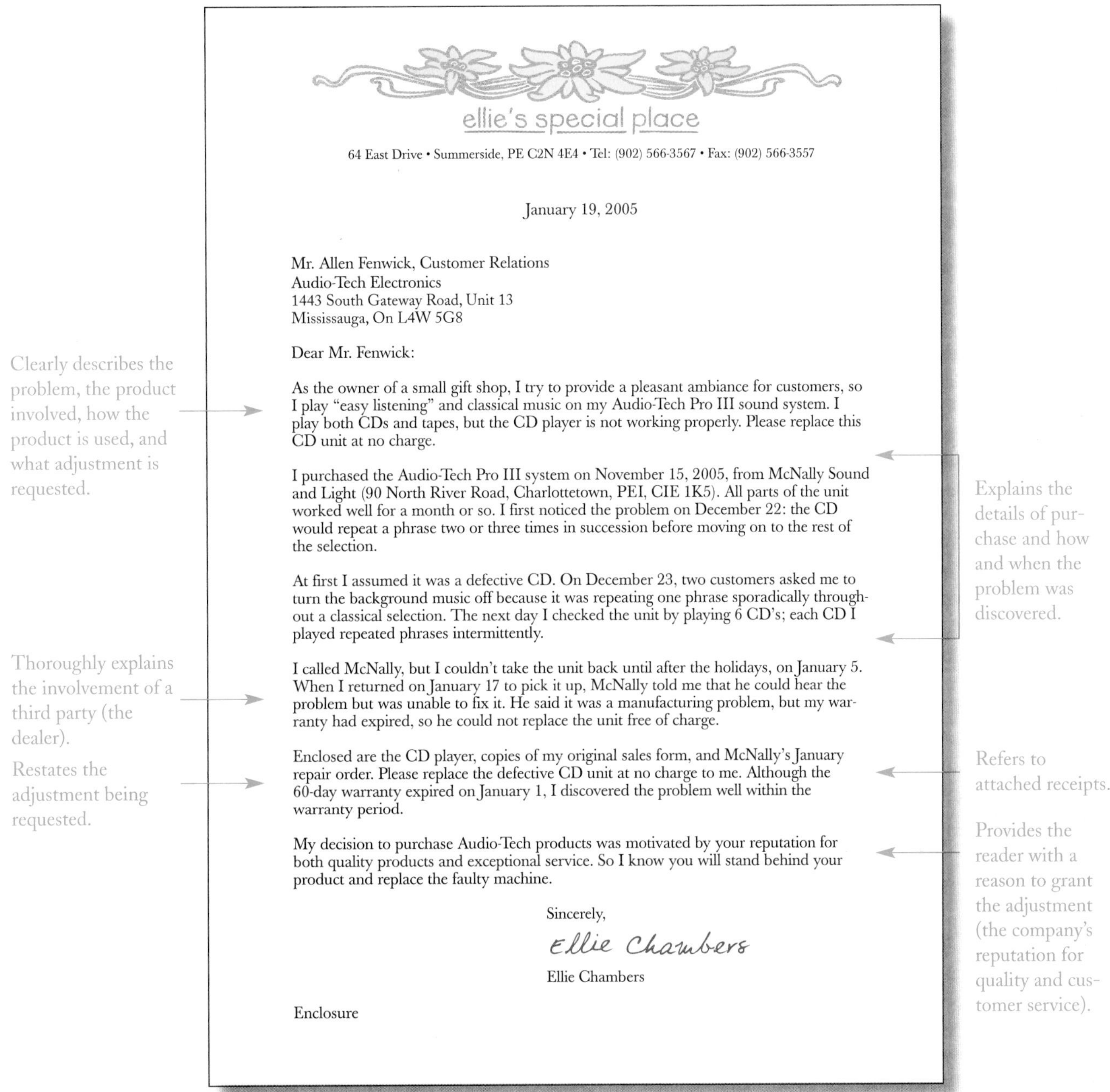

ellie's special place
64 East Drive • Summerside, PE C2N 4E4 • Tel: (902) 566-3567 • Fax: (902) 566-3557

January 19, 2005

Mr. Allen Fenwick, Customer Relations
Audio-Tech Electronics
1443 South Gateway Road, Unit 13
Mississauga, On L4W 5G8

Dear Mr. Fenwick:

As the owner of a small gift shop, I try to provide a pleasant ambiance for customers, so I play "easy listening" and classical music on my Audio-Tech Pro III sound system. I play both CDs and tapes, but the CD player is not working properly. Please replace this CD unit at no charge.

I purchased the Audio-Tech Pro III system on November 15, 2005, from McNally Sound and Light (90 North River Road, Charlottetown, PEI, CIE 1K5). All parts of the unit worked well for a month or so. I first noticed the problem on December 22: the CD would repeat a phrase two or three times in succession before moving on to the rest of the selection.

At first I assumed it was a defective CD. On December 23, two customers asked me to turn the background music off because it was repeating one phrase sporadically throughout a classical selection. The next day I checked the unit by playing 6 CD's; each CD I played repeated phrases intermittently.

I called McNally, but I couldn't take the unit back until after the holidays, on January 5. When I returned on January 17 to pick it up, McNally told me that he could hear the problem but was unable to fix it. He said it was a manufacturing problem, but my warranty had expired, so he could not replace the unit free of charge.

Enclosed are the CD player, copies of my original sales form, and McNally's January repair order. Please replace the defective CD unit at no charge to me. Although the 60-day warranty expired on January 1, I discovered the problem well within the warranty period.

My decision to purchase Audio-Tech products was motivated by your reputation for both quality products and exceptional service. So I know you will stand behind your product and replace the faulty machine.

Sincerely,

Ellie Chambers

Ellie Chambers

Enclosure

FIGURE 9–4 In-Depth Critique: Letter Making a Persuasive Claim

All these decisions depend on the audience you're trying to reach—their characteristics and their likely acceptance of or resistance to your message. You must analyze your audience and focus on their needs, interests, and emotional concerns—just as you would for any persuasive message. Try to form a mental image of the typical buyer for the product you wish to sell. But in addition to the usual questions, also ask yourself: What might audience members want to know about this product? How can your product help them? Are they driven by bottom-line pricing, or is quality more important to them?

In order to make campaign decisions, you need to know your audience.

In addition to learning about your product, performing a more in-depth audience analysis, and planning your sales campaign, you need a few other sales letter strategies: You need to determine selling points and benefits; you want to be sure that you stay within the law; and you must know how to use action terms, talk about price, and support your claims. In addition, it helps to know how each phase of the AIDA plan differs in sales letters.

Checklist: Persuasive Claims and Requests for Adjustments

Attention

- ✓ For your opening, use one of the following: sincere compliment, rhetorical question, agreeable comment or assertion, statement of the basic problem, or brief review of what has been done about the problem.
- ✓ At the beginning, state something that you and the audience can agree on or what you wish to convince the audience about.

Interest and Desire

- ✓ Provide a description that shows the members of your audience that their firm is responsible for the problem.
- ✓ Make your request factual, logical, and reasonable.
- ✓ Appeal to the audience's sense of fair play, desire for customer goodwill, need for a good reputation, or sense of legal or moral responsibility.
- ✓ Emphasize your goal of having the adjustment granted.
- ✓ Present your case in a calm, logical manner.
- ✓ Tell the audience how you feel; your disappointment with the products, policies, or services provided may well be the most important part of your argument.

Action

- ✓ Make sure the action request is a logical conclusion based on the problem and the stated facts.
- ✓ State the request specifically and confidently.
- ✓ Specify a deadline for action (when desirable).
- ✓ State the main audience benefit as a reminder of benefits in earlier statements.

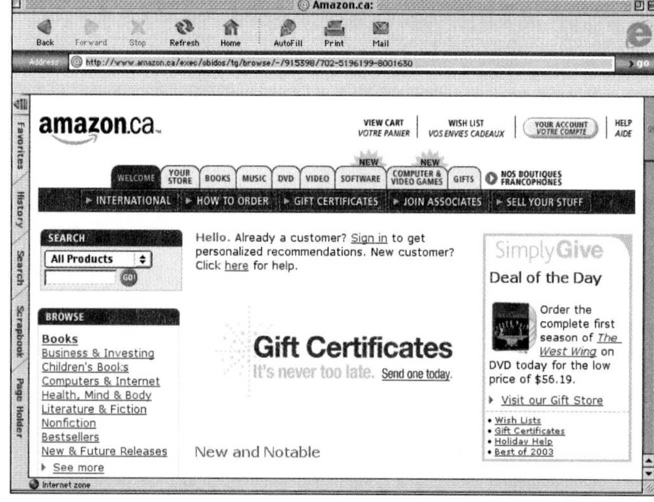

Amazon.com's CEO Jeffrey Bezos knows how to to persuade customers that the Internet superstore is convenient. His aim is to re-create that small-town store experience, where the owner knows you and knows what you like. To keep customers returning, the Web site is personalized. It suggests new products to you on the basis of what you have previously purchased, and it helps you provide friends accessing the site with a list of what you've already bought and what you want to buy.
© 2002 Amazon.com, Inc. All rights reserved. Amazon, Amazon.ca logo are trademarks or registered trademarks of Amazon.com, Inc.

Selling points focus on the product; benefits focus on the user.

DETERMINING SELLING POINTS AND BENEFITS

Sales letters require you to know your product's selling points and how each one benefits your particular audience. You'll need to highlight these points when you compose your persuasive message. As Table 9–2 below shows, selling points are the most attractive features of an idea or product; benefits are the particular advantages that readers will realize from those features. Selling points focus on the product. Benefits focus on the user. For example, if you say that your shovel has "an ergonomically designed handle," you've described a good feature. But to persuade someone to buy that shovel, say "the ergonomically designed handle will reduce your risk of back injury." That's a benefit. For your letter and your overall sales efforts to be successful, your product's distinguishing benefit must correspond to your readers' primary needs or emotional concerns.

Take a look at Figure 9-5 on page 250. The sales letter for SecureAbel Alarms uses the AIDA plan to persuade students to buy its dorm-room alarm system. The features of the system are that it can be installed with a screwdriver, has an activator that hooks to your key chain or belt loop, and has a blinking red light to warn intruders to stay away. The benefits are ease of installation, ease of activation, and a feeling of safety and security—all obtainable without investing in a full-blown permanently installed alarm system. When composing sales messages, be sure to focus on relatively few product benefits. Ultimately, you'll single out one benefit, which will become the hallmark of your campaign. Safety seems to be the key benefit emphasized by SecureAbel Alarms.

TABLE 9-2 Features versus Benefits

Product Feature (Selling Point)	Consumer Benefit
No money down, no interest payments for 24 months.	You can buy what you want right now at no additional costs.
This printer prints 17 pages per minute.	This printer can turn out one of your 100-page proposals in six minutes.
Our shelter provides 100 adult beds and 50 children's beds for the needy.	Your donation will provide temporary housing for 100 women who don't want to return to abusive husbands.
Your corporate sponsorship of the seminar will pay for the keynote speaker's travel and lodging.	Your corporate sponsorship of the seminar will allow your site manager a five-minute introduction at the beginning of the program to summarize your services.

SELLING ETHICALLY

Whether you're selling a good, a service, or your company's image, you want to write sales letters of the highest ethical character, so focus on solving your readers' problem rather than on selling your product. You must be able to do what you say you can do. So avoid even implying offers or promises that you can't deliver. Misrepresenting the price, quality, or performance of a product in a sales letter is fraud. Fraud also includes using a testimonial by a person misrepresented as being an expert. Making a false statement in a sales letter is fraud if the recipient can prove the following:

You can avoid both legal and ethical pitfalls by being genuinely concerned about your audience's needs, but you must also know the law.

- You intended to deceive.
- You made your statement regarding a fact (not an opinion or a speculation).
- The recipient was justified in relying on your statement.
- The recipient was damaged by your statement (in a legal sense).

To sell ethically, you must also respect people's privacy. Using a person's name, photograph, or other identity in a sales letter without permission constitutes invasion of privacy—with some exceptions. Using a photo of the members of a local softball team in a chamber of commerce mailer may be perfectly legal if team members are public figures in the community and if using the photo doesn't falsely imply their endorsement. On the other hand, using a photo of your provincial premier, without consent, on a letter about the profits to be made in worm farming could be deemed an invasion of privacy.

In addition, publicizing a person's private life in a sales letter can result in legal problems. For example, stating that the president of a local company (mentioned by name) served six months in prison for income tax evasion is a potentially damaging fact that may be considered an invasion of privacy. You would also risk a lawsuit by publicizing another person's past-due debts or by publishing without consent another person's medical records or x-rays.

When you sell online, you should be familiar with proper electronic business practices to avoid serious legal problems (see "Promoting Workplace Ethics—Selling Ethically Online" on page 251).

USING ACTION TERMS

Action words give strength to any business message, but they are especially important in sales letters. Compare the following:

To give force to a message
- Use action terms
- Use colourful verbs and adjectives

INSTEAD OF THIS	WRITE THIS
The NuForm desk chair is designed to support your lower back and relieve pressure on your legs.	The NuForm desk chair supports your lower back and relieves pressure on your legs.

The second version expresses the same idea in fewer words and emphasizes what the chair does for the user ("supports") rather than the intentions of the design team ("is designed to support").

1 Planning

Analyze: The purpose here is to persuade readers to buy the portable alarm system. The audience will be neutral—or even resistant.

Investigate: Gather information on product's features and benefits, as well as on audience needs.

Adapt: Use a typical sales letter format.

2 Writing

Organize: Make safety the central selling point. Follow the indirect AIDA approach. Important to get the reader's attention right away.

Compose: Use both logical and emotional appeals. Use a friendly, conversational tone. Include a response card to make reader action easy.

3 Completing

Revise: Don't emphasize emotional appeals. The point is to help readers, not threaten them. Edit for focus and clarity.

Produce: Use a simple design for the letter and any brochures (in line with reasonable pricing).

Proofread: Be accurate. Remove all typographical distractions.

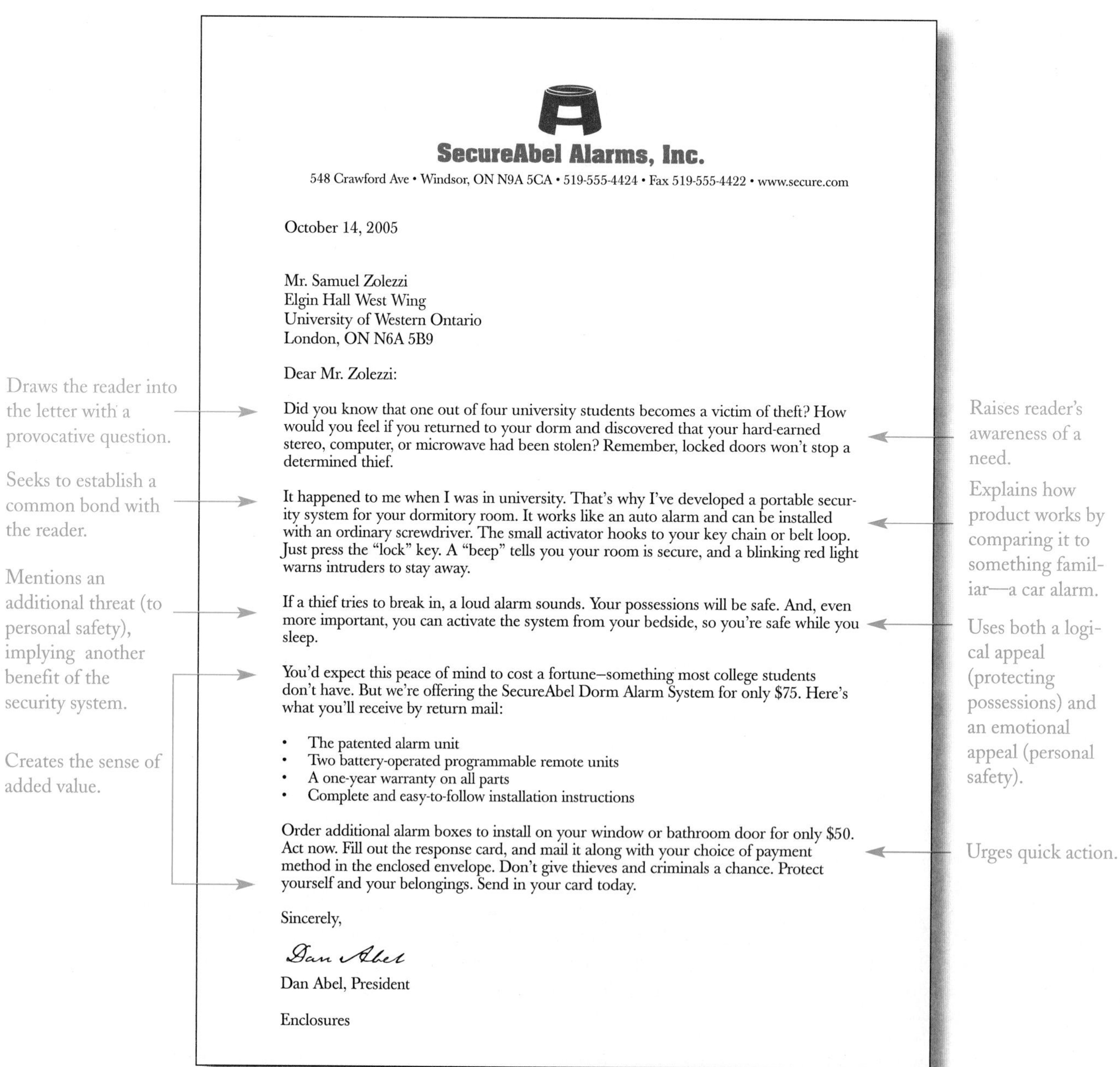

SecureAbel Alarms, Inc.

548 Crawford Ave • Windsor, ON N9A 5CA • 519-555-4424 • Fax 519-555-4422 • www.secure.com

October 14, 2005

Mr. Samuel Zolezzi
Elgin Hall West Wing
University of Western Ontario
London, ON N6A 5B9

Dear Mr. Zolezzi:

Did you know that one out of four university students becomes a victim of theft? How would you feel if you returned to your dorm and discovered that your hard-earned stereo, computer, or microwave had been stolen? Remember, locked doors won't stop a determined thief.

It happened to me when I was in university. That's why I've developed a portable security system for your dormitory room. It works like an auto alarm and can be installed with an ordinary screwdriver. The small activator hooks to your key chain or belt loop. Just press the "lock" key. A "beep" tells you your room is secure, and a blinking red light warns intruders to stay away.

If a thief tries to break in, a loud alarm sounds. Your possessions will be safe. And, even more important, you can activate the system from your bedside, so you're safe while you sleep.

You'd expect this peace of mind to cost a fortune–something most college students don't have. But we're offering the SecureAbel Dorm Alarm System for only $75. Here's what you'll receive by return mail:

- The patented alarm unit
- Two battery-operated programmable remote units
- A one-year warranty on all parts
- Complete and easy-to-follow installation instructions

Order additional alarm boxes to install on your window or bathroom door for only $50. Act now. Fill out the response card, and mail it along with your choice of payment method in the enclosed envelope. Don't give thieves and criminals a chance. Protect yourself and your belongings. Send in your card today.

Sincerely,

Dan Abel

Dan Abel, President

Enclosures

Draws the reader into the letter with a provocative question.
Seeks to establish a common bond with the reader.
Mentions an additional threat (to personal safety), implying another benefit of the security system.
Creates the sense of added value.
Raises reader's awareness of a need.
Explains how product works by comparing it to something familiar—a car alarm.
Uses both a logical appeal (protecting possessions) and an emotional appeal (personal safety).
Urges quick action.

FIGURE 9–5 In-Depth Critique: Letter Selling a Product

PROMOTING WORKPLACE ETHICS

Selling Ethically Online

Before you sell products online, become familiar with the *Canadian Code of Practice for Consumer Protection in Electronic Commerce*. Developed by professional associations such as the Retail Council of Canada, federal and provincial government agencies, and corporations, its intent is to protect consumers during any online transaction. By subscribing to these guidelines, you will conduct your business ethically and avoid complaints and lawsuits.

- **Provide complete and current contact and policy information.** Customers often need to contact companies to ask questions, learn about their warranties, change orders, customer support services, and complain. Your Web site should include all contact information (postal address, e-mail address, phone and fax numbers) and details regarding payment methods, return policy, warranties, and complaint process. You should also state your policies on privacy and unsolicited e-mail. As the *Code of Practice* states, all information should be "clearly presented in plain language, truthful, conspicuous and easily accessible ... at appropriate stages of consumers' decision making, particularly before consumers confirm transactions or provide any personal information."
- **Describe products fully.** Customers want to know what they are buying. You should describe your products accurately and in detail, and include any information that customers would see if they bought the product in a store, such as health and safety warnings or suggestions for parental supervision. If you neglect to fully disclose product information, or deliver a product materially different from that described, you must honour any refund request, including charges the buyer incurred for returning the product.
- **Respect consumers' right to privacy.** As an online vendor, you must make your privacy policy easily accessible on your Web site. Tell your customers the kind of information you collect, its purpose, how it will be used, and to whom it may be disclosed. Consumers must know how they can review their personal information, and, when necessary, how they can correct or remove it. You cannot require your customers to disclose personal data as a condition of sale beyond that needed to complete the transaction. Your customer's right to privacy also extends to unsolicited e-mail. The *Code of Practice* notes that online vendors should not send e-mail to customers without their consent, and that marketing messages should include a provision, in plain language, for removal from electronic marketing messages, with a return e-mail address for that purpose.

You can learn more about the *Canadian Code of Practice for Consumer Protection in Electronic Commerce* at **strategis.ic.gc.ca/SSG/ca01861e.html**.

CAREER APPLICATIONS

1. Review two Web sites that sell products online, such as **www.canadiantire.com** or **www.mec.com** (Mountain Equipment Co-op). In what areas do they follow the guidelines set for in the *Canadian Code of Practice for Consumer Protection in Electronic Commerce*? How can these Web sites be improved in terms of consumer protection?
2. Do you think that following the guidelines in the *Canadian Code of Practice for Consumer Protection in Electronic Commerce* improves the potential of commercial Web sites to sell products? Justify your answer.

Use colourful verbs and adjectives that convey a dynamic image. Be careful, however, not to overdo it: "Your factory floors will sparkle like diamonds" is hard to believe and may prevent your audience from believing the rest of your message.

TALKING ABOUT PRICE

The price that people are willing to pay for a product depends on several factors: the prices of similar products, the general state of the economy, and the psychology of the buyer. Price is a complicated issue and often a sensitive one. So you need to be careful whenever you talk about price in your sales messages.

Whether you highlight or downplay the price of your product, prepare your readers for it. Words such as *luxurious* and *economical* provide unmistakable clues about how your price compares with that of competitors. Such words help your readers accept your price when you finally state it. Here's an example from a sales letter offering a product at a bargain price:

You can prepare readers for your product's price by subtle choice and arrangement of words.

> ***All the Features of Name-Brand Sunglasses at Half the Price!***
> Why pay for a designer name when you can enjoy wearing stylish sunglasses with polarized lenses for $29.99?

If the price is an attractive feature, emphasize it by displaying it prominently.

To de-emphasize price
- Bury actual figures in the middle of a paragraph near the end.
- Mention benefits and favourable money matters before the actual price.
- Break a quantity price into units.
- Compare the price with the cost of some other product or activity.

In this excerpt the price falls right at the end of the paragraph, where it stands out. In addition, the price issue is featured in a bold headline. This technique may even be used as the opening of a letter, if (1) the price is the most important feature and (2) the audience for the letter is value conscious.

If price is not a major selling point, you can handle it in several ways. You could leave the price out altogether or mention it only in an accompanying brochure. You could de-emphasize the price by putting the actual figures in the middle of a paragraph that comes close to the end of your sales letter, well after you've presented the benefits and selling points.

Emphasizing the rarity of the edition signals value and thus prepares the reader for the big-ticket price that follows.

The actual price is buried in the middle of a sentence and is tied in with another reminder of the exclusivity of the offer.

> Only 100 prints of this exclusive, limited-edition lithograph will be created. On June 15, they will be made available to the general public, but you can reserve one now for only $350, the special advance reservation price. Simply rush the enclosed reservation card back today so that your order is in before the June 15 publication date.

The pros also use two other techniques for minimizing price. One technique is to break a quantity price into units. Instead of saying that a case of wine costs $144, you might say that each bottle costs $12. The other technique is to compare your product's price with the cost of some other product or activity: "The cost of owning your own spa is less than you'd pay for a health-club membership." Your aim is to make the cost seem as small and affordable as possible, thereby eliminating price as a possible objection.

SUPPORTING YOUR CLAIMS

You can't assume that people will believe what you say about your product just because you've said it in writing. You'll have to prove your claims. Support is especially important if your product is complicated, costs a lot, or represents some unusual approach.

Types of support for product claims:
- Samples
- Brochures
- Examples
- Testimonials
- Statistics
- Guarantees

Support for your claims may take several forms. Samples and brochures, often with photographs, are enclosed in a sales package and are referred to in the letter. The letter also describes or typographically highlights examples of how the product has benefited others. It includes testimonials (quotations from satisfied customers) or cites statistics from scientific studies of the product's performance. Guarantees of exchange or return privileges may be woven into the letter or set off in a special way, indicating that you have faith in your product and are willing to back it up.

It's almost impossible to provide too much support. Try to anticipate every question your audience may want to ask. Put yourself in your audience's place so that you can discover, and solve, all the "what if" scenarios.[18]

USING THE AIDA PLAN IN SALES MESSAGES

Most sales letters are prepared according to the AIDA plan used for any persuasive message. You begin with an attention-getting device, generate interest by describing some of the product's unique features, increase the desire for your product by highlighting the benefits that are most appealing to your audience, and close by suggesting the action you want the audience to take.

Getting Attention Like other persuasive messages, sales letters start with an attention-getting device; however, the emphasis of the attention phase is slightly different. Sales-letter professionals use some common techniques to attract their audience's attention. One popular technique is opening with a provocative question. Look closely at the following three examples. Which seems most interesting to you?

> How would you like straight A's this semester?
> Get straight A's this semester!
> Now you can get straight A's this semester, with ...

If you're like most people, you'll find the first option the most enticing. The question invites your response—a positive response designed to encourage you to read on. The second option is fairly interesting too, but its commanding tone may make you wary of the claim. The third option is acceptable, but it certainly conveys no sense of excitement. Its quick introduction of the product may lead you to a snap decision against reading further.

Other techniques can also help you open your sales letters with excitement. You can grab your audience's attention by emphasizing

Certain tried-and-true attention-getting devices are used in sales letters for a wide variety of products.

- **A piece of genuine news.** "In the past 60 days, mortgage rates have fallen to a 30-year low."
- **A personal appeal to the reader's emotions and values.** "The only thing worse than paying taxes is paying taxes when you don't have to."
- **Your product's most attractive feature along with the associated benefit.** "New control device ends problems with employee pilferage!"
- **An intriguing number.** "Here are three great secrets of the world's most-loved entertainers."
- **A sample of the product.** "Here's your free sample of the new Romalite packing sheet."
- **A concrete illustration with story appeal.** "In 1990 Earl Colbert set out to find a better way to process credit applications. After 10 years of trial and error, he finally developed a procedure so simple and yet thorough that he was cited for service to the industry by the North American Creditors Association."
- **A specific trait shared by the audience.** "Busy executives need another complicated 'time-saving' device like they need a hole in the head!"
- **A challenge.** "Don't waste another day wondering how you're going to become the success you've always wanted to be!"
- **A solution to a problem.** "Tired of arctic air rushing through the cracks around your windows? Stay warm and save energy with StormSeal Weather-stripping."

Look at your own mail to see how many sales messages use these few techniques. Such attention-getting devices will give your sales letters added impact. Look back at Figure 9-5 on page 250 for a typical example.

Choose an attention-getter that encourages the reader to read more.

Sales-message professionals know that textual openings aren't the only way to get attention. Advertisements and catalogues, such as those produced by Patagonia, the outdoor gear and apparel company, capture attention and heighten emotional desire by featuring lush, vibrant photographs of nature. Professionals also use a variety of formatting devices to get attention. You can grab your audience by using personalized salutations, special sizes or styles of type, underlining, bullets, colour, indentations, and so on (see Figure 9-6 below). Even so, not all attention-getting devices are equally effective. The best is the one that makes your audience read the rest of your message.

To determine your product's central selling point, ask

- What does the competition offer?
- What is special about my product?
- What are potential buyers really looking for?

Building Interest In the interest section of your message, highlight your product's key selling point. Say that your company's alarm device is relatively inexpensive, durable, and tamperproof. Although these are all attractive features, you want to focus on only one. Ask what the competition has to offer, what most distinguishes your product, and what most concerns potential buyers. The answers to these questions will help you select the central selling point, the single point around which to build your sales message. Build your audience's interest by highlighting this point, and make it stand out through typography, design, or high-impact writing.[19]

Determining the central selling point will also help you define the benefits to potential buyers. Perhaps your company built its new alarm to overcome competing products' susceptibility to tampering. Being tamperproof is the feature you choose as your central selling point, and its benefit to readers is that burglars won't be able to break in so easily.

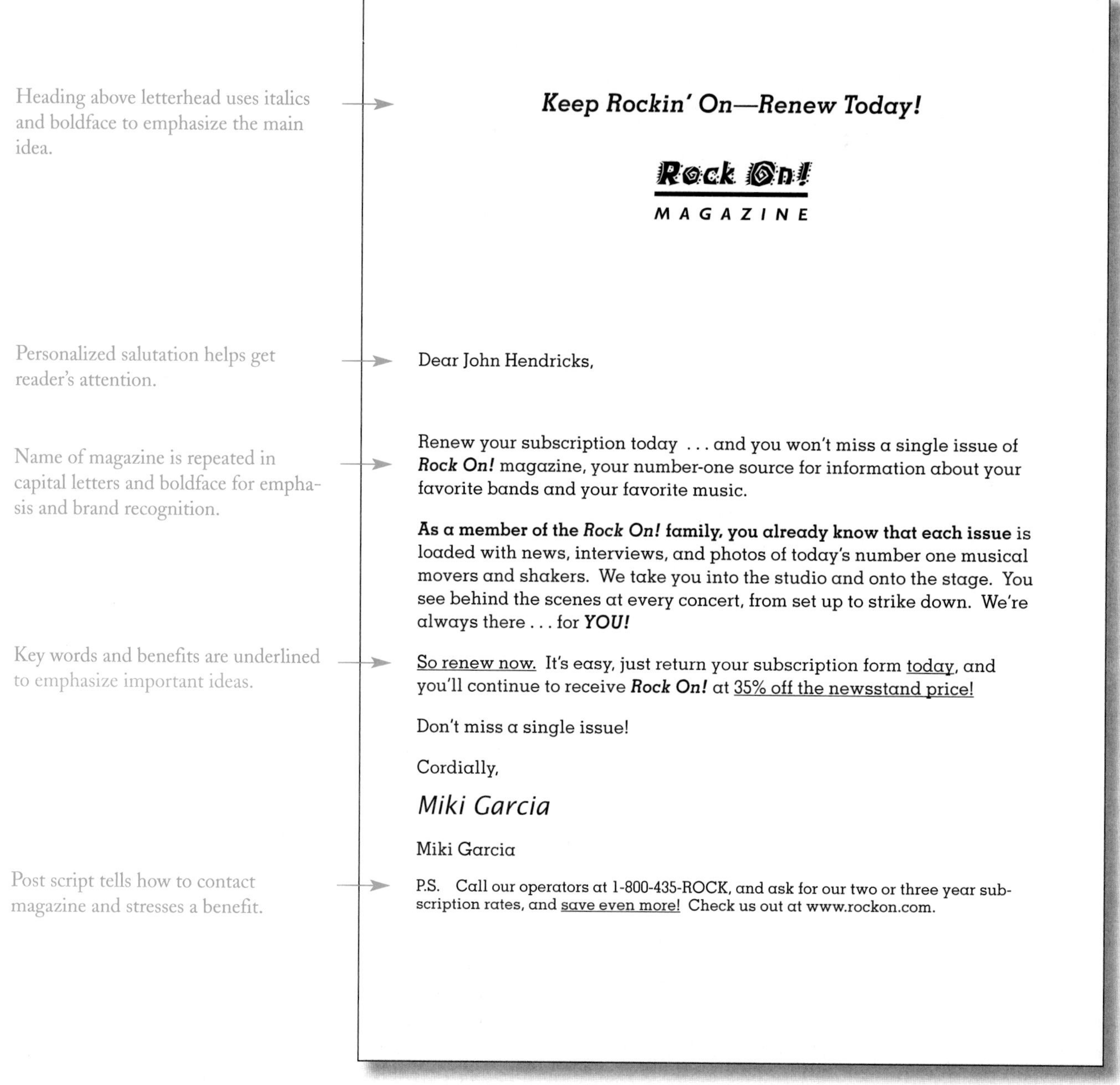

Keep Rockin' On—Renew Today!

Rock On!
MAGAZINE

Dear John Hendricks,

Renew your subscription today . . . and you won't miss a single issue of ***Rock On!*** magazine, your number-one source for information about your favorite bands and your favorite music.

As a member of the *Rock On!* family, you already know that each issue is loaded with news, interviews, and photos of today's number one musical movers and shakers. We take you into the studio and onto the stage. You see behind the scenes at every concert, from set up to strike down. We're always there . . . for ***YOU!***

So renew now. It's easy, just return your subscription form today, and you'll continue to receive ***Rock On!*** at 35% off the newsstand price!

Don't miss a single issue!

Cordially,

Miki Garcia

Miki Garcia

P.S. Call our operators at 1-800-435-ROCK, and ask for our two or three year subscription rates, and save even more! Check us out at www.rockon.com.

Heading above letterhead uses italics and boldface to emphasize the main idea.
Personalized salutation helps get reader's attention.
Name of magazine is repeated in capital letters and boldface for emphasis and brand recognition.
Key words and benefits are underlined to emphasize important ideas.
Post script tells how to contact magazine and stresses a benefit.

FIGURE 9–6 In-Depth Critique: Sales Letter with Formatting Devices

To increase desire, expand your main benefit while adding others.

Increasing Desire In the desire section, mention your main benefit repeatedly, expanding and explaining as you go. Use both words and pictures, if possible. This main benefit is what will entice recipients to read on and take further action.

As you continue to stress your main benefit, weave in references to other benefits. ("You can get this worry-free protection for much less than you might think," and "The same technology that makes it difficult for burglars to crack your alarm system makes the device durable, even when it must be exposed to the elements.") Remember, sales letters reflect the "you" attitude through references to benefits, so always phrase the selling points in terms of what your product's features can do for potential customers.

Keep in mind that you don't need to provide every last detail as you explain product benefits. The best letters are short (preferably one but no more than two pages). They include enough detail to spur the reader's interest, but they don't try to be the sole source of information. Also, remember to use bullet points to highlight details whenever possible. You have to assume that your readers are pressed for time and are interested only in what matters most to them.[20]

Motivating Action In the last section, you explain clearly how to take the next step. After all, the overriding purpose of a sales letter is to get your reader to do something. Many consumer products sold through the mail simply ask for a cheque—in other words, an immediate decision to buy. On the other hand, companies selling big-ticket and more complex items frequently ask for just a small step toward the final buying decision, such as sending for more information or authorizing a call by a sales representative.

Aim to get the reader to act as soon as possible.

Whatever you ask readers to do, try to persuade them to do it right away. Convince them that they must act now, perhaps to guarantee a specific delivery date. If there's no particular reason to act quickly, many sales letters offer discounts for orders placed by a certain date or prizes or special offers to, say, the first 500 people to respond. Others suggest that purchases be charged to a credit card or be paid off over time. Still others offer a free trial, an unconditional guarantee, or a no-strings request card for information—all in an effort to overcome readers' natural inertia.

Of course, adding a P.S. (post script) is one of the most effective ways to boost audience response (see Figure 9-6 on page 254). This is the place to make your final impression, so be sure the information is noteworthy. Use the P.S. to reiterate your primary benefit, make an additional offer, or compel the reader to act quickly by emphasizing a deadline.[21]

Finally, use good judgment when distributing your messages to would-be customers, especially when using e-mail. Unwanted e-mail, or "spam," is annoying and will deter people from buying your products. It's been estimated that in a company of 100 workers, the cost of productivity to deleting spam can exceed $250 000 U.S. per year, a figure that will grow as spam continues to fill e-mail boxes.[22]

Strategies for Fundraising Messages

Fundraising letters use many of the same techniques that are used in sales letters.

Motivating action is a challenge for the best sales letters. Even more of a challenge is motivating action when you're trying to raise funds. Most of the techniques used to write sales letters can also be used to write fundraising letters, as long as your techniques match your audience, your goals, and the cause or organization you're representing. Be careful to establish value in the minds of your donors. Above all, don't forget to include the "what's in it for me?" information: for example, telling your readers how good they'll feel by making a donation.[23] "In fund raising," says direct-mail expert Dean Reick, "emotions are important because, unlike the marketing of products and services, there is no tangible, personal benefit in the transaction. Fund raising is all about triggering and channeling emotional responses."[24] To make sure that your fundraising letters outshine the competition's letters, take some time to plan your message before you actually begin writing.[25] You can begin by reading the mail you receive from donors. Learn as much as you can about your audience by noting the tone of these letters, the language used, and the concerns raised. This exercise will help you write letters that donors will both understand and relate to.

You might also keep a file of competing fundraising letters. Study these samples to find out what other fundraisers are doing and what new approaches they're taking. Most important, find out what works and what doesn't. Then you can continue with your other research efforts, such as conducting interviews, holding focus groups, and reading trade journals to find out what people are concerned about, what they're interested in, and what gets their attention.

Finally, before you start writing, know whose benefits to emphasize. Make a two-column list; on one side, list what your organization does, and on the other side, list what your donors want. You'll discover that the two columns are quite different. Make sure that the benefits you emphasize are related to what your donors want,

Be sure to focus on the concerns of your readers, who want to know how their donations will be used. Human interest stories are the best way to interest your readers in fundraising letters.

not to what your organization does. Then you can work on stating those donor benefits in specific detail. For example: "Your donation of $100 will provide 15 people with a Thanksgiving dinner."

PERSONALIZING FUNDRAISING MESSAGES

Because fundraising letters depend so heavily on emotional appeals, keep your message personal. A natural, real-life lead-in usually gets your reader emotionally involved in your cause. Storytelling is perfect when your narrative is unforced and goes straight to the heart of the matter; relevant human-interest stories present the faces of the people donors are helping.[26] Your fundraising messages should sound like one individual writing to another: don't make a sales pitch, but talk to your reader in a warm and personal way. You want to make a personal connection.[27] Also consider personalizing the appearance of your message: instead of using a word-processed font throughout, consider including a brief, handwritten paragraph. The personalized appearance of a partially handwritten section can raise the number of donations: one nonprofit organization that used this strategy more than tripled its income.[28]

Personalize fundraising letters by helping your readers identify with recipients.

It's also up to you to help your donors identify with recipients. A busy company executive may not be able to identify with the homeless person she passes on the street every day. But every human being understands pain; we've all felt it. So do your best to portray that homeless person's pain using words that the busy executive can understand.[29]

STRENGTHENING FUNDRAISING MESSAGES

OBJECTIVE 6 List eight guidelines that will help you strengthen your fundraising messages.

The best fundraising letters do four things: (1) thoroughly explain a specific need, (2) show how important it is for readers to help, (3) spell out exactly what amount of help is being requested, and (4) describe in detail the benefits of helping.[30] To help you accomplish these four major tasks, here are some fundraising guidelines:[31]

Strong fundraising letters
- Explain a specific need thoroughly
- Show how important it is for readers to help
- Spell out exactly what amount of help is being requested
- Describe in detail the benefits of helping

- **Interest your readers immediately.** If you don't catch your readers' interest at the absolute beginning of your letter, you never will. And keep in mind that the envelope is a critical tool for getting your donor to read the message. A brief attention-getting statement, such as news about your cause, a call for help, or a short introduction to a person described in your message, will motivate readers to open the envelope, learn about your cause, and discover how they can help.[32]
- **Use simple language.** Tell your story with simple, warm, and personal language. Nothing else is as effective in getting people to empathize.
- **Give readers an opportunity to accomplish something important.** Donors want to feel needed. They want the emotional fulfillment of coming to your rescue. Educate your readers about your cause.[33]
- **Make it hard to say "no."** Make the need so urgent and strong that your readers will find it difficult to turn you down. Use details to humanize your appeal. Your reader should become familiar with individuals described in your message and with your organization and its activities.
- **Make your needs clear.** Leave no doubt about the amount of money that you want. Be absolutely clear, and be sure the amount requested is appropriate for your audience. Explain why the money is needed as soon as possible. Many fundraisers offer donors different contribution levels in their messages or the option to spread out payments. Giving donors a choice of options will make a donation more likely.[34]
- **Feel free to write two-page letters.** Don't believe donors will read only one-page messages. If you need to develop your story onto a second page, do so.[35] Often, longer messages are best for fundraising. Just keep sentences and paragraphs short, maximize content, and minimize wordiness.
- **Make your reply form complete and thorough.** Include all the basics: your name, address, and telephone number; a restatement of your request and the gift amount; your donor's name and address (or space enough for a label); information on payment options (cheque or credit card); and information on tax deductibility. Also

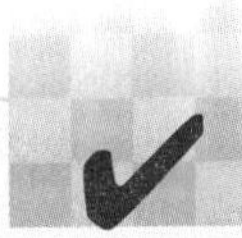

Checklist: Composing Sales and Fundraising Letters

Attention

✓ Design a positive opening that awakens a favourable association with the product, need, or cause.

✓ Write the opening so that it's appropriate, fresh, honest, interesting, specific, and relevant.

✓ Promise a benefit to the reader.

✓ Keep the first paragraph short, preferably two to five lines, and sometimes only one.

✓ For sales letters, get attention with a provocative question, a significant/startling fact, a solution to a problem, a special offer/gift, a testimonial, a current event, an illustration, a comparison, an event in the reader's life, a problem the reader may face, or a quotation.

✓ For fundraising letters, design an attention-getter that uses a human-interest story.

Interest

✓ State information clearly, vividly, and persuasively, and relate it to the reader's concerns.

✓ Develop the central selling point.

✓ Feature the product or charitable need in two ways: physical description and reader benefits.

✓ Place benefits first, or interweave them with a physical description.

✓ Describe objective details of the need or product (size, shape, colour, scent, sound, texture, etc.).

✓ Use psychological appeals to present the sensation, satisfaction, or pleasure readers will gain.

✓ Blend cold facts with warm feelings.

Desire

✓ Enlist one or more appeals to support the central idea (selling point or fundraising goal).

✓ If the product is valued mainly because of its appearance, describe its physical details.

✓ If the product is machinery or technical equipment, describe its sturdy construction, fine crafting, and other technical details in terms that help readers visualize themselves using it.

✓ Include technical sketches and meaningful pictures, charts, and graphs, if necessary.

✓ For sales letters, provide test results from recognized experts, laboratories, or authoritative agencies.

✓ To raise funds, detail how donations are spent, using recognized accounting/auditing firms.

✓ To elicit donations, use strong visual details, good narrative, active verbs, and limited adjectives.

✓ Emphasize reader benefits.

✓ Anticipate and answer the reader's questions.

✓ Use an appropriate form of proof.

✓ Include verifiable reports/statistics about users' experience what the product or organization.

✓ Provide names (with permission only) of satisfied buyers, users, or donors.

✓ Present unexaggerated testimonials from persons or firms whose judgment readers respect.

✓ In sales letters, offer a free trial or a guarantee, and refer to samples if they are included.

✓ Note any enclosures in conjunction with a selling point or a reader benefit.

Action

✓ Clearly state the action you desire.

✓ Provide specific details on how to order the product, donate money, or reach your organization.

✓ Ease action with reply cards, pre-addressed envelopes, phone numbers, follow-up phone calls.

✓ Offer a special inducement to act now: time limit or situation urgency, special price for a limited time, premium for acting before a certain date, gift for acting, free trial, no obligation to buy with more information or demonstration, easy payments with no money down, credit-card payments.

✓ Supply a final reader benefit.

✓ In a postscript, convey important donation information or an important sales point (if desired).

consider secure payment on your organization's Web site as a convenient way for the donor to send the donation.

➤ **Use interesting enclosures.** Enclosures that simply give more information will decrease returns. Instead, use enclosures that are helpful or that give the donor something to do, sign, return, or keep. The War Amps of Canada, for example, include a uniquely numbered key tag on a chain to ensure the return of lost car keys.

These guidelines should help you reach the humanity and compassion of your readers by focusing on specific reader benefits, detailing the unique need, emphasizing the urgency of the situation, and spelling out the exact help needed.

Rita Gomez, the director of PETsMART Charities, has the task of raising millions of dollars to help save the lives of and find families for hundreds of thousands of homeless pets; this program began operating in Canada in 1999.[36]

Like sales letters, fundraising letters are simply particular types of persuasive messages. Both categories have their unique requirements, some of which only professional writers can master. (See this chapter's "Checklist: Composing Sales and Fundraising Letters" on page 257 as a reminder of the tasks involved in writing these messages.)

Summary of Learning Outcomes

1 Discuss the planning tasks that need extra attention when preparing persuasive messages. Because persuasive messages can be complicated and sensitive, several planning tasks need extra attention. You'll be persuading people to take action that they probably wouldn't have taken without your message, so analyzing your purpose is crucial. In addition, audience analysis may be more detailed for persuasive messages, gauging psychological and social needs in addition to cultural differences. Also, when persuading a skeptical audience, your credibility must be unquestionable, so you may need to spend some extra effort to establish it. Since your attempts to persuade could be viewed by some as manipulative, you need to strive for the highest ethical standards.

2 Distinguish between emotional and logical appeals, and discuss how to balance them. Emotional appeals call on human feelings, using arguments that are based on audience needs or sympathies. However, these appeals aren't effective by themselves. Logical appeals call on human reason (whether using analogy, induction, or deduction). If you're careful to avoid faulty logic, you can use logic together with emotion, thereby supplying rational support for an idea that readers have already embraced emotionally. In general, logic will be your strongest appeal, with only subtle emotion. However, when persuading someone to purchase a product, join a cause, or make a donation, you can heighten emotional appeals a bit.

3 Describe the AIDA plan for persuasive messages. When using the AIDA plan, you open your message by getting *attention* with a reader benefit, a problem, a stimulating question, a piece of news, or an unexpected statement. You build *interest* with facts, details, and additional reader benefits. You increase *desire* by providing more evidence and reader benefits and by anticipating and answering possible objections. You conclude by motivating a specific *action,* emphasizing the positive results of that action, and making it easy for the reader to respond.

4 Explain the best way to overcome resistance to your persuasive message, and list four common mistakes. The best way to overcome resistance is to think of all the objections your audience could possibly have and then explain the pros and cons of all sides. Provide solutions to all the problems your audience might perceive. In addition, make sure you do not (1) use an up-front hard sell, (2) rule out compromise, (3) rely solely on great arguments while ignoring how you present them, and (4) assume your persuasive attempt is a one-time effort.

5 Compare sales messages with fundraising messages. Sales messages are used by for-profit companies to persuade readers to make a purchase for themselves. In contrast, fundraising messages are used by nonprofit organizations to persuade readers to donate their time or their money to help others. However, these two types of persuasive messages have a lot in common. Primarily, they both try to persuade readers to "buy" (with time or money) the value that is being offered (the product or the cause). In addition, both types of persuasive message generally use the AIDA plan.

6 List eight guidelines that will help you strengthen your fundraising messages. To strengthen your fundraising messages, follow these guidelines: (1) interest your readers immediately, (2) use simple language, (3) give your readers the chance to do something important, (4) make it hard to say no, (5) make your needs clear, (6) write no longer than you have to, (7) make your reply form complete and thorough, (8) use interesting enclosures.

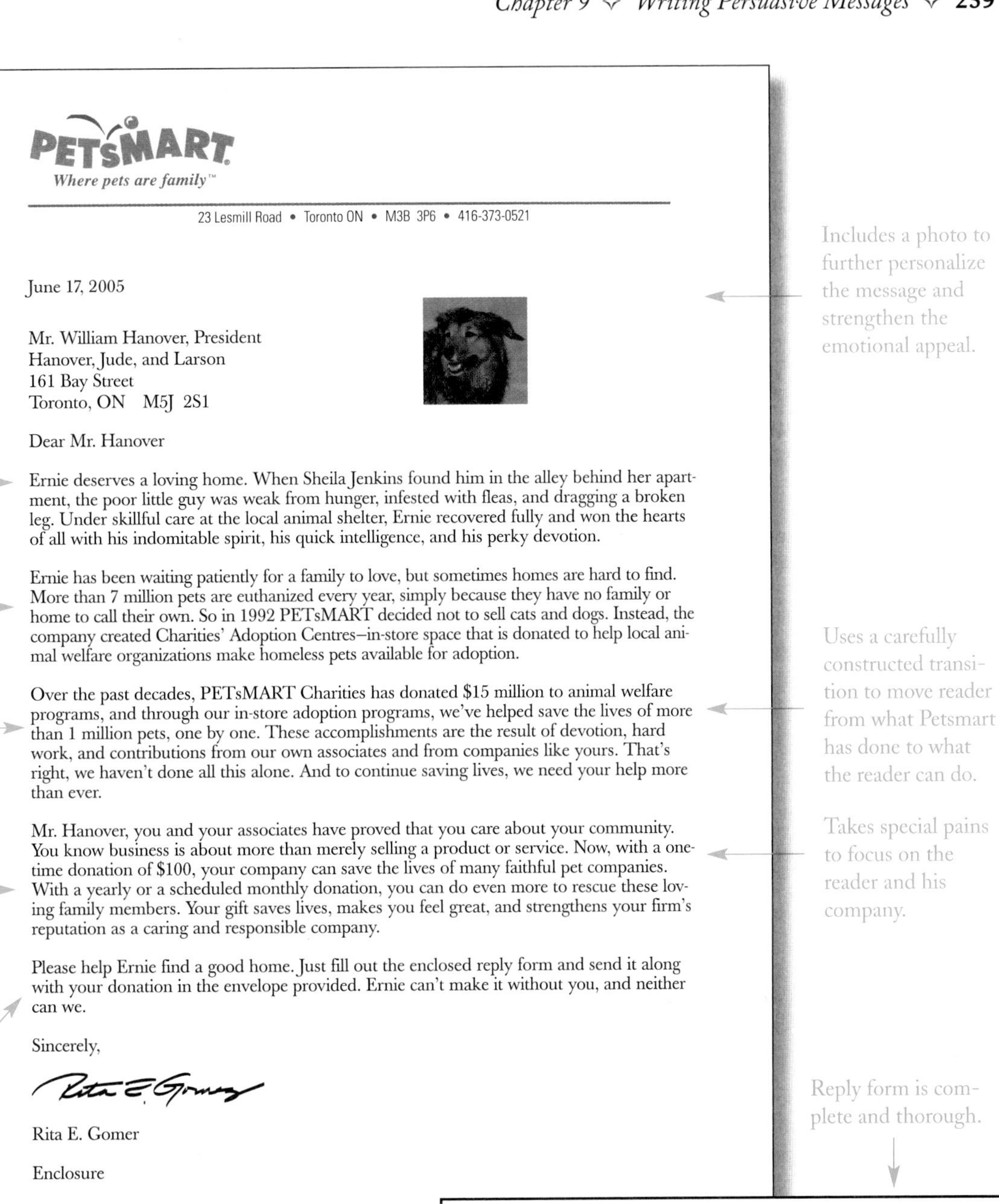

PETsMART
Where pets are family™

23 Lesmill Road • Toronto ON • M3B 3P6 • 416-373-0521

June 17, 2005

Mr. William Hanover, President
Hanover, Jude, and Larson
161 Bay Street
Toronto, ON M5J 2S1

Dear Mr. Hanover

Ernie deserves a loving home. When Sheila Jenkins found him in the alley behind her apartment, the poor little guy was weak from hunger, infested with fleas, and dragging a broken leg. Under skillful care at the local animal shelter, Ernie recovered fully and won the hearts of all with his indomitable spirit, his quick intelligence, and his perky devotion.

Ernie has been waiting patiently for a family to love, but sometimes homes are hard to find. More than 7 million pets are euthanized every year, simply because they have no family or home to call their own. So in 1992 PETsMART decided not to sell cats and dogs. Instead, the company created Charities' Adoption Centres–in-store space that is donated to help local animal welfare organizations make homeless pets available for adoption.

Over the past decades, PETsMART Charities has donated $15 million to animal welfare programs, and through our in-store adoption programs, we've helped save the lives of more than 1 million pets, one by one. These accomplishments are the result of devotion, hard work, and contributions from our own associates and from companies like yours. That's right, we haven't done all this alone. And to continue saving lives, we need your help more than ever.

Mr. Hanover, you and your associates have proved that you care about your community. You know business is about more than merely selling a product or service. Now, with a one-time donation of $100, your company can save the lives of many faithful pet companies. With a yearly or a scheduled monthly donation, you can do even more to rescue these loving family members. Your gift saves lives, makes you feel great, and strengthens your firm's reputation as a caring and responsible company.

Please help Ernie find a good home. Just fill out the enclosed reply form and send it along with your donation in the envelope provided. Ernie can't make it without you, and neither can we.

Sincerely,

Rita E. Gomer

Rita E. Gomer

Enclosure

Includes a photo to further personalize the message and strengthen the emotional appeal.

Gains attention by personalizing the message with a real-life story.

Increases interest by providing hard (even painful) numbers and details of just what Petsmart Charities does.

Uses a carefully constructed transition to move reader from what Petsmart has done to what the reader can do.

Creates a desire to be involved by sharing specific successes of the program.

Takes special pains to focus on the reader and his company.

Makes the request by stating the benefits of the reader's donation to others as well as to the reader.

Closes by echoing the real-life story that opened the message and repeating the request for specific action.

Reply form is complete and thorough.

TO HELP PETsMART CHARITIES SAVE LIVES

______________________ (company)
______________________ (address)

WISHES TO DONATE

❑ $100
❑ $____ each year
❑ $____ a month (for 12 months)

❑ By cheque (enclosed)
❑ By credit card:
____ Visa ____ Mastercard ____ Discover

Card No.: ______________
Signature: ______________
Position: ______________

FIGURE 9–7 In-Depth Critique: Letter to Raise Funds

ON THE JOB

Solving a Communication Dilemma at the Young Entrepreneurs' Association

Since its founding in 1992, the Young Entrepreneurs' Association has helped hundreds of young Canadians to start and develop their businesses. Students who join the YEA have opportunities to make contacts and discuss their plans with peers and mentors. YEA meetings are conducted in an environment where members can "comfortably share their triumphs and challenges, ideas, experiences and knowledge." Members may attend programs such as the "Successful Entrepreneurs' Series," "Presidents' Roundtables," the "Business Expert Series," and "Breakfast Brainstorming." Growing quickly in Ontario, the YEA began to expand nationally in 1997 and now has chapters established in Victoria, Vancouver, Halifax, and St. John's and under development in Kelowna, Calgary, Regina, Winnipeg, Moncton, and Fredericton. A non-profit organization, the YEA is assisted by such established companies as Royal Bank, MediaRidge Communicaitons, and Sporg Internet Corporation, and is eager to receive any kind of help that will enable them to further their goals.

Your Mission: As a member of the YEA's Board of Directors, one of your duties is to contact the chairpersons of business programs at Canadian universities and colleges, seeking their support for YEA activities and programs. Use your knowledge of persuasive messages to choose the *best* alternative in each of the following situations. Be prepared to explain why your choice is the most effective one.

1 You have been allocated the job of drafting a form letter to be sent to the chairpersons of business programs in Canada where new chapters of the Young Entrepreneurs' Association are established, but the members don't yet have a designated office. The chairpersons are already familiar with the work of the YEA. Which of the following versions is the best attention-getter for this letter?

a No, this isn't a letter asking for a financial contribution. We know are looking for a valuable resource you may be able to share with us: a few hundred square feet of unused office space.

b Don't let that unused office space go to waste! Let the YEA take that space off your hands. We're looking for a vacant room in your department. If you let us have any office space you're not using, you'll be giving your students a chance to meet with their fellow YEA members.

c If you could put your empty office space to productive use by helping your students, wouldn't you be interested? Donate some of your department's unused space to the Young Entrepreneurs' Association chapter at your school. You'll gain the satisfaction of helping your students by giving them a central place to meet and to learn from the success of other young business people.

2 Which of the following versions is the most effective interest and desire section for your letter?

a You may have one medium-sized office, or even a portion of an open work space, that you no longer use. Just 121-square metres would allow the chapter president and secretary to have enough space to maintain a place where they can perform administrative work and hold meetings with members. We would be able to adapt any empty office to our needs, regardless of its location. We would supply our own computers, printer, fax machine, and furniture. By donating space to your school's chapter of the Young Entrepreneurs' Association, you will be able to enhance your students' studies by providing a location where they can share ideas and information in a relaxed atmosphere. You will see them take into the classroom the enthusiasm they've developed from seeing how entrepreneurs started their own businesses and became successful.

b The officers of your school's YEA branch can work productively in as little as 121-square metres of office space. So please look around. Check every nook and cranny in your facility. See whether you have a large office, or a portion of an open work area you no longer use that may be suitable.

You will be proud of your department's donation, which will help the YEA serve your students. Help us educate the next generation of entrepreneurs by donating your unused office space today!

c The Young Entrepreneurs' Association needs your help. Any office space—as little as 121-square metres—will help us put local representatives near the students they serve. Please take a moment to see whether you have one large office, or a portion of an open work area, that you no longer use.

If you donate this empty space, we'll take care of the details. We'll both benefit. You'll unload space you don't need, and we'll be able to have a place to operate. But the people who will benefit most will be your students.

3 Which of the following versions would be the best action section for your letter?

a Your donation of unused office space will make a real difference to the YEA and to the students we serve. If you have any questions about donating office space, please call me at 905-555-6541. I'd be happy to discuss the details with you.

b Your donation of free office space for our local chapter of the YEA would be much appreciated. If you have any space that you are able to donate, call me immediately at 905-555-6541 and I will be ready to answer any questions about donating space that you have.

c If you can donate unused office space, you will help your student members of the YEA immeasurably. If you are willing to donate space, please take a moment to call me at 905-555-6541. I will try to answer any questions you have about donating space.

4 University and college newspapers managed and written by students are common on many campuses. Imagine that the YEA has put together an advertisement they would like to place in as many of these newspapers as possible, but because of limited funds, they would like the advertising space to be donated. Which of the following appeals to your audience would be most effective in a letter seeking free advertising space?

a An entirely emotional appeal stressing the needs of the YEA and the satisfaction of helping a worthy cause.

b An entirely logical appeal stressing that the advertisements can be inserted whenever the newspapers have unused space, thus saving editors the trouble of rearranging articles and other advertisements to make the page look good, or using meaningless filler.

c A combination of emotional and logical appeals, stressing both the satisfaction of helping a worthy cause and the rationale behind printing the advertisement whenever the editors have available space.[37]

Test Your Knowledge

Review Questions

1 How do emotional appeals differ from logical appeals?
2 What is the AIDA plan, and how does it apply to persuasive messages?
3 What are four common mistakes to avoid when developing a persuasive message to overcome resistance?
4 What are the similarities and differences between sales messages and fundraising messages?
5 What are some similarities between sales messages and bad-news messages?
6 What are some questions to ask when gauging the audience's needs during the planning of a persuasive message?
7 What role do demographics and psychographics play in audience analysis during the planning of a persuasive message?
8 What are four of the ways you can build credibility with an audience when planning a persuasive message?
9 What three types of reasoning can you use in logical appeals?
10 How can semantics affect a persuasive message?
11 How do benefits differ from features?

Interactive Learning 

Use This Text's Online Resources

Visit our Companion Web site at **www.pearsoned.ca/thill**, where you can use the interactive Study Guide to test your chapter knowledge and get instant feedback. Additional resources link you to the sites mentioned in this text and to additional sources of information on chapter topics.

Also check out the resources on the Mastering Business Communication CD, including "Perils of Pauline," an interactive presentation of the business communication challenges within a fictional company. For Chapter 9, see in particular the episode "Writing Persuasive Messages".

Apply Your Knowledge

Critical Thinking Questions

1 Why is it important to present both sides of an argument when writing a persuasive message to a potentially hostile audience?
2 How are persuasive messages different from routine messages?
3 When is it appropriate to use the direct organizational approach in persuasive messages?
4 As an employee, how many of your daily tasks require persuasion? List as many as you can think of. Who are your audiences, and how do their needs and characteristics affect the way you develop your persuasive messages at work?
5. **Ethical Choices** Are emotional appeals ethical? Why or why not?

Practice Your Knowledge

Documents for Analysis

Read the following documents, then (1) analyze the strengths and weaknesses of each sentence and (2) revise each document so that it follows this chapter's guidelines.

Document 9.A: Writing Persuasive Requests for Action

At Tolson Auto Repair, we have been in business for over 25 years. We stay in business by always taking into account what the customer wants. That's why we are writing. We want to know your opinions to be able to better conduct our business.

Take a moment right now and fill out the enclosed questionnaire. We know everyone is busy, but this is just one way we have of making sure our people do their job correctly. Use the enclosed envelope to return the questionnaire.

And again, we're happy you chose Tolson Auto Repair. We want to take care of all your auto needs.

Document 9.B: Writing Persuasive Claims and Requests for Adjustment

Dear Gateway:

I'm writing to you because of my disappointment with my new TelePath X2 Faxmodem. The modem works all right, but the volume is set wide open and the volume knob doesn't turn it down. It's driving us crazy. The volume knob doesn't seem to be connected to anything but simply spins around. I can't believe you would put out a product like this without testing it first.

I depend on the modem to run my small business and want to know what you are going to do about it. This reminds me of every time I buy electronic equipment from what seems like any company. Something is always wrong. I thought quality was supposed to be important, but I guess not.

Anyway, I need this fixed right away. Please tell me what you want me to do.

Document 9.C: Writing Sales and Fundraising Letters

We know how awful dining hall food can be, and that's why we've developed the "Mealaweek Club." Once a week, we'll deliver food to your dormitory or apartment. Our meals taste great. We have pizza, buffalo wings, hamburgers and curly fries, veggie roll-ups, and more!

When you sign up for just six months, we will ask what day you want your delivery. We'll ask you to fill out your selection of meals. And the rest is up to us. At "Mealaweek," we deliver! And payment is easy. We accept MasterCard and VISA or a personal check. It will save you money especially when compared with eating out.

Just fill out the enclosed card and indicate your method of payment. As soon as we approve your credit or check, we'll begin delivery. Tell all your friends about Mealaweek. We're the best idea since sliced bread!

Exercises

9–1 What type of reasoning is at work in the following statement: "We've lost money on 48 of the 52 power plants we've constructed in South America in the last 10 years. It's obvious that it's impossible to turn a profit in that market." In which persuasive messages would this type of reasoning be appropriate?

9–2 **Teamwork** With another student, analyze the persuasive memo at Host Marriott (Figure 9–3 on page 245) by answering the following questions:

a What techniques are used to capture the reader's attention?
b Does the writer use the direct or the indirect organizational approach? Why?
c Is the subject line effective? Why or why not?
d Does the writer use an emotional or a logical appeal? Why?
e What reader benefits are included?
f How does the writer establish credibility?
g What tools does the writer use to reinforce his position?

9–3 Compose effective subject lines for the following persuasive memos:

a A request to your supervisor to purchase a new high-speed laser printer for your office. You've been outsourcing quite a bit of your printing to AlphaGraphics and you're certain this printer will pay for itself in six months.
b A direct mailing to area residents soliciting customers for your new business "Meals à la Car," a carryout dining service that delivers from most local-area restaurants. All local restaurant menus are on the Internet. Mom and Dad can dine on egg rolls and chow mein while the kids munch on pepperoni pizza.
c A special request to the company president to allow managers to carry over their unused vacation days to the following year. Apparently, many managers cancelled their fourth-quarter vacation plans to work on the installation of a new company computer system. Under their current contract, vacation days not used by December 31 aren't accruable.

9–4 **Ethical Choices** Your boss has asked you to draft a memo asking everyone in your department to donate money to the company's favourite charity, an organization that operates a special summer camp for physically challenged children. You wind up writing a three-page memo packed with facts and heartwarming anecdotes about the camp and the children's experiences. When you must work that hard to persuade your audience to take an action such as donating money to a charity, aren't you being manipulative and unethical? Explain.

9–5 Determine whether the following sentences focus on features or benefits; rewrite as necessary to focus all the sentences on benefits.

a All-Cook skillets are coated with a durable, patented nonstick surface.

b You can call anyone and talk as long you like on Saturdays and Sundays with this new mobile telephone service.

c We need to raise $25 to provide each needy child with a backpack filled with school supplies.

9–6 Internet Visit the *Canadian Consumer Handbook* Web site at **strategis.ic.gc.ca/SSG/ca01136e.html**. Read the section on fraud (p. 21). Select one or two sales letters you've recently received and see whether they contain any of the suspicious content mentioned in the warnings. What does the *Canadian Consumer Handbook* suggest you do before you buy (p. 13)?

Cases

Applying the Three-Step Writing Process to Cases

Apply each step to the following cases, as assigned by your instructor.

1 Planning Cases

Analyze

1 What is your general purpose?
2 What is your specific purpose?
3 What do you want readers to do?
4 Who are your readers? (Who is the primary audience? Who is the secondary audience? What do readers have in common? What is their general background? How will they react?)

Investigate

5 What information do readers need?
6 What facts must you gather?

Adapt

7 How will you establish credibility?

2 Writing Cases

Organize

1 What is your main idea?
2 Will you use the direct or indirect approach? Why?

Compose

3 Will your tone be informal or more formal?
4 Draft the message as discussed in the "Your Task" section of the case.

3 Completing Cases

Revise

1 Use the "Checklist for Revising Business Messages" in Chapter 6 to edit and revise your message for clarity.

Produce

2 What's the best way to distribute your message? By fax? By e-mail? By sealed envelope?

Proofread

3 Proofread your message for errors in layout, spelling, and mechanics.

Persuasive Requests for Action

1 Selling an idea: E-mail message to your instructor You went browsing the Web to find out about the Toulmin model for reasoning. You were intrigued by what you found at **www.unl.edu/speech/comm109/Toulmin**. Spend a few minutes exploring the site. Do you think that this Web site is useful for learning how to develop persuasive messages?

Your Task: Write an e-mail message to your instructor to persuade her or him of your opinion.

2 Helping out: Persuasive memo to Good Eats store managers Good Eats is a chain of organic food stores with locations in Ottawa. The stores are big and well lit, like their more traditional grocery store counterparts. They are also teeming with a wide variety of attractively displayed foods and related products.

However, Good Eats is different from the average supermarket. Its products include everything from granola sold in bulk to environmentally sensitive household products. The meats sold come from animals that were never fed antibiotics, and the cheese is from cows said to be raised on small farms and treated humanely.

Along with selling these products to upscale shoppers, the company has been giving food to homeless shelters. Every third weekend, Good Eats donates non-perishable food to three soup kitchens downtown. Company executives believe they are in a unique position to help others.

You work for the Chief Operating Officer (COO) of Good Eats. You've been asked to find ways to expand the donation program by involving the company's eight branches, most of which are in the suburbs. Ideally, the company would be able to increase the number of people it helps and to get more of its employees involved.

You don't have a great deal of extra money for the program, so the emphasis has to be on using resources already available to the stores. One idea is to use trucks from suburban branches to make the program mobile. Another idea is to join forces with a retailing chain to give food and clothing to individuals. The key is to be original and not exclude any idea, no matter how absurd it might seem. The only stipulation is to keep ideas politically neutral. Good Eats executives do not want to be seen as supporting any party or candidate. They just want to be good corporate citizens.

Your Task: Send persuasive memos to all managers at Good Eats, requesting ideas to expand the program. Invite employees to contribute ideas, for this or any other charitable project for the company.[38]

3 Ouch, that hurts! Persuasive memo at Technology One requesting equipment retrofit Mike Andrews leaves your office, shutting the door behind him. The pain in his arm is reflected on his face. He's about to file a worker's compensation claim—your third this month. As human resources director for Technology One, a major software development firm, you're worried not only about costs but also about the well-being of your employees.

Mike's complaints are much the same as those already reported by two other computer technicians: sharp pains in the wrist, numbness, and decreased range of motion. You know that the average technician spends at least six hours a day working on the computer, yet you've never had this many complaints in a short time, and the severity of the symptoms seems to be increasing.

You decide to seek the advice of experts. A local sports and orthopedic medicine clinic gives you a detailed description of repetitive strain injuries, or RSIs. The symptoms they describe are virtually identical to those exhibited by your technicians. You're distressed to learn that, if the cause of these injuries is not found and corrected, your technicians could require surgery or could even become permanently disabled.

The physical therapist at the clinic believes that exercises and wrist splints may help relieve symptoms and could even prevent new injuries. However, she also recommends that you consult an ergonomic analyst who can evaluate the furniture and equipment your technicians are using.

On her advice, you bring in an analyst who spends an entire day at your facility. After measuring desk and chair height, watching technicians at work, and conducting a detailed analysis of all your equipment, he makes two recommendations: (1) throw out all your computer keyboards and replace them with ergonomic keyboards, and (2) replace every mouse with a trackball. Suddenly you realize that the RSI complaints began shortly after your controller and purchasing manager bought a truckload of new computer equipment at a local merchant's going-out-of-business sale. You begin to wonder about the quality and design of that equipment, and you ask the analyst what benefits the changes will provide.

The ergonomic keyboard actually splits the traditional rows of keys in half and places the rows of keys at different angles, allowing the wrists to stay straight and relieving pressure on the forearm. The repetitive motions involved in using a mouse further aggravate the symptoms created by use of the traditional keyboard. Using a trackball does not require the repetitive clicking motion of the forefinger.

Your Task: You know that replacing peripheral equipment on more than 50 computers will be costly, especially when the existing equipment is nearly new. However, increasing RSIs and disability claims could be even more costly. Write a persuasive memo to Katherine Wilson, your controller, and convince her of the immediate need to retrofit the technicians' computer equipment.[39]

4 Travel turnaround: E-mail message at Travelfest convincing your boss to expand client services As a successful travel agent with Travelfest, Inc., you have been both amazed and troubled by the recent changes in the travel industry. The upset started more than a year ago, when airlines stopped paying the customary 10 percent commission on airline tickets. Instead, airlines paid a flat $25 on one-way domestic flights and $50 on round-trip domestic flights. International flights were not affected.

Travelfest is located in Montreal. It has four offices and more than 80 employees. Headquarters are in the centre of downtown, in the lobby of a 35-storey office tower. The other three offices are located in major shopping centres in upscale suburbs. The company's business is made up of about 70 percent corporate and business travel and 30 percent leisure travel. However, much of the leisure business comes from corporate customers.

Your boss, Narindar Pradeep, has been working night and day to make up for declining revenues brought about by the loss of airline commissions. He has tried everything, from direct-mail campaigns to discount coupons to drawings for cruises and weekend getaways. Still, revenues remain flat, and there seems to be no solution in sight.

You've been doing some research and analysis of your office's existing customer profiles. You find that many of your customers are middle- to high-income sophisticated travellers and that, with the expansion of the global economy, foreign travel has increased dramatically in the past 12 months. Your research has triggered some ideas that you believe could substantially increase your revenue from existing customers.

You envision turning your suburban mall office into a travel supermarket. First, since there's such a growth in foreign travel, you'd like to sell videos and audiotape courses in Spanish, Japanese, French, and other languages. You'd like to introduce a line of travel products, including luggage, maps, travel guides, and electronics. You visualize a room with computer terminals where customers would have direct access to the Internet so that they could obtain up-to-date weather reports, currency-exchange rates, and other important information about travel destinations. You're even thinking about a special area for kids, with videos and other educational materials.

You realize your ideas won't generate a lot of direct profit. However, you believe they will get customers in the door, where you and other agents can sell them travel, particularly leisure travel to foreign destinations. If Pradeep is willing to try it in your office and it works, he may want to do the same in his other two locations.

Your Task: E-mail Narindar Pradeep at Travelfest's downtown office. Outline your ideas and suggest a meeting to discuss them further and determine what market research he'd like you to perform. Pradeep's e-mail address is npradeep@travelfest.com.[40]

5 The glass bicycle: Persuasive letter from Owens-Corning requesting bids for manufacturing rights A student design group from Brazil's University of São Paulo has come up with the winning bicycle design in the Global Design Challenge. Sponsored by Owens-Corning, the competition called on teams from eight top design and engineering schools in the United States, Canada, Europe, Asia, and South America to design a bicycle that would cost less than $100 and would incorporate mainly glass-fibre composites in the construction. The winning entry is called the Kangaroo. Its framework is made of polyester reinforced with glass fibre, and its estimated manufacturing cost is $82. Moreover, some unique features make it a product of truly worldwide potential. An adjustable wheelbase can be shortened to allow easy manoeuvring in city traffic, and the seat and handlebars can be adjusted within a range to suit 95 percent of the world's population. Since more than half of the people on the globe depend on bicycles as their primary means of transportation, and since bicycles require no fossil fuel for operation, this product has tremendous potential in countries from Abu Dhabi to Zimbabwe.

As Owens-Corning's North American licensing manager, your job is to sign up companies to produce and market the Kangaroo bicycle for the Canadian, Mexican, and U.S. markets. A manufacturing deal has been arranged with a Chinese producer who can deliver the bicycles to any West Coast NAFTA port for $86, including shipping, taxes, and tariffs. Your problem is that you have no distribution system to handle bicycles, so you must find a marketing partner who will licence the rights to distribute and market the Kangaroo in North America. Your preference is to find a single marketer to serve the entire region, and priority will be given to companies such as Schwinn, Nishiki, and Cannondale Bicycles who are currently using Owens-Corning materials in their products. You are planning to licence the marketing rights for a five-year term for an initial payment of $350 000 plus 8 percent of the gross sales.

Your Task: Write a persuasive letter to Mr. Gregg Bagni, Marketing Director, Schwinn Bicycle & Fitness (1690 38th Street, Boulder, CO 80301-2602), requesting a bid on the North American marketing rights and offering him first refusal. Point out the features that you think will make the Kangaroo a widespread success, and be sure to spell out the financial terms. He can then determine whether the deal makes sense from his perspective. But don't give him too much time—ask for a response within ten days.[41]

6 Life's little hassles: Request for satisfaction It's hard to go through life without becoming annoyed at the way some things work. You have undoubtedly been dissatisfied with a product you've bought, a service you've received, or an action of some elected official or government agency.

Your Task: Write a three- to five-paragraph persuasive request expressing your dissatisfaction in a particular case. Specify the action you want the reader to take.

7 Point, click, recruit: Persuasive memo about e-cruiting at Rock Construction More than 60 percent of computer-related companies are recruiting over the Internet, but only 2 percent of the companies in the building industry have tried it. You think Rock Construction should join those "e-cruiting" pioneers. After all, you've got projects all over the province needing skilled workers, both in the field and behind the desk. As vice-president, you're responsible for keeping costs down, and you're convinced that e-cruiting could save a bundle, while snatching talent from your competitors.

Display ads in the Sunday newspapers have always been the standby for your human resources director, Sheila Young. They typically cost $1000 or more per job. On the other hand, major Internet career sites such as monster.com, hotjobs.com, or careermosaic.com may charge only $100 to $300 a month to list openings. Plus, since newspapers charge by the word, the amount of information you can put in an ad is limited, but online space is not. You can fully describe Rock Construction's appeal to talented workers: its status as a major builder, its longevity, and its reputation for good benefits, safe working conditions, and upward mobility. *Air Conditioning, Heating, and Refrigeration News* says that in one survey, the average cost per hire via the web was $183, compared to $1383 for traditional hiring.

Creating a Web site with a careers page is another good recruiting tactic, but you want to wait until you've tried the job boards. You've read that some 30 000 to 100 000 Internet sites are devoted to recruiting. In the U.S. alone, there are 148.8 million Internet users. Last year, 74 percent of those over the age of 18 used the Internet to look for a job. That means your pool of potential candidates could be huge, certainly much larger than the local newspaper can attract. And there are no geographical limitations online. If they're willing to relocate, you might land good employees you'd never have met otherwise.

Some companies claim they've started receiving résumés within moments of posting an opening. Hiring decisions that once took six weeks are now being made within the hour, these companies report. No more waiting for snail mail. Using available software, you can search through online résumés using keywords to prescreen candidates for certain qualifications or experience.

Of course, you won't totally abandon traditional hiring. E-cruiting can't do everything. For instance, you won't be able to see online applicants in person. And you could miss "passive" candidates, the type who are happily employed, highly qualified, and fought over by recruiters because they're often willing to take a good offer. But they rarely post résumés online. On the other hand, passive candidates might respond to an online job posting.

Overall, you think e-cruiting offers advantages that will make the effort worthwhile. Bank of Montreal claims to be saving more than $1 million by e-cruiting this year; other large companies say they've even hired executives using Internet tools.

Your Task: Write a memo to Sheila Young, director of human resources, persuading her to try e-cruiting for Rock's next job openings. You don't want this message to be an order, so use the AIDA plan to convince her that the advantages outweigh the drawbacks.[42]

8 Caribbean Recognition: E-mail to city council The request seems simple enough: members of the Caribbean Business Association of your city have asked the city council to erect two signs designating the neighbourhood where many Caribbean businesses are located as the Caribbean Business District. The area has been home to your family's restaurant, the *Island Tastes*, for many years.

But some members of the community complained when the issue was brought up during a city council session. "We should be focusing on unifying the community as a whole and its general diversity," they argued, "not dividing the city up into small ethnic districts." Some of the council members had been intrigued, however, by the prospect of creating a new tourist destination by marking the Caribbean Business District officially—that's what it actually is and has been for as long as you can remember. However, the issue was tabled for later consideration.

As the manager of your family's restaurant, you agree with those council members who think the designation would attract visitors. Moreover, the Caribbean Business Association has returned to the city council with an offer to pay for the cement structures which will designate the neighbourhood as the Caribbean Business District. The Association is willing to spend up to $30 000 for the design and installation of the signs.

Your Task: As a member of the Caribbean Business Association, you've been asked to support the request with an e-mail message to Cathy Stanford, your city's deputy mayor, at **cstandford@council.yc**.[43]

9 Power pioneers: Sales letter touting Ballard Power Systems fuel cells If you can turn water (H_2O) into hydrogen and oxygen by running an electrical current through it (electrolysis), can you produce an electrical current by combining hydrogen and oxygen? A British lawyer, Sir William Robert Grove, proved in 1839 that you could. He produced the world's first electricity-generating fuel cell. But until recently, no one could produce a commercially viable version of Grove's invention.

The simple device is somewhat like a battery; it produces an electrical current by means of an electrochemical reaction. It's also like a combustion or turbine engine; it continues to operate as long as it's supplied with fuel (some form of hydrogen and oxygen). Best of all, the fuel cell's only by-products are water, heat, and, if certain fuels are used, carbon dioxide.

Analysts predict that two decades from now fuel cells will account for 15 percent of growth in the global power-producing industry. Burnaby, B.C.'s Ballard Power Systems develops and manufactures fuel cells to power buses, cars, and trucks. They also produce stationary fuel-cell power generators, which could supply enough power to meet the electricity needs of homes and businesses. In 1999 Ballard introduced the Xcellsis Fuel Cell Engine, manufactured by their associated company Xcellsis. These engines were used on three buses operated with TransLink in Vancouver and three buses operated by the Chicago Transit Authority during two-year field trials, which concluded successfully in 2000. These trials showed that fuel cells make engines for mass transportation cleaner and environmentally more friendly than conventionally powered ones.

Your Task: If the trials were so successful in Vancouver, why not hold a trial in your city or town? Write a letter selling the idea of a fuel-cell trial to the head of your local transit service. Plan to enclose Ballard Power Systems's most recent annual report, which will give your reader more information about fuel cell technology.[44]

Persuasive Requests for Claims and Adjustments

10 Phone frustration: Persuasive letter to Western Tel requesting resolution of telephone service overcharges You are a freelance business researcher, and your time is valuable, especially when you're using online research facilities. These valuable resources are becoming more and more important in your work, so you can't afford to sit around waiting for your Internet searches to download files at 56 000 bits per second (56 kbps). You often deal with massive files that can take forever to transfer at these rates. You determined that an ISDN (Integrated Services Digital Network) connection would be a faster alternative for your online work. You contacted Western Tel in November and requested residential ISDN service (you work from home).

When the confirming work order arrived, you discovered that Western Tel had your account set up as business service, so you called the service representative to change it to the lower residential rate. As a result, your business service was disconnected, and it took Western Tel two weeks to reconnect you. On top of that, when the initial bill arrived, there was a $125 charge for disconnecting the business service, and another $75 charge for reinstallation, but no credit for the two weeks of downtime. You have made at least 13 calls to the customer service department, both locally and at Western Tel headquarters in Edmonton. You even left a message on the customer feedback section of Western Tel's Internet Web site. But none of these actions have resolved the situation.

Your Task: Compose a persuasive letter to Ms. Claire Abell (Western Tel's director of consumer affairs at Western Tel, Edmonton, AB T5A 1B0), explaining your frustration with this billing problem and asking for immediate adjustment.[45]

11 Endless trouble: Claim letter to Abe's Pool Installation As chief administrator, you worked hard to convince the board of directors of Westlake Therapy and Rehabilitation Centre that a small, 2.5-by-4.5-metre Endless Pool would be a wonderful addition to the facility. Because the pool produces an adjustable current flow, a swimmer can swim "endlessly" against it, never reaching the pool's edge. With this new invention by a Philadelphia manufacturer, your patients could experience a complete range of water therapy, in a year-round, indoor pool small enough to fit in a standard living room! The board agreed, choosing the optional two-metre depth, which would allow for additional therapeutic uses but would require (1) a special platform and (2) installation in a room with a high ceiling. The old gymnasium would become your new

Water Therapy Pavilion. Total cost with custom features: $20 080, plus $8000 budgeted for installation.

According to the manufacturer, "The Endless Pool has been designed as a kit for bolt-together assembly. It can be assembled by two reasonably handy people with no prior installation experience following detailed procedural videos." You can do it yourself, they proclaim, or hire a local contractor.

You've hired Abe's Pool Installation, which will build the special access platform and install the pool. You passed along the instructional videos, along with the manufacturer's hotline numbers. They've offered a pre-installation engineering consultation for your customized pool, without additional charge, as you told Abe. They'll also be glad to help determine whether the planned site can handle the pool's 10-tonne filled weight. Abe nodded and told you not to worry.

Finally, Abe's crew completed the platform and amid much excitement from your staff, assembled the galvanized steel pool. At a grand, ribbon-cutting dedication ceremony, you personally flipped the switch.

Immediately the hydraulic motor began moving 140 000 litres of water per minute through a grill at the front, which smoothes and straightens the current. Everyone's excitement grew as the first wave of water washed down the centre of the pool. But instead of entering the turning vane arrays (which were supposed to recirculate the water through hidden channels back to the front of the pool), the water kept going, splashing out the back of the pool onto the platform and the gathered onlookers ... at 140 000 litres per minute. Panic and shouts erupted as you fumbled quickly to turn the thing off.

Final damage included a collapsed platform, a ruined floor, an incorrectly installed pool, and numerous dry-cleaning bills from onlookers. Fortunately, no one was hurt. Estimated cost, including floor repair: $10 000. Abe is not returning your phone calls. But local reporters are coming to film the damage tomorrow, and it's your job to conduct their tour.

Your Task: Write a claim letter to Abe Hanson, Owner, Abe's Pool Installation, 7650 Fort Sheppard Dr., Nelson, British Columbia, V1L 6A5.[46]

12 Cow-spotty text: Letter to Gateway requesting warranty extension Words Unlimited is a "microbusiness"—just two owners and you, the all-round office assistant. From a small office with two computers, you three provide editorial services to businesses.

When your employers, Tom and Miranda Goodman, decided to add a third computer, they ordered a Professional S1300 business system from Gateway, with a flat screen monitor that was supposed to offer superior visual display. They didn't realize that the monitor, recommended by salesman Chris Swanson, uses liquid crystal display (LCD) technology. That's great for graphics, but text is produced as disconnnected dots that are hard on the eyes. What they really need is an old-fashioned CRT monitor that displays text as a solid line.

They returned to the store and found one with a fast refresh rate, costing only $20 more, under Gateway's 30-day exchange program. But when they got to the register, they discovered that their 30-day exchange period had run out five days before. Gateway wouldn't take back the LCD monitor, and the Goodmans would have to pay full price for the CRT.

"How did the time run out?" you ask when they return.

"Remember how Swanson forgot to include a modem in our original order and we had to wait for it to be delivered from the factory?" Tom says. "Then UPS delivered the package to the wrong address. When we finally retrieved it, the installation technician was out sick and we had to wait for his return."

Miranda adds, "And then it took Tom forever to set up the new system, between phone calls and other jobs. By the time we saw the flat screen in action, our 30 days had already elapsed."

"At least Swanson apologized," Tom adds. "He thinks his manager will extend our 30-day exchange period if we write her a letter."

Your Task: Since your bosses are busy, they've asked you to draft the persuasive letter to Ann Cameron, Manager, Gateway Country Store, 2900 Pine Lake Rd., Lincoln, NE 68516. So far Gateway employees have been courteous, quick, and eager to help, despite the mix-ups. You all have high hopes.[47]

Sales and Fundraising Messages

13 Greener cleaners: Letter promoting "environmentally sound" franchise When you told everyone you aspired to work for an environmentally responsible business, you didn't imagine you'd be hanging your hat in the dry-cleaning business. But now that you are director of franchise development for Hangers Cleaners, you go home every night with a "clean conscience" (your favorite new pun).

Micell Technologies, Inc., in Raleigh, North Carolina, is the parent company of the new Hangers chain. Co-founders Joseph DeSimone, James McClain, and Timothy Romack established Micell in 1995 after research resulted in the first breakthrough in dry-cleaning technology in nearly 50 years. They developed a cleaning process, now called Micare, which uses liquid carbon dioxide (CO_2) and specially developed detergents to clean clothes. There's no heat required, and no further need for the toxic perchloroethylene (perc) or petroleum traditionally used in dry cleaning.

Hangers franchise owners don't have to deal with regulatory paperwork, zoning restrictions, or expensive insurance and taxes for hazardous waste disposal. And unlike petroleum-based solvents, the CO_2 that Micare uses is noncombustible. It's the same substance that carbonates beverages, and it's captured from the waste stream of industries that produce it as a by-product. Moreover, 98 percent of the CO_2 used in a Hangers outlet is recycled and used again, which helps keep prices competitive.

You've already sold franchises in 23 states and three provinces. Customers love the fact that their clothes don't carry toxic fumes after cleaning, and employees are happy to be working in a safe and cool environment. The process is actually gentler on clothes (no strong solvents or heat), reducing fading and shrinking and helping them last longer. You aren't dry cleaners; you're "garment care specialists." And in addition to giving customers what they want, Micell executives talk about the "triple bottom line," a standard for success that emphasizes profit, ecology, and social responsibility.

And beyond the progressive corporate atmosphere, you simply love the design of Hangers stores. Micell hired dry-cleaning experts and architects alike to come up with a sleek, modern, high-end retail "look" that features a cool, clean, light-filled interior and distinctive signage out front. It's more akin to a Starbucks than the overheated, toxic-smelling storefront most customers associate with dry cleaning. This high-end look is making it easier to establish Hangers as a national brand, attracting investors and franchisees rapidly as word spreads about the new "greener cleaner."

Your Task: Develop a sales letter that can be mailed in response to preliminary inquiries from potential franchise owners. You'll include brochures covering franchise agreements and Micare specifics, so focus instead on introducing and promoting the unique benefits of Hangers Cleaners. Your contact information is Micell Technologies Franchise Development Department, Micell Technologies, Inc., 7516 Precision Drive, Raleigh, NC 27617, 919-313-2102, Ext. 129, or **www.micell.com**.[48]

14 The bride wore hiking boots: Persuasive letter to "We Do" bridal superstore When Shari and Randy Almsburg of Burnaby, B.C., decided to tie the knot, they knew just what they wanted. "We always enjoyed hiking. In fact, we met each other on a hike. That's why we wanted to wrap our wedding plans around our favourite hobby." Enter Tie the Knot, a one-owner company specializing in bizarre wedding plans.

"Actually, the bride wearing a white dress and a pair of hiking boots was *not* our most unusual wedding," says owner and wedding consultant, Todd Dansing (whose own wedding took place a mile high just before the happy couple plunged to Earth by parachute). "We recently helped plan an underwater wedding in a shark tank at the aquarium for two marine biologists whose work involved feeding the fish. Our main problem there was this huge turtle that kept bumping into the preacher." Dansing tells you of other unusual weddings that took place in airplanes, on boats, underwater, and in exotic locations such as Alberta's Badlands. Whatever your wedding plans, Todd believes he can find the necessary resources and save you time and money in the process.

Todd's marketing efforts to date have involved mostly word of mouth and free press coverage of his unusual weddings (although reporters kept their distance when two snake handlers from the zoo tied the knot). But his brother-in-law has invested capital in the business, so Todd hires you to help him tell the world about his services. You suggest that he consider affiliating with an established wedding service or store. You and Todd visit We Do, a bridal superstore located in Winnipeg, Manitoba, and you help Todd see the potential for marketing his unusual, offbeat wedding service to this large company. We Do is a 26 000-square-foot matrimonial Mecca that sells 600 styles of bridal gowns and everything else traditional couples need for a wedding. The franchise hopes to open 40 stores eventually, so if Todd can strike a deal with We Do, his future profit potential will be high.

Your Task: Write a letter for Todd's signature to Carol Feinberg, CEO of We Do. Suggest that Tie the Knot would make a great consultant for couples with offbeat wedding tastes. Emphasize Todd's experience, and point out the ways this venture will provide additional market share for We Do. Think of possible objections, such as Todd's lack of capital and small company size, and try to assure Feinberg that Tie the Knot is the right business to help capitalize on a unique opportunity.[49]

15 Finding money creatively: Fund-raising letter from Bel Canto Opera Bel Canto Opera is a small, creative opera company, renowned for its daring, sometimes offbeat, performances. Located in a major metropolitan area, it has been hampered by having to compete with larger, more affluent opera companies that have large followings and budgets to match.

Despite the competition, Bel Canto Opera has benefited from critical acclaim, and it has built a small but loyal following since its premier performance more than 18 years ago. Now the company is at a crossroads. Most recently it mounted a production of *Elegy for Young Lovers.* However, the show had to close after only a week because of poor attendance. Bills continue to come in, and the bank account is bare. The creative director won't even discuss continuing the season unless a solution can be found.

Out of the darkness comes an angel. A local university with a brand-new performing arts centre would like to form an alliance with Bel Canto Opera. Although the university isn't offering large sums of cash, its board members are willing to let the company use the performing arts centre and other campus facilities at no cost. They would also consider some joint ventures in money-making educational events such as lectures and exhibitions. These events would be fairly easy and inexpensive to produce, and they could generate some immediate cash flow.

But the *coup de théâtre* for Bel Canto Opera would be access to the university's key donors, alumni, and supporters of the arts. The company's management team believes that, properly cultivated, this group could provide the sound financial base the company needs for future operations. Everyone on the team is excited.

The chairperson of the opera's board, the creative director, the development director, and the head of the university's fine arts department recently held a strategy session. After agreeing in principle to finalize the alliance between Bel Canto Opera and the university, all agreed that the first order of business is to raise funds. It was generally agreed that business and community leaders should be informed and invited to lend their financial support to the new venture.

A symposium is planned, at which the new venture will be introduced. The symposium will include musical previews of Bel Canto's upcoming season, a presentation by the creative director, and messages from key university staff. The goal of the symposium is to raise $500 000 in pledges.

Your Task: As development director of Bel Canto Opera, you have been asked to draft a letter to community and business leaders. Your goals are to convince them of the opera's viability, get them to attend the symposium, and convince them to pledge their financial support.[50]

16 Buses for seniors: Fundraising letter from King County Senior Centre The King County Senior Centre is one of Nova

Scotia's oldest non-profit institutions for the elderly. Over the past 50 years, it has relied on financial support from government, businesses, and individuals.

Unfortunately, recent provincial cutbacks have dug into the organization's budget. In addition, in the last five years two of the county's largest companies, Hardwick Industries and McCarthy Electrical Motors, have moved offshore and shut down local operations. Both businesses were supporters of the centre, as were many of the workers who lost jobs.

However, the needs of the centre keep growing. For many of the county's roughly 1000 seniors who live alone, it's the only place where they can meet their peers, use a special library, avoid extreme weather, or get a well-balanced meal. The centre is not a nursing home and has no overnight facilities. Most individuals get to the facility on one of the three shuttle-type vans belonging to the centre. The buses are also used for various day trips to museums, plays, and similar functions. Occasionally, they are used to help the temporarily disabled get to doctors' offices or pharmacists.

Each van is more than eight years old. Although not unsafe, the vans are showing their age. The constant repairs are stopgap measures at best, and most weeks at least one of the vehicles is inoperable. Monthly repairs are averaging a total of $600 for the three vehicles. In addition, when the vans aren't working, the clients, staff, and budget all suffer. Seniors can't get to the centre, trips are cancelled, and drivers are sometimes paid for coming to work even though they weren't able to drive.

Conservatively, it would cost about $42 000 to replace each van with a new one: $126 000 total. This includes estimates on how much the centre could gain from selling the old vans. It's a fair amount of money, but in the opinion of your board of directors, buying new vans would be better than continuously repairing the old ones or risking the purchase of used ones.

Your Task: As director of the centre, draft a fund-raising letter to send to all of the businesses in the county. Stress the good work the centre does and the fact that this is a special fund-raising effort. Mention that all the money collected will go directly toward the purchase of the vans.

Going Online Exercises

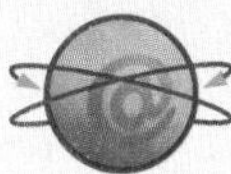

Lobby Your Leaders, found on page 244 of this chapter

Follow the links to the home page of one of your MPs from the "how Canada is governed" Web site. Draft and send a persuasive but short e-mail message about an issue that concerns you. Be sure to apply the best persuasive strategy you've learned in this chapter for writing your message.

1 Discuss why businesses need reports and the factors that affect how reports are prepared

2 Distinguish between informational and analytical reports

3 Explain the difference between a problem statement and a statement of purpose, and then identify five other elements often included in a formal work plan

4 Describe six tasks necessary to doing research for business reports

5 Define *informational interviews,* and list four types of interview questions

6 Clarify what it means to adapt your report to your audience

Planning Business Reports and Proposals

ON THE JOB

Facing a Communication Dilemma at Dell Inc.

Staying on Top of the Computer World

www.dell.com

Since Michael Dell founded Dell Inc. in 1984, his business has become the largest computer manufacturer in the United States and the fastest-growing computer systems company in the world. Dell began selling in Canada in 1998, and now Dell Inc. ranks third in overall PC shipments and second in the desktop and server market.

However, as his company doubled in size every year throughout the 1990s, Michael Dell learned some hard lessons. At one point, technological advancements in memory chips decreased the value and usefulness of his company's existing inventory. Dell was stuck with a large inventory of chips that nobody wanted, which crystallized the company's need to establish inventory controls, and especially, to analyze developments in the computer industry. Later, Dell's company briefly experimented with selling computers in retail outlets. But after studying retail sales reports that were based on careful data analysis, Dell was able to determine that selling directly to consumers was the most profitable approach for his company.

Dell pulled out of the retail market and focused on selling desktop and notebook computers directly to consumers around the world through the company's international Web sites. Now Dell faces two challenges: (1) attracting new customers and (2) satisfying the needs of existing clients. To succeed, Dell must constantly track and understand industry innovations. He must be able to inform customers about new products and trends, determine customer preferences, and respond to these preferences with appropriate products and services. He needs information. But "information in its raw form doesn't present itself in neat and tidy packages," notes Dell. "When a customer says, 'I want a notebook computer that lasts the whole day,' we have to translate that desire into relevant technology."

The reports at Dell Inc. must do more than simply summarize and present carefully researched data. These reports must analyze the data to identify and discuss pertinent issues. Suppose you were in charge of writing reports for Michael Dell—reports on issues such as industry trends, inventory control, customer preferences, and employee needs. How would you go about planning these reports? What steps would you take to define each problem? Conduct the research? Analyze the data?[1]

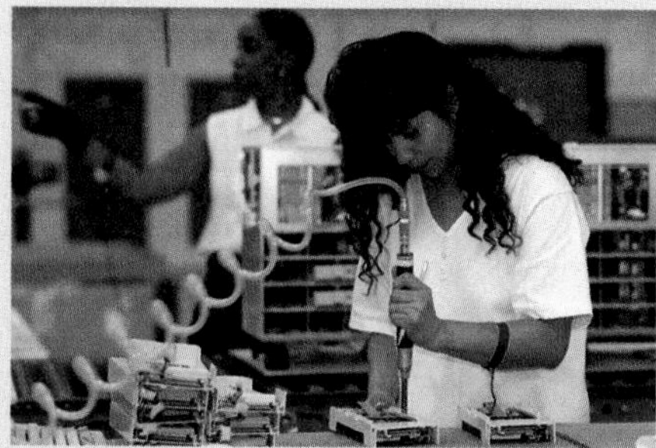

Dell Inc. is the world's leading direct computer systems company. It designs, manufactures, and customizes products and services to customer requirements, offering an extensive selection of hardware, software, and peripherals. In the fast-paced world of computer technology, the company relies on reports to keep up with current industry trends, statistics, and issues.

Why Businesses Need Reports

OBJECTIVE 1 **Discuss why businesses need reports and the factors that affect how reports are prepared.**

Even the most capable managers, such as Michael Dell, must rely on other people to observe events or collect information for them. Some managers are often too far away to oversee everything themselves; some are responsible for preparing the reports needed by others. Whether you prepare or receive them, reports are the basis of effective decisions and solutions.

Reports are like bridges, spanning time and space. Organizations use them to provide a formal, verifiable link between people, places, and times. Some reports are for internal communication; others are for corresponding with outsiders. Some serve as a permanent record; others solve an immediate problem or answer a passing question. Many reports travel upward to help managers monitor various organizational units; some travel downward to explain managerial decisions to the employees responsible for day-to-day operations.

Business reports help companies make decisions and solve business problems.

Because business reports are intended to inform and to aid the decision-making and problem-solving process, they must be accurate, complete, and unbiased. Your goal in writing reports is to make your information as clear and convenient to use as possible. Time is precious, so tell your readers what they need to know—no more, no less—and present the information in a way that is geared to their needs.

Make your business reports
- Accurate
- Complete
- Unbiased
- Clear
- Convenient to use
- Relevant

Reports come in all shapes and sizes, from formal three-volume bound manuscripts to a fleeting image on a computer screen. Like other messages in business, reports are strongly influenced by the advances in technology. Look at annual reports that corporations such as Bell Canada (www.bell.ca) post on their Web sites. Interactive versions show a table of contents as an instant navigation guide. Each page includes a sequential listing of headings highlighting where readers are in the report, and by clicking on the headings, the reader can quickly move to different sections. "Living" annual reports feature video presentations by CEOs and links to current financial information.[2]

No matter whether the report is electronic or paper, report preparation varies according to the following factors:

Reports may be
- Voluntary or authorized
- Routine or special
- Internal or external
- Short or long
- Informational or analytical

- **Source (who initiates the report).** *Voluntary reports* are prepared on your own initiative, whereas *authorized reports* are prepared at the request of someone else. For a voluntary report, you need to provide more background on the subject and to explain your purpose more carefully than for an authorized report, which responds directly to the reader's request.
- **Frequency (how often the report is needed).** *Routine (or periodic) reports* are submitted on a recurring basis (daily, weekly, monthly, quarterly, annually), at times requiring little more than filling in a preprinted or computerized form or perhaps formatting information in a standard way. These routine reports need less introductory and transitional material than *special reports,* which are nonrecurring and present the results of specific, onetime studies or investigations.
- **Target audience (where the report is being sent).** Because they are used within an organization, *internal reports* are generally less formal than *external reports,* which are sent outside the organization. Many internal reports are written in memo format, especially those under ten pages. External reports may be in letter format (if no longer than five pages) or in manuscript format (if they exceed five pages).
- **Length (how much detail the report contains).** *Short reports* (generally one to nine pages) differ from *long reports* (ten pages or more) in scope, research, and timetable. A long report examines a problem in detail and generally requires more extensive research and preparation time. A short report may discuss just one part of the problem and may not require formal research.
- **Intent (whether the report is meant to educate or to draw conclusions).** *Informational reports* focus on facts and are intended mainly to explain something or to educate readers. *Analytical reports* are intended to solve problems by

TABLE 10–1 Intent, Type, and Purpose of Business Reports

Intent	Type	Purpose
Informational	**1. Monitor/control reports**	To oversee and manage company operations
	2. Policy/procedure reports	To carry out company rules and ways of doing things
	3. Compliance reports	To obey government and legal requirements
	4. Progress reports	To inform others of what's been done on a project
Analytical	**5. Problem-solving reports**	To guide decisions on particular issues
	6. Proposals	To get products, plans, or projects accepted by others

showing how the data, analysis, and interpretation justify the conclusions and recommendations. The information in analytical reports plays a supporting role; it is a means to an end, not an end in itself.

A single report may encompass all these factors. For instance, a monthly sales report is generally authorized, routine, internal, short, and informational, whereas a market analysis is generally authorized, special, internal, long, and analytical. Whatever factors are involved in a business report, most reports usually fall into one of six general categories (which are listed in Table 10.1 above). Being familiar with the various types of reports will help you plan your own reports more effectively, so let's take a closer look.

Informational Reports

OBJECTIVE 2 Distinguish between informational and analytical reports.

Informational reports are used to educate and inform, not to persuade. Their uses and topics are innumerable. However, we focus here on three types: those for monitoring and controlling operations, implementing policies and procedures, and documenting progress.

REPORTS FOR MONITORING AND CONTROLLING OPERATIONS

Monitor/control reports help managers find out what's happening in the operations under their control.

Managers rely on reports to find out what is happening to the operations under their control. These *monitor/control reports* focus on data, so they require special attention to accuracy, thoroughness, and honesty of content. Don't cover up bad news and emphasize only accomplishments. Such distortion defeats the purpose of these reports. Be objective. The problems will show up eventually, so you should get them out in the open. Following are three examples of reports used for monitoring and controlling operations.

Plans help managers
- Coordinate the various activities of a business
- Guide the distribution of resources
- Motivate employees

Plans Plans establish guidelines for future action. Strategic plans document an organization's overall goals and the methods it will use to reach them.[3] Business plans help companies obtain financing or contract for managerial support services.[4] Marketing plans identify a firm's customers and detail how to serve them. Other plans include annual budgets, five-year plans, sales plans, recruiting plans, production plans, and so on. Internal audiences generally use such plans (1) to improve organizational coordination, (2) to guide the distribution of money and material, and (3) to motivate employees. However, plans are also written for external audiences.

Operating Reports Operating reports provide managers with detailed information from a management information system (MIS), which captures statistics about everything happening in the organization (sales, production, inventory, shipments, backlogs, costs, personnel, etc.). The MIS is usually computerized, but operating reports can also be created manually. Information can be included in its raw state or analyzed and reported in paragraph form.

Periodic operating reports describe what's happened during a particular period. A real estate director for a coffee retailer prepared the report in Figure 10–1 below. It presents information that will help the company make good decisions when it selects new store locations. The writer avoids burdening his manager with details about every potential site by making his report concise and presenting information in summary format.

Personal Activity Reports Personal activity reports describe what occurred during a conference, convention, trip, or other activity. They're intended to provide important information or decisions that emerged during the activity. These reports also

Going Online

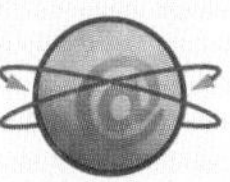

Pointers for Business Plans

What's involved in a business plan? BizPlanIt.Com offers tips and advice, consulting services, a free e-mail newsletter, and a sample virtual business plan. You'll find suggestions on what details and how much information to include in each section of a business plan. You can explore the site's numerous links to business plan books and software; online magazines; educational programs; government resources; women and minority resources; funding sources; and even answers to your business plan questions.

www.bizplanit.com

To link directly to this site, visit our Companion Web site at **www.pearsoned.ca/thill** *and look for the Chapter 10 resources.*

MEMORANDUM

TO: Joan Chen, V.P.
New Business Development

DATE: August 2, 2005

FROM: Roger Watson,
Real Estate Director

SUBJECT: July location scouting

During the last two weeks of July, I scouted four Calgary locations for our coffee outlets. George Spindle recommended these sites in his business development report (which is on the intranet under "Regional reports"). All four sites are in existing office buildings.

HOW THE CALGARY SITES COMPARE

Here's a quick look at the basic aspects of each site. Lease rates are comparable at all four locations, ranging from $34 to $38 a square foot.

Site	Space	Availability	Competition	Visibility
Bridgeland	260 square feet	Now	Starbucks has begun construction 4 blocks north; no other stores within a 16-block radius	None; on the second of two retail floors in this building
Victoria Park	525 square feet; with additional 150 square feet in one year	January	2 Starbucks (2 blocks south and 8 blocks west); Second Cup (across street, but poor visibility)	Superb corner location; windows on both streets
Mount Royal	420 square feet	December	JavaLand 3 blocks east; Starbucks 4 blocks south	Good visibility but little evening/weekend traffic
University of Calgary	Two options: 340 square feet, 655 square feet	Now for the smaller site; March for the larger	Five independents in the immediate area; Starbucks on campus (2 blocks west)	Good visibility, both locations near university library

SCOUTING PLANS FOR SEPTEMBER

Our schedule has been pretty tight for the last six months. Following are the plans for our efforts in September:

Calgary: I'll contract Shure Research to conduct foot traffic counts at all four sites (we should have those numbers in 10 days). I've asked George's team to do a permits search to study future building plans in each location. I'll be talking with Melissa Hines next week about construction restrictions. (She's the Smith, Allen broker who helped us with the Grand Junction sites last year.)

Saskatoon: Jean-Luc Goddard wants us to review several sites he's had his eye on. I'll send Sue or visit them myself if my schedule permits.

Orients the reader but doesn't waste time with unnecessary explanations.

Headings stand out to make report easy to read.

Table organizes summary information in a time-saving format.

Data is thorough and accurate, giving all the news, not just the good news.

Details of upcoming efforts help the reader maintain a timely overview of the progress.

FIGURE 10–1 In-Depth Critique: Periodic Operating Report

Personal activity reports describe the facts and decisions that emerge during conversations, trips, and business meetings.

help companies track what's happening in the marketplace or with customers. Examples include sales-call and expense reports.

Figure 10–2 below is a personal activity report prepared by a human resources manager of a small insurance firm. Her report summarizes the highlights of a seminar she attended on legal issues in employee recruiting and interviewing.

REPORTS FOR IMPLEMENTING POLICIES AND PROCEDURES

Policy/procedure reports help managers communicate the company's standards.

Reports for implementing policies and procedures are necessary because managers can't talk firsthand with everyone in an organization. Written reports are available to anyone with a question. These reports present their information in a straightforward manner. Some policy/procedure reports are preserved as lasting guidelines; others are one-time position papers.

MEMORANDUM

TO:	Jeff Balou; all members of HR staff	DATE:	March 14, 2005
FROM:	Carrie Andrews	SUBJECT:	Recruiting and hiring seminar

States Andrews's reason for attending the seminar.

As we all know, legal considerations frame the process of recruiting, screening, and hiring new employees. Because we don't have an in-house lawyer to advise us in our hiring decisions, it is critical for all of us to be aware of acceptable practice.

Last week I attended a Canadian Management Centre seminar on this subject. I got enough useful information to warrant updating our online personnel handbook and perhaps developing a training session for all interviewing teams. First, here's a quick look at the knowledge I gained.

Organized around the three areas of knowledge gained by Andrew, thus helping readers focus on what is important.

Highlights new knowledge with bullets for easy reader reference.

AVOIDING LEGAL MISTAKES

- How to write recruiting ads that accurately portray job openings and that meet employment equity guidelines
- How to use an employment agency effectively and safely (without risk of legal entanglements)

SCREENING AND INTERVIEWING MORE EFFECTIVELY

- How to sort through résumés more efficiently (including looking for telltale signs of false information)
- How to avoid interview questions that are legally questionable
- When and how to check criminal records

MEASURING APPLICANTS

- Which types of pre-employment tests have proven most effective
- Which drug-testing issues and recommendations affect us

The report does not waste time on unimportant activities such as how many sessions were offered during the seminar or what was served for lunch.

As you can see, the seminar addressed a lot of important information. We cover the basic guidelines for much of this process already, but a number of specific recommendations and legal concepts should be emphasized.

One eye-opening part of the seminar was learning about the mistakes other companies have made. Some companies have lost millions of dollars in employment-discrimination lawsuits. The risks are significant, and violating human rights during the hiring process can have considerable consequences for us.

Presents pertinent material: (1) the information needed by department members and (2) the plans for how to disseminate it.

It will take me two weeks to get the personnel handbook updated; as you know, we don't have any hiring plans for the foreseeable future. I'll keep the seminar handouts and my notes on my desk, in case you want to review them. After I've updated the handbook, we can get together and decide whether we need to train the interviewing team members and how we will approach doing this.

If you have any questions in the meantime, don't hesitate to e-mail me or drop by for a chat.

FIGURE 10–2 In-Depth Critique: Personal Activity Report

Lasting Guidelines Lasting guidelines comprise the rules of an organization. For example, the production supervisor might develop guidelines for standardizing quality-control procedures, or the office manager might issue a memo explaining how to reserve the conference room for special meetings. Such policy/procedure reports then become part of the company's large body of lasting guidelines for following practices in a certain way. Figure 10-3 below explains a building access policy for a firm where many of the scientists work irregular hours, especially when a deadline approaches or when experiments need constant monitoring.

Some policies and procedures provide lasting "recipes" for how practices should be executed.

Position Papers In contrast to lasting guidelines, position papers treat less-permanent issues. They explain management's views on particular nonrecurring issues or problems as they arise. For example, an office manager might write a report on the need for extra security precautions after a rash of burglaries in the area.

Other policies and procedures explain management's position on passing events.

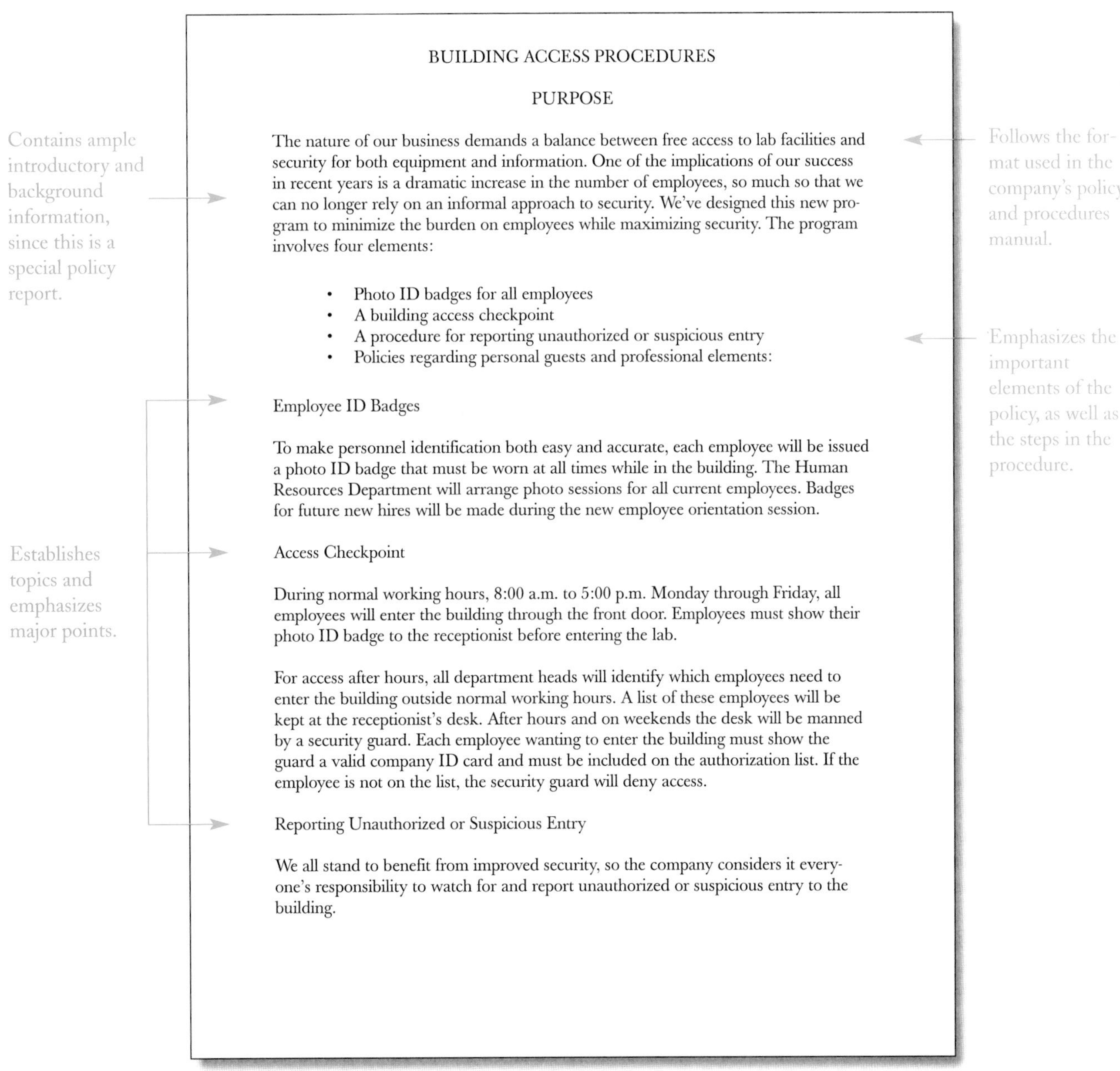

BUILDING ACCESS PROCEDURES

PURPOSE

The nature of our business demands a balance between free access to lab facilities and security for both equipment and information. One of the implications of our success in recent years is a dramatic increase in the number of employees, so much so that we can no longer rely on an informal approach to security. We've designed this new program to minimize the burden on employees while maximizing security. The program involves four elements:

- Photo ID badges for all employees
- A building access checkpoint
- A procedure for reporting unauthorized or suspicious entry
- Policies regarding personal guests and professional elements:

Employee ID Badges

To make personnel identification both easy and accurate, each employee will be issued a photo ID badge that must be worn at all times while in the building. The Human Resources Department will arrange photo sessions for all current employees. Badges for future new hires will be made during the new employee orientation session.

Access Checkpoint

During normal working hours, 8:00 a.m. to 5:00 p.m. Monday through Friday, all employees will enter the building through the front door. Employees must show their photo ID badge to the receptionist before entering the lab.

For access after hours, all department heads will identify which employees need to enter the building outside normal working hours. A list of these employees will be kept at the receptionist's desk. After hours and on weekends the desk will be manned by a security guard. Each employee wanting to enter the building must show the guard a valid company ID card and must be included on the authorization list. If the employee is not on the list, the security guard will deny access.

Reporting Unauthorized or Suspicious Entry

We all stand to benefit from improved security, so the company considers it everyone's responsibility to watch for and report unauthorized or suspicious entry to the building.

Contains ample introductory and background information, since this is a special policy report.
Establishes topics and emphasizes major points.
Follows the format used in the company's policy and procedures manual.
Emphasizes the important elements of the policy, as well as the steps in the procedure.

FIGURE 10-3 In-Depth Critique: Building Access Policy (Excerpt)

Reports documenting progress on a contract provide all the information the client needs.

Projects or jobs that take place over time must provide regular updates in the form of progress reports.

At the end of the project, a final report provides a wrap-up of results.

REPORTS FOR DOCUMENTING PROGRESS

Whether you're writing a progress report for a client or for your manager, you need to anticipate your reader's needs and provide the required information clearly and tactfully. Progress reports are generally submitted on a regular basis. They may be required monthly or weekly, or they may be keyed to phases of the project. Interim progress reports give an idea of the work that has been accomplished to date (see Figure 10.4 below): the writer states what tasks have been completed, identifies problems, outlines future steps, and summarizes important findings.

In many cases these interim reports are followed by a final report at the conclusion of the contract or project. Final reports are generally more elaborate than interim reports and serve as a permanent record of what was accomplished. They focus on final results rather than on progress along the way.

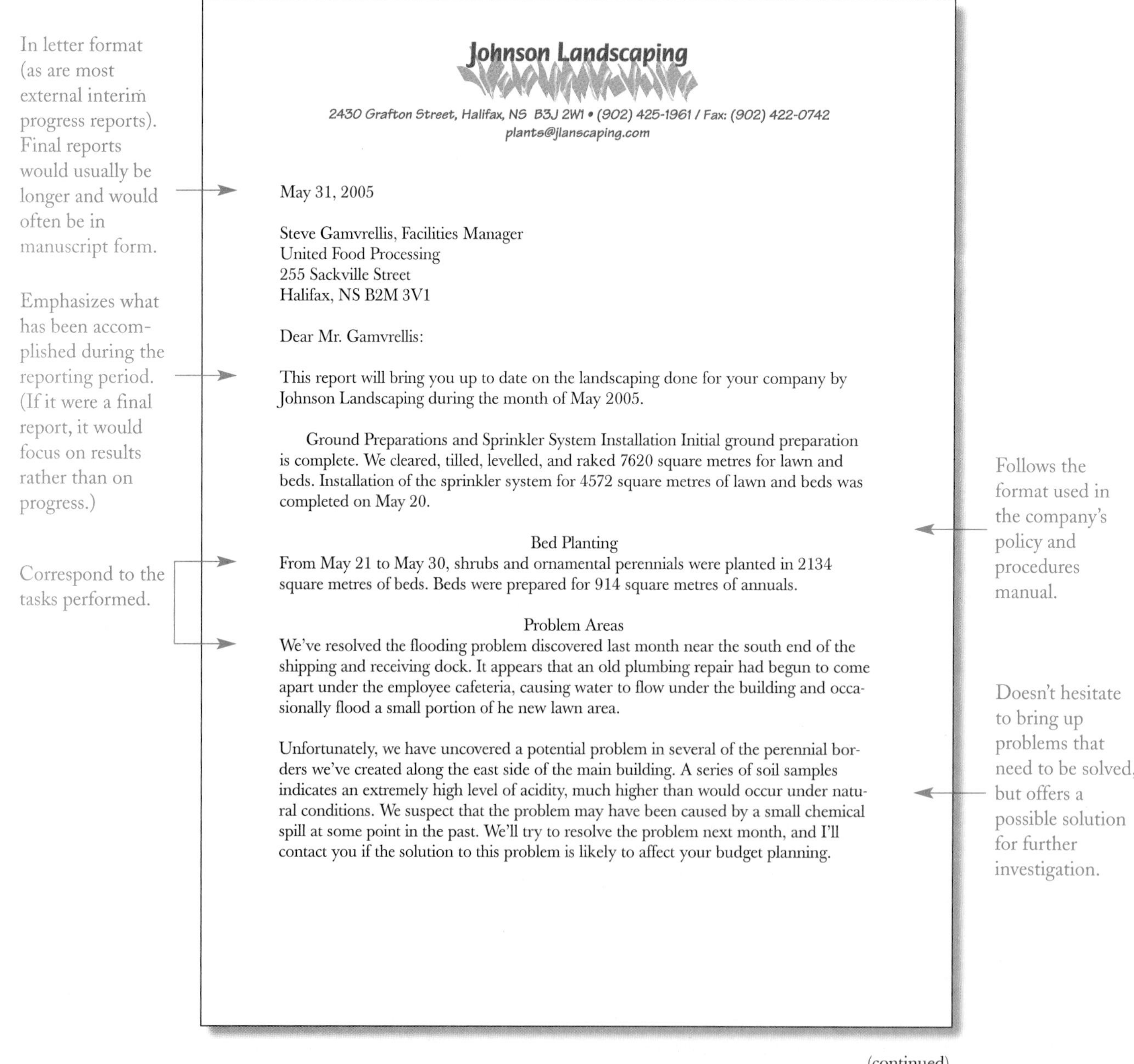

In letter format (as are most external interim progress reports). Final reports would usually be longer and would often be in manuscript form.

Emphasizes what has been accomplished during the reporting period. (If it were a final report, it would focus on results rather than on progress.)

Correspond to the tasks performed.

Follows the format used in the company's policy and procedures manual.

Doesn't hesitate to bring up problems that need to be solved, but offers a possible solution for further investigation.

Johnson Landscaping

2430 Grafton Street, Halifax, NS B3J 2W1 • (902) 425-1961 / Fax: (902) 422-0742
plants@jlanscaping.com

May 31, 2005

Steve Gamvrellis, Facilities Manager
United Food Processing
255 Sackville Street
Halifax, NS B2M 3V1

Dear Mr. Gamvrellis:

This report will bring you up to date on the landscaping done for your company by Johnson Landscaping during the month of May 2005.

Ground Preparations and Sprinkler System Installation Initial ground preparation is complete. We cleared, tilled, levelled, and raked 7620 square metres for lawn and beds. Installation of the sprinkler system for 4572 square metres of lawn and beds was completed on May 20.

Bed Planting

From May 21 to May 30, shrubs and ornamental perennials were planted in 2134 square metres of beds. Beds were prepared for 914 square metres of annuals.

Problem Areas

We've resolved the flooding problem discovered last month near the south end of the shipping and receiving dock. It appears that an old plumbing repair had begun to come apart under the employee cafeteria, causing water to flow under the building and occasionally flood a small portion of he new lawn area.

Unfortunately, we have uncovered a potential problem in several of the perennial borders we've created along the east side of the main building. A series of soil samples indicates an extremely high level of acidity, much higher than would occur under natural conditions. We suspect that the problem may have been caused by a small chemical spill at some point in the past. We'll try to resolve the problem next month, and I'll contact you if the solution to this problem is likely to affect your budget planning.

(continued)

FIGURE 10–4 In-Depth Critique: Interim Progress Report (Excerpt)

Mr. Steve Gamvrellis May 31, 2005 Page 2

Plans for June

1. Distribute beauty bark and plant remaining annuals.
2. Resolve the soil quality issue in the perennial bed and make soil amendments as needed.
3. Monitor and adjust the automated sprinkling system to ensure adequate watering.

Outlines plans for the coming period.

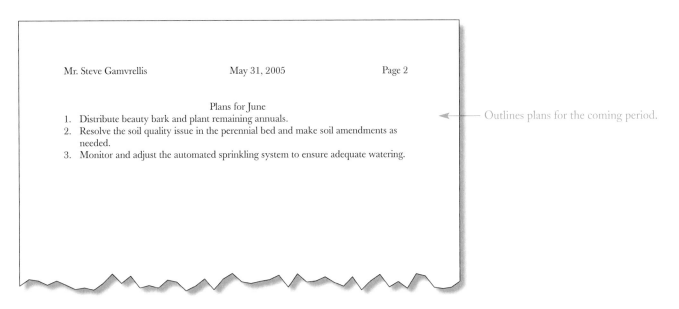

FIGURE 10-4 (Continued)

REPORTS FOR SUMMARIZING INFORMATION

Business summaries communicate and organize information that is needed in business.

Businesspeople are bombarded with masses of information, and at one time or another, everyone in business relies on someone else's summary of a situation, publication, or document. To write a summary report, gather the information (whether by reading, talking with others, or observing circumstances), organize that information, and then present it in your own words. Although summarizing may seem a simple skill, it's actually more complex than it appears. A well-written summary is accurate in relaying facts and opinions, comprehensive, and balanced. To help colleagues or supervisors make a decision, include all the information necessary for readers to understand the situation, problem, or proposal. Present all sides of the issue fairly and equitably, and include all the information necessary. Even though summaries are intended to be as brief as possible, your readers need a minimum amount of information to grasp the issue being presented.

Analytical Reports

Analytical reports are intended to convince readers that its conclusions and recommendations are valid.

When making major decisions, Michael Dell and his management team must rely on analytical reports for information, analysis, and recommendations. Analytical reports require a strong foundation of facts combined with good insight and excellent communication skills on the part of the writer. When you prepare one of these reports, you have the chance to present your skills to top management. Naturally, you'll want to give these assignments your best effort.

Although analytical reports vary greatly, all of them tend to ask "should we or shouldn't we" questions: Should we expand into this market? Should we reorganize the research department? Should we invest in new equipment? Some of the more common examples of analytical reports are those for solving problems, justifying a project or a course of action, and getting products, plans, or projects accepted by others (usually called *proposals*).

REPORTS FOR SOLVING PROBLEMS

Problem-solving reports provide management with background information and analysis of options.

When making decisions, managers need both basic information and detailed analysis of the various options. Most problem-solving reports require research or internal information that may cover topics such as product demand, growth projections, competitor profiles, company strengths and weaknesses, and so on. If the report is distributed as an e-mail attachment, it might include financial models that allow

SHARPENING YOUR CAREER SKILLS

Seven Errors in Logic That Can Undermine Your Reports

For your report to be effective, it must be logical. If you learn how to think logically, you'll also write more logically. Here are some common errors to avoid.

1. **Lack of objectivity.** Seeing only the facts that support your views and ignoring any contradictory information:

   "Although half the survey population expressed dissatisfaction with our current product, a sizable portion finds it satisfactory."
   (You may be tempted to ignore the dissatisfied half instead of investigating the reasons for their dissatisfaction.)

2. **Hasty generalizations.** Forming judgments on the basis of insufficient evidence or special cases:

   "Marketing strategy Z increased sales 13 percent in St. John's supermarkets. Let's try it in Kelowna."
   (St. John's and Kelowna are probably vastly different markets.)

3. **Hidden assumptions.** Hiding a questionable major premise:

   "We are marketing product X in trade journals because we marketed product Y in trade journals."
   (Who says product X and product Y should be marketed the same way?)

4. **Either-or scenarios.** Setting up two alternatives and not allowing for others:

   "We must open a new plant by spring, or we will go bankrupt."
   (Surely there are other ways to avoid bankruptcy.)

5. **False causal relationships.** Assuming that event A caused event B merely because A preceded B:

   "Sales increased 42 percent as soon as we hired the new sales director."
   (Something besides the new sales director might have been responsible for increased sales.)

6. **Begged questions.** Assuming as proven what you are seeking to prove:

   "We need a standard procedure so that we will have standard results."
   (But why is standardization important?)

7. **Personal attacks or appeals to popular prejudice.** Insulting people or ideas you don't like by chaining them to irrelevant but unpopular actions or ideas:

   "Ellen mishandled the budget last year, so she can't be expected to motivate her staff."
   (Ellen's accounting ability may have nothing to do with her ability to motivate a staff.)

   "It's not the Canadian way to impose government regulations." *(Regulations are unpopular, but they do exist in Canada.)*

CAREER APPLICATIONS

1. Discuss some newsworthy business problem that arose from errors in logic. For example, Huffy tried to sell a combination mountain-and-racing bicycle through Kmart and other large stores that sold Huffy bicycles. Unfortunately, Huffy's logic was faulty. The company had no reason to assume that this special bike (which was priced higher than other Huffy models) could be sold by salespeople who weren't knowledgeable about bicycles. Huffy lost $5 million on the product.
2. Go through the "Letters to the Editor" columns in recent newspapers or newsmagazines. Examine the arguments made, and point out errors in logic.

Adapted from Christopher Power, "Flops," *Business Week* 16 Aug. 1993: 79; Mary Munter, *Guide to Managerial Communication*, 2nd ed. (Upper Saddle River, N.J.: Prentice Hall, 1982) 31. Adapted by permission of Prentice Hall, Inc., Upper Saddle River, NJ.

managers to compare various scenarios by plugging in different assumptions and projections.

Troubleshooting reports are one type of problem-solving report. Whenever a problem exists, somebody has to investigate it and propose a solution. Regardless of the specific problem at hand, these troubleshooting reports deal with the same basic research questions: How did this problem arise, what's the extent of the damage, and what can we do about it? These reports usually start with some background information on the problem, then analyze alternative solutions, and finally recommend the best approach.

REPORTS FOR JUSTIFYING A PROJECT OR COURSE OF ACTION

A justification report is a proposal to upper-level management from lower- or middle-level management.

Justification reports (or feasibility reports) are used to persuade upper-level management to approve a project or course of action. These reports may be written about acquiring capital assets, reorganizing a department, revising recruiting procedures, changing the company's training programs, or improving operations in hundreds of other ways.

A good justification report explains why a project or course of action is needed, what it will involve, how much it will cost, and what the benefits will be. Also, even if a justification report is intended to persuade others to do something, it must always be unbiased. Look at the report in Figure 10-5 below. Shandel Cohen manages the customer-response section of the marketing department at a personal computer manufacturer. Her section sends out product information requested by customers and the field sales force. Cohen has observed that the demand for information increases when a new product is released and diminishes as a product matures. This fluctuating demand causes drastic changes in her section's workload.

Cohen's report proposes to install an automatic mail-response system. Because the company manufactures computers, she knows that her boss won't object to a computerized solution. Also, since profits are always a concern, her report emphasizes the financial benefits of her proposal. Her report describes the problem, her proposed solutions, and the benefits to the company.

PROPOSALS FOR OBTAINING NEW BUSINESS OR FUNDING

Proposals are reports written to get products, plans, or projects accepted by outside business or government clients.

A **proposal** is a special type of analytical report designed to get products, plans, or projects accepted by outside business or government agencies. Proposals to outsiders are similar to the justification reports that solicit approval of projects within an organi-

MEMO

TO: Jamie Engle
FROM: Shandel Cohen
DATE: July 8, 2005
SUBJECT: Proposed automatic mail-response system

THE PROBLEM:
SLOW RESPONSE TO CUSTOMER REQUESTS FOR INFORMATION

Describes the problem carefully in a positive light (in terms of the company's success).

Our new product line has been very well received, and orders have surpassed our projections. This very success, however, has created a shortage of printed catalogues and data sheets, as well as considerable overtime for people in the customer response centre. As we introduce upgrades and new options, our printed materials quickly become outdated. If we continue to rely on printed materials for customer information, we have two choices: Distribute existing materials (even though they are incomplete or inaccurate) or discard existing materials and print new ones.

THE SOLUTION:
AUTOMATED MAIL-RESPONSE SYSTEM

With minor modifications to our current computer system and very little additional software, we can set up an automated mail-response system to respond to customer requests for information. This process can save us time and money and can keep our distributed information current.

Automated mail-response systems have been tested and proven effective. Many companies already use this method to respond to customer information requests, so we won't have to worry about relying on untested technology. Both customer and company responses have been positive.

Uses headings to highlight the benefits of the solution.

Ever-Current Information

Rather than discard and print new materials, we would need to update only the electronic files. We would be able to provide customers and our field sales organization with up-to-date, correct information as soon as the upgrades or options are available.

Instantaneous Delivery

Within a short time of requesting information, customers would have that information in hand. Electronic delivery would be especially advantageous for our international customers. Regular mail to remote locations sometimes

(continued)

FIGURE 10-5 In Depth Critique: Justification Report

2

takes weeks to arrive, by which time the information may already be out of date. Both customers and field salespeople will appreciate the automatic mail-response system.

Minimized Waste

With our current method of sending printed information, we discard virtually tons of obsolete catalogues, data sheets, and other materials.

By maintaining and distributing the information electronically, we would eliminate this waste. We would also free up a considerable amount of floor space and shelving that is required for storing printed materials.

Of course, some of our customers may still prefer to receive printed materials, or they may not have access to electronic mail. For these customers we could simply print copies of the files when we receive requests.

Lower Overtime Costs

Besides savings in paper and space, we would also realize considerable savings in wages. Because of the increased interest in our new products, we must continue to work overtime or hire new people to meet the demand. An automatic mail-response system would eliminate this need, allowing us to deal with fluctuating interest without a fluctuating work force.

Setup and Operating Costs

Carefully explains the costs of the proposal.

The necessary equipment and software costs approximately $15,000. System maintenance and upgrades are estimated at $5000 per year.

We expect the following annual savings from eliminating printed information:

$100,000	Printing costs
25,000	Storage costs
5,000	Postage
20,000	Wages
$150,000	

Justifies the cost by detailing projected annual savings.

3

CONCLUSION

Closes by offering to answer any questions management may have, rather than trying to anticipate management's questions and including unnecessary detail.

I will be happy to answer any questions you have about this system. I believe that this system would greatly benefit our company, in terms of both cost and customer satisfaction. If you approve the system, we can have it installed and running in six weeks.

FIGURE 10-5 (Continued)

zation. However, proposals are different from justification reports in an important way: although justification reports may compete for company dollars, time, or resources, they don't compete for business. Proposals try to convince readers that your organization is the best source of a product or service. Thus, you devote considerable space to explaining your experience, qualifications, facilities, and equipment. Moreover, you show that you clearly understand your reader's problem or need.[5]

Proposals can be one or two pages, or they can be hundreds of pages if they involve large, complex jobs. Regardless of the size and scope, these special types of reports analyze an audience's problem, present a solution, and persuade the audience that the solution presented is the best approach. Proposals are usually read by people in positions of authority.

The two basic types of proposal are those invited by a prospective client and those sent without a specific invitation from a prospective client.

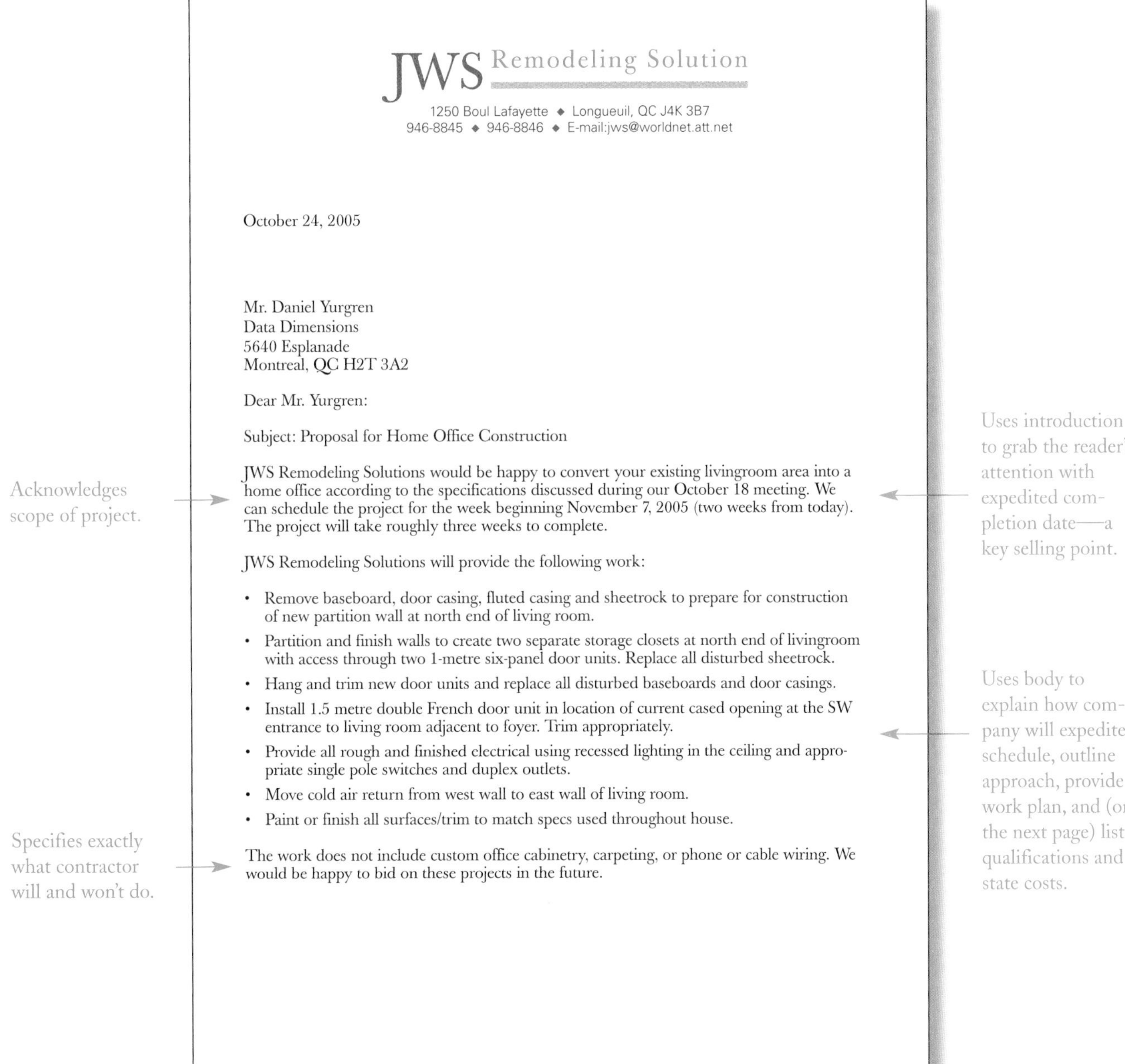

JWS Remodeling Solution

1250 Boul Lafayette ◆ Longueuil, QC J4K 3B7
946-8845 ◆ 946-8846 ◆ E-mail:jws@worldnet.att.net

October 24, 2005

Mr. Daniel Yurgren
Data Dimensions
5640 Esplanade
Montreal, QC H2T 3A2

Dear Mr. Yurgren:

Subject: Proposal for Home Office Construction

JWS Remodeling Solutions would be happy to convert your existing livingroom area into a home office according to the specifications discussed during our October 18 meeting. We can schedule the project for the week beginning November 7, 2005 (two weeks from today). The project will take roughly three weeks to complete.

JWS Remodeling Solutions will provide the following work:

- Remove baseboard, door casing, fluted casing and sheetrock to prepare for construction of new partition wall at north end of living room.
- Partition and finish walls to create two separate storage closets at north end of livingroom with access through two 1-metre six-panel door units. Replace all disturbed sheetrock.
- Hang and trim new door units and replace all disturbed baseboards and door casings.
- Install 1.5 metre double French door unit in location of current cased opening at the SW entrance to living room adjacent to foyer. Trim appropriately.
- Provide all rough and finished electrical using recessed lighting in the ceiling and appropriate single pole switches and duplex outlets.
- Move cold air return from west wall to east wall of living room.
- Paint or finish all surfaces/trim to match specs used throughout house.

The work does not include custom office cabinetry, carpeting, or phone or cable wiring. We would be happy to bid on these projects in the future.

(continued)

FIGURE 10-6 External Proposal, Solicited

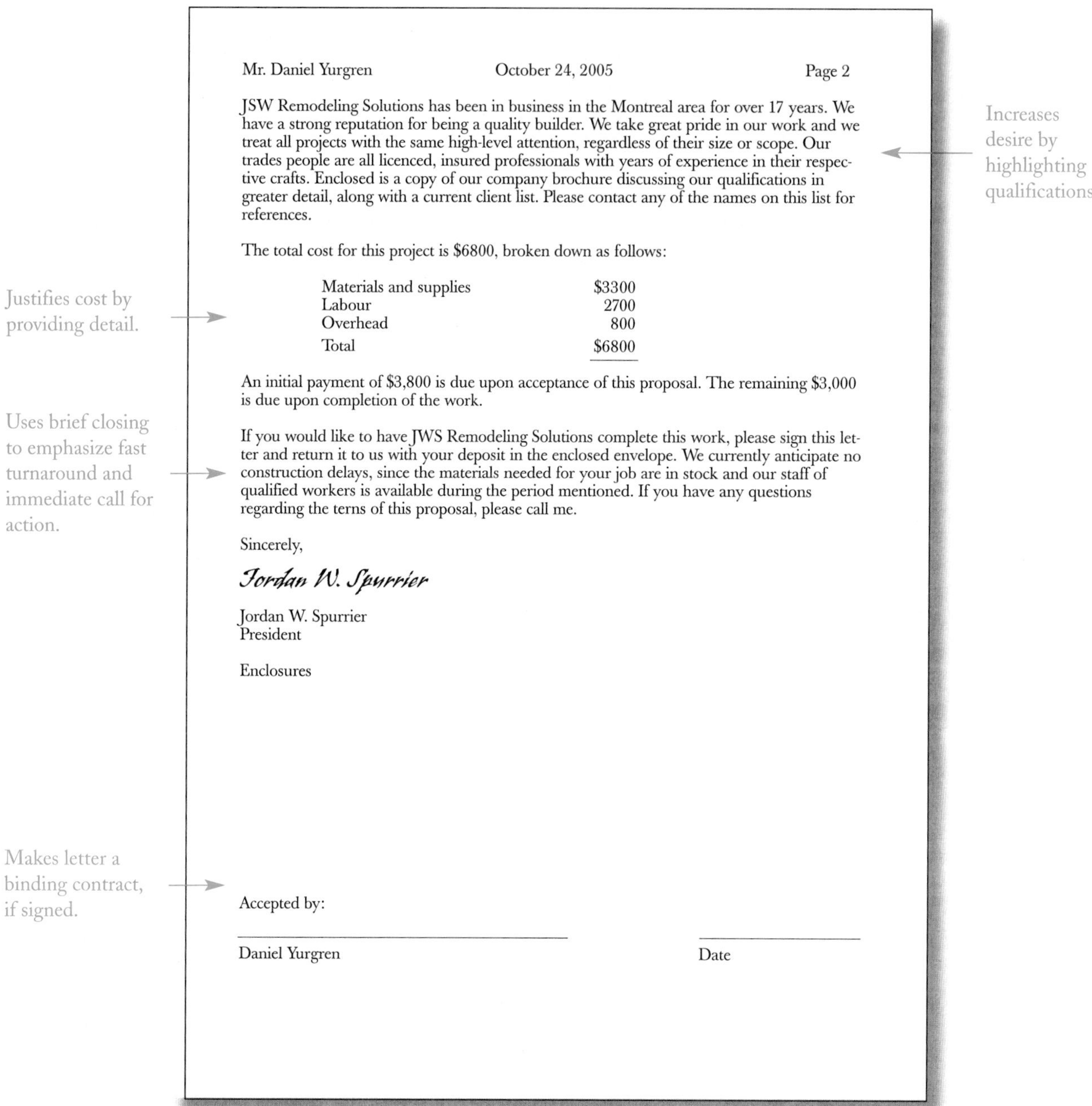

Mr. Daniel Yurgren October 24, 2005 Page 2

JSW Remodeling Solutions has been in business in the Montreal area for over 17 years. We have a strong reputation for being a quality builder. We take great pride in our work and we treat all projects with the same high-level attention, regardless of their size or scope. Our trades people are all licenced, insured professionals with years of experience in their respective crafts. Enclosed is a copy of our company brochure discussing our qualifications in greater detail, along with a current client list. Please contact any of the names on this list for references.

The total cost for this project is $6800, broken down as follows:

Materials and supplies	$3300
Labour	2700
Overhead	800
Total	$6800

An initial payment of $3,800 is due upon acceptance of this proposal. The remaining $3,000 is due upon completion of the work.

If you would like to have JWS Remodeling Solutions complete this work, please sign this letter and return it to us with your deposit in the enclosed envelope. We currently anticipate no construction delays, since the materials needed for your job are in stock and our staff of qualified workers is available during the period mentioned. If you have any questions regarding the terns of this proposal, please call me.

Sincerely,

Jordan W. Spurrier

Jordan W. Spurrier
President

Enclosures

Accepted by:

Daniel Yurgren Date

Increases desire by highlighting qualifications
Justifies cost by providing detail.
Uses brief closing to emphasize fast turnaround and immediate call for action.
Makes letter a binding contract, if signed.

FIGURE 10–6 (Continued)

A solicited proposal demonstrates that your organization is better qualified than competitors to handle a particular contract.

Solicited Proposals Solicited proposals are prepared at the request of clients who need something done. The invitation to bid on the contract is called a request for proposal (RFP). Such an invitation includes instructions that specify the exact type of work to be performed, along with guidelines on how and when the company wants the work completed. For example, if a city transportation agency is seeking a supplier of intra-city buses, the agency will prepare an RFP that specifies the needs and requirements. You respond by preparing a proposal that shows how you would meet the potential customer's needs.

When a company gets an RFP, the managers decide whether they're interested in the job and whether they have a reasonable chance of winning the contract. When the proposal effort actually begins, the company reviews the requirements, defines the scope of the work, determines the methods and procedures to be used, and estimates time requirements, personnel requirements, and costs. Then the proposal writers put it all on paper—exactly as specified in the RFP, following the exact format it requires and responding meticulously to every point it raises.[6] Most proposals begin with an introductory section that states the purpose of the proposal, defines the scope of the work, presents background information, and explains any restrictions that might apply to the contract. The body of the proposal gives details on the proposed effort and specifies what the anticipated results will be. The discussion covers the methods, schedule, facilities, equipment, personnel, and costs that will be involved in the contract. A final section generally summarizes the key points of the proposal and asks for a decision from the client. In Figure 10–6 on page 281, a construction company explains how its staff will renovate a potential client's home office.

When renovating, homeowners usually seek three bids from contractors. What criteria do you think homeowners use when evaluating a firm to work on their houses?

Unsolicited Proposals Unsolicited proposals are initiated by organizations attempting to obtain business or funding without a specific invitation from a potential client. In other words, with an unsolicited proposal, the writer makes the first move. Unsolicited proposals differ from solicited proposals in one important respect: the recipient has to be convinced of the benefits of buying (or funding) something. Unsolicited proposals generally devote considerable space to explaining why readers should take action and convincing them of the benefits of the project or plan. For example, a university seeking funding for a specific research project might submit an unsolicited proposal to a large local corporation. To be convincing, the proposal should show how the research could benefit the corporation, and it should demonstrate that the university has the resources and expertise to conduct the research.[7] Or, an entrepreneur seeking funding for a new business would create a proposal showing potential investors the benefits of investing in that venture.

An unsolicited proposal establishes the value of funding your project.

Planning Business Reports—Analysis

OBJECTIVE 3 Explain the difference between a problem statement and a statement of purpose, and then identify five other elements often included in a formal work plan.

As with other business messages, when writing reports and proposals, you benefit from following the three-step writing process (see Figure 10-7 on page 284). In this chapter we focus on Step 1, "Planning Business Reports." Step 2 is discussed in Chapter 11, "Writing Business Reports and Proposals," and Step 3 is the subject of Chapter 12, "Completing Formal Business Reports and Proposals."

The planning tasks for reports fall into the three familiar categories: analysis, investigation, and adaptation. However, certain tasks have a special importance for business reports and proposals. For example, when analyzing your purpose, you'll want to put particular effort into defining the problem, limiting the scope of the study, outlining the issues for investigation, developing the statement of purpose, and preparing the work plan.

When writing reports, pay special attention to analysis tasks such as the following:

- Defining the problem
- Limiting the scope
- Outlining the issues
- Developing the statement of purpose
- Preparing the work plan

Defining the Problem

If you're writing an informational report, your assignment may be as simple as gathering last month's sales figures and submitting them to management in a table format. Most informational reports don't go beyond submitting the facts. However, if you're writing an analytical report, your assignment will likely involve solving a problem, so begin by developing a **problem statement** that defines the problem you need to resolve.

This problem can be negative or positive—it may deal with shrinking sales or the need for more childcare facilities. Just be careful not to confuse a simple topic (campus parking) with a problem (the lack of enough campus parking). If you're the only person who thinks this issue is a problem, your audience won't be very interested in your solution, so be sure to focus on your audience, consider your organization's perspective, and keep in mind the needs of the people who will read your report.[8] You may have to spend some time convincing your readers that a problem exists.

Limiting the Scope of the Study

Linda Moreno is the cost accounting manager for Electrovision, a high-technology company. She was asked to find ways of reducing employee travel and entertainment costs (her complete report appears in Chapter 12). As in Moreno's case, the person who authorizes the report often defines the problem for the writer. To ensure that she understands exactly what is required of her, Moreno begins by discussing the objectives of her report with the person who requested and authorized the investigation. Specifically, she tries to answer the following questions:

One way to limit the scope of your study is to verify your assignment with the person authorizing your report.

- What needs to be determined?
- Why is this issue important?
- Who is involved in the situation?
- Where is the trouble located?
- When did it start?
- How did the situation originate?

Not all these questions apply in every situation, but asking them helps limit the scope of the problem and clarify the boundaries of the investigation. You can then draft a written statement that will serve as a guide to whatever problem you're trying to solve or whatever question you're trying to answer in the report.[9]

Another way to limit the scope of your study is to factor the problem.

Besides asking such general questions, you can also limit the scope of your study by breaking down the problem into a series of logical, connected questions that try to identify cause and effect. This process is sometimes called **problem factoring.** You probably subconsciously approach most problems this way. When your car's engine won't start, what do you do? You use the available evidence to organize your investigation, to start a search for cause-and-effect relationships. For example, if the engine doesn't turn over at all, you might suspect a dead battery. If the engine does turn over but won't fire, you can conclude that the battery is okay but perhaps you're out of gas. When you speculate on the cause of a problem, you're forming a **hypothesis,** a potential explanation that needs to be tested. By subdividing a problem and forming hypotheses based on available evidence, you can tackle even the most complex situations.

Studies that focus on problem solving may be structured around hypotheses that the report writer plans to prove or disprove during the investigation.

Linda Moreno used the factoring process to structure her investigation into ways of reducing travel and entertainment costs at Electrovision. "I began with a two-part question," says Moreno. "Why have our travel costs grown so dramatically, and how can we reduce them? Then I factored that question into two subquestions: Do we have adequate procedures for tracking and controlling costs? Are these procedures being followed?"

1 Planning

Analyze: Study the audience and analyze your purpose: Define the problem, limit the scope, outline the investigation, write the statement of purpose, and prepare the work plan.

Investigate: Research secondary or primary sources.

Adapt: Establish a good audience relationship and choose the right medium.

2 Writing

Organize: Decide format, length, order, and structure. Prepare the final outline, and organize any visual aids.

Compose: Control your style through level of formality and tone. Establish a time perpective and help readers find their way with devices such as headings, lists, and transitions.

3 Completing

Revise: Evaluate content and review readability, editing and rewriting for conciseness and clarity.

Produce: Use effective design elements. Include all required formal components.

Proofread: Review text and visuals for errors in layout, spelling, and mechanics.

FIGURE 10–7 The Three-Step Writing Process for Reports

Looking into cost-control procedures, I speculated that the right kind of information was not reaching the executives who were responsible for these costs. From there, the questioning naturally led to the systems and procedures for collecting this information. If we didn't have the right procedures in place or if people weren't following procedures, the information wouldn't reach the people in charge.

Once Moreno had determined what was wrong with Electrovision's cost-control system, she could address the second part of the main question: the problem of recommending improvements. This factoring process, or breaking a problem into a series of subproblems, enabled Moreno and her colleagues to approach the task methodically.

You don't have to become an expert on every subject you undertake, but you must learn enough about the subject you are exploring to pose intelligent questions, just as detectives do when they investigate a case.

Outlining the Issues for Investigation

As you go through the factoring process, you may want to use an outline format to represent your ideas. For example, if your problem is to determine why your company is having trouble hiring secretaries, you'll begin by speculating on the causes. Then you'll collect information to confirm or disprove each reason. Your outline of the major issues might look something like this:

Use an outline format when factoring complex problems.

Why are we having trouble hiring secretaries?

1. Are salaries too low?
   a. What do we pay our secretaries?
   b. What do comparable companies pay their secretaries?
   c. How important is pay in influencing secretaries' job choices?
2. Is our location poor?
   a. Are we accessible by public transportation and major roads?
   b. Is the area physically attractive?
   c. Are housing costs affordable?
   d. Is crime a problem?
3. Is the supply of secretaries diminishing?
   a. How many secretaries were available five years ago as opposed to now?
   b. What was the demand for secretaries five years ago as opposed to now?

When writing headings for outlines, use the same grammatical form for items of the same level. Parallel construction shows that the ideas are related, of similar importance, and on the same level of generality. When wording outlines, you must also choose between descriptive (topical) and informative (talking) headings. Descriptive headings label the subject that will be discussed, whereas informative headings (in either question or summary form) suggest more about the meaning of the issues.

Although outlines with informative headings take a little longer to write, they're generally more useful in guiding your work, especially if written in terms of the questions you plan to answer during your investigation. They're also easier for others to review. If other people are going to comment on your outline, they may not have a very clear idea of what you mean by the descriptive heading "Advertising." However, they will get the main idea if you use the informative heading "Did Cuts in Ad Budget Cause Sales to Decline?"

Informative outline headings are useful in guiding your work.

The way you outline your investigation may differ from the final outline of your resulting report. That's because solving a problem is one thing, and "selling" the solution is another. During your investigation, you might analyze five possible causes of a problem and discover that only two are relevant. In your report, you might not even introduce the three unrelated causes. (Chapter 4 discusses common outline forms, and Chapter 11 discusses the benefits of preparing a final outline.) If a few notes are enough to guide you through a short, informal report in memo form, an outline might not be necessary.

The outline for investigation differs from the final outline of the report.

Developing the Statement of Purpose

The **statement of purpose** defines the objective of your report.

Once you've determined the problem and limited its scope, you're ready to develop a **statement of purpose**, which defines the objective of the report. In contrast to the problem statement, which defines *what* you are going to investigate, the statement of purpose defines *why* you are preparing the report (see Table 10–2 below).

The most useful way to phrase your purpose is to begin with an infinitive phrase. For instance, in an informational report, your statement of purpose can be as simple as these:

- To update clients on the progress of the research project (interim progress report)
- To develop goals and objectives for the coming year (strategic plan)
- To identify customers and explain how the company will service them (marketing plan)
- To submit monthly sales statistics to management (periodic operating report)
- To summarize what occurred at the annual sales conference (personal activity report)
- To explain the building access procedures (policy implementation report)
- To submit required information to the SEC (compliance report)

Using an infinitive phrase (*to* plus a verb) encourages you to take control and decide where you're going before you begin. When you choose an infinitive phrase—*to inform, to confirm, to analyze, to persuade, to recommend*—you pin down your general goal in preparing the report.

Statements of purpose for analytical reports are often more complex than are those for informational reports.

The statement of purpose for analytical reports is often more comprehensive. Look at Linda Moreno's statement of purpose. Because she was supposed to suggest specific ways of reducing costs, she phrased her statement like this:

> ... to analyze the T&E [travel and entertainment] budget, evaluate the impact of recent changes in airfares and hotel costs, and suggest ways to tighten management's control over T&E expenses.

If Moreno had been given an informational assignment instead, she might have stated her purpose this way:

> To summarize Electrovision's spending on travel and entertainment.

You can see from these two examples how much influence the purpose statement has on the scope of your report. If Moreno's manager had expected her to suggest ways to reduce costs but Moreno had collected only cost data, her report would have failed to meet expectations. Because she was assigned an analytical report rather than an informational report, Moreno had to go beyond merely collecting data to drawing conclusions and making recommendations.

Remember, the more specific your purpose, the more useful it will be as a guide to planning your report. Furthermore, always double-check your statement of purpose

TABLE 10–2 Problem Statements versus Statement of Purpose

Problem Statement	Statement of Purpose
Our company's market share is steadily declining.	To explore different ways of selling our products and to recommend the ones that will most likely increase our market share.
Our current computer network system is inefficient and cannot be upgraded to meet our future needs.	To analyze various computer network systems and to recommend the system will best meet our company's current and future needs.
We need $2 million to launch our new product.	To convince investors that our new business would be a sound investment so that we can obtain desired financing.
Our current operations are too decentralized and expensive.	To justify the closing of the St. John's plant and the transfer of East Coast operations to a single Western location in order to save the company money.

with the person who authorized the report. Seeing the purpose written down in black and white, the authorizer may decide that the report needs to go in a different direction.

Prepare a written statement of your purpose; then review it with the person who authorized the study.

Preparing the Work Plan

Once you've defined the problem and the purpose of your report, you are ready to establish a work plan. In business, most reports have a firm deadline and finite resources. You not only have to produce quality reports, but you have to do so quickly and efficiently. A carefully thought-out work plan is the best way to make sure you produce quality work on schedule.

If you are preparing the work plan for yourself, it can be relatively informal: a simple list of the steps you plan to take, an estimate of their sequence and timing, and a list of the sources of information you plan to use. If you're conducting a lengthy, formal study, however, you'll want to develop a detailed work plan that can guide the performance of many tasks over a span of time. Most proposals require a detailed work plan, which becomes the basis for a contract if the proposal is accepted. A formal work plan might include the following elements (especially the first two):

Whether you prepare an informal work plan for yourself or a detailed work plan for your team, be sure it identifies all the tasks that must be performed.

- **Statement of the problem.** The problem statement clarifies the challenge you face, helps you and anyone working with you to stay focused on the core problem, and helps everyone avoid the distractions that are likely to arise during report preparation.
- **Statement of the purpose and scope of your investigation.** The purpose statement describes what you plan to accomplish with this report and, thus, the boundaries of your work. Stating which issues you will cover and which issues you won't cover is especially important with complex, lengthy investigations.
- **Discussion of tasks to be accomplished.** Be sure to indicate your sources of information, the research necessary, and any constraints (on time, money, personnel, or data). For simple reports, the list of tasks to be accomplished will be short and probably obvious. However, longer reports and complex investigations require an exhaustive list so that you can reserve time with customers, executives, or outside services such as pollsters or print shops.
- **Description of any products that will result from your investigation.** In many cases, the only product of your efforts will be the report itself. In other cases, you may need to produce something beyond a report, perhaps a new marketing plan or even a tangible product. Clarify these expectations at the outset, and be sure to schedule enough time and resources to get the job done.
- **Review of project assignments, schedules, and resource requirements.** Indicate who will be responsible for what, when tasks will be completed, and how much the investigation will cost. If more than one person will be involved, you may also want to include a brief section on coordinating report writing and production. (Collaborative writing is discussed in detail in Chapter 2. Also see "Give Others Specific, Constructive Criticism," in Chapter 6.)
- **Working outline.** Some work plans include a tentative outline of the report, as does the plan in Figure 10-8 on page 289. This plan was developed for a report on whether to launch a company newsletter.
- **Plans for following up after delivering the report.** Follow-up can be as simple as making sure people received the information they needed or as complex as conducting additional research to evaluate the outcome of the recommendations you made. Even informal follow-up can help you improve your future reports. It certainly signals that you care about your work's effectiveness and its impact on the organization.

With a plan in place, you're ready to get to work, which in some cases means starting with research.

Planning Business Reports—Gathering Information

OBJECTIVE 4 Describe six tasks necessary to doing research for business reports.

Like Michael Dell, you may someday need to gather information on specific companies, industries, trends, issues, or people. This may seem like an overwhelming task considering the amount of information available today. But if you sharpen your research strategy, you'll find that looking for business information can be a rewarding experience.

Sharpening your research strategy will help you find all the business information you need.

Over the years, your instructors have assigned carefully designed projects to help you develop and practice good research skills. This chapter will build on those skills by explaining a research strategy that you can use for the remainder of your business studies (including this course), on the job, or whenever you're looking for information. In addition, some popular resources that you'll need in business will be introduced, and it will be explained where to find them, how to use them, and how to evaluate them.

When it comes to finding information, many people go to the library, log on to a database or the Internet, type in some key words, produce almost endless resources, and immediately begin taking notes on whatever comes up under their topic. Resist the temptation. If your research strategy is weak, any business decisions based on your research will also be weak.

Complete six tasks to find, evaluate, and process information effectively and efficiently.

Adopt an organized approach to research by: (1) finding and accessing secondary information, (2) gathering necessary primary information, (3) evaluating and finalizing your sources, (4) processing your information, (5) analyzing your data, and (6) interpreting your data. In most cases you'll perform these tasks in order; however, the amount of time you spend on a single task will depend on the nature and amount of information you need, as well as on the purpose of your research. Conducting research often requires jumping around, branching off, or looping back; that is, your discoveries may lead you to additional questions, which require further research, and so on. What's important is to become competent in each task and to complete all six of them.

Find and Access Secondary Information

You conduct secondary research by locating information that has already been collected, usually in the form of books, periodicals, and reports.[10] In most cases, you'll be unfamiliar with your research topic, so you'll need to learn something about your subject before you begin your research in earnest.

Begin your research effort by becoming familiar with your topic.

The best way to learn about something new is to browse through materials on your topic. Leaf through some books and periodicals, conduct some loosely structured interviews, or log on to a database (either at the library or on the Internet) and see what comes up. You may even want to visit your favourite bookstore (whether physical or online, such as Amazon.ca), gather some business books on your topic, and scan their table of contents. Once you have a better understanding of your topic, you're ready to begin your research.

KNOWING WHAT TO LOOK FOR

To research a company, first find out whether it's public or private. You can also look in the *Canadian Index* and the *Financial Post Investment Reports: Industry Reports* to find information related to the industry.

If you're looking for information about a specific company, you'll need to know whether the company is public (sells shares of stock to the general public) or private. Public companies generally have more information available than private companies. You can find a list of Canadian public companies on the SEDAR (System for Electronic Document Analysis and Retrieval) Web site. For U.S. companies, look in the *Directory of Companies Required to File Annual Reports with the Securities and Exchange Commission*, which is available at most public libraries.

If you need industry information, look at the *Canadian Index* (check *industry* as a topic in the index) and the *Financial Post Investment Reports: Industry Reports*. To

States problem clearly enough for anyone to understand without background research.

STATEMENT OF THE PROBLEM
The rapid growth of our company over the past five years has reduced the sense of community among our staff. People no longer feel like part of an intimate organization where they matter as individuals.

Lays out the tasks to be accomplished and does so in clear, simple terms.

Delineates exactly what will be covered in the report.

PURPOSE AND SCOPE OF WORK
The purpose of this study is to determine whether a company newsletter would help rebuild employee identification with the organization. The study will evaluate the impact of newsletters in other companies and will attempt to identify features that might be desirable in our own newsletter. Such variables as length, frequency of distribution, types of articles, and graphic design will be considered. Costs will be estimated for several approaches. In addition, the study will analyze the personnel and the procedures required to produce a newsletter.

SOURCES AND METHODS OF DATA COLLECTION
Sample newsletters will be collected from 50 companies similar to ours in size, group rate, and types of employees. The editors will be asked to comment on the impact of their publication on employee morale. Our own employees will be surveyed to determine their interest in a newsletter and their preferences for specific features. Production procedures and costs will be analyzed through conversations with newsletter editors and printers.

Presents preliminary outline for guidance, even though no description of the end product is included.

PRELIMINARY OUTLINE
I. Do newsletters affect morale?
  A. Do people read them?
  B. How do employees benefit?
  C. How does the company benefit?
II. What are the features of good newsletters?
  A. How long are they?
  B. What do they contain?
  C. How often are they published?
  D. How are they designed?
III. How should a newsletter be produced?
  A. Should it be written, edited, and printed internally?
  B. Should it be written internally and printed outside?
  C. Should it be totally produced outside?
IV. What would a newsletter cost?
  A. What would the personnel costs be?
  B. What would the materials costs be?
  C. What would outside services cost?
V. Should we publish a company newsletter?
IV. If so, what approach should we take?

Includes no plans for following up.

States the assignments and the schedules for completing them.

WORK PLAN

Collect/analyze newsletter	09/01–09/14
Interview editors by phone	09/16–09/20
Survey employees	09/14–09/28
Develop sample	09/28–10/05
Develop cost estimates	10/07–10/10
Prepare report	10/10–10/24
Submit final report	10/25

FIGURE 10-8 In-Depth Critique: Work Plan for a Formal Study

do research on U.S. industries, you'll need to know the North American Industry Classification System (NAICS) code of that particular industry. The U.S. government requires all companies, from sole proprietorships to corporations, to assign themselves a six-digit industry number that classifies their business by the type of product or service they provide. The NAICS codes are available on the Internet and in business reference books.

You may need to find information on company and industry statistics, economic forecasts, business concerns, legal issues, competition, and industry performance ratios and averages. Figure 10-9 on pages 291 to 293 lists some of the more popular resources for company and industry information (many of which are available in both print and electronic database format). One of the best places to begin your search for secondary information is the nearest public or university library.

FINDING INFORMATION IN THE LIBRARY

Reference librarians are there to assist you with your research efforts.

At the library, you can find most of the information you need either in print format, in databases or other electronic media, or on microfilm.

Libraries are where you'll find business books, databases, periodicals, and other helpful materials. In addition, you'll find your most important resource: librarians. Reference librarians are trained in research techniques, and are highly skilled at managing information and helping people find materials. They can show you how to use the library's many databases and they can help you find obscure information. Whether you're trying to locate information in printed materials, on databases, or on microfilm, each type of resource serves a specific function.

Business Books Books are less timely than journal articles, but they provide in-depth coverage of a variety of business topics. Because of budgetary constraints, libraries must be selective about the books they put on their shelves, so you will have better luck finding specialized information at central or district libraries, rather than smaller neighbourhood branches. You will also have a better chance of finding specialized material at company libraries or at a college or university library (assuming the school offers courses in those subjects).

Electronic databases contain journal articles that are more timely than books.

Electronic Databases An **electronic database** is a computer-searchable collection of information, often categorized by subject areas such as business, law, science, technology, and education. When using an electronic database, try to get a list of the periodicals or publications it includes, as well as the time period it covers. Then fill in the gaps for any important resources not in the database.

Newspapers can be one of the more up-to-date resources.

Newspapers Libraries subscribe to only a select number of newspapers and store only a limited number of back issues in print. However, they frequently subscribe to databases containing newspaper articles in full text (available online, on CD-ROM, or on microfilm). In addition, most newspapers today offer full-text or limited editions of their papers on the Internet.

Periodicals are another timely resource for business information.

Periodicals Most periodicals fall into one of four categories: (1) popular magazines (not intended for business, professional, or academic use), (2) trade journals (providing news and other facts about particular professions, industries, and occupations), (3) business magazines (covering all major industries and professions), and (4) academic journals (publishing data from professional researchers and educators). To locate a certain periodical, check your library's database.

Directories offer basic information on organizations and companies.

Directories Directories cover everything from accountants to zoos. Many include membership information for all kinds of special-interest groups. For instance, business directories provide entries for companies, products, and individuals, and they include the name of key contact persons. Directories are considered invaluable for marketers, job seekers, and others who need to establish a prospect list.

Almanacs offer statistics about countries, politics, and more.

Almanacs and Statistical Resources Almanacs are handy guides to factual and statistical information about countries, politics, the labour force, and so on. Also check

COMPANY, INDUSTRY, AND PRODUCT RESOURCES (PRINT AND CD-ROM)

- ***Blue Book of Canadian Business.*** Detailed profiles of over 50 Canadian companies. Electronic database includes more than 2500 of Canada's largest firms.
- ***Brands and Their Companies/Companies and Their Brands.*** Data on over 281 000 consumer products and 51 000 manufacturers, impo
- ***Corporate and Industry F*** Collection of industry repo analysts for investment pu includes industry profitabili market share, profits, and f
- ***Directory of Canadian-m*** Canadian suppliers with na experience. Information on trade experience, and tech
- ***Directory of Canadian Ma*** Information on contacts and
- ***Directory of Companies F Reports with the Securiti Commission.*** Listing of U.S
- ***Dun's Directory of Servic*** 205 000 U.S. service comp
- ***Financial Post Data Grou Reports.*** Background infor companies.
- ***Financial Post 500.*** Contac information on Canada's lar
- ***Financial Post Investment*** Company, product, and fina
- ***Financial Services Canad*** financial services industry.
- ***Forbes.*** Annual Report on A first January issue of each y
- ***Fraser's Canadian Trade D*** Canadian companies, produ
- ***Hoover's Handbook of Am*** over 500 public and private c
- ***Manufacturing USA.*** Data s companies, including detaile manufacturing industries.
- ***Market Share Report.*** Data service categories originating newsletters, and magazines.
- ***Moody's Industry Review.*** D about 150 industries. Ranks five financial statistics (reven cash and marketable securiti includes key performance rat
- ***Moody's Manuals.*** Weekly m each of six business areas: in public utilities, banks finance, industrials.
- ***Report on Business Magazi*** financial, and product informa corporations.
- ***Scott's Industrial Directory.*** of Canadian companies. Includes list of companies by NAICS code.
- ***Service Industries USA.*** Comprehensive data on 2100 services grouped into over 150 industries.
- ***Small Business Profiles for Canadian Provinces and Territories.*** Financial and employment data on small business in Canada. CD-ROM format.
- ***dustry Surveys.*** Concise broad range of industries. ith a focus on current situation ne summary data on major ry.
- ***ster of Corporations, Directors*** f major U.S. and international s, products, sales volume, and
- ***merican Manufacturers.*** of U.S. manufacturers indexed oduct.
- Annual profiles of several es. Each industry report covers s tables, graphs, and charts how an industry compares with g important component growth c measures.
- ory of leading private orate affiliations.

, AND PRODUCT E)

- **bilities** ccc/engdoc/homepage.html. n businesses, by d product-specific business
- w.ctidectory.com. Searchable description, and keyword. nd exporters.
- cial and management corporate documents of over s.
- com. Brief profiles of the 500 .S.
- vers.com. Profiles of publicly d on major stock exchanges rivate companies. Search by ne, location, industry, or sales.
- ent.com. (requires s for over 10 000 U.S. 7 000 annual reports from ur to five years of annual mpany.
- .gov/epcd/naics/naicstb2.txt. ssification System.
- dgarhp.htm. SEC filings l reports, and prospectuses

FIGURE 10–9 Major Business R

(continued)

INTERNATIONAL TELEPHONE CODES

Use this method whenever you need to spell your name or address over the phone:

A as in Adam	J as in James	S as in Susan
B as in Baker	K as in Kind	T as in Thomas
C as in Charlie	L as in Lewis	U as in Union
D as in David	M as in Mary	V as in Victor
E as in Edward	N as in Nancy	W as in William
F as in Frank	O as in Otto	X as in X-ray
G as in George	P as in Peter	Y as in Yankee
H as in Henry	Q as in Queen	Z as in Zebra
I as in Ida	R as in Robert	

- ***SEDAR (System for Electronic Document Analysis and Retrieval)***. Annual reports, securities information for public companies and mutual funds within Canadian securities regulatory agencies.
- **Yahoo!** dir.yahoo.com/Business. More than 50 categories of information with dozens of links.

DIRECTORIES AND INDEXES (PRINT)

- ***Associations Canada.*** Lists more than 19 000 Canadian associations and many foreign associations active in Canada or of interest to Canadians.
- ***Books in Print.*** Index of 425 000 books in 62 000 subject categories currently available from U.S publishers. Indexed by author and title.
- ***Canadian Books in Print.*** Index of more than 48 000 titles in 800 different subject categories. Author and title index are cross-referenced.
- ***Directories in Print.*** Information on over 16 000 business and industrial directories.
- ***Encyclopedia of Associations.*** Index of thousands of associations listed by broad subject category, specific subject, association, and location.
- ***Reader's Guide to Periodical Literature.*** Periodical index categorized by subject and author.
- ***Ulrich's International Periodicals Directory.*** Listings by title, publisher, editor, phone, and address of over 140 000 publications such as popular magazines, trade journals, government documents, and newspapers. Great for locating hard-to-find trade publications.

PEOPLE (PRINT)

- ***Dun & Bradstreet's Reference Book of Corporate Management.*** Professional histories of people serving as the principal officers and directors of more than 12 000 U.S. companies.
- ***Who's Who in America.*** Biographies of living U.S. citizens who have gained prominence in their fields. Related book, *Who's Who in the World*, covers global achievers.
- ***Who's Who in Canadian Business.*** Includes more than 15 000 biographical sketches of Canadian businesspeople.

TRADEMARKS (PRINT AND ONLINE)

- **Canadian Patents Database** wysiwyg://88/http://patentsl.ic.gc.ca/intro-e:html. Database contains more than 75 years of patent descriptions and images, in over 1.5 million documents.
- **Canadian Trademarks Database** wysiwyg://http://strategis.ic.gc.ca/cipo/trademarks/search/tmSearch.do. Trademark information, including designs, wares and services.
- **Official Gazette of the United States Patent and Trademark Office.** Weekly publication (one for trademarks and one for patents) providing official record of newly assigned trademarks and patents, product descriptions and product names.
- **United States Patent and Trademark Office** www.uspto.gov. Trademark and patent information records.

STATISTICS AND FACTS (PRINT AND CD-ROM)

- ***Dun & Bradstreet Canadian Industry Norms and Key Ratios.*** Canadian industry, performance, and performance ratios.
- ***Industry Norms and Key Business Ratios (Dun & Bradstreet).*** Industry, financial, and performance ratios.
- ***Information Please Almanac.*** Compilation of broad-range statistical data with strong focus on labor force.
- ***Robert Morris Associates' Annual Statement Studies.*** Industry, financial, and performance ratios.
- ***Statistical Abstract of the United States.*** U.S. economic, social, political, and industrial statistics.
- ***Statistics Canada Publications.*** Large collection of comprehensive business, census, and other data.
- ***The World Almanac and Book of Facts.*** Facts on economic, social, educational, and political events for major countries.

STATISTICS AND FACTS (ONLINE)

- **Canadian Almanac & Directory** http://library/usask.ca/dbs.cad.html. (requires subscription). Wide-ranging statistics and facts about Canada, including financial institutions, media, transportation, and Canada's chief trading partners.
- **Canadian Human Rights Commission** www.chrc-ccdp.ca. Legislation and policies regarding employment equity and other human rights legislation.
- **Bureau of Economic Analysis** www.bea.doc.gov. Large collection of economic and government data.
- **Canadian Legislature** www.parl.gc.ca. Information about bills, committees, and the Canadian Parliament.
- **FedStats** www.fedstats.gov. Access to full range of statistics and information from over 70 U.S. government agencies.
- **Human Resources Development Canada** www.hrdc-drhc.gc.ca. Comprehensive labour and employment information.
- **Industry Canada** http://strategis.ic.gc.ca. Wide-ranging information about the Canadian economy, business, and employment. Includes company directories and consumer information.
- **Statistics Canada** www.statcan.ca. Online collection of comprehensive business, census, and other data.
- **STAT-USA** www.stat.usa.gov. Large collection of economic and government data.
- **U.S. Census Bureau** www.census.gov. Demographic data on both consumers and businesses based on 1990 census.
- **U.S. Bureau of Labor Statistics** www.bls.gov. Extensive national and regional information on labour and business, including employment, industry growth, productivity, Consumer Price index (CPI), and overall U.S. economy.

FIGURE 10–9 (Continued)

(continued)

INTERNATIONAL BUSINESS RESOURCES (PRINT)

- ***Bank of Canada Review.*** Includes charts and statistics on external trade.
- ***D&B International Businesses.*** Company information, annual sales of about 50 000 leading businesses worldwide. Produced annually.
- ***Dictionary of International Business Terms.*** Definitions relating to international dimensions of accounting, business policy and strategy, information systems and technology, marketing, management, finance, and trade.
- ***Emerging Markets Handbook.*** Company information, key business activities, key financial ratios of over 1000 major companies in the world's emerging markets.
- ***Inter-Corporate Ownership.*** Index of which corporation owns and/or controls other corporations in Canada. Data includes country of residence, country of control, and percentage of voting rights held.
- ***International Directory of Business Information Sources.*** Contact and company information relating to businesses in 46 of the world's major economies.
- ***World Development Report.*** Analyzes major international economic conditions and trends for International Monetary Fund and World Bank countries. Produced annually.

COMMERCIAL DATABASES (REQUIRE SUBSCRIPTIONS)

- **ABI Inform.** Database of over 1500 scholarly and trade journals in business, management, industry, and economics (full text and abstracts).
- **CBCA—Canadian Business & Current Affairs.** Database of over 700 Canadian industry and professional periodicals and newsletters. Covers business, science, and technology.
- **CPI.Q—Canadian Periodical Index.** Citations, abstracts, and full-text articles from periodicals published in or providing major coverage of Canadian business, technology, arts, and other areas.
- **Dialog.** Over 900 main databases that include areas such as business and finance, news and media, medicine, pharmaceuticals, reference, social sciences, government and regulation, science and technology, and more.
- **Electric Library.** Hundreds of full-text newspaper, magazine, and newswire articles, plus maps and photographs.
- **LEXIS-NEXIS.** More than 1.4 billion documents in more than 8000 databases.
- **UMI ProQuest Direct.** More than 5000 journals, magazines, newspapers, and other information sources.

FIGURE 10-9 (Continued)

out the various Canadian government Web sites, such as Statistics Canada, Human Resources Development Canada, and Industry Canada. These resources contain statistics about life, work, government, population patterns, business, and the environment.

Government Publications For information on a law, a court decision, or current population patterns and business trends, consult government documents. A librarian can direct you to the information you want. You'll need the name of the government agency you're interested in and some identification for the specific information you need (employment equity or the latest census figures). If you know the date and name of a specific publication, the search will be easier.

The government tracks legal, population, and business trends.

FINDING INFORMATION ON THE INTERNET

The most popular source of company and industry information today is the Internet, with business information that ranges from current news and industry trends to company-related data on financial performance, products, goals, and employment. (See Table 10-3 on page 294) You must remember that anyone (including you) can post anything on a Web site. No one filters it, checks it for accuracy, or screens authors about why they are placing it on the Internet (See "Sharpening Your Career Skills: Evaluating World Wide Web Resources" on page 295). Before you seriously surf the Web for business information, learn a bit about your topic from journals, books, and commercial databases. You'll be able to detect skewed or erroneous information, and you can be more selective about which Web sites and documents you choose to use as resources.

When doing research on the Internet you need to be selective, because anyone can publish anything and no one checks the information for accuracy.

One good place to start on the Web is the Internet Public Library at **www.ipl.org**. Modelled after a real library, this site provides you with a carefully selected collection of links to high-quality business resources. If you are looking for specific company information, your best source may be the company's Web site (if it maintains one). Company sites generally include detailed information about the firm's products,

You can find all kinds of information about a company on its Web site.

TABLE 10-3 Best of Internet Searching

Major Search Engines	
AllTheWeb	www.alltheweb.com Remains one of the largest indexes of the web
Alta Vista	www.altavista.com Indexes data from millions of webpages and articles from thousands of Usenet newsgroups
Ask Jeeves	www.ask.com Finds answers to natural-language questions such as "Who won Super Bowl XXV?"
Excite	www.excite.com Is an all-purpose site loaded with options
Fedstats	www.fedstats.gov/search.html Simultaneously queries 14 federal agencies (U.S.) for specified statistics and numerical data
Google	www.google.com Is a simple directory that is especially useful for finding homepages of companies and organizations
LookSmart	www.looksmart.com Remains the closest rival to Yahoo! in terms of being a human-compiled directory (Choose "Your Town" for local directories)
Open Directory	http://dmoz.org Is the largest, most comprehensive human-edited directory of the Web (maintained by a vast, global community of volunteer editors)
Teoma	www.teoma.com Offers a "refine" feature, which gives suggested topics to explore after you do a search
WebBrain	www.webbrain.com Lets you search the web visually, so you can explore a dynamic picture of related information
WebCrawler	www.webcrawler.com Allows you to either search the entire site or browse any of the preselected categories
WiseNut	www.wisenut.com Automatically generates WiseGuide categories that are semantically related to the words in your query
Yahoo!	www.yahoo.com Is the oldest major website directory, listing over 500,000 sites

Multiple Search Engine Sites—Metacrawlers	
Dogpile	www.dogpile.com Lets you enter one query and then sniffs through FTP files, Usenet message boards, and Web sites (despite the silly name)
IXQuick	www.ixquick.com Searches up to 14 search engines at the same time, ranking by relevancy
Kartoo	www.kartoo.com Gathers the results, compiles them, and presents them graphically in a series of interactive maps
Mamma	www.mamma.com Claims to be the "Mother of All Search Engines" (this multilegged spider queries the major search engines for fast results)
ProFusion	www.profusion.com Retrieves only the "best" results from selected search engines (the University of Kansas spider)
Vivisimo	www.vivisimo.com Organizes results with document-clustering technology, which provides users with lists of documents in meaningful groups
Zworks	www.zworks.com Ranks results based on the cumulative score of all the engines used in the search, so duplicate results

SHARPENING YOUR CAREER SKILLS:

Evaluating World Wide Web Resources

Anyone who has gone online will agree that the Web offers the benefits of high speed and enormous scope for people who want both convenience and wide access to a variety of information sources. A quick entry into an online search engine may harvest dozens, hundreds, or thousands of hits, confronting Web researchers with data ranging from essential to just plain worthless. If you are just starting to acquire research skills, or wish to refine them further, developing a critical sense of Web resources will help you become a better researcher. Your reports could be more credible and beneficial to your audiences.

Analyzing the reliability of your Web information is not that much different from determining the trustworthiness of your secondary print sources, a topic already discussed in this chapter (see *Evaluate and Finalize Your Sources* on page 301). You must consider the source's reputation and potential bias. You must determine where your sources got their information, thereby providing yourself with a further check for reliability. You must also see if you can verify your source's information independently and if your source's claims meet the test of thoughtful scrutiny—in other words, do they make sense? With information you have accessed electronically, you should also ask yourself the following questions:

- **What is the URL (Universal Resource Locator)?** If the URL is a corporation or a political party, the information on the Web site may be particularly slanted. For example, if you are doing a study of the popularity of a certain snack food, the manufacturer's Web site will likely not include information you should know about competing products. And if the URL is a personal Web page, the information is more likely to be opinion than fact.
- **Who is the author? What are the author's qualifications?** An unsolicited book review downloaded from a major online bookseller, such as Chapters.Indigo.ca, may be written by a fan of the author, or even a friend, who wants to promote the book by writing a favourable review. If you have obtained an article from a private or organizational Web site, look for a biography of the author and a list of her or his publications and affiliations. Check these carefully for clues to the author's attitudes and interests, which may betray a particular viewpoint. Sometimes the author is anonymous, often a clue that the information may not be reliable.
- **Who is the audience?** Noting the URL and investigating the Web site and its links will help you determine if the information is directed toward a particular group of people with common interests. If it is, the information you have obtained may be slanted. For example, information on Web sites established by environmental associations or associations that promote the interests of the tobacco industry should be analyzed carefully for signs of bias.
- **Is the information in its original format? If not, is the original source cited?** You must try to determine if the information is taken out of context, different from the original, or plagiarized. If the source isn't documented, it may not be trustworthy.
- **Has the information been filtered?** Filtering means that an author's article has undergone review by external readers. The author's peers, a publisher, or an editor has read it and probably asked the author for improvements in content and writing style. Look for an author's acknowledgements of reviewers and editors. Acknowledgements suggest that the work was submitted to this kind of quality control, which results in a more authoritative and reliable electronic document than one that wasn't.
- **How current is the Web site?** Web sites include a "last updated" feature that indicates the last time the site was revised. Stale-dated sites may contain out-of-date information. Be aware of the site's date, which can usually be found on the Web site's first page.

For information that is current and has undergone the peer-review process, your best bet is to search your school library's electronic journals or those located at your public library. Spending the time analyzing your Web sources will help you to become a credible and reliable researcher and writer. Your audiences will value your skills and respect you for your integrity.

CAREER APPLICATIONS

1. Look at two Web sites for manufacturers of your favourite products. What kinds of bias to you see on these sites? How is the bias displayed?
2. You are writing a research paper on the advantages and disadvantages of snack foods. How can you use information you find through commercial databases to evaluate information on company Web sites?

Sources: Esther Grassian, *Thinking Critically about World Wide Web Resources*, <http://www.library.ucla.edu/libraries/college/ help/critical/index.htm> (2 Feb. 2001); Elizabeth E. Kirk, *Evaluating Information Found on the Internet*, <http://milton.mse.jhu.edu:8001/ research/education/net.html> (2 February 2001); Hope N. Tillman, *Evaluating Quality on the Net*, <http://www.hopetillman.com/findqual.html> (2 February 2001); and *Why We Need to Evaluate What We Find on the Internet*, <http:// thorplus.lib.purdue.edu/~techman/eval.html> (2 February 2001).

services, history, mission, strategy, financial performance, and employment needs. Many sites provide links to related company information, such financial reports, press releases, and more.

You can obtain press releases and general company news from news release sites such as PRNewswire **www.prnewswire.com** and Business Wire **www.businesswire.com**. These sites offer free databases of news releases from companies subscribing to their services. If you subscribe to a commercial online database system, you can also use the Internet to access information from the provider's database.

Press releases and general news about companies are also available at news release sites and through online databases.

The Web doesn't have everything. There may be nothing about small organizations, or perhaps just their address and phone number. And even if the information exists on the Web, you may not be able to find it. Web pages number over 320 million, but even the best search engines index only 100 million of those pages.[11]

Searchers can get the most dependable results from well-known, commercially backed search engines, which are likely to be well maintained and upgraded (see Table 10–3 on page 294). Most have simple or advanced search features, plus extras such as interactive maps and weather, travel information, phone and e-mail directories, and company profiles.

SEARCHING A DATABASE

By following a few guidelines, you can improve your database search results.

Even if search engines turn up what you're looking for, they'll also turn up a mountain of stuff you don't need. Narrow your results by following these tips to conduct an effective database search:[12]

- **Select appropriate databases.** You'll want a good business database. However, journals on your topic may be in a database that also includes journals on psychology, computers, or medicine.
- **Use multiple search engines.** Not all search engines are the same. Don't limit yourself to a single search engine, especially if you're looking for less-popular topics. To improve your results, read the help file and learn how the search engine works.
- **Translate concepts into key words and phrases.** For instance, if you want to determine the "effect of TQM on company profits," you should select the key words *TQM, total quality management, profits, sales, companies,* and *corporations.* Remember, use synonyms or word equivalents whenever possible, and use quotation marks around phrases to look for the entire phrase instead of separate words.
- **Use a short phrase or single term rather than a long phrase.** Search engines look for the words exactly as you key them in. If the words occur in an entry but not in the same order, you may miss relevant hits.
- **Do not use stopwords.** *Stopwords* are words the computer disregards and will not search for. Database documentation will identify any stopwords in addition to the common ones: *a, an, the, of, by, with, for,* and *to.*
- **Use variations of your terms.** Use abbreviations (*CEO, CA*), synonyms (*man, male*), related terms (*child, adolescent, youth*), different spellings (*dialog, dialogue*), singular and plural forms (*man, men*), nouns and adjectives (*manager, management, managerial*), and open and compound forms (*online, on line, on-line*).
- **Specify a logical relationship between the key words.** Must the document contain both *companies* and *corporations,* or is either one fine? Must it contain both *profits* and *companies,* or should it contain *TQM* or *total quality management* and *profits* or *sales?*
- **Evaluate the precision and quality of your results to refine your search if necessary.** If you end up with more than 60 to 100 links to sort through, refine your search. If your first page of results doesn't have something of interest, you've entered the wrong words or too few words. Also pay attention to whether you're searching in the title, subject, or document field of the database. Each will return different results.
- **Use Boolean operators.** Narrow or broaden your search by including AND, OR, or NOT (see Table 10–4 on page 297). Many search engines automatically include Boolean operators in their strategies even though you can't see them on the screen, so either insert your own (which should override automatic operators) or review the instructions for your search engine.
- **Use proximity operators.** To specify how close one of your key words should be to another, use a proximity operator such as NEAR. For example, the search phrase "marketing NEAR/2 organizations" means that *marketing* must be within two words of *organizations.*

➤ **Use wildcards.** Wildcard characters help you find plurals and alternate spellings of your key words. For example, by using a question mark in the word *organi?ations,* you'll find documents with both *organisations* (British spelling) and *organizations.* Similarly, by using an asterisk at the end of *chair*,* you'll find *chairman, chairperson, chairs,* and *chairlift.*

KEEPING TRACK OF YOUR PROGRESS

The goal of your initial note taking is to keep track of your sources so that you can select the best ones to use.

As you find and review your secondary source materials, take some brief notes to keep track of your progress. These are not the detailed notes you'll be taking later, but you'll need enough information to evaluate and finalize your sources. For instance, write down enough information to distinguish one source from the next. Identify the main idea or theme of each source, and perhaps write a brief comment about which subquestion the article addresses and whether the information was helpful. For example: "Discusses current franchise trends with statistics on number of new franchises started each year," or "Chapter 3 gives itemized steps for investigating franchise opportunities."

When using the Internet, note relevant Web sites by bookmarking, downloading, or printing out the actual Web pages. If the library database you're using includes material in full text, print out helpful articles; otherwise print out a copy of your search results and ask the librarian for assistance in finding the articles listed.

To record your comments, use note cards or Post-It Notes, or write on a printout or photocopy of the actual material. Develop a system that works for you. In addition, prepare a detailed bibliography of each source you intend to use later. Adopt one of the systems explained in Appendix B, "Documentation of Report Sources." If you photocopy an article, be sure to record on the photocopy all the bibliographic material you'll need to properly cite that source later on.

Conduct primary research by collecting basic information yourself.

TABLE 10-4 Improving Your Search Results

Search Operator	Effect	Strategy	Results
AND	Narrows results. Searches for records containing both the words it separates. Words separated by AND may be anywhere in the document—and far away from each other.	Rock AND roll	Music
OR	Broadens results. Searches for records containing either of the words it separates. A scattergun search that turns up a lot of matches. Not particularly precise.	Rock OR Roll	Igneous rocks; gemstones; crescent rolls; music
NOT	Limits results. Searches for records containing the first word(s) but not the second one.	Snow skiing NOT water skiing	Snow skiing; cross-country skiing
NEAR OR WITHIN	Proximity operator. Searches for words that all appear in a specified word range.	Snow NEAR 2 skiing	Results in which *skiing* is within two words of *snow*
ADJ	Adjacency operator. Searches for records in which second word immediately follows first word (two words are next to each other).	Ski ADJ Patrol	Ski patrol
?	Wildcard operator for single character. Matches any one character.	Ski?	Skit; skid; skin; skip
*	Wildcard operator for string of characters. Matches any number of characters.	Ski*	Ski; skiing; skies; skill; skirt; skit; skinny; skimpy
""	Exact match. Searches for string of words placed within quotation marks.	"1999 budget deficit"	1999 budget deficit

Gather Primary Information

Conduct primary research by collecting basic information yourself.

Sometimes the information you need is not available from secondary sources, or you may need information beyond what is covered in secondary sources. In that case, you must go out into the real world to gather the necessary information yourself. Five methods of collecting primary data are examining documents, making observations, conducting experiments, surveying people, and conducting interviews.

DOCUMENTS, OBSERVATIONS, AND EXPERIMENTS

Documentary evidence and historical records are sources of primary data.

Often the most useful primary references are internal sources, such as company sales reports, memos, balance sheets, income statements, policy statements, brochures, newsletters, annual reports, correspondence with customers or suppliers, and contracts. A great deal of information is often stored in company databases; by scouring company files, you can often piece together an accurate, factual, historical record from the tidbits of evidence revealed in various letters, memos, and reports.

A single document may be both a secondary source and a primary source. For example, when citing summaries of financial and operational data from an annual report, you're using the report as a secondary source; that is, somebody has already summarized the information for you. However, the same annual report would be considered a primary source if you were analyzing its design features, comparing it with annual reports from other years, or comparing it with reports from other companies.

Observation applies your five senses and your judgment to the investigation.

Making informal observations is another method of gathering primary information in business. For instance, you can observe people performing their jobs or observe other business operations. Observation is a useful technique when you're studying objects, physical activities, processes, the environment, or human behaviour. However, it can be expensive and time consuming, and the value of the observation depends on the reliability of the observer.

Experiments can be effective, but they are expensive.

Experiments can be an excellent source of primary information. This method is far more common in technical fields than in general business. That's because an experiment requires extensive, accurate, and measurable manipulation of the factors involved—not only tweaking those variables being tested but also controlling those variables that aren't being tested. This sort of experiment management is often expensive.

SURVEYS

One of the best ways to get information is to ask people with relevant experience and opinions. Surveys include everything from the one-time, one-on-one interview to the distribution of thousands of questionnaires. When prepared and conducted properly, surveys will tell you what a cross section of people think about a given topic.

Surveys are only useful when they're reliable and valid. A survey is *reliable* if it produces identical results when repeated. A survey is *valid* if it measures what it's intended to measure. One of the most crucial elements of a survey is the questionnaire.

Developing an effective survey questionnaire requires care and skill.

Begin developing your questionnaire by making a list of the points you need to determine. Then break these points into specific questions, choosing an appropriate type of question for each point. (Figure 10–10 shows various types of survey questions.) The following guidelines will help you produce results that are both valid and reliable:[13]

- **Provide clear instructions.** Respondents need to know exactly how to fill out your questionnaire.
- **Keep the questionnaire short and easy to answer.** Ask only questions that are relevant to your research. Remember that people are most likely to respond if they can complete your questionnaire within 10 to 15 minutes.
- **Formulate questions that provide easily tabulated or analyzed answers.** Remember, numbers and facts are easier to summarize than opinions.
- **Avoid leading questions.** Questions that lead to a particular answer bias your survey. If you ask, "Do you prefer that we stay open in the evenings for customer

convenience?" you'll get a "yes" answer. Instead, ask, "What time of day do you normally do your shopping?"

- **Ask only one question at a time.** A compound question such as "Do you read books and magazines regularly?" doesn't allow for respondents who read one but not the other.
- **Pretest the questionnaire.** Have a sample group identify questions that are subject to misinterpretation.

If you're mailing your questionnaire rather than administering it in person, include a persuasive cover letter that explains why you're conducting the research. You must convince your readers that responding is important. Remember that even under the best of circumstances, you may get no more than a 10 to 20 percent response.

QUESTION TYPE	EXAMPLE
Open-ended	How would you describe the flavour of this ice cream?
Either-or	Do you think this ice cream is too rich? _____ Yes _____ No
Multiple choice	Which description best fits the taste of this ice cream? (Choose only one.) a. Delicious b. Too fruity c. Too sweet d. Too intensely flavoured e. Bland f. Stale
Scale	Please mark an X on the scale to indicate how you perceive the texture of this ice cream. ←————————————————→ Too light Light Creamy Too creamy
Checklist	Which flavours of ice cream have you had in the past 12 months? (Check all that apply.) _____ Vanilla _____ Chocolate _____ Strawberry _____ Chocolate chip _____ Coffee
Ranking	Rank these flavours in order of your preference, from 1 (most preferred) to 5 (least preferred): _____ Vanilla _____ Cherry _____ Maple nut _____ Chocolate ripple _____ Coconut
Short-answer	In the past month how many times did you buy ice cream in the supermarket? __________ In the past month how many times did you buy ice cream in ice cream shops? __________

FIGURE 10–10 Types of Survey Questions

Internet surveys
- Cost less
- Reach large numbers of people quickly
- Improve response rates

An increasingly popular vehicle for conducting surveys or polling customers is the Internet. Online surveys offer distinct benefits: They cost less to conduct than traditional surveys, they reach large numbers of people quickly and economically, and their response rates are higher. For example, Harris Interactive conducted an online survey of 100 000 people concerning their online shopping habits. The survey took only 17 days to complete and cost $150 000. Harris estimates that the same survey by phone could have taken one year and cost about $5 million.[14]

INTERVIEWS

OBJECTIVE 5 Define *informational interviews* and list four types of interview questions.

An **interview** is any planned conversation that has a specific purpose and involves two or more people.

Getting information straight from an expert can be a great way to research a report. **Interviews** are planned conversations with a predetermined purpose that involve asking and answering questions. Although they are frequently overlooked, interviews are an effective method of gathering information. However, before you decide to do one, ask yourself whether an interview is really the best way to get the information you need.

In a typical information interview, the interviewer seeks facts that bear on a decision or that contribute to basic understanding. The interviewer controls the action by asking a list of questions designed to elicit information from the interviewee. When you are conducting an interview, it's important to decide in advance what kind of information you want and how you will use it. This sort of planning saves you time and builds goodwill with the people you interview.

Effective interviewers develop a communication plan.

Planning Interviews Planning an interview is similar to planning any other form of communication. You begin by analyzing your purpose, learning about the other person, and formulating your main idea. Then you decide on the length, style, and organization of the interview.

Organize an interview much as you would organize a written message.

Sometimes you'll want to provide a list of questions several days before the interview.

Good interviews have an opening, a body, and a close. The opening establishes rapport and orients the interviewee to the remainder of the session. You might begin by introducing yourself, asking a few polite questions, and then explaining the purpose and ground rules of the interview. The body of the interview is used for asking questions. In the close of the interview you summarize the outcome, preview what will come next, and underscore the rapport that has been established.

Four basic types of interview questions:
- Open-ended questions
- Direct open-ended questions
- Closed-ended questions
- Restatement questions

Preparing Interview Questions The answers you receive are influenced by the types of questions you ask, by the way you ask them, and by your subject's cultural and language background. Race, gender, age, educational level, and social status are all influential factors, so know your subject before you start writing questions.[15] In addition, be aware of ethical implications. For example, asking someone to divulge personal information about a co-worker may be asking that person to make an unethical choice. Always be careful about confidentiality, politics, and other sensitive issues.

Consider providing a list of questions a day or two before the interview, especially if you'd like to quote your subject in writing or if your questions might require your subject to conduct research or think extensively about the answers. Receiving your questions early will give your subject time to prepare more complete (and therefore more helpful) answers. Consider tape-recording the interview if your topic is complex or if you plan to quote or paraphrase the interviewee in a written document.

Interview questions can be categorized into four types. **Open-ended questions** invite the interviewee to offer an opinion, not just a yes, a no, or a one-word answer: "What do you think your company wants most from suppliers?" Such questions help you learn the reasons behind a decision rather than just the facts. However, they diminish your control of the interview.

Direct open-ended questions suggest a response: "What have you done about smoothing out the intercultural clashes in your department?" These questions give you more control while still giving the interviewee some freedom in framing a response.

Closed-ended questions require yes or no answers or call for short responses: "Did you meet your sales quota?" Such questions produce specific information, save time, require less effort from the interviewee, and eliminate bias and prejudice in answers. On the other hand, they also limit the respondent's initiative and may prevent important information from being revealed.

Restatement questions mirror a respondent's previous answer and invite the respondent to expand on that answer: "You said you dislike sales quotas. Is that correct?" They also signal to the interviewee that you're paying attention.

The following guidelines will help you come up with an effective set of interview questions:[16]

- **Think about sequence.** Arrange your questions in a way that helps uncover layers of information or that helps the subject tell you a complete story.
- **Rate your questions and highlight the ones you really need answers to.** If you start to run out of time during the interview, you may have to skip less important questions.
- **Ask smart questions.** If you ask a question that your subject perceives to be less than intelligent, the interview could deteriorate in a hurry.
- **Use a mix of question types.** Vary the pacing of your interview by using open-ended, direct open-ended, closed-ended, and restatement questions.
- **Limit the number of questions.** Don't try to cover more questions than you have time for. People can speak at a rate of about 125 to 150 words (about one paragraph) per minute. If you're using a mix of question types, you can probably handle about 20 questions in a half-hour. Remember that open-ended questions take longer to answer than other types do.
- **Edit your questions.** Try to make your questions as neutral and as easy to understand as possible. Then practice them several times to make sure you're ready for the interview.

Processing Interview Information When you've concluded the interview, take a few moments to write down your thoughts, go over your notes, and organize your material. Look for important themes, helpful facts or statistics, and direct quotes. Fill in any blanks while the interview is fresh in your mind. If you made a tape recording, transcribe it (take down word for word what the person said) or take notes from the tape just as you would while listening to someone in person.

Carefully review your interview notes immediately after the interview and fill in the gaps before you forget.

Interviews don't necessarily have to take place in person. As more and more people come online, e-mail interviews are becoming more common. Perhaps one of the biggest advantages of an e-mail interview is that it gives subjects a chance to think through their responses thoroughly, rather than rushing to fit the time constraints of an in-person interview.[17] (As a reminder of the tasks involved in interviews, see this chapter's "Checklist: Conducting Effective Information Interviews" on page 302.)

Conducting interviews by e-mail is becoming increasingly popular.

Evaluate and Finalize Your Sources

Be selective when choosing your actual sources from the piles of material you've just gathered. Avoid dated or biased material. If possible, check on who collected the data, the methods they used, their qualifications, and their professional reputations.[18] Common sense will help you judge the credibility of the sources you plan to use.

Ask questions about the reference works you use, such as

- Who collected the data? How?
- What are the authors' qualifications and reputations?
- Is the source up to date?
- Is the information objective?

To make the best selections, ask yourself the following questions about each piece of material:

- **Does the source have a reputation for honesty and reliability?** Naturally, you'll feel more comfortable using information from a publication that has a reputation for accuracy. But don't let your guard down completely; even the finest reporters and editors make mistakes. Find out how the publication accepts articles and whether it has an editorial board.

- **Is the source potentially biased?** Depending on what an organization stands for, its messages may be written with a certain bias—which is neither bad nor unethical. The Tobacco Institute and the Canadian Association of Retired Persons have their own points of view. In order to interpret an organization's information, you need to know its point of view. Its source of funding may also influence its information output.
- **Where did the source get its information?** Many secondary sources get their information from other sources, removing you even further from the original data. If a newspaper article says that pollutants in a local river dropped by 50 percent since last year, the reporter probably didn't measure those pollutants directly. That information was obtained from someone else.
- **Can you verify the material independently?** A good way to uncover bias or a mistake is to search for the same information from another source. Verification can be particularly important when the information goes beyond simple facts to include projections, interpretations, and estimates.
- **Is the material current?** Check the publication date of a source, and make sure you are using the most current information available. Timeliness is especially important if you are using statistics or citing law.
- **Is the author credible?** Find out whether the person or the publisher is well known in the field. Is the author an amateur? Merely someone with an opinion to air?
- **What is the purpose of the material?** Was the material designed to inform others of new research, summarize existing research, advocate for a position, or stimulate discussion? Was it designed to promote or sell a product? Be sure to distinguish between advertising and informing.
- **Is the material complete?** Determine whether the information you have is the entire text or a selection from another document. If it's a selection, which parts were excluded? Do you need more detail?

Checklist: Conducting Effective Information Interviews

Preparing Your Interview

- ✓ Analyze your purpose, goals, and audience.
- ✓ Determine the needs of your interviewee and gather background information.
- ✓ Outline your interview on the basis of your goals, audience, and interview category.
- ✓ Set the level of formality.
- ✓ Choose a structured or an unstructured approach.
- ✓ Formulate questions as clearly and concisely as possible.
- ✓ Ask questions in an order that helps your subject tell you a complete story.
- ✓ Ask intelligent questions that show you've done your homework.
- ✓ Use a mix of question types.
- ✓ Select a time and a site.
- ✓ Inform the interviewee of the nature of the interview and the agenda to be covered.
- ✓ Provide a list of questions in advance if the interviewee will need time to research and formulate quality answers.

Conducting Your Interview

- ✓ Be on time for the interview appointment.
- ✓ Remind the interviewee of the purpose and format.
- ✓ Clear the taking of notes or the use of a tape recorder with the interviewee.
- ✓ Use your ears and eyes to pick up verbal and nonverbal cues.
- ✓ Follow the stated agenda, but be willing to explore relevant subtopics.
- ✓ Close the interview by restating the interviewee's key ideas and by reviewing the actions, goals, and tasks that each of you has agreed to.

Following Up

- ✓ Write a thank-you memo or letter that provides the interviewee with a record of the meeting.
- ✓ Review notes and revise them while the interview is fresh in your mind.
- ✓ Transcribe tape recordings.
- ✓ Monitor progress by keeping in touch with your interviewee.

- **Do the source's claims stand up to scrutiny?** Step back and ask yourself whether the information makes sense. If a researcher claims that the market for a particular product will triple in the next five years, ask yourself what would have to happen for that prediction to come true. Will three times as many customers buy the product? Will existing customers buy three times more than they currently buy? Why? Is this information relevant to your needs?

You probably won't have time to conduct a thorough background check on all your sources, so focus your efforts on the most important or most suspicious pieces of information.

At the end of your evaluation, you should have two piles of information: those sources you want to use and those you have eliminated. Now review the pile of information you intend to use and ask yourself several questions: Do I have enough of the right kind of information to answer all my questions? Do I need more? What type of information am I missing?

How will you know when you have enough information? You have enough when (1) you can answer all the questions that began the research project and (2) you begin noticing that sources are becoming redundant.[19] Too much information can frustrate your note-taking and processing efforts.

Stop when you reach the point at which additional effort provides little new information.

Process Your Information

Once you have selected your sources, it's time to start using what you've found. In some cases you may only need to read the material carefully and meet with your supervisor to discuss your findings—for example, when you're looking for the answer to a simple question. However, in most cases, you'll be asked to submit a written report or give an oral presentation on your findings. That means you'll need to go through your research and take some extensive notes.

READING THE MATERIAL AND TAKING NOTES

Before you start taking notes, organize your research into a logical order. For instance, you might divide the material by subquestions and then divide it chronologically within each grouping. This approach will enable you to focus on a specific topic and read the most current information first. Afterward you can read earlier documents to fill in the history, gather background material, or find older statistics to analyze trends.

When you read a document to take notes, you need not read every word. Read the topic sentences first (generally the first sentence of a business article) to decide whether the paragraph may contain useful information. If it does, then read the entire paragraph.

Decide whether a document contains useful information before reading it carefully to take notes.

When your information is a computer printout or a photocopy, feel free to mark up these documents. Highlight key phrases, facts, or segments, and write comments in the margins. Then record your notes on cards or enter them directly into a computer.

The recording system that most students use (and many instructors recommend) is taking notes on three-by-five-inch index cards. Note cards are easy to use, carry, sort, and arrange. You can also take notes by computer. By recording notes in electronic format instead of on handwritten cards, the researcher can easily search for words (using the "find" function), sort the notes by column headings, and copy information directly into the document draft.

You may find that the best solution is using a combination of index cards (to capture information while you're reading it) and computer software (to manage the information once you've captured it or to take notes directly from the source). Whichever method you choose, be sure to take complete notes so that you can avoid backtracking to look up something you've forgotten.

When deciding whether to use note cards or computer software for taking notes, select whichever system works best for you.

On each note card write only one fact. Indicate whether the information is your own idea, a paraphrase of someone else's idea, or a direct quote (by using quotation

Each note card or computer entry should contain
- Only one fact
- A subject heading
- Complete source information or a cross-reference to bibliography cards

marks, ellipses, and brackets as necessary). For your own reference and sorting purposes, write at the top of the card the general subject of the material (either a simple phrase or identifying numbers from your outline). Finally, carefully record bibliographic information so that you can cite the source later. If you are collecting several pieces of information from each source, you might prepare a bibliography card for each source, number the source, and then use the numbers to cross-reference your note cards. Thus notes taken from source 75 will be written on notecards numbered 75.1, 75.2, and so on.

QUOTING AND PARAPHRASING

Use direct quotations when the original language will enhance your argument or when rewording the passage would lessen its impact. However, try not to quote sources at great length. Too much quoting creates a choppy patchwork of varying styles and gives the impression that you've lost control of your material.

Express material in your own words unless quoting the original language will have a greater impact.

One way to avoid such choppiness is to **paraphrase** material, or express it in your own words. When you paraphrase, you present information to your reader in a fresh, condensed manner that demonstrates your complete understanding of the material. In fact, paraphrasing may actually increase your comprehension of the source material, because when you recast a passage, you have to think carefully about its meaning—more carefully than if you merely copied it word for word.[20]

To paraphrase effectively, follow these tips:[21]

- Reread the original passage until you fully understand its meaning.
- Record your paraphrase on a note card or in an electronic format.
- Use business language and jargon that your audience is familiar with.
- Check your version with the original source to verify that you have not altered the meaning.
- Use quotation marks to identify any unique terms or phrases you have borrowed exactly from the source.
- Record the source (including the page number) on your note card so that you can give proper credit if you use this material in your report.

In short, good paraphrasing accomplishes three goals: (1) It's shorter than the original text, (2) it's presented in your own words, and (3) it does not alter or distort the meaning of the original text.[22]

Whether you paraphrase or use direct quotes, maintain your credibility and ethics by giving proper credit to the original source.

DOCUMENTING SOURCES AND GIVING CREDIT

Always give proper credit when you use someone else's material or ideas.

Whenever you quote or paraphrase, you are using someone else's words or ideas. Doing so without proper credit is **plagiarism**. You can avoid plagiarism by documenting the original source using one of the systems explained in Appendix B, "Documentation of Report Sources." Documenting your sources through footnotes, endnotes, or some similar system is necessary for books, articles, tables, charts, diagrams, song lyrics, scripted dialogue, letters, speeches—anything that you take from someone else. Even if you paraphrase the material, it's best to give credit to the person from whom you obtained the original information.

It's not necessary to give source credit for material that is general knowledge.

However, you do not have to cite a source for general knowledge or for specialized knowledge that's generally known among your readers. For example, it's common knowledge that 1867 is the year of Confederation. You can say so on your own authority, even if you've read an article in which the author says the same thing. Moreover, even though copyright law covers printed materials, audiovisual material, many forms of artistic expression, computer programs, maps, mailing lists, and even answering machine messages, it does not protect

- Titles, names, short phrases, and slogans
- Familiar symbols or designs
- Lists of ingredients or contents

- Ideas, procedures, methods, systems, processes, concepts, principles, discoveries, or devices (although it does cover their description, explanation, or illustration)

A work is considered copyrighted as soon as it's put into fixed form, even if it hasn't been registered.[23]

Crediting the source is not always enough. According to the fair use doctrine you can use other people's work only as long as you don't unfairly prevent them from benefiting as a result. For example, if you reproduce someone else's copyrighted questionnaire in a report you're writing, even if you identify the source thoroughly you're preventing the author from selling a copy of that questionnaire to your readers.

The fair use doctrine offers guidelines for determining how copyrighted material may be used.

In general, avoid relying to such a great extent on someone else's work. However, when you can't avoid it, contact the copyright holder (usually the author or publisher) for permission to reprint. You'll usually be asked to pay a fee.

Analyze Your Data

By themselves, the data you've collected won't offer much meaning or insight. You'll need to search for relationships among the facts and the bits of evidence you've compiled. This analysis allows you to interpret your findings and thus answer the questions or solve the problem that instigated your report.

Analyze your results by calculating statistics, drawing reasonable and logical conclusions, and, if appropriate, developing a set of recommendations.

Much of the information you compile during the research phrase will be in numerical form. However, such statistical information in its raw state is of little practical value. It must be manipulated so that you and your readers can interpret its significance. Look at the data from various angles and try to detect patterns by fitting pieces together to form tentative conclusions. This process enables you to answer the questions you generated when defining the problem. As you proceed with your analysis, either verify or reject your conclusions.

One useful way of looking at numerical data is to find the **average**, which is a number that represents a group of numbers. Three useful averages are shown in Table 10–5 below. The **mean** is the sum of all the items in the group divided by the number of items in that group. The **median** is the "middle of the road" average, or the midpoint of a series (with an equal number of items above and below). The **mode** is the number that occurs more often than any other in your sample. It's the best average for answering a question such as "What is the usual amount?"

The same set of data can be used to produce three kinds of averages: mean, median, and mode.

It's also helpful to look for a **trend**, a steady upward or downward movement in a pattern of events taking place over time. Trend analysis is common in business. By looking at data over a period of time, you can detect patterns and relationships that will help you answer important questions.

Trend analysis involves examining data over time in order to detect patterns and relationships.

Once you have identified a trend, you'll want to look for a cause. To do this, you could look for a **correlation**, a statistical relationship between two or more variables. For example, if the salespeople with the largest accounts consistently produced higher sales,

A **correlation** is a statistical relationship between two or more variables.

Table 10–5 Three Types of Average: Mean, Median, and Mode

Salesperson	Sales	
Wilson	$3000	
Green	5000	
Carrick	6000	
Wimper	7000	Mean
Keeble	7500	Median
Kemble	8500	Mode
O'Toole	8500	Mode
Mannix	8500	Mode
Caruso	9000	
Total	**$63 000**	

you might assume that those two factors were related in a predictable way. However, your conclusion might be wrong. Correlations are useful evidence, but they do not necessarily prove a cause-and-effect relationship. To be certain that factors are correlated, you might have to collect more evidence.

Interpret Your Data

Now your data is in a form that both you and your readers can understand. But you're not finished yet. Once you have thoroughly analyzed your information, your next step is to draw conclusions and, if requested, develop recommendations.

DRAWING CONCLUSIONS

Conclusions are interpretations of the facts.

A **conclusion** is a logical interpretation of the facts in your report. Reaching good conclusions based on the evidence at hand is one of the most important skills you can develop in your business career. A sound conclusion

- **Must fulfill the original statement of purpose.** After all, drawing a conclusion is why you took on the project in the first place.
- **Must be based strictly on the information included in the rest of the report.** Consider all the information in your report. Don't ignore anything—even if it doesn't support your conclusion. Moreover, don't introduce any new information in your conclusion. (After all, if something is that important, it should be in the body of your report.)
- **Must be logical.** A logical conclusion is one that follows accepted patterns of reasoning.

Check the logic that underlies your conclusions.

Even though conclusions need to be logical, they may not automatically flow from the evidence. Most business decisions require assumptions and judgment; relatively few are based strictly on the facts. Your personal values or the organization's values may also influence your conclusions; just be sure that you're aware of how these biases affect your judgment. Also, don't expect all team members to examine the evidence and arrive at the same conclusion. One of the reasons for bringing additional people into a decision is to gain their unique perspectives and experiences.

DEVELOPING RECOMMENDATIONS

Recommendations are suggestions for action.

Whereas a conclusion interprets the facts, a **recommendation** suggests what to do about the facts. The difference between a conclusion and a recommendation can be seen in the following example:

CONCLUSION	RECOMMENDATION
I conclude that, on the basis of its track record and current price, this company is an attractive buy.	I recommend that we write a letter to the president offering to buy the company at a 10 percent premium over the market value of its stock.

Good recommendations are
- Practical
- Acceptable to readers
- Explained in enough detail for readers to take action

When you've been asked to take the final step and translate your conclusions into recommendations, be sure to make the relationship between them clear. Recommendations are inappropriate in a report when you're not expected to supply them. But when you do develop recommendations of your own, try not to let your assumptions and personal values influence them. To be credible, recommendations must be based on logical analysis and sound conclusions. They must also be practical and acceptable to your readers, the people who have to make the recommendations work. Finally, when making a recommendation be certain that you have adequately described the steps that come next. Don't leave your readers scratching their heads and saying, "This all sounds good, but what do I do on Monday morning?"

Planning Business Reports—Adaptation

Now you're ready to think about how you want to present your findings to others. In one respect, reports are no different from other business messages: You need to establish a good relationship with your audience, and you must select a channel and medium that are appropriate to your audience and your purpose.

OBJECTIVE 6 Clarify what it means to adapt your report to your audience.

Establish a Good Relationship with Your Audience

Even though reports are meant to be factual, objective, and logical, you still need to focus on your audience to help your reports succeed. To help your audience accept what you're saying, remember the following advice:

- **Use the "you" attitude.** Show readers how your report answers *their* questions and solves *their* problems.
- **Emphasize the positive.** Even if your report recommends a negative action, remember to state the facts and make your recommendations positively. Instead of using a negative tone, "The only way we'll ever strengthen our cash position is to reduce employee spending," use a positive, forthright one: "Reducing employee spending will strengthen our cash position."
- **Establish your credibility.** One of the best ways to gain your audience's trust is to be thorough, research all sides of your topic, and document your findings with credible sources.
- **Be polite.** Earn your audience's respect by being courteous, kind, and tactful.
- **Use bias-free language.** Avoid unethical and embarrassing blunders in language related to gender, race, ethnicity, age, and disability.
- **Project the company's image.** Whether your report is intended for people inside or outside the company, be sure to plan how you will adapt your style and your language to reflect the image of your organization.

Establishing a good relationship with an audience is the same for reports as for other business messages.

Select the Appropriate Channel and Medium

As with other business messages, you'll need to select the best format for conveying your report. In some cases a simple letter, memo, or e-mail message will do. At other times you'll need to write a formal report or discuss your findings in an oral presentation. Remember, the medium you choose may be dictated by your report's classification—whether it's authorized, routine, or internal.

See this chapter's "Checklist: Planning Business Reports" on page 308 to review the tasks and concepts just discussed. Chapter 11 discusses how to organize and write reports and how to incorporate visuals. Chapter 12 explains how to assemble and format formal reports and proposals. Finally, Chapter 13 discusses how to present information orally.

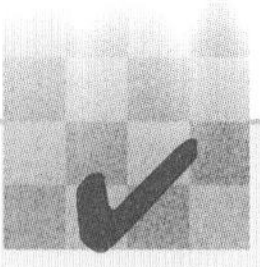

Checklist: Planning Business Reports

Analyzing Business Reports

✓ Define the problem and develop a problem statement.

✓ Limit the scope of your study by clarifying your assignment, factoring the problem, and forming a hypothesis.

✓ Outline issues for investigation, using informative headings in parallel construction.

✓ Develop a statement of purpose that specifically defines why you're preparing the report.

✓ Prepare a work plan to clarify the tasks to be accomplished; describe any products to result from the investigation; review all project assignments, schedules, and resource requirements; and plan for following up after the report has been delivered.

Investigating Business Reports

✓ Find and access secondary information by searching libraries, the Internet, and databases.

✓ Know what you're looking for and keep track of your progress.

✓ Gather primary information from company documents, casual observations, controlled experiments, surveys, and interviews.

✓ Evaluate and finalize your sources by avoiding dated or biased material and by using only credible and reliable sources.

✓ Fill in any information holes by conducting more research as necessary.

✓ Process your information by reading your final sources and taking careful notes.

✓ Document all quoted and paraphrased material.

✓ Analyze your data so that you can interpret your findings.

✓ Draw conclusions that fulfill your original statement of purpose, that are based strictly on the information in your report, and that are logical.

✓ Carefully develop recommendations about how to solve the problem in your report (only if requested to do so).

Adapting Business Reports

✓ Establish a good relationship with your audience, using the "you" attitude, emphasizing the positive, establishing your credibility, being polite, using bias-free language, and projecting the company image.

✓ Select the appropriate channel and medium for your report, whether printed, electronic, or oral.

Summary of Learning Outcomes

1 Discuss why businesses need reports and the factors that affect how reports are prepared. Business reports provide the information that allows internal and external users to make effective decisions and solve business problems. Business reports may travel up or down the organizational hierarchy to link managers with employees. Successful reports are accurate, complete, and unbiased. To be useful, they must present exactly the right kind and amount of information in a clear and convenient manner. Whether printed or electronic, report preparation varies according to five factors: (1) the source of the report (or who initiates it); (2) frequency (reports may be routine or special); (3) target audience; and (4) intent (whether the report is meant to educate or draw conclusions).

2 Distinguish between informational and analytical reports. Informational reports focus on facts and are intended mainly to inform and educate readers, not to persuade them. Informational reports include those for monitoring and controlling operations (plans, operating reports, personal activity reports), implementing policies and procedures (lasting guidelines, position papers), complying with government regulations, documenting progress (interim progress reports, final reports), and summarizing information. On the other hand, analytical reports analyze and interpret data, summarize the data in logical conclusions, and sometimes make recommendations based on the data. Many analytical reports are intended to persuade readers to accept a decision, action, or recommendation, so information plays a supporting role in these documents. Analytical reports tend to ask "should we or shouldn't we" questions, and they include reports for solving problems, justifying a project or course of action, and obtaining new business or funding (proposals).

3 Explain the difference between a problem statement and a statement of purpose, and then identify five other elements often included in a formal work plan. A problem statement defines *what* you're going to investigate, whereas a statement of purpose defines *why* you are preparing your report. Other work plan elements include (1) the tasks to be accomplished and the sequence in which they should be performed; (2) a description of any product that will result from your study; (3) a review of responsibilities, assignments, schedules, and resource requirements; (4) a working outline; and (5) plans for following up after delivering the report.

4 Describe six tasks necessary to doing research for business reports. When investigating business reports, you need to complete six basic tasks. (1) Find and access secondary information by knowing what to look for and where to look (in libraries, on the Internet, and in databases). (2) Gather primary information from company documents, casual observations, formal experiments, surveys, or interviews. (3) Evaluate and finalize your sources by judging their relevance and credibility. (4) Process your information by reading the materials you've gathered, quoting and paraphrasing your sources, and giving credit to those sources. (5) Analyze your data by searching for relationships among the facts and evidence you've gathered. (6) Interpret your data by drawing conclusions and developing recommendations when appropriate.

5 Define *informational interviews*, and list four types of interview questions. Interviews are planned conversations with a predetermined purpose that involve asking and answering questions. The interviewer seeks information that may broaden understanding or aid decision-making. Interview questions are of four types: (1) open-ended questions (which invite the person being interviewed to offer an opinion), (2) direct open-ended questions (which suggest a response), (3) closed-ended questions (which require little more than yes or no answers), and restatement questions (which mirror a respondent's previous answer and invite the person to expand on that answer).

6 Clarify what it means to adapt your report to your audience. As with other business messages, adapting a report to an audience involves establishing a good relationship and selecting the appropriate channel and medium. When preparing business reports, plan to use the "you" attitude, emphasize the positive, establish your own credibility, be polite, use bias-free language, and project the company's image. Then decide whether to convey your report in a letter, memo, or e-mail message or whether you should emphasize formality with a report that's in the form of a manuscript or an oral presentation.

ON THE JOB

Solving a Communication Dilemma at Dell Inc.

To maintain his company's leading edge in the computer industry, founder Michael Dell and his management team need mountains of information, much of it in the form of reports. These reports must be well planned, must define each problem, and must not only present carefully researched data but also analyze that data. Such reports greatly influence Dell Inc.

During the 1990s, Dell learned the value of gathering and examining information for establishing inventory procedures. He now analyzes average discount rates and inventory turnover, and with the help of his managers, Dell sets up daily reports for suppliers to provide timely communication about orders and delivery times. In addition, to boost quality standards and limit the number of defective parts, Dell's managers provide regular progress reports to suppliers with quality evaluations.

Reports also play a key role in Dell's e-commerce efforts, selling directly to customers over the Internet. Before setting a goal of selling 50 percent of the company's products through the Web, Dell gathered and analyzed information on overall market growth, the potential of online purchases, and the potential for his company's products. Once he had completed his analysis, Dell was able to introduce customers to the idea of ordering custom-built computers online—and he quickly achieved his Internet sales goals.

Knowing the value of reports, Dell makes sure that his Web site now offers much more than an online ordering centre for customers. Through dell.com, company managers can track customer satisfaction levels, measure customer responses, monitor complaint resolutions, and prepare performance reports. In addition, the site enables managers and customer service representatives to establish and maintain direct links with consumers. Consumers can obtain quick responses to e-mail queries and technical questions, find timely information on new products and new technology, and track the progress of their orders at Dell Premier Pages (an Internet-based system customized for each client).

Reports also influence Dell's decisions about entering new markets and offering new products. For example, before expanding into a new country, Dell examines his company's market share, country-by-country and product-by-product, and evaluates the growth potential of the market under consideration. By collecting and analyzing data on customers and products from countries around the world, Dell can forecast potential market penetration and sales force productivity.

Dell also analyzes employee needs to anticipate the company's demand for new workers. He depends on his human resources staff to produce reports that measure turnover and productivity, identify key job openings, define training needs, and map out organizational charts. Dell also analyzes the key qualities of successful employees so that he can spot similar qualities in prospective job candidates.

Overall, Dell depends on more than 4000 types of analysis to keep his operation running smoothly and to keep his company at the top of the computer industry. "To say that we have become a data-driven company is almost an understatement," Dell says. "Data is the engine that keeps us on track."

Your Mission Michael Dell realizes that to stay on top, Dell Inc. must continue to improve customer service at its various country-specific sites. You are a manager in customer relations, and Dell has asked you to plan a report that will outline ways to increase customer service and satisfaction at dell.ca. You'll need to conduct the necessary research, analyze the findings, and present your recommendations. From the following, choose the best responses, and be prepared to explain why your choices are best.

1 Which of the following represents the most appropriate statement of purpose for this study?

a The purpose of this study is to identify any customer service problems at dell.ca.

b This study answers the following question: "What improvements in customer service can dell.ca make in order to increase overall customer satisfaction?"

c This study identifies the dell.com customer service representatives who are most responsible for poor customer satisfaction.

d This study identifies steps that Dell's customer service representatives should take to change customer service practices at dell.ca.

2 You have tentatively identified the following factors for analysis:

I To improve customer service, we need to hire more customer service representatives.
  A Compute competitors' employee-to-sales ratio.
  B Compute our employee-to-sales ratio.

II To improve customer service, we need to hire better customer service representatives.
  A Assess skill level of competitors' customer service representatives.
  B Assess skill level of our customer service representatives.

III To improve customer service, we need to retrain our customer service representatives.
  A Review competitors' training programs.
  B Review our training programs.

IV To improve customer service, we need to compensate and motivate our people differently.
  A Assess competitors' compensation levels and motivational techniques.
  B Assess our compensation levels and motivational techniques.

Should you proceed with the investigation on the basis of this preliminary outline, or should you consider other approaches to factoring the problem?

a Proceed with this outline.

b Do not proceed. Factor the problem by asking customers how they perceive current customer service efforts at dell.ca. In addition, ask customer service representatives what they think should be done differently.

c Do not proceed. Factor the problem by surveying nonbuyers to find out if current customer service efforts influenced their decision not to buy at dell.ca. In addition, ask nonbuyers what they think should be done differently.

d Do not proceed. Factor the problem by asking customer service representatives for suggestions on how to improve customer service. In addition, ask nonbuyers and current customers what they think should be done differently.

3 Which of the following work plans is the best option for guiding your study of ways to improve customer service?

a Version One

Statement of Problem: As part of Dell Inc.'s continuing efforts to offer the most attractive computers in the world, Michael Dell wants to improve customer service at dell.ca. The challenge here is to identify service improvements that are meaningful and valuable to the customer without being too expensive or time consuming.

Purpose and Scope of Work: The purpose of this study is to identify ways to increase customer satisfaction by improving customer service at dell.ca. A four-member study team, composed of the vice-president of customer relations and three customer service representatives, has been appointed to prepare a written service-improvement plan. To accomplish this objective, this study will survey customers to learn what changes they'd like to see in terms of customer service at dell.ca. The team will analyze these potential improvements in terms of cost and time requirements and then will design new service procedures that customer service representatives can use to better satisfy customers.

Sources and Methods of Data Collection and Analysis: The study team will assess current customer service efforts by (1) querying customer service representatives regarding their customer service, (2) observing representatives in action dealing with customers through e-mail responses and telephone calls, (3) surveying current Dell owners regarding their purchase experiences, and (4) surveying visitors to dell.ca who decide not to purchase from Dell (by intercepting a sample of these people as they leave the Web site). The team will also visit competitive Web sites to determine firsthand how they treat customers, and the team will submit online questionnaires to a sample of computer owners and classify the results by brand name. Once all these data have been collected, the team will analyze them to determine where buyers and potential buyers consider customer service to be lacking. Finally, the team will design procedures to meet their expectations.

Schedule:

Jan 10–Jan 30:	Query customer service representatives. Observe representatives in action. Survey current Dell owners. Survey nonbuyers at dell.ca.
Jan 31–Feb 15:	Visit competitive Web sites. Conduct online survey of computer owners.
Feb 15–Mar 15:	Analyze data. Draft new procedures.
Mar 16–Mar 25:	Prepare final report.
Mar 28:	Present to management/customer service committee.

b Version Two

Statement of Problem: Dell's customer service representatives need to get on the ball in terms of customer service, and we need to tell them what to do in order to fix their customer service shortcomings.

Purpose and Scope of Work: This report will address how we plan to solve the problem. We'll design new customer service procedures and prepare a written report that customer service representatives can learn from.

Sources and Methods of Data Collection: We plan to employ the usual methods of collecting data, including direct observation and surveys.

Schedule:

Collect data	Jan 10–Feb 15
Analyze data	Feb 15–Mar 1
Draft new procedures	Mar 2–Mar 15
Prepare final report	Mar 16–Mar 25
Present to management/ customer service committee	Mar 28

c Version Three

Task 1—Query customer service representatives: We will interview a sampling of customer service representatives to find out what steps they take to ensure customer satisfaction. Dates: Jan 10–Jan 20

Task 2—Observe representatives in action: We will observe a sampling of customer service representatives as they work with potential buyers and current owners, in order to learn firsthand what steps employees typically take. Dates: Jan 21–Jan 30

Task 3—Survey current Dell owners: Using a sample of names from Dell's database of current owners, we'll ask owners how they felt about the purchase process when they bought their computer and how they feel they've been treated since then. We'll also ask them to suggest steps we could take to improve service. Dates: Jan 15–Feb 15

Task 4—Survey nonbuyers at dell.ca: While we are observing customer service representatives, we will also approach visitors at dell.ca who leave the site without making a purchase. As visitors exit the site, we'll present a quick online survey, asking them what they think about Dell's customer service policies and practices and whether these had any bearing on their decisions not a buy a Dell product. Dates: Jan 21–Jan 30

Task 5—Visit competitive Web sites: Under the guise of shoppers looking for new computers, we will visit a selection of competitive Web sites to discover how they treat customers and whether they offer any special service that Dell doesn't. Dates: Jan 31–Feb 15

Task 6—Conduct online survey of computer owners: Using Internet-based technology, we will survey a sampling of computer owners (of all brands). We will then sort the answers by brand of computer owned to see which dealers are offering which services. Dates: Jan 15–Feb 15

Task 7—Analyze data: Once we've collected all these data, we'll analyze them to identify (1) services that customers would like to see Dell offer, (2) services offered by competitors that aren't offered by Dell, and (3) services currently offered by Dell that may not be all that important to customers. Dates: Feb 15–Mar 1

Task 8—Draft new procedures: From the data we've analyzed, we'll select new services that should be considered by dell.ca. We'll also assess the time and money burdens that these services are likely to present, so that management can see whether each new service will yield a positive return on investment. Dates: Mar 2–Mar 15

Task 9—Prepare final report: This is essentially a documentation task, during which we'll describe our work, make our recommendations, and prepare a formal report. Dates: Mar 16–Mar 25

Task 10—Present to management/customer relations committee: We'll summarize our findings and recommendations and will make the full report available to dealers at the quarterly meeting. Date: Mar 28

d Version Four

Problem: To identify meaningful customer service improvements that can be implemented by Dell Inc. at dell.ca.

Data Collection: Use direct observation and online surveys to gather details about customer service at dell.ca and at competing Web sites. Have the study team survey current Dell owners and people who visited dell.ca but did not buy, and send an online questionnaire to computer owners.

Schedule:

Step 1: Data collection. Work will begin on January 10 and end on February 15.

Step 2: Data analysis. Work will start on February 15 and end on March 1.

Step 3: Drafting new procedures. Work will start on March 2 and end on March 15.

Step 4: Preparation of the final report. Work will start on March 16 and end on March 25.

Step 5: Presentation of the final report. The report will be presented to management and the customer service committee on March 28.[24]

Test Your Knowledge

Review Questions

1 What factors affect how reports are prepared?
2 How do informational reports differ from analytical reports?
3 What is a problem statement, and how does it differ from a statement of purpose?
4 What is included in a work plan for a report, and why is it important?
5 How does primary information differ from secondary information?
6 What four types of questions can be posed during an interview?
7 What is paraphrasing, and what is its purpose?
8 What are the characteristics of a sound conclusion?
9 How does a conclusion differ from a recommendation?
10 Why do writers use the "you" attitude in their reports?

Interactive Learning 

Use This Text's Online Resources

Visit our Companion Web site at **www.pearsoned.ca/thill**, where you can use the interactive Study Guide to test your chapter knowledge and get instant feedback. Additional resources link you to the sites mentioned in this text and to additional sources of information on chapter topics.

Also check out the resources on the Mastering Business Communication CD, including "Perils of Pauline," an interactive presentation of the business communication challenges within a fictional company.

Apply Your Knowledge

Critical Thinking Questions

1 If your report includes only factual information, is it objective? Please explain.
2 After an exhaustive study of an important problem, you have reached a conclusion that you believe your company's management will reject. What will you do? Explain your answer.
3 Why do you need to evaluate your sources?
4 How is the evaluation of Web sites different from periodical sources? How is it similar?
5 Put yourself in the position of a manager who is supervising an investigation but doing very little of the research personally. Why would a work plan be especially useful to the manager? To the researcher? Explain.
6 **Ethical Choices** If you want to make a specific recommendation in your report, should you include information that might support a different recommendation? Explain.

Practice Your Knowledge

Documents for Analysis

Assume that your university's vice-president of student affairs has received many student complaints about campus parking problems. You are appointed to chair a student committee organized to investigate the problems and report on recommended solutions. The president gives you the file labelled "Parking: Complaints from Students," and you jot down the essence of the complaints as you inspect the contents. Your notes look like this:

- Inadequate student spaces at critical hours
- Poor night lighting near the computer centre
- Inadequate attempts to keep resident neighbours from occupying spaces
- Dim marking lines
- Motorcycles taking up full spaces
- Discourteous security officers
- Spaces (usually empty) reserved for university officials
- Relatively high parking fees
- Full fees charged to night students even though they use the lots only during low-demand periods
- Vandalism to cars and a sense of personal danger
- Inadequate total space
- Resident harassment of students parking on the street in front of neighbouring houses

Your first job is to organize these complaints into four or five general categories for your committee to discuss and analyze before preparing its report. Choose the main headings for your outline, and group these specific complaints under them.

Exercises

10–1 **Understanding Business Reports and Proposals: How Companies Use Reports** Interview several people working in a career you might like to enter, and ask them about the written reports they receive and prepare. How do these reports tie in to the decision-making process? Who reads the reports they prepare? Summarize your findings in writing, give them to your instructor, and be prepared to discuss them with the class.

10–2 **Understanding Business Reports and Proposals: Report Classification** Using the information presented in this chapter, identify the purpose of the following reports. In addition, write a brief paragraph about each, explaining who the audience is likely to be, what type of data would be used, and whether conclusions and recommendations would be appropriate.

a A statistical study of the pattern of violent crime in a large city during the last five years
b A report prepared by a seed company demonstrating the benefits of its seed corn for farmers
c A report prepared by an independent testing agency evaluating various types of cold remedies sold without prescription
d A trip report submitted at the end of a week by a travelling salesperson
e A report indicating how 45 acres of undeveloped land could be converted into an industrial park

f An annual report to be sent to the shareholders of a large corporation
g A formal report by a police officer who has just completed an arrest

10–3 Internet Visit Industry Canada's Publishing Toolbox site at **icnet.ic.gc.ca/publication/english/index_e.html**. What information is available on this site? Who is the audience for this site? What sorts of information on this site can help businesspeople plan reports and proposals?

10–4 Planning Reports: Procedures You're the vice-president of operations for a Montreal fast-food chain. In the aftermath of a major snowstorm, you're drafting a report on the emergency procedures to be followed by personnel in each restaurant when heavy snowfall warnings are in effect. Answer who, what, when, where, why, and how, and then prepare a one-page draft of your report.

10–5 Planning Reports: Secondary Information You're getting ready to write a research paper on a topic of your choice. You decide to search for information using both the library databases and the Internet. Develop a search strategy.
a What are some key words and phrases you might use?
b Which Boolean operators would you use to narrow your search?
c Which wildcard operators might you use?

10–6 Planning Reports: Primary Information Deciding how to collect primary data is an important part of the research process. Which one or more of the five methods of data collection (examining documents, making observations, surveying people, conducting experiments, and performing interviews) would you use if you were researching these questions?
a Has the litter problem on campus been reduced since the cafeteria began offering fewer take-out choices this year than in past years?
b Has the school attracted more transfer students since it waived the formal application process and allowed students at other colleges to send in transcripts with a one-page letter of application?
c Have the number of traffic accidents at the school's main entrance been reduced since a traffic light was installed?
d Has student satisfaction with the campus bookstore improved now that students can order their books over the Internet and pick them up at several campus locations?

10–7 Planning Reports: Surveys You work for a movie studio that is producing a young director's first motion picture, the story of a group of unknown musicians building a reputation in a competitive industry. Unfortunately, some of the director's friends leave the first complete screening saying that the 132-minute movie is simply too long. Others can't imagine any more editing cuts. Your boss wants to test the movie on a regular audience and ask viewers to complete a questionnaire that will help the director decide whether edits are needed and, if so, where. Design a questionnaire you can use to solicit valid answers for a report to the director about the audience's reaction to the movie.

10–8 Planning Reports: Data Analysis Your boss has asked you to analyze and report on your division's sales for the first nine months of this year. Using the following data from company invoices, calculate the mean for each quarter and all averages for the year to date. Then identify and discuss the quarterly sales trends.

January	$24 600	**April**	$21 200	**July**	$29 900
February	25 900	**May**	24 600	**August**	30 500
March	23 000	**June**	26 800	**September**	26 600

10–9 Planning Reports: Secondary Information Using online, database, or printed sources, find the following information. Be sure to properly cite your source using the formats discussed in Appendix B. (*Hint:* Start with Figure 10-9, Major Business Resources.)
a Contact information for the Canadian Management Association
b Median weekly earnings of men and women by occupation
c Current market share for Perrier water
d Performance ratios for office supply retailers
e Annual stock performance for Bank of Montreal.
f Number of franchise outlets in Canada.
g Composition of the Canadian workforce by profession

10–10 Planning Reports: Library Sources Businesspeople have to know where to look for secondary information when they research a report. Prepare a list of the most important magazines and professional journals in the following fields:
a Marketing/advertising
b Insurance
c Communications
d Accounting

10–11 Planning Reports: Industry Information Locate the NAICS codes for the following industries:
a Hotels and motels
b Breakfast cereals
c Bottled water
d Automatic vending machines

10–12 Planning Reports: Company Information Select any public company and find the following information:
a Names of the company's current officers
b List of the company's products or services
c Current issues in the company's industry
d Outlook for the company's industry as a whole

10–13 Planning Reports: Study Scope Your boss has asked you to do some research on franchising. Actually, he's thinking about purchasing a few Subway franchises and he needs some information. Visit **www.amazon.ca** and review the site. On the home page, perform a key word search on "franchise." Explore some of the books by clicking on "read more about this title."
a Use the information to develop a list of subquestions to help you narrow your focus.
b Write down the names of three books you might purchase for your boss.
c How can this Web site assist you with your research efforts?

10–14 Planning Reports: Unsolicited Proposal You're getting ready to launch a new lawn-care business that offers mowing, fertilizing, weeding, and other services. The lawn surrounding a nearby shopping centre looks as if it could use better care, so you target that business for your first sales proposal. To help prepare this proposal, write your answers to these questions:

a What problem statement and statement of purpose would be most appropriate? (Think about the reader's viewpoint.)

b What questions will you need answered before you can write a proposal to solve the reader's problem? Be as specific as possible.

c What conclusions and recommendations might be practical, acceptable to the reader, and specific enough for the shopping centre to take action? (Think about the purpose of the report.)

10–15 Planning Reports: Work Plan Now turn the situation around and assume that you're the shopping centre's facilities manager. You report to the general manager, who must approve any new contracts for lawn service. Before you contract for lawn care, you want to prepare a formal study of the current state of your lawn's health. The report will include conclusions and recommendations for your boss's consideration. Draft a work plan, including the problem statement, the statement of purpose and scope, a description of what will result from your investigation, the sources and methods of data collection, and a preliminary outline.

10–16 Teamwork The university administration has asked you to head a student committee that will look into how the bookstore can ease the long lines during the first two weeks of every term, when students need to buy books. Select two other students to serve on your committee and help plan a feasibility study and an analytical report showing your recommendations. As a first step, your committee should prepare a brief memo to the administration. The memo should accomplish the following:

a Identify the problem (problem statement) and the purpose (statement of purpose).

b Identify two or three likely alternatives to be investigated.

c Clearly identify the criteria for selecting among the options.

d Identify the primary and secondary sources of information to be used in the study.

10-17 Finding Information: Interviews Plan to conduct an informational interview with a professional working in your chosen field of study. Plan the structure of the interview and create a set of interview questions. Conduct the interview. Using the information you gathered, write a memo to another student describing the tasks, advantages, and disadvantages of jobs in this field of study. (Your reader is a person who also plans to pursue a career in this field of study.)

10-18 Teamwork: Evaluating Sources Break into small groups and surf the Internet to find Web sites that provide business information such as company or industry news, trends, analysis, facts, or performance data. Using the criteria discussed under "Evaluate and Finalize Your Sources" on page 301 and "Sharpening Your Career Skills: Evaluating World Wide Web Resources" on page 295, evaluate the credibility of the information presented at these Web sites.

10-19 Quoting and Paraphrasing Select an article from a business journal such as *Canadian Business, Report on Business Magazine,* or *Fortune*. Read the article and highlight the article's key points. Summarize the main idea of the article, paraphrasing the key points.

10-20 Ethical Choices Your company operates a Web site featuring children's games and puzzles. The vice-president of marketing needs to know more about the children who visit the site so she can plan new products. She has asked you to develop an online survey questionnaire to collect the data. What ethical issues do you see in this situation? What should you do?

Going Online Exercises

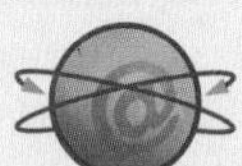

Pointers for Business Plans, found on page 273 of this chapter

What are the components of a business plan? What do readers of a plan look for? What common mistakes should you avoid? For answers to these questions and advice for planning a business plan, log on to BizPlanIt.Com.

1 Why is the executive summary such an important section of a plan? What kind of information is contained in the executive summary?
2 What is the product/service section? What information should it contain? List some of the common errors to avoid when planning this part.
3 What type of business planning should you describe in the exit strategy section? Why?

Writing Business Reports and Proposals

1 Discuss the structure of informational reports

2 Explain the structure of analytical reports

3 List the most popular types of visuals and discuss when to use them

4 Clarify five principles of graphic design to remember when preparing visuals

5 Identify and briefly describe five tools that writers can use in long reports to help readers stay on track

ON THE JOB

Facing a Communication Dilemma at FedEx

Delivering On Time, Every Time

www.fedex.com

Imagine collecting, transporting, and delivering more than five million letters and packages every day. Now imagine that every one of these parcels absolutely, positively has to arrive at its destination when expected. That's the standard against which Federal Express managers—and customers—measure performance. Living up to this exacting standard day in and day out presents founder and CEO Frederick W. Smith and his entire management team with a variety of communication challenges.

When FedEx began operations in 1973, its services covered 22 U.S. cities. Today it delivers throughout the United States and Canada, and to 211 countries around the world. FedEx operates nearly 600 airplanes, maintains a fleet of 38 500 trucks and vans, and employs more than 137 000 people. In Canada, Federal Express employs more than 5000 people in 63 facilities, and maintains over 1000 drop-off locations and three call centres (in Vancouver, Toronto, and Montreal), which respond to 36 500 calls a day. Making sure that all these people have the information they need in the form they need it is tough enough, but the challenge doesn't stop there.

FedEx must also battle a host of rivals, including United Parcel Service (UPS), Purolator (owned by Canada Post), Airborne Express, DHL, and other delivery companies. Competition is fierce, so FedEx is constantly on the lookout for information on competitors and on innovative ways to serve its own customers better. The firm offers a host of online business tools, including address books, an address checker, complete international shipping documents, and customizable portals where Fedex customers can track shipments and access signature proofs of delivery. Businesses can also add common Fedex functions to their retail Web sites and link directly to their own order management systems.

With competitors offering more and customers expecting more, Smith and his management team have their work cut out for them. Monitoring and controlling company operations, training new employees, tracking competitor service and performance, making a host of decisions about how to serve customers better—all these activities require the communication of timely, accurate information, and much of that information comes in the form of reports. To keep the business running smoothly, maintain satisfied customers, and hold competitors at bay, FedEx managers receive and prepare reports of all kinds. So how do Smith and his managers use reports for internal communication? How can FedEx writers make their reports readable and convenient to use? What makes one report better than another?[1]

At FedEx, reports of all kinds are used to track both system and employee performance, as well as to assemble information needed for making managerial decisions. Not only does Frederick Smith read innumerable reports, he wrote a very famous one which detailed the idea of his air express delivery service and persuaded investors to fund him.

Consultants consider reports essential to keep their clients up to date with projects and to communicate information and advice.

Organizing Business Reports and Proposals

Before composing a business report or proposal, organize the material collected, arranging it in a logical order that meets your audience's needs. High-level managers like Frederick Smith would advise to carefully choose the format, length, order, and structure for a report before drafting even the first word.

Deciding on Format and Length

At times, the person who requests the report will make the decision about format and length for you. Such guidance is often the case with monitor/control reports, justification reports, proposals, progress reports, and compliance reports. The more routine the report, the less flexibility you have in deciding format and length. Monthly status reports, for example, are usually routine, and will have the same basic appearance and structure. Within that framework, however, there is room for flexibility, depending on the nature of the information being reported.

Organizing means arranging your material in an order that is logical and that meets your audience's needs.

Periodic reports are usually written in memo format and don't need much of an introduction: two or three sentences orienting the reader to the purpose and scope of the report are often sufficient. They should follow the same general format and organization from period to period. Personal activity reports are also written in memo format, but because they're nonrecurring documents, they require more introduction than periodic reports do; for example, you may need to include some background information in your opening remarks.

You may present a report in one of four formats: preprinted, letter, memo, or manuscript form.

When you do have some leeway in length and format, base your decisions on your readers' needs. Your goal is to present your information in a format suitable for your audience and purpose. When selecting a format for your report, you have four options:

- **Preprinted form.** Used for fill-in-the-blank reports. Most are relatively short (five or fewer pages) and deal with routine information, often mainly numerical. Use this format when the person authorizing the report requests it.
- **Letter.** Commonly used for reports of five or fewer pages that are directed to outsiders. These reports include all the normal parts of a letter, but they may also have headings, footnotes, tables, and figures.
- **Memo.** Commonly used for short (fewer than 10 pages) informal reports distributed within an organization. Like longer reports, they often have internal headings and sometimes include visual aids. Memos exceeding 10 pages are sometimes referred to as *memo reports* to distinguish them from briefer memos.
- **Manuscript.** Commonly used for reports that require a formal approach, whether a few pages or several hundred. As length increases, reports in manuscript format require more elements before (prefatory parts) and after (supplementary parts) the text. Chapter 12 explains these elements and includes a checklist for preparing formal reports.

Appendix A, "Format and Layout of Business Documents," contains more specific guidelines for physically preparing reports.

Length depends on
- Your subject
- Your purpose
- Your relationship with your audience

The length of your report obviously depends on your subject and purpose, but it's also affected by your relationship with your audience. When your readers are relative strangers, if they are skeptical or hostile, if the material is nonroutine or controversial, you will usually have to explain your points in greater detail, which results in a longer document. However, you can afford to be brief if you are on familiar terms with your readers, if they are likely to agree with you, and if the information is routine or uncomplicated. Short reports are more common in business than long ones, and you'll probably write many more 5-page memos than 250-page formal reports.

Choosing the Direct or Indirect Approach

What order is best for your audience and purpose? As Chapter 5 explains, when an audience is considered either receptive or open-minded, use the direct approach: lead off with a summary of your key findings, conclusions, and recommendations. This "up-front" arrangement is by far the most popular and convenient order for business reports. It saves time and makes the rest of the report easier to follow. For those who have questions or want more information, later parts of the report provide complete findings and supporting details. The direct approach also produces a more forceful report. You sound sure of yourself when you state your conclusions confidently at the outset.

However, confidence may sometimes be misconstrued as arrogance. If you're a junior member of a status-conscious organization or if your audience is skeptical or hostile, you may want to use the indirect approach: introduce your complete findings and discuss all supporting details before presenting your conclusions and recommendations. The indirect approach gives you a chance to prove your points and gradually overcome your audience's reservations. By deferring the conclusions and recommendations to the end of the report, you imply that you've weighed the evidence objectively without prejudging the facts. You also imply that you're subordinating your judgment to that of the audience, whose members are capable of drawing their own conclusions when they have access to all the facts.

The indirect approach helps overcome resistance by withholding the main idea until later in the report.

Although the indirect approach has its advantages, some report readers will always be in a hurry to get to the recommendations and turn to them immediately, thus defeating your purpose. In general, the longer the message, the less effective an indirect approach is likely to be. Furthermore, an indirect argument is harder to follow than a direct one. Therefore, carefully consider report length before deciding on the direct or indirect approach.

Because both direct and indirect approaches have merit, businesspeople often combine them. They reveal their conclusions and recommendations as they go along, rather than putting them either first or last. Figure 11–1 on page 318 presents the introductions from two reports with the same general outline. In the direct version, a series of statements summarize the conclusion reached in relation to each main topic in the outline. In the indirect version, the same topics are introduced in the same order without drawing any conclusions about them. The conclusions appear within the body of the report instead. So is this second report direct or indirect? Business reports are often difficult to classify.

Businesspeople often combine the direct and indirect approaches.

Regardless of the format, length, or order used, you must still deal with the question of how your ideas will be subdivided and developed. Suppose you're writing a controversial report recommending that your company revise its policy on who reports to whom. You know that some of your readers will object to your ideas, so you decide to use indirect order. How do you develop your argument? Your job is to choose the most logical structure—the one that suits your topic and goals and that makes the most sense to your audience.

Structuring Informational Reports

OBJECTIVE 1 Discuss the structure of informational reports.

Informational reports are the easiest to organize because they provide nothing more than facts. When writing informational reports, reader reaction is not usually an issue. Most readers will presumably respond unemotionally to your material, so you can use the direct approach. What you do need to be concerned about, however, is reader comprehension. The information must be presented logically and accurately so that your audience will understand exactly what is meant and will be able to use your information easily.

Reader reaction is rarely an issue in informational reports.

FIGURE 11-1 Direct Approach versus Indirect Approach in an Introduction

THE DIRECT APPROACH

Since the company's founding 25 years ago, we have provided regular repair service for all our electric appliances. This service has been an important selling point as well as a source of pride for our employees. However, we are paying a high price for our image. Last year, we lost $500 000 on our repair business.

Because of your concern over these losses, you have asked me to study the pros and cons of discontinuing our repair service. With the help of John Hudson and Susan Lefkowitz, I have studied the issue for the past two weeks and have come to the conclusion that we have been embracing an expensive, impractical tradition.

By withdrawing from the electric appliance repair business, we can substantially improve our financial performance without damaging our reputation with customers. This conclusion is based on three basic points that are covered in the following pages:

- It is highly unlikely that we will ever be able to make a profit in the repair business.
- Sevice is no longer an important selling point with customers.
- Closing down the service operation will create few internal problems.

THE INDIRECT APPROACH

Since the company's founding 25 years ago, we have provided repair service for all our electric appliances. This service has been an important selling point as well as a source of pride for our employees. However, the repair business itself has consistently lost money.

Because of your concern over these losses, you have asked me to study the pros and cons of discontinuing our repair service. With the help of John Hudson and Susan Lefkowitz, I have studied the issue for the past two weeks. The following pages present my findings for your review. Three basic questions are addressed:

- What is the extent of our losses, and what can we do to turn the business around?
- Would withdrawal hurt our sales of electrical appliances?
- What would be the internal repercussions of closing down the repair business?

Topical organization is arranging material in order of importance, sequence, chronology, spatial relationships, location, or categories.

When writing an informational report let the nature of whatever you're describing dictate the structure. For example, when describing a machine, each component can correspond to a part of your report. When describing an event, approach the discussion chronologically. And when explaining how to do something, describe the steps in the process. Informational reports use a **topical organization**, arranging material according to one of these following topics:

- **Importance.** When reviewing five product lines, you might organize a study according to the sales for each product line, beginning with the line that produces the most revenue and proceeding to the one that produces the least.
- **Sequence.** When studying a process, discuss it step by step—1, 2, 3, and so on.
- **Chronology.** When investigating a chain of events, organize the study according to what happened in January, what happened in February, and so on.
- **Spatial orientation.** When explaining how a physical object works, describe it left to right (or right to left in some cultures), top to bottom, outside to inside.
- **Geography.** When location is important, organize a study according to geography, perhaps by region of the country or by area of a city.
- **Category.** When asked to review several distinct aspects of a subject, look at one category at a time, such as sales, profit, cost, or investment.

There are other bases for organization. Because some informational reports, especially compliance reports and internal reports, are prepared on preprinted forms, they are organized according to instructions supplied by the person requesting the information. In addition, many proposals conform to an outline specified in the request for proposal that is issued by the client. The client's request might include a statement of the problem, some background information, the scope of work involved, applicable restrictions, recommended sources and methods, a work schedule, required personnel qualifications, available facilities, anticipated costs, and expected results.

TABLE 11–1 Common Ways to Structure Analytical Reports

Structures to Use:	Focus on Conclusions	Focus on Recommendations	Focus on Logical Argument		
			2 + 2 = 4	Scientific	Yardstick
When readers are ...	Likely to accept	Likely to accept	Skeptical and need to be convinced of logic	Skeptical and need to be convinced of the best solution	Skeptical and need to be convinced with criteria
When the order is ...	Direct	Direct	Indirect	Indirect	Indirect
When your credibility is ...	High	High	Low	Low	Low
Advantages: Structure allows readers to ...	Quickly grasp recommendations	Quickly grasp conclusions	Follow writer's thinking process	Draw their own conclusions	Measure alternatives against the same standards (criteria)
Drawbacks: Structure can make the report ...	Seem too simple	Seem too simple	Longer	Very long, by discussing each alternative	Very long (often boring) by measuring each item against each criteria (also requires readers to agree on criteria)

Structuring Analytical Reports

OBJECTIVE 2 Explain the structure of analytical reports.

For analytical reports, your choice of structural approach depends on the reaction anticipated. When expecting your audience to agree with you, use a structure that focuses attention on conclusions and recommendations. When expecting your audience to disagree with you or to be hostile, use a structure that focuses attention on the reasons behind your conclusions and recommendations. The three most common approaches to structuring analytical reports are (1) focusing on conclusions, (2) focusing on recommendations, and (3) focusing on logical argument (see Table 11–1).

The structure of analytical reports depends on audience reaction.

Three popular ways to organize analytical reports:

- By conclusions
- By recommendations
- By logical arguments

FOCUSING ON CONCLUSIONS: A RESEARCH AND ANALYSIS REPORT

When writing an analytical report for people from your own organization who have asked you to study something, you're writing for your most receptive readers. They may know from experience that you'll do a thorough job, and they may trust your judgment. If they're likely to accept your conclusions, you can structure your report around conclusions or recommendations using a direct approach.

Analytical reports may be organized around conclusions and recommendations (direct approach) when the audience is receptive.

However, the direct approach does have some drawbacks. If your readers have reservations either about you or about your material, strong statements at the beginning may intensify their resistance. Also, focusing on conclusions and recommendations may make everything seem too simple. Your readers could criticize your report as being superficial: "Why didn't you consider this option?" or "Where did you get this number?" You're generally better off taking the direct approach in a report only when your credibility is high—when your readers trust you and are willing to accept your conclusions and recommendations.

The direct approach has some drawbacks.

Figure 11–2 on page 320 presents an outline of a report analyzing the success of an outsourced training program. The writer's company decided to have a consulting company handle its employee training. The writer, a human resources specialist, was asked to evaluate the arrangement a year after it was established. Her analysis

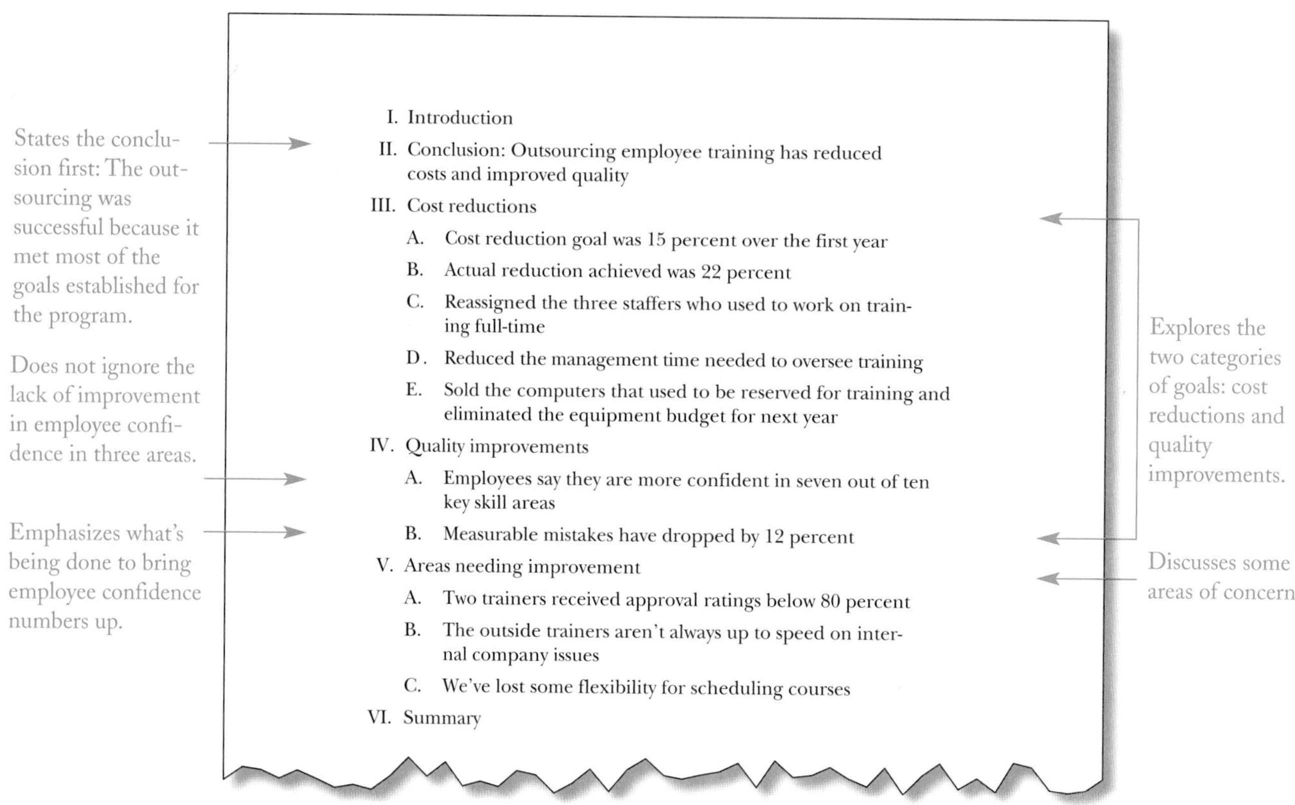

States the conclusion first: The outsourcing was successful because it met most of the goals established for the program.
Does not ignore the lack of improvement in employee confidence in three areas.
Emphasizes what's being done to bring employee confidence numbers up.
Explores the two categories of goals: cost reductions and quality improvements.
Discusses some areas of concern.

I. Introduction
II. Conclusion: Outsourcing employee training has reduced costs and improved quality
III. Cost reductions
  A. Cost reduction goal was 15 percent over the first year
  B. Actual reduction achieved was 22 percent
  C. Reassigned the three staffers who used to work on training full-time
  D. Reduced the management time needed to oversee training
  E. Sold the computers that used to be reserved for training and eliminated the equipment budget for next year
IV. Quality improvements
  A. Employees say they are more confident in seven out of ten key skill areas
  B. Measurable mistakes have dropped by 12 percent
V. Areas needing improvement
  A. Two trainers received approval ratings below 80 percent
  B. The outside trainers aren't always up to speed on internal company issues
  C. We've lost some flexibility for scheduling courses
VI. Summary

FIGURE 11-2 In-Depth Critique: Outline of a Research Report Focusing on Conclusions

shows that the outsourcing experiment was very beneficial. She structured her report in three main sections, as the outline illustrates.

Use a similar structure whenever you're asked to analyze a problem or an opportunity. Readers who are interested mainly in your conclusions can grasp them quickly, and readers who want to know more about your analysis can look at the data you provide.

When the reader is concerned with conclusions, use them as the main points.

FOCUSING ON RECOMMENDATIONS: A JUSTIFICATION REPORT

A slightly different approach is useful when readers want to know what they ought to do (as opposed to what they ought to conclude). You'll often be asked to solve a problem rather than just study it. The actions you want your readers to take become the main subdivisions of your report.

When the reader is concerned about what action to take, use recommendations as the main points.

When structuring a report around recommendations, follow five steps:

1. Establish the need for action in the introduction, generally by briefly describing the problem or opportunity.
2. Introduce the benefit that can be achieved, without providing any details.
3. List the steps (recommendations) required to achieve the benefit, using action verbs for emphasis.
4. Explain each step more fully, giving details on procedures, costs, and benefits.
5. Summarize the recommendations.

Figure 11-3 on page 321 shows a report written by a business development manager at a retail chain. She was asked by the company's board of directors to suggest whether the firm should set up a retailing site on the World Wide Web and, if so, how to implement the site. Setting up shop on the Internet was a major decision for the

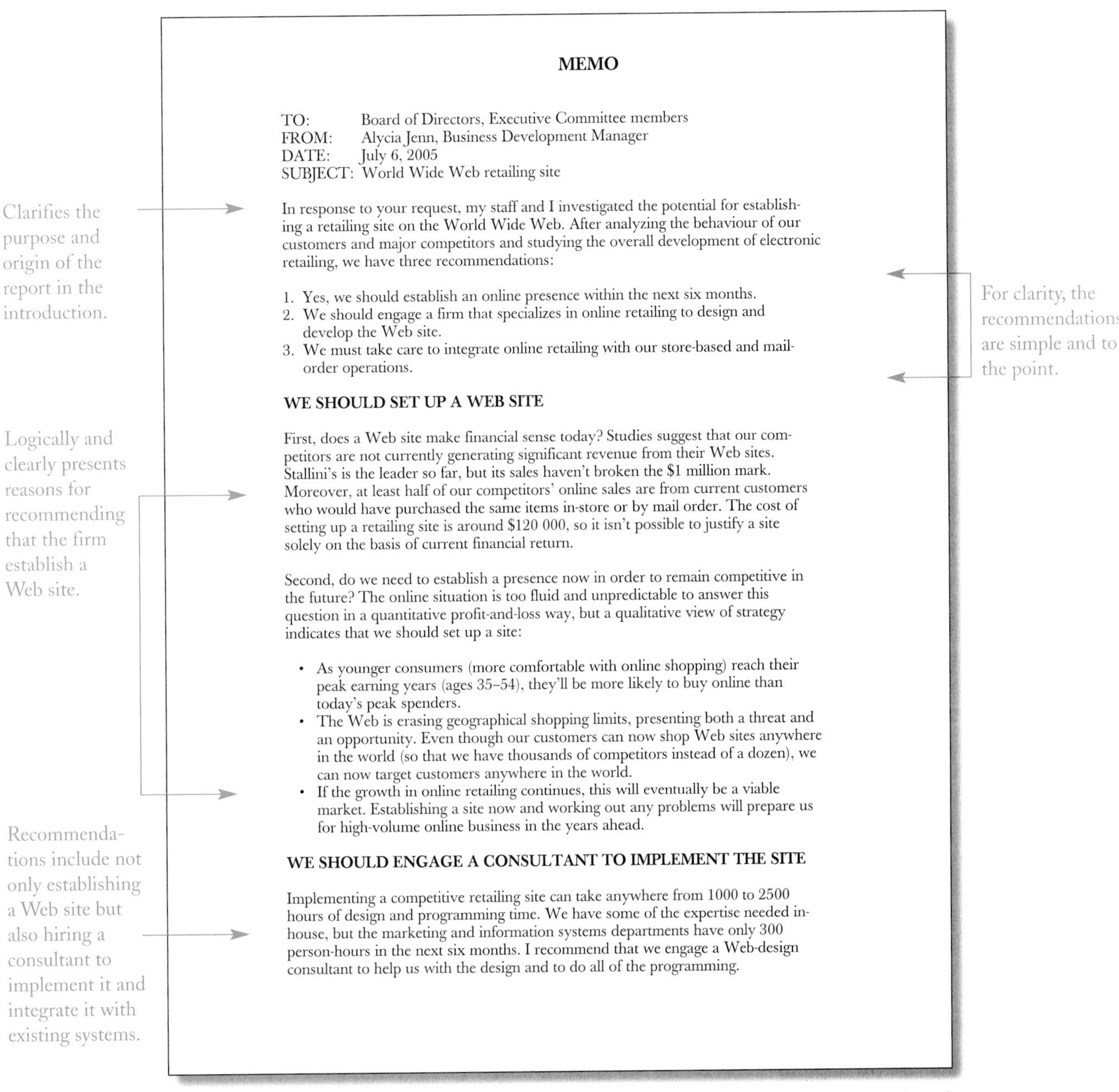

MEMO

TO: Board of Directors, Executive Committee members
FROM: Alycia Jenn, Business Development Manager
DATE: July 6, 2005
SUBJECT: World Wide Web retailing site

In response to your request, my staff and I investigated the potential for establishing a retailing site on the World Wide Web. After analyzing the behaviour of our customers and major competitors and studying the overall development of electronic retailing, we have three recommendations:

1. Yes, we should establish an online presence within the next six months.
2. We should engage a firm that specializes in online retailing to design and develop the Web site.
3. We must take care to integrate online retailing with our store-based and mail-order operations.

WE SHOULD SET UP A WEB SITE

First, does a Web site make financial sense today? Studies suggest that our competitors are not currently generating significant revenue from their Web sites. Stallini's is the leader so far, but its sales haven't broken the $1 million mark. Moreover, at least half of our competitors' online sales are from current customers who would have purchased the same items in-store or by mail order. The cost of setting up a retailing site is around $120 000, so it isn't possible to justify a site solely on the basis of current financial return.

Second, do we need to establish a presence now in order to remain competitive in the future? The online situation is too fluid and unpredictable to answer this question in a quantitative profit-and-loss way, but a qualitative view of strategy indicates that we should set up a site:

- As younger consumers (more comfortable with online shopping) reach their peak earning years (ages 35–54), they'll be more likely to buy online than today's peak spenders.
- The Web is erasing geographical shopping limits, presenting both a threat and an opportunity. Even though our customers can now shop Web sites anywhere in the world (so that we have thousands of competitors instead of a dozen), we can now target customers anywhere in the world.
- If the growth in online retailing continues, this will eventually be a viable market. Establishing a site now and working out any problems will prepare us for high-volume online business in the years ahead.

WE SHOULD ENGAGE A CONSULTANT TO IMPLEMENT THE SITE

Implementing a competitive retailing site can take anywhere from 1000 to 2500 hours of design and programming time. We have some of the expertise needed in-house, but the marketing and information systems departments have only 300 person-hours in the next six months. I recommend that we engage a Web-design consultant to help us with the design and to do all of the programming.

Clarifies the purpose and origin of the report in the introduction.
For clarity, the recommendations are simple and to the point.
Logically and clearly presents reasons for recommending that the firm establish a Web site.
Recommendations include not only establishing a Web site but also hiring a consultant to implement it and integrate it with existing systems.

(continued)

FIGURE 11–3 In-Depth Critique: Sample Justification Report Focusing on Recommendations

company, as it didn't have a large computer-systems staff that could maintain the site. However, dismissing the option of online business could hurt the company's profits, as Internet shopping continues to grow in popularity. In her memo, the writer uses her recommendations to structure her thoughts. She also maintains a formal and respectful tone for her audience.

FOCUSING ON LOGICAL ARGUMENTS

Analytical reports may be organized around logical arguments (indirect approach) when the audience is unreceptive.

Focusing on conclusions or recommendations is the most forceful and efficient way to structure an analytical report, but it isn't the best solution for every situation. You

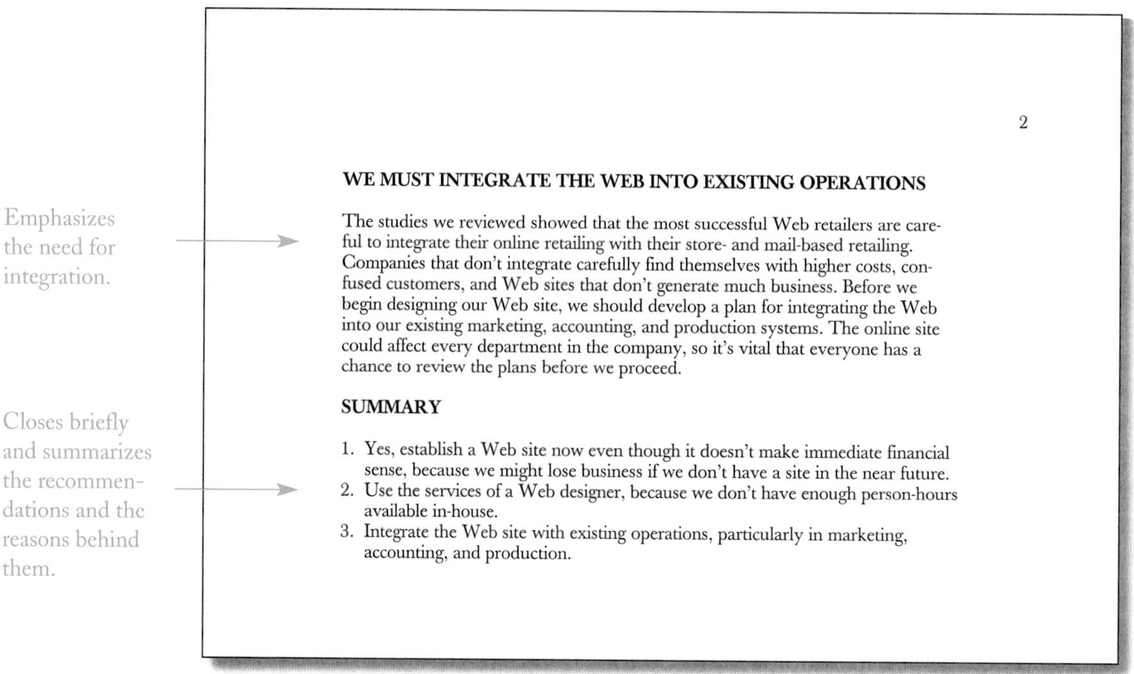

2

WE MUST INTEGRATE THE WEB INTO EXISTING OPERATIONS

The studies we reviewed showed that the most successful Web retailers are careful to integrate their online retailing with their store- and mail-based retailing. Companies that don't integrate carefully find themselves with higher costs, confused customers, and Web sites that don't generate much business. Before we begin designing our Web site, we should develop a plan for integrating the Web into our existing marketing, accounting, and production systems. The online site could affect every department in the company, so it's vital that everyone has a chance to review the plans before we proceed.

SUMMARY

1. Yes, establish a Web site now even though it doesn't make immediate financial sense, because we might lose business if we don't have a site in the near future.
2. Use the services of a Web designer, because we don't have enough person-hours available in-house.
3. Integrate the Web site with existing operations, particularly in marketing, accounting, and production.

Emphasizes the need for integration.
Closes briefly and summarizes the recommendations and the reasons behind them.

FIGURE 11-3 In-Depth Critique: Sample Justification Report Focusing on Recommendations (Continued)

can sometimes achieve better results by encouraging readers to weigh all the facts before you present your conclusions or recommendations.

When your purpose is to collaborate with your audience and solve a problem or persuade them to take a definite action, your structural approach must highlight logical arguments or focus the audience's attention on what needs to be done. When you want your audience to concentrate on why your ideas make sense, use a **logical organization**: arrange your ideas around the reasoning behind your report's conclusions and recommendations. Organize your material to reflect the thinking process that will lead readers to your conclusions.

Three organizational approaches are useful for convincing skeptical readers that your conclusions and recommendations are well founded: the 2 + 2 = 4 approach, the scientific method, and the yardstick approach.

Three basic structural approaches may be used to argue your case: the 2 + 2 = 4 approach, the scientific method, and the yardstick approach. Bear in mind that these three approaches are not mutually exclusive. Choose an approach that matches the reasoning process used to arrive at the conclusion. This way you can lead readers along the same mental pathways you used in hopes they will follow you to the same conclusions.

In a long report, particularly, you may find it convenient to use differing organizational approaches for various sections. In general, however, simplicity of organization is a virtue. You need a clear, comprehensible argument in order to convince skeptical readers to accept your conclusions or recommendations.

The 2 + 2 = 4 approach works well when you have many reasons for your point of view but no single reason is overwhelming.

The 2 + 2 = 4 Approach: A Troubleshooting Report The 2 + 2 = 4 approach essentially convinces readers of your point of view by demonstrating that everything adds up. The main points in your outline are the major reasons behind your conclusions and recommendations. Support each reason with the evidence collected during analysis.

Figure 11-4 shows a troubleshooting report. Written by a national sales manager of a sporting goods company, the author was concerned about his firm's ability to sell to its largest customers. His superior, the vice-president of marketing, shared these concerns and instructed the writer to analyze the situation and recommend a solution.

MEMORANDUM

TO: Robert Mendoza, Vice-President of Marketing
FROM: Binh Phan, National Sales Manager
DATE: September 12, 2005
SUBJECT: Major accounts sales problems

INTRODUCTION

This report outlines the results of my investigation into the recent slowdown in sales to major accounts and the accompanying rise in sales- and service-related complaints from some of our largest customers.

As we discussed at last quarter's management retreat, major account sales dropped 12 percent over the last four quarters, whereas overall sales were up 7 percent. During the same time, we've all noticed an increase in both formal and informal complaints from larger customers regarding how confusing and complicated it has become to do business with us.

My investigation started with in-depth discussions with the four regional sales managers, first as a group and then individually. The tension I felt in the initial meeting eventually came to the surface during my meetings with each manager. Staff members in each region are convinced that other regions are booking orders they don't deserve, with one region doing all the legwork only to see another region get credited with the sale and, naturally, the commission and quota credit.

I followed up the sales manager discussions with informal talks and e-mail exchanges with several sales reps from each region. Virtually everyone who is involved with our major national accounts has a story to share. No one is happy with the situation, and I sense that some reps are walking away from major customers because the process is so frustrating.

ORGANIZATIONAL ISSUES

When we divided the national sales force into four geographical regions last year, the idea was to focus our sales efforts and clarify responsibilities for each prospective and current customer. The regional managers have gotten to know their market territories very well, and sales have increased beyond even our most optimistic projections.

Unfortunately, while solving one problem, we seem to have created another. In the past 12 to 18 months, several regional customers have grown to national status. In addition, a few national retailers have taken on (or expressed interest in) our products. As a result, a significant portion of both our current sales and our future opportunities lie with these large national accounts.

I uncovered more than a dozen cases in which sales reps from two or more regions found themselves competing with each other by pursuing the same customer from different locations.

Moreover, the complaints from our major accounts about overlapping or nonexistent account coverage are a direct result of the regional organization. In some cases,

Begins by discussing report's purpose and scope, background, and methods of research instead of summarizing recommendations.

Main points are the very reasons for the recommendations.

Presents facts and observations in an objective tone, without revealing writer's point of view.

(continued)

FIGURE 11–4 In-Depth Critique: Sample Troubleshooting Report Using the 2 + 2 = 4 Approach

The report recommends that the company should establish separate sales teams for major accounts, rather than continuing to service them through the company's four regional divisions. However, the sales manager knew his plan would be controversial because it required a significant change in the company's organization and in the way sales reps are paid. His thinking had to be clear and easy to follow, so he used the 2 + 2 = 4 approach to focus on his reasons.

Because of its naturalness and versatility, the 2 + 2 = 4 approach is generally the most persuasive and efficient way to develop an analytical report for skeptical readers. When writing your own reports, try this structure first. You'll find that your arguments usually fall naturally into this pattern. However, not every problem or reporting situation can be handled with this organizational approach.

2

customers aren't sure which of our reps they're supposed to call with problems and orders. In others, no one has been in contact with them for several months.

An example should help illustrate the problem. CanSport, with retail outlets in the Maritimes and the west coast, was being pitched by reps from our West, Central, and East regions. Because we give our regional offices a lot of negotiating freedom, the three reps were offering the client different prices. But all of CanSport's buying decisions are made at their headquarters in Montreal, so all we did was confuse the customer.

The irony of this situation is that we're often giving our weakest selling and support efforts to the largest customers in the country.

COMMISSION ISSUES

The regional organization issues are compounded because of the way we assign commissions and quota credit. Salespeople in one region can invest a lot of time in pursuing a sale, only to have the customer place the order in another region. So a sales rep in the second region ends up with the commission on a sale that was partly or even entirely earned by someone in the first region.

Each main point is supported with concrete evidence.

Also, sales reps sometimes don't pursue leads in their regions if they think that a rep in another region will get the commission. For example, Athletic Express, with outlets in four provinces spread across all regions, finally got so frustrated with us that the company president called our headquarters. Athletic Express has been trying to place a large order for tennis and golf accessories, but none of our local reps seem interested in paying attention. I spoke with the rep responsible for Winnipeg, where the company is headquartered, and asked her why she wasn't working the account more actively. Her explanation was that last time she got involved with Athletic Express, the order was actually placed from their Vancouver regional office, and she didn't get any commission after more than two weeks of selling time.

RECOMMENDATION

Saves recommendation for the fourth section, where writer adds up the reasons (2 + 2 = 4).

Our sales organization should reflect the nature of our customer base. To accomplish that goal, we need a group of reps who are free to pursue accounts across regional borders–and who are compensated fairly for their work. The most sensible answer is to establish a national accounts group. Customers whose operations place them in more than one region would automatically be assigned to the national group.

The recommendation is a logical culmination of the main points that have been presented so carefully.

Further, we need to modify our commission policy to reward people for team selling. I'll talk with the sales managers to work out the details, but in general, we'll need to split commissions whenever two or more reps help close a sale. This policy will also involve a "finder's fee" for a rep who pulls in leads at the regional level that are passed on to the national account team.

FIGURE 11–4 In-Depth Critique: Sample Troubleshooting Report Using the 2 + 2 = 4 Approach (Continued)

When organizing a report to reflect the scientific method, you discuss, one by one, hypothetical solutions to the problem.

The Scientific Method: A Proposal When you're trying to discover whether an explanation is true, whether an option will solve your problem, or which one of several solutions will work best, you're likely to find the scientific method useful. Every day hundreds of managers ask themselves, "What's wrong with this operation, and what should we do about it?" They approach the problem by coming up with one or several possible solutions (hypotheses) and then conducting experiments or gathering information to find the most effective one.

Reports based on the scientific method begin with a statement of the problem and a brief description of the hypothetical solution or a list of possible solutions. The body of the report discusses each alternative in turn and offers evidence that will either confirm the alternative or rule it out. Because many problems have multiple causes

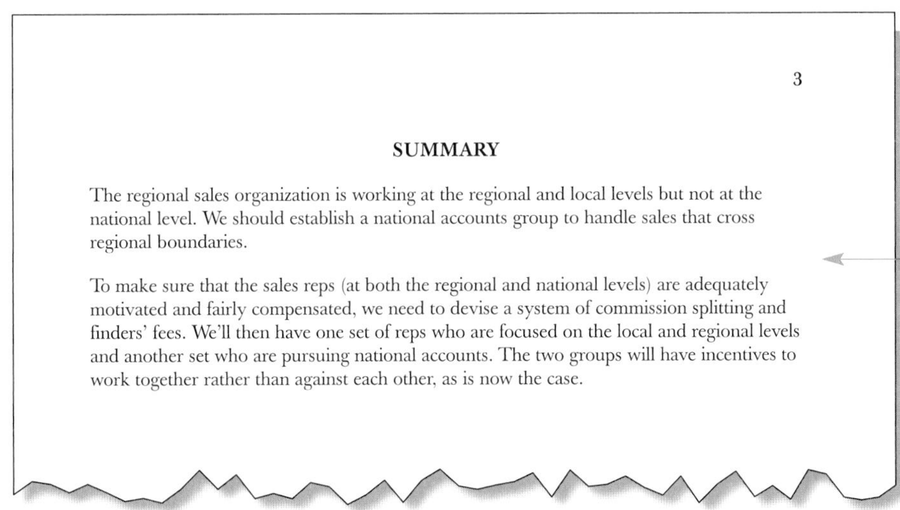

3

SUMMARY

The regional sales organization is working at the regional and local levels but not at the national level. We should establish a national accounts group to handle sales that cross regional boundaries.

To make sure that the sales reps (at both the regional and national levels) are adequately motivated and fairly compensated, we need to devise a system of commission splitting and finders' fees. We'll then have one set of reps who are focused on the local and regional levels and another set who are pursuing national accounts. The two groups will have incentives to work together rather than against each other, as is now the case.

Clearly and succinctly recaps the reccommendation and the reasons for it.

FIGURE 11-4 In-Depth Critique: Sample Troubleshooting Report Using the 2 + 2 = 4 Approach (Continued)

and complex solutions, several alternatives may be relevant. The final section of the report summarizes the findings and indicates which solution or solutions are valid. The report concludes with recommendations for solving the problem or eliminating the causes.

The outline in Figure 11-5 on page 326 is the basis of a proposal recommending an investment in a franchise operation. The proposal uses a variation of the scientific method. Prepared by an executive from a restaurant management firm, the proposal intends to help the company decide in which of four franchise operations to invest. By analyzing each alternative, the writer hoped to unify a divided audience for this major investment decision. The chances of bringing about a consensus are much better when the strengths and weaknesses of all the ideas are shown. The main drawback is that many of the alternatives may turn out to be irrelevant or unproductive, but they all must still be discussed. The more ideas you discuss, the more confused readers may become and the more trouble they may have comparing pros and cons.

The Yardstick Approach: A Problem-Solving Report One way to reduce the confusion presented by having several alternatives is to review all alternatives against the same standard (or yardstick). Begin by discussing the problem, as with the scientific method, but then set up the conditions that must be met in order to solve the problem. These are the criteria against which all possible solutions are evaluated. In the body of the report, evaluate each alternative in relation to the criteria. The main points of the outline are either the criteria themselves or the alternatives.

With the yardstick approach, the report is organized around criteria; the solution is the alternative that best meets the criteria.

Yardstick reports are similar in some respects to those based on the scientific method, but in criteria-based reports, all the alternatives are reviewed against the same standards. Another distinction is that criteria-based reports can be used to prove the need for action: the current situation can be measured against the criteria and shown to be wanting.

The yardstick approach is useful for certain kinds of proposals because the client who requests the proposal often provides a list of criteria that the solution must meet. Say that your company has been asked to bid on a contract to install a computer system for a large corporation. The client has listed the requirements (criteria) for the system, and you've developed a preliminary design to meet them. In the body of your proposal, you could use the client's list of requirements as the main headings and under each one explain how your preliminary design meets the requirement.

Some proposals are best organized by using the client's criteria as the main points.

Covers two major steps: (1) establishing the decision criteria and (2) testing each of four alternatives against those criteria.

Assigns each of the four alternatives to an appropriate subdivision: description, pros, cons, and conclusion (priority).

Main Idea: We should purchase the 45 franchises currently for sale in the Burger World chain.

I. Statement of problem and purpose of this proposal
II. Scope of the investigation
III. Method used to compare the business opportunities
  A. Establish decision criteria
  B. Get input from consultants
  C. Gather secondary research
  D. Conduct market surveys for primary research
  E. Meet with franchisor management teams
  F. Analyze quantitative and qualitative data
  G. Prioritize and select the best opportunity
IV. Analysis of the four franchise operations
  A. Wacky Taco
    1. Description: Low-fat Mexican food; most locations in malls
    2. Pros: 58 units available within a year; consultants believe the concept has significant growth potential; operations easy to manage
    3. Cons: Company recently hit with employment discrimination lawsuit; franchise fees are 30 percent above average
    4. Conclusion: Priority = 3; lawsuit may be indicative of mismanagement; fees too high
  B. Thai in the Sky
    1. Description: Thai food served in New Age settings
    2. Pros: Healthy and interesting food; unusual theme concept; no franchised competition
    3. Cons: Complexity of food preparation; only 40 franchises a vailable; franchisor's top management team replaced only six months ago
    4. Conclusion: Priority = 4; too risky and not enough units available
  C. Dog Tower
    1. Description: Gourmet hot dogs
    2. Pros: No nationwide competition; more than 60 franchises available within a year; easy to manage; fees lower than average
    3. Cons: Limited market appeal; many stores need updating
    4. Conclusion: Priority = 2; needs too much investment
  D. Burger World
    1. Description: Mainstream competitor to McDonald's and Burger King

Presents each alternative objectively even though the decision can never be black and white.

    2. Pros: Aggressive franchisor willing to invest in national marketing; start-up costs are low; unique demographic target (teenagers and young adults; not a little kids' place)
    3. Cons: Fierce competition in burgers overall; some units in unproved locations
    4. Conclusion: Priority = 1; finances look good; research shows that teenagers will support a chain that doesn't cater to small children
V. Summary
VI. Appendixes
  A. Financial data
  B. Research results

FIGURE 11–5 In-Depth Critique: Outline of a Proposal Using the Scientific Method

Figure 11–6 below is an outline of a yardstick report that was written by a market analyst for a large company that makes irrigation equipment for farms and ranches. Because the company was successful in the agricultural market, they started to run out of customers to sell to. To keep the company growing, the firm needed to find another market. Two alternatives considered were commercial buildings and residences. The author of the report was determined to make careful recommendations because, even though she didn't make the final decision, the information and the professional opinions that she provided weighed heavily in the decision process.

One drawback of the yardstick approach is that it can be a little boring. You may find yourself saying the same things over and over again: "Opportunity A has high growth potential, opportunity B has high growth potential, opportunity C has high growth potential," and so on. One way to minimize the repetition is to compare the options in tables and then highlight the more unusual or important aspects of each alternative in the text so that you get the best of both worlds. This allows all the alternatives to be compared against the same yardstick but calls attention to the most significant differences among them.

Tables are useful in the yardstick approach
- To avoid repetition
- To make the options easier to compare

Another drawback is that all readers must agree on which criteria to use. In the case of the report shown in Figure 11-6, the criteria had been agreed to before the writer began her investigation. She included them in her report to remind her readers and make it easy for them to evaluate the options available.

For the yardstick approach to work, readers must accept your criteria.

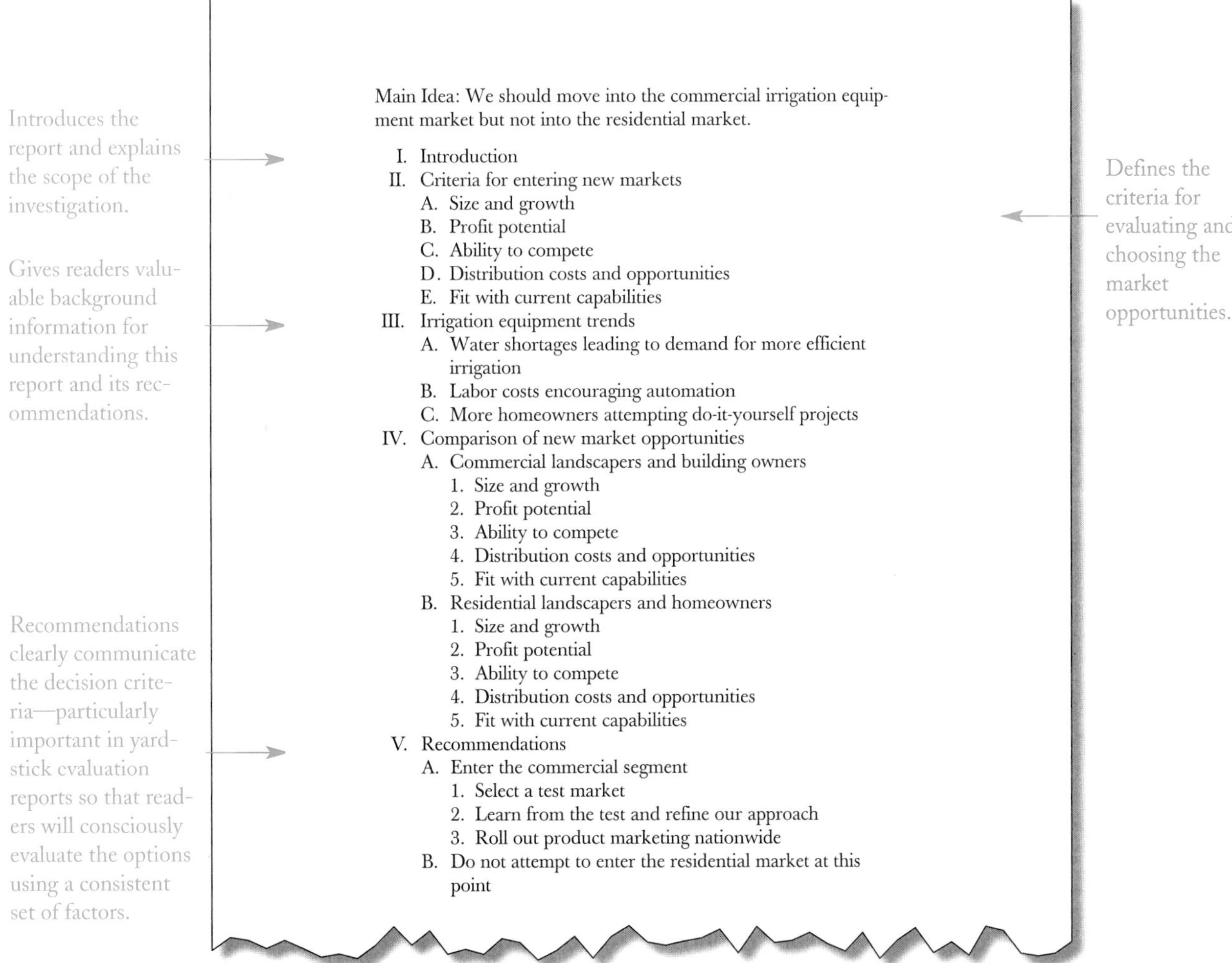

Introduces the report and explains the scope of the investigation.
Gives readers valuable background information for understanding this report and its recommendations.
Recommendations clearly communicate the decision criteria—particularly important in yardstick evaluation reports so that readers will consciously evaluate the options using a consistent set of factors.
Defines the criteria for evaluating and choosing the market opportunities.
Main Idea: We should move into the commercial irrigation equipment market but not into the residential market.
I. Introduction
II. Criteria for entering new markets
A. Size and growth
B. Profit potential
C. Ability to compete
D. Distribution costs and opportunities
E. Fit with current capabilities
III. Irrigation equipment trends
A. Water shortages leading to demand for more efficient irrigation
B. Labor costs encouraging automation
C. More homeowners attempting do-it-yourself projects
IV. Comparison of new market opportunities
A. Commercial landscapers and building owners
1. Size and growth
2. Profit potential
3. Ability to compete
4. Distribution costs and opportunities
5. Fit with current capabilities
B. Residential landscapers and homeowners
1. Size and growth
2. Profit potential
3. Ability to compete
4. Distribution costs and opportunities
5. Fit with current capabilities
V. Recommendations
A. Enter the commercial segment
1. Select a test market
2. Learn from the test and refine our approach
3. Roll out product marketing nationwide
B. Do not attempt to enter the residential market at this point

FIGURE 11-6 In-Depth Critique: Outline of a Research Report Using the Yardstick Approach

Preparing the Final Outline

Before writing your report, you may have to revise the outline you used to guide your research effort.

Once the proper structure for your material has been decided, prepare a final report outline.[2] A final outline gives a visual diagram of the report, its important points, the order in which they will be discussed, and the detail to be included. Sometimes the preliminary outline that guided your research can be used as a final blueprint for the report. More often, however, you have to rework the preliminary outline to take into account your purpose, your audience's probable reactions, and what you learned during your study. Furthermore, include only the items you plan to discuss in your report (your research outline may have additional topics).

Aside from guiding you in the writing effort, preparing a final outline forces you to reevaluate the information you have selected to include and the order in which you present it. You may notice once you look at the outline, that your discussion is too light in one area or too heavy in another. You may decide to use an indirect approach instead of a direct one because now that you see your conclusions up front, you think it might be too forceful for your audience. Think of your final report outline as a working draft that you'll revise and modify as you go along.

A final outline is a work in progress.

Phrase your final outline so that the points on the outline can serve as headings that appear in the report (report headings are discussed later in this chapter). Bear in mind that the way you phrase outline headings will affect the tone of the report. If you want a hard-hitting, direct tone use, informative phrasing. If you prefer an objective, indirect tone, use descriptive phrasing. Be sure to use parallel construction when wording the points on the outline.

You can soften the force of controversial points by using descriptive (not informative) headings.

Once you've prepared a final outline, you can begin to identify which points should be illustrated with visual aids, such as tables, graphs, drawings, flowcharts, and so on.

A visual aid is an illustration in tabular, graphic, schematic, or pictorial form.

Organizing Visual Aids for Business Reports

Many report writers prefer to plan out and organize their visual aids before composing textual material.

Businesspeople include graphs and other visuals in their reports and proposals mainly to convey an important idea. But which should be prepared first, visuals or text? Although fitting visual aids to completed text makes some sense, many experienced businesspeople prefer to begin with the visual aids. Doing so has three advantages. First, much of the fact finding and analytical work is already in tabular or graphic form, so sorting through and refining your visuals will help you decide exactly what you're going to say. Second, by starting with the visual aids, you develop a graphic story line that can be used for the written report. Finally, because your text will explain and refer to any tables, charts, and graphs you include, save time by having them ready before beginning to compose the text, particularly if you plan to use quite a few visuals.

Gaining an Advantage with Visuals

Carefully prepared visuals can make a report or presentation more interesting. But even more important, pictures are an effective way to communicate with diverse audiences. In addition, in the numbers-oriented world of work, people rely heavily on images. They think in terms of trend lines, distribution curves, and percentages. An upward curve means good news in any language. Finally, visual aids attract and hold people's attention.

Visual aids help communicators get through to an audience.

Despite their value, use visual aids selectively and include only those elements that support your primary message. Use visuals to supplement the written word, not to replace it. Restrict the use of visual aids to situations in which they do the most good. Table 11–2 helps you identify those situations.

TABLE 11–2 When to Use Visuals

Purpose	Application
To clarify	Support text descriptions of "graphic" topics: quantitative or numerical information, explanations of trends, descriptions.
To simplify	Break complicated descriptions into components that can be depicted with conceptual models, flowcharts, organization charts, or diagrams.
To emphasize	Call attention to particularly important points by illustrating them with line, bar, and pie charts.
To summarize	Review major points in the narrative by providing a chart or table that sums up the data.
To reinforce	Present information in visual and written form to increase reader's retention.
To attract	Make material seem more interesting by decorating the cover or title page and by breaking up the text with visual aids.
To impress	Build credibility by putting ideas into visual form to convey the impression of authenticity and precision.
To unify	Depict the relationship among points—for example, with a flowchart.

"Visualizing" Information

When planning and organizing visual aids

- Decide what you want to say.
- Pick out the points that can best be made visually.
- Judge whether you have too many or too few graphics.

When you begin to compose a report or a presentation, you usually have a lot of raw data that can be moulded into any number of messages. As you sort through the information compiled during the research phase, you begin to see relationships and draw conclusions. The following steps help you decide how many and what type of visuals to include in your report:

- **Decide which points require visual support.** Some information, such as figures, is confusing and tedious in paragraph form. You will find that tables and graphs conveniently organize and display facts and numbers, and flowcharts, drawings, and photographs clarify detailed descriptions of physical relationships or procedures. In addition, you may simply want to draw attention to a particular fact or detail by reinforcing the message visually.
- **Maintain a balance between illustrations and words.** The ideal blend of words and pictures depends on the nature of your subject. Illustrating every point dilutes the effectiveness of your visuals and can confuse readers who assume that the amount of space allocated to a topic indicates its relative importance. Also, if you know that your audience prefers either words or pictures, you can adjust your balance accordingly.
- **Consider your production schedule.** If you're producing your report without the help of an art department or appropriate computer-graphics tools, you may want to restrict the number of visuals in your report. Making charts and tables takes time, particularly if you're inexperienced. In addition, constructing visual aids requires a good deal of imagination and attention to detail.

Deciding on the appropriate type of graph is always a challenge. Keep in mind that most types of graphs are not interchangeable. As we see in the next section, different types of graphs best depict different types of data.

OBJECTIVE 3 **List the most popular types of visuals and discuss when to use them.**

Selecting the Right Graphic for the Job

Choose the type of graphic that best presents your message.

Once you've selected which points to illustrate graphically, the next step is to select the type of graph that will present your data most clearly and effectively to your audience:

- To present detailed, exact values, use tables.
- To illustrate trends over time, use a line chart or a bar chart.

- To show frequency or distribution, use a pie chart, segmented bar chart, or area chart.
- To compare one item with another, use a bar chart.
- To compare one part with the whole, use a pie chart.
- To show correlations, use a line chart, a bar chart, or a scatter (dot) chart.
- To show geographic relationships, use a map.
- To illustrate a process or a procedure, use a flowchart or a diagram.

Here's a closer look at each of these graphic types.

TABLES

Use tables to help your audience understand detailed information.

When you have to present detailed, specific information, choose a **table**, a systematic arrangement of data in columns and rows. Tables are ideal when the audience needs the information that would be either difficult or tedious to handle in the main text.

Most tables contain the standard parts illustrated in Table 11–3. Every table includes vertical columns and horizontal rows, with helpful headings along the top and side. Tables projected onto a screen during an oral presentation should be limited to three column heads and six row heads; tables presented on paper may include from one or two heads to a dozen or more. If the table has too many columns to fit comfortably between the margins of the page, turn the paper horizontally and insert it in the report with the top toward the binding.

Although formal tables set apart from the text are necessary for complex information, you can present some data more simply within the text. You make the table, in essence, a part of the paragraph, typed in tabular format. Such text tables are usually introduced with a sentence that leads directly into the tabulated information. Here's an example:

Use word tables
- To summarize survey results
- To compare items with some standard

The following table shows steel producer Dofasco's fixed assets in 2002 and 2001:

(in millions)	2002		2001	
	Cost	Accumulated Depreciation	Cost	Accumulated Depreciation
Land	$ 46.8	$ —	$ 46.8	$ —
Buildings	764.8	472.6	743.7	420.8
Equipment and machinery	4,655.7	3,300.4	4,457.9	2,995.7
Construction in progress	64.5	—	152.4	—
	$5,531.8	$3,773.0	$5,400.0	$3,416.5
Net book value		$1,758.8		$1,984.3

Source of the table is documented in a source note

Source: Dofasco Inc., *2002 Annual Report*. 58.

Although many tables are strictly numerical, tables that also use words can be just as useful. Some tables contain no numbers at all. They are particularly appropriate for presenting survey findings or for comparing various items against a specific standard.

When preparing a numerical table, be sure to

- Use common, understandable units, and clearly identify the units used: dollars, percentages, price per ton, or whatever.
- Express all items in a column in the same unit, and round off for simplicity.
- Label column headings clearly, and use a subhead if necessary.
- Separate columns or rows with lines or extra space to make the table easy to follow.
- Provide column-to-row totals or averages when relevant.
- Document the source of the data below the table using the same format as a text footnote (see Appendix B).

TABLE 11–3 Parts of a Table

Multicolumn Head*				
Stub Head	**Subhead**	**Subhead**	**Single-column head**	**Single-column head**
Row head	XXX	XXX	XX	XX
Row head				
Subhead	XX	XXX	XX	X
Subhead	XX	XXX	XX	XX
Total	XXX	XXX	XX	XX

Source: (In the same format as a text footnote; see Appendix B.)

*Footnote (for explanation of elements in the table; a superscript number or small letter may be used instead of an asterisk or other symbol).

LINE AND SURFACE CHARTS

Use line charts
- To indicate changes over time
- To plot the relationship of two variables

A line chart illustrates trends over time or plots the relationship of two variables. In line charts showing trends, the vertical, or y, axis shows the amount, and the horizontal, or x, axis shows the time or the quantity being measured. Ordinarily, both scales begin at zero and proceed in equal increments; however, in Figure 11–7 the vertical axis is broken to show that some of the increments have been left out. A broken axis is appropriate when the data are plotted far above zero, but be sure to clearly indicate the omission of data points.

A simple line chart may be arranged in many ways. One of the most common is to plot several lines on the same chart for comparative purposes, as shown in Figure 11–8 on page 332. Try to use no more than three lines on any given chart, particularly if the lines cross. Another variation of the simple line chart has a vertical axis with both positive and negative numbers (see Figure 11–9 on page 332). This arrangement is handy when you have to illustrate losses.

A surface chart is a kind of line chart showing a cumulative effect.

A **surface chart**, also called an **area chart**, is a form of line chart with a cumulative effect; all the lines add up to the top line, which represents the total (see Figure 11–10 on page 332). This form of chart helps you illustrate changes in the composition of something over time. When preparing a surface chart, put the most important segment against the baseline, and restrict the number of strata to four or five.

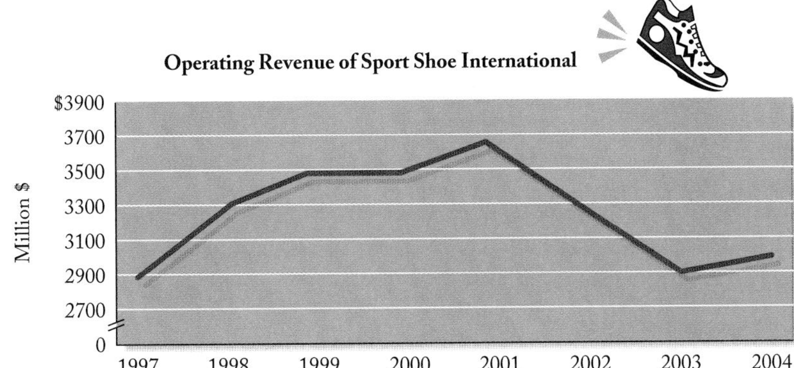

FIGURE 11–7 Line Chart with Broken Axis

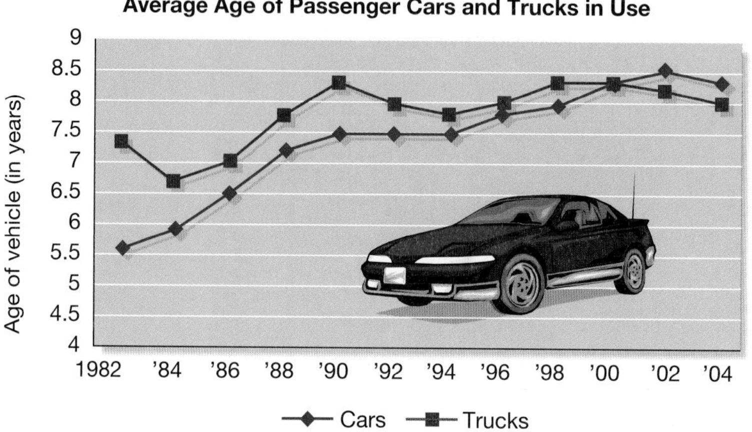

FIGURE 11–8 Line Chart with Multiple Lines

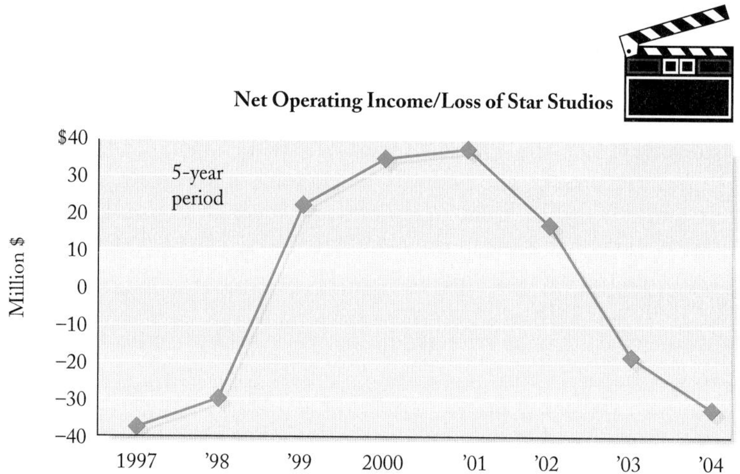

FIGURE 11–9 Line Chart with Positive and Negative Values on Vertical Axis

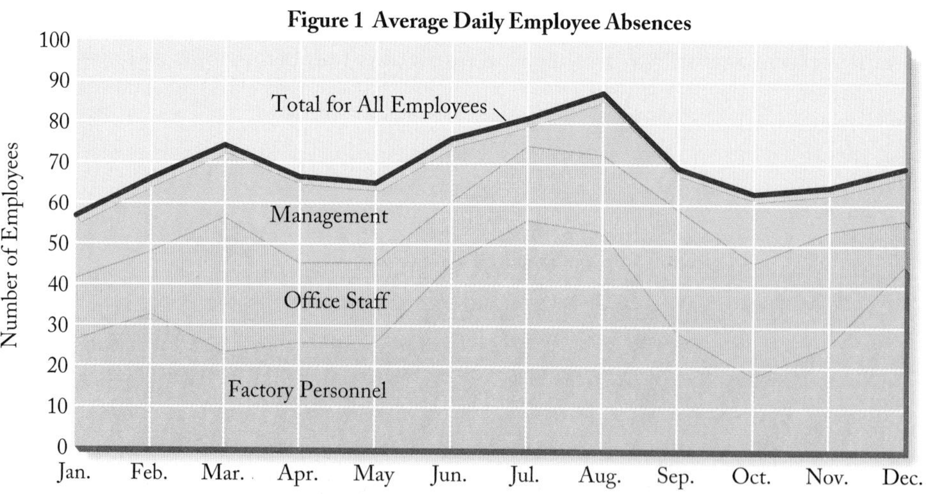

FIGURE 11–10 Surface Chart

BAR CHARTS

A **bar chart** portrays numbers by the height or length of its rectangular bars, making a series of numbers easy to read or understand. Bar charts are particularly valuable when you want to

Bar charts, in which numbers are visually portrayed by rectangular bars, can take a variety of forms.

- Compare the size of several items at one time
- Show changes in one item over time
- Indicate the composition of several items over time
- Show the relative size of components of a whole

As Figure 11–11 on pages 334–335 shows, bar charts can be singular (Where the University Students Are), grouped (Eating Occasions), segmented (Targeted Newscasts), or a combination of chart types (Commercial Superhighway—line and bar). Grouped bar charts compare more than one set of data (using a different colour or pattern for each set). Segmented bar charts, also known as stacked bar charts, show how individual components contribute to a total number (using a different colour or pattern for each component). Combination bar and line charts compare quantities that require different intervals.

You can be creative with bar charts in several ways. You might align the bars either vertically or horizontally or you might even use bar charts to show both positive and negative quantities. Be careful, however, to keep all the bars in the chart the same width; different widths could suggest a relative importance to the viewer. In addition, space the bars evenly and place them in a logical order, such as chronological or alphabetical. Keep in mind that most computer software (such as Microsoft Excel) will generate charts from data tables. The software will place the data in a graph based on the order that is used in the table. So plan ahead, and if you don't like the way the computer interprets your data graphically, go back to the data table and adjust the order there first.

PIE CHARTS

Like segmented bar charts and area charts, a pie chart shows how parts of a whole are distributed. Each segment represents a slice of a complete circle, or pie. As you can see in Figure 11–12 on page 336, pie charts are an effective way to show percentages or to compare one segment with another. You can combine pie charts with tables to expand the usefulness of such visuals.

Use pie charts to show the relative sizes of the parts of a whole.

When composing pie charts, try to restrict the number of slices in the pie. Otherwise, the chart looks cluttered and is difficult to label. If necessary, combine the smallest pieces together in a "miscellaneous" category. Ideally, the largest or most important slice of the pie, the segment you want to emphasize, is placed at the twelve o'clock position; the rest are arranged clockwise either in order of size or in some other logical progression.

You can use different colours or patterns to distinguish the various pieces. If you want to draw attention to the segment that is of the greatest interest to your readers, use a brighter colour for that segment, draw an arrow to the segment, or explode it; that is, pull the segment away from the rest of the pie. In any case, label all the segments and indicate their value in either percentages or units of measure so that your readers will be able to judge the value of the wedges. Remember, the segments must add up to 100 percent if percentages are used or to the total number if numbers are used.

FLOWCHARTS AND ORGANIZATIONAL CHARTS

If you need to show physical or conceptual relationships rather than numerical ones, you might want to use a flowchart or an organizational chart. A **flowchart** illustrates a sequence of events from start to finish. It is indispensable when illustrating processes, procedures, and sequential relationships. The various elements in the process you want to portray may be represented by pictorial symbols or geometric shapes, as shown in Figure 11–13 on page 336.

Use flowcharts

- To show a series of steps from beginning to end
- To show sequential relationships

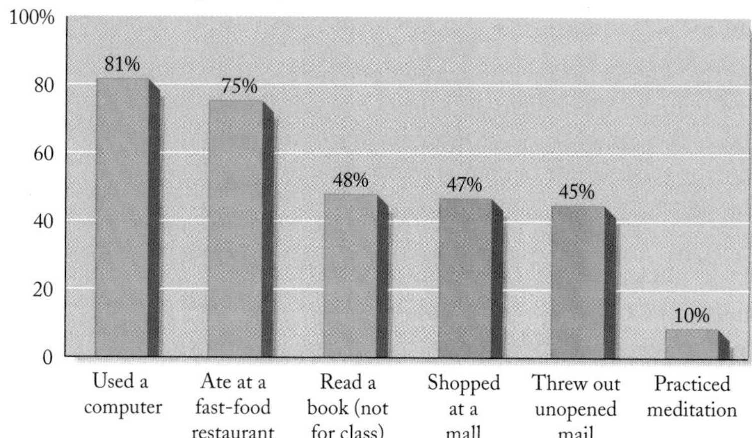

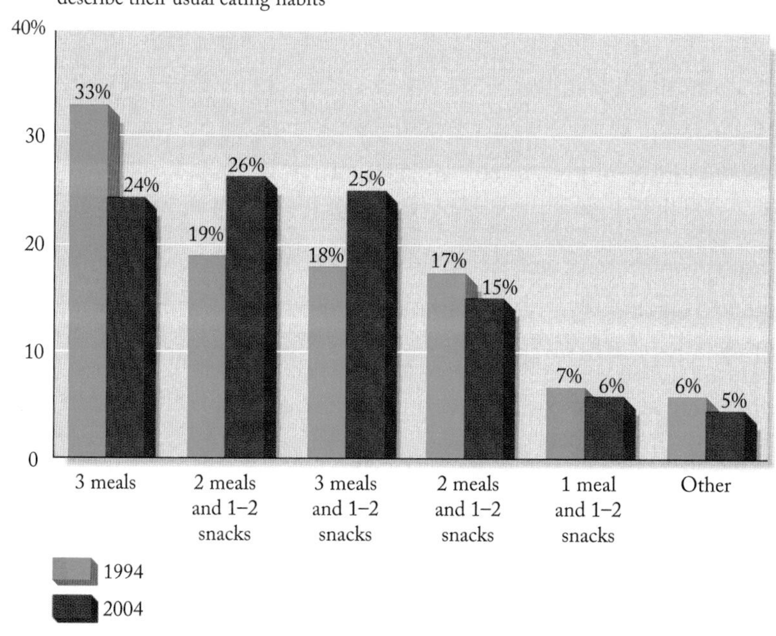

FIGURE 11-11 The Versatile Bar Chart

Use organizational charts to depict the interrelationships among the parts of an organization.

An **organizational chart**, as the name implies, illustrates the positions, units, or functions of an organization and the way they interrelate. An organization's normal communication channels are almost impossible to describe without the benefit of a chart like that in Figure 11-14 on page 337.

MAPS

Use maps
- To represent statistics by geographic area
- To show locational relationships

For certain applications, maps are ideal. One of the most common uses is to show concentrations of something, such as fast food outlets or banks, by geographic area. Maps are popular features of annual reports; where they allow multinational companies to show the global nature of their operations, see the Bata world map in Chapter 3 (Figure 3-2). In your own reports, you might use maps to show regional differences in variables such as your company's sales of a product, or you might indicate proposed plant sites and their relationship to key markets.

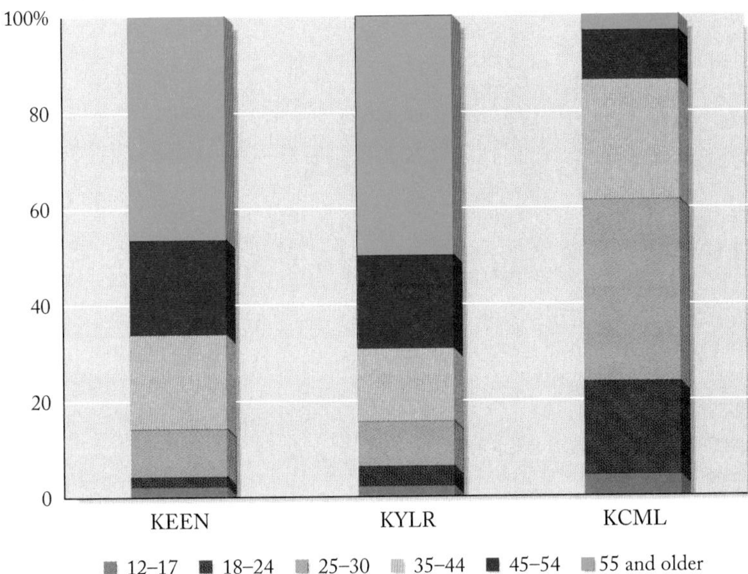

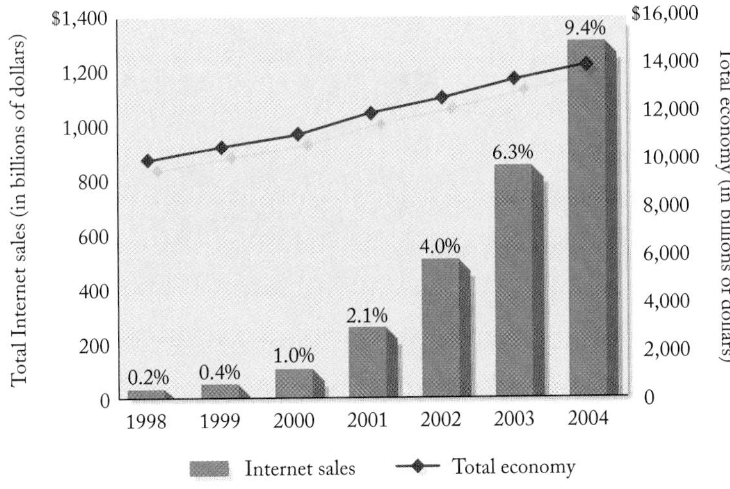

FIGURE 11–11 The Versatile Bar Chart (Continued)

Most office-supply stores carry blank maps of various regions of world. You can illustrate these maps to suit your needs, using dots, shading, colour, labels, numbers, and symbols. In addition, popular programs such as Excel and CorelDraw! come with regional, country, and world map templates. You just insert the columns of data and assign the data to a state or a country; the software will do the rest.

DRAWINGS, DIAGRAMS, AND PHOTOGRAPHS

Although less commonly used than other visual aids, drawings, diagrams, and photographs can also be valuable elements in business reports and presentations. Drawings and diagrams are most often used to show how something looks or operates. Figure 11–15 (on page 337) was prepared using Visio software and explains the benefits of converged communication networks over traditional networks. Diagrams can be much clearer than words alone when it comes to giving your audience an idea of

Use drawings and diagrams to show
- How something looks or works
- How something is made or used

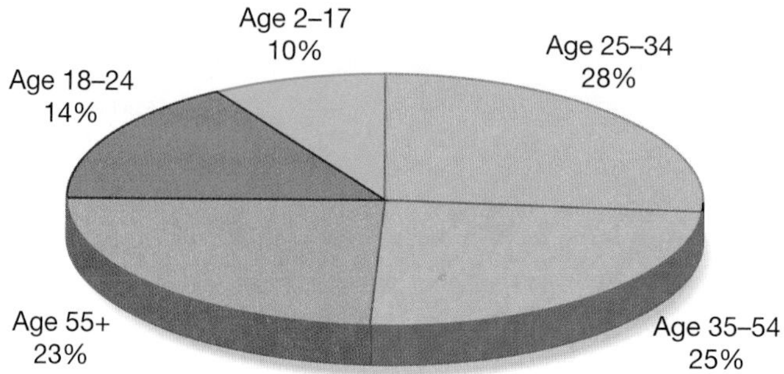

FIGURE 11-12 Pie Chart

how an item looks or can be used. In industries such as engineering and architecture, computer-aided design (CAD) systems produce detailed diagrams and drawings. A variety of widely available software programs provide a file of symbols and pictures of various types that can be used to add a decorative touch to reports and presentations. However, be sure to employ these images sparingly, as overuse will detract from the impact of your documents.

Use photographs
- For visual appeal
- To show exact appearance

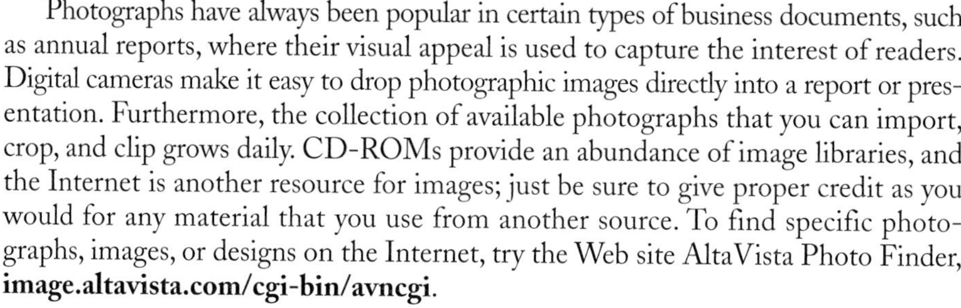

Photographs have always been popular in certain types of business documents, such as annual reports, where their visual appeal is used to capture the interest of readers. Digital cameras make it easy to drop photographic images directly into a report or presentation. Furthermore, the collection of available photographs that you can import, crop, and clip grows daily. CD-ROMs provide an abundance of image libraries, and the Internet is another resource for images; just be sure to give proper credit as you would for any material that you use from another source. To find specific photographs, images, or designs on the Internet, try the Web site AltaVista Photo Finder, **image.altavista.com/cgi-bin/avncgi**.

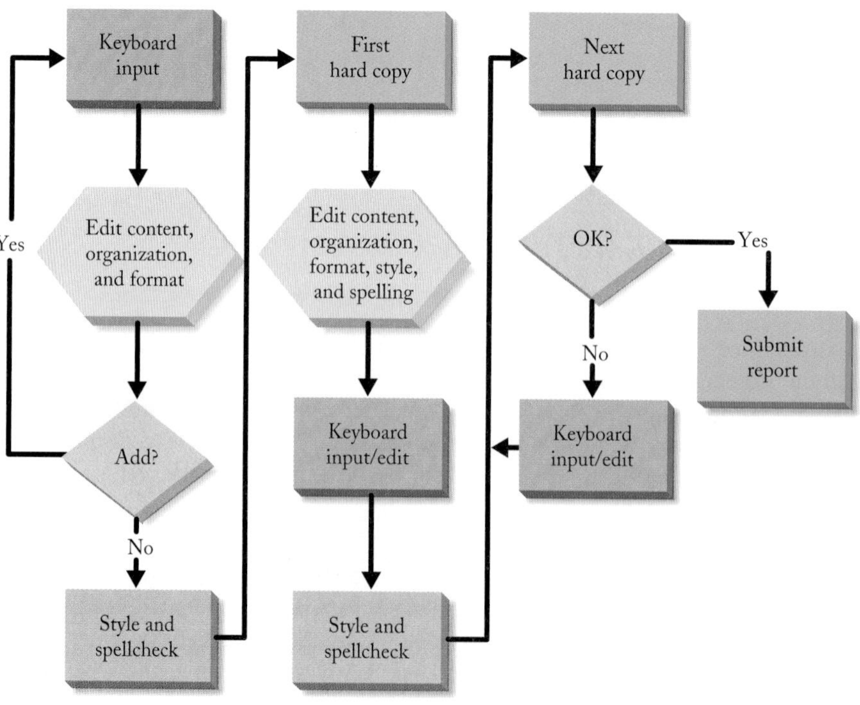

FIGURE 11-13 Flowchart

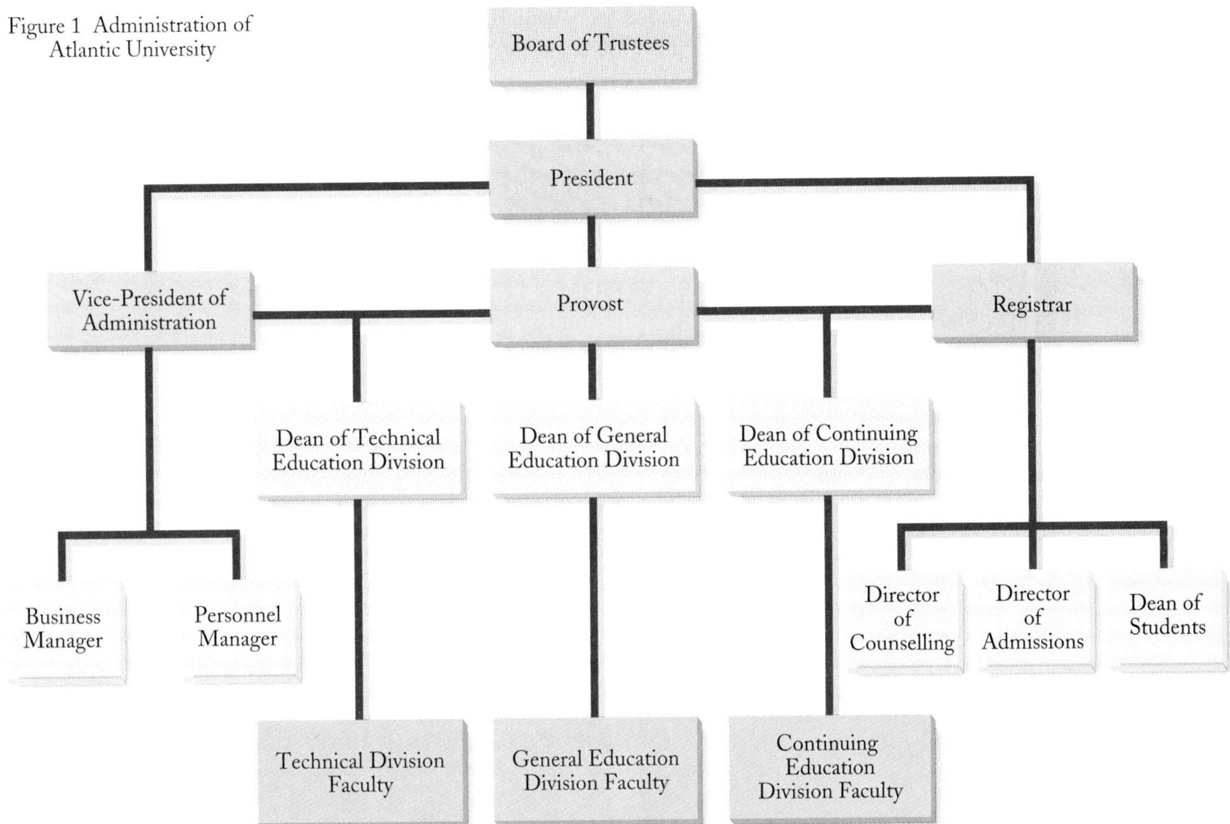

FIGURE 11–14 Organizational Chart

Nothing can demonstrate the exact appearance of a new facility, a piece of property or equipment, or a new product the way a photograph can. However, in some situations a photograph may show too much detail. This is one of the reasons that repair manuals frequently use drawings instead of photos. With a drawing, you can select how much detail to show and focus the reader's attention on particular parts or places.

Although technology has made it easier to use photographs in reports and presentations, it also presents an important ethical concern. Software tools such as Photoshop and CorelDraw! make it easy for computer users to make dramatic changes

Today's technology for altering photos raises serious ethical questions.

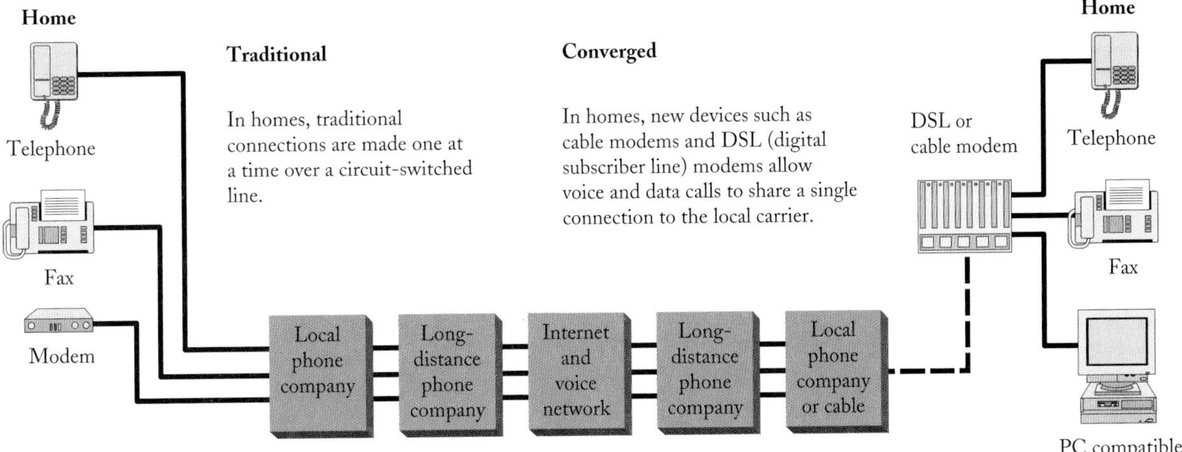

FIGURE 11–15 Diagram

Going Online

Exploring Computer Graphics

From Mambo you can visit more than 65 Web sites that contain some colourful examples and lots of information on computer graphics. You'll find links to various software companies, government, and university labs that introduce the world of imaginative computer graphics. You can go to the site for conference announcements and answers to frequently asked questions—or you can just explore the resources to discover the creative uses of computer graphics. As you learn more about computer graphics, you may get ideas for designing effective graphics to enhance one of your business reports.

mambo.ucsc.edu/psl/cg.html

To link directly to this site, visit our Companion Website at **www.pearsoned.ca/thill** and look for the Chapter 11 resources.

OBJECTIVE 4 Clarify five principles of graphic design to remember when preparing visuals.

When designing visual aids, observe the principles of continuity, contrast, emphasis, simplicity, and experience.

to photos—without leaving a clue that they've been altered. Making small changes to photos has been possible for a long time (more than a few people have blemishes airbrushed out of their yearbook photos), but computers make drastic changes easy and undetectable. You can remove people from photographs, put Person A's head on Person B's body, and make products look more attractive than they really are. As when using other technological tools, stop and ask yourself where the truth lies before you start making changes.[3]

Designing Graphics for Reports

Computer technology has made it easy to produce professional-looking graphics. Before you take advantage of any computer-graphics tools, think about the kind of image you want to project. The style of your visual aids communicates a subtle message about your relationship with the audience. A simple, hand-drawn diagram is fine for a working meeting but inappropriate for a formal presentation or report. On the other hand, elaborate, full-colour visuals may be viewed as extravagant for an informal memo but may be entirely appropriate for a message to top management or influential outsiders. The image you want to project should determine the visual aid you create.

UNDERSTANDING GRAPHIC DESIGN PRINCIPLES

Few of us have studied the "language" of line, mass, space, size, colour, pattern, and texture. When arranged in certain ways, these elements of visual design are pleasing to the eye. More important for the business communicator, design elements have a meaning of their own. A thick line implies more power than a thin one; a bold colour suggests strength; a solid mass seems substantial. To create effective visual aids, become aware of both the aesthetic and the symbolic aspects of graphic art so that you won't send the wrong message. Here are a few principles to remember:

- **Continuity.** Readers view a series of visual aids as a whole, assuming that design elements will be consistent from one page to the next. For instance, if your first chart shows results for division A in blue, readers will expect division A to be shown in blue throughout the report. You'll confuse people by arbitrarily changing colour, shape, size, position, scale, or typeface.
- **Contrast.** Readers expect visual distinctions to match verbal ones. To emphasize differences, depict items in contrasting colours: red and blue, black and white. But to emphasize similarities, make colour differences subtler. In a pie chart, you might show two similar items in two shades of blue and a dissimilar item in yellow. Accent colours draw attention to key elements, but they lose their effect if overdone.
- **Emphasis.** Readers assume the most important point will receive the most visual emphasis. So present the key item on the chart in the most prominent way—through colour, position, size, or whatever. Visually downplay less important items. Avoid using strong colours for unimportant data, and de-emphasize background features such as the grid lines on a chart.
- **Simplicity.** Limit the number of colours and design elements you use in reports. Also avoid chart junk, the decorative elements that clutter documents (and confuse readers) without adding any relevant information.[4] The two charts in Figure 11–16 show the same information, but the second one is cluttered with useless decoration.
- **Experience.** Culture and education condition people to expect things to look a certain way, including report visuals. A red cross on a white background stands for emergency medical care in many countries. But the cross is also a Christian symbol; the red crescent is the logo used by the International Federation of Red Cross and Red Crescent Societies in Islamic countries.[5]

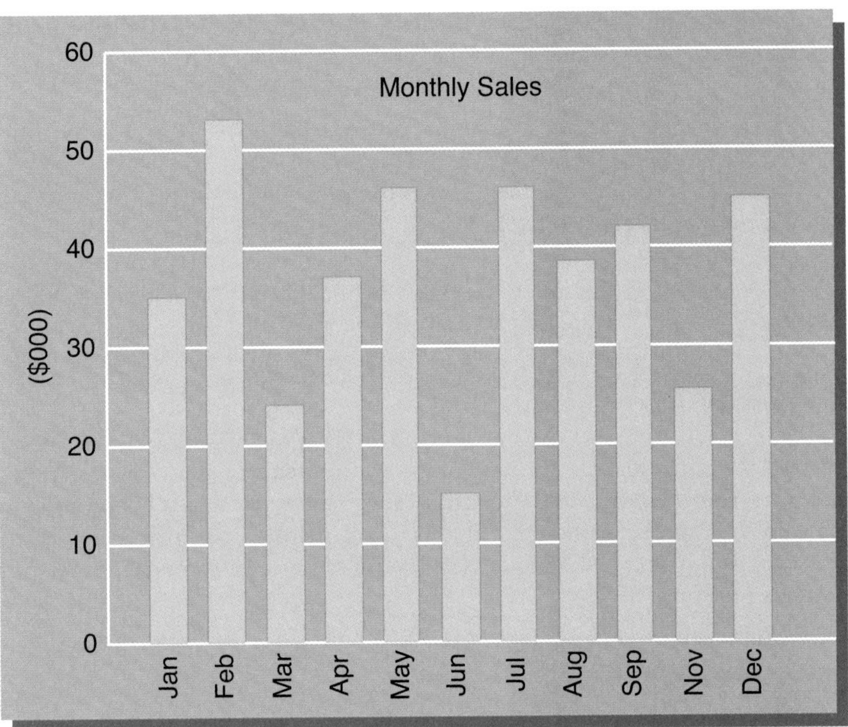

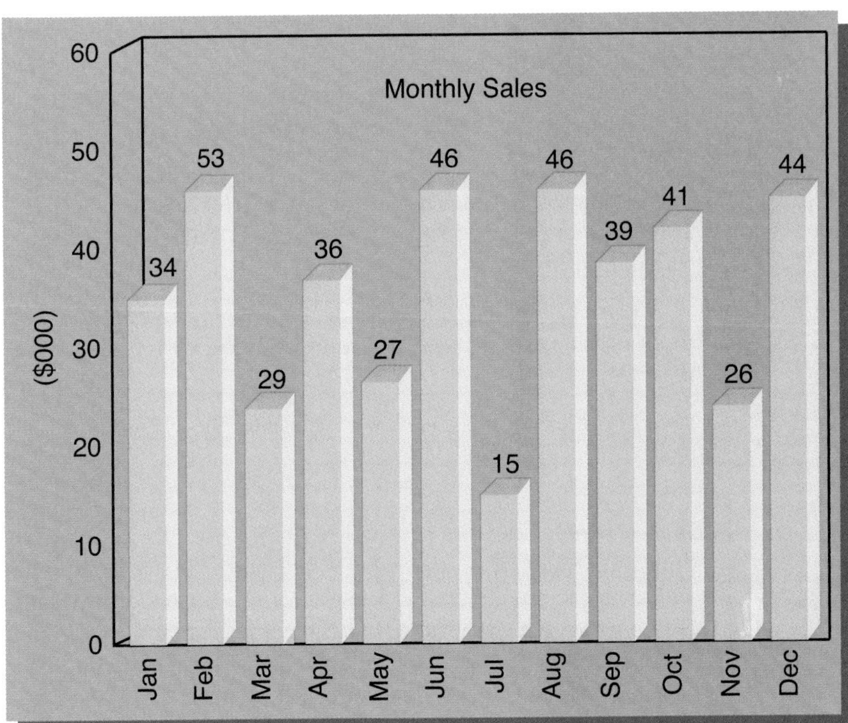

FIGURE 11-16 Simplify Graphics to Avoid Clutter and Confusion

The best time to think about the principles of good design is before preparing your visual aids; making changes after the fact increases the amount of time required to produce them.

FITTING GRAPHICS INTO THE TEXT

To tie visual aids to your text
- Introduce them in the text.
- Place them near the points they illustrate.
- Choose a meaningful title and legend for each one.

Because visuals clarify your text, tie them closely to the discussion. Integrate your visuals into text in a manner that is convenient for your audience and practical for you to do.

Introduce Visuals in the Text Every visual used should be clearly referred to by number in the text of your report. Some report writers refer to all visual aids as exhibits and number them consecutively throughout the report; many others number tables and figures separately (everything that isn't a table is regarded as a figure). In a long report with numbered chapters (as in this book), visuals may have a double number (separated by a period, hyphen, or dash) representing the chapter number and the individual illustration number within that chapter.

Help your readers understand the significance of any visual aids by referring to them before they appear in the text. The reference helps readers perceive why the table or chart is important. The following examples show how you can make this connection in the text:

> Figure 1 summarizes the financial history of the motorcycle division over the past five years, with sales broken into four categories.
>
> Total sales were steady over this period, but the mix of sales by category changed dramatically (see Figure 2).
>
> The underlying reason for the remarkable growth in our sales of low-end fax machines is suggested by Table 4, which provides data on fax machine sales in Canada by region and model.

Put a visual aid as close as possible to its in-text reference to help readers understand the illustration's relevance.

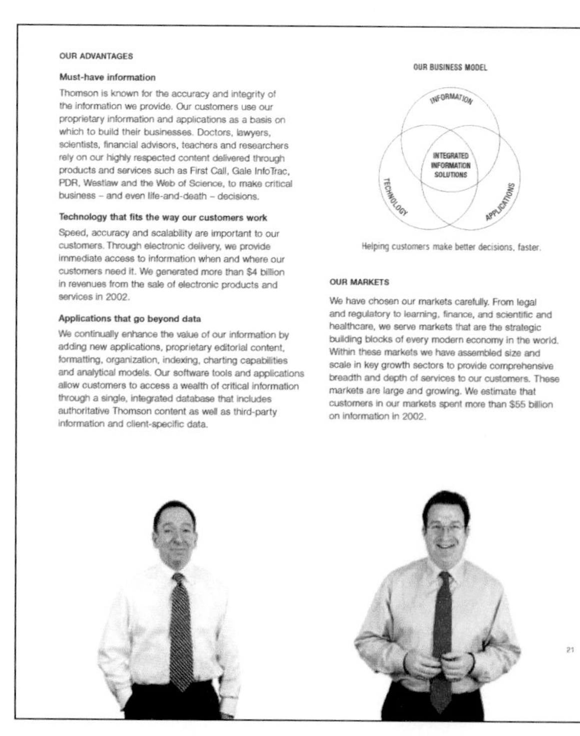

OUR ADVANTAGES

Must-have information

Thomson is known for the accuracy and integrity of the information we provide. Our customers use our proprietary information and applications as a basis on which to build their businesses. Doctors, lawyers, scientists, financial advisors, teachers and researchers rely on our highly respected content delivered through products and services such as First Call, Gale InfoTrac, PDR, Westlaw and the Web of Science, to make critical business – and even life-and-death – decisions.

Technology that fits the way our customers work

Speed, accuracy and scalability are important to our customers. Through electronic delivery, we provide immediate access to information when and where our customers need it. We generated more than $4 billion in revenues from the sale of electronic products and services in 2002.

Applications that go beyond data

We continually enhance the value of our information by adding new applications, proprietary editorial content, formatting, organization, indexing, charting capabilities and analytical models. Our software tools and applications allow customers to access a wealth of critical information through a single, integrated database that includes authoritative Thomson content as well as third-party information and client-specific data.

OUR MARKETS

We have chosen our markets carefully. From legal and regulatory to learning, finance, and scientific and healthcare, we serve markets that are the strategic building blocks of every modern economy in the world. Within these markets we have assembled size and scale in key growth sectors to provide comprehensive breadth and depth of services to our customers. These markets are large and growing. We estimate that customers in our markets spent more than $55 billion on information in 2002.

As this page shows, graphics play an imprtant role in the Thomson Corporation 2002 annual report. Charts present information in a way that is easily understandable as the reader reviews company operations. Photographs show readers the human face of the company.

When describing the data shown in your visual aids, be sure to emphasize the main point you are trying to make. Don't make the mistake of simply repeating the data to be shown. Paragraphs like this are guaranteed to put the reader to sleep:

> Among women who replied to the survey, 17.4 percent earn less than $10 per hour; 35.8 percent earn $10–$12; 33.7 percent, $13–$17; 18.0 percent, $18–$249 9.6 percent, $30–$54; and 2.9 percent earn $55 and over.

The visual will provide these details; there is no need to repeat them in the text. Instead, use round numbers that sum up the message:

> Over two-thirds of the women who replied earn less than $17 per hour.

Place Visual Aids near the Points They Illustrate Try to position your visual aids so that your audience won't have to flip back and forth too much between the visuals and the text. Ideally, it is best to place each visual aid right beside or right after the paragraph it illustrates so that readers can consult the explanation and the visual at the same time. Make sure each visual is clearly and correctly referred to in the text. If you have four or more visual aids, prepare a separate list of them that can be placed with the table of contents at the front of the report. Some writers list tables separately from figures. The two lists should start on separate pages unless both lists will fit on the same page.

If the visual aid is too large to fit on a page with the text it illustrates, place it on a separate page right after the page referring to the visual, and not at the end of the report. With this arrangement, your readers will look at the visual aid the context you have prepared.

Choose Titles and Legends with a Message One of the best ways to tie your visual aids to the text is to choose titles (or captions) and descriptions (or legends) that reinforce the point you want to make. This precaution is especially necessary when the visual aids are widely separated from the text.

Titles and legends should
- Reinforce the point you want to make
- Be specific

The title of a visual aid, when combined with labels and legends on the piece itself, should be complete enough to tell the reader what the content is. The title "Petroleum Tanks in Canada" is sufficient if it's the title of a line chart labelled "Year" along the horizontal axis and "Number (in thousands)" along the vertical axis. However, if the visual aid is a map overlaid with dots of different sizes, the title needs to explain a bit more: "Concentrations of Petroleum Tanks in Canada in 2003." A legend might then explain how many petroleum tanks each size of dot represents.

When placing a visual aid next to the text discussion that pertains to it, clear labelling and a good title are usually enough; the text can explain the visual aid's significance and details. However, when you place a visual aid elsewhere or when the illustration requires considerable explanation that would disrupt the flow of the text, you may need to add a description (or legend). Legends are generally written as one or more complete sentences, and they do more than merely repeat what's already clear from the title and figure labels. It's better to be too specific than too general when you're identifying the content of an illustration. As a check, ask yourself whether you've covered the who, what, when, where, why, and how of the illustration.

Legends identify specific content of visual aids.

When using informative headings in your report, carry this style over into the titles and legends. Instead of using a descriptive title, which identifies the topic of the illustration, call attention to the conclusion that ought to be drawn from the data by using an informative title. Here's the difference:

DESCRIPTIVE TITLE	INFORMATIVE TITLE
Relationship Between Petroleum Demand and Refinery Capacity in Canada	Shrinking Refinery Capacity Results from Stagnant Petroleum Demand

Regardless of whether titles and legends are informative or descriptive, phrase them consistently throughout the report. At the same time, be consistent in the format. If the title of the first visual aid is typed entirely in capital letters, type all the remaining titles that way as well. Although an employer may specify the placement of titles, as a general rule place all table titles at the top. Figure titles may be placed at the top or the bottom. When using legends, make them all roughly the same length. For a review of the important points to remember when creating visual aids, see "Checklist: Creating Effective Visual Aids" on page 342.

Composing Business Reports and Proposals

Once you've organized the text and visuals for your report, you're nearly ready to begin composing it. However, to ensure your report's success, you need to make several decisions that will affect the way it's received and understood by readers. You must set the degree of formality, establish a consistent time perspective, and insert appropriate structural clues.

Checklist: Creating Effective Visual Aids

Preparation

- ✓ Select the proper types of graphics for the data and for the objective of the message.
- ✓ Be sure the visual aid contributes to overall understanding of the subject.
- ✓ Depict data accurately.
- ✓ Portray information honestly.
- ✓ Give proper credit, if required, and follow proper bibliographic form.
- ✓ Make sure that the material is appropriate for the intended audience.

Design

- ✓ Make design elements consistent.
- ✓ Make sure that design elements meet audience expectations.
- ✓ Use colour effectively.
- ✓ Emphasize important points.
- ✓ Make visuals simple and easy to understand.
- ✓ Make headings, labels, titles, and legends clear, whether descriptive or informative.
- ✓ Use space appropriately.
- ✓ Clearly identify data units so that they are easily understandable.
- ✓ Use typefaces and fonts that are clear and readable.
- ✓ Use clip art sparingly.

Layout

- ✓ Balance words and visuals.
- ✓ Clearly reference illustrations in text.
- ✓ Assign each illustration a number or letter.
- ✓ Place visuals close to the points they illustrate.
- ✓ Make sure that visuals appear balanced on the page.
- ✓ Make captions short, precise, and informative.

Choosing the Proper Degree of Formality

For informal reports, adopt a personal style, using the pronouns *I* and *you*.

The issue of formality is closely related to considerations of format, length, and organization. If you know your readers reasonably well and if your report is likely to meet with their approval, you can generally adopt a fairly informal tone. You can speak to readers in the first person, referring to yourself as *I* and to your readers as *you*. This personal approach is often used in brief memo or letter reports, although there are many exceptions.

Longer reports, especially those dealing with controversial or complex information, are traditionally written using a more formal tone. You'll also write more formally when your report will be sent to other parts of the organization or to customers or suppliers. Communicating with people in other cultures often calls for more formality, for two reasons. First, the business environment outside Canada and the U.S. tends to be more formal in general, and that formality must be reflected in your communication style. Second, the techniques used to make a document informal, such as humour and idiomatic language, are the hardest to transfer from culture to culture. Reducing formality in these cases increases the risk of offending people and miscommunicating.

Achieve a formal tone by using the impersonal style, eliminating all references to *I* (including *we*, *us*, and *our*) and *you*. However, be careful that avoiding personal pronouns doesn't lead to overuse of phrases such as *there is* and *it is*, which are both dull and wordy. Avoiding personal pronouns makes it easier to slip into passive voice, which can also be dull and wordy. Instead of saying "I think we should buy TramCo," you might end up saying "It is recommended that the company buy TramCo."

When writing in a formal style, you impose a certain distance between you and your readers. You remain businesslike, unemotional, and objective. You eliminate your own opinions and perceptions and retain only the provable facts You use no jokes, similes, or metaphors, and very few colourful adjectives or adverbs. You can easily destroy your credibility by exaggerating and using overblown language. Consider the following example:

> The catastrophic collapse in sales, precipitated by cutthroat pricing on the part of predatory and unscrupulous rivals, has jeopardized the very survival of the once-soaring hot-air balloon division.

Although this sentence contains no personal references, the colourful adjectives make its objectivity highly questionable.

Nor does the formal style guarantee objectivity of content. The selection of facts is far more important than the way they're phrased. If you omit crucial evidence, you're not being objective, even though you're using an impersonal style.

Despite its drawbacks, the impersonal style is a tradition in many business organizations. You can often tell what tone is appropriate for your readers by looking at other reports of a similar type in your company. If all the other reports on file are impersonal, you should probably adopt the same tone yourself, unless you're confident that your readers prefer a more personal style. However, most organizations expect an unobtrusive, impersonal writing style for business reports.

Establishing a Time Perspective

Be consistent in the verb tense you use.

In what time frame will your report exist? Will you write in the past or present tense? The person who wrote this paragraph never decided:

> Of those interviewed 25 percent <u>report</u> that they <u>are</u> dissatisfied with their present brand. The wealthiest participants <u>complained</u> most frequently, but all income categories <u>are</u> interested in trying a new brand. Only 5 percent of the interviewees <u>say</u> they <u>had</u> no interest in alternative products.

By switching from tense to tense when describing the same research results, you only confuse your readers. They wonder whether the shift is significant or whether you are just being sloppy. Eliminate such confusion by using tense consistently.

Follow a proper chronological sequence in your report.

Also be careful to observe the chronological sequence of events in your report. If you're describing the history or development of something, start at the beginning and cover each event in the order of its occurrence. If you're explaining the steps in a process, take each step in proper sequence.

OBJECTIVE 5 Identify and briefly describe five tools that writers can use in long reports to help readers stay on track.

Helping Readers Find Their Way

As you begin to compose the text for your report, remember that readers have no concept of how the various pieces of your report relate to one another. Because you have done the work, you have a sense of your document's wholeness and can see how each page fits into the overall structure. But readers see the report one page at a time. Experienced report writers know that good writers give their readers a preview, or road map, of a report's structure, clarifying how the various parts are related. These directions are particularly important for people from other cultures and countries, whose language skills and business expectations may differ from yours.

Your readers' perspective differs from yours, so without help from you, they may not see your overall organization, and they may not understand how all the pieces fit together.

In a short report, readers are in little danger of getting lost. As the length of a report increases, however, so do readers' opportunities for becoming confused and losing track of the relationships among ideas. If you want readers to understand and accept your message, help them avoid confusion. Five tools are particularly useful for giving readers a sense of the overall structure of your document and for keeping them on track as they read along: the opening, headings and lists, smooth transitions, previews and reviews, and the ending.

In the opening, tell readers what to expect, tell them why your subject is important, and orient them toward your organizational approach.

THE OPENING

As the name suggests, the **opening** is the first section in any report. A good opening accomplishes at least three things:

- Introduces the subject of the report.
- Indicates why the subject is important.
- Previews the main ideas and the order in which they

Failure to provide readers with these clues to the structure of your report means that they could read aimlessly and miss important points.

If your audience is skeptical, the opening should downplay the controversial aspects of your message while providing the necessary framework for understanding your report. Here's a good example of an indirect opening, taken from the introduction of a memo on why a new line of luggage has failed to sell well. The writer's ultimate goal is to recommend a shift in marketing strategy.

> The performance of the Venturer line can be improved. In the two years since its introduction, this product line has achieved a sales volume lower than we expected, resulting in a drain on the company's overall earnings. The purpose of this report is to review the luggage-buying habits of consumers in all markets where the Venturer line is sold so that we can determine where to put our marketing emphasis.

This paragraph quickly introduces the subject (disappointing sales), tells why the problem is important (drain on earnings), and indicates the main points to be addressed in the body of the report (review of markets where the Venturer line is sold), without revealing what the conclusions and recommendations will be.

SHARPENING YOUR CAREER SKILLS

Writing Headings That Grab Your Reader

Headings help readers follow the main points of your report, but when carefully developed they also do much more. By capturing interest, they make readers want to read your entire report. By showing how your document is organized, they save readers time. By labelling the parts of your document, they help readers find the most important or most relevant parts. Moreover, headings help you organize your writing.

Each heading offers you an opportunity to make an important point. For example, instead of "Introduction," your opening section might be called "An Insight into the Need for Better Communication." This heading gets attention and sparks interest. The heading "Chart of Proposed Organization" gains impact when reworded as "Organizing for Results." So does "Cost Considerations" when retitled "A New Way to Cut Costs."

Headings fall into two categories. Descriptive (topical) headings, such as "Cost Considerations," identify a topic but do little more. However, they are fine in routine reports and in controversial reports, where they may defuse emotional reactions. Informative (talking) headings, such as "A New Way to Cut Costs," convey more information about the main idea of the report. They help readers think about your topic in a certain way. For more effective reports, concentrate on developing informative headings rather than descriptive ones. However, be aware that informative headings are more difficult to create.

Try to avoid vague headings. In a chronological history of your company, headings such as "The Dawning of a New Era" and "The Times They Are a-Changin'" may sound distinguished or cute, but readers will have no idea what period you are discussing. Preferable headings would be "The War Years: Bombardier's Military Vehicles" or "The 1990s See International Expansion."

Whatever headings you choose, try to keep them grammatically parallel. For example, this series of headings is parallel: "Cutting Costs," "Reducing Inventory," "Increasing Profits." This series of headings is not: "Cutting Costs," "Inventory Reduction," "How to Increase Profits."

CAREER APPLICATIONS

1. Think about newspaper headlines. What functions do they perform? How are they usually phrased? What can you learn from journalistic headlines that would apply to report writing?
2. For practice in writing headings, collect some brochures, newsletters, or similar items and rewrite the headings to convey more information about the theme or main idea.

HEADINGS AND LISTS

A **heading** is a brief title at the start of a subdivision within a report. Headings cue readers about the content of the section that follows. Headings are essential markers for clarifying the framework of a report. They visually indicate shifts from one idea to the next, and when *subheadings* (lower-level headings) and headings are both used, they help readers see the relationship between subordinate and main ideas. In addition, busy readers can quickly understand the essentials of a document simply by scanning the headings. (See "Sharpening Your Career Skills—Writing Headings That Grab Your Reader.")

Use headings to give readers the gist of your report.

Within a given section, headings of the same level should be phrased in parallel form, as they are in outlines. If one heading begins with a verb, all same-level headings in that section should begin with a verb. If one is phrased as a question, all same-level headings in that section should also be questions. For example, imagine you work in a computer store and the owner has asked you to create a flyer for customers that would help them to select a home computer. The outline you create to organize your thoughts might look like this:

Phrase all same-level headings within a section in parallel terms.

Title: Selecting a desktop computer

I. Understand your requirements
    A. What will you use the computer for?
        1. Business
        2. School
        3. Recreation
    B. What is your price range?
II. Learn about different products
    A. Read product reviews
    B. Consult with friends and colleagues
III. Narrow down your choices
    A. Compare features
        1. Processor speed
        2. Memory
        3. Optical drives
        4. Monitor resolution
    B. Compare prices and warranties

All first level headings begin with verbs.

All headings of the same level within a specific section are grammatically parallel (either beginning with verbs or phrased as questions in this example).

Putting comparable ideas in similar terms tells readers that the ideas are related. The only exception might be descriptive headings such as "Introduction" at the beginning of a report and "Conclusions" and "Recommendations" at the end. Many companies specify a format for headings. If yours does, use that format. Otherwise, you can use the scheme shown in Figure 11–17 on page 346.

Lists are another effective way to set off important ideas and provide the reader with clues. (Bullets and lists are discussed in detail in Chapter 5.) Like headings, lists are phrased in parallel form. A list that uses bullets or letters instead of numbers indicates choices without implying order or hierarchy:[5]

Use lists to set off important ideas and to show sequence.

A. Convert an existing conference room.
B. Build an add-on room.
C. Lease space in an existing daycare centre.

When you use lists, introduce them clearly so that people know what they're about to read. Moving your readers smoothly into and out of lists requires careful use of transitions—the subject of the next section.

TRANSITIONS

Phrases such as *to continue the analysis*, *on the other hand*, and *an additional benefit* are another type of structural clue. These are examples of transitions, words or phrases that tie ideas together within a report and help readers understand the train of thought.

Use transitions consisting of a single word, a few words, or a whole paragraph to provide additional structural clues.

TITLE

The title is centred at the top of the page in all-capital letters, usually boldfaced (or underlined if typewritten), often in a large font (type size), and often using a sans serif typeface. When the title runs to more than one line, the lines are usually double-spaced and arranged as an inverted pyramid (longer line on the top).

FIRST-LEVEL HEADING

A first-level heading indicates what the following section is about, perhaps by describing the subdivisions. All first-level headings are grammatically parallel, with the possible exception of such headings as "Introduction," "Conclusions," and "Recommendations." Some text appears between every two headings, regardless of their levels. Still boldfaced and sans serif, the font may be smaller than that used in the title but still larger than the typeface used in the text and still in all capital letters.

Second-Level Heading

Like first-level headings, second-level headings indicate what the following material is about. All second-level headings within a section are grammatically parallel. Still boldfaced and sans serif, the font may either remain the same or shrink to the size used in the text, and the style is now initial capitals with lower case. Never use only one second-level heading under a first-level heading. (The same is true for every other level of heading.)

Third-Level Heading

A third-level heading is worded to reflect the content of the material that follows. All third-level headings beneath a second-level heading should be grammatically parallel.

Fourth-Level Heading. Like all the other levels of heading, fourth-level headings reflect the subject that will be developed. All fourth-level headings within a subsection are parallel.

Fifth-level headings are generally the lowest level of heading used. However, you can indicate further breakdowns in your ideas by using a list:

1. *The first item in a list.* You may indent the entire item in block format to set it off visually. Numbers are optional.
2. *The second item in a list.* All lists have at least two items. An introductory phrase or sentence may be italicized for emphasis, as shown here.

FIGURE 11–17 Heading Format for Reports

Good writers use transitions to help readers move from one section of a report to the next, from one paragraph to the next, and even from one sentence to the next. Here is a list of transitions frequently used to guide readers smoothly between sentences and paragraphs:

Additional detail	moreover, furthermore, in addition, besides, first, second, third, finally
Causal relationship	therefore, because, accordingly, thus, consequently, hence, as a result, so
Comparison	similarly, here again, likewise, in comparison, still

Contrast	yet, conversely, whereas, nevertheless, on the other hand, however, but, nonetheless
Condition	although, if
Illustration	for example, in particular, in this case, for instance
Time sequence	formerly, after, when, meanwhile, sometimes
Intensification	indeed, in fact, in any event
Summary	in brief, in short, to sum up
Repetition	that is, in other words, as I mentioned earlier

Although transitional words and phrases are useful, they're not sufficient in themselves to overcome poor organization. Your goal is first to put your ideas in a strong framework and then to use transitions to link them even more strongly.

Consider using a transitional device whenever it might help readers understand your ideas and follow you from point to point. You can use transitions inside paragraphs to tie related points together and between paragraphs to ease the shift from one distinct thought to another. In longer reports, transitions that link major sections or chapters are often complete paragraphs that serve as mini-introductions to the next section or as summaries of the ideas presented in the section just ending. Here's an example:

> Given the nature of this problem, the alternatives are limited. As the previous section indicates, we can stop making the product, improve it, or continue with the current model. Each of these alternatives has advantages and disadvantages. The following section discusses pros and cons of each of the three alternatives.

PREVIEWS AND REVIEWS

Throughout your report, introduce topics with previews, and summarize them with reviews.

Use *preview sections* before and *review sections* after important material in your report. Previews introduce a topic: they help readers get ready for new information. Previews are particularly useful when the information is complex or unexpected. You don't want readers to get halfway into a section before figuring out what it's about. Review sections that come after a body of material and summarize the information for your readers. Reviews help readers absorb details while keeping track of the big picture. Long reports and reports dealing with complex subjects can often benefit from multiple review sections, not just a single review at the very end.

Whenever you've had your readers immersed in detail for any length of time, bring them back to the main ideas with a review section so that they can get their bearings again.

THE ENDING

Reemphasize your main ideas in the ending.

The **ending** of the final section of a report leaves a strong and lasting impression. That's why it's important to use the ending to emphasize the main points of your message. In a report written in direct order, you may want to remind readers once again of your key points or your conclusions and recommendations. If your report is written in indirect order, end with a summary of key points (except in short memos). In analytical reports, end with conclusions and recommendations as well as key points.

Be sure to summarize the benefits to the reader in any report that suggests a change from common practice or some other action. In general, the ending refers back to all the key ideas in the report body and reminds readers how those ideas fit together. It provides a final opportunity to emphasize your central message. Furthermore, it gives you one last chance to make sure that your report says what you intended.[7] To review the tasks involved in writing reports, see "Checklist: Writing Business Reports and Proposals" on page 348.

Checklist: Writing Business Reports and Proposals

Format and Style

✓ For brief external reports, use letter format, including a title or a subject line after the reader's address that clearly states the subject of the document.

✓ For brief internal reports, use memo or manuscript format.

✓ Single-space the text.

✓ Double-space between paragraphs.

✓ Use headings where helpful, but try not to use more than three levels of headings.

✓ Call attention to significant information by setting it off visually with lists or indention.

✓ Include visual aids to emphasize and clarify the text.

✓ Use an informal style (*I* and *you*) for letter and memo reports (unless company prefers impersonal third person).

✓ Use an impersonal style for more formal short reports in manuscript format.

✓ Maintain a consistent time frame by writing in either the present or the past tense, using other tenses only to indicate prior or future events.

✓ Give each paragraph a topic sentence.

✓ Link paragraphs by using transitional words and phrases.

✓ Strive for readability by using short sentences, concrete words, and appropriate terminology.

✓ Be accurate, thorough, and impartial in presenting the material.

✓ Avoid including irrelevant and unnecessary details.

✓ Document for all material quoted or paraphrased from secondary sources.

Opening

✓ For short, routine memos, use the subject line of the memo form and the first sentence or two of the text as the introduction.

✓ For all other short reports, cover these topics in the introduction: purpose, scope, background, restrictions (in conducting the study), sources of information and methods of research, and organization of the report.

✓ If using direct order, place conclusions and recommendations in the opening.

Body (Direct or Indirect Order)

✓ Use direct order for informational reports to receptive readers, developing ideas around subtopics (chronologically, geographically, categorically).

✓ Use direct order for analytical reports to receptive readers, developing points around conclusions or recommendations.

✓ Use indirect order for analytical reports to skeptical or hostile readers, developing points around logical arguments.

Ending

✓ In informational reports summarize major findings at the end, if you wish.

✓ Summarize points in the same order in which they appear in the body.

✓ In analytical reports using indirect order, list conclusions and recommendations at the end.

✓ Be certain that conclusions and recommendations follow logically from facts presented in the text.

✓ Consider using a list format for emphasis.

✓ Avoid introducing new material in the summary, conclusions, or recommendations.

Summary of Learning Objectives

1 Discuss the structure of informational reports. Because reader reaction is rarely an issue for informational reports, structure is dictated by the nature of your topic. Of utmost concern is reader comprehension, so informational reports must be both logical and accurate. Topical organization allows you to structure your report in six common arrangements. When basing your structure on importance, cover the most important facts first and the least important last. When using sequence, cover a process step by step. When basing your structure on chronology, cover facts as a chain of events occurring in time. When using spatial orientation, detail physical aspects from right to left, left to right, top to bottom, or outside to inside. To base your structure on geography, cover facts by location. And to use category as your structural basis, cover facts as distinct aspects that can be classified into groups.

2 Explain the structure of analytical reports. Because the structure of analytical reports depends on anticipated audience reaction, use either a structure that focuses attention on conclusions and recommendations (for receptive audiences) or one that focuses attention on the rationale behind your conclusions and recommendations (for skeptical or hostile audiences). Focusing directly on conclusions or recommendations can intensify resistance or even make your solution seem too simple. When you want your audience to focus on why your ideas will work, you need to draw attention to the logic of your argument. There are three popular approaches to a logical organization. The 2 + 2 = 4 approach demonstrates that everything in your report adds up. The scientific method reveals the most effective solution, or hypothesis, by showing evidence that either proves or disproves each alternative. The yardstick approach establishes conditions, or criteria, against which all possible solutions are measured.

3 List the most popular types of visuals and discuss when to use them. Various types of information are best depicted in various types of visuals. For example, tables communicate facts and detail in an easy-to-read format. Line charts illustrate trends over time or plot the relationships of two or more variables. Surface charts illustrate the cumulative effect of trends. Bar charts portray numbers by the height or length of their rectangular bars and facilitate comparisons of size in addition to showing changes over time. Pie charts show percentages or how the parts of a whole are distributed. Flowcharts illustrate a sequence of events. Organizational charts illustrate positions and functions in an organization. Maps show concentrations by geographic area. Drawings and diagrams show how something looks or operates.

4 Clarify five principles of graphic design to remember when preparing visuals. To design the most effective visuals for business reports, keep five principles in mind. First, continuity: to avoid confusing readers, be consistent in your use of design elements such as colour, shape, size, position, scale, and typeface. Second, contrast: use contrasting colours to show difference and subtle colours to show similarity. Third, emphasis: use design elements to draw attention to key points and to visually downplay less important ones. Fourth, simplicity: avoid clutter and chart junk. Fifth, experience: take into account your audience's culture, education, and other background experiences.

5 Identify and briefly describe five tools that writers can use in long reports to help readers stay on track. Readers see reports one page at a time, so in long reports, they may have difficulty seeing the overall structure and just how various report sections fit together. To help readers navigate the long reports, five tools are available. The opening introduces the subject of the report, indicates why it's important, and previews the key points in the order they will be discussed. Headings and lists set off important ideas and provide the reader with clues. Transitions tie ideas together and keep readers moving along. Previews and reviews prepare readers for new information and summarize previously discussed information. The ending summarizes the key points, conclusions, or recommendations.

ON THE JOB

Solving a Communication Dilemma at FedEx

Entrepreneur Frederick Smith was sure that his new transportation network would increase Federal Express's efficiency and decrease the cost of moving packages across the U.S. and Canada. From a central hub in Memphis, Tennessee, Smith wanted to sort packages and fly them to their final destinations. When raising money for this venture, Smith used business reports as a tool. Business reports have remained important through the years as he and his managers have built Federal Express into a global business with $22 billion in annual revenues.

Because of Federal Express's heavy orientation toward customer satisfaction, the company has a strong emphasis on training. Training costs money, and reports are used to justify training expenditures. One of those expenditures might be for computer-networking equipment to support the company's interactive training program. Before managers buy equipment, these items are thoroughly and objectively investigated and analyzed. Then managers can read through special, non-recurring reports, study the justification for each major purchase, and weigh the pros and cons.

Reports are also important to the company's internal auditors, who are charged with studying how the company controls its finances, operations, and legal compliance. Internal auditors visit the departments they are assigned to examine, conduct their investigations, and then write reports to communicate their findings and any ideas for improvement. The analytical reports that Federal Express's auditors prepare contain recommendations as well as conclusions.

The human resources and internal audit departments are only two of the many Federal Express departments that prepare and receive reports. As Frederick Smith and his managers strive against competitors, work toward customer satisfaction, and keep the business running smoothly, business reports are sure to continue to play a key role at Federal Express.

Your Mission You have recently been hired as Frederick Smith's administrative assistant to help him with a variety of special projects. In each of the following situations, choose the best communication alternative from among those listed, and be prepared to explain why your choice is best.

1 To keep track of the industry, Smith has asked you to research two online services offered by FedEx's top competitors: online pickup requests and online package tracking. How should you introduce your report? Choose the best opening from the four shown below.

a Begin by introducing the purpose of the study (to review what online services competitors are offering) and making recommendations about how FedEx can better compete with these offerings.

b Begin by introducing the purpose of the study (to review what online services competitors are offering) and outlining how you will present your data.
c Begin by giving a brief history of the rivalry between FedEx and its top three competitors.
d Begin by summarizing FedEx efforts to stay on top of the technology wave and how important such technology will be to the future of the company.

2 As you work on your report about competitor's online services, you want to include a visual that compares FedEx's online statistics with those of its major competitors. For example, you know that FedEx.com receives 3 million visitors each month and gets 1.1 million tracking requests per day. Once you have located the same information for all major competitors, what is the best way to present it?

a Use a table to present the numbers for each company.
b Use a line chart to present the numbers for each company.
c Use a bar chart to present the numbers for each company.
d Use a pie chart to present the numbers for each company.

3 Smith wants to celebrate the company's thirty-fifth anniversary by creating a special advertising insert on FedEx's history. He wants to distribute this insert inside the April issue of a national business magazine. The magazine's publisher is excited about the concept and has asked Smith to send her "something in writing." Smith asks you to draft the proposal, which should be no more than ten pages long. Which of the following outlines should you use?

a First version

I. An overview of FedEx's history
  A. How company was founded
  B. Overview of company services
  C. Overview of markets served
  D. Overview of transportation operations
II. The FedEx magazine insert
  A. Historic events to be included
  B. Employees to be interviewed
  C. Customers to be discussed
  D. Production schedule
III. Pros and cons of FedEx magazine insert
  A. Pros: Make money for magazine, draw new customers for FedEx
  B. Cons: Costs, questionable audience interest

b Second version

I. Introduction: Overview of the FedEx special insert
  A. Purpose
  B. Content
  C. Timing
II. Description of the insert
  A. Text
    1. Message from CEO
    2. History of FedEx
    3. Interviews with employees
    4. Customer testimonials
  B. Advertising
    1. Inside front and back covers
    2. Colour spreads
    3. Congratulatory ads placed by customers
III. Next steps
IV. Summary

c Third version

Who:	FedEx
What:	Special magazine insert
When:	Inserted in April issue
Where:	Coordinated by magazine's editors
Why:	To celebrate FedEx's anniversary
How:	Overview of content, production responsibilities, and schedule

d Fourth version

I. Introduction: The rationale for producing a magazine insert promoting FedEx
  A. Insert would make money for magazine
  B. Insert would boost morale of FedEx employees
  C. Insert would attract new customers
II. Insert description
  A. Interview with founder Frederick Smith
  B. Interviews with employees
  C. Description of historic moments
  D. Interviews with customers
  E. Advertisements
III. Production plan
  A. Project organization
  B. Timing and sequence of steps
  C. FedEx's responsibilities
  D. Magazine's responsibilities
IV. Detailed schedule
V. Summary of benefits and responsibilities

4 Smith has asked you to think about ways of attracting new customers that need FedEx's expertise in managing international parts and parcel distribution. You have talked with executives at Laura Ashley and National Semiconductor, two current customers, and discovered that they care most about the time needed to process orders and deliver parts to stores or factories. FedEx can cut the delivery time from as much as twenty-one days to as little as four days after ordering. You believe that an advertising campaign featuring testimonials from these two satisfied customers will give FedEx a tremendous advantage over competitors. As a relatively junior person at FedEx, you are a little apprehensive about suggesting your idea. You don't want to seem presumptuous, but on the other hand, you think your idea is good. You have decided to raise the issue with Smith. Which of the following approaches is preferable?

a Instead of writing a report, arrange a meeting to discuss your ideas with Smith, the advertising manager, and an executive from the company's advertising agency. This allows you to address the issues and ideas firsthand in an informal setting.

b You write the following short report:
You recently asked me to give some thought to how FedEx might attract new customers for its international parts distribution business. I decided to sound out two of our largest customers to get a feel for why they hired us to handle this operation. Interestingly, they didn't choose FedEx because they wanted to reduce their shipping costs. Rather, they were interested in reducing the time needed to process and ship orders to stores and factories.

Many companies are in the same situation as Laura Ashley and National Semiconductor. They're not just looking for the carrier with the lowest prices, they're looking for the carrier with the proven ability to process orders and get shipments to their destinations as quickly as possible. Instead of waiting as long as twenty-one days for shipments to reach their destination, these companies can promise delivery in four days.

Clearly, our track record with Laura Ashley and National Semiconductor is the key to capturing the attention of other global companies. After all, how many competitors can show they have the ability to cut as much as seventeen days off the time needed to process and deliver an order? Of course, companies might be skeptical if we made this claim on our own, but they would be more likely to accept it if our customers told their own stories. That's why FedEx should ask executives from Laura Ashley and National Semiconductor to offer testimonials in an advertising campaign.

c You write the following short report:
In response to your request, I have investigated ways in which FedEx might attract new customers for its international parts distribution business. In conducting this investigation, I have talked with executives at two of our largest customers, Laura Ashley and National Semiconductor, and discussed the situation with our advertising manager and our advertising agency. All agreed that companies are interested in more than merely saving money on international shipments.

Typically, a global company has to keep a lot of parts or materials on hand and be ready to ship these whenever a store or factory places an order. As soon as an order arrives, the company packages the parts and ships it out. The store or factory doesn't want to wait a long time because it, in turn, has to keep a lot of money tied up in parts to be sure it doesn't run out before the new shipment arrives. Thus, if the company can cut the time between ordering and delivery, it will save its stores or factories a lot of money and, at the same time, build a lot of customer loyalty.

As a result, shipping costs are less important than the need to process orders and get shipments to their destinations as quickly as possible. Instead of delivery in twenty-one days, these companies can promise deliveries in four days. If we can show global companies how to do this, we will attract many more customers.

d You write the following short report:
This report was authorized by Frederick W. Smith on May 7. Its purpose is to analyze ways of attracting more customers to FedEx's international parts distribution business.

Laura Ashley and National Semiconductor are two large, global companies that use our international parts distribution service. Both companies are pleased with our ability to cut the time between ordering and parts delivery. Both are willing to give testimonials to that effect.

These testimonials will help attract new customers if they are used in newspaper, magazine, and television advertising. A company is more likely to believe a satisfied customer than someone who works for FedEx. If the advertising department and the advertising agency start working on this idea today, it could be implemented within two months.[8]

Test Your Knowledge

Review Questions

1 What are your options for structuring an informational report?
2 What are your options for structuring an analytical report?
3 How does topical organization differ from logical organization?
4 When is it appropriate to use tables, line charts, surface charts, and pie charts in a report?
5 What five principles apply to effective visuals for business reports?
6 How does a flowchart differ from an organizational chart?
7 What tools can you use to help readers follow the structure and flow of information in a long report?
8 What ethical issue is raised by the use of technology to alter photographs in reports?
9 What is the purpose of adding titles and legends to visual aids in reports?
10 How do writers use transitions in reports?

Interactive Learning 

Use This Text's Online Resources

Visit our Companion Website at **www.pearsoned.ca/thill**, where you can use the interactive Study Guide to test your chapter knowledge and get instant feedback. Additional resources link you to the sites mentioned in this text and to additional sources of information on chapter topics.

Also check out the resources on the Mastering Business Communication CD, including "Perils of Pauline," an interactive presentation of the business communication challenges within a fictional company.

Apply Your Knowledge

Critical Thinking Questions

1 Should a report always explain the writer's method of gathering evidence or solving a problem? Why or why not?

2 Would you use the direct or indirect approach to document inventory shortages at your manufacturing plant? To propose an employee stock-option plan? Why?

3 What tense is better for most business reports, past or present? Explain.

4 Besides telling readers why an illustration is important, why must you refer to it in the text of your document?

5 **Ethical Choices** What should you consider when using colour to accentuate key points in visual aids?

Practice Your Knowledge

Documents for Analysis

Document 11.A

Examine the pie charts in Figure 11–18 below and point out any problems or errors you notice.

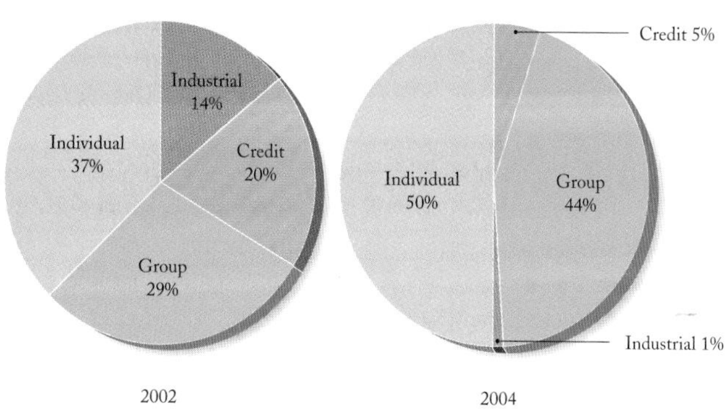

FIGURE 11–18 Pie Charts for Analysis (Document 11.A)

Document 11.B

Examine the line chart in Figure 11–19 below and point out any problems or errors you notice.

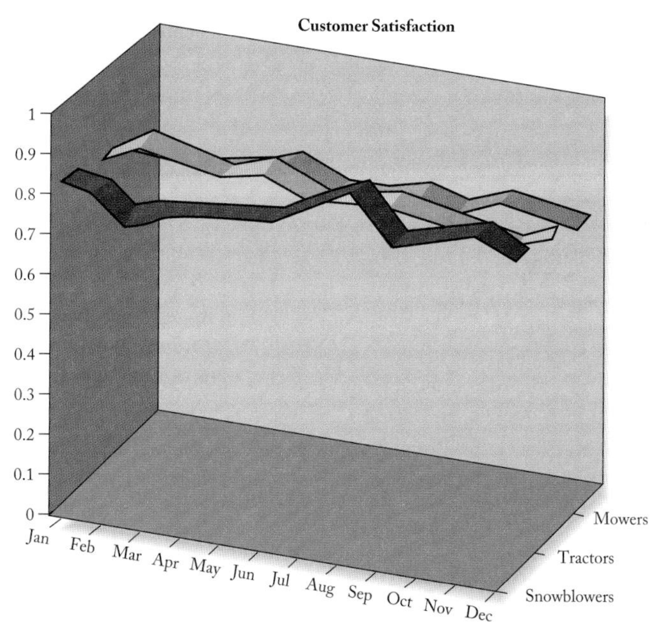

FIGURE 11–19 Line Chart for Analysis (Document 11.B)

Exercises

11–1 Writing Reports: Organizational Approach Of the organizational approaches introduced in the chapter, which is best suited for reporting on each of the following problem statements? Briefly explain why.

a In which market segment—root beer, cola, or lemon-lime—should Fizz Drinks, Inc., introduce a new soft drink to take advantage of its enlarged research and development budget?

b Should Major Manufacturing, Inc. close down operations of its antiquated St. John's, Newfoundland plant despite the adverse economic impact on the town that has grown up around the plant?

c Should you and your partner adopt a new accounting method to make your financial statements look better to potential investors?

d Should Johnson Chemicals buy disposable test tubes to reduce labour costs associated with cleaning and sterilizing reusable test tubes?

e What are some reasons for the recent data loss at the college computer centre, and how can we avoid similar problems in the future?

11–2 Internet Visit the Internet site **www.sedar.ca** and review the annual reports recently released by two corporations in the same industry (go to the "public company documents" search page). Analyze each report and be prepared to discuss the following questions in class:

@

a What differences do you see in the way each corporation reports its financial data? Are the data presented clearly so that shareholders can draw conclusions about each corporation's financial results?

b What goals, challenges, and plans do top managers emphasize in their discussion of results?

c How do the format and organization of each report enhance or detract from the information being presented?

11–3 Writing Reports: Visual Aids As a market researcher for a province-wide chain of car dealerships, you're examining car and truck ownership and lease patterns among single drivers in various age groups. By discovering which age groups have the highest percentages of owners, you will be better able to target advertising that promotes the leasing option. Using the following information, prepare a bar graph comparing the number of owners with the number of leasers in each age category. Be sure to label your graph, and include combined totals for owners and leasers ("total drivers"). Then prepare a pie chart showing the proportion of owners and leasers in the one age group that you think holds the most promise for leasing a new vehicle. Write a sentence that prepares your company's management for the information shown in the pie chart.

Age group	Number of owners (in 000s)	Number of leasers (in 000s)
18–24	1830	795
25–29	1812	1483
30–34	1683	1413
35–44	1303	1932
45–54	1211	1894
55–64	1784	1435
65–74	3200	1142
75+	3431	854

11–4 Writing Reports: Pie Charts As director of new business development for a growing advertising agency, you're interested in how companies spend their advertising dollars. Create a pie chart based on the following information, which shows national advertising spending by media category. Summarize these findings (in two or three sentences) for publication in a report to top management.[9]

Media type	Expenditure (in $billions)
Television	42.5
Newspaper	38.4
Direct mail	38.4
Miscellaneous	22.6
Radio	12.3
Yellow Pages	10.8
Magazines	9.0
Business papers	3.8
Outdoor	1.3
Total	$179.1

11–5 Writing Reports: Line Charts The pet food manufacturer you work for is interested in the results of a recent poll of U.S. pet-owning households. Look at the statistics that follow and decide on the most appropriate scale for a chart; then create a line chart of the trends in cat ownership. What conclusions do you draw from the trend you've charted? Draft a paragraph or two discussing the results of this poll and the potential consequences for the pet food business. Support your conclusions by referring readers to your chart.

In 1990, 22 million U.S. households owned a cat.
In 1995, 24 million households owned a cat.
In 2000, 28 million households owned a cat.
In 2005, 32 million households owned a cat.

11–6 Writing Reports: Visual Aid Selection You're preparing the annual report for FretCo Guitar Corporation. For each of the following types of information, what form of visual aid would you choose to illustrate the text? Explain your choices.

a Data on annual sales for the past 20 years

b Comparison of FretCo sales, product by product (electric guitars, bass guitars, amplifiers, acoustic guitars), for this year and last year

c Explanation of how a FretCo acoustic guitar is manufactured

d Explanation of how the FretCo Guitar Corporation markets its guitars

e Data on sales of FretCo products in each of 12 countries

f Comparison of FretCo sales figures with sales figures for three competing guitar makers over the past 10 years

11–7 Teamwork Team up with a classmate to design graphics based on a comparison of the total tax burden of the Canadian taxpayer with that of people in other nations. One teammate should sketch a horizontal bar chart and the other should sketch a vertical one from the estimates that follow. Then exchange visual aids and analyze how well each conveys the situation of the Canadian taxpayer. Would the bar chart look best with vertical or horizontal bars? Why? What scale is best? How does the direction used in the bar chart enhance or obscure the meaning or impact of the data? What suggestions can you make for improving your teammate's visual aid?

Estimates show that Swedish taxpayers spend 51 percent of their incomes on taxes, British taxpayers spend 48 percent, French taxpayers spend 37 percent, Japanese taxpayers spend 28 percent, and U.S. taxpayers spend 27 percent.

11–8 Writing Reports: Graphics Design The following table shows last year's sales figures for the appliance and electronics megastore where you work. Construct visual aids based on these figures that will help you explain to the store's general manager how sales fluctuate by season in each department. Then write a title and legend for each visual aid.

TABLE 11–4 Store Sales in 2004 (in thousands)

Month	Home Electronics	Computers	Appliances
January	$68	$39	$36
February	72	34	34
March	75	41	30
April	54	41	28
May	56	42	44
June	49	33	48
July	54	31	43
August	66	58	39
September	62	58	36
October	66	44	33
November	83	48	29
December	91	62	24

11–9 Teamwork With a team of three or four other students, brainstorm and then sketch at least three types of visual aids you can use to compare the populations of all ten provinces and three territories in Canada. You can use any of the graphic ideas presented in this chapter, as well as any ideas or examples you find from other sources.

11–10 Composing Reports: Report Content You are writing an analytical report on the Canadian sales of your newest product. Of the following topics, identify those that should be covered in the report's opening, body, and closing. Briefly explain your decisions:

a Regional breakdowns of sales across the country
b Date the product was released in the marketplace
c Sales figures from competitors selling similar products worldwide
d Predictions of how the U.S. economy will affect sales over the next six months
e Method used for obtaining the above predictions
f The impact of similar products being sold in the United States by Japanese competitors
g Your recommendation as to whether the company should sell this product internationally
h Actions that must be completed by year end if the company decides to sell this product internationally

11–11 Composing Reports: Navigational Clues Review a long business article in a journal or newspaper. Highlight examples of how the article uses heading, transitions, and previews and reviews to help the readers find their way.

11–12 Ethical Choices If you create a new visual aid using data drawn from a visual aid posted on a Web site or printed in a magazine, must you indicate the source of the original data? Explain your answer.

Cases

Informal Informational Reports

1 My progress to date: Interim progress report on your academic career As you know, the bureaucratic process involved in getting a degree or certificate is nearly as challenging as any course you could take.

Your Task: Prepare an interim progress report detailing the steps you've taken toward completing your graduation or certification requirements. After examining the requirements listed in your school catalogue, indicate a realistic schedule for completing those that remain. In addition to course requirements, include steps such as completing the residency requirement, filing necessary papers, and paying necessary fees. Use memo format for your report, and address it to anyone who is helping or encouraging you through school.

2 Gavel to gavel: Personal activity report of a meeting Meetings, conferences, and conventions abound in the academic world, and you have probably attended your share.

Your Task: Prepare a personal activity report on a meeting, convention, or conference that you recently attended. Use memo format, and direct the report to other students in your field who were not able to attend.

3 Check that price tag: Informational report on trends in university costs Are tuition costs going up, going down, or remaining the same? Your university's administration has asked you to compare your university's tuition costs with those of a university in another province and determine which has risen more quickly. Research the trend by checking your university's annual tuition costs for each of the most recent four years. Then research the four-year tuition trends for a neighboring university. For both university's, calculate the percentage change in tuition costs from year to year and between the first and fourth year.

Your Task: Prepare an informal report (using letter format) presenting your findings and conclusions to the president of your college. Include graphics to explain and support your conclusions.

4 Sampling success: Operating report on a program to promote a new cracker To help food manufacturers promote their new products, Sample Canada offers supermarket shoppers bite-size samples of everything from cheese and ice cream to pretzels and cookies. This month Sample Canada gave away a total of 12 800 samples of Cheezy sesame crackers in 11 Toronto supermarkets. The Cheezy Company wants Sample Canada to give away 14 000 sesame cracker samples in 13 Vancouver supermarkets during the coming month. However, one large supermarket chain hasn't yet agreed to let Sample Canada set up a tasting booth.

Your Task: As the Western regional manager for Sample Canada, you send your clients a monthly operating report on results and future sampling plans. Prepare this month's report to Jacques D'Aprix, the director of marketing at the Cheezy Company. Be sure to include future plans as well as any problems that may affect next month's activities.

Informal Analytical Reports

5 My next career move: Justification report organized around recommendations If you've ever analyzed your career objectives, you'll be quite comfortable with this project.

Your Task: Write a memo report directed to yourself and signed with a fictitious name. Indicate a possible job that your education will qualify you for, mention the advantages of the position in terms of your long-range goals, and then outline the actions you must take to get the job.

6 Staying the course: Proposal using the 2 + 2 = 4 approach Think of a course you would love to see added to the core curriculum at your school. Conversely, if you would like to see a course offered as an elective rather than being required, write your e-mail report accordingly.

Your Task: Write a short e-mail proposal using the 2 + 2 = 4 approach. Prepare your proposal to be submitted to the academic dean by e-mail. Be sure to include all the reasons supporting your idea.

7 Planning my program: Problem-solving report using the scientific method Assume that you will have time for only one course next term.

Your Task: List the pros and cons of four or five courses that interest you, and use the scientific method to settle on the course that is best for you to take at this time. Write your report in memo format, addressing it to your academic adviser.

8 "Would you carry it?" Unsolicited sales proposal recommending a product to a retail outlet. Select a product you are familiar with, and imagine that you are the manufacturer trying to get a local retail outlet to carry it.

Your Task: Write a sales proposal in letter format to the owner (or manager) of the store, proposing that the item be stocked. Making up some reasonable figures, tell what the item costs, what it can be sold for, and what services your company provides (return of unsold items, free replacement of unsatisfactory items, necessary repairs, and so on).

9 Get a move on it: Lasting guidelines for moving into college dormitories Moving into a university dormitory is one experience you weren't quite prepared for. In addition to lugging your belongings up four flights of stairs in 30-degree heat, channelling electrical cords to the one electrical outlet tucked in the corner of the room, and negotiating with your roommate over who gets the bigger closet, you had to hug your parents goodbye in the parking lot in front of the entire freshman class—or so it seemed. Now that you're a pro, you've offered to write some lasting guidelines for future first-year students so that they know what is expected of them on moving day.

Your Task: Prepare an informational report for future first-year classes outlining the rules and procedures to follow when moving into a university dorm. Lay out the rules such as starting time, handling trash and empty boxes, items permitted and not permitted in dorm rooms, common courtesies, and so on. Be sure to mention what the policy is for removing furniture from the room, and overloading electrical circuits. Of course, any recommendations on how to handle disputes with roommates would be helpful. So would some brief advice on how to cope with anxious parents. Direct your memo report to the university director of housing.

10 Restaurant review: Troubleshooting report on a restaurant's food and operations Visit any restaurant, possibly your school cafeteria. The workers and fellow customers will assume that you are an ordinary customer, but you are really a spy for the owner.

Your Task: After your visit, write a short report to the owner, explaining (a) what you did and what you observed, (b) any violations of policy that you observed, and (c) your recommendations for improvement. The first part of your report (what you did and what you observed) will be the longest. Include a description of the premises, inside and out. Tell how long it took for each step of ordering and receiving your meal. Describe the service and food thoroughly. You are interested in both the good and bad aspects of the establishment's decor, service, and food. For the second section (violations of policy), use some common sense. If all the servers but one have their hair covered, you may assume that policy requires hair to be covered; a dirty window or restroom obviously violates policy. The last section (recommendations for improvement) involves professional judgment. What management actions will improve the restaurant?

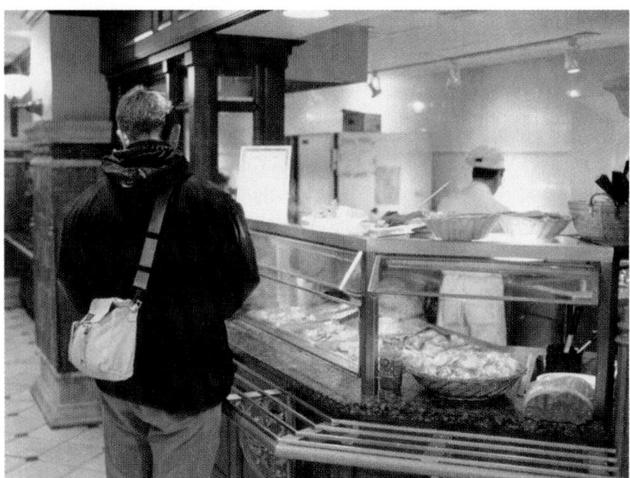

11 On the books: Troubleshooting report on improving the campus bookstore Imagine that you are a consultant hired to improve the profits of your campus bookstore.

Your Task: Visit the bookstore and look critically at its operations. Then draft a memo offering recommendations to the bookstore manager that would make the store more profitable, perhaps suggesting products it should carry, hours that it should remain open, or added services that it should make available to students. Be sure to support your recommendations.

12 Press one for efficiency: Unsolicited proposal on a telephone interviewing system How can a firm be thorough yet efficient when considering dozens of applicants for each position? One tool that just may help is IntelliView, a 10-minute question-and-answer session conducted by Touch-Tone telephone. The company recruiter dials up the IntelliView computer and then leaves the room. The candidate punches in answers to roughly 100 questions about work attitudes and other issues. In a few minutes, the recruiter can call Pinkerton, which offers the service, and find out the results. On the basis of what the IntelliView interview revealed, the recruiter can delve more deeply into certain areas and, ultimately, have more information on which to base the hiring decision.

Your Task: As a recruiter for Curtis Box and Crate, you think that IntelliView might help your firm. Write a brief memo to Wallace Jefferson, the director of human resources, in which you suggest a test of the IntelliView system. Your memo should tell your boss why you believe your firm should test the system before making a long-term commitment.[10]

13 Day and night: Problem-solving report on stocking a 24-hour convenience store When a store is open all day, every day, when's the best time to restock the shelves? That's the challenge at Store 24, a retail chain that never closes. Imagine you're the assistant manager of a Store 24 branch that just opened near your campus. You want to set up a restocking schedule that won't conflict with prime shopping hours. Think about the number of customers that you're likely to serve in the morning, afternoon, evening, and overnight hours. Consider, too, how many employees you might have during these four periods.

Your Task: Using the scientific approach, write a problem-solving report in letter form to the store manager (Isabel Chu) and the regional manager (Eric Angstrom), who must agree on a solution to this problem. Discuss the pros and cons of each of the four periods, and include your recommendation for restocking the shelves.

Going Online Exercises

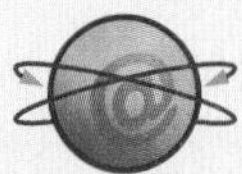

Exploring Computer Graphics, found on page 338 of this text

How can you add effectively designed visual aids to a report or proposal to emphasize an important point, reinforce an idea, and create interest in the text? Computer graphics can create surprising, eye-catching visual information to supplement the written text. Log on to Mambo and visit the Perceptual Science Lab and its many links to build on what you've learned in this chapter about computer graphics.

1 What type of computer graphics did you find? Tell how you could use these graphics (or ideas from them) to create a visual that would enhance a business report or proposal. If you did not get any ideas, explain why.
2 Describe what new information you learned about computer graphics at the PSL (or one of its links).
3 What new resources did you discover at the PSL (or one of its links)? If you didn't find the site or its links useful, explain why.

Completing Formal Reports and Proposals

1. List the three tasks involved in completing business reports and proposals and briefly explain what's involved in revising them
2. Explain the 10 prefatory parts of a formal report
3. Describe four important functions of a formal report's introduction and identify the possible topics it might include
4. Discuss the four areas of specific information that must be covered in the body of a proposal
5. Explain the four questions to ask when proofing visual aids

ON THE JOB

Facing a Communication Dilemma at Dofasco

Placing a High Value on Reports

www.dofasco.ca

Effective communication is one of Dofasco's fundamental values, affecting everything from personal interactions to community relations. In the team-based culture of the Hamilton, Ontario steelmaker, employees are entrusted to suggest ways to improve procedures, product quality, customer service, and profits. As a company sensitive to the impact of its operations on the community and the environment, Dofasco also "has a long history of communicating with external stakeholders," says Ian Hamilton, one of the firm's corporate communications managers.

One way that Dofasco communicates is through reports. Hamilton prepares the company's *Environmental and Energy Report*, an annual document that describes Dofasco's environmental policies and management. The report's audience includes environmental organizations, government officials at both the federal and provincial levels, members of Dofasco's local communities, employees, shareholders, financial analysts, the media, and other companies in the steel industry. Dofasco's E & E report, explains Hamilton, is "a forum in which we communicate our progress to all stakeholders, outline our priorities, and demonstrate our commitment." To complete the task successfully, Hamilton and his team make sure the report is clear and well organized, and contains all the elements necessary to promote easy understanding.

If you worked with Hamilton, how would you approach the challenge of communicating complex ideas and issues? What steps would you take to make sure an audience gets what it needs from long reports? What features would you include to help readers find and understand the information?[1]

Dofasco's environmental performance reports are the result of careful planning and research, and the collaboration of many employees.

Revising Formal Reports and Proposals

Experienced businesspeople realize that writing a formal report or proposal is a demanding and time-consuming task, and doesn't end with a first draft. To complete a successful report, you still need to carefully edit, rewrite, produce, and then proofread your final version.

Just as you would do for any other business message, revise formal reports and proposals by evaluating content and organization. Make sure not only that you've said what you want to say, but also that you've said it clearly, concisely, in the most logical order, and in a way that responds to your audience's needs. Refresh your memory about revising business messages by referring back to Chapter 6. The revision process is basically the same for reports, but it may take longer, depending on the length of your report or proposal. However, you will see that there are differences between producing formal reports and proposals, and shorter business documents.

Producing Formal Reports and Proposals

Personal computers can handle many of the mechanical aspects of report preparation.

Once you are satisfied with your revision, the next step is to format and produce your report by incorporating the design elements discussed in Chapter 6. Typographical devices (such as capital letters, italics, and boldface type), margins, line justifications, and white space are just some of the techniques and tools you can use to present your material effectively. Also useful are visual aids to illustrate and emphasize major points, as well as preview and review statements to frame sections of your text. Many organizations have format guidelines that make your design decisions easier, but your goal is always to focus reader attention on major points and the flow of ideas.

Be sure to schedule enough time to turn out a document that looks professional.

Make sure that you schedule enough time for formatting and production. When working on reports (or any other business document) remember unexpected technological problems may occur: corrupted disk files, printing problems, and other glitches can consume hours. When preparing a long, formal report, you will need extra time to prepare and assemble all the various prefatory and supplementary parts.

OBJECTIVE 1 List the three tasks involved in completing business reports and proposals, and briefly explain what's involved in revising them.

Components of a Formal Report

A formal report's manuscript format and impersonal tone convey an impression of professionalism. A formal report can be either short (fewer than 10 pages) or long (10 pages or more). It can be informational or analytical, direct or indirect. It may be directed to readers inside or outside the organization. What sets it apart from other reports is its polish.

The parts included in a report depend on the type of report you are writing, the requirements of your audience, the organization you're working for, and the report's length. At Dofasco, Ian Hamilton and other writers in the corporate communications department pay close attention to their readers' needs, whether they are employees, customers, or members of the community. From the style of the report to the language used. Hamilton and the communications team target their readers' preferences and knowledge, and include only the parts that are appropriate for each audience. The components listed in Figure 12–1 fall into three categories, depending on where they are found in a report: prefatory parts, the text of the report, and supplementary parts. For an illustration of how the various parts fit together, see the Electrovision report in "Report Writer's Notebook—In-Depth Critique: Analyzing a Formal Report," beginning on page 360 of this chapter.

The three basic divisions of a formal report:

- Prefatory parts
- Text
- Supplementary parts

Many of the components in a formal report start on a new page, but not always. Inserting page breaks consumes more paper and adds to the bulk of your report (which may be a significant financial concern if you plan to distribute many copies).

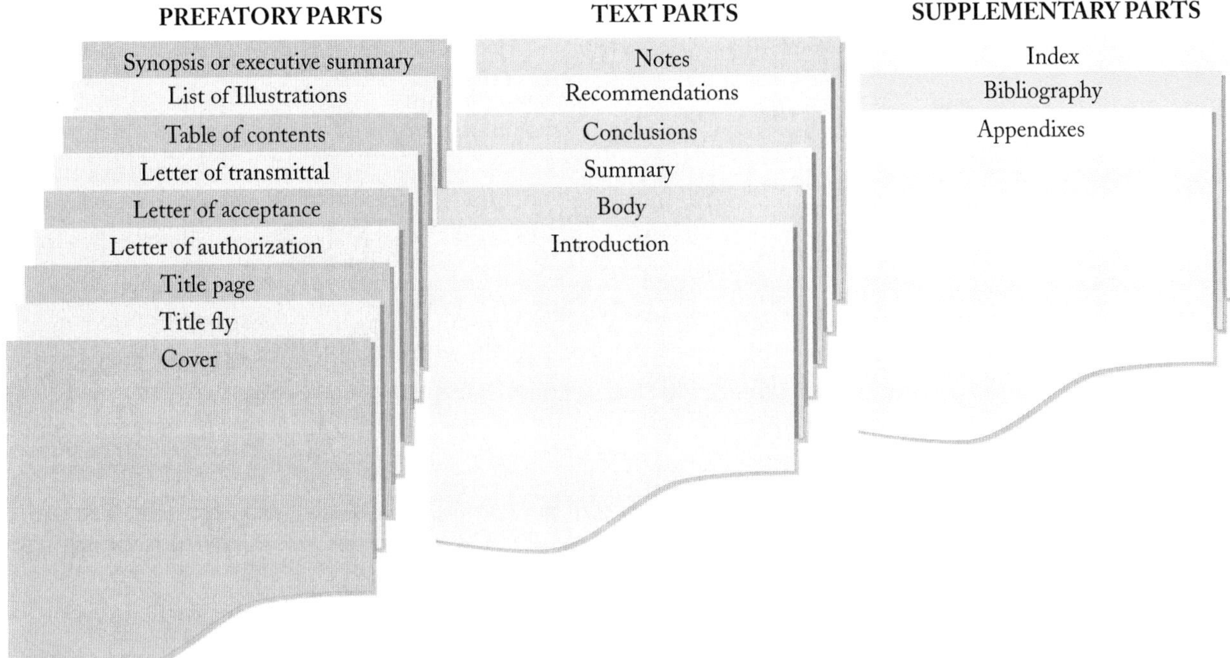

FIGURE 12–1 Parts of a Formal Report

On the other hand, starting a section on a new page helps your readers navigate the report and recognize transitions between major sections or features.

Most prefatory parts (such as the table of contents) should be placed on their own pages. However, the various parts in the report text are often run together and seldom stand alone. If your introduction is only a paragraph long, don't bother with a page break before moving into the body of your report. If the introduction runs longer than a page, however, a page break can signal the reader that a major shift is about to occur in the flow of the report.

Only about 30 years ago, report writers commonly prepared their reports on manual or electric typewriters. What are the differences between using old-fashioned typewriters to prepare reports and using computers with wordprocessing software? Are there any advantages to typewriters? Any disadvantages to using computers? What are they?

PREFATORY PARTS

Prefatory parts are front-end materials that provide key preliminary information so that readers can decide whether (and how) to read the report.[2] Although the prefatory parts are placed before the text of the report, you may not want to write them until after you've written the text. Many of these parts—such as the table of contents, list of illustrations, and executive summary—are easier to prepare after the text has been completed because they directly reflect the contents. Other parts can be prepared at almost any time.

OBJECTIVE 2 Explain the 10 prefatory parts of a formal report.

Prefatory parts may be written after the text has been completed.

Cover Many companies have standard covers for reports, usually made of heavy paper and imprinted with the company's name and logo. Report titles are either printed on these covers or attached with labels. If your company has no standard covers, you can usually find something suitable in a good stationery store. Look for a cover that is attractive, convenient, and appropriate to the subject matter. Also, make sure it can be labelled with the report title, the writer's name (optional), and the submission date (also optional).

REPORT WRITER'S NOTEBOOK

In-Depth Critique: Analyzing a Formal Report

The report presented in the following pages was prepared by Linda Moreno, manager of the cost accounting department at Electrovision, a high-tech company. Electrovision's main product is optical character recognition equipment, which is used by postal services throughout the world for sorting mail. Moreno's job is to help analyze the company's costs. She has this to say about the background of the report:

"For the past three or four years, Electrovision has been very successful. Our A-12 optical character reader was a real breakthrough, and postal services grabbed up as many as we could make. Our sales and profits kept climbing, and morale was fantastic. Everybody seemed to think that the good times would last forever. Unfortunately, everybody was wrong. When one of our major clients announced that it was postponing all new equipment purchases because of cuts in its budget, we woke up to the fact that we are essentially a one-product company. At that point, management started scrambling around looking for ways to cut costs until we could diversify our business a bit.

"The vice-president of operations, Dennis McWilliams, asked me to help identify cost-cutting opportunities in the travel and entertainment area. On the basis of his personal observations, he felt that Electrovision was overly generous in its travel policies and that we might be able to save a significant amount by controlling these costs more carefully. My investigation confirmed his suspicion.

"I was reasonably confident that my report would be well received. I've worked with Dennis for several years and know what he likes: plenty of facts, clearly stated conclusions, and specific recommendations for what should be done next. I also knew that my report would be passed on to other Electrovision executives, so I wanted to create a good impression. I wanted the report to be accurate and thorough, visually appealing, readable, and appropriate in tone."

When writing the analytical report that follows, Moreno used an organization based on conclusions and recommendations, presented in direct order. The first two sections of the report correspond to Moreno's two main conclusions: That Electrovision's travel and entertainment costs are too high and that cuts are essential. The third section presents recommendations for achieving better control over travel and entertainment expenses. As you review the report, analyze both the mechanical aspects and the way Moreno presents her ideas. Be prepared to discuss the way the various components convey and reinforce the main message.

Put a title on the cover that is informative but not too long.

Think carefully about the title you put on the cover. A business report is not a mystery novel, so give your readers all the information they need: the who, what, when, where, why, and how of the subject. At the same time, try to be reasonably concise. You don't want to intimidate your audience with a title that's too long or awkward. You can reduce the length of your title by eliminating phrases such as *A Report of, A Study of,* or *A Survey of.*

The title page usually includes four blocks of information.

Title Fly and Title Page The title fly is a plain sheet of paper with only the title of the report on it. It's not essential, but it adds a touch of formality.

The **title page** includes four blocks of information, as shown in the Electrovision report: (1) the title of the report; (2) the name, title, and address of the person, group, or organization that authorized the report (usually the intended audience); (3) the name, title, and address of the person, group, or organization that prepared the report; and (4) the date on which the report was submitted. On some title pages the second block of information is preceded by the words *Prepared for* or *Submitted to,* and the third block of information is preceded by *Prepared by* or *Submitted by.* In some cases the title page serves as the cover of the report, especially if the report is relatively short and intended solely for internal use.

A letter of authorization usually follows the direct-request plan.

Letter of Authorization (or memo of authorization) If you received written authorization to prepare the report, you may want to include that letter or memo in your report (and you may sometimes even include the letter or memo of acceptance). The

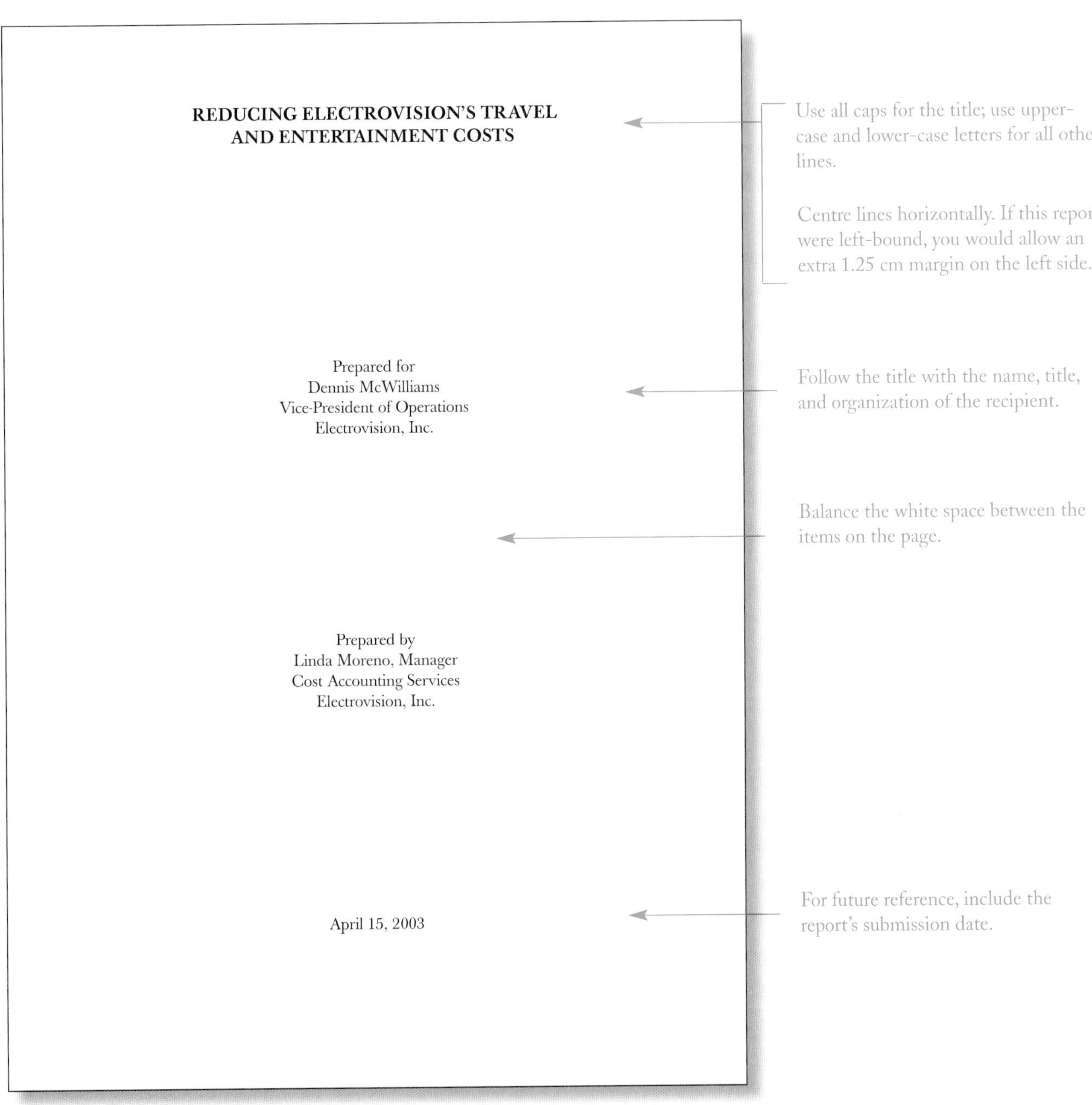

REDUCING ELECTROVISION'S TRAVEL
AND ENTERTAINMENT COSTS
Prepared for
Dennis McWilliams
Vice-President of Operations
Electrovision, Inc.
Prepared by
Linda Moreno, Manager
Cost Accounting Services
Electrovision, Inc.
April 15, 2003
Use all caps for the title; use upper-case and lower-case letters for all other lines.
Centre lines horizontally. If this report were left-bound, you would allow an extra 1.25 cm margin on the left side.
Follow the title with the name, title, and organization of the recipient.
Balance the white space between the items on the page.
For future reference, include the report's submission date.

The "how to" tone of Moreno's title is appropriate for an action-oriented report that emphasizes recommendations. A more neutral title, such as "An Analysis of Electrovision's Travel and Entertainment Costs," would be more suitable for an informational report.

Use memo format for transmitting internal reports, letter format for transmitting external reports.

Present the main conclusion or recommendation right away if you expect a positive response.

Use an informal, conversational style for the letter or memo of transmittal.

Acknowledge any help that you have received.

Close with thanks, an offer to discuss results, and an offer to assist with future projects, if appropriate.

MEMORANDUM

TO: Dennis McWilliams, Vice-President of Operations

FROM: Linda Moreno, Manager of Cost Accounting Services

DATE: April 15, 2003

SUBJECT: Reducing Electrovision's Travel and Entertainment Costs

Here is the report you requested March 3 on Electrovision's travel and entertainment costs.

Your suspicion was right. We are spending far too much on business travel. Our unwritten policy has been very open, leaving us with no real control over T&E expenses. Although this hands-off approach may have been understandable when Electrovision's profits were high, we can no longer afford the luxury of going first class.

The solution to the problem seem rather clear. We need to have someone with centralized responsibility for travel and entertainment costs, a clear statement of policy, an effective control system, and a business-oriented travel service that can optimize our travel arrangements. We should also investigate alternatives to travel, such as videoconferencing. Perhaps more important, we need to change our attitude. Instead of viewing travel funds as a bottomless supply of money, all travelling employees need to act as though they were paying the bills themselves.

Getting people to economize is not going to be easy. In the course of researching this issue, I've found that our employees are deeply attached to their first-class travel privileges. We'll need a lot of top management involvement to persuade people of the need for moderation. One thing is clear: People will be very bitter if we create a two-class system in which top executives get special privileges while the rest of the employees make the sacrifices.

I'm grateful to Mary Lehman and Connie McIlvain for their help in gathering and sorting through five years' worth of expense reports. I cannot praise them enough for the effort they put into this time-consuming task.

Thank you for giving me the opportunity to work on this assignment. I appreciate gaining insight into Electrovision's T&E issues. If you have any questions about the report, please call or e-mail me.

In this report Moreno decided to write a brief memo of transmittal and include a separate executive summary. Short reports (fewer than ten pages) often combine the synopsis or executive summary with the memo or letter of transmittal.

CONTENTS

iii

Include no element that appears before the "Contents" page.

Word the headings exactly as they appear in the text.

Include only the first page number of each section.

Moreno included only first- and second-level headings in her table of contents, even though the report contains third-level headings. She prefers a shorter table of contents that focuses attention on the main divisions of thought. She used informative titles, which are appropriate for a report to a receptive audience.

Number figures consecutively throughout the report.

Number the contents pages with lower-case Roman numerals centred at the bottom margin.

LIST OF ILLUSTRATIONS

iv

Because figures and tables were numbered separately in the text, Moreno listed them separately here. If all had been labelled as exhibits, a single list of illustrations would have been appropriate.

EXECUTIVE SUMMARY

This report analyzes Electrovision's travel and entertainment (T&E) costs and presents recommendations for reducing those costs.

Travel and Entertainment Costs Are Too High

Travel and entertainment is a large and growing expense category for Electrovision. The company spends over $16 million per year on business travel, and these costs have been increasing by 12 percent annually. Company employees make roughly 1880 trips each year at an average cost per trip of $8500. Airfares are the biggest expense, followed by hotels, meals, and rental cars.

The nature of Electrovision's business does require extensive travel, but the company's costs appear to be excessive. Every year Electrovision employees spend almost 3 times more on T&E than the average business traveller. Although the location of the company's facilities may partly explain this discrepancy, the main reason for Electrovision's high costs is the firm's philosophy and managerial style. Electrovision's tradition and its hands-off style almost invite employees to go first class and pay relatively little attention to travel costs.

Cuts Are Essential

Although Electrovision has traditionally been casual about travel and entertainment expenses, management now recognizes the need to gain more control over this element of costs. The company is currently entering a period of declining profits, prompting management to look for every opportunity to reduce spending. At the same time, rising airfares and hotel rates are making travel and entertainment expenses more important to the bottom line.

Electrovision Can Save $6 Million per Year

Fortunately, Electrovision has a number of excellent opportunities for reducing its travel and entertainment costs. Savings of up to $6 million per year should be achievable, judging by the experience of other companies. Corporate Travel Link, a consulting company that trains in-house personnel to act as the firm's travel agent, says that a sensible travel management program can save companies 25 to 35 percent a year (McDougall, "How to Get There from Here 46). Given that we purchase many more first-class tickets than the average company, we should be able to achieve even greater savings. The first priority should be to hire a director of travel and entertainment to assume overall responsibility for T&E spending. This individual should establish a written travel and entertainment policy and create a budget and a cost-control system. The director should also retain a nationwide travel agency to handle our reservations and should lead an investigation into electronic alternatives to travel.

v

Begin by stating the purpose of the report.

Present the points in the executive summary in the same order as they appear in the report.

Use subheadings that summarize the content of the main sections of the report without repeating those that appear in the text.

Type the synopsis or executive summary in the same font as the text of the report. Use single spacing if the report is single spaced, and use the same format as used in the text for margins, paragraph indentions, and headings.

Moreno decided to include an executive summary because her report was aimed at a mixed audience. She knew that some readers would be interested in the details of her report and some would prefer to focus on the big picture. The executive summary was aimed at the group that favoured the overview. Moreno wanted to give these readers enough information to make a decision without burdening them with the task of reading the entire report.

The frank tone of this executive summary is appropriate for a receptive audience. A more neutral approach would be better for hostile or skeptical readers.

At the same time, Electrovision should make employees aware of the need for moderation in travel and entertainment spending. People should be encouraged to forgo any unnecessary travel and to economize on airline tickets, hotels, meals, rental cars, and other expenses.

In addition to economizing on an individual basis, Electrovision should look for ways to reduce costs by negotiating preferential rates with travel providers. Once retained, a travel agency should be able to accomplish this.

Finally, we should look into alternatives to travel. Although we may have to invest money in video-conferencing systems or other equipment, we should be able to recover these costs through decreased travel expenses. I recommend that the new travel director undertake this investigation to make sure it is well integrated with the rest of the travel program.

These changes, although necessary, are likely to hurt morale, at least in the short term. Management will need to make a determined effort to explain the rationale for reduced spending. By exercising moderation in their own travel arrangements, Electrovision executives can set a good example and help other employees accept the changes. On the plus side, cutting back on travel with video conferencing or other alternatives will reduce the travel burden on many employees and help them balance their business and personal lives much better.

Number the pages of the executive summary with lowercase roman numerals centred about 1 inch from the bottom of the page.

vi

This executive summary is written in an impersonal style, which adds to the formality of the report. Some writers prefer a more personal approach. You should gear your choice of style to your relationship with the readers. Moreno chose the formal approach because several members of her audience were considerably higher up in the organization. She did not want to sound too familiar. In addition, she wanted the executive summary and the text to be compatible, and her company prefers the impersonal style for formal reports.

REDUCING ELECTROVISION'S TRAVEL AND ENTERTAINMENT COSTS

Centre the title of the report on the first page of the text, 5 centimetre from the top of the page 6.2 centi metres.

INTRODUCTION

Electrovision has always encouraged a significant amount of business travel, believing that it is an effective way of operating. To compensate employees for the inconvenience and stress of frequent trips, management has authorized generous travel and entertainment (T&E) allowances. This philosophy has been good for morale, but the company has paid a price. Last year Electrovision spent $16 million on T&E–$7 million more than it spent on research and development.

Begin the introduction by establishing the need for action.

This year the cost of travel and entertainment will have a bigger impact on profits, owing to changes in airfares and hotel rates. The timing of these changes is unfortunate because the company anticipates that profits will be relatively weak for a variety of other reasons. In light of these profit pressures, Dennis McWilliams, Vice-President of Operations, has asked the accounting department to take a closer look at the T&E budget.

Purpose, Scope, and Limitations

The purpose of this report is to analyze the T&E budget, evaluate the impact of recent changes in airfares and hotel costs, and suggest ways to tighten management's control over T&E expenses. Although the report outlines a number of steps that could reduce Electrovision's expenses, the precise financial impact of these measures is difficult to project. The estimates presented in the report provide a "best-guess" view of what Electrovision can expect to save. Until the company actually implements these steps, however, we won't know exactly how much the travel and entertainment budget can be reduced.

Sources and Methods

In preparing this report, the Accounting department analyzed internal expense reports for the past five years to determine how much Electrovision spends on travel and entertainment. These figures were then compared with travel business costs compiled by investigating fee structures of air carriers, hotels, and car rental agencies; we also investigated average corporate meal expense accounts reported in the American Express Survey of Canadian Business Travel Management. We analyzed trends discussed in the American Express publication *Trends & Forecasts for the Canadian Business Travel Industry* (2002) and studied suggestions published in a variety of business journal articles to see how other companies are coping with the high cost of business travel.

Mentioning sources and methods increases the credibility of a report and gives readers a complete picture of the study's background.

1

Use the Arabic numeral 1 for the first page of the report; centre the number about 1 inch from the bottom of the page.

In a brief introduction like this one, some writers would omit the subheadings within the introduction and rely on topic sentences and on transitional words and phrases to indicate that they are discussing such subjects as the purpose, scope, and limitations of the study. Moreno decided to use headings because they help readers scan the document. Also, to conserve space, Moreno used single spacing and one-inch side margins.

Using Arabic numerals, number the second and succeeding pages of the text in the upper right-hand corner where the top and right-hand margins meet.

2

Report Organization

This report reviews the size and composition of Electrovision's travel and entertainment expenses, analyzes trends in travel costs, and recommends steps for reducing the T&E budget.

THE HIGH COST OF TRAVEL AND ENTERTAINMENT

Although many companies view travel and entertainment as an "incidental" cost of doing business, the dollars add up. At Electrovision the bill for airfares, hotels, rental cars, meals, and entertainment totalled $16 million last year. Our T&E budget has increased by 12 percent per year for the past 5 years. Compared to the average Canadian business traveller in our industry, Electrovision's expenditures are high, largely because of management's generous policy on travel benefits.

$16 Million per Year Spent on Travel and Entertainment

Electrovision's annual budget for travel and entertainment is only 8 percent of sales. Because this is a relatively small expense category compared with such things as salaries and commissions, it is tempting to dismiss T&E costs as insignificant. However, T&E is Electrovision's third-largest controllable expense, directly behind salaries and information systems.

Last year Electrovision personnel made about 1880 trips at an average cost per trip of $8500. The typical trip involved a round-trip flight of 8000 km, meals and hotel accommodations for four or five days, and a rental car. Roughly 80 percent of the trips were made by 20 percent of the staff–top management and sales personnel travelled most, averaging 17 trips per year.

Place the visual aid as close as possible to the point it illustrates.

Figure 1 illustrates how the travel and entertainment budget is spent. The largest categories are airfares and lodging, which together account for $7 out of every $10 that employees

Make placement of visual-aids titles consistent throughout a report. Options for placement include above, below, or beside the visual.

Give each visual aid a title that clearly indicates what it's about.

FIGURE 1
Airfares and Lodging Account for Over Two-Thirds of Electrovision's Travel and Entertainment Budget.

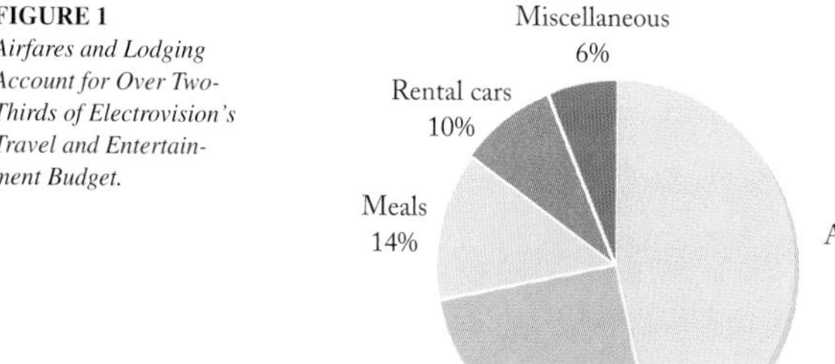

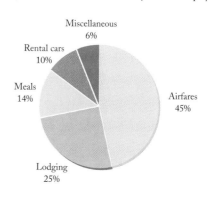

Moreno opened the first main section of the body with a topic sentence that introduces an important fact about the subject of the section. Then she oriented the reader to the three major points developed in the section.

3

spend on travel and entertainment. This spending breakdown has been relatively steady for the past five years and is consistent with the distribution of expenses experienced by other companies.

Although the composition of the T&E budget has been consistent, its size has not. As mentioned earlier, these expenditures have increased by about 12 percent per year for the past 5 years, roughly twice the rate of the company's growth in sales (see Figure 2). This rate of growth makes T&E Electrovision's fastest-growing expense item.

Introduce visual aids before they appear, and indicate what readers should notice about the data.

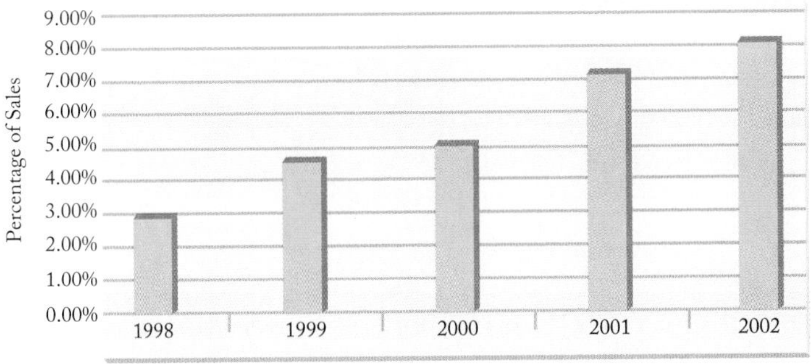

FIGURE 2
Travel and Entertainment Expenses Have Increased as a Percentage of Sales.

Number the visual aids consecutively, and refer to them in the text by their numbers. If your report is a book-length document, you may number the visual aids by chapter: Figure 4–2, for example, would be the second figure in the fourth chapter.

Electrovision's Travel Expenses Exceed National Averages

Much of our travel budget is justified. Two major factors contribute to Electrovision's high travel and entertainment budget:

- With our headquarters in Kanata, Ontario, and our major customers in the U.S., Central and South America, and Western Europe, we naturally spend a lot on international flights.
- A great deal of travel takes place between our headquarters here in Kanata and the manufacturing operations in Salt Lake City, Utah; Seattle, Washington; and Dublin, Ireland. Corporate managers and division personnel make frequent trips to coordinate these disparate operations.

However, even though a good portion of Electrovision's travel budget is justifiable, our travellers spend considerably more on travel and entertainment than the average business traveller (see Figure 3).

Moreno originally drew the bar chart in Figure 2 as a line chart, showing both sales and T&E expenses in absolute dollars. However, the comparison was difficult to interpret because sales were so much greater than T&E expenses. Switching to a bar chart expressed in percentage terms made the main idea much easier to grasp.

4

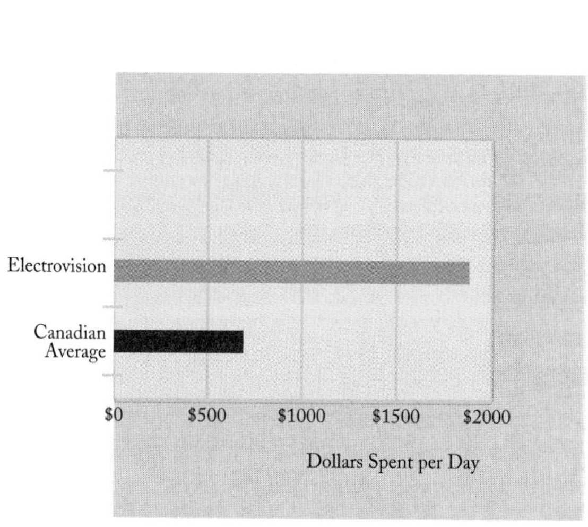

FIGURE 3
Electrovision People Spend Almost Three Times More than the Average Business Traveller
Source: American Express (Cuthbert C15) and company records.

Basing my calculations on information in the March 2002 American Express report, *Trends & Forecasts for the Canadian Business Travel Industry*,* Canadian companies spend on average $2,900 for each traveller, based on airfare, hotel rates, meals, and rental car rates. For a 4.5 day trip, the daily rate is about $644 per day. In contrast, Electrovision's average daily expense over the past year has been about $1,888 per day, or about three times higher than average. This figure is based on the average trip cost of $8,500 listed earlier and an average trip length of 4.5 days.

Leaving a bit more white space above a heading than below it helps readers associate that heading with the text it describes.

Spending Has Been Encouraged

Although a variety of factors may contribute to this differential, Electrovision's relatively high T&E costs are at least partially attributable to the company's philosophy and management style. Because many employees do not enjoy business travel, management has tried to make the trips more pleasant by authorizing first-class airfare, luxury hotel accommodations, and full-size rental cars. The sales staff is encouraged to entertain clients at top restaurants and to invite them to cultural and sporting events.

The cost of these privileges is easy to overlook, given the weakness of Electrovision's system for keeping track of T&E expenses:

Include notes that clarify your discussion (called "substantive notes") on the bottom of the page. Direct your readers to the substantive notes with symbols such as asterisks.

* Airfares are based on full economy fares.

The chart in Figure 3 is very simple, but it creates an effective visual comparison. Moreno included just enough data to make her point. Moreno was as careful about the appearance of her report as she was about its content.

5

- The monthly financial records provided to management do not contain a separate category for travel and entertainment; the information is buried under Cost of Goods Sold and Selling, General, and Administrative Expenses.
- Each department head is given authority to approve any expense report, regardless of how large it may be.
- Receipts are not required for expenditures of less than $100.
- Individuals are allowed to make their own travel arrangements.
- No one is charged with the responsibility for controlling the company's total spending on travel and entertainment.

Bulleted lists make it easy for readers to identify and distinguish related points.

GROWING IMPACT ON THE BOTTOM LINE

During the past three years, the company's healthy profits have resulted in relatively little pressure to push for tighter controls over all aspects of the business. However, as we all know, the situation is changing. We're projecting flat to declining profits for the next two years, a situation that has prompted all of us to search for ways to cut costs. At the same time, rising airfares and hotel rates have increased the impact of T&E expenses on the company's financial results.

Lower Profits Underscore the Need for Change

The next two years promise to be difficult for Electrovision. After several years of steady increases in spending, many of our clients are tightening procurement policies for automated mail-handling equipment. As a consequence, the marketing department expects sales to drop by 15 percent. Although Electrovision is negotiating several promising R&D contracts with non-government clients, the marketing department does not foresee any major procurements for the next two to three years.

At the same time, Electrovision is facing cost increases on several fronts. As we've known for several months, the new production facility now under construction in Montreal is behind schedule and over budget. Labour contracts in Salt Lake City and Seattle expire within the next six months, and plant managers there anticipate that significant salary and benefits concessions may be necessary to avoid strikes. Moreover, marketing and advertising costs are expected to increase as we attempt to strengthen these activities to better cope with competitive pressures. Given the expected decline in revenues and increase in costs, the Executive Committee's prediction that profits will fall by 12 percent in the coming fiscal year does not seem overly pessimistic.

Informative headings focus reader attention on the main points of the report. Thus they are most appropriate when the report is in direct order and is aimed at a receptive audience. Descriptive headings are more effective when a report is in indirect order and the readers are less receptive.

Airfares and Hotel Rates Are Rising

Business travellers have grown accustomed to frequent fare wars and discounting in the travel industry in recent years. Excess capacity and aggressive price competition, particularly in the airline business, made travel a relative bargain.

Because airfares represent Electrovision's biggest T&E expense, Moreno included a subsection that deals with the possible impact of trends in the airline industry. Airfares are rising, so it is especially important to gain more control over employees' air travel arrangements.

Documenting the facts adds weight to Moreno's argument.

Pointing out both the benefits and risks of taking action gives recommendations an objective flavour.

6

However, that situation has changed as weaker competitors have been forced out and the remaining players have grown stronger and smarter. Airlines and hotels are better at managing inventory and keeping occupancy rates high, and high occupancy translates into higher prices because suppliers have less reason to compete on price. Last year saw some of the steepest rate hikes in years. Business airfares (tickets most likely to be purchased by business travellers) jumped over 40 percent in many markets. The trend is expected to continue, with rates increasing another 5 to 6 percent overall (*Trends & Forecasts* 2). Hotel and meal rates are expected to grow 2 to 3 percent, and car rental charges 4 to 5 percent (Fitzpatrick FP7).

Given the fact that air and hotel costs account for 70 percent of Electrovision's T&E budget, the trend toward higher prices in these two categories will have serious consequences on the company's expenses unless management takes action to control these costs.

METHODS FOR REDUCING TRAVEL AND ENTERTAINMENT COSTS

By implementing a number of reforms, management can expect to reduce Electrovision's T&E budget by 25 to 35 percent a year (McDougall, How to Get There from Here 46). This estimate is based on the general assessment made by Corporate Travel Link, a travel consulting company that trains employees to handle staff travel (McDougall, "How to Get There from Here" 46) and the fact that we have an opportunity to significantly reduce air travel costs by reducing or eliminating first-class travel. However, these measures are likely to be unpopular with employees. To gain acceptance for such changes, management will need to sell employees on the need for moderation in travel and entertainment allowances.

Four Ways to Trim Expenses

By researching what other companies are doing to curb travel and entertainment expenses, the accounting department has identified four prominent opportunities that should enable Electrovision to save about $6 million annually in travel-related costs.

Institute Tighter Spending Controls

A single individual should be appointed director of travel and entertainment to spearhead the effort to gain control of the T&E budget. According to American Express Canada, 48 percent of Canadian companies employ travel managers in an effort to keep costs in line ("Expanding Markets" 52–53). The director should be familiar with the travel industry and should be well versed in both accounting and information technology. The director should also report to the vice-president of Operations. The director's first priorities should be to establish a written travel and entertainment policy and to implement a system for controlling travel and entertainment costs.

Moreno created a forceful tone by using action verbs in the third-level subheadings of this section. This approach is appropriate considering the nature of the study and the attitude of the audience. However, in a status-conscious organization, the imperative verbs might sound a bit too presumptuous coming from a junior member of the staff.

7

Electrovision currently has no written policy on travel and entertainment, a step widely recommended by air travel experts (Green 47–48; "Amex Canada Sees Travel Turnaround" 11–12; Sharkey C16). Creating a policy would clarify management's position and serve as a vehicle for communicating the need for moderation. At a minimum, the policy should include the following provisions:

- All travel and entertainment should be strictly related to business and should be approved in advance.
- Except under special circumstances to be approved on a case-by-case basis, employees should travel economy class and stay in mid-range hotels.
- The travel and entertainment policy should apply equally to employees at all levels in the organization. No special benefits should be allowed for top executives.

Bulleted-list format not only calls attention to important points but also adds visual interest. You can also use visual aids, headings, and direct quotations to break up large, solid blocks of print.

To implement the new policy, Electrovision will need to create a system for controlling travel and entertainment expenses. Each department should prepare an annual T&E budget as part of its operating plan. These budgets should be presented in detail so that management can evaluate how travel and entertainment dollars will be spent and recommend appropriate cuts.

Specifies the steps required to implement recommendations.

To help management monitor performance relative to these budgets, the director of travel and entertainment should prepare monthly financial statements showing actual travel and entertainment expenditures by department. The system for capturing this information should be computerized and capable of identifying individuals who consistently exceed approved spending levels. The recommended average should range between $3500 and $4200 per month for each professional employee, depending on the individual's role in the company. Because they make frequent trips, sales and top management personnel can be expected to have relatively high travel expenses.

The director of travel should also be responsible for retaining a business-oriented travel service that will schedule all employee business trips and look for the best travel deals, particularly in airfares. In addition to centralizing Electrovision's reservation and ticketing activities, the agency will negotiate reduced group rates with hotels and rental car agencies. By consolidating its travel planning in this way, Electrovision can increase its control over costs and achieve economies of scale. This is particularly important in light of the dizzying array of often wildly different airfares available between some cities. It's not uncommon to find dozens of fares along commonly travelled routes ("Pricing for Profit" 47).

The director should also work with the agency to explore low-cost alternatives, such as buying tickets from airfare consolidators (the air-travel equivalent of factory outlet malls). In addition, the director can help coordinate travel across the company to secure group discounts whenever possible (Sharkey C16).

Moreno decided to single space her report to create a formal, finished look; however, double spacing can make the text of a long report somewhat easier to read, and it provides more space for readers to write comments.

8

Reduce Unnecessary Travel and Entertainment

One of the easiest ways to reduce expenses is to reduce the amount of travelling and entertaining that occurs. An analysis of last year's expenditures suggests that as much as 30 percent of Electrovision's travel and entertainment is discretionary. The professional staff spent $2.8 million attending seminars and conferences last year. Although some of these gatherings are undoubtedly beneficial, the company could save money by sending fewer representatives to each function and by eliminating some of the less useful seminars.

Similarly, Electrovision could economize on trips between headquarters and divisions by reducing the frequency of such visits and by sending fewer people on each trip. Although there is often no substitute for face-to-face meetings, management could try to resolve more internal issues through telephone conferences, video-conferences, online chats, and written communication.

Electrovision can also reduce spending by urging employees to economize. Instead of flying first class, employees can fly tourist class or take advantage of discount fares. Instead of taking clients to dinner, Electrovision personnel can hold breakfast meetings, which tend to be less costly. Rather than ordering a $75 bottle of wine, employees can select a less expensive bottle or dispense with alcohol entirely. People can book rooms at moderately priced hotels and drive smaller rental cars. In general, employees should be urged to spend the company's money as though it were their own.

Obtain Lowest Rates from Travel Providers

Apart from urging individual employees to economize, Electrovision can also save money by searching for the lowest available airfares, hotel rates, and rental car fees. Currently, few Electrovision employees have the time or specialized knowledge to seek out travel bargains. When they need to travel, they make the most convenient and comfortable arrangements. However, if Electrovision contracts with a professional travel service, the company will have access to professionals who can more efficiently obtain the lower rates from travel providers.

Judging by the experience of other companies, Electrovision may be able to trim as much as 30 to 40 percent from the travel budget by looking for bargains in airfares and negotiating group rates with hotels and rental car companies. Electrovision should be able to achieve these economies by analyzing its travel patterns, identifying frequently visited locations, and selecting a few hotels that are willing to reduce rates in exchange for guaranteed business. At the same time, the company should be able to save up to 40 percent on rental car charges by negotiating a corporate rate.

Note how Moreno made the transition from one section to the next. The first sentence under the second heading on this page refers to the subject of the previous paragraph and signals a shift in thought.

The possibilities for economizing are promising, but it's worth noting that making the best arrangements is a complicated undertaking, requiring many trade-offs such as the following:

- The best fares might not always be the lowest. Indirect flights are often less expensive than direct flights, but they take longer and may end up costing more in lost work time.
- The cheapest tickets may have to be booked 30 days in advance, often impossible for us.
- Discount tickets may be non-refundable, which is a real drawback if the trip has to be cancelled at the last minute.

Pointing out possible difficulties demonstrates that you have considered all the angles and builds reader confidence in your judgment.

Electrovision is currently ill-equipped to make these and other trade-offs. However, by employing a business-oriented travel service, the company will have access to computerized systems that can optimize its choices.

Replace Travel with Technological Alternatives

We might be able to replace a significant portion of our interdivisional travel with electronic meetings that utilize video conferencing, real-time document sharing through the Internet, and other alternatives. Naturally, we don't want to reduce employee or team effectiveness, but many companies use these tools to cut costs and reduce wear and tear on employees.

Rather than make specific recommendations in this report, I suggest that the new travel and entertainment director conduct an in-depth study of the company's travel patterns as part of an overall cost-containment effort. A thorough analysis of why employees travel and what they accomplish will highlight any opportunities for replacing face-to-face meetings. Part of this study should include limited-scope tests of various communication systems as a way of measuring their impact on both workplace effectiveness and overall costs.

The Impact of Reforms

By implementing tighter controls, reducing unnecessary expenses, negotiating more favourable rates, and exploring "electronic travel," Electrovision should be able to reduce its travel and entertainment budget significantly. As Table 1 illustrates, the combined savings should be in the neighbourhood of $6 million, although the precise figures are somewhat difficult to project.

Note how Moreno calls attention in the last paragraph to items in the following table, without repeating all the information in the table.

10

TABLE 1

Electrovision Can Trim Travel and Entertainment Costs by an Estimated $6 Million per Year

Source of Savings	Amount Saved
Switching from first-class to coach airfare	$2 300 000
Negotiating preferred hotel rates	940 000
Negotiating preferred rental car rates	460 000
Systematically searching for lower airfares	375 000
Reducing interdivisional travel	675 000
Reducing seminar and conference attendance	1 250 000
TOTAL POTENTIAL SAVINGS	**$6 000 000**

To achieve the economies outlined in the table, Electrovision will incur expenses for hiring a director of travel and entertainment and for implementing a T&E cost-control system. These costs are projected at $95 000: $85 000 per year in salary and benefits for the new employee and a one-time expense of $10 000 for the cost-control system. The cost of retaining a full-service travel agency is negligible because agencies normally receive a commission from travel providers rather than a fee from clients.

The measures required to achieve these savings are likely to be unpopular with employees. Electrovision personnel are accustomed to generous travel and entertainment allowances, and they are likely to resent having these privileges curtailed. To alleviate their disappointment

- management should make a determined effort to explain why the changes are necessary.
- the director of corporate communication should be asked to develop a multifaceted campaign that will communicate the importance of curtailing travel and entertainment costs.
- management should set a positive example by adhering strictly to the new policies.
- the limitations should apply equally to employees at all levels in the organization.

The informative title is consistent with other headings. This is appropriate for a report to a receptive audience. The complete sentence helps readers to see the point immediately.

Even though estimated savings may be difficult to project, including dollar figures helps management envision the impact of your suggestions.

The table on this page puts Moreno's recommendations in perspective. Note how she called attention in the text to the most important sources of savings and also spelled out the costs required to achieve these results.

11

CONCLUSIONS AND RECOMMENDATIONS

Use a descriptive heading for the last section of the text. In informational reports, this section is generally called "Summary"; in analytical reports, it is called "Conclusions" or "Conclusions and Recommendations."

Electrovision is currently spending $16 million per year on travel and entertainment. Although much of this spending is justified, the company's costs appear to be high relative to competitors', mainly because Electrovision has been generous with its travel benefits.

Electrovision's liberal approach to travel and entertainment was understandable during years of high profitability; however, the company is facing the prospect of declining profits for the next several years. Management is therefore motivated to cut costs in all areas of the business. Reducing T&E spending is particularly important because the impact of these costs on the bottom line will increase as a result of fare increases in the airline industry.

Electrovision should be able to reduce travel and entertainment costs by as much as 40 percent by taking 4 important steps:

Emphasize the recommendations by presenting them in list format if possible.

1. *Institute tighter spending controls.* Management should hire a director of travel and entertainment who will assume overall responsibility for T&E activities. Within the next six months, this director should develop a written travel policy, institute a T&E budget and a cost-control system, and retain a professional, business-oriented travel agency that will optimize arrangements with travel providers.

2. *Reduce unnecessary travel and entertainment.* Electrovision should encourage employees to economize on travel and entertainment spending. Management can accomplish this by authorizing fewer trips and by urging employees to be more conservative in their spending.

3. *Obtain lowest rates from travel providers.* Electrovision should also focus on obtaining the best rates on airline tickets, hotel rooms, and rental cars. By channelling all arrangements through a professional travel agency, the company can optimize its choices and gain clout in negotiating preferred rates.

4. *Replace travel with technological alternatives.* With the number of computers already installed in our facilities, it seems likely that we could take advantage of desktop video conferencing and other distance-meeting tools. This won't be quite as feasible with customer sites, since these systems require compatible equipment at both ends of a connection, but it is certainly a possibility for communication with Electrovision's own sites.

Do not introduce new facts in this section of the text.

Because these measures may be unpopular with employees, management should make a concerted effort to explain the importance of reducing travel costs. The director of corporate communication should be given responsibility for developing a plan to communicate the need for employee cooperation.

Because Moreno organized her report around conclusions and recommendations, readers have already been introduced to them. Thus she summarizes her conclusions in the first two paragraphs. A simple list is enough to remind readers of the four main recommendations. In a longer report she might have divided the section into subsections, labelled "Conclusions" and "Recommendations," to distinguish between the two. If the report had been organized around logical arguments, this would have been a reader's first exposure to the conclusions and recommendations, and Moreno would have needed to develop them more fully.

List references alphabetically by the author's last name or, when the author is unknown, by the title of the reference. See Appendix B for additional details on preparing reference lists.

12

WORKS CITED

American Express. *Trends & Forecasts for the Canadian Business Travel Industry.* March 2002. American Express Consulting.

"Amex Canada Sees Travel Turnaround: Buying Pros Help Control Costs." *Purchasing B2B,* Apr. 2002: 11-12.

"Expanding Markets: Growth in Canadian Business Travel to be Filled by Mid-Sized Companies." *CMA Management* 74.5 (2000): 52-53.

Fitzpatrick, Peter. "Business Travel on the Rebound: AMEX Survey: $12B Budget in 2002." *Financial Post* (*National Post*) 20 Mar. 2002: FP1, FP7.

Green, Carolyn. "Mandated Travel Policies: Wave of the Future?" *CMA Management* 76.2 (Apr. 2002): 47-48.

McDougall, Diane. "How to Get There from Here." *CMA Management* 76.6 (Sept. 2002): 46.

_____. "Travel Costs on the Rise." *CMA Management* 76.1 (Mar. 2002): 53.

"Pricing For Profit: With Corporate Travellers Refusing to Pay Top Dollar to Fly Anymore, Airlines are Finally Listening." *Air Transport World* 40.2 (Feb. 2003): 47.

Sharkey, Joe. "Companies Continue to Tighten Up on Expenses, Sometimes by Enforcing Long-Dormant Policies." *New York Times,* 15 Nov. 2000: C16.

Moreno's list of references follows the style recommended in the *MLA Style Manual.*

letter of authorization (or memo of authorization) is a document requesting that a report be prepared. It normally follows the direct-request plan described in Chapter 5, and it typically specifies the problem, scope, time and money restrictions, special instructions, and due date.

You may sometimes want to include the **letter or memo of acceptance**, which acknowledges the assignment to conduct the study and prepare the report. Following the good-news plan, the acceptance confirms time and money restrictions and other pertinent details. This document is rarely included in reports.

Use the good-news plan for a letter of acceptance.

Letter of Transmittal The letter of transmittal (or memo of transmittal) conveys your report to your audience. (In a book, this section is called the preface.) The letter of transmittal says what you'd say if you were handing the report directly to the person who authorized it, so the style is less formal than the rest of the report. For example, the letter would use personal pronouns (*you, I, we*) and conversational language. Moreno's Electrovision report includes a one-page transmittal memo from Moreno to her boss (the person who requested the report).

Use a less-formal style for the letter of transmittal than for the report itself.

The transmittal letter usually appears right before the table of contents. If your report will be widely distributed, however, you may decide to include the letter of transmittal only in selected copies so that you can make certain comments to a specific audience. If your report discusses layoffs or other issues that affect people in the organization, you might want to discuss your recommendations privately in a letter of transmittal to top management. If your audience is likely to be skeptical of or even hostile to something in your report, the transmittal letter is a good opportunity to acknowledge their concerns and explain how the report addresses the issues they care about.

The letter of transmittal follows the routine and good-news plans described in Chapter 7. Begin with the main idea, officially conveying the report to the readers and summarizing its purpose. Such a letter typically begins with a statement such as "Here is the report you asked me to prepare on ..." The rest includes information about the scope of the report, the methods used to complete the study, and the limitations that became apparent. In the body of the letter you may also highlight important points or sections of the report, make comments on side issues, give suggestions for follow-up studies, and offer any details that will help readers understand and use the report. You may also wish to acknowledge help given by others. The concluding paragraph is a note of thanks for having been given the report assignment, an expression of willingness to discuss the report, and an offer to assist with future projects.

Use the good-news plan for a letter of transmittal.

If the report does not have a synopsis, the letter of transmittal may summarize the major findings, conclusions, and recommendations. This material would be placed after the opening of the letter.

The synopsis of short reports is often included in the letter of transmittal.

Table of Contents The table of contents indicates in outline form the coverage, sequence, and relative importance of the information in the report. The headings used in the text of the report are the basis for the table of contents. Depending on the length and complexity of the report, your contents page may show only the top two or three levels of headings or only first-level headings. The exclusion of some levels of headings may frustrate readers who want to know where to find every subject you cover. On the other hand, a simpler table of contents helps readers focus on the major points. No matter how many levels you include, make sure readers can easily distinguish between them (see Figure 11–16 for examples of various levels of headings).

The **table of contents** outlines the text and lists prefatory and supplementary parts.

The table of contents is prepared after the other parts of the report have been typed so that the beginning page numbers for each heading can be shown. The headings should be worded exactly as they are in the text of the report. Also listed on the contents page are the prefatory parts (only those that follow the contents page) and the supplementary parts. If you have fewer than four visual aids, you may wish to list them in the table of contents, too; but if you have four or more visual aids, create a separate list of illustrations.

Be sure the headings in the table of contents match up perfectly with the headings in the text.

Put the lists of figures and tables on separate pages if they won't fit on one page with the table of contents.

List of Illustrations For simplicity's sake, some reports refer to all visual aids as illustrations or exhibits. In other reports, as in Moreno's Electrovision report, tables are labelled separately from other types of visual aids, which are called figures. Regardless of the system used to label visual aids, the list of illustrations gives their titles and page numbers.

If you have enough space on a single page, include the list of illustrations directly beneath the table of contents. Otherwise, put the list on the page after the contents page. When tables and figures are numbered separately, they should also be listed separately. The two lists can appear on the same page if they fit; otherwise, start each list on a separate page.

Provide a brief overview of the report in a synopsis.

Synopsis or Executive Summary A synopsis is a brief overview (one page or less) of a report's most important points, designed to give readers a quick preview of the contents. It's often included in long informational reports dealing with technical, professional, or academic subjects and can also be called an abstract. Because it's a concise representation of the whole report, it may be distributed separately to a wide audience; then interested readers can request a copy of the entire report.

An informative synopsis summarizes the main ideas; a descriptive synopsis states what the report is about.

The phrasing of a synopsis can be either informative or descriptive, depending on whether the report is in direct or indirect order. In an informative synopsis, you present the main points of the report in the order in which they appear in the text. A descriptive synopsis, on the other hand, simply tells what the report is about, using only moderately greater detail than the table of contents; the actual findings of the report are omitted. Here are examples of statements from each type:

INFORMATIVE SYNOPSIS	DESCRIPTIVE SYNOPSIS
Sales of super-premium ice cream make up 11 percent of the total ice cream market.	This report contains information about super-premium ice cream and its share of the market.

Use a descriptive synopsis for a skeptical or hostile audience, an informative synopsis for most other situations.

The way you handle a synopsis reflects the approach you use in the text. If you're using an indirect approach in your report, you're better off with a descriptive synopsis. An informative synopsis, with its focus on conclusions and key points, may be too confrontational if you have a skeptical audience. You don't want to spoil the effect by providing a controversial beginning. No matter which type of synopsis you use, be sure to present an accurate picture of the report's contents.[3]

Put enough information in an executive summary so that an executive can make a decision without reading the entire report.

Many business report writers prefer to include an **executive summary** instead of a synopsis or an abstract. Whereas a synopsis is a prose table of contents that outlines the main points of the report, an executive summary is a fully developed "mini" version of the report itself, intended for readers who lack the time or motivation to study the complete text. An executive summary is more comprehensive than a synopsis, often as much as 10 percent as long as the report itself.

Unlike a synopsis, an executive summary may contain headings, well-developed transitions, and even visual aids. It is often organized in the same way as the report, using a direct or an indirect approach, depending on the audience's receptivity. However, executive summaries can also deviate from the sequence of material in the remainder of the report.

Linda Moreno's Electrovision report provides one example of an executive summary. After reading the summary, audience members know the essentials of the report and are in a position to make a decision. Later, when time permits, they may read certain parts of the report to obtain additional detail. However, from daily newspapers to Web sites, businesspeople are getting swamped with more and more data and information. They are looking for ways to cut through all the clutter, and reading executive summaries is a popular shortcut. Because you can usually assume that many of your readers will not read the main text of your report, make sure you cover all your important points (along with significant supporting information) in the executive summary.

Many reports require neither a synopsis nor an executive summary. Length is usually the determining factor. Most reports of fewer than 10 pages either omit such a preview or combine it with the letter of transmittal. However, if your report is over 30 pages long, you'll probably include either a synopsis or an executive summary as a convenience for readers. Which one you'll provide depends on the traditions of your organization.

TEXT OF THE REPORT

Apart from deciding on the fundamental issues of content and organization, you must also make decisions about the design and layout of your report. You can use a variety of techniques to present your material effectively. Many organizations have format guidelines that make your decisions easier, but the goal is always to focus the reader's attention on major points and the flow of ideas. Headings, typographical devices (such as capital letters, italics, and boldface type), and white space are useful tools, as are visual aids. Also, as discussed in Chapter 11, you can use preview and review statements to frame sections of your text. This strategy keeps your audience informed and reinforces the substance of your message.

Aids to understanding the text of a report:
- Headings
- Typographical devices
- Visual aids
- Preview and summary statements

OBJECTIVE 3 Describe four important functions of a formal report's introduction and identify the possible topics it might include.

Introduction The introduction of a report serves a number of important functions:

- puts the report in a broader context by tying it to a problem or an assignment
- tells readers the purpose of the report
- previews the contents and organization of the report
- establishes the tone of the report and the writer's relationship with the audience

An introduction has a number of functions and covers a wide variety of topics.

The length of the introduction depends on the length of the report. In a relatively brief report, the introduction may be only a paragraph or two and may not be labelled with a heading of any kind. On the other hand, the introduction to a major formal report may extend to several pages and can be identified as a separate section by the first-level heading "Introduction." (See Linda Moreno's Electrovision report.)

Here's a list of topics to consider covering in an introduction, depending on your material and your audience:

- **Authorization.** When, how, and by whom the report was authorized; who wrote it; and when it was submitted. This material is especially important when no letter of transmittal is included.
- **Problem/Purpose.** The reason for the report's existence and what is to be accomplished as a result.
- **Scope.** What is and what isn't going to be covered in the report. The scope indicates the report's size and complexity.
- **Background.** The historical conditions or factors that led up to the report. This section enables readers to understand how the problem developed, and what has been done about it so far.
- **Sources and methods.** The primary and secondary sources of information used. This section explains how samples were selected, how questionnaires were constructed (which should be included in an appendix with any cover letters), what follow-up was done, and so on. This section builds reader confidence in the work and in the sources and methods used.
- **Definitions.** A brief statement introducing a list of terms and their definitions. This section is unnecessary if readers are familiar with the terms you've used in your report. Moreno's Electrovision report doesn't use unfamiliar terminology, so no list of definitions is included. However, if you have any question about reader knowledge, define any terms that might be misinterpreted. Terms may also be defined in the body, explanatory notes, or glossary.

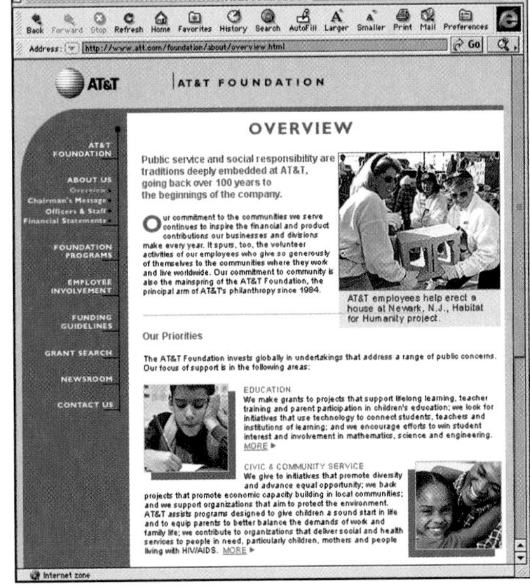

A report's introduction gives readers just a brief overview of the main points covered. Readers who want more information must then flip back to the table of contents to locate the right page within the body. On the Web, however, your introduction can include links to bring readers directly to the report sections covering main points. For example, when the AT&T Foundation **www.att.com/foundation** posted an executive summary of its philanthropic activities on the Web, it added links labelled "more" to encourage readers to click for more details on each activity.

➢ **Limitations.** Factors beyond your control that affect report quality, such as a budget too small to do needed work, a schedule too short to do needed research, and unreliable or unavailable data. Includes doubts about any aspect of your report. Such candour may lead readers to question results, but it also helps them assess those results, and it builds your report's integrity. Even so, limitations do not excuse a poor study or a bad report.

Some of these items may be combined in the introduction; some may not be included at all. You can decide what to include by figuring out what kind of information will help your readers understand and accept your report. Also give some thought to how the introduction relates to the prefatory parts of the report. In longer reports you may have a letter of transmittal, a synopsis or an executive summary, and an introduction—all of which cover essentially the same ground. To avoid redundancy, balance the various sections. For example, if the letter of transmittal and the synopsis are fairly detailed, you might make the introduction relatively brief.

Avoid repeating in the introduction the material that has already been covered in other prefatory parts.

However, because some people may barely glance at prefatory parts, be sure your introduction is detailed enough to provide an adequate preview of your report. If you believe that your introduction must repeat information that has already been covered in one of the prefatory parts, simply use different wording.

Body The body of the report follows the introduction. It consists of the major sections or chapters (with various levels of headings) that present, analyze, and interpret the information gathered during your investigation. These chapters contain the "proof," the evidence, or the detailed information necessary to support your conclusions and recommendations. (See the body of Linda Moreno's Electrovision report.)

One of the decisions to make when writing the body of your report is how much detail to include. Your decision depends on the nature of your information, the purpose of your report, and the preferences of your audience. Some situations call for detailed coverage; others lend themselves to shorter treatment. Provide only enough detail in the body to support your conclusions and recommendations; put additional detail in tables, charts, and appendixes.

Restrict the body to those details necessary to prove your conclusions and recommendations.

You can also decide whether to put your conclusions in the body or in a separate section or both. If the conclusions seem to flow naturally from the evidence, you'll almost inevitably cover them in the body. However, if you want to give your conclusions added emphasis, you can include a separate section to summarize them. Having a separate section is particularly appropriate in long reports; the reader may lose track of the conclusions if they're given only in the body.

Summary, Conclusions, and Recommendations The final section of the report text tells readers what has been said. In a short report, this final wrap-up may be only a paragraph or two. A long report generally has separate sections labelled "Summary," "Conclusions," and "Recommendations." Here's how the three differ:

Summaries, conclusions, and recommendations serve different purposes.

➢ **Summary.** The key findings of your report, paraphrased from the body and stated or listed in the order in which they appear in the body.
➢ **Conclusions.** An analysis of what the findings mean. These are the answers to the questions that led to the report.
➢ **Recommendations.** Opinions about the course of action that should be taken—always based on reason and logic. In the Electrovision report, Moreno lists four specific steps the company should take to reduce travel costs.

If the report is organized in direct order, the summary, conclusions, and recommendations are presented before the body and are reviewed only briefly at the end. If the report is organized in indirect order, these sections are presented for the first time at the end and are covered in detail. Many report writers combine the conclusions and recommendations under one heading because it seems like the natural thing to do. It is often difficult to present a conclusion without implying a recommendation. (See the Electrovision report.)

In action-oriented reports, put all the recommendations in a separate section, and spell out precisely what should happen next.

Whether you combine them or not, if you have several conclusions and recommendations, you may want to number and list them. An appropriate lead-in to such a list might be, "The findings of this study lead to the following conclusions." A statement that could be used for a list of recommendations might be, "Based on the conclusions of this study, the following recommendations are made." New findings are not presented in the conclusions or in the recommendations section.

In reports that are intended to lead to action, the recommendations section is particularly important; it spells out exactly what should happen next. It brings all the action items together in one place and gives the details about who should do what, when, where, and how. Readers may agree with everything you say in your report but still fail to take any action if you're vague about what should happen next. Your readers must understand what's expected of them and must have some appreciation of the difficulties that are likely to arise. Providing a schedule and specific task assignments is helpful because concrete plans have a way of commanding action.

Source Documentation You have an ethical and a legal obligation to give other people credit for their work. Acknowledging your sources also enhances the credibility of your report. By citing references in the text, you demonstrate that you have thoroughly researched your topic. Mentioning the names of well-known or important authorities on the subject also helps build credibility for your message. It's often a good idea to mention a credible source's name several times if you need to persuade your audience.

Give credit where credit is due.

On the other hand, you don't want to make your report read like an academic study, moving along from citation to citation. The source references should be handled as conveniently and inconspicuously as possible. One approach, especially for internal reports, is simply to mention a source in the text:

> According to Dr. Lewis Morgan of Northwestern Hospital, hip replacement operations account for 7 percent of all surgery performed on women age 65 and over.

However, if your report will be distributed to outsiders, include additional information on where you obtained the data. Most university and college students are familiar with citation schemes suggested by the Modern Language Association (MLA) or the American Psychological Association (APA). *The Chicago Manual of Style* is a reference often used by editors and publishers. All of these encourage the use of in-text citations (inserting the author's last name and a year of publication or a page number directly into the text). An alternative is to use numbered footnotes (bottom of the page) or endnotes (end of the report). (Linda Moreno's Electrovision report uses the author-date system, whereas this textbook uses endnotes.) For more information on citing sources, see Appendix B, "Documentation of Report Sources."

SUPPLEMENTARY PARTS

Supplementary parts follow the text of the report and include the appendixes, bibliography, and index. They are more common in long reports than in short ones.

An **appendix** contains materials related to the report but not included in the text because they're too lengthy or bulky or because they lack direct relevance. However, be sure not to include too much ancillary material. Keep your reports straightforward and concise.

Put into an appendix materials that are
- Bulky or lengthy
- Not directly relevant to the text

Frequently included in appendixes are sample questionnaires and cover letters, sample forms, computer printouts, and statistical formulas; a glossary may be put in an appendix or may stand as a separate supplementary part. The best place to include visual aids is in the text body nearest the point of discussion. If any graphics are too large to fit on one page or are only indirectly relevant to your report, they too may be put in an appendix. Some organizations specify that all visual aids be placed in an appendix.

Each type of material deserves a separate appendix. Identify the appendixes by labelling them, for example, "Appendix A: Questionnaire," "Appendix B: Computer Printout of Raw Data," and so on. All appendixes should be mentioned in the text and listed in the table of contents.

Going Online

Research Reports and Learning by Example

A good way to get ideas for the best style, organization, and format of a report is by looking at professional business reports. To find samples of different types of reports, you can use a metasearch engine, such as Ixquick Metasearch. Ixquick searches many engines simultaneously; in addition to searching in English, you can conduct your search in five other languages. See what Ixquick produces when you enter the phrase "business reports." Choose from various titles or descriptions to compare different kinds of reports. This research could result in your preparing better reports and proposals.

www.ixquick.com

To link directly to this site, visit our Companion Website at **www.pearsoned.ca/thill** *and look for the Chapter 12 resources.*

A **bibliography** is a list of secondary sources consulted when preparing the report. The Electrovision report bibliography is labelled "Works Cited" and it lists only the works that were mentioned in the report. You might call this section "Sources" or "References" if it includes works consulted but not mentioned in your report. The construction of a bibliography is shown in Appendix B.

An **index** is an alphabetical list of names, places, and subjects mentioned in the report, along with the pages on which they occur (see the index for this book). An index is rarely included in unpublished reports.

Components of a Formal Proposal

Certain analytical reports are called proposals, including bids to perform work under a contract and pleas for financial support from outsiders. Such bids and pleas are always formal. The goal of a proposal is to impress readers with your professionalism and to make your service and your company stand out. This goal is best achieved through a structured and deliberate approach.

Formal proposals contain many of the same components as other formal reports (see Figure 12–2). The difference lies mostly in the text, although a few of the prefatory parts are also different. With the exception of an occasional appendix, most proposals have few supplementary parts.

PREFATORY PARTS

Formal proposals contain most of the same prefatory parts as other formal reports.

The cover, title fly, title page, table of contents, and list of illustrations are handled the same as in other formal reports. However, other prefatory parts are handled quite differently, such as the copy of the RFP, the letter of transmittal, and the synopsis or executive summary.

Copy of the RFP Instead of having a letter of authorization, a formal proposal may have a copy of the request for proposal (RFP), which is a letter or memo soliciting a proposal or a bid for a particular project. The RFP is issued by the client to whom the proposal is being submitted, and it outlines what the proposal should cover. If the RFP includes detailed specifications, it may be too long to bind into the proposal; in that case, you may want to include only the introductory portion of the RFP. Another option is to omit the RFP and simply refer to it in your letter of transmittal.

Letter of Transmittal The way you handle the letter of transmittal depends on whether the proposal is solicited or unsolicited. If the proposal is solicited, the transmittal letter follows the pattern for good-news messages, highlighting those aspects of your proposal that may give you a competitive advantage. If the proposal is unsolicited, the transmittal letter takes on added importance; it may be all the client reads. The letter must persuade the reader that you have something worthwhile to offer, something that justifies the time required to read the entire proposal. The transmittal letter for an unsolicited proposal follows the pattern for persuasive messages (see Chapter 9).

Most proposals do not require a synopsis or an executive summary.

Synopsis or Executive Summary Although you may include a synopsis or an executive summary for your reader's convenience if your proposal is quite long, these components are often less useful in a formal proposal than they are in a formal report. If your proposal is unsolicited, your transmittal letter will already have caught the reader's interest, making a synopsis or an executive summary pointless. It may also be pointless if your proposal is solicited, because the reader is already committed to studying your proposal to find out how you intend to satisfy the terms of a contract. The introduction to a solicited proposal would provide an adequate preview of the contents. However, in some cases, an executive summary can serve you well.

Bruce Rogow was an engineering student when he was first struck by the idea of leading a team of students to design, build, and race a solar car at the World Solar

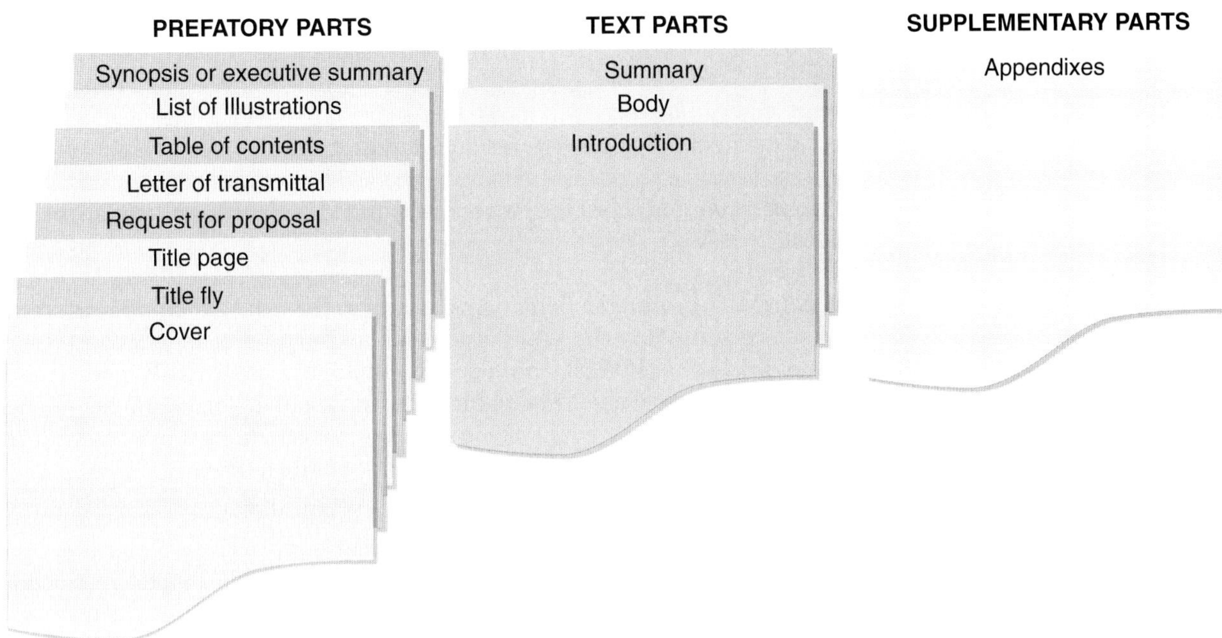

FIGURE 12–2 Parts of a Formal Proposal

Challenge Race across the Australian outback. The race itself would be the least of Rogow's challenges: first he had to convince students and faculty of the project's benefits; then he had to keep them motivated (and working long, hard hours) while he tackled administrative and engineering roadblocks that even he couldn't predict.

Ultimately, Rogow's Solar Car Project succeeded, drawing involvement from various academic departments, dozens of student volunteers, several corporate benefactors, and many news organizations. Rogow challenged science, engineering, and computer students to design and test *Suntrakker* (as the car was named). But he also challenged business students to come up with a proposal that would help him raise the support *Suntrakker* required.

"We needed to raise $145 000," Rogow recalls. "And since we had no faculty support in the beginning, we had to have something that would give us credibility. The proposal gave us much more than that."

Three students from an entrepreneurship class agreed to work with Rogow on a proposal that eventually filled over 70 pages. "The proposal mapped out every detail of our project, from start to finish, and made us look at things we had not considered. It also earned us respect from the faculty and was responsible for a $5000 donation from our local power company." Rogow now believes that the proposal made the difference between "thriving and just surviving."

A proposal is both a selling tool and a contractual commitment.

Figure 12–3 on page 387 shows an excerpt from the executive summary that Rogow included in his unsolicited proposal. The proposal presents the benefits up front and the financial information at the close. Detailed and thorough, it includes sections describing the vehicle, the management team, and even "Critical Risks." Appendixes include an organizational chart, résumé, design schematics, letters of support, lists of volunteers and contributors, and a telemarketing script.

TEXT OF THE PROPOSAL

The text of a proposal performs two essential functions: it persuades readers to award you a contract, and it spells out the terms of that contract. The challenge is to sell your audience on your ideas without making promises that you will not be able to fulfill later.

Follow the instructions presented in the RFP.

If your proposal is unsolicited, you have some latitude in arranging the text. However, the organization of a solicited proposal is governed by the request for the proposal. Most RFPs spell out precisely what you should cover, and in what order, so that all bids will be similar in form. This uniformity enables the client to evaluate the competing proposals in a systematic way. In many organizations a team of evaluators splits up the proposals and looks at various sections. An engineer might review the technical portions of all the proposals submitted, and an accountant might review the cost estimates.

In the introduction, establish the need for action and summarize the key benefits of your proposal.

Introduction The introduction orients readers to the rest of your proposal. It identifies your organization and your purpose, and outlines the remainder of the text. If your proposal is solicited, the introduction should refer to the RFP, if not, it should mention any factors that led you to submit your proposal. You might mention mutual acquaintances, or you might refer to previous conversations you've had with readers. Subheadings in the introduction often include the following:

In some proposals, introductions include subheads.

- **Background or statement of the problem.** Briefly reviews the reader's situation, and establishes a need for action. Readers may not perceive a problem or opportunity the same way you do. You must convince them that a problem or opportunity exists before you can convince them to accept your solution. In a way that is meaningful to your reader, discuss the current situation and explain how things could be better.
- **Overview of approach.** Highlights your key selling points and their benefits, showing how your proposal will solve the reader's problem. The heading for this section might also be "Preliminary Analysis" or some other wording that will identify this section as a summary of your solution.
- **Scope.** States the boundaries of the proposal—what you will and will not do. This brief section may also be labelled "Delimitations."
- **Report organization.** Orients the reader to the remainder of the proposal and calls attention to the major divisions of thought.

OBJECTIVE 4 Discuss the four areas of specific information that must be covered in the body of a proposal.

Body The core of the proposal is the body, which has the same purpose as the body of other reports. In a proposal, however, the body must cover some specific information:

In the approach section, demonstrate the superiority of your ideas, products, or services.

Use the work plan to describe the tasks to be completed under the terms of the contract.

In the qualifications section, demonstrate that you have the personnel, facilities, and experience to do a competent job.

The more detailed your cost proposal is, the more credibility your estimates will have.

- **Proposed approach.** May also be titled "Technical Proposal," "Research Design," "Issues for Analysis," or "Work Statement." This section describes what you have to offer: your concept, product, or service. To convince readers that your proposal has merit, focus on the strengths of your offer in relation to reader needs. Point out any advantages that you have over your competitors.
- **Work plan.** Describes how you'll accomplish what must be done (unless you'll provide a standard, off-the-shelf item). Explain the steps you'll take, their timing, the methods or resources you'll use, and the person(s) responsible. Also indicate completion dates for critical portions of the work. If your proposal is accepted, the work plan is contractually binding, so don't promise to deliver more than you can realistically achieve within a given period.
- **Statement of qualifications.** Describes your organization's experience, personnel, and facilities—all in relation to readers' needs. If you work for a large company that frequently submits proposals, you might borrow much of this section intact from previous proposals. However, be sure to tailor any boilerplate material to suit the situation. The qualifications section can be an important selling point, and it deserves to be handled carefully.
- **Costs.** Has few words and many numbers but can make or break your proposal. A high price can lose the bid; however, a low price could doom you to losing money on the project. Estimating costs is difficult, so prove that your costs are realistic—break them down in detail so that readers can see how you got your numbers: so much for labour, so much for materials, so much for overhead.

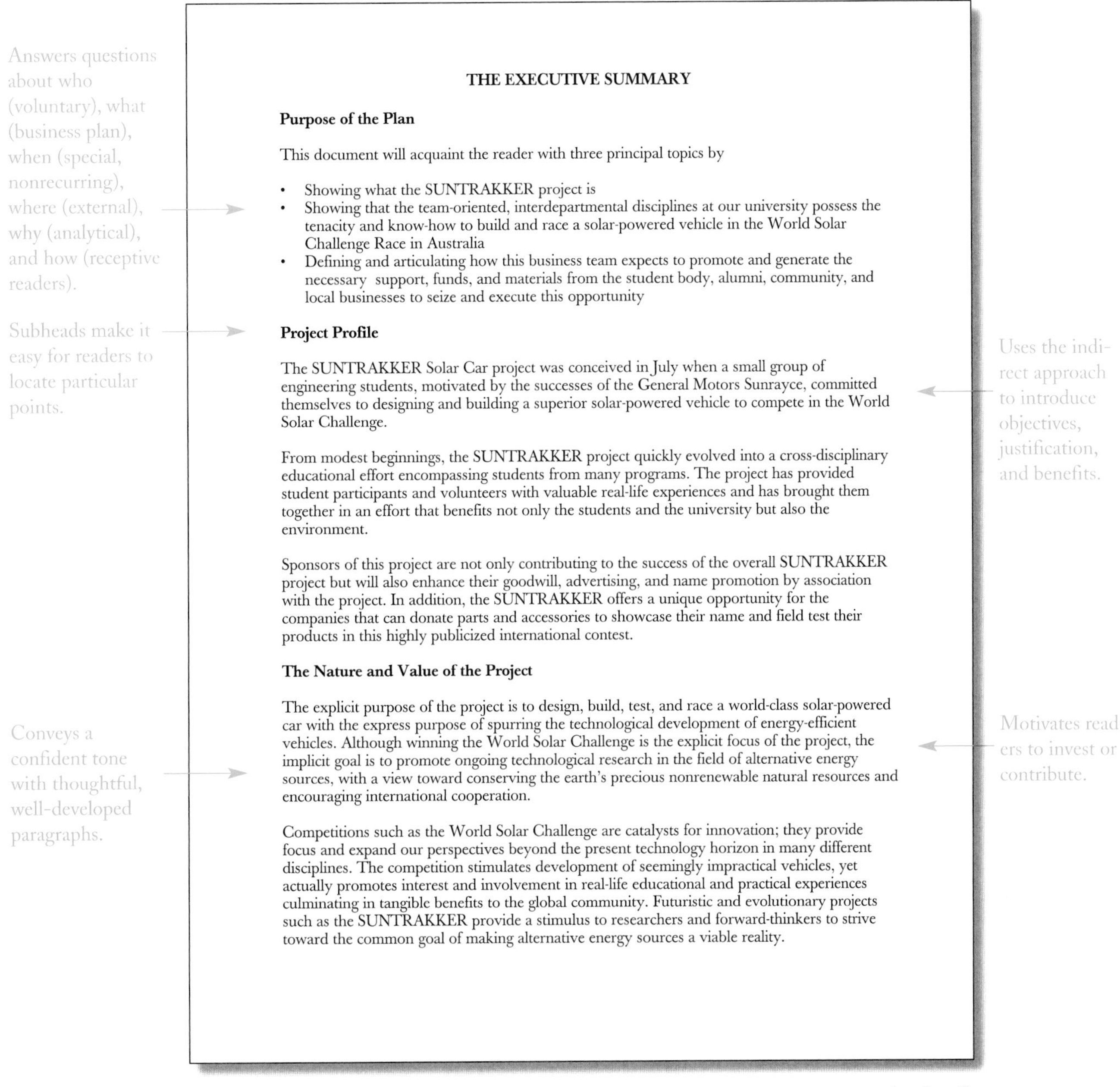

Answers questions about who (voluntary), what (business plan), when (special, nonrecurring), where (external), why (analytical), and how (receptive readers).

Subheads make it easy for readers to locate particular points.

Uses the indirect approach to introduce objectives, justification, and benefits.

Conveys a confident tone with thoughtful, well-developed paragraphs.

Motivates readers to invest or contribute.

THE EXECUTIVE SUMMARY

Purpose of the Plan

This document will acquaint the reader with three principal topics by

- Showing what the SUNTRAKKER project is
- Showing that the team-oriented, interdepartmental disciplines at our university possess the tenacity and know-how to build and race a solar-powered vehicle in the World Solar Challenge Race in Australia
- Defining and articulating how this business team expects to promote and generate the necessary support, funds, and materials from the student body, alumni, community, and local businesses to seize and execute this opportunity

Project Profile

The SUNTRAKKER Solar Car project was conceived in July when a small group of engineering students, motivated by the successes of the General Motors Sunrayce, committed themselves to designing and building a superior solar-powered vehicle to compete in the World Solar Challenge.

From modest beginnings, the SUNTRAKKER project quickly evolved into a cross-disciplinary educational effort encompassing students from many programs. The project has provided student participants and volunteers with valuable real-life experiences and has brought them together in an effort that benefits not only the students and the university but also the environment.

Sponsors of this project are not only contributing to the success of the overall SUNTRAKKER project but will also enhance their goodwill, advertising, and name promotion by association with the project. In addition, the SUNTRAKKER offers a unique opportunity for the companies that can donate parts and accessories to showcase their name and field test their products in this highly publicized international contest.

The Nature and Value of the Project

The explicit purpose of the project is to design, build, test, and race a world-class solar-powered car with the express purpose of spurring the technological development of energy-efficient vehicles. Although winning the World Solar Challenge is the explicit focus of the project, the implicit goal is to promote ongoing technological research in the field of alternative energy sources, with a view toward conserving the earth's precious nonrenewable natural resources and encouraging international cooperation.

Competitions such as the World Solar Challenge are catalysts for innovation; they provide focus and expand our perspectives beyond the present technology horizon in many different disciplines. The competition stimulates development of seemingly impractical vehicles, yet actually promotes interest and involvement in real-life educational and practical experiences culminating in tangible benefits to the global community. Futuristic and evolutionary projects such as the SUNTRAKKER provide a stimulus to researchers and forward-thinkers to strive toward the common goal of making alternative energy sources a viable reality.

(continued)

FIGURE 12–3 In-Depth Critique: Executive Summary for a Proposal (Excerpt)

In a formal proposal it pays to be as thorough and accurate as possible. Carefully selected detail enhances your credibility, as does successful completion of any task you promise to perform.

Summary or Conclusion You may want to include a summary or conclusion section because it's your last opportunity to persuade readers to accept your proposal. Summarize the merits of your approach, reemphasize why you and your firm are the ones to do the work, and stress the benefits. Make this section relatively brief, assertive, and confident.

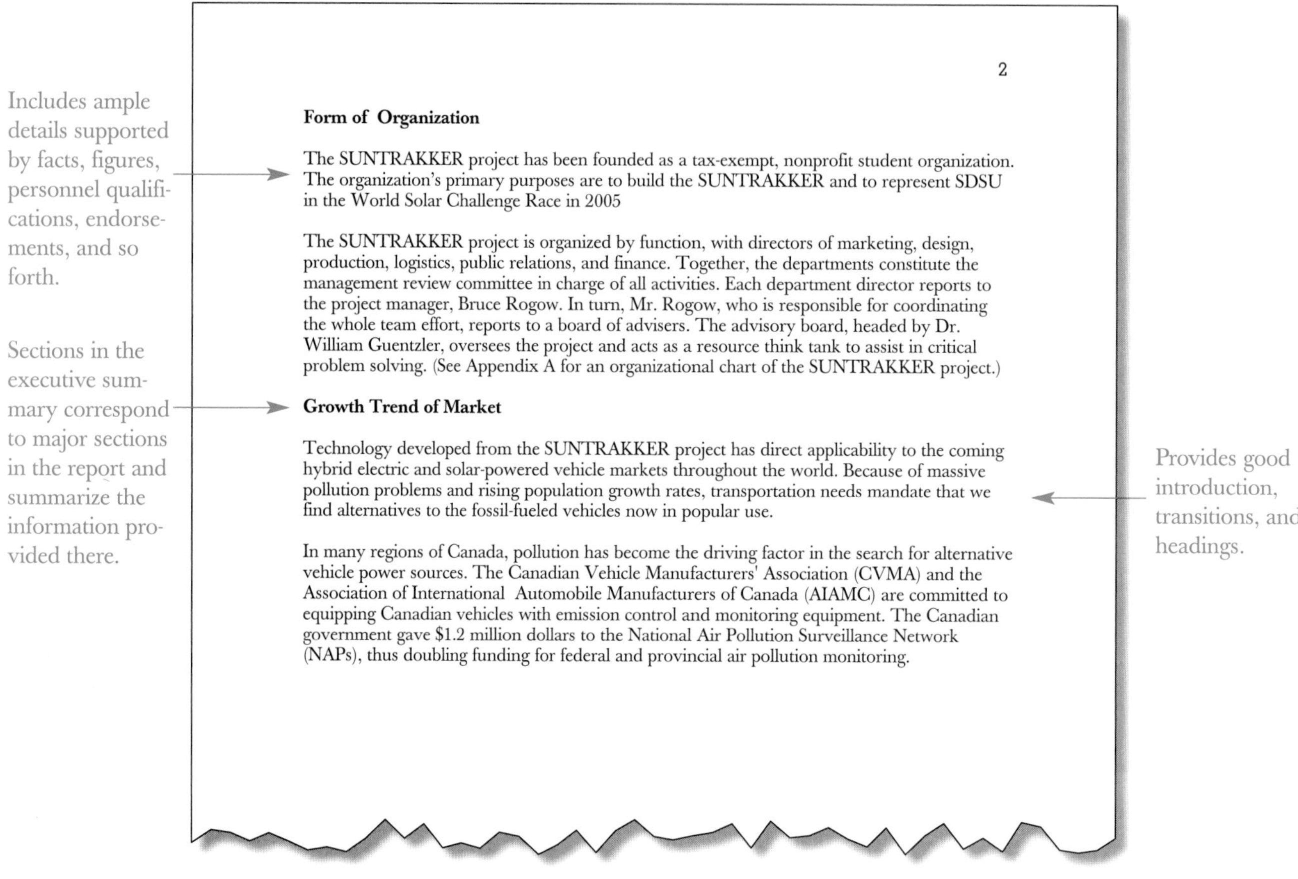
Includes ample details supported by facts, figures, personnel qualifications, endorsements, and so forth.
Sections in the executive summary correspond to major sections in the report and summarize the information provided there.
Provides good introduction, transitions, and headings.

2

Form of Organization

The SUNTRAKKER project has been founded as a tax-exempt, nonprofit student organization. The organization's primary purposes are to build the SUNTRAKKER and to represent SDSU in the World Solar Challenge Race in 2005

The SUNTRAKKER project is organized by function, with directors of marketing, design, production, logistics, public relations, and finance. Together, the departments constitute the management review committee in charge of all activities. Each department director reports to the project manager, Bruce Rogow. In turn, Mr. Rogow, who is responsible for coordinating the whole team effort, reports to a board of advisers. The advisory board, headed by Dr. William Guentzler, oversees the project and acts as a resource think tank to assist in critical problem solving. (See Appendix A for an organizational chart of the SUNTRAKKER project.)

Growth Trend of Market

Technology developed from the SUNTRAKKER project has direct applicability to the coming hybrid electric and solar-powered vehicle markets throughout the world. Because of massive pollution problems and rising population growth rates, transportation needs mandate that we find alternatives to the fossil-fueled vehicles now in popular use.

In many regions of Canada, pollution has become the driving factor in the search for alternative vehicle power sources. The Canadian Vehicle Manufacturers' Association (CVMA) and the Association of International Automobile Manufacturers of Canada (AIAMC) are committed to equipping Canadian vehicles with emission control and monitoring equipment. The Canadian government gave $1.2 million dollars to the National Air Pollution Surveillance Network (NAPs), thus doubling funding for federal and provincial air pollution monitoring.

FIGURE 12–3 In-Depth Critique: Executive Summary for a Proposal (Excerpt) (continued)

Proofreading Formal Reports and Proposals

Don't forget to proofread everything one last time.

Finally, you have the final version of your report or proposal. You've revised the content for clarity and conciseness, and you've assembled all the various components. You've designed the document to please readers, and you've produced it in its final form. Now you need to review everything thoroughly one last time.

Checking Over Textual Materials

As you proofread your report, check for typos, spelling errors, and mistakes in punctuation. Make sure your text is laid out on the page in a clear, uncluttered fashion. Make sure that nothing has been left out or overlooked, and be certain that every word contributes to your report's purpose.

OBJECTIVE 5 Explain the four questions to ask when proofing visual aids.

If you need specific tips on proofreading your report, look back at Chapter 6. Proofreading the textual part of your report is pretty much the same as proofreading any business message. However, reports often have elements that may not be included in other messages, so don't forget to review your visual aids thoroughly.

Checking Over Visual Aids

Any visuals that you have included are present to help your readers absorb, understand, and accept your message. Their appearance is crucial to your message's success, so be sure to check visuals for mistakes such as typographical errors, inconsistent colour treatment, and misaligned elements. Also take a few extra minutes to make sure that your visuals are necessary, absolutely accurate, properly documented, and honest.

IS THE VISUAL NECESSARY?

A few well-placed visual aids can clarify and dramatize your message, but too many illustrations may bury it. Avoid the temptation to overload your reports with unnecessary tables, graphs, and charts. Remember that your audience is busy. Don't give people information they don't need simply because you want to impress them or because you've fallen in love with your computer's graphics capabilities.

Make sure the visual serves a specific purpose.

IS THE VISUAL ACCURATE?

Make sure that every number is correct. Verify that every line is plotted accurately and that every scale is drawn to reflect reality. Be sure that every bit of information included in a visual is consistent with what is said in the text. When you're proofreading, be sure to check each visual's source notes and content notes for accuracy.

Proof visuals as carefully as you proof text.

IS THE VISUAL PROPERLY DOCUMENTED?

You may be the creator of the actual graphic design, but if you use someone else's data, you need to give credit by citing the source of any data you use in creating a visual. Identify the actual source of data (such as the name of the journal the information came from) or refer simply to the nature of the information (for example, "interviews with 50 soybean farmers"). If the data displayed in a visual are "primary" (you gathered the information for your own purposes), then say so. To avoid cluttering your graphic, you could use a shortened citation on the graphic itself and include a complete citation elsewhere in the report.

Don't forget to document your visuals.

IS THE VISUAL HONEST?

In visuals, you can have all the numbers right and still give your audience a false impression; graphs and charts tend to oversimplify some numerical relationships.

Make your report ethical by keeping your visuals honest.

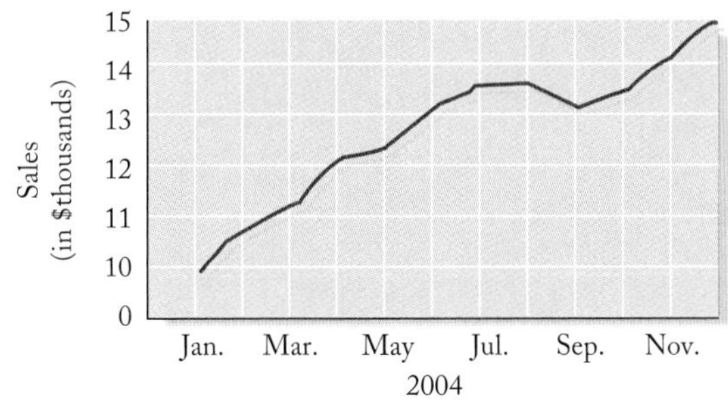

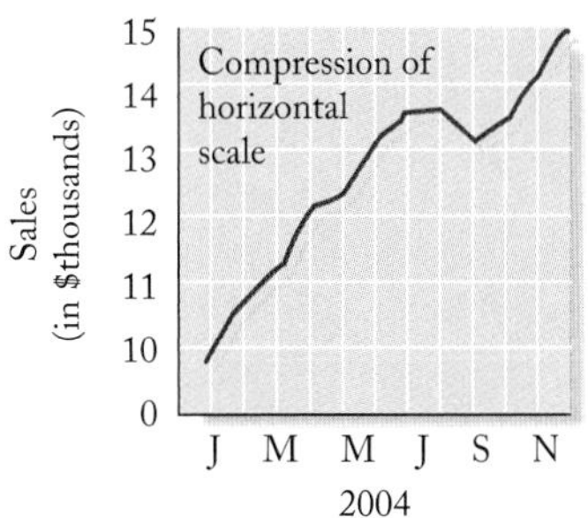

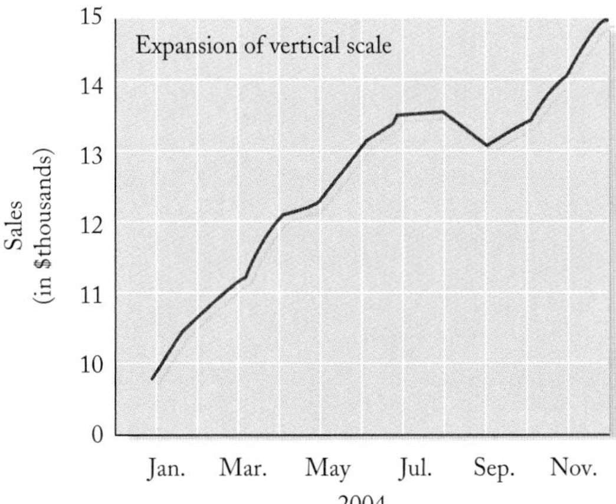

FIGURE 12-4 The Impact of Scale on the Slope of a Curve

But deliberately leaving out important information is highly unethical. Don't leave out data points that don't fit your needs. And don't omit any outside influences on the data you're portraying.

The scale of a graph or chart can also introduce distortion. As Figure 12–4 on page 389 illustrates, you can transform modest results into dramatic ones by compressing the horizontal scale or by expanding the vertical scale. But when you do so, you abandon good business ethics and mislead your audience in the process. So choose a scale that conveys a realistic picture of what's happening. Likewise, maintain the same scale in successive charts comparing the same factors.

Getting Feedback from Formal Reports and Proposals

Ask for feedback, and learn from your mistakes.

Once you've completed your formal report and sent it off to your audience, you'll naturally expect a positive response, and quite often you'll get one—but not always. You may get half-hearted praise or no action on your conclusions and recommendations. Even worse, you may get some serious criticism. Try to learn from these experiences. Sometimes you won't get any response at all. If you don't hear from your readers within a week or two, you might want to ask politely whether the report arrived. In hopes of stimulating a response, you might also offer to answer any questions or provide additional information. To review the ideas presented in this chapter, consult "Checklist: Producing Formal Reports and Proposals."

Checklist: **Producing Formal Reports and Proposals**

Prepare Sturdy, Attractive Cover

✓ Label the cover clearly with the title of the document.

✓ Use a title that tells the audience exactly what the document is about.

Prepare Title Page

✓ List title; recipient's name, title, affiliation; author's name, title, affiliation; date of submission.

✓ Balance the information in blocks on the page.

Include Copy of Letter of Authorization or Request for Proposal, If Appropriate

✓ Prepare Letter or Memo of Transmittal

✓ Include only in some copies if it contains sensitive information suitable for some but not all readers.

✓ Convey the document officially to the readers.

✓ Refer to authorization and discuss purpose, scope, background, source and methods, and limitations.

✓ Acknowledge everyone who was especially helpful in preparing the document.

✓ Close with thanks, offer to be of further assistance, and suggest future projects, if appropriate.

Prepare Table of Contents

✓ Include all first- and second-level headings (perhaps all third-level headings).

✓ Give the page number of each heading.

✓ Word all headings exactly as they appear in the text.

✓ Include the synopsis (if there is one) and supplementary parts.

✓ Number table of contents and all prefatory pages with lower-case roman numerals (bottom centre).

Prepare List of Illustrations If You Have Four or More Visual Aids

✓ Put the list in the same format as the table of contents.

✓ Identify visuals either directly under table of contents or on a separate page under its own heading.

Develop Synopsis or Executive Summary (for Long, Formal Documents)

✓ Tailor the synopsis or executive summary to the document's length and tone.

✓ Condense the document's main points, using either the informative or the descriptive approach.

✓ Present the points in a synopsis in the same order as they appear in the document.

✓ An executive summary can deviate from the order of points appearing in the report.

Prepare Introduction to Text

✓ Leave a five-cm margin at the top of the page, and centre the title of the document.

✓ In a long document, type the first-level heading "Introduction" three lines below title.

✓ In a short document, omit "Introduction" heading and begin typing three lines below title.

✓ Discuss the authorization (unless already covered in a letter of transmittal), purpose, scope, background, sources and methods, definitions, limitations, and text organization.

Prepare Body of Document

✓ Number all pages with arabic numerals in the upper right-hand corner (except for the first page, where the number is centred 2.5 cm from the bottom).

Prepare Conclusion of Document

✓ Wrap up the text of reports and proposals with a summary.

✓ If appropriate, include conclusions and recommendations.

Prepare Appendixes, If Necessary

✓ Give each appendix a title.

✓ For multiple appendixes, number or letter them consecutively in the order the text refers to them.

Prepare Reference List (Bibliography) Under Three Conditions

✓ If you used secondary sources that need to be identified.

✓ If it seems that readers would benefit.

✓ If the document would gain credibility.

Summary of Learning Objectives

1 List the three tasks involved in completing business reports and proposals, and briefly explain what's involved in revising them. To complete business reports and proposals, you need to revise, produce, and proofread the document, just as you would with any other business message. Revising reports and proposals involves evaluating content and organization, reviewing style and readability, and editing for conciseness and clarity.

2 Explain the 10 prefatory parts of a formal report. Depending on readers' preferences and familiarity, formal reports may include as many as nine of the ten possible prefatory parts: (1) The cover includes at least the report's title and maybe the writer's name and submission date. (2) The title fly is a blank sheet of paper that adds a touch of formality. (3) The title page includes the report title; the name, title, and address of the person or group that authorized the report; the name, title, and address of the person or group that prepared the report; and the date of submission. (4) The letter (or memo) of authorization is the document requesting a report be written. (5) The letter (or memo) of acceptance acknowledges the assignment and is rarely included in reports. (6) The letter (or memo) of transmittal conveys the report to the audience and may appear in only selected copies of the report. (7) The table of contents lists report headings in outline form with page numbers. (8) The list of illustrations gives the titles and page numbers of visual aids. (9) A synopsis (or abstract) is a brief (one page or less) review of the report's most important points. (10) The executive summary is a fully developed "mini" version of the report that may contain headings and even visual aids. The executive summary would replace the synopsis, since both components would never be included in the same report.

3 Describe four important functions of a formal report's introduction and identify the possible topics it might include. Four important functions of introductions are (1) putting the report in a broader context by tying it to a problem or an assignment, (2) telling readers the report's purpose, (3) previewing the report's contents and organization, and (4) establishing the tone of the report and the writer's relationship with the audience. To accomplish these functions, an introduction might address topics such as authorization, scope, background, sources and methods, definitions, limitations, and organization.

4 Discuss the four areas of specific information that must be covered in the body of a proposal. The body of a proposal must cover four specific areas of information. First, describe your proposed approach—your concept, product, or service. In this section, focus on how your approach satisfies reader needs and on any advantages you have over competitors. Second, describe your work plan—how you'll accomplish the task. Be clear about the steps you'll take, as well as when you'll take them and how. Clearly identify the person(s) responsible for the work and the completion dates for important portions of the work. Third, describe your qualifications to do the work. Include your organization's experience, personnel, and facilities, and make sure this material relates directly to the reader's particular situation. Fourth, describe the cost of the work. Break down all estimated costs so that readers can see how you arrived at your overall figure.

5 **Explain the four questions to ask when proofing visual aids.** As you check over visual aids, ask yourself four questions: (1) Is the visual necessary? Avoid overloading your report with unnecessary illustrations. Include as much information as readers need, but no more. (2) Is the visual accurate? Make sure that every number, word, and data point is consistent with the text of the report. Check carefully for typos, colour inconsistencies, and misaligned elements. (3) Is the visual properly documented? Whether you include the full citation on the graphic or elsewhere in the report, you need to give credit for the information you include in your visual. (4) Is the visual honest? Make sure that your visual not only contains all the correct information but also projects the right impression. To ensure that your visual makes the right impression, be sure you haven't oversimplified data, omitted information, or chosen an unrealistic scale.

ON THE JOB

Solving a Communication Dilemma at Dofasco

Dofasco's Environmental and Energy report is written by one person, but requires the input of numerous employees. Accordingly, this complex document, an artful combination of text, graphics, and photographs, demands a finely tuned overall plan to see the document from conception to completion. One individual has the project-management function, making him responsible for the budget, creating the critical paths that focus the report and drive it to publication, delegating work and responsibilities, and keeping the external suppliers, such as the printer and designer, in touch and on schedule.

Determining the overall theme is a first step in the planning process, and is critical, says corporate communications manager, Ian Hamilton, "as it sets the tone for the coming year." The theme is developed collaboratively by Dofasco's director of communications and public affairs, senior communications staff, outside designers, and consultants. The ultimate approval comes from senior management.

Much of the research is primary. Employees involved in the report process interview Environment and Energy staff who have responsibility for specific areas, such as air, water, waste, and energy. These staff members are asked to contribute important "stories," Hamilton explains, such as "new projects, accomplishments and/or shortcomings, as well as context for the stories. At these meetings, images and photos are also discussed."

Another step in creating the E & E Report is to develop the design concepts by bringing in the expertise of external designers and printers. Designers also help with the outline and pagination. Visual support is another essential part of the document, such as the graphics and charts, "which can communicate complex information in a couple of square inches," Hamilton remarks. The relevant department prepares these; for example, finance prepares the financial charts. Photography is also a necessary component; a single photograph can transmit a complicated concept, such as "growth," "confidence," or "direction." Photos also "put a human face on the company, and in showing, not telling, what we do," says Hamilton.

As the annual *Environmental and Energy Report* moves toward completion, its overall format and appearance are determined. As Hamilton observes, "structural considerations are a part of every long report. Introductions, theme pages, visuals, highlight and summary sections, sidebars, and other features are used throughout to provide a lot of explanation in a confined space, as well as to maintain reader interest by being both visually engaging and possessing a logical flow."

Ian Hamilton notes that Dofasco's position is simply this: we will be honest, forthright, and open to dialogue with our stakeholders, whether they are industry peers or a group of concerned local citizens. In our reports, we try to paint an accurate picture of where we are, how we're performing, and, importantly, where we're going."

Your Mission As an intern in Dofasco's corporate communications department, you are learning how to prepare formal reports. One of your most important tasks is helping to prepare the current *Environmental and Energy Report*, which is distributed both online and in printed form. Study the following questions, select the best answer in each case, and be prepared to support your choices.

1 Just about everybody—employees, business leaders, government regulators, and community members—is overwhelmed with data and information. Because people have too much information to digest and too little time to read, the executive summary has become a particularly important part of corporate reports. Which of the following approaches would you take with the executive summary in this year's E&E report?

a Use the executive summary to provide a quick score card for the company's performance in each of the areas addressed by E&E report. Readers may be tempted to skip the detail contained in the body of the report, but at least they'll get the highlights in the executive summary.

b Use the executive summary to highlight changes in the report from previous years. You believe that the report is widely read by all its audiences every year, so people will need guidance to understand how this year's content and organization differ from that of past reports.

c Do not use an executive summary at all. This report is made available to everyone interested in reading it, not just a handful of executives, so an executive summary is not appropriate.

2 Much of the information you've collected from your interviews with Dofasco employees is difficult or impossible to represent numerically. However, you believe that readers would appreciate a brief summary of the interview results. For one issue, you posed the following open-ended question "How would you describe our progress toward limiting Dofasco's impact on the environment this year?" The responses range from simple, one-sentence answers to long, involved essays complete with examples. All together, the responses fill 13 pages. What's the best way of summarizing your findings?
   a Pick a half dozen responses that in your opinion represent the range of responses. For example, you might include one that says "we have not succeeded in controlling our impact on the environment this year," one that says "I believe we've been very successful at limiting harmful emissions into the atmosphere," and four more that fall between these two extremes.
   b Create a five-step measurement scale that ranges from "little or no progress" to "completely successful." Together with a few experienced members of your staff, review each response and decide in which of the five categories it belongs. Then create a chart that shows how the responses are distributed among the five categories. Explain how you developed the chart, and offer to provide a complete listing of the responses to any reader who requests one.
   c Since the information is not quantitative, it's impossible to summarize and boil down to a few facts and figures. It would, therefore, be inappropriate to summarize the information at all. Simply include all 13 pages of responses as an appendix in your report.

3 One of the questions you asked employees was to rate their feelings about the company's response to employee complaints about how Dofasco is controlling its energy use. You provided a scale that included five choices: 1 (very satisfied), 2 (satisfied), 3 (no opinion), 4 (unsatisfied), and 5 (very unsatisfied). A staff member illustrated this data in a line chart, but during the revision process, you've realized that a line chart is not a good choice. (It attempts to show trends in the relationship between two variables, but you have five data points, and you need to show how many employees chose each one.) What would be the best visual to replace the original?
   a A bar chart with five bars that indicate the number of responses in each category.
   b A surface chart with one line for each choice, which shows the sum of all five lines.
   c A pie chart with five slices that indicate the number of responses in each category.[4]

Test Your Knowledge

Review Questions

1 What are the tasks involved in revising a report or proposal?
2 What are the 10 prefatory parts of a formal report?
3 How do writers use an introduction in a formal report?
4 What four questions do writers need to ask when checking visual aids for a report?
5 What information is included on the title page of a report?
6 What is a letter of transmittal, and where is it positioned within a report?
7 How does a synopsis differ from an executive summary?
8 How does the summary section of a report differ from the conclusions section?
9 What are three supplementary parts often included in formal reports?
10 Why is the work plan a key component of a proposal?

Interactive Learning

Use This Text's Online Resources

To link directly to this site, visit our Companion Website at **www.pearsoned.ca/thill** and look for the Chapter 13 resources.

Also check out the resources on the Mastering Business Communication CD, including "Perils of Pauline," an interactive presentation of the business communication challenges within a fictional company.

Apply Your Knowledge

Critical Thinking Questions

1 Under what circumstances would you include more than one index in a lengthy report?

2 If you were submitting a solicited proposal to build an indoor pool, would you include as references the names and addresses of other clients for whom you recently built similar pools? Would you include these references in an unsolicited proposal? Where

in either proposal would you include these references? Why?

3 If you were writing an analytical report about your company's advertising policies, where would you include your recommendations—in the beginning of the report or at the end? Why?

4 If you included a bibliography in your report, would you also need to include in-text citations? Please explain.

5 **Ethical Choices** How would you report on a confidential survey in which employees rated their managers' capabilities? Both employees and managers expect to see the results. Would you give the same report to employees and managers? What components would you include or exclude for each audience? Explain your choices.

Practice Your Knowledge

Document for Analysis

Visit the Citizenship and Immigration Canada reports page at **www.cic.gc.ca/english/srr/review/reports-c.html**, and follow the link to *Evaluation of Canada's War Crimes Program: Final Report*. Read the report's introduction (Section 1.0). Using the information in this chapter, analyze the introduction and offer specific suggestions for revising it.

Exercises

12–1 **Teamwork** You and a classmate are helping Linda Moreno prepare her report on Electrovision's travel and entertainment costs (see "Report Writer's Notebook," beginning on page 360). This time, however, the report is to be informational rather than analytical, so it will not include recommendations. Review the existing report and determine what changes would be needed to make it an informational report. Be as specific as possible. For example, if your team decides the report needs a new title, what title would you use? Now draft a transmittal memo for Moreno to use in conveying this informational report to Dennis McWilliams, Electrovision's vice-president of operations.

12–2 **Producing Reports: Letter of Transmittal** You are president of the Friends of the Library, a nonprofit group that raises funds and provides volunteers to support your local library. Every February, you send a report of the previous year's activities and accomplishments to the County Arts Council, which provides an annual grant of $1000 toward your group's summer reading festival. Now it's February 6, and you've completed your formal report. Here are the highlights:

- Back-to-school book sale raised $2000.
- Holiday craft fair raised $1100.
- Promotion and prizes for summer reading festival cost $1450.
- Materials for children's program featuring local author cost $125.
- New reference databases for library's career centre cost $850.
- Bookmarks promoting library's Web site cost $200.

Write a letter of transmittal to Erica Maki, the council's director. Because she is expecting this report, you can use the direct approach. Be sure to express gratitude for the council's ongoing financial support.

12–3 **Internet** Follow the step-by-step hints and examples for writing a funding proposal at **www.learnerassociates.net/proposal**. Review the writing hints and the entire sample proposal online. What details did the author decide to include in appendixes? Why was this material placed in the appendixes and not the main body of the report?

12–4 **Ethical Choices** Your boss has asked you to proofread his yearly report on consumer accidents due to household chemicals. Chart A (Figure 12–5 below) catches your eye. Does the scale on this line graph leave the right impression about insecticide accident levels? What revisions, if any, would you suggest to ensure that this chart offers a realistic picture of the situation?

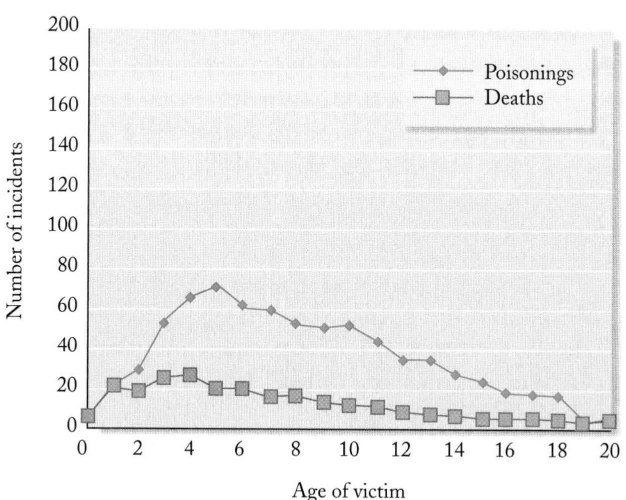

Figure 12–5

Cases

Short, Formal Report Requiring No Additional Research

1 Sailing past the sunsets: Report using statistical data to suggest a new advertising strategy. As manager of Distant Dreams, a travel agency in Halifax, Nova Scotia, you are interested in the information in Table 12–1. Dollar income seems to be shifting toward the 35–44 age group. Tables 12–2 and 12–3 are also broken down by age group. Your agency has traditionally concentrated its advertising on people nearing retirement—people who are closing out successful careers and now have the time and money to vacation abroad. Having examined the three sets of data, however, you realize that it's time for a major shift in emphasis.

Your Task: Write a report to Mary Henderson, who writes your advertisements, explaining why future ads should still be directed to people who want to explore far reaches of the world but to people in other age groups as well as those in their fifties and sixties. Justify your explanation by referring to the data you have examined.

2 Giving it the online try: Report analyzing the advantages and disadvantages of corporate online learning As the newest member of the corporate training division of Paper Products, Inc., you have been asked to investigate and analyze the merits of establishing Internet courses (e-learning) for the company's employees. The president of your company thinks e-learning might be a good employee benefit as well as a terrific way for employees to learn new skills that they can use on the job. You've already done your research and here's a copy of your notes:

- Online courses open up new horizons for working adults, who often find it difficult to juggle conventional classes with jobs and families.
- Adults over 25 now represent nearly half of higher-ed students; most are employed and want more education to advance their careers.
- Some experts believe that online learning will never be as good as face-to-face instruction.
- Online learning requires no commute and is appealing for employees who travel regularly.
- Enrollment in courses offered online by postsecondary institutions is expected to increase from 2 million students in 2001 to 5 million students in in 2006.
- E-learning is a cost-effective way to get better-educated employees.
- Corporate spending on e-learning is expected to more than quadruple by 2005, to $18 billion.
- At IBM, some 200 000 employees received education or training online last year, and 75 percent of the company's Basic Blue course for new managers is online. E-learning cut IBM's training bill by $350 million last year—mostly because online courses don't require travel.
- There are no national statistics, but a recent report from the *Chronicle of Higher Education* found that institutions are seeing dropout rates that range from 20 to 50 percent for online learners. The research does not adequately explain why the dropout rates for e-learners are higher.
- A recent study of corporate online learners reported that employees want the following things from their online courses: college credit or a certificate; active correspondence with an online facilitator who has frequent virtual office hours; access to 24-hour, seven-day-a-week technical support; and the ability to start a course anytime.

TABLE 12–1 Percentage of Total Canadian Household Income Earned by Various Age Groups

Age Group	1994	1999	2004
25–34	23%	24%	26%
35–44	22	25	28
45–54	22	21	19
55–64	19	17	15
Over 65	14	13	12

TABLE 12–2 Preferences in Travel Among Various Age Groups

Age Group Travel Interests	18–34	35–54	55+
I am more interested in excitement and stimulation than rest and relaxation.	67%	42%	38%
I prefer to go where I haven't been before.	62	58	48
I like adventurous travel.	62	45	32
I love foreign and exotic things.	41	25	21
Vacation is a time for self-indulgence, regardless of the cost.	31	16	14
I don't see the need for a travel agent.	67	63	52

TABLE 12–3 Basic Desire for Travel Among Various Age Groups

Age Group Attitude Toward Travel	18–34	35–54	55+
Travel is one of the most rewarding and enjoyable things one can do.	71%	69%	66%
I love the idea of travelling and do so at every opportunity.	66	59	48
I often feel the need to get away from everything.	56	55	33

- Corporate e-learners said that their top reason for dropping a course was lack of time. Many had trouble completing courses from their desktops because of frequent distractions caused by co-workers. Some said they could only access courses through the company's Intranet, so they couldn't finish their assignments from home.
- Besides lack of time, corporate e-learners cited the following as e-learning disadvantages: lack of management oversight; lack of motivation; problems with technology; lack of student support; individual learning preferences; poorly designed courses; substandard/inexperienced instructors.
- A recent study by GE Capital found that finishing a corporate online course was dependent on whether managers gave reinforcement on attendance, how important employees were made to feel, and whether employee progress in the course was tracked.
- Sun Microsystems found that interactivity can be a critical success factor for online courses. Company studies showed that only 25 percent of employees finish classes that are strictly self-paced. But 75 percent finish when given similar assignments and access to tutors through e-mail, phone, or threaded discussion.
- Too often companies dump courses on their employees and wonder why they don't finish them.
- Company managers must supervise e-learning just as they would any other important initiative.
- For online learning to work, companies must develop a culture that takes online learning just as seriously as classroom training.
- For many e-learners, studying at home is optimal. Whenever possible, companies should offer courses through the Internet or provide Intranet access at home. Having employees studying on their own time will more than cover any added costs.
- Corporate e-learning has flared into a $2.3 billion market, making it one of the fastest-growing segments of the education industry.
- Rather than fly trainers to 7000 dealerships, General Motors University now uses interactive satellite broadcasts to teach salespeople the best way to highlight features on the new Buick.
- Fast and cheap, e-training can shave companies' training costs while it saves employees travel time.
- Pharmaceutical companies such as Merck are conducting live, interactive classes over the Web, allowing sales reps to learn about the latest product information at home rather than fly them to a conference centre.
- McDonald's trainers can log into Hamburger University to learn such skills as how to assemble a made-to-order burger or properly place the drink on a tray.
- One obstacle to the spread of online corporate training is the mismatch between what employees really need—customized courses that are tailored to a firm's products and its unique corporate culture—and what employers can afford.
- Eighty percent of companies prefer developing their own online training courses in-house. But creating even one customized e-course can take months, involve armies of experts, and cost anywhere from $25 000 to $50 000.
- Thus, most companies either stick with classroom training or buy generic courses on such topics as how to give performance appraisals, understanding basic business ethics, and so on. Employers can choose from a wide selection of non-customized electronic courses.

For online learning to be effective, content must be broken into short "chunks" with lots of pop quizzes, online discussion groups, and other interactive features that let students demonstrate what they've learned. For instance, Circuit City's tutorial on digital camcorders consists of three 20-minute segments. Each contains audio demonstrations of how to handle customer product queries, tests on terminology, and "try-its" that propel trainees back onto the floor to practice what they've learned.

Your Task: Write a short (3–5 pages) memo report to the director of human resources, Kerry Simmons, presenting the advantages and disadvantages of e-learning and making a recommendation as to whether Paper Products, Inc., should invest time and money in training its employees this way. Be sure to organize your information so that it is clear, concise, and logically presented. Simmons likes to read the "bottom line" first, so be direct: Present your recommendation up front and support your recommendation with your findings.[5]

Short, Formal Reports Requiring Additional Research

3 Picking the better path: Research report assisting a client in a career choice You are employed by Open Options, a career-counselling firm, where your main function is to help clients make career choices. Today a client with the same name as yours (a truly curious coincidence!) came to your office and asked for help deciding between two careers, careers that you yourself had been interested in (an even greater coincidence!).

Your Task: Do some research on the two careers and then prepare a short report that your client can study. Your report should compare at least five major areas, such as salary, working conditions, and education required. Interview the client to understand her or his personal preferences regarding each of the five areas. For example, what is the minimum salary the client will accept? By comparing the client's preferences with the research material you collect, such as salary data, you will have a basis for concluding which of the two careers is best. The report should end with a career recommendation.

4 Selling overseas: Research report on the prospects for marketing a product in another country Select (a) a product and (b) a country. The product might be a novelty item that you own (an inexpensive but accurate watch or clock, a desk organizer, or a coin bank). The country should be one that you are not now familiar with. Imagine that you are with the international sales department of the company that manufactures and sells the novelty item and that you are proposing to make it available in the country you have selected.

The first step is to learn as much as possible about the country in which you plan to market the product. Check almanacs and encyclopedias for the most recent information, paying particular attention to descriptions of the social life of the inhabitants and their economic conditions. If your library carries the *Yearbook of International Trade Statistics, Monthly Bulletin of Statistics,* or *Trade Statistics* (all published by the United Nations), you may want to consult them. Check the card catalogue and recent periodical indexes for sources of additional information; look for (among other matters) cultural traditions that would encourage or discourage use of the product. If you have online access, check both Web sites and any relevant databases you can find.

Your Task: Write a short report that describes the product you plan to market abroad, briefly describes the country you have selected, indicates the types of people in this country who would find the product attractive, explains how the product would be transported into the country (or possibly manufactured there if materials and labour are available), recommends a location for a regional sales centre, and suggests how the product should be sold. Your report is to be submitted to the chief operating officer of the company, whose name you can either make up or find in a corporate directory. The report should include your conclusions (how the product will do in this new environment) and your recommendations for marketing (steps the company should take immediately and those it should develop later).

5 The new way to advertise: Report summarizing Internet demographics The number of Internet users continues to grow rapidly in North America and around the world. For marketers, the Internet represents a veritable gold mine of potential customers. Unlike traditional print and broadcast media, an Internet site can be seen around the world at any time. The trick is to get your target customers to take the time to visit your page.

As marketing strategist for a specialty foods mail-order company, you have been toying with the idea of going online for quite some time. Your company, Martha's Kitchen, has been selling its cakes, cheeses, fruit, and candy in printed catalogues for a little over a decade and has built up a loyal clientele. Most of your customers are affluent adults age 30 and over, and 75 percent of them are women. Large portions of your sales come during the holidays.

As more and more customers ask about ordering on the Internet, you feel compelled to establish an Internet presence. Nevertheless, you have heard conflicting reports about whether companies actually make any money by selling over the Internet. Moreover, developing a top-notch Web site will likely cost a lot of money. How can you sort through the hype to find real answers?

Your Task: Write a short formal report to the director of marketing explaining whether Martha's Kitchen should develop an Internet presence. You will need some solid figures about the demographics of Internet users, their surfing habits, the types of products they purchase online, and growth trends in online commerce. The following are good resources to help you get started.

- **www.emarketer.com/estats/welcome.html**
- **www.cyberatlas.internet.com**
- **www.ad-guide.com**

(Hint: Type "Canada" in the search box.)

These sites also contain links to other sites with additional useful information. As background, you may also find it helpful to look at some competitors' sites, such as Harry and David **www.harryanddavid.com** and Norm Thompson **www.normthompson.com**.

On the basis of your findings, how do you think an Internet site will improve the company's bottom line? Use your imagination to fill in the details about the company.

Long, Formal Reports Requiring No Additional Research

6 Customer service crisis: Report summarizing and explaining customer service problems You are the operations manager for Continental Security Systems (CSS), a mail-order supplier of home-security systems and components. Your customers are do-it-yourself homeowners who buy a wide range of motion sensors, automatic telephone dialers, glass breakage detectors, video cameras, and other devices.

The company's aggressive pricing has yielded spectacular growth in the last year, and everyone is scrambling to keep up with the orders arriving every day. Unfortunately, customer service has often taken a back seat to filling those orders. Your boss, the company's founder and president, knows that service is slipping, and she wants you to solve the problem. You started with some internal and external surveys to assess the situation. Some of the most significant findings from the research are presented in Tables 12–4, 12–5, and 12–6.

TABLE 12–4 Customer Complaints over the Last 12 Months

Type of Complaint	Number of Occurrences	Percentage of Total
Delays in responding	67	30%
Product malfunction	56	25
Missing parts	45	20
No answer when calling for help	32	14
Rude treatment	18	8
Overcharge	5	2

Note: Percentages don't add to 100 because of rounding.

Long, Formal Reports Requiring Additional Research

7 Is there any justice? Report critiquing legislation Plenty of people complain about their legislators, but few are specific about their complaints. Here's your chance.

Your Task: Write a long formal report about a law that you believe should not have been enacted or should be enacted. Be objective.

TABLE 12–5 Customer Perceptions And Opinions

Statement	Agree	Disagree
CSS offers a competitive level of customer service.	12%	88%
I recommended CSS to friends and colleagues.	4	96
I plan to continue buying from CSS.	15	85
I enjoy doing business with CSS.	9	91

TABLE 12–6 How Complaints Were Resolved

Resolution	Percentage
Employee receiving the phone call	20% solved the problem
Employee referred customer to manager	30
Customer eventually solved the problem by himself/herself	12
Unable to solve problem	23
Resolution unknown	15

Write the report using specific facts to support your beliefs. Reach conclusions and offer your recommendation at the end of the report. As a final step, send a copy of the report to an appropriate federal or provincial official or legislator.

8 Travel opportunities: Report comparing two destinations You are planning to take a two-week trip abroad sometime within the next year. Because there are a couple of destinations that appeal to you, you are going to have to do some research before you can make a decision.

Your Task: Prepare a lengthy comparative study of two countries that you would like to visit. Begin by making a list of important questions you will need to answer. Do you want a relaxing vacation or an educational experience? What types of services will you require? What will your transportation needs be? Where will you have the least difficulty with the language? Using resources in your library, the Internet, and perhaps travel agencies, analyze the suitability of these two destinations with respect to your own travel criteria. At the end of the report, recommend the better country to visit this year.

9 Doing business abroad: Report summarizing the social and business customs of a foreign country Your company would like to sell its products overseas. Before they begin negotiating on the international horizon, however, management must have a clear understanding of the social and business customs of the foreign countries where they intend to do business.

Your Task: Choose a non-English-speaking country, and write a long formal report summarizing the country's social and business customs. Review Chapter 3 and use that chapter's "Checklist: Doing Business Abroad" as a guide for the types of information you should include in your report.

Formal Proposals

10 Creative marketing: Proposal to sell educational/advertising materials to schools Reaching children poses significant challenges to marketers because children typically don't listen to the radio or read magazines or newspapers. They do watch television, but television ads can be expensive. However, marketers have a new opportunity to get their messages out to children, thanks to Jeff Lederman. His company, Planet Report, targets youngsters by placing ads where they are most likely to be noticed—in the classroom. The ads are part of teaching materials that Planet Report distributes free to schools. These materials usually take the form of posters displaying information about current events. Each month, the company sends teachers a new poster containing tidbits of current news items and facts about science, politics, and culture. Along with this information are attractive ads for Disney movies, YTV television programs, Vans sneakers, and other products that appeal to young consumers. Lederman and an employee create two versions of each poster, one aimed at high-school students and the other at elementary or middle-school students. Teachers who use the posters also receive prepared questions they can use to test the students on the information in the posters. Besides questions about the factual information on the posters, the tests contain questions about the ads. Planet Report also distributes bookmarks with ads printed on them that teachers can give out as prizes or awards.

At a time when schools are facing tough financial constraints, Planet Report's strategy can be a real win-win situation. "Teachers get something they can use and a marketing purpose is served," says Lederman. Many teachers like the posters because they encourage students to read and learn. As one teacher who uses the posters says, "Whatever we can get that encourages voluntary reading is a plus."

However, not everyone supports the idea. Critics say that ads don't belong in the classroom. They complain that the posters distract students from their studies and encourage a commercial culture. Moreover, including test questions on the commercial content of the posters may cause confusion about what is most important for students to learn. One fourth-grade teacher points out that his students rarely miss questions about the ads, but they are likely to forget some of the other information.

Your Task: Write a proposal that Jeff Lederman can use to convince school administrators to adopt Planet Report's posters in their schools. Provide details such as how the posters will benefit students. Keep in mind that not everyone supports the idea of advertising in schools, even if it is linked to effective learning materials. How will you address the concerns of your critics and convince your audience that your product is good for both students and schools?

11 Brewing up sales: Proposal to supply coffee to Peter's Doughnuts You are the president of Lighthouse Roasters, a small but growing coffee-roasting company. The company has made a name for itself by offering fresh, dark-roasted gourmet coffees. Unlike Starbuck's and other competitors, Lighthouse Roasters does not operate its own stores. Instead, it sells roasted gourmet coffee beans to retailers such as restaurants, bakeries, and latte carts. These retailers then use the Lighthouse beans to make their coffee beverages.

Lighthouse's total cost to produce a kilogram of roasted gourmet coffee is $5.50. The company wholesales its roasted gourmet beans for an average price of $9.00 per kilogram. Competitors who sell non-gourmet variety coffees typically charge about $6.00 per kilogram. However, the average price of a gourmet coffee beverage is $1.50, about 50¢ more than beverages made with regular coffee (including both brewed coffee and espresso drinks). Each pound of coffee yields about 40 beverages.

Peter's Doughnuts, which owns 76 doughnut shops in 6 provinces, has seen its sales decline in recent months after Starbucks began opening stores in Peter's markets. Starbucks not only sells gourmet coffee but also carries a selection of delicious pastries that offer alternatives to doughnuts. Peter's management figures that by offering gourmet coffee, it will win back customers who like doughnuts but who also want darker-roasted coffees. Peter's has invited you to submit a proposal to be its exclusive supplier of coffee. Peter's anticipates that it will need 200 kilograms of coffee a month during the colder months (October–March) and 150 kilograms during the warmer months (April–September). The company has said it wants to pay no more than $6.50 per kilogram for Lighthouse coffee.

Your Task: Using your imagination in devising the details, write a proposal describing your plan to supply the coffee. Considering your costs, will you meet Peter's pricing demands, or will you attempt to gain a higher price?

Going Online Exercises

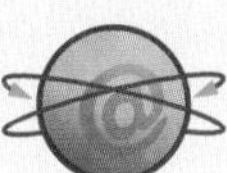

Research Reports and Learning by Example, found on page 384 of this chapter

One way to learn how to write more skillfully and effectively is by reading other writers' work. Look at different examples of professional business reports, and skim their contents to reinforce what you've learned in this chapter about structure, style, and organization. Let Ixquick Metasearch work for you.

1. What is the purpose of the report you read? Who is its target audience? Explain why the structure and style of the report make it easy or difficult to follow the main idea.
2. What type of report did you read? Briefly describe the main message. Is the information well organized? If you answer "yes," explain how you can use the report as a guide for a report you might write. If you answer "no," explain why the report is not helpful.
3. Drawing on what you know about the qualities of a good business report, review a report and describe what features contribute to its readability.

To link directly to this site, visit our Companion Website at **www.pearsoned.ca/thill** and look for the Chapter 12 resources.

1 Illustrate how planning presentations differs from planning written documents

2 Describe the five tasks that go into organizing presentations

3 Delineate the tasks involved in developing the opening, body, and close of your oral presentation

4 Explain why using visuals in an oral presentation is a good idea, and list six types of visuals commonly used with oral presentations

5 Identify six ways to make your text slides more effective and six ways to make your graphic slides more effective

6 Relate nine ways to overcome your anxiety and feel more confident

Giving Oral Presentations

ON THE JOB

Facing a Communication Dilemma

Canadian Soccer Association

www.canadasoccer.com

Scoring Goals and Sponsors

David Bedford's job requires getting the sponsors that keep kids and adults playing the sport they love—soccer. In 2002, total Canadian soccer registration reached 790 000, surpassing 2001 figures by almost 32 000, and more than 40 percent above 10 years earlier. Demographically, almost 40 percent of 2002 soccer players were female, and 87 percent were under the age of 18.

In 2003 the Canadian Soccer Association received less than 7 percent of its funding from Sport Canada, threatening the health of an organization whose mission is to promote "the growth and development of soccer for all Canadians at all levels." The remaining support must be obtained through the private sector, and it is the job of professionals such as David Bedford to help keep the sport going. As managing director of Soccer Canada Properties, a unit created by the CSA in partnership with IMG Canada, a sports management firm, Bedford and his team solicit and administer sponsorship for the CSA's amateur activities.

Research and planning play a critical part in finding a sponsor, and when a meeting is arranged, Bedford and his team deliver a presentation about the benefits of sponsoring the CSA. To deliver their presentations successfully, Bedford and his colleagues must focus their purpose, analyze their audience, and prepare supporting materials that will reinforce his information and engage their listeners. Because each audience is different, each presentation is tailored to the specific situation.

If you worked with David Bedford, how would you approach planning and developing presentations for the Canadian Soccer Association? How would you prepare your text and visual support? And how would you work on an effective delivery style and confident platform manner?[1]

The goal of the Canadian Soccer Association is to sustain and promote the game in Canada. To deliver their programs, the organization must seek private support. Oral presentations are a critical medium for persuading companies to sponsor CSA activities.

The Three-Step Oral Presentation Process

Chances are you'll have many opportunities to deliver oral presentations throughout your career. You may not speak before large audiences of employees or the media, but you'll certainly be expected to present ideas to your colleagues, make sales presentations to potential customers, or engage in other kinds of spoken communication. For instance, if you're in the human resources department, you may give orientation briefings to new employees or explain company policies, procedures, or benefits at assemblies. If you're a department supervisor, you may conduct training programs. Or, if you're a problem solver or consultant, you may give analytical presentations on the merits of various proposals.

Regardless of your job or the purpose of your presentation, you will be more effective if you adopt an oral presentation process that follows these three steps (see Figure 13–1):

1. Plan your presentation.
2. Write your presentation.
3. Complete your presentation.

The three-step oral presentation process is quite similar to the three-step writing process.

Step 1: Planning Oral Presentations

OBJECTIVE 1 Illustrate how planning presentations differs from planning written documents.

Planning oral presentations is much like planning any other business message. It requires analyzing your purpose and your audience, gathering necessary information, and adapting your message to the occasion and audience so that you can establish a good relationship. However, adjusting your technique to an oral communication channel presents both opportunities and challenges.

The major opportunity lies in the interaction that is possible between you and your audience. When you speak before a group, you can receive information as well as transmit it. Instead of simply expressing your ideas, you can draw ideas from your audience and then reach a mutually acceptable conclusion. You also have the opportunity to reinforce your message with nonverbal cues. Audiences receive much richer stimuli during a speech than while reading a written report.

1 Planning

Analyze: Study your purpose, lay out your schedule, and profile your audience.

Investigate: Gather needed information through formal or informal research methods.

Adapt: Adapt your presentation to the occasion and your audience, then establish a good relationship with your audience.

2 Writing

Organize: Define your main idea, limit the scope, choose your approach, prepare your outline, and decide on style.

Develop: Compose your speech, ensuring that the introduction, body, close, and question-and-answer period all accomplish the necessary tasks for an oral medium.

3 Completing

Revise: Edit content for conciseness and clarity.

Produce: Design effective visuals.

Proofread: Review all for typos and errors.

Deliver: Practice, check location, overcome anxiety, present visuals effectively, and field questions responsibly.

FIGURE 13–1 The Three-Step Oral Presentation Process

The major challenge of using an oral communication channel is being able to control what happens. The more you expect to interact with your audience, the less control you'll have. As you plan each part of your presentation, think about how you will deliver the information. Halfway through your presentation, a comment from someone in the audience might force you to shift topics, organization, or even style of delivery. Try to anticipate such shifts, so that you don't lose control by being caught off guard.

Planning presentations requires some special adjustments to the communication channel.

Because your presentation is a onetime event, your audience cannot leaf back through printed pages to review something you said earlier. To make sure that your audience will hear what you say and remember it, you must you must pay special attention to defining your purpose clearly and learning about your audience's needs.

Defining Your Purpose

The content and style of speeches and presentations vary, depending on your purpose.

You usually give a speech for one of four purposes.

The four basic purposes for giving a presentation are to inform, to persuade, to motivate, and to entertain. Many of your presentations or speeches will be informative, a straightforward statement of the facts. However, you can convey straightforward information in a memo or a report. Speaking in front of an audience is an interactive process, affording you tremendous opportunity to persuade your listeners.[2] Quite a few of your presentations will probably be persuasive, based on the organizational and writing techniques discussed in Chapter 9. Motivational speeches tend to be more specialized, so many companies bring in outside professional speakers to handle this type of presentation. Entertainment speeches are perhaps the rarest in the business world; they are usually limited to after-dinner speeches and to speeches at conventions or retreats. Here are sample statements of purpose for business speeches:

- To inform the accounting department of the new remote data-access policy
- To explain to the executive committee the financial ramifications of OmniGroup's takeover offer
- To persuade potential customers that our bank offers the best commercial banking services for their needs
- To motivate the sales force to increase product sales by 10 percent.

Regardless of your purpose, you will be more effective if you keep your audience interested in your message. To do so, you must understand who your audience members are and what they need.

Developing an Audience Profile

If you're involved in selecting the audience or speaking to a group of peers at work, you'll certainly have information about their characteristics. But in many cases, you'll be speaking to a group of people you know little about, so you'll want to investigate their needs and characteristics before showing up to speak. As Soccer Canada's David Bedford can tell you, analyzing your audience is a particularly important element of your preparation because you'll be gearing the style and content of your speech to your audience's needs and interests. Analyzing your audience is particularly important when addressing people from other cultures (see "Achieving Intercultural Communication—Five Tips for Making Presentations Around the World" on page 423). Be sure to review the discussion of audience analysis presented in Chapter 4.

You can ask your host or some other contact person for help with audience analysis, and you can supplement that information with some educated estimates of your own. For a reminder of how to analyze an audience, review Chapter 4's "Develop an Audience Profile." Also take a look at this chapter's "Checklist: Audience Analysis." For even more insight into audience evaluation (including emotional and cultural issues), consult a good public-speaking textbook.

Checklist: Audience Analysis

Determine Audience Size and Composition

✓ Estimate how many people will attend.

✓ Consider whether they have some political, religious, professional, or other affiliation in common.

✓ Analyze the mix of men and women, age ranges, socioeconomic and ethnic groups, occupations, and geographic regions represented.

Predict the Audience's Probable Reaction

✓ Analyze why audience members are attending the presentation.

✓ Determine the audience's general attitude toward the topic: interested, moderately interested, unconcerned, open-minded, or hostile.

✓ Analyze the mood that people will be in when you speak to them.

✓ Find out what kind of backup information will most impress the audience: technical data, historical information, financial data, demonstrations, samples, and so on.

✓ Consider whether the audience has any biases that might work against you.

✓ Anticipate possible objections or questions.

Gauge the Audience's Level of Understanding

✓ Analyze whether everybody has the same background and experience.

✓ Determine what the audience already knows about the subject.

✓ Decide what background information the audience will need to better understand the subject.

✓ Consider whether the audience is familiar with your vocabulary.

✓ Analyze what the audience expects from you.

✓ Think about the mix of general concepts and specific details you will need to present.

Step 2: Writing Oral Presentations

OBJECTIVE 2 Describe the five tasks that go into organizing presentations.

You may not ever actually write out a presentation word for word. But that doesn't mean that preparing your presentation will be any easier or quicker than preparing a written document. Speaking intelligently about a topic may actually involve more work and more time than writing about the same topic.

Organizing Your Presentation

Every facet of organizing your presentation is driven by what you know about your audience. For example, if you're organizing a sales presentation, focus on how much your product will benefit the people in your audience, not on how great the product is. If you're explaining a change in medical benefits for company employees, address the concerns your audience is likely to have, such as cost and quality of care. You should organize an oral message just as you would organize a written message, by focusing on your audience as you define your main idea, limit your scope, choose your approach, prepare your outline, and decide on the most effective style for your presentation.

DEFINE THE MAIN IDEA

The main idea points out how the audience can benefit from your message.

What is the one message you want your audience to walk away with? What do you want them to do after listening to you? Look for a one-sentence generalization that links your subject and purpose to your audience's frame of reference, much as an advertising slogan points out how a product can benefit consumers. Here are some examples:

Going Online

Speak with Flair

The Virtual Presentation Assistant offers abundant resources with related links. You can go to other public speaking sites that contain useful articles, reviews, or supplemental materials for planning presentations. You can also connect to popular media and library pages with worldwide research information. You'll find examples of speech types, suggestions for selecting and focusing your topic, tips on audience analysis, delivery, using visual aids, and various other guidelines to help you prepare and deliver an effective presentation. If you need inspiration, check out this site.

www.ukans.edu/cwis/units/coms2/vpa/vpa.htm

To link directly to this site, visit our Companion Website at **www.pearsoned.ca/thill** *and look for the Chapter 13 resources.*

- Convince department members that reorganizing the data-processing unit will imporve customer service and reduce employee turnover
- Convince board members that we should build a new plant in New Brunswick to eliminate manufacturing bottlenecks and improve production quality
- Address employee concerns about a new healthcare plan by showing how the plan will reduce their costs and improve the quality of their care

Each of these statements puts a particular slant on the subject, one that directly relates to the audience's interests. This sort of "you" attitude helps keep your audience's attention and convinces people that your points are relevant. For example, a group of new employees will be much more responsive to your discussion of plant safety procedures if you focus on how the procedures can save a life rather than on how the rules conform to occupational health and safety guidelines.

LIMIT YOUR SCOPE

You'll need to tailor your material to the time allowed, which is often strictly regulated. Use your outline to estimate how much time that your speech or presentation will take. The average speaker can deliver about 125 to 150 words a minute (or roughly 7500 to 9000 words an hour), which corresponds to 20 to 25 double-spaced, typed pages of text per hour. The average paragraph is about 125 to 150 words in length, so most of us can speak at a rate of about one paragraph per minute.

Say you want to make three basic points. In a ten-minute speech, you could take about two minutes to explain each point, using roughly two paragraphs for each. If you devoted a minute each to the introduction and the conclusion, you would have two minutes left over to interact with the audience. If you had an hour, however, you could spend the first five minutes introducing the presentation, establishing rapport with the audience, providing background information, and giving an overview of your topic. In the next thirty to forty minutes, you could explain each of the three points, spending about ten to thirteen minutes on each one (the equivalent of five or six typewritten pages). Your conclusion might take another three to five minutes. The remaining ten to twenty minutes would then be available for responding to questions and comments from the audience.

Which is better, the ten-minute speech or the hour-long presentation? If your speech doesn't have to fit into a specified time slot, the answer depends on your subject, your audience's attitude and knowledge, and the relationship you have with your audience. For a simple, easily accepted message, ten minutes may be enough. On the other hand, if your subject is complex or your audience is skeptical, you'll probably need more time. Don't squeeze a complex presentation into a period that is too brief, and don't spend any more time on a simple talk than necessary.

CHOOSE YOUR APPROACH

Structure a short presentation like a letter or a memo.

With a well-defined main idea to guide you, and a clear idea about the scope of your presentation, you can begin to arrange your message. If you have ten minutes or less to deliver your message, organize your speech much as you would a letter or a brief memo: use the direct approach if the subject involves routine information or good news, and use the indirect approach if the subject involves bad news or persuasion.

Longer presentations are organized like reports. If the purpose is to entertain, motivate, or inform, use direct order and a structure imposed naturally by the subject (importance, sequence, chronology, spatial orientation, geography, or category—as discussed in Chapter 11). If your purpose is to analyze, persuade, or collaborate, organize your material around conclusions and recommendations or around a logical argument. Use direct order if the audience is receptive and indirect if you expect resistance.

Organize longer presentations like formal reports.

You may have to adjust your organization in response to feedback from your audience, especially if your purpose is to collaborate. You can plan ahead by thinking of several organizational possibilities (based on "what if" assumptions about your audience's reactions). If someone says something that undercuts your planned approach, you can switch smoothly to another one.

Oral communication demands simplicity of organization. If listeners lose the thread of your comments, they'll have a hard time catching up and following the remainder of your message. They can't review a paragraph or flip pages back and forth, as they can when reading. So look for the most obvious and natural way to organize your ideas, using a direct order of presentation whenever possible.

Explain at the beginning how you've organized your material, and try to limit the number of main points to three or four—even when the presentation is rather long. Include only the most useful, interesting, and relevant supporting evidence. And at the end of each section, reorient the audience by summarizing the point you've just made and explaining how it fits into your overall framework.

PREPARE AN OUTLINE

A carefully prepared outline can be more than just the starting point for composing a speech or presentation—it will help you stay on task. You can use your outline to make sure your message accomplishes its purpose to help you keep your presentation both audience centred and within the allotted time. Prepare your outline in several stages:

- **State your purpose and main idea.** As you develop your outline, check frequently to be sure that the points, organization, connections, and title relate to your purpose and main idea.
- **Organize your major points and subpoints.** Express each major point as a single, complete sentence to help you keep track of the one specific idea you want to convey in that point. Then look at the order of points to make sure their arrangement is logical and effective.
- **Identify your opening, body, and close.** Start with the body, numbering each major point and subpoint according to its level in your outline. Then lay out the points for your opening (or introduction) and close (or conclusion). Be sure you begin your numbering system anew for each section—opening, body, and close.
- **Show your connections.** Write out in sentence form the transitions you plan to use to move from one part to the next. Remember to include additional transitions between major points in the body of your presentation. Don't number transitions; position each one on a separate line between the two sections and enclose it in parentheses.
- **Show your sources.** Prepare your bibliography, making sure that it is easy to read, follows a consistent format, and includes all the details to identify your various sources.
- **Choose a title.** Not all speeches need or have a title. However, a title can be useful if your speech will be publicized ahead of time or introduced by someone else.

Use a clear, direct organization to accommodate your listeners' limitations.

You'll use your outline for multiple tasks, including:
- Composing your presentation
- Staying on task
- Ensuring your presentation accomplishes its purpose
- Keeping your presentation audience-centered
- Keeping your presentation within the allowed time
- Serving as your final script

Figure 13-2 is an outline for a 30-minute analytical presentation. It is organized around conclusions and presented in direct order. This outline is based on Chapter 12's Electrovision report, written by Linda Moreno.

To sound as natural as possible, plan to deliver your presentation from notes rather than from written text, and use your outline as your final "script." When your outline will serve as your speaking notes, its purpose is merely to prompt your memory about what you plan to say and in what order. Therefore, you put much less detail into your speaking outline than you have in your planning outline (see Figure 13-3 on page 408.[3] To prepare an effective speaking outline, follow these steps:[4]

- **Follow the planning outline.** Follow the same format as you used for your planning outline (so that you can see at a glance where you are in your speech and how each part and point relates to the one before and after). However, strip away anything you don't plan to say to your audience (statements of general purpose, specific purpose, main idea, bibliography, etc.)

When you use your outline as speaking notes, you'll make some special alterations.

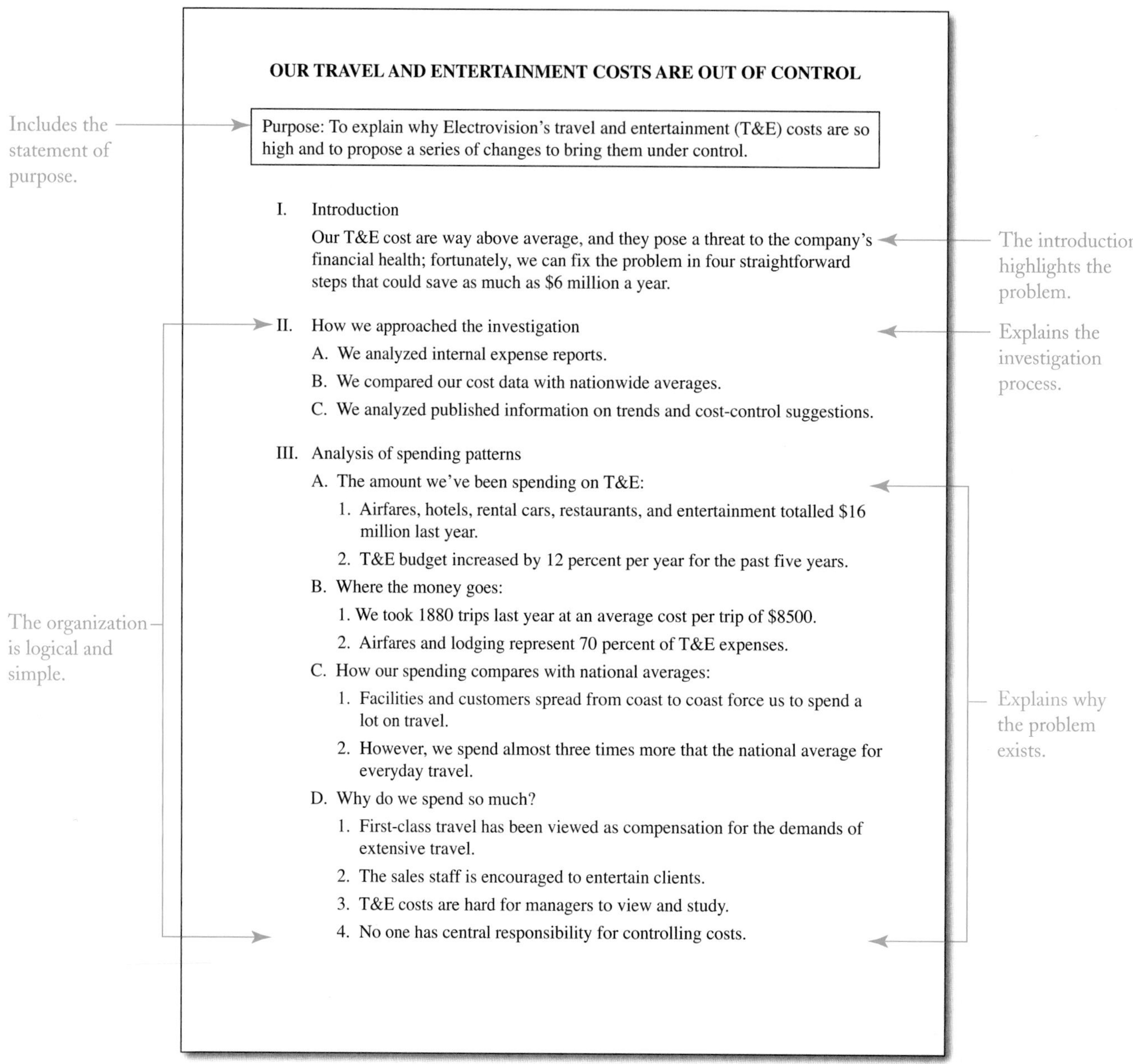
OUR TRAVEL AND ENTERTAINMENT COSTS ARE OUT OF CONTROL

Purpose: To explain why Electrovision's travel and entertainment (T&E) costs are so high and to propose a series of changes to bring them under control.

I. Introduction

Our T&E cost are way above average, and they pose a threat to the company's financial health; fortunately, we can fix the problem in four straightforward steps that could save as much as $6 million a year.

II. How we approached the investigation

A. We analyzed internal expense reports.

B. We compared our cost data with nationwide averages.

C. We analyzed published information on trends and cost-control suggestions.

III. Analysis of spending patterns

A. The amount we've been spending on T&E:

1. Airfares, hotels, rental cars, restaurants, and entertainment totalled $16 million last year.
2. T&E budget increased by 12 percent per year for the past five years.

B. Where the money goes:

1. We took 1880 trips last year at an average cost per trip of $8500.
2. Airfares and lodging represent 70 percent of T&E expenses.

C. How our spending compares with national averages:

1. Facilities and customers spread from coast to coast force us to spend a lot on travel.
2. However, we spend almost three times more that the national average for everyday travel.

D. Why do we spend so much?

1. First-class travel has been viewed as compensation for the demands of extensive travel.
2. The sales staff is encouraged to entertain clients.
3. T&E costs are hard for managers to view and study.
4. No one has central responsibility for controlling costs.

Includes the statement of purpose.
The introduction highlights the problem.
Explains the investigation process.
The organization is logical and simple.
Explains why the problem exists.

FIGURE 13–2 In-Depth Critique: Effective Outline for a 30-Minute Presentation (continued)

- **Condense points and transitions to keywords.** Choose words that will prompt you to remember what each point is about so that you can speak fluently. However, write out statistics, quotations, and other specifics so that you don't stumble over them. You may also want to write complete sentences for transitions that connect main points or for critical points in your opening or your close. Aim for the shortest outline you can comfortably use.
- **Add delivery cues.** During rehearsals, note the places in your outline where you plan to enhance your meaning by pausing, speaking more slowly, using visual aids, and so on. You might use coloured ink to highlight your cues. But avoid cluttering your outline; just show the most important cues.
- **Arrange your notes.** Whether you handprint or type your speaking outline on paper or note cards, make sure your final version is legible and accessible so that you can refer to it as you speak. Number your cards (or sheets of paper) so that you can keep them in order.

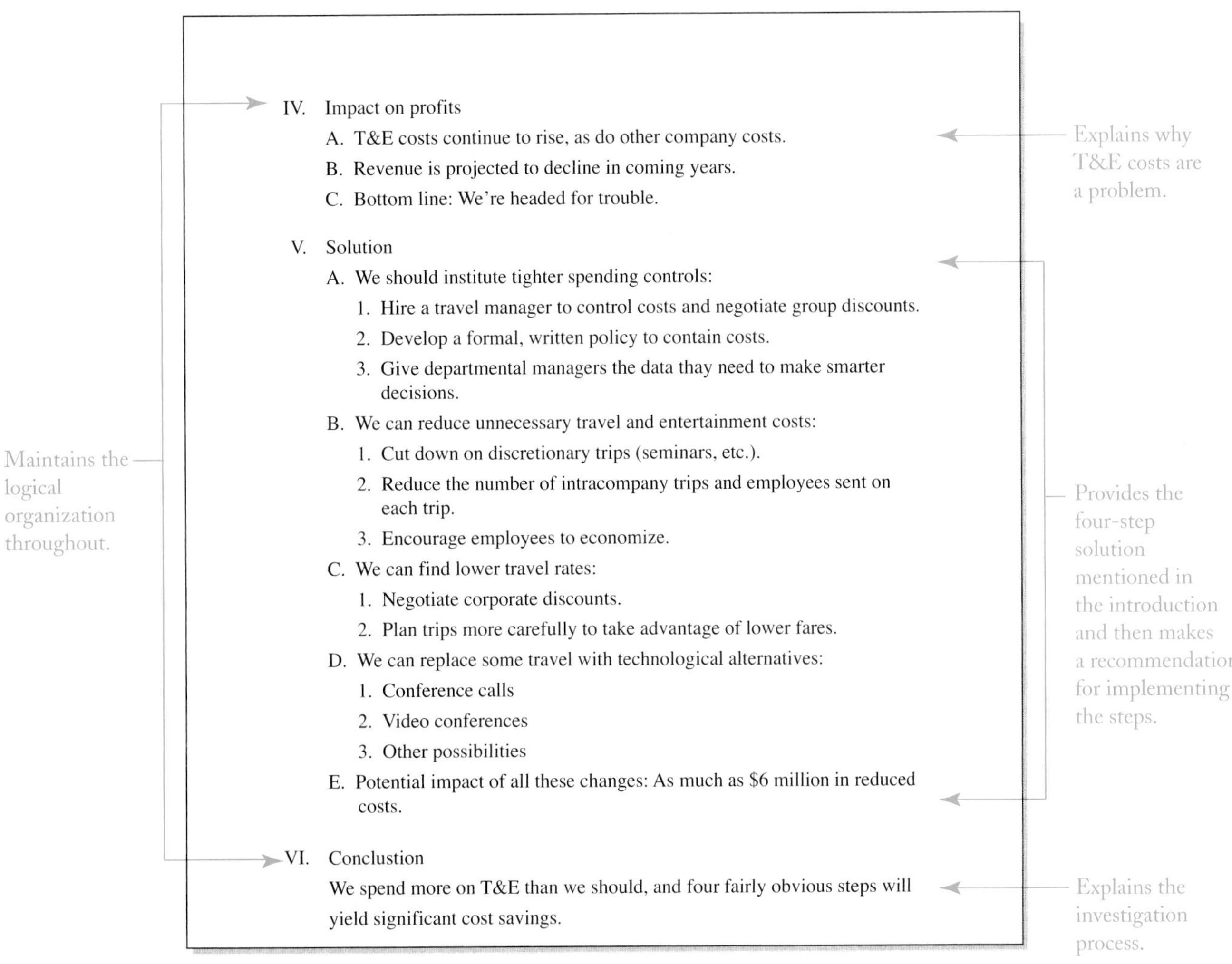
IV. Impact on profits
A. T&E costs continue to rise, as do other company costs.
B. Revenue is projected to decline in coming years.
C. Bottom line: We're headed for trouble.
V. Solution
A. We should institute tighter spending controls:
1. Hire a travel manager to control costs and negotiate group discounts.
2. Develop a formal, written policy to contain costs.
3. Give departmental managers the data thay need to make smarter decisions.
B. We can reduce unnecessary travel and entertainment costs:
1. Cut down on discretionary trips (seminars, etc.).
2. Reduce the number of intracompany trips and employees sent on each trip.
3. Encourage employees to economize.
C. We can find lower travel rates:
1. Negotiate corporate discounts.
2. Plan trips more carefully to take advantage of lower fares.
D. We can replace some travel with technological alternatives:
1. Conference calls
2. Video conferences
3. Other possibilities
E. Potential impact of all these changes: As much as $6 million in reduced costs.
VI. Conclusion
We spend more on T&E than we should, and four fairly obvious steps will yield significant cost savings.
Maintains the logical organization throughout.
Explains why T&E costs are a problem.
Provides the four-step solution mentioned in the introduction and then makes a recommendation for implementing the steps.
Explains the investigation process.

FIGURE 13–2 (Continued)

DECIDE ON AN APPROPRIATE STYLE

Another important element in your preparation is style. Will you present a formal speech in an impressive setting, with professionally produced visual aids? Or will you lead a casual, roll-up-your-sleeves working session? Choose your style to fit the occasion. Your audience's size, your subject, your purpose, your budget, and the time available for preparation all influence your style.

Use a casual style for small groups; use a formal style for large groups and important events.

If you're speaking to a relatively small group, you can use a casual style that encourages audience participation. A small conference room, with your audience seated around a table, may be appropriate. Use simple visual aids, and invite your audience to interject comments. Deliver your remarks in a conversational tone, using notes to jog your memory if necessary.

If you're addressing a large audience and the event is an important one, you'll want to establish a more formal atmosphere. A formal style is well suited to announcements about mergers or acquisitions, new products, financial results, and other business milestones. During formal presentations, speakers are often located on a stage or platform, standing behind a lectern and are often accompanied by slides and other visual aids showcasing major products, technological breakthroughs, and other information that the speakers want audience members to remember.

Whether you're delivering a formal or an informal presentation, never try to impress your audience with obscure or unfamiliar vocabulary. Make sure you can define all the words you use. And keep things simple. If you repeatedly stumble over a word as you rehearse, use a different one.[5]

In both formal and informal presentations, keep things simple.

Developing the Opening of Your Presentation

OBJECTIVE 3 Delineate the tasks involved in developing the opening, body, and close of your oral presentation.

A good opening arouses the audience's interest in your topic, establishes your credibility, and prepares the audience by previewing what will follow. That's a lot to pack in the first few minutes of your presentation. Of the total time you allocate to writing your oral presentation, plan on spending a disproportionate amount on developing your opening.

The opening must capture attention, inspire confidence, and preview the contents.

AROUSING AUDIENCE INTEREST

To capture attention, connect your topic to your listeners' needs and interests.

Some subjects are naturally more interesting than others. If you will be discussing a matter of profound significance that will personally affect the members of your audience, chances are they'll listen regardless of how you begin. All you really have to do is announce your topic ("Today I'm announcing the reorganization of the information systems department").

Other subjects call for more imagination. How do you get people to listen if you're explaining the pension program to a group of new clerical employees, none of whom will be full participants for another five years and most of whom will probably leave the company within two? The best approach to dealing with an uninterested audience is to appeal to human nature and encourage people to take the subject personally. Show them how they'll be affected as individuals. For example, you might begin addressing the new clerical employees like this:

> If somebody offered to give you $200 000 in exchange for $5 per week, would you be interested? That's the amount you can expect to collect during your retirement years if you choose to contribute to the voluntary pension plan. During the next two weeks, you will have to decide whether you want to participate. Although retirement is many years away for most of you, it is an important financial decision. During the next 20 minutes, I hope to give you the information you need to make that decision intelligently.

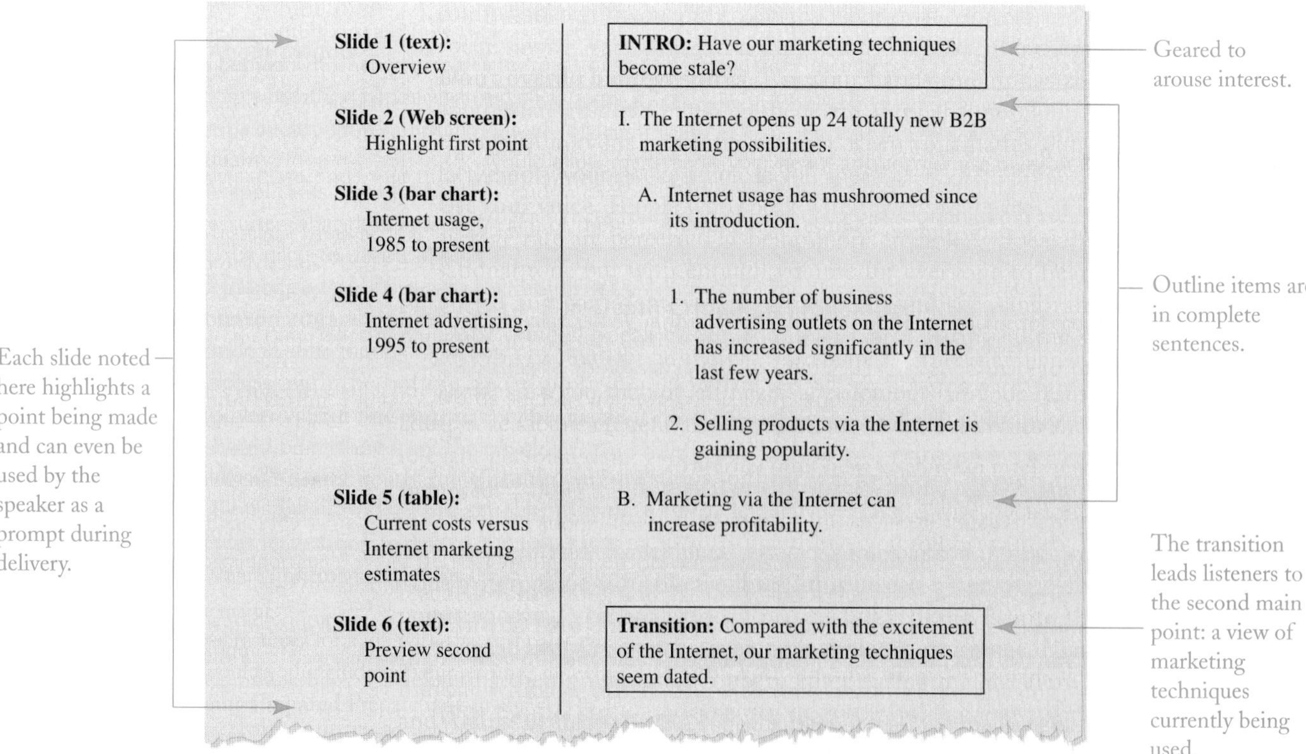

FIGURE 13-3 In-Depth Critique: Excerpt from Sample Outline with Delivery Notes

Another way to arouse audience interest is to draw out ideas and encourage comments from listeners throughout your presentation. Of course, this technique works better with a small group of co-workers than it does when you're addressing a large audience—particularly if the members of that large audience are hostile or unknown to you. During a presentation to a large group or a speech that covers controversial material, responding to questions and comments can interrupt the flow of information, weaken your argument, and reduce your control of the situation. In such situations, it's best to ask people to hold their questions until after you have concluded your remarks. Just be sure to allow ample time for audience questions at the end of your presentation, as this chapter discusses later.

Some speakers grab attention by drawing comments from audience members.

Table 13–1 suggests several techniques you can use to arouse audience interest and keep listeners involved. Regardless of which technique you choose, always make sure that the opening matches the tone of your presentation. If the occasion is supposed to be fun, you may begin with something light; but if you're talking business to a group of executives, don't waste their time with cute openings. Avoid jokes and personal anecdotes when you're discussing a serious problem. If you're giving a routine oral report, don't be overly dramatic. Most of all, be natural. Nothing turns off the average audience faster than a trite, staged beginning.

Match the introduction to the tone of your speech or presentation.

Although many techniques will arouse audience interest, avoid staged beginnings.

BUILDING YOUR CREDIBILITY

You want your audience to like you as a person and respect your opinion. Use your opening to establish your credentials—and quickly; people will decide within a few minutes whether you're worth listening to.[6] But to establish this sort of credibility, you need to lay the groundwork while you're developing your speech. Achieving credibility with a familiar, open-minded audience is relatively easy. The difficulty comes when you try to earn the confidence of strangers, especially those predisposed to be skeptical or antagonistic.

You have only a few minutes to establish your credibility.

One way to build credibility is to let someone else introduce you. That person can present your credentials so that you won't appear boastful. Just make sure that the person introducing you doesn't exaggerate your qualifications. If you're introducing yourself, plan to keep your comments simple, but don't be afraid to mention your accomplishments. Your listeners will be curious about your qualifications, so tell them briefly who you are and why you're there. You need mention only a few aspects of your background: your position in an organization, your profession, and the name of your company. You might plan to say something like this:

To build credibility, you can let someone else introduce you or you can introduce yourself—explaining (without boasting) why you are qualified to speak on the subject.

TABLE 13–1 Five Ways to Get Atention and Keep It

Use humour	Even though the subjects of most business presentations are serious, including a light comment now and then can perk up the audience. Just be sure the humour is relevant to the presentation and not offensive to the audience.
Tell a story	Slice-of-life stories are naturally interesting and can be compelling. Be sure your story illustrates an important point.
Pass around a sample	Psychologists say that you can get people to remember your points by appealing to their senses. The best way to do so is to pass around a sample. If your company is in the textile business, let the audience handle some of your fabrics. If you sell chocolates, give everybody a taste.
Ask a question	Asking questions will get the audience actively involved in your presentation and, at the same time, will give you information about them and their needs.
State a startling statistic	People love details. If you can inject an interesting statistic, you can often wake up your audience.

> I'm Karen Whitney, a market research analyst with Information Resources Corporation. For the past five years, I've specialized in studying high technology markets. Your director of engineering, Jean LaBarre, has asked me to brief you on recent trends in computer-aided design so that you'll have a better idea of how to direct your research efforts.

This speaker established credibility by tying her credentials to the purpose of her presentation. By mentioning her company's name, her specialization and position, and the name of the audience's boss, she let her listeners know immediately that she was qualified to tell them something they needed to know. She connected her background to their concerns.

PREVIEWING YOUR PRESENTATION

Let the audience know what lies ahead.

Giving your audience a preview of what's ahead adds to your authority and, more important, helps them understand your message. A reader can get an idea of the structure of a report by looking at the table of contents and scanning the headings. In an oral presentation, however, the speaker provides that framework. Without cues from the speaker, the audience may be unable to figure out how the main points of the message fit together.

Your preview should summarize your main idea, identify the supporting points, and indicate the order in which you will develop those points. Tell your listeners in so many words, "This is the subject, and these are the points I will cover." Once you've established the framework, you can be confident that the audience will understand how the individual facts and figures are related to your main idea as you move into the body of your presentation.

Developing the Body of Your Presentation

Limit the body to three or four main points.

The bulk of your speech or presentation is devoted to a discussion of the three or four main points in your outline. Use the same organizational patterns you'd use in a letter, memo, or report, but keep things simple. Your goals are to make sure that (1) the organization of your speech or presentation is clear and (2) your speech keeps your audience's attention.

CONNECTING YOUR IDEAS

Help your audience follow your presentation by using clear transitions between sentences and paragraphs, as well as between major sections.

To show how ideas are related, a written report uses typographical and formatting clues: headings, paragraph indentions, white space, and lists. However, an oral presentation relies on words to link various parts and ideas.

For the small links between sentences and paragraphs, use one or two transitional words: *therefore, because, in addition, in contrast, moreover, for example, consequently, nevertheless,* or *finally.* To link major sections of the speech or presentation, use complete sentences or paragraphs, such as "Now that we've reviewed the problem, let's take a look at some solutions." Every time you shift topics, be sure to stress the connection between ideas. Summarize what's been said, and then preview what's to come.

Emphasize your transitions by repeating key ideas, using gestures, changing your tone of voice, or introducing a visual aid.

The longer your presentation, the more important transitions become. If you will be presenting many ideas, audience members may have trouble absorbing them and seeing the relationship among them. Your listeners need clear tran-

Mark Swartz is a career consultant, speaker, and author of *Get Wired, You're Hired*, a guide to using the Internet for job searches. He stresses that effective speakers take into account the needs of the audience, stick to the agenda and time limits, and maintain a platform manner and speaking style that helps the audience understand and retain the message.

sitions to guide them to the most important points. Furthermore, they need transitions to pick up any ideas they may have missed. By repeating key ideas in your transitions, you can compensate for lapses in your audience's attention. When you actually deliver your presentation, you might also want to call attention to the transitions by using gestures, changing your tone of voice, or introducing a visual aid.

HOLDING YOUR AUDIENCE'S ATTENTION

Make a special effort to capture wandering attention.

To communicate your points effectively, you must do more than connect your ideas with clear transitions. You also have to hold your audience's attention. Here are a few helpful tips for developing memorable presentations:

- **Relate your subject to the audience's needs.** People are interested in things that affect them personally. Plan to present every point in light of the audience's needs and values.
- **Anticipate your audience's questions.** Prepare for as many questions as you can think of and address them in the body of your presentation. Also prepare and reserve additional material to use during the question-and-answer period, should the audience ask for greater detail.
- **Use clear, vivid language.** People become bored quickly when they don't understand the speaker. If your presentation will involve abstract ideas, plan to show how those abstractions connect with everyday life. Use familiar words, short sentences, and concrete examples.
- **Explain the relationship between your subject and familiar ideas.** Plan to show how your subject is related to ideas that audience members already understand so that you give people a way to categorize and remember your points.[7]

Many effective speakers involve audience members by asking for opinions or pausing occasionally for questions or comments. Audience feedback helps you determine whether your listeners understand a key point before you launch into another section. Feedback also gives your audience a chance to switch for a time from listening to participating. Plan your pauses, even going so far as to note them in your outline so that you won't forget to pause once you're on stage.

Developing the Close of Your Presentation

The close should leave a strong and lasting impression.

The close of a presentation is almost as important as the beginning, because audience attention peaks at this point. Plan to devote about 10 percent of your total time for the ending. Tell listeners that you're about to finish so that they'll make one final effort to listen intently. Don't be afraid to sound obvious; consider saying something like "in conclusion" or "to sum it all up." You want people to know that this is the home stretch. In your close, you need to accomplish three important tasks: review the points you've made, make sure everyone knows what to do next, and leave listeners with a statement that will help them remember the subject of your talk.

RESTATING YOUR MAIN POINTS

Summarize the main idea and restate the main points.

Once you've decided how to announce your close, plan on repeating your main idea. Be sure to emphasize what you want your audience to do or think, and state the key motivating factor. Finally, reinforce your theme by repeating the three or four main supporting points. A few sentences are generally enough to refresh people's memories.

DESCRIBING THE NEXT STEPS

Be certain that everyone agrees on the outcome and understands what should happen next.

Some presentations require the audience to reach a decision or to agree to take specific action. In such cases, the close provides a clear wrap-up. If the audience agrees on an issue covered in the presentation, plan to review the consensus in a sentence or two. If they don't agree, make the lack of consensus clear by saying something such as, "We seem to have some fundamental disagreement on this question." Then you'll be ready to suggest a method of resolving the differences.

If you expect any action to occur as a result of your presentation, you must explain who is responsible for doing what. One effective technique is to list the action items, with an estimated completion date and the name of the person responsible. You can present this list in a visual aid, and ask each person on the list to agree to accomplish his or her assigned task by the target date. This public commitment to action is the best insurance that something will happen. If the required action is likely to be difficult, make sure that everyone understands the problems involved. You don't want people to leave the presentation thinking their tasks will be easy, only to discover later that the jobs are quite demanding. You'll want everyone to have a realistic attitude and to be prepared to handle whatever arises.

ENDING ON A POSITIVE NOTE

Your audience will be more likely to remember your final words if those words are enthusiastic and upbeat.

Make sure that your final remarks are encouraging and memorable. After summarizing the key points of your presentation, conclude with a quote, a call to action, or some encouraging words. You might stress the benefits of action or express confidence in your listeners' ability to accomplish the work ahead. An alternative is to end with a question or a statement that will leave your audience thinking.

One speaker ended a presentation on the company's executive compensation program by repeating his four specific recommendations and then concluding with a memorable statement that would motivate his audience to take action:

> We can all be proud of the way our company has grown. If we want to continue that growth, however, we will have to adjust our executive compensation program to reflect competitive practices. If we don't, our best people will look for opportunities elsewhere.
>
> In summary, our survey has shown that we need to do four things to improve executive compensation:
>
> - Increase the overall level of compensation
> - Install a cash bonus program
> - Offer a variety of stock-based incentives
> - Improve our health insurance and pension benefits
>
> By making these improvements, we can help our company cross the threshold of growth into the major leagues.

Remember that your final words round out the presentation. Your task is to leave the audience with a satisfied feeling, a feeling of completeness. The close is not the place to introduce new ideas or to alter the mood of the presentation. Even if parts of your presentation are downbeat, you want to close on a positive note. Avoid using a staged finale—keep it natural. As with everything else in your speech, plan your closing remarks carefully. You don't want to wind up on stage with nothing to say but, "Well, I guess that's it."

OBJECTIVE 4 Explain why using visuals in an oral presentation is a good idea, and list six types of visuals commonly used with oral presentations.

Using Visual Aids in Oral Presentations

The ability to create and deliver an effective presentation is a vital skill in today's workplace. Good content and a smooth delivery are not enough. As David Bedford and his colleagues know, audiences will also expect you to use visual aids in your oral presentations.

Visual aids can improve the quality and impact of your oral presentation by creating interest, illustrating points that are difficult to explain in words alone, adding variety, and increasing the audience's ability to absorb and remember information. Studies of behavioural research have shown that visual aids can improve learning by up to 400 percent because humans can process visuals 60 000 times faster than text.[8]

Visual aids help the audience remember important points.

As a speaker, you'll find that visual aids can help you remember the details of your message (no small feat in a lengthy presentation). They can also improve your professional image, since speakers who use visuals generally appear to be better prepared and more knowledgeable than speakers who do not do. To enhance oral presentations, today's speakers can select from a variety of visual aids:

Effective speakers can choose from a variety of visual aids.

- **Overhead transparencies.** For decades, transparencies have been the standard visual aid. An **overhead transparency** is a piece of clear plastic with text or some other image on it. You show a transparency by placing it on an overhead projector that reflects the image or text onto a screen. You can create transparencies by using word-processing or electronic-slide-presentation software, and you can even prepare them by hand. Because their content and design elements are similar to electronic slides, we sometimes refer to transparencies as slides for purposes of this chapter.

Overheads transparencies and electronic presentations are the most popular types of visual aids.

- **Electronic presentations.** In most business situations today, the visual aid of choice is the **electronic presentation** or *slide show.* It consists of **electronic slides** that you can create using software such as Microsoft PowerPoint, Lotus Freelance Graphics, or CorelDraw. These slides can incorporate photos, sound, video, graphics, and animation to capture and engage your audience like no other visual. Special projection equipment grabs images from your computer monitor and displays them on the same screen used for viewing transparencies. You can create, display, and modify your electronic slides as your speech unfolds.[9]
- **35-millimeter slides.** The content of 35-millimetre slides may be text, graphics, or pictures. If you're trying to create a polished, professional atmosphere, you might find this approach worthwhile, particularly if you'll be addressing a crowd and don't mind speaking in a darkened room. If you choose this visual aid, you will need to coordinate your slides with your speech and appoint someone to operate the projector.
- **Chalkboards and whiteboards.** Because content for chalkboards and whiteboards is produced on the spot, they offer flexibility. They are effective tools for recording points made during small-group brainstorming sessions; however, they're too informal for some situations.
- **Flip charts.** Large sheets of paper attached at the top like a tablet can be propped on an easel so that you can flip the pages as you speak, with each chart illustrating or clarifying a point. You might have a few lines from your outline on one, a graph or diagram on another, and so on. By using felt-tip markers of various colors, you can also record ideas generated during a discussion.
- **Other visual aids.** A sample of a product or material allows an audience to experience your subject directly. Models built to scale conveniently represent an object. Audiotapes may be used to supplement a slide show or to present a precisely worded and timed message. Movies and filmstrips can capture audience attention with colour and movement. Television and videotapes are good for showing demonstrations, interviews, and other events. Plus, film strips, movies, television, and videos can be used as stand-alone vehicles (independent of a speaker) to communicate with dispersed audiences at various times.

Because the two most popular types of visual aids are overhead transparencies and electronic presentations, we will focus on them in the remainder of this section. Even though these two visual aids differ in the features they offer and in the way they are delivered, both consist of a collection of slides that must be well written and well designed to be effective. Once the slides are created, they are either printed on clear plastic sheets (acetates) for overhead transparencies or stored electronically and further embellished with multimedia effects for electronic presentations.

CHOOSING OVERHEAD TRANSPARENCIES OR ELECTRONIC PRESENTATIONS

Both overhead transparencies and electronic slides have advantages and disadvantages. Many businesspeople prefer to use overhead transparencies, because they are inexpensive, easy to create, and simple to use. You can prepare high-quality overheads

Simplicity, availability, and affordability are key advantages of overhead transparencies.

using a computer and a high-resolution colour inkjet or laser printer. Moreover, they require little extra equipment to show: Most conference rooms or classrooms have overhead projectors and a table large enough to stack transparencies. And, because transparency images can be projected in full daylight, speakers can maintain eye contact with the audience. They can also use special markers to write on transparencies as they present information.

Overhead transparencies are fragile, difficult to modify, and clumsy to use.

Despite these advantages, transparencies have a number of drawbacks. First, because they are in a permanent printed format, they must be replaced if their content changes. You cannot erase or change a word, colour, or graph on a transparency as you can on an electronic slide. Second, each time you add or remove a transparency from a sequence, you must manually renumber the batch. Third, transparencies are fragile: They chip, flake, scratch, and tear easily. You can protect transparencies with cardboard or plastic frames or with transparent sleeves, but these protectors are costly and are bulky to store or transport. Fourth, overhead projectors can be noisy and a challenge to talk over. Finally, transparencies must be aligned carefully on the overhead projector (one at a time). This requirement limits the presenter's ability to move freely about the room.

Electronic slides offer more features and benefits than overhead transparencies.

Electronic presentations are another story. Their biggest advantage is their computerized format, which makes real-time manipulation of data easy. You can change a graphic, add a bulleted phrase, and even alter the sequence of your slides with a simple click of the mouse. You can add animation, video clips, sound, hypertext, and other multimedia effects to slides—turning them into dazzling professional presentations. You can even preprogram and automate the release of text and graphical elements. Furthermore, electronic presentations are easy to store, transport, and customize for different audiences.

Another advantage of electronic presentations is the slide sorter view, which lets you see a file's entire batch of slides at once (see Figure 13–4 below). This view makes it relatively easy to add and delete slides, reposition them, and check them for design consistency. You can also use this view to preview animation and transition effects and experiment with design elements.

Electronic presentations require expensive, complicated equipment, which can tempt presenters to pay too much attention to technical components and special effects.

However, electronic presentations have disadvantages, too. First, electronic slides require more expensive display equipment than overhead transparencies—especially if you are presenting to large audiences. This equipment can be complicated to use and may not be available in all situations. Second, most people spend too much time focusing on the technical components of an electronic presentation—they pay more attention to the animation and special effects of their slide shows than they do to the content of their message. Third, inexperienced presenters tend to pack too many special effects into their electronic slides, creating a visual feast of pictures and graphics that dazzle the audience but blur the key message.

Electronic equipment can fail, so be sure to have a backup plan.

Electronic presentations can and often do go awry. When planning an electronic presentation, ensure success even in the face of equipment failure by following these tips:[10]

- **Set up in advance.** Schedule plenty of time to set up and test your equipment before your speech. You don't want to troubleshoot hardware glitches in front of your audience.
- **Bring two of everything.** Borrow backup laptop computers, display panels or projectors, modems, or any other hardware you plan to use.
- **Back up your programs.** Save a copy of your show on a floppy disk, Zip drive, CD, or other storage medium so that you'll have it if you need it.
- **Have backup technical support available.** Line up an expert who you can call if something doesn't work.
- **Avoid real-time use of the Internet.** When using the Internet during a presentation, you may encounter slow phone connections, downed Web sites, and general frustration. You can save the sites you want on your hard drive and then access them offline. (Consult your browser's help menu.)

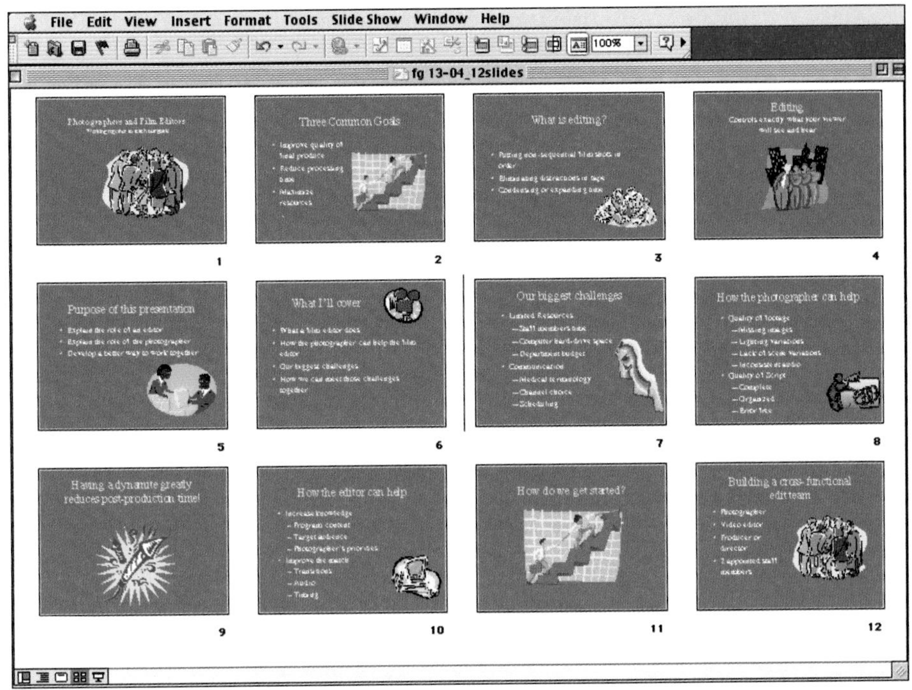

Examining thumbnails of slides on one screen is the best way to check the overall design of your final product. Note how each slide in this group looks uncluttered (not overburdened with text) and uses consistent colours and design elements.

FIGURE 13-4 Slide Sorter View

- **Have a contingency plan.** Take along copies of key exhibits prepared as handouts or overhead transparencies. These back-ups may be less glamorous, but if your electronic equipment fails, they are certainly better than nothing.

CREATING EFFECTIVE SLIDES FOR ORAL PRESENTATIONS

OBJECTIVE 5 **Identify six ways to make your text slides more effective and six ways to make your graphic slides more effective.**

Too many people design their slides before preparing the slides' content. Although design is an important element, it is secondary to a well-organized, well-developed, audience-centred message. Plan what each slide is going to say and organize the content, as you would for any written message. Then write and polish the written content before focusing on the slide's design elements. Your primary focus when creating text or graphic slides is to create content that is simple and readable: select design elements that enhance your message without overshadowing it, keep your design selections consistent, and use special effects selectively.

Plan slide content before making design decisions.

Creating Simple, Readable Content Text visuals (frequently called "bullet charts") help the audience follow the flow of ideas. They are simplified outlines of your presentation that summarize and preview your message or that signal major shifts in thought. Don't overload them with too much information. Keep your messages short and simple. When writing text slides, do the following:

Text slides are most effective when they are simple.

- Limit each slide to one thought, concept, or idea.
- Limit the content to about 40 words—with no more than 6 lines of text containing about 6 or 7 words per line.
- Write short bulleted phrases rather than long sentences or paragraph-length blocks of text.
- Phrase list items in grammatical form and use telegraphic wording ("Profits Soar," for example) without being cryptic ("Profits").

- Make your slides easy to read by using the active voice.
- Include short informative titles.

Figure 13–4 on page 415 is a good example of text slides that have been revised according to these principles to make their content more readable.

Graphic visuals can be an effective way to clarify a concept, show a process, or highlight important information (see Figure 13–6 below). In addition to increasing audience interest and retention, they can help the audience absorb information in a short time. Chapter 11 discusses how to create effective graphics such as charts, diagrams, maps, drawings, and tables for written documents. When using such graphics in oral presentations, your first task is to simplify them. Create effective graphic visuals by following these guidelines:

Graphics used in oral presentations should be simplified versions of those used in written reports.

- **Reduce the detail.** Eliminate anything that is not absolutely essential to the message. Show only key numbers on a chart. If people need to see only trends, then show only the trend line and not the numbers. If necessary, break information into more than one graphic illustration.
- **Avoid repeating text.** Don't repeat the same word five times. Minimize repetition by including the word in a title, subtitle, label, or legend.

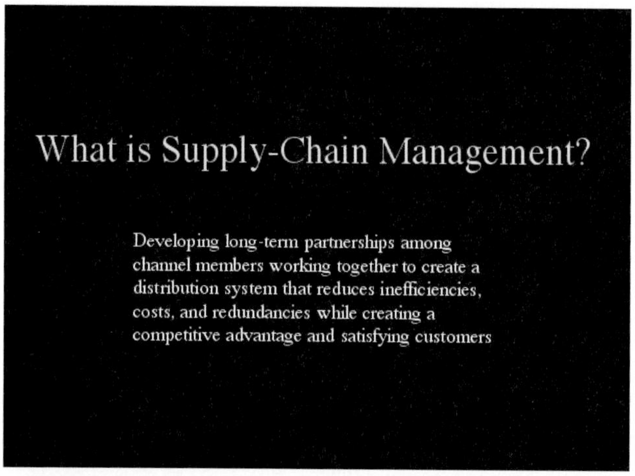

What is Supply-Chain Management?

Developing long-term partnerships among channel members working together to create a distribution system that reduces inefficiencies, costs, and redundancies while creating a competitive advantage and satisfying customers

FIGURE 13-5A Inappropriate paragraph style

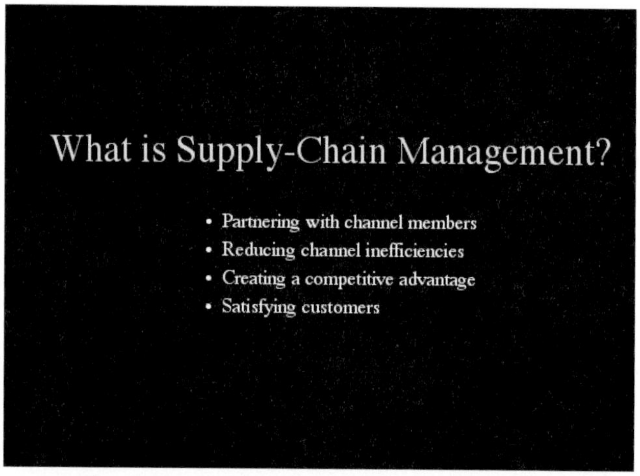

What is Supply-Chain Management?

- Partnering with channel members
- Reducing channel inefficiencies
- Creating a competitive advantage
- Satisfying customers

FIGURE 13-5B Appropriate bulleted phrases

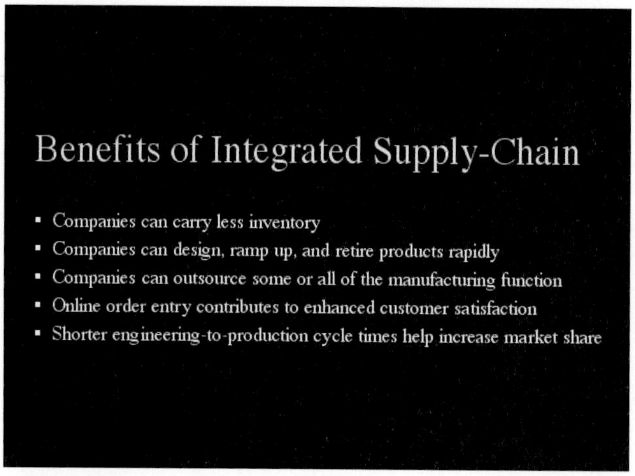

Benefits of Integrated Supply-Chain

- Companies can carry less inventory
- Companies can design, ramp up, and retire products rapidly
- Companies can outsource some or all of the manufacturing function
- Online order entry contributes to enhanced customer satisfaction
- Shorter engineering-to-production cycle times help increase market share

FIGURE 13-5C Wordy bullets

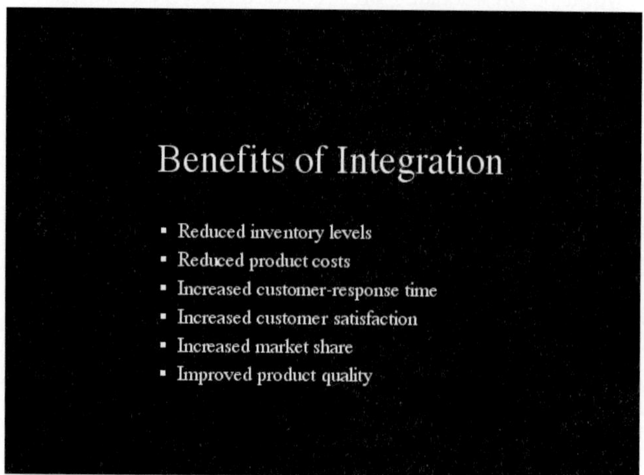

FIGURE 13-5D Concise bullets

FIGURE 13-5 Writing Readable Content

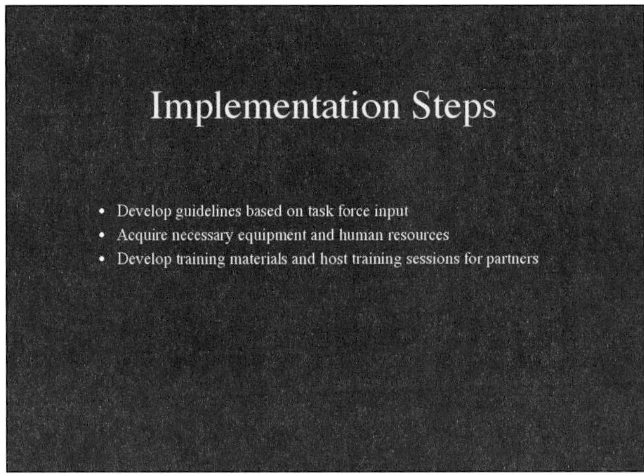

FIGURE 13-6A Steps in written format

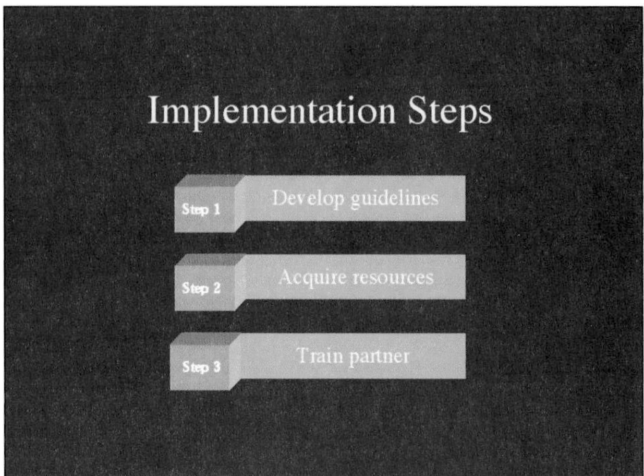

FIGURE 13-6B Steps in graphic format

- **Shorten numbers.** On graphs, use 04 for the year 2004; round off numbers such as $12 500.72 to $12 or $12.5, and then label the axis to indicate thousands.
- **Limit data.** Don't put more than five lines or five sets of bars on one chart.
- **Highlight key points.** Use arrows, boldface type, and colour to direct your audience's eyes to the main point of a visual. Summarize the intent of the graphic in one clear phrase or sentence, such as "Earnings have increased by 15 percent."
- **Adjust the size and design.** Modify the size of the graphic to accommodate the size of a slide. Leave plenty of white space (area with no text or graphics) so that the audience members can view and interpret content from a distance. Use colours that stand out from the slide's background, and choose a font that's clear and easy to read.

Selecting Design Elements Once you've composed the text and graphic elements of your slides, you're ready to focus on their design. Chapter 11 highlights five principles of effective design: continuity, contrast, emphasis, simplicity, and experience. Pay close attention to these principles as you select the color, background design, artwork, fonts, and typestyles for your slides. To make your slides as effective as possible, handle the following design elements carefully:

Colour can increase the appeal and impact of your slides.

- **Colour.** Limit colour choices to a few complementary ones. Some colours work better together than others; for example, contrasting colours increase readability. So when selecting colour for backgrounds, titles, and text, avoid colours that are close in hue (yellow text on a white background, brown on green, blue on black).[11] Because electronic presentations are usually shown in a dark room, use darker colours (such as blue) for the background, midrange brightness for illustrations, and light colors for text. To show overhead transparencies in a well-lit room, reverse the scheme: use light colours for background and dark colors for text (see Figure 13.7 on page 418).[12]

Your choice of background design and clip art sends a message to the audience.

- **Background designs and clip art.** If you are not using a custom company background design, choose one that is simple, is appropriate for the subject, and will appeal to the audience—nothing too busy or too colourful. You don't want to use a blue-jean background when the audience is wearing pin-striped suits. Similarly, clip art that is inappropriate, improperly sized, or overpowering can detract from a slide's message. Use art to help explain the main idea of your message and draw attention to key parts of your slide. Make sure it fits the slide's overall design, and place it carefully so that it doesn't compete with text or other design elements.

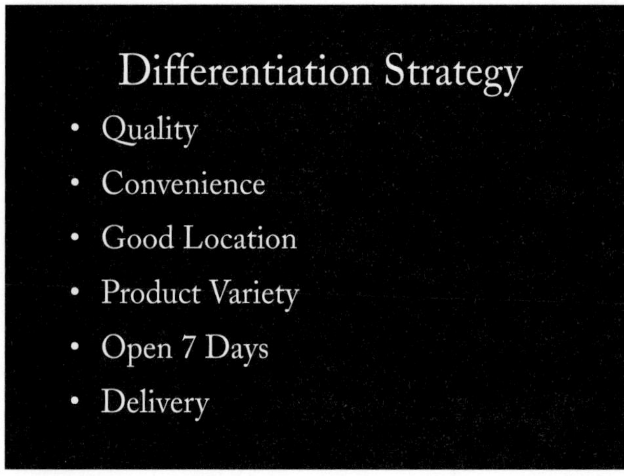

FIGURE 13–7A Electronic Slide

Differentiation Strategy

- Quality
- Convenience
- Good Location
- Product Variety
- Open 7 Days
- Delivery

FIGURE 13–7B Overhead Transparency

FIGURE 13–7 Adjusting Colour for Lighting Differences

Test your font and typeface selections by viewing slides from the back of a room.

- **Fonts and type styles.** When selecting fonts and type styles for slides, avoid script or decorative fonts. Limit your fonts to one or two per slide (if two fonts are used, reserve one for headings and the other for bulleted items). Using boldface type for electronic slides will keep letters from looking washed out. Be sure to avoid italicized type; it is difficult to read when projected. Use both uppercase and lowercase letters, with extra white space between lines of text. For electronic presentations, use type that is between 24 and 36 points, reserving the larger size for titles and the smaller for bullet items. Use the same font, type size, and colour for headings of the same level of importance.

Be consistent in designing slides.

- **Consistency.** Graphic elements such as borders, backgrounds, and company logos should repeat on every visual. Consistency of design makes your slides easier to read and gives your presentation a clean, professional look. You can also achieve design consistency by using the layout templates that are included with most presentation software packages. As Figure 13–8 shows, each layout contains placeholders for specific slide elements such as a title, a piece of graphic art, or bulleted text. The templates use a landscape orientation, which minimizes the amount of text wrapping to the next line. When possible, place bulleted text toward the top of the slide, where it is easier to read from a distance.

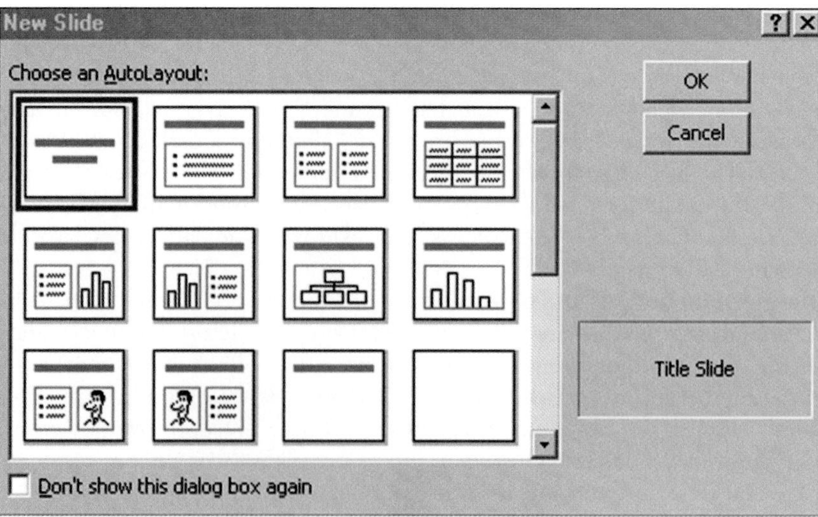

FIGURE 13–8 PowerPoint's Predefined Layouts

Adding Animation and Special Effects Electronic slide shows can utilize a number of special effects, including sound, animation, and video You can even automate your program to move from one slide to the next without the speaker's intervention. Automation is especially useful for running electronic presentations on television monitors in large places such as conventions and trade shows, where the slide show is, in effect, the only information present. Some common special effects include the following:

You can add sound, animation, and video to electronic slides.

- **Transitions.** By controlling how one electronic slide replaces another on screen, transitions can make your presentation flow smoothly from slide to slide. Most electronic software packages include a number of effective transition effects.
- **Builds.** Builds control the release of text, graphics, and other elements on slides. You can make your bullet points appear one at a time rather than having all of them appear on a slide at once. This special effect helps draw the audience's attention to the point being discussed and prevents the audience from reading ahead.
- **Hyperlinks.** Hyperlinks make your electronic slides interactive. When you click on a slide's hyperlink, you are transported to a different slide in your presentation, to other files on a computer, or even to a web page. Hyperlinks are a great tool for illustrating fine details without having to incorporate each detail into a slide.

As with design elements, use the same transitions and builds throughout your presentation. Don't introduce text that builds left to right on one slide and from top to bottom on the next.

A major challenge to those new to creating presentations is overcoming the tendency to use too many of these features. Excessive special effects overwhelm and distract audiences. Used sparingly, however, special effects can add punch to an oral presentation. So before you add animation or special effects to your presentation, ask yourself, Will the special effect support and enhance the message? If not, don't use it. For online resources offering PowerPoint tips, visit the following sites:

Don't overdo special effects.

- Microsoft: **www.microsoft.com/education/default.asp?ID=PPTTutorial**
- Indiana University—Purdue University, Indianapolis: **www.iupui.edu/~webtrain/tutorials/powerpoint2000_basics.html**
- University of Maryland: **www.education.umd.edu/blt/tcp/resetpp.html**

CREATING EFFECTIVE HANDOUTS

Handouts are a terrific way to offer your audience additional material without overloading your slides with information. Candidates for good handout material include complex charts and diagrams, company reports, magazine articles, case studies, Web sites, and copies of presentation slides.[13] Other good handout materials include brochures, pictures, outlines, and a copy of the presentation agenda.

Good handouts keep the audience informed without overwhelming them with information.

A well-prepared handout is the best way to jog someone's memory and make sure the hard work you put into your presentation is not wasted. Plan handouts together with your presentation. Think of handouts as a place to store information overflow. Include "need to know" information in your presentation and save "nice to know" information for your handouts. But be selective. Once you've assembled material for your handouts, sort through it to eliminate duplicate material and to minimize information overkill. Make sure handout information directly supports the goal of your presentation.[14]

Timing the distribution of handouts is a difficult decision. You must base that decision on the content of your handouts, the nature of your presentation, and your personal preference. Some speakers distribute handout materials—perhaps copies of slides, with space for taking notes—before the presentation begins. The drawback of doing so is that it allows your audience to read ahead instead of listening to you. Other speakers simply advise the audience of the types of information they are including in handouts but delay distributing anything until they have finished speaking.

Handouts can be both useful and distracting.

Step 3: Completing Oral Presentations

Review and revise your slides as you would any written message.

To complete your oral presentation, you will need to evaluate the content of your message and edit your remarks for clarity and conciseness as you would for any business message. Besides these tasks, three additional areas require your special attention: mastering the art of delivery, overcoming anxiety, and handling questions responsively.

Mastering the Art of Delivery

Not all methods of delivery are ideal.

Once you've planned, written, and developed visuals for your presentation you're ready to begin practicing your delivery. You have a variety of delivery methods to choose from, some of which are more effective than others are.

- **Memorizing.** Avoid memorizing your speech, especially a long one. You're likely to forget your lines, you will speak in a monotone, and your speech will sound stilted. Besides, you will often need to address audience questions during your speech, so you must be flexible enough to adjust your speech as you go. However, memorizing a quotation, an opening paragraph, or a few concluding remarks can bolster your confidence and strengthen your delivery.
- **Reading.** If you're delivering a technical or complex presentation, you may want to read it. Policy statements by government officials are sometimes read because the wording may be critical. If you choose to read your speech, practice enough so that you can still maintain eye contact with your audience. Triple-spaced copy, wide margins, and large type will help. You might even want to include stage cues, such as *pause, raise hands, lower voice.*

Speaking from notes is generally the best way to handle delivery.

Regardless of which delivery mode you use, be sure that you're thoroughly familiar with your subject. Knowing what you're talking about is the best way to build your self-confidence. Don't read your slides to the audience.

- **Speaking from notes.** Making a presentation with the help of an outline, note cards, or visual aids is probably the most effective and easiest delivery mode. This approach gives you something to refer to and still allows for eye contact and interaction with the audience. If your listeners look puzzled, you can expand on a point or rephrase it. Generally, note cards are preferable to sheets of paper, because nervousness is easier to see in shaking sheets of paper.
- **Impromptu speaking.** Unrehearsed speaking is what you do during a job interview, when you are called on to speak unexpectedly, or when you have agreed to speak but neglected to prepare your remarks. When you're asked to speak "off the cuff," take a moment to consider carefully what you will say. Organize your thoughts, and think of a general introduction. Use transitions to move from point to point. Be sure to stay focused, avoiding the temptation to ramble. Although impromptu speaking presents special challenges for novice speakers, with practice you will become comfortable when speaking without preparation.

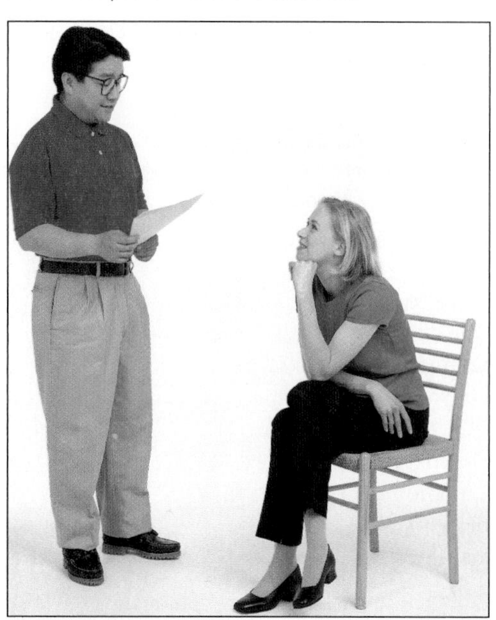

Practicing your oral presentation with a co-worker or a friend is a very effective way to polish your public speaking skills in a relaxed setting.

The most common mistake people make when delivering a presentation is reading their slides. When speakers read bulleted points to the audience word for word, they lose contact with the audience and lose voice inflection. As a result, the listeners become bored and eventually stop paying attention. Moreover, people who read slides insult the audience's intelligence. Audiences expect speakers to add valuable information that is not included on slides. To do so, however, speakers must know enough about the subject of their presentation to elaborate on each bulleted point. They must do their research and practice.

PRACTICING YOUR DELIVERY

When practicing your presentation, run through it about five times using your electronic slides or overhead transparencies. Your credibility is dramatically enhanced when you move seamlessly through your presentation. Practicing helps keep you on track, helps you maintain a conversational tone with your audience, and boosts your confidence and composure.

As you practice, try not to be so dependent on your slides that you're unable to function without them. Some people are quite capable of delivering a perfect presentation without notes. But for those who require notes, electronic software gives you an added advantage. Speaker's notes (as shown in Figure 13–9) are a helpful tool included with most popular electronic presentation software packages. You can display these notes along with a scaled-down version of your slide on a computer screen so that only you can see the notes. Use speaker's notes to list important facts or to remind yourself of supporting comments you should make as you present the slide. For instance, you might input such notes as "Don't forget to explain the impact of last year's bad weather on sales."

Use speaker's notes to jog your memory.

Practicing in front of a mirror is always a good idea, especially if your primary concern is the mechanics of the presentation. But if you're concerned about the content of your presentation and the effectiveness of your slides, you will find it best to practice in front of people who are willing to stop you when they don't understand your message or when they need you to clarify a point on your slide.

Practicing in front of a live audience is the best way to perfect your presentation.

Introducing Slides All visual aids must be properly introduced. Effective speakers verbally introduce the next visual aid before they show it. They don't say, "The next slide illustrates ..." Instead, they match their words to the slide and let the audience make the proper connection:

"We can get started with this new program by introducing these policies ..."

"The next segment of my presentation discusses ..."

"The three most significant issues facing our company are ..."

If you are using overhead transparencies, the best approach is to introduce the next overhead as you remove the old one and position the new one on the projector. Immediately cover all but the first bulleted phrase with a sheet of paper to prevent the audience from reading ahead. Then step aside to give the audience about five seconds to look it over before you start discussing it. As you advance through your discussion, you can move the paper down the transparency to uncover the next bullet item, waiting a few seconds for the audience to find your point of reference. When you are finished using the transparency, it's often a good idea to cover it until you're ready to introduce a new slide.

Introduce your slides before you show them.

Practice placing overhead transparencies on a projector so that it becomes second nature.

If you are using electronic slides, the best approach is to introduce the slide before you show it and then give the audience a few seconds to view the title and design ele-

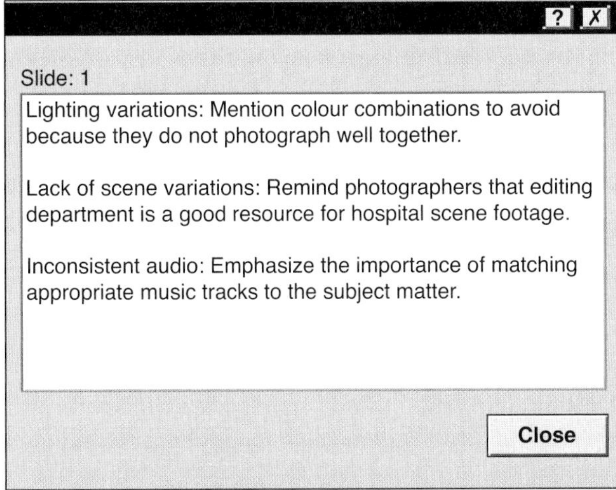

FIGURE 13–9A Speaker's Notes

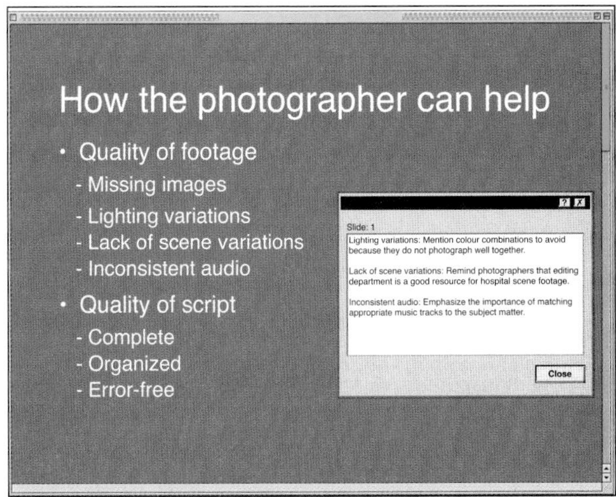

FIGURE 13–9B Corresponding Slide

FIGURE 13–9 Speaker's Notes

ments. With electronic slides, you can release bulleted points or sections of a graph as you discuss them. This control gives you more flexibility to move about the room—something you don't have with overheads.

You are not tied to the projector or front of the room with electronic slides.

If you're using a pointer, keep in mind that it's a tool meant to guide the audience to a specific part of a visual. It is not a riding crop, conductor's baton, leg scratcher, or walking stick. Use the pointer only at the time you need it, then fold it and remove it from sight. If you are using a laser pointer that puts a focused dot of light on the desired part of your visual, don't overdo it. A laser pointer is an excellent tool if used judiciously, but in the hands of the overzealous presenter, it can become a distraction.[15]

Limiting the Number of Slides Even if you produce an outstanding set of slides, they won't do you any good if you can't complete your presentation in the allotted time. Having too many visuals can detract from your message. It forces you either to rush through a presentation or to skip slides—some of which may be critical to your message.

Limit the number of slides to a few good ones.

Gauging the correct number of slides to include depends on the length of your presentation and the complexity of the subject matter. If you are using electronic slides, you must also factor in the time it takes for the special effects. As a general guideline, try to average 1 slide for every 90 seconds you speak. For a 30-minute presentation, you should create about 20 slides.[16] Of course, you may spend more time discussing some slides than others, so the best way to find the "right" number is to time your presentation as you practice.

Delete slides that take too long to discuss, either because they are too complex or because they cover too much information. Similarly, if you discover that you're taking only a few seconds to discuss a slide, it may be a clue that the slide is too elementary.[17]

As you time your presentation, keep in mind that it is much better to cover less information in a relaxed style than to cover too much information in a hurried and disorganized state. No one likes to listen to someone who keeps saying, "I just don't have enough time."[18] Build enough time in your presentation for a smile, an anecdote, or further illustration of a point. Audiences won't be angry if you let them out early, but they might be upset if you keep them late.

PREPARING TO SPEAK

In addition to knowing your material and practicing your delivery, you can build confidence in other ways. First, know that your location is ready and that you will have everything you'll need. Second, make sure you're prepared to address audiences from other cultures.

Before you speak, prepare the location.

Whenever you can, check the location for your presentation in advance. Check the seating arrangements to make sure they're appropriate for your needs. If you want audience members to sit at tables, be sure tables are available. Check the room for any outlets you'll need for a projector or microphone. Locate light switches and dimmers. If you need a flip-chart easel or a chalkboard, be sure it's on hand. Check for chalk, an eraser, a pointer, extension cords, and any other small but crucial items you might need. If at all possible, practice giving your presentation in the room where you will be speaking.

If you're addressing an audience that doesn't speak your language, consider using an interpreter. Working with an interpreter does constrain your presentation somewhat—you must speak slowly enough for the interpreter to keep up with you but not so slowly that the rest of your audience loses interest. Send your interpreter a copy of your speech and any visual aids as far in advance as possible.

Consider cultural differences and whether you need to use an interpreter.

Any time you deliver an oral presentation to people from other cultures, you may need to adapt the content of your presentation (see "Five Tips for Making Presentations Around the World"). It is also important to take into account any cultural differences in appearance, mannerisms, and other customs. Your interpreter will be able to suggest appropriate changes for a specific audience or particular occasion.

ACHIEVING INTERCULTURAL COMMUNICATION 

Five Tips for Making Presentations Around the World

In any successful presentation, getting your message across to an audience requires clear communication. But how can you communicate successfully with members of an international audience—especially if their fluency in your language ranges from expert to novice?

1. **Speak slowly and distinctly.** The most common complaint of international audiences is that English speakers talk too fast. If you speak too rapidly, your less-fluent listeners will be lost. Articulate every word carefully. Emphasize consonants for clarity, and pause frequently so that the audience will have time to absorb each key point.
2. **Repeat key words and phrases.** When audiences are less familiar with your language, they need to hear important information more than once. In addition, they may not be familiar with synonyms, so refer to key points in the same way throughout your presentation. If you introduce the concept of *benefits,* for example, continue to use the same word. Don't refer to *advantages* later on.
3. **Aim for clarity.** Keep your message simple. Eliminate complex sentence structure, abbreviations, and acronyms. Avoid two-word verbs such as *look over* and *check out.* Such verbs are confusing because the definition of each separate word differs from the meaning of the two words combined. For clearer communication, use one specific term (substitute *review* for *look over; examine* for *check out; write* for *jot down; return* for *drop by*). Stay away from cultural idioms, such as "once in a blue moon," which may be unfamiliar to an international audience.
4. **Communicate with body language.** Establish a relationship with your audience through strong eye contact. And don't forget to smile! Smiles and other facial expressions are universally recognized. Moreover, multilingual audiences pay close attention to a speaker's body language to get clues about the meanings of unfamiliar words. For example, prepositions can often be confusing to multilingual listeners, so use gestures to illustrate the meaning of words such as up, down, or under.
5. **Support your oral message with visual aids.** For most audiences, visual messages support and clarify spoken words. Develop handouts, flip charts, or slides for your presentation, using simple words to describe your key points. To eliminate problems with rapid speech, unclear pronunciations, or strange accents, prepare captions both in English and in your audience's native language. Avoid confusion about quantities by presenting numbers in graphs or pie charts and by converting financial figures into local currency.

CAREER APPLICATIONS

1. As marketing director for an international corporation, you will be making a presentation to the company's marketing representatives in Germany. How will you communicate company goals and sales projections clearly?
2. Make a list of ten two-word verbs. How does the meaning of each separate word differ from the definition of the combined words? Replace each two-word verb with a single, specific word that will be clearer to an international audience.

Adapted from Eric J. Adams, "Management Focus: User-Friendly Presentation Software," *World Trade,* March 1995, 92.

Overcoming Anxiety

OBJECTIVE 6 Relate nine ways to overcome your anxiety and feel more confident.

If you're nervous about facing an audience, you're not alone. Even speakers with years of experience feel some anxiety about getting up in front of an audience. Although you might not be able to make your nervous feelings disappear, you can learn to cope with your anxiety.

FEELING MORE CONFIDENT

Nervousness shows that you care about your audience, your topic, and the occasion. If your palms get wet or your mouth goes dry, don't think of nerves, think of excitement. Such stimulation can give you the extra energy you need to make your presentation sparkle. Harness your nervous energy to become a more confident speaker:[19]

Several techniques can help you become a more confident speaker.

- **Prepare more material than necessary.** Combined with a genuine interest in your topic, extra knowledge will reduce your anxiety.
- **Rehearse.** The more familiar you are with your material, the less panic you'll feel.
- **Think positively.** See yourself as polished and professional, and your audience will too.
- **Visualize your success.** Use the few minutes before you actually begin speaking to tell yourself you're on and you're ready.

- **Take a few deep breaths.** Before you begin to speak, remember that your audience is silently wishing you success.
- **Be ready.** Have your first sentence memorized and on the tip of your tongue.
- **Be comfortable.** If your throat is dry, drink some water.
- **Don't panic.** If you feel that you're losing your audience during your speech, try to pull them back by involving them in the action; ask for their opinions or pause for questions.
- **Keep going.** Your comfort level increases as you continue.

Perhaps the best way to overcome stage fright and to feel more confident is to concentrate on your message and on your audience, not on yourself. When you're busy thinking about your subject and observing your audience's response, you tend to forget your fears.

APPEARING MORE CONFIDENT

The best technique for overcoming your anxiety is to concentrate on your listeners and on their needs, rather than focusing on yourself.

As you deliver your presentation, try to be aware of the nonverbal signals you're transmitting. Regardless of how you feel inside, your effectiveness greatly depends on how you look and sound.

- **Don't rush.** Well-delivered presentations start with your first minute at the podium. As you approach the speaker's lectern, walk slowly, breathe deeply, and stand up straight. Face your audience, adjust the microphone, count to three slowly, and then survey the room. When you find a friendly face, make eye contact and smile. Count to three again, and then begin your presentation.[20] This slow, controlled beginning will help you establish rapport.
- **Maintain eye contact.** Once your presentation is under way, pick out several people positioned around the room and shift your gaze from one to another. Looking directly at your listeners will make you appear sincere, confident, and trustworthy. It also helps you get an idea of the impression you're creating.
- **Stand tall.** Your posture is important in projecting more confidence. Stand with your weight on both feet and your shoulders back. Avoid gripping the lectern. In fact, you might step out from behind the lectern to help your audience feel more comfortable with you and to express your own comfort and confidence in what you're saying. Vary your facial expressions to make your message more dynamic.
- **Don't overdo hand gestures.** Use your hands to emphasize your remarks with appropriate gestures, but keep them still at other times. Don't distract your audience with nervous hand movements. Keep your hands out of your pockets; in fact, empty your pockets before you speak.
- **Use your voice.** People who speak with lower vocal tones at a slightly faster than average rate are perceived as being more credible.[21] Speak in a normal, conversational tone but with enough volume for everyone to hear you. Try to sound poised and confident, varying your pitch and speaking rate to add emphasis. Don't ramble. Speak clearly and crisply, articulating all the syllables, and sound enthusiastic about what you're saying. Use silence instead of meaningless filler words such as *um, you know, okay,* and *like.*

Handling Questions Responsively

Be ready with answers so that you can
- Emphasize your most important points
- Refer to material that didn't fit in the formal presentation
- Overcome audience resistance

The question-and-answer period is a valuable part of an oral presentation. In addition to giving you valuable feedback, this period gives you a chance to emphasize points you made earlier, work in material that didn't fit into the formal presentation, and identify and try to overcome audience resistance. Many speakers do well delivering their presentation, only to falter during the question-and-answer period.

Since you've already spent time anticipating these questions, you are ready with answers. Some experts recommend that you hold back some dramatic statistics as ammunition for the question-and-answer session.[22] If your message is unpopular, you should also be prepared for hostile questions. Treat them as legitimate requests for information. Maintaining your professionalism will improve your credibility.

FOCUS ON THE QUESTIONER

When someone poses a question, focus your attention on that individual. Pay attention to body language and facial expression to help determine what the person really means. Nod your head to acknowledge the question; then repeat it aloud to confirm your understanding and to ensure that the entire audience has heard it. If the question is vague or confusing, ask for clarification; then give a simple, direct answer. If you're asked to choose between two alternatives, don't feel you must do so. Offer your own choice instead, if that makes more sense.[23]

Use body language to emphasize the fact that you're listening to the questioner.

RESPOND APPROPRIATELY

Be sure to answer the question you're asked. Don't sidestep it, ignore it, or laugh it off. Furthermore, don't say more than you need to: you want to have enough time to cover all the questions. If giving an adequate answer would take too long, simply say, "I'm sorry, we don't have time to get into that issue right now, but if you'll see me after the presentation, I'll be happy to discuss it with you." If you don't know the answer, don't pretend that you do. Instead, say something like, "I don't have those figures. I'll get them for you as quickly as possible." You don't have to answer every question that is asked.

Keep your answers short and to the point.

- ***Maintain Control*** Before you begin, try suggesting a time limit, announcing a question limit per person, or asking people to identify themselves before asking a question. Such ground rules will protect you from questioners who try to engage you in a heated exchange, monopolize the floor, or mount their own soapbox. Give as many audience members as possible a chance to participate by calling on people from different parts of the room. If the same person keeps angling for attention, you might admit that you and the questioner have differing opinions, offer to get back to someone once you've done more research, or simply respond with a brief answer that avoids lengthy debate or more questions.[24]

During meetings, polished speakers use question-and-answer sessions to reinforce their ideas and credibility.

- ***Survive the Hot Seat*** If a question ever puts you on the hot seat, remember to be honest, but keep your cool. Look the person in the eye, answer the question as well as you can, and try not to show your feelings. Don't get into an argument. Defuse hostility by paraphrasing the question and asking the questioner to confirm that you've understood it correctly. Break long, complicated questions into parts that you can answer simply. State your response honestly, accurately, and factually; then move on to the next question. Avoid postures or gestures that might seem antagonistic. Maintain a businesslike tone of voice and a pleasant expression.[25] Help audience members ask you questions.
- ***Motivate Questions*** In case your audience is too timid or hostile to ask questions, you might want to plant some of your own. If a friend or the meeting organizer gets the ball rolling, other people in the audience will probably join in. You might ask a question yourself: "Would you like to know more about..." If someone in the audience answers, act as if the question came from that person in the first place. When all else fails, say something like, "I know from experience that most questions are asked after the question period. So I'll be around afterward to talk."[26]

Respond unemotionally to tough questions.

Checklist: Oral Presentations

Planning your oral presentation

✓ Define your purpose.

✓ Analyze your audience.

Writing the oral presentation

✓ Organize your presentation: define your main idea, limit your scope, choose an appropriate approach, prepare your outline, and decide on an appropriate style.

✓ Develop the opening: arousing audience interest, building credibility, and previewing the main points.

✓ Develop the body: connecting your ideas and holding audience interest.

✓ Develop the close: restating the main points, describing the next steps, and ending on a strong note.

✓ Prepare for the question-and-answer period: Figure out how to control the situation, and anticipate questions and objections.

✓ Prepare visual aids.

✓ Create effective slides: creating simple, readable content; selecting design elements; and adding animation and special effects.

✓ Create effective handouts.

✓ Have a back-up plan in case of equipment failure.

Completing the oral presentation

✓ Decide which delivery method to use: memorizing, reading, speaking from notes, or speaking impromptu.

✓ Practice delivery elements: don't read slides, use speaker's notes, practice in front of someone willing to stop you for clarification, introduce each slide before showing it, use pointers judiciously, and don't include too many slides.

✓ Check out the room ahead of time, and make sure the equipment works.

✓ Consider using an interpreter for audiences who don't speak your language.

✓ Control your anxiety by using your nervousness as a tool.

✓ Try to feel more confident: prepare more material than necessary, rehearse, think positively, visualize your success, take a few deep breaths, be ready, be comfortable, don't panic, and keep going.

✓ Try to appear more confident: don't rush, maintain eye contact, stand tall, don't overdo hand gestures, and use your voice.

✓ Handle questions responsively: focus on the questioner, respond appropriately, maintain control, survive the hot seat, and motivate questions

✓ Conclude your presentation gracefully: announce that you're presentation is ending, summarize your main idea, thank people for listening, look around the room (making eye contact), gather your notes, and leave the podium.

Concluding Your Presentation

Finish up on time—even if people are enthusiastic to continue.

When the time allotted for your presentation is up, call a halt to the question-and-answer session, even if more people want to talk. Prepare the audience for the end by saying: "Our time is almost up. Let's have one more question." After you've made your reply, summarize the main idea of the presentation and thank people for their attention. Conclude the way you opened: by looking around the room and making eye contact. Then gather your notes and leave the podium, shoulders straight, head up. (The above "Checklist: Oral Presentations" is a reminder of the tasks involved in oral communication.)

Summary of Learning Objectives

1 Illustrate how planning presentations differs from planning written documents. Unlike a written document, an oral presentation is a one-time event, so audience members cannot browse through the speaker's comments to verify something said earlier. Unlike document writers, presenters must find a way to capture audience attention and keep it so listeners will remember what is said. To capture attention, presenters must be especially careful to define the purpose of their presentations (to inform, explain, persuade, or motivate) and to develop accurate audience profiles (to specifically address audience needs and interests).

2 Describe the five tasks that go into organizing oral presentations. When you organize an oral presentation, you need to complete five tasks: (1) When you define the main idea, you create a one-sentence generalization that first states the one message you want your audience to walk away with and then relates that message to your audience's needs. (2) When you limit your scope, you make sure that your presentation fits into the time allowed for it and that the time allowed is enough for the complexity of your subject. (3) When you choose your approach, you arrange your presentation in the order that is most appropriate for your audience's receptivity and for the purpose and duration of your speech. (4) When you prepare an outline of your presentation, you use it to compose your speech, to stay on task as you proceed, to make sure your presentation accomplishes your purpose, and sometimes to serve as speaking notes. (5) When you decide on an appropriate style, you match the occasion of your speech—anything from a formal presentation before a large audience to a casual working session around a conference table.

3 Delineate the tasks involved in developing the opening, body, and close of your oral presentation. As you develop each part of your presentation, you must make sure that you accomplish specific tasks. In the introduction, you must arouse audience interest, build your credibility, and preview your presentation. In the body, you must connect your ideas and hold your audience's attention. In the close, you must restate your main points, describe the next steps, and end on a positive note.

4 Explain why using visuals in an oral presentation is a good idea and list six types of visuals commonly used with oral presentations. When a speaker makes an oral presentation, visuals create interest and clarify important points. They help listeners absorb the information being presented. They help the speaker remember the details of a speech, and thus they help the speaker appear more professional and better prepared. Types of visuals commonly used in presentations include overhead transparencies, electronic slides, 35-millimeter slides, chalkboards and whiteboards, and flipcharts.

5 Identify six ways to make your text slides more effective and six ways to make your graphic slides more effective. Simplicity is the key to your text slides. To make them effective, (1) limit each slide to one idea; (2) limit the content to about 40 words; (3) write short, bulleted points, not long sentences; (4) phrase list items in grammatical form and use telegraphic wording; (5) use active voice; and (6) include short informative titles. Simplicity is also the key to effective graphic slides: (1) reduce the detail, by eliminating anything not relevant to the message; (2) minimize repetitive vocabulary; (3) round off numbers; (4) limit charts to five lines or five sets of bars on one chart; (5) highlight key points with arrows, boldface type, or colour to focus your audience's attention on the main point; and (6) leave lots of white space and choose complementary colours to make slide content easy to see.

6 Relate nine ways to overcome your anxiety and feel more confident. To overcome anxiety and feel more confident as a speaker, prepare more material than necessary so that the extra knowledge will reduce your nervousness. Rehearse your speech to become as familiar as possible with your topic. Think positively and see yourself as a polished professional. Right before speaking, visualize your success and tell yourself you're ready. Take a few deep breaths and remember that your audience actually wants you to succeed. Be ready by memorizing your first sentence. Be comfortable by sipping some water. If you feel you're losing your audience, don't panic; instead, pull them back by asking for their opinions or questions and involving them in the action. Keep going no matter what because you'll get better as you go.

ON THE JOB

Solving a Communication Dilemma at the Canadian Soccer Association

"Soccer is the most popular game in the world, and the CSA is the keeper of that trust in Canada," says David Bedford, managing director of Soccer Canada Properties. The sponsorship funds he raises, or products or services that he persuades companies to donate, are earmarked for such activities as 13 different national team programs, national championships involving domestic clubs, mini-soccer festivals, and coaching development.

Presentations are a key tool for fulfilling Bedford's purpose of gaining sponsorship for the Canadian Soccer Association's activities. During the planning stage, Bedford and his team will develop an audience profile. "We pick the targets that we think have the most affinity to soccer and its demographics, or we target services or products for which the CSA has a need—Air Canada, for instance."

Bedford and his colleagues will investigate a potential company's market, analyzing such areas as a firm's target audience, competitors, sales-distribution channels, and pricing. They will also meet with potential sponsors to understand their objectives, budgets, and timing. Preparing a detailed audience profile helps Bedford understand how a company will fit with the CSA. He explains that fast-food giant McDonald's is a "natural fit" with the mini-soccer programs because of its appeal to kids and families. "Some leads come from a company's natural association with soccer, either via equipment sponsorship—Adidas, for instance, or by virtue of the company's involvement in other jurisdictions." One example here is JVC, an electronics leader, which provides sponsorship to both FIFA (Federation of International Football Associations) and the CSA.

With an audience profile nailed down, Bedford next works on his presentation. His main idea is to convince potential sponsors that "an integrated soccer sponsorship package will work for them." Building credibility into his presentation is essential. In his opening, he highlights the credibility of the CSA, the organization he represents, by demonstrating the overwhelming popularity of the sport in Canada through telling statistics. His audiences learn, for example, how many more kids play soccer than hockey, including 38 percent young women as compared to 7 percent in hockey.

Bedford's presentations are often delivered by a team, typically formed by Bedford with corporate sales and marketing representatives from IMG Canada, the sports management firm that works with the CSA. Thorough rehearsal ensures smooth delivery of the content. Their presentations include multimedia, incorporating video, pictures, and logos; and the visual support, like the speech text, is tailored to each to each distinct audience.

Persuading companies to sponsor CSA activities is rarely easy. But through careful planning and practice, Bedford delivers presentations that bring in new sponsors and more programs for the Canadian Soccer Association's amateur athletes.

Your Mission As a member of the IMG Canda's marketing team, you help David Bedford plan some of the presentations he delivers to potential Canadian Soccer Association sponsors. For the following assignments, choose the best solution and be prepared to explain your choice.

1 David Bedford will be giving a 20-minute presentation in Vancouver to the executive management of a fast-food chain. Which of the following purposes do you think Bedford should try to accomplish?
  a To inform the audience about the history of soccer in Canada.
  b To inspire members of the audience to sponsor CSA youth programs.
  c To entertain the audience with stories about victories of CSA teams.
  d To analyze the impact of soccer on Canadian youth and adults.

2 Bedford has asked you to help plan a 10-minute speech that he can give to Canadian Soccer Association officers, division managers, and coaches. He expects up to 30 people to attend. His topic is "innovative ways to gain sponsors" and his purpose is to persuade his audience of ways they can personally convince companies to sponsor CSA activities. His main idea is that the CSA needs their own officers and coaches, rather than professional fundraisers like Bedford, to give presentations to potential sponsors. How should he handle audience questions?
  a To get his audience to agree with his idea, Bedford should state early in his speech that he would be happy to accept questions at any time during the speech.
  b Since his audience is not accustomed to giving presentations to raise sponsorship funding, and feel uncomfortable about being asked to take on this role, Bedford should be prepared to answer every single question, even if he ends up running over his allotted time.
  c To make sure he understands a questioner's meaning, he should focus on the questioner, paying attention to body language and facial expression.
  d Bedford should prepare enough material beforehand to be able to answer all questions immediately, without needing extra time or further research.

3 You are helping Bedford prepare a presentation on the CSA for a potential sponsor. He wants to talk about CSA programs for female players. Which visual aid should he use to emphasize growth in the number of female players?
  a An electronic slide showing a match between two Canadian women's soccer teams.
  b A short video clip showing a match between two Canadian women's soccer teams.
  c An overhead transparency showing a line graph of the growth of female soccer players.
  d A professionally prepared booklet of handouts that include copies of slides used in (a) and (b), along with other relevant information.

4 In his speech to a high-tech company interested in sponsoring CSA activities, Bedford wants to present some statistics that compare enrollment in amateur soccer programs to enrollment in amateur hockey programs. How should he handle the quantitative details for this high-tech audience?
  a Bedford should prepare handouts that summarize the financial data in tabular and graphic form. Everyone in the audience should receive a copy of the handout to refer to during the speech.
  b Bedford should write the information on a blackboard while he delivers the speech.
  c Bedford should prepare simple overhead transparencies to use during the speech. As he concludes his remarks, he should tell the audience that detailed financial statements are available at the door for those who are interested.
  d Given the technical knowledge of the audience, he should show an electronic slide show that summarizes the financial information in tabular and graphic format. The slide show should be professionally prepared to ensure its quality.[27]

Test Your Knowledge

Review Questions

1 What are the three steps in planning an oral presentation?
2 What is the purpose of defining the main idea of a speech?
3 Why do you have to limit your scope when planning a presentation?
4 What do you want to achieve with the introduction to your speech? With the close of your speech?
5 What types of visuals are commonly used in presentations?
6 What are six key rules for designing effective text visuals? Graphic visuals?
7 How does the delivery method of impromptu speaking differ from the delivery method of speaking from notes?
8 As a speaker, what nonverbal signals can you send to appear more confident?

9 What can speakers do to maintain control during the question-and-answer period of a presentation?

10 Why is simplicity of organization important in oral communication?

Interactive Learning 

Use This Text's Online Resources

Visit our Companion Website at **www.pearsoned.ca/thill**, where you can use the interactive Study Guide to test your chapter knowledge and get instant feedback. Additional resources link you to the sites mentioned in this text and to additional sources of information on chapter topics.

Also check out the resources on the Mastering Business Communication CD, including "Perils of Pauline," an interactive presentation of the business communication challenges within a fictional company. For Chapter 13, see in particular the episode "Giving a Formal Speech."

Apply Your Knowledge

Critical Thinking Questions

1. Would you rather (a) give a presentation to an outside audience, (b) be interviewed for a news story, or (c) make a presentation to a departmental meeting? Why? How do the communication skills differ among those situations? Explain.
2. How might the audience's attitude affect the amount of audience interaction during or after a presentation? Explain your answer.
3. What are some of the advantages and disadvantages of distributing handouts before a presentation and what can you do to minimize the disadvantages?
4. From the speaker's perspective, what are the advantages and disadvantages of responding to questions from the audience throughout a speech or presentation rather than just afterward? From the listener's perspective, which approach would you prefer? Why?
5. **Ethical Choices** What ethical concerns are raised by a speech that encourages audience members to take illegal or questionable actions?

Practice Your Knowledge

Document for Analysis

Pick a speech from *Vital Speeches of the Day,* a publication containing recent speeches on timely and topical subjects. As an alternative, select a speech from an online source such as a Canadian corporation (many post executive speeches online). Examine both the introduction and the close; then analyze how these two sections work together to emphasize the main idea. What action does the speaker want the audience to take?

Next, identify the transitional sentences or phrases that clarify the speech's structure for the listener, especially those that help the speaker shift between supporting points. Using these transitions as clues, list the main message and supporting points; then indicate how each transitional phrase links the current supporting point to the succeeding one. Now, prepare a brief (two- to three-minute) oral presentation summarizing your analysis for your class.

Exercises

13–1 **Internet** For many years, Toastmasters has been dedicated to helping its members give speeches. Instruction, good speakers as models, and practice sessions aim to teach members to convey information in lively and informative ways. Visit the Toastmasters Web site at **www.toastmasters.org** and carefully review the linked pages about listening, speaking, voice, and body. Evaluate the information and outline a three-minute presentation to your class telling why Toastmasters and its Web site would or would not help you and your classmates write and deliver an effective presentation.

13–2 **Mastering Delivery: Analysis** Attend a speech at your school or in your area, or watch a speech on television. Categorize the speech as one that motivates or entertains, one that informs or analyzes, or one that persuades or urges collaboration. Then compare the speaker's delivery and use of visual aids with this chapter's "Checklist: Oral Presentations" on page 426. Write a two-page report analyzing the speaker's performance and suggesting improvements.

13–3 **Mastering Delivery: Nonverbal Signals** Observe and analyze the delivery of a speaker in school, at work, or other setting. What type of delivery did the speaker use? Was this delivery appropriate for the occasion? What nonverbal signals did the speaker use to emphasize key points? Were these signals effective? Which nonverbal signals would you suggest to further enhance the delivery of this speech—and why?

13–4 **Ethical Choices** Think again about the speech you observed and analyzed in Exercise 13–3. How could the speaker have used nonverbal signals to unethically manipulate the audience's attitudes or actions?

13–5 Teamwork You've been asked to give an informative ten-minute talk on vacation opportunities in your province. Draft your introduction, which should last no more than two minutes. Then pair off with a classmate and analyze each other's introductions. How well do these two introductions arouse the audience's interest, build credibility, and preview the presentation? Suggest how these introductions might be improved.

13–6 Writing Oral Presentations: Visuals Which types of visual aids would you use to accompany each of the following speeches? Explain your answers.

a An informal 10-minute speech explaining the purpose of a new training program to 300 assembly-line employees
b An informal 10-minute speech explaining the purpose of a new training program to 5 vice-presidents
c A formal 5-minute presentation explaining the purpose of a new training program to the company's 12-member board of directors
d A formal 5-minute speech explaining the purpose of a new company training program to 35 members of the press

13–7 Creating Effective Slides: Content and Design You've been asked to give an informative ten-minute talk to a group of conventioneers on great things to see and do while visiting your hometown. To keep them interested, you've decided to whip up a couple of slides for your oral presentation. Write the content for two or three slides. Then think about the design elements for your slides. Which colours, clip art, and other design elements will you use to enhance your slides?

13–8 Creating Effective Slides: Design Elements Word-processing software packages include a large selection of fonts. Review the fonts available to you and select three to five fonts suitable for electronic slides or overhead transparencies. Explain the criteria you used for your selections.

13–9 Completing Speeches: Self-Assessment How good are you at planning, writing, and delivering presentations? Rate yourself on each of the following elements of the oral presentation process. Then examine your ratings to identify where you are strongest and where you can improve, using the tips in this chapter.

Element of Presentation Process	Always	Frequently	Occasionally	Never
1 I start by defining my purpose.	______	______	______	______
2 I analyze my audience before writing a presentation.	______	______	______	______
3 I match my presentation length to the allotted time.	______	______	______	______
4 I begin my presentations with an attention-getting introduction.	______	______	______	______
5 I look for ways to build credibility as a speaker.	______	______	______	______
6 I cover only a few main points in the body of my presentation.	______	______	______	______
7 I use transitions to help listeners follow my ideas.	______	______	______	______
8 I review main points and describe next steps in the close.	______	______	______	______
9 I choose visual aids appropriate for the audience and occasion.	______	______	______	______
10 I design simple visual aids to supplement my presentation.	______	______	______	______
11 I practice my speech, with visuals, before the presentation.	______	______	______	______
12 I prepare in advance for questions and objections.	______	______	______	______
13 I conclude presentations by summarizing my main idea.	______	______	______	______

Going Online Exercises

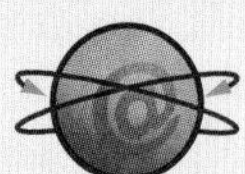

Speak with Flair, found on page 404 of this chapter

Do you need new ideas for a speech that you're planning to deliver or material for an oral presentation? When you log on to the Virtual Presentation Assistant, you'll find examples of speeches, advice on delivery, and plentiful resources to help you prepare or improve a speech.

1. Suppose you have been asked to prepare a speaking project on a business issue currently in the news. How could you use what you've discovered at the VPA site to help you select a topic? How could you use this site to find additional information or supplementary materials related to your project?
2. List some reasons that visual aids are an important aspect of oral presentations. Describe two practical tips on preparing effective visual aids that you discovered using the VPA site or its links.
3. What topics or information will entice you to return to this site or its links? (If you don't find the Virtual Presentation Assistant useful, explain why.)

To link directly to this site, visit our Companion Website at **www.pearsoned.ca/thill** and look for the Chapter 13 resources.

Writing Résumés and Application Letters

1 Discuss three ways that you can adapt to today's changing workplace

2 Describe the six ways to prepare for and successfully complete your search for employment.

3 Discuss how to choose the appropriate organization for your résumé and list the advantages or disadvantages of the three options

4 List the major sections of a traditional résumé

5 Describe the process involved in adapting your résumé to an electronic format

6 Define the purpose of application letters and explain how to apply the AIDA organizational approach to them

ON THE JOB

Facing a Communication Dilemma

Looking for People Who Never Stop Learning

www.ford.com

"If you're an active learner, you'll find you fit in at Ford Motor Company," says chair and CEO Bill Ford (great grandson of founder Henry Ford). Ford Motor Company makes vehicles with such brands as Aston Martin, Ford, Jaguar, Lincoln, Mercury, and Volvo. The company owns a controlling 33 percent stake in Mazda, has purchased BMW's Land Rover SUV operations, and owns Hertz rental cars. Ford offers numerous, challenging assignments, not only in design and manufacturing but also in marketing, sales and service, purchasing, finance, information technology, and other areas.

Ford looks for particular qualities in employment candidates. The company hopes to find well-rounded individuals who have high academic standing, leadership potential, the ability to work well with others, and achievements in extracurricular activities. Successful candidates exhibit characteristics showing that they behave with honour and dignity, have a passion for excellence, and can sustain relationships by fostering teamwork, connecting with customers, committing to community.

Building Toward a Career

As Bill Ford will tell you, getting the job that's right for you takes more than sending out a few résumés and application letters. Before entering the workplace, you need to learn as much as you can about your own capabilities and about the job marketplace.

Understanding Today's Changing Workplace

Numerous forces are changing today's workplace.

The workplace today is changing constantly.[2] The attitudes and expectations of both employers and employees are being affected not only by globalization, technology, diversity, and teams but also by deregulation, shareholder activism, corporate downsizing, mergers and acquisitions, outsourcing, and entrepreneurism (people starting their own business or buying a franchise).[3] This constant change is affecting the job search in several ways:

- **How often people look for work.** Rather than looking for lifelong employees, many employers now hire temporary workers and consultants on a project-by-project basis. Likewise, rather than staying with one employer for their entire careers, growing numbers of employees are moving from company to company.
- **Where people find work.** Large companies are creating fewer jobs. One expert predicts that soon 80 percent of the labour force will be working for firms employing fewer than 200 people. Moreover, self-employment seems to be an increasingly attractive option for many former employees.[4]
- **The type of people who find work.** Employers today are looking for people who are able and willing to adapt to diverse situations and who continue to learn throughout their careers. Companies want team players with strong work records, leaders who are versatile, and employees with diversified skills and varied job experience.[5] Plus, most employers expect employees to be sensitive to intercultural differences.[6]

Adapting to the Changing Workplace

Today, employment is viewed as more flexible, with much less focus on life long employment.

Before you limit your employment search to a particular industry or job, do some preparation. Analyze what you have to offer, what you hope to get from your work, and how you can make yourself more valuable to potential employers. This preliminary analysis will help you identify employers who are likely to want you and vice versa.

ANALYZE WHAT YOU HAVE TO OFFER

OBJECTIVE 1 **Discuss three ways that you can adapt to today's changing workplace.**

What you have to offer:
- Functional skills
- Education and experience
- Personality traits

When seeking employment, you must tell people about who you are. You need to know what talents and skills you have. You'll need to explain how these skills will benefit potential employers. Here are some suggestions to help your self-analysis:

- **Jot down 10 achievements you're proud of.** Did you learn to ski, take a prize-winning photo, tutor a child, edit your school paper? Think about what skills these achievements demanded (leadership qualities, speaking ability, and artistic talent may have helped you coordinate a winning presentation to your school's administration). You'll begin to recognize a pattern of skills, many of which might be valuable to potential employers.
- **Look at your educational preparation, work experience, and extracurricular activities.** What do your knowledge and experience qualify you to do? What have you learned from volunteer work or class projects that could benefit you on the job? Have you held any offices, won any awards or scholarships, mastered a second language?

- **Take stock of your personal characteristics.** Are you aggressive, a born leader? Or would you rather follow? Are you outgoing, articulate, great with people? Or do you prefer working alone? Make a list of what you believe are your four or five most important qualities. Ask a relative or friend to rate your traits as well.

Your college or university placement office may be able to administer a variety of tests to help you identify interests, aptitudes, and personality traits. These tests won't reveal your "perfect" job, but they'll help you focus on the types of work best suited to your personality.

DECIDE WHAT YOU WANT TO DO

Knowing what you *can* do is one thing. Knowing what you *want* to do is another. Don't lose sight of your own values. Discover the things that will bring you satisfaction and happiness on the job. Ask yourself some questions:

What you want from your career is as important as what you have to offer employers.

- **What would you like to do every day?** Talk to people in various occupations about their typical workday. You might consult relatives, local businesses, or former graduates (through your school's alumni relations office). Read about various occupations. Start with your school library or placement office.
- **How would you like to work?** Consider how much independence you want on the job, how much variety you like, and whether you prefer to work with products, machines, people, ideas, figures, or some combination thereof. Do you like physical work, mental work, or a mix? Constant change or a predictable role?
- **What specific compensation do you expect?** What do you hope to earn in your first year? What kind of pay increase do you expect each year? What's your ultimate earnings goal? Would you be comfortable getting paid on commission, or do you prefer a steady paycheque? Are you willing to settle for less money in order to do something you really love?
- **Can you establish some general career goals?** Consider where you'd like to start, where you'd like to go from there, and the ultimate position you'd like to attain. How soon after joining the company would you like to receive your first promotion? Your next one? What additional training or preparation will you need to achieve them?
- **What size company would you prefer?** Do you like the idea of working for a small, entrepreneurial operation? Or would you prefer a large corporation?
- **What type of operation is appealing to you?** Would you prefer to work for a profit-making company or a non-profit organization? Are you attracted to service businesses or manufacturing operations? Do you want regular, predictable hours, or do you thrive on flexible, varied hours? Would you enjoy a seasonally varied job such as education (which may give you summers off) or retailing (with its selling cycles)?
- **What location would you like?** Would you like to work in a city, a suburb, a small town, an industrial area, or an uptown setting? Do you favour a particular part of the country? A country abroad? Do you like working indoors or outdoors?
- **What facilities do you envision?** Is it important to you to work in an attractive place, or will simple, functional quarters suffice? Do you need a quiet office to work effectively, or can you concentrate in a noisy, open setting? Is access to public transportation or freeways important?
- **What sort of corporate culture are you most comfortable with?** Would you be happy in a formal hierarchy with clear reporting relationships? Or do you prefer less structure? Are you looking for a paternalistic firm or one that fosters individualism? Do you like a competitive environment? One that rewards teamwork? What qualities do you want in a boss?

MAKE YOURSELF MORE VALUABLE TO EMPLOYERS

Take positive steps toward building your career. Before you graduate from college or university or while you are seeking employment, you can still do a lot. The following suggestions will help potential employers recognize the value of hiring you:

- **Keep an employment portfolio.** Get a three-ring notebook and a package of plastic sleeves that open at the top. Collect anything that shows your ability to perform (classroom or work evaluations, certificates, awards, papers you've written). Your portfolio is a great resource for writing your résumé, and it gives employers tangible evidence of your professionalism.

Your chances of getting a job are increased by career-building efforts.

- **Consider an e-portfolio.** You can think of an e-portfolio as a multimedia presentation about your skills and experiences. It's an extensive résumé that links to an electronic collection of your student papers, problem-solving situations, pictures from study-abroad stints, internship projects, and anything else that demonstrates your accomplishments and activities. Although such portfolios are usually stored on college or university Web sites, students can make copies on CD-ROMs and send them out instead of résumés.[7]
- **Take interim assignments.** As you search for a permanent job, consider temporary or freelance work. Also gain a competitive edge by participating in an internship program. These temporary assignments not only help you gain valuable experience and relevant contacts but also provide you with important references and with items for your portfolio.[8]
- **Work on polishing and updating your skills.** Whenever possible, join networks of professional colleagues and friends who can help you keep up with your occupation and industry. While waiting for responses to your résumé, take a computer course, or seek out other educational or life experiences that would be hard to get while working full-time.

Even after you're hired, you can increase your value to employers by continuing to improve your skills. Lifelong learning will distinguish you from your peers, help you advance within a company, and help you follow opportunities with other employers. To reach your personal goals in the workplace, become a lifelong learner by doing the following.[9]

Your career-building efforts don't stop after you are hired.

- Obtain as much technical knowledge as you can.
- Learn to accept and adapt to change.
- Regularly read publications such as *Canadian Business, The Globe and Mail Report on Business, The Wall Street Journal, Business Week,* and *U.S. News & World Report.*
- View each job as an opportunity to learn more and to expand your knowledge, experience, and social skills.
- Take on as much responsibility as you can (listening to and learning from others while actively pursuing new or better skills).
- Stay abreast of what's going on in your organization and industry.
- Share what you know with others.
- Understand the big picture. Be familiar with national and world events and the economy.

As with other business messages, the three-step writing process can help you plan, write, and complete your résumé and other employment messages.

Seeking Employment in the Changing Workplace

The search for employment is a process.

Look at Figure 14–1 below for an idea of what an employment search entails. The first two tasks are discussed in this chapter; the rest are discussed in Chapter 15. Gather as much information as you can, narrowing it as you go until you know precisely the companies you want to approach.

Find out where the job opportunities are.

Begin by finding out where the job opportunities are, which industries are strong, which parts of the country are booming, and which specific job categories offer the best prospects for the future. From there you can investigate individual organizations, doing your best to learn as much about them as possible. To prepare for and successfully complete your search for employment, do the following:

- **Stay abreast of business and financial news.** Subscribe to a major newspaper (print or online) and scan the business pages every day. Watch some of the television programs that focus on business, such as *ROBTV* and *Wall Street Week.* Consult Human Resources Development Canada publications, such as *Job Futures*

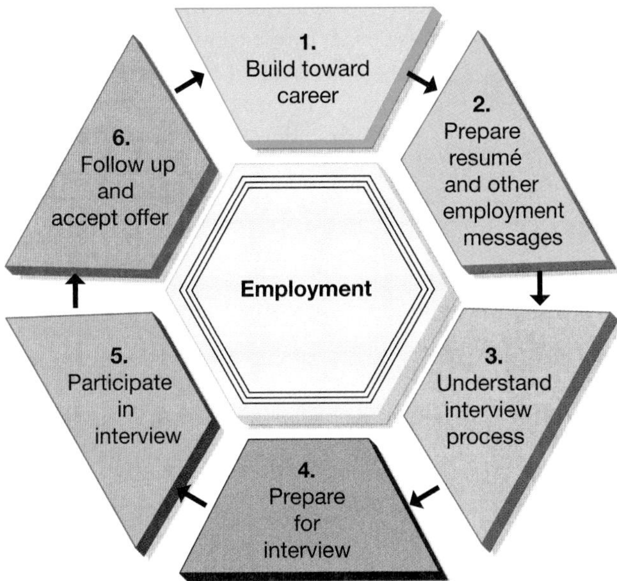

FIGURE 14-1 The Employment Search

(available online at **jobfutures.ca/en/home.sthml**) and the National Occupational Classification (NOC) **www.hrdc-drhc.gc.ca/hrib-prh/noc**. Also explore the *Dictionary of Occupational Titles* (U.S. Employment Service), the employment publications of Science Research Associates, and the *Occupational Outlook Handbook* (U.S. Bureau of Labor Statistics—in print and online at **www.bls.gov/oco**).

OBJECTIVE 2 Describe six ways to prepare for and successfully complete your search for employment.

- **Research specific companies.** Compile a list of specific organizations that appeal to you (by consulting directories of employers at your school library, at your career centre, or on the Web). Consult company profiles, press releases, financial information, and information on employment opportunities. Find out about a company's mission, products, annual reports, and employee benefits. Send an e-mail request for annual reports, brochures, or newsletters.
- **Look for job openings.** Check company Web sites for job openings, or find sites that list openings from multiple companies—many of which allow you to search by region, industry, job title, company, skills, or requirements (see "Netting a Job on the Web" on page 438). And don't forget to look in newspapers and sign up for campus interviews.
- **Respond to job openings.** You can respond directly to job listings by posting tailor-made résumés (that match required qualifications) and by sending e-mail résumés and focused cover letters directly to the people doing the hiring. Since companies receive thousands of electronic résumés a day, also consider a printed letter or a phone call.[10]
- **Network.** Find people in your field by participating in student business organizations (such as the American Marketing Association or the American Management Association, both of which have Canadian branches). Visit organizations, contact their personnel departments, and talk with key employees. On the Web, locate and communicate with potential employers using discussion groups, Usenet groups (where you can post messages on electronic bulletin boards) and listservs (where e-mail messages are sent to every member). Once you locate a potential contact, send an e-mail requesting information about the company or about job openings.
- **Find career counselling.** College and university placement offices offer counselling, credential services, job fairs, on-campus interviews, and job listings. They provide workshops in job-search techniques, résumé preparation, interview techniques,

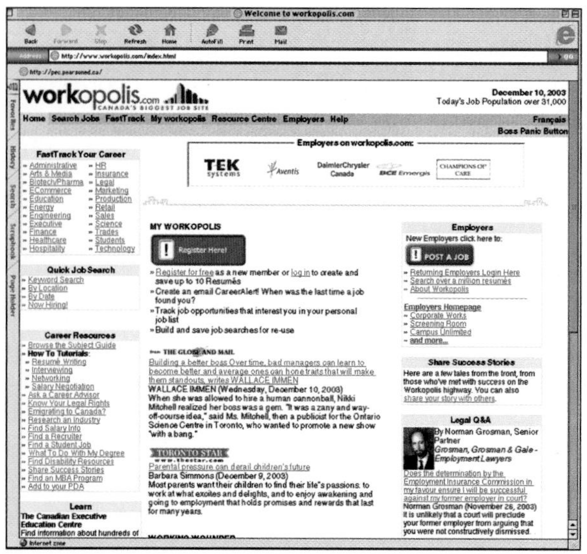

Workopolis.com is just one of the many Web sites that job seekers turn to for career advice, as well as for employer information and company job postings.

and more.[11] College- and university-run online career centres are excellent. Commercial career centres (online and off) range from award winning to depressing, so find those with advice that is both useful and sensible.

While looking for employment, you'll need to send out messages such as résumés and application letters. Whenever you send out such employment messages, you have an opportunity to showcase your communication skills—skills valued highly by the majority of employers, such as Bill Ford. So write these messages carefully by following the three-step writing process (see Figure 14–2 on page 437).

Planning Your Résumé

A **résumé** is a structured, written summary of a person's education, employment experience, and job qualifications. Many people have misconceptions about the value and function of résumés (see Table 14–1 on page 437). As with other business messages, planning a résumé means analyzing your purpose and audience, gathering information, and adapting the document to your purpose and audience:

Your résumé is a structured, written summary of your education and employment background and shows your qualifications for a job.

Begin preparing your résumé by planning carefully.

- **Analyze your purpose and audience.** Your résumé must be more than a simple list of jobs you've held. It is a form of advertising intended to stimulate an employer's interest in you—in meeting you and learning more about you. With this purpose in mind, put yourself in your audience's position and tailor your résumé to satisfy audience needs.
- **Gather pertinent information.** Gather every scrap of pertinent personal history you can and have it at your fingertips: all details of previous jobs (dates, duties, accomplishments), all relevant educational experience (formal degrees, skill certificates, academic or civic awards), all relevant information about personal endeavours (dates of membership in an association, offices you held in a club or organization, presentations you made to a community group).
- **Adapt your résumé to your audience.** Your résumé must make an impression quickly. Focus on your audience. Ask yourself what key qualifications this employer will be looking for. Decide which qualifications are your greatest strengths. Choose three or four of your most relevant accomplishments and what resulted from these accomplishments. A good résumé is flexible and can be customized for various situations and employers.

Think in terms of an image or "theme" you'd like to project. Are you academically gifted? A campus leader? A well-rounded person? A creative genius? A technical wizard? Avoid exaggerating, altering the past, or claiming skills you don't have. However, don't dwell on negatives. By knowing yourself and your audience, you'll focus successfully on the strengths needed by potential employers.

Writing Your Résumé

To write a successful résumé, you need to convey seven qualities that employers seek. You want to show that you (1) think in terms of results, (2) know how to get things done, (3) are well rounded, (4) show signs of progress, (5) have personal standards of excellence, (6) are flexible and willing to try new things, and (7) possess strong communication skills. As you organize and compose your résumé, think about how you can convey those seven qualities.

1 Planning

Analyze: Study your purpose and your audience to tailor your message for maximum effect.

Gather Information: Gather relevant information about you and about the employer you're targeting.

Adapt: Establish a good relationship by highlighting those skills and qualifications that match each employer.

2 Writing

Organize: Use the AIDA approach in letters and choose the most appropriate résumé format to highlight your strongest points.

Compose: Make your letters friendly, businesslike, and slightly more formal than usual. For résumés, use action verbs and make your style direct, brief, and crisp.

3 Completing

Revise: Evaluate content, revising for both clarity and conciseness.

Produce: Ensure a clean, sharp look whether your message is printed, e-mail, or online.

Proofread: Look carefully for errors in spelling and mechanics that can detract from your professionalism.

FIGURE 14–2 Three-Step Writing Process for Employment Messages

TABLE 14–1 Fallacies and Facts about Résumés

Fallacy	Fact
The purpose of a résumé is to list all your skills and abilities.	The purpose of a résumé is to kindle employer interest and generate an interview.
A good résumé will get you the job you want.	All a résumé can do is get you in the door.
Your résumé will be read carefully and thoroughly by an interested employer.	Your résumé probably has less than 45 seconds to make an impression.
The more good information you present about yourself in your résumé the better.	Too much information on a résumé may actually kill the reader's appetite to know more.
If you want a really good résumé, have it prepared by a résumé service.	Prepare your own résumé—unless the position is especially high-level or specialized. Even then, you should check carefully before using a service.

Organize Your Résumé Around Your Strengths

OBJECTIVE 3 Discuss how to choose the appropriate organization for your résumé, and list the advantages or disadvantages of the three options.

Although you may want to include a little information in all categories, emphasize the information that has a bearing on your career objective, and minimize or exclude any that is irrelevant or counterproductive. Call attention to your best features and downplay your weaknesses—but be sure you do so without distorting or misrepresenting the facts.[12] To focus attention on your strongest points, adopt the appropriate organizational approach—chronological, functional, or a combination of the two. The "right" choice depends on your background and goals.

THE CHRONOLOGICAL RÉSUMÉ

In a **chronological résumé**, the work-experience section dominates and is placed in the most prominent slot, immediately after the name, your contact information, and the objective (if one is included). You develop this section by listing your jobs sequentially in reverse order, beginning with the most recent position and working backward toward earlier jobs. Under each listing, describe your responsibilities and accomplishments, giving the most space to the most recent positions. Within this format, try to make the chronology clear, use bulleted lists effectively, and emphasize important points

USING THE POWER OF TECHNOLOGY 

Netting a Job on the Web

Can the Web provide the answer to all your employment dreams? Perhaps ... or perhaps not. As the Web grows, the employment information it provides is constantly expanding. And you're fortunate, because you don't have to start from scratch like some intrepid adventurer. For helpful hints and useful Web addresses, you can turn to books such as *What Color Is Your Parachute?* by Richard Nelson Bolles. Other places to check out online include the following:

- **Job Bank** (Human Resources Development Canada **www.jobbank.gc.ca/prov-en.asp**. A Government of Canada job bank, this site contains all full-time, part-time, and temporary jobs posted through HRDC for all of Canada. Create your own profile, and save it on the site with a personalized service code. French and English.
- **Job Listings** (Communications Canada **www.jobsetc.ca/toolbox/job_search**. Lists Canadian job postings sites. French and English.
- **Job-Search-Engine.com. www.jobsearchengine.com**. Search several Canadian job posting sites at a single time.
- **Canada WorkinfoNet www.workinfonet.ca**. Includes job postings and recruiting campaigns. Information on the labour market and outlook. Also find guidance on self-employment. French and English.
- **WORKink Job Postings www.workink.com/workink/national/oppsbyregion.htm**. This site is operated by the Canadian Council on Rehabilitation and Work. Browse jobs by location or link to human resources departments of companies committed to employment equity.
- **Monster Canada english.monster.ca**. Find jobs in Canada and around the world. Set up a job search agent with My Monster to receive e-mail job alerts.
- **Careers.ca www.careers.ca/job_listings.html**. Lists all jobs in newspapers for that day. Covers all provinces, Nunavut and Northwest Territories.
- **AllJobSearch.com www.alljobsearch.com**. Searches over 1000 popular job sites, newspapers, or newsgroups. Use for Canada, United States, and Great Britain. Search by job type, posting date, and category, as well as location.
- **Flipdog.com www.flipdog.com**. Posts jobs that it finds on employer Web sites. For Canadian jobs, choose "Find Jobs by Country" on Jobs page. Choose status level for privacy when posting résumé online.
- **Hot Jobs www.hotjobs.ca**. Search for jobs by keyword or browse by city or by company. Use HotBlock to control access to your posted résumé.
- **JobSearcher.ca www.jobsearcher.ca**. This engine searches several sites at once and displays results from each site.
- **workopolisCampus.com campus.workopolis.com/index.html**. Job search for new graduates. Includes government and private-sector positions and on-campus jobs. English and French.

CAREER APPLICATIONS

1. Surfing the Web can chew up a disproportionate amount of your job-seeking time. Explain how you can limit the amount of time you spend on the Web and still make it work for you.
2. When posting your résumé on the World Wide Web, you're revealing a lot of information about yourself that could be used by people other than employers (salespeople, people competing for similar positions, con artists). What sort of information might you leave off your Web résumé that would certainly appear on a traditional résumé?

Source: Adapted from Richard N. Bolles, "Career Strategizing or, What Color Is Your Web Parachute?" Yahoo! *Internet Life*, May 1998, 116, 121; Tara Weingarten, "The All-Day, All-Night, Global, No-Trouble Job Search," *Newsweek*, 6 April 1998, 17; Michele Himmelberg, "Internet an Important Tool in Employment Search," *San Diego Union-Tribune*, 7 September 1998, D2; Gina Imperato, "35 Ways to Land a Job Online," *Fast Company*, August 1998, 192–197; Roberta Maynard, "Casting the Net for Job Seekers," *Nation's Business*, March 1997, 28–29.

Most recruiters prefer the chronological plan: a historical summary of your education and work experience.

The chronological approach is the most common way to organize a résumé, and many employers prefer it. This approach has three key advantages: (1) employers are familiar with it and can easily find information, (2) it highlights growth and career progression, and (3) it highlights employment continuity and stability.[13]

The chronological approach is especially appropriate if you have a strong employment history and are aiming for a job that builds on your current career path. This is the case for Roberto Cortez, whose résumé appears in Figure 14-3 on page 440.

THE FUNCTIONAL RÉSUMÉ

A **functional résumé** focuses attention on your areas of competence.

A **functional résumé** emphasizes a list of skills and accomplishments, identifying employers and academic experience in subordinate sections. This pattern stresses individual areas of competence, so it is useful for people who are just entering the job market, want to redirect their careers, or have little continuous career-related experience. The functional approach also has three advantages: (1) without having to read through job descriptions, employers can see what you can do for them, (2) you can emphasize earlier job experience, and (3) you can de-emphasize any lack of career progress or lengthy unemployment.

Figure 14–4 on page 441 illustrates how Glenda Johns uses the functional approach to showcase her qualifications for a career in retail. Although she has not held any paid, full-time positions in retail sales, Johns has participated in work-experience programs, and she knows a good deal about the profession from research and from talking with people in the industry. She organized her résumé in a way that demonstrates her ability to handle such a position. Bear in mind, however, that many seasoned employment professionals are suspect of this résumé style. They assume that candidates who use it are trying to hide something.[14]

THE COMBINATION RÉSUMÉ

A **combination résumé** includes the best features of the chronological and functional approaches. Nevertheless, it is not commonly used, and it has two major disadvantages: (1) it tends to be longer, and (2) it can be repetitious if you have to list your accomplishments and skills in both the functional section and the chronological job descriptions.[15] When Erica Vorkamp developed her résumé, she chose not to use a chronological pattern, which would focus attention on her lack of recent work experience. As Figure 14–5 on page 442 shows, she used a combination approach to emphasize her abilities, skills, and accomplishments while also including a complete job history.

A **combination résumé** is a hybrid of the chronological and functional résumés.

Compose Your Résumé to Impress

To save your readers time and to state your information as forcefully as possible, write your résumé using a simple and direct style. Use short, crisp phrases instead of whole sentences, and focus on what your reader needs to know. Avoid using the word *I*. Instead, start your phrases with impressive action verbs such as the ones listed in Table 14–2. For instance, you might say, "Coached a Little League team to the regional playoffs" or "Managed a fast-food restaurant and four employees." Here are some additional examples of how to phrase your accomplishments using active statements that show results:

To capture attention quickly, leave out the word *I*, and begin your phrases with strong, action verbs.

Avoid Weak Statements	Use Active Statements
Responsible for developing a new filing system	Developed a new filing system that reduced paperwork by 50 percent
I was in charge of customer complaints and all ordering problems	Handled all customer complaints and resolved all product order discrepancies
Won a trip to Europe for opening the most new customer accounts in my department	Generated the highest number of new customer accounts in my department
Member of special campus task force to resolve student problems with existing cafeteria assignments	Assisted in implementing new campus dining program that allows students to eat at any dorm

TABLE 14–2 Action Verbs to Use in Résumés

accomplished	coordinated	initiated	participated	set up
achieved	created	installed	performed	simplified
administered	demonstrated	introduced	planned	sparked
approved	developed	investigated	presented	streamlined
arranged	directed	joined	proposed	strengthened
assisted	established	launched	raised	succeeded
assumed	explored	maintained	recommended	supervised
budgeted	forecasted	managed	reduced	systematized
chaired	generated	motivated	reorganized	targeted
changed	identified	operated	resolved	trained
compiled	implemented	organized	saved	transformed
completed	improved	oversaw	served	upgraded

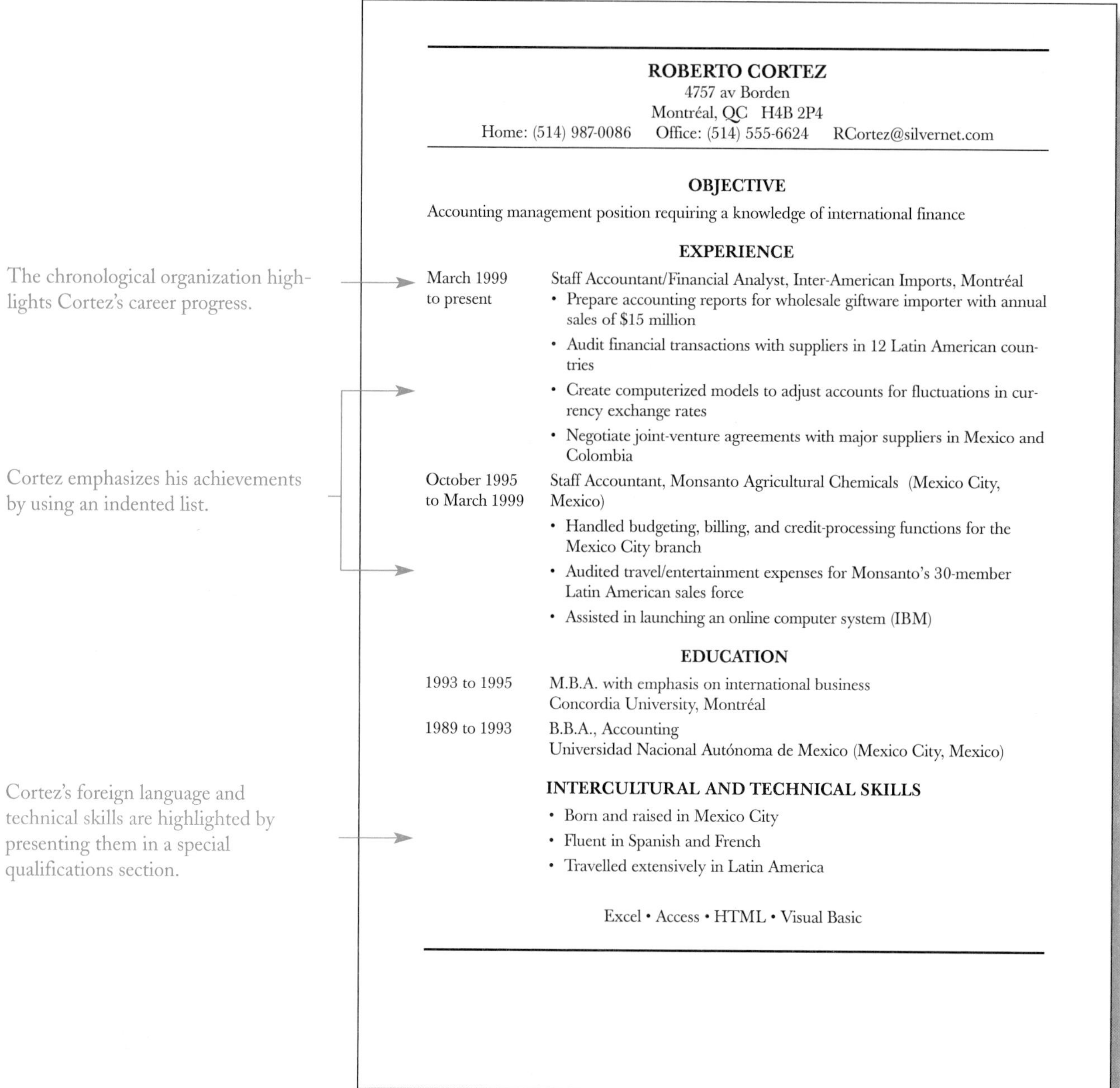

The chronological organization highlights Cortez's career progress.
Cortez emphasizes his achievements by using an indented list.
Cortez's foreign language and technical skills are highlighted by presenting them in a special qualifications section.

ROBERTO CORTEZ
4757 av Borden
Montréal, QC H4B 2P4
Home: (514) 987-0086 Office: (514) 555-6624 RCortez@silvernet.com

OBJECTIVE

Accounting management position requiring a knowledge of international finance

EXPERIENCE

March 1999 to present — Staff Accountant/Financial Analyst, Inter-American Imports, Montréal
- Prepare accounting reports for wholesale giftware importer with annual sales of $15 million
- Audit financial transactions with suppliers in 12 Latin American countries
- Create computerized models to adjust accounts for fluctuations in currency exchange rates
- Negotiate joint-venture agreements with major suppliers in Mexico and Colombia

October 1995 to March 1999 — Staff Accountant, Monsanto Agricultural Chemicals (Mexico City, Mexico)
- Handled budgeting, billing, and credit-processing functions for the Mexico City branch
- Audited travel/entertainment expenses for Monsanto's 30-member Latin American sales force
- Assisted in launching an online computer system (IBM)

EDUCATION

1993 to 1995 — M.B.A. with emphasis on international business
Concordia University, Montréal

1989 to 1993 — B.B.A., Accounting
Universidad Nacional Autónoma de Mexico (Mexico City, Mexico)

INTERCULTURAL AND TECHNICAL SKILLS
- Born and raised in Mexico City
- Fluent in Spanish and French
- Travelled extensively in Latin America

Excel • Access • HTML • Visual Basic

FIGURE 14–3 In-Depth Critique: Chronological Résumé

Most potential employers expect to see certain items in any résumé. The bare essentials are name and address, academic credentials, and employment history.

Make sure you include all necessary elements in your résumé: your name and address, academic credentials, employment history, activities and achievements, and relevant personal data.

OBJECTIVE 4 List the major sections of a traditional résumé.

NAME AND ADDRESS

The first thing an employer needs to know is who you are and where you can be reached: your name, address, and phone number (as well as your e-mail address or URL, if you have one). If you have contact information at school and at home, you can include both. Similarly, if you have a work phone and a home phone, list both and indicate which is which. Many résumé headings are nothing more than the name and address centred at the top of the page. You don't really need to include the word *résumé.* Just make sure the reader can tell in an instant who you are and how to communicate with you.

Glenda S. Johns

Home:	688 Crescent Rd. Newmarket, ON L3Y 2C2 (905) 555-5971	School:	66 Bernick Drive Barrie, ON L4M 2V6 (705)111-5254

OBJECTIVE

Retailing position that utilizes my experience in housewares

RELEVANT SKILLS

- Personal Selling/Retailing
  - Led housewares department in fewest mistakes while cashiering and balancing register receipts
  - Created end-cap and shelf displays for special housewares promotions
  - Sold the most benefit tickets during college fund-raising drive for local community centre
- Public Interaction
  - Commended by housewares manager for resolving customer complaints amicably
  - Performed in summer theatre productions in Newmarket
- Managing
  - Trained part-time housewares employees in cash register operation and customer service
  - Reworked housewares employee schedules as assistant manager
  - Organized summer activities for children 6–12 years old in Barrie–including reading programs, sports activities, and field trips

Because she is a recent graduate, the applicant describes her skills first, based on details of her limited experience.

The use of action verbs and specific facts enhances this résumé's effectiveness.

EDUCATION

- Certificate in Retail Management (3.81 GPA / 4.0 scale), Georgian College, Barrie, June 2004
- In addition to required retailing, buying, marketing, and merchandising courses, completed electives in visual merchandising, business information systems, principles of management, and business math

WORK EXPERIENCE

- Assistant manager, housewares, at The Bay store during off-campus work experience program, Barrie (winter 2003–spring 2004)
- Sales clerk, housewares, at The Bay store during off-campus work experience program, Barrie (winter 2002–spring 2003)
- Assistant director, Summer Recreation Program, Barrie (summer 2001)
- Actress, Resurgence Players, Newmarket (summer 2000)

The applicant's sketchy work history is described but not emphasized.

REFERENCES AND SUPPORTING DOCUMENTS

Available from Placement Office, Georgian College, Barrie, ON L4M 3X9

FIGURE 14–4 In-Depth Critique: Functional Résumé

CAREER OBJECTIVE OR SUMMARY OF QUALIFICATIONS

Experts disagree about the need to state a career objective on your résumé. Some argue that your objective is obvious from your qualifications. Some also maintain that such a statement only limits you as a candidate (especially if you want to be considered for a variety of openings) because it labels you as being interested in only one type of work. Other experts argue that employers will try to categorize you anyway, so you might as well make sure they attach the right label. Your goal is to generate interest immediately. If you decide to state your objective, make it effective by being as specific as possible about what you want to do:

Stating your objective or summarizing your qualifications helps the recruiter categorize you.

> A software sales position in a growing company requiring international experience
>
> Advertising assistance with print media emphasis requiring strong customer-contact skills

Erica Vorkamp

67 Garfield St., Moncton, NB E1C 3Z2
(506) 555-2153

OBJECTIVE

To obtain a position as a special events coordinator that will utilize my skills and experience

CAPABILITIES

- Plan and coordinate large-scale public events
- Develop community support for concerts, festivals, and entertainment
- Manage publicity for major events
- Coordinate activities of diverse community groups
- Establish and maintain financial controls for public events
- Negotiate contracts with performers, carpenters, electricians, and suppliers

SPECIAL EVENT EXPERIENCE

- Arranged 2004's week-long Arts and Entertainment Festival for the Moncton Public Library, involving performances by 25 musicians, dancers, actors, magicians, and artists
- Supervised the 2002 PTA Halloween Carnival, an all-day festival with game booths, live bands, contests, and food service that raised $7600 for the PTA
- Organized the 2003 Atlantic convention for 300 members of the YWCA, which extended over a three-day period and required arrangements for hotels, meals, speakers, and special tours
- Served as chair for the 2003 Children's Home Society Fashion Show, a luncheon for 150 that raised $3000 for orphans and abused children

EDUCATION

- B.A., Psychology, Mount Allison University (Sackville, NB), First Class Honours

WORK HISTORY

- Bank of Nova Scotia, June 1992 to October 1994, personnel counsellor/campus recruiter; scheduled and conducted interviews with graduating M.B.A. students on 5 Atlantic campuses; managed orientation program for recruits hired for bank's management trainee staff
- Mount Allison University, November 2000 to June 2002, part-time research assistant; helped Professor Paul Harangozo conduct behavioural experiments using rats trained to go through mazes

All capabilities and achievements are related to the specific job target, giving a very selective picture of the candidate's abilities.

Includes event attendance and fund-raising results to qualify accomplishments.

This work history has little bearing on the candidate's job target, but she felt that recruiters would want to see evidence that she has held a paid position.

FIGURE 14–5 In-Depth Critique: Combination Résumé

If you have different types of qualifications (such as a certificate in secretarial science and two years' experience in retail sales), prepare separate résumés, each with a different objective. If your immediate objective differs from your ultimate one, combine the two in a single statement:

> A marketing position with an opportunity for eventual managerial status

> Proposal writer, with the ultimate goal of becoming a contracts administrator

Instead of stating your objective, you might summarize your qualifications in a brief statement that highlights your strongest points, particularly if you have had a good deal of varied experience. Use a short, simple phrase:

> Summary of qualifications: Ten years of experience in commission selling with track record of generating new customer leads through creative advertising and community leadership positions

The career objective or summary may be the only section read fully by the employer, so if you include either one, make it strong, concise, and convincing.

EDUCATION

If you are still in school, education is probably your strongest selling point. Present your educational background in depth, choosing facts that support your "theme." Give this section a heading such as "Education," "Professional College Training," or "Academic Preparation." Then, starting with the school you most recently attended, list the name and location of each one, the term of your enrollment (in months and years), your major and minor fields of study, significant skills and abilities you've developed in your course work, and the degrees or certificates you've earned. If you're working on an unfinished degree, include in parentheses the expected date of completion. Showcase your qualifications by listing courses that have directly equipped you for the job you are seeking, and indicate any scholarships, awards, or academic honours you've received.

If education is your strongest selling point, discuss it thoroughly and highlight it visually.

The education section also includes off-campus training sponsored by business or government. Include any relevant seminars or workshops you've attended, as well as the certificates or other documents you've received. Mention high school or military training only if the associated achievements are pertinent to your career goals. Whether you list your grades depends on the job you want and the quality of your grades. If you choose to show a grade-point average, be sure to mention the scale, especially if a five-point scale is used instead of a four-point scale.

Education is usually given less emphasis in a résumé after you've worked in your chosen field for a year or more. If work experience is your strongest qualification, save the section on education for later in the résumé and provide less detail.

WORK EXPERIENCE, SKILLS, AND ACCOMPLISHMENTS

Like the education section, the work experience section focuses on your overall theme. Tailor your description to highlight the relationship between your previous responsibilities and your target field. Call attention to skills you've developed and your progression from jobs of lesser to greater responsibility.

The work experience section lists all the related jobs you've had:

- Name and location of employer
- What the organization does (if not clear from its name)
- Your functional title
- How long you worked there
- Your duties and responsibilities
- Your significant achievements or contributions

When describing your work experience, list your jobs in chronological order, with the current or last one first. Include any part-time, summer, or intern positions, even if unrelated to your current career objective. Employers will see that you have the ability to get and hold a job—an important qualification in itself. If you have worked your way through school, say so. Employers interpret this as a sign of character.

Each listing includes the name and location of the employer. If readers are unlikely to recognize the organization, briefly describe what it does. When you want to keep the name of your current employer confidential, identify the firm by industry only ("a large film-processing laboratory") or use the name but request confidentiality in the application letter or in an underlined note ("Résumé submitted in confidence") at the top or bottom of the résumé. If an organization's name or location has since changed, state the current name and location and then "formerly ..."

Before or after each job listing, state your functional title, such as "clerk typist" or "salesperson." If you were a dishwasher, say so. Don't try to make your role seem more important by glamourizing your job title, functions, or achievements. Employers are checking on candidates' backgrounds more than they used to, so inaccuracies are likely to be exposed sooner or later. Also state how long you worked on each job, from month/year to month/year. Use the phrase "to present" to denote current employment. If a job was part-time, say so.

Devote the most space to the jobs that are related to your target position. If you were personally responsible for something significant, be sure to mention it ("Devised a new collection system that accelerated payment of overdue receivables"). Facts about your skills and accomplishments are the most important information you can give a prospective employer, so quantify them whenever possible:

Designed a new ad that increased sales by 9 percent

Raised $2500 in 15 days for cancer research

Include miscellaneous facts that are related to your career objective:
- Command of other languages
- Computer expertise
- Date you can start working

You may also include a section describing other aspects of your background that pertain to your career objective. If you were applying for a position with a multinational organization, you would mention your command of another language or your travel experience. Other skills you might mention include the ability to operate a computer, word processor, or other specialized equipment. You might title a special section "Computer Skills" or "Language Skills" and place it near your "Education" or "Work Experience" section.

If samples of your work might increase your chances of getting the job, insert a line at the end of your résumé offering to supply them on request. You may put "references available upon request" at the end of your résumé, but doing so is not necessary; the availability of references is usually assumed. Don't include actual names of references. List your references on a separate sheet and take them to your interview.

ACTIVITIES AND ACHIEVEMENTS

Non-paid activities may provide evidence of work-related skills.

Your résumé should also describe any volunteer activities that demonstrate your abilities. List projects that require leadership, organization, teamwork, and cooperation. Emphasize career-related activities such as "member of the Student Marketing Association." List skills you learned in these activities, and explain how these skills are related to the job you're applying for. Include speaking, writing, or tutoring experience; participation in athletics or creative projects; fund-raising or community-service activities; and offices held in academic or professional organizations. (However, mention of political or religious organizations may be a red flag to someone with different views, so use your judgment.)

Note any awards you've received. Again, quantify your achievements whenever possible. Instead of saying that you addressed various student groups, state how many and the approximate audience sizes. If your activities have been extensive, you may want to group them into divisions such as "University Activities," "Community Service," "Professional Associations," "Seminars and Workshops," and "Speaking Activities." An alternative is to divide them into two categories: "Service Activities" and "Achievements, Awards, and Honours."

PERSONAL DATA

Provide only the personal data that will help you get the job.

Experts advise you to leave personal interests off your résumé—unless including them enhances the employer's understanding of why you would be the best candidate for the job.[16] For instance, candidates applying to Mountain Equipment Co-op, a retailer of outdoor gear and apparel, may want to list outdoor activities as a personal interest. Someone applying for a bodyguard position with a security company may want to list martial arts achievements among their personal interests. Such information shows how a candidate will fit in with the organization's culture.

Some information should be excluded from your résumé. Human rights legislation prohibits employers from discriminating on the basis of gender, marital or family status, age, race, colour, religion, national origin, and physical or mental disability. So be sure to exclude any items that could encourage discrimination. Experts also recommend excluding salary information, reasons for leaving jobs, and names of previous supervisors; save these items for the interview, and offer them only if the employer specifically requests them. Supply your social insurance number only when you are offered the job and are completing the required Revenue Canada and company benefit forms.

If military service is relevant to the position, you may list it here (or under "Education" or "Work Experience"). List the date of induction, the branch of service, where you served, the highest rank you achieved, any accomplishments related to your career goals, and the date you were discharged.

Avoid Résumé Deception

Do not misrepresent your background or qualifications.

In an effort to put your best foot forward, you may be tempted to skirt a few points that could raise questions about your résumé. Although statistics on the prevalence of résumé inflation are difficult to gather, the majority of recruiters agree that distortion is common. Avoid the most frequent forms of deception:[17]

- **Do not claim educational credits you don't have.** Candidates may state (or imply) that they earned a degree when, in fact, they never attended the school or they attended but never completed the regular program. A typical claim might read, "Majored in commerce at the University of Toronto."
- **Do not inflate your grade-point average.** Students who feel pressured to impress employers with their academic performance may claim a higher GPA than they actually achieved.
- **Do not stretch dates of employment to cover gaps.** Many candidates try to camouflage gaps in their work history by giving vague dates of employment. For example, a candidate who left a company in January 2002 and joined another in December 2003 might cover up by showing that the first job ended in 2002 and the next began in 2003.
- **Do not falsely claim to be self-employed.** Another common way people cover a period of unemployment is by saying that they were "self-employed" or a "consultant." The candidate claims to have operated an independent business during the period in question.
- **Do not claim to have worked for companies that are out of business.** Candidates who need to fill a gap in their work record sometimes say they worked for a firm that has gone out of business. Checking such claims is difficult because the people who were involved in the disbanded business are hard to track down.
- **Do not omit jobs that might cause embarrassment.** Being fired from one or two jobs is understandable when corporate mergers and downsizing are commonplace. However, a candidate who has lost several jobs in quick succession may seem a poor employee to recruiters. To cover a string of job losses, candidates may decide to leave out a few positions and stretch the dates of employment for the jobs held before and after.
- **Do not exaggerate expertise or experience.** Candidates often inflate their accomplishments by using verbs somewhat loosely. Words such as *supervised, managed, increased, improved,* and *created* imply that the candidate was personally responsible for results that, in reality, were the outcome of a group effort.

Think twice before trying one of these ploys yourself. If you misrepresent your background and your résumé raises suspicion, you will probably get caught, and your reputation will be damaged. A deceptive résumé can seriously affect your ability to get hired and pursue your career.

Experienced recruiters are familiar with the games that candidates play to enhance their image. Many employers fire people who lied on their résumés, and companies today are hiring highly skilled investigators who can access much-improved databases to seek the truth. Sure, it's fine to present your strongest, most impressive qualifications and to minimize your weaknesses. But don't exaggerate, alter the past, or claim to have skills you don't have (see Table 14–3 on page 446).

Completing Your Résumé

The last step in the Three-Step Writing Process is no less important than the other two. As with any other business message, you need to revise your résumé, produce it in an appropriate form, and proofread it for any errors. For résumés, you'll also be concerned with submitting electronic versions and building online versions.

Revising Your Résumé

The key to writing a successful résumé is to adopt the "you" attitude and focus on your audience. Think about what the prospective employer needs, and then tailor your résumé accordingly. People at organizations such as the Ford Motor Company read

The "perfect" résumé responds to the reader's needs and preferences and avoids some common faults.

TABLE 14–3 How Far Can You Go To Make Your Résumé Strong and Positive?

Do	Don't
Tell the truth. If you lie, you will almost certainly get caught, and the damage to your career could be significant.	**Fabricate.** Fake academic degrees and nonexistent jobs are checked first and will cost you the job, before or after you're hired.
Make your story positive. Most blemishes on your record can be framed in a positive way.	**Make blatant omissions.** Failing to disclose a job that didn't work out is almost as bad as making one up.
Sanitize your record. Clear up unresolved issues such as tax liens and lawsuits.	**Exaggerate successes.** Be ready to prove any claim about your accomplishments.
	Go overboard. There's usually no need to disclose career or personal history that's more than 15 years old. If asked directly, answer truthfully—but with a minimum of elaboration.

thousands of résumés every year and they complain about the following common problems:

- **Too long.** The résumé is not concise, relevant, and to the point.
- **Too short or sketchy.** The résumé does not give enough information for a proper evaluation of the applicant.
- **Hard to read.** A lack of "white space" and of devices such as indentions and boldfacing makes the reader's job more difficult.
- **Wordy.** Descriptions are verbose, with numerous words used for what could be said more simply.
- **Too slick.** The résumé appears to have been written by someone other than the applicant, which raises the question of whether the qualifications have been exaggerated.
- **Amateurish.** The applicant appears to have little understanding of the business world or of a particular industry, as revealed by including the wrong information or presenting it awkwardly.
- **Poorly reproduced.** The print is faint and difficult to read.
- **Misspelled and ungrammatical throughout.** Recruiters conclude that candidates who make such mistakes lack good verbal skills, which are important on the job.
- **Boastful.** The overconfident tone makes the reader wonder whether the applicant's self-evaluation is realistic.
- **Dishonest.** The applicant claims to have expertise or work experience that he or she does not possess.
- **Gimmicky.** The words, structure, decoration, or material used in the résumé depart so far from the usual as to make the résumé ineffective.

Compare the final version of your own with the suggestions in this chapter's "Checklist: Writing Résumés" on page 448.

Producing Your Traditional Résumé

With less than a minute to make a good impression, your résumé needs to look sharp and grab a recruiter's interest in the first few lines. A typical recruiter devotes 45 seconds to each résumé before tossing it into either the "maybe" or the "reject" pile.[18] Most recruiters skim a résumé rather than read it from top to bottom. If yours doesn't stand out, chances are the recruiter won't look at it long enough to judge your qualifications.

The key characteristics of a good résumé are

- Neatness
- Simplicity
- Accuracy
- Honesty

To give your printed résumé the best appearance possible, use a clean typeface on high-grade, letter-size bond paper (in white or some light earth tone). Make sure that your stationery and envelope match. Leave ample margins all around, and make sure that any corrections are unnoticeable. Avoid italic typefaces, which are difficult to read, and use a quality laser printer.

The length of your résumé depends on how much space you need in order to show what you can do. For entry-level positions, a one-page résumé may be just right. If you have a great deal of experience and are applying for a higher-level position, you may need to prepare a somewhat longer résumé. The rule guiding length is to have enough space to present a persuasive, but accurate, portrait of your skills and accomplishments.

Lay out your résumé to make information easy to grasp.[19] Break up the text with headings that call attention to various aspects of your background, such as work experience and education. Underline or capitalize key points, or set them off in the left margin. Use lists to itemize your most important qualifications, and leave plenty of white space, even if doing so forces you to use an extra page.

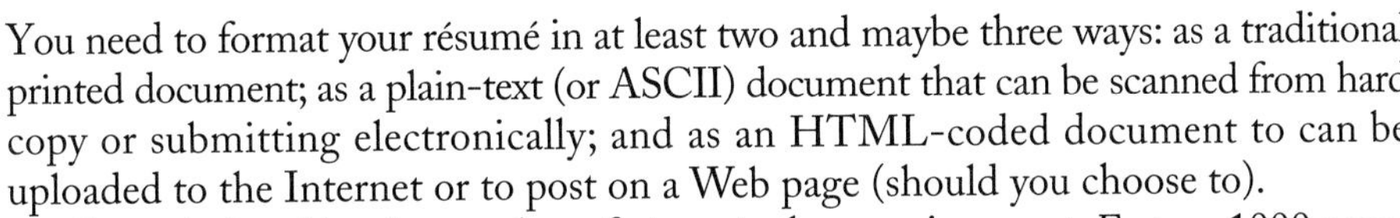

Job recruiters can receive hundreds of résumés a month. A well-formatted résumé makes their job easier and helps yours get noticed.

Converting Your Résumé to an Electronic Format

OBJECTIVE 5 Describe the process involved in adapting your résumé to an electronic format.

You need to format your résumé in at least two and maybe three ways: as a traditional printed document; as a plain-text (or ASCII) document that can be scanned from hard copy or submitting electronically; and as an HTML-coded document to can be uploaded to the Internet or to post on a Web page (should you choose to).

Doing an electronic version of your résumé is helpful if it will be scanned or if you will be posting it on the Internet or submitting it via e-mail.

Overwhelmed by the number of résumés they receive, most *Fortune* 1000 companies encourage applicants to submit electronic (scannable) résumés. Scannable résumés convey the same information as traditional résumés, but the format must be changed to one that is computer friendly, because scannable résumés are not intended to be read by humans. During the scanning process, special hardware and software are used to convert a paper résumé into an image on the employer's computer, which can be searched and sorted by keywords, criteria, or almost anything the employer wants (see Figure 14–6 on page 449).

To make your traditional résumé a scannable one, format it as a plain-text (ASCII) document, improve its look, and modify its content slightly by providing a list of keywords and by balancing common language with current jargon.[20]

PREPARE YOUR RÉSUMÉ AS AN ASCII DOCUMENT

To make your résumé scannable
- Save it as an ASCII file
- Provide a list of key words
- Balance clear language with up-to-date jargon

ASCII is a common plain-text language that allows your résumé to be read by any scanner and accessed by any computer, regardless of the wordprocessing software you used to prepare the document. All wordprocessing programs allow you to save files as plain text. To convert your résumé to an ASCII plain-text file, do the following:

- ➤ Remove all formatting (boldfacing, underlining, italics, centring, bullets, graphic lines, etc.) and all formatting codes such a tab settings or tables.
- ➤ Remove shadows and reverse print (white letters on black background).
- ➤ Remove graphics and boxes.
- ➤ Use scannable typefaces (such as Helvetica, Futura, Optima, Univers, Times New Roman, Palatino, New Century Schoolbook, and Courier).
- ➤ Use a font size of 10 to 14 points.
- ➤ Remove multicolumn formats that resemble newspapers or newsletters.
- ➤ Save your document under a different name by using your word processor's "save as" option and selecting "text only with line breaks."

IMPROVE THE LOOK OF YOUR SCANNABLE RÉSUMÉ

Simple formatting improves the appearance of ASCII documents.

Résumés in ASCII format (without special formatting) look ugly in comparison to traditional résumés. Use the following formatting techniques (which are acceptable for scannable résumés) to enhance the résumé's overall look and effectiveness:[21]

Checklist: Writing Résumés

Planning Your Résumé

✓ Analyze your purpose and audience (both the organization and the individuals there).

✓ Gather all pertinent information, including work history (specific dates, duties, and accomplishments), educational experience, and personal endeavors.

✓ Adapt your résumé to your audience, combining your experiences into a straightforward message that communicates what you can do for your potential employer.

Organizing Your Résumé

✓ Use the chronological approach unless you have a weak employment history.

✓ Use the functional approach if you are new to the job market, want to redirect your career, or have gaps in your employment history.

✓ Use the combined approach to maximize the advantages of both chronological and functional résumés, but only when neither of the other two formats will work.

Composing Your Résumé in a Simple, Direct Style

✓ Use short noun phrases and action verbs, not whole sentences.

✓ Use facts, not opinions.

✓ Adopt a "you" attitude.

✓ Omit personal pronouns (especially *I*).

✓ Omit the date of preparation, desired salary, and work schedule.

✓ Use parallelism when listing multiple items.

✓ Use positive language and simple words.

✓ Use white space, quality paper, and quality printing.

Opening Your Résumé

✓ Include contact information (name, address).

✓ Include a career objective or a skills summary, if desired.

✓ Make your career objective specific and interesting.

✓ Prepare two separate résumés if you can perform two unrelated types of work.

✓ In a skills summary, present your strongest qualifications first.

Presenting Your Educational Background

✓ List the name and location of every post-secondary school you've attended (with dates, and with degrees/certificates obtained).

✓ Indicate your college or university major (and minor).

✓ Indicate numerical scale (4.0 or 5.0) if you include your grade-point average.

✓ List other experiences (seminars, workshops), with dates and certificates obtained.

Presenting Your Work Experience, Skills, and Accomplishments

✓ List all relevant work experience (paid employment, volunteer work, internships).

✓ List full-time and part-time jobs.

✓ Provide name and location of each employer (with dates of employment).

✓ List job title and describe responsibilities.

✓ Note on-the-job accomplishments and skills; quantify them whenever possible.

Describing Activities and Achievements

✓ List all relevant offices and leadership positions.

✓ List projects you have undertaken.

✓ Show abilities such as writing or speaking, and list publications and community service.

✓ List other information, such as your proficiency in languages other than English.

✓ Mention ability to operate special equipment, including technical, computer, and software skills.

Including Personal Data

✓ Omit personal details that might be seen as negative or used to discriminate against you.

✓ Leave personal interests off unless they enhance your value to potential employers.

✓ List a reference only with permission to do so.

Converting Your Traditional Résumé to an Electronic One

✓ Eliminate graphics, boldface, underlines, italics, small print, tabs, and all format codes.

✓ Save the file in plain-text (ASCII) format.

✓ Add blank spaces, align text, and use asterisks for bullets.

✓ Add a "Keyword Summary," listing nouns to define skills, experience, education, and professional attributes.

✓ Mirror the job description when possible.

✓ Add job-related jargon, but don't overdo it.

Building Your Online Résumé

✓ Provide your URL and e-mail address.

✓ Use a keyword hyperlink to an ASCII version so that employers can download it.

✓ Use a keyword hyperlink to a fully formatted résumé that can be read online and printed.

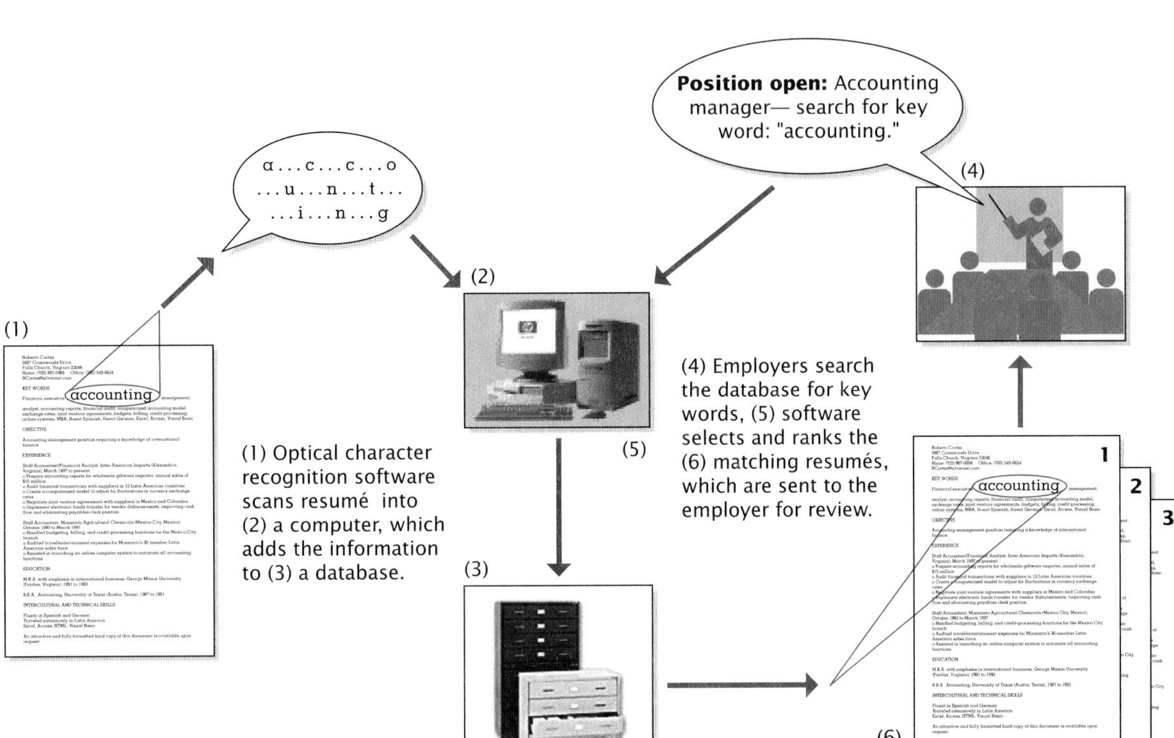

FIGURE 14–6 Understanding the Scanning Process

- Align text by adding some blank spaces (rather than tabs).
- Create headings and separate paragraphs by adding a few blank lines.
- Indicate bullets with an asterisk or the lowercase letter *o*.
- Use white space so that scanners and computers can tell when one topic ends and another begins.
- Do not condense the spacing between letters.
- Use all capital letters for section headings (as long as the letters do not touch each other).
- Put your name at the top of each page on its own line (with no text appearing above or beside your name).
- Use the standard address format below your name.
- List each phone number on its own line.
- Use white or light-coloured 21.5-by-27.5-cm paper, printing on one side only.

Because scannable résumés are designed to be read by computers, it's fine to submit multiple pages—but don't get carried away. To increase your chances of a quality scan, do not fold or staple the résumé and do not send a photocopy. Provide a printed original, if possible.

PROVIDE A LIST OF KEY WORDS

When converting your résumé to a scannable format, emphasize certain key words to help potential employers select your résumé from the thousands they scan. Employers generally search for nouns (since verbs tend to be generic rather than specific to a particular position or skill). To maximize the number of matches (or hits) include a key word summary of 20 to 30 words and phrases that define your skills, experience, education, professional affiliations, and so on. Place this list right after your name and address. Here's an example of a possible key word summary for an accountant:

Going Online

Post an Online Résumé

At CareerBuilder, you'll find sample résumés, tips on preparing different types of résumés (including scannable ones), links to additional articles, and expert advice on creating résumés that bring positive results. After you've polished your résumé-writing skills, you can search for jobs online using the site's numerous links to national and international industry-specific Web sites. You can access the information at CareerBuilder to develop your résumé and then post it with prospective employers—all free of charge. Take advantage of what this site offers, and get ideas for writing or improving a résumé.

www.careerbuilder.com/ gh–res–htg–tips.html

To link directly to this site, visit our Companion Website at **www.pearsoned.ca/thill/** *and look for the Chapter 14 resources.*

Key words help potential employers sort through an entire database of résumés.

Key Word Summary

Accountant, Corporate Controller, Fortune 1000, Receivables, Payables, Inventory, Cash Flow, Financial Analysis, Payroll Experience, Corporate Taxes, Activity-Based Accounting, Problem Solving, Computer Skills, Excel, Access, Networks, HTML, Peachtree, Quick Books, BA Ryerson University—Business Management, CA, Honours, Team Player, Flexible, Willing to Travel, Fluent French.

One way to identify which key words to include in your electronic summary is to underline all the skills listed in ads for the types of jobs you're interested in. Make sure these ads match your qualifications and experience. Although most employers search for key words that tell whether you *can* do the job, some employers also look for key words that tell whether you *will* do the job. These *interpersonal key words* tell what kind of person you are (see Table 14–4 below).

Some job candidates try to beat the system by listing every conceivable skill and by guessing which words the computer is likely to be looking for. But that strategy seldom works. The computer may be looking for a Rotman Business School graduate who once worked at National Bank Financial and now lives in Kamloops. If you went to Concordia University, worked at McCain Foods, and live in Whitehorse, you're out of luck.[22]

Use words your employer will understand by including some jargon specific to your field.

Balance Common Language with Current Jargon Another way to maximize hits on your résumé is to use words that potential employers will understand (for example, say *keyboard*, not *input device*). Also, use abbreviations sparingly (except for common ones such as B.A. or M.B.A.). At the same time, learn and use the important buzzwords in your field. Look for current jargon in the want ads of major newspapers such as *The Globe and Mail*, the *National Post*, and *The Wall Street Journal* and in other résumés in your field that are posted online. Be careful to check and recheck the spelling, capitalization, and punctuation of any jargon you include, and use only those words you see most often.

Roberto Cortez created an electronic résumé by changing his formatting and adding a list of key words. However, the information remains essentially the same and appears in the same order, as you can see in Figure 14–7. Now his target employers can scan his résumé into a database, and Cortez can submit his résumé via e-mail or post it on the Internet.

E-mail is the best way to transmit your plain-text résumé.

Proofread Your Résumé

Your résumé is a concrete example of how you will prepare material on the job. In every format, remember to pay close attention to mechanics and details. Check all headings and lists for parallelism, and be sure that your grammar, spelling, and punctuation are correct.

TABLE 14–4 Interpersonal Keywords

ability to delegate	communication skills	follow instructions	open minded	self-accountable
ability to implement	competitive	follow through	oral communication	self-managing
ability to plan	conceptual ability	follow up	organizational skills	sensitive
ability to train	creative	high energy	persuasive	setting priorities
accurate	customer oriented	industrious	problem solving	supportive
adaptable	detail minded	innovative	public speaking	takes initiative
aggressive work	empowering others	leadership	results oriented	team player
analytical ability	ethic	multitasking	risk taking	tenacious
assertive	flexible	open communication	safety conscious	willing to travel

Roberto Cortez
4757 av Borden
Montréal, QC H4B 2P4

Home: (514) 987-0086 Office: (514) 555-6624

RCortez@silvernet.com

KEY WORDS

Financial executive, accounting management, international finance, financial analyst, accounting reports, financial audit, computerized accounting model, exchange rates, joint-venture agreements, budgets, billing, credit processing, online systems, M.B.A., fluent Spanish, fluent French, Excel, Access, Visual Basic, team player, willing to travel

OBJECTIVE

Accounting management position requiring a knowledge of international finance

EXPERIENCE

Staff Accountant/Financial Analyst, Inter-American Imports (Montréal)
March 1999 to present

o Prepare accounting reports for wholesale importer, annual sales of $15 million
o Audit financial transactions with suppliers in 12 Latin American countries
o Create computerized models to adjust for fluctuations in currency exchange rates
o Negotiate joint-venture agreements with suppliers in Mexico and Colombia

Staff Accountant, Monsanto Agricultural Chemicals (Mexico City)
October 1995 to March 1999

o Handled budgeting, billing, credit-processing functions for the Mexico City branch
o Audited travel/entertainment expenses for Monsanto's 30-member Latin American sales force
o Assisted in launching an online computer system (IBM)

EDUCATION

M.B.A. with emphasis on international business, Concordia University (Montréal) 1993 to 1995

B.B.A., Accounting, Universidad Nacional Autónoma de Mexico (Mexico City) 1989 to 1993

INTERCULTURAL QUALIFICATIONS

Born and raised in Mexico City
Fluent in Spanish and French
Travelled extensively in Latin America
Excel, Access, HTML, Visual Basic

Formatted résumé available on request

Remove all boldfacing, rules, bullets, and two-column formatting.

Includes carefully selected key words that describe Cortez's skills and accomplishments.

Key words also include specific attributes such as "team player" and "willing to travel" to single Cortez out from the crowd.

Uses a lowercase letter *o* in his indented lists.

Uses ample white space to make his plain-text résumé appear more readable.

The final note informs the reader of the availability of a fully formatted version of this electronic résumé.

FIGURE 14–7 In-Depth Critique: Electronic Résumé

Once your résumé is complete, update it continuously. As already mentioned, employment is becoming much more flexible these days, so it's likely you'll want to change employers at some point. Besides, you'll also need your résumé to apply for membership in professional organizations and to work toward a promotion. Keeping your résumé updated is a good idea.

Keep your résumé up to date.

Submitting Scannable Résumés

If an employer gives you an option of submitting a scannable résumé by mail, by fax, or by e-mail, choose e-mail. E-mail puts your résumé directly into the employer's database, bypassing the scanning process. If you send your résumé in a paper format by regular mail or by fax, you run the risk that an OCR scanning program will

E-mail is the best way to submit your plain-text résumé.

SuperJobs.net is a leading job-search site for university and entry-level professional positions, with résumé matching and daily e-mails to students.

create an error when reading it. In fact, increasing numbers of job applicants are submitting both a traditional and a scannable résumé, explaining in their cover letter that the scannable résumé is for downloading into a database if the company desires.[23]

When submitting your résumé by e-mail, find out how the company wants to receive it. Many human resources departments won't accept attached files; they're concerned about computer viruses. If preferred, you can paste your résumé into the body of your e-mail message. Whenever you know a reference number or a job ad number, include it in your e-mail subject line.

If you're posting a scannable résumé to an employer's online résumé builder, copy and paste the appropriate sections from your electronic file directly into the employer's form. This method avoids rekeying and eliminates errors.

If you fax your scannable résumé, set your machine to "fine" mode (to ensure a high-quality printout on the receiving end). If you're mailing a résumé, you may want to send both a well-designed traditional résumé and a scannable one. Simply attach Post-it notes, labelling one "visual résumé" and the other "scannable résumé."

Building an Online Résumé

One advantage of posting your résumé on your Web site is the opportunity to use hyperlinks.

If you wish to post your résumé on your Web page, provide employers with your URL; most recruiters won't take the time to use search engines to find your site.[24] As you design your Web site résumé, think of important key words to use as hyperlinks—words that will grab an employer's attention and make the recruiter want to click on that hyperlink to learn more about you. You can make links to papers you've written, recommendations, and sound or video clips. Don't distract potential employers from your credentials by using hyperlinks to organizations or other Web sites.

To post your résumé with an index service, you must convert it to an electronic format (see page 447) and transmit it by mail, fax, modem, or e-mail. Once your résumé is in the service's database, it is sent to employers who match the key words you've listed.

Do not use photos, and avoid providing information that reveals your age, gender, race, marital status, or religion. Because a Web site is a public access area, you should also leave out the names of references and previous employers. Either mention that references are available on request, or say nothing. Finally, include an ASCII version of your résumé on your Web page so prospective employers can download it into their company's database.

OBJECTIVE 6 Define the purpose of application letters, and explain how to apply the AIDA organizational approach to them.

Preparing Other Types of Employment Messages

Although your résumé will take the greatest amount of time and effort, you will need to prepare other employment messages as well, including application letters, job-inquiry letters, and application follow-ups.

Application Letters

Whenever you submit your résumé, accompany it with a cover, or application, letter to let readers know what you're sending, why you're sending it, and how they can benefit from reading it. Because your application letter is in your own style (rather than the choppy, shorthand style of your résumé), it gives you a chance to show your communication skills and some personality.

Always send your résumé and application letter together, because each has a unique job to perform. The purpose of your résumé is to get employers interested enough to contact you for an interview. The purpose of your application letter is to get the reader interested enough to read your résumé.

Application letters are intended to get readers interested enough to read your résumé.

Before drafting a letter, learn something about the organization you're applying to. Then focus on your audience so that you can show you've done your homework. Imagine yourself in the recruiter's situation, and show how your background and talents will solve a particular problem or fill a specific need of the company. The more you can learn about the organization, the better you'll be able to capture the reader's attention and convey your desire to join the company.[25] During your research, find out the name, title, and department of the person you're writing to. Reaching and addressing the right person is the most effective way to gain attention. Avoid phrases such as "To Whom It May Concern" and "Dear Sir."

When putting yourself in your reader's shoes, remember that this person's in-box is probably overflowing with résumés and cover letters. So respect your reader's time. Steer clear of gimmicks, which almost never work, and be sure your cover letter interprets your résumé, rather than repeats it word-for-word. Keep your letter straightforward, fact based, short, upbeat, and professional. Some quick tips for cover letters include the following:[26]

Write the most effective application letter you can.

- **Be specific.** Avoid general objectives. Be as clear as possible about the kind of opportunity and industry you're looking for.
- **Include salary.** If you've been working in your field, include your current salary, but make sure your reader understands that this information is not a demand but intended to inform and assist.
- **Make e-mail covers even shorter.** When sending a cover letter by e-mail, make it a bit shorter than traditional application letters. Remember, e-mail readers want the gist very quickly.
- **Aim for high quality.** Meticulously check your spelling, mechanics, and grammar. Recruiters complain about the declining quality of written communication, including cover letters.

Maintain a friendly yet conversational tone, and highlight the specific points the company is looking for. To sell the employer on you, show that you know the job.

If you're sending a **solicited application letter**—in response to an announced job opening—you'll usually know what qualifications the organization is seeking. You'll also have more competition because hundreds of other job seekers will have seen the listing and may be sending applications too. The letter in Figure 14–8 on page 454 was written in response to a help-wanted ad. Kenneth Sawyer highlights his chief qualifications and mirrors the requirements specified in the ad. He actually grabs attention by focusing on the phrase "proven skills" used in the ad: he elaborates on his own proven skills throughout the letter, and even mentions the term in the closing paragraph.

You write a solicited application letter in response to an announced job opening.

In some respects, an **unsolicited letter**—sent to an organization that has not announced an opening—stands a better chance of being read and receiving individualized attention. Glenda Johns wrote the unsolicited application letter in Figure 14–9 on page 455. She manages to give a snapshot of her qualifications and skills without repeating what is said in her résumé (which appears in Figure 14–3 on page 440). She gains attention by focusing on the needs of the employer.

You write an unsolicited application letter to an organization that has not announced a job opening.

Like your résumé, your application letter is a form of advertising, so organize it as you would a sales letter: Use the AIDA approach, focus on your audience, and emphasize reader benefits (as discussed in Chapter 9). Make sure your style projects confidence. To sell a potential employer on your merits, you must believe in them and sound as though you do.

Follow the AIDA approach when writing your application letter: attention, interest, desire, action.

Both solicited and unsolicited letters present your qualifications similarly. The main difference is in the opening paragraph. In a solicited letter, you need no special

States the reason for writing and links the writer's experience to stated qualifications.

Discusses how specific skills apply to the job sought, showing that Sawyer understands the job's responsibilities.

Asks for an interview and facilitates action.

Kenneth Sawyer

2141 Michelle Cres., Kelowna, BC V1Z 2W2

February 2, 2005

Ms. Angela Singh
Director of Administration
Cummings and Welbane, Inc.
260 Harvey Ave., Suite 333
Kelowna, BC V1Y 7S5

Dear Ms. Singh:

In the January 31 issue of the *Daily Courier,* your ad mentioned "proven skills." I believe I have what you are looking for in an administrative assistant. In addition to experience in a variety of office settings, I am familiar with the computer software that you use in your office.

I recently completed a three-course sequence at the University College of the Cariboo in Kamloops, on Microsoft Word and PowerPoint. I learned how to apply those programs to speed up letter- and report-writing tasks. A workshop on "Writing and Editing with the Unix Processor" gave me experience with other valuable applications such as composing and formatting sales letters, financial reports, and presentation slides.

These skills were invaluable to me as assistant to the director of UCC food-training (please refer to my résumé). I'm particularly proud of the order-confirmation system I designed, which has sharply reduced the problems of late shipments and depleted inventories.

Because "proven skills" are best explained in person, I would appreciate an interview with you. Please phone me any afternoon between 3 and 5 p.m. at (250) 555-6139 to let me know the day and time most convenient for you.

Sincerely,

Kenneth Sawyer

Kenneth Sawyer

Enclosure: Résumé

FIGURE 14–8 In-Depth Critique: Sample Solicited Application Letter

attention- getter because you have been invited to apply. In an unsolicited letter, you need to start by capturing the reader's attention and interest.

GETTING ATTENTION

Table 14–5 on page 456 highlights some important ways to spark interest and grab attention in your opening paragraph. All these examples demonstrate the "you" attitude, and many indicate how the applicant can serve the employer.

The opening of an application letter captures attention, gives the reason you're writing, and states which job you're applying for.

The opening paragraph of your application letter must also state your reason for writing and the position you are applying for:

> Please consider my application for an entry-level position in technical writing.
>
> Your firm advertised a fleet sales position (on September 23, 2005, in the *St. John's Evening Telegram*).

655 Crescent Rd.
Newmarket, ON L3Y 2C2
June 16, 2005

Ms. Patricia Downings, Store Manager
Zellers Inc.
Orillia Square Mall
Orillia, ON L3V 6H6

Dear Ms. Downings:

You want retail clerks and managers who are accurate, enthusiastic, and experienced. You want someone who cares about customer service, who understands merchandising, and who can work with others to get the job done. When you're ready to hire a manager trainee or a clerk who is willing to work toward promotion, please consider me for the job.

Gains attention in the first paragraph.

Working as clerk and then as assistant department manager in a large department store has taught me how challenging a career in retailing can be. Moreover, my certificate in retailing (including work in such courses as retailing, marketing, and business information systems) will provide your store with a well-rounded associate. Most important, I can offer Zellers' Orillia store more than my two years of study and field experience. You'll find that I'm interested in every facet of retailing, eager to take on responsibility, and willing to continue learning throughout my career. Please look over my résumé to see how my skills can benefit your store.

Points out personal qualities that aren't specifically stated in her résumé.

I understand that Zellers prefers to promote its managers from within the company, and I would be pleased to start out with an entry-level position until I gain the necessary experience. Do you have any associate positions opening up soon? Could we discuss my qualifications? I will phone you early next Wednesday to arrange a meeting at your convenience.

Interests reader with knowledge of the company's policy toward promotions.

Focuses on the audience and displays the "you" attitude, even though the last paragraph uses the word *I*.

Sincerely,

Glenda Johns

Glenda Johns

Enclosure

FIGURE 14–9 In-Depth Critique: Sample Unsolicited Application Letter

With my 16 months of new-car sales experience, won't you consider me for that position?

Open a solicited application letter by mentioning how you found out about the position.

Another way to state your reason for writing is to use a title at the opening of your letter:

Subject: Application for bookkeeper position

BUILDING INTEREST AND INCREASING DESIRE

The middle section of your application letter presents your strongest selling points in terms of their potential benefit to the organization, thereby building interest in you and creating a desire to interview you. If you already mentioned your selling points in the opening, don't repeat them. Simply give supporting evidence. Be careful not to repeat the facts presented in your résumé; simply interpret those facts for the reader. Spell

After getting your reader's attention, you can begin emphasizing how hiring you will benefit the organization.

TABLE 14–5 Tips for Getting Attention in Application Letters

Tip	Example
Unsolicited Application Letters	
· Show how your strongest skills will benefit the organization. A 20 year old in her third year of college might begin like this:	When you need a secretary in your export division who can take shorthand at 125 words a minute and transcribe notes at 70—in English, Spanish, or Portuguese—call me.
· Describe your understanding of the job's requirements and then show how well your qualifications fit them.	Your annual report states that Suncor runs employee training about work-force diversity. The difficulties involved in running such programs can be significant, as I learned while tutoring inner-city high school students last summer. My 12 pupils were enrolled in vocational training programs and came from diverse ethnic and racial backgrounds. The one thing they had in common was a lack of familiarity with the typical employer's expectations. To help them learn the "rules of the game," I developed exercises that cast them in various roles: boss, customer, new recruit, and coworker. Of the 12 students, 10 subsequently found full-time jobs and have called or written to tell me how much they gained from the workshop.
· Mention the name of a person known to you and highly regarded by the reader.	When Janice McHugh of your franchise sales division spoke to our business communication class last week, she said you often need promising new marketing graduates at this time of year.
· Refer to publicized company activities, achievements, changes, or new procedures.	Today's issue of the *The Winnipeg Free Press* reports that you need the expertise of computer programmers versed in robotics when your Lansing tire plant automates this spring.
· Use a question to demonstrate your understanding of organization's needs.	Can your fast-growing market research division use an interviewer with 1-1\2 years of field-survey experience, a B.A. in public relations, and a real desire to succeed? If so, please consider me for the position.
· Use a catch-phrase opening if the job requires ingenuity and imagination.	*Haut monde*—whether said in French, Italian, or Arabic, it still means "high society." As an interior designer for your Yorkville showroom, not only could I serve and sell to your distinguished clientele, but I could do it in all these languages. I speak, read, and write them fluently.
Solicited Application Letters	
· Identify the publication in which the ad ran; then describe what you have to offer.	Your ad in the April issue of *Travel & Leisure* for a cruise social director caught my eye. My eight years of experience as a social director in the travel industry would allow me to serve your new Caribbean cruise division well.

out a few of your key qualifications, and back up your assertions with some convincing evidence of your ability to perform:

Poor: I completed three courses in business communication, earning an A in each course, and have worked for the past year at Imperial Construction.

Improved: Using the skills gained from three semesters of training in business communication, I developed a collection system for Imperial Construction that reduced its 2003 bad-debt losses by 3.7 percent, or $9902, over those of 2002. Instead of using time worn terminology, the new system's collection letters offered discount incentives for speedy payment.

Improved: Experience in customer relations and university courses in public relations have taught me how to handle the problem-solving tasks that arise in a leading retail clothing firm like yours. Such important tasks include identifying and resolving customer complaints, writing letters that build good customer relations, and above all, promoting the organization's positive image.

When writing a solicited letter in response to an advertisement, be sure to discuss each requirement specified in the ad. If you are deficient in any of these requirements, stress other solid selling points to help strengthen your overall presentation.

The middle of your application letter also demonstrates a few significant job-related qualities, such as your diligence or your ability to work hard, learn quickly, handle responsibility, or get along with people:

The middle section of an application letter

- Summarizes your relevant qualifications
- Emphasizes your accomplishments
- Suggests desirable personal qualities
- Justifies salary requirements
- Refers to your résumé

> While attending university full-time, I trained three hours a day with the varsity track team. In addition, I worked part-time during the school year and up to 60 hours a week each summer in order to be totally self-supporting while in university. I can offer your organization the same level of effort and perseverance.

You might also bring up your salary requirements in this section—but *only* if the organization has asked you to state them. Unless you know approximately what the job pays, suggest a salary range, or indicate that the salary is negotiable or open. You might consult Human Resources Development Canada Web site **www.labourmarketinformation.ca** to get an idea of the salary range for various job classifications and geographic areas. If you do state a target salary, tie it to the benefits you would bring to the organization (much as you would handle price in a sales letter):

> For the past two years, I have been helping a company similar to yours organize its database. I would therefore like to receive a salary in the same range (the mid-30s) for helping your company set up a more efficient customer database.

Toward the end of this section, refer the reader to your résumé by citing a specific fact or general point covered there:

> You will find my people skills an asset. As you can see in the attached résumé, I've been working part-time with a local publisher since my second year in university, and during that time I have successfully resolved more than a few "client crises."

MOTIVATING ACTION

The final paragraph of your application letter has two important functions: to ask the reader for a specific action and to make a reply easy. In almost all cases, the action you request is an interview. However, don't demand it; try to sound natural and appreciative. Offer to come to the employer's office at a convenient time or, if the firm is some distance away, to meet with its nearest representative. Make the request easy to fulfill by stating your phone number and the best time to reach you—or, if you wish to be in control, by mentioning that you will follow up with a phone call in a few days. Refer again to your strongest selling point and, if desired, your date of availability:

Close by asking for an interview and making the interview easy to arrange.

> After you have reviewed my qualifications, could we discuss the possibility of putting my marketing skills to work for your company? Because I will be on spring break the week of March 8, I would like to arrange a time to talk then. I will call in late February to schedule a convenient time when we could discuss employment opportunities at your company.

Once you have edited and proofread your application letter, mail it and your résumé promptly, especially if they have been solicited.

ADAPTING STYLE AND APPROACH TO CULTURE

The AIDA approach isn't appropriate for job seekers in every culture. If you're applying for a job abroad or want to work with a subsidiary of an organization based in another country, you may need to adjust your tone. Blatant self-promotion is considered bad form in some cultures. Other cultures stress group performance over individual contributions. As for format, recruiters in some countries (including France) prefer handwritten letters to printed or typed ones. So research a company carefully before drafting your application letter.

You may need to vary your approach according to your reader's culture.

For Canadian and U.S. companies, let your letter reflect your personal style. Be yourself, but be businesslike too; avoid sounding cute. Don't use slang or a gimmicky

Checklist: Writing Application Letters

Attention (Opening Paragraph)

✓ Open the letter by capturing the reader's attention in a businesslike way.

✓ Use your strongest skills, the job's requirements, an employee's name, company activities, a question that demonstrates your understanding of the company's needs, and so on.

✓ State that you are applying for a job, and identify the position or the type of work you seek.

Interest and Desire, or Evidence of Qualifications (Next Several Paragraphs)

✓ Present your key qualifications for the job, highlighting what is on your résumé: job-related education and training; relevant work experience; and related activities, interests, and qualities.

✓ Adopt a mature, businesslike tone.

✓ Eliminate boasting and exaggeration.

✓ Back up your claims by citing specific achievements in educational, work, and outside settings.

✓ Demonstrate your knowledge of the organization by citing its operations or trends in the industry.

✓ Link your education, experience, and personal qualities to the job requirements.

✓ Relate aspects of your training or work experience to those of the target position.

✓ Outline your educational preparation for the job.

✓ Provide evidence that you can learn quickly, work hard, handle responsibility, and get along with others.

✓ Show that you possess personal qualities and work attitudes that are desirable for job performance.

✓ If asked to state salary requirements in your letter, state current salary or a desired salary range, and link it to the benefits of hiring you.

✓ Refer the reader to the enclosed résumé.

Action (Closing Paragraph)

✓ Request an interview at the reader's convenience.

✓ Request a screening interview with the nearest regional representative, if company headquarters is some distance away.

✓ Make it easy to comply with your request by providing your phone number (with area code) and stating the best time to reach you, or mention a time when you will be calling to set up an interview.

✓ Express your appreciation for an opportunity to have an interview.

✓ Repeat your strongest qualification to reinforce your claim that you can contribute to the organization.

layout. The only time to be unusually creative in content or format is when the job you're seeking requires imagination, such as a position in advertising. Compare your own letters with the tasks in the "Checklist: Writing Application Letters" above.

Job-Inquiry Letters

Use a job-inquiry letter to request an application form, which is a standardized data sheet that simplifies comparison of applicants' credentials.

Before considering you for a position, some organizations require you to fill out and submit an **application form**, a standardized data sheet that simplifies the comparison of applicants' qualifications. To request such a form, send a job-inquiry letter and include enough information about yourself in the letter to show that you have at least some of the requirements for the position you are seeking:

> Please send me an application form for work as an interior designer in your home furnishings department. For my certificate in design, I took courses in retail merchandising and customer relations. I have also had part-time sales experience at Capwell's department store.

Instead of writing a letter of this kind, you may want to drop in at the office you're applying to. You probably won't be able to talk to anyone other than the receptionist or a human resources assistant, but you can pick up the form, get an impression of the organization, and demonstrate your initiative and energy.

Organizations will use your application form as a convenient one-page source for information about your qualifications. So try to be thorough and accurate when filling it out. Have your résumé with you to remind you of important information, and if you can't remember something and have no record of it, provide the closest estimate possible. If you cannot provide some information because you have no such background (military experience, for example), write "Not applicable." When filling out applications, use a pen (unless specifically requested to use a pencil) and print legibly.

Your care in filling out application forms suggests to the employer that you will be thorough and careful in your work.

Application forms rarely give you enough space or ask you the right questions to reflect your skills and abilities accurately. Nevertheless, show your cooperation by doing your best to fill out the form completely. If you get an interview, you'll have an opportunity to fill in the gaps. You might also ask whether you might submit a résumé and an application letter along with the application.

Application Follow-Ups

If your application letter and résumé fail to bring a response within a month or so, follow up with a second letter to keep your file active. This follow-up letter also gives you a chance to update your original application with any recent job-related information:

Use a follow-up letter to let the employer know you're still interested in the job.

> Since applying to you on May 3 for an executive secretary position, I have completed a course in office management at Coquitlam College. I received straight As in the course. I now am a proficient user of MS Word, including macros and other complex functions.
>
> Please keep my application in your active file, and let me know when you need a skilled executive secretary.

Even if you've received a letter acknowledging your application and saying that it will be kept on file, don't hesitate to send a follow-up letter three months later to show that you are still interested:

> Three months have elapsed since I applied to you for an underwriting position, but I want to let you know that I am still very interested in joining your company.
>
> I recently completed a four-week temporary work assignment at a large local insurance agency. I learned several new verification techniques and gained experience in using the online computer system. This experience could increase my value to your underwriting department.
>
> Please keep my application in your active file, and let me know when a position opens for a capable underwriter.

Unless you state otherwise, the human resources office is likely to assume that you've already found a job and are no longer interested in the organization. Moreover, requirements change. A follow-up letter can demonstrate that you're sincerely interested in working for the organization, that you're persistent in pursuing your goals, and that you're upgrading your skills to make yourself a better employee. And it might just get you an interview.

Summary of Learning Objectives

1 Discuss three ways that you can adapt to today's changing workplace. Today's workplace is changing constantly. Adapt by (1) analyzing what you have to offer, noting your functional skills, education and experience, and personality traits; (2) decide what you want to do, by considering how and where you'd like to work, for example; and (3) make yourself more valuable to employers, by keeping an employment protfolio, taking interim assignments, and updating your skills.

2 Describe six ways to prepare for and successfully complete your search for employment. The employment search is a process.

To prepare for and complete your search, (1) stay abreast of business and financial news, by reading newspapers, watching television shows that focus on business, and consulting government publications; (2) research specific companies by consulting company profiles and reading such material as press releases and annual reports; (3) look for job openings on company Web sites, in the newspapers, or on campus recruiting days; (4) respond to job openings by sending e-mail or hard copy résumés; (5) network through student business organizations or joining online discussion groups; and (6) find career counselling at school career placement offices or commercial career centres.

3 Discuss how to choose the appropriate organization for your résumé and list the advantages or disadvantages of the three options. Each organizational approach emphasizes different strengths. If you have a lot of employment experience, you would choose the chronological approach because it focuses on your work history. The advantages of the chronological résumé are (1) it helps employers easily locate necessary information, (2) it highlights your professional growth and career progress, and (3) it emphasizes continuity and stability in your employment background. The functional approach focuses on particular skills and competencies you've developed. The advantages of the functional résumé are (1) it helps employers easily see what you can do for them, (2) it allows you to emphasize earlier job experience, and (3) it lets you downplay any lengthy periods of unemployment or a lack of career progress. The combination approach uses the best features of the other two, but it has two disadvantages: (1) it tends to be longer, and (2) it can be repetitious if you must list accomplishments and skills in the functional section as well as in the individual job descriptions.

4 List the major sections of a traditional résumé. Your résumé must include three sections: (1) your name and address, (2) your educational background (with related skills and accomplishments), and (3) your work experience (with related skills and accomplishments). Options include listing your career objective or summary of qualifications, describing related activities and achievements, and perhaps (although not necessarily recommended) explaining relevant personal data.

5 Describe the process involved in adapting your résumé to an electronic format. Begin by eliminating all fancy printing, graphics, and formatting such as boldface, italics, and tabs. Save the résumé as a plain-text (ASCII) document, adding some blank spaces, blank lines, and asterisks to make it more readable. Finally, provide a list of key words (nouns) that define your skills, experience, and education. Make sure it also includes important jargon that is characteristic of the language in your field.

6 Define the purpose of application letters and explain how to apply the AIDA organizational approach to them. The purpose of an application letter is to convince readers to look at your résumé. This makes application letters a type of sales letter, so you'll want to use the AIDA organizational approach. Get attention in the opening paragraph by showing how your work skills could benefit the organization, by explaining how your qualifications fit the job, or by demonstrating an understanding of the organization's needs. Build interest and desire by showing how you can meet the job requirements, and be sure to refer your reader to your résumé near the end of this section. Finally, motivate action by making your request easy to fulfill and by including all necessary contact information.

ON THE JOB

Solving a Communication Dilemma Ford Motor Company

CEO Bill Ford says, "Employees are the only sustainable competitive advantage that any company has. I want the company to succeed, and to do that, we need to get the best people." Ford's hiring process involves two steps. The first is initial recruiting. Through the company's Web site, on campus, or at a career fair, you can find out about career programs, see whether Ford's environment fits your style, read about Ford people, and find out what it's like to work at Ford. To apply for a position, you answer an online questionnaire and paste in your résumé. If your online assessment and résumé are what Ford is looking for, the company may invite you to a leadership conference. Don't be discouraged if you aren't invited right away. You are given a personal Web page on Ford's career Web site, and the company continues to consider you for openings, unless it notifies you otherwise.

The second step is the leadership conference, an expenses-paid event at a Ford facility. You and other guests meet and interact with Ford people. Through activities such as workshops, interviews, problem-solving teams, and tours, both you and the company have ample opportunity to learn about and evaluate each other. As you interact with Ford people, they give you meaningful feedback on how you're doing, where you would best fit in at Ford, and where you are in the process. Finally, you choose whether to receive your assessment results in person at the conference or later on by letter.

To help you gain experience and knowledge, Ford offers a range of student programs, including a summer intern program, a co-op program that lets you alternate semesters between school and work, and full-time programs for university graduates and experienced professionals. As employees continue on with their education, Ford reimburses their tuition fees.

Your Mission As a member of Ford's human resources department, you regularly review résumés that are attached to the Web-based personal assessments. You have received assessments and résumés from four people. Give your team leader your best advice about the following applicants, and be prepared to explain your recommendations.

1. Of the career objectives that were listed on these résumés, which of the following is the most effective?
   a An entry-level management position in a large company
   b To invest my management talent and business savvy in shepherding Ford Motor Company toward explosive growth
   c A management position in which my degree in business administration and my experience in managing personnel will be useful
   d To learn all I can about personnel management in an exciting environment with a company whose reputation is as outstanding as Ford's

2. Of the education sections included in the résumés, which of the following is the most effective?
   a **University of Calgary, Calgary, AB 1998-2002** Received B.A. degree with a major in Business Administration and a minor in Finance. Graduated with a 3.65 grade-point average. Played varsity football and basketball. Worked 15 hours per week in the library. Coordinated the local student chapter of the Canadian Management Association. Member of Alpha Phi Alpha social fraternity.
   b I attended Mohawk College in Hamilton for two years and then transferred to Ryerson University, Toronto where I completed my studies. My program of study was economics, but I also took many business management courses, including human resources, small business administration, introduction to marketing, and organizational behaviour. I selected courses based on the professors' reputation for excellence, and I received mostly A's and B's. Unlike many students, I viewed the acquisition of knowledge—rather than career preparation—as my primary goal. I believe I have received a well-rounded education that has prepared me to approach management situations as problem-solving exercises.
   c **St. Francis Xavier University, Antigonish, NS.** Graduated with a B.A. degree in 2001. Majored in Physical Education. Minored in Business Administration. Graduated with a 2.85 average.
   d **University of Regina, Regina, Saskatchewan.** Received B.A. and M.B.A. degrees. I majored in business as an undergraduate and concentrated in manufacturing management during my M.B.A. program. Received a special $2500 scholarship offered by Rotary international recognizing academic achievement in business courses. I also won the MEGA award in 1999. Honour student.

3. Based only on their experience, which of the following four candidates would you recommend to your team leader?
   a <u>McDonald's, The Pas, MB 1998-2000. Part-time cook.</u> Worked 15 hours per week while attending high school. Prepared hamburgers, chicken nuggets, and french fries. Received employee-of-the-month award for outstanding work habits.
   <u>University Grill, Sasakatoon, SK 1995-1998. Part-time cook.</u> Worked 20 hours per week while attending university. Prepared hot and cold sandwiches. Helped manager purchase ingredients. Trained new kitchen workers. Prepared work schedules for kitchen staff.
   b Although I have never held a full-time job, I have worked part-time and during summer vacations throughout my high school and university years. During my first and second years in high school, I bagged groceries at the Safeway store three afternoons a week. The work was not terribly challenging, but I liked the customers and the other employees. During my third and fourth years, I worked at the YMCA as an after-school counsellor for elementary school children. The kids were really sweet, and I still get letters from some of them. During summer vacations while I was in university, I did construction work for a local homebuilder. The job paid well, and I also learned a lot about carpentry. The guys I worked with were a mixed bag who expanded my vocabulary and knowledge of the world. I also worked part-time in university in the student cafeteria, where I scooped food onto plates. This did not require much talent, but it taught me a lot about how people behave when standing in line. I also learned quite a bit about life from my boss, Sam "the man" Benson, who has been managing the student cafeteria for 25 years.
   c <u>The Broadway Department Store, Moncton NB. Summers, 1999-2002. Sales Consultant, Furniture Department.</u> I interacted with a diverse group of customers, including suburban matrons, teenagers, career women, and professional couples. I endeavoured to satisfy their individual needs and make their shopping experience memorable, efficient, and enjoyable. Under the direction of the sales manager, I helped prepare employee schedules and fill out departmental reports. I also helped manage the inventory, worked the cash register, and handled a variety of special orders and customer complaints with courtesy and aplomb. During the 2002 annual storewide sale, I sold more merchandise than any other salesperson in the entire furniture department.
   d <u>Medicine Hat, AB. Civilian Member of Public Safety Committee, January–December 2002.</u>

   - Organized and promoted a lecture series on vacation safety and home security for the residents of Medicine Hat; recruited and trained seven committee members to help plan and produce the lectures; persuaded local businesses to finance the program; designed, printed, and distributed fliers; wrote and distributed press releases; attracted an average of 120 people to each of three lectures
   - Developed a questionnaire to determine local residents' home security needs; directed the efforts of 10 volunteers working on the survey; prepared written report for city council and delivered oral summary of findings at town meeting; helped persuade city to fund new home security program
   - Initiated the Business Security Forum as an annual meeting at which local business leaders could meet to discuss safety and security issues; created promotional flyers for the first forum; convinced 19 business owners to fund a business security survey; arranged press coverage of the first forum

4. You've received the following résumé. What action will you take?

Maria Martin
911 Alfred Ave
Winnipeg MB R2X 0V1

Career Objective: To build a management career in a growing Canadian company

Summary of Qualifications: As a student at the University of Manitoba in Winnipeg, carried out various assignments that have required skills related to a career in management. For example:

Planning Skills. As president of the university's foreign affairs forum, organized six lectures and workshops featuring 36 speakers from 16 foreign countries within a nine-month period. Identified and recruited the speakers, handled their travel arrangements, and scheduled the facilities.

Interpersonal Skills. As chairman of the parade committee for homecoming weekend, worked with the city of Winnipeg to obtain approval, permits, and traffic control for the parade. Also encouraged local organizations such as the Lion's Club, the Kiwanis Club, and the Boy Scouts to participate in the parade. Coordinated the efforts of the 15 fraternities and 18 sororities that entered floats in the parade. Recruited 12 marching bands from surrounding communities and coordinated their efforts with the university's marching band. Also arranged for local auto dealers to provide cars for the 10 homecoming queen candidates.

Communication Skills. Wrote over 25 essays and term papers dealing with academic topics. Received an A on all but two of these papers. As a senior, wrote a 20-page analysis of the paper products industry, interviewing the five top executives at the Abitibi Paper company. Received an A on this paper.

a Definitely recommend that Ford take a look at this outstanding candidate.

b Turn down the candidate. She doesn't give enough information about when she attended university, what she majored in, or where she has worked.

c Review the candidate's Web-based personal assessment. If the assessment contains the missing information and the candidate sounds promising, recommend her to your team leader. If vital information is still missing, send the candidate an e-mail (or place a message on her personal page at Ford), requesting additional information. Make the decision once you receive all necessary information.

d Consider the candidate's qualifications relative to those of other applicants. Recommend her to your team leader if you do not have three or four other applicants with more directly relevant qualifications.[27]

Test Your Knowledge

Review Questions

1. What is the purpose of maintaining an employment portfolio?
2. What is a résumé, and why is it important to adopt a "you" attitude when preparing one?
3. In what ways can job-seekers use the Internet during their career and employment search?
4. How does a chronological résumé differ from a functional résumé, and when is each appropriate?
5. What elements are commonly included in a résumé?
6. What are some of the most common problems with résumés?
7. Why is it important to provide a key word summary in a scannable or electronic résumé?
8. What advantages do résumés sent by e-mail have over résumés sent by fax or by mail?
9. How does a solicited application letter differ from an unsolicited letter?
10. How does the AIDA approach apply to an application letter?

Interactive Learning

Use This Text's Online Resources

Visit our Companion Website at **www.pearsoned.ca/thill**, where you can use the interactive Study Guide to test your chapter knowledge and get instant feedback. Additional resources link you to the sites mentioned in this text and to additional sources of information on chapter topics.

Also check out the resources on the Mastering Business Communication CD, including "Perils of Pauline," an interactive presentation of the business communication challenges within a fictional company. For Chapter 14, see in particular the episode "Successful Résumés."

Apply Your Knowledge

Critical Thinking Questions

1 According to experts in the job-placement field, the average job seeker relies too heavily on the résumé and not enough on other elements of the job search. Which elements do you think are most important? Please explain.

2 One of the disadvantages of résumé scanning is that some qualified applicants will be missed because the technology isn't perfect. However, more companies are using this approach. Do you think that résumé scanning is a good idea? Please explain.

3 Stating your career objective on a résumé or application might limit your opportunities by labelling you too narrowly. Not stating your objective, however, might lead an employer to categorize you incorrectly. Which outcome is riskier? Do summaries of qualifications overcome such drawbacks? If so, how? Explain briefly.

4 When writing a solicited application letter and describing the skills requested in the employer's ad, how can you avoid using *I* too often? Explain and give examples.

5 **Ethical Choices** Between your third and fourth years in university, you quit school for a year to earn the money to finish school. You worked as a clerk in a finance company, checking references on loan applications, typing, and filing. Your manager made a lot of the fact that he had never attended university. He seemed to resent you for pursuing your education, but he never criticized your work, so you thought you were doing okay. After you'd been working there for six months, he fired you, saying that you failed to be thorough enough in your credit checks. You were actually glad to leave, and you found another job right away at a bank doing similar duties. Now that you've graduated from university, you're writing your résumé. Will you include the finance company job in your work history? Please explain.

Practice Your Knowledge

Documents for Analysis

Read the following documents; then (1) analyze the strengths or weaknesses of each document and (2) revise each document so that it follows the guidelines presented in this chapter.

Document 14.A: Writing a Résumé

Sylvia Manchester
23 Rustic Ridge
Bedford, Nova Scotia B3Z 1L4
902-831-3687
smanchester@sympatico.ca

PERSONAL: Single, excellent health, 5'8", 136 lbs.; hobbies include cooking, dancing, and reading.

JOB OBJECTIVE: To obtain a responsible position in marketing or sales with a good company.

Education: B.A. degree in biology, Acadia University. Graduated with a 3.0 average. Member of the varsity cheerleading squad. President of the Canadian-Caribbean Club. Homecoming queen.

WORK EXPERIENCE

Fisher Scientific Instruments, 2003 to Present, Field Sales Representative. Responsible for calling on customers and explaining the features of Fisher's line of laboratory instruments. Also responsible for writing sales letters, attending trade shows, and preparing weekly sales reports.

Fisher Scientific Instruments, 2000–2002, Customer Service Representative. Was responsible for handling incoming phone calls from customers who had questions about delivery, quality, or operation of Fisher's line of laboratory instruments. Also handled miscellaneous correspondence with customers.

Medical Electronics, Inc. 1997–2000. Administrative Assistant to the Vice-President of Marketing. In addition to handling typical secretarial chores for the vice-president of marketing, I was in charge of compiling the monthly sales reports, using figures provided by members of the field sales force. I also was given responsibility for doing various market research activities.

Halifax Convention and Visitors Bureau. 1994–1995, Summers. Tour Guide. During the summers of my university years, I led tours of Halifax for tourists visiting the city. My duties included greeting conventioneers and their spouses at hotels, explaining the history and features of the city during an all-day sight-seeing tour, and answering questions about Halifax and its attractions. During my fourth summer with the bureau, I was asked to help train the new tour guides.

I prepared a handbook that provided interesting facts about the various tourist attractions and answers to the most commonly asked tourist questions. The Bureau was so impressed with the handbook they had it printed up so that it could be given as a gift to visitors.

Arcadia University. 1994–1997. Part–Time Clerk in Admissions Office. While I was a student in university, I worked 15 hours a week in the admissions office. My duties included filing, processing applications, and handling correspondence with high school students and administrators.

Document 14.B: Writing an Application Letter

I'm writing to let you know about my availability for the brand manager job you advertised. As you can see from my enclosed résumé, my background is perfect for the position. Even though I don't have any real job experience, my grades have been outstanding considering that I went to a top-ranked business school.

I did many things during my undergraduate years to prepare me for this job:

- Earned a 3.4 out of a 4.0 with a 3.8 in my business courses
- Elected representative to the student governing association
- Selected to receive the Lamar Franklin Award
- Worked to earn a portion of my tuition

I am sending my résumé to all the top firms, but I like yours better than any of the rest. Your reputation is tops in the industry, and I want to be associated with a business that can pridefully say it's the best.

If you wish for me to come in for an interview, I can come on a Friday afternoon or anytime on weekends when I don't have classes. Again, thanks for considering me for your brand manager position.

Document 14.C: Writing Application Follow-Up Messages

Did you receive my résumé? I sent it to you at least two months ago and haven't heard anything. I know you keep résumés on file, but I just want to be sure that you keep me in mind. I heard you are hiring healthcare managers and I certainly would like to be considered for one of those positions.

Since I last wrote you, I've worked in a variety of positions that have helped prepare me for management. To wit, I've become lunch manager at the restaurant where I work, which involved a raise in pay. I now manage a wait-staff of 12 girls and take the lunch receipts to the bank every day.

Of course, I'd much rather be working at a real job, and that's why I'm writing again. Is there anything else you would like to know about me or my background? I would really like to know more about your company. Is there any literature you could send me? If so, I would really appreciate it.

I think one reason I haven't been hired yet is that I don't want to leave Sherbrooke. So I hope when you think of me, it's for a position that wouldn't require moving. Thanks again for considering my application.

Exercises

14–1 Teamwork Working with another student, change the following statements to make them more effective for a traditional résumé by using active verbs.
 a Have some experience with database design.
 b Assigned to a project to analyze the cost accounting methods for a large manufacturer.
 c I was part of a team that developed a new inventory control system.
 d Am responsible for preparing the quarterly department budget.
 e Was a manager of a department with seven employees working for me.
 f Was responsible for developing a spreadsheet to analyze monthly sales by department.
 g Put in place a new program for ordering supplies.

14–2 Résumé Preparation: Work Accomplishments Using your team's answers to Exercise 14–1, make the statements stronger by quantifying them (make up any numbers you need).

14–3 Ethical Choices Assume that you achieved all the tasks shown in Exercise 14–1 not as an individual employee, but as part of a team. In your résumé, must you mention other team members? Explain your answer.

14–4 Résumé Preparation: Electronic Version Using your revised version of Document for Analysis 14.A on page 463, prepare a fully formatted print résumé. What formatting changes would Sylvia Manchester need to make if she were sending her résumé electronically? Develop a key-word summary and make all the changes needed to complete this electronic résumé.

14–5 Work-Related Preferences: Self-Assessment What work-related activities and situations do you prefer? Evaluate your preferences in each of the following areas. Use the results as a good start for guiding your job search.

Activity or Situation	**Strongly Agree**	**Agree**	**Disagree**	**No Preference**
1 I want to work independently.	_______	_______	_______	_______
2 I want variety in my work.	_______	_______	_______	_______
3 I want to work with people.	_______	_______	_______	_______
4 I want to work with products or machines.	_______	_______	_______	_______
5 I want physical work.	_______	_______	_______	_______
6 I want mental work.	_______	_______	_______	_______
7 I want to work for a large organization.	_______	_______	_______	_______
8 I want to work for a nonprofit organization.	_______	_______	_______	_______
9 I want to work for a small family business.	_______	_______	_______	_______
10 I want to work for a service business.	_______	_______	_______	_______
11 I want regular, predictable work hours.	_______	_______	_______	_______

Activity or Situation	Strongly Agree	Agree	Disagree	No Preference
12 I want to work in a city location.	_____	_____	_____	_____
13 I want to work in a small town or suburb.	_____	_____	_____	_____
14 I want to work in another country.	_____	_____	_____	_____
15 I want to work outdoors.	_____	_____	_____	_____
16 I want to work in a structured environment.	_____	_____	_____	_____

14–6 Internet Based on the preferences you identified in the self-assessment (Exercise 14–5) and the academic, professional, and personal qualities you have to offer, perform an Internet search for an appropriate career, using any of the Web sites listed in "Using the Power of Technology—Netting a Job on the Web" on page 438. Draft a brief report indicating how the careers you select and job openings you find match your strengths and preferences.

Cases

Thinking About Your Career

1 Taking stock and taking aim: Application package for the right job Think about yourself. What are some things that come easily to you? What do you enjoy doing? In what part of the country would you like to live? Do you like to work indoors? Outdoors? A combination of the two? How much do you like to travel? Would you like to spend considerable time on the road? Do you like to work closely with others or more independently? What conditions make a job unpleasant? Do you delegate responsibility easily, or do you like to do things yourself? Are you better with words or numbers? Better at speaking or writing? Do you like to work under fixed deadlines? How important is job security to you? Do you want your supervisor to state clearly what is expected of you, or do you like the freedom to make many of your own decisions?

Your Task: After answering these questions, gather information about possible jobs that suit your profile by consulting reference materials (from your college or university library or placement centre) and by searching the Internet (using some of the search strategies discussed in Chapter 11). Next, choose a location, a company, and a job that interests you. With guidance from your instructor, decide whether to apply for a job you're qualified for now or one you'll be qualified for with additional education. Then, as directed by your instructor, write one or more of the following: (a) a job-inquiry letter, (b) a résumé, (c) a letter of application, (d) a follow-up letter to your application letter.

2 Scanning the possibilities: Résumé for the Internet In your search for a position, you discover that *Career Magazine* is a Web site that lists hundreds of companies advertising on the Internet. Your chances of getting an interview with a leading company will be enhanced if you submit your résumé and cover letter electronically. On the Web, explore **www.careermag.com**.

Your Task: Prepare a scannable résumé that could be submitted to the site that best fits your qualifications, experience, and education. Print out the résumé for your instructor.

3 Online application: Electronic cover letter introducing a résumé *Motley Fool* **www.fool.com** is a "Generation X" online magazine accessed via the World Wide Web. Although its founders and writers are extremely creative and motivated, they lack business experience and need a fellow "Xer" to help them manage the business. Among articles in a recent edition was one titled "The Soul of the Dead," about the influence of the Grateful Dead on more than one generation of concert-goers. Other articles deal with lifestyle issues, pop movies, music, and "trends for an old-young generation."

Your Task: Write an e-mail message that will serve as your cover letter, and attach your résumé as a file to be downloaded. Address your message to Louis Corrigan, Managing Editor. Try to limit your message to one screen (about 23 lines). You'll need a creative "hook" and a reassuring approach that identifies you as the right person to help Motley Fool become financially viable.

Writing a Résumé and an Application Letter

4 "Help wanted": Application for a job listed in the classified section Among the jobs listed in today's *Province* (200 Granville Street, Vancouver, BC V6C 3N3) are the following:

Accounting Assistant
Established leader in the vacation ownership industry has immediate opening in its Nelson corp. accounting dept. for an Accounting Assistant. Responsibilities include: bank reconciliation, preparation of deposits, and cash receipt posting. Join our fast-growing company and enjoy our great benefits package. Flex work hours, medical, dental insurance. Fax résumé to Lisa: 604-564-3876.

Administrative Assistant
Fast-paced Burnaby office seeks professional with strong computer skills. Proficient in MS Word & Excel, PowerPoint a plus. Must be detail oriented, able to handle multiple tasks, and possess strong communication skills. Excellent benefits, salary, and work environment. Fax résumé to 604-350-8649.

Customer Service
A nationally known computer software developer has an exciting opportunity in customer service and inside sales support in its fast-paced downtown Vancouver office. You'll help resolve customer problems over the phone, provide information, assist in account management, and administer orders. If you're friendly, self-motivated, energetic, and have two years of experience, excellent problem-solving skills, organizational, communication, and PC skills, and communicate well over the phone, send résumé to J. Haber, 2359 Venable St, Vancouver BC V5L 2J5.

Sales-Account Manager
MidCity Baking Company is seeking an Account Manager to coordinate our programs with major accounts in the Vancouver market. The candidate should possess strong analytical and selling skills and demonstrate computer proficiency. Previous sales experience with major account level assignment desired. A degree in business or equivalent experience preferred. For confidential consideration please mail résumé to Steven Crane, Director of Sales, MidCity Baking Company, PO Box 23727, Vancouver, BC V7B 1X9

Your Task: Send a résumé and an application letter to one of these potential employers.

Writing Other Types of Employment Messages

5 Crashing the last frontier: Letter of inquiry about jobs in the Yukon. Your friend can't understand why you would want to move to the Yukon. So you explain: "What really decided it for me was that I'd never seen the northern lights."

"But what about the bears? The 60-degree-below winters? The permafrost?" asks your friend.

"No problem. Whitehorse doesn't get much colder than Saskatoon does. It is just windier and wetter. Anyhow, I want to live in the wilderness, by the famous Yukon River. Whitehorse has lots of small businesses, like a frontier town. I think I'd be able to buy a tract on the outskirts and build my own cabin there."

"Your plans seem a little hasty," your friend warns. "Maybe you should write for information before you just take off. How do you know you could get a job?"

Your Task: Take your friend's advice and write to the Chamber of Commerce, City of Whitehorse, 2121 2nd Avenue, Whitehorse, Yukon, Y1A 1C2. Ask what types of employment are available to someone with your education and experience, and ask who specifically is hiring year-round employees.

Going Online Exercises

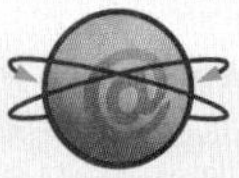

Post an Online Résumé, found on page 449 of this chapter

Your résumé is like a letter of introduction: it should make a good first impression. It must be organized, error-free, and in an appropriate format. In today's electronic business world, you should know how to prepare a résumé to post on the Internet or to send by e-mail. Learn this and more by logging on to CareerBuilder.

1. Before writing a new résumé, make a list of action verbs that describe your skills and experience.
2. Describe the advantages and disadvantages of chronological and functional résumé formats. Do you think a combination résumé would be an appropriate format for your new résumé? Explain why or why not.
3. List some of the tips you learned for preparing an electronic résumé.

To complete this exercise, log on to this text's Web site at **www.pearsoned.ca/thill**. Select Chapter 14, then select "Student Resources," click on the name of the featured Web site, and follow the detailed navigational directions.

Interviewing for Employment and Following Up

1 Explain the typical sequence of interviews

2 Identify and briefly describe the most common types of job interviews

3 List six tasks you need to complete to prepare for a successful job interview

4 Explain the three stages of a successful employment interview

5 Name six common employment messages that follow an interview and state briefly when you would use each one

ON THE JOB

Facing a Communication Dilemma at IBM

Winning the Interview with Big Blue

www.ibm.com

Are you looking for a company that cares about people? You might try IBM. *Fortune* magazine ranked IBM number 1 in its "Top Ten Most Admired Companies—Computer Industry," and number 38 (among 1000 firms) in its 2003 list of the 100 best companies to work for. *Working Mother* magazine has honoured IBM as one of the top U.S. employers of minority women for fifteen years running, and *Chief Executive* magazine has ranked the high-tech giant as the best company for developing executive talent. IBM prides itself on providing ongoing employee training and offers flexible work arrangements.

When IBM recruiters interview a job candidate, they look at the person's education and experience, but they also look for something else: the ability to get along with others. Interviewers want to know why job candidates want to work for IBM, what they can bring to the company, and what the company can give to them. Teamwork is what makes IBM successful as the world's largest information technology company, with almost 316 000 employees working in more than 160 countries.

The challenge facing IBM recruiters when they interview job candidates—be they students looking for co-op positions, summer jobs, or their first career position; or seasoned professionals seeking a change—is determining if they will fit with the IBM culture. The challenge facing candidates is how to prepare for a job interview. What would you do? How would you behave during an interview? Is there anything you could do after the interview has ended?[1]

IBM's recruiters look at a candidate's education and experience, but even more important is the candidate's personality. It's the company's number one objective to find people who can operate in the company's team-based environment.

Understanding the Interviewing Process

An **employment interview** is a formal meeting in which both employer and applicant ask questions and exchange information to learn more about each other.

An interview helps both the interviewer and the applicant achieve their goals.

Most recruiters, like those at IBM, have a list of qualities and accomplishments they are looking for in job candidates. Good interviewers aren't attempting to intimidate or scare anyone; they're simply trying to learn as much as they can about each candidate. An **employment interview** is a formal meeting during which both employer and applicant ask questions and exchange information. These meetings have a dual purpose: (1) the organization wants to find the applicant best suited to the job and the company, and (2) the applicant wants to find the job best suited to his or her goals and capabilities. While recruiters are trying to decide whether you are right for them, you must decide whether the company is right for you.

Because interviewing takes time, begin seeking jobs well in advance of the date you want to start work. Some students begin their job search as early as nine months before graduation. During downturns in the economy, early planning is even more crucial. Since many employers have become more selective and many corporations have reduced their campus visits and campus hiring programs, more of the job-search burden now falls on you. It can take an average of 10 interviews to get 1 job offer, so if you hope to have several offers to choose from, expect to go through 20 or 30 interviews during your job search.[2] Also plan on facing a series of interviews, each with a different purpose.

The Typical Sequence of Interviews

In a typical job search, you can expect to have many interviews before you accept a job offer.

Not all organizations interview potential candidates the same way. However, most employers interview an applicant two or three times before deciding to make a job offer.

OBJECTIVE 1 Explain the typical sequence of interviews.

THE SCREENING STAGE

The preliminary *screening stage* may be held on campus or on company premises to help employers screen out unqualified applicants. These interviews are fairly structured: Applicants are often asked roughly the same questions so that all candidates will be measured against the same criteria. In some cases, technology has transformed the initial, get-to-know-you interview, allowing employers to screen candidates by phone, video interview, or computer.[3]

Most organizations interview an applicant several times before extending a job offer:

- Screening stage
- Selection stage
- Final stage

Your best approach to the screening stage is to follow the interviewer's lead. Keep your responses short and to the point. Time is limited, so talking too much can work against you. However, your goal is to differentiate yourself from other candidates. Without resorting to gimmicks, call attention to one key aspect of your background. Then the recruiter can say, "oh yes, I remember Kim—she explained her senior corporate communications project." Just be sure the trait you accentuate is relevant to the job in question. Also be ready to demonstrate a particular skill (perhaps problem solving), if asked to do so. Candidates who meet the company's requirements are invited to participate in additional interviews.

During the screening stage of interviews, try to differentiate yourself from other candidates by presenting a memorable headline.

THE SELECTION STAGE

During the selection stage of interviews, you may interview with several people, perhaps even all at once.

The next stage of interviews helps the organization narrow the field a little further. Typically, if you're invited for additional interviews, you will talk with several people: a member of the human resources department, one or two potential colleagues, and your potential supervisor. By noting how you listen, think, and express yourself, interviewers can decide how likely you are to get along with colleagues.

Your best approach during this *selection stage* of interviews is to show interest in the job, relating your skills and experience to the organization's needs. Broaden your sales pitch. Instead of telegraphing the headline, give the interviewer the whole story. Touch briefly on all your strengths, but explain three or four of your best qualifications.

At the same time, probe for information that will help you evaluate the position objectively. As important as it is to get an offer, it's also important to learn whether the job is right for you. Be sure to listen attentively, ask insightful questions, and display enthusiasm. If the interviewer believes that you're a good candidate, you may receive a job offer, either on the spot or a few days later by phone or mail.

OBJECTIVE 2 Identify and briefly describe the most common types of job interviews.

FINAL STAGE

You may be invited back for a final evaluation by a higher-ranking executive with the authority to make an offer and negotiate terms. This person may already have concluded that your background is right and may be more concerned with sizing up your personality. You both need to see whether there is a good psychological fit, so be honest about your motivations and values. If the interview goes well, your goal is to clinch the deal on the best possible terms. An underlying objective of the *final stage* is often to sell you on the advantages of joining the organization.

During the final stage, the interviewer may try to sell you on working for the firm.

Types of Interviews

Organizations use different types of interviews to discover as much as possible about applicants.

- **Structured interviews.** Generally used in the screening stage, structured interviews are controlled by the employer, who asks a series of prepared questions in a set order. All answers are noted. Although useful in gathering facts, the structured interview is generally a poor measure of an applicant's personal qualities. Nevertheless, some companies use structured interviews to create uniformity in their hiring processes.[4]

A structural interview is controlled by the interviewer to gather facts.

- **Open-ended interviews.** Less formal and unstructured, these interviews can have a relaxed format. To bring out a candidate's personality and test professional judgment, the interviewer asks broad, open-ended questions, encouraging the applicant to talk freely. However, some candidates reveal too much, rambling on about personal details or family problems, so try to strike a balance between being friendly and remembering that you're in a business situation.

In an open-ended interview, the recruiter encourages the candidate to speak freely.

- **Panel interviews.** These interviews allow multiple members of the staff to meet and question each candidate. Panels usually consist of three to six members, perhaps including a supervisor, a person from human resources, a co-worker, and maybe someone from a division or department that you would often be required to interact with. Each panel member may ask you a prepared list of questions and may take copious notes on your response.

Panel interviews let you meet more members of the staff.

- **Group interviews.** To judge interpersonal skills, some employers meet with several candidates simultaneously to see how they interact. The Walt Disney Company uses group interviews when hiring people for its theme parks. During a 45-minute session, the Disney recruiter watches how three candidates relate to one another. Do they smile? Are they supportive of one another's comments?[5] Do they try to score points at each other's expense?[6]

Group interviews help recruiters see how candidates interact with one another.

- **Stress interviews.** Some employers set up stress interviews to see how a candidate handles pressure (an important qualification for some jobs, such as consulting, investment banking, or any job that subjects you to stressful situations). To irk or unsettle you, the interviewer might ask you pointed questions, subject you to long periods of silence, criticize your appearance, deliberately interrupt you, and react abruptly or even with hostility.

Stress interviews determine how candidates deal with pressure.

- **Video interviews.** To cut travel costs, many large companies use video conferencing systems. You need to prepare a bit differently for a video interview: (1) request a preliminary phone conversation to establish rapport with the interviewer, (2) arrive early enough to get used to the equipment and setting, (3) speak clearly but no more slowly than normal, (4) sit straight (looking up but not down), and (5) show some animation (but not so much that you blur your appearance to the interviewer).[7]

Video interviews require some special preparation.

In situational interviews, candidates must explain how they would handle a specific set of circumstances.

➤ **Situational interviews.** Many companies claim that interviewing is about the job, not about a candidate's five-year goals, weaknesses or strengths, challenging experiences, or greatest accomplishments. An interviewer describes a situation and asks, "How would you handle this?" So the situational interview is a hands-on, at-work meeting between an employer who needs a job done and a worker who must be fully prepared to do the work.

Regardless of the type of interview you may face, a personal interview is vital because your résumé can't show whether you're lively and outgoing or subdued and low-key, able to take direction or able to take charge. Each job requires a different mix of personality traits. The interviewer's task is to find out whether you will be effective on the job.

Preparing for a Job Interview

OBJECTIVE 3 List six tasks you need to complete to prepare for a successful job interview.

For a successful interview, preparation is mandatory. Recruiters at IBM can tell you that it's perfectly normal to feel a little anxious before an interview. But good preparation will help you perform well. Be sure to consider any cultural differences when preparing for interviews, and base your approach on what your audience expects. The advice in this chapter is most appropriate for companies and employers in Canada and the United States. Before an interview, know what employers look for in applicants, do some follow-up research, think ahead about questions, bolster your confidence, polish your interview style, plan to look good, and be ready when you arrive.

What Employers Look For

Just as written messages need planning, employment interviews need preparation.

Every job has basic qualifications. Employers want candidates who will fit in with the organization, who can handle a specific job, and who perform well during pre-employent testing.

A GOOD FIT WITH THE ORGANIZATION

Compatibility with the organization is judged on the basis of personal background, attitudes, and style.

Interviewers try to decide whether a candidate will be compatible with the other people in the organization. Some interviewers use personal background as a clue to a candidate's fit, so they will ask about your interests, hobbies, awareness of world events, and so forth. To anticipate such questions, have broad reading habits, try to meet new people, and participate in discussion groups, seminars, and workshops. Some interviewers may also take into account a candidate's personal style, so try to be open, enthusiastic, interested, courteous, and sincere. Try to show that you're positive, self-confident, and willing to learn. (See Chapter 2 for how to emphasize your personal style nonverbally.)

QUALIFICATIONS FOR THE JOB

Suitability for the specific job is judged on the basis of
- Academic preparation
- Work experience
- Job-related personality traits

When you're invited to interview for a position, the interviewer may already have some idea of whether you have the right qualifications, based on a review of your résumé. But during the interview, you'll be asked to describe your education and previous jobs in more depth so that the interviewer can determine how well your skills match the requirements. In many cases, the interviewer will be seeking someone with the flexibility to apply diverse skills in several areas.[8] When describing your skills, be honest. If you don't know how to do something, say so.

PRE-EMPLOYMENT TESTING

To defray the costs of hiring, some employers require tests. The most common tests measure competency or specific abilities needed to do a job. Psychological tests (usually questionnaires) assess overall intellectual ability, work attitudes, interests, managerial potential, and so on. Pre-employment drug testing for a drug or alcohol dependency in a public service or federally regulated workplace is prohibited by the Canadian Human Rights act. (This policy does not affect corporate employers.)[9]

Do Some Follow-Up Research

When planning your employment search, you probably already researched the companies to which you sent your résumé. But now that you've been invited for an interview, you'll want to fine-tune your research and brush up on the facts you've collected (see Table 15–1 on page 472). You can review Chapter 14 for ideas on where to look for information.

Today's companies expect serious candidates to demonstrate an understanding of the company's operations, its market, and its strategic and tactical problems.[10] Learning about the organization and the job enables you to show the interviewer just how you will meet the organization's particular needs. With a little research, for instance, you would discover that McCain Foods is both upgrading and doubling the size of its Grand Falls, New Brunswick pizza plant to meet increasing sales. Knowing this fact might help you pinpoint aspects of your background (such as your ability to manage new customer accounts) that would appeal to McCain recruiters.[11]

Think Ahead about Questions

Planning ahead for questions is one of the best ways to prepare. Planning will help you handle the interviewer's questions intelligently. (See "Sharpening Your Career Skills—Interview Strategies: Answering the 16 Toughest Questions" on page 474.) Moreover, you'll be able to prepare intelligent questions of your own.

PLANNING FOR THE EMPLOYER'S QUESTIONS

Employers usually gear their interview questions to specific organizational needs.

You can expect to be asked about your skills, achievements, and goals, as well as about your attitude toward work and school, your relationships with others (work supervisors, colleagues, and fellow students), and occasionally, your hobbies and interests. Candidates might be asked to collaborate on a decision or to develop a group presentation. Trained observers evaluate the candidates' performance using predetermined criteria and then advise management on how well each person is likely to handle the challenges normally faced on the job.[12]

For a look at the types of questions often asked, see Table 15–2 on page 473. Jot down a brief answer to each one. Then read the answers over until you feel comfortable with each of them. You may want to tape record your answers and then listen to make sure they sound clear and convincing.

Although practicing your answers will help you feel prepared and confident, you don't want to memorize responses or sound over-rehearsed. You might also give a list of interview questions to a friend or relative and have that person ask you various questions at random. This method helps you learn to articulate answers and to look at the person as you answer.

PLANNING QUESTIONS OF YOUR OWN

In an interview the questions you ask are just as important as the answers you provide. By asking intelligent questions, you demonstrate your understanding of the organization, and you can steer the discussion into those areas that allow you to present your qualifications to peak advantage. Before the interview, prepare a list of about a dozen questions you need answered in order to evaluate the organization and the job.

Going Online

Planning for a Successful Interview

How can you practice for a job interview? What are some questions that you might be asked, and how should you respond? What questions are you not obligated to answer? **Job-interview.net** provides mock interviews based on actual job openings. It provides job descriptions, questions and answers for specific careers and jobs, and links to company guides and annual reports. You'll find a step-by-step plan that outlines key job requirements, lists practice interview questions, and helps you put together practice interviews. The site offers tips on the key words to look for in a job description that will help you narrow your search and anticipate the questions you might be asked on your first or next job interview.

www.job-interview.net

To link directly to this site, visit our Companion Website at **www.pearsoned.ca/thill** *and look for the Chapter 15 resources.*

Practice answering interview questions.

Be prepared to relate your qualifications to the organization's needs.

The library is an excellent place to learn about the job search.

TABLE 15-1 Finding Out About the Organization and the Job

Where to Look for Information	
· Annual report	Summarizes operations; describes products, lists events, names key personnel
· In-house magazine or newspaper	Reveals information about company operations, events, personnel
· Product brochure or publicity release	Gives insight into firm's operations and values (obtain from public relations office)
· Stock research report	Helps assess stability and growth prospects (obtain online or from stockbroker)
· Newspapers (business or financial)	Contain news items about organizations, current performance figures
· Periodicals indexes	Contain descriptive listings of magazine/newspaper articles about firms (obtain from library)
· Better Business Bureau and Chamber of Commerce	Distribute information about some local organizations
· Former and current employees	Have insight into job and work environment
· College and university placement office	Collects information on organizations that recruit and also on job qualifications and salaries
What to Find Out About the Organization	
· Full Name	How the firm is officially known (e.g., BMO is Bank of Montreal)
· Location	Where the organization's headquarters, branch offices, and plants are
· Age	How long the organization has been in business
· Products	What goods and services the organization produces and sells
· Industry position	What the organization's current market share, financial position, and profit picture are
· Earnings	What the trends in the firm's stock prices and dividends are (if the firm is publicly held)
· Growth	How the firm's earnings/holdings have changed in recent years and prospects for expansion
· Organization	What subsidiaries, divisions, and departments make up the whole
What to Find Out About the Job	
· Job title	What you will be called
· Job functions	What the main tasks of the job are
· Job qualifications	What knowledge and skills the job requires
· Career path	What chances for ready advancement exist
· Salary range	What the firm typically offers and what is reasonable in this industry and geographic area
· Travel opportunities	How often, long, and far you'll be allowed (or required) to travel
· Relocation opportunities	Where you might be allowed (or required) to move and how often

You are responsible for deciding whether the work and the organization are compatible with your goals and values.

Don't limit your questions to those you think will impress the interviewer, or you won't get the information you'll need to make a wise decision if and when you're offered the job. Here's a list of some things you might want to find out:

- **Are these my kind of people?** Observe the interviewer, and if you can, arrange to talk with other employees.
- **Can I do this work?** Compare your qualifications with the requirements described by the interviewer.
- **Will I enjoy the work?** Know yourself and what's important to you. Will you find the work challenging? Will it give you feelings of accomplishment, of satisfaction, and of making a real contribution?

TABLE 15-2 Twenty-Five Common Interview Questions

Questions About College and University
1. What courses did you like most? Least? Why?
2. Do you think your extracurricular activities were worth the time you spent on them? Why or why not?
3. When did you choose your area of concentration? Did you ever change it? If so, why?
4. Do you feel you did the best scholastic work you are capable of?
5. Which of your college and university years was the toughest? Why?
Questions About Employers and Jobs
6. What jobs have you held? Why did you leave?
7. What percentage of your college and university expenses did you earn? How?
8. Why did you choose your particular field of work?
9. What are the disadvantages of your chosen field?
10. Have you served in the military? What rank did you achieve? What jobs did you perform?
11. What do you think about how this industry operates today?
12. Why do you think you would like this particular type of job?
Questions About Personal Attitudes and Preferences
13. Do you prefer to work in any specific geographic location? If so, why?
14. How much money do you hope to be earning in five years? In ten years?
15. What do you think determines a person's progress in a good organization?
16. What personal characteristics do you feel are necessary for success in your chosen field?
17. Tell me a story.
18. Do you like to travel?
19. Do you think employers should consider grades? Why or why not?
Questions About Work Habits
20. Do you prefer working with others or by yourself?
21. What type of boss do you prefer?
22. Have you ever had any difficulty getting along with colleagues or supervisors? With instructors? Other students?
23. Would you prefer to work in a large or small organization? Why?
24. How do you feel about overtime work?
25. What have you done that shows initiative and willingness to work?

- **Is the job what I want?** You may never find a job that fulfills all your wants, but the position you accept should satisfy at least your primary ones. Will it make use of your best capabilities? Does it offer a career path to the long-term goals you've set?
- **Does the job pay what I'm worth?** By comparing jobs and salaries before you're interviewed, you'll know what's reasonable for someone with your skills in your industry.
- **What kind of person would I be working for?** If the interviewer is your prospective boss, watch how others interact with that person, tactfully query other employees, or pose a careful question or two during the interview. If your prospective boss is someone else, ask for that person's name, job title, and responsibilities. Try to learn all you can.
- **What sort of future can I expect with this organization?** How healthy is the organization? Can you look forward to advancement? Does the organization offer insurance, pension, vacation, or other benefits?

SHARPENING YOUR CAREER SKILLS

Interview Strategies: Answering the 16 Toughest Questions

The answers to challenging interview questions can reveal a lot about a candidate. You can expect to face several such questions during every interview. If you're prepared with thoughtful answers that are related to your specific situation, you're bound to make a good impression. Here are 16 tough questions and guidelines for planning answers that put your qualities in the best light.

1 **What was the toughest decision you ever had to make?** Be prepared with a good example, explaining why the decision was difficult and how you decided.

2 **Why do you want to work for this organization?** Show that you've done your homework, and cite some things going on in the company that appeal to you.

3 **Why should we employ you?** Emphasize your academic strengths, job skills, and enthusiasm for the firm. Tie specific skills to the employer's needs, and give examples of how you can learn and become productive quickly. Cite past activities to prove you can work with others as part of a team.

4 **If we hire you, what changes would you make?** No one can know what to change in a position before settling in and learning about the job and company operations. State that you would take a good hard look at everything the company is doing before making recommendations.

5 **Can we offer you a career path?** Reply that you believe so, but you need to know more about the normal progression within the organization.

6 **What are your greatest strengths?** Answer sincerely by summarizing your strong points: "I can see what must be done and then do it" or "I'm willing to make decisions" or "I work well with others."

7 **What are your greatest weaknesses?** Describe a weakness so that it sounds like a virtue—honestly revealing something about yourself while showing how it works to an employer's advantage. If you sometimes drive yourself too hard, explain that it has helped when you've had to meet deadlines.

8 **What didn't you like about previous jobs you've held?** State what you didn't like and discuss what the experience taught you. Avoid making slighting references to former employers.

9 **How do you spend your leisure time?** Instead of focusing on just one, mention a cross section of interests—active and quiet, social and solitary.

10 **Are there any weaknesses in your education or experience?** Take stock of your weaknesses before the interview, and practice discussing them in a positive light. You'll see they're minor when discussed along with the positive qualities you have to offer.

11 **Where do you want to be five years from now?** This question tests (1) whether you're merely using this job as a stopover until something better comes along and (2) whether you've given thought to your long-term goals. Saying that you'd like to be company president is unrealistic, and yet few employers want people who are content to sit still. Your answer should reflect your long-term goals and the organization's advancement opportunities.

12 **What are your salary expectations?** If you're asked this at the outset, say, "Why don't we discuss salary after you decide whether I'm right for the job?" If the interviewer asks this after showing real interest in you, speak up. Do your homework, but if you need a clue about salary levels, say, "Can you discuss the salary range with me?"

13 **What would you do if ...** This question tests your resourcefulness. For example: "What would you do if your computer broke down during an audit?" Your answer is less important than your approach to the problem—and a calm approach is best.

14 **What type of position are you interested in?** Job titles and responsibilities vary from firm to firm. So state your skills ("I'm good with numbers") and the positions that require those skills ("accounts payable").

15 **Tell me something about yourself.** Answer that you'll be happy to talk about yourself, and ask what the interviewer wants to know. If this point is clarified, respond. If it isn't, explain how your skills can contribute to the job and the organization. This is a great chance to sell yourself.

16 **Do you have any questions about the organization or the job?** Employers like candidates who are interested in the organization. Convey your interest and enthusiasm.

Be sure that your answers are sincere, truthful, and positive. Take a moment to compose your thoughts before responding so that your answers are to the point.

CAREER APPLICATIONS

1 What makes an effective answer to an interviewer's question? Consider some of the ways answers can vary: specific versus general, assertive versus passive, informal versus formal.

2 Think of four additional questions that pertain specifically to your résumé. Practice your answers.

Adapted from "Career Strategies," *Black Enterprise,* February 1986, 122. Copyright © 1986, *Black Enterprise Magazine,* The Earl Graves Publishing Company, Inc., New York, NY. All rights reserved.

Types of questions to ask during an interview:

- Warm-up
- Open-ended
- Indirect

Rather than bombarding the interviewer with these questions the minute you walk in the room, use a mix of formats to elicit this information. Start with a warm-up question to help break the ice. You might ask an IBM recruiter, "What departments usually hire new graduates?" After that, you might build rapport by asking an open-ended question that draws out the interviewer's opinion ("How do you think

Internet sales will affect IBM's continued growth?"). Indirect questions can elicit useful information and show that you've prepared for the interview ("I'd really like to know more about IBM's plans for expanding its presence globally" or "The information in the annual report on IBM's sponsorship of cancer research was very interesting"). Any questions you ask should be in your own words so that you don't sound like every other candidate. For a list of other good questions you might use as a starting point, see Table 15–3.

Write your list of questions on a notepad and take it to the interview. If you need to, jot down brief notes during the meeting, and be sure to record answers in more detail afterward. Having a list of questions should impress the interviewer with your organization and thoroughness. It will also show that you're there to evaluate the organization and the job as well as to sell yourself.

Bolster Your Confidence

If you feel shy or self-conscious, remember that recruiters are human too.

By building your confidence, you'll make a better impression. The best way to counteract any apprehension is to remove its source. You may feel shy or self-conscious because you think you have some flaw that will prompt others to reject you.

If some aspect of your appearance or background makes you uneasy, correct it or offset it by exercising positive traits such as warmth, wit, intelligence, or charm. Instead of dwelling on your weaknesses, focus on your strengths so that you can emphasize them to an interviewer. Make a list of your good points and compare them with what you see as your shortcomings. And bear in mind, however, that you're much more conscious of your limitations than other people are.

Remember that you're not alone. All the other candidates for the job are just as nervous as you are. Even the interviewer may be nervous.

TABLE 15–3 Fifteen Questions to Ask the Interviewer

Questions About the Job
1. What are the job's major responsibilities?
2. What qualities do you want in the person who fills this position?
3. Do you want to know more about my related training?
4. What is the first problem that needs the attention of the person you hire?
5. Would relocation be required now or in the future?
6. Why is this job now vacant?
7. What can you tell me about the person I would report to?
Questions About the Organization
8. What are the organization's major strengths? Weaknesses?
9. Who are your organization's major competitors, and what are their strengths and weaknesses?
10. What makes your organization different from others in the industry?
11. What are your organization's major markets?
12. Does the organization have any plans for new products? Acquisitions?
13. How would you define your organization's managerial philosophy?
14. What additional training does your organization provide?
15. Do employees have an opportunity to continue their education with help from the organization?

WHAT EMPLOYERS DON'T LIKE TO SEE IN CANDIDATES

- ☑ Poor personal appearance
- ☑ Overbearing, overaggressive, conceited demeanour; a "superiority complex"; "know-it-all" attitude
- ☑ Inability to express ideas clearly; poor voice, diction, grammar
- ☑ Lack of knowledge or experience
- ☑ Poor preparation for the interview
- ☑ Lack of interest in the job
- ☑ Lack of planning for career; lack of purpose, goals
- ☑ Lack of enthusiasm; passive and indifferent demeanour
- ☑ Lack of confidence and poise; appearance of being nervous and ill at ease
- ☑ Insufficient evidence of achievement
- ☑ Failure to participate in extracurricular activities
- ☑ Overemphasis on money; interest only in the best dollar offer
- ☑ Poor scholastic record; just got by
- ☑ Unwillingness to start at the bottom; expecting too much too soon
- ☑ Tendency to make excuses
- ☑ Evasive answers; hedges on unfavourable factors in record
- ☑ Lack of tact
- ☑ Lack of maturity
- ☑ Lack of courtesy; ill-mannered
- ☑ Condemnation of past employers
- ☑ Lack of social skills
- ☑ Marked dislike for schoolwork
- ☑ Lack of vitality
- ☑ Failure to look interviewer in the eye
- ☑ Limp, weak handshake

FIGURE 15–1 Marks Against Applicants (in general order of importance)

Polish Your Interview Style

Confidence helps you walk into an interview, but once you're there, you want to give the interviewer an impression of poise, good manners, and good judgment. Some job seekers hire professional coaches and image consultants to create just the right impression. Charging anywhere from $125 to $500 an hour, these professionals spend most of their time teaching clients how to assess communication styles by using role playing, videotaping, and audiotaping.[13] You can use these techniques too.

You can develop an accomplished style by staging mock interviews with a friend. After each practice session, try to identify opportunities for improvement. Have your friend critique your performance, using the list of interview faults shown in Figure 15–1 above. You can tape-record or videotape these mock interviews and then evaluate them yourself. The taping process can be intimidating, but it helps you work out any problems before you begin actual job interviews.

Staging mock interviews with a friend is a good way to hone your style.

As you stage your mock interviews, pay particular attention to your nonverbal behaviour. In Canada and the United States, you are more likely to have a successful interview if you maintain eye contact, smile frequently, sit in an attentive position, and use frequent hand gestures. These nonverbal signals convince the interviewer that you're alert, assertive, dependable, confident, responsible, and energetic.[14] Many companies based in Canada and the United States are owned and managed by people from other cultures, so during your research find out about the company's cultural background and preferences regarding nonverbal behaviour.

The sound of your voice can also have a major impact on your success in a job interview.[15] You can work with a tape recorder to overcome voice problems. If you tend to speak too rapidly, practice speaking more slowly. If your voice sounds too loud or too soft, practice adjusting it. Work on eliminating speech mannerisms such as *you know, like,* and *um,* which might make you sound inarticulate.

Nonverbal behaviour has a significant effect on the interviewer's opinion of you.

Plan To Look Good

Physical appearance is important because clothing and grooming reveal something about a candidate's personality and professionalism. When it comes to clothing, the best policy is to dress conservatively. Wear the best-quality businesslike clothing you can, preferably in a dark, solid colour. Select an outfit you have worn before and are comfortable wearing.[16] Avoid flamboyant styles, colours, and prints. Even in companies where interviewers may dress casually, it's important to show good judgment by dressing (and acting) in a professional manner.

The way you speak is almost as important as what you say.

Company Web sites may give you information on what to wear to interviews. You might try checking things out for yourself: A few days before your interview, wear something you believe to be appropriate and visit the company to pick up its annual report or company newsletter. While you're there, take a good look at what people are wearing and dress that way on the day of the interview.[17]

To look like a winner
- Dress conservatively
- Be well groomed
- Smile when appropriate

Good grooming makes any style of clothing look better. Make sure your clothes are clean and unwrinkled, your shoes unscuffed and well shined, your hair neatly styled and combed, your fingernails clean, and your breath fresh. If possible, check your appearance in a mirror before entering the room for the interview. Finally, remember that one of the best ways to look good is to smile at appropriate moments.

Be Ready When You Arrive

When preparing for a job interview, plan to take a small notebook, a pen, a list of the questions you want to ask, two copies of your résumé (protected in a folder). You may want to take five or more résumés, just in case your interview turns out to be a panel interview or you're asked to participate in multiple interviews that day with different people. Also take along an outline of what you have learned about the organization, and any past correspondence about the position. You may also want to take a small calendar, a transcript of your college or university grades, a list of references, and a portfolio containing samples of your work (when relevant), performance reviews, and certificates of achievement. In an era when many people exaggerate their qualifications, visible proof of your abilities carries a lot of weight.[18]

When recruiters interview potential employees, they look for people who communicate well. Part of good communication is being prepared with résumés and, when relevant, work samples; another part is knowing how to look. Applicants show more than their job skills. They also demonstrate their ability to communicate and their concern for a professional appearance.

Be sure you know when and where the interview will be held. The worst way to start any interview is to be late. Check the route you will take, even if it means phoning the interviewer's secretary to ask. Find out how much time it takes to get there; then plan to arrive early. Allow a little extra time in case you run into a problem on the way.

Once you arrive, relax. You may have to wait a little while, so bring along something to read or occupy your time (the less frivolous or controversial, the better). If company literature is available, read it while you wait. In any case, be polite to the interviewer's assistant. If the opportunity presents itself, ask a few questions about the organization or express enthusiasm for the job. Refrain from smoking before the interview (non-smokers can smell smoke on the clothing of interviewees), and avoid chewing gum in the waiting room. Anything you do or say while you wait may well get back

Be prepared for the interview by
- Taking proof of your accomplishments
- Arriving on time
- Waiting graciously

to the interviewer, so make sure your best qualities show from the moment you enter the premises. That way you'll be ready for the interview itself once it actually begins.

Interviewing for Success

OBJECTIVE 4 Explain the three stages of a successful employment interview.

As discussed at the beginning of this chapter, how you handle a particular interview depends on where you stand in the interview process. Is this your first interview in the screening process? Have you made it to the selection interview or even the final interview? Regardless of where you are in the interview process, every interview will proceed through three stages: the warm-up, the question-and-answer session, and the close.

The Warm-Up

The first minute of the interview is crucial.

Of the three stages, the warm-up is the most important, even though it may account for only a small fraction of the time you spend in the interview. Psychologists say that 50 percent of an interviewer's decision is made within the first 30 to 60 seconds, and another 25 percent is made within 15 minutes. If you get off to a bad start, it's extremely difficult to turn the interview around.[19]

Body language is important at this point. Because you won't have time to say much in the first minute or two, you must sell yourself nonverbally. Begin by using the interviewer's name if you're sure you can pronounce it correctly. If the interviewer extends a hand, respond with a firm but gentle handshake, then wait until you are asked to be seated. Let the interviewer start the discussion, and listen for cues that tell you what he or she is interested in knowing about you as a potential employee.

The Question-and-Answer Stage

Questions and answers will consume the greatest part of the interview. The interviewer will ask you about your qualifications and discuss many of the points mentioned in your résumé. You'll also be asked whether you have any questions of your own.

DEALING WITH QUESTIONS

Tailor your answers to emphasize your strengths.

Let the interviewer lead the conversation, and never answer a question before he or she has finished asking it. Surprisingly, the last few words of the question might alter how you respond. As questions are asked, tailor your answers to make a favourable impression. Don't limit yourself to yes or no answers. If you're asked a difficult question, be sure you pause to think before responding.

If you periodically ask a question or two from the list you've prepared, you'll not only learn something but also demonstrate your interest. Probe for what the company is looking for in its new employees so that you can show how you meet the firm's needs. Also try to zero in on any reservations the interviewer might have about you so that you can dispel them.

LISTENING TO THE INTERVIEWER

Paying attention to both verbal and nonverbal messages can help you turn the question-and-answer stage to your advantage.

Paying attention when the interviewer speaks can be as important as giving good answers or asking good questions. Recruiters suggest that listening should make up about half the time you spend in an interview.[20] For tips on becoming a better listener, see Chapter 2.

The interviewer's facial expressions, eye movements, gestures, and posture may tell you the real meaning of what is being said. Be especially aware of how your comments are received. Does the interviewer nod in agreement or smile to show approval? If so, you're making progress. If not, you might want to introduce another topic or modify your approach.

FIELDING DISCRIMINATORY QUESTIONS

Remember that employers cannot legally discriminate against a job candidate on the basis of race, colour, gender, age, marital status, religion, national origin, or disability. In general, the following topics should not be directly or indirectly introduced by an interviewer:[21]

Some topics should not be broached by interviewers.

- Your religious affiliation or organizations and lodges you belong to
- Your national origin, ethnic origin, race, colour, and citizenship
- Your age, marital status, family status, and same-sex partnership status
- Your spouse, spouse's employment or salary, dependents, children, or child-care arrangements
- Your height, weight, gender, pregnancy, or any health conditions or disabilities that are not reasonably related to job performance
- A prior criminal record

If your interviewer asks these personal questions, you might (1) ask how the question is related to your qualifications, (2) explain that the information is personal, (3) respond to what you think is the interviewer's real concern, or (4) answer both the question and the concern. However, be aware that you are under no obligation to answer a question that violates the Canadian Human Rights Code. If you believe an interviewer's questions are unreasonable, unrelated to the job, or an attempt to discriminate, you may complain to your provincial human rights commission, which is entrusted with enforcing its human rights code.

Think about how you might respond if you are asked to answer unlawful interview questions.

The Close

Like the opening, the end of the interview is more important than its duration would indicate. In the last few minutes, you need to evaluate how well you've done. You also need to correct any misconceptions the interviewer might have.

CONCLUDING GRACEFULLY

You can generally tell when the interviewer is trying to conclude the session. The interviewer may ask whether you have any more questions, sum up the discussion, change position, or indicate with a gesture that the interview is over. When you get the signal, respond promptly, but don't rush. Be sure to thank the interviewer for the opportunity and express an interest in the organization. If you can do so comfortably, try to pin down what will happen next, but don't press for an immediate decision.

Conclude the interview with courtesy and enthusiasm.

If this is your second or third visit to the organization, the interview may culminate with an offer of employment. You have two options: Accept it or request time to think it over. The best course is usually to wait. If no job offer is made, the interviewer may not have reached a decision yet, but you may tactfully ask when you can expect to know the decision.

DISCUSSING SALARY

If you do receive an offer during the interview, you'll naturally want to discuss salary. However, let the interviewer raise the subject. If asked your salary requirements, say that you would expect to receive the standard salary for the job in question. If you have added qualifications, point them out: "With my 18 months of experience in the field, I would expect to start in the middle of the normal salary range." Some applicants find the Internet an excellent resource for salary information.

Be realistic in your salary expectations and diplomatic in your negotiations.

If you don't like the offer, you might try to negotiate, provided you're in a good bargaining position and the organization has the flexibility to accommodate you. You'll be in a fairly strong position if your skills are in short supply and you have several other offers. It also helps if you're the favourite candidate and the organization is growing. However, many organizations are relatively rigid in their salary practices, particularly at the entry level. In Canada, the United States, and some European countries

Negotiating salary can be tricky.

Negotiating benefits may be one way to get more value from an employment package.

it is perfectly acceptable to ask, "Is there any room for negotiation?" Use your research to help you negotiate a higher salary if the employer is willing to discuss the matter with you.

OBJECTIVE 5 Name six common employment messages that follow an interview and state briefly when you would use each one.

Interview Notes

Six types of follow-up messages:

1. Thank-you message
2. Inquiry
3. Request for a time extension
4. Letter of acceptance
5. Letter declining a job offer
6. Letter of resignation

If yours is a typical job search, you'll have many interviews before you accept an offer. For that reason, keeping a notebook or binder of interview notes can help you refresh your memory of each conversation. As soon as the interview ends, find a quiet place to relax, have a snack, and jot down the names and titles of the people you met. Briefly summarize the interviewer's answers to your questions. Then quickly evaluate your performance during the interview, listing what you handled well and what you didn't. Going over these notes can help you improve your performance in the future.[22] In addition to improving your performance during interviews, interview notes will help you keep track of any follow-up messages you'll need to send. Whenever you need to review important tips, consult this chapter's "Checklist: Succeeding with Job Interviews" on page 481.

It's good practice to jot down the questions you were asked, and your answers, while the interview is fresh in your mind. You may even consider transferring your handwritten notes into a computer file. This material will help your performance at future interviews, whether they are next week or in two or three years.

Following Up After the Interview

Touching base with the prospective employer after the interview, either by phone or in writing, shows that you really want the job and are determined to get it. Following up brings your name to the interviewer's attention once again and reminds him or her that you're waiting for the decision.

The two most common forms of follow-up are the thank-you message and the inquiry. These messages are generally handled by letter, but an e-mail or a phone call can be just as effective, particularly if the employer seems to favour a casual, personal style. Other types of follow-up messages are sent only in certain cases—letters requesting a time extension, letters of acceptance, letters declining a job offer, and letters of resignation. These four employment messages are best handled in writing to document any official actions relating to your employment.

Thank-You Message

Express your thanks within two days after the interview, even if you feel you have little chance for the job. Acknowledge the interviewer's time and courtesy, and be sure to restate the specific job you're applying for. Convey your continued interest, then ask politely for a decision.

A note or phone call thanking the interviewer

- Is organized like a routine message
- Closes with a request for a decision or future consideration

Keep your thank-you message brief (less than five minutes for a phone call or only one page for a letter), and organize it like a routine message. Demonstrate the "you" attitude, and sound positive without sounding overconfident. The following sample thank-you letter shows how to achieve all this in three brief paragraphs:

Reminds the interviewer of the reasons for the meeting and graciously acknowledges the consideration shown to the applicant. →

> After talking with you yesterday, touring your sets, and watching the television commercials being filmed, I remain very enthusiastic about the possibility of joining your staff as a television/film production assistant. Thanks for taking so much time to show me around.

Indicates the writer's flexibility and commitment to the job if hired. →

> During our meeting, I said that I would prefer not to relocate, but I've reconsidered the matter. I would be pleased to relocate wherever you need my skills in set decoration and prop design.

Reminds the recruiter of special qualifications. →

> Now that you've explained the details of your operation, I feel quite strongly that I can make a contribution to the sorts of productions you're lining up. You can also

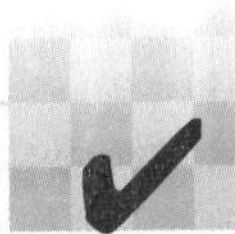

Checklist: Succeeding with Job Interviews

Preparation

- ✓ Fine-tune the research you already conducted before sending your résumé to the company (determine the requirements and general salary range of the job; review the organization's products, structure, financial standing, and prospects for growth; determine the interviewer's name, title, and status in the firm).
- ✓ Prepare (but don't over-rehearse) answers for the questions you are likely to be asked.
- ✓ Develop relevant questions to ask.
- ✓ Work on increasing your confidence level.
- ✓ Dress in a businesslike manner, regardless of the mode of dress preferred within the organization.
- ✓ Take a briefcase or portfolio—with a pen, paper, a list of questions, résumés, and work samples.
- ✓ Double-check the location and time of the interview, mapping out the route beforehand.
- ✓ Plan to arrive 10 to 15 minutes early; allow 10 to 15 minutes for possible problems en route.

The Warm-Up Stage of the Interview

- ✓ Greet the interviewer by name, with a smile and direct eye contact.
- ✓ Offer a firm (not crushing) handshake if the interviewer extends a hand.
- ✓ Take a seat only after the interviewer invites you to be seated or has taken his or her own seat.
- ✓ Listen for cues about what the questions are trying to reveal about you and your qualifications.
- ✓ Assume a calm and poised attitude (avoiding gum chewing, smoking, and other signs of nerves).

The Question-and-Answer Stage of the Interview

- ✓ Display a genuine (not artificial) smile, when appropriate.
- ✓ Convey interest and enthusiasm.
- ✓ Listen attentively so that you can give intelligent responses (taking few notes).
- ✓ Relate your knowledge and skills to the position and stress your positive qualities.
- ✓ Keep responses brief, clear, and to the point.
- ✓ Avoid exaggeration, and convey honesty and sincerity.
- ✓ Avoid slighting references to former employers.

The Close of the Interview

- ✓ Watch for signs that the interview is about to end.
- ✓ Tactfully ask when you will be advised of the decision on your application.
- ✓ If you're offered the job, either accept or ask for time to consider the offer.
- ✓ Let the interviewer initiate the discussion of salary, but put it off until late in the interview if possible.
- ✓ If asked, state that you would like to receive the standard salary for the position.
- ✓ With a warm smile and a handshake, thank the interviewer for meeting with you.

> count on me to be an energetic employee and a positive addition to your crew. Please let me know your decision as soon as possible.

Closes on a confident, "you"-oriented noted.

Ends with a request for decision.

Even if the interviewer has said that you are unqualified for the job, a thank-you message may keep the door open.

Letter of Inquiry

If you're not advised of the interviewer's decision by the promised date or within two weeks, you might make an inquiry. A letter of inquiry is particularly appropriate if you've received a job offer from a second firm and don't want to accept it before you have an answer from the first. The following letter follows the general plan for a direct request; the writer assumes that a simple oversight, and not outright rejection, is the reason for the delay:

An inquiry about a hiring decision follows the plan for a direct request.

> When we talked on April 7 about the fashion coordinator position in your York Avenue showroom, you said you would let me know your decision before May 1. I would still like the position very much, so I'm eager to know what conclusion you've reached.

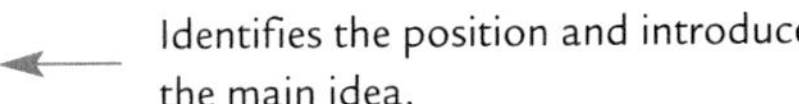

Identifies the position and introduces the main idea.

Places the reason for the request second.

To complicate matters, another firm has now offered me a position and has asked that I reply within the next two weeks.

Makes a courteous request for specific action last, while clearly stating a preference for this organization.

Because your company seems to offer a greater challenge, I would appreciate knowing about your decision by Thursday, May 12. If you need more information before then, please let me know.

Request for a Time Extension

If you receive a job offer while other interviews are still pending, you'll probably want more time to decide, so write to the offering organization and ask for a time extension. Employers understand that candidates often interview with several companies. They want you to be sure you're making the right decision, so most are happy to accommodate you with a reasonable extension.

A request for a time extension follows the plan for a direct request but pays extra attention to easing the reader's disappointment.

Preface your request with a friendly opening. Ask for more time, stressing your enthusiasm for the organization. Conclude by allowing for a quick decision if your request for additional time is denied. Ask for a prompt reply confirming the time extension if the organization grants it. This type of letter is, in essence, a direct request. However, because the recipient may be disappointed, be sure to temper your request for an extension with statements indicating your continued interest. The letter in Figure 15–2 is a good example.

Letter of Acceptance

A letter of acceptance follows the good-news plan.

When you receive a job offer that you want to accept, reply within five days. Begin by accepting the position and expressing thanks. Identify the job that you're accepting. In the next paragraph, cover any necessary details. Conclude by saying that you look forward to reporting for work. As always, a good-news letter should convey your enthusiasm and eagerness to cooperate:

Confirms the specific terms of the offer with a good-news statement at the beginning.

I'm delighted to accept the graphic design position in your advertising department at the salary of $3450 per month.

Covers miscellaneous details in the middle.

Enclosed are the health benefits forms you asked me to complete and sign. I've already given notice to my current employer and will be able to start work on Monday, January 18.

Closes with another reference to the good news and a look toward the future.

The prospect of joining your firm is very exciting. Thank you for giving me this opportunity for what I'm sure will be a challenging future.

Written acceptance of a job offer is legally binding.

Be aware that a job offer and a written acceptance of that offer constitute a legally binding contract, for both you and the employer. Before you write an acceptance letter, be sure you want the job.

Letter Declining a Job Offer

A letter declining a job offer follows the bad-news plan.

After all your interviews, you may find that you need to write a letter declining a job offer. The bad-news plan is ideally suited to this type of letter. Open warmly, state the reasons for refusing the offer, decline the offer explicitly, and close on a pleasant note, expressing gratitude. By taking the time to write a sincere, tactful letter, you leave the door open for future contact.

Makes the opening paragraph a buffer.

One of the most interesting interviews I have ever had was the one last month at your Halifax shipping company. I'm flattered that you would offer me the computer analyst position that we talked about.

Precedes the bad news with tactfully phrased reasons from the applicant's unfavourable decision, and leaves the door open.

During my job search, I applied to five highly rated firms like your own, each one a leader in its field. Both your company and another offered me a position. Because my desire to work abroad can more readily be satisfied by the other company, I have accepted that job offer.

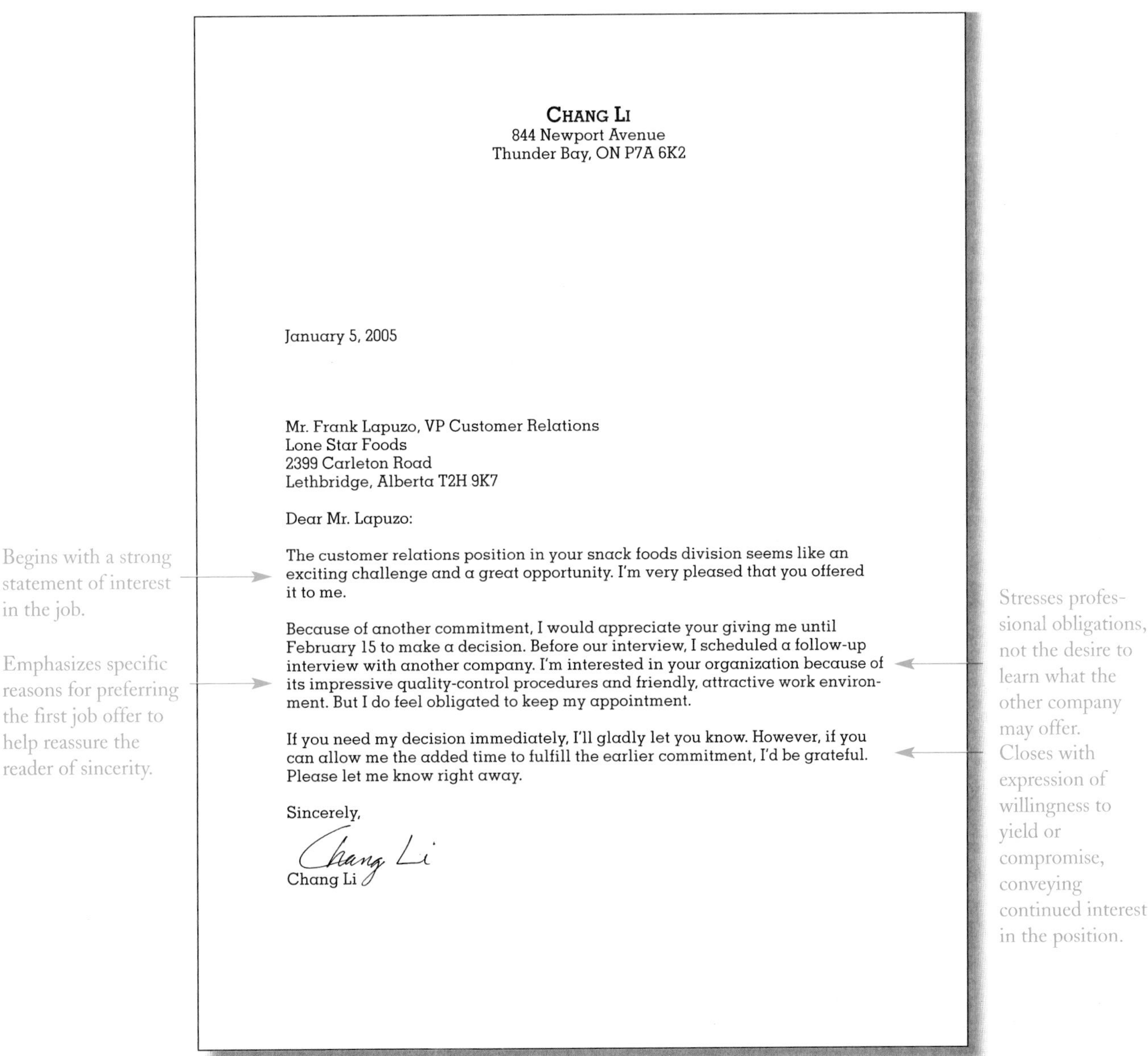

CHANG LI
844 Newport Avenue
Thunder Bay, ON P7A 6K2

January 5, 2005

Mr. Frank Lapuzo, VP Customer Relations
Lone Star Foods
2399 Carleton Road
Lethbridge, Alberta T2H 9K7

Dear Mr. Lapuzo:

The customer relations position in your snack foods division seems like an exciting challenge and a great opportunity. I'm very pleased that you offered it to me.

Because of another commitment, I would appreciate your giving me until February 15 to make a decision. Before our interview, I scheduled a follow-up interview with another company. I'm interested in your organization because of its impressive quality-control procedures and friendly, attractive work environment. But I do feel obligated to keep my appointment.

If you need my decision immediately, I'll gladly let you know. However, if you can allow me the added time to fulfill the earlier commitment, I'd be grateful. Please let me know right away.

Sincerely,

Chang Li

Begins with a strong statement of interest in the job.
Emphasizes specific reasons for preferring the first job offer to help reassure the reader of sincerity.
Stresses professional obligations, not the desire to learn what the other company may offer.
Closes with expression of willingness to yield or compromise, conveying continued interest in the position.

FIGURE 15–2 In-Depth Critique: Request for a Time Extension

> I deeply appreciate the hour you spent talking with me. Thank you again for your consideration and kindness.

Lets the reader down gently with a sincere and cordial ending.

Letter of Resignation

If you get a job offer and are currently employed, you can maintain good relations with your current employer by writing a letter of resignation to your immediate supervisor. Follow the bad-news plan, and make the letter sound positive, regardless of how you feel. Say something favourable about the organization, the people you work with, or what you've learned on the job. Then state your intention to leave and give the date of your last day on the job. Be sure you give your current employer at least two weeks' notice.

A letter of resignation also follows the bad-news plan.

> My sincere thanks to you and to all the other Emblem Corporation employees for helping me learn so much about serving the public these past 11 months. You have given me untold help and encouragement.

Uses an appreciative opening as a buffer.

States reasons before the bad news itself, using tactful phrasing to help keep the relationship friendly, should the writer later want letters of recommendation.

You may recall that when you first interviewed me, my goal was to become a customer relations supervisor. Because that opportunity has been offered to me by another organization, I am submitting my resignation. I regret leaving all of you, but I can't pass up this opportunity.

Discusses necessary details in an extra paragraph.

I would like to terminate my work here two weeks from today but can arrange to work an additional week if you want me to train a replacement.

Tempers any disappointment with a cordial close.

My sincere thanks and best wishes to all of you.

Compare your messages with the suggestions in this chapter's "Checklist: Writing Follow-up Messages" on the next page.

Checklist: Writing Follow-Up Messages

Thank-You Message

✓ Write a thank-you letter within two days of the interview (keeping it to one page).

✓ If you have no alternative, thank the interviewer by phone (in less than five minutes).

✓ In the opening, express thanks and identify the job and the time and place of the interview.

✓ Use the middle section for supporting details.

✓ Express your enthusiasm about the organization and the job.

✓ Add any new facts that may help your chances.

✓ Try to repair any negative impressions you may have left during the interview.

✓ Use an action ending.

Letter of Inquiry

✓ Make an inquiry—by letter, phone, or e-mail, if you aren't informed of the decision by the promised date.

✓ Follow the plan for direct requests: main idea, necessary details, specific request.

Requests for a Time Extension

✓ Request an extension if you have pending interviews and need time to decide about an offer.

✓ Open with an expression of warmth.

✓ In the middle, explain why you need more time and express continued interest in the company.

✓ In the close, promise a quick decision if your request is denied, and ask for a confirmation if your request is granted.

Letter of Acceptance

✓ Send this message within five days of receiving the offer.

✓ State clearly that you accept the offer, identify the job you're accepting, and include vital details.

✓ Conclude with a statement that you look forward to reporting for work.

Letter Declining a Job Offer

✓ Open a letter of rejection warmly.

✓ Explain why you are refusing the offer, and express your appreciation.

✓ End on a sincere, positive note.

Letter of Resignation

✓ Send a letter of resignation to your current employer as soon as possible.

✓ Begin with an appreciative buffer.

✓ In the middle section, state your reasons for leaving, and actually state that you are resigning.

✓ Close cordially.

Summary of Learning Objectives

1 Explain the typical sequence of interviews. Most companies interview a candidate two or three times before making the job offer. The first stage in the sequence is the screening stage, when applicants are asked the same questions so that they are all measured against the same criteria. The second is the selection stage: here, applicants will meet with several interviewers, who will decide if you are a good fit with the organization. The final interview stage further determines if you will get along with your future colleagues learning more about your personality. Here, your interviewers will try to persuade you to join the company if they want to hire you.

2 Identify and briefly describe the most common types of job interviews. Applicants may encounter seven types of job interviews. Mainly used in the screening stage, the (1) structured interview is employer-controlled: the applicant is asked a series of prepared questions in a pre-determined order. Useful for gathering factual information about the applicant, structured interviews are poor for learning about the applicant's personality. (2) Open-ended interviews are less formal than the structured interview: they are intended to bring out an applicant's personality and test professional judgment through broad, open-ended questions. (3) During panel interviews, the candidate meets with several staff members; each person asks prepared questions. (4) Group interviews are intended to judge interpersonal skills; in this situation, employers meet with several applicants simultaneously to see how they interact. (5) Stress interviews test how a candidate handles pressure by subjecting the applicant to pointed questions and rudeness. (6) Video interviews use video conferencing equipment to evaluate candidates in distant locations: applicants should control their movements and look straight at the camera in this situation. (7) Situational interviews ask applicants to describe how they would handle a specific task.

3 List six tasks you need to complete to prepare for a successful job interview. To prepare for a successful job interview, begin by (1) refining the research you did when planning your résumé. Knowing as much as you can about the company and its needs helps you highlight the aspects of your background and qualifications that will appeal to the organization. (2) Next, think ahead about questions—both those you'll need to answer and those you'll want to ask. (3) Bolster your confidence by focusing on your strengths to overcome any apprehension. (4) Polish your style by staging mock interviews and paying close attention to nonverbal behaviours, including voice problems. (5) Plan to look your best with businesslike clothing and good grooming. (6) Arrive on time and ready to begin.

4 Explain the three stages of a successful employment interview. All employment interviews have three stages. The warm-up stage is the most important because first impressions greatly influence an interviewer's decision. The question-and-answer stage is the longest, during which you will answer and ask questions. Listening carefully and watching the interviewer's nonverbal clues help you determine how the interview is going. The close is also important because you need to evaluate your performance to see whether the interviewer has any misconceptions that you must correct.

5 Name six common employment messages that follow an interview and state briefly when you would use each one. The two most common types of follow-up messages are usually in letter form but can also be effective by phone or e-mail. You send the *thank-you* message within two days after your interview to show appreciation, express your continued interest in the job, and politely ask for a decision. You send an *inquiry* if you haven't received the interviewer's decision by the date promised or within two weeks of the interview—especially if you've received a job offer from another firm. The remaining four employment messages are best sent in letter form, to document any official action. You request a *time extension* if you receive a job offer while other interviews are pending and you want more time to complete those interviews before making a decision. You send a *letter of acceptance* within five days of receiving a job offer that you want to take. You send a *letter declining a job offer* when you want to refuse an offer tactfully and leave the door open for future contact. You send a *letter of resignation* when you receive a job offer that you want to accept while you are currently employed.

ON THE JOB

Solving a Communication Dilemma at IBM

IBM recruiters work year-round arranging career fairs, booking speaking engagements, and responding to inquiries—all to attract the best students for the company. Whether at the IBM Information Day or any other career fair, be aware that the interview process begins when you step up to a company representative. Recruiters will want to see a résumé and learn about your background and interests. If they think you might fit with IBM's needs, they will set up a longer interview, lasting from 30 minutes to an hour with a manger.

You will be asked about your technical background, likes and dislikes. The ability to communicate is a key qualification; former IBM CEO Lou Gerstner has said that IBM "will need some new translators." These are the people who "can stand between the scientific community and the world at large and bridge the awesome technological possibilities to the rest of society."

You'll be asked questions based on behaviour, about how you applied your technical skills and abilities. You will also be asked to recount your interpersonal relationships on previous jobs; a common question is: "Could you relate an incident when you had a difference of opinion with a colleague and tell me how you resolved it?" You will also be asked about your achievements, technical and personal strengths, what value you will bring to IBM, and why you want to work for the company. Interviewers are seeking specific qualities, and they want specific and honest answers, ideally with examples that illustrate your strengths and areas for improvement. The company wants to place you in the role that best suits your abilities.

You interviewer will also listen to the questions you ask. To prepare your questions, IBM recommends learning everything you can about the company and the operations that especially interest you, such as marketing, project management, or information technology. They also suggest staging mock interviews with a friend, analyzing your own strengths and weaknesses, and practicing your answers to commonly asked questions (such as "Over the next three to five years, what sort of role do you see yourself in?").

The interviewer's goal is for applicants to leave the interview feeling positive about IBM and knowing when they will learn the outcome.

Your Mission As a member of IBM's human resources department, you are responsible for screening job candidates and arranging for candidates to interview with members of IBM's professional staff. Your responsibilities include the development of interview questions and evaluation forms for use by company employees involved in the interview process. You also handle all routine correspondence with job candidates. In each of the following situations, choose the best alternative, and be prepared to explain why your choice is best.

1 IBM has decided to establish a management-training program for recent university graduates. The program will groom people for careers in strategic planning, marketing, administration, and general management. To recruit people for the program, the firm will conduct on-campus interviews at several universities. You and the other IBM interviewers will be talking with 30 or 40 applicants on campus. You will have 20 minutes for each interview. Your goal is to identify the candidates who will be invited to come to the office for evaluation interviews. You want the preliminary screening process to be as fair and objective as possible, so how will you approach the task?

a Meet with all the IBM interviewers to discuss the characteristics that successful candidates will exhibit. Allow each interviewer to use his or her individual approach to identify these characteristics in applicants. Encourage the interviewers to ask whatever questions seem most useful in light of the individual characteristics of each candidate.

b Develop a list of 10 to 15 questions that will be posed to all candidates. Instruct the interviewers to adhere strictly to the list so that all applicants will respond to the same questions and be evaluated on the same basis.

c Develop a written evaluation form for measuring all candidates against criteria such as academic performance, relevant experience, capacity for teamwork, and communication skills. For each criterion, suggest four or five questions that interviewers might use to evaluate the candidate. Instruct the interviewers to cover all the criteria and to fill out the written evaluation form for each applicant immediately after the interview.

d Design a questionnaire for candidates to complete prior to their interviews. Then ask the interviewers to outline the ideal answers they would like to see a candidate offer for each item on this questionnaire. These ideal answers give you a standard against which to measure actual candidate answers.

2 During the on-campus screening interviews, you ask several candidates, "Why do you want to work for IBM?" Of the following responses, which would you rank the highest?

a "I'd like to work here because I'm interested in the computer business. I've always been fascinated by computers. In addition to studying computer systems, I have taken courses in marketing and finance. I also have some personal experience in building computers. I enjoy helping my friends construct computer systems for their needs."

b "I'm an independent person with a lot of internal drive. I do my best work when I'm given a fairly free reign to use my creativity. From what I've read about your corporate culture, I think my working style would fit very well with your management philosophy. I'm also the sort of person who identifies very strongly with my job. For better or worse, I define myself through my affiliation with my employer. I get a great sense of pride from being part of a first-rate operation, and I think IBM is first-rate. I've read about your selection as one of America's most admired companies. The articles say that IBM is a well-managed company. I think I would learn a lot working here, and I think my drive and creativity would be appreciated."

c "There are several reasons why I'd like to work for IBM Canada. For one thing, I have family and friends in Montreal, and I'd like to stay in the area. Also, I have friends who work for IBM, and they both say it's terrific. I've also heard good things about your compensation and benefits."

d "My ultimate goal is to start my own company, but first I need to learn more about managing a business. I read in *Fortune* that IBM is one of North America's most admired corporations. I think I could learn a lot by joining your management training program and observing your operations."

3 You are preparing questions for the professional staff to use when conducting follow-up interviews at IBM's Canadian headquarters in Montreal. You want a question that will reveal something about the candidates' probable loyalty to the organization. Which of the following questions is the best choice?

a If you knew you could be one of the world's most successful people in a single occupation, such as music, politics, medicine, or business, what occupation would you choose? If you knew you had only a 10 percent chance of being so successful, would you still choose the same occupation?

b We value loyalty among our employees. Tell me something about yourself that demonstrates your loyalty as a member of an organization.

c What would you do if you discovered that a co-worker routinely made personal, unauthorized long-distance phone calls from work?

d What other companies are you interviewing with?

4 In concluding an evaluation interview, you ask the candidate, "Do you have any questions?" Which of the following answers would you respond most favourably to?

a "No. I can't think of anything. You've been very thorough in describing the job and the company. Thank you for taking the time to talk with me."

b "Yes. I have an interview with one of your competitors, next week. How would you sum up the differences between your two firms?"

c "Yes. If I were offered a position here, what would my chances be of getting promoted within the next 12 months?"

d "Yes. Do you think IBM will be a better or worse company 15 years from now?"[23]

Test Your Knowledge

Review Questions

1 How does a structured interview differ from an open-ended interview and a situational interview?
2 What typically occurs during a stress interview?
3 Why do employers conduct pre-employment testing?
4 Why are the questions you ask during an interview as important as the answers you give to the interviewer's questions?
5 What are the three stages of every interview, and which is the most important?
6 How should you respond if an interviewer at a company where you want to work asks you a question that seems too personal or unethical?
7 What should you say in a thank-you message after an interview?
8 What is the purpose of sending a letter of inquiry after an interview?
9 What is the legal significance of a letter of acceptance?
10 What organizational plan is appropriate for a letter of resignation, and why?

Interactive Learning

Use This Text's Online Resources

Visit our Companion Website at **www.pearsoned.ca/thill**, where you can use the interactive Study Guide to test your chapter knowledge and get instant feedback. Additional resources link you to the sites mentioned in this text and to additional sources of information on chapter topics.

Also check out the resources on the Mastering Business Communication CD, including "Perils of Pauline," an interactive presentation of the business communication challenges within a fictional company. For Chapter 15, see in particular the episode "The Job Interview."

Apply Your Knowledge

Critical Thinking Questions

1 How can you distinguish yourself from other candidates in a screening interview and still keep your responses short and to the point? Explain.
2 What can you do to make a favourable impression when you discover that an open-ended interview has turned into a stress interview? Briefly explain your answer.
3 If you want to switch jobs because you can't work with your supervisor, how can you explain this situation to a prospective employer? Give an example.
4 During a group interview you notice that one of the other candidates is trying to monopolize the conversation. He's always the first to answer, his answer is the longest, and he even interrupts the other candidates while they are talking. The interviewer doesn't seem to be concerned about his behaviour, but you are. You would like to have more time to speak so that the interviewer could get to know you better. What should you do?
5 **Ethical Choices** Why is it important to distinguish unethical or illegal interview questions from acceptable questions? Explain.

Practice Your Knowledge

Documents for Analysis

Read the following documents; then (1) analyze the strengths or weaknesses of each document and (2) revise each document so that it follows this chapter's guidelines.

Document 15.A: Thank-You Message

Thank you for the really marvelous opportunity to meet you and your colleagues at Starret Engine Company. I really enjoyed touring your facilities and talking with all the people there. You have quite a crew! Some of the other companies I have visited have been so rigid and uptight that I can't imagine how I would fit in. It's a relief to run into a group of people who seem to enjoy their work as much as all of you do.

I know that you must be looking at many other candidates for this job, and I know that some of them will probably be more experienced than I am. But I do want to emphasize that my two-year hitch in the Navy involved a good deal of engineering work. I don't think I mentioned all my shipboard responsibilities during the interview.

Please give me a call within the next week to let me know your decision. You can usually find me at my dormitory in the evening after dinner (phone: 614-877-9080).

Document 15.B: Letter of Inquiry

I have recently received a very attractive job offer from the Warrington Company. But before I let them know one way or another, I would like to consider any offer that your firm may extend. I was quite impressed with your company during my recent interview, and I am still very interested in a career there.

I don't mean to pressure you, but Warrington has asked for my decision within 10 days. Could you let me know by Tuesday whether you plan to offer me a position? That would give me enough time to compare the two offers.

Document 15.C: Letter Declining a Job Offer

I'm writing to say that I must decline your job offer. Another company has made me a more generous offer, and I have decided to accept. However, if things don't work out for me there, I will let you know. I sincerely appreciate your interest in me.

Exercises

15–1 **Teamwork** Divide the class into two groups. Half the class will be recruiters for a large national chain of stores looking to fill manager trainee positions (there are 15 openings). The other half of the class will be candidates for the job. The company is specifically looking for candidates who demonstrate these three qualities: initiative, dependability, and willingness to assume responsibility.
- a Have each recruiter select and interview an applicant for 10 minutes.
- b Have all the recruiters discuss how they assessed the applicant against each of the three desired qualities. What questions did they ask or what did they use as an indicator to determine whether the candidate possessed the quality?
- c Have all the applicants discuss what they said to convince the recruiters that they possessed each of these qualities.

15–2 **Internet** Select a large company (one that you can easily find information on) where you might like to work. Use Internet sources to gather some preliminary research on the company.
- a What did you learn about this organization that would help you during an interview there?
- b What Internet sources did you use to obtain this information?
- c Armed with this information, what aspects of your background do you think might appeal to this company's recruiters?
- d If you choose to apply for a job with this company, what key words would you include on your résumé, and why?

15–3 **Interviews: Being Prepared** Prepare written answers to 10 of the questions listed in Table 15–2, "Twenty-Five Common Interview Questions" on page 473.

15–4 **Ethical Choices** You have decided to accept a new position with a competitor of your company. Write a letter of resignation to your supervisor announcing your decision.
- a Will you notify your employer that you are joining a competing firm? Please explain.
- b Will you use the direct or the indirect approach? Please explain.
- c Will you send your letter by e-mail, by regular mail, or place it on your supervisor's desk?

15–5 **Interviews: Understanding Qualifications** Write a short memo to your instructor discussing what you believe are your greatest strengths and weaknesses from an employment perspective. Next, explain how interviewers evaluating your qualifications would view these strengths and weaknesses.

Cases

Interviewing with Potential Employers

1 Interviewers and interviewees: Classroom exercise in interviewing Interviewing is clearly an interactive process involving at least two people. The best way to practice for interviews is to work with others.

Your Task: You and all other members of your class are to write letters of application for an entry-level or management-trainee position requiring a pleasant personality and intelligence but a minimum of specialized education or experience. Sign your letter with a fictitious name that conceals your identity. Next polish (or prepare) a résumé that accurately identifies you and your educational and professional accomplishments.

Now, three members of the class who volunteer as interviewers divide among themselves all the anonymously written application letters. Then each interviewer selects a candidate who seems the most pleasant and convincing in his or her letter. At this time the selected candidates identify themselves and give the interviewers their résumés.

Each interviewer then interviews his or her chosen candidate in front of the class, seeking to understand how the items on the résumé qualify the candidate for the job. At the end of the interviews, the class may decide who gets the job and discuss why this candidate was successful. Afterward, retrieve your letter, sign it with the right name, and submit it to the instructor for credit.

2 Internet interview: Exercise in interviewing Using Google (or another search engine), locate the home page of a company you would like to work for. Then identify a position within the company for which you would like to apply. Study the company using any of the online business resources discussed in Chapter 11, and prepare for an interview with that company.

Your Task: Working with a classmate, take turns interviewing each other for your chosen positions. Interviewers should take notes during the interview. Once the interview is complete, critique each other's performance (interviewers should critique how well candidates prepared for the interview and answered the questions; interviewees should critique the quality of the questions asked). Write a follow-up letter thanking your interviewer and submit the letter to your instructor.

Following Up After the Interview

3 A slight error in timing: Letter asking for delay of an employment decision You botched up your timing and applied for your third-choice job before going after what you really wanted. What you want to do is work in retail marketing with Holt Renfrew in Vancouver; what you have been offered is a similar job with Zellers in Regina.

You review your notes. Your Regina interview was three weeks ago with the human resources manager, R. P. Bronson, a congenial person who has just written to offer you the position. His address is PO Box 79801, Regina, SK S4N 0A0. Mr. Bronson notes that he can hold the position open for ten days. You have an interview scheduled with Holt Renfrew next week, but it is unlikely that you will know the store's decision within this ten-day period.

Your Task: Write to R. P. Bronson, requesting a reasonable delay in your consideration of his job offer.

4 Job hunt: Set of employment-related letters to a single company Where would you like to work? Pick a real or an imagined company, and assume that a month ago you sent your résumé and application letter. Not long afterward, you were invited to go in for an interview, which seemed to go very well.

Your Task: Use your imagination to write the following: (a) a thank-you letter for the interview, (b) a note of inquiry, (c) a request for more time to decide, (d) a letter of acceptance, and (e) a letter declining the job offer.

Going Online Exercises

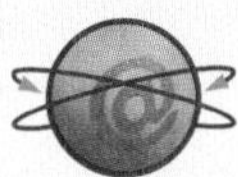

Planning for a Successful Interview, page 471

If you have not interviewed recently (or ever) for a job, do you have an idea of the kind of questions you might be asked? How can you prepare for an interview so that you'll appear knowledgeable about the job and confident in your skills? At **Job-interview.net** you'll get advice and ideas to make your next interview successful.

1 What are some awkward questions you might be asked during a job interview? How would you handle these questions?
2 Choose a job title from the list and read more about it. What did you learn that could help during an actual interview for the job you selected?
3 Developing an "interview game plan" ahead of time helps you make a strong, positive impression during an interview. What are some of the things you can practice to help make everything you do during an interview seem to come naturally?

To link directly to this site, visit our Companion Website at **www.pearsoned.ca/thill** and look for the Chapter 15 resources.

Format and Layout of Business Documents

Few hard-and-fast rules govern the format and layout of business documents. The cosmetics of letters, memos, and reports vary from country to country, and many Canadian organizations adapt standard forms to suit their own needs, modifying styles for the types of messages they send and for the kinds of audiences that receive them. The formats described here are more common than others. Whether you handle all your own communication on your computer or rely on someone else to handle it for you, knowing both the proper form for your documents and how to make them attractive to your readers are crucial to conveying the right image.

First Impressions

Your documents tell readers a lot about you and about your company's professionalism. All your documents must look neat, present an image of competence, and be easy to read. Your audience's first impression of a document comes from the quality of its paper, the way it is customized, and its general appearance.

Paper

To give a quality impression, businesspeople consider carefully the paper they use. Several aspects of paper contribute to the overall impression:

- **Weight.** Paper quality is judged by the weight of 4 reams (each a 500-sheet package) of letter-size paper. The weight most commonly used by Canadian and U.S. business organizations is 20-pound paper, but 16- and 24-pound versions are also used.
- **Cotton content.** Paper quality is also judged by the percentage of cotton in the paper. Cotton doesn't yellow over time the way wood pulp does, and it's both strong and soft. For letters and reports going to outsides, use paper with a 25 percent cotton content. For memos and other internal documents, you can use a lighter-weight paper with lower cotton content. Airmail-weight paper may save money for international correspondence, but make sure it isn't too flimsy.[1]
- **Size.** In Canada and the United States, the standard paper size for business documents is $8^1/_2$ by 11 inches. Standard legal documents are $8^1/_2$ by 14 inches. Executives sometimes have heavier 7-by-10-inch paper on hand (with matching envelopes) for personal messages such as congratulations and recommendations.[2] They may also have a box of note cards imprinted with their initials and a box of plain folded notes for condolences or for acknowledging formal invitations.
- **Colour.** White is the standard colour for business purposes, although neutral colours such as ivory and gray are sometimes used. Memos can be produced on pastel-coloured paper to distinguish them from external correspondence. In addition, memos are sometimes produced on various colours of paper for routing to separate departments. Light-coloured papers are appropriate, but bright or dark colours make reading difficult and may appear too frivolous.

Customization

For letters to outsiders, Canadian businesses commonly use letterhead stationery, which may be either professionally printed or designed in-house using word-processing templates and graphics. The letterhead includes the company's name and address, usually at the top of the page but sometimes along the left side or even at the bottom. Other information may be included in the letterhead as well: the company's telephone number, fax number, website address, cable address, product lines, date of establishment, officers and directors, slogan, and logo. Well-designed letterhead gives readers[3]

- Pertinent reference data
- A favourable image of the company
- A good idea of what the company does

For as much as it's meant to communicate, the letterhead should be as simple as possible. Too much information makes the page look cluttered, occupies space needed for the message, and might become outdated before all the stationery can be used. If you correspond frequently with people abroad, your letterhead must be intelligible to foreigners.

It must include the name of your country in addition to your cable, telex, e-mail, or fax information.

In Canada, businesses always use letterhead for the first page of a letter. Successive pages are usually plain sheets of paper that match the letterhead in colour and quality. Some companies use a specially printed second-page letterhead that bears only the company's name. Other countries have other conventions.

Many companies also design standardized forms for memos and frequently written reports that always require the same sort of information (such as sales reports and expense reports). These standardized forms are often created with word-processing or spreadsheet programs. Employees can complete and save them electronically, and e-mail copies to supervisors and colleagues.[4] These forms may also be printed in sets for use with carbon paper or in carbonless-copy sets that produce multiple copies automatically.

Appearance

Produce almost all of your business documents using either a laser printer (which gives a sharper resolution than an ink-jet printer) or a typewriter. Certain documents, such as a short informal memo or a note of condolence, should be handwritten. Be sure to handwrite, print, or type the envelope to match the document. However, even a letter on the best-quality paper with the best-designed letterhead may look unprofessional if it's poorly produced. So pay close attention to all the factors affecting appearance, including the following:

- **Margins.** Canadian companies ensure that documents are centered on the page, with margins of at least an inch all around. Using word-processing software, you can achieve this balance simply by defining the format parameters. When using a typewriter, either establish a standard line length (usually about 6 inches) or establish a "picture frame."
- **Line length.** Lines are rarely full-justified, because the resulting text looks too much like a form letter and can be hard to read (even with proportional spacing). Varying line length makes the document look more personal and interesting. Pica type (12 points) gives you 60 characters in a line; elite type (10 points) gives you 72 characters in a line.
- **Line spacing.** You can adjust the number of blank lines between elements (such as between the date and the inside address) to ensure that a short document fills the page vertically or that a longer document extends at least two lines of the body onto the last page.
- **Character spacing.** Use proper spacing between characters and after punctuation. For example, Canadian and U.S. conventions include leaving one space after commas, semicolons, and colons. Documents look best with two spaces after sentence-ending periods. Each letter in a person's initials is followed by a period and a single space. However, abbreviations such as U.S.A. or MBA may or may not have periods, but they never have internal spaces.
- **Special symbols.** When using a computer, use appropriate symbols to give your document a professional look (see Table A–1 for examples). When using a typewriter, use a hyphen for the en dash, and use two hyphens (with no space before, between, or after) for the em dash. Find other details of this sort in your company's style book or in most secretarial handbooks.
- **Corrections.** Messy corrections are obvious and unacceptable in business documents. Reprint or retype any letter, report, or memo requiring a lot of corrections. Word-processing software and self-correcting typewriters can produce correction-free documents at the push of a button.

TABLE A.1 Special Symbols on Computer

	Computer symbol	Typed symbol
Case fractions	½	1/2
Copyright	©	(c)
Registered trademark	®	(R)
Cents	¢	None
British pound	£	None
Paragraph	¶	None
Bullets	●, ◆, ■, □, ✓,☐,⊗	*, #, 0
Em dash	—	-- (two hyphens)
En dash	–	- (one hyphen)

Letters

All business letters have certain elements in common. Several of these elements appear in every letter; others appear only when desirable or appropriate. In addition, these letter parts are usually arranged in one of three basic formats.

Standard Letter Parts

The letter in Figure A–1 shows the placement of standard letter parts. The writer of this business letter had no letterhead available but correctly included a heading. All business letters typically include these seven elements.

HEADING

Letterhead (the usual heading) shows the organization's name, full address, telephone number, World Wide Web and e-mail address (often). Executive letterhead also bears the name of an individual within the organization.

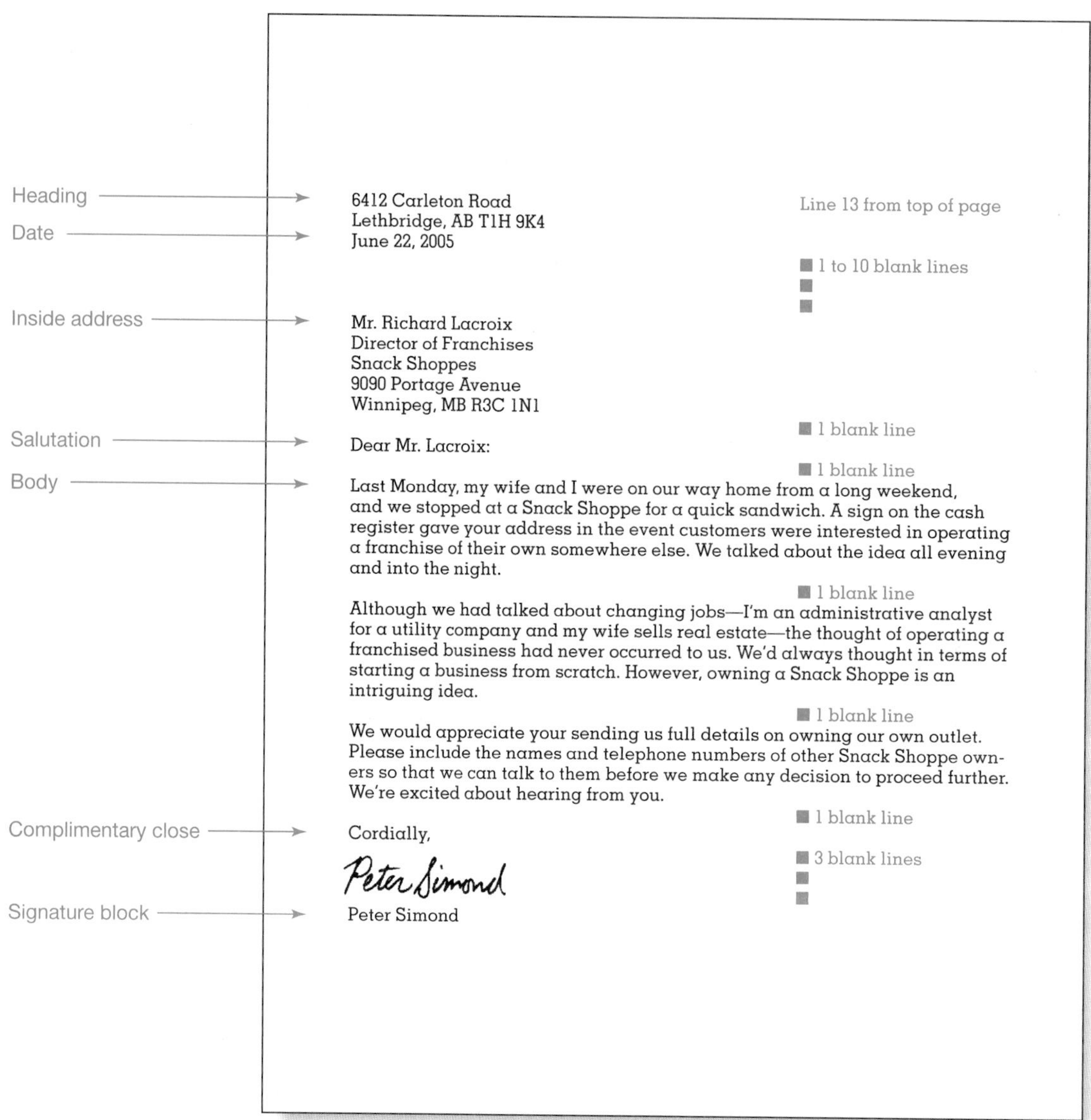

FIGURE A–1 Standard Letter Parts

Computers allow you to design your own letterhead (either one to use for all correspondence or a new one for each piece of correspondence). If letterhead stationery is not available, the heading includes a return address (but no name) and starts 13 lines from the top of the page, which leaves a two-inch top margin.

DATE

If you're using letterhead, place the date at least one blank line beneath the lowest part of the letterhead. Without letterhead, place the date immediately below the return address. The standard method of writing the date in Canada uses the full name of the month (no abbreviations), followed by the day (in numerals, without *st, nd, rd,* or *th*), a comma, and then the year: July 14, 2005 (7/14/05). Some organizations follow other conventions (see Table A–2). To maintain the utmost clarity in international correspondence, always spell out the name of the month in dates.[5]

When communicating internationally, you may also experience some confusion over time. Some Canadian companies refer to morning (a.m.) and afternoon (p.m.), dividing a 24-hour day into 12-hour blocks so that they refer to 4 o'clock in the morning (4:00 a.m.) or 4 o'clock in the afternoon (4:00 p.m.). The Canadian military and European companies refer to one 24-hour period so that 0400 hours (4:00 a.m.) is always in the morning and 1600 hours (4:00 p.m.) is always in the afternoon.[6] Make sure your references to time are as clear as possible, and be sure you clearly understand your audience's time references.

TABLE A–2 Common Date Forms

Convention	Description	Date—Mixed	Date—All Numerals
Canadian standard	Month (spelled out) day, year	July 14, 2005	7/14/05
Canadian government and some Canadian industries	Day (in numerals) month (spelled out) year	14 July 2005	14/7/05
European	Replace Canadian solidus (diagonal line) with periods	14 July 2005	14.7.2005
International standard	Year month day	2005 July 14	2005,7,14

INSIDE ADDRESS

The inside address identifies the recipient of the letter. For U.S. correspondence, begin the inside address at least one line below the date. Precede the addressee's name with a courtesy title, such as *Dr.*, *Mr.*, or *Ms.* The accepted courtesy title for women in business is *Ms.*, although a woman known to prefer the title *Miss* or *Mrs.* is always accommodated. If you don't know whether a person is a man or a woman (and you have no way of finding out), omit the courtesy title. For example, *Terry Smith* could be either a man or a woman. The first line of the inside address would be just *Terry Smith*, and the salutation would be *Dear Terry Smith*. The same is true if you know only a person's initials, as in *S. J. Adams*.

Spell out and capitalize titles that precede a person's name, such as *Professor* or *General* (see Table A–3 for the proper forms of address). The person's organizational title, such as *Director*, may be included on this first line (if it is short) or on the line below; the name of a department may follow. In addresses and signature lines, don't forget to capitalize any professional title that follows a person's name:

Mr. Ray Johnson, Dean
Ms. Patricia T. Higgins, Assistant Vice President

However, professional titles not appearing in an address or signature line are capitalized only when they directly precede the name.

President Kenneth Johanson will deliver the speech.

Maria Morales, president of ABC Enterprises, will deliver the speech.

The Honourable Ethel Blondin-Andrew, member of Parliament for Western Arctic, Northwest Territories, will deliver the speech.

If the name of a specific person is unavailable, you may address the letter to the department or to a specific position within the department. Also, be sure to spell out company names in full, unless the company itself uses abbreviations in its official name.

Other address information includes the treatment of buildings, house numbers, and compass directions (see Table A–4). The following example shows all the information that may be included in the inside address and its proper order for Canadian correspondence:

Dr. H. C. Armstrong
Research and Development
Commonwealth Mining Consortium
The Chelton Building, Suite 301
585 Second Street SW
Calgary, Alberta T2P 2P5

U.S. addresses are similar:

Ms. Linda Rodriguez, Vice President
Corporate Planning Department
Midwest Airlines
Kowalski Building, Suite 21-A
7279 Bristol Avenue
Toledo, OH 43617

The order and layout of address information vary from country to country. So when addressing correspondence for other countries, carefully follow the format and information that appear in the company's letterhead. However, when you're sending mail from Canada, be sure that the name of the destination country appears on the last line of the address in capital letters. Use the English version of the country name so that your mail is routed from Canada to the right country. Then, to be sure your mail is routed correctly within the destination country, use the foreign spelling of the city name (using the characters and diacritical marks that would be commonly used in the region). For example, the following address uses *Köln* instead of *Cologne*:

H. R. Veith, Director	Addressee
Eisfieren Glaswerk	Company Name
Blaubachstraße 13	Street address
Postfach 10 80 07	Post office box
D-5000 Köln I	District, city
GERMANY	Country

For additional examples of international addresses, see Table A–5.

Be sure to use organizational titles correctly when addressing international correspondence. Job designations vary around the world. In England, for example, a managing director is often what a Canadian company would call its chief executive officer or president, and a British deputy is the equivalent of a vice president. In France, responsibilities are assigned to individuals without regard to title or

TABLE A–3 Forms of Address

Person	In Address	In Salutation
Personal Titles		
Man	Mr. [first & last name]	Dear Mr. [last name]:
Woman (marital status unknown)	Ms. [first & last name]	Dear Ms. [last name]:
Woman (single)	Ms. *or* Miss [first & last name]	Dear Ms. *or* Miss [last name]:
Woman (married)	Ms. *or* Mrs. [wife's first & last name] or Mrs. [husband's first & last name]	Dear Ms. *or* Mrs. [last name]:
Woman (widowed)	Ms. *or* Mrs. [wife's first name & last name]	Dear Ms. *or* Mrs. [last name]:
Woman (separated or divorced)	Ms. *or* Mrs. [first & last name]	Dear Ms. *or* Mrs. [last name]:
Two men (or more)	Mr. [first & last name] and	Dear Mr. [last name] and Mr. [last name]
	or	
	Mr. [first & last name]	Messrs. [last name] and [last name]:
Two women (or more)	Ms. [first & last name] and	Dear Ms. [last name] and Ms. [last name]
	or	
	Ms. [first & last name]	Mses. [last name] and [last name]:
	or	
	Mrs. [first & last name] and Mrs. [first & last name]	Dear Mrs. [last name] and Mrs. [last name]: *or* Dear Mesdames [last name] and [last name] or Mesdames:
	Miss [first & last name] Mrs. [first & last name]	Dear Miss [last name] and Mrs. [last name]:
One woman and one man	Ms. [first & last name] and Mr. [first & last name]	Dear Ms. [last name] and Mr. [last name]:
Couple (married)	Mr. and Mrs. [husband's first & last name]	Dear Mr. and Mrs. [last name]:
Couple (married with different last names)	[title] [first & last name of husband] [title] [first & last name of wife]	Dear [title] [husband's last name] and [title] [wife's first & last name]:
Couple (married professionals with same title and same last name)	[title in plural form] [husband's first name] and [wife's first & last name]	Dear [title in plural form] [last name]:
Couple (married professionals with different titles and same last name)	[title] [first & last name of husband] and [title] [first & last name of wife]	Dear [title] and [title] [last name]:

organizational structure, and in Chin a the title *project manager* has meaning, but the title *sales manager* may not.

To make matters more complicated, businesspeople in some countries sign correspondence without their names typed below. In Germany, for example, the belief is that employees represent the company, so it's inappropriate to emphasize personal names.[7] Use the examples in Table A.5 as guidelines when addressing correspondence to countries outside Canada.

SALUTATION

In the salutation of your letter, follow the style of the first line of the inside address. If the first line is a person's name, the salutation is *Dear Mr.* or *Ms. Name.* The formality of the salutation depends on your relationship with the addressee. If in conversation you would say "Mary," your letter's salutation should be *Dear Mary,* followed by a colon. Otherwise, include the courtesy title and last name, followed by a colon. Presuming to write *Dear Lewis* instead of *Dear Professor Chang* demonstrates a disrespectful familiarity that the recipient will probably resent.

If the first line of the inside address is a position title such as *Director of Personnel,* then use *Dear Director*. If the addressee is unknown, use a polite description, such as *Dear Alumnus, Dear SPCA Supporter,* or *Dear Voter.* If the first line is plural (a department or company), then use *Ladies and Gentlemen* (look again at Table A–3). When you do not know whether you're writing to an individual or a group

TABLE A.3 Continued

Person	In Address	In Salutation
Professional Titles		
President of a college or university (doctor)	Dr. [first & last name], President	Dear Dr. [last name]:
Dean of a school of college	Dean [first & last name] *or* Dr., Mr., Mrs., *or* Miss [first & last name] Dean of (title)	Dear Dean [last name]: Dear Dr., Mr., Ms., Mrs., *or* Miss [last name]:
Professor	Professor [first & last name]	Dear Professor [last name]:
Physician	[first & last name], M.D.	Dear Dr. [last name]:
Lawyer	Mr., Ms., Mrs., *or* Miss [first & last name]	Dear Mr., Ms., Mrs., *or* Miss [last name]:
Service personnel	[full rank, first & last name, abbreviation of service designation] (add Retired if applicable)	Dear [rank] [last name]:
Company or corporation	[name of organization]	Ladies and Gentlemen or Gentlemen and Ladies
Governmental Titles		
Prime Minister of Canada	The Right Honourable [name]	Dear Prime Minister
Federal Minister	The Honourable [name], MP	Dear Mr. *or* Ms. [name] or Dear Minister
Member of Parliament	Mr. *or* Mrs. [name], MP	Dear Mr. *or* Mrs. [last name]
Judge	The Honourable [name] Dear Madame Justice [last name]	Dear Mr. Justice [last name]
Mayor	Mayor [name]	Dear Mr. *or* Ms.Mayor
Councillor	Councillor [name]	Dear Mr. *or* Ms. [name]
		Thank you, Mr. Brown, Salutopening for your prompt payment of your bill. Body Congratulations, Ms. Lake! Salutopening Your promotion is well deserved. Body

(for example, when writing a reference or a letter of recommendation), use *To whom it may concern.*

In Canada and the U.S. some letter writers use a "salutopening" on the salutation line. A salutopening omits *Dear* but includes the first few words of the opening paragraph along with the recipient's name. After this line, the sentence continues a double space below as part of the body of the letter, as in these examples:

Whether your salutation is informal or formal, be especially careful that names are spelled right. A misspelled name is glaring evidence of carelessness, and it belies the personal interest you're trying to express.

TABLE A-4 Inside Address Information

Description	Example
Capitalize building names.	Royal Bank Plaza
Capitalize locations within buildings (apartments, suites, rooms).	Suite 1073
Use numerals for all house or building numbers, except the number one.	One Trinity Lane 637 Adams Ave., Apt. 7
Spell out compass directions that fall within a street address	1074 West Connover St.
Abbreviate compass directions that follow the street address	783 Main St., N.E., Apt. 27

TABLE A–5 International Addresses and Salutations

Country	Postal Address	Address Elements	Salutations
Argentina	Sr. Juan Pérez Editorial Internacional S.A. Av. Sarmiento 1337, 8° P. C C1035AAB BUENOS AIRES - CF ARGENTINA	S.A. = Sociedad Anónima (corporation) Av. Sarmiento (name of street) 1337 (building number) 8° = 8th. P = Piso (floor) C (room or suite) C1035AAB (postcode 1 city) CF = Capital Federal (federal capital)	Sr. = Señor (Mr.) Sra. = Señora (Mrs.) Srta. = Señorita (Miss) Don't use given names except with people you know well.
Australia	Mr. Roger Lewis International Publishing Pty.Ltd. 166 Kent Street, Level 9 GPO Box 3542 SYDNEY NSW 2001 AUSTRALIA	Pty.Ltd. = Proprietory Limited (corp.) 166 (building number) Kent Street (name of street) Level (floor) GPO Box (post office box) city 1 state (abbrev.) 1 postcode	Mr. and Mrs. used on first contact. Ms. not common (avoid use). Business is informal—use given name freely.
Austria	Herrn Dipl.-Ing.J.Gerdenitsch International Verlag Ges.m.b.H. Glockengasse 159 1010 WIEN AUSTRIA	Herrn = To Mr. (separate line) Dipl.-Ing. (engineering degree) Ges.m.b.H. (a corporation) Glockengasse (street name) 159 (building number) 1010 (postcode + city) WIEN (Vienna)	Herr (Mr.) Frau (Mrs.) Fräulein (Miss) obsolete in business, so do not use. Given names are almost never used in business.
Brazil	Ilmo. Sr. Gilberto Rabello Ribeiro Editores Internacionais S.A. Rua da Ajuda, 228-6° Andar Caixa Postal 2574 20040-000 RIO DE JANEIRO - RJ BRAZIL	Ilmo. = Ilustrissimo (honorific) Ilma. = Ilustrissima (hon.female) S.A. = Sociedade Anônima (corporation) Rua = street, da Ajuda (street name) 228 (building number) 6° = 6th. Andar (floor) Caixa Postal (P.O. box) 20040-000 (postcode + city) - RJ (state abbrev.)	Sr. = Senhor (Mr.) Sra. = Senhora (Mrs.) Srta. = Senhorita (Miss) Family name at end, e.g., Senhor Ribeiro (Rabello is mother's family—as in Portugal) Given names readily used in business.
China	Xia Zhiyi International Publishing Ltd. 14 Jianguolu Chaoyangqu BEIJING 100025 CHINA	Ltd. (limited liability corporation) 14 (building number) Jianguolu (street name), lu (street) Chaoyangqu (district name) (city + postcode)	Family name (single syllable) first. Given name (2 syllables) second, sometimes reversed. Use Mr. or Ms. at all times (Mr. Xia).
France	Monsieur LEFÈVRE Alain Éditions Internationales S.A. Siège Social Immeuble Le Bonaparte 64–68, av. Galliéni B.P. 154 75942 PARIS CEDEX 19 FRANCE	S.A. = Société Anonyme Siège Social (head office) Immeuble (building + name) 64–68 (building occupies 64, 66, 68) av. = avenue (no initial capital) B.P. = Boîte Postale (P.O. box) 75942 (postcode) CEDEX (postcode for P.O. box)	Monsieur (Mr.) Madame (Mrs.) Mademoiselle (Miss) Best not to abbreviate. Family name is sometimes in all caps with given name following.
Germany	Herrn Gerhardt Schneider International Verlag GmbH Schillerstraße 159 44147 DORTMUND GERMANY	Herrn = To Herr (on a separate line) GmbH (inc.—incorporated) -straße (street—'ß' often written 'ss') 159 (building number) 44147 (postcode + city)	Herr (Mr.) Frau (Mrs.) Fräulein (Miss) obsolete in business, so do not use. Business is formal: (1) do not use given names unless invited, and (2) use academic titles precisely.

TABLE A-5 Continued

Country	Postal Address	Address Elements	Salutations
India	Sr. Shyam Lal Gupta International Publishing (Pvt.) Ltd. 1820 Rehaja Centre 214, Darussalam Road Andheri East BOMBAY - 400049 INDIA	(Pvt.) (privately owned) Ltd. (limited liability corporation) 1820 (possibly office #20 on 18th floor) Rehaja Centre (building name) 214 (building number) Andheri East (suburb name) (city + hyphen + postcode)	Shri (Mr.), Shrimati (Mrs.) but English is common business language, so use Mr., Mrs., Miss. Given names are used only by family and close friends.
Italy	Egr. Sig. Giacomo Mariotti Edizioni Internazionali S.p.A. Via Terenzio, 21 20138 MILANO ITALY	Egr. = Egregio (honorific) Sig. = Signor (not nec. a separate line) S.p.A. = Società per Azioni (corp.) Via (street) 21 (building number) 20138 (postcode + city)	Sig. = Signore (Mr.) Sig.ra = Signora (Mrs.) Sig.a (Ms.) Women in business are addressed as Signora. Use given name only when invited.
Japan	Mr. Taro Tanaka Kokusai Shuppan K.K. 10-23, 5-chome, Minamiazabu Minato-ku TOKYO 106 JAPAN	K.K. = Kabushiki Kaisha (corporation) 10 (lot number) 23 (building number) 5-chome (area #5) Minamiazabu (neighborhood name) Minato-ku (city district) (city + postcode)	Given names not used in business. Use family name + job title. Or use family name + "-san" (Tanaka-san) or more respectfully, add "-sama" or "-dono."
Korea	Mr. KIM Chang-ik International Publishers Ltd. Room 206, Korea Building 33-4 Nonhyon-dong Kangnam-ku SEOUL 135-010 KOREA	English company names common Ltd. (a corporation) 206 (office number inside the building) 33-4 (area 4 of subdivision 33) -dong (city neighbourhood name) -ku (subdivision of city) (city + postcode)	Family name is normally first but sometimes placed after given name. A two-part name is the given name. Use Mr. or Mrs. in letters, but use job title in speech.
Mexico	Sr. Francisco Pérez Martínez Editores Internacionales S.A. Independencia No.322 Col. Juárez 06050 MEXICO D.F.	S.A. = Sociedad Anónima (corporation) Independencia (street name) No. = Número (number) 322 (building number) Col. = Colonia (city district) Juárez (locality name) 06050 (postcode + city) D.F. = Distrito Federal (federal capital)	Sr. = Señor (Mr.) Sra. = Señora (Mrs.) Srta. = Señorita (Miss) Family name in middle: e.g., Sr. Pérez (Martínez is mother's family). Given names are used in business.
South Africa	Mr. Mandla Ntuli International Publishing (Pty.) Ltd. Private Bag X2581 JOHANNESBURG 2000 SOUTH AFRICA	Pty. = Proprietory (privately owned) Ltd. (a corporation) Private Bag (P.O. Box) (city + postcode) or (postcode + city)	Mnr = Meneer (Mr.) Mev. = Mevrou (Mrs.) Mejuffrou (Miss) is not used in business. Business is becoming less formal, so the use of given names is possible.
United Kingdom	Mr. N. J. Lancaster International Publishing Ltd. Kingsbury House 12 Kingsbury Road EDGEWARE Middlesex HA8 9XG ENGLAND	N. J. (initials of given names) Ltd. (limited liability corporation) Kingsbury House (building name) 12 (building number) Kingsbury Road (name of street/road) EDGEWARE (city—all caps) Middlesex (county—not all caps) HA8 9XG (postcode—after 6 spaces, or on a separate line)	Mr. and Ms. used mostly. Mrs. and Miss sometimes used in North and by older women. Given names—(first names)—are used in business after some time. Wait to be invited.

BODY

The body of the letter is your message. Almost all letters are single-spaced, with one blank line before and after the salutation or salutopening, between paragraphs, and before the complimentary close. The body may include indented lists, entire paragraphs indented for emphasis, and even subheadings. If it does, all similar elements should be treated in the same way. Your department or company may select a format to use for all letters.

COMPLIMENTARY CLOSE

The complimentary close begins on the second line below the body of the letter. Alternatives for wording are available, but currently the trend seems to be toward using one-word closes, such as *Sincerely* and *Cordially.* In any case, the complimentary close reflects the relationship between you and the person you're writing to. Avoid cute closes, such as *Yours for bigger profits.* If your audience doesn't know you well, your sense of humor may be misunderstood.

SIGNATURE BLOCK

Leave four blank lines for a written signature below the complimentary close, and then include the sender's name (unless it appears in the letterhead). The person's title may appear on the same line as the name or on the line below:

Cordially,

Raymond Dunnigan
Director of Personnel

Your letterhead indicates that you're representing your company. However, if your letter is on plain paper or runs to a second page, you may want to emphasize that you're speaking legally for the company. The accepted way of doing that is to place the company's name in capital letters a double space below the complimentary close and then include the sender's name and title four lines below that:

Sincerely,

WENTWORTH INDUSTRIES
(Mrs.) Helen B. Yamaguchi
President

If your name could be taken for either a man's or a woman's, a courtesy title indicating gender should be included, with or without parentheses. Also, women who prefer a particular courtesy title should include it:

Mrs. Nancy Winters
(Miss) Juana Flores
Ms. Pat Li
(Mr.) Jamie Saunders

Additional Letter Parts

Letters vary greatly in subject matter and thus in the identifying information they need and the format they adopt. The letter in Figure A–2 shows how these additional parts should be arranged. The following elements may be used in any combination, depending on the requirements of the particular letter:

- **Addressee notation.** Letters that have a restricted readership or that must be handled in a special way should include such addressee notations as *Personal, Confidential,* or *Please Forward.* This sort of notation appears a double space above the inside address, in all-capital letters.
- **Attention line.** Although not commonly used today, an attention line can be used if you know only the last name of the person you're writing to. It can also direct a letter to a position title or department. Place the attention line on the first line of the inside address and put the company name on the second.[8] Match the address on the envelope with the style of the inside address. An attention line may take any of the following forms or variants of them:

  Attention Dr. McHenry
  Attention Director of Marketing
  Attention Marketing Department

- **Subject line.** The subject line tells recipients at a glance what the letter is about (and indicates where to file the letter for future reference). It usually appears below the salutation, either against the left margin, indented (as a paragraph in the body), or centered. It can be placed above the salutation or at the very top of the page, and it can be underscored. Some businesses omit the word *Subject,* and some organizations replace it with *Re:* or *In re:* (meaning "concerning" or "in the matter of"). The subject line may take a variety of forms, including the following:

  Subject: RainMaster Sprinklers
  About your February 2, 2005, order
  FALL 2004 SALES MEETING
  Reference Order No. 27920

- **Second-page heading.** Use a second-page heading whenever an additional page is required. Some companies have second-page letterhead (with the company name and address on one line and in a smaller typeface). The heading bears the name (person or organization) from the first line of the inside address, the page number, the date, and perhaps a reference number. Leave two blank lines before the body. Make sure that at least two lines of a continued paragraph appear on the first and second pages. Never allow the closing lines to appear alone on a continued page. Precede the complimentary close or signature lines with at least two lines of the body. Also, don't hyphenate the last word on a page. All the following are acceptable forms for second-page headings:

Ms. Melissa Baker
May 10, 2005
Page 2

Ms. Melissa Baker, May 10, 2005, Page 2

Ms. Melissa Baker -2- May 10, 2005

- **Company name.** If you include the company's name in the signature block, put it all in capital letters a double space below the complimentary close. You usually include the company's name in the signature block only when the writer is serving as the company's official spokesperson or when letterhead has not been used.
- **Reference initials.** When businesspeople keyboard their own letters, reference initials are unnecessary, so they are becoming rare. When one person dictates a letter and another person produces it, reference initials show who helped prepare it. Place initials at the left margin, a double space below the signature block. When the signature block includes the writer's name, use only the preparer's initials. If the signature block includes only the department, use both sets of initials, usually in one of the following forms: *RSR/sm, RSR:sm,* or *RSR:SM* (writer/ preparer). When the writer and the signer are different people, at least the file copy should bear both their initials as well as the typist's: *JFS/RSR/sm* (signer/writer/preparer).
- **Enclosure notation.** Enclosure notations appear at the bottom of a letter, one or two lines below the reference initials. Some common forms include the following:

Enclosure

Enclosures (2)

Enclosures: Résumé
Photograph
Attachment

- **Copy notation.** Copy notations may follow reference initials or enclosure notations. They indicate who's receiving a *courtesy copy* (*cc*). Some companies indicate copies made on a photocopier (*pc*), or they simply use *copy* (*c*). Recipients are listed in order of rank or (rank being equal) in alphabetical order. Among the forms used are the following:

cc: David Wentworth, Vice President
pc: Dr. Martha Littlefield
Copy to Peter Simond
6412 Carleton Rd.
Lethbridge, AB T1H 9K4
c: Joseph Martinez with brochure and
technical sheet

- When sending copies to readers without other recipients knowing, place *bc, bcc,* or *bpc* ("blind copy," "blind courtesy copy," or "blind photocopy") along with the name and any other information only on the copy, not on the original.
- **Mailing notation.** You may place a mailing notation (such as *Special Delivery* or *Registered Mail*) at the bottom of the letter, after reference initials or enclosure

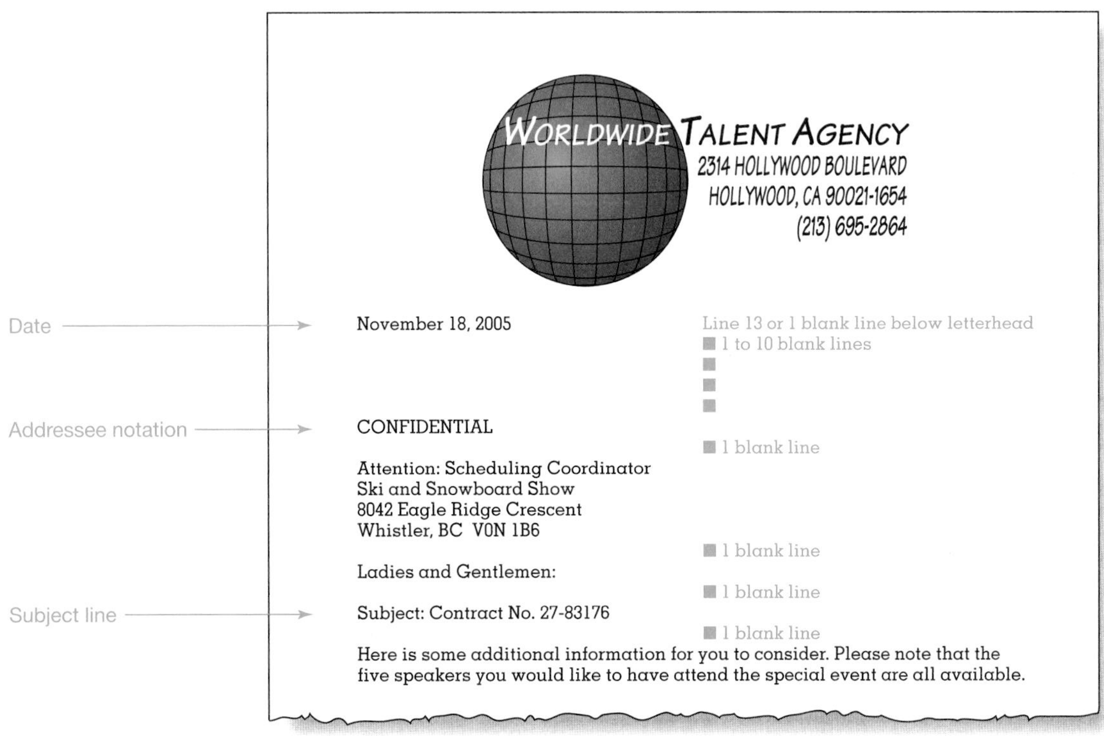

WORLDWIDE TALENT AGENCY
2314 HOLLYWOOD BOULEVARD
HOLLYWOOD, CA 90021-1654
(213) 695-2864

November 18, 2005

CONFIDENTIAL

Attention: Scheduling Coordinator
Ski and Snowboard Show
8042 Eagle Ridge Crescent
Whistler, BC V0N 1B6

Ladies and Gentlemen:

Subject: Contract No. 27-83176

Here is some additional information for you to consider. Please note that the five speakers you would like to have attend the special event are all available.

FIGURE A–2 Additional Letter Parts

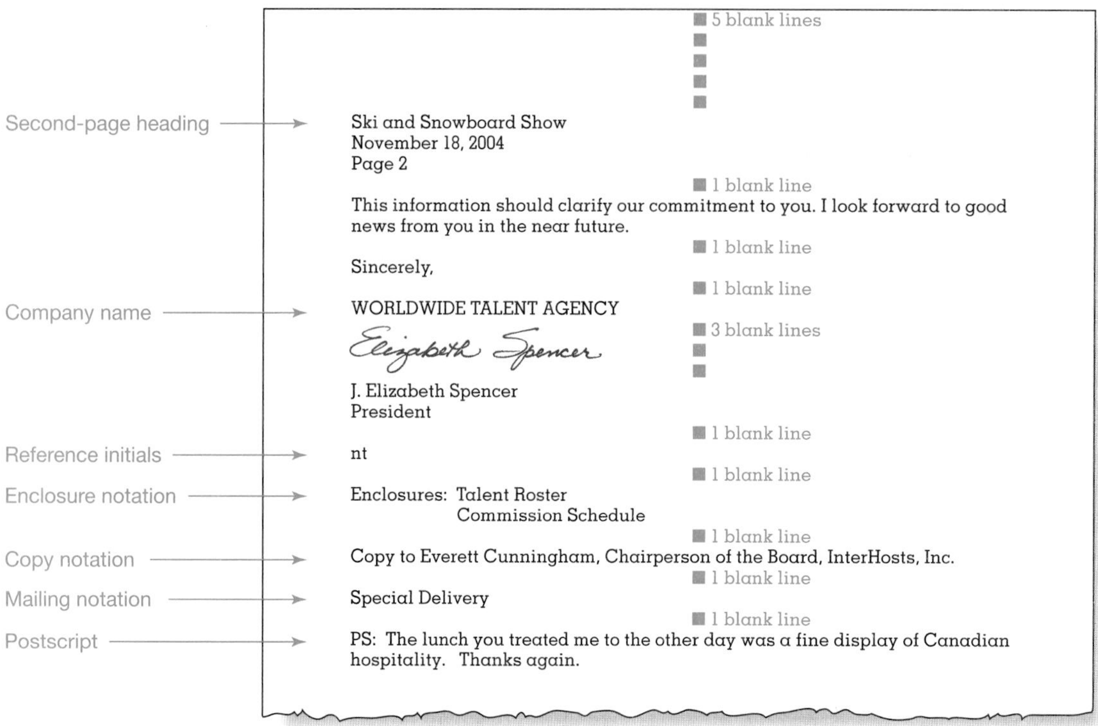

FIGURE A–2 Continued

notations (whichever is last) and before copy notations. Or you may place it at the top of the letter, either above the inside address on the left side or just below the date on the right side. For greater visibility, mailing notations may appear in capital letters.

➤ **Postscript.** A postscript is an afterthought to the letter, a message that requires emphasis, or a personal note. It is usually the last thing on any letter and may be preceded by *P.S., PS., PS:,* or nothing at all. A second afterthought would be designated *P.P.S.* (post postscript). Since postscripts usually indicate poor planning, generally avoid them. However, they're common in sales letters as a punch line to remind readers of a benefit for taking advantage of the offer.

Letter Formats

A letter format is the way of arranging all the basic letter parts. Sometimes a company adopts a certain format as its policy; sometimes the individual letter writer or preparer is allowed to choose the most appropriate format. In Canada, three major letter formats are commonly used:

➤ **Block format.** Each letter part begins at the left margin. The main advantage is quick and efficient preparation (see Figure A–3 on page 501).

➤ **Modified block format.** Same as block format, except that the date, complimentary close, and signature block start near the center of the page (see Figure A–4 on page 502). The modified block format does permit indentions as an option. This format mixes preparation speed with traditional placement of some letter parts. It also looks more balanced on the page than the block format does.

➤ **Simplified format.** Instead of using a salutation, this format often weaves the reader's name into the first line or two of the body and often includes a subject line in capital letters (see Figure A–5 on page 503). With no complimentary close, your signature appears after the body, followed by your printed (or typewritten) name (usually in all-capital letters). This format is convenient when you don't know the reader's name; however, some people object to it as mechanical and impersonal (a drawback you can overcome with a warm writing style). Because certain letter parts are eliminated, some line spacing is changed.

These three formats differ in the way paragraphs are indented, in the way letter parts are placed, and in some punctuation. However, the elements are always separated by at least one blank line, and the printed (or typewritten) name is always separated from the line above by at least three blank lines to allow space for a signature. If paragraphs are indented, the indention is normally five spaces. The most common formats for intercultural business letters are the block style and the modified block style.

In addition to these three letter formats, letters may also be classified according to their style of punctuation. *Standard,* or *mixed, punctuation* uses a colon after the salutation (a comma if the letter is social or personal) and a comma after the complimentary close. *Open punctuation* uses no colon or comma after the salutation or the complimentary close. Although the most popular style in business communication

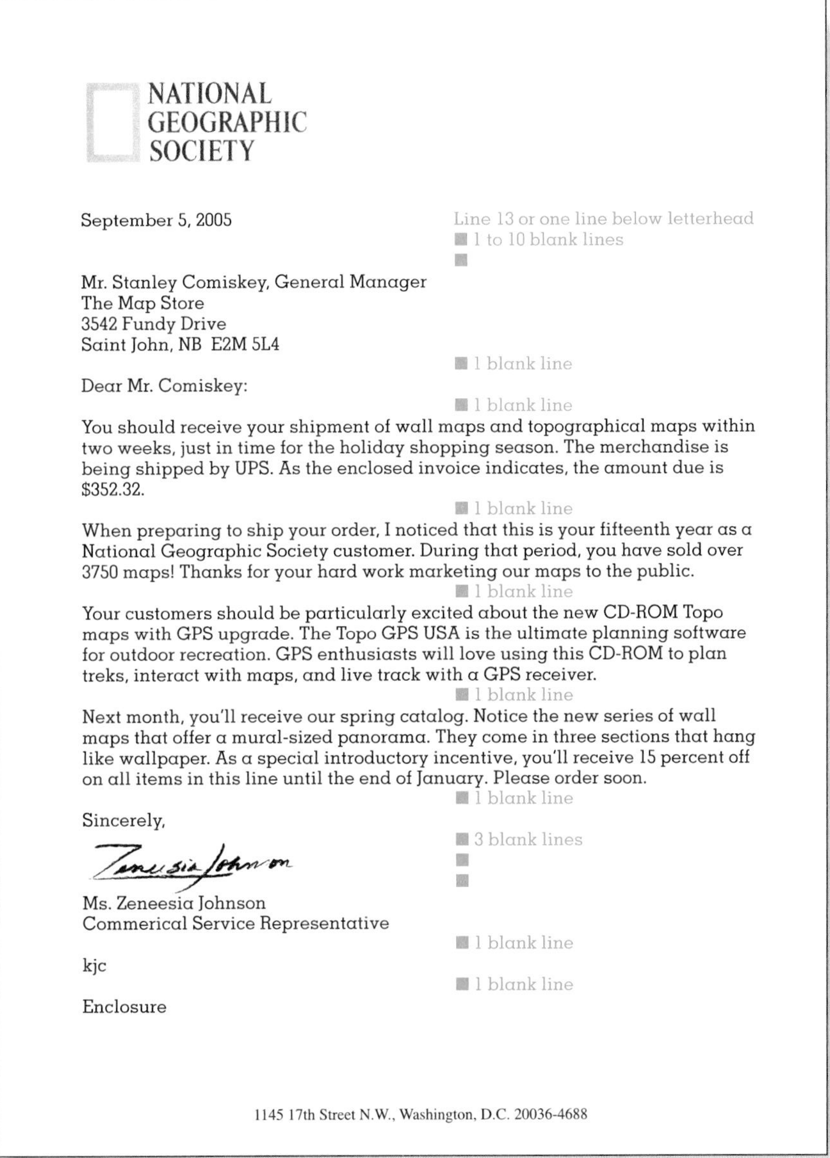

NATIONAL
GEOGRAPHIC
SOCIETY

September 5, 2005

Mr. Stanley Comiskey, General Manager
The Map Store
3542 Fundy Drive
Saint John, NB E2M 5L4

Dear Mr. Comiskey:

You should receive your shipment of wall maps and topographical maps within two weeks, just in time for the holiday shopping season. The merchandise is being shipped by UPS. As the enclosed invoice indicates, the amount due is $352.32.

When preparing to ship your order, I noticed that this is your fifteenth year as a National Geographic Society customer. During that period, you have sold over 3750 maps! Thanks for your hard work marketing our maps to the public.

Your customers should be particularly excited about the new CD-ROM Topo maps with GPS upgrade. The Topo GPS USA is the ultimate planning software for outdoor recreation. GPS enthusiasts will love using this CD-ROM to plan treks, interact with maps, and live track with a GPS receiver.

Next month, you'll receive our spring catalog. Notice the new series of wall maps that offer a mural-sized panorama. They come in three sections that hang like wallpaper. As a special introductory incentive, you'll receive 15 percent off on all items in this line until the end of January. Please order soon.

Sincerely,

Zeneesia Johnson

Ms. Zeneesia Johnson
Commerical Service Representative

kjc

Enclosure

1145 17th Street N.W., Washington, D.C. 20036-4688

FIGURE A_3 Block Letter Format

is mixed punctuation, either style of punctuation may be used with block or modified block letter formats. Because the simplified letter format has no salutation or complimentary close, the style of punctuation is irrelevant.

Envelopes

For a first impression, the quality of the envelope is just as important as the quality of the stationery. Letterhead and envelopes should be of the same paper stock, have the same colour ink, and be imprinted with the same address and logo. Most envelopes used by Canadian businesses are No. 10 envelopes ($9^1/_2$ inches long), which are sized for an $8^1/_2$-by-11-inch piece of paper folded in thirds. Some occasions call for a smaller, No. $6^3/_4$, envelope or for envelopes proportioned to fit special stationery. Figure A–6 on page 504 shows the two most common sizes.

Addressing the Envelope

No matter what size the envelope, the address is always single-spaced with all lines aligned on the left. The address on the envelope is in the same style as the inside address and presents the same information. The order to follow is from the smallest division to the largest:

Fashion Sense

April 12, 2002

Ms. Clara Simpson, President
Young Volunteers Association
1295 Martindale Crescent
Brampton, ON L6X 3T1

Dear Ms. Simpson:

Thank you for inviting us to participate in the Young Volunteers Association Fashion Show. We will be delighted to provide some clothing samples for the May 15 event.

You indicated that you would like us to supply about 12 outfits from our designer collection, six in size 10 and six in size 12. We can certainly accommodate your request. To give your audience a representative overview of our merchandise, I suggest we provide the following: three tailored daytime dresses or pant suits, two dressy dresses, one formal ball gown, four casual weekend outfits, and two active sports outfits.

Please give me a call to schedule a "shopping" trip for you and your committee members. Together, I'm sure we can find exactly what you need to stage a well-rounded show. In the meantime, you might enjoy looking through the enclosed catalogue. It will introduce you to some of the options.

Sincerely,

Vera O'Donnell

(Mrs.) Vera O'Donnell
Special Events Manager

bcg

Enclosure

Fashion Sense, 1853 Queen Street, Brampton, ON L6X 3K8

□ One blank space

* Variable space depending on length of letter

FIGURE A–4 Modified Block Letter Format

1. Name and title of recipient
2. Name of department or subgroup
3. Name of organization
4. Name of building
5. Street address and suite number, or post office box number
6. City, province, and postal code; or city, state, and zip code
7. Name of country (if the letter is being sent abroad)

Canada Post's optical scanning equipment can read both handwritten and typed addresses, and their addressing guidelines accommodate the requirements of French and English and the preferences of mailers. Businesses can use upper and lower case letters and accents when addressing envelopes and spell out and punctuate all addressing elements if they desire. However, Canada Post does encourage customers to follow specific formats because their mail will be handled more efficiently. For example, when a civic number suffix is present, there is no space when it is a letter (123A), and there is one space when it is a fraction (123 1/2). (A civic

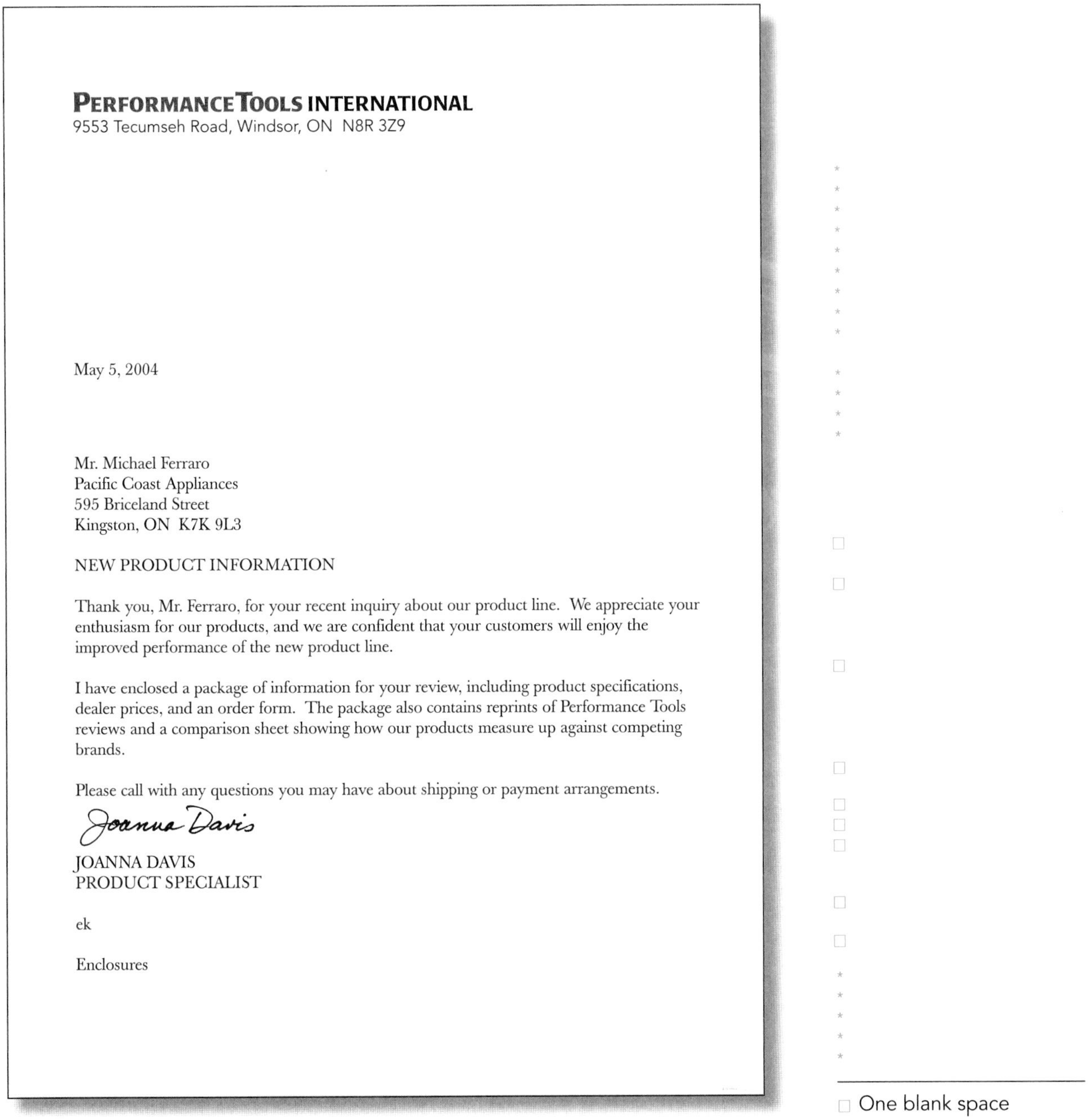

PERFORMANCE TOOLS INTERNATIONAL
9553 Tecumseh Road, Windsor, ON N8R 3Z9

May 5, 2004

Mr. Michael Ferraro
Pacific Coast Appliances
595 Briceland Street
Kingston, ON K7K 9L3

NEW PRODUCT INFORMATION

Thank you, Mr. Ferraro, for your recent inquiry about our product line. We appreciate your enthusiasm for our products, and we are confident that your customers will enjoy the improved performance of the new product line.

I have enclosed a package of information for your review, including product specifications, dealer prices, and an order form. The package also contains reprints of Performance Tools reviews and a comparison sheet showing how our products measure up against competing brands.

Please call with any questions you may have about shipping or payment arrangements.

Joanna Davis

JOANNA DAVIS
PRODUCT SPECIALIST

ek

Enclosures

□ One blank space

· Variable space depending on length of letter

FIGURE A–5 Simplified Letter Format

number is the official number a municipality assigns to an address.) Canada Post prefers that common abbreviations be used for street types (such as ST and AVE), and directs that the only street types that may be translated are ST (RUE), AVE (AV), and BLVD (BOUL). A French street type is always placed before the street name, unless it is ordinal (1er, 2e) or cardinal (PREMIÈRE, DEUXIÈME). The street name is the official name recognized by each municipality and cannot be translated (for example, "Main" is not "Principale").

Canada Post also prefers that a province be written using the recognized two-letter symbol (see Figure A–6 on page 504) and requires that the postal code be in upper case and placed two spaces to the right of the province, with one space between the first three and the last three characters. Review the Canada Postal Guide (**www.canadapost.com/business/tools/pg/downloads.down01-e.asp**) for the details governing address format.

Follow U.S. Postal Service guidelines when addressing envelopes to customers in the United States. Like Canada

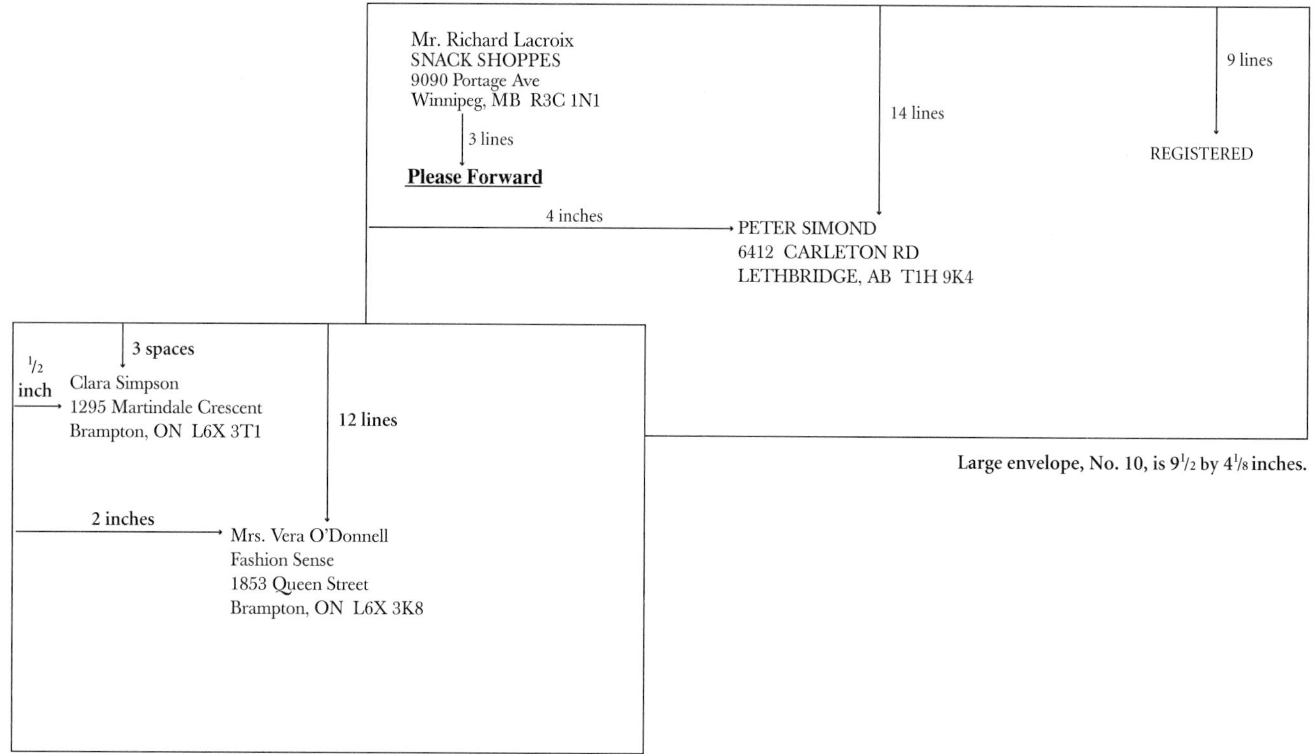

Large envelope, No. 10, is 9½ by 4⅛ inches.

Small envelope, No. 6¾, is 6½ by 3⅝ inches.

FIGURE A–6 Prescribed Envelope Format

Post, the U.S. Postal Service prefers the two-character state abbreviation over the full state name. The ZIP code must be separated from the state abbreviation by two spaces. The ZIP code may be five or nine digits. A hyphen separates the fifth and sixth digits. For example,

Mr. Damon Smith
1277 Morris Ave., Apt. 6-B
Bronx, NY 10451-4598

Folding to Fit

The way a letter is folded also contributes to the recipient's overall impression of your organization's professionalism. When sending a standard-size piece of paper in a No. 10 envelope, fold it in thirds, with the bottom folded up first and the top folded down over it (see Figure A–7 on page 506); the open end should be at the top of the envelope and facing out. Fit smaller stationery neatly into the appropriate envelope simply by folding it in half or in thirds. When sending a standard-size letterhead in a No. 6¾ envelope, fold it in half from top to bottom and then in thirds from side to side.

International Mail

Postal service differs from country to country. It's usually a good idea to send international correspondence by airmail and to ask that responses be sent that way as well. Also, remember to check the postage; rates for sending mail to most other countries differ from the rates for sending mail within your own country.

Canada Post offers three methods for sending mail internationally:

- Purolator International, the most expensive service, offers next-day delivery to the U.S. and timely delivery to 220 countries
- Xpresspost International, delivers between 4 and 9 business days to major centres in selected countries
- Air parcels, a medium-priced option, provides 6 to 10 day delivery to available destinations
- Surface parcel, the economy service, offers 4 to 6 weeks delivery to most international destinations

When preparing material for international destinations, follow Canada Post's instructions, available at **www.canadapost.com/business/tools/pg/downloads/down01-e.asp**, for detailed information about size and weight limitations of letters and packages. Canada Post stresses that the name of the country must be spelled in full (for example, UK is not acceptable; UNITED KINGDOM is). In addition, observe customs requirements to avoid delays; you can access Revenue Canada Customs & Revenue at **www.ccra-adrc.gc.ca/customs/business/menu-e.html/**

TABLE A.-6 Two-Letter Mailing Abbreviations for Canada and the United States

Province/ Territory/ State	Abbreviation	Province/ Territory/ State	Abbreviation	Province/ Territory/ State	Abbreviation
Canada		Connecticut	CT	New Hampshire	NH
Alberta	AB	Delaware	DE	New Jersey	NJ
British Columbia	BC	District of Columbia	DC	New Mexico	NM
Labrador	LB	Florida	FL	New York	NY
Manitoba	MB	Georgia	GA	North Carolina	NC
New Brunswick	NB	Guam	GU	North Dakota	ND
Newfoundland	NL	Hawaii	HI	Northern Mariana	CM
Northwest Territories	NT	Idaho	ID	Ohio	OH
Nova Scotia	NS	Illinois	IL	Oklahoma	OK
Nunavut	NU	Indiana	IN	Oregon	OR
Ontario	ON	Iowa	IA	Pennsylvania	PA
Prince Edward Island	PE	Kansas	KS	Puerto Rico	PR
Quebec	PQ	Kentucky	KY	Rhode Island	RI
Saskatchewan	SK	Louisiana	LA	South Carolina	SC
Yukon Territory	YT	Maine	ME	South Dakota	SD
United States		Maryland	MD	Tennessee	TN
Alabama	AL	Massachusetts	MA	Trust Territories	TT
Alaska	AK	Michigan	MI	Texas	TX
American Samoa	AS	Minnesota	MN	Utah	UT
Arizona	AZ	Mississippi	MS	Vermont	VT
Arkansas	AR	Missouri	MO	Virginia	VA
California	CA	Montana	MT	Virgin Islands	VI
Canal Zone	CZ	Nebraska	NE	Washington	WA
colourado	CO	Nevada	NV	West Virginia	WV

Memos

Many organizations have memo forms preprinted, with labeled spaces for the recipient's name (or sometimes a checklist of all departments in an organization or all persons in a department), the sender's name, the date, and the subject (see Figure A–8 on page 506). If such forms don't exist, you can use a memo template (which comes with word-processing software and provides margin settings, headings, and special formats), or you can use plain paper.

On your document, include a title such as *MEMO* or *INTER-OFFICE CORRESPONDENCE* (all in capitals) centered at the top of the page or aligned with the left margin. Also at the top, include the words *To*, *From*, *Date*, and *Subject*—followed by the appropriate information—with a blank line between, as shown here:

MEMO

TO:
FROM:
DATE:
SUBJECT:

Sometimes the heading is organized like this:

MEMO

TO:	DATE:
FROM:	SUBJECT:

You can arrange these four pieces of information in almost any order. The date sometimes appears without the head ing *Date*. The subject may be presented with the letters *Re:* (in

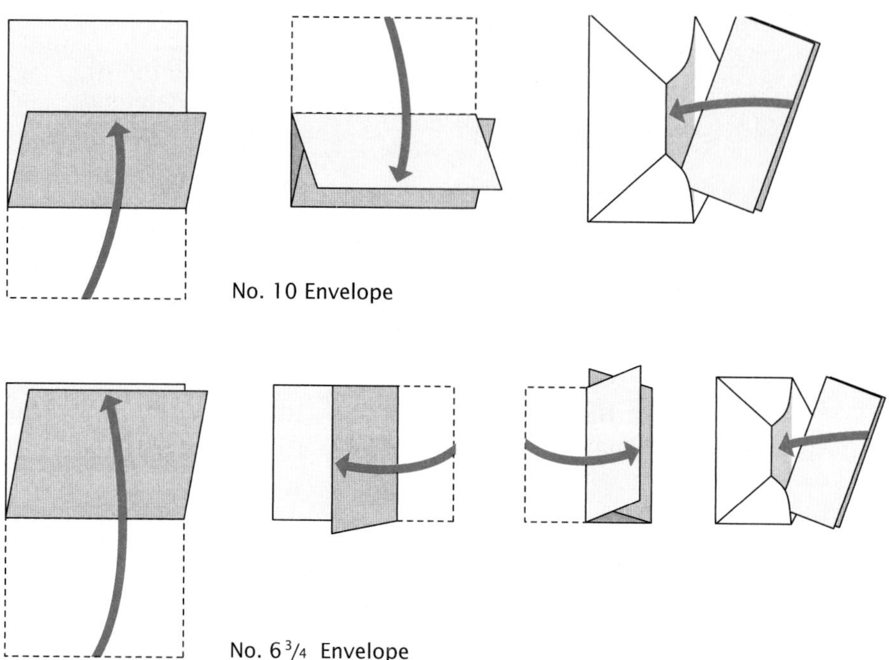

FIGURE A–7 Folding Standard-Size Letterhead

place of *SUBJECT:*) or may even be presented without any heading (but in capital letters so that it stands out clearly). You may want to include a file or reference number, introduced by the word *File.*

The following guidelines will help you effectively format specific memo elements:

- **Addressees.** When sending a memo to a long list of people, include the notation *See distribution list* or *See below* in the *To* position at the top; then list the names at the end of the memo. Arrange this list alphabetically, except when high-ranking officials deserve more prominent placement. You can also address memos to groups of people—*All Sales Representatives, Production Group, New Product Team.*
- **Courtesy titles.** You need not use courtesy titles anywhere in a memo; first initials and last names, first names, or even initials alone are often sufficient. However, use a courtesy title if you would use one in a face-to-face encounter with the person.
- **Subject line.** The subject line of a memo helps busy colleagues quickly find out what your memo is about. Although the subject "line" may overflow onto a second line, it's most helpful when it's short (but still informative).
- **Body.** Start the body of the memo on the second or third line below the heading. Like the body of a letter, it's usually single-spaced with blank lines between paragraphs. Indenting paragraphs is optional. Handle lists, important passages, and subheadings as you do in letters. If the memo is very short, you may double-space it.
- **Second page.** If the memo carries over to a second page, head the second page just as you head the second page of a letter.
- **Writer's initials.** Unlike a letter, a memo doesn't require a complimentary close or a signature, because your name is already prominent at the top. However, you may initial the memo—either beside the name appearing at the top of the memo or at the bottom of the memo—or you may even sign your name at the bottom, particularly if the memo deals with money or confidential matters.

MEMO

TO: ______________________

DEPT: ______________________ FROM: ______________________

DATE: ______________________ TELEPHONE: ______________________

SUBJECT: ______________________ *For your* ☐ APPROVAL ☐ INFORMATION ☐ COMMENT

FIGURE A–8 Preprinted Memo Form

- **Other elements.** Treat elements such as reference initials, enclosure notations, and copy notations just as you would in a letter.

Memos may be delivered by hand, by the post office (when the recipient works at a different location), or through inter-office mail. Inter-office mail may require the use of special reusable envelopes that have spaces for the recipient's name and department or room number; the name of the previous recipient is simply crossed out. If a regular envelope is used, the words *Inter-office Mail* appear where the stamp normally goes, so that it won't accidentally be stamped and mailed with the rest of the office correspondence.

Informal, routine, or brief reports for distribution within a company are often presented in memo form (see Chapter 10). Don't include report parts such as a table of contents and appendixes, but write the body of the memo report just as carefully as you'd write a formal report.

E-Mail

Because e-mail messages can act both as memos (carrying information within your company) and as letters (carrying information outside your company and around the world), their format depends on your audience and purpose. You may choose to have your e-mail resemble a formal letter or a detailed report, or you may decide to keep things as simple as an inter-office memo. A modified memo format is appropriate for most e-mail messages.[9] All e-mail programs include two major elements: the header and the body (see Figure A–9).

Header

The e-mail header depends on the particular program you use. Some programs even allow you to choose between a shorter and a longer version. However, most headers contain similar information.

- **To:** Contains the audience's e-mail address (see Figure A–10). Most e-mail programs also allow you to send mail to an entire group of people all at once. First, you create a distribution list. Then you type the name of the list in the *To:* line instead of typing the addresses of every person in the group.[10] The most common e-mail addresses are addresses such as

  info@gallery.ca (National Gallery of Canada)
  info@shimmel-piano.de (Schimmel Piano, Braunschweig, Germany)
  kraftkitchens@customer-info.net (customer information service at Kraft Canada)
  advqueries@nationalpost.com (print advertising sales at the *National Post*)

- **From:** Contains your e-mail address.
- **Date:** Contains the day of the week, date (day, month, year), time, and time zone.
- **Subject:** Describes the content of the message and presents an opportunity for you to build interest in your message.
- **Cc:** Allows you to send copies of a message to more than one person at a time. It also allows everyone on the list to see who else received the same message.
- **Bcc:** Lets you send copies to people without the other recipients knowing—a practice considered unethical by some.[11]
- **Attachments:** Contains the name(s) of the file(s) you attach to your e-mail message. The file can be a word-processing document, a digital image, an audio or video message, a spreadsheet, or a software program.[12]

Most e-mail programs now allow you the choice of hiding or revealing other lines that contain more detailed information, including

- **Message-Id:** The exact location of this e-mail message on the sender's system
- **X-mailer:** The version of the e-mail program being used
- **Content type:** A description of the text and character set that is contained in the message
- **Received:** Information about each of the systems your e-mail passed through en route to your mailbox.[13]

Body

The rest of the space below the header is for the body of your message. In the *To:* and *From:* lines, some headers actually print out the names of the sender and receiver (in addition to their e-mail addresses). Other headers do not. If your mail program includes only the e-mail addresses, you might consider including your own memo-type header in the body of your message, as in Figure A.9. The writer even included a second, more specific subject line in his memo-type header. Some recipients may applaud the clarity of such second headers; however, others will criticize the space it takes. Your decision depends on how formal you want to be.

Do include a greeting in your e-mail. As pointed out in Chapter 5, greetings personalize your message. Leave one line space above and below your greeting to set it off from the rest of your message. You may end your greeting with a colon (formal), a comma (conversational), or even two hyphens (informal)—depending on the level of formality you want.

Your message begins one blank line space below your greeting. Just as in memos and letters, skip one line space between paragraphs and include headings, numbered lists, bulleted lists, and embedded lists when appropriate. Limit your line lengths to a maximum of 80 characters by inserting a hard return at the end of each line.

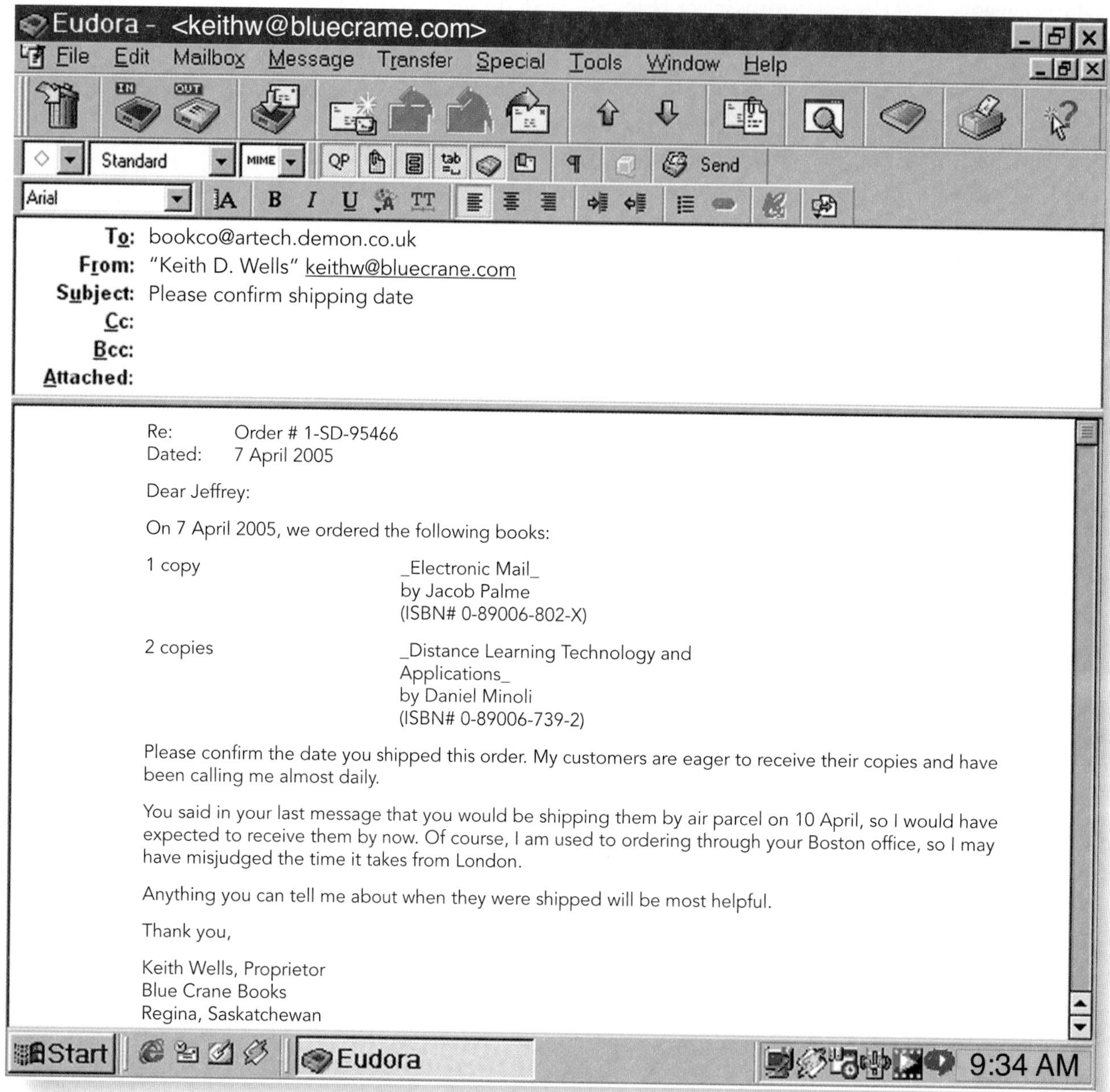

Eudora - <keithw@bluecrame.com>

To: bookco@artech.demon.co.uk
From: "Keith D. Wells" keithw@bluecrane.com
Subject: Please confirm shipping date
Cc:
Bcc:
Attached:

Re: Order # 1-SD-95466
Dated: 7 April 2005

Dear Jeffrey:

On 7 April 2005, we ordered the following books:

1 copy _Electronic Mail_
by Jacob Palme
(ISBN# 0-89006-802-X)

2 copies _Distance Learning Technology and Applications_
by Daniel Minoli
(ISBN# 0-89006-739-2)

Please confirm the date you shipped this order. My customers are eager to receive their copies and have been calling me almost daily.

You said in your last message that you would be shipping them by air parcel on 10 April, so I would have expected to receive them by now. Of course, I am used to ordering through your Boston office, so I may have misjudged the time it takes from London.

Anything you can tell me about when they were shipped will be most helpful.

Thank you,

Keith Wells, Proprietor
Blue Crane Books
Regina, Saskatchewan

FIGURE A–9 A Typical E-Mail Message

One blank line space below your message, include a simple closing, often just one word. A blank line space below that, include your signature. Whether you type your name or use a signature file, including your signature personalizes your message.

Reports

Enhance your report's effectiveness by paying careful attention to its appearance and layout. Follow whatever guidelines your organization prefers, always being neat and consistent throughout. If it's up to you to decide formatting questions; the following conventions may help you decide how to handle margins, headings, spacing and indention, and page numbers.

Margins

All margins on a report page are at least 1 inch wide. For double-spaced pages, use 1-inch margins; for single-spaced pages, set margins between $1^1/_4$ and $1^1/_2$ inches. The top, left, and right margins are usually the same, but the bottom margins can be $1^1/_2$ times deeper. Some special pages also have deeper top margins. Set top margins as deep as 2 inches for pages that contain major titles: prefatory parts

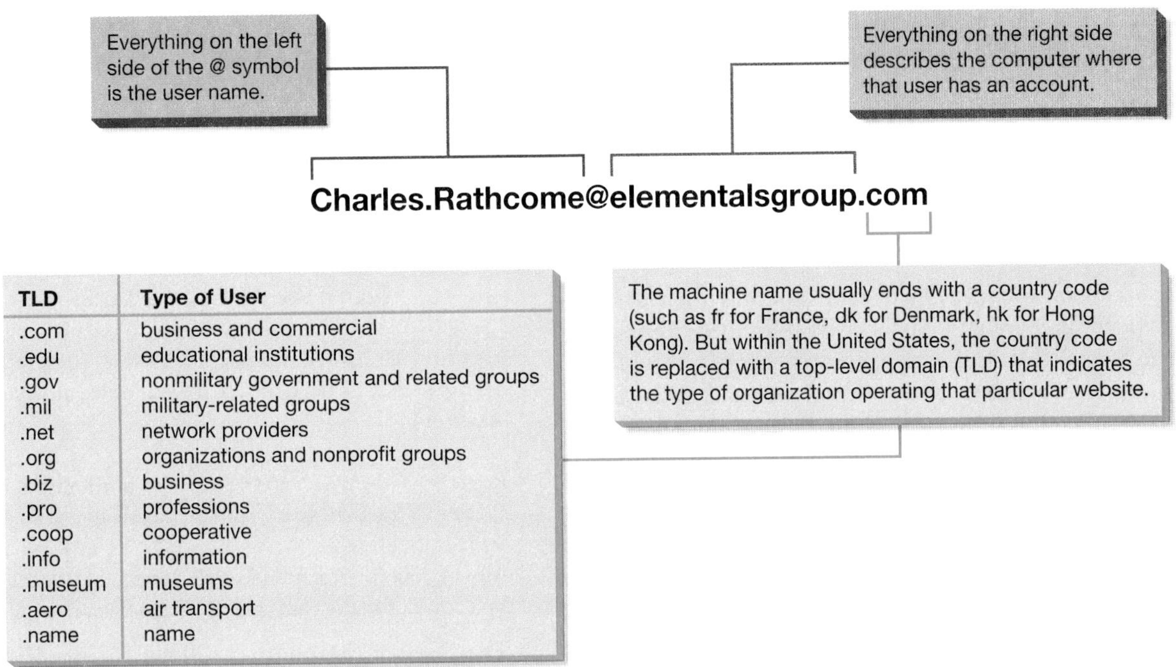

Everything on the left side of the @ symbol is the user name.
Everything on the right side describes the computer where that user has an account.
Charles.Rathcome@elementalsgroup.com
The machine name usually ends with a country code (such as fr for France, dk for Denmark, hk for Hong Kong). But within the United States, the country code is replaced with a top-level domain (TLD) that indicates the type of organization operating that particular website.
TLD
Type of User
.com
business and commercial
.edu
educational institutions
.gov
nonmilitary government and related groups
.mil
military-related groups
.net
network providers
.org
organizations and nonprofit groups
.biz
business
.pro
professions
.coop
cooperative
.info
information
.museum
museums
.aero
air transport
.name
name

FIGURE A–10 Anatomy of an E-Mail Address

(such as the table of contents or the executive summary), supplementary parts (such as the reference notes or bibliography), and textual parts (such as the first page of the text or the first page of each chapter).

If you're going to bind your report at the left or at the top, add half an inch to the margin on the bound edge (see Figure A–12). The space taken by the binding on left-bound reports makes the centre point of the text a quarter inch to the right of the centre of the paper. Be sure to centre headings between the margins, not between the edges of the paper. Computers can do this for you automatically. Other guidelines for report formats are in the Chapter 12 samples.

Headings

Headings of various levels provide visual clues to a report's organization. Figure 11–16 illustrates one good system for showing these levels, but many variations exist. No matter which system you use, be sure to be consistent.

Spacing and Indentions

If your report is double-spaced (perhaps to ease comprehension of technical material), indent all paragraphs five character spaces (or about 1/2 inch). In single-spaced reports, block the paragraphs (no indentions) and leave one blank line between them.

Make sure the material on the title page is centred and well balanced, as on the title page of the sample report in Chapter 12. When using a typewriter, proper spacing takes some calculation. To center text in left-bound reports, start a quarter inch to the right of the paper's center. From that point, backspace once for each two letters in the line. The line will appear centred once the report is bound.

To place lines of type vertically on the title page, follow these steps:

1 Count the number of lines in each block of copy, including blank lines.
2 Subtract that total from 66 (the number of lines on an 11-inch page); the result is the number of unused lines.
3 Divide the number of unused lines by the number of blank areas (always one more than the number of blocks of copy). The result is the number of blank lines to allocate above, between, and below the blocks of copy.

A word-processing program will do these calculations for you automatically.

Page Numbers

Remember that every page in the report is counted; however, not all pages show numbers. The first page of the report, normally the title page, is unnumbered. All other pages in the prefatory section are numbered with a lower-case roman numeral, beginning with *ii* and continuing with *iii, iv, v,* and so on. The unadorned (no dashes, no period) page number is centred at the bottom margin.

Number the first page of the text of the report with the unadorned arabic numeral 1, centered at the bottom margin (double- or triple-spaced below the text). In left-bound reports, number the following pages (including the supplementary parts) consecutively with unadorned arabic numerals (2, 3, and so on), placed at the top right-hand margin (double- or triple-spaced above the text). For top-bound reports and for special pages having 2-inch top margins, centre the page numbers at the bottom margin.

Meeting Documents

The success of any meeting depends on how thoroughly participants prepare and on the follow-up measures they take to implement decisions or to seek information after the meeting. Meeting documents—agendas and minutes—aid this process by putting the meeting plan and results into permanent, written form. Although small informal meetings may not require a written agenda, any meeting involving a relatively large number of people or covering a lot of ground will run more smoothly if an agenda is distributed in advance. A written agenda helps participants prepare by telling them what will be discussed, and it helps keep them on track once the meeting begins. The typical agenda format (shown in Figure A–12) may seem stiff and formal, but it helps structure a meeting so that as little time as possible is wasted. It also provides opportunities for discussion.

The presentation, a special form of meeting that allows for relatively little group interaction, may also require an agenda or a detailed outline. Visual aids such as computer-based slides help attendees grasp the message, and copies are often provided for future reference. After a meeting the secretary who attended prepares a set of minutes for distribution to all attendees and to any other interested parties (shown in Figure A.13). The minutes are prepared in much the same format as a memo or letter, except for the heading, which takes this form:

MINUTES
PLANNING COMMITTEE MEETING
MONDAY, AUGUST 22, 2005

Present: [All invited attendees who were present are listed here, generally by rank, in alphabetical order, or in some combination.]

Regrets: [All invited attendees who notified the convener ahead of time that they would be unable to attend.]

Absent: [All invited attendees who were not present and neglected to notify the convener are listed here, in similar order.]

The body of the minutes follows the heading, and it notes the times the meeting started and ended, all major decisions reached at the meeting, all assignments of tasks to meeting participants, and all subjects that were deferred to a later meeting. In addition, the minutes objectively summarize important discussions, noting the names of those who contributed major points. Outlines, subheadings, and lists help organize the minutes, and additional documen-

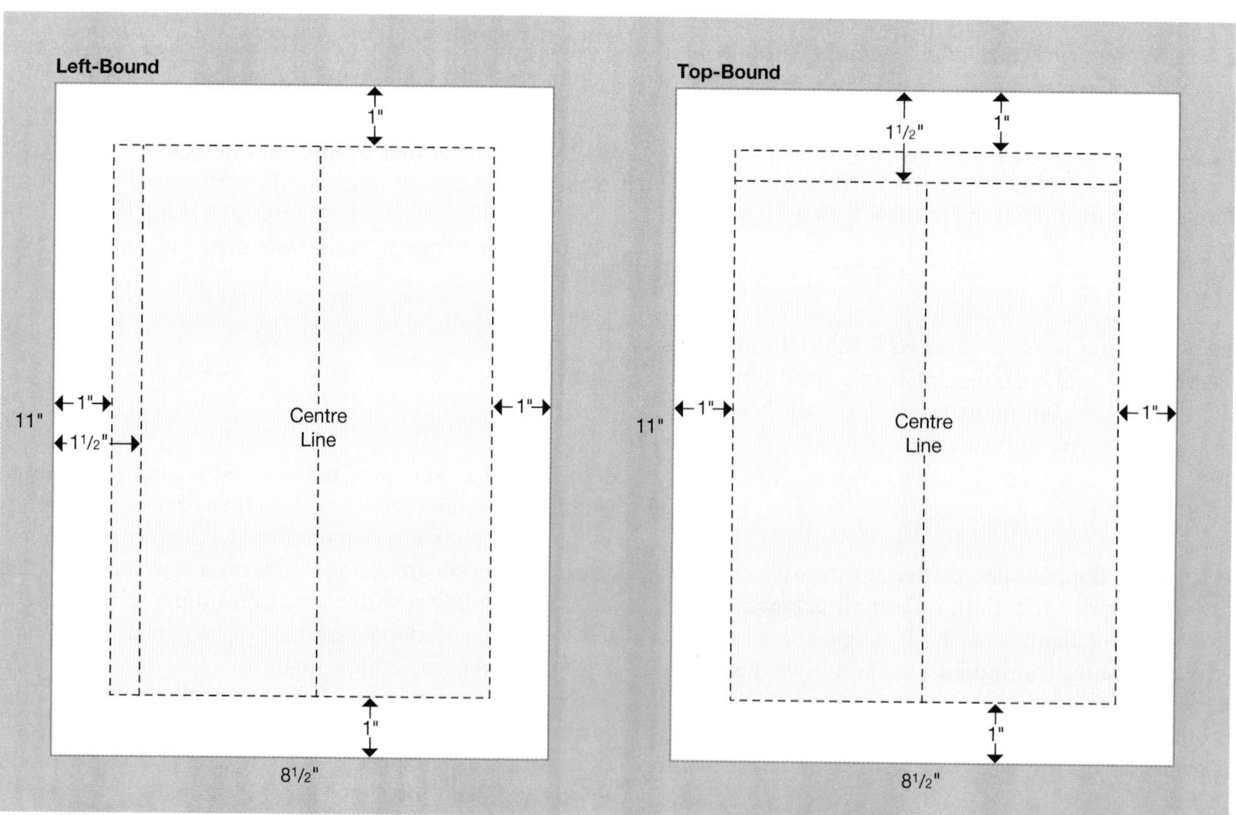

FIGURE A–11 Margins for Formal Reports

tation (such as tables or charts submitted by meeting participants) are noted in the minutes and attached.

At the end of the minutes, the words *Submitted by* should be added, followed by blank lines for a signature and then the signer's printed (or typed) name and title (if appropriate). If the minutes have been written by one person and prepared by another, the preparer's initials should be added, as in the reference initials on a letter or memo.

An informal meeting may not require minutes. Attendees simply pencil their own notes onto their copies of the agenda. Follow-up is then their responsibility, although the meeting leader may need to remind them via an e-mail, phone call, or face-to-face chat.

ALIYA FINANCIAL SERVICES, INC.

PRESENTATION PLANNING MEETING

THURSDAY, JUNE 17, 2005

10:00 A.M., ROOM 400A

A G E N D A

1.0 Adoption of Minutes, previous meeting (Thursday, June 3, 2005)

2.0 Business arising from Minutes

3.0 Report from Andrew Abolafia, Financial Products

4.0 Report from Miriam Saring, Event Planning

5.0 Report from David Maxwell, Art Department

6.0 Other Business

7.0 Adjournment

FIGURE A–12 Agenda Format

MINUTES OF PLANNING MEETING OF JUNE 17, 2005

Present: Andrew Obolafia, Financial Products
Miriam Saring, Event Planning
David Maxwell, Art Department
John Arthur, Manager, Customer Services
Eleanor Mentz, P.A., Meeting recorder

1. Andrew Abolofia reviewed his ideas for the presentations he believes should be delivered in 2006. He discussed forecasts by Bill Gunning, a bank economist, for winter 2006. Andrew believes his presentations should focus on RSP contributions and mutual funds as an investment option. Andrew would like to give GICs secondary consideration in his presentations.

2. John Arthur suggested that Andrew start working on two separate presentations, one about RSPs themselves, and the other about mutual funds.

   ACTION: Andrew will prepare two outlines for discussion, one on RSPs, the other on mutual funds.

3. Miriam Saring discussed the venues for last year's educational seminars. She noted that at two of the three locations (the branch at Laurier Ave. and Steele St., and the Finchurst Hotel) attendance was very low. She suggested that these locations be re-evaluated, and, in light of the findings, perhaps new ones be found.

   ACTION: Miriam will prepare a report on attendance at these locations for the team.

4. David Maxwell reported that the look of the visual aids will be updated this year. He has investigated new presentation software and hardware on the market, and would like to see more use of multimedia. He showed examples of last year's promotional material, and mock-ups of a new look he would like to see used.

5. John noted that the issue of poor attendance was a serious one. He suggested that Miriam prepare a presentation on the problem to be given at a meeting in about two weeks, to executive staff.

   ACTION: Miriam will prepare a presentation on the attendance problem, to be given the week of July 1.

6. The meeting ended at 11:15 a.m.

FIGURE A–13 Example of Meeting Minutes

Documentation of Report Sources

Documenting a report is too important a task to undertake haphazardly. By providing information about your sources, you improve your own credibility as well as the credibility of the facts and opinions you present. Documentation gives readers the means for checking your findings and pursuing the subject further. Also, documenting your report is the accepted way to give credit to the people whose work you have drawn from.

What style should you use to document your report? Experts recommend various forms, depending on your field or discipline. Moreover, your employer or client may use a form different from those the experts suggest. Don't let this discrepancy confuse you. If your employer specifies a form, use it; the standardized form is easier for colleagues to understand. However, if the choice of form is left to you, adopt one of the styles described here. Whatever style you choose, be consistent within any given report, using the same order, punctuation, and format from one reference citation or bibliography entry to the next.

A wide variety of style manuals provide detailed information on documentation. Here is a brief annotated list:

- American Psychological Association, *Publication Manual of the American Psychological Association,* 5th ed. (Washington, DC: American Psychological Association, 2001). Details the author-date system, which is preferred in the social sciences and often in the natural sciences as well.
- *The Chicago Manual of Style,* 15th ed. (Chicago: University of Chicago Press, 2003). Often referred to only as *Chicago* and widely used in the publishing industry; provides detailed treatment of documentation in Chapters 16 and 17.
- Joseph Gibaldi, *MLA Handbook for Writers of Research Papers,* 6th edition (New York: Modern Language Association, 1998). Serves as the basis for the note and bibliography style used in much academic writing and is recommended in many college textbooks on writing term papers; provides a lot of examples in the humanities.
- Andrew Harnack, *Online! A Reference Guide to Using Internet Sources—2003* (New York: St. Martin's Press, 2003). Offers an approach to style for citing online references.

Although many schemes have been proposed for organizing the information in source notes, all of them break the information into parts: (1) information about the author (name), (2) information about the work (title, edition, volume number), (3) information about the publication (place, publisher), (4) information about the date, and (5) information on relevant page ranges.

In the following sections, we summarize the major conventions for documenting sources in three styles: *The Chicago Manual of Style* (Chicago), the *Publication Manual of the American Psychological Association* (APA), and the *MLA Style Manual* (MLA).

Chicago Humanities Style

The Chicago Manual of Style recommends two types of documentation systems. The *documentary-note,* or *humanities,* style gives bibliographic citations in notes—either footnotes (when printed at the bottom of a page) or endnotes (when printed at the end of the report). The humanities system is often used in literature, history, and the arts. The other system strongly recommended by *Chicago* is the *author-date* system, which cites the author's last name and the date of publication in the text, usually in parentheses, reserving full documentation for the reference list (or bibliography). For the purpose of comparing styles, we will concentrate on the humanities system, which is described in detail in *Chicago.*

In-Text Citation—Chicago Humanities Style

To document report sources in text, the humanities system relies on superscripts—arabic numerals placed just above the line of type at the end of the reference:

> Toward the end of his speech, Myers sounded a note of caution, saying that even though the economy is expected to grow, it could easily slow a bit.[10]

The superscript lets the reader know how to look for source information in either a footnote or an endnote (see Figure B–1 on the following page). Some readers prefer

NOTES

Journal article with volume and issue numbers	1. Patrick Tuohey, "10 Things Every Annual Report Writer Should Know," *Public Relations Tactics* 8, no. 4 (2001): 32.
Brochure	2. Seimens AG, *A56 User Guide* (San Diego: Seimens Information and Communication Mobile LLC, 2002), p. 33.
Newspaper article, no author	3. "A Misspelling Proves Costly," *The New York Times,* 23 November 1991, 29.
Annual report	4. Suncor, *2003 Annual Report* (Calgary: Suncor Inc., 2004), 3.
Magazine article	5. Danny Kucharsky, "Navigating Quebec's Promo Regulations," *Marketing Magazine*, 3 April 2000, 20–21
Television broadcast	6. Wendy Mesley, "Telemarketing," *Marketplace* (Toronto: CBC, 26 November 2002).
World Wide Web	7. "Polishing Your Presentation," 3M Meeting Network, <www.mmm.com/meeting network/readingroom/meetingguide_pres.html> (8 June 2001).
Book, component parts	8. Julia C. Gluesing, Tara C. Alcordo, and Margaret A. Neale, "The Development of Global Virtual Teams," in *Virtual Teams that Work: Creating Conditions for Virtual Team Effectiveness,* ed. Cristina B. Gibson and Susan G. Cohen (San Francisco: Jossey-Bass, 2003), 356.
Unplublished dissertation or thesis	9. Changhui Zhou, "Transnational Flow of Knowledge in Multinational Corporations: R&D Co-Practice as an Integrating Force" (Ph.D. diss. University of Western Ontario, 2002), 34–43.
Paper presented at a meeting	10. Ava Cross, " The Written Communication Needs of the Nonprofit and Voluntary Sector: A Pilot Study", paper presented at the Association for Business Communication Eastern Division Conference, Toronto, ON, April 2003.
Online magazine article	11. Meredith Levinson, "How To Find, Fix Or Fire Your Poor Performers," *CIO Magazine* [online], 1 November 2003, <www.cio.com/archive/110103/poor.html> (9 November 2003).
Article from an electronic database	12. Steven V. Davis and Andrew Gilman, "Communication Coordination," *Risk Management* 49, no. (2002): 39, Proquest, Document ID 148778291 (27 October 2003).
CD-ROM encyclopedia article, one author	13. Robert Parkings, "George Eastman," *The Concise Columbia Encyclopedia* (New York: Columbia University Press, 1997) [CD-ROM].
Interview	14. Ian Hamilton, Manager, Corporate Communications, Dofasco Inc., e-mail interview by author, 15 January 2002.
Newspaper article, one author	15. Diane Francis, "Work is a Warm Puppy," *National Post,* 27 May 2000, W20.
Book, two authors	16. Paul A. Argenti and Janis Forman, *The Power of Corporate Communication: Crafting the Voice and Image of Your Business* (New York: McGraw Hill, 2002), 102–103.
Government publication	17. Office of Consumer Affairs, Industry Canada, *Canadian Consumer Handbook* (Ottawa: Office of Consumer Affairs: 2002), 8.

FIGURE B–1 Sample Endnotes—Chicago Humanities Style

footnotes so that they can simply glance at the bottom of the page for information. Others prefer endnotes so that they can read the text without a clutter of notes on the page. Also, endnotes relieve the writer from worrying about how long each note will be and how much space it will take away from the page. Both footnotes and endnotes are handled automatically by today's word-processing software.

For the reader's convenience, you can use footnotes for **content notes** (which may supplement your main text with asides about a particular issue or event, provide a cross-reference to another section of your report, or direct the reader to a related source). Then you can use endnotes for **source notes** (which document direct quotations, paraphrased passages, and visual aids). Consider which type of note is most common in your report, and then choose whether to present these notes all as endnotes or all as footnotes. Regardless of the method you choose for referencing textual information in your report, notes for visual aids (both content notes and source notes) are placed on the same page as the visual.

Bibliography—Chicago Humanities Style

The humanities system may or may not be accompanied by a bibliography (because the notes give all the necessary

BIBLIOGRAPHY

Newspaper article, no author	"A Misspelling Proves Costly," *New York Times*, 23 November 1991, 29.
Book, two authors	Argenti, Paul A. and Janis Forman. *The Power of Corporate Communication: Crafting the Voice and Image of Your Business.* New York: McGraw Hill, 2002.
Paper presented at a meeting	Cross, Ava. "The Written Communication Needs of the Nonprofit and Voluntary Sector: A Pilot Study." Paper presented at the Association for Business Communication Eastern Division Conference, Toronto, ON, April 2003.
Article from an electronic database	Davis, Steven V. and Andrew Gilman. "Communication Coordination." *Risk Management* 49, no. 8 (2002): 38-43. Proquest, Document ID 148778291 (27 October 2003).
Newspaper article, one author	Francis, Diane. "Work is a Warm Puppy." *National Post,* 27 May 2000, W20.
Book, component parts	Gluesing, Julia C., Tara C. Alcordo, and Margaret A. Neale, "The Development of Global Virtual Teams." In *Virtual Teams that Work: Creating Conditions for Virtual Team Effectiveness*, edited by Cristina B. Gibson and Susan G. Cohen. San Francisco: Jossey-Bass, 2003.
Interview	Cited in text only, not in the list of references.
Magazine article	Kucharsky, Danny. "Navigating Quebec's Promo Regulations." *Marketing Magazine*, (3 April 2000), 20–21.
Online magazine article	Levinson, Meridith. "How To Find, Fix Or Fire Your Poor Performers." *CIO Magazine* [online], 1 November 2003, < www.cio.com/archive/110103/poor.html> (9 November 2003).
Television broadcast	Mesley, Wendy. "Telemarketing," *Marketplace.* Toronto: CBC, 26 November 2002.
Government publication	Office of Consumer Affairs, Industry Canada. *Canadian Consumer Handbook.* Ottawa: Office of Consumer Affairs: 2002.
CD-ROM encyclopedia article, one author	Parkings, Robert. "George Eastman." *The Concise Columbia Encyclopedia.* New York: Columbia University Press, 1998. [CD-ROM].
World Wide Web	"Polishing Your Presentation," 3M Meeting Network, <www.mmm.com/meetingnetwork/ readingroom/meetingguide_pres.html> , (8 June 2001).
Brochure	Seimens AG, *A56 User Guide.* San Diego: Seimens Information and Communication Mobile LLC, 2002.
Annual report	Suncor. *2003 Annual Report.* Calgary: Suncor Inc., 2004.
Journal article with volume and issue numbers	Tuohey, Patrick. "10 Things Every Annual Report Writer Should Know." *Public Relations Tactics* 8, no. 4 (2001): 32.
Unpublished dissertation	Zhou, Changhui. "Transnational Flow of Knowledge in Multinational Corporations: R&D Co-Practice as an Integrating Force." Ph.D. diss, University of Western Ontario, 2002.

FIGURE B–2 Sample Bibliography—Chicago Humanities Style

bibliographic information). However, endnotes are arranged in order of appearance in the text, so an alphabetical bibliography can be valuable to your readers. The bibliography may be titled *Bibliography, Reference List, Sources, Works Cited* (if you include only those sources you actually cited in your report), or *Works Consulted* (if you include uncited sources as well). This list of sources may also serve as a reading list for those who want to pursue the subject of your report further, so you may want to annotate each entry—that is, comment on the subject matter and viewpoint of the source, as well as on its usefulness to readers. Annotations may be written in either complete or incomplete sentences. (See the annotated list of style manuals at the beginning of this appendix.) A bibliography may also be more manageable if you subdivide it into categories (a classified bibliography), either by type of reference (such as books, articles, and unpublished material) or by subject matter (such as government regulation, market forces, and so on). Figure B–2 shows the major conventions for developing a bibliography according to *Chicago* style.

- Exclude any page numbers that may be cited in source notes, except for journals, periodicals, and newspapers.
- Alphabetize entries by the last name of the lead author (listing last name first). The names of second and succeeding authors are listed in normal order. Entries without an author name are alphabetized by the first important word in the title.
- Format entries as hanging indents (indent second and succeeding lines three to five spaces).
- Arrange entries in the following general order: (1) author name, (2) title information, (3) publication information, (4) date, (5) periodical page range.
- Use quotation marks around the titles of articles from magazines, newspapers, and journals—capitalizing the first and last words, as well as all other important words (except prepositions, articles, and coordinating conjunctions).
- Use italics to set off the names of books, newspapers, journals, and other complete publications—capitalizing the first and last words, as well as all other important words.
- For journal articles, include the volume number and the issue number (if necessary). Include the year of publication inside parentheses and follow with a colon and the page range of the article: *Public Relations Tactics* 8, no. 4 (2001): 32. (In this source, the volume is 8, the number is 4, and the page is 32.)
- Use brackets to identify all electronic references: [Online database] or [CD-ROM].
- Explain how electronic references can be reached: Available from www.spaceless.com/WWWVL.
- Give the retrieved date for online references in parentheses: (23 August 2002).

APA Style

The American Psychological Association (APA) recommends the author-date system of documentation, which is popular in the physical, natural, and social sciences. When using this system, you simply insert the author's last name and the year of publication within parentheses following the text discussion of the material cited. Include a page number if you use a direct quote. This approach briefly identifies the source so that readers can locate complete information in the alphabetical reference list at the end of the report. The author-date system is both brief and clear, saving readers time and effort.

In-Text Citation—APA Style

To document report sources in text using *APA* style, insert the author's surname and the date of publication at the end of a statement. Enclose this information in parentheses. If the author's name is referred to in the text itself, then the name can be omitted from parenthetical material.

> Organizations that prepare annual reports must be aware of their reader's financial knowledge (Tuohey, 32).

> Argenti and Forman (2002) explain how the media unrelentingly casts its electronic eye on business through television, radio, and the Internet.

Personal communications and interviews conducted by the author would not be listed in the reference list at all. Such citations would appear in the text only.

> Relating to all stakeholders is high on the list of Dofasco's Environmental and Energy reports, according to Ian Hamilton, a Dofasco corporate communications manager (personal communication, January 15 2002).

List of References—APA Style

For *APA* style, list only those works actually cited in the text (so you would not include works for background or for further reading). Report writers must choose their references judiciously. Following are the major conventions for developing a reference list according to *APA* style (see Figure B–3):

- Format entries as hanging indents.
- List all author names in reversed order (last name first), and use only initials for the first and middle names.
- Arrange entries in the following general order: (1) author name, (2) date, (3) title information, (4) publication information, (5) periodical page range.
- Follow the author name with the date of publication in parentheses.
- List titles of articles from magazines, newspapers, and journals without underlines or quotation marks. Capitalize only the first word of the title, any proper nouns, and the first word to follow an internal colon.
- Italicize titles of books, capitalizing only the first word, any proper nouns, and the first word to follow a colon.
- Italicize names of magazines, newspapers, journals, and other complete publications—capitalizing all the important words.
- For journal articles, include the volume number (in italics) and, if necessary, the issue number (in parentheses). Finally, include the page range of the article: *Public Relations Tactics 8,* (4), 32. (In this example, the volume is 8, the number is 4, and the page is 32.
- Include personal communications (such as letters, memos, e-mail, and conversations) only in text, not in reference lists.
- Electronic references include author, date of publication, title of article, name of publication (if one), volume, date of retrieval (month, day, year), and the source.
- For electronic references, indicate the actual year of publication, and the exact date of retrieval.
- For electronic references, specify the URL, leave periods off the ends of URLs.

	REFERENCES
Newspaper article, no author	A misspelling proves costly. (1991, November 13), *The New York Times*, p. 29.
Book, two authors	Argenti, P. & Forman, J. (2002). *The power of corporate communication: crafting the voice and image of your business.* New York: McGraw Hill.
Paper presented at a meeting	Cross, A. (2002 April). *The written communication needs of the nonprofit and voluntary sector: A pilot study.* Paper presented at the Association for Business Communication Eastern Division Conference, Toronto, ON.
Article from an electronic database	Davis, S. & Gilman, A. (2002 August). Communication coordination. *Risk Management, 49*(8), 38–43. Retrieved October 27, 2003, from Proquest database.
Newspaper article, one author	Francis, D. (2000, May 27). Work is a warm puppy. *National Post,* p. W20.
Book, component parts	Gluesing, J., Alcordo, T., & Neale, M. (2003). "The development of global virtual teams." In C.B. Gibson & S.G. Cohen (Eds.), *Virtual teams that work: Creating conditions for virtual team effectiveness* (pp. 353–380). San Francisco: Jossey-Bass.
Government publication	Industry Canada. Office of Consumer Affairs. (2002). *Canadian consumer handbook.* Ottawa: Office of Consumer Affairs.
Interview	Cited in text only, not in the list of references.
Magazine article	Kucharsky, D. (2002, April 13). Navigating Quebec's promo regulations. *Marketing Magazine, 105*(13), 20–21.
Online magazine article	Levinson, M. (2003, November 1). How to find, fix or fire your poor performers. *CIO Magazine.* Retrieved November 9, 2002, from //www.cio.com/archive/110103/poor.html.
Television broadcast	Mesley, W. (2002, November 26). Telemarketing. *Marketplace* [Television broadcast]. Toronto: CBC.
CD-ROM encyclopedia article, one author	Parkings, R. (1998). George Eastman. *The concise Columbia encyclopedia.* [CD-ROM]. New York: Columbia University Press.
Internet—World Wide Web	3M Meeting Network. *Polishing your presentation.* Retrieved June 8, 2001, from www.mmm.com/meetingnetwork/readingroom/meetingguide_pres.html
Brochure	Seimens AG. (2002). *A56 user guide.* [Brochure]. San Diego: Seimens Information and Communication Mobile LLC.
Annual report	Suncor. (2004). *2003 annual report.* Calgary: Suncor Inc.
Journal article with volume and issue numbers	Tuohey, P. (2001, October). 10 things every annual report writer should know. *Public Relations Tactics 8*(4), 32.
Unpublished dissertation	Zhou, C. (2002). *Transnational flow of knowledge in multinational corporations: R&d co-practice as an integrating force.* Unpublished doctoral dissertation, University of Western Ontario.

FIGURE B–3 Sample References—APA Style

MLA Style

The style recommended by the Modern Language Association of America is used widely in the humanities, especially in the study of language and literature. Like *APA* style, *MLA* style uses brief parenthetical citations in the text. However, instead of including author name and year, *MLA* citations include author name and page reference.

In-Text Citation—MLA Style

To document report sources in text using *MLA* style, insert the author's last name and a page reference inside parentheses following the cited material: (Matthews 63). If the author's name is mentioned in the text reference, the name can be omitted from the parenthetical citation: (63). The citation indicates that the reference came from page 63 of a work by Matthews. With the author's name, readers can find complete publication information in the alphabetically arranged list of works cited that comes at the end of the report.

> Organizations that prepare annual reports must be aware of their reader's financial knowledge (Tuohey 32).

> Argenti and Forman (209-15) explain how the media unrelentingly casts its electronic eye on business through television, radio, and the Internet.

	WORKS CITED
Newpaper article, no author	"A Misspelling Proves Costly," *New York Times* 23 Nov. 1991: 29.
Book, two authors	Argenti, Paul A., and Janis Forman. *The Power of Corporate Communication: Crafting the Voice and Image of Your Business.* New York: McGraw Hill, 2002.
Paper presented at a meeting	Cross, Ava. "The Written Communication Needs of the Nonprofit and Voluntary Sector: A Pilot Study." Association for Business Communication Eastern Division Conference. Toronto, ON. 5 Apr. 2003.
Article from an electronic database	Davis, Steven V., and Andrew Gilman. "Communication Coordination." *Risk Management* 49.8 (2002): 38–43. *Proquest.* Ryerson U. Lib. Toronto. 27 Oct. 2003.
Newspaper article, one author	Francis, Diane. "Work is a Warm Puppy." *National Post* 27 May 2000: W20.
Book, component parts	Gluesing, Julia C., Tara C. Alcordo, and Margaret A. Neale, "The Development of Global Virtual Teams." In "*Virtual Teams that Work: Creating Conditions for Virtual Team Effectiveness.*" Ed. Cristina B. Gibson and Susan G. Cohen. San Francisco: Jossey-Bass, 2003. 353–380.
interview	Hamilton, Ian. Manager, Corporate Communications, Dofasco Inc. E-mail interview, 15 Jan. 2002.
Magazine article	Kucharsky, Danny. "Navigating Quebec's Promo Regulations." *Marketing Magazine* 3 Apr. 2000: 20–21.
Online magazine article	Levinson, Meridith. "How To Find, Fix Or Fire Your Poor Performers." *CIO Magazine* 1 Nov. 2003. 9 November 2003 < www.cio.com/archive/110103/poor.html>.
Television broadcast	Mesley, Wendy. "Telemarketing," *Marketplace.* CBC, Toronto. 26 Nov. 2002.
Government publication	Office of Consumer Affairs, Industry Canada. *Canadian Consumer Handbook.* Ottawa: Office of Consumer Affairs, 2002.
CD-ROM encyclopedia article, one author	Parkings, Robert. "George Eastman." *The Concise Columbia Encyclopedia.* CD-ROM. New York: Columbia UP, 1998.
Internet—World Wide Web	"Polishing Your Presentation," *3M Meeting Network.* 8 June 2001 <www.mmm.com/meetingnetwork/readingroom/meetingguide_pres.html>.
brochure	Seimens AG. *A56 User Guide.* San Diego: Seimens Information and Communication Mobile LLC, 2002.
Annual report	Suncor. *2003 Annual Report.* Calgary: Suncor Inc., 2004.
Journal article with volume and issue numbers	Tuohey, Patrick. "10 Things Every Annual Report Writer Should Know." *Public Relations Tactics* 8.4 (2001): 32.
Unpublished dissertation	Zhou, Changhui. "Transnational Flow of Knowledge in Multinational Corporations: R&D Co-Practice as an Integrating Force." Diss. U of Western Ontario, 2002.

FIGURE B–4 Sample Works Cited—MLA Style

List of Works Cited—*MLA* Style

The *MLA Style Manual* recommends preparing the list of works cited first so that you will know what information to give in the parenthetical citation (for example, whether to add a short title if you're citing more than one work by the same author, or whether to give an initial or first name if you're citing two authors who have the same last name). The list of works cited appears at the end of your report, contains all the works that you cite in your text, and lists them in alphabetical order. Following are the major conventions for developing a reference list according to *MLA* style (see Figure B–4).

- Format entries as hanging indents.
- Arrange entries in the following general order: (1) author name, (2) title information, (3) publication information, (4) date, (5) periodical page range.
- List the lead author's name in reverse order (last name first), using either full first names or initials. List second and succeeding author names in normal order.
- Use quotation marks around the titles of articles from magazines, newspapers, and journals—capitalize all important words.
- Italicize the names of books, newspapers, journals and other complete publications, capitalizing all main words in the title.

- For journal articles, include the volume number and the issue number (if necessary). Include the year of publication inside parentheses and follow with a colon and the page range of the article: *Public Relations Tactics* 8.4 (2001): 32. (In this source, the volume is 8, the number is 4, and the page is 32.)
- Electronic sources are less fixed than print sources, and they may not be readily accessible to readers. So citations for electronic sources must provide more information. Always try to be as comprehensive as possible, citing whatever information is available.
- The date for electronic sources should contain both the date assigned in the source and the date accessed by the researcher.
- The URL for electronic sources must be as accurate and complete as possible, from access-mode identifier (http, ftp, gopher, telnet) to all relevant directory and file names. Be sure to enclose this path inside angle brackets: <www.mmm.com/meetingnetwork/readingroom/meetingguide_pres.html>

Fundamentals of Grammar and Usage

Grammar is nothing more than the way words are combined into sentences, and usage is the way words are used by a network of people—in this case, the community of business people who use English. You'll find it easier to get along in this community if you know the accepted standards of grammar and usage. What follows is a review of the basics of grammar and usage, which you've probably learned but may have forgotten. Without a firm grasp of these basics, you risk not only being misunderstood but also damaging your company's image, losing money for your company, and possibly even losing your job.

1.0 Grammar

The sentence below looks innocent, but is it really?

> We sell tuxedos as well as rent.

You might sell rent, but it's highly unlikely. Whatever you're selling, some people will ignore your message because of a blunder like this. The following sentence has a similar problem:

> Vice President Eldon Neale told his chief engineer that he would no longer be with Avix, Inc., as of June 30.

Is Eldon or the engineer leaving? No matter which side the facts are on, the sentence can be read the other way. You may have a hard time convincing either person that your simple mistake was not a move in a game of office politics. Now look at this sentence:

> The year before we budgeted more for advertising sales were up.

Confused? Perhaps this is what you meant:

> The year before, we budgeted more for advertising. Sales were up.

Maybe you meant this:

> The year before we budgeted more for advertising, sales were up.

The meaning of language falls into bundles called sentences. A listener or reader can take only so much meaning before filing a sentence away and getting ready for the next one. So, as a writer, you have to know what a sentence is. You need to know where one ends and the next one begins.

If you want to know what a thing is, you have to find out what goes into it, what its ingredients are. Luckily, the basic ingredients of an English sentence are simple. They're called the parts of speech, and the content-bearing ones are nouns, pronouns, verbs, adjectives, and adverbs. They combine with a few functional parts of speech to convey meaning. Meaning is also transmitted by punctuation, mechanics, and vocabulary.

1.1 Nouns

A noun names a person, place, or thing. Anything you can see or detect with one of your other senses has a noun to name it. Some things you can't see or sense are also nouns—ions, for example, or space. So are things that exist as ideas, such as accuracy and height. (You can see that something is accurate or that a building is tall, but you can't see the idea of accuracy or the idea of height.) These names for ideas are known as abstract nouns. The simplest nouns are the names of things you can see or touch: car, building, cloud, brick.

1.1.1 PROPER NOUNS AND COMMON NOUNS

So far, all the examples of nouns have been common nouns, referring to general classes of things. The word *building* refers to a whole class of structures. Common nouns such as *building* are not capitalized.

If you want to talk about one particular building, however, you might refer to the Glazier Building. The name is capitalized, indicating that *Glazier Building* is a proper noun.

Here are three sets of common and proper nouns for comparison:

COMMON	PROPER
city	Saskatoon
company	Blaisden Company
store	Books Galore

1.1.2 PLURAL NOUNS

Nouns can be either singular or plural. The usual way to make a plural noun is to add *s* to the singular form of the word:

SINGULAR	PLURAL
rock	rocks
picture	pictures
song	songs

Many nouns have other ways of forming the plural. Letters, numbers, and words used as words are sometimes made plural by adding an apostrophe and an *s*. Very often, *'s* is used with abbreviations that have periods, lowercase letters that stand alone, and capital letters that might be confused with words when made into plurals:

Spell out all *St.*'s and *Ave.*'s.

He divided the page with a row of *x*'s.

Sarah will register the *A*'s through the *I*'s at the convention.

In other cases, however, the apostrophe may be left out:

They'll review their *ABC*s.

The stock market climbed through most of the 1980s.

Circle all *the*s in the paragraph.

In these examples, the letters used as letters and words used as words *are italicized* (discussed later).

Other nouns, such as those below, are so-called irregular nouns; they form the plural in some way other than simply adding *s:*

SINGULAR	PLURAL
tax	taxes
specialty	specialties
cargo	cargoes
shelf	shelves
child	children
woman	women
tooth	teeth
mouse	mice
parenthesis	parentheses
son-in-law	sons-in-law
editor-in-chief	editors-in-chief

Rather than memorize a lot of rules about forming plurals, use a dictionary. If the dictionary says nothing about the plural of a word, it's formed the usual way: by adding *s*. If the plural is formed in some irregular way, the dictionary shows the plural or has a note something like this: *ples.*

Exercise

Circle the nouns in the following sentences. Determine whether each is proper/common, singular/plural, and fill in the chart accordingly.

Basketball, one of the world's most popular sports, was invented by a Canadian. Dr. James Naismith was born in Ontario in 1861. While working at the YMCA Training School in Springfield, Massachusetts, Naismith was faced with the problem of finding a sport which his students could play indoors during the long winters. In 1891, the inaugural game of basketball was played with a soccer ball and two peach baskets serving as goals. Basketball was introduced at the Olympics in 1936.

	common	proper
singular		
plural		

1.1.3 POSSESSIVE NOUNS

A noun becomes possessive when it's used to show the ownership of something. Then you add *'s* to the word:

the man's car the woman's apartment

However, ownership does not need to be legal:

the secretary's desk

the company's assets

Also, ownership may be nothing more than an automatic association:

a day's work

a job's prestige

An exception to the rule about adding *'s* to make a noun possessive occurs when the word is singular and already has two *s* sounds at the end. In cases like the following, an apostrophe is all that's needed:

crisis' dimensions

Mr. Moses' application

When the noun has only one *s* sound at the end, however, retain the *'s:*

Chris's book

Carolyn Nuss's office

With hyphenated nouns (compound nouns), add *'s* to the last word:

HYPHENATED NOUN	POSSESSIVE NOUN
mother-in-law	mother-in-law's
mayor-elect	mayor-elect's

To form the possessive of plural nouns, just begin by following the same rule as with singular nouns: add *'s*. However, if the plural noun already ends in an *s* (as most do), drop the one you've added, leaving only the apostrophe:

> the clients'~~s~~ complaints employees'~~s~~ benefits

Exercise

Form the possessive case of each word in parentheses.

1. Currently specializing in (ladies) lingerie, the company hopes to diversify into (children) clothing.
2. Her (father-in-law) opinion is that the assignment will be (child) play.
3. (Shakespeare) poetry is moving, but Tai-Cheung feels (Keats) is more melodic.
4. The (goddess) festival takes place at harvest time.
5. The (goddesses) festival brings the entire community together.
6. The (people) prayers were long and touching.
7. The (prayers) meaning was hard to discern.
8. The (drug) effect was instantaneous.
9. The (consultants) appraisal was discouraging.
10. (James) performance evaluation is impressive, but (Chris) shows several areas needing improvement.
11. The (women) movement has long roots.
12. (Clients) expectations have risen considerably.
13. The (duchess) complexion was perfect.
14. (Science) impact on our country is incalculable.
15. The (sciences) problem is a naïve faith in objectivity.
16. (North America) beauty is breathtaking.
17. (North Americans) manners leave much to be desired.
18. The (hurricanes) ravages were devastating.
19. The (Chans) daughter is charming.
20. (Manitobans) driving is more aggressive than (Newfoundlanders).
21. The (Winnipeg Blue Bombers) passing statistics are superior to the (Calgary Stampeders).
22. The (men) blood pressures were higher than the (women).
23. The twelve (jurors) decision differed from the (judge).
24. The (business) clientele is growing.
25. The (businesses) solution was to form a coalition.

1.2 Pronouns

A pronoun is a word that stands for a noun; it saves repeating the noun:

> *Drivers* have some choice of weeks for vacation, but *they* must notify this office of *their* preference by March 1.

The pronouns *they* and *their* stand in for the noun *drivers*. The noun that a pronoun stands for is called the antecedent of the pronoun; *drivers* is the antecedent of *they* and *their*.

When the antecedent is plural, the pronoun that stands in for it has to be plural; *they* and *their* are plural pronouns because *drivers* is plural. Likewise, when the antecedent is singular, the pronoun has to be singular:

> We thought the *contract* had been signed, but we soon learned that *it* had not been.

1.2.1 MULTIPLE ANTECEDENTS

Sometimes a pronoun has a double (or even a triple) antecedent:

> Kathryn Boettcher and Luis Gutierrez went beyond *their* sales quotas for January.

Kathryn Boettcher, if taken alone, is a singular antecedent. So is *Luis Gutierrez*. However, when together they are the antecedent of a pronoun, they're plural and the pronoun has to be plural. Thus the pronoun is *their* instead of *her* or *his*.

Exercise

Circle each pronoun in the following paragraph. If relevant, identify the pronoun's antecedent.

> When we think of millionaires, we often picture palatial homes, designer clothes, and exotic cars. In reality, experts say that most self-made millionaires cultivate a low-key existence. Rather than flaunting his or her wealth, the typical millionaire drives an old but reliable car, and lives in a modest house in a middle-class neighbourhood. In fact, you may know a low-profile millionaire or two without even realizing it: statistics suggest that one out of every 85 Canadians has $1 million or more in financial assets.

1.2.2 UNCLEAR ANTECEDENTS

In some sentences the pronoun's antecedent is unclear:

> Sandy Wright sent Jane Brougham *her* production figures for the previous year. *She* thought they were too low.

To which person does the pronoun *her* refer? Someone who knew Sandy and Jane and knew their business relationship might be able to figure out the antecedent for *her*. Even with such an advantage, however, a reader might receive the wrong meaning. Also, it would be nearly impossible for any reader to know which name is the antecedent of *she*.

The best way to clarify an ambiguous pronoun is usually to rewrite the sentence, repeating nouns when needed for clarity:

> Sandy Wright sent her production figures for the previous year to Jane Brougham. *Jane* thought they were too low.

The noun needs to be repeated only when the antecedent is unclear.

Exercise

Rewrite the following sentences to eliminate unclear antecedents.

1. Mr. Ashat asked Mr. Lo to review his performance evaluation.
2. Because he felt Imola was more hard-working than Savita, he asked her to stay late.
3. Before I sold perfumes, I used to walk past the department-store displays, amazed at their variety.
4. We visit the Gaspé Peninsula every year, which I always enjoy.

1.2.3 GENDER-NEUTRAL PRONOUNS

The pronouns that stand for males are *he, his,* and *him.* The pronouns that stand for females are *she, hers,* and *her.* However, you'll often be faced with the problem of choosing a pronoun for a noun that refers to both females and males:

> Each manager must make up (his, her, his or her, its, their) own mind about stocking this item and about the quantity that (he, she, he or she, it, they) can sell.

This sentence calls for a pronoun that's neither masculine nor feminine. The issue of gender-neutral pronouns responds to efforts to treat females and males evenhandedly. Here are some possible ways to deal with this issue:

> Each manager must make up *his* ...

(Not all managers are men.)

> Each manager must make up *her* ...

(Not all managers are women.)

> Each manager must make up *his or her* ...

(This solution is acceptable but becomes awkward when repeated more than once or twice in a document.)

> Each manager must make up *her* ... Every manager will receive *his* ... A manager may send *her* ...

(A manager's gender does not alternate like a windshield wiper!)

> Each manager must make up *their* ...

(The pronoun can't be plural when the antecedent is singular.)

> Each manager must make up *its* ...

(*It* never refers to people.)

The best solution is to make the noun plural or to revise the passage altogether:

> Managers must make up *their* minds ... Each manager must decide whether ...

Be careful not to change the original meaning.

Exercise

If necessary, suggest gender-neutral alternatives to the following sentences.

1. At the end of the year, the top student will have his name in the local newspaper.
2. Each employee is asked to read her benefits package carefully.
3. Any client left off the list will have to submit his claim later.
4. Wireless technology is evolving so quickly that developers must continually update their skills.
5. Each salesperson has his own tried-and-true strategies.

1.2.4 CASE OF PRONOUNS

The case of a pronoun tells whether it's acting or acted upon:

> *She* sells an average of five packages each week.

In this sentence *she* is doing the selling. Because *she* is acting, *she* is said to be in the nominative case. Now consider what happens when the pronoun is acted upon:

> After six months Ms. Browning promoted *her.*

In this sentence the pronoun *her* is acted upon. The pronoun *her* is thus said to be in the objective case.

Contrast the nominative and objective pronouns in this list:

NOMINATIVE	OBJECTIVE
I	me
we	us
he	him
she	her
they	them
who	whom
whoever	whomever

Objective pronouns may be used as either the object of a verb (such as *promoted*) or the object of a preposition (such as *with*):

> Rob worked with *them* until the order was filled.

In this example *them* is the object of the preposition *with* because Rob acted upon—worked with—them.

Here's a sample sentence with three pronouns, the first one nominative, the second the object of a verb, and the third the object of a preposition:

> *He* paid *us* as soon as the cheque came from *them.*

He is nominative; *us* is objective because it's the object of the verb *paid; them* is objective because it's the object of the preposition *from.*

Every writer sometimes wonders whether to use *who* or *whom:*

> (Who, Whom) will you hire?

Because this sentence is a question, it's difficult to see that *whom* is the object of the verb *hire*. You can figure out which pronoun to use if you rearrange the question and temporarily try *she* and *her* in place of *who* and *whom:* "Will you hire *she?*" or "Will you hire *her?*" *Her* and *whom* are both objective, so the correct choice is "*Whom* will you hire?" Here's a different example:

(Who, Whom) logged so much travel time?

Turning the question into a statement, you get:

He logged so much travel time.

Therefore, the correct statement is:

Who logged so much travel time?

Exercise

Select the correct pronoun in parentheses.

1. There is a rift between the office manager and _____ (*me, I*).
2. It's a private matter concerning only the CEO and _____ (*he, him*).
3. The strength of ____ (*we, us*) Canadians is an ability to recognize our weaknesses.
4. ___ (*We, Us*) Canadians possess an ability to recognize our weaknesses.
5. ___ (*Who, Whom*) is responsible for the fourth-quarter performance evaluations?
6. Since we had little sales experience, Jean-Claude and ____ (*I, me*) expected Ellen and ___ (*she, her*) to meet the quota first.
7. Wendy and _____ (*I, me*) summarized Gerald Schwartz's proposal for ____ (*they, them*).
8. If you do not understand the assignment, please see the project manager or ___ (*me, I*).
9. Java training will be given to __________ (*whoever, whomever*) requires it.
10. (*She, her*) _____ and Max disagree about _____ (*who, whom*) should initiate negotiations.

1.2.5 POSSESSIVE PRONOUNS

Possessive pronouns are like possessive nouns in the way they work: They show ownership or automatic association.

her job	their preferences
his account	its equipment

However, possessive pronouns are different from possessive nouns in the way they are written. That is, possessive pronouns never have an apostrophe.

POSSESSIVE NOUN	POSSESSIVE PRONOUN
the woman's estate	her estate
Roger Franklin's plans	his plans
the shareholders' feelings	their feelings
the vacuum cleaner's attachments	its attachments

The word *its* is the possessive of *it*. Like all other possessive pronouns, *its* doesn't have an apostrophe. Some people confuse *its* with *it's*, the contraction of *it is*. Contractions are discussed later.

Exercise

Fill in the blanks with the possessive "its" or the contraction "it's."

1. The Ontario Securities Commission has as _____ mandate to protect the integrity of the capital markets.
2. _____ paramount that the commission treat all of _____ constituents fairly.
3. Part of the OSC's responsibility is to communicate with a company in order to review _____ transactions and disclosures.
4. _____ important for participants in the capital markets to adhere strictly to securities law.
5. _____ the responsibility of each public company to ensure that ____ actions fall within the parameters of securities law.
6. The company's duty to _____ shareholders includes providing them with full and timely disclosure.

1.3 Verbs

A verb describes an action:

They all *quit* in disgust.

It may also describe a state of being:

Working conditions *were* substandard.

The English language is full of action verbs. Here are a few you'll often run across in the business world:

verify	perform	fulfill
hire	succeed	send
leave	improve	receive
accept	develop	pay

You could undoubtedly list many more.

The most common verb describing a state of being instead of an action is *to be* and all its forms:

I am, was, or will be; you are, were, or will be

Other verbs also describe a state of being:

It *seemed* a good plan at the time.

She *sounds* impressive at a meeting.

These verbs link what comes before them in the sentence with what comes after; no action is involved. (See Section 1.7.5 for a fuller discussion of linking verbs.)

1.3.1 VERB TENSES

English has three simple verb tenses: present, past, and future.

PRESENT: Our branches in Newfoundland *stock* other items.

PAST: When we *stocked* Purquil pens, we received a great many complaints.

FUTURE: Rotex Tire Stores *will stock* your line of tires when you begin a program of effective national advertising.

With most verbs (the regular ones), the past tense ends in *ed;* the future tense always has *will* or *shall* in front of it. But the present tense is more complex:

SINGULAR	PLURAL
I stock	we stock
you stock	you stock
he, she, it stocks	they stock

The basic form, *stock,* takes an additional *s* when *he, she,* or *it* precedes it.

In addition to the three simple tenses, there are three perfect tenses using forms of the helping verb *have.* The present perfect tense uses the past participle (regularly the past tense) of the main verb, *stocked,* and adds the present-tense *have* or *has* to the front of it:

(I, we, you, they) *have stocked.*

(He, she, it) *has stocked.*

The past perfect tense uses the past participle of the main verb, *stocked,* and adds the past-tense *had* to the front of it:

(I, you, he, she, it, we, they) *had stocked.*

The future perfect tense also uses the past participle of the main verb, *stocked,* but adds the future-tense *will have:*

(I, you, he, she, it, we, they) *will have stocked.*

Keep verbs in the same tense when the actions occur at the same time:

When the payroll checks *came* in, everyone *showed* up for work.

We *have found* that everyone *has pitched* in to help.

Of course, when the actions occur at different times, you may change tense accordingly:

A shipment *came* last Wednesday, so when another one *comes* in today, please return it.
The new employee *had been* ill at ease, but now she *has become* a full-fledged member of the team.

1.3.2 IRREGULAR VERBS

Many verbs don't follow in every detail the patterns already described. The most irregular of these verbs is *to be:*

TENSE	SINGULAR	PLURAL
PRESENT:	I *am*	we *are*
	you *are*	you *are*
	he, she, it *is*	they *are*
PAST:	I *was*	we *were*
	you *were*	you *were*
	he, she, it *was*	they *were*

The future tense of *to be* is formed in the same way that the future tense of a regular verb is formed.

The perfect tenses of *to be* are also formed as they would be for a regular verb, except that the past participle is a special form, *been,* instead of just the past tense:

PRESENT PERFECT: you have been

PAST PERFECT: you had been

FUTURE PERFECT: you will have been

Here's a sampling of other irregular verbs:

PRESENT	PAST	PAST PARTICIPLE
begin	began	begun
shrink	shrank	shrunk
know	knew	known
rise	rose	risen
become	became	become
go	went	gone
do	did	done

Dictionaries list the various forms of other irregular verbs.

Exercise

Place the underlined verbs in the appropriate boxes in the table on the following page.

Ted Nolan's life has been a series of sharp ups and downs. A native Canadian, Nolan grew up on a reserve in a family of 12. Around him he saw lives ravaged by poverty, alcohol and violence. Hockey was his means of escape: hard work and dedication made him an NHL winger. However, an injury ended his playing days when he was 28. Indomitable, he changed careers: if he had been a good hockey player, he was to be a great hockey coach. His superb work with the Buffalo Sabres led him to be named the NHL coach of the year at the age of 39. Strangely, though, he then lost his position, and many feel that racism has hampered his NHL coaching career.

Ted Nolan, however, is not to be daunted by adversity. Long a supporter of native youth, he has created Team Indigenous, a hockey club of Canadian aboriginal males. No one knows whether Nolan will ever return to the NHL, but it hardly matters any more; a hero to his players, he instills hope, motivation and pride in aboriginal youth. At the end of his career, he will have made a difference not just on the ice, but also in the hearts and minds of the native peoples he has never forgotten.

1.3.3 TRANSITIVE AND INTRANSITIVE VERBS

Many people are confused by three particular sets of verbs:

lie/lay sit/set rise/raise

Using these verbs correctly is much easier when you learn the difference between transitive and intransitive verbs.

Transitive verbs convey their action to an object; they "transfer" their action to an object. Intransitive verbs do not. Here are some sample uses of transitive and intransitive verbs:

simple past	simple present	simple future	past perfect	present perfect	future perfect

INTRANSITIVE	TRANSITIVE
We should include in our new offices a place to *lie* down for a nap.	The workers will be here on Monday to *lay* new carpeting.
Even the way an interviewee *sits* is important.	That crate is full of stemware, so *set* it down carefully.
Salaries at Compu-Link Inc., *rise* swiftly.	They *raise* their level of production every year.

The workers *lay* carpeting, you *set* down the crate, they *raise* production; each action is transferred to something. In the intransitive sentences, one *lies* down, an interviewee *sits*, and salaries *rise* without (at least grammatically) affecting anything else. Intransitive sentences are complete with only a subject and a verb; transitive sentences are not complete unless they also include an object, or something to transfer the action to.

Tenses are a confusing element of the *lie/lay* problem:

PRESENT	PAST	PAST PARTICIPLE
I *lie*	I *lay*	I have *lain*
I *lay* (something down)	I *laid* (something down)	I have *laid* (something down)

The past tense of *lie* and the present tense of *lay* look and sound alike, even though they're different verbs.

Exercise

Select the correct verb in parentheses.

1. (*Lay, Lie*) your cards on the table: you're not pleased with the new intern's productivity.
2. He does tend to (*lie, lay*) around the office drinking coffee a little too much. Yesterday I had to (*lay, lie*) down company policy to him in no uncertain terms.
3. However, when I (*set, sit*) him a complex task, he often (*rises, raises*) to the challenge; he could be a first-class employee if he were to (*rise, raise*) his general level of productivity.

1.3.4 VOICE OF VERBS

Verbs have two voices, active and passive:

ACTIVE: The buyer paid a large amount.

PASSIVE: A large amount was paid by the buyer.

The passive voice uses a form of the verb *to be*.

Also, the passive-voice sentence uses eight words, whereas the active-voice sentence uses only six words to express the same idea. The words *was* and *by* are unnecessary to convey the meaning of the sentence. In fact, extra words usually clog meaning. So be sure to opt for the active voice when you have a choice.

At times, however, you have no choice:

Several items *have been taken*, but so far we don't know who took them.

The passive voice becomes necessary when you don't know (or don't want to say) who performed the action; the active voice is bolder and more direct.

Exercise

Where possible, transform the following sentences from the passive voice to the active voice.

1. The invoice was faxed by the shipping department.
2. An explanatory letter will be sent to all customers.
3. The final cost of the Halifax project had been wildly underestimated by the consultants.
4. This task must be delegated by the vice-president of corporate affairs.
5. The national lacrosse team plays well under pressure.

1.3.5 MOOD OF VERBS

You have three moods to choose from, depending on your intentions. Most of the time you use the indicative mood to make a statement or to ask a question:

The secretary *mailed* a letter to each supplier.

Did the secretary *mail* a letter to each supplier?

When you wish to command or request, use the imperative mood:

Please mail a letter to each supplier.

Sometimes, especially in business, a courteous request is stated like a question; in that case, however, no question mark is required.

> Would you *mail* a letter to each supplier.

The subjunctive mood, most often used in formal writing or in presenting bad news, expresses a possibility or a recommendation. The subjunctive is usually signalled by a word such as *if* or *that.* In these examples, the subjunctive mood uses special verb forms:

> If the secretary *were to mail* a letter to each supplier, we might save some money.

> I suggested that the secretary *mail* a letter to each supplier.

Although the subjunctive mood is not used as often as it once was, it's still found in such expressions as *Come what may* and *If I were you.* In general, it is used to convey an idea that is contrary to fact: If iron *were* lighter than air.

Exercise

Identify the mood of each underlined verb.

1. In Spain let a handshake last five to seven strokes; pulling away too soon may be interpreted as rejection. In France, however, the preferred handshake is a single stroke.
2. Don't give a gift of liquor in Arab countries. If you were to give such a gift, offence would be taken.
3. In Pakistan don't be surprised when business people excuse themselves in the middle of a meeting to conduct prayers. Muslims pray five times a day.
4. Allow plenty of time to get to know the people you're dealing with in Africa; they are suspicious of people who are in a hurry.

1.4 Adjectives

An adjective modifies (tells something about) a noun or pronoun:

an *efficient* staff	a *heavy* price
brisk trade	*poor* you

Each of these phrases says more about the noun or pronoun than the noun or pronoun would say alone.

Adjectives always tell us something we wouldn't know without them. So you don't need to use adjectives when the noun alone, or a different noun, will give the meaning:

> a *company* employee

(An employee ordinarily works for a company.)

> a *crate-type* container

(*Crate* gives the entire meaning.)

At times, adjectives pile up in a series:

> It was a *long, hot,* and *active* workday.

Such strings of adjectives are acceptable as long as they all convey a different part of the phrase's meaning.

Verbs in the *ing* (present participle) form can be used as adjectives:

> A *boring* job can sometimes turn into a *fascinating* career.

So can the past participle of verbs:

> A freshly *painted* house is a *sold* house.

Adjectives modify nouns more often than they modify pronouns. When adjectives do modify pronouns, however, the sentence usually has a linking verb:

They were *attentive.*	It looked *appropriate.*
He seems *interested.*	You are *skilful.*

Most adjectives can take three forms: simple, comparative, and superlative. The simple form modifies a single noun or pronoun. Use the comparative form when comparing two items. When comparing three or more items, use the superlative form.

SIMPLE	COMPARATIVE	SUPERLATIVE
hard	harder	hardest
safe	safer	safest
dry	drier	driest

The comparative form adds *er* to the simple form, and the superlative form adds *est.* (The *y* at the end of a word changes to *i* before the *er* or *est* is added.)

A small number of adjectives are irregular, including these:

SIMPLE	COMPARATIVE	SUPERLATIVE
good	better	best
bad	worse	worst
little	less	least

When the simple form of an adjective is two or more syllables, you usually add *more* to form the comparative and *most* to form the superlative:

SIMPLE	COMPARATIVE	SUPERLATIVE
useful	more useful	most useful
exhausting	more exhausting	most exhausting
expensive	more expensive	most expensive

The most common exceptions are two-syllable adjectives that end in *y:*

SIMPLE	COMPARATIVE	SUPERLATIVE
happy	happier	happiest
costly	costlier	costliest

If you choose this option, change the *y* to *i,* and tack *er* or *est* onto the end.

1.5 Adverbs

An adverb modifies a verb, an adjective, or another adverb:

MODIFYING A VERB: Our marketing department works efficiently.

MODIFYING AN ADJECTIVE: She was not dependable, although she was *highly* intelligent.

MODIFYING ANOTHER ADVERB: His territory was *too* broadly diversified, so he moved *extremely* cautiously.

Most of the adverbs mentioned are adjectives turned into adverbs by adding *ly*, which is how many adverbs are formed:

ADJECTIVE	ADVERB
efficient	efficiently
high	highly
extreme	extremely
special	specially
official	officially
separate	separately

Some adverbs are made by dropping or changing the final letter of the adjective and then adding *ly:*

ADJECTIVE	ADVERB
due	duly
busy	busily

Other adverbs don't end in *ly* at all. Here are a few examples of this type:

often	fast	too
soon	very	so

Exercise

Identify each adverb and adjective in the following sentences. Note any examples of the comparative and superlative.

1. Given her high profile, Pamela Wallin is surprisingly accessible and engaging.
2. He duly noted that Mr. Wu felt that direct marketing, though initially costlier, would in the long run prove more efficient.
3. The best solution to declining morale is a policy which rewards the most innovative initiatives and the most effective trouble-shooting.

1.6 Other Parts of Speech

Nouns, pronouns, verbs, adjectives, and adverbs carry most of the meaning in a sentence. Four other parts of speech link them together in sentences: prepositions, conjunctions, articles, and interjections.

1.6.1 PREPOSITIONS

Prepositions are words like these:

of to for with at by from about

They most often begin prepositional phrases, which function like adjectives and adverbs by telling more about a pronoun, noun, or verb:

of a type *by* Friday *to* the point *with* characteristic flair

1.6.2 CONJUNCTIONS, ARTICLES, AND INTERJECTIONS

Conjunctions are words that usually join parts of a sentence. Here are a few:

and but because yet although if

Using conjunctions is discussed in sections 1.7.3 and 1.7.4.

Only three articles exist in English: *the, a,* and *an.* These words are used, like adjectives, to specify which item you are talking about.

Interjections are words that express no solid information, only emotion:

Wow! Well, well! Oh no! Good!

Such purely emotional language has its place in private life and advertising copy, but it only weakens the effect of most business writing.

Exercise

Identify the prepositions, conjunctions and articles in the following sentences.

1. He admires her skills, but told her in no uncertain terms that she must improve her ability to work with others.
2. Jatinder will have his associate chart profits to the end of the quarter.
3. The volatility of tech stocks is a concern, yet Binah feels that the company's risk-management strategies are adequate.
4. If she handles the situation with her usual tact, Vanita will successfully negotiate a compromise with the various parties.

Exercise

Place the underlined words in the appropriate boxes in the table on the following page.

The Canadian Ski Marathon began in 1967 when Olympic Nordic Ski Team member Don MacLeod decided to celebrate Canada's hundredth birthday by organizing a gruelling, 200-kilometre cross-country ski marathon. He chose as his starting point a shopping centre in suburban Montreal; since no one owned a gun, organizers signalled the start of the race by smashing an air-filled paper bag. The inaugural marathon presented unforeseen challenges: thanks to local pranksters who had removed trail markers, almost all the skiers got lost.

Warm temperatures in the marathon's second year brought much riskier adventures. Many skiers broke through ice, and the Canadian army, ski patrol, police and marathon organizers had to rescue dozens of hypothermic skiers.

Astonishingly, there were no fatalities. One might think that such a disaster would signal the marathon's

common noun	proper noun	pronoun	verb	adjective	adverb	preposition	conjunction	article

demise, but instead word spread about the event, and the following year drew more sponsors and skiers. This ultimate winter challenge is still going strong, and has never missed a year since its 1967 inception.

1.7 Sentences

Sentences are constructed with the major building blocks, the parts of speech.

> Money talks.

This two-word sentence consists of a noun (*money*) and a verb (*talks*). When used in this way, the noun works as the first requirement for a sentence, the subject, and the verb works as the second requirement, the predicate. Now look at this sentence:

> They merged.

The subject in this case is a pronoun (*they*), and the predicate is a verb (*merged*). This is a sentence because it has a subject and a predicate. Here is yet another kind of sentence:

> The plans are ready.

This sentence has a more complicated subject, the noun *plans* and the article *the;* the complete predicate is a state-of-being verb (*are*) and an adjective (*ready*).

Without these two parts, the subject (who or what does something) and the predicate (the doing of it), no collection of words is a sentence.

Exercise

Rewrite the following paragraph to make it more effective, succinct, and stylistically pleasing. The paragraph is largely composed of simple sentences; you may find it useful to use some compound and complex sentences in your revisions.

> Rick Mercer is one of the stars of a popular CBC show. This show is called *This Hour Has 22 Minutes.* This show is produced by Salter Street Films. This show is shot in Halifax. The other stars are Mary Walsh, Cathy Jones and Greg Thomey. Rick Mercer is one of Canada's most beloved comics. He does one of the show's funniest and most popular segments. This segment is called "Talking to Americans." Mercer did his first episode of "Talking to Americans" in 1998. One episode was particularly memorable. Mercer was in Iowa. Mercer spoke to several Americans. He spoke about Canada's 20-hour clock. He said for centuries Canada had operated on the 20-hour clock. He said that a Canadian hour was actually 75 American minutes. He said this system was confusing to American tourists visiting Canada. He said many tourists missed their buses, etc. He said Canada was finally switching to the 24-hour clock. He asked the Iowans' opinion. Most thought this was a sensible idea. They offered their congratulations to Canada for finally switching to American time.

1.7.1 COMMANDS

In commands, the subject (always *you*) is only understood, not stated:

> (You) Move your desk to the better office.

> (You) Please try to finish by six o'clock.

1.7.2 LONGER SENTENCES

More complicated sentences have more complicated subjects and predicates, but they still have a simple subject and a predicate verb. In the following examples, the simple subject is underlined once, the predicate verb twice:

> Marex and Contron enjoy higher earnings each quarter.

(Marex [and] Contron did something; enjoy is what they did.)

> My interview, coming minutes after my freeway accident, did not impress or move anyone.

(Interview is what did something. What did it do? It did [not] impress [or] move.)

> In terms of usable space, a steel warehouse, with its extremely long span of roof unsupported by pillars, makes more sense.

(Warehouse is what makes.)

These three sentences demonstrate several things. First, in all three sentences the simple subject and predicate verb are the "bare bones" of the sentence, the parts that carry the core idea of the sentence. When trying to find the simple subject and predicate verb, disregard all prepositional phrases, modifiers, conjunctions, and articles.

Second, in the third sentence the verb is singular (*makes*) because the subject is singular (*warehouse*). Even though the plural noun *pillars* is closer to the verb, *warehouse* is the subject. So *warehouse* determines whether the verb is singular or plural. Subject and predicate must agree.

Third, the subject in the first sentence is compound (*Marex* [and] *Contron*). A compound subject, when connected by *and,* requires a plural verb (*enjoy*). Also in the second sentence, compound predicates are possible (*did* [not] *impress* [or] *move*).

Fourth, the second sentence incorporates a group of words—*coming minutes after my freeway accident*—containing a form of a verb (*coming*) and a noun (*accident*). Yet this group of words is not a complete sentence for two reasons:

- Accident is not the subject of coming. Not all nouns are subjects.
- A verb that ends in *ing* can never be the predicate of a sentence (unless preceded by a form of *to be,* as in *was coming*). Not all verbs are predicates.

Because they don't contain a subject and a predicate, the words *coming minutes after my freeway accident* (called a phrase) can't be written as a sentence. That is, the phrase can't stand alone; it can't begin with a capital letter and end with a period. So a phrase must always be just one part of a sentence.

Sometimes a sentence incorporates two or more groups of words that do contain a subject and a predicate; these word groups are called clauses.

> My interview, because it came minutes after my freeway accident, did not impress or move anyone.

The independent clause is the portion of the sentence that could stand alone without revision:

> My interview did not impress or move anyone.

The other part of the sentence could stand alone only by removing *because:*

> (because) It came minutes after my freeway accident.

This part of the sentence is known as a dependent clause; although it has a subject and a predicate (just as an independent clause does), it's linked to the main part of the sentence by a word (*because*) showing its dependence.

In summary, the two types of clauses—dependent and independent—both have a subject and a predicate. Dependent clauses, however, do not bear the main meaning of the sentence and are therefore linked to an independent clause. Nor can phrases stand alone, because they lack both a subject and a predicate. Only independent clauses can be written as sentences without revision.

1.7.3 SENTENCE FRAGMENTS

An incomplete sentence (a phrase or a dependent clause) that is written as though it were a complete sentence is called a fragment. Consider the following sentence fragments:

> Marilyn Sanders, having had pilferage problems in her store for the past year.
>
> Refuses to accept the results of our investigation.

This serious error can easily be corrected by putting the two fragments together:

> Marilyn Sanders, having had pilferage problems in her store for the past year,
>
> refuses to accept the results of our investigation.

Not all fragments can be corrected so easily. Here's more information on Sanders's pilferage problem.

> Employees a part of it. No authority or discipline.

Only the writer knows the intended meaning of these two phrases. Perhaps the employees are taking part in the pilferage. If so, the sentence should read:

> Some employees are part of the pilferage problem.

On the other hand, it's possible that some employees are helping with the investigation. Then the sentence would read:

> Some employees are taking part in our investigation.

It's just as likely, however, that the employees are not only taking part in the pilferage but are also being analyzed:

> Those employees who are part of the pilferage problem will accept no authority or discipline.

In fact, even more meanings could be read into these fragments. Because fragments can mean so many things, they mean nothing. No well-written memo, letter, or report ever demands the reader to be an imaginative genius.

One more type of fragment exists, the kind represented by a dependent clause. Note what *because* does to change what was once a unified sentence:

> Our stock of sprinklers is depleted.
>
> Because our stock of sprinklers is depleted.

Although the second version contains a subject and a predicate, adding *because* makes it a fragment. Words such as *because* form a special group of words called subordinating conjunctions. Here's a partial list:

since	though	whenever
although	if	unless
while	even if	after

When a word of this type begins a clause, the clause is dependent and cannot stand alone as a sentence. However, if a dependent clause is combined with an independent clause, it can convey a complete meaning. The independent clause may come before or after the dependent clause:

> We are unable to fill your order because our stock of sprinklers is depleted.

> Because our stock of sprinklers is depleted, we are unable to fill your order.

Another remedy for a fragment that is a dependent clause is to remove the subordinating conjunction. That solution leaves a simple but complete sentence:

> Our stock of sprinklers is depleted.

The actual details of a transaction will determine the best way to remedy a fragment problem.

The ban on fragments has one exception. Some advertising copy contains sentence fragments, written knowingly to convey a certain rhythm. However, advertising is the only area of business in which fragments are acceptable.

1.7.4 FUSED SENTENCES AND COMMA SPLICES

Just as there can be too little in a group of words to make it a sentence, there can also be too much:

> All our mail is run through a postage meter every afternoon someone picks it up.

This example contains two sentences, not one, but the two have been blended so that it's hard to tell where one ends and the next begins. Is the mail run through a meter every afternoon? If so, the sentences should read:

> All our mail is run through a postage meter every afternoon. Someone picks it up.

Perhaps the mail is run through a meter at some other time (morning, for example) and is picked up every afternoon:

> All our mail is run through a postage meter. Every afternoon someone picks it up.

The order of words is the same in all three cases; sentence division makes all the difference. Either of the last two cases is grammatically correct. The choice depends on the facts of the situation.

Sometimes these so-called fused sentences have a more obvious point of separation:

> Several large orders arrived within a few days of one another, too many came in for us to process by the end of the month.

Here the comma has been put between two independent clauses in an attempt to link them. When a lowly comma separates two complete sentences, the result is called a comma splice. A comma splice can be remedied in one of three ways:

- ➤ Replace the comma with a period and capitalize the next word: " ... one another. Too many ... "
- ➤ Replace the comma with a semicolon and do not capitalize the next word: " ... one another; too many ... " This remedy works only when the two sentences have closely related meanings.
- ➤ Change one of the sentences so that it becomes a phrase or a dependent clause. This remedy often produces the best writing, but it takes more work.

The third alternative can be carried out in several ways. One is to begin the blended sentence with a subordinating conjunction:

> Whenever several large orders arrived within a few days of one another, too many came in for us to process by the end of the month.

Another way is to remove part of the subject or the predicate verb from one of the independent clauses, thereby creating a phrase:

> Several large orders arrived within a few days of one another, too many for us to process by the end of the month.

Finally, you can change one of the predicate verbs to its *ing* form:

> Several large orders arrived within a few days of one another, too many coming in for us to process by the end of the month.

At other times a simple coordinating conjunction (such as *or, and,* or *but*) can separate fused sentences:

> You can fire them, *or* you can make better use of their abilities.

> Margaret drew up the designs, *and* Matt carried them out.

> We will have three strong months, *but* after that sales will taper off.

Be careful using coordinating conjunctions: Use them only to join simple sentences that express similar ideas.

Also, because they say relatively little about the relationship between the two clauses they join, avoid using coordinating conjunctions too often: *and* is merely an addition sign; *but* is just a turn signal; *or* only points to an alternative. Subordinating conjunctions such as *because* and *whenever* tell the reader a lot more.

Exercise

Rewrite the following paragraph to make it more effective, succinct, and stylistically pleasing. Make sure that each sentence is complete and correct.

> Evelyn Lau is one of Canada's exciting young writers, she was born in 1971, her hometown is Vancouver. She lived

on the streets as a teen, she wrote about her harrowing experiences with prostitution and drugs in *Runaway: Diary of A Street Kid.* Having become a bestseller. Made into a T.V. movie. In the candid article "An Insatiable Emptiness" Evelyn writes about an aspect of her life little mentioned in *Runaway* her painful struggle with bulimia lasted many years. A moving piece of writing. She eventually came to a realization. The cause of her eating disorder not so much concern with her weight, but rather her troubled relationship with her parents.

1.7.5 SENTENCES WITH LINKING VERBS

Linking verbs were discussed briefly in the section on verbs (Section 1.3). Here you can see more fully the way they function in a sentence. The following is a model of any sentence with a linking verb:

A (verb) B.

Although words such as *seems* and *feels* can also be linking verbs, let's assume that the verb is a form of *to be:*

A *is* B.

In such a sentence, A and B are always nouns, pronouns, or adjectives. When one is a noun and the other is a pronoun, or when both are nouns, the sentence says that one is the same as the other:

She is president.

Rachel is president.

When one is an adjective, it modifies or describes the other:

She is forceful.

Remember that when one is an adjective, it modifies the other as any adjective modifies a noun or pronoun, except that a linking verb stands between the adjective and the word it modifies.

Exercise

Circle the linking verbs in the following sentences.

Tamara is president of the student council. She seems a good choice for the job, since she is a charming individual who can exert authority when necessary.

1.7.6 MISPLACED MODIFIERS

The position of a modifier in a sentence is important. The movement of *only* changes the meaning in the following sentences:

Only we are obliged to supply those items specified in your contract.

We are obliged *only* to supply those items specified in your contract.

We are obliged to supply *only* those items specified in your contract.

We are obliged to supply those items specified *only* in your contract.

In any particular set of circumstances, only one of these sentences would be accurate. The others would very likely cause problems. To prevent misunderstanding, place modifiers such as *only* as close as possible to the noun or verb they modify.

For similar reasons, whole phrases that are modifiers must be placed near the right noun or verb. Mistakes in placement create ludicrous meanings:

Antia Information Systems has bought new computer chairs for the programmers *with more comfortable seats.*

The anatomy of programmers is not normally a concern of business writers. Obviously, the comfort of the chairs was the issue:

Antia Information Systems has bought new computer chairs *with more comfortable seats* for the programmers.

Here is another example:

I asked him to file all the letters in the cabinet *that had been answered.*

In this ridiculous sentence the cabinet has been answered, even though no cabinet in history is known to have asked a question. *That had been answered* is too far from *letters* and too close to *cabinet.* Here's an improvement:

I asked him to file in the cabinet all the letters *that had been answered.*

In some cases, instead of moving the modifying phrase closer to the word it modifies, the best solution is to move the word closer to the modifying phrase.

Exercise

Correct any misplaced or dangling modifiers in the following sentences.

1. The pastries were served to the royals on fine crystal.
2. Frivolous, predictable and unrealistic, most females have lost patience with the typical women's magazine.
3. At the Juno and Genie Awards, several women are always snapped by photographers wearing daring evening gowns.
4. Professional and exacting, Peter Mansbridge is integral to the success of CBC's *The National.*
5. Waiting for the rescuers, a bat skimmed by my head.

2.0 Punctuation

On the highway, signs tell you when to slow down or stop, where to turn, when to merge. In similar fashion, punctuation helps readers negotiate your prose. The proper use of punctuation keeps readers from losing track of your meaning.

2.1 Periods

Use a period (1) to end any sentence that is not a question, (2) with certain abbreviations, and (3) between dollars and cents in an amount of money.

2.2 Question Marks

Use a question mark after any direct question that requests an answer:

> Are you planning to enclose a cheque, or shall we bill you?

Don't use a question mark with commands phrased as questions for the sake of politeness:

> Will you send us a cheque today.

2.3 Exclamation Points

Use exclamation points after highly emotional language. Because business writing almost never calls for emotional language, you will seldom use exclamation points.

2.4 Semicolons

Semicolons have three main uses. One is to separate two closely related independent clauses:

> The outline for the report is due within a week; the report itself is due at the end of the month.

A semicolon should also be used instead of a comma when the items in a series have commas within them:

> Our previous meetings were on November 11, 1999; February 20, 2000; and April 28, 2002.

Finally, a semicolon should be used to separate independent clauses when the second one begins with a word such as *however, therefore,* or *nevertheless* or a phrase such as *for example* or *in that case:*

> Our supplier has been out of part D712 for 10 weeks; however, we have found another source that can ship the part right away.

> His test scores were quite low; on the other hand, he has a lot of relevant experience.

Section 4.4 has more information on using transitional words and phrases.

2.5 Colons

Use a colon (1) after the salutation in a business letter, (2) at the end of a sentence or phrase introducing a list or (sometimes) a quotation, and (3) to separate two closely related independent clauses not joined by *and, but,* or *or.*

> Our study included the three most critical problems: insufficient capital, incompetent management, and inappropriate location.

In some introductory sentences, phrases such as *the following* or *that is* are implied by using a colon.

A colon should not be used when the list, quotation, or idea is a direct object or part of the introductory sentence:

> We are able to supply
> - staples
> - wood screws
> - nails
> - toggle bolts

> This shipment includes 9 videotapes, 12 CDs, and 14 cassette tapes.

2.6 Commas

Commas have many uses; the most common is to separate items in a series:

> He took the job, learned it well, worked hard, and succeeded.

> Put paper, pencils, and paper clips on the requisition list.

Company style often dictates omitting the final comma in a series. However, if you have a choice, use the final comma; it's often necessary to prevent misunderstanding.

A second place to use a comma is between independent clauses that are joined by a coordinating conjunction (*and, but,* or *or*) unless one or both are very short:

> She spoke to the sales staff, and he spoke to the production staff.

> I was advised to proceed and I did.

A third use for the comma is to separate a dependent clause at the beginning of a sentence from an independent clause:

> Because of our lead in the market, we may be able to risk introducing a new product.

However, a dependent clause at the end of a sentence is separated from the independent clause by a comma only when the dependent clause is unnecessary to the main meaning of the sentence:

> We may be able to introduce a new product, although it may involve some risk.

A fourth use for the comma is after an introductory phrase or word:

> Starting with this amount of capital, we can survive in the red for one year.

> Through more careful planning, we may be able to serve more people.

> Yes, you may proceed as originally planned.

However, with short introductory prepositional phrases and some one-syllable words (such as *hence* and *thus*), the comma is often omitted:

Before January 1 we must complete the inventory.

Thus we may not need to hire anyone.

In short the move to Tulsa was a good idea.

Fifth, commas are used to surround nonrestrictive phrases or words (expressions that can be removed from the sentence without changing the meaning):

The new owners, the Kowacks, are pleased with their purchase.

Sixth, commas are used between adjectives modifying the same noun (coordinate adjectives):

She left Monday for a long, difficult recruiting trip.

To test the appropriateness of such a comma, try reversing the order of the adjectives: *a difficult, long recruiting trip.* If the order cannot be reversed, leave out the comma (*a good old friend* isn't the same as *an old good friend*). A comma is also not used when one of the adjectives is part of the noun. Compare these two phrases:

a distinguished, well-known figure

a distinguished public figure

The adjective-noun combination of *public* and *figure* has been used together so often that it has come to be considered a single thing: *public figure.* So no comma is required.

Seventh, commas should precede *Inc., Ltd.,* and the like:

Cloverdell, Inc.   Beamer, Ltd.

In a sentence, a comma also follows such abbreviations:

Belle Brown, Ph.D., is the new tenant.

Eighth, commas are used both before and after the year in sentences that include month, day, and year:

It will be sent by December 15, 2005, from our Moncton plant.

Some companies write dates in another form: 15 December 2005. No commas should be used in that case. Nor is a comma needed when only the month and year are present (December 2005).

Ninth, a comma may be used after an informal salutation in a letter to a personal friend. (In business letters, however, the salutation is followed by a colon.)

Tenth, a comma is used to separate a quotation from the rest of the sentence:

Your warranty reads, "These conditions remain in effect for one year from date of purchase."

However, the comma is left out when the quotation as a whole is built into the structure of the sentence:

He hurried off with an angry "Look where you're going."

Finally, a comma should be used whenever it's needed to avoid confusion or an unintended meaning. Compare the following:

Ever since they have planned new ventures more carefully.
Ever since, they have planned new ventures more carefully.

Exercise

Punctuate the following paragraph as necessary.

The most basic form of communication is **nonverbal communication** all the cues gestures vocal qualities spatial relationships and attitudes toward time that allow us to communicate without words Anthropologists theorize that long before human beings used words to talk things over our ancestors communicated with one another by using their bodies They gritted their teeth to show anger they smiled and touched one another to indicate affection Although we have come a long way since those primitive times we still use nonverbal cues to express superiority dependence dislike respect love and other feelings

2.7 Dashes

Use a dash to surround a comment that is a sudden turn in thought:

Membership in the IBSA—it's expensive but worth it—may be obtained by applying to our New York office.

A dash can also be used to emphasize a parenthetical word or phrase:

Third-quarter profits—in excess of $2 million—are up sharply.

Finally, use dashes to set off a phrase that contains commas:

All our offices—Toronto, Vancouver, and Regina—have sent representatives.

Don't confuse a dash with a hyphen. A dash separates and emphasizes words, phrases, and clauses more strongly than a comma or parentheses can; a hyphen ties two words so tightly that they almost become one word.

When typing a dash, type two hyphens with no space before, between, or after.

Exercise

Add dashes to the following sentences as appropriate.

1. I had hoped to visit Sabrina an old and dear friend if time permitted.
2. My favourite movies *The Terminator, The Matrix,* and *Crouching Tiger, Hidden Dragon* all have superb action sequences.

3. Inflation to no one's surprise appears to be rising again.

2.8 Hyphens

Hyphens are mainly used in three ways. The first is to separate the parts of compound words beginning with such prefixes as self-, ex-, quasi-, and all:

self-assured	quasi-official
ex-wife	all-important

However, hyphens are usually left out and the words closed up in words that have such prefixes as *pro*, *anti*, *non*, *un*, *inter*, and *extra:*

prolabour	nonunion
antifascist	interdepartmental

Exceptions occur when (1) the prefix occurs before a proper noun or (2) the vowel at the end of the prefix is the same as the first letter of the root word:

pro-Republican	anti-American
anti-inflammatory	extra-atmospheric

When in doubt, consult your dictionary.

Hyphens are also used in some compound adjectives, which are adjectives made up of two or more words. Specifically, you should use hyphens in compound adjectives that come before the noun:

an interest-bearing account   well-informed executives

However, you need not hyphenate when the adjective follows a linking verb:

This account is interest bearing.

Their executives are well informed.

You can shorten sentences that list similar hyphenated words by dropping the common part from all but the last word:

Check the costs of first-, second-, and third-class postage.

Finally, hyphens may be used to divide words at the end of a typed line. Such hyphenation is best avoided, but when you have to divide words at the end of a line, do so correctly (see Section 3.4). A dictionary will show how words are divided into syllables.

Exercise

Add hyphens to the following words as needed.

exhusband	quasiceremonial
thankyou letter	allconsuming
prolabour faction	previous boyfriend
intercontinental	

2.9 Apostrophes

Use an apostrophe in the possessive form of a noun (but not in a pronoun):

On *his* desk was a reply to *Bette Ainsley's* application for the *manager's* position.

Apostrophes are also used in place of the missing letter(s) of a contraction:

WHOLE WORDS	CONTRACTION
we will	we'll
do not	don't
they are	they're

Exercise

Add apostrophes to the following as necessary.

Dont tell me that you cant help. I know perfectly well that youre tutoring Stephens child, so why shouldnt you spend some time with Bobbys as well?

2.10 Quotation Marks

Use quotation marks to surround words that are repeated exactly as they were said or written:

The collection letter ended by saying, "This is your third and final notice."

Remember: (1) When the quoted material is a complete sentence, the first word is capitalized. (2) The final comma or period goes inside the closing quotation marks.

Quotation marks are also used to set off the title of a newspaper story, magazine article, or book chapter:

You should read "Legal Aspects of the Collection Letter" in *Today's Credit.*

The book title is shown here in italics. When typewritten, the title is underlined. The same treatment is proper for newspaper and magazine titles. (Appendix B explains documentation style in more detail.)

Quotation marks may also be used to indicate special treatment for words or phrases, such as terms that you're using in an unusual or ironic way:

Our management "team" spends more time squabbling than working to solve company problems.

When using quotation marks, take care to put in both sets, the closing marks as well as the opening ones.

Although periods and commas go inside any quotation marks, colons and semicolons go outside them. A question mark goes inside the quotation marks only if the quotation is a question:

All that day we wondered, "Is he with us?"

If the quotation is not a question but the entire sentence is, the question mark goes outside:

> What did she mean by "You will hear from me"?

2.11 Parentheses

Use parentheses to surround comments that are entirely incidental:

> Our figures do not match yours, although (if my calculations are correct) they are closer than we thought.

Parentheses are also used in legal documents to surround figures in arabic numerals that follow the same amount in words:

> Remittance will be One Thousand Two Hundred Dollars ($1200).

Be careful to put punctuation (period, comma, and so on) outside the parentheses unless it is part of the statement in parentheses.

2.12 Ellipses

Use ellipsis points, or dots, to indicate that material has been left out of a direct quotation. Use them only in direct quotations and only at the point where material was left out. In the following example, the first sentence is quoted in the second:

> The Dow Jones Industrial Average, which skidded 38.17 points in the previous five sessions, gained 4.61 to end at 2213.84.

> According to the the *National Post,* "The Dow Jones Industrial Average … gained 4.61" on June 10.

The number of dots in ellipses is not optional; always use three. Occasionally, the points of ellipsis come at the end of a sentence, where they seem to grow a fourth dot. Don't be fooled: One of the dots is a period.

2.13 Underscores and Italics

Usually a line typed underneath a word or phrase either provides emphasis or indicates the title of a book, magazine, or newspaper. If possible, use italics instead of an underscore. Italics (or underlining) should also be used for defining terms and for discussing words as words:

> In this report *net sales* refers to after-tax sales dollars.

> The word *building* is a common noun and should not be capitalized.

Exercise

Make any necessary corrections to the following sentences.

1. Does he prefer the National Post or The Globe and Mail.
2. I asked him that same question, and he replied, "I don't have sufficient familiarity with the newer paper to be able to make a judgment.
3. My own opinion (for what it's worth) is that both national papers are kept on their toes by having such fierce competition.
4. According to one source I read, "Competition combats complacency [….] and fosters excellence in journalism, as in so many other fields".
5. Still, my friend John, who's taking journalism at a local college, feels that the country can only support one national newspaper. As few individuals buy two papers.
6. It is the case—and I know this from personal experience—that some readers buy the papers alternately.
7. My own father a long-time Globe reader, buys the weekend National Post because he enjoys reading Saturday Night, the magazine now included (at no extra charge).
8. My brother Stanley told me recently that he: "prefers to read the Sun, since the tone is more informal and engaging."
9. My brother Joseph—always an appreciator of the female form—likes the Sun for other reasons; though he claims to buy it only for the sports coverage.

3.0 Mechanics

The most obvious and least tolerable mistakes that a business writer makes are probably those related to grammar and punctuation. However, a number of small details, known as writing mechanics, demonstrate the writer's polish and reflect on the company's professionalism.

3.1 Capitals

You should, of course, capitalize words that begin sentences:

> *Before* hanging up, he said, "*We'll* meet here on Wednesday at noon."

A quotation that is a complete sentence should also begin with a capitalized word.

Capitalize the names of particular persons, places, and things (proper nouns):

> We sent *Ms. Larson* an application form, informing her that not all *applicants* are interviewed.

> Let's consider opening a branch in the *West*, perhaps at the *west* end of *Vancouver, British Columbia.*

> As office buildings go, the Kinney Building is a pleasant setting for TDG Office Equipment.

Ms. Larson's name is capitalized because she is a particular applicant, whereas the general term *applicant* is left uncapitalized. Likewise, *West* is capitalized when it refers to a particular place but not when it means a direction. In the same way, *office* and *building* are not capitalized when they are general terms (common nouns), but they are capitalized when they are part of the title of a particular office or building (proper nouns).

Titles within families, governments, or companies may also be capitalized:

> My *Uncle David* offered me a job, but I wouldn't be comfortable working for one of my *uncles.*

> We've never had a *president* quite like *President Sweeney.*

In addition, always capitalize the first word of the salutation and complimentary close of a letter:

> *Dear* Mr. Andrews: *Yours* very truly,

Finally, capitalize the first word after a colon when it begins a complete sentence:

> Follow this rule: *When* in doubt, leave it out.

Otherwise, the first word after a colon should not be capitalized (see Section 2.5).

Exercise

Add capital letters to the following as appropriate.

> silicon valley's staggering success is due in large part to its ability to attract the best and brightest minds. canada is a rich source for such minds: an estimated 250 000 to 350 000 canadians reside in the valley, forming the bay area's largest invisible minority. at gatherings of these ex-pats, conversation frequently turns to hockey, tim hortons coffee, and canadian high-tech heroes like rob burgess and jeff skoll.

3.2 Abbreviations

Abbreviations are used heavily in tables, charts, lists, and forms. They're used sparingly in prose paragraphs, however. Here are some abbreviations often used in business writing:

ABBREVIATION	FULL TERM
b/l	bill of lading
ca.	circa (about)
dol., dols.	dollar, dollars
etc.	et cetera (and so on)
Inc.	Incorporated
L.f.	Ledger folio
Ltd.	Limited
mgr.	manager
NSF or N/S	not sufficient funds
P&L or P/L	profit and loss
reg.	regular
whsle.	wholesale

Because *etc.* contains a word meaning *and,* never write *and etc.*

Exercise

Write out the full term for each of the following common abbreviations.

1. ca.
2. etc.
3. Ltd.
4. mgr.
5. whsle.

3.3 Numbers

Numbers may correctly be handled many ways in business writing, so follow company style. In the absence of a set style, however, generally spell out all numbers from one to ten and use arabic numerals for the rest.

There are some exceptions to this general rule. First, never begin a sentence with a numeral:

> *Twenty* of us produced *641* units per week in the first *12* weeks of the year.

Second, use numerals for the numbers one through ten if they're in the same list as larger numbers:

> Our weekly quota rose from *9* to *15* to *27.*

Third, use numerals for percentages, time of day (except with *o'clock*), dates, and (in general) dollar amounts.

> Our division is responsible for *7* percent of total sales.

> The meeting is scheduled for *8:30* a.m. on August *2.*

> Add *$3* for postage and handling.

When writing dollar amounts, use a decimal point only if cents are included. In lists of two or more dollar amounts, use the decimal point either for all or for none:

> He sent two cheques, one for *$67.92* and one for *$90.00.*

Exercise

Correct the use of numbers in the following.

> 20 or so times a year, I like to get together with my friends for lunch at a new restaurant. Last week, we chose a Sri Lankan restaurant that proved surprisingly expensive. My meal cost $42.50; one of my friend's cost $80. We generally tip around fifteen to twenty %.

3.4 Word Division

In general, avoid dividing words at the ends of lines. When you must, follow these rules:

- Don't divide one-syllable words (such as *since, walked,* and *thought*); abbreviations (*mgr.*); contractions (*isn't*); or numbers expressed in numerals (*117 500*).
- Divide words between syllables, as specified in a dictionary or word-division manual.

- ➤ Make sure that at least three letters of the divided word are moved to the second line: *sin-cerely* instead of *sincere-ly.*
- ➤ Do not end a page or more than three consecutive lines with hyphens.
- ➤ Leave syllables consisting of a single vowel at the end of the first line (*impedi-ment* instead of *imped-iment*), except when the single vowel is part of a suffix such as *-able, -ible, -ical,* or *-ity* (*respons-ible* instead of *responsi-ble*).
- ➤ Divide between double letters (*tomor-row*), except when the root word ends in double letters (*call-ing* instead of *cal-ling*).
- ➤ Divide hyphenated words after the hyphen only: *anti-independence* instead of *anti-inde-pendence.*

Exercise

Correct any of the following words which are incorrectly divided.

jog-ged
fal-low
undoubted-ly
fall-ing
anti-quated

4.0 Vocabulary

Using the right word in the right place is a crucial skill in business communication. However, many pitfalls await the unwary.

4.1 Frequently Confused Words

Because the following sets of words sound similar, be careful not to use one when you mean to use the other:

WORD	MEANING
accede exceed	to comply with to go beyond
accept except	to take to exclude
access excess	admittance too much
advice advise	suggestion to suggest
affect effect	to influence the result
allot to a lot	distribute much or many
all ready already	completely prepared completed earlier
born borne	given birth to carried

WORD	MEANING
capital capitol	money; chief city a government building
cite sight site	to quote a view a location
complement compliment	complete amount; to go well with to flatter
corespondent correspondent	party in a divorce suit letter writer
council counsel	a panel of people advice; a lawyer
defer differ	to put off until later to be different
device devise	a mechanism to plan
die dye	to stop living; a tool to colour
discreet discrete	careful separate
envelop envelope	to surround a covering for a letter
forth fourth	forward number four
holey holy wholly	full of holes sacred completely
human humane	of people kindly
incidence incidents	frequency events
instance instants	example moments
interstate intrastate	between states within a state
later latter	afterward the second of two
lead led	a metal guided
lean lien	to rest at an angle a claim
levee levy	embankment tax
loath loathe	reluctant to hate

WORD	MEANING
loose	free; not tight
lose	to mislay
miner	mineworker
minor	underage person
moral	virtuous; a lesson
morale	sense of well-being
ordinance	law
ordnance	weapons
overdo	to do in excess
overdue	past due
peace	lack of conflict
piece	a fragment
pedal	a foot lever
peddle	to sell
persecute	to torment
prosecute	to sue
personal	private
personnel	employees
precedence	priority
precedents	previous events
principal	sum of money; chief; main
principle	general rule
rap	to knock
wrap	to cover
residence	home
residents	inhabitants
right	correct
rite	ceremony
write	to form words on a surface
role	a part to play
roll	to tumble; a list
root	part of a plant
rout	to defeat
route	a traveller's way
shear	to cut
sheer	thin, steep
stationary	immovable
stationery	paper
than	as compared with
then	at that time
their	belonging to them
there	in that place
they're	they are
to	a preposition
too	excessively; also
two	the number

WORD	MEANING
waive	to set aside
wave	a swell of water; a gesture
weather	atmospheric conditions
whether	if

In the preceding list only enough of each word's meaning is given to help you distinguish between the words in each group. Several meanings are left out entirely. For more complete definitions, consult a dictionary.

Exercise

Select the appropriate word in parentheses.

1. In this (*instance, instants*), the (*effect, affect*) of the decision was immediate.
2. (*Discrete, Discreet*) employees (*accept, except*) the confidentiality requirements of (*there, their, they're*) firm.
3. As a matter of (*principle, principal*), the (*personal, personnel*) department is unwilling to (*wave, waive*) the educational requirement.
4. The president (*complimented, complemented*) the Montreal branch on the sound (*council, counsel*) it had offered concerning (*capital, capitol*) gains.
5. (*Allot, A lot*) of employees (*lose, loose*) sight of the importance of avoiding (*excess, access*) stress.
6. A (*wholly, holy, holey*) inappropriate mission statement would (*affect, effect*) company (*moral, morale*) more (*then, than*) individual productivity.

4.2 Frequently Misused Words

The following words tend to be misused for reasons other than their sound. Reference books (including the *Canadian Oxford English Dictionary*; *The Canadian Style: A Guide to Writing and Editing,* revised and expanded edition; and Fowler's *Modern English Usage*) can help you with similar questions of usage.

a lot: When the writer means "many," *a lot* is always two separate words, never one.

correspond with: Use this phrase when you are talking about exchanging letters. Use *correspond to* when you mean "similar to." Use either *correspond with* or *correspond to* when you mean "relate to."

disinterested: This word means "fair, unbiased, having no favourites, impartial." If you mean "bored" or "not interested," use *uninterested.*

etc.: This is the abbreviated form of a Latin phrase, *et cetera.* It means "and so on" or "and so forth." The current tendency among business writers is to use English rather than Latin.

imply/infer: Both refer to hints. Their great difference lies in who is acting. The writer *implies;* the reader *infers,* sees between the lines.

lay: This is a transitive verb. Never use it for the intransitive *lie.* (See Section 1.3.3.)

less: Use *less* for uncountable quantities (such as amounts of water, air, sugar, and oil). Use *fewer* for countable quantities (such as numbers of jars, saws, words, pages, and humans). The same distinction applies to *much* and *little* (uncountable) versus *many* and *few* (countable).

like: Use *like* only when the word that follows is just a noun or a pronoun. Use *as* or *as if* when a phrase or clause follows:

She looks *like* him.

She did just *as* he had expected.

It seems *as if* she had plenty of time.

many/much: See *less.*

regardless: The *less* ending is the negative part. No word needs two negative parts, so it is illiterate to add *ir* (a negative prefix) at the beginning.

to me/personally: Use these phrases only when personal reactions, apart from company policy, are being stated (not often the case in business writing).

try: Always follow with *to,* never *and.*

verbal: People in the business community who are careful with language frown on those who use *verbal* to mean "spoken" or "oral." Many others do say "verbal agreement." Strictly speaking, *verbal* means "of words" and therefore includes both spoken and written words. Be guided in this matter by company usage.

Exercise

Select the appropriate word in parentheses.

1. What was he (*implying, inferring*) when he said that he wished certain employees claimed (*fewer, less*) expenses?
2. I would (*imply, infer*) that he feels you are abusing your employee privileges.
3. Try (*and, to*) understand his point of view: just (*like, as*) you have to justify your expenses to him, he has to justify his to upper management.
4. In my (*disinterested, uninterested*) opinion, you do tend to use your business credit card somewhat too freely.
5. Since he receives (*a lot, alot*) of international inquiries, Atul corresponds (*with, to*) the Vancouver legal firm frequently.

4.3 Frequently Misspelled Words

All of us, even the world's best spellers, sometimes have to check a dictionary for the spelling of some words. People who have never memorized the spelling of commonly used words must look up so many that they grow exasperated and give up on spelling words correctly.

Don't expect perfection, and don't surrender. If you can memorize the spelling of just the words listed here, you'll need the dictionary far less often and you'll write with more confidence.

absence
absorption
accessible
accommodate
accumulate
achieve
advantageous
affiliated
aggressive
alignment
aluminum
ambience
analyze
apparent
appropriate
argument
asphalt
assistant
asterisk
auditor

bankruptcy
believable
brilliant
bulletin

calendar
campaign
category
ceiling
changeable
clientele
collateral
committee
comparative
competitor
concede
congratulations
connoisseur
consensus
convenient
convertible
corroborate
criticism

definitely
description
desirable
dilemma
disappear
disappoint
disbursement
discrepancy
dissatisfied
dissipate

eligible
embarrassing
endorsement
exaggerate
exceed
exhaust
existence
extraordinary

fallacy
familiar
flexible
fluctuation
forty

gesture
grievous

haphazard
harassment
holiday

illegible
immigrant
incidentally
indelible
independent
indispensable
insistent
intermediary
irresistible

jewellery
judgment
judicial

labelling
legitimate
leisure
litigation

maintenance
mathematics
mediocre
minimum

necessary
negligence
negotiable
newsstand
noticeable

occurrence
omission

parallel
pastime
peaceable
permanent
perseverance
persistent
personnel
persuade
possesses
precede
predictable
preferred
privilege
procedure
proceed
pronunciation
psychology
pursue

questionnaire

receive
recommend
repetition
rescind
rhythmical
ridiculous

saleable
secretary
seize
separate
sincerely
succeed
suddenness
superintendent
supersede
surprise

tangible
tariff
technique
tenant
truly

unanimous
until

vacillate
vacuum
vicious

Exercise

Correct the misspelled words in the following paragraphs.

1. I have recieved your most recent letter and the enclosed questionaire. Let me say that I admire your perserverence in trying to contact disatisfied customers. However, your agressive approach and your persistant attempts to minimize your own blame have exausted my patience; I will consider it harrassment if you try to contact me again.

   Yours truely, Dr. D. Chow
2. Many companies are conseding that the standard minimim fourty-hour work week is inconveniant for parents with young children. These companies now try to accomodate their employees' needs by offering a flexable scheduling option. Those familier with pyschology will not be surprised to learn that this arrangement often proves advantagous to the employers. Appreciative of the positive working ambiance, employees show their gratitude by producing brillient, independant work, and often become indispensible to the company.
3. Since our competiter is now offering lower prices on jewlery, it is desireable for us to find new ways of attracting clientel. Our company would risk bankrupcy if we were to undersell our competiter. However, we sinserely believe that we can offer priviliged customers a shopping experience that will exseed their expectations. We recomend that a commitee be struck to analize the situation and suggest an apropriate action plan.
4. The new assistent's handwriting is nearly illegeble. Moreover, standard operating prosedures remain a mystery to him, and he posesses an unerring instinct for mispelling even the simplest legal terms. You may think I exagerate, but many can coroborate what I say: it is apparant to all who work with him that the personel department made a greivous error in hiring him. The general concensus is that to avoid the company any further embarassment, we must ensure that he is removed from the department by the end of the calender year.

4.4 Transitional Words and Phrases

The following two sentences don't co`mmunicate as well as they might because they lack a transitional word or phrase:

> Production delays are inevitable. Our current lag time in filling orders is one month.

A semicolon between the two sentences would signal a close relationship between their meanings, but it wouldn't even hint at what that relationship is. Here are the sentences, now linked by means of a semicolon, with a space for a transitional word or phrase:

> Production delays are inevitable; _______ , our current lag time in filling orders is one month.

Now read the sentence with *nevertheless* in the blank space. Now try *therefore, incidentally, in fact,* and *at any rate* in the blank. Each substitution changes the meaning of the sentence.

Here are some transitional words (called conjunctive adverbs) that will help you write more clearly:

accordingly	furthermore	moreover
anyway	however	otherwise
besides	incidentally	still
consequently	likewise	therefore
finally	meanwhile	

The following transitional phrases are used in the same way:

as a result	in other words
at any rate	in the second place
for example	on the other hand
in fact	to the contrary

When one of these words or phrases joins two independent clauses, it should be preceded by a semicolon and followed by a comma, as shown here:

> The consultant recommended a complete reorganization; moreover, she suggested that we drop several products.

Exercise

Supply the appropriate transitional word or phrase. In some cases, more than one possibility exists.

1. John's interview was by far the best; __________, I will be recommending that we hire him.
2. Suzette will be leaving soon on maternity leave; _________, I would have offered her this plum assignment.
3. Francesco's skill set is outdated. _______________, he lacks the familiarity with XML necessary to this project.
4. Mario has limited experience in sales; ________, he is such an engaging individual that I feel he will soon be meeting quotas.
5. Timothy has written the bar exam three times. ___________, success has crowned his efforts.

Proofreading Marks

Symbol	Meaning	Symbol Used in Context	Corrected Copy
	Align horizontally	meaningful result	meaningful result
	Align vertically	1. Power cable 2. Keyboard	1. Power cable 2. Keyboard
	Capitalize	Pepsico, Inc.	PepsiCo, Inc.
	Center	Awards Banquet	Awards Banquet
	Close up space	self- confidence	self-confidence
	Delete	harrassment and abuse	harassment
ds	Double-space	text in first line text in second line ds	text in first line text in second line
	Insert	tirquoise shirts (u, and white)	turquoise and white shirts
	Insert apostrophe	our teams goals	our team s goals
	Insert comma	a, b and c	a, b, and c
	Insert hyphen	third quarter sales	third-quarter sales
	Insert period	Harrigan et al	Harrigan et al.
	Insert quotation marks	This team isn t cooperating.	This team isn t cooperating.
#	Insert space	realestate testcase	real estate test case
/	Lower case	TULSA, South of here	Tulsa, south of here
	Move down	Sincerely,	Sincerely,
	Move left	Attention: Security	Attention: Security
	Move right	February 2, 2004	February 2, 2004
	Move up	THIRD-QUARTER SALES	THIRD-QUARTER SALES
STET	Restore	staff talked openly and frankly STET	staff talked openly
	Run lines together	Manager, Distribution	Manager, Distribution
ss	Single space	ss text in first line text in second line	text in first line text in second line
	Spell out	COD	cash on delivery
sp	Spell out	sp Assn. of Biochem. Engrs.	Association of Biochemical Engineers
	Start new line	Marla Fenton, Manager, Distri- bution	Marla Fenton, Manager, Distribution
¶	Start new paragraph	¶ The solution is easy to determine but difficult to implement in a competitive environment like the one we now face.	The solution is easy to determine but difficult to implement in a competitive environment like the one we now face.
	Transpose	airy, light, casaul tone	light, airy, casual tone
bf	Use boldface	Recommendations bf	**Recommendations**
ital	Use italics	Quarterly Report ital	*Quarterly Report*

Endnotes

Chapter 1

1. Suncor Energy, *Suncor 2001 Annual Report*. No date. 19 Feb. and 1 Apr. 2003. <www.suncor.com/bins/ content_page.asp?cid=8-7-515>; Suncor Energy, Suncor *2001. Report on Sustainability*. No date. 19 Feb. and 1 Apr. 2003. <www.suncor.com/bins/ content_page.asp?cid=4-18-1777>; Sue Lee, "How Human Resources, Communications Help Drive Corporate Growth," *Canadian Speeches* 12.9 (Jan.-Feb. 1999): 65-71; Andrew Nikiforuk, "Saint or Sinner? Rick George Has Engineered a Dramatic Turnaround At Suncor, While Making Peace with the Greens," *Canadian Business* 13 May 2002: 54-56, 59+.

2. Joan L. Milne, "Do You Hear What I Hear? Survey Finds Poor Communication Devours Nearly Eight Workweeks Per Year," *Canadian Manager* 24.1 (1999): 5.

3. Milne, "Do You Hear What I Hear?" 5.

4. "Interpersonal Skills Are Key in Office of the Future," *TMA Journal* 19.4 (1999): 53.

5. Information drawn from the Canadian Telework Association. 1 Mar. 2003 <www.ivc.ca/studies/canadian studies.htm>.

6. "Interpersonal Skills Are Key in Office of the Future," *TMA Journal* 19.4 (1999): 53.

7. Lillian H. Chaney and Jeanette S. Martin, *Intercultural Business Communications* (Upper Saddle River, N.J.: Prentice Hall, 2000) 1–2.

8. "World at Home," *Maclean's* 3 Feb. 2003: 13.

9. "Canada's Multiculturalism Aids Trade Efforts, Pettigrew Says," *Canadian Press Newswire Online* 25 May 2000. 8 Mar. 2003 <cbca1.micromedia/ca>.

10. James M. Citrin and Thomas J. Neff, "Digital Leadership," *Strategy and Business,* First Quarter 2000: 42–50; Gary L. Neilson, Bruce A. Pasternack, and Albert J. Viscio, "Up the E-Organization," *Strategy and Business* First Quarter 2000: 52–61.

11. "How to Improve Communications," *Control Engineering* 45.12 (1998): 23.

12. "Did You Hear It Through the Grapevine?" *Training and Development* 48:10 (1994): 20.

13. Sierra, "Tell It to the Grapevine," *Communication World* 19.4 (2002): 28.

14. Adapted from Gina Connell, "Communicating in a Crisis," *Communication World* 19.6 (2002): 18-21; Peter V. Stanton, "Ten Communication Mistakes You Can Avoid When Managing a Crisis," *Public Relations Quarterly* 47.2 (2002): 19-22; Loretta Ucelli, "The CEO's 'how to' Guide to Crisis Communication," *Strategy & Leadership* 30.2 (2002): 21-24.

15. Some material adapted from, Courtland L. Bovée, et al. *Management* (New York: McGraw-Hill, 1993) 537–538.

16. Gillian Flynn, "Pillsbury's Recipe Is Candid Talk," *Workforce* Feb. 1998: 556–571.

17. Louise Kehoe, "Management Tools Slowly Taking Care of e-Mail Overload," *Financial Post (National Post)* 24 Jan. 2001: C8.

18. Bruce W. Speck, "Writing Professional Codes of Ethics to Introduce Ethics in Business Writing," *Bulletin of the Association for Business Communication* 53.3 (1990): 21–26; H.W. Love, "Communication, Accountability and Professional Discourse: The Interaction of Language Values and Ethical Values," *Journal of Business Ethics* 11 (1992): 883–892; Kathryn C. Rentz and Mary Beth Debs, "Language and Corporate Values: Teaching Ethics in Business Writing Courses," *Journal of Business Communication* 24.3 (1987): 37–48.

19. Hymonwitz, "If the Walls Had Ears You Wouldn't Have Any Less Privacy," *Wall Street Journal* 19 May 1998: B1.

20. Francis, "Work is a Warm Puppy," *National Post* 27 May 2000: W20; Hilary Davidson, "My Company is the Coolest," *Profit* Nov. 1999: 46–52; Jan Ravensbergen, "Software Firm Plays Hardball," *The Gazette (Montreal)* Dec. 1999: C1.

21. Kenneth Hein, "Hungry for Feedback," *Incentive* Sept. 1997: 91.

22. Suncor *2001 Report on Sustainability*; Nikoforuk, "Saint or Sinner?"

23. Michael H. Mescon et al., *Business Today,* 9th ed. (Upper Saddle River, N.J.: Prentice-Hall, 1999) 214.

24. Thomas A. Young, "Ethics in Business: Business of Ethics," *Vital Speeches* 15 Sept. 1992: 725–730.

25. David Grier, "Confronting Ethical Dilemmas: The View from Inside—A Practitioner's Perspective," *Vital Speeches* 1 Dec. 1989: 100–104.

26. Joseph L. Badaracco, Jr., "Business Ethics: Four Spheres of Executive Responsibility," *California Management Review* Spring 1992: 64–79; Kenneth Blanchard and Norman Vincent Peale, *The Power of Ethical Management (*New York: Ballantine Books, 1996) 7–17.

27. Blanchard and Peale, *The Power of Ethical Management* 7–17; Badaracco, "Business Ethics: Four Spheres of Executive Responsibility": 64–79.

28. Jules Harcourt, "Developing Ethical Messages: A Unit of Instruction for the Basic Business Communication Course," *Bulletin of the Association for Business Communication* 53.3 (1990): 17–20; John D. Pettit, Bobby Vaught, and Kathy J. Pulley, "The Role of Communication in Organizations," *Journal of Business Communication* 27.3 (1990): 233–249; Kenneth R. Andrews,

"Ethics in Practice," *Harvard Business Review* Sept.–Oct. 1989: 99–104; Priscilla S. Rogers and John M. Swales, "We the People? An Analysis of the Dana Corporation Policies Document," *Journal of Business Communication* 27.3 (1990): 293–313; Larry Reynolds, "The Ethics Audit," *Business Ethics* July–Aug. 1991: 120–122; Katherine Macklem, "Crooks in the Boardroom: Canadians Have Lost Their Confidence in Business Leaders," *Maclean's* 30 Dec. 2002: 30-31.

29. See note 1.

Chapter 2

1. Adapted from Royal Bank Financial Group Web site. Facts about Royal Bank. No date. 22 Feb. 2003. <www.royalbank.com.aboutus/index.html>; Royal Bank Financial Group Web site. *Royal Bank, 2001 Community Report*. No date. 22 Feb. 2003. <www.royalbank.com.aboutus.fastfacts.html>; Charles Coffey, executive vice-president, government & community affairs. RBC Financial Group, "Investing in People: Work/Life Solutions," speech delivered to the Robert Half International Breakfast Session, Toronto, ON, 15 Jan. 2003. 22 Feb. 2003. <www.rbc.com/newsroom/20030115coffey_1.html>; Kristi Nelson, "Royal Bank of Canada Optimizes Work Force," *Bank Systems + Technology* 39.6 (2002): 42.

2. Michael H. Mescon, Courtland L. Bovée, and John V. Thill, *Business Today* (Upper Saddle River, N.J.: Prentice-Hall, 1999) 203.

3. "Office Trends: More Teamwork, Less Personal Time," *Worklife Report* 13.3 (2001): 338.

4. "Teamwork Translates Into High Performance," *HR Focus* July 1998: 7.

5. Greg Crone, "Welcome to the Other Web: Loose Clusters, Not Rigid Contracts, Are the Future in Business," *Financial Post* 22 Jan. 1998: 11.

6. Glenn Parker, "Leading a Team of Strangers: Most Teams Now are Diverse or Virtual," *T&D* 57.2 (2003): 21.

7. Blaize Horner and Michelle L. Kaarst-Brown, "Seeding Innovation: IT Staff Can Make Even Better Business Partners by Sharing Their Knowledge," *National Post* 15 May 2001: M12.

8. Ellen Neuborne, "Companies Save, But Workers Pay," *USA Today* 25 Feb. 1997: B2; Richard L. Daft, *Management,* 4th ed. (Fort Worth: Dryden, 1997) 338; Richard Moderow, "Teamwork Is the Key to Cutting Costs," *Modern Healthcare* 29 Apr. 1996: 138.

9. Stephen P. Robbins, *Essentials of Organizational Behavior,* 6th ed. (Upper Saddle River, N.J.: Prentice Hall, 2000) 109.

10. Richard L. Daft, *Management,* 4th ed. (Fort Worth: Dryden, 1997) 612–615.

11. Robbins, *Essentials of Organizational Behavior* 98; Jean C. Baird and James J. Maroney, "When Are Two Auditors Better than One? Group Decision Making in Auditing," *CPA Journal* 70.2 (2000): 56.

12. John Alan Cohan, "'I Didn't Know' and 'I Was Only Doing My Job': Has Corporate Governance Careened Out Of Control? A Case Study of Enron's Information Myopia," *Journal of Business Ethics* 40.13 (2002): 275 (25pp.).

13. Mike Verespej, "Drucker Sours on Teams," *Industry Week* 6 Apr. 1998: 16+.

14. Aubrey B. Fisher, *Small Group Decision Making: Communication and the Group Process,* 2nd ed. (New York: McGraw-Hill, 1980) 145–149; Robbins and De Cenzo, *Fundamentals of Management* 334–335; Daft, *Management* 602–603.

15. Lawrence Magid, "Groupthink Can Be Fatal," *Information Week* 14 Apr. 1997: 114.

16. Lynda McDermott, Bill Waite, and Nolan Brawley, "Executive Teamwork," *Executive Excellence* May 1999: 15.

17. Larry Cole and Michael Cole, "Why Is the Teamwork Buzz Word Not Working?" *Communication World* Feb.-Mar. 1999: 29; Patricia Buhler, "Managing in the 90s: Creating Flexibility in Today's Workplace," *Supervision* Jan. 1997: 24+; Allison W. Amason, Allen C. Hochwarter, Wayne A. Thompson, and Kenneth R. Harrison, "Conflict: An Important Dimension in Successful Management Teams," *Organizational Dynamics* Autumn 1995: 20+.

18. Thomas K. Capozzoli, "Conflict Resolution—A Key Ingredient in Successful Teams," *Supervision* Nov. 1999: 14–16.

19. Daft, *Management* 609–612.

20. Amason, Hochwarter, Thompson, and Harrison, "Conflict: An Important Dimension in Successful Management Teams."

21. Jesse S. Nirenberg, *Getting Through to People* (Paramus, N.J.: Prentice-Hall, 1973) 134–142; Daniel Grigg and Jennifer Newman, "How to Harness Runaway Teams," *National Post (Financial Post)* 14 Apr. 2003: BE2.

22. Nirenberg, *Getting Through to People* 134–142.

23. Nirenberg, *Getting Through to People* 134–142.

24. William P. Galle Jr., Beverly H. Nelson, Donna W. Luse, and Maurice F. Villere, *Business Communication: A Technology-Based Approach* (Chicago: Irwin, 1996) 260.

25. Mary Beth Debs, "Recent Research on Collaborative Writing in Industry," *Technical Communication* Nov. 1991: 476–484.

26. Ruth G. Newman, "Communication: Collaborative Writing with Purpose and Style," *Personnel Journal* Apr. 1988: 37–38; Galle, Nelson, Luse, and Villere, *Business Communication* 256.

27. Jon Hanke, "Presenting as a Team," *Presentations* Jan. 1998: 74–82.

28. Julia Lawlor, "Videoconferencing: From Stage Fright to Stage Presence," *New York Times* 27 Aug. 1998: D6.

29. Heath Row, "The Joys of Togetherness," *Webmaster* June 1997: 44–48.

30. Vijay Govindarajan and Anil K. Gupta, "Building an Effective Global Business Team," *MIT Sloan Management Review* 42.4 (2001): 63.

31. Carla Joinson, "Managing Virtual Teams: Keeping Members on the Same

Page without Being in the Same Place Poses Challenges for Managers," *HR Magazine* 47.62: 68.

32. Joinson, "Managing Virtual Teams": 69.

33. Hanke, "Presenting as a Team": 74–82.

34. Robyn D. Clarke, "Do You Hear What I Hear?" *Black Enterprise* May 1998: 129; Dot Yandle, "Listening to Understand," *Pryor Report Management Newsletter Supplement* 15.8 (1998): 13.

35. Clarke, "Do You Hear What I Hear?"

36. Augusta M. Simon, "Effective Listening: Barriers to Listening in a Diverse Business Environment," *Bulletin of the Association for Business Communication* 54.3 (1991): 73–74.

37. Jennifer J. Salopek, "Is Anyone Listening," *Training & Development* 53.9 (1999): 58.

38. Bob Lamons, "Good Listeners Are Better Communicators," *Marketing News* 11 Sept. 1995: 13+; Phillip Morgan and H. Kent Baker, "Building a Professional Image: Improving Listening Behavior," *Supervisory Management* Nov. 1985: 35–36.

39. "An Added Joy of E-Mail: Fewer Face-to-Face Meetings," *Wall Street Journal* 14 July 1998: A1.

40. Laura Fowlie, "Gauging Success by One's Attributes, Not Resume: More Companies are Using the Competency Profile as a Benchmark In Assessing an Employee's Performance," *Financial Post* 17 Oct. 1998: R8.

41. "Listening: Hearing Better at Meetings," *Communication Briefings* 18.11 (1999): 2.

42. Ronald B. Adler and George Rodman, *Understanding Human Communication,* 8th ed. (New York: Oxford University Press, 2003) 124-132.

43. Adler and Rodman, *Understanding Human Communication* 126-130.

44. Adler and Rodman, *Understanding Human Communication* 132-133.

45. Adler and Rodman, *Understanding Human Communication* 135-145.

46. Sherwyn P. Morreale and Courtland L. Bovée, *Excellence in Public Speaking* (Orlando, Fla.: Harcourt Brace, 1998) 72–76; Lyman K. Steil, Larry L. Barker, and Kittie W. Watson, *Effective Listening: Key to Your Success* (Reading, Mass.: Addison-Wesley, 1983) 21–22.

47. Patrick J. Collins, *Say It with Power and Confidence (*Upper Saddle River, N.J.: Prentice-Hall, 1997) 40–45.

48. Collins, *Say It with Power and Confidence* 40–45.

49. Ann Warfield, "Do You Speak Body Language?" *Training & Development* 55.4 (2001): 60.

50. David Lewis, *The Secret Language of Success* (New York: Carroll & Graf, 1989) 67, 170; James Poon Teng Fatt, "Nonverbal Communication and Business Success," *Management Research News* 21.4/5: 1+; Warfield, "Do You Speak Body Language?" 60.

51. Dave Zielinski, "Body Language: What You Think You Know about Body Language May Be Hurting Your Career," *Presentations* 15.4 (2001): 36+.

52. Dale G. Leathers, *Successful Nonverbal Communication: Principles and Applications (*New York: Macmillan, 1986) 19.

53. Gerald H. Graham, Jeanne Unrue, and Paul Jennings, "The Impact of Nonverbal Communication in Organizations: A Survey of Perceptions," *Journal of Business Communication* 28.1 (1991): 45–62.

54. Zielinski, "Body Language: What You Think You Know about Body Language May Be Hurting Your Career" 36+.

55. Zielinski, "Body Language: What You Think You Know about Body Language May Be Hurting Your Career," 36+.

56. "Better Meetings Benefit Everyone: How to Make Yours More Productive," *Working Communicator Bonus Report* July 1998.

57. William C. Waddell and Thomas A. Rosko, "Conducting an Effective Off-Site Meeting," *Management Review* Feb. 1993: 40–44.

58. "Better Meetings Benefit Everyone: How to Make Yours More Productive," *Working Communicator Bonus Report* July 1998.

59. Kathy E. Gill, "Board Primer: Parliamentary Procedure," *Association Management* 1993: L-39.

60. See note 1.

Chapter 3

1. Based on information from the Malkam Cross-Cultural Training Web site. 4 July 2000 <www.malkam.com. news/KnowingMe.html>; 31 Mar. 2003 <www.malkam.com/news/cultural_taboos. htm>; 18 May 2003 <www.malkam.com/ CultureShock/Issue09.html>; Janet Baine, "Softening the Culture Shock: As Companies Begin Recruiting Abroad, the Need for Cultural Trainers is on the Rise," *SVN Canada* 6.6 (2001): B25; "Sharpening One's Soft Skills," *Computing Canada* 24 Aug. 2001: 25.

2. "Canada's Multiculturalism Aids Trade Efforts, Pettigrew Says," *Canadian Press Newswire* 25 May 2000. 8 Mar. 2003 <cbca1.micromedia/ca>.

3. Citizenship and Immigration Canada. "The Mirror" newsletter. Spring 2003. 18 May, 2003. <cicnet.ci.gc.ca/english/ monitor/issue01/02-immigrants.html>. The other countries in this list are Iran, South Korea, Romania, the United States, Sri Lanka, and the United Kingdom.

4. Hed N.Seelye and Alan Seelye-James, *Culture Clash (*Chicago: NTC Business Books, 1995) xv, xviii.

5. Sari Kalin, "The Importance of Being Multiculturally Correct," *Computerworld* 6 Oct. 1997: G16–G17.

6. Renee Huang, "The Fine Art of Canadian Conversation: More Firms are Offering On-Site Language Classes for Immigrant Staff," *The Globe and Mail* 17 Mar. 2003: C3.

7. Huang, "The Fine Art of Canadian Conversation" C3.

8. Baine, "Softening the Culture Shock" B25.

9. Philip R. Harris, and Robert T. Moran, *Managing Cultural Differences,*

3d ed. (Houston: Gulf, 1991) 394–397, 429–430.

10. William H. Chaney, and Jeanette S. Martin, *Intercultural Business Communication (*Upper Saddle River, N.J.: Prentice-Hall, 2000) 6.

11. Stephanie Strom, "Breaking from Tradition: Change Trickles Down the Ranks as Workers Rethink Benefit Plans," *Chicago Tribune* 5 July 1998: sec. G, 1, 3; Carley H. Dodd, *Dynamics of Intercultural Communication,* 3rd ed.: (Dubuque, I.A.: Brown, 1991) 50; Philip R. Harris and Robert T. Moran, *Managing Cultural Differences,* 3rd ed.: 140; David J. Stanley, "Japan's Uncertain Future: Key Trends and Scenarios," *Futurist* 36.2 (2002): 48-53.

12. Larry A. Samovar and Richard E. Porter, eds., "Basic Principles of Intercultural Communication," in *Intercultural Communication: A Reader,* 6th ed. (Belmont, C.A.: Wadsworth, 1991) 12.

13. Chaney and Martin, *Intercultural Business Communication* 11.

14. Gus Tyler, "Tokyo Signs the Paychecks," *The New York Times Book Review* 12 Aug. 1990: 7.

15. Chaney and Martin, *Intercultural Business Communication* 159.

16. Jennifer Campbell, "Firm Helps Worker, Employer Blend Cultures," *Ottawa Citizen* 16 Nov. 1998: D3.

17. Linda Beamer, "Teaching English Business Writing to Chinese-Speaking Business Students," *Bulletin of the Association for Business Communication* 57.1 (1994): 12–18.

18. Larry A. Samovar and Richard, E. Porter, eds., Edward T. Hall, "Context and Meaning" in *Intercultural Communication* 46–55.

19. Beamer, "Teaching English Business Writing to Chinese-Speaking Business Students."

20. Dodd, *Dynamics of Intercultural Communication:* 69–70; Iris Varner and Lisa Beamer, *Intercultural Communication in the Global Workplace (*Chicago: Irwin, 1995) 18; "Colombian Negotiating" (International Snapshot feature), *Sales & Marketing Management* 154.6 (2002): 64.

21. Chaney and Martin, *Intercultural Business Communication* 206–211.

22. Varner and Beamer, *Intercultural Communication in the Global Workplace* 229.

23. Varner and Beamer, *Intercultural Communication in the Global Workplace* 100.

24. James Wilfong and Toni Seger, *Taking Your Business Global* (Franklin Lakes, N.J.: Career Press, 1997) 277–278.

25. Harris and Moran, *Managing Cultural Differences* 260.

26. Skip Kaltenheuser, "Bribery Is Being Outlawed Virtually Worldwide," *Business Ethics* May–June 1998: 11; Thomas Omestad, "Bye-Bye to Bribes." *U.S. News & World Report,* 22 Dec. 1997: 39, 42–44.

27. Karen P. H. Lane, "Greasing the Bureaucratic Wheel," *North American International Business* Aug. 1990: 35–37; Arthur Aronoff, "Complying with the Foreign Corrupt Practices Act," *Business America* 11 Feb. 1991: 10–11; Bill Shaw, "Foreign Corrupt Practices Act: A Legal and Moral Analysis," *Journal of Business Ethics* 7, (1988): 789–795; Claudia Cattaneo, "An Exporter of Ethics," *Financial Post (National Post)* 13 Feb. 1999: D1, D6; Neville Nankivell, "New Legislation Forces Companies to Take Foreign Bribery Seriously: But Enforcing Anti-Corruption Law Will Be Tricky," *Financial Post (National Post)* 11 Feb. 1999: C7; Mike Trickery, "Code of Ethics for Conduction Business Overseas Developed by Group of Canadian Firms," *Calgary Herald* 5 Sept. 1997, final ed.: D6.

28. Guo-Ming Chen, and William J. Starosta, *Foundations of Intercultural Communication* (Boston: Allyn & Bacon, 1998) 288–289.

29. Sharon Ruhly, *Intercultural Communication,* 2d ed. MODCOM (Modules in Speech Communication) (Chicago: Science Research Associates, 1982) 14.

30. Robert O. Joy, "Cultural and Procedural Differences That Influence Business Strategies and Operations in the People's Republic of China," *SAM Advanced Management Journal* (1989): 29–33.

31. "Home Away from Home," *Ottawa HR.* July 2000. 18 May 2003. <www. malkam.com/news/homeaway.htm>.

32. Varner and Beamer, *Intercultural Communication in the Global Workplace* 156-157.

33. Varner and Beamer, *Intercultural Communication in the Global Workplace* 186.

34. Chaney and Martin, *Intercultural Business Communication* 122–123.

35. Chaney and Martin, *Intercultural Business Communication* 122–123.

36. Varner and Beamer, *Intercultural Communication in the Global Workplace* 154.

37. Dawn MacKeen, "Signs, Signs, Everywhere the Signs: In the World of International Business, Notes Author Roger E. Axtell," in "Innocuous Thumbs-Up Gesture Can Ruin a Deal," *The Globe and Mail* 9 Dec. 1998: B4.

38. Laray M. Barna, "Stumbling Blocks in Intercultural Communication," in *Intercultural Communication,* eds. Samovar and Porter, 345–352; Jean A. Mausehund, Susan A. Timm, and Albert S. King, "Diversity Training: Effects of an Intervention Treatment on Nonverbal Awareness," *Business Communication Quarterly* 38. 1 (1995): 27–30.

39. Chaney and Martin, *Intercultural Business Communication* 9.

40. Chen and Starosta, *Foundations of Intercultural Communication* 39–40.

41. Samovar and Porter, eds. Richard W. Brislin, "Prejudice in Intercultural Communication," *Intercultural Communication* 366–370.

42. James Culvert Scott, "Differences in American and British Vocabulary: Implications for International Business Communication," *Business Communication Quarterly* 63.4 (2000): 27.

43. Chaney and Martin, *Intercultural Business Communication* 130.

44. Varner and Beamer, *Intercultural Communication in the Global Workplace* 143-144.

45. Fawzia Sheikh, "Something Lost in the Translation," *Marketing* 24 Feb. 1997: 14.

46. Wilfong and Seger, *Taking Your Business Global* 232.

47. Vijay Govindarajan and Anil K.Gupta, "Building an Effective Global Business Team." *MIT Sloan Management Review* 42.4 (2001): 63+.

48. Varner and Beamer, *Intercultural Communication in the Global Workplace* 151.

49. Jensen J. Zhao and Calvin Parks, "Self-Assessment of Communication Behavior: An Experiential Learning Exercise for Intercultural Business Success," *Business Communication Quarterly* 58.1 (1995): 20–26; Dodd, *Dynamics of Intercultural Communication:* 142–143, 297–299; Stephen P. Robbins, *Organizational Behavior,* 6th ed. (Paramus, N.J.: Prentice-Hall, 1993) 345.

50. Mona Casady and Lynn Wasson, "Written Communication Skills of International Business Persons," *Bulletin of the Association for Business Communication* 57.4 (1994): 36–40.

51. Laura Morelli, "Writing for a Global Audience on the Web," *Marketing News* 17 Aug. 1998: 16; Yuri Radzievsky and Anna Radzievsky, "Successful Global Web Sites Look Through Eyes of the Audience," *Advertising Age's Business Marketing* Jan. 1998: 17; Sari Kalin, "The Importance of Being Multiculturally Correct," *Computerworld* 6 Oct. 1997: G16–G17; B.G. Yovovich, "Making Sense of All the Web's Numbers," *Editor & Publisher* Nov. 1998: 30–31; Sandra Mingail, "Cultural Context Lost in E-Sales," *Financial Post (National Post)* 8 Sept. 1999: E5.

52. "Cultural Context Lost in E-sales," *Financial Post (National Post)* 8 Sept. 1999: E5.

53. See note 1.

54. Michael Copeland, specialist, international training, personal communication, Jan. 1990.

Chapter 4

1. Adapted from The Forzani Group 2002 annual report; Ian Portsmouth, "Get in the Game," *Profit, the Magazine for* Apr. 2002: 27-28; Norman Ramage, "Forzani Covers the Field," *Marketing* Sept. 9, 2002: 14-15; Rhea Seymour, "Touchdown! John Forzani of Forzani Group Ltd," *Profit Magazine* Nov. 2001: 12.

2. Sanford Kaye, "Writing Under Pressure," *Soundview Executive Book Summaries* 10.12, part 2 (Dec. 1988): 1–8.

3. Peter Bracher, "Process, Pedagogy, and Business Writing," *Journal of Business Communication* 24.1 (1987): 43–50; Elizabeth Blackburn-Brockman, "Prewriting, Planning, and Professional Communication," *English Journal* (2001): 51-53; Thomas Clark, "Encouraging Critical Thinking in Business Memos," *Business Communication Quarterly* 61.3 (1998): 71-74.

4. Mahalingham Subbiah, "Adding a New Dimension to the Teaching of Audience Analysis: Cultural Awareness," *IEEE Transactions on Professional Communication* 35.1 (1992): 14–19; Ronald E. Dulek, John S. Fielden, and John S. Hill, "International Communication: An Executive Primer," *Business Horizons* Jan.–Feb. 1991: 20–25; Frances J. Ranney and Kevin M. McNeilly, "International Business Writing Projects: Learning Content through Process," *Business Communication Quarterly* 59.9 (1996): 9-17; Dwight W. Stevenson, "Audience Analysis Across Cultures," *Journal of Technical Writing and Communication* 13.4 (1983): 319–330.

5. Laurey Berk and Phillip G. Clampitt, "Finding the Right Path in the Communication Maze," *IABC Communication World* Oct. 1991: 28–32; Jenny C. McCune, "Working Together, but Apart," *Management Review* 87.8 (1998): 45-47.

6. Iris I. Varner, "Internationalizing Business Communication Courses," *Bulletin of the Association for Business Communication* 50.4 (1987): 7–11.

7. Berk and Clampitt, "Finding the Right Path in the Communication Maze."

8. Raymond M. Olderman, *10 Minute Guide to Business Communication* (New York: Alpha Books, 1997) 19–20.

9. Mohan R. Limaye and David A. Victor, "Cross-Cultural Business Communication Research: State of the Art and Hypotheses for the 1990s," *Journal of Business Communication* 28.3 (1991): 277–299.

10. Berk and Clampitt, "Finding the Right Path in the Communication Maze."

11. Berk and Clampitt, "Finding the Right Path in the Communication Maze."

12. Mike Bransby, "Voice Mail Makes a Difference," *Journal of Business Strategy* Jan.–Feb. 1990: 7–10.

13. D. Biersdorfer, "To Nail the Sale, E-Mail's Too Slow," *The New York Times,* 13 June 2001: 3; Heather Newman, "Instant Messaging a Communications Revolution," *San Diego Union-Tribune* 12 June 2001: 4.

14. Tim McCollum, "The Net Result of Computer Links," *Nation's Business* Mar. 1998: 55–58.

15. Elizabeth Blackburn and Kelly Belanger, "You-Attitude and Positive Emphasis: Testing Received Wisdom in Business Communication," *Bulletin of the Association for Business Communication* 56.2 (June 1993): 1–9.

16. Annette N. Shelby and N. Lamar Reinsch, Jr., "Positive Emphasis and You Attitude: An Empirical Study," *Journal of Business Communication* 32.4 (1995): 303–322.

17. Judy E. Pickens, "Terms of Equality: A Guide to Bias-Free Language," *Personnel Journal* Aug. 1985: 24.

18. Lisa Taylor, "Communicating About People with Disabilities: Does the Language We Use Make a Difference?" *Bulletin of the Association for Business Communication* 53.3 (1990): 65–67.

19. See note 1.

Chapter 5

1. Adapted from McCain Web site. 27 May 2003. <www.maccain.com/McCainWorldWide>; <www.maccain.com/McCainWorldWide/History>; <www.mccain.com/Faq/MakingOfaFrenchFry/MFF1.htm>; Steve Hemsley, "Extra Sensory Perception: There's Much More to Sampling than the Free Portions of Cheese on the Deli Counter," *Marketing Week* (Special Report: Field Marketing) 21 Nov. 2002: 41-42; Adam Pletch, "They Might Be Giants: Processors of the Century," *Food in Canada* 60.1 (2000): 16-20; Jill Vardy, "Fries From a Vending Machine McCain Shoestrings in Seconds," *National Post (Financial Post)* 27 Mar. 2002: FP1, FP11.

2. Susan Hall and Theresa Tiggeman, "Getting the Big Picture: Writing to Learn in a Finance Class," *Business Communication Quarterly* 58.1 (1995): 12–15.

3. Ernest Thompson, "Some Effects of Message Structure on Listener's Comprehension," *Speech Monographs* 34 (Mar. 1967): 51–57.

4. Based on the Pyramid Model developed by Barbara Minto of McKinsey & Company, management consultants.

5. Mi Young Park, W. Tracy Dillon, and Kenneth L. Mitchell, "Korean Business Letters: Strategies for Effective Complaints in Cross-Cultural Communications," *Journal of Business Communication* 35.3 (1998): 328-346.

6. Philip Subanks, "Messages, Models, and the Messy World of Memos," *Bulletin of the Association for Business Communication* 57.1 (1994): 33–34.

7. Mary A. DeVries, *Internationally Yours* (Boston: Houghton Mifflin, 1994) 61.

8. Anon. "In Plain View," *Saturday Night.* Sept. 1999: 11.

9. Anon. "Big Spin=Big Losses," *Research* 26.5 (May 2003): 22.

10. Peter Crow, "Plain English: What Counts Besides Readability?" *Journal of Business Communication* 25.1 (1988): 87–95.

11. Portions of this section are adapted from Courtland L. Bovée, *Techniques of Writing Business Letters, Memos, and Reports (*Sherman Oaks, C.A.: Banner Books International, 1978) 13–90.

12. Robert Hartwell Fiske, *Thesaurus of Alternatives to Worn-Out Words and Phrases* (Cincinnati: Writer's Digest Books, 1994) 171.

13. Iris I. Varner, "Internationalizing Business Communication Courses, "*Bulletin of the Association for Business Communication* 50.4 (1987): 7–11.

14. Jill H. Ellsworth and Matthew V. Ellsworth, *The Internet Business Book* (New York: Wiley, 1994) 91; Mary Munter, Priscilla S. Rogers, and Jone Rymer, "Business E-Mail: Guidelines for Users," *Business Communication Quarterly* 66.1: 27-40; Phillip Vassallo, "Egad! Another E-Mail: Using E-Mail Sensibly" (book review), *ETC: A Review of General Semantics* 59.4 (2002): 448-453.

15. Munter, Rogers, and Rymer, "Business E-mail: Guidelines for Users": 27.

16. Louise Kehoe, "Management Tools Slowly Taking Care of E-Mail Overload," *Financial Post* (*National Post*) 24 Jan. 2001: C8; Harold Taylor, "E-Mail is a Great Time Save, But—It Could also Become Too Much of Good Thing," *Canadian Manager* 26.3 (2001): 16, 28.

17. Vassallo, "Egad! Another E-Mail: Using E-mail Sensibly" 448-453.

18. Munter, Rogers, and Rymer, "Business E-Mail: Guidelines for Users" 31.

19. Vassallo. "Egad! Another E-Mail: Using E-Mail Sensibly" 448-453.

20. Munter, Rogers, and Rymer. "Business E-Mail: Guidelines for Users" 30.

21. Lance Cohen, "How to Improve Your E-Mail Messages," <galaxy.einet/galaxy/Business-and-Commerce/Management/Communications/How_to_Improve_Your Email.html>; Munter, Rogers, and Rymer, "Business E-Mail: Guidelines for Users" 31-32.

22. Jack Powers, Electric Pages, "Writing for the Web, Part I," 28 June 2000. <www.electric-pages.com/articles/wftw1.htm>.

23. Stephen H. Wildstrom, "You, Too, Can be a Webmaster," *Business Week* 3 Feb. 2003: 29+.

24. Nielsen, "Reading on the Web."

25. Reid Goldsborough, "Words for the Wise," *Link-Up* Sept.–Oct. 1999: 25–26.

26. Jakob Nielsen, "Failure of Corporate Websites," 23 April 2000. <www.useit.com/alertbox/981018. html>.

27. Holtz, "Writing for the Wired World" 72–73.

28. Holtz, "Writing for the Wired World" 95.

29. "Web Writing: How to Avoid Pitfalls," *Investor Relations Business* 1 Nov. 1999: 15.

30. Lerner, "Building Worldwide Websites."

31. Morkes and Nielsen, "How to Write for the Web."

32. Holstead, "Three Steps to Web-Smart Editing."

33. See note 1.

34. Based on Milton Moskowitz, Michael Katz, and Robert Levering, eds., *Everybody's Business: An Almanac* (San Francisco: Harper & Row, 1980) 131.

35. Randolph H. Hudson, Gertrude M. McGuire, and Bernard J. Selzler, *Business Writing: Concepts and Applications* (Los Angeles: Roxbury, 1983) 27.

36. Susan Benjamin, *Words at Work* (Reading, Mass.: Addison-Wesley, 1997) 121.

Chapter 6

1. Based on interview with Anna MacDonald Publicist, Confederation Centre of the Arts, email interview with author, 12 Dec. 2003; Confederation Centre of the Arts Web site. 11 June 2003. <www.confederationcentre.ca/press.asp>; <www.confederationcentre.ca/history/asp>; <www.confederationcentre.ca/news.asp>.

2. Varner, "Internationalizing Business Communication Courses,": 7–11.

3. Kevin T. Stevens, Kathleen C. Stevens, and William P. Stevens, "Measuring the Readability of Business Writing: The Cloze Procedure versus Readability Formulas," *Journal of Business Communication* 29.4 (1992): 367–382; Alinda Drury, "Evaluating Readability," *IEEE Transactions on Professional Communication* PC-28 (1985): 11; Cynthia Crossen, "If You Can Read This, You Most Likely are a High-School Grad—Software Gauging Readability Goes for Short Sentences and Not So Many Syllables," *The Wall Street Journal* 1 Dec. 2000: A1.

4. Susan Benjamin, *Words at Work* (Reading, Mass.: Addison-Wesley, 1997) 71.

5. William Zinsser, *On Writing Well,* 5th ed. (New York: HarperCollins, 1994) 126.

6. Mary A. DeVries, *Internationally Yours* (Boston: Houghton Mifflin, 1994) 160.

7. Zinsser *On Writing Well* vii–12.

8. Zinsser *On Writing Well* 9.

9. Joel Haness, "How to Critique a Document," *IEEE Transactions on Professional Communication* PC-26 1 (March 1983): 15–17.

10. Charles E. Risch, "Critiquing Written Material," *Manage* 35.4 (1983): 4–6.

11. Risch, "Critiquing Written Material."

12. Portions of the following sections are adapted from Roger C. Parker, *Looking Good in Print,* 2d ed. (Chapel Hill, N.C.: Ventana Press, 1990).

13. Raymond W. Beswick, "Designing Documents for Legibility," *Bulletin of the Association for Business Communication* 50.4 (1987): 34–35.

14. Patsy Nichols, "Desktop Packaging," *Bulletin of the Association for Business Communication* 54.1 (1991): 43–45; Beswick, "Designing Documents for Legibility."

15. Beswick, "Designing Documents for Legibility."

16. "The Process Model of Document Design," *IEEE Transactions on Professional Communication* PC-24 4 (1981): 176–178.

17. William Wresch, Donald Pattow, and James Gifford, *Writing for the Twenty-First Century: Computers and Research Writing* (New York: McGraw-Hill, 1988) 192–211; Melissa E. Barth, *Strategies for Writing with the Computer* (New York: McGraw-Hill, 1988) 108–109, 140, 172–177.

18. Mary Munter, Priscilla S. Rogers, and Jone Rymer, "Business E-Mail: Guidelines for Users," *Business Communication Quarterly* 66.1: 27-40; Philip, Vassallo, "Egad! Another E-Mail: Using E-Mail Sensibly" (book review), *ETC: A Review of General Semantics* 59.4 (2002): 448-453.

19. Susan Avery, "More Reliable than E-Mail, Fax Delivers Peace of Mind," *Purchasing* 132.7 (2003): 49-50.

20. Munter, Rogers, and Rymer, "Business E-Mail: Guidelines for Users" 35-40.

21. See note 1.

Chapter 7

1. Based Indigo Books and Music Web site. Home Page. 24 Aug. 2000, 23 June 2003 <www.indigo.ca>; Paul Brent, "High-Stakes Holiday: The Chapters and Indigo Bookstore Chains are Spending Millions to Take Their Main Street Rivalry into Electronic Commerce," *Financial Post* 13 Nov. 1999: D1; Mikala Folb, "Online Book Boom: Canadian Booksellers Aren't About to Equal Amazon.com's Revenues, but Sales of up to $50 million this Year ain't Shabby," *Marketing Magazine* 25 Jan. 1999: 15–16; Geoff Kirbyson, "Bookseller has More than 200 Employees, Annual Revenues of $15 Million," *Winnipeg Free Press* 15 Sept. 2000: B5; John Lorinc, "The Indigo Way: Stylish and Savvy, Canada's #2 Chain Marches to Its Own Beat," *Quill & Quire* 66.2 (2000): 22–23; Katherine Macklem, "The Book Lady," *Maclean's* 26 Feb. 2001: 40-45; Hollie Shaw, "Amazon Not in Breach of Book Sale Laws: Canadian Heritage Rules in Favor of U.S. Internet Giant," *Financial Post (National Post)* 11 July 2002: FP1, FP10; Kate MacNamara, "Big-Box Book Emporia Are Losing their Lustre," *Financial Post (National Post)* 18 Feb. 2003: FP7; "Sales, Earnings Increase at Indigo." *Publishers Weekly* 9 June 2003: 22.

2. Julie McAlpine, "10 Steps for Reducing Exposure to Wrongful Dismissal," *Canadian HR Reporter* 6 May 2002: 8.

3. Daniel P. Finkelman and Anthony R. Goland, "Customers Once Can Be Customers for Life," *Information Strategy: The Executive's Journal* (1990): 5–9.

4. *Techniques for Communicators* (Chicago: Lawrence Ragan Communication, 1995) 34, 36.

5. Donna Larcen, "Authors Share the Words of Condolence," *Los Angeles Times* Dec. 20, 1991: E11.

6. See note 1.

7. Adapted from Floorgraphics Web site. 18 June 2001. <www.floor graphics.com>; John Grossman, "It's an Ad, Ad, Ad, Ad World," *Inc.* Mar. 2000: 23–26; David Wellman, "Floor 'Toons," *Supermarket Business* 15 Nov. 1999: 47; "Floorhsow," *Dallas Morning News* 4 Sept. 1998: 11D.

8. Eben Shapiro, "Blockbuster Rescue Bid Stars Viacom Top Guns," *The Wall Street Journal* 7 May 1997: B1, B10.

9. Adapted from Michael M. Phillips, "Carving Out an Export Industry, and Hope, in Africa," *The Wall Street Journal* 18 July 1996: A8.

10. Based on Canada's SchoolNet Web site. 11 Dec. 2000. <www.schoolnet.ca>.

11. "Entrepreneurs across America," *Entrepreneur Magazine Online,* 12 June 1997 <www.entrepreneurmag.com/ entmag/50states5.hts>.

12. Adapted from Barbara Carton, "Farmers Begin Harvesting Satellite Data to Boost Yields," *The Wall Street Journal* 11 July 1996: B4.

13. "Entrepreneurs across America," *Entrepreneur Magazine Online,* 12 June 1997 <www.entrepreneurmag.com/ entmag/50states5.hts#top>.

14. Sal D. Rinalla and Robert J. Kopecky, "Recruitment: Burger King Hooks Employees with Educational Incentives," *Personnel Journal* Oct. 1989: 90–99.

15. Adapted from Bernard Weinraub, "New Harry Potter Book Becoming a Publishing Phenomenon," *The New York Times* 3 July 2000. 12 July 2000. <www.nytimes.com/ library/books>.

16. Based on Sal D. Rinalla and Robert J. Kopecky, "Recruitment: Burger King Hooks Employees with Educational Incentives," *Personnel Journal* Oct. 1989: 90–99.

17. Based on ABC Canada Literacy Foundation Web site, 18 Dec. 2000 <www.abc-canada.org>.

18. Based on Ace Canada Web site, 15 Dec. 2000 <www.acecanada.ca>.

Chapter 8

1. Based on Wal-Mart Web site. 19 Dec. 2000, 30 June 2003. <www.walmart stores.com/wmstores/wmstores/Mainsu pplier.jsp?>; Kevin Libin, "The Last Retailer in Canada?" *Canadian Business* 18 Mar. 2002: 30 (9pp.); Hollie Shaw, "Wal-Mart bring Sam's Club to Canada," *National Post* 23 Nov. 2002: FP1.

2. Mark H. McCormack, *On Communicating* (Los Angeles: Dove Books 1998) 87.

3. James Calvert Scott and Diana J. Green, "British Perspectives on Organizing Bad-News Letters: Organizational Patterns Used by Major U.K. Companies," *Bulletin of the Association for Business Communication* 55.1 (1992): 17–19.

4. Ram Subramanian, Robert G. Insley, and Rodney D. Blackwell, "Performance and Readability: A Comparison of Annual Reports of Profitable and Unprofitable Corporations," *Journal of Business Communication* 30.2 (1993): 49–61.

5. Subramanian, Insley, and Blackwell, "Performance and Readability: A Comparison of Annual Reports of Profitable and Unprofitable Corporations": 49–61.

6. See "Case Notes," *Focus on Canadian Employment & Equality Rights* 5.24 (1999): 188; Stacey Ball, "Employers Should Exercise Care When Writing References for Former Employees," *Financial Post* 1-3 June 1996: 21; Howard Levitt, "If You Can't Say Something Good, Say Something Bad," *Financial Post (National Post)* 27 Nov. 1998: C17; "Employers Layoffs and Terminations Across Canada," *Employers Online.* 29 Dec. 2000 <employers.gc.ca>.

7. "Protecting Your Firm," *Canadian HR Reporter* 24 Mar. 2003: 5.

8. David Smith, "When Called for a Reference," *Computing Canada* 26 May 2000: 35.

9. Ball, "Employers Should Exercise Care When Writing References for Former Employees" 21.

10. Judi Brownell, "The Performance Appraisal Interviews: A Multipurpose Communication Assignment," *The Bulletin of the Association for Business Communication* 57.2 (1994): 11–21; Tom Davis and Michael J. Landa, "A Contrary Look at Employee Performance Appraisals," *Canadian Manager* 24.3 (1999): 18–19; Laura Fowlie, "Make Your Next Performance Review Count: Much of the Anxiety Surrounding the Dreaded Meeting Can Be Minimized With a Bit of Preparation," *Financial Post* 11/13 Apr. 1998: R14; Laura Ramsay, "Time to Examine the Exam: Mostly Everyone Dreads a Performance Appraisal, and for Good Reasons," *Financial Post (National Post)* 18 Oct. 1999: C15; Lauren M. Bernardi, "Powerful Performance Evaluations [Excerpts from *Powerful Employment Policies*]," *Canadian Manager* 26.1 (2001): 18-20+; John Joynor, "Performance Reviews: A Blueprint for Growth," *Computing Canada* 29 June 2001: 24.

11. Brownell, "The Performance Appraisal Interviews"; Bernardi, "Powerful Performance Evaluations [Excerpts from *Powerful Employment Policies*]"; Sandy French, "Conversations that Matter: Communicating Effectively in Difficult Situations." *Canadian HR Reporter* 28 Jan. 2002: 12.

12. Stephanie Gruner, "Feedback from Everyone," *Inc.* Feb. 1997: 102–103.

13. Bernardi, "Powerful Performance Evaluations [Excerpts from *Powerful Employment Policies*]."

14. Patricia A. McLagan, "Advice for Bad-News Bearers: How to Tell Employees They're Not Hacking It and Get Results," *Industry Week* 15 Feb. 1993: 42; Michael Lee Smith, "Give Feedback, Not Criticism," *Supervisory Management* 1993: 4; "A Checklist for Conducting Problem Performer Appraisals," *Supervisory Management* Dec. 1993: 7–9; French, "Conversations that Matter: Communicating Effectively in Difficult Situations": 12; Bernardi, "Powerful Performance Evaluations [Excerpts from *Powerful Employment Policies*]."

15. See note 1.

16. "Swimmer Invents Pool Tool," *The Coast News* 13 Aug. 1998: A-15.

17. Adapted from Craftopia.com print advertisement, 31 July 2000; Craftopia.com Web site. 24 Aug. 2000 <www.craftopia.com/ shop/promo/martha3.asp>; Claire Furia Smith, "West Chester Start-up Tries to Become a Crafters' Utopia," *Philadelphia Inquirer* 26 June 2000. 24 August 2000 <www. craftopia.com/shop/features/ about_us_mc_6_26_00_ inquirer.asp>; Laura M. Naughton, Crafting a Niche," *Daily Local News* 8 Mar. 2000. 24 Aug. 2000 <www.craftopia.com/shop/features/ about_us_mc_3_8_00_dailylocal.asp>

18. Adapted from Wolf Blitzer, "More Employers Taking Advantage of New Cyber-Surveillance Software," *CNN.com.* 10 July 2000. 11 July 2000 <www.cnn.com/2000/US/07/10/ workplace.eprivacy/index.html>, Stephen Mill, "Creating Corporate E-Mail Policies: Guidelines Must Promote a Productive Work Environment, but Not Make Employees Feel Monitored," *Computing Canada* 27.23 (2001): 23.

19. Based on Michelle Higgins, "The Ballet Shoe Gets a Makeover, But Few Yet See the Pointe," *The Wall Street Journal* 8 Aug. 1998: A1, A6.

20. Adapted from Robert Johnson, "Your Little Monkey Is So Cuddly. Here, Let Me—OUCH!" *The Wall Street Journal* 2 Dec. 1991: A1, A14.

21. Adapted from Michael H. Mescon, Courtland L. Bovée, and John V. Thill. *Business Today,* 10th ed. (Upper Saddle River, N.J.: Prentice-Hall, 2002) 369; Bruce Upbin, "Profit in a Big Orange Box," *Forbes* 24 Jan. 2000. 2 Aug. 2001 <www.forbes.com/forbes/2000/0124/6502122a.html>.

22. Pascal Zachary, "Sun Microsystems Apologizes in Letter for Late Payments," *The Wall Street Journal* 11 Oct. 1989: B4.

23. Based on "Campbell Pulls School Program," *Marketing Magazine* 6 Mar. 2000: 1; Danny Kucharsky, "Navigating Quebec's Promo Regulations," *Marketing Magazine* 3 Apr. 2000: 20–21; Campbell's Web site. 17 Dec. 2000 <www. campbellsoup.ca>.

24. Based on "No cell calls on Nfld. roads." *The Gazette* (Montreal) 24 Aug. 2003: A4; Ellen van Wangeningen, "Fatal Driver Pleads Guilty." *Windsor Star* 25 Feb. 2003: A5.

25. Adapted from Associated Press, "Children's Painkiller Recalled." CNN.com/Health Web site. 16 August 2001. 22 August 2001 <www.cnn.com/2001/HEALTH/parenting/08/16/kids.drug.recalled.ap/index.html>; Perrigo Company Web site. 29 August 2001 <www.perrigo.com>.

Chapter 9

1. Based on Young Entrepreneurs' Association Web site, 15 Dec. 2000. 15 July 2003 <www.yea.ca>.

2. Jay A. Conger, "The Necessary Art of Persuasion," *Harvard Business Review* May–June 1998: 84–95; Jeanette W. Gisldorf, "Write Me Your Best Case for . . ." *Bulletin of the Association for Business Communication* 54.1 (1991): 7–12.

3. Anne Fisher, "Success Secret: A High Emotional IQ," *Fortune* 16 Oct. 1998: 293–298.

4. Mary Cross, "Aristotle and Business Writing: Why We Need to Teach Persuasion," *Bulletin of the Association for Business Communication* 54.1 (1991): 3–6.

5. Based on Susan Pinker, "Poor People Skills Can Wreak Havoc," (Problem-Solving Column) *The Globe and Mail* 16 July 2003: C2.

6. Robert T. Moran, "Tips on Making Speeches to International Audiences," *International Management* Apr. 1980: 58–59.

7. Conger. "The Necessary Art of Persuasion."

8. Gilsdorf, "Write Me Your Best Case for . . ."

9. Raymond M. Olderman, *10-Minute Guide to Business Communication* (New York: Macmillan Spectrum/Alpha Books, 1997) 57–61.

10. Gilsdorf. "Write Me Your Best Case for . . ."

11. John D. Ramage and John C. Bean, *Writing Arguments: A Rhetoric with Readings,* 3d ed. (Boston: Allyn & Bacon, 1995) 430–442.

12. Conger, "The Necessary Art of Persuasion."

13. Dianna Booher, *Communicate with Confidence* (New York: McGraw-Hill, 1994) 110.

14. Tamra B. Orr, "Persuasion without Pressure," *Toastmaster* Jan. 1994: 19–22; William Friend, "Winning Techniques of Great Persuaders," *Association Management* Feb. 1985: 82–86; Patricia Buhler, "How to Ask For—and Get—What You Want!" *Supervision* Feb. 1990: 11–13.

15. Booher, *Communicate with Confidence* 102.

16. Conger, "The Necessary Art of Persuasion."

17. Robert L. Hemmings, "Think Before You Write," *Fund Raising Management* Feb. 1990: 23–24.

18. William North Jayme, quoted in Albert Haas Jr., "How to Sell Almost Anything by Direct Mail," *Across the Board* Nov. 1986: 50; "How to Adapt Mail to Boost Response," *Marketing* 10 Jan. 2002: 23; "Direct Mail Showcase," *Marketing* 3 Oct. 2002: 25.

19. Teri Lammers, "The Elements of Perfect Pitch," *Inc.* Mar. 1992: 53–55; "How to Adapt Mail to Boost Response," *Marketing*.

20. Kimberly Paterson, "The Writing Process—Sales Letters That Work," *Rough Notes* Apr. 1998: 59–60.

21. Paterson, "The Writing Process."

22. Lynn Greiner, "Spamming Should Be a Crime," *Computing Canada* 14 Mar. 2003: 20; Jonathan Fowlie, "Ottawa Looking for Way to Can the Spam," *The Globe and Mail* 24 Jan. 2003: A1.

23. Hemmings, "Think Before You Write."

24. Dean Reick, "Using an Emotional Appeal to Boost Your Direct Mail Response," *Fund Raising Management* 31.3 (2000): 24.

25. Hemmings, "Think Before You Write"; Jenny Printz and Dwight Maltby, "Beyond Personalization: When Handwriting Makes a Difference," *Fund Raising Management* 28.3 (1997): 16-20.

26. Conrad Squires, "How to Write a Strong Letter, Part Two: Choosing a Theme," *Fund Raising Management* Nov. 1991: 65–66; Dean Reick, "Powerful Fund Raising Letters—From A to Z (part 1)," *Fund Raising Management* 29.2 (1998): 25-29.

27. Reick, "Powerful Fund Raising Letters."

28. Printz and Maltby, "Beyond Personalization: When Handwriting Makes a Difference."

29. Constance L. Clark, "25 Steps to Better Direct Mail Fundraising," *Nonprofit World* July–Aug. 1989: 11–13.

30. Conrad Squires, "Why Some Letters Outpull Others," *Fund Raising Management* 21.11 (1991): 67, 72.

31. Squires, "Why Some Letters Outpull Others"; Clark, "25 Steps to Better Direct Mail Fundraising"; Jerry Huntsinger, "My First 29 1/2 Years in Direct-Mail Fund Raising: What I've Learned," *Fund Raising Management* 22.11 (1992): 40–43.

32. Roscos Barnes III, "Letter-Opening Copy: What TV Journalists Can Teach Us About Teasing Donors, and Getting Them to Open Our Mail," *Fund Raising Management* 32.5 (2001): 36.

33. Reick, "Powerful Fund Raising Letters."

34. Nicole Rivard, "Facilitating Fundraising," *University Business* 6.6 (2003): 68.

35. Jerry Huntsinger, "It's Not Contagious," *The Non-Profit Times* 15 July 2001: 22.

36. 21 July 2003, <www.petsmart.com/charities/petsmart_charities/about_petsmart_charities.shtml>.

37. See note 1.

38. Adapted from Andrew Ferguson, "Supermarket of the Vanities," *Fortune* 10 June 1996: 30, 32.

39. Kevin M. Savetz, "Preventive Medicine for the Computer User," *Multimedia Online* 2.2 (1996): 58–60.

40. Adapted from John Case and Jerry Useem, "Six Characters in Search of a Strategy," *Inc.* Mar. 1996: 46–49.

41. Adapted from Peter Coy, "Peddling Better Bike Designs," *Business Week* 1 July 1996: 103.

42. Adapted from Mescon, Bovée, and Thill, *Business Today* 306-307; John R. Hall, "Recruiting via the Internet," *Air Conditioning, Heating & Refrigeration News*, 9 April 2001: 26; Kim Peters, "Five Keys to Effective E-cruiting," *Ivey Business Journal* (London, ON), Jan.-Feb. 2001: 8-10; C. Glenn Pearce and Tracy L. Tuten, "Internet Recruiting in the Banking Industry," *Business Communication Quarterly* (Mar.) 64.1: 9-18; Christopher Caggiano, "The Truth About Internet Recruiting," *Inc.* Dec. 1999: 156.

43. Adapted from Cathy Werblin, "Korean Business Owners Want Signs to Mark Area," *Los Angeles Times* 29 Mar. 1997: B3.

44. Adapted from Karen E. Klein and Steve Scauzillo, "The Fuel Cell Future," *The World & I* Apr. 1994: 192–99; Ballard Power Systems Web site. Home Page. *1999 Ballard Power Systems Annual Report*. 1 May 2001 <www.ballard.com>.

45. Adapted from Steve Bass, "ISDN Not; The Agony, the Ecstasy, the Migraines," *Computer Currents* 7 May 1996: 9.

46. Adapted from advertisement, *The Atlantic Monthly* Jan. 2000: 119; Endless Pools, Inc. Web site. Home Page. 31 August 2000 <www.endlesspools.com>.

47. Adapted from Gateway Web site. Home Page. 2 Oct. 2001 <www.gateway.com>; Gateway customer service sales representative, 1-800-GATEWAY, personal interview, 10 Oct. 2001.

48. Adapted from Charles Fishman, "The Greener Cleaners," *Fast Company* 36: 54. 11 July 2000 <fastcompany.com/online/36/greenclean.html>; Micell Technologies Web site. 1 Sept. 2000 <www.micell.com/08142000.htm>; Hangers Cleaners Web site. 1 Sept. 2000 <www.hangersdrycleaners.com/about/corp/triplebottom line.htm>.

49. Adapted from "Down These Aisles Is Matrimonial Bliss," *Los Angeles Times* 22 Mar. 1996: D3.

50. Adapted from Chris Pasles, "Long Beach Opera Cancels Rest of Season as Deal Nears," *Los Angeles Times* 16 May 1996: F4, F9.

Chapter 10

1. Adapted from Dell Computer Corporation's Web site. Home Page. 22 March 2000 <www.dell.com>; Neel Chowdhury, "Dell Cracks China," *Fortune* 21 June 1999: 120–124; Michael Dell with Catherine Fredman, *Direct from Dell* (New York: HarperCollins Publishers, 1999) 8–15, 36–38, 66–80, 92–101, 133, 144, 175–182, 186, 196–197, 208; Louise Fickel, "Know Your Customer," *CIO* 15 Aug. 1999: 62–72; Interview: E-commerce Drives Dell Computer's Success," *IT Cost Management Strategies* June 1999: 4–6; Carla Joinson, "Moving at the Speed of Dell," *HRMagazine* Apr. 1999: 50–56; Daniel Roth, "Dell's Big New Act," *Fortune* 6 Dec. 1999: 152–156; Vawn Himmelbach, "Dell Eyes First Place," *Computer Dealer News* 21 Apr. 2000: 1-2.

2. Shin-Lin Chan, "Testing the Limits of Online Annual Reports," *National Post* 3 June 2000: E1.

3. Dan Steinhoff and John F. Burgess, *Small Business Management Fundamentals,* 5th ed. New York: (McGraw-Hill, 1989) 37.

4. Joan F. Vesper and Karl H. Vesper, "Writing a Business Plan: The Total Term Assignment," *Bulletin of the Association for Business Communication* 56.2 (1993): 29–32.

5. Tom Sant, *Persuasive Business Proposals,* New York: American Management Association, 1992, summarized in *Soundview Executive Book Summaries* 14.10, pt. 2 (Oct. 1992): 3.

6. Iris T. Varner, *Contemporary Business Report Writing,* 2nd ed. (Chicago: Dryden Press, 1991) 170.

7. Varner, *Contemporary Business Report Writing* 178.

8. Bruce McComiskey, "Defining Institutional Problems: A Heuristic Procedure," *Business Communication Quarterly* 58.4 (1995): 21–24.

9. Varner, *Contemporary Business Report Writing:* 135.

10. Information for this section was obtained from "Finding Industry Information," 3 Nov. 1998 <www.pitt.edu/~buslibry/industries.htm>; Thomas P. Bergman, Stephen M. Garrison, and Gregory M. Scott, *The Business Student Writer's Manual and Guide to the Internet* (Upper Saddle River, N.J.: Prentice Hall, 1998) 67–80; Ernest L. Maier, et al., *The Business Library and How to Use It* (Detroit: Omnigraphics, 1996) 53–76; Sherwyn P. Morreale and Courtland L. Bovée, *Excellence in Public Speaking* (Fort Worth: Harcourt Brace College Publishers, 1998) 166–171.

11. "The Research Site's Fairy Godmother Report," *What Color Is Your Parachute Online*. 10 Oct. 1998 <www.washingtonpost.com/wp~adv/classifieds/careerpost/parachute/reseajhg.htm>.

12. Ernest L. Maier, et al., *The Business Library and How to Use It* (Detroit: Omnigraphics, 1996) 84–97; Matt Lake, "Desperately Seeking Susan OR Suzie NOT Sushi," *The New York Times* 3 Sept. 1998: D1, D7.

13. "How to Design and Conduct a Study," *Credit Union Magazine* Oct. 1983: 36–46; see also Arlene Fink, *How to Design Surveys* (Thousand Oaks, C.A.: Sage, 1995).

14. Erin White, "Market Research on the Internet Has Its Drawbacks," *The Wall Street Journal* 2 Mar. 2000: B4.

15. Sherwyn P. Morreale and Courtland L. Bovée, *Excellence in Public Speaking*: 177.

16. Morreale and Bovée, *Excellence in Public Speaking* 178–180.

17. Morreale and Bovée, *Excellence in Public Speaking* 182.

18. David A. Aaker and George S. Day, *Marketing Research,* 2d ed. (New York: Wiley, 1983) 88–89; Esther Grassian, *Thinking Critically about World Wide Web Resources.* 2 Feb. 2001 <www.library.ucla.edu/libraries/college/help/critical/index.htm>.

19. Robert E. Cason, *Writing for the Business World* (Upper Saddle River, N.J.: Prentice-Hall, 1997) 102.

20. Thomas P. Bergman, Stephen M. Garrison, and Gregory M. Scott, *The Business Student Writer's Manual and Guide to the Internet,* (Upper Saddle River, N.J.: Prentice-Hall, 1998) 65.

21. *How to Paraphrase Effectively: 6 Steps to Follow.* Research paper.com. 26 October 1998 <www.researchpaper.com/writing_center/30.html>.

22. Cason, *Writing for the Business World* 71–72.

23. Dorothy Geisler, "How to Avoid Copyright Lawsuits," *IABC Communication World* June 1984: 34–37; see <canada.justice.gc.ca/en/cons/jeh/britt.html> 31 July 2003.

24. See note 1.

Chapter 11

1. Adapted from Federal Express Web site. 27 October 1997. 1 Aug. 2003 <www.fedex.com/ca_english/business tools/toolsbyplatform>; <www.fedex.com/ca_english/businesstools/tools byfunction>; UPS Web site. Home Page. 27 Oct. 1997. 19 Jan. 2001 <www.ups.com>; DHL Web site. Home Page. 27 Oct. 1997. 19 Jan. 2001 <www.dhl.com>; Airborne Express Web site. Home Page. 27 Oct. 1997. 19 Jan. 2001 <www.airborne.com>; Hoover's Online. 27 Oct. 1997. 19 Jan. 2001 <www.hoovers.com>; "All Strung Up," *The Economist* 17 Apr. 1993: 70; Gary M. Stern, "Improving Verbal Communications," *Internal Auditor* Aug. 1993: 49–54; Gary Hoover, Alta Campbell, and Patrick J. Spain, *Hoover's Handbook of American Business 1994* (Austin, TX: Reference Press, 1993) 488–489; "Pass the Parcel," *The Economist* 21 Mar. 1992: 73–74; "Federal Express," *Personnel Journal* Jan. 1992: 52.

2. This section is based on John V. Thill and Courtland L. Bovée, *Excellence in Business Communication,* 4th ed. (Upper Saddle River, N.J.: Prentice-Hall, 1999) 314.

3. Sheri Rosen, "What Is Truth?" *IABC Communication World* Mar. 1995: 40.

4. Edward R. Tufte, *The Visual Display of Quantitative Information* (Cheshire, Conn.: Graphic Press, 1983) 113.

5. Courtland L. Bovée, Michael J. Houston, and John V. Thill, *Marketing,* 2d ed. (New York: McGraw-Hill, 1995) 250.

6. Eleanor Rizzo, "Document Design Basics," *Technical Communication* Fourth Quarter (1992): 645.

7. A.S.C. Ehrenberg, "Report Writing—Six Simple Rules for Better Business Documents," *Admap* June 1992: 39–42.

8. See note 1.

9. *Advertising Age* 29 Sept. 1997: S63.

10. Adapted from Bob Smith, "The Evolution of Pinkerton," *Management Review* Sept. 1993: 54–58.

11. See note 1.

Chapter 12

1. Adapted from <www.dofasco.ca/NEWS/mediakit.html> 17 Aug. 2003; <www.dofasco.ca/CORPORATE_PROFILE/sustain.html> 18 Aug. 2003; *Dofasco Inc. 2002 Annual Report*; Ian Hamilton, Manager, Corporate Communications, Dofasco, e-mail, 15 Jan. 2002; Monika Rola, "Dofasco Retools to Create 'Communities of Practice,'" *Compute Canada* 11 Apr. 2003: 6.

2. Oswald M. T. Ratteray, "Hit the Mark with Better Summaries," *Supervisory Management* Sept. 1989: 43–45.

3. See note 1.

4. Adapted from William C. Symonds, "Giving It the Old Online Try," *Business Week* 3 Dec. 2001: 76–80; Karen Frankola, "Why Online Learners Drop Out," *Workforce* Oct. 2001: 52–60; Mary Lord, "They're Online and on the Job; Managers and Hamburger Flippers Are Being E-Trained at Work," *U.S. News & World Report* 15 Oct. 2001: 72–77.

5. Based on Denis Gellene, "Marketers Target Schools by Offering Facts and Features," *Los Angeles Times* 4 June 1998: D1.

Chapter 13

1. Based on <www.soccercanada.com/eng/about>; <www.soccercanada.com/eng/docs/blueprint>; <www.soccercanada.com/eng/stadium>; Canadian Soccer Association, *2002 Demographics Report*; Canadian Soccer Association, *2002 Annual Report.*

2. Jim Barlow, "PowerPoint Talks Can Be Sparkling," *Houston Chronicle* 28 Nov. 2000: C1+.

3. Sherwyn P. Morreale and Courtland L. Bovée, *Excellence in Public Speaking* (Fort Worth: Harcourt Brace, 1998) 234–237.

4. Morreale and Bovée, *Excellence in Public Speaking* 230.

5. Morreale and Bovée, *Excellence in Public Speaking* 241–243.

6. "Choose and Use Your Words Deliberately," *Soundview Executive Book Summaries* 20.6 pt. 2 (June 1998): 3.

7. Walter Kiechel III, "How to Give a Speech," *Fortune* 8 June 1987: 180.

8. *Communication and Leadership Program* (Santa Ana, C.A.: Toastmasters International, 1980) 44, 45.

9. "Polishing Your Presentation." 3M Meeting Network. 8 June 2001 <www.mmm.com/meetingnetwork/readingroom/meetingguide_pres.html>.

10. Kathleen K. Weigner, "Visual Persuasion," *Forbes* 16 Sept. 1991: 176; Kathleen K. Weigner, "Showtime!" *Forbes* 13 May 1991: 118.

11. Donald B. Adler and Jeanne Marquardt Elmhorst, *Communicating at Work* (Boston: McGraw-Hill, 2002) 379.

12. Jon Hanke, "Five Tips for Better Visuals," 3M Meeting Network. 8 June 2001 <www.mmm.com/meeting network/presentations/pmag_better_ visuals.html>.

13. Hanke, "Five Tips for Better Visuals."

14. Ted Simons "Handouts That Won't Get Trashed," *Presentations* Feb. 1999: 47–50.

15. Simons, "Handouts That Won't Get Trashed": 47–50; David Green, Personal communication. 13 July 2001; "Help 'Em Remember with Handouts," Idea Café: Handouts for Your Business Presentations, 4 Oct. 2001 <www.idea cafe.com/fridge/spotlight/spothandouts. html>; Bob Lamons, "Good Listeners Are Better Communicators," *Marketing News* 11 Sept. 1995: 13+; Phillip Morgan and H. Kent Baker, "Building a Professional Image: Improving Listening Behavior," *Supervisory Management* Nov. 1985: 35–36.

16. Patrick J. Collins, *Say It with Power and Confidence* (Upper Saddle River, N.J.: Prentice-Hall, 1997) 122–124.

17. Allbee, personal communication, 13 July 2001.

18. Ed Bott and Woody Leonard, *Special Edition—Using Microsoft Office 2000.* (Indianapolis: Que Corporation, 1999) 907.

19. Mary Munter, *Guide to Managerial Communication,* 5th ed. (Upper Saddle River, N.J.: Prentice-Hall, 2000) 59.

20. Morreale and Bovée, *Excellence in Public Speaking* 24–25.

21. Judy Linscott, "Getting On and Off the Podium," *Savvy* Oct. 1985: 44.

22. Iris R. Johnson, "Before You Approach the Podium," *MW* Jan.–Feb. 1989: 7.

23. Sandra Moyer, "Braving No Woman's Land," *The Toastmaster* Aug. 1986: 13.

24. Control the Question-and-Answer Session," *Soundview Executive Book Summaries* 20.6, pt. 2 (June 1998): 4.

25. Control the Question-and-Answer Session."; Teresa Brady, "Fielding Abrasive Questions During Presentations," *Supervisory Management* February 1993: 6.

26. Robert L. Montgomery, "Listening on Your Feet," *The Toastmaster* July 1987: 14–15.

27. Adapted from Ronald L. Applebaum and Karl W. E. Anatol, *Effective Oral Communication: For Business and the Professions* (Chicago: Science Research Associates, 1982) 240–244.

28. See note 1.

Chapter 14

1. James Cox and David Kiley, "Ford Jr. Takes on Role He Was Born to Plan," *USA Today* 31 Oct. 2001. 10 Sept. 2002 <usatoday.com>; "Ford Motor Company Capsule," *Hoover's Online* 10 Sept. 2002 <www.hoovers.com>; Betsy Morris, Noshua Watson, and Patricia Neerings, "Idealist On Board: This Ford is Different," *Fortune* 3 Apr. 2000. 11 Sept. 2002 <www.fortune.com/indexw.jhtml? channel=artcol.jhtml&doc_id=00001487>; Ford Company, *2001 Annual Report.* 10 Sept. 2002. 11 Oct. 2003 <www.mycareer. ford.com/HOWEEHIRE>.

2. Camille DeBell, "Ninety Years in the World of Work in America," *Career Development Quarterly* 50.1 (2001): 77–88.

3. John A. Challenger, "The Changing Workforce: Workplace Rules in the New Millenium," *Vital Speeches of the Day* 67.23 (2001): 721–728.

4. Marvin J. Cetron and Owen Davies, "Trends Now Changing the World: Technology, the Workplace, Management, and Institutions," *Futurist* 35.1 (2001): 27–42.

5. Amanda Bennett, "GE Redesigns Rungs of Career Ladder," *The Wall Street Journal* 15 Mar. 1993: B1, B3; Joan L. Milen, "Hiring Managers Value Personality, Multi-Tasking, and the Ability to Learn," *Canadian Manager* 27.1 (2002): 5.

6. Robin White Goode, "International and Foreign Language Skills Have an Edge," *Black Enterprise* May 1995: 53.

7. Jeffrey R. Young "'E-Portfolios'" Could Give Students a New Sense of Their Accomplishments," *The Chronicle of Higher Education* 8 Mar. 2002: A31.

8. Nancy M. Somerick, "Managing a Communication Internship Program," *Bulletin of the Association for Business Communication* 56.3 (1993): 10–20.

9. Joan Lloyd, "Changing Workplace Requires You to Alter Your Career Outlook," *Milwaukee Journal Sentinel* 4 July 1999: 1; DeBell, "Ninety Years in the World of Work in America."

10. Stephanie Armour, "Employers: Enough Already with the E-Résumés," *USA Today* 15 July 1999: 1B.

11. Cheryl L. Noll, "Collaborating with the Career Planning and Placement Center in the Job-Search Project," *Business Communication Quarterly* 58.3 (1995): 53–55.

12. Pam Stanley-Weigand, "Organizing the Writing of Your Resume," Bulletin of the *Association for Business Communication* 54.3 (1991): 11–12.

13. Richard H. Beatty and Nicholas C. Burkholder, *The Executive Career Guide for MBAs* (New York: Wiley, 1996) 133.

14. Beatty and Burkholder, *The Executive Career Guide for MBA:* 151.

15. Rockport Institute, "How to Write a Masterpiece of a Résumé."

16. Rockport Institute, "How to Write a Masterpiece of a Résumé."

17. Anne Field, "Coach, Help Me Out with This Interview," *Business Week* 22 Oct. 2001: 134E4, 134E6; Joan E. Rigdon, "Deceptive Résumés Can Be Door-Openers but Can Become an Employee's Undoing," *The Wall Street Journal* 17 June 1992: B1; Diane Cole, "Ethics: Companies Crack Down on Dishonesty," *Managing Your Career* Spring 1991: 8–11; Nancy Marx Better, "Résumé Liars," *Savvy* Dec. 1990–Jan. 1991: 26–29.

18. Beverly Culwell-Block and Jean Anna Sellers, "Résumé Content and Format—Do the Authorities Agree?" *Bulletin of the Association for Business Communication* 57.4 (1994): 27–30.

19. Janice Tovey, "Using Visual Theory in the Creation of Résumés: A Bibliography," *Bulletin of the Association* *for Business Communication* 54.3 (1991): 97–99.

20. Bronwyn Fryer, "Job Hunting the Electronic Way," *Working Woman* Mar. 1995: 59–60, 78; Joyce Lane Kennedy and Thomas J. Morrow, *Electronic Resume Revolution,* 2nd ed. (New York: Wiley, 1995) 30–33; Mary Goodwin, Deborah Cohn, and Donna Spivey, *Netjobs: Use the Internet to Land Your Dream Job* (New York: Michael Wolff, 1996) 149–150; Zane K. Quible, "Electronic Résumés: Their Time Is Coming," *Business Communication Quarterly* 58.3 (1995): 5–9; Alfred Glossbrenner and Emily Glossbrenner, *Finding a Job on the Internet* (New York: McGraw-Hill, 1995) 194–197; Pam Dixon and Silvia Tiersten, *Be Your Own Headhunter Online* (New York: Random House, 1995) 80–83.

21. Quible, "The Electronic Resume: An Important New Job-Search Tool."

22. Pollock, "Sir: Your Application for a Job Is Rejected."

23. Quible, "The Electronic Resume: An Important New Job-Search Tool."

24. Pontow, "Electronic Résumé Writing Tips."

25. William J. Banis, "The Art of Writing Job-Search Letters," *CPC Annual.* 36th ed. no. 2 (1992): 42–50.

26. Toni Logan, "The Perfect Cover Story," *Kinko's Impress* 2 (2000): 32, 34.

27. See note 1.

Chapter 15

1. Adapted from IBM Canada. 12 Oct. 2003 <www.can.ibm.com/hr/faq.html; www.can.ibm/hr.training.html> <www-8.ibm.com/employment/sg/life/principles.html>; <www.-8.ibm.com/employment/sg.life/goals.html>; <www-8.ibm.com/employment/in/positions/interview.html>; <www-1.ibm.com/press>; L. V. Gerstner, Speech to University of Notre Dame Mendoza College of Business Commencement, May 20, 2001, South Bend, Indiana. "Lou Gerstner Speeches," 13 Oct. 2003 <www.ibm.com/lvg.0521.phtml>; John V. Thill and Courtland L. Bovée, *Excellence in Business Communication*, 4th ed. (Upper Saddle River, N.J.: Prentice-Hall, 1999) 466-467.

2. Sylvia Porter, "Your Money: How to Prepare for Job Interviews," *San Francisco Chronicle* 3 Nov. 1981: 54.

3. Stephanie Armour, "The New Interview Etiquette," *USA Today* 23 Nov. 1999: B1, B2.

4. Samuel Greengard, "Are You Well Armed to Screen Applicants?" *Personnel Journal* Dec. 1995: 84–95.

5. Charlene Marmer Solomon, "How Does Disney Do It?" *Personnel Journal* Dec. 1989: 53.

6. Marcia Vickers, "Don't Touch That Dial: Why Should I Hire You?" *The New York Times* 13 Apr. 1997: F11.

7. Nancy K. Austin, "Goodbye Gimmicks," *Incentive* May 1996: 241.

8. Joel Russell, "Finding Solid Ground," *Hispanic Business* Feb. 1992: 42–44, 46.

9. "Alberta's Suncor Says It's Reviewing Drug Testing After Human Rights Ruling," *Canadian Press Newswire* 12 July 2002; "CHRC New Policy on Alcohol and Drug Testing," *Human Resources Advisor Newsletter Ontario Edition* Sept.-Oct. 2002: 3; "CHRC Revises Testing Policy," *Worklife Reporter* 14.2 (2002): 13; "Five Steps to a Drug-Free Workplace," *Canadian HR Reporter* 6 May 2002: 11; Asha Tomlinson, "No Clear Cut Answer to Drug Testing," *Canadian HR Reporter* 6 May 2002: 1, 11.

10. Austin, "Goodbye Gimmicks."

11. "Major Pizza Plant Expansion." News release 7 July 2003. 14 Oct. 2003 <www.mccain.com/MediaDesk>.

12. Peter Rea, Julie Rea, and Charles Moonmaw, "Training: Use Assessment Centers in Skill Development," *Personnel Journal* Apr. 1990: 126–131; Greengard, "Are You Well Armed to Screen Applicants?"

13. Anne Field, "Coach, Help Me Out with This Interview," *Business Week* 22 Oct. 2001: 134E2, 134E4.

14. Robert Gifford, Cheuk Fan Ng, and Margaret Wilkinson, "Nonverbal Cues in the Employment Interview: Links Between Applicant Qualities and Interviewer Judgments," *Journal of Applied Psychology* 70.4 (1985): 729.

15. Dale G. Leathers, *Successful Nonverbal Communication* (New York: Macmillan, 1986) 225.

16. Leslie Plotkin, "Dress for Success," *Work Tree*, 29 May 2003 <www.work tree.com/tb/IN_dress.cfm>.

17. Lynne Waymon, "Don't Stress Over Interview Dress," *The Industrial Physicist* Sept. 1998. 29 May 2003 <www.aip.org/tip/0998.html>.

18. Shirley J. Shepherd, "How to Get That Job in 60 Minutes or Less," *Working Woman* Mar. 1986: 119.

19. Shepherd, "How to Get That Job in 60 Minutes or Less": 118.

20. Herman-Miller, Home Page. 9 Nov. 1997. <www.hermanmiller.com>; Hoover's Online. 23 Jan. 1997 <www.hoovers.com>; A.J. Vogl, "Risky Work," *Across the Board* July–August 1993: 27–31; Kenneth Labich, "Hot Company, Warm Culture," *Fortune* 27 Feb. 1989: 74–78; George Melloan, "Herman Miller's Secrets of Corporate Creativity," *The Wall Street Journal* 3, May 1988: A31; Beverly Gerber, "Herman Miller: Where Profits and Participation Meet," *Training* Nov. 1987: 62–66; Robert J. McClory, "The Creative Process at Herman Miller," *Across the Board* May 1985: 8–22; Tom Peters and Nancy Austin, *A Passion for Excellence (*New York: Random House, 1985) 204–205.

21. "Quotable" [Editorial]. *Focus on Canadian Employment & Equality Rights* 5.15 (Mar. 1999): 1+.

22. Harold H. Hellwig, "Job Interviewing: Process and Practice," *Bulletin of the Association for Business Communication* 55.2 (1992): 8–14.

23. See note 1.

Appendix A

1. Mary A. DeVries, *Internationally Yours* (Boston: Houghton Mifflin, 1994) 9.

2. Patricia A. Dreyfus, "Paper That's Letter Perfect," *Money*, May 1985: 184.

3. "When Image Counts, Letterhead Says It All," *The Advocate and Greenwich Time*, 10 Jan. 1993: F4.

4. Mel Mandell, "Electronic Forms Are Cheap and Speedy," *DB Reports*, July–Aug. 1993: 44–45.

5. Linda Driskill, *Business & Managerial Communication: New Perspectives* (Orlando, Fla.: Harcourt Brace Jovanovich, 1992) 470.

6. Driskill, *Business & Managerial Communication* 470.

7. Lennie Copeland and Lewis Griggs, *Going International: How to Make Friends and Deal Effectively in the Global Marketplace*, 2d ed. (New York: Random House, 1985) 24–27.

8. DeVries, *Internationally Yours*, 8.

9. Copeland and Griggs, *Going International*, 24–27.

10. Renee B. Horowitz and Marian G. Barchilon, "Stylistic Guidelines for E-Mail," *IEEE Transactions on Professional Communications* 37.4 (1994): 207–212.

11. Jill H. Ellsworth and Matthew V. Ellsworth, *The Internet Business Book* (New York: Wiley, 1994) 93.

12. Bill Eager, *Using the Internet* (Indianapolis, Ind.: Que, 1994) 11.

Acknowledgements

Text, Figures, and Tables

4 Courtesy of Spitz Sales Inc. **6** (Figure 1.3): From David J. Rachman and Michael Mescon, *Business Today*, 5th edition, p. 27, 1987. McGraw-Hill. **8** (Figure 1.5) Letterhead courtesy of Swift Canoe and Kayak. **11** (Figure 1.6) Adapted from Allan D. Frank, *Communicating on the Job* (Glenview, Ill.: Scott Foresman, 1982). **27** (Table 2.1) Adapted from Phillip Morgan and H. Kent Baker, "Building a Professional Image: Improving Listening Behavior." Reprinted by permission of the publisher, from *Supervisory Management*, November 1985, 34. © 1987 McGraw-Hill Inc. **32** (Figure 2.1) Copyright, Dr. Lyman K. Steil, President, Communication Development, Inc., St. Paul, Minn. Prepared for the Sperry Corporation. Reprinted with permission of Dr. Steil and Unisys Corporation. **34** (Table 2.2) Adapted from Phillip Morgan and H. Kent Baker, "Building a Professional Image: Improving Listening Behavior." Reprinted by permission of the publisher, from *Supervisory Management*, November, 1985, 34 © 1987 McGraw-Hill Inc. **35** (Table 2.3) Adapted from J. Michael Sproule. *Communication Today* (Glenview, Ill.: Scott, Foresman, 1981), by permission of J. Michael Sproule. Copyright J. Michael Sproule. **54** (Table 3.1) Gary P. Ferraro, The Cultural Dimension of International Business, 4th ed. (Upper Saddle River, NJ.: Prentice Hall, 2002), 58; Mary O'Hara-Devereaux and Robert Johansen, *Global Work: Bridging Distance, Culture and Time* (San Francisco: Jossey-Bass, 1994), 55, 59. **57** (Figure 3.1) Sam Ward, "Atlanta Committee for Olympic Games," *USA Today*, taken from Ben Brown, "Atlanta Out to Mind its Manners," *USA Today*, March 14, 1996. **59** (Table 3.2) Guo-Ming Chen and William J. Starosta, *Foundations of Intercultural Communication* (Boston: Allyn and Bacon, 1998), 66. **79** (Figure 4.3) Courtesy of Cadbury Beverages Canada Inc. **84** (Figure 4.5) Courtesy of Yukon Brewing Company. **119** (Figure 5.7) Courtesy of Microsoft; **124** (Figure 5.8) Courtesy of Textile Outfitters Inc., Calgary, Alberta. **129** Courtesy of www.orbitz.com. **137** (On the Job: Facing a Communication Dilemma at the Confederation Centre of the Arts) Courtesy of Anna MacDonald, Publicist, Confederation Centre of the Arts.**142** (Figure 6.3) Adapted from Robert Gunning, *The Technique of Clear Writing* (New York: McGraw-Hill, rev. ed., 1973). Used with permission of copyright owners, Gunning-Mueller Clear Writing Institute, Inc. **149** (Figure 6.5) Courtesy of the Royal Ontario Museum. **159** Courtesy of David McKenzie, Chief Executive Officer of The Confederation Centre of the Arts. **181** Courtesy of Dampp-Chaser Corporation. **186** (Figure 7.9) Courtesy of Bell Canada. **240** (Figure 9.2) Letterhead courtesy of Host Mariott. **294** (Table 10.3) Search Engines Fact and Fun [accessed 11 March 1998] searchenginewatch.com/facts/major.html; Getting started – What you need to Know to Begin Using the Internet," *Fortune Technology Buyer's Guide*, Winter 1998, 232-240; Matt Lake, "Desperately Seeking Susan OR Suzie NOT Shushi," *New York Times*, 3 September 1998, D1, D7; "Notable Websites," *Fortune Technology Buyer's Guide*, Winter 1999, 238, 240. **329** (Table 11.2) Adapted from Robert Lefferts, *Elements of Graphics*, pp. 18-35. Copyright 1981 by Robert Lefferts, Harper and Rowe. **330** *Dofasco Inc. 2002 Annual Report*, p. 58. **331** (Figure 11-7) *Adapted from Standard and Poor's Industry Surveys– Footware*, 1 December 1998, 26. **332** (Figure 11.8) *Adapted from Standard and Poor's Industry Surveys – Autos*, 5 March, 1998, 16. **332** (Figure 11.9) *Adapted from Standard and Poor's Industry Surveys – Movies*, 12 November 1998, 30. **334** (Figure 11.11) F11.11-a (Where the college students are): Adapted from *American Demographics*, March 1998, 47; F11.11-b (Eating occasions): *Adapted from American Demographics*, January 1998, 52. F11.11-c (Targeted Talks): *Adapted from American Demographics*, February, 1998, 52. F11.11-d (Commercial Superhighway): *Wall Street Journal*, 7 December 1998, R4. **337** (Figure 11.14) From John M. Lannon, *Technical Writing*, 3rd edition. Copyright © 1985 by John M. Lannon. Reprinted by permission of Addison Wesley Educational Publishers, Inc. **337** (Figure 11.15) "How the Networks Deliver the Goods," *Business Week*, 6 April 1998, 91-92. **394** (Figure 12.5) Adapted from A.S.C. Ehrenberg, "The Problem of Numeracy," *Admap*, February 1992, 37-40; Mary S. Auvil and Kenneth W. Auvil, *Introduction to Business Graphics: Concepts and Applications* (Cincinnati: South-Western, 1992), 40, 192-193; Peter H. Selby, *Using Graphics and Tables: A Self-Teaching Guide* (New York: Wiley, 1979) 8-9. **395** (Table 12.1) Adapted from Robert Lefferts, *How to Prepare Charts and Graphs for Effective Reports* (New York: Harper and Row, Publishers, Inc., 1981) **395** (Table 12.2) Adapted from Robert Lefferts, *How to Prepare Charts and Graphs for Effective Reports* (New York: Harper and Row, Publishers, Inc., 1981) **418** (Figure 13.8) Microsoft PowerPoint 2000 software. **439** (Table 14.2) Rockport Institute, "How to Write a Masterpiece of a Resume" [accessed 16 October 1998], www.rockportinstitute.com/resumes.html. **446** (Table 14.3) Anne Field, "Coach Help Me Out with This Interview," *Business Week*, 22 October 2001, 134E4, 134E6; Joan E. Rigdon, "Deceptive Resumes Can Be Door-Openers But Can Become an Employee's Undoing," *Wall Street Journal* , 17 June 1992, B1; Diane Cole, "Ethics: Companies Crack Down on Dishonesty," *Managing Your Career*, Spring 1991, 8-11; Nancy Marx Better, "Resume liars," *Savvy*, December 1990-January 1991, 26-29. **450** (Table 14.4) Joyce Lain Kennedy and Thomas J. Morrow, *Electronic Resume Revolution* (New York: Wiley, 1994). **472** (Table 15.1) Adapted from *The NorthWestern Endicott Report* (Evanston: Ill.: Northwestern University Placement Centre). **473** (Table 15.2) Adapted from *The NorthWestern Endicott Report* (Evanston: Ill.: Northwestern University Placement Centre). **475** (Table 15.3) Adapted from H. Lee Rust, *Job Search: The Completion Manual for Jobseekers* (New York: American Management Association, 1979), 56. **509** (Figure A-10) Adapted from Jill H. Ellsworth and Matthew V. Ellsworth, *The Internet Business Book* (New York: Wiley, 1994), 93.

Photographs

2 Courtesy of Suncor Energy Inc. **3** © Steve Chenn.CORBIS/MAGMA. **7** Courtesy of TELUS. **11** Tom McCarthy/PhotoEdit. **13** CBC Photo Gallery. **17** Courtesy of Falconbridge

Limited. **23** Steve Smith/Getty Images. **25** Jeffery Greenberg/Photo Researchers Inc. **30** Andy Freeberg Photography. **33** © Dorling Kindersley. **38** © Dorling Kindersley. **41** Library of Parliament/Stephen Fenn. Bibliotheque du Parlement/Stephen Fenn. **49** Courtesy of Laraine Kaminsky. **51** Pearson Education/PH College. **52** Paul Chesley/Getty Images. **56** Courtesy of Bata Ltd. **58** ©Bojan Brecelj/CORBIS/Magmaphoto.com. **59** Courtesy of Dalton Chemical Laboratories, Inc. **72** © Dorling Kindersley. **74** Rob Lewine/CORBIS/Magmaphoto.com. **77** Courtesy of the Aboriginal Banking Unit of the Business Development Bank of Canada. **87** Courtesy of Ballard Power Systems. **100** Courtesy McCain Foods Limited. **101** Wendy MacNair. Courtesy of Marie Delorme. **110** Churchill & Klehr Photography. **129** Courtesy of Orbitz. **137** Courtesy of Confederation Centre of the Arts, Charlottetown, Prince Edward Island. **146** Nick Daly/Getty Images. **153** Courtesy of Logitech. **155** Reprinted by permission from IBM Annual Report copyright 2002 by International Business Machines Corporation. **164** Courtesy of Indigo. **165** Picturesque Stock Photo. **171** Darryl Estrine/Outline Press Syndicate, Inc. **178** © Dorling Kindersley. **187** Cancer Care Ontario. **196** D. Young Wolf, PhotoEdit. **198** Deere & Company. **201** © Ralf-Finn Hestoft/CORBIS/Magmaphoto.com. **202** John Riley/Getty Images. **205** ©Dick Hemmingway. **206** Rogers Communications Inc. **226** Suzanne Plunkett, AP/Wide World Photos. **227** Courtesy of Sherry Torchinsky. **232** Paul Barton/CORBIS/MAGMA. **238** Getty Images/Photodisc. **245** Courtesy of Habitat for Humanity. **248** ©2002 Amazon.com, Inc. All rights reserved. Amazon, Amazon.ca logo are trademarks or registered trademarks of Amazon.com, Inc. **264** ML Sinibaldi, Corbis/Stock Market. **269** Clarksburg Exponent Telegram, Bob Shaw, AP/Wide World Photos. **270** Bob Daemmrich Photography, Inc. **283** Michael Newman/PhotoEdit. **285** ©Rob Bartee/Maxximages.com. **315** George Disario. **316** Real Life/Getty Images. **354** Charles Rex Arbogast, AP/WideWorld Photos. **356** Churchill & Klehr photography. **359** Photodisc/Getty Images. **360** SuperStock, Inc. **381** Xerox Corporation. **399** Photo by Peter Thompson/Permission granted by Judith A. Walsh on behalf of Amy Walsh. **400** Frank Oberle, ImageQuest. **410** Courtesy of Mark Swartz. **420** © Dorling Kindersley. **425** Mark Richards. **436** workopolis.com screen shot courtesy of Workopolis. **447** © Dorling Kindersley. **452** Claude Gelinas, WebMaster. **467** Monkmeyer Press. **471** The Image Works. **477** Darryl Estrine, Corbis/Outline. **480** PhotoLibrary.com.

Name Index

Subject Index

D

P

Y

"AS IS" LICENSE AGREEMENT AND LIMITED WARRANTY

READ THIS LICENSE CAREFULLY BEFORE OPENING THIS PACKAGE. BY OPENING THIS PACKAGE, YOU ARE AGREEING TO THE TERMS AND CONDITIONS OF THIS LICENSE. IF YOU DO NOT AGREE, DO NOT OPEN THE PACKAGE. PROMPTLY RETURN THE UNOPENED PACKAGE AND ALL ACCOMPANYING ITEMS TO THE PLACE YOU OBTAINED THEM. ***THESE TERMS APPLY TO ALL LICENSED SOFTWARE ON THE DISK EXCEPT THAT THE TERMS FOR USE OF ANY SHAREWARE OR FREEWARE ON THE DISKETTES ARE AS SET FORTH IN THE ELECTRONIC LICENSE LOCATED ON THE DISK:***

1. GRANT OF LICENSE and OWNERSHIP: The enclosed computer programs ("Software") are licensed, not sold, to you by Pearson Education Canada Inc. ("We" or the "Company") in consideration of your adoption of the accompanying Company textbooks and/or other materials, and your agreement to these terms. You own only the disk(s) but we and/or our licensors own the Software itself. This license allows instructors and students enrolled in the course using the Company textbook that accompanies this Software (the "Course") to use and display the enclosed copy of the Software for academic use only, so long as you comply with the terms of this Agreement. You may make one copy for back up only. We reserve any rights not granted to you.

2. USE RESTRICTIONS: You may <u>not</u> sell or license copies of the Software or the Documentation to others. You may <u>not</u> transfer, distribute or make available the Software or the Documentation, except to instructors and students in your school who are users of the adopted Company textbook that accompanies this Software in connection with the course for which the textbook was adopted. You may <u>not</u> reverse engineer, disassemble, decompile, modify, adapt, translate or create derivative works based on the Software or the Documentation. You may be held legally responsible for any copying or copyright infringement which is caused by your failure to abide by the terms of these restrictions.

3. TERMINATION: This license is effective until terminated. This license will terminate automatically without notice from the Company if you fail to comply with any provisions or limitations of this license. Upon termination, you shall destroy the Documentation and all copies of the Software. All provisions of this Agreement as to limitation and disclaimer of warranties, limitation of liability, remedies or damages, and our ownership rights shall survive termination.

4. DISCLAIMER OF WARRANTY: THE COMPANY AND ITS LICENSORS MAKE <u>NO</u> WARRANTIES ABOUT THE SOFTWARE, WHICH IS PROVIDED "<u>AS-IS</u>." IF THE DISK IS DEFECTIVE IN MATERIALS OR WORKMANSHIP, YOUR ONLY REMEDY IS TO RETURN IT TO THE COMPANY WITHIN 30 DAYS FOR REPLACEMENT UNLESS THE COMPANY DETERMINES IN GOOD FAITH THAT THE DISK HAS BEEN MISUSED OR IMPROPERLY INSTALLED, REPAIRED, ALTERED OR DAMAGED. THE COMPANY DISCLAIMS ALL WARRANTIES, EXPRESS OR IMPLIED, INCLUDING WITHOUT LIMITATION, THE IMPLIED WARRANTIES OF MERCHANTABILITY AND FITNESS FOR A PARTICULAR PURPOSE. THE COMPANY DOES NOT WARRANT, GUARANTEE OR MAKE ANY REPRESENTATION REGARDING THE ACCURACY, RELIABILITY, CURRENTNESS, USE, OR RESULTS OF USE, OF THE SOFTWARE.

5. LIMITATION OF REMEDIES AND DAMAGES: IN NO EVENT, SHALL THE COMPANY OR ITS EMPLOYEES, AGENTS, LICENSORS OR CONTRACTORS BE LIABLE FOR ANY INCIDENTAL, INDIRECT, SPECIAL OR CONSEQUENTIAL DAMAGES ARISING OUT OF OR IN CONNECTION WITH THIS LICENSE OR THE SOFTWARE, INCLUDING, WITHOUT LIMITATION, LOSS OF USE, LOSS OF DATA, LOSS OF INCOME OR PROFIT, OR OTHER LOSSES SUSTAINED AS A RESULT OF INJURY TO ANY PERSON, OR LOSS OF OR DAMAGE TO PROPERTY, OR CLAIMS OF THIRD PARTIES, EVEN IF THE COMPANY OR AN AUTHORIZED REPRESENTATIVE OF THE COMPANY HAS BEEN ADVISED OF THE POSSIBILITY OF SUCH DAMAGES. SOME JURISDICTIONS DO NOT ALLOW THE LIMITATION OF DAMAGES IN CERTAIN CIRCUMSTANCES, SO THE ABOVE LIMITATIONS MAY NOT ALWAYS APPLY.

6. GENERAL: THIS AGREEMENT SHALL BE CONSTRUED AND INTERPRETED ACCORDING TO THE LAWS OF THE PROVINCE OF ONTARIO. This Agreement is the complete and exclusive statement of the agreement between you and the Company and supersedes all proposals, prior agreements, oral or written, and any other communications between you and the company or any of its representatives relating to the subject matter.

Should you have any questions concerning this agreement or if you wish to contact the Company for any reason, please contact in writing: Editorial Manager, Pearson Education Canada, 26 Prince Andrew Place, Don Mills, Ontario, M3C 2T8.

Use of this CD-ROM is restricted to the purchasing (or acquiring) institution or to situations under the auspices of the institution. No copying, alteration, broadcast, cable distribution, digital delivery, or sale is permitted, and the video content included herein may not be transferred to any other source.